T0336690

Reconfigurable Embedded Control Systems:
Applications for Flexibility and Agility

Mohamed Khalgui
Xidian University, China

Hans-Michael Hanisch
Martin Luther University, Germany

INFORMATION SCIENCE REFERENCE

Hershey · New York

Director of Editorial Content:	Kristin Klinger
Director of Book Publications:	Julia Mosemann
Acquisitions Editor:	Lindsay Johnston
Development Editor:	Joel Gamon
Publishing Assistant:	Casey Conapitski
Typesetter:	Milan Vracarich Jr.
Production Editor:	Jamie Snavely
Cover Design:	Lisa Tosheff

Published in the United States of America by
　　Information Science Reference (an imprint of IGI Global)
　　701 E. Chocolate Avenue
　　Hershey PA 17033
　　Tel: 717-533-8845
　　Fax: 717-533-8661
　　E-mail: cust@igi-global.com
　　Web site: http://www.igi-global.com

Library of Congress Cataloging-in-Publication Data

Reconfigurable embedded control systems : applications for flexibility and
agility / Mohamed Khalgui and Hans-Michael Hanisch, editors.
　　p. cm.
　Includes bibliographical references and index.
　　ISBN 978-1-60960-086-0 (hardcover) -- ISBN 978-1-60960-088-4 (ebook) 1.
Programmable controllers. 2. Embedded computer systems. 3. Digital control
systems. I. Khalgui, Mohamed. II. Hanisch, Hans-Michael.
　TJ223.P76R43 2011
　629.8'95--dc22
　　　　　　　　　　　2010042276

British Cataloguing in Publication Data
A Cataloguing in Publication record for this book is available from the British Library.

All work contributed to this book is new, previously-unpublished material. The views expressed in this book are those of the authors, but not necessarily of the publisher.

Table of Contents

Detailed Table of Contents

Chapter 1

Mohamed Khalgui, Xidian University, China

The chapter deals with reconfigurable embedded control systems following component-based technologies and/or Architecture Description Languages used today in industry. The author defines Control Components as software units to support control tasks of the system which is assumed to be a network of components with precedence constraints. The author defines an agent-based architecture to handle automatic reconfigurations under well-defined conditions by creating, deleting or updating components to bring the whole system into safe and optimal behaviors. To cover all reconfiguration forms, the agent is modelled by nested state machines such that states correspond to other state machines. Several complex networks can implement the system where each one is executed at a given time when a corresponding reconfiguration scenario is automatically applied by the agent. To check the correctness of each one of them, we apply in several steps a refinement-based approach that automatically specifies feasible Control Components according to NCES. The model checker SESA is automatically applied in each step to verify deadlock properties of new generated components, and it is manually used to verify CTL-based properties according to user requirements. The author implements the reconfiguration agent by three modules that allow interpretations of environment evolutions, decisions of useful reconfiguration scenarios and finally their applications. Two Industrial Benchmark Production Systems FESTO and EnAS available in the author's research laboratory are applied to explain the paper contribution.

Chapter 2

Jason Agron, University of Arkansas, USA
David Andrews, University of Arkansas, USA
Markus Happe, University of Paderborn, Germany
Enno Lübbers, University of Paderborn, Germany
Marco Platzner, University of Paderborn, Germany

Embedded and Real-Time (ERTS) systems have continued to expand at a vigorous rate. Designers of ERTS systems are continually challenged to provide new capabilities that can meet the expanding requirements and increased computational needs of each new proposed application, but at a decreasing price/performance ratio. Conventional solutions using general purpose processors or custom ASICs are less and less able to satisfy the contradictory requirements in performance, flexibility, power, development time, and cost. This chapter introduces the concept of generating semi-custom platforms driven from a traditional multithreaded programming model. This approach offers the advantage of achieving productivity levels close to those associated with software by using an established programming model but with a performance level close to custom hardware through the use of a flexible hardware platform capable of adapting to specialized application requirements. We discuss the underlying concepts, requirements and advantages of multithreading in the context of reconfigurable hardware, and present two approaches which provide multithreading support to hardware and software components at the operating system level.

Thomas Strasser, Austrian Institute of Technology, Austria
Alois Zoitl, Vienna University of Technology, Austria
Martijn Rooker, PROFACTOR GmbH, Austria

Future manufacturing is envisioned to be highly flexible and adaptable. New technologies for efficient engineering of reconfigurable systems and their adaptations are preconditions for this vision. Without such solutions, engineering adaptations of Industrial Process Measurement and Control Systems (IPMCS) will exceed the costs of engineered systems by far and the reuse of equipment will become inefficient. Especially the reconfiguration of control applications is not sufficiently solved by state-of-the-art technology. This paper chapter gives an overview of the use of reconfiguration applications for zero-downtime system reconfiguration of control applications on basis of the standard IEC 61499 which provides a reference model for distributed and reconfigurable control systems. A new approach for the reconfiguration of IEC 61499 based control application and the corresponding modeling is discussed. This new method significantly increases engineering efficiency and reuse in component-based IPMCS.

Christian Plessl, University of Paderborn, Germany
Marco Platzner, University of Paderborn, Germany

Numerous research efforts in reconfigurable embedded processors have shown that augmenting a CPU core with a coarse-grained reconfigurable array for application-specific hardware acceleration can greatly increase performance and energy-efficiency. The traditional execution model for such reconfigurable co-processors however requires the accelerated function to fit onto the reconfigurable array as a whole, which restricts the applicability to rather small functions.

In our the authors' research presented in this chapter, we the authors have studied hardware virtualization approaches that overcome this restriction by leveraging dynamic reconfiguration. We They present two different hardware virtualization methods, virtualized execution and temporal partitioning, and introduce the Zippy reconfigurable processor architecture that has been designed with specific hardware virtualization support. Further, we the authors outline the corresponding hardware and software tool flows. Finally, we the authors demonstrate the potential provided by hardware virtualization with two case studies and discuss directions for future research.

Chapter 5

    Raimund Kirner, University of Hertfordshire, UK
    Sven Bünte, Technische Universität Wien, Austria
    Michael Zolda, Technische Universität Wien, Austria

Reconfigurable embedded computing opens many interesting possibilities for efficiency and reliability improvement. Still, it is necessary to verify whether the reconfigurable embedded computer system fulfills its timing requirements. Purely static worst-case execution time (WCET) analysis is not the best choice for verifying the timing behavior of reconfigurable embedded computer systems, as frequent re-modeling of different hardware configurations is not practicable. We describe measurement based timing analysis as an approach that is better applicable for reconfigurable applications. Measurement-based timing analysis is a hybrid approach that combines static program analysis techniques, borrowed from static WCET analysis, with empirical learning of the application's timing behavior by performing systematic measurements. But even the MBTA approach is challenged by the reconfigurable computing paradigm by the need for adequate coverage of the reconfigurable fabric.

Chapter 6

    C. Valderrama, University of Mons, Belgium
    L. Jojczyk, University of Mons, Belgium
    P. Possa, University of Mons, Belgium

This chapter presents reconfigurable embedded systems by looking closely at three different but interrelated aspects: design tools, methodologies and architectures, paying special attention at reconfigurable interconnections. We The authors will start having a closer look at the evolution of the latest design strategies, tools and methodologies facing challenges and user requirements. Reconfigurable interconnections will be analyzed, examining topologies, drawbacks, and capabilities, specially focusing on the reconfiguration potential. From the application point of view, we the authors will resume with a case study regarding embedded systems, a Software-Defined Radio application highlighting the most significant technical features and design choices.

Chapter 7

    Laurent George, University of Paris-Est – Val de Marne, France
    Pierre Courbin, LACSC – ECE Paris, France

In this paper chapter we the authors focus on the problem of reconfiguring embedded real-time systems. Such reconfiguration can be decided either off-line to determine if a given application can be run on a different platform, while preserving the timeliness constraints imposed by the application, or on-line, where a reconfiguration should be done to adapt the system to the context of execution or to handle hardware or software faults. The task model considered in this paper chapter is the classical sporadic task model defined by a Worst Case Execution Time (WCET), a minimum inter-arrival time (also denoted the minimum Period) and a late termination deadline. We The authors consider two preemptive scheduling strategies: Fixed Priority highest priority first (FP) and Earliest Deadline First (EDF). We They propose a sensitivity analysis to handle reconfiguration issues. Sensitivity analysis aims at determining acceptable deviations from the specifications of a problem due to evolutions in system characteristics (reconfiguration or performance tuning). We They present a state of the art for sensitivity analysis in the case of WCETs, Periods and Deadlines reconfigurations and study to what extent sensitivity analysis can be used to decide on the possibility of reconfiguring a system.

The continuous increase in the degree of design complexity in the design of modern digital hardware systems, come into being due to the increasing demand of more and more functionality under strict design constraints, has led to designers to try to alleviate this complexity by increasing the level of abstraction when describing the functionality of a system. Recent proposals in the field of Electronic Design Automation intend to use common programming languages, like C, C++, and Java, or dialects derived from them, to describe the behavior of a digital hardware system and then generate a lower-level representation, closer to the hardware implementation platform, from such description. This phenomenon led us to firmly believe that the process of describing the functionality of a digital circuit resembles more and more the process of developing software; and, thus, it is possible to experiment with the application of the latest trends in software engineering, like the Model-Driven Engineering (MDE) paradigm, to design digital hardware systems. In this chapter we describe the basic principles of MDE, and provide some hints about the kind of languages and transformation tools needed to design algorithms in the domain of digital control that could be transformed into a digital circuit. We intend to open doors and encourage the research on the design of digital control systems at higher levels of abstraction and their implementations in different kinds of hardware platforms, including reconfigurable devices.

Massive parallel processing systems, particularly Single Instruction Multiple Data architectures, play a crucial role in the field of data intensive parallel applications. One of the primary goals in using these systems is their scalability and their linear increase in processing power by increasing the number of processing units. However, communication networks are the big challenging issue facing researchers. One of the most important networks on chip for parallel systems are the multistage interconnection networks. In this paper, we propose a design methodology of multistage interconnection networks for massively parallel systems on chip. The framework covers the design step from algorithm level to RTL. We first develop a functional formalization of MIN-based on-chip network at a high level of abstraction. The specification and the validation of the model have been defined in the logic of ACL2 proving system. The main objective in this step is to provide a formal description of the network that integrates architectural parameters which have a huge impact on design costs. After validating the functional model, step 2 consists in the design and the implementation of the Delta multistage networks on chip dedicated to parallel multi-cores architectures on reconfigurable platforms FPGA. In the last step, we propose an evaluation methodology based on performance and cost metrics to evaluate different topologies of dynamic network through data parallel applications with different number of cores. We also show in the proposed framework that multistage interconnection networks are cost-effective high performance networks for parallel SOCs.

Chapter 10

    Mohamed Khalgui, Xidian University, China
    Olfa Mosbahi, Martin Luther University, Germany

The chapter deals with distributed multi-agent reconfigurable embedded control systems following the component-based International Industrial Standard IEC61499 in which a Function Block (abbreviated by FB) is an event-triggered software component owning data and a control application is a distributed network of Function Blocks that have classically to satisfy functional and to meet temporal properties described in user requirements. We The authors define a new reconfiguration semantic where a crucial criterion to consider is the automatic improvement of the system's performance at run-time, in addition to its protection when hardware faults occur. To handle all possible cases in industry, we the authors classify thereafter the reconfiguration scenarios into three forms before we the authors define an architecture of reconfigurable multi-agent systems where a Reconfiguration Agent is affected to each device of the execution environment to apply local reconfigurations, and a Coordination Agent is proposed for any coordination between devices in order to guarantee safe and adequate distributed reconfigurations. A Communication Protocol is proposed in our research work to handle coordinations between agents by using well-defined Coordination Matrices. We The authors specify both the reconfiguration agents to be modelled by nested state machines, and the Coordination Agent according to the formalism Net Condition/Event Systems (Abbreviated by NCES) which is an extension of Petri nets. To verify the whole architecture, we the author check by applying the model checker SESA in each device functional and temporal properties described in the temporal logic ""Computation Tree Logic"", but we the authors have also to check any coordination between devices by verifying that whenever a reconfiguration is applied in a device, the Coordination Agent and other concerned devices should react as described in user requirements. The chapter's contributions are applied to two Benchmark Production Systems available in our research laboratory.

Chapter 11

Slim Ben Othman, National Institute of Applied Sciences and Technology (INSAT), Tunisia
Ahmed Karim Ben Salem, National Institute of Applied Sciences and Technology (INSAT), Tunisia
Slim Ben Saoud, National Institute of Applied Sciences and Technology (INSAT), Tunisia

The performances of System on Chip (SoC) and the Field Programmable Gate Array (FPGA) particularly, are increasing continually. Due to the growing complexity of modern embedded control systems, the need of more performance digital devices is evident. Recent FPGA technology makes it possible to include processor cores into the FPGA chip, which ensures more flexibility for digital controllers. Indeed, greater functionality of hardware and system software, Real-Time (RT) platforms and distributed subsystems are demanded. In this chapter, design concept of FPGA based controller with Hardware/ Software (Hw/Sw) codesign is proposed. It is applied for electrical machine drives. There are discussed different MultiProcessor SoC (MPSoC) architectures with Hw peripherals for the implementation on FPGA-based embedded processor cores. Hw accelerators are considered in the design to enhance the controller speed performance and reduce power consumption. Test and validation of this control system are performed on RT motor emulator implemented on the same FPGA. Experimental results, carried on a real prototyping platform, are given in order to analyze the performance and efficiency of discussed architecture designs helping to support hard RT constraints.

Chapter 12

Alba Cristina Magalhaes Alves de Melo, University of Brasilia, Brazil
Nahri Moreano, Federal University of Mato Grosso do Sul, Brazil

The recent and astonishing advances in Molecular Biology, which led to the sequencing of an unprecedented number of genomes, including the human, would not have been possible without the help of Bioinformatics. Bioinformatics can be defined as a research area where computational tools and algorithms are developed to help biologists in the task of understanding the organisms. Some Bioinformatics applications, such as pairwise and sequence-profile comparison, require a huge amount of computing power and, therefore, are excellent candidates to run in FPGA platforms. This chapter discusses in detail several recent proposals on FPGA-based accelerators for these two Bioinformatics applications, highlighting the similarities and differences among them. At the end of the chapter, research tendencies and open questions are presented.

Chapter 13

Osman Hasan, National University of Science and Technology (NUST), Pakistan
Sofiène Tahar, Concordia University, Canada

Real-time systems usually involve a subtle interaction of a number of distributed components and have a high degree of parallelism, which makes their performance analysis quite complex. Thus, traditional techniques, such as simulation, or state-based formal methods usually fail to produce reasonable results. The main limitation of these approaches may be overcome by conducting the performance analysis of real-time systems using higher-order-logic theorem proving. This chapter is mainly oriented towards this emerging trend and it provides the details about analyzing both functional and performance related properties of real-time systems using a higher-order-logic theorem prover (HOL). For illustration purposes, the Stop-and-Wait protocol, which is a classical example of real-time systems, has been considered as a case-study.

Chapter 14

Olfa Mosbahi, Nancy University, France & Martin Luther University, Germany
Mohamed Khalgui, Xidian University, China

This chapter deals with the use of two verification approaches: theorem proving and model checking. We The authors focus on the Event-B method by using its associated theorem proving tool (Click_n_Prove), and on the language TLA+ by using its model checker TLC. By considering the limitation of the Event-B method to invariance properties, we the authors propose to apply the language TLA+ to verify liveness properties on a software behavior. We The authors extend first the expressivity and the semantics of a B model (called temporal B model) to deal with the specification of fairness and eventuality properties. Second, we they give transformation rules from a temporal B model into a TLA+ module. We The authors present in particular, our their prototype system called B2TLA+, that we they have developed to support this transformation; then we they can verify these properties thanks to the model checker TLC on finite state systems. For the verification of infinite-state systems, we they propose the use of the predicate diagrams. We The authors illustrate our their approach on a case study of a parcel sorting system.

Chapter 15

Chunfu Zhong, Xidian University, People's Republic of China
Zhiwu Li, Xidian University, People's Republic of China

In flexible manufacturing systems, deadlocks usually occur due to the limited resources. To cope with deadlock problems, Petri nets are widely used to model these systems. This chapter focuses on deadlock prevention for flexible manufacturing systems that are modeled with S4R nets, a subclass of generalized Petri nets. The analysis of S4R leads us to derive an iterative deadlock prevention approach. At each iteration step, a non-max-controlled siphon is derived by solving a mixed integer linear programming. A monitor is constructed for the siphon such that it is max-controlled. Finally, a liveness-enforcing Petri net supervisor can be derived without enumerating all the strict minimal siphons.

Chapter 16

Abderrazak Jemai, National Institute of Applied Science and Technology, Tunisia

This chapter provides a comparative study between recent operating systems, designed for embedded systems. Our study focuses, in particular, on systems designed for Multiprocessors implementations called MPSoC. An OS can be seen as abstract layer or an interface between the embedded application and the underlying hardware. In this chapter, we give a comparative study of main operating systems used in embedded systems. The originality of this chapter is that we specially focus on the OS ability to be optimized to support and manage a multiprocessor architecture. A multiprocessor system-on-chip is software driven and mastering the development complexity of the software part of MPSoC, is the key to reduce developing time factor. This opportunity could be reached through the use of a document giving a detailed description and analysis for criteria related to MPSoC. The wide diversity of existing operating systems, the huge complexity to develop an application specific or a general purpose, and the aggressive evolution of embedded systems makes the development of such a system a so difficult task. These considerations lead to the realization that a work that provides guidance for the MPSoC designers will be very beneficial for these communities.

Chapter 17

The chapter presents a specification technique borrowing features from two classes of specification methods, formal and semi-formal ones. Each of the above methods have been proved to be useful in the development of real-time and critical systems and widely reported in different papers (Bruel, 1996; Clarke & Wing, 1996; Cohen, 1994; Fitzgerald & Larsen, 1994; Ghezzi, Mandrioli & Morzenti, 1990). Formal methods are based on mathematical notations and axiomatic which induce verification and validation. Semi-formal methods are, in the other hand, graphic, structural and uer-friendly. Each method is applied on a suitable case study, that we regret some missing features we could find in the other class. This remark has motivated our work. We are interested in the integration of formal and semi-formal methods in order to lay out a specification approach which combines the advantages of these two classes of methods. The proposed technique is based on the integration of the semi-formal method STATEMATE (Harel, 1997; Harel, 1987) and the temporal logic FNLOG (Sowmya & Ramesh, 1997). This choice is justified by the fact that FNLOG is formal, deals with quantitative temporal properties and that these two approaches have a compatibility which simplifies their integration (Sowmya & Ramesh, 1997). The proposed integration approach uses the notations of STATEMATE and FNLOG, defines various transformation rules of a STATEMATE specification towards FNLOG and extends the axiomatics of the temporal logic FNLOG by new lemmas to deal with duration properties. The paper chapter presents the various steps of our integration approach, the proposed extentions and illustrates it over a case of critical real-time systems : the gas burner system (Ravn, Rishel & Hansen, 1993).

Chapter 18

The research presented in this chapter deals with the design and implementation of Real-Time (RT) control systems applying advanced Field Programmable Gate Array (FPGAs). The chapter proposes a promising flexible architecture that uses RT Operating System (RTOS) and ready-to-use Intellectual Properties (IPs). The authors detail an approach that uses software closed control loop function blocks (FB), running on embedded processor cores. These FBs implement the different control drive sub-modules into RTOS tasks of the execution environment, where each task has to be executed under well defined conditions. Two RTOSes are evaluated: μC-OS/II and Xilkernel. The FPGA embedded processor cores are combined with reconfigurable logic and dedicated resources on the FPGA. This System-on-Chip (SoC) has been applied to electric motors drive. A comparative analysis, in terms of speed and cost, is carried-out between various hardware/software FPGA-based architectures, in order to enhance flexibility without sacrificing performance and increasing cost. Case studies results validate successfully the feasibility and the efficiency of the flexible approach for new and more complex control algorithms. The performance and flexibility of FPGA-based motor controllers are enhanced with the reliability and modularity of the introduced RTOS support.

Chapter 19
    Julien Delange, TELECOM ParisTech, France
    Laurent Pautet, TELECOM ParisTech, France
    Fabrice Kordon, Université P. & M. Curie, France

Aircraft manufacturers have been moving toward the Integrated Modular Avionics (IMA) approach to reduce the number of dedicated boxes in the aircraft. Standards such as as DO178B or ARINC 653 must be followed during design, configuration or certification of IMA systems. Productivity and costs must also be improved while preserving conformance to standards. For instance, development process of avionics systems involves several system representations and representation transformations are done manually. Moreover, the complexity of new generation of safety-critical systems has also increased the complexity of their development. The authors present their component-based approach which relies on an appropriate modeling language (AADL) combined with modeling patterns to represent, configure and deploy an IMA system. It reduces costs by detecting errors earlier and prevents specifications revisions. Their code generator reduces memory footprint and improves code coverage. One last benefit is a possible automatic certification.

Chapter 20
    Goh Kiah Mok, Singapore Institute of Manufacturing Technology, Singapore
    Benny Tjahjono, Cranfield University, UK
    Ding Wei, Penn State University, USA

Developing an embedded software solution can be time consuming and challenging especially for non-software trained engineers. This is because traditionally, embedded software is programmed manually in proprietary computer languages such as C, C++, Java and assembly languages, meaning that the developers have to be familiar with at least one of these languages. In addition, most of the embedded software design environments do not cater for both microprocessors-based and Field Programmable

Gate Array (FPGA) based embedded computing environments, making the development process even more difficult without the assistance of a common method. This paper chapter proposes a design of a new embedded system code generator framework which is based on the International Electrotechnical Commission (IEC) 61499 Function Block, XML and EBNF. Along with this code generator, an Iterative Knowledge Based Code Generator (IKBCG) is presented to improve the accuracy of the target codes.

Preface

Nowadays, embedded control systems are widely used in many industrial sectors such as consumer electronics like personal digital assistants, mp3 and DVD players, videogame consoles, digital cameras, fax and printers, GPS receivers, and mobile phones. In addition, many household devices such as washing machines, intelligent alarms, dishwashers, microwave ovens, new televisions are based on embedded control systems for control and surveillance. In Transport, systems from flight, maritime to automobiles, motorcycles and bikes increasingly use embedded systems especially for safety. Future electric vehicles are increasingly using embedded software to maximize efficiency and reduce pollution. Telecommunication systems employ also embedded systems from telephone switches to mobile phones at the end-user. Moreover, ventilating, heating and air conditioning systems use networked thermostats to control temperature that can change by time of day and season. Many automated systems use wired- and wireless-networking that can be used to control lights, security, surveillance, climate etc., all of which use embedded control devices for sensing and controlling. Medical equipments are increasingly using today more and more embedded control systems for vital signs monitoring, electronic stethoscopes for amplifying sounds, and various medical imaging for non-invasive internal inspections.

Although embedded control systems are widely used anywhere, their development process is not easy in several cases because a failure can be critical for the safety of human beings (e.g. air and railway traffic control, nuclear plant control, aircraft and car control). They classically should satisfy according to user requirements, functional and temporal properties, but their time to market should be shorter and shorter than ever. A new generation of these systems is addressing new criteria as flexibility and agility. To reduce their cost, these systems should be changed and adapted to their environment without disturbances. Several interesting academic and industrial research works have been made last years to develop reconfigurable embedded control systems. We distinguish in these works two reconfiguration policies: static and dynamic reconfigurations such that static reconfigurations are applied off-line to apply changes before the system cold start, whereas dynamic reconfigurations are dynamically applied at run-time. Two cases exist in the last policy: manual reconfigurations applied by users and automatic reconfigurations applied by Intelligent Agents. The system is modeled therefore in the functional level by different networks of software components such that only one network should be executed when a well-defined reconfiguration scenario is manually-automatically or statically applied. In the operational level, each network is assumed as a set of OS tasks under real-time constraints in some cases. We are interested in this book in the development of reconfigurable embedded control systems: from modeling to final deployment.

Chapter 1 deals with reconfigurable embedded control systems following component-based technologies and/or Architecture Description Languages. The author defines Control Components as software units to support control tasks of the system which is assumed to be a network of components with precedence constraints. An agent-based architecture is proposed to handle automatic reconfigurations under well-defined conditions by creating, deleting or updating components to bring the whole system into safe and optimal behaviors. To cover all reconfiguration forms, the agent is modeled by nested state machines such that states correspond to other state machines. Several complex networks can implement the system where each one is executed at a given time when a corresponding reconfiguration scenario is automatically applied by the agent. To check the correctness of each one of them, a refinement-based approach is defined to automatically specify feasible Control Components in several steps according to NCES. The model checker SESA is automatically applied in each step to verify deadlock properties of new generated components, and is manually used to verify CTL-based properties according to user requirements. The chapter implements the reconfiguration agent by three modules that allow interpretations of environment evolutions, decisions of useful reconfiguration scenarios and finally their applications.

Embedded and Real-Time Systems (ERTS) have continued to expand at a vigorous rate. Designers of ERTS systems are continually challenged to provide new capabilities that can meet the expanding requirements and increased computational needs of each new proposed application, but at a decreasing price/performance ratio. Conventional solutions using general purpose processors or custom ASICs are less and less able to satisfy the contradictory requirements in performance, flexibility, power, development time, and cost. Chapter 2 introduces an approach to generate semi-custom platforms driven from a traditional multithreaded programming model of an embedded real-time system. This approach offers the advantage of achieving productivity levels close to those associated with software by using an established programming model, but with a performance level close to custom hardware through the use of a flexible hardware platform capable of adapting to specialized application requirements. The authors discuss the underlying concepts, requirements and advantages of multithreading in the context of reconfigurable hardware, and present two approaches which provide multithreading support to hardware and software components at the operating system level.

Future manufacturing is envisioned to be highly flexible and adaptable. New technologies for efficient engineering of reconfigurable systems and their adaptations are preconditions for this vision. Without such solutions, engineering adaptations of Industrial Process Measurement and Control Systems (IPMCS) will exceed the costs of engineered systems by far and the reuse of equipment will become inefficient. Especially the reconfiguration of control applications is not sufficiently solved by state-of-the-art technology. Chapter 3 gives an overview of the use of reconfiguration applications for zero-downtime system reconfiguration of control applications on basis of the standard IEC 61499 which provides a reference model for distributed and reconfigurable control systems. A new approach for the reconfiguration of IEC 61499 based control application and the corresponding modeling is discussed. This new method significantly increases engineering efficiency and reuse in component-based IPMCS.

Numerous research efforts in reconfigurable embedded processors have shown that augmenting a CPU core with a coarse-grained reconfigurable array for application-specific hardware acceleration can greatly increase performance and energy-efficiency. The traditional execution model for such reconfigurable co-processors however requires the accelerated function to fit onto the reconfigurable array as a whole, which restricts the applicability to rather small functions. Chapter 4 studies hardware virtualization approaches that overcome this restriction by leveraging dynamic reconfiguration. It presents two different hardware virtualization methods, virtualized execution and temporal partitioning, and introduces the Zippy reconfigurable processor architecture that has been designed with specific hardware virtualization support. Further, the authors outline the corresponding hardware and software tool flows. Finally, they demonstrate the potential provided by hardware virtualization with two case studies and discuss directions for future research.

Reconfigurable embedded computing opens many interesting possibilities for efficiency and reliability improvement. Still, it is necessary to verify whether the reconfigurable embedded computer system fulfills its timing requirements. Purely *static worst-case execution time* (WCET) analysis is not the best choice for verifying the timing behavior of reconfigurable embedded computer systems, as frequent re-modeling of different hardware configurations is not practicable. Chapter 5 describes *measurement-based timing analysis* as an approach that is better applicable for reconfigurable applications. Measurement-based timing analysis is a hybrid approach that combines static program analysis techniques, borrowed from static WCET analysis, with empirical learning of the application's timing behavior by performing systematic measurements. But even the MBTA approach is challenged by the reconfigurable computing paradigm by the need for adequate coverage of the reconfigurable fabric.

Chapter 6 presents reconfigurable embedded systems by looking closely at three different but inter-related aspects: design tools, methodologies and architectures, paying special attention at reconfigurable interconnections. The authors start by having a closer look at the evolution of the latest design strategies, tools and methodologies facing challenges and user requirements. Reconfigurable interconnections will be analyzed, examining topologies, drawbacks, and capabilities, specially focusing on the reconfiguration potential. From the application point of view, the authors resume with a case study regarding embedded systems, a Software-Defined Radio application highlighting the most significant technical features and design choices.

Chapter 7 deals with the problem of reconfiguring embedded real-time systems. Such reconfiguration can be decided either off-line to determine if a given application can be run on a different platform, while preserving the timeliness constraints imposed by the application, or on-line, where a reconfiguration should be done to adapt the system to the context of execution or to handle hardware or software faults. The task model considered in this chapter is the classical sporadic task model defined by a Worst Case Execution Time (WCET), a minimum inter-arrival time (also denoted the minimum Period) and a late termination deadline. The authors consider two preemptive scheduling strategies: Fixed Priority highest priority first (FP) and Earliest Deadline First (EDF). They propose a sensitivity analysis to handle reconfiguration issues. Sensitivity analysis aims at determining acceptable deviations from the specifications of a problem due to evolutions in system characteristics (reconfiguration or performance tuning). The chapter presents a state of the art for sensitivity analysis in the case of WCETs, Periods and Deadlines reconfigurations and study to what extent sensitivity analysis can be used to decide on the possibility of reconfiguring a system.

The continuous increase in the degree of design complexity in the design of modern digital hardware systems, come into being due to the increasing demand of more and more functionality under strict design constraints, has led to designers to try to alleviate this complexity by increasing the level of abstraction when describing the functionality of a system. Recent proposals in the field of Electronic Design Automation intend to use common programming languages, like C, C++, and Java, or dialects derived from them, to describe the behavior of a digital hardware system and then generate a lower-level representation, closer to the hardware implementation platform, from such description. This phenomenon led us to firmly believe that the process of describing the functionality of a digital circuit resembles more and more the process of developing software; and, thus, it is possible to experiment with the application of the latest trends in software engineering, like the Model-Driven Engineering (MDE) paradigm, to design digital hardware systems. Chapter 8 describes the basic principles of MDE, and provides some hints about the kind of languages and transformation tools needed to design algorithms in the domain of digital control that could be transformed into a digital circuit. The authors intend to open doors and encourage the research on the design of digital control systems at higher levels of abstraction and their implementations in different kinds of hardware platforms, including reconfigurable devices.

Massive parallel processing systems, particularly Single Instruction Multiple Data Architectures, play a crucial role in the field of data intensive parallel applications. One of the primary goals in using these systems is their scalability and their linear increase in processing power by increasing the number of processing units. However, communication networks are the big challenging issue facing researchers. One of the most important networks on chip for parallel systems are the multistage interconnection networks. Chapter 9 proposes a design methodology of multistage interconnection networks for massively parallel systems on chip. The framework covers the design step from algorithm level to RTL. The authors first develop a functional formalization of MIN-based on-chip network at a high level of abstraction. The specification and the validation of the model have been defined in the logic of ACL2 proving system. The main objective in this step is to provide a formal description of the network that integrates architectural parameters which have a huge impact on design costs. After validating the functional model, step 2 consists in the design and the implementation of the Delta multistage networks on chip dedicated to parallel multi-cores architectures on reconfigurable platforms FPGA. In the last step, an evaluation methodology based on performance and cost metrics is proposed to evaluate different topologies of dynamic network through data parallel applications with different number of cores. The authors also show in the proposed framework that multistage interconnection networks are cost-effective high performance networks for parallel SOCs.

Chapter 10 deals with distributed multi-agent reconfigurable embedded control systems following the component-based International Industrial Standard IEC61499 in which a Function Block (abbreviated by FB) is an event-triggered software component owning data and a control application is a distributed network of Function Blocks that have classically to satisfy functional and to meet temporal properties described in user requirements. The authors define a new reconfiguration semantic where a crucial criterion to consider is the automatic improvement of the system's performance at run-time, in addition to its protection when hardware faults occur. To handle all possible cases in industry, the authors classify thereafter the reconfiguration scenarios into three forms before they define an architecture of reconfigurable multi-agent systems where a Reconfiguration Agent is affected to each device of the execution environment to apply local reconfigurations, and a Coordination Agent is proposed for any coordination between devices in order to guarantee safe and adequate distributed reconfigurations. A Communication Protocol is proposed to handle any coordination between agents by using well-defined Coordination Matrices. The authors specify both the reconfiguration agents to be modeled by nested state machines, and the Coordination Agent according to the formalism Net Condition/Event Systems (Abbreviated by NCES) which is an extension of Petri nets. To verify the whole architecture, the model checker SESA is applied in each device to verify functional and temporal properties described in the temporal logic"Computation Tree Logic", but any coordination between devices should also be checked by verifying that whenever a reconfiguration is applied in a device, the Coordination Agent and other concerned devices should react as described in user requirements.

The performances of System on Chip (SoC) and the Field Programmable Gate Array (FPGA) particularly, are increasing continually. Due to the growing complexity of modern embedded control systems, the need of more performance digital devices is evident. Recent FPGA technology makes it possible to include processor cores into the FPGA chip, which ensures more flexibility for digital controllers. Indeed, greater functionality of hardware and system software, Real-Time (RT) platforms and distributed subsystems are demanded. In Chapter 11, design concept of FPGA based controller with Hardware/Software (Hw/Sw) co-design is proposed. It is applied for electrical machine drives. There are discussed different MultiProcessor SoC (MPSoC) architectures with Hw peripherals for the implementation on FPGA-based embedded processor cores. Hw accelerators are considered in the design to enhance the controller speed performance and reduce power consumption. Test and validation of this control system are performed on RT motor emulator implemented on the same FPGA. Experimental results, carried on a real prototyping platform, are given in order to analyze the performance and efficiency of discussed architecture designs helping to support hard RT constraints.

The recent and astonishing advances in Molecular Biology, which led to the sequencing of an unprecedented number of genomes, including the human, would not have been possible without the help of Bioinformatics. Bioinformatics can be defined as a research area where computational tools and algorithms are developed to help biologists in the task of understanding the organisms. Some Bioinformatics applications, such as pairwise and sequence-profile comparison, require a huge amount of computing power and, therefore, are excellent candidates to run in FPGA platforms. Chapter 12 discusses in detail several recent proposals on FPGA-based accelerators for these two Bioinformatics applications, highlighting the similarities and differences among them. At the end of the chapter, research tendencies and open questions are presented.

Real-time systems usually involve a subtle interaction of a number of distributed components and have a high degree of parallelism, which makes their performance analysis quite complex. Thus, traditional techniques, such as simulation, or state-based formal methods usually fail to produce reasonable results. The main limitation of these approaches may be overcome by conducting the performance analysis of real-time systems using higher-order-logic theorem proving. Chapter 13 is mainly oriented towards this emerging trend and provides the details about analyzing both functional and performance related properties of real-time systems using a higher-order-logic theorem prover (HOL). For illustration purposes, the Stop-and-Wait protocol, which is a classical example of real-time systems, has been considered as a case-study.

Chapter 14 deals with the use of two verification approaches: theorem proving and model checking. The authors focus on the Event-B method by using its associated theorem proving tool (Click_n_Prove), and on the language TLA+ by using its model checker TLC. By considering the limitation of the Event-B method to invariance properties, the authors propose to apply the language TLA+ to verify liveness properties on a software behavior. They extend first the expressivity and the semantics of a B model (called temporal B model) to deal with the specification of fairness and eventuality properties. Second, they give transformation rules from a temporal B model into a TLA+ module. The chapter presents in particular, a prototype system called B2TLA+ that supports this transformation; then these properties can be verified thanks to the model checker TLC on finite state systems. For the verification of infinite-state systems, the authors propose the use of the predicate diagrams.

In flexible manufacturing systems, deadlocks usually occur due to limited resources. To cope with deadlock problems, Petri nets are widely used to model these systems. The chapter 15 focuses on deadlock prevention for flexible manufacturing systems that are modeled with S^4R nets, a subclass of generalized Petri nets. The analysis of S^4R leads us to derive an iterative deadlock prevention approach. At each iteration step, a non-max-controlled siphon is derived by solving a mixed integer linear programming.

A monitor is constructed for the siphon such that it is max-controlled. Finally, a liveness-enforcing Petri net supervisor can be derived without enumerating all the strict minimal siphons.

Chapter 16 provides a comparative study between recent operating systems, designed for embedded systems. The study focuses, in particular, on systems designed for Multiprocessors implementations called MPSoC. An OS can be seen as abstract layer or an interface between the embedded application and the underlying hardware. In this chapter, the authors give a comparative study of main operating systems used in embedded systems. The originality of this chapter is that it specially focuses on the OS ability to be optimized to support and manage a multiprocessor architecture. A multiprocessor system-on-chip is software driven and mastering the development complexity of the software part of MPSoC, is the key to reduce developing time factor. This opportunity could be reached through the use of a document giving a detailed description and analysis for criteria related to MPSoC. The wide diversity of existing operating systems, the huge complexity to develop an application specific or a general purpose, and the aggressive evolution of embedded systems makes the development of such a system a so difficult task. These considerations lead to the realization that a work that provides guidance for the MPSoC designers will be very beneficial for these communities.

Chapter 17 presents a specification technique borrowing features from two classes of specification methods, formal and semi-formal ones. Each of the above methods have been proved to be useful in the development of real-time and critical systems and widely reported in different papers. Formal methods are based on mathematical notations and axiomatic which induce verification and validation. Semi-formal methods are, in the other hand, graphic, structural and uer-friendly. Each method is applied on a suitable case study, that the author regrets some missing features she could find in the other class. This remark has motivated the work. The chapter is interested in the integration of formal and semi-formal methods in order to lay out a specification approach which combines the advantages of theses two classes of methods. The proposed technique is based on the integration of the semi-formal method STATEMATE and the temporal logic FNLOG. This choice is justified by the fact that FNLOG is formal, deals with quantitative temporal properties and that these two approaches have a compatibility which simplifies their integration. The proposed integration approach uses the notations of STATEMATE and FNLOG, defines various transformation rules of a STATEMATE specification towards FNLOG and extends the axiomatics of the temporal logic FNLOG by new lemmas to deal with duration properties. The chapter presents the various steps of the integration approach, the proposed extensions and illustrates it over a case of critical real-time systems : the gas burner system.

The research presented in Chapter 18 deals with the design and implementation of Real-Time (RT) control systems applying advanced Field Programmable Gate Array (FPGAs). The chapter proposes a promising flexible architecture that uses RT Operating System (RTOS) and ready-to-use Intellectual Properties (IPs). The authors detail an approach that uses software closed control loop function blocks (FB), running on embedded processor cores. These FBs implement the different control drive sub-modules into RTOS tasks of the execution environment, where each task has to be executed under well defined conditions. Two RTOSes are evaluated: μC-OS/II and Xilkernel. The FPGA embedded processor cores are combined with reconfigurable logic and dedicated resources on the FPGA. This System-on-Chip (SoC) has been applied to electric motors drive. A comparative analysis, in terms of speed and cost, is carried-out between various hardware/software FPGA-based architectures, in order to enhance flexibility without sacrificing performance and increasing cost. Case studies results validate successfully the feasibility and the efficiency of the flexible approach for new and more complex control algorithms.

The performance and flexibility of FPGA-based motor controllers are enhanced with the reliability and modularity of the introduced RTOS support.

Aircraft manufacturers have been moving toward the Integrated Modular Avionics (IMA) approach to reduce the number of dedicated boxes in the aircraft. Standards such as as DO178B or ARINC 653 must be followed during design, configuration or certification of IMA systems. Productivity and costs must also be improved while preserving conformance to standards. For instance, development process of avionics systems involves several system representations and representation transformations are done manually. Moreover, the complexity of new generation of safety-critical systems has also increased the complexity of their development. Chapter 19 presents a component-based approach which relies on an appropriate modeling language (AADL) combined with modeling patterns to represent, configure and deploy an IMA system. It reduces costs by detecting errors earlier and prevents specifications revisions. The proposed code generator reduces memory footprint and improves code coverage. One last benefit is a possible automatic certification.

Finally, developing an embedded software solution can be time consuming and challenging especially for non-software trained engineers. This is because traditionally, embedded software is programmed manually in proprietary computer languages such as C, C++, Java and assembly languages, meaning that the developers have to be familiar with at least one of these languages. In addition, most of the embedded software design environments do not cater for both microprocessors-based and Field Programmable Gate Array (FPGA) based embedded computing environments, making the development process even more difficult without the assistance of a common method. The chapter 20 proposes a design of a new embedded system code generator framework which is based on the International Electrotechnical Commission (IEC) 61499 Function Block, XML and EBNF. Along with this code generator, an Iterative Knowledge Based Code Generator (IKBCG) is presented to improve the accuracy of the target codes.

These different chapters, prepared in different known research laboratories, address many interesting topics that can be considered in Industry. We hope that the scientific and technical contributions of the book will satisfy researchers, and will be useful for new generations of embedded control systems.

Mohamed Khalgui
Xidian University, China

Hans-Michael Hanisch
Martin Luther University, Germany

xxiv

Acknowledgment

We want to thank IGI Global that provides us the opportunity to publish this scientific and technical book, we thank in particular Mr. Joel Gamon for patience, valuable and useful services to finish this work. We want also to thank all the authors of chapters for their collaborations and interesting contributions.

We are very grateful also to Martin Luther University and Alexander Von Humboldt Foundation in Germany for their technical and financial supports and encouragements. We thank also all the members of the Research Laboratory on Automation Technology of Prof. Dr. Hans-Michael Hanisch for their encouragements, collaborations and services.

- **Technical Supporter:** Martin Luther University, Germany,
- **Financial Supporter:** Alexander Von Humboldt Foundation – Germany.

The book was made between February 2009 and December 2010, officially in Halle Germany.

Mohamed Khalgui
Xidian University, China

Hans-Michael Hanisch
Martin Luther University, Germany

Chapter 1
Multi–Agent Reconfigurable Embedded Systems:
From Modelling to Implementation

Mohamed Khalgui
Xidian University, China

ABSTRACT

The chapter deals with reconfigurable embedded control systems following component-based technologies and/or Architecture Description Languages used today in industry. The author defines Control Components as software units to support control tasks of the system which is assumed to be a network of components with precedence constraints. The author defines an agent-based architecture to handle automatic reconfigurations under well-defined conditions by creating, deleting or updating components to bring the whole system into safe and optimal behaviors. To cover all reconfiguration forms, the agent is modelled by nested state machines such that states correspond to other state machines. Several complex networks can implement the system where each one is executed at a given time when a corresponding reconfiguration scenario is automatically applied by the agent. To check the correctness of each one of them, we apply in several steps a refinement-based approach that automatically specifies feasible Control Components according to NCES. The model checker SESA is automatically applied in each step to verify deadlock properties of new generated components, and it is manually used to verify CTL-based properties according to user requirements. The author implements the reconfiguration agent by three modules that allow interpretations of environment evolutions, decisions of useful reconfiguration scenarios and finally their applications. Two Industrial Benchmark Production Systems FESTO and EnAS available in the author's research laboratory are applied to explain the paper contribution.

DOI: 10.4018/978-1-60960-086-0.ch001

INTRODUCTION

The development of safe and critical embedded control systems is not an easy activity because they have classically to satisfy functional and to meet temporal properties defined in user requirements, in addition to their time to market that should be more and more shorter than ever (Goessler, Graf, Majster-Cederbaum, Martens, & Sifakis, 2007; Lee & Villasenor, 2009; Acharya & Mahapatra, 2008; Song, Kim & Karray, 2008; Tsui, Masmoudi, Karray, Song & Masmoudi, 2008; Pagilla, Dwivedula & Siraskar, 2007). To meet all these constraints, different component-based technologies (Crnkovic & Larsson, 2002) and Architecture Description Languages (abbr. ADL) (Dissaux, Filali Amine, Michel, & Vernadat, 2005) have been proposed last years to reuse already developed components and to follow modular approaches for specification and verification. The Architecture Description Languages define components as independent software units of computations to be connected by well-defined connectors (McKenzie, Petty, & Xu, 2004). ADL examples include Darwin, Aesop, Unicon, Wright, Rapide, Acme, AADL, UML,..etc (Dissaux, Filali Amine, Michel, & Vernadat, 2005). Among all industrial technologies, the International Standard IEC61499 (IEC61499-1, 2003; Khalgui & Hanisch, 2008) is a Component-based technology extending the previous well-known Standard IEC61131 which used for developments of Centralized Programmable Logic Controllers (IEC61131, 1993). This technology defines a Function Block as an event triggered component owning data and composed of an interface as well as an implementation. The interface contains data/event inputs and outputs for external interactions with the environment. Events are responsible for activations of the block while data contain valued information. The implementation consists of internal data and algorithms to implement block's functionalities. Today in academia and also in industry, rich books have been written (Vyatkin, 2007), several research

works have been made (Khalgui & Thramboulidis, 2008; Khalgui, Rebeuf, & Simonot-Lion, 2007; Khalgui & Rebeuf, 2008), useful tools have been developed (Rockwell, 2006) and various manufacturing platforms are completely deployed according to this technology: (i) a footwear factory that we simulated in (Hanisch, Khalgui & Carpanzano, 2008) is developed in Italy while following the Function Block technology, (ii) two Benchmark Production Systems FESTO and EnAS are developed according to this standard in our research laboratory at Martin Luther University in Germany. We present in Figure 1 a simple example of an IEC61499 control application named Temperature Regulator to regulate the temperature of an oven in a factory (detailed descriptions are available in (Lewis, 2002)). This regulator is composed of two interface Function Blocks (Input1 and Output1) and a regulation block PID1 which reads data from a sensor before regulations of the temperature (by applying the well-known PID algorithm (Ben Jmaa Derbel, 2007),) and activations of the corresponding actuator.

The Carnegie Mellon university proposes also its own concept of components named Port Based Objects to develop industrial control applications in robotics (Stewart, Volpe & Khosla, 1997). A PBO component is a particular case of a Function Block by containing three different interfaces as well as an implementation. The main first interface contains data inputs and outputs for external interactions with other components. A second parameterization interface is used to update internal data and algorithms. Finally, a third interface is used for interactions with physical processes. We present in Figure 2 Speed Regulator as a simple example of PBO components to regulate the speed of a vehicle. The component cyclic periodically sends desired values to Regulate which regulates measured values from Interface (Stewart, Volpe & Khosla, 1997). We note finally that a rich library is available today to develop applications following this industrial technology (Stewart, Volpe & Khosla, 1997).

Figure 1. A FB Component: Temperature Regulator

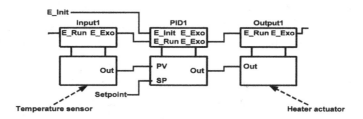

Figure 2. A PBO Component: Speed Regulator

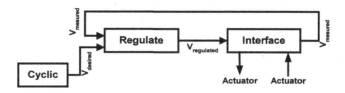

Figure 3. A Rubus Component: BrakeSystem

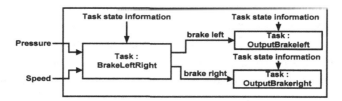

The Arcticus Systems propose also another component model called "Rubus" which is characterized by an implementation and an interface (Arcticus, 2009). The interface classically defines data inputs and outputs for external interactions with the environment, and the implementation is a set of algorithms to provide component's functionalities. In this rich technology, functional and temporal properties of components can be assumed. We present in Figure 3 BrakeSystem as a simple example of Rubus components to use in a vehicle. The component BrakeLeftRight allows to brake left or right by considering the pressure and also the speed of the vehicle. Detailed descriptions of this example are available in (Crnkovic & Larsson, 2002).

The Philips company proposes also its own concept of component called Koala (Van Ommer-

ing, 2002) which is classically composed of interfaces and an implementation. Two different interfaces exist, provided interfaces and required interfaces. The first offer services of the component for the environment, while the second offer services from the environment for the component. The implementation is classically composed of algorithms to support component's functionalities. We note that (Philips, 2009) provides a Koala compiler that reads Koala descriptions and generates C codes and header files. The Pecos international project proposes also a particular model of components to develop real-time embedded systems (Pecos-project, 2006) where a component is classically characterized by an interface and an implementation. The interface classically defines data inputs and outputs for external interactions with the environment. A control application is then a composition of components thanks to well-defined connectors. We note finally that (Pecos-project, 2006) defines a component run-time environment allowing the development of control systems.

Although these different technologies are rich and very useful in industry, we want in our research work to be independent of any one of them for the development of embedded control systems. We define the general concept of Control Components as software units to be composed of interfaces for external interactions and implementations to support their functionalities. A Control Component in this chapter can be a Function Block according to the Standard IEC61499, a Koala component according to the Koala technology, a software component according to any ADL..., etc. It checks and interprets the Environment's evolution (i.e. user new commands, evolution of corresponding physical processes or execution of other previous components) by reading data from sensors before any possible reaction by activating corresponding actuators in the plant which is assumed in this chapter to be composed of different physical processes under precedence constraints that define the production order. This plant is formalized by sets of sensors and actuators under precedence constraints to control corresponding physical processes.

The new generation of industrial control systems is addressing new criteria as flexibility and agility. To reduce their cost, these systems should be changed and adapted to their environment without disturbances. Several interesting academic and industrial research works have been made last years to develop reconfigurable control systems (Gehin & Staroswiecki, 2008; Zhuo & Prasanna, 2008; Lysne, Montanana, Flich, Duato, Pinkston & Skeie, 2008; Jigang, Srikanthan & Wang, 2007; Ahmadinia, Bobda, Fekete, Teich & Van Der Veen, 2007; Takahashi, Yamaguchi, Sekiyama & Fukuda, 2009; Minghui, Shugen, Bin & Yuechao, 2009; Tang, Weng, Dong & Yan, 2009). We distinguish in these works two recon-

figuration policies: static and dynamic policies where static reconfigurations are applied off-line to apply changes before any system cold start (Angelov, Sierszecki & Marian, 2005), whereas dynamic reconfigurations are applied dynamically at run-time. Two cases exist in the last policy: manual reconfigurations applied by users (Rooker, Sunder, Strasser, Zoitl, Hummer & Ebenhofer, 2007). and automatic reconfigurations applied by intelligent agents (Al-Safi, & Vyatkin, 2007). We are interested in this research work in automatic reconfigurations of multi-agent embedded control system that can be implemented by different complex networks of Control Components such that only one is executed at a given time when a corresponding reconfiguration scenario is automatically applied at run-time under well-defined conditions. The agent checks the environment's evolution and considers user requirements before applying reconfigurations by creating, deleting or updating Control Components to bring the whole control system into optimal and safe behaviors. It is composed of three units: Architecture Unit that creates/removes components, Control Unit that updates composition of components or their internal behaviors and Data Unit that applies light reconfigurations by updating data. We model the agent by nested state machines where states correspond to other machines in order to cover all possible forms of reconfigurations. An approach for the specification and verification of reconfiguration agents is proposed in a second chapter of this book. We specify in the current chapter the different networks of Control Components that correspond to different reconfiguration scenarios to be automatically applied by the agent. We want in this case to apply a model checking for automatic and manual verifications of functional properties of such complex networks (Hsiung, Chen & Lin, 2007). By considering that this verification is difficult to do in complex cases like our reconfigurable benchmark embedded systems FESTO and EnAS, we apply in this work a refinement-based technique that automatically models and checks in several steps each network of components according to the formalism Net Condition/Event Systems (Rausch & Hanisch, 1995) which is an extension of Petri nets (Li, Zhou & Jeng, 2008; Hu, & Li, 2009; Tan, Fan & Zhou, 2009). An abstract model of the network is defined in the first step according to this formalism. It is automatically refined step by step thereafter to automatically generate in each step NCES-based models of Control Components to be automatically checked by the model checker SESA in order to verify deadlock properties. We manually verify in addition functional properties to be described according to the temporal logic "Computation Tree Logic" (abbr. CTL) in order to check the correct behavior of the new generated components in each step (Roch, 2000; Roch, 2000). If the refinement-based specification and verification of Control Components is feasible in different steps, Then the correctness of their network is deduced. The safety of the whole reconfigurable embedded system is confirmed if all networks of Control Components are correct. Once the whole reconfigurable system is specified and checked, the next step to be addressed is the implementation of the agent which is composed of three modules: (i) Interpreter, (ii) Reconfiguration Engine, (iii) Converter. The first interprets the environment's evolution by detecting hardware problems or by checking parameters that allow improvements of the system's performances into optimal states. It forwards any useful information to the Reconfiguration Engine which is the main agent module that defines new scenarios to be applied according to such environment's evolution. The engine contains the three reconfiguration units: (i) Architecture unit, (ii) Control unit, (iii) Data unit. Once a scenario is fixed by the engine, the third module Converter sends desired reconfiguration commands in forms of XML code blocks to well-defined Management Control Components that apply such scenario by exploiting an available library to create, change and delete system components. To explain the

different contributions of the paper, the systems FESTO and EnAS are taken in the following as running examples.

In the next Section, we present a background to describe FESTO and EnAS before we present the formalism Net Condition/Event Systems and the temporal logic "Computation Tree Logic". We formalize the plant in Section 3 before we propose the concept of Control Components in Section 4, and we present the agent architecture in Section 5. We propose in Section 6 the refinement-based approach to specify and verify different networks of Control Components that correspond to different reconfiguration scenarios. We propose in Section 7 an XML-based implementation of the reconfiguration agent and we present finally in Section 8 the conclusion and our future work.

BACKGROUND

We present in this section the case studies to be followed in the chapter, before we describe the formalism Net Condition/Event Systems and the temporal logic "Computation Tree Logic".

Benchmark Production Systems

We use in this section the Benchmark Production Systems FESTO and EnAS developed in the research laboratory led by Prof. Hans-Michael Hanisch at Martin Luther University in Germany.

FESTO Manufacturing System

The Benchmark Production System FESTO is a well-documented demonstrator used as a running example in the context of this paper. FESTO is composed of three units: the Distribution, Test and Processing units. The Distribution unit is composed of a pneumatic Feeder and a Converter. It forwards cylindrical work pieces from a stack to the Test unit which is composed of the Detector, the Tester and the Elevator. This unit performs

Figure 4. Functional operations of the FESTO system

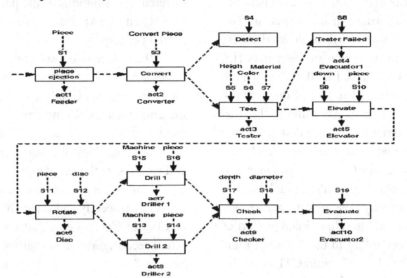

checks on work pieces for height, material type and color. Work pieces that successfully pass this check are forwarded to the rotating Disk of the Processing unit, where the drilling of the work piece is performed. We assume in this research work two drilling machines Drill_machine1 and Drill_machine2 to drill pieces. The result of the drilling operation is next checked by the checking machine and the work piece is forwarded to another mechanical unit. We present in Figure 4 the sequence of functional operations in the system such that each operation needs required data from sensors to activate corresponding actuators. In our research laboratory, three production modes of FESTO are considered according to the rate of input pieces denoted by number_pieces into the system (i.e. ejected by the feeder): (i) Case1: High production. If number_pieces≥ Constant1, Then the two drilling machines are used simultaneously to accelerate the production. In this case, the Distribution and the Testing units have to forward two successive pieces to the rotating disc before starting the drilling with Drill_machine1 AND Drill_machine2. For this production mode, the periodicity of input pieces is p = 11seconds. (ii) Case2: Medium production. If Constant2

≤ number_pieces < Constant1, Then we use Drill_machine1 OR Drill_machine2 to drill work pieces. For this production mode, the periodicity of input pieces is p = 30seconds. (iii) Case3: Light production. If number_pieces < Constant2, Then only the drilling machine Drill_machine1 is used. For this production mode, the periodicity of input pieces is p = 50seconds. If one of the drilling machines is broken at run-time, Then we have to only use the other one. In this case, we reduce the periodicity of input pieces to p = 40 seconds. The system is completely stopped in the worst case if the two drilling machines are broken. The dynamic reconfiguration of FESTO is useful to:

- protect the whole system if hardware faults occur at run-time. Indeed, If Drill_machine1 (resp, Drill_machine2) is broken, Then the drilling operation will be supported by Drill_machine2 (resp, Drill_machine1),
- improve the system productivity. Indeed, If the rate of input pieces is increased, Then we improve the production from Light to the Medium or from the Medium to High mode. This first example shows the new reconfiguration semantic in industry: we

Figure 5. Functional operations of the EnAS system

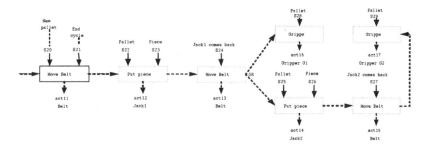

can change the system configuration to improve performances even if there are no faults.

EnAS System

The Benchmark Production System EnAS is assumed to transport pieces from the production system FESTO to storing units. It places pieces inside tins to close with caps afterwards. Two different production strategies can be applied : we place in each tin one or two pieces according to production rates of pieces, tins and caps. We denote respectively by nb_{pieces}, $nb_{tins+caps}$ the production number of pieces and tins (as well as caps) per hour and by *Threshold* a variable (defined in user requirements) to choose the adequate production strategy. The EnAS system is mainly composed of a belt, two Jack stations (J1 and J2) and two Gripper stations (G1 and G2). The Jack stations place new drilled pieces from FESTO and close tins with caps, whereas the Gripper stations remove charged tins from the belt into storing units.

Initially, the belt moves a particular pallet containing a tin and a cap into the first Jack station J1. We distinguish two cases according to production parameters: (i) First Production Policy: If (nb_{pieces} /$nb_{tins+caps}$ ≤ Threshold), Then the Jack station J1 places from FESTO a new piece and closes the tin with the cap. In this case, the Gripper station G1 removes the tin from the belt to the storing station St1. (ii) Second Production Policy: If (nb_{pieces} /$nb_{tins+caps}$ > Threshold), Then the Jack

station J1 places just a piece in the tin which is moved thereafter to the second Jack station to place a second new piece. Once J2 closes the tin with a cap, the belt moves the pallet to the Gripper station G2 in order to remove the tin (with two pieces) to the second storing station St2. We present in Figure 5 the sequence of functional operations of EnAS such that each operation needs required data from sensors to activate corresponding actuators.

Net Condition/Event Systems

The formalism of Net Condition/Event Systems (NCES) is an extension of the well-known Petri net formalism. It was introduced by Rausch and Hanisch in (Rausch & Hanisch, 1995) and further developed through last years, in particular in (Hanisch & Luder, 1999), according to which a completely composed NCES is a Place-Transition Net formally represented as follows (Figure 6):

$S = \{PTN; CN; W_{CN}; I; W_I; EN; em\}$ where:

- PTN = $(P; T; F; K; W_F)$ is a classic Place/Transition Net,
- $CN \subseteq (P \times T)$ is a set of condition arcs,
- $W_{CN}: CN \rightarrow N^+$ defines a weight for each condition arc,
- $I \subseteq (P \times T)$ is a set of inhibitor arcs
- $W_I: I \rightarrow N^+$ defines a weight for each inhibitor arc,
- $EN \subseteq (T \times T)$ is a set of event arcs free of circles, which means:
  - $\nexists (t_1; t_2) \in EN: (t_1 = t_2)$,

Figure 6. A module of Net Condition/Event Systems

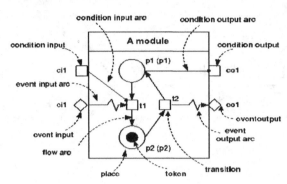

○ $\not\exists$ $(t_1; t_2); \ldots ; (t_{i-1}; t_i): (t_{i-1}; t_i) \in EN$
with $2 \leq l \leq i \wedge (t_1 = t_i)$.

•   em: $T \rightarrow \{\vee, \wedge\}$ is an event mode for every transition (i.e. if $\wedge$ then the corresponding events have to occur simultaneously before the transition firing, else if $\vee$ then one of them is enough).

NCES are defined by the firing rules of transitions. There are several conditions to be fulfilled to enable a transition to fire. First, as it is in ordinary Petri nets, an enabled transition has to have a token concession. That means that all pre-places have to be marked with at least one token. In addition to the flow arcs from places, a transition in NCES may have incoming condition arcs from places and event arcs from other transitions. A transition is enabled by condition signals if all source places of the condition signals are marked by at least one token. The other type of influence on the firing can be described by event signals which come to the transition from some other transitions. Transitions having no incoming event arcs are called spontaneous, otherwise forced. A forced transition is enabled if it has token concession and it is enabled by condition and event signals (Rausch & Hanisch, 1995). We note finally that the model-checker SESA is a useful tool available in our research laboratory to verify functional and temporal properties of NCES (Vyatkin &

Hanisch, 2003). We apply it in our work to check safe reconfigurable embedded control systems.

Temporal Logic

The "Computation Tree Logic" CTL offers facilities for specifications of properties to be fulfilled by the system behavior (Roch, 2000; Roch, 2000). In this section, we briefly present this logic, its extension "Extended Computation Tree Logic" (denoted by eCTL) and the "Timed Computation Tree Logic" (denoted by TCTL).

Computation Tree Logic

In CTL, all formulae specify behaviors of the system starting from an assigned state in which the formula is evaluated by taking paths (i.e. sequence of states) into account. The semantics of formulae is defined with respect to a reachability graph where states and paths are used for the evaluation. A reachability graph M consists of all global states that the system can reach from a given initial state. It is formally defined as a tuple $M = [Z, E]$ where,

• Z is a finite set of states,
• E is a finite set of transitions between states, i.e. a set of edges (z, z_0), such that z, $z_0 \in Z$ and $z0$ is reachable from z.

In CTL, paths play the key role in the definition and evaluation of formulae. By definition, a path starting in the state z_0 is a sequence of states $(z_i) = z_0, z_1, ...$ such that for all $j \geq 0$ it holds that there is an edge $(z_j, z_{j+1}) \in E$. In the following, we denote by (z_i) such path. The truth value of CTL formulae is evaluated with respect to a certain state of the reachability graph. Let $z_0 \in Z$ be a state of the reachability graph and φ a CTL formula, then the relation $\vDash$ for CTL formulae is defined inductively.

- Basis:
  - $z_0 \vDash \varphi$ iff the formula φ holds in z_0,
  - $z_0 \vDash true$ always holds,
  - $z_0 \vDash false$ iff never holds,
- Steps:
  - $z_0 \vDash EF \varphi$ iff there is a path (z_i) and $j \geq 0$ such that $z_j \vDash \varphi$,
  - $z_0 \vDash AF \varphi$ iff for all paths (z_i) there exists $j \geq 0$ such that $z_j \vDash \varphi$,
  - $z_0 \vDash AG \varphi$ iff for all paths (z_i) and for all $j \geq 0$ it holds $z_j \vDash \varphi$,

Extended Computation Tree Logic

In CTL, it is rather complicated to refer to information contained in certain transitions between states of a reachability graph. A solution is given in (Roch, 2000; Roch, 2000) for this problem by proposing an extension of CTL called Extended Computation Tree Logic eCTL. A transition formula is introduced in eCTL to refer to a transition's information contained in the edges of the reachability graph. Since it is wanted to refer not only to state information but also to steps between states, the structure of the reachability graph M = [Z, E] is changed as follows:

- Z is a finite set of states,
- E is a finite set of transitions between states, i.e. a set of labeled edges (z,s,z′), such that $z, z′ \in Z$ and $z′$ is reachable from z by executing the step s.

Let $z_0 \in Z$ be a state of the reachability graph, τ a transition formula and φ an ECTL formula. The relation $\vDash$ for ECTL formulae is defined inductively:

- $z_0 \vDash E \tau X \varphi$: iff there exists a successor state z_1 such that there is an edge $(z_0, s, z_1) \in E$ where $(z_0, s, z_1) \vDash \tau$ and $z_1 \vDash \varphi$ holds,
- $z_0 \vDash A \tau X \varphi$: iff $z_1 \vDash \varphi$ holds for all successors states z_1 with an edge $(z_0, s, z_1) \in E$ such that $(z_0, s, z_1) \vDash \tau$ holds,

Timed Computation Tree Logic

TCTL is an extension of CTL to model qualitative temporal assertions together with time constraints. The extension essentially consists in attaching a time bound to the modalities. We note that a good survey can be found in (Alur, & Dill, 1994). For a reachability graph M = [Z, E], the state delay D is defined as a mapping D: $Z \rightarrow N0$ and for any state z = [m, u] the number D(z) is the number of time units which have to elapse at z before firing any transition from this state. For any path (z_i) and any state $z \in Z$ we put:

- $D[(z_i), z] = 0$, if $z_0 = z$,
- $D[(z_i), z] = D(z_0) + D(z_1) + ... + D(z_{k-1})$, if $z_k = z$ and $z_0, ..., z_{k-1} \neq z$.

With other words, $D[(z_i), z]$ is the number of time units after which the state z on the path (z_i) is reached the first time, i.e. the minimal time distance from z_0. Let $z_0 \in Z$ be a state of the reachability graph and φ a TCTL formula. The relation $\vDash$ for TCTL is defined as follows:

- $z_0 \vDash EF[l,h] \varphi$, iff there is a path (z_i) and a $j > 0$ such that $z_j \vDash \varphi$ and $l \leq D((z_i), z_j) \leq h$,
- $z_0 \vDash AF[l,h] \varphi$, iff for all paths (z_i), there is a $j > 0$ such that $z_j \vDash \varphi$ and $l \leq D((z_i), z_j) \leq h$.

PLANT FORMALIZATION

We denote in the following by Sys the control system that controls, by reading data from sensors and activating corresponding actuators, the plant which is classically composed of a set of physical processes denoted by "*Plant*". Let $\alpha_{sensors}$ and $\alpha_{actuators}$ be respectively the set of sensors and actuators in the plant. For each sensor *sens* $\in$ $\alpha_{sensors}$, we assume that any data reading by Sys is an event *ev = event(sens)*, and for each actuator *act* $\in$ $\alpha_{actuators}$, we define a couple of events *(activ, cf) = activation(act)* that corresponds to the activation of and the confirmation from act. Let $\varphi_{sensors}$ be the set of events to occur when data are read from sensors of $\alpha_{sensors}$ and let $\varphi_{actuators}$ be the set of couples of events when actuators of $\alpha_{actuators}$ are activated.

$\varphi_{sensors}$ = { ev/ $\exists$ sens $\in$ $\alpha_{sensors}$, ev = event(sens) }

$\varphi_{actuators}$ = {(activ, cf)/ $\exists$ act $\in$ $\alpha_{actuators}$, (activ, cf) = activation(act)}

We characterize each process $\phi \in$ *Plant* by (i) a set denoted by *sensors(ϕ)* of sensors that provide required data by Sys before the activation of ϕ; (ii) a set of actuators denoted by *actuators(ϕ)* and activated by the system under well-defined conditions. The control of the different physical processes of "*Plant*" has to satisfy a partial order that we characterize as follows for each actuator *act* $\in$ $\alpha_{actuators}$: (i) *prev(act)*: a set of actuators to be activated just before the activation of *act*, (ii) *follow(act)*: a set of actuator sets such that only one set has to be activated between all sets in a particular execution scenario when the activation of *act* is done, (iii) *sensor(act)*: a set of sensors that provide required data by *Sys* before any activation of *act*. We denote in the following by *first($\alpha_{actuators}$)* (resp. *last($\alpha_{actuators}$)*) the set of actuators with no predecessors in the plant: they are the first (resp. last) to be activated by the system.

Running Example. In the Benchmark Production System FESTO, 11 physical processes of *Plant* are distinguished: Feeder, Converter, Detector, Tester, Evacuator1, Elevator, Disc, Driller1, Driller2, Checker, and Evacuator2. The actuators act6 and act7 are characterized in particular as follows:

prev(act6) = { act5 } ; follow(act6) = {{ act7 }, { act8 }} ;

sensor(act7) = { S15, S16 }.

Before the activation of act7, Sys has to know if a piece is available in Drill_machine1 (i.e. information to be provided by the sensor S16) and also if this machine is ready (i.e. information provided by S15). Note that act1 (resp. act10) is the only actuator without predecessors (resp. successors) in FESTO: *act1* $\in$ *first($\alpha_{actuators}$)* and *act10* $\in$ *last($\alpha_{actuators}$)*. The EnAS Benchmark Production System is composed of 7 physical processes. We characterize the actuator act13 corresponding to the Belt as follows: (i) prev(act13) = {act12}; (ii) follow(act13) = {{act14}, {act16}}, (iii) sensor(act13) = {S24}. Note that act11 (resp. act16 and act17) is (resp. are) the only actuator(s) without predecessors (resp. successors) in EnAS: (i) *act11* $\in$ *first($\alpha_{actuators}$)*, (ii) *act16* $\in$ *last($\alpha_{actuators}$)*, (iii) $_{act17}$ $\in$ $_{last(\alpha actuators)}$.

CONTROL COMPONENTS

We define the concept of "Control Component" to develop embedded control systems following different component- based technologies and/or Architecture Description Languages (ADL) in order to reduce their time to market by reusing already developed components available in rich libraries and by exploiting execution environments used today in industry. A Control Component in our case can be a Function Block according to the IEC61499 technology, or a Koala block according to the Koala technology..etc. We assume an embedded control system as a network of components with precedence constraints allowing the control of physical processes by reading and interpreting data from sensors before reactions and activations of corresponding actuators. To check the whole system behavior when errors occur at run-time, NCES-based models are proposed thereafter for these components.

Formalization

We define a Control Component *CC* as an event-triggered software unit of Sys to control physical processes of the plant. It is composed of an interface for external interactions with the environment (the plant or other Control Components), and an implementation which is a set of algorithms for interpretations of input data from sensors of $\alpha_{sensors}$ before activations of corresponding actuators of $\alpha_{actuators}$. The system Sys is assumed to be a set of Control Components with precedence constraints where each component should start its control task of the plant when its predecessors finish their executions. We define event flows exchanged between system's components to order their executions according to their precedence constraints. We denote in the following by $\phi(CC)$ the set of Control Components of Sys where each component is characterized as follows:

CC = { pred, succ, sens, act }, where:

(i) *pred(CC):* the set of Control Components that have to be executed before the activation of *CC*, (ii) *succ(CC):* the set of Control Components to be activated when the execution of *CC* is well-finished, (iii) *sens(CC):* the set of sensors that provide required data for *CC*, (iv) *act(CC):* the set of actuators to be activated by *CC*.

Specification

We specify the behavior of a Control Component CC by a NCES-based model that has only one initial place and it is characterized by a set of

traces such that each trace *tr* contains the following transitions: (i) *i(CC, sensors_set)*: a transition of the *CC's* model that allows data readings from a subset of sensors *sensors_set* $\subseteq \alpha$ *sensors*, (ii) *a(CC, act_set)*: a transition of the *CC's* model that allows the activation of the subset *act_set* $\subseteq \alpha$ *actuators*, (iii) *cf(CC, act_set):* a transition allowing a final confirmation from actuators of *act_set* once the corresponding physical processes finish their executions.

Running Example. In our Benchmark Production Systems FESTO and EnAS, the Control Components are assumed to be Function Blocks according to the Standard IEC61499. We show in Figure 7 a NCES-based model of the Control Component CC_Jack1 that controls in EnAS the Jack station J1. This component has to read required data from the sensors S22 (i.e. the pallet is in front of J1) and S23 (i.e. a new piece is ready to be put in the tin) before the activation of the actuator act12.

AGENT-BASED ARCHITECTURE FOR SAFETY EMBEDDED CONTROL SYSTEMS

Different errors can occur in embedded control systems and bring their behaviors at run-time to critical scenarios. At the occurrence of each one of them that we assume in the paper as a hardware error, the system should be immediately reconfigured in order to avoid any risk. The reconfiguration can be applied in addition to improve or to decrease the productivity under well-defined conditions. We define in this section an agent-based architecture where the agent analyzes the environment's evolution and applies automatic reconfigurations of Control Components to bring the whole system into safe and optimal behaviors. We model the agent by Nested State Machines to cover all reconfiguration forms that can be applied by the agent at run-time.

Figure 7. Interactions between the Control Component CC_Jack1 and the plant's sensors S22 and S23 before the activation of act12

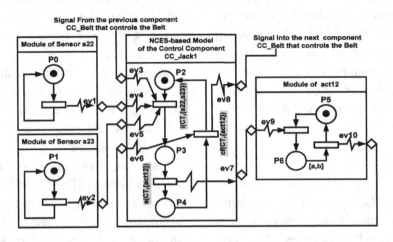

We define the following units that belong to three hierarchical levels of the agent architecture: (i) First level: (Architecture Unit) this unit checks the system behavior and changes its architecture (adds/removes Control Components) when particular conditions are satisfied, (ii) Second level: (Control Unit) for a particular loaded architecture, this unit checks the system behavior and reconfigures compositions or internal behaviors of Control Components, (iii) Third level: (Data Unit) this unit updates data if particular conditions are satisfied. We design the agent by nested state machines where the Architecture Unit is specified by an Architecture State Machine (denoted by ASM) in which each state corresponds to a particular architecture of the system. Therefore, each transition of the ASM corresponds to the load (or unload) of Control Components into (or from) the memory. We construct for each state S of the ASM a particular Control State Machine (denoted by CSM) in the Control Unit. This state machine specifies all reconfiguration forms to possibly apply when the system architecture corresponding to the state S is loaded (i.e. modification of compositions of components or of their internal behaviors). Each transition of any CSM should be fired if particular conditions are satisfied. Finally, Data Unit is specified also by Data State Machines

(denoted by DSMs) where each one corresponds to a state of a CSM or the whole ASM.

Notation. we denote in the following by, (i) n_{ASM} the number of states in the ASM state machine (i.e. the number of possible architectures implementing the system). ASM_a ($i \in [1, nASM]$) denotes a state of ASM to encode a particular architecture (i.e. particular FB network). This state corresponds to a particular CSM state machine that we denote by CSM_a ($a \in [1, n_{ASM}]$), (ii) n_{CSMa} the number of states in CSM_a and let $CSM_{a,b}$ ($b \in [1, nCSMa]$) be a state of CSM_a, (iii) n_{DSM} the number of Data State Machines corresponding to all possible reconfiguration scenarios of the system. Each state $CSM_{a,b}$ ($b \in [1, n_{CSMa}]$) is associated to a particular DSM state machine DSM_c ($c \in [1, n_{DSM}]$). We define Data() the function supporting such association (i.e. Data($CSM_{a,b}$) = DSM_c), (iv) n_{DSMc} the number of states in DSM_c. $DSM_{c,d}$ ($d \in [1, n_{DSMc}]$) denotes a state of the state machine DSM_c which can correspond to one of the following cases: one or more states of a CSM state machine, more than one CSM state machine or all the ASM state machines. The agent automatically applies at run-time different reconfiguration scenarios where each scenario denoted by *Reconfiguration$_{a,b,c,d}$* corresponds to a particular network of Control Components $Net_{a,b,c,d}$ as fol-

Figure 8. Specification of the FESTO Agent by nested state machines

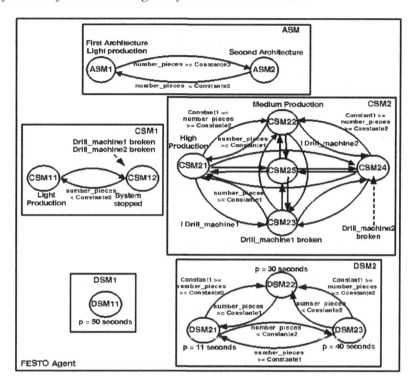

lows: (i) the architecture ASM_a is loaded in the memory, (ii) the control policy is fixed in the state $CSM_{a,b}$, (iii) the data configuration corresponding to the state $DSM_{c,d}$ is applied.

Running example. We present in Figure 8 the nested state machines of our FESTO agent. The ASM state machine is composed of two states ASM1 and ASM2 corresponding to first (i.e. Light Production Mode) and the second (High and Medium modes) architectures. The state machines CSM1 and CSM2 correspond to the states ASM1 and ASM2. In CSM2 state machine, the states CSM21 and CSM22 correspond respectively to High and Medium production modes (where the second architecture is loaded). To fire a transition from CSM21 to CSM22, the value of number_pieces has to be in [Constant2, Constant1[. We note that the states CSM12 and CSM25 correspond to the blocking problem where the two drilling machines are broken. Finally the state machines DSM1 and DSM2 correspond to the

state machines CSM1 and CSM2. In particular, the state DSM21 encodes the production periodicity when we apply High production mode (i.e. the state CSM21 of CSM2), and the state DSM22 encodes the production periodicity when we apply Medium mode (i.e. CSM22 of CSM2). Finally, the state DSM23 corresponds to CSM23 and CSM24 and encodes the production periodicity when one of the drilling machines is broken. We design the agent of our EnAS Benchmark Production System by nested state machines as depicted in Figure 9. The first level is specified by the ASM where each state defines a particular architecture of the system (i.e. a particular composition of blocks to load in the memory). The state ASM1 (resp. ASM2) corresponds to the second (resp. first) policy where the stations J1, J2 and G2 (resp. only J1 and G1) are loaded in the memory. We associate for each one of these states a CSM in the Control unit. Finally, the data unit is specified with a DSM defining the values that Threshold

Figure 9. Specification of the EnAS Agent by nested state machines

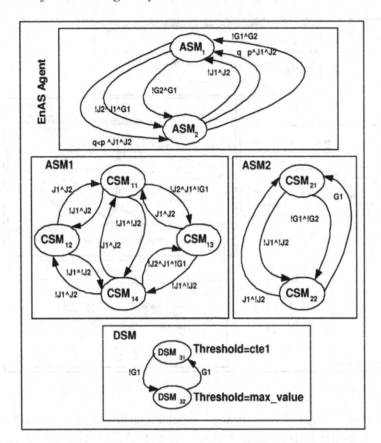

takes under well-defined conditions. Note that if we follow the second production policy (state ASM 1) and the gripper G2 is broken, then we have to change the policy and also the system architecture by loading the block G1_CTL to remove pieces into Belt1. On the other hand, we associate in the second level for the state ASM1 the CSM CSM1 defining the different reconfiguration forms to apply when the first architecture is loaded in the memory. In particular, when the state CSM11 is active and the Jack station J1 is broken, then we activate the state CSM12 in which the Jack station J2 is running alone to place only one piece in the tin. In this case, the internal behavior of the block Belt _CT L has to be changed (i.e. the tin has to be transported directly to the station J 2).

In the same way, if we follow the same policy in the state CSM11 and the Jack station J2 is broken, then we have to activate the state CSM 13 where the J1 behavior has to be changed to place a piece in the tin that has to be closed too (i.e. the ECC structure of the block J1_CTL has to be reconfigured). Finally, we specify in the data unit a DSM where we change the value of Threshold when the Gripper G1 is broken (we suppose as an example that we are not interested in the system performance when the Gripper G1 is broken). By considering this specification of the agent, we specify all possible reconfiguration scenarios that can be applied in a system: Add-Remove (first level) or Update the structure of blocks (second level) or just update data (third level).

AUTOMATIC REFINEMENT_BASED SPECIFICATION AND VERIFICATION OF NETWORKS OF CONTROL COMPONENTS

We are interested in the model checking of all Control Components that implement each network of Sys to be executed after a well-defined reconfiguration scenario. We check step by step each network $Net_{a,b,c,d}$ ($a \in [1, n_{ASM}]$, $b \in [1, n_{CSMa}]$, $c \in [1, n_{DSM}]$, $d \in [1, n_{DSMc}]$) by applying a refinement-based strategy to control the verification complexity. We define at first time a NCES-based abstract model for each $Net_{a,b,c,d}$ which is automatically refined in several steps where NCES-based models of Control Components are automatically generated. The model checker SESA is automatically applied in each step to verify deadlock properties of the new generated components, and it is manually applied to verify in addition CTL-based functional properties according to user requirements. The whole control system is feasible if each network $Net_{a,b,c,d}$ of Control Components is correct and safe.

Refinement-Based Specification and Verification of a Network of Control Components

Let $Net_{a,b,c,d}$ be a network of Control Components that implement the system under well-defined conditions described in user requirements. We specify at first time this network by a NCES-based abstract model (denoted initially by $M1_{a,b,c,d}$) in which:

- data are read from sensors to activate actuators of *first($\alpha_{actuators}$)*,
- all the actuators of *last($\alpha_{actuators}$)* are activated.

The Control Components composing this network are automatically modeled in several steps according to the formalism NCES, and are automatically and manually checked in each step by our model checker SESA as follows:

Step 1. Initial Step. First models of Control Components of $Net_{a,b,c,d}$ are automatically generated as follows:

- $M^1_{a,b,c,d}$ is refined to define the first set $set^1_{a,b,c,d}$ of NCES-based models for Control Components activating actuators of *first($\alpha_{actuators}$)*,
- A new abstract model $M^2_{a,b,c,d}$ is automatically generated from $M^1_{a,b,c,d}$ where: (i) sensors (resp. actuators) to be read (resp. to be activated) by components of $set^1_{a,b,c,d}$ are moved from $M^2_{a,b,c,d}$, (ii) sensors used to activate actuators succeeding those activated by components of $set^1_{a,b,c,d}$ are added to $M^2_{a,b,c,d}$,
- The model checker SESA is automatically applied to verify deadlock properties of the new generated NCES-based models of Control Components of $set^1_{a,b,c,d}$ with $M^2_{a,b,c,d}$. It is manually applied in addition to verify CTL-based functional properties.

If these components are safe (no deadlock is possible)) and correct Then:

If $M^2_{a,b,c,d}$ is not empty Then it is automatically refined in Step2,

Else the network of Control Components $Net_{a,b,c,d}$ is correct and safe.

Else The whole system is not feasible because $Net_{a,b,c,d}$ is not safe.

In each **Step i (i > 1)**, Control Components are recursively modeled and checked as follows:
Step i.

- The abstract model $M^i_{a,b,c,d}$ is automatically refined by generating a new set $set^i_{a,b,c,d}$ of NCES-based models of Control Components,
- A new abstract model $M^{i+1}_{a,b,c,d}$ is automatically generated from $M^i_{a,b,c,d}$,

Figure 10. The abstract model M1{ 2,1,2,1 } ; { 1,1,0,0 } of FESTO and EnAS systems

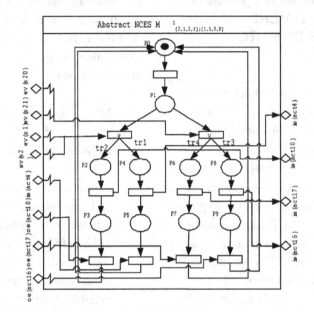

- The model checker SESA is automatically applied to verify deadlock properties of Control Components of $set^i_{a,b,c,d}$ with $M^{i+1}_{a,b,c,d}$. It is manually applied in addition to verify CTL-based functional properties.

If the new generated Control Components are safe and correct Then:

If $M^{i+1}_{a,b,c,d}$ is not empty Then it is automatically refined in Step$i+1$,

Else the network of Control Components $Net_{a,b,c,d}$ is safe.

Else The whole system is not feasible because $Net_{a,b,c,d}$ is not safe.

Running example. In the Benchmark Production Systems FESTO and EnAS, we show in Figure 10 the abstract NCES-based model $M^1_{\{2,1,2,1\};\{1,1,0,0\}}$ where High Production Mode is followed in the first system (i.e. Reconfiguration$_{2,1,2,1}$ is applied and $Net_{2,1,2,1}$ is executed) and the Second Production Policy is followed in the second one (i.e. Reconfiguration$_{1,1,0,0}$ is applied and $Net_{1,1,0,0}$ is executed). This model contains the following four abstract traces of states:

- First trace tr1: this abstract trace is followed by FESTO when the test of the workpiece is failed. tr1 is characterized as follows:
  - It reads data from the sensors S1 and S2 to activate thereafter the actuator act1,
  - It allows the activation of the actuator act4 to evacuate the failed workpiece (act4 $\in$ last($\alpha_{actuators}$)).
- Second trace tr2: this abstract trace is followed by FESTO when the test of the workpiece is succeeded. tr2 is characterized as follows:
  - It reads data from the sensors S1 and S2 to activate thereafter the actuator act1,
  - It allows the activation of the actuator act10 to evacuate the workpiece once the drilling operation is done (act10 $\in$ last($\alpha_{actuators}$)).
- Third trace tr3: this abstract trace is followed by EnAS when the first production policy is applied. tr3 is characterized as follows:

Figure 11. The first Step of an automatic refinement process

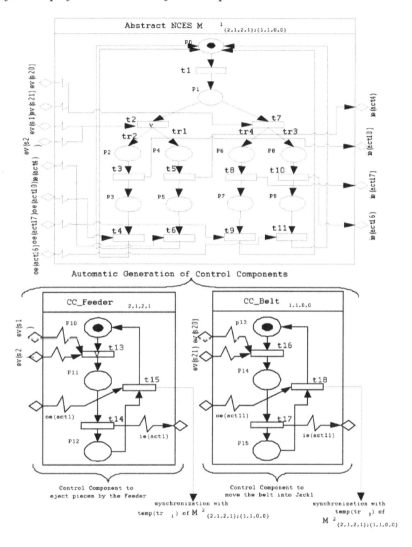

○ It reads data from the sensors S20 and S21 to activate thereafter the actuator act11,

○ It allows the activation of the actuator act16 to send the piece into the storing unit St1 (act16 ∈ last($\alpha_{actuators}$)).

• Fourth trace tr4: this abstract trace is followed by EnAS when the second production policy is applied. tr4 is characterized as follows:

○ It reads data from the sensors S20 and S21 to activate thereafter the actuator act11,

○ It allows the activation of the actuator act17 to send the piece into the storing unit St2.

We present in Figure 11 the first step of the refinement process to automatically generate NCES-based models of CC_Feeder$_{2,1,2,1}$ and CC_Belt$_{1,1,0,0}$ that respectively control the Feeder in FESTO and the Belt in EnAS. The model checker SESA is automatically applied in this step to check the safety of these components (i.e. no deadlock is possible). We present in Figure 12 the second refinement step to automatically generate CC_Convert$_{2,1,2,1}$

Figure 12. The second Step of an automatic refinement process

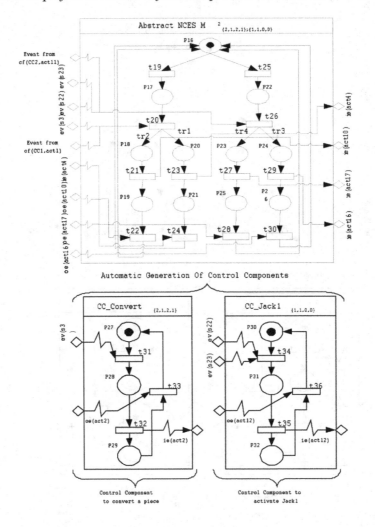

and $CC\_Jack1_{1,1,0,0}$ that respectively control the Converter in FESTO and the first Jack station in EnAS. We present in Figure 13 the last steps to automatically generate $CC\_Checker_{2,1,2,1}$ and $CC\_Evac_{2,1,2,1}$ that respectively control Checker and Evacuator2 in FESTO.

Formalization

We formalize the automatic refinement-based specification and verification of Control Components that implement the whole control system. We denote by $\Sigma^i_{a,b,c,d}$ the set of actuators that have to be considered for the refinement of the abstract model $M^i_{a,b,c,d}$ (when the reconfiguration scenario Reconfiguration$_{a,b,c,d}$ is well-applied by the agent) and by first($\Sigma^i_{a,b,c,d}$) a subset of actuators of $\Sigma^i_{a,b,c,d}$ with no predecessors in $\Sigma^i_{a,b,c,d}$.

$\forall$ act $\in$ first($\Sigma^i_{a,b,c,d}$), prev(act) $\subset \alpha_{actuators} \setminus \Sigma^i_{a,b,c,d}$

Let simul_set$^i_{a,b,c,d}$ be a subset of actuators to be activated simultaneously in first($\Sigma^i_{a,b,c,d}$). We denote in addition by sensor(simul_set$^i_{a,b,c,d}$) the set of sensors that provide required data before any activation of simul_set$^i_{a,b,c,d}$ and we denote by set_follow(simul_set$^i_{a,b,c,d}$) the following set:

set_follow(simul_set$^i_{a,b,c,d}$) = {act_set $\subset \alpha_{actuators}$ / $\exists$ act $\in$ simul_set$^i_{a,b,c,d}$, act_set $\in$ follow(act)}

Figure 13. The last Steps of an automatic refinement process

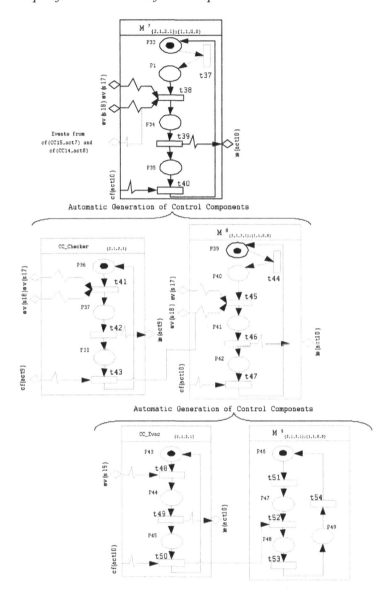

The automatic refinement-based specification and verification of Control Components is applied as shown in Box 1.

Running Example. In our FESTO and EnAS Benchmark Production Systems and according to Figure 11, first($\Sigma^1_{\{2,1,2,1\};\{1,1,0,0\}}$) = {act1, act11}.

We refine therefore the abstract NCES-based model $M^1_{\{2,1,2,1\};\{1,1,0,0\}}$ into two Control Components $CC\_Feeder_{2,1,2,1}$ and $CC\_Belt_{1,1,0,0}$ that activate respective the actuators act1 and act11.

In addition, a new abstract model $M^2_{\{2,1,2,1\};\{1,1,0,0\}}$ is automatically generated from $M^1_{\{2,1,2,1\};\{1,1,0,0\}}$ where first($\Sigma^2_{\{2,1,2,1\};\{1,1,0,0\}}$) = {act2, act12}.

Verification of CTL-based Properties with SESA

In addition to automatic verifications of deadlock properties, we manually verify in each refinement step eCTL-based properties of the Benchmark

Box 1. Algorithm. Step-By-Step

- For each Step i corresponding to the refinement of the NCES-based abstract model $M^i_{a,b,c,d}$:
    - For each $simul\_set^i_{a,b,c,d} \subset first(\Sigma^i_{a,b,c,d})$:
        - Create Control Component *CC*,
        - For each $act \in simul\_set^i_{a,b,c,d}$,
            - add i(CC, sensor(act)) to CC,
            - add a(CC, act),
            - add cf(CC, act),
        - $I \leftarrow simul\_set^i_{a,b,c,d} \cap last(\alpha_{actuators})$,
        - For each $act_0 \in I$,
            - $M^i_{a,b,c,d} \leftarrow M^i_{a,b,c,d} \setminus i(M^i_{a,b,c,d}, sensor(act0))$,
            - $M^i_{a,b,c,d} \leftarrow M^i_{a,b,c,d} \setminus a(M^i_{a,b,c,d}, act0)$,
            - $M^i_{a,b,c,d} \leftarrow M^i_{a,b,c,d} \setminus cf(M^i_{a,b,c,d}, act0)$,
        - $simul\_set^i_{a,b,c,d} \leftarrow simul\_set^i_{a,b,c,d} \setminus I$,
        - If($simul\_set^i_{a,b,c,d}$)
            - For each $act0 \in simul\_set^i_{a,b,c,d}$,
                - $M^i_{a,b,c,d} \leftarrow M^i_{a,b,c,d} \setminus i(M^i_{a,b,c,d}, sensor(act0))$,
            - For each $set0 \in set\_follow(simul\_set^i_{a,b,c,d})$, For each $act0 \in set0$,
                - $M^i_{a,b,c,d} \leftarrow M^i_{a,b,c,d} \cup i(M^i_{a,b,c,d}, sensor(act0))$
- If SESA automatically finds a deadlock in the current step, or manually proves that a CTL-based property is not satisfied,
    - Then Stop the automatic construction,
    - Else
        - $\Sigma^{i+1}_{a,b,c,d} \leftarrow \Sigma^i_{a,b,c,d} \setminus first(\Sigma^i_{a,b,c,d})$,
        - $M^{i+1}_{a,b,c,d} \leftarrow M^i_{a,b,c,d}$,
        - If($\Sigma^{i+1}_{a,b,c,d}$)
            - Then apply Step i+1 to refine the NCES-based model $M^{i+1}_{a,b,c,d}$,
        - Else display(System is safe).

End Algorithm.

Production Systems FESTO and EnAS in order to check if the generated Control Components satisfy user requirements. In particular, the precedence constraint between the actuators act1 and act2 (resp. act11 and act12) is manually verified in the first refinement step when the NCES-based models of the components $CC\_Feeder_{\{2,1,2,1\}}$ and $CC\_Convert_{\{2,1,2,1\}}$ are generated. We propose the following eCTL formula:

$$z0 \models AGA\ t20\ X\ P10\ (resp.\ z0 \models AGA\ t26\ X\ P13)$$

Indeed, whenever a state transition of the reachability graph that fulfills the transition t20 (resp. t26) of the abstract model $M^2_{\{2,1,2,1\};\{1,1,0,0\}}$ i.e. The Plant Control System reads data from the sensor S3 (resp. sensors S22 and S23) is possible, this transition should lead to a successor state in which P10 (resp. P13) holds true i.e. the actuator act1 (resp. act11) is already activated. These properties are proven to be True by the model checker SESA. On the other hand, the behavior of each new Control Component has to be checked: it reads data from sensors before it activates and waits the confirmation of the corresponding actuator. We propose the following formula to check the behavior of the Control Component $CC\_Checker_{\{2,1,2,1\}}$ (resp. $CC\_Evac_{\{2,1,2,1\}}$) in the 7th (resp. 8th) refinement step.

Box 2. Algorithm. Specify_Verify

- For each Architecture ASM_a, $i \in [1, n_{ASM}]$
  - For each Control policy $CSM_{a,b}$, $b \in [1, n_{CSMa}]$
    - For each Data configuration $DSM_{c,d}$, $d \in [1, n_{DSMc}]$ such that $DSM_c = Data(CSM_{a,b})$

      Step-By-Step($Net_{a,b,c,d}$);

      If a deadlock occurs or a CTL-based property is not satisfied in Stepi, $i \geq 1$

      Then Stop Algorithm; Display (system is infeasible);

      Display(System is feasible);

End.

$z0 \models$ AGA t41 X AF E t42 XAF E t43X TRUE

$z0 \models$ AGA t48 X AF E t49 XAF E t50X TRUE

Indeed, we verify that the Control Component $CC\_Checker_{\{2,1,2,1\}}$ reads data from the sensors S17 and S18 before the activation and the confirmation of the actuator act9. This formula is proven to be True by the model checker SESA.

Generalization: Refinement-Based Specification and Verification of a Reconfigurable System

We apply as follows the proposed refinement-based technique to automatically specify different networks of Control Components that can probably implement the whole embedded system after well-defined reconfiguration scenarios to be applied by the agent in Box 2.

We developed and tested in our research laboratory these algorithms by checking the safety and correctness of different networks that can probably implement our Benchmark Production Systems FESTO and EnAS. If each network that corresponds to a particular reconfiguration scenario is correctly specified and verified, Then the correctness of these demonstrators is deduced. The complexity of these algorithms is as follows: let n be an upper bound of n_{ASM}, $max\{n_{CSMa}, a \in [1, n_{ASM}]\}$ and $max\{n_{DSMc}, c \in [1, n_{DSM}]\}$, and let

β be the biggest number of steps to generate in one of the considered scenarios, the complexity is then in $O(n^3.\beta)$. In FESTO and EnAS, 49 reachability graphs are automatically generated by SESA to check the feasibility of Control Components in seven different networks corresponding to seven reconfiguration scenarios. We present in Figure 14 the number of states generated in each one of these graphs. By applying the proposed refinement-based approach, the sum of states generated by SESA after the verification of these different networks is 3736 states, whereas the number of states is about 10^{14} when we applied a classic approach without refinement for the verification of these demonstrators (Figure 15). This comparison shows the significance of our contributions in this study.

Running Example. We show in Figure 17 a reachability graph which is automatically generated by SESA in a last refinement step when $Reconfiguration_{2,1,2,1}$ (i.e. High Production Policy) is applied in FESTO and $Reconfiguration_{1,1,0,0}$ (i.e. Second Production Mode) is applied in EnAS, to check the Control Components $CC\_Checker_{2,1,2,1}$ and $CC\_Evacuator_{2,1,2,1}$ that control respectively the physical processes Checker and Evacuator2 in FESTO. We show in Figure 18 another reachability graph which is automatically generated by SESA in Step6 when $Reconfiguration_{1,1,1,1}$ (i.e. Light Production Policy) is applied in FESTO and $Reconfiguration_{2,1,0,0}$ (i.e. First Production Mode)

Figure 14. Refinement-based Verification of FESTO and EnAS Benchmark Production Systems

Steps		1	2	3	4	5	6	7
FESTO: Reconfiguration $_{2,1,2,1}$ EnAS: Reconfiguration $_{1,1,0,0}$	States Number	121	35	71	191	94	144	16
FESTO: Reconfiguration $_{2,2,2,2}$ EnAS: Reconfiguration $_{1,1,0,0}$	States Number	123	36	74	183	91	36	16
FESTO: Reconfiguration $_{1,1,1,1}$ EnAS: Reconfiguration $_{2,1,0,0}$	States Number	119	37	75	187	33	12	16
FESTO: Reconfiguration $_{2,3,2,3}$ EnAS: Reconfiguration $_{2,1,0,0}$	States Number	131	38	73	186	31	24	16
FESTO: Reconfiguration $_{2,4,2,3}$ EnAS: Reconfiguration $_{1,1,0,0}$	States Number	124	34	72	185	92	36	16
FESTO: Reconfiguration $_{1,1,1,1}$ EnAS: Reconfiguration $_{1,2,0,0}$	States Number	128	35	77	189	31	12	16
FESTO: Reconfiguration $_{1,1,1,1}$ EnAS: Reconfiguration $_{1,3,0,0}$	States Number	118	37	78	188	29	14	16

Figure 15. (a) Number of states automatically generated by SESA for the refinement-based specification and verification of 7 different networks of Control Components. (b) Number of states generated by SESA for the specification and verification of 7 networks of Control Components without applying any refinement

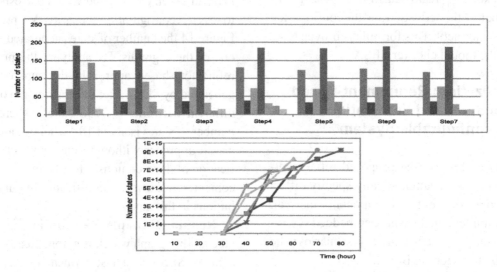

Figure 16. A reachability graph generated by SESA in Step7 when Reconfiguration$_{2,1,2,1}$ is applied in FESTO andReconfiguration$_{1,1,0,0}$ is applied in EnAS

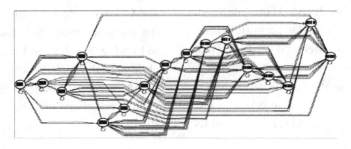

is applied in EnAS, to check the Control Component CC_Drill1$_{2,1,2,1}$ that controls Drill_machine1 in FESTO. We show finally in Figure 19 a reachability graph generated in Step6, when Reconfiguration$_{2,2,2,2}$ (i.e. Medium Production Mode) is applied in FESTO and Reconfiguration$_{1,1,0,0}$ (First Production Mode) is applied in EnAS, to check the Control Components CC_Drill2$_{2,2,2,2}$ and CC_G2$_{1,1,0,0}$ that control respectively Drill_ma-

chine2 in FESTO and the second Gripper station in EnAS.

IMPLEMENTATION OF AGENTS

We define in this section an implementation of a reconfigurable agent to be composed of three modules: Interpreter, Reconfiguration Engine and

Figure 17. A reachability graph generated by SESA in Step6 when Reconfiguration$_{1,1,1,1}$ is applied in FESTO and Reconfiguration$_{2,1,0,0}$ is applied in EnAS

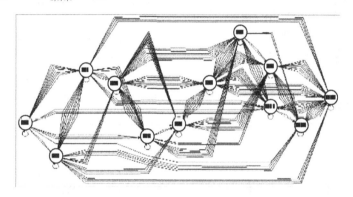

Figure 18. A reachability graph generated by SESA in Step6 when Reconfiguration$_{2,2,2,2}$ is applied in FESTO and Reconfiguration$_{1,1,0,0}$ is applied in EnAS

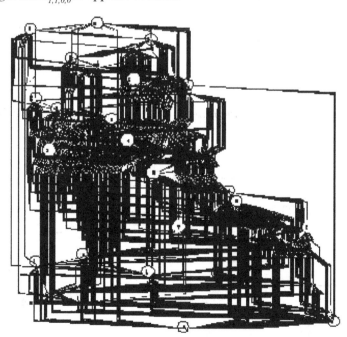

Figure 19. Interaction between the Agent and the Embedded Control System

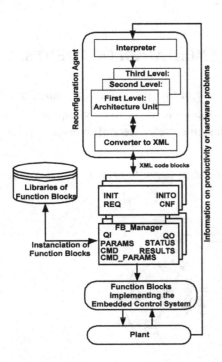

Converter. The second as the main module decides any reconfigurations to be applied at run-time, whereas the others support interactions with the plant and/or Control Components implementing the system Sys.

Agent Interpreter

To guarantee a high reactivity of the agent, Interpreter ensures by sensors the detection of any hardware problems that disturb the normal execution, and it ensures in addition the evaluation of production parameters for any optimization of system performances.

Running Example. In our EnAS Benchmark Production System where Control Components are Function Blocks according to the Standard IEC61499, Interpreter has to detect by sensors any hardware problems in the plant in order to apply thereafter by the agent required reconfigurations that guarantee a safe behavior of the whole system (Figure 20). In addition, it has to count the numbers of pieces nb_{pieces} (as well as caps) $nb_{tins + caps}$ per hour. We present in Figure 21 an IEC61499-based implementation of Interpreter where the Function Block FB_Inventory counts such numbers and FB_Evaluate evaluates each hour if First or Second production policy should be followed (evaluation of $nb_{pieces} / (nb_{tins + caps} \times Threshold)$).

Reconfiguration Engine

The reconfiguration engine is the agent mind that receives notifications from Interpreter to decide and apply thereafter automatic reconfigurations

Figure 20. Function Blocks-based implementation of the agent interpreter in the EnAS system

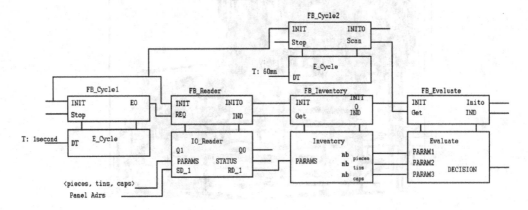

of the whole system. It contains the Architecture, the Control and the Data units (Figure 20).

Agent Converter

To handle interactions between the agent and the system Control Components, we use as a technical solution a management Control Component "Manager" to apply the desired reconfiguration scenarios. Indeed, when a scenario is fixed by the engine (i.e. ASM, CSM and DSM state machines) according to environment's evolutions, the converter has to send this decision in forms of XML code blocks to "Manager" which effectively apply such reconfiguration by exploiting a well-defined library to automatically create, update or delete system Control Components. The module Converter is technically based on a conversion table that defines for each scenario to be fixed by the engine, the XML file that contains the correspond-

ing XML code blocks. In this table, each entry [< $i1, i2$ >, <$j1, j2$ >, <$k1, h1, k2, h2$ >, <@Manager >, < @XML − F ile >] defines the addresses of "Manager" and the XML file that contains the XML code blocks when the engine reconfigures the system from Reconfiguration$_{i1,j1,k1,h1}$ to the scenario Reconfiguration$_{i2,j2,k2,h2}$ (the ASM state machine evolutes from the state ASM$_{i1}$ to ASM$_{i2}$, the CSM state machine evolutes from the state CSM$_{i1,j1}$ to CSM$_{i2,j2}$ and the DSM state machine evolutes from DSM$_{k1,h1}$ to DSM$_{k2,h2}$).

Running Example. In our EnAS Benchmark Production System, Control Components are Function Blocks. According to (Lewis, 2002), the Standard IEC61499 defines a Standardized Management Function Block "Manager" (Figure 19 and Figure 21) that offers rich services to Create (load), Initiate, Start, Stop and Delete Function Blocks at run-time (Figure 22). This block can be used by specifying different values for the CMD

Figure 21. Management Function Block"

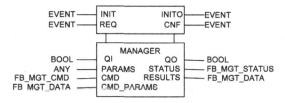

Figure 22. Management Services offered by the Function Block "Manager"

Service Function	Description
Create	Create data type definitions, function block types, instances and connections between function blocks. This will involve downloading definitions from a source, e.g. copying across a network, copying in from a memory smart card.
Initialise	Initialise data type definitions, function block types, instances and connections between function blocks. This concerns setting up function blocks and connections into a runnable state and will include resetting variables to their default initial values.
Start	The Start function triggers the execution of function block networks within a resource. Typically it will start the resource scheduling function and start to run SI function blocks that generate timing events. These in turn trigger chains of events that cause function block execution.
Stop	The Stop service causes all execution to cease by suspending the resource scheduling function.
Delete	The Delete service can be used to delete the definition of any data type, function block or connection.

Figure 23. Reconfiguration of the EnAS system to activate the first from the second production policy

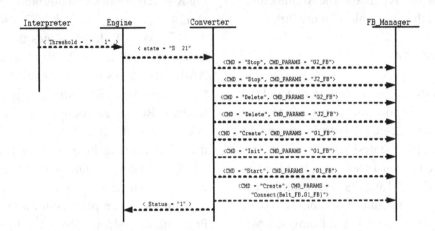

input that allows various service functions which are characterized by the value of the CMD_ PARAMS input. The response to each form of service functions is given by the value returned in the Status output.

Examples.

- CMD = CREAT E,
- CMD_PARAMS = fb_instance_definition,
- P ARAMS = fb_instance_definition data,
- RESULT = fb_instance_ reference.

This operation allows "Manager" to create an instance fb_instance_definition in the control system. We note that data types for values (for the inputs PARAMS and RESULT) are not defined in IEC61499 and are regarded as implementation specific. However, the standard has defined a data exchange format for porting function block definitions based on the XML language which is chosen as a file ex-change format for IEC61499 library elements, for example, for exchanging function block definitions between engineering support systems and other IEC61499 compliant applications. The proposed Agent Converter is based on a conversion table containing 18 entries that correspond to different reconfiguration cases to be fixed by the engine. The EnAS agent behaves as follows:

- If nb_{pieces} + $nbtins+caps$ ≤ *Threshold* and no hardware problems occur,
- Then Interpreter signals the Control Unit CSM2 (of the Reconfiguration Engine) to apply the First production policy by activating the state S21. In this case, Converter sends XML code blocks to the Function Block "Manager" as follows (Figure 23):
- Stops the Function Blocks J2_FB and G2_FB,
- Deletes from the memory these blocks,
- Creates the block G1_FB to implement the First production policy,
- Initializes and Connects this block to the rest of the FBs network before starting its execution.
- Else If nb_{pieces} + $nb_{tins+caps}$ >Threshold, Then Interpreter informs the Control Unit CSM1 in order to apply the Second production policy by activating the state S11. In this case, Converter sends XML code blocks into the Function Block "Manager" as follows (Figure 24):
- Stops the Function Blocks G1_F B that controls the Gripper station G1,
- Deletes this block from the memory,
- Creates the block J2_FB and G2_FB that controls respectively J2 and G2 in order to implement the Second production policy,

Figure 24. Reconfiguration of the EnAS system to activate the second from the first production policy

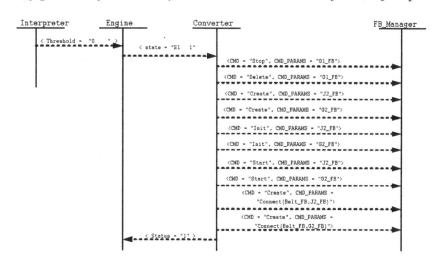

- Initializes and Connects these blocks to the rest of the FBs network before starting its execution.

CONCLUSION

This paper deals with reconfigurable embedded control systems following different component-based technologies and/or Architecture Description Languages to reduce their time to market by exploiting rich execution environments and also rich libraries available today in industry. We define the general concept of "Control Component" as an event-triggered software unit composed of an interface for external interactions and an implementation to support control actions of physical processes. A Control Component checks and interprets the environment's evolution by reading data from sensors before reacting and activating corresponding actuators in the plant. It is modeled according to the formalism Net Condition/Event Systems. We define an agent-based architecture where the agent controls the plant and applies automatic reconfigurations by creating, deleting or updating Control Components to bring the system into safe behaviors. It is specified by nested state machines where states correspond to other states.

The system is implemented by different complex networks of components such that only one is executed at a given time when a corresponding reconfiguration scenario is applied by the agent. To check that no deadlocks are possible in these networks, we propose a refinement-based technique that automatically specifies and checks step by step each network. In addition, CTL-based properties of Control Components are manually verified to check their correctness. The whole system is correct if all networks are well-checked and verified. We implement the agent by three modules: Interpreter, Reconfiguration Engine and Converter where the first interprets environment evolutions, the second decides new reconfiguration scenarios to be applied, and the third sends desired reconfiguration commands in forms of XML code blocks to well-defined Management Control Components that apply such scenarios by exploiting an available library to create, change and delete system components. To explain the paper contribution, the systems FESTO and EnAS are followed as examples where technical solutions are given to implement their reconfiguration agents. In our future work, we plan simulations of embedded control systems which is not an exhaustive approach. In this case, an approach based on injections of faults should be proposed to optimize such a posteriori verification (Khalgui, Carpanzano & Hanisch, 2008).

REFERENCES

Acharya, S., & Mahapatra, R.-N. (2008). A dynamic slack management technique for real-time distributed embedded systems. *IEEE Transactions on Computers, 57*(2).

Ahmadinia, A., Bobda, C., Fekete, S.-P., Teich, J., & Van Der Veen, J.-C. (2007). Optimal free-space management and routing-conscious dynamic placement for reconfigurable devices. *IEEE Transactions on Computers, 56*(5).

Al-Safi, Y., & Vyatkin, V. (2007). An ontology-based reconfiguration agent for intelligent mechatronic systems. In *Third International Conference on Industrial Applications of Holonic and Multi-Agent Systems*. Berlin: Springer-Verlag.

Alur, R., & Dill, D. (1994). A theory of Timed Automata. *Theoretical Computer Science, 126*(2), 183–235.

Angelov, C., Sierszecki, K., & Marian, N. (2005). *Design models for reusable and reconfigurable state machines.* In L.T. Yang et al (Eds.), *EUC 2005 International Federation for Information Processing*, (LNCS 3824, pp. 152-163).

Arcticus. (2009). *Rubus OS Reference Manual.* Retrieved from Arcticus Systems, http://www.arcticus-systems.com/

Crnkovic, I., & Larsson, M. (2002). *Building reliable component-based software systems.* Boston: Artech House.

Ben Jmaa Derbel, H., (2007). On the pid control of systems with large delays. *International Journal of Modelling, Identification and Control (IJMIC), 2*(1).

Dissaux, P., Filali Amine, M., Michel, P., & Vernadat, F. (Eds.). (2005). Architecture Description Languages. In *IFIP TC-2 Workshop on Architecture Description Languages (WADL), World Computer Congress,* (Vol. 176).

Gehin, A-L., & Staroswiecki, M., (2008). Reconfiguration analysis using generic component models. *IEEE Transactions on Systems, Machine and Cybernetics, 38*(3).

Goessler, G., Graf, S., Majster-Cederbaum, M., Martens, M., & Sifakis, J. (2007). An approach to modeling and verification of component based systems. In *Current Trends in Theory and Practice of Computer Science, SOFSEM'07, (LNCS 4362).* Berlin: Springer.

Hanisch, H.-M., & Luder, A. (1999), *Modular modelling of closed-loop systems.* In *Colloquium on Petri Net Technologies for Modelling Communication Based Systems,* (pp. 103-126), Germany.

Hsiung, P.-A., Chen, Y.-R., & Lin, Y.-H. (2007). Model checking safety-critical systems using safecharts. *IEEE Transactions on Computers, 56*(5).

Hu, H.-S., & Li, Z.-W. (2009). Clarification on the computation of liveness-enforcing supervisor for resource allocation systems with uncontrollable behavior. *IEEE Transactions on Automation Science and Engineering, 6*(2).

IEC61131. (1993). 3. In *International Standard IEC 1131-3. Bureau Central de la commission Electrotechnique Internationale.* Switzerland: Programmable Controllers Part.

IEC61499-1. (2003). *Function Blocks for Industrial Process Measurements and Control Systems.* International Standard IEC-TC65-WG6.

Jigang, W., Srikanthan, T., & Wang, X. (2007). Integrated row and column rerouting for reconfiguration of vlsi arrays with four-port switches. *IEEE Transactions on Computers, 56*(10).

Khalgui, M., & Rebeuf, X. (2008). An approach to implement a programmable logic controller from real-time software components. *International Journal of Industrial and Systems Engineering, 3*(6).

Khalgui, M., Rebeuf, X., & Simonot-Lion, F., (2007). A deployment method of component based applications on distributed industrial control systems. *European Jounal of Automated Systems, 41*(6).

Khalgui, M., & Hanisch, H.-M. (2008). Automatic specification of feasible Control Tasks in Benchmark Production Systems. In IEEE International Conference on *Emerging Technologies and Factory Automation, ETFA08.*

Khalgui, M., & Thramboulidis, K. (2008). A n IEC61499-based Development Approach for the Deployment of Industrial Control Applications. *International journal of Modelling* [IJMIC]. *Identification and Control, 4*(2), 186–204.

Khalgui, M., Carpanzano, E., & Hanisch, H.-M. (2008). An optimised simulation of component-based embedded systems in manufacturing industry. *International Journal of Simulation and Process Modelling, 4*(2), 148–162.

Lee, D.-U., & Villasenor, J.-D. (2009). Optimized custom precision function evaluation for embedded processors. *IEEE Transactions on Computers, 58*(1).

Lewis, R.-W. (2002). *Modelling control systems using iec 61499, Applying function blocks to distributed systems, (Control Engineering Series).* Stevenage, UK: Institution Of Engineering and Technology.

Li, Z.-W., Zhou, M.-C., & Jeng, M.-D. (2008). A maximally permissive deadlock prevention policy for fms based on Petri net siphon control and the theory of regions. *IEEE Transactions on Automation Science and Engineering, 5*(1).

Lysne, O., Montanana, J.-M., Flich, J., Duato, J., Pinkston, T.-M., & Skeie, T. (2008). An efficient and deadlock-free network reconfigurable protocol. *IEEE Transactions on Computers, 57*(6).

Hanisch, H.-M., Khalgui, M., & Carpanzano, E. (2008). An optimised simulation of component-based embedded systems in manufacturing industry. *International Journal of Simulation and Process Modelling, 4*(2).

McKenzie, F-D., Petty, M-D. & Xu, Q. (2004). Usefulness of software architecture description languages for modeling and analysis of federates and federation architectures. *SCS Simulation journal.*

Minghui, W., Shugen, M., Bin, L., & Yuechao, W. (2009). Reconfiguration of a group of wheel-manipulator robots based on msv and csm. *IEEE Transactions on Mechatronics, 14*(2).

Pagilla, P-R., Dwivedula, R-V. & Siraskar, N-B. (2007). A decentralized model reference adaptive controller for large-scale systems. *IEEE Transactions on Mechatronics, 12*(2).

Pecos-project. (2006). Retrieved from www.pecos-project.org/publications.html

Philips. (2009). Retrieved from http://www.philips.com/

Rausch, M., & Hanisch, H.-M. (1995). Net condition/event systems with multiple condition outputs. In *Symposium on Emerging Technologies and Factory Automation,* (Vol.1, pp.592-600).

Roch, S. (2000). Extended computation tree logic. In *Proceedings of the CESP2000 Workshop,* (Vol. 140, pp. 225-234). Berlin: Informatik Berichte.

Roch, S. (2000). Extended computation tree logic: Implementation and application. In *Proceedings of the AWPN2000 Workshop,* Germany.

Rockwell. (2006). *Rockwell automation.* Retrieved from http://www.holobloc.com

Rooker, M.-N., Sunder, C., Strasser, T., Zoitl, A., Hummer, O., & Ebenhofer, G. (2007). Zero downtime reconfiguration of distributed automation systems: The εcedac approach. In *Third International Conference on Industrial Applications of Holonic and Multi-Agent Systems*. Berlin: Springer-Verlag.

Song, I., Kim, S., & Karray, F., (2008). A real-time scheduler design for a class of embedded systems. *IEEE Transactions on Mechatronics, 13*(1).

Stewart, D.-B., Volpe, R.-A., & Khosla, P.-K. (1997). Design of dynamically reconfigurable real-time software using port-based objects. *IEEE Transactions on Software Engineering, 23*(12), 759–776.

Takahashi, J., Yamaguchi, T., Sekiyama, K., & Fukuda, T. (2009). Communication timing control and topology reconfiguration of a sink-free meshed sensor network with mobile robots. *IEEE Transactions on Mechatronics, 14*(2).

Tan, W., Fan, Y., & Zhou, M. (2009). A Petri net-based method for compatibility analysis and composition of web services in business process execution language. *IEEE Transactions on Automation Science and Engineering, 6*(1).

Tang, H., Weng, L., Dong, Z-Y., & Yan, R., (2009). Adaptive and learning control for si engine model with uncertainties. *IEEE Transactions on Mechatronics, 14*(1).

Tsui, W., Masmoudi, M-S., Karray, F., Song, I., & Masmoudi, M. (2008). Soft-computing-based embedded design of an intelligent wall/lane-following vehicle. *IEEE Transactions on Mechatronics, 13*(1).

Van Ommering, R. (2002). Building product populations with software components. In *Proceedings of the 24th international Conference on Software engineering*, (pp. 255-265). New York: ACM Press.

Vyatkin, V. (2007). *IEC61499 Function Blocks for Embedded and Distributed Control Systems Design*. Research Triangle Park, NC: ISA Publisher.

Vyatkin, V., & Hanisch, H.-M. (2003). Verification of distributed control systems in intelligent manufacturing. *International Journal of Manufacturing, 14*(1), 123–136.

Zhuo, L., & Prasanna, V.-K. (2008). High-performance designs for linear algebra operations on reconfigurable hardware. *IEEE Transactions on Computers, 57*(8).

Chapter 2
Multithreaded Programming of Reconfigurable Embedded Systems

Jason Agron
University of Arkansas, USA

David Andrews
University of Arkansas, USA

Markus Happe
University of Paderborn, Germany

Enno Lübbers
University of Paderborn, Germany

Marco Platzner
University of Paderborn, Germany

ABSTRACT

Embedded and Real-Time (ERTS) systems have continued to expand at a vigorous rate. Designers of ERTS systems are continually challenged to provide new capabilities that can meet the expanding requirements and increased computational needs of each new proposed application, but at a decreasing price/performance ratio. Conventional solutions using general purpose processors or custom ASICs are less and less able to satisfy the contradictory requirements in performance, flexibility, power, development time, and cost. This chapter introduces the concept of generating semi-custom platforms driven from a traditional multithreaded programming model. This approach offers the advantage of achieving productivity levels close to those associated with software by using an established programming model but with a performance level close to custom hardware through the use of a flexible hardware platform capable of adapting to specialized application requirements. We discuss the underlying concepts, requirements and advantages of multithreading in the context of reconfigurable hardware, and present two approaches which provide multithreading support to hardware and software components at the operating system level.

DOI: 10.4018/978-1-60960-086-0.ch002

INTRODUCTION

Embedded and Real-Time (ERT) systems continue to expand at a vigorous rate. From personal electronics, through transportation, and into the telecommunications industries, ERT systems continue to redefine our personal and professional lifestyles. With each new application and usage, the designers of ERT systems are continually faced with the challenge of fielding systems with expanding performance and capabilities, but within constricting price/performance ratios. Designers are now turning to modern Field Programmable Gate Arrays (FPGAs) to help resolve these conflicting requirements. FPGAs have long held the promise of allowing designers to create systems with performance levels close to custom circuits but with the ability to reconfigure gates with software-like levels of flexibility. While the performance of FPGA-based systems are now very impressive, productivity levels for helping guide the building of FPGA-based systems has historically remained closer to those associated with designing hardware.

In this chapter we show how we have enabled the multithreaded programming model to close the productivity gap and guide the development of systems on programmable chip (SopCs). To aid in design productivity and reduce design time, the application can first be created as a group of threads, and run and tested for functional correctness on a standard desktop PC. Once tested, the threads can then be profiled and evaluated to determine the specific type of computational component required to meet timing and performance requirements.

Using this abstraction, designers are free to implement the individual threads on appropriate combinations of commercially available or custom soft IP cores within FPGA. The soft cores can be general purpose programmable CPUs, more powerful Digital Signal Processing Units (DSPs), semi-custom and extensible processors, or fully custom hardware accelerators.

Important for both designer efficiency and system correctness, the high level communication and synchronization primitives defined by the model to co-ordinate interactions between threads are provided through a standard set of Application Programmer Interfaces (APIs). The use of APIs allows the separation of policy and mechanism. The API calls are provided to the designer for use within the application program and are independent of the computational components on which the threads execute. Only the lower level implementations of the model's calls are platform specific. We provide these implementations as linkable libraries for general threads that are run on purpose processors, and as includable VHDL for threads that are turned into custom hardware accelerators.

In the remainder of this section we provide an introduction to the generalized multithreaded programming model. We then provide an overview of the relationship between fabrication advancements for FPGA components and corresponding developments in software infrastructure and design abstractions. We finish this section by showing how the multithreaded programming model can be used to help create a complete multiprocessor system on chip. In Section 3, we show how the standard policies of the model are provided through two separate operating systems for FPGAs; Hthreads and ReconOS. Both operating systems provide designers with the same policies but through different mechanisms. Section 4 concludes the chapter with projections on how FPGAs and the multithreaded programming model are moving towards supporting systems with heterogeneous multiprocessor systems on chip.

BACKGROUND

The Multithreaded Programming Model

Although the multithreading *programming model* has become widely popular within the last few decades, the concept of multithreading was common much earlier, as exhibited in the CDC 6600 in the early 1960's. During this earlier era, multithreading referred to the time multiplexing of a single fast CPU between multiple slower peripheral processors running I/O operations. The early concept of time multiplexing hardware resources between different threads of software was once again adopted within more modern programming models to enable users to write concurrent programs. For systems with a single processor the multiple threads must time-slice on the shared CPU. When ported to a machine with multiple processors, the threads can be executed in parallel. The popularity of the multithreaded programming model has led to the definition of a platform independent operating system standard with well-defined synchronization primitives and APIs for implementing portable multithreaded systems (POSIX).

The multithreaded programming model has proven to be convenient for client server applications, where requests from different clients can be executed as independent threads, and time-sliced on a server to increase processor utilization and overall performance. The model has also gained acceptance in real-time control systems with its ability to model parallel operations that are executed reactively when new input data arrives. It is widely supported in contemporary embedded operating systems such as VxWorks (Wind River, 2007), RTXC (Quadros Systems, 2007), eCos (eCosCentric, 2008), and QNX Neutrino (QNX Software Systems, 2009). In reactive systems, input data (such as produced by sensors) causes the initiation of processing. The processed data is then typically used to control actuators or output drivers within the system under control. When modeling an embedded control system, the multithreaded programming model allows an application to be partitioned into separate input, processing, and output threads that are invoked, execute, and synchronize based on available input, or specific timing requirements. An input

thread can block until new data is available, at which point the input thread executes to acquire new data samples. The synchronization primitives of the model then allow the input thread to signal, or unblock, the processing threads. When a processing thread completes, it in turn wakes the data output thread. Thus, each thread executes independently, and signals its succeeding thread with operations defined by the programming model. For systems with multiple computational resources, the threads can execute in parallel and overlap their operations to increase throughput and resource efficiency.

The multithreaded programming model defines the necessary *policies* required to create, manage, schedule, share data and synchronize multiple threads. The model does not define the *mechanisms* or low level implementation of the policies. Languages such as Java have the policies built into the language. C, on the other hand, provides no support and instead relies on additional middleware libraries such as Pthreads. The multithreaded systems described in this chapter are based on C and the Pthreads libraries. Table 1 lists the more common APIs provided by the pthreads standard. A complete listing of the pthreads APIs can be found in (Butenhoff, 1997).

The primitives provided by the middleware layer can then be used to specify all interactions between the threads of the application. Figure 1 illustrates an example control application with several threads communicating and synchronizing using message queues, shared memory, and semaphores.

FPGAs: From Co-Processors to Reconfigurable Systems-on-Chip

Field Programmable Gate Array (FPGA) chips have progressed through four rapid technology generations (Trimberger, 2007). The first two generations offered steady increases in gate densities. As the gate densities grew, the use of FPGAs as simple replacement parts for glue logic

Table 1. PThreads APIs

Type	Example	Description
Thread Management	pthread_create	Creates a thread
Synchronization	pthread_join	Waits for thread completion
	sem_post	Synchronization primitive
	sem_wait	
	mutex_(un)lock	Mutual exclusion primitive
	pthread_cond_wait	Synchronization and Barrier for Multiple Threads
Communication	pthread_mq_send	Message transfer primitive
	pthread_mq_recv	

Figure 1. Multithreaded Programming Model {FILE: prog_model_example.tiff}

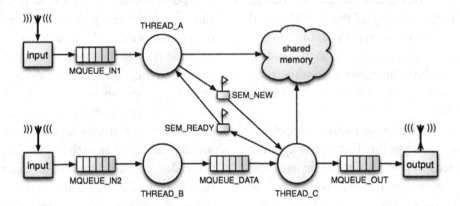

on mother boards expanded into a new role as a co-processor accelerator for speeding up portions of an application program. Figure 2 shows this use case. The section of code to be replaced with an accelerator had to be identified, lifted out, and coded by hand in a synthesizable hardware description language (HDL). Designers were also responsible for creating a custom HW/SW interface between the software program running on the CPU and the accelerator running in the FPGA. Data had to be transferred into the accelerator, typically using FIFO and Queue structures, and then the accelerator had to be started. Once the accelerator completed, the program then read the results back out of a FIFO or Queue into memory or the CPU's register set.

To ease the task of hardware development and open the potential of the FPGA to software programmers, new high level language to gates (HLL to gates) translators began to appear as alternatives to working in an HDL (Wazlowski, Agarwal, Lee, Smith, Lam, Athanas, Silverman & Ghosh, 1993), (Celoxica, n.d.), (Najjar, Bohm, Draper, Hammes, Rinker, Beveridge, Chawathe & Ross, 2003), (ImpulseC, n.d.), (Guo, Buyukkurt, Na jjar & Vissers, 2005), (Gupta, Dutt & Nicolau, 2003). The majority of these efforts as typified by HandelC (Celoxica, n.d.) and ImpulseC (ImpulseC, n.d.) sought to provide a more C like environment with abstract data types and familiar programming language syntax. The designers of these languages quickly faced the same issues that designers of parallel programming languages for paral-

Figure 2. FPGAs as Co-Processors {FILE: early_fpga_design_flow.tiff}

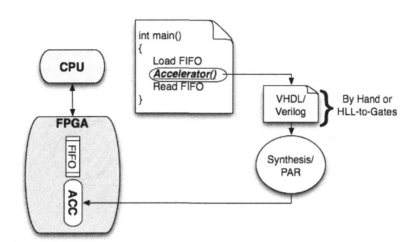

lel processing faced a decade earlier: how best to represent and exploit parallelism within an inherently sequential language (Edwards, 2006). Optimizing compilers adopted techniques developed earlier for unrolling loops to implicitly expose parallelism for creating the accelerator. Most languages provided new constructs within the source language to be used by the designer to explicitly expose parallelism.

The last two generations of FPGAs led to devices with gate densities that scaled in size past what was required to host a single application accelerator. These generations also integrated diffused Intellectual Property (IP) such as SRAM memories, multipliers, and general purpose microprocessor cores within the denser and bigger reconfigurable fabric. The increased capabilities of the FPGAs allowed designers to create complete systems, including multiple processors, on a programmable Chip (SoPCs). To open the potential of these new chips, we began investigating how to enable appropriate system level software frameworks such as operating systems and middleware to bring the multiple computational components implemented within the FPGA fabric under a unifying and familiar programming model. From a programmers perspective, each thread created

within a multithreaded program represents a virtual CPU. In systems with traditional microprocessors the virtual CPU's are simply time-multiplexed on a physical CPU. The concept of a virtual CPU is also convenient for guiding the creation of parallel physical resources. Instead of being compiled, the body of a thread can alternatively serve as a specification for synthesizing an independent custom accelerator. The body of the thread can be represented in VHDL, or can be coded in any of the prior C to gates languages and automatically translated into VHDL. Regardless of the synthesis method, the programming model provides APIs that allow the thread to seamlessly interact with the other threads independent of their implementation method. Conceptually, the designer can create a virtual multiprocessor with more custom accelerators by simply increasing the number of application threads. This capability can be useful to increase system throughput by carefully decomposing the application program into an appropriate set of physical parallel threads. After the threads have been defined, a custom system can be synthesized specifically for the application. Figure 3 shows how parallel threads from a single multithreaded program can be synthesized and mapped within

Figure 3. Multiprocessor System-on-Chip on an FPGA {FILE: soc_abstract.tiff}

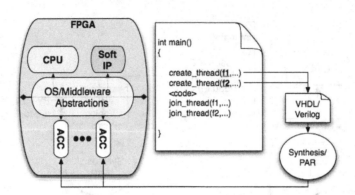

the FPGA, where they communicate using abstractions provided by an operating system layer.

The HW/SW specific application code and data queues required during earlier generations is now replaced by our standard APIs that are linked into the source code. Equivalent mechanisms for hardware threads in the form of finite state machines replace traditional software binary libraries underneath the APIs. The software libraries and finite state machines form the OS/ Middleware abstraction layer shown in Figure 3 to hide the CPU/FPGA boundary from the application developer.

The fundamental policies of the pthreads multithreaded programming model are represented by APIs set by a standards committee. As we will show in the next section, it is possible to create different implementations of these policies to meet particular system requirements.

OPERATING SYSTEMS FOR MULTITHREADED RECONFIGURABLE SYSTEMS-ON-CHIP

In this section we present *hthreads* and *ReconOS* and show how they both support the multithreaded paradigm but with different implementations. The objective of the hthreads system was to provide

very low latency primitives with constant delay times to support precise real-time system requirements. The objective of the ReconOS system was to provide maximum flexibility and portability across different processor families. At a very broad brush level, the main differences between the two systems are in how and where the core operating system services are implemented. The hthreads system follows a microkernel approach that partitions operating system functions into parallel, independent service groups. Many of the key service groups are then migrated into hardware for performance. ReconOS stays with the more popular monolithic kernel approach with a set of centralized services running on a general purpose processor. This approach allows ReconOS to enhance portability across platforms through building on top of two existing operating systems kernels; eCos and Linux. Independent of the organization and location of the core operating system services both systems adopt an abstraction layer that sits between threads synthesized as hardware accelerators and the other operating system components. This abstraction layer is in the form of a finite state machine to provide operating system services to hardware accelerators. ReconOS then provides remote procedure type calls between the abstraction layer and centralized services. Hthreads directs requests to one of the hardware based microkernel services.

Figure 4. hthreads Architecture

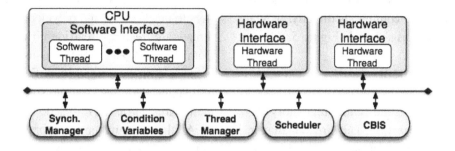

Hthreads

Hthreads, originally known as HybridThreads, provides a comprehensive set of OS primitives that are uniformly accessible to both software and hardware threads as shown in Figure 4 [4],[3]. Software threads are traditional threads that execute on a CPU, whereas hardware threads are hardware-based components that do not require CPU resources for execution. In hthreads, all hardware threads make use of a Hardware Thread Interface (HWTI) abstraction layer for all system-level interactions and system calls. The OS primitives in hthreads are implemented as a set of independent IP cores; where each component provides a separate OS service. The major core services within hthreads include:

- Thread Management
- Scheduling
- Mutex-based Synchronization
- Condition Variables
- Interrupt Scheduling

Each OS core exposes a memory-mapped interface to allow any component capable of mastering the system bus to make use of the core's services. This architecture enables uniform access to OS services from both CPU-based software threads and hardware-based threads. Each core encapsulates all of the necessary state required to perform its services. This information is kept

in a combination of registers and Block RAM, and access to all stored information is mediated by the core itself.

Commands associated with an OS core can be invoked through traditional load/store operations. When a core is targeted by a load/store command, the bus logic associated with the core detects an active transaction and invokes the necessary core logic to process and acknowledge the command. Commands that require no return value can be implemented as traditional store commands, whereas commands that require a return value or status update can be fully implemented in a single load operation. A single load operation has two phases, the first being address formation and request, and the second being acknowledgement with a return value. The process of address formation for an hthreads core command uses an encoding process that embeds all operands and opcodes for an operation into the address field of a load operation. The receiving core decodes this information from the address field, performs the requested operation, and returns the result on the data lines of the bus. The entire process is atomic, as each hthreads OS core is capable of delaying an acknowledgement until the requested operation is complete. This allows traditional read-modify-write style operations to be embedded in a single atomic load transaction. This is a key feature of the hthreads OS, and enables atomic access to OS services in a heterogeneous system-on-chip environment. Software threads are able to request

OS services directly via CPU-based loads/stores, while hardware threads are able to do the same using bus read/write commands directly, or via the hthreads HWTI as shown in Figure 5.

Thread Management

The thread manager is the central repository for all thread state information. The thread manager is responsible for the creation and allocation of thread identifiers, internal thread state, and inter-thread relationships. Status information is stored on a per-thread basis in embedded Block RAMs (BRAMs) and contains data concerning:

- Thread Status - Joinable or detached.
- Thread Existence - Thread identifier used or un-unused.
- Thread Exited - Currently exited or not.

The core manages a thread identifier (TID) allocation stack that allows for fresh thread identifiers to be allocated and recycled at run-time. As threads are created, thread identifiers are removed from the stack and marked as used. As threads begin to exit, the thread identifiers are recycled by placing them back on the stack and marking their status entries as un-used.

All thread management operations are shown in Table 2. Sets of these operations are used to construct higher-level POSIX operating system APIs, such as pthread_create and pthread_join. While most of these operations are solely concerned with management operations, some directly result in the invocation of scheduling operations; for instance thread creation leads to the invocation of a scheduling operation in order to add the newly created thread to the scheduler's ready-to-run queue. This relationship between thread management and scheduling operations resulted in the need for a dedicated command interface between the

Figure 5. hthreads OS Interfaces {FILES: hthread_arch.tiff, thread_interfaces.tiff }

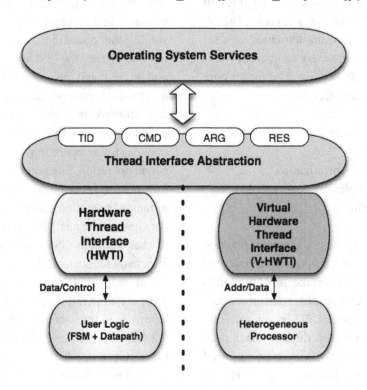

Table 2. Thread Management Operations

Operation	Type	Description
Add_Thread	Read-only, depth = T	Adds a threads to the scheduling queue.
Current_Thread	Read-only, depth = 1	Returns the TID of the thread currently running on the CPU.
Next_Thread	Read-only, depth = 1	Operation that "consumes" a scheduling decision If a valid scheduling decision exists, then that TID will be placed in the current_thread_ID register.
Create_Thread (Detached)	Read-only, depth = 1	Creates a new managment thread structure for a detached thread and returns the TID of the new thread.
Create_Thread (Joinable)	Read-only, depth = 1	Creates a new managment thread structure for a joinable thread and returns the TID of the new thread.
Clear_Thread	Read-only, depth = T	De-allocates a thread managment structure for a given thread so that it's TID can be recycled.
Yield_Thread	Read-only, depth = 1	Voluntary yield operation that places the currently running thread back in the ready-to-run queue, makes a new scheduling decision (if possible) so that a different TID can be placed in the current_thread_ID register.
Exit_Thread	Read-only, depth = 1	Notifies the manager that a thread has terminated (exited). If the thread is joinable, then threads that have joined on this thread are added to the scheduling queue.
Join_Thread	Read-only, depth = T	Allows a parent thread to "block" on a child thread until it has exited.
Detach_Thread	Read-only, depth = T	Operation that changes a thread's status from joinable to detached.

thread manager and the scheduler. The interface allows the thread manager to have fast access to scheduler functionality, and eliminates the need for the thread manager to use a more complicated master interface. The raw timing results for thread management operations are shown in Table 3.

Thread Scheduling

All scheduling and ready-to-run queue operations are handled by the the thread scheduling core. The core manages a partitioned O(1) ready-to-run queue that allows for constant-time enqueue, dequeue, and scheduling decision operations. The ready-to-run queue is implemented using a set of Block RAMs to form a set of independent doubly-linked lists, where each list contains the threads resident in a given priority level. The structure of the hthreads scheduler allows for extremely low-overhead and low-jitter scheduling decisions

Table 3. Raw (HW-only) Timing Results of Thread Management Operations

Operation	Time (clock cycles)
Add_Thread	10 + ENQ
Clear_Thread	10
Create_Thread_Joinable	8
Create_Thread_Detached	8
Current_Thread	3
Detach_Thread	10
Exit_Thread	17
Join_Thread	10
Next_Thread	10 + DEQ
Yield_Thread	10 + ENQ + DEQ

to be made in parallel with the execution of application threads.

The scheduler currently supports up to 256 threads and 128 different priority levels with built-in support for round-robin and preemptive-priority scheduling operations. The core contains support for dynamically changing thread priority levels, however support for automatic aging of thread priorities has been left out in order to conserve hardware resources. However, dynamic aging policies can be easily implemented in software.

The hthreads scheduler is unique in that it is purpose-built for scheduling in a heterogeneous environment. Each thread has a scheduling parameter that signifies whether or not it is a software- or hardware-thread. Software threads are traditional CPU-bound threads that are time-multiplexed over one or many CPUS (Agron, Peck, Anderson, Andrews, Komp, Sass, Baijot, & Stevens, 2006). On the other hand, hardware threads are dedicated computational units that do not require time-multiplexing. Hardware threads cannot be preempted, as their resources are dedicated towards the execution of a specific task. When a hardware thread can resume execution immediately after it has been created or when it becomes un-blocked, as it does not have to fight for shared execution resources.

The scheduler has two distinct interfaces: (1) BUSCom; a bus interface for generalized access to scheduling operations, and (2) TMCom; a dedicated interface for thread management related operations. The scheduling operations available through the TMCom and BUSCom interfaces are shown in Tables 4 and 5 respectively. Priority is given to TMCom commands, as they are the result of a currently outstanding thread management request, and therefore should be completed as

quickly as possible. The raw timing performance of the scheduling primitives are shown in Table 6.

Thread Synchronization

All low-level synchronization mechanisms are encapsulated within the synchronization management core. The core provides mutex primitives available in three POSIX-compatible forms:

- **Fast:** No error condition notifications
- **Error Checking:** Tracks state of mutex and records error conditions
- **Recursive:** Enables recursive locking behavior

The mutex primitives are easily accessible from any computational component capable of producing a master transaction on a bus, and does not rely on the use of specialized atomic operations and coherency protocols. Instead, the core's interface makes use of traditional load/store operations, allowing it to be readily used in heterogeneous environments where processors and other components may have incompatible atomic operations. The synchronization manager itself is a centralized repository of mutex information, completely eliminating the need for coherency protocols to distribute up-to-date mutex information between processors and other computational components.

The synchronization management operations are shown in Table 7. These operations allow con-

Table 4. Scheduler Operations Available Through TMCom

Operation	Parameter(s)	Description
Enqueue	TID to enqueue	Adds a thread to the R2RQ, updates the next scheduling decision, and performs a preemption check if necessary
Dequeue	TID to dequeue	Removes a thread from the R2RQ and updates the next scheduling decision
Is_Queued	TID to query	Returns a status bit indicating whether or not a thread is currently in the R2RQ
Is_Empty	NONE	Returns a status bit indicating whether or not the R2RQ in empty

Table 5. Scheduler Operations Available Through BUSCom

Operation	Type	Description
Toggle_Preemption	Write-only, depth = 1	Enable/disable the scheduler's preemption interrupt. The bit will be set to the value of the MSB of the data being written. A '1' represents an enabled interrupt, while a '0' disables the interrupt.
Set_SchedParam	Write-only, depth = T	Updates a thread's scheduling parameter. A value between 0 and 127 signifies a priority-level for a SW thread, and a value greater than 127 represents the base address of a HW thread.
Get_SchedParam	Read-only, depth = T	Returns the 32-bit scheduling parameter for a thread.
Check_SchedParam	Read-only, depth = T	Performs an safety check on the thread's scheduling parameter. If a thread is not queued, then the call is guaranteed to pass. However, if the thread is queued, then a check is performed to make sure that thread's scheduling parameter is in the valid range for SW threads (0 to 127).
Set_Idle_Thread	Read-only, depth = T	Sets up the thread ID of the idle thread, and Sets the internal idle_thread_valid flag.
Get_Idle_Thread	Read-only, depth = T	Returns the TID of the idle thread as well as the internal idle_thread_valid flag.

figuration of the type (kind) of individual mutex objects, ability to lock/unlock mutexes, and the ability to query mutex state (ower, count, kind). The synchronization core stores all mutex state in embedded Block RAMs: including individual blocked-lists for threads waiting on mutex objects. The core adds waiting threads to its internal blocked-list upon lock unsuccessful lock operations; a lock operation that occurs when a mutex is already owned by another thread. Additionally, the core automatically unblocks threads by sending requests to the thread manager upon mutex unlock requests. All blocked-list management operations are handled by the synchronization manager FSM. Every mutex operation completes in less than 5 clock cycles and each is fully deterministic, leading to very low overhead and low jitter synchronization operations as shown in Table 8.

Interrupt Scheduling

In most CPU-based systems, interrupts are special in that they have the ability to preempt any task running on the processor, regardless of that task's priority. This is allowed to happen, as an OS must first invoke the top-half of an interrupt handler in

order to check what type of interrupt is occurring. Unfortunately, this means that interrupts are in a separate priority class of ∞ that always trumps any and all application tasks.

The effect of asynchronous interrupts with priority levels of ∞ can wreak havoc on the determinicity of application programs. Currently, the only way to prevent interrupt events from preempting user-level tasks is to disable inter-

Table 6. Raw (HW-only) Timing Results of Scheduling Operations

Operation	Time (clock cycles)
Enqueue(SWthread)	28
Enqueue(HWthread)	20 + (1 Bus Transaction)
Dequeue	24
Get_Entry	10
Is_Queued	10
Is_Empty	10
Set_Idle_Thread	10
Get_Sched_Param	10
Check_Sched_Param	10
Set_Sched_Param(NotQueued)	10
Set_Sched_Param(Queued)	50

Table 7. Synchronization Operations

Operation	Type	Description
Lock	Read-only, depth = MxT	Attempts to lock a mutex for a given thread.
Try-lock	Read-only, depth = MxT	Attempts to try-lock a mutex for a given thread.
Unlock	Read-only, depth = M	Unlocks a mutex.
Owner	Read-only, depth = M	Returns the current owner's TID of a given mutex.
Kind	Read/Write, depth = M	Returns or updates the kind of a given mutex. Where kind is one of the following: FAST, RECURSIVE, or ERROR.
Count	Read-only, depth = M	Returns the current lock count of a given mutex. Only valid for RECURSIVE mutexes.

Table 8. HW Timing of Synchronization Operations

Operation	Time (cycles)
Lock Mutex	4
Unlock Mutex	5
Try Lock Mutex	3
Get Mutex Owner	3
Get Mutex Count	3
Get/Set Mutex Kind	3

rupts all together. This is quite dangerous to do, as this can prevent any future interrupts from being serviced for long periods of time. If interrupts are left enabled, repetitive interrupt events can cause a program to be preempted over and over again. While the program will still be able to make progress, the interrupt events will destroy the timeliness characteristics of the task. This is especially concerning for real-time and embedded systems, where determinicity and timeliness are a first-class concern.

Hthreads has implemented an interrupt-scheduling core, known as the CPU-Bypass Interrupt Scheduler (CBIS), that is able to pre-screen interrupt events before interrupting the CPU. The core works by allowing a programmer to make associations between interrupts and application threads as opposed to traditional interrupt service routines.

The associated threads, which are referred to as interrupt service threads (ISTs) (Kreuzinger, Schulz, Pfeffer, Ungerer, Brinkschulte & Krakowski, 2000), are fully schedulable computations that have priority levels in the range of all other application threads. This allows interrupt events to be prioritized and scheduled without having to needlessly interrupt the CPU.

The CBIS acts a translator; turning pulses on interrupt lines into add_thread requests to the HW-based thread manager core. This translation process occurs in hardware, concurrently with application execution. Preemption of a thread running on the CPU *only* happens when a scheduled interrupt has best priority in the system. Otherwise, the thread will remain in the ready-to-run queue waiting to execute. Interrupt events can also be transparently associated with heterogeneous threads, such as hardware threads. The operations supported by the CBIS are shown in Table 9. The association operation of the CBIS requires only a single bus transaction to cause a thread to wait until a future interrupt event. Additionally, the wake-up process only requires a single bus transaction to add the associated thread back to the system ready-to-run queue.

Table 9. CBIS Operations

Operation	Type	Description
Interrupt_Associate	Read-only, depth = IxT	Associates a thread with a specific interrupt. This causes the calling thread to block until an event occurs on the associated interrupt line.
Interrupt_Clear	Read-only, depth = I	Clears any thread associations for a specific interrupt.

Integrated Performance

The OS services of Hthreads are uniformly accessible from any computational component, including traditional software threads, hardware threads, and heterogeneous processing units. Additionally, the OS cores themselves have been parallelized to provide extremely low-overhead and low-jitter operations. This structure results in extremely predictable and efficient system calls for computations on either side of the HW/SW boundary. As an example, timing results for mutex-based synchronization operations for software-, hardware-, and heterogeneous-computations are shown in Table 10. Hardware-based mutex operations are actually faster than software as the hardware thread interface's invocation mechanism is able to use combinational logic instead of a sequential system call handler, and does not distinguish between user and privileged modes of operation. The software-based mutex operations, which are only slightly slower, incur additional overhead due to the system call *trap* mechanism and the invocation of the system call handler. The uniformity of these operations simplifies the process of changing a thread's implementation style, as it aids in eliminating drastic performance differences when migrating a thread from software to hardware or vice-versa.

ReconOS

The ReconOS project extends the multithreaded programming model across the hardware/software

Table 10. Integrated performance of hthreads synchronization primitives

Operation	Execution Time (Cycles)
SW lock	450
SW unlock	357
HW lock	39
HW unlock	39
Hetero lock	288
Hetero unlock	295

boundary, just as hthreads. Instead of implementing the required operating system functionality as dedicated hardware modules, ReconOS tries to re-use much of the functionality already provided by existing software operating system kernels, and makes it available to reconfigurable hardware. As a consequence, any hardware platform that intends to support ReconOS must consist of at least one microprocessor, or CPU, to execute the operating system kernel, and platform-specific logic as an operating system interface (OSIF) between the kernel and the reconfigurable fabric. There are two ReconOS implementations, one based on the embedded configurable operating system eCos, and the other based on the wide-spread operating system Linux, which also partly illustrates the different focus of ReconOS compared to hthreads. Figure 6(a) shows an example for the decomposition of a ReconOS system.

A prominent feature of ReconOS is to preserve low-level languages for design entry for hardware threads. These can either be generated from more abstract languages, e.g. from MATLAB or (aug-

Figure 6. ReconOS architecture {FILES: reconf_arch.tiff, reconos_arch.tiff} ((a) architectural overview) ((b) hardware architecture)

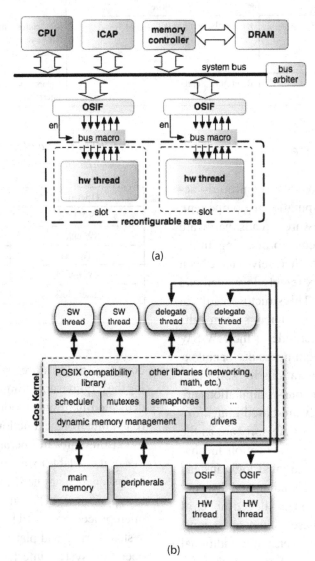

(a)

(b)

mented) C, via high-level synthesis tools, or be specified directly in a hardware description language. To this end, ReconOS provides methods for facilitating operating system interactions from within hardware modules described in a low-level language, such as VHDL. The required structure and design methods for ReconOS hardware threads are outlined in Section 3.2.1.

The reconfigurable fabric is split into *slots* of arbitrary size, position, and shape, each of

which represents the execution environment for a hardware thread. The current implementation of the ReconOS hardware architecture is shown in Figure 6(b), and is independent from the employed host operating system. Hardware threads are connected to the system via their OS interfaces, which, in turn, are connected to the system's buses. ReconOS systems employ two different buses: a memory bus and a control communication bus (not shown in Figure 6(b)). The memory bus is used by the CPU and the hardware threads to access the memory controller and other system peripherals. All control communication between the OS kernel and the threads' OS interfaces is routed across a separate control bus. This separation of control and data communications provides improved latency and independence from the employed data communication topology.

Being a portable extension to existing software OS kernels, ReconOS has been implemented on various host operating systems and processor architectures. We provide prototype implementations for eCos on PowerPC (ReconOS/eCos-PPC), Linux on PowerPC (ReconOS/Linux-PPC), as well as Linux on a MicroBlaze soft-core CPU (ReconOS/Linux-MicroBlaze). Section 3.2.4 evaluates the respective OS overheads for these prototypes.

Hardware Thread Programming

In contrast to the sequential execution semantics of a software thread, hardware threads are implicitly parallel. They do not have a single control flow and therefore no apparent notion of calling an operating system function. Consequently, typical hardware description languages, such as VHDL or VeriLog, offer no built-in mechanism to implement *blocking calls*.

In order to extend the multithreaded programming model towards hardware, we structure the description of a hardware thread in a particular way. A single sequential state machine manages all interactions with the operating system by using VHDL procedures from an operating system function library, e.g., reconos_sem_wait(). Together with the operating system interface, a separate synchronizing logic module serving as the connection between the hardware thread and the OS, these procedures are able to establish the semantics of blocking calls in VHDL. Typically, a hardware thread comprises at least two VHDL processes: the synchronization state machine and the actual user logic. The state transitions in the

synchronization state machine are always dependent on control signals from the OSIF; only after a previous operating system call returns, the next state can be reached. Thus, the communication with the operating system is purely sequential, while the processing of the hardware thread itself can be highly parallel. It is up to the programmer to decompose a hardware thread into a collection of user logic modules and one synchronization state machine. Besides the increased complexity due to the parallel nature of hardware, this process is no different from programming a software thread.

The source code for a synchronization state machine of an example hardware thread is given in Listing 1. In the example, the thread retrieves a message *m* from the message box *MB_IN*, adds a constant value to it, and forwards the modified value to the message box *MB_OUT*.

Listing 1: Example synchronization state machine

```
case state is
    when STATE_GET =>
        reconos_mbox_get([...], MB_
START, m);
        next_state:- STATE_WAIT;
    when STATE_ADD =>
        m:= m + SOME_CONSTANT;
        next_state:= STATE_PUT;
    when STATE_PUT =>
        reconos_mbox_put([...], MB_
DONE, m);
        next_state:= STATE_GET;
end case;
```

Table 11 shows an overview of the operating system objects and their related ReconOS and POSIX API calls, as used by hardware and software threads, respectively. Most of the hardware functions are direct counterparts to the POSIX software API, as outlined in Section 2.1. Notable exceptions include mailboxes, which provide separate sets of calls for blocking and non-blocking put and get operations, and memory accesses, which can

Table 11. Overview of ReconOS API functions

OS object	POSIX API (software)	ReconOS API (hardware)
semaphores	sem_post()	reconos_sem_post()
	sem_wait()	reconos_sem_wait()
mutexes	pthread_mutex_lock()	reconos_mutex_lock()
	pthread_mutex_unlock()	reconos_mutex_unlock()
condition variables	pthread_cond_wait()	reconos_cond_wait()
	pthread_cond_signal()	reconos_cond_signal()
	pthread_cond_broadcast()	reconos_cond_broadcast()
message queues /		reconos_mq_send()
mail boxes	mq_send()	reconos_mbox_put()
		reconos_mbox_tryput()
		reconos_mq_receive()
	mq_receive()	reconos_mbox_get()
		reconos_mbox_tryget()
shared memory		reconos_write()
		reconos_write_burst()
		reconos_read()
		reconos_read_burst()
threads	pthread_exit()	reconos_thread_exit()
	pthread_create()	—

explicitly request single-word or burst transfers. Currently, the ReconOS hardware API supports the most important subset of the calls available in POSIX. The incorporation of additional functions, such as calls for thread creation or scheduler control, requires only minimal extensions to the execution environment.

OS integration

Every hardware thread is connected to the rest of the system by its operating system interface (OSIF). The task of the OSIF is to handle operating system calls from the hardware threads by either executing them directly, if they can be processed in hardware, or by relaying them to the CPU. At the same time, the OSIF also handles all control communication from the OS to the reconfigurable

hardware, such as reset, state save/restore, or reconfiguration commands.

On one side, the OSIF connects to the hardware thread's OS synchronization state machine and local RAM. On the other side, the OSIF provides an interface to two bus systems, the system memory bus (PLB) and the OS control bus (DCR). Further, the OSIF requires an interrupt line to the CPU's interrupt controller and features optional ports to connect to FIFO cores. The OSIF itself is built from several modules whose tasks are described in the following. Figure 7 gives an overview of the OSIF's structure and its interfaces.

Thread Supervision and Control

The mechanisms that govern the OS call request-response interactions between the OSIF and the hardware thread are controlled by the *command*

Figure 7. OSIF overview and interfaces {FILE: osif_connections.tiff}

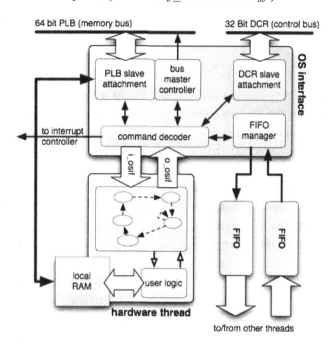

decoder module. This module receives OS call requests from the hardware thread, decodes them and initiates the appropriate processes to fulfill that request. This may involve, for example, raising an interrupt with the system CPU, initiating a bus master transfer or feeding data into a FIFO.

Since the operating system executing on the CPU cannot process OS calls within one clock cycle, the OSIF needs a means to suspend state transitions of the thread's OS synchronization state machine. This is achieved by having the OS synchronization state machine routinely check input signals (*busy* and *blocking*) from the OSIF before setting its next state. This way, the OSIF can block the part of the hardware thread that interacts with the operating system, which effectively implements the semantics of blocking calls in VHDL.

OS Call Relaying

The OSIF relays all services that are not handled in hardware to the OS kernel running on the CPU.

Once the command decoder receives such a request from the hardware thread, it places the command and associated arguments in software-accessible registers on the DCR bus, and raises an interrupt with the CPU. This interrupt is forwarded to the software delegate thread associated with the hardware thread (see below), which retrieves the command and arguments from the registers and executes the software OS call on behalf of the hardware thread. Any return values are placed in the OSIF's DCR registers, which pass the values on to the hardware thread. For completeness, it should be noted that the parallel user processes inside the thread may continue their execution during an OS call.

Data Communication Routing

Due to the substantial overhead involved in relaying OS requests to software, all high-throughput data communications should be handled in hardware without involving the CPU. The ReconOS OSIF features hardware support for several different communication primitives that provides the basis for any efficient, high-bandwidth thread-to-thread communication:

- **Bus Master Access** The memory bus attachment logic encapsulates the logic for direct memory access to the system's entire physical address space. Using the OSIF's capabilities, an attached hardware thread can access shared memory by means of convenient single word access or high-throughput burst transfers, both for read and write operations. Additionally, the DMA facilities of the OSIF permit efficient and CPU-autonomous data transfer for message queues.

- **Hardware FIFOs** To allow for bus-independent thread-to-thread data communication, the ReconOS run-time environment provides dedicated FIFO buffers implemented in hardware. Two threads connected by such a FIFO module can transfer data without interrupting the CPU or increasing bus load. When a hardware thread signals a pending read or write access to such a FIFO, the OSIF's command decoder passes the request to the *FIFO manager* (see Figure 7), which controls the handshake lines of the FIFO modules.

Delegate Threads

Once a OS request originating from a hardware thread has been relayed to the CPU, it needs to be translated into an actual software OS system call to the operating system kernel. To this end, ReconOS creates a separate software thread, the *delegate*, for every hardware thread. This delegate thread executes the operating system calls on behalf of its hardware thread and relays any return values back to the corresponding OSIF. This approach has three distinct advantages:

- *Transparency.* For the kernel, operating system calls initiated in hardware cannot be distinguished from calls initiated by software threads, which provides the aforementioned transparency with respect to a thread's execution context (hardware or software).

- *Portability.* Since a delegate thread is executed as a regular software thread (e.g. in user space, for systems that distinguish execution privileges for application and kernel code), no modifications to the operating system kernel apart from a generic OSIF driver are necessary. This makes the ReconOS approach easily adaptable to other operating systems.

- *Flexibility.* Making additional operating system calls available to hardware threads involves relatively small changes to the delegate thread, again without necessitating any changes to the kernel.

Dynamic Partial Reconfiguration

As mentioned before, the decomposition of an application into separate threads provides suitable separate modules for both parallel execution as well as for better resource utilization through multithreading. In the case of reconfigurable hardware, multithreading is implemented through the use of partial reconfiguration. A ReconOS slot, as introduced in Section 3.2, provides the area in which hardware threads can be (re-)configured. Because every slot is connected to exactly one OSIF, there can only be one hardware thread in every slot at a given time. Bus macros embedded in the interface between hardware thread and OSIF (as depicted in Figure 6(b)) provide for configuration-invariant routing and glitchless reconfiguration when exchanging hardware threads.

Partial reconfiguration allows two execution techniques with related, but distinctively different advantages. When placed under application control through the already established thread creation and termination API, the hardware/software partitioning can be changed during run-time to allow for changing performance requirements brought about by, for example, varying input data characteristics. Because the unified thread interface and programming model, the system can decide to replace a software thread with a hardware thread and vice versa, thereby possibly trading one performance parameter (e.g., execution time) for another (e.g., power consumption or area). This is the approach taken by the application case study presented in Section 3.3.

The second technique involves integrating the reconfiguration control for hardware threads into the operating system's scheduler together with preemption techniques for hardware threads. This allows to adapt the system's hardware thread composition both to external conditions as well as to the hardware thread's execution patterns. Idle hardware threads that are waiting on resources which are being held by other threads could be replaced by other threads which are ready to execute, thus raising the utilization of the system's reconfigurable resources. This mechanism is mostly transparent to the designer, as it operates on the established threading model. The current implementation of ReconOS employs a cooperative scheduling method for hardware threads (Luebbers & Platzner, 2009).

Performance and Overheads

To evaluate the performance of the various communication and synchronization primitives, we have conducted experimental measurements for both OS call overheads and communication throughputs. The results are listed in Tables 12 and 13.

While ReconOS offers a simple and flexible way of providing operating system services to hardware threads, the experiments demonstrate clearly that there is a penalty involved. Nevertheless, designers are more likely to use the precious logic resources for heavy data-parallel processing

rather than implementing synchronization-intensive control dominated code. Under this premise the synchronization latencies are well within reasonable bounds.

Application Case Study

To demonstrate how our proposed modeling approach can be implied on a real world example, we have developed a multithreaded framework for tracking the system state inside a dynamic non-linear environment over time using Sequential Monte Carlo (SMC) methods (Happe, Leubbers, & Platzner, 2009). SMC methods have a wide range of applications in the embedded and real-time domain, such as network packet processing or navigation systems. They estimate the system state based on a statistical approach where the prob-

Table 12. Performance of ReconOS synchronization primitives

	eCos/PPC	Linux/PPC	Linux/Micro-Blaze
mutex (raw OS calls)			
SW lock	83	821	9178
SW unlock	171	551	9179
HW lock	959	7769	35855
HW unlock	679	2636	22360
mutex (turnaround)			
SW SW	453	8821	83657
SW HW	629	9824	90515
HW SW	1449	14371	121673
HW HW	1460	14102	126668
semaphore (raw OS calls)			
SW post	73	598	13180
HW post	695	1972	22116
semaphore (turnaround)			
SW SW	305	9094	203221
SW HW	528	9575	207824
HW SW	908	12291	145924
HW HW	1114	12196	154013
All values given in bus cycles (1 cycle = 10 ns)			

Table 13. Performance of ReconOS communication primitives

Operation	[μs]	[MB/s]
MEMHW (burst read)	4.574	17.080
HWMEM (burst write)	4.054	19.271
MEMSWMEM (memcopy)	13.251	
HWHW (mailbox)	6.142	12.720
SWHW (mailbox)	58500	13
HWSW (mailbox)	58510	13
SWHW (message queue)	47.200	1.655
HWSW (message queue)	48.231	1.620
All operations were run for 8 kBytes of data		

Figure 8. Object tracking in a video sequence (soccer) {FILES: frame.tiff}*

(a) Frame 5

(b) Frame 90

(c) Frame 150

(d) Frame 260

ability distribution over all possible system states is approximated by a large number of samples (particles), which are iteratively compared with (possibly noisy) measurements to compute an approximation of the the current state probability distribution. In this section, we will illustrate our framework's operation on an example implementation of a video tracking system.

Our implementation relies on a modified Sampling-Importance-Resampling (SIR) approach that operates in a loop covering four stages: *Sampling* (S) for estimating the distribution based on a defined system model, *Observation* (O) for extracting observations from given measurements, *Importance* (I) for weighing the new particles according to the extracted observations, and *Resampling* (R) for eliminating or duplicating individual particles according to their weights to form a new probability distribution for the system's state.

Figure 8 depicts the video object tracking problem implemented as a application using the SMC framework. Here, the system state is modeled by the current object position, its velocity and its scaling factor. The system dynamics are

represented by a simple first-order model, which moves the system state according to the tracked object's current velocity. Colored histograms are used as observations for the importance stage, where a particle's histogram gets compared to the color histogram of the initially-selected object.

For each stage, a hardware and a software implementation is available to the framework in the form of hardware and software threads. The processing of a stage can be performed by one or multiple threads of arbitrary HW/SW distribution. Especially the S, O, and I stages can benefit from parallel execution, as the particles are independent of each other.

Multiple HW/SW partitionings were implemented and measured, as can be seen in Figure 9(a). The measurements were observed for the soccer video sequence, shown in Figure 8, on a Avnet Virtex-4 FX100 development board, with the CPU running at 300 MHz and the hardware threads at 100 MHz and using ReconOS as programming model. In the sequence, the soccer player moves into the background, thus reducing the number of pixels contributing to the histogram calculations. It can be seen that a HW thread for the I-stage

Figure 9. Runtime in of static and adaptive partitionings. Each index i and index o represent the use of a corresponding hw thread. Hence, is a partitioning with two hw threads for the O-stage and one hw thread for the I-stage. sw represents a partitioning without any hw thread. {FILES: measurements*.tiff}

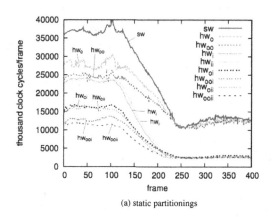

(a) static partitionings

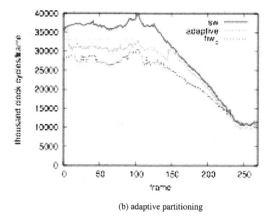

(b) adaptive partitioning

always improves the runtime by a constant value, while HW threads for the O-stage benefit the system only in cases where many pixels need to be computed (i.e. in the first 100 frames). This is a prime example for input-data dependent performance characteristics which warrant a run-time change of the HW/SW partitioning, as described in Section 3.2.3.

First results are depicted in Figure 9(b), which shows a single HW thread for the observation stage being reconfigured into the system's only HW slot at the first frame (vertical line) to achieve a given performance. After 144 frames, this thread is again removed from the slot, where the perfor-

mance can be attained without the support of an additional HW slot, which can then be used for other more critical processing threads.

OUTLOOK AND FUTURE DIRECTIONS

Recently, the wide-spread use of multithreaded programming in software-based systems has enabled the exploitation of modern multi-core processors both in the desktop and the embedded domain. While multithreading is a viable design methodology of and by itself, it is also often used as the implementation vehicle for higher-level parallel languages employing monitors, coroutines, or other paradigms for explicitly and implicitly exploiting the increasingly parallel nature of modern computer systems. By supporting multithreading on reconfigurable hardware, this segment is opened up for substantial improvements in handling system complexity, design productivity, and system performance. At the same time, modeling heterogeneous processing environments such as platform FPGAs using the multithreaded programming model raises important research questions regarding the scheduling of interdependent processes on such a system, possibly while observing real-time constraints. On homogeneous multi-core processors, an often used approach to scheduling is directly based on existing single-processor scheduling techniques, which are employed on partitions of the original task set that are mapped onto single processing units. Here, basically any thread exhibits the same execution characteristics regardless of the processor it has been scheduled to. The introduction of heterogeneous processing elements such as soft processor cores or specific hardware threads introduces additional complexities not reflected in current established multi-processor scheduling techniques.

Apart from mapping threads onto specialized hardware accelerators within the reconfigurable fabric, both hthreads and ReconOS support the inclusion of hard- and soft-core microprocessors with varying ISAs into the mix of available processing elements. Hardware threads, as introduced in this chapter, can also be seen as a specialized hardware processor capable of executing one particular thread. Thus, a modern platform FPGA with dedicated hard processor cores, synthesized soft-core processors, and hardware threads, can be modeled as a heterogeneous multi-processor system.

CPU/FPGA hybrid chips have become extremely important components contributing to the creation of a family of commercial off the shelf (COTS) hardware platforms for future ERT systems. These chips continue to mature with each new generation offering faster and denser components. The current generation of platform FPGA's is already capable of supporting a complete Multiprocessor System on Programmable Chip (MPSoPC). As these chips continue on their current growth path, vendors are now encouraging designers to view the processor as the smallest design quantum instead of the transistor. This viewpoint carries with it an important implication for creating high performance system designs; designers can switch from time consuming hardware design of custom accelerators towards creating systems with scalable numbers of programmable cores. This switch happened during the 1980's for embedded systems when off the shelf programmable DSP chips and faster general purpose processors became viable replacements for costly custom ASIC designs. As this paradigm shift occurs, providing a higher level parallel programming model in which users can write parallel programs to run on scalable numbers of cores will gain in importance. hthreads and ReconOS provide important frameworks that can help designers transition into this new era. The abstract programming model provided by these projects is not limited by the numbers or types of processor units included within the FPGA. The advancements these projects have made in abstracting the CPU/FPGA boundary provide important directions for next generation operating systems that need to provide uniform services across programmable processors with potentially different instruction sets. These types of systems are now termed *heterogeneous many-cores*.

Future ERT systems will be deployed in highly dynamic environments with changing requirements on, for example, performance and energy. Additionally, future ERT systems will have to deal with varying resources due to increasingly unreliable components and the need for thermal management. This emerging level of dynamics asks for a new breed of self-aware ERT systems that model both their environment and inner system state to autonomously predict and self-adapt to changes.

REFERENCES

Andrews, D., Niehaus, D., & Ashenden, P. J. (2004). Programming Models for Hybrid CPU/FPGA Chips. *IEEE Computer*, *37*(1), 118–120.

Andrews, D., Sass, R., Anderson, E., Agron, J., Peck, W., & Stevens, J. (2008, January). Achieving Programming Model Abstractions For Reconfigurable Computing. *IEEE Transactions on Very Large Scale Integration (VLSI). Systems*, *16*(1), 34–44.

Butenhof, D. R. (1997). *Programming with POSIX threads*. Boston: Addison-Wesley Longman Publishing Co. eCosCentric. (2008). *eCos*. Retrieved from http://ecos.sourceware.org

Celoxica. (n.d.). Retrieved from http://www. celoxica.com

Edwards, S. A. (2006). The Challenges of Synthesizing Hardware from C-Like Languages. *IEEE Design & Test of Computers*, *23*(5), 375–386. doi:10.1109/MDT.2006.134

Guo, Z., Buyukkurt, B., Najjar, W., & Vissers, K. (2005 March). *Optimized Generation of Data-Path from C Codes*., Agron, J., Peck, W., Anderson, E., Andrews, D., Komp, E., Sass, R., Baijot, F., & Stevens, J. (2006, December). Run-Time Services for Hybrid CPU/FPGA Systems On Chip. In *Proceedings of the 27th IEEE International Real-Time Systems Symposium (RTSS)*.

Gupta, S., Dutt, N. D., Gupta, R. K., & Nicolau, A. (2003, January). SPARK: A High-Level Synthesis Framework For Applying Parallelizing Compiler Transformations. In *International Conference on VLSI Design*, (pp. 461–466).

Happe, M., Luebbers, E., & Platzner, M. (2009 December). An Adaptive Sequential Monte Carlo Framework with Runtime HW/SW Repartitioning. In *Proceedings of the 2009 International Conference on Field-Programmable Technology (FPT)*.

ImpulseC. (n.d.). Retrieved from http://www. impulsec.com

Kreuzinger, J., Schulz, A., Pfeffer, M., Ungerer, T., Brinkschulte, U., & Krakowski, C. (2000, December). Real-time Scheduling on Multithreaded Processors. In *Proceedings of the 7th International Conference on Real-Time Computing Systems and Applications (RTCSA)*, (pp. 155–159), Cheju Island, South Korea.

Luebbers, E., & Platzner, M. (2009, August). Cooperative Multithreading in Dynamically Reconfigurable Systems. In *Proceedings of the 19th International Conference on Field Programmable Logic and Applications (FPL)*.

Najjar, W. A., Bohm, W., Draper, B. A., Hammes, J., Rinker, R., Beveridge, J. R., et al. (2003, August). High-Level Language Abstraction for Reconfigurable Computing. In *IEEE Computer*, (pp. 63–69).

QNX Software Systems. (2009). *QNX Neutrino RTOS Overview*. Retrieved from http://www.qnx. com/products/neutrino_rtos/

Quadros Systems Inc. (2007). *RTXC 3.2 real-time kernel*. Retrieved from http://www.quadros.com/ products/operating-systems/rtxc-32/, Trimberger, S. (2007). *FPL 2007 Xilinx Keynote Talk - Redefining the FPGA*. Retrieved from http://ce.et.tudelft. nl/FPL/trimbergerFPL2007.pdf

Wazlowski, M., Agarwal, L., Lee, T., Smith, A., Lam, E., Athanas, P., et al. (1993). PRISM-II Compiler and Architecture. In *Proceedings of the IEEE Workshop on FPGAs for Custom Computing Machines*, (pp. 9–16).

Wind River. (2007). *VxWorks 6.x*. Retrieved from http://www.windriver.com/products/run-time_technologies/Real-Time_Operating_Systems/VxWorks_6x/

Chapter 3
Zero–Downtime Reconfiguration of Distributed Control Logic in Industrial Automation and Control

Thomas Strasser
Austrian Institute of Technology, Austria

Alois Zoitl
Vienna University of Technology, Austria

Martijn Rooker
PROFACTOR GmbH, Austria

ABSTRACT

Future manufacturing is envisioned to be highly flexible and adaptable. New technologies for efficient engineering of reconfigurable systems and their adaptations are preconditions for this vision. Without such solutions, engineering adaptations of Industrial Process Measurement and Control Systems (IPMCS) will exceed the costs of engineered systems by far and the reuse of equipment will become inefficient. Especially the reconfiguration of control applications is not sufficiently solved by state-of-the-art technology. This chapter gives an overview of the use of reconfiguration applications for zero-downtime system reconfiguration of control applications on basis of the standard IEC 61499 which provides a reference model for distributed and reconfigurable control systems. A new approach for the reconfiguration of IEC 61499 based control application and the corresponding modeling is discussed. This new method significantly increases engineering efficiency and reuse in component-based IPMCS.

INTRODUCTION

The decisive factor for the market success of the manufacturing industry (e.g. auto manufacturers and part makers, process industry etc.) is a fast and flexible reaction to changing customer demands— companies must show a high degree of change-ability. New paradigms like "Flexible production up to small lot-sizes", "Mass Customization" or

DOI: 10.4018/978-1-60960-086-0.ch003

"Zero-Downtime Production" will achieve these requirements but demand completely new technologies for its realization (European Commission, 2004). Changeability, which describes the ability of companies being flexible concerning customer demands, impacts all levels of product manufacturing. In particular these are the agility at a strategic level, the transformability at a factory level and the reconfigurability at the manufacturing system and machine level (Koren, 1999).

The state-of-the-art in manufacturing systems is inadequate to meet the above mentioned requirements. Current manufacturing systems are either tailored towards a specific product at high volume production and thus they can hardly be adapted to new products or they are flexible and programmable but technology specific and only for single item or small batch production. Another relatively new approach which is flexible and programmable but less technology specific but also hardly adoptable concerning the above mentioned requirements is the usage of "Multi Machining Technology Integration Production Systems" (Abele, 2005) which are characterized by the static implementation and combination of different technologies within one production system. The major drawback of this approach is that it is very resource consuming and therefore it can hardly be ported to small and resource constrained embedded controllers which are often used in modern industrial automation and control systems.

To reach the above mentioned changeability at the manufacturing systems and machine level it can be postulated that a change from product and technology rigid manufacturing systems towards product and technology flexible, modular, easy to setup component-based production systems is necessary. Following consequently this trend means that future plants will produce their products on manufacturing systems and machines which will be designed and setup just prior to production of goods since they are constructed on basic building blocks. Such building blocks are in general smart mechatronic components with embedded intelligence. These building blocks are designed in a way that they provide a specific manufacturing and/or automation functionality and they are not reconfigurable in general. Machining, assembly and transport systems of such production systems are also designed and set up by the utilization of various flexible autonomous and intelligent mechatronic components just before usage within the production line.

The consequences of the above mentioned attempt are extensive and many technological breakthroughs will be necessary. Beside others the development of an adequate automation system for heavily interacting distributed real-time systems can be seen as a major task. Current architectures of IPMCS do not conceptually support reconfiguration and distribution which are necessary to fulfill the requirements for the above mentioned systems (Sünder, 2006). Distributed embedded real–time systems for industrial automation and control of plants that evolve towards zero-downtime adaptable systems will play a key role to realize the roadmaps towards adaptive manufacturing (Koren, 1999) of products, goods and services in 2020. Most value will then be added in engineering and performing a system transition or reconfiguration (the change from one system state to another) rather than in engineering and performing "normal operation".

The challenge and aim of this chapter is to present an approach for modeling of reconfiguration control applications based on the IEC 61499 standard which provide an adequate engineering methodology for programmed system reconfiguration (i.e. system reconfiguration executed by a special control application). The first section discusses general reconfiguration issues. The next section gives an overview of state-of-the-art in reconfiguration of control applications. After that a summary of the main features and characteristics of IEC 61499 as the reference model for distributed automation and control systems with special focus of the management capabilities for reconfiguration is given. Furthermore an enhanced IEC 61499 Device Management is introduced which is used for the proposed approach for the controlled reconfiguration of control applications as the main topic of this chapter. Especially the modeling of reconfiguration control applications based on the IEC 61499 reference model is topic of this chapter. Tests at the Odo Struger Laboratory at Vienna University of Technology (Automation and Control Institute) and at PROFACTOR are also presented. The summary of this work concludes this chapter.

BACKGROUND: GENERAL CONSIDERATIONS ABOUT RECONFIGURATION

In industrial informatics, reconfiguration of software modules and components has been discussed many times, for instance (Brennan, 2002; Bussmann, 1999; Burmester, 2004). Agile software processes like the extreme programming method recognize change as an essential part of the software life–cycle (Mens, 2005).

Basic vs. Dynamic Reconfiguration

Within the scope of this chapter reconfiguration is described best as altering a system's operation in order to meet changes in requirements. Quite a simple reconfiguration method—hence further denoted as basic reconfiguration—is to stop current operation, apply all necessary changes to the system and restart the desired operation again (coldstart). But this approach is not sufficient to meet the constraints mentioned in the introduction.

Brinkschulte et al. (2005) define dynamic reconfiguration as reconfiguration of an application while it is running. What therefore further distinguishes dynamic from basic reconfiguration is provision for timeliness constraints (Brennan, 2002). Dynamic reconfiguration considers timeliness as a crucial facet of correctness. With respect

to control applications this means that timeliness requirements put on the whole application must be preserved while parts of it are modified.

Classification of Dynamic Reconfiguration

Within the topic of dynamic reconfiguration a big variety of opportunities arises. This especially demands means of classification for the different approaches within this field. Wermelinger (1997) has formulated 3 essential questions that have to be answered for dynamic reconfiguration:

1. What kind of modifications can be done?
2. How are they performed?
3. When may the changes be performed?

The first two questions concern the reconfiguration model (model of system architecture and modification process) as well as the features of the underlying operating system and/or the runtime environment. Question 3 is of special interest. The answer to this question is that those parts of an automation system that will undergo changes have to be in a consistent state before. But consistency is not only is a prerequisite for reconfiguration. Quite on the contrary, consistency is an important attribute of systems that must be preserved over reconfiguration in order to avoid unnecessary disruption to the system environment. This requires transfer of state information from the current system state to the desired state after reconfiguration.

Rasche and Polze (2005) give an idea of how consistent state information can be ensured in the context of different use cases of reconfiguration, illustrated in Figure 1. Adaptation at runtime (upper part of the figure) either requires transfer (save/transmit/load) of state information (update, migration) or gathering state information via input processing (transitional reconfiguration). On the other hand failure recovery (lower part of figure) must be able to restore a consistent state either by

Figure 1. State consistency and reconfiguration

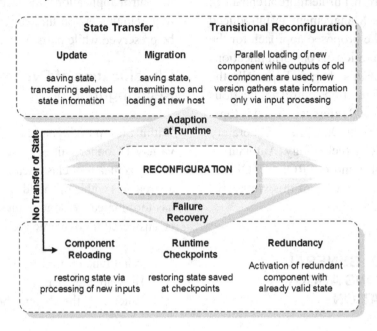

loading saved state information (runtime check-points) or input processing (component reloading) or by activating redundant components (which already have gathered valid state information).

State-of-the-Art Reconfiguration Approaches

This section briefly outlines current reconfiguration approaches relevant for industrial automation. Today common automation systems predominantly rely on the programming paradigms of the standard IEC 61131–3 (IEC, 2003) dedicated to systems based on programmable logic controllers (PLCs). The common paradigm within IEC 61131 is a device centered engineering methodology. Aspects of distribution (cooperation of several devices within an overall application) have to be considered from the beginning of the engineering phase.

Current IEC 61131–3 based engineering tools such as (kirchner SOFT, 2009) already enable online code exchange—called instant-reload—for single devices at task level, including transfer of

variable values. Their product logi,CAD already provides some basic support for reconfiguration of applications (i.e. of programs, resources and configurations; this keywords are used in terms of IEC 61131) in the programming system logi.CAD as well as in kirchner SOFT's target system implementations (i.e. Soft-PLCs). Their reconfiguration approach is centered on managing changes for a single IEC 61131-3 resource at a time. Changing applications at runtime without stopping them is fully supported for the user. Unfortunately using such a resource-centered approach has some disadvantages when changes for too many different applications running in different resources have to be applied simultaneously. In addition there exist also some other drawbacks of this approach like undeterministic switching points in time (due to cyclic execution policy), lack of fine granularity (reconfiguration at task level), jitter effects (task reconfiguration influences other tasks) or the possibility of inconsistent states (e.g. leading to deadlocks) (Sünder, 2006).

The International Electrotechnical Commission (IEC) addresses these issues by the standard

IEC 61499 (IEC, 2005), which extend the Function Block (FB) model of IEC 61131-3 in order to meet the requirements of engineering distributed automation systems. The most important concepts of IEC 61499 are an event–driven execution model; a management interface capable of basic reconfiguration support and the application centered engineering methodology. The major benefit of this approach is a separation of concerns: first the whole application is programmed as a function block network like in centralized systems; afterwards the components of this network (the function blocks) are mapped to the devices of the real system where they shall be executed. Doing so e.g. facilitates the movement of functionality from one controller to another as mentioned in section I, since only the mapping is concerned while the original application remains unchanged. A more detailed description of IEC 61499 and its aptitude for reconfiguration purposes can be found in (Strasser, 2005).

Various researchers have developed reconfiguration methodologies based on IEC 61499: the research project TORERO (Lorentz, 2006) focuses on plug–and–play and self–(re)configuration of field devices in a so–called total lifecycle approach utilizing IEC 61499 for modeling control logic. The main objective of this project was on the creation of a total lifecycle web-integrated control design architecture and methodology for distributed control systems for industrial and factory automation. The major focus and research was on the development of a self-configuring and maintaining control infrastructure with automated distribution support. One of the major drawbacks of the TORERO approach is the fact that a device hast to be stopped for the deployment of code and afterwards it has to be restarted.

Thramboulidis et al. (2004) use Realtime–UML (Unified Modeling Language) as a meta model between the design models of IEC 61499 and their implementation models to support dynamic reconfiguration of control applications.

Brennan et al. (2002) propose an agent–based reconfiguration approach, extending the IEC 61499 function block model: they introduce a second state–machine within the basic function block together with a reconfiguration agent and a second event and data flow for reconfiguration purposes. All these reconfiguration approaches rely on technology that is outside the scope of IEC 61499 (e.g. Universal Plug and Play, agents or Realtime–UML), they do not consider utilizing the basic reconfiguration functionality provided by the IEC 61499 management model outlined in the next section.

IEC 61499 as Reference Model for Reconfigurable Distributed Control

The new standard IEC 61499 (IEC, 2005) serves as a reference architecture that has been developed for distributed, modular, and flexible control systems. It specifies an architectural model for distributed applications in IPMCS in a very generic way and extends the function block model of its predecessor IEC 61131-3 (Function Block Diagram - FBD) with additional event handling mechanisms and concepts for distributed systems.

The standard builds a good basis to overcome the above mentioned problems according to reconfiguration processes in current IPMCS. The following sections describe some fundamental issues of IEC 61499 that make this standard suitable as a reference architecture for building zero-downtime IPMCS by using the concept of reconfiguration applications. More detailed information is available from (Christensen, 2009; Lastra, 2004; Lewis, 2001).

Figure 2 provides a brief overview of the most important concepts and models of the IEC 61499 standard. In the following we briefly explain important aspects of the reference model in order to better understand this standard. For more details about definitions, concepts and models we refer to the IEC standard (IEC, 2005).

Figure 2. The IEC 61499 reference model for distributed automation and control

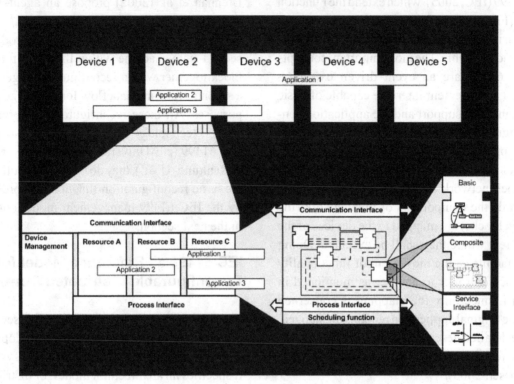

Execution Control by Events

The function block model of IEC 61499 defines function blocks that are characterized by the occurrence of two Input/Output (I/O) types: events and data. The execution is triggered by events, needed data have to be valid at the inputs of the FB before an event arrives (denoted as the WITH construct in IEC 61499, i.e. the vertical lines between event and data inputs or outputs as shown in Figure 3a). Only if an event occurs at a FB input, the runtime environment has to process the execution of this FB. Therefore it is obvious and clearly understandable whether an application is active or not and even exactly which part is currently processed. Compared to PLC-based approaches like IEC 61131-3 the IEC 61499 approach doesn't define any time base nor has a cyclic-based execution approach

Distribution Model

One of the main intentions of IEC 61499 is enabling distributed applications. The system model consists of devices connected by a communication network and applications. These applications may be distributed within devices. Moreover the IEC 61499 standard allows in addition the separation of devices into independent resources which are execution containers for function block networks. This concept allows a local distribution of an application part of a specific device into several resources of this device. The engineering process starts with the top-level functionality that has to be realized without reference to the concrete hardware structure. By use of libraries of software components, the user models the needed applications. The last step within the engineering cycle is the mapping of the applications to concrete hardware components; independent of whether the applica-

Figure 3. Generic management function block type

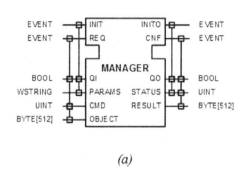

(a)   *(b)*

tion is executed by one device or distributed to several devices.

Management Interface of IEC 61499 Devices

The configuration of a distributed automation and control system based on IEC 61499 can be enabled by the use of management functions which can be included in each device. For this purpose the standard defines a management application, represented by a management FB (the generic interface is depicted in Figure 3a). By using this FB combined with a remote application, mutual access between different IEC 61499 compliant devices is possible. The IEC 61499 Compliance Profile for Feasibility Demonstrations (available from Christensen (2009)) describes a concrete interface of a management FB and an appropriate remote application. The following standardized management functions can be used to interact with a device (IEC, 2005, Part 1-Table 6, 8). For illustration examples of possible actions are added.

- **CREATE:** FB instance, data or event connection
- **DELETE:** FB instance, data or event connection
- **START:** FB instance, application
- **STOP:** FB instance, application
- **READ:** FB instance data outputs

- **WRITE:** FB instance data inputs
- **KILL:** FB instance
- **QUERY:** FB types, FB instance, data or event connection

Especially the management of software components (i.e. FBs) regarding to their execution is a very important issue in reconfiguration processes. A FB instance operates according to a state machine (IEC 2005, Part 1-Figure 24) that includes an initialization and operation state controlled by management commands: Create, Start, Stop/Kill and Delete.

Verification and Validation

A very important feature of a control modeling language is the possibility to proof correctness. The basic function block of IEC 61499 includes an event-triggered state machine (Execution Control Chart, ECC) that provides the connection between an incoming event and the execution of algorithms and outgoing events. This basic model enables the conversion of IEC 61499 applications to mathematical models like Petri Nets to provide verification and validation. Different approaches to this topic are already available, for instance Net Condition/Event Systems (Vyatkin, 1999), timed automata (Stanica, 2004) or Signal/Net Systems (Schnakenbourg, 2002).

ENHANCED IEC 61499 DEVICE MANAGEMENT FOR DOWNTIMELESS RECONFIGURATION

In the case of dynamic reconfiguration of control applications or application parts it is necessary to define several (re-)configuration services, which provide enough functionality to vary FB parameters, to change the behavior of FBs or Function Block Networks (FBN) and to create or delete instances of FBs and Resources. This section describes the necessity of an enhanced set of (re-)configuration services based on the IEC 61499 standard. As mentioned in the previous section the IEC 61499 standard already provides a basis set of (re-)configuration services but it lacks a method and an implementation how these services can be efficiently applied for the reconfiguration of control applications. Therefore the aim of this approach is to make extensions to the IEC 61499 standard to simplify the reconfiguration process. This will be explained in the next sub-sections.

Considerations on Enhanced (Re-)Configuration Services

The following list displays possible reconfiguration scenarios for IEC 61499 based FBNs:

- **Instance reconfiguration:** regards to the exchange, adding or removal of a certain instance of IEC 61499 types (FB, Data, Resource, and Device). In case of an exchange of FB instances there exists the possibility with and without the adoption of internal FB variable values.
- **Type reconfiguration / runtime set-up:** the supported IEC 61499 types (Function Block, Data, Resource and Device) have to be exchanged; added or removed from a runtime system (i.e. this issue is mainly related to the change in the structure and

elements of the type library of the runtime system).

- **Parameter reconfiguration:** the parameterization of Function Blocks, Resource or Device instances has to be adapted.
- **Application structure reconfiguration:** the logical configuration of the control applications has to be adapted. This is mainly related to the change of event and data connections or the type instances in IEC 61499 based control applications.
- **System reconfiguration:** the structure of the IEC 61499 system (i.e. the device and communication structure) is adapted to new requirements. This issue means that the IEC 61499 system configuration (i.e. the system model as represented in Figure 2) will be changed. Such changes can be the addition or deletion of devices and/or resources or even the exchange of existing devices with other once. Moreover it is also possible to (ex-)change the communication system similar to the (ex-)change of the device configuration.

Categorization of Basic Reconfiguration Services

Based on the device management commands introduced by IEC 61499 and the analysis of general reconfiguration tasks the following set of basic reconfiguration services are identified and categorized:

- **Structural services:** These services are mainly related to the modification/change of the logical configuration/structure of control applications and their behavior. IEC 61499 already provides a very rudimentary set of services that allow to create and delete FBs, resources and connections and to write parameters of FBs and resources. This rudimentary set of IEC 61499 configuration services is extended with additional features to form a more comprehensive set of basic structural reconfiguration services.

- **Execution control services:** These services allow interaction with the currently executing control application. In this case IEC 61499 provides a start, stop and kill mechanism for FBs. By extending these mechanisms with an additional restart service and also using these services for event and data connections the reconfiguration process provides more possibilities to manage and change the execution of Function Block Networks (i.e. IEC 61499 applications). This especially enables a more efficient rewiring of FBs without use of extra computational power compared to the standard execution control services (i.e. start, stop and kill) provides by the IEC 61499 standard. The execution of only one management service (i.e. restart) is necessary compared to the execution of the service sequence stop FB and start FB. The restart service can be implemented more efficiently in a runtime environment. Fulfilling this requirement is essential if running control applications are reconfigured. In the case of reconfiguration of running control applications high effort has to be put into keeping the interruption of the running system as short as possible.

- **State interaction services:** These services retrieve and set internal states of FBs. The IEC 61499 standard does not clearly define these services. Such services are mainly needed for providing transition management, which takes care that the process is also under stable control during the reconfiguration phase (i.e. instabilities during the reconfiguration phase have to be avoided). The FBs are just components without access to anything outside their interface. In the case of reconfiguration full access to internal FB states and data is necessary

to force the FB to a defined state avoiding reinitializing the FB.

- **Query services:** These services are necessary to acquire the current state of the distributed control application running on several devices. Especially during dynamic reconfiguration the system state will change several times. Because of that, query services are necessary in order to obtain the actual systems state and moreover also consistency checks are necessary to during dynamic reconfiguration. A consistent state after a reconfiguration is very important in industrial automation and control systems because inconsistent system states can lead to catastrophic faults. Another fact is that the execution of reconfiguration applications is characterized by a time span between engineering and execution. Within a multi user system, the reconfiguration has to ensure that the considered system part has not changed between this time span. The query mechanisms provided by IEC 61499 can serve as basis for this service.

- **Library services:** These services allow adding or removing IEC 61499 types such as Function Blocks, Event, Data or Resources to or from the runtime library of the control device respectively. They are also not clearly defined within IEC 61499. The main description of FBs is defined by the use of the Extended Mark-up Language (XML), but e.g. the description language for algorithms within FBs is still not defined. The capability of device independent type libraries needs a full new specification.

In addition to the above mentioned basic reconfiguration services it is often necessary to define further services that will be used in many reconfiguration applications (e.g. rewire a connection). To simplify reconfiguration applications and to reduce their size, it is envisaged to provide

Figure 4. Enhanced Reconfiguration Service of IEC61499 Device Management

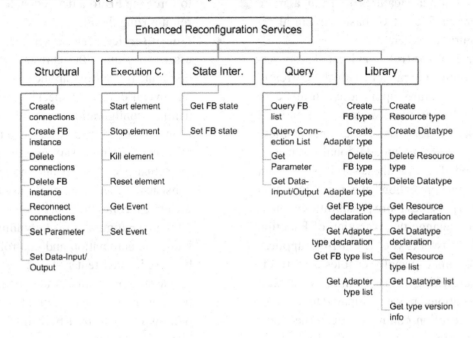

also more sophisticated reconfiguration services in addition to the basic services whereby a trade-off between reconfiguration application size and runtime environment complexity has to be found. Figure 4 gives an overview of the set of identified basic reconfiguration services based on the above categorization.

The above-presented enhanced services are either implemented as IEC 61499 XML commands or as special management FBs.

Reconfiguration of Control Applications

The reconfiguration can be initiated from a user via configuration tools (see Figure 5) or as a special control application—herein referred as Reconfiguration Control Application (RCA)—as depicted in Figure 6.

Therefore in both cases an underlying runtime system has to provide the necessary (enhanced) services for reconfiguration which are presented above. The reconfiguration steps can also be di-

rectly implemented into the control application but the RCA is especially used to encapsulate these reconfiguration steps into a separate application. This makes the presented approach for a control engineer more useable otherwise the control application will be overloaded with reconfiguration parts. The RCA is built of special IEC 61499 compliant management FB types that encapsulate the above mention reconfiguration services for dynamic reconfiguration of control application in a distributed system. The trigger to execute the RCA can either be initiated by the user, the control application or by the underlying controlled process.

AN ENGINEERING METHOD FOR RECONFIGURATION OF IPMCS APPLICATIONS

To overcome the limitations of current embedded industrial automation and control engineering methods, we propose an application centered

Figure 5. Reconfiguration via configuration tool

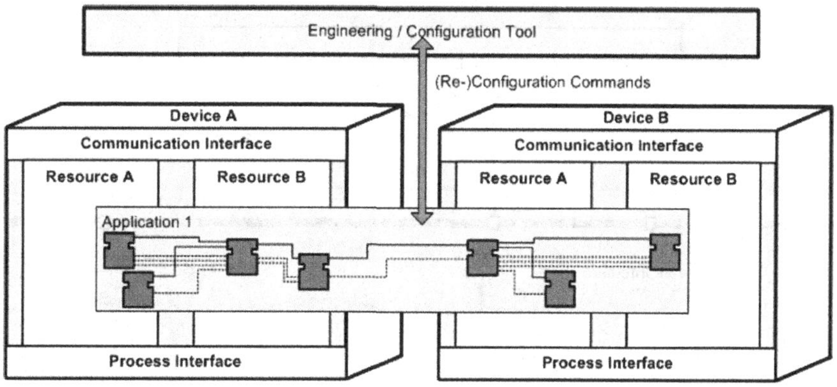

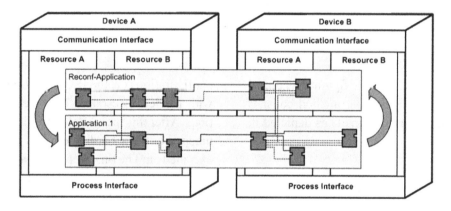

Figure 6. Reconfiguration Control Application

engineering method for efficient component-based modeling of applications for controlled reconfiguration of IPMCS. The execution of a reconfiguration will become a normal operational state of such systems, while dependability and Quality of Service (QoS) of the reconfigured system are not endangered and migration is cost–efficient. Thus important steps towards Adaptive Manufacturing will be realized.

An Approach for Controlled Reconfiguration

The top–level approach focuses on replacing state–of–the–art "ramp down—stop—download—re-start—ramp up" methods with a zero-downtime system reconfiguration, which is controlled by a

reconfiguration control application that is modeled with components in the same way as control applications are. Zero-downtime means in this context to perform the controlled reconfiguration during runtime without the need to stop the execution of a runtime system. Reconfiguration control can be either executed from an engineering environment or it can be distributed to different controllers (as shown in Figure 7).

Modeling Cycle for Control and Reconfiguration Control Applications

The following engineering process provides a method for handling system reconfiguration of IPMCS by an efficient support for engineering of

Figure 7. Controlled reconfiguration of control applications

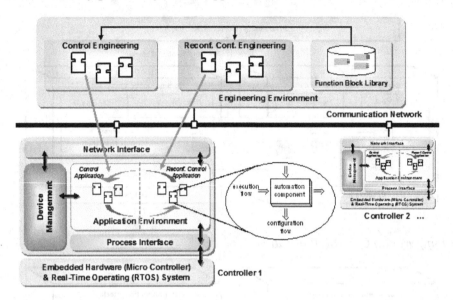

control applications and reconfiguration control applications. This engineering method consists of the following four major parts as depicted in Figure 8.

1. Acquire Current System State (Acquire existing application)

Collect all data necessary for describing the current system state and deliver it as input to the application modeling. The data consists of the system model including applications currently running in the system, the hardware configuration of the system (used devices and network structure), the mapping of the applications to the different devices and the hardware capability descriptions.

2. Model New Control Application (Application Modeling)

Modeling of the new control application based on the existing ones by adding/removing components, their interconnections and specification of application properties (e.g. real–time constraints). The next step is the configuration of the system

configuration (i.e. the IEC 61499 system model) with Devices, Resources and Network connections. After this the modeled application parts are mapped to the according devices they should be executed on. The final step is a formal verification and validation of the control application n order to determine if the specified application constraints will be met or not. For this verification and validation step approaches like Net Condition/Event Systems (Vyatkin, 1999), timed automata (Stanica, 2004) or Signal/Net Systems (Schnakenbourg, 2002) can be applied.

3. Model Reconfiguration Control Application (Reconfiguration Engineering)

Differences between the current running control application and the newly modeled control application are determined with the Delta Analysis. These differences serve as input and starting point for the modeling of the reconfiguration control application that will change the existing application to the new one. The reconfiguration control properties and parameters are specified in the same way as control application properties (according

Figure 8. Modeling cycle for control and reconfiguration control applications

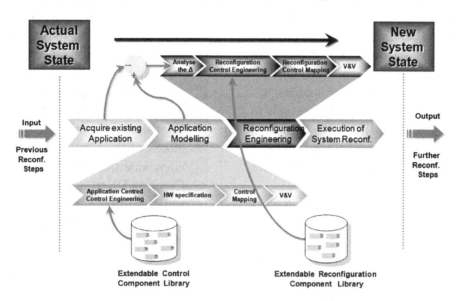

to step 2). Similar to the mapping of the control application the reconfiguration application parts are mapped to the devices. The final step is the verification of the reconfiguration control application together with device capabilities in order to determine if reconfiguration constraints (e.g. the timeframe in which a reconfiguration can take place or how long a reconfiguration can take place, etc.) will be met and the running application is disturbed as little as possible.

4.   Execute Reconfiguration Control Application (Execution of System Reconfiguration)

To execute reconfiguration control applications the utilization of basic reconfiguration services at runtime platforms based on IEC 61499 management commands is necessary. The first step is to instantiate the reconfiguration control application on the according devices. Next the execution of the reconfiguration control application is done, i.e. the currently running control application is transformed into the new control application. This is achieved through basic reconfiguration services proving real–time constraint execution

of reconfiguration processes at device level. The main services are:

- Control application component load/ remove
- Connect/disconnect
- Query parameters
- Write parameters
- Query component state
- Write component state

To finish the reconfiguration procedure the reconfiguration control application will be removed after it has successfully executed all commands and all changes are finished.

Reconfiguration Methodology

The process of reconfiguring an automation system without downtimes sets high demands on the underlying concepts and methodologies: Applications within the automation system have to work without disturbances; the reconfiguration process has to be adapted to the special environmental conditions of the affected application part.

Any fault during the reconfiguration process has to be managed at least to such a degree, that the system is left in a defined state. As described in the introduction the standard IEC 61499 already includes basic management commands for configuration and reconfiguration of applications. This section now proposes useful extensions to the management model of IEC 61499 enhancing the reconfiguration abilities of IEC 61499 with special regard to remaining compliant to the ideas of the standard.

The main idea of this new methodology is to control the reconfiguration of control logic (part of the control application) by an application, the so called reconfiguration application. The reconfiguration application does not differ from any other application and can therefore be modeled in the same manner. But it will have an impact on the control application, which means that it will include management commands that influence FBs and their interconnections in a defined manner. The basic idea of reconfiguration applications is described by Sünder et al. (2006). The presented engineering methodology builds on these results, particularly with regard to the setup and characteristics of reconfiguration applications.

Reconfiguration Control Terminology and Definitions

At this point it is suitable to define a few terms used later on for the development of an appropriate engineering methodology for dynamic reconfiguration processes:

- **Region of Interest (ROI):** this is a specific part of an IEC 61499 application that will be target for a specific reconfiguration. A reconfiguration application is assigned to this specific part. The definition of this region is given by the following cases of system changes:
- **Creating/Deleting a function block:** the suggested ROI is the function block itself plus the connected event as well as data inputs and outputs, since there is a significant temporal order of operations (a function block cannot be deleted unless all of its connections have been deleted).
- **Creating/Deleting a connection:** the suggested ROI consists of the corresponding halves of source and target function blocks of the connection along with their interconnections.
- **Creating/Deleting a parameter (i.e. a parameter in the context of IEC 61499 is a fixed value on a data input of a Function Block):** quite similar to connections, but without a source function block. So the suggested ROI only consists of the left half of the target FB and the parameter itself.
- **System reconfiguration:** the whole process of transforming the current control application in an IPMCS into the desired control application (instead of the state–of–the–art method "ramp down—stop—download—restart—ramp up"). Usually such a process is carried out by a number of reconfiguration applications on a number of ROIs. Reconfiguration takes place in four phases as depicted above (see Figure 8).
- **Reconfiguration Execution Control Function Blocks (RECFB):** special function blocks encapsulating reconfiguration functionality (e.g. a whole reconfiguration application). Within the execution of *RECFB* 3 reconfiguration control execution phases can be distinguished (see Figure 9; the vertical connections of the event as well as data inputs and outputs denote that only such data inputs and outputs are sampled which are connected to a specific event; this is a general concept of the IEC 61499 Function Block model; more details are explained in the IEC 61499 standard (IEC, 2005)):

Figure 9. Reconfiguration Execution Control Function Block (RECFB)

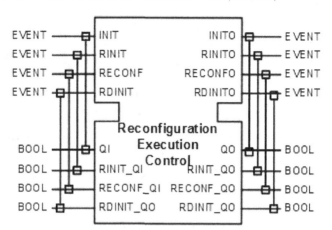

- **INIT Sequence:** is needed in order to start-up and to configure the RECFB and the underlying runtime environment.
- **RINIT Sequence:** contains all preparation work that is needed to enable a controlled change of applications (for instance new FBs will be instantiated and interconnected).
- **RECONF Sequence:** encapsulates all operations necessary to change from the old state to the new one. This for instance includes reading of internal states, calculation of the new internal states and writing the internal state to the new FB in case of a simple FB exchange with awareness to consistency. The final step of this sequence is the switch to the new FB.
- **RDINIT Sequence:** responsible for cleaning up after reconfiguration (e.g. deleting connections and function blocks not needed anymore). One *RECFB* belongs to one ROI, there is a one to one relation between them.
- **Reconfiguration Control Application:** application (i.e. a special IEC 61499 based function block network) built of *RECFBs*, that carries out the whole system reconfiguration process on an ordinary IEC 61499 system.

Reconfiguration Engineering Method

Reconfiguration applications define and describe the controlled reconfiguration within a ROI during runtime. The main intentions for the introduction of a reconfiguration engineering method handling these reconfiguration applications are:

- **Complexity:** The use of reconfiguration applications includes a reasonable amount of engineering complexity. The bigger the ROI is the more complex the whole reconfiguration application will be. This can lead to hardly understandable reconfiguration control applications which make the development and maintenance of them more complex. By using small or smaller ROIs, the engineering complexity keeps quite low.
- **Scalability:** There has to be a way to compose larger reconfiguration scenarios from several smaller reconfiguration steps. The RECFBs give the possibility to build composite RECFBs in the same way as in "normal" control applications using the same means (i.e. the models and concepts of the IEC 61499 standard).
- **Reusability:** As scaling is possible, the use of libraries for often used scenarios

Figure 10. Regions of interest during the reconfiguration process

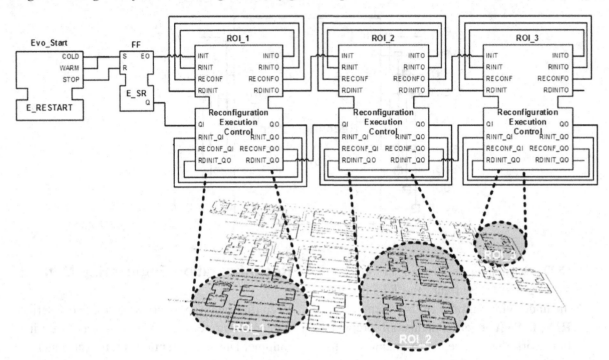

within typical application scopes will be useful. The concept enables such standardized RECFBs and their simple usage within composite RECFBs, again in the same way as in "normal" applications. The main idea of the proposed approach is to maintain the fundamental principles of IEC 61499 (application centered engineering, component-based architecture, event–driven execution and the management model) for reconfiguration engineering. Figure 10 illustrates a reconfiguration control application containing 3 RECFBs. Each of these RECFBs contains a reconfiguration application performing reconfiguration on the associated ROI in the IEC 61499 application shown in the lower part of the figure. The interconnection of the RECFBs defines the way of executing the three steps. In the shown example only one RECFB is active at the same time (serial execution). In detail, each RECFB runs

through the three phases of Initialization, Reconfiguration and Deinitialization before the next RECFB is triggered. By using the QI and QO data variables of the RECFBs, the internal sequences of the RECFBs communicate in a very simple manner. If one sequence fails, the next step will not be executed. Of course this communication can be enhanced according to the reconfiguration purpose. For instance, the coupling of two or more RECFBs is also possible.

The presented engineering methodology handles the two main tasks of reconfiguration applications according to Figure 1 in the following way:

• It performs runtime adaptations on the control application of a distributed automation system, corresponding to the upper half of Figure 1. This includes transfer of state information from one system state to another, if necessary to avoid disruption to the system.

- It performs runtime–checks during execution to ensure correct operation. In case of failures at least the system must be left in a tolerable state, this may include undo functionality for abortive reconfiguration steps. Such failure recovery strategies also require backup and restore mechanisms for state information, corresponding to the lower half of Figure 1. In our approach these topics are handled on different levels. First of all within one reconfiguration application (an ROI represented by an RECFB) the issues of recovery or undo have to be handled internally of a RECFB. Second also within reconfiguration control applications this issue has to be modeled explicitly. The example in Figure 10 only provides a very simple failure handling. If an error occurs in one of the RECFB instances (i.e. instance names ROI_1, ROI_2 and ROI_3) then the QO data outputs (i.e. RINT_QO, RECONF_QO and RDINIT_QO) are set to false. This is an indication that a failure has occurred and the reconfiguration of a ROI will not take place. But of course more sophisticated error handling procedure can be defined as this simple once.

Another important aspect for reconfiguration is real-time constrained execution. IEC 61499 leaves issues such as timeliness open and delegate's appropriate specifications to compliance profiles and runtime implementations respectively. There exists no barrier to apply such a capability of the runtime environment to the presented engineering methodology. So if the underlying runtime system features timeliness (i.e. deterministic behavior), it can also be applied to the reconfiguration process (doing so certainly the complexity is further increasing).

Reconfiguration Patterns

Based on the above presented reconfiguration method enhanced system reconfiguration the following reconfiguration patterns have been defined in order to provide design rules for reconfiguration processes to the control engineer. These patterns cover the following scenarios:

- Moving of function block instances between IEC 61499 Resources at one device,
- Moving of function blocks instances between different IEC 64199 Devices,
- Moving of resource configurations between IEC 61499 Devices,
- Exchange of Function Block types (same and different interface), and
- Exchange of Resource types.

All of these patterns have in common that they are using RECFBs to describe the reconfiguration process.

Fault Handling During the Reconfiguration Process

In order to manage possible errors or faults during the reconfiguration process the following error scenarios for the zero-downtime system reconfiguration have been covered:

- **Creation of the reconfiguration control application fails:** This situation can be caused by download errors and initialization errors during the deployment phase of the reconfiguration control application. Download errors comprise connection faults, i.e. loss of connection from the engineering environment to the device management (possible reasons might be network or device failure), and device management exceptions.

- **RINIT phase of a reconfiguration step fails:** This situation again comprises connection faults, device management exceptions and initialization errors. Possible reasons are for creating the reconfiguration control application, except network failure, since the reconfiguration application or parts of it are executed locally on the Device.

- **RECONF phase of a reconfiguration step fails:** This category consists of reconfiguration errors and application faults. Reconfiguration errors again comprise connections faults and device management exceptions. Application faults can be characterized as follows: all reconfiguration tasks terminated successfully, but the overall behavior of the new application is faulty.

- **RDINIT phase of a reconfiguration step fails:** The reasons why the RDINIT phase can fail are quite similar to those of the RINIT phase in. The only differences are that device management exceptions can occur upon deleting FBs or connections (reasons remain the same) and that initialization errors are replaced by de-initialization errors possible for all FBs requiring an INIT-event.

In order to handle these error scenarios the following error handling and fallback strategies have been developed:

- **Error handling during download of the reconfiguration application (RINIT phase):** The error scenarios and therefore the possible handling strategies are the same for these two phases. Connection faults might be recoverable by a simple RETRY; since these errors are time-uncrit-

ical it could also prove useful to wait for a short time before retry as a busy network might recover meanwhile. Unrecoverable connection faults terminate the whole reconfiguration process, cleanup is thereby impossible for devices with unreachable manager. Initialization errors can be handled likewise, except that upon failed RETRY of INIT+ the targets should be cleaned up. Device management errors will not be automatically recoverable in general. Already a single unrecoverable error terminates the whole reconfiguration process. Two approaches seem feasible: (i) Terminate upon the first error, which is primitive but rather safe; (ii) Let the user interact (e.g. let him download missing FB types or delete instances already present) and continue if the error could be resolved that way, which is advanced, but dangerous. Upon any termination the targets should be cleaned up.

- **Error handling during RECONF phase:** First of all, error handling during RECONF is time-critical. Upon connection faults two cases must be distinguished: (i) No structural change has been made to the application (only transfer of internal states has occurred so far). If the device is still operational no damage has been caused, otherwise within modern plants emergency measures will be activated if the failed device is a critical one. RETRY, although possible, is a dangerous option to handle connection faults during RECONF, since a faulted connection indicates problems; (ii) At least one structural change has been made already. The system is in an inconsistent state, RETRY is imperative (try to reach a consistent state by all means). If RETRY fails this is the worst case, all that can be done is give alarm and let emergency measures take control.

Also application faults can be divided in two categories: (i) Uncritical faults, e.g. the process are under control in desired manner, but a display is not updated. In this situation it is possible to keep the new application, perform RDINIT as scheduled and resolve the remaining problem by means of another reconfiguration. Certainly error handling strategies below might also be applied here, in doubt the user should be notified to decide how to continue; (ii) Critical faults → the new application is unusable, control over the process might be lost. Several possibilities exist to cope with this situation: UNDO of all changes until a tolerable state is reached; pre-modeled scenarios in the reconfiguration control application could enable reaching a "failsafe" state by further reconfiguration steps or the new application already contains alternative branches along with appropriate switching logic. If the favored branch fails, the second-best solution is tried and so on. Note: this is not real error handling anymore; such a fallback strategy rather belongs to the domain of fault tolerance of the (new) application.

Device management exceptions during RECONF can be treated like critical application faults. In general the RDINIT phase cannot be executed as scheduled if critical errors have occurred during RECONF. Hence the RDINIT phase must either be blocked or adjusted properly (e.g. FB instances planned for removal must not be deleted if still active due to UNDO).

- **Error handling during RDINIT:** Error handling in this phase is quite similar to the RINIT phase, with a few exceptions: errors do not terminate the whole process anymore (e.g. continue with cleanup measures, even if a certain FB could not be deleted, as long as it is safe). De-initializing errors are also candidates for RETRY; caution is advised if de-initializing of an FB fails. In this case it might cause the system to become unstable if such a FB is deleted.

TESTS AND CONCEPT VALIDATION

Engineering Prototype

The following section gives an overview of a prototypic implementation of the proposed reconfiguration engineering method. Based on Eclipse SDK and the Graphical Editing Framework (GEF) (Gamma, 2003) the engineering environment supporting the definition of RECFBs is realized as a set of different plug-in for Eclipse. Eclipse is an open source community whose projects are focused on providing an extensible development platform and application frameworks for building software which is very suitable for the engineering of the proposed reconfiguration approach. Figure 11 shows the prototypic implementation.

The main parts of the tool are the Application, the Hardware Configuration Editor, the System (Project) Manager, the Reconfiguration Application Editor and the Function Block and Device Libraries. The Application Editor is used to specify and define function block networks (i.e. IEC61499 applications). Usability and aid for the user are main goals of the editor. Functions like copy/paste or undo/redo are supported by the tool. Checks during drawing of connections are performed in order to avoid programming errors in a very early stage. Functions like zooming helps the user developing larger function block networks. The Outline View provides an overview of the developed control application. Furthermore connections are drawn by a dotted line if connected function blocks are mapped to different devices. This shows the user that communication links have to be configured (see Figure 11).

The Hardware Configuration Editor is responsible for the modeling of the automation hardware (incl. communication network and devices as defined by the IEC 61499 standard). The network can be split into more parts for structuring. Each of these parts can be opened with the editor. Within this editor a function block can be mapped to a device. Mapping means that a function block gets

Figure 11. Engineering Prototype

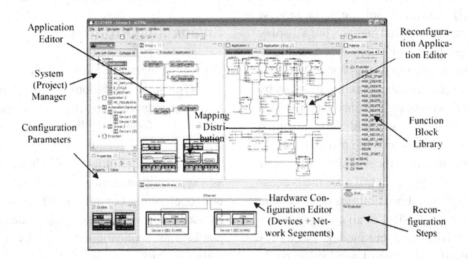

assigned to a device or to a resource if the device has more resources (execution environments for function blocks according to IEC 61499). The system manager gives an overview of different automation projects and can be use to navigate through these projects.

Within the Reconfiguration Application Editor the reconfiguration control applications are modeled based on existing control applications according to the approach presented in this chapter. The tool supports the control engineer in the definition of the reconfiguration control application. It shows the old and the new application and provides also a Delta Analysis as shown in Figure 8. In addition the tool provides also a support to partly generate a RECFB based on some user interaction. For example if a control engineer wants to exchange a function block of a control application he has to drop the new function block over the old one in the Reconfiguration Application Editor. The tool replaces the function block and generates a RECFB and makes also some configurations of this block based on the reconfiguration templates as explained in the previous section.

Servo Drive Controller Configuration

First tests in the "Testbed for Highly Distributed Control" for the proposed reconfiguration concept have been performed at the Odo Struger Laboratory of the Automation and Control Institute (ACIN), Vienna University of Technology. These tests gave us the possibility of validating our reconfiguration concepts. In detail, reconfiguration of a prototypic implementation of an execution environment with enhanced (re-)configuration services as explained above, a linear servo drive, has been performed during operation, in this example the movement of the axis according to a position profile.

The control program for the linear servo drive consists of the velocity closed-loop control and the position closed-loop control. The tests have been provided for both of these two parts of the control program. For instance a proportional control algorithm has been exchanged by a new one including also an integral part or in addition a derivative part. The scenario for the velocity closed-loop control was the exchange of the control algorithm without changes in the control hardware. So the ROI for this scenario was restricted to the FB including the control algorithm and its surrounding. During

Figure 12. Reconfiguration with output-fitting at time 0.75 s

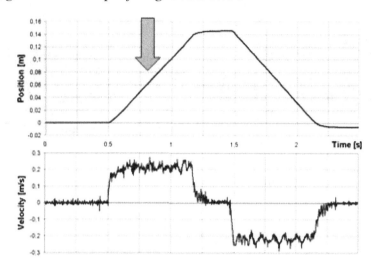

the RECONF sequence an appropriate algorithm has to be applied to avoid disturbances, in this example the output fitting method has been used (Guler, 2003). In the second scenario the position closed-loop control has been exchanged and also the hardware configuration has been changed. An additional controller has been introduced and the new position controller has been applied to the new controller. The results of the second scenario are presented in Figure 12.

The linear axis performs a ramp. During the ramp up sequence the reconfiguration takes place, depicted by the arrow in Figure 12. In the lower part of Figure 12 the corresponding velocity of the linear axis gives an impression of the performance of the reconfiguration. There is no influence visible in the velocity graph (of course also in the position graph), although the control algorithm of the position controller has been changed and the position controller itself has been moved to another device within the network. This first result provides first evidence that the proposed reconfiguration approach is sufficient for providing dynamic reconfiguration of lower level control applications in distributed IPMCS. In the provided example the reconfiguration took place only

in a few microseconds which is normally fast enough for control tasks in IPMCS.

Communication Reconfiguration

Additional tests for the proposed reconfiguration concept have been also performed by PROFACTOR. To show how a controlled reconfiguration, as explained above, works an example has been created that uses two embedded control boards (DIGI ConnectME development boards, DIGI, 2009) called DIGI1 and DIGI2. Both embedded boards are equipped with the Net+OS 6.3 real-time operating systems (which is based on the ThreadX open source project) and an IEC 61499 compliant runtime environment with enhanced reconfiguration services. The initial control application performs the following steps:

1)   A HMI device (e.g. PC) sends a user input (a number) to the DIGI1 device over Ethernet.
2)   DIGI1 device sends data to DIGI2 device over Ethernet.
3)   The DIGI2 device sends the data to the HMI device over Ethernet and this device displays the result to the user

Figure 13. Two DIGI ConnectME embedded controller connected via serial link

Figure 14. Part of the application in the DIGI1 device

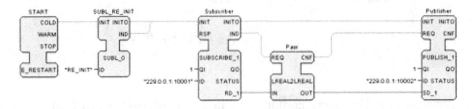

All communication in this application is over Ethernet, but this can be changed online by a reconfiguration application. This application has been designed such that it changes Step 2 from a communication over Ethernet to a communication over a serial link (for hardware layout see Figure 13).

Figure 14 shows the part of the application that is mapped to the DIGI1 device. The simplified reconfiguration application has to change the PUBLISH_1 FB instance to a SERCOMM_1_0 FB instance and performs the following steps:

1) Create SERCOMM_1_0 FB with name "Serial"
2) Start "Serial"
3) Set parameter "Serial.QI" to value "1"
4) Set parameter "Serial.ID" to value "COM1"
5) Set parameter "Serial.BAUD" to value "1200"
6) Reconnect[1] "Publisher.INIT" to "Serial. INIT"
7) Reconnect "Publisher.REQ" to "Serial. REQ"
8) Reconnect "Publisher.SD_1" to "Serial. SD_1"

9) Stop "Publisher"
10) Delete "Publisher"
11) Send INIT event to "Serial"

All these steps can be mapped to the above mentioned special management FBs that are available. Figure 15 shows these steps graphically. Similar steps have to be taken to change the part of the application in device DIGI2.

FUTURE RESEARCH DIRECTIONS

The next steps in our research work are to implement reconfiguration services in an advanced IEC 61499 based runtime environment which is capable of executing reconfiguration control applications. Furthermore a validation of the above described approach will be carried out over a wide range of different control scenarios and applications in the future. Moreover we will also focus our work on an enhanced engineering environment supporting the design and implementation of reconfiguration control applications.

Figure 15. Reconfiguration steps in the DIGI1 device

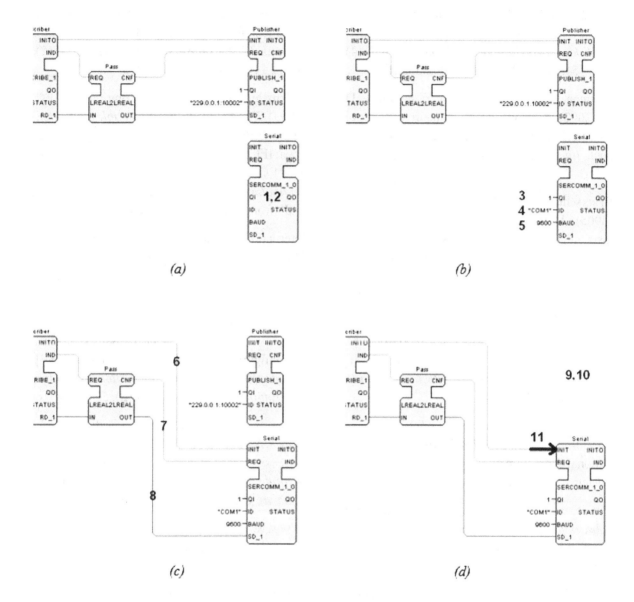

(a)

(b)

(c)

(d)

CONCLUSION

This chapter presents an approach for structured modeling of reconfiguration control applications of IPMCS based on the IEC 61499 standard. It has been shown that the concept and elements of the IEC 61499 standard's management model, with little extensions, are sufficient for dynamic reconfiguration of distributed applications.

REFERENCES

Abele, E., Wörn, A., Stroh, C., & Elzenheimer, J. (2005). *Multi Machining Technology Integration in RMS*. Proceedings of the CIRP sponsored 3rd Conference on Reconfigurable Manufacturing, University of Michigan, Ann Arbor, MI, USA.

Brennan, R. W., Fletcher, M., & Norrie, D. H. (2002). An agent-based approach to reconfiguration of real-time distributed control systems. *IEEE Journal on Robotics and Automation, 18*(4), 444–451. doi:10.1109/TRA.2002.802211

Brennan, R. W., Zhang, X., Xu, Y., & Norrie, D. H. (2002). A reconfigurable concurrent function block model and its implementation in real-time java. *Integrated Computer-Aided Engineering, 9*, 263–279.

Brinkschulte, U., Schneider, E., & Picioragá, F. (2005). Dynamic real-time reconfiguration in distributed systems: timing issues and solutions. In *Proceedings of the Eighth IEEE International Symposium on Object-Oriented Real-Time Distributed Computing, ISORC 2005*, Seattle, WA, (pp. 174–181).

Burmester, S. (2004). Modeling reconfigurable mechatronic systems with mechatronic UML. *MDAFA - Model Driven Architecture: Foundations and Applications.*

Bussmann, S., & McFarlane, D. (1999). *Rationales for Holonic Manufacturing Control*. In 2nd International Workshop on Intelligent Manufacturing Systems. New York: Leuven.

Christensen, J. H. (2009). *Holobloc Inc. - Resources for the New Generation of Automation and Control*. Retrieved November 2, 2009 from http://www.holobloc.com

DIGI. (2009). *DIGI Connect ME development boards*. Retrieved November 2, 2009 from http://www.digi.com

European Commission. (2004). *MANUFUTURE A Vision for 2020*. Report of the High-Level Group.

Gamma, E., & Beck, K. (2003). *Contributing to Eclipse: Principles, Patterns, and Plugins* (1st ed.). Boston: Addison-Wesley Professional.

Guler, M., Clement, S., Wills, L. M., Heck, B. S., & Vachtsevanos, G. J. (2003). Transition management for reconfigurable hybrid control systems. *IEEE Control Systems Magazine, 23*(1). doi:10.1109/MCS.2003.1172828

International Electrotechnical Commission - IEC. (2003). *IEC 61131-3: Programmable controllers - Part 3: Programming languages*, (2nd Ed.). Geneva: IEC Press, International Standard. kirchner SOFT GmbH. (2009). *logiCAD - The IEC 61131 Technology Platform*. Retrieved November 2, 2009 from http://www.logicals.com

International Electrotechnical Commission - IEC. (2005). *IEC 61499: Function Blocks - Part 1,2, &3* (1st ed.). Geneva: IEC Press, International Standard.

Koren, Y., Heisel, U., Jovane, F., Moriwaki, T., Pritshow, G., Ulsoy, G., & van Brussel, H. (1999). Reconfigurable Manufacturing Systems. [CIRP]. *Annals of the International Institution for Production Engineering Research, 48*(2), 527–539.

Lastra, J. Martinez, Lobov, A. Godinho, & L. Nunes, A. (2004). *Function Blocks for Industrial-Process Mesaurement and Control Systems. Institute of Production Engineering*, Report 67. Tampere University of Technology.

Lewis, R. W. (2001). *Modeling control systems using IEC 61499*. Washington, DC: IEE Publishing.

Lorentz, K. (2006). *Torero newsletter no. 2, TORERO Consortium*. Retrieved March 3, 2006 from http://www.uni-magdeburg.de/iaf/cvs/torero

Mens, T., Wermelinger, M., Ducasse, S., Demeyer, S., Hirschfeld, R., & Jazayeri, M. (2005). Challenges in software evolution. In *Proceedings of the Eighth International Workshop on Principles of Software Evolution*, (pp. 13–22).

Rasche, A., & Polze, A. (2005). Dynamic reconfiguration of component-based real-time software. In *Proceedings of the 10th IEEE International Workshop on Object-Oriented Real-Time Dependable Systems, WORDS 2005,* Sedona, Arizona, (pp. 347–354).

Schnakenbourg, C., Faure, J.-M., & Lesage, J.-J. (2002). Towards IEC 61499 function block diagrams verification. In *Proceedings of the IEEE International Conference on Systems, Man and Cybernetics,* Nashville, TN.

Stanica, M., & Guèguen, H. (2004). Using Timed Automata for the Verification of IEC 61499 Applications. In *Proceedings of the Workshop on Discrete Event Systems,* Reims, France.

Strasser, T., Zoitl, A., Auinger, F., & Sünder, C. (2005). *Towards engineering methods for reconfiguration of distributed automation systems based on the reference model of IEC 61499.* Proceedings of the 2nd International Conference on Industrial Applications of Holonic and Multi-Agent Systems. Copenhagen, Denmark, Aug. 22–24.

Sünder, C., Zoitl, A., Favre-Bulle, B., Strasser, T., Steininger, H., & Thomas, S. (2006). Towards reconfiguration applications as basis for control system evolution in zero-downtime automation systems. *Proceedings of the IPROMS NoE Virtual International Conference on Intelligent Production Machines and Systems, IPROMS, 2006*(June), 3–14.

Thramboulidis, K., Doukas, G., & Frantzis, A. (2004). Towards an implementation model for FB-based reconfigurable distributed control applications. In *Proceedings of the 7th IEEE International Symposium on Object-Oriented Real-Time Distributed Computing,* Vienna, Austria, (pp. 193–200).

Vyatkin, V., & Hanisch, H.-M. (1999). *A Modeling Approach for Verification of IEC1499 Function Blocks using Net Condition/Event Systems.* Proceedings of IEEE International Conference on Emerging Technologies and Factory Automation, ETFA 1999, Barcelona, Spain.

Wermelinger, M. (1997). A hierarchic architecture model for dynamic reconfiguration. In *Proceedings of the Second International Workshop on Software Engineering for Parallel and Distributed Systems,* Boston, (pp. 243–254).

Zoitl, A. (2008). *Real-Time Execution for IEC 61499.* Research Triangle Park, NC: International Society of Automation - ISA, ISA Press.

ADDITIONAL READING

Al-Safi, Y., & Vyatkin, V. (2009). Ontology-based Reconfiguration Agent for Intelligent Mechatronic Systems in Flexible Manufacturing. *International Journal of Robotics and Computer Integrated Manufacturing.*

Black, G., & Vyatkin, V. (2010). Intelligent Component - based Automation of Baggage Handling Systems with IEC 61499. *IEEE Transactions on Automation Science and Engineering.*

Brennan, R., Vrba, P., Tichy, P., Zoitl, A., Sünder, C., Strasser, T., & Marik, V. (2008). *Developments in Dynamic and Intelligent Reconfiguration of Industrial Automation. Computers in Industry – An International, Application Oriented Research Journal.* Elsevier Editorial.

Cengic, G. (2009), Fuber - FUnction Block Execution Runtime. Retrieved November 2, 2009 from http://sourceforge.net/projects/fuber

Christensen, J. H. (2009), IEC 61499 - A Standard for Software Reuse in Embedded, Distributed Control Systems. Retrieved November 2, 2009 from http://knol.google.com/k/james-christensen/iec-61499#

4DIAC Consortium. (2009), 4DIAC - Framework for Distributed Industrial Automation and Control. Retrieved November 2, 2009 from http://www.fordiac.org

Dubinin, V., & Vyatkin, V. (2009). *Refactoring of Execution Control Charts in Basic Function Blocks of the IEC 61499 Standard*. IEEE Transactions on Industrial Informatics.

Ferrarini, L., & Lorentz, K. (2003). *A case study for modeling and design of distributed automation systems*. Procedings of the IEEE/ASME International Conference on Advanced Intelligent Mechatronics. Port Island, Kobe, Japan. pp. 1043–1048.

Fletcher, M., & Norrie, D. (2001). *Realtime Reconfiguration using an IEC 61499 Operating System*. Proceedings of the 15th International Parallel and Distributed Processing Symposium (IPDPS'01) Workshops. IPDPS'01. San Francisco. CA, USA.

Higgins, N., Vyatkin, V., Nair, N., & Schwarz, K. (2009). *Intelligent Decentralised Power Distribution Automation with IEC 61850, IEC 61499 and Holonic Control*. IEEE Transactions on Systems, Machine and Cybernetics, Part C.

Marik, V., Brennan, R., & Pechoucek, M. (Eds.). (2005). *Holonic and Multi-Agent Systems for Manufacturing*. Proceedings of the 2nd International Conference on Industrial Applications of Holonic and Multi-Agent Systems. HoloMAS 2005. Vol. 3593, Lecture Notes in Computer Science. Springer. ISBN: 978-3-540-28237-2.

Marik, V., McFarlane, D., & Valckenares, P. (Eds.). (2003). *Holonic and Multi-Agent Systems for Manufacturing*. Proceedings of the 1st International Conference on Industrial Applications of Holonic and Multi-Agent Systems. HoloMAS 2003. Lecture Notes in Computer Science. Vol. 2744. Springer. ISBN: 978-3-540-40751-5.

Marik, V., Strasser, T., & Zoitl, A. (Eds.). (2009). *Holonic and Multi-Agent Systems for Manufacturing*. Proceedings of the 4th International Conference on Industrial Applications of Holonic and Multi-Agent Systems. HoloMAS 2009. Lecture Notes in Computer Science. Vol. 5696. Springer. ISBN: 978-3-642-03666-8.

Marik, V., Vyatkin, V., & Colombo, V. (Eds.). (2007). *Holonic and Multi-Agent Systems for Manufacturing*. Proceedings of the 3rd International Conference on Industrial Applications of Holonic and Multi-Agent Systems. HoloMAS 2007. Lecture Notes in Computer Science. Vol. 4659. Springer. ISBN: 978-3-540-74478-8.

O³neida. (2009a). IEC 61499 Compliance Profile - Execution Models of IEC 61499 Function Block Applications. Retrieved March 2, 2009 from http://www.oooneida.org/standards_development_Compliance_Profile.html

O³neida. (2009b). O³neida - Network of Networks to Advance Distributed Industrial Automation. Retrieved November 2, 2009 from http://www.oooneida.org

Sardesai, A. R., Mazharullah, O., & Vyatkin, V. (2006). *Reconfiguration of mechatronic systems enabled by IEC 61499 function blocks*. Proceedings of the Australasian Conference on Robotics and Industrial Automation. ACRA 2006. Auckland, New Zealand.

Strasser, T., Fessl, K., Hämmerle, A., & Ankerl, M. (2005). *Rapid Reconfiguration of Machine-Tools for Holonic Manufacturing Systems*. Proceedings of the 16th IFAC World Congress. Prague, Czech Republic.

Strasser. T., Rooker, M., & Ebenhofer, G. (2010). An IEC 61499 Distributed Control Concept for Recongurable Robots. Accepted for publication. *International Journal Computer Aided Engineering and Technology*.

Sünder, C., Vyatkin, V., & Favre-Bulle, B. (2008). *Proving Feasibility and Estimating Parameters of Dynamic Reconfiguration in IEC 61499 Controllers using Formal Modelling. International Journal of Mechatronics and Manufacturing Systems*. IJMMS.

Thramboulidis, K. (2009), CORFU ESS - Engineering Support System. Retrieved November 2, 2009 from http://seg.ece.upatras.gr/Corfu

Vyatkin, V. (2007). *IEC 61499 Function Blocks for Embedded and Distributed Control Systems Design. International Society of Automation - ISA*. ISA Press.

Vyatkin, V. (2009). *The IEC 61499 Standard and its Semantics*. IEEE Industrial Electronics Magazine.

Zoitl, A., Auinger, F., Vyatkin, V., & Martinez Lastra, J. L. (2004). *Towards basic real-time reconfiguration services for next generation zero-downtime automation systems*. Proceedings of the International IMS Forum 2004: Global Challenges in Manufacturing. Como, Italy.

Zoitl, A., Strasser, T., Hall, K. H., Staron, R., Sünder, C., & Favre-Bulle, B. (2007). *The Past, Present, and Future of IEC 61499*. Proceedings of the 3rd International Conference on Industrial Applications of Holonic and Multi-Agent Systems. HoloMAS 2007. Regensburg, Germany.

Zoitl, A., Strasser, T., Sünder, C., & Baier, T. (2009). *IEC 61499 and IEC 61131-3 in Perfect Harmony?* IEEE Industrial Electronics Magazine.

KEY TERMS AND DEFINITIONS

ACIN: Automation and Control Institute.

EC: Embedded Controller.

ECC: Execution Control Chart.

FB: Function Block.

FBN: Function Block Network.

GEF: Graphical Editing Framework.

IPC: Industrial PC.

IEC: International Electrotechnical Commission.

I/O: Input/Output.

IEC 61131: standard for PLCs.

IEC 61499: reference model for distributed and reconfigurable automation and control systems.

IPMCS: Industrial Process Measurement and Control Systems.

PC: Personal Computer.

PLC: Programmable Logic Controller.

QoS: Quality of Service.

RCA: Reconfiguration Control Application.

RECFB: Reconfiguration Execution Control Function Blocks.

Reconfiguration: arrange into a new PLC/EC configuration.

ROI: Region of Interest.

SDK: Software Development Kit

UML: Unified Modeling Language.

XML: Extended Mark-up Language.

ENDNOTE

[1]   Reconnect in this context means disconnect the event connection from "Publisher.INIT" and connect it to "Serial.INIT"

Chapter 4
Hardware Virtualization on Dynamically Reconfigurable Processors

Christian Plessl
University of Paderborn, Germany

Marco Platzner
University of Paderborn, Germany

ABSTRACT

Numerous research efforts in reconfigurable embedded processors have shown that augmenting a CPU core with a coarse-grained reconfigurable array for application-specific hardware acceleration can greatly increase performance and energy-efficiency. The traditional execution model for such reconfigurable co-processors however requires the accelerated function to fit onto the reconfigurable array as a whole, which restricts the applicability to rather small functions. In the authors' research presented in this chapter, the authors have studied hardware virtualization approaches that overcome this restriction by leveraging dynamic reconfiguration. They present two different hardware virtualization methods, virtualized execution and temporal partitioning, and introduce the Zippy reconfigurable processor architecture that has been designed with specific hardware virtualization support. Further, the authors outline the corresponding hardware and software tool flows. Finally, the authors demonstrate the potential provided by hardware virtualization with two case studies and discuss directions for future research.

INTRODUCTION

In this chapter, we present results from the Zippy research project (Plessl, 2006, Plessl, Platzner, & Thiele, 2006, Enzler, Plessl, & Platzner, 2005, Plessl & Platzner, 2005, Enzler, Plessl, & Platzner, 2003b, 2003a, Enzler, 2004) that was started at ETH Zurich in 2001 and was continued later at University of Paderborn. At the center of the Zippy project stands the novel Zippy reconfigurable processor architecture, which comprises an embedded CPU core and an attached coarse-grained multi-context reconfigurable array. Zippy has been

DOI: 10.4018/978-1-60960-086-0.ch004

designed to support rapid dynamic reconfiguration at runtime as the prime feature of the architecture. The key objective of the Zippy research effort is to identify the potential of rapid reconfiguration in an embedded computing context. In particular, we have studied *hardware virtualization* as one particularly interesting application domain for dynamic reconfiguration which allows for exploring new performance versus chip-size versus energy trade-offs in the architecture design phase. For increasing the efficiency of hardware virtualization, we have augmented the Zippy architecture with specific hardware components that implement the execution models required for hardware virtualization directly in hardware.

This chapter is structured as follows. In Section BACKGROUND we present an overview of the area of reconfigurable processors. We present related work and discuss the motivation and need for hardware virtualization as a new approach to balance performance, energy efficiency and chip size in embedded processors. We introduce two hardware virtualization approaches denoted as *virtualized execution* and *temporal partitioning* that we have explored in our work. In Section ZIPPY DYNAMICALLY RECONFIGURABLE PROCESSOR ARCHITECTURE we present the architecture of the Zippy reconfigurable processor and point out the dedicated hardware units for efficient hardware virtualization. In Section TOOL FLOWS we briefly introduce the hardware tool flow for mapping hardware accelerators to the reconfigurable array and the compilation tool chain. Section SYSTEM-LEVEL CYCLE-ACCURATE CO-SIMULATION introduces our system-level co-simulation environment that allows us to accurately evaluate a broad variety of reconfigurable processor architectures. In Section SYSTEM-LEVEL CYCLE-ACCURATE CO-SIMULATION we explain how the hardware virtualization techniques outlined in Section BACKGROUND are supported by the Zippy architecture and we present two detailed case studies that demonstrate and evaluate the benefits of hardware virtualization on our architecture. Finally, we present an outlook

on future trends in Section FUTURE TRENDS and summarize the conclusions from our work in Section CONCLUSIONS.

BACKGROUND

The design and implementation of embedded systems is generally challenging due to the stringent performance, power and cost constraints. It has been shown for many applications that co-processors based on field-programmable reconfigurable hardware devices, such as FPGAs, allow for significant speedups, cost and energy savings over embedded systems based on general-purpose microprocessors or microcontrollers. However, mapping complete applications rather than kernels to a reconfigurable device is difficult and often inefficient. It is useful to offload the performance hungry and latency sensitive application kernels to a reconfigurable coprocessor, while relying on a comparatively simple CPU core for handling the system management and control tasks that are not performance critical. Hence a processor architecture that combines reconfigurable hardware with a general-purpose CPU core in an integrated device is an attractive platform for building embedded systems. These architectures, denoted as *reconfigurable processors* have received increasing attention in the last years and a number of architectures have been introduced both in academic research and in the commercial marketplace.

Another trend that has emerged in recent years is the exploration of coarse-grained reconfigurable architectures. While fine-grained FPGAs are suitable for accelerating bit-oriented and custom operations, coarse-grained architectures operate on word-sized data and are particularly suitable for arithmetically intensive digital signal processing applications, as they occur in many embedded computing applications. Around the year 2000, a number of academic research projects have been started to study the potential of coarse-grained arrays in reconfigurable processors (Singh et al., 2000, Miyamori & Olukotun, 1999, Baumgarte, May, Nückel, Vorbach, & Weinhardt, 2001, Salefski & Caglar, 2001). These projects have shown that even rather small coarse-grained reconfigurable arrays can substantially improve the performance and energy-efficiency of an embedded system-on-chip. In contrast to competing technologies, such as ASICs, reconfigurable processors are fully programmable and hence allow to implement a wide range of application-specific co-processors, which can even be changed at runtime using dynamic reconfiguration.

While these results are highly encouraging, reconfigurable processors architectures still pose a number of challenges that delay the adoption of these architectures in the industrial practice. One particular area we have studied in our research presented here is finding ways of weakening the strong mutual dependence of the hardware accelerator circuits and the reconfigurable array architecture. While we take it for granted that the instruction set abstraction makes CPUs compatible, that is, the same binary code can be executed on any device in a processor family, configurations for reconfigurable accelerators are targeted to one specific device in a family without any compatibility on the binary (bitstream) level. Similarly, we take it for granted that CPUs can execute programs of arbitrary size by virtue of virtual memory, while the maximum size of a hardware accelerator circuit is strictly limited by the hardware resources provided by a specific reconfigurable array.

To overcome these limitations and to achieve a higher level of device independence of hardware accelerators and reconfigurable devices, researchers have studied approaches to transfer ideas from virtual memory to hardware and have coined the term *hardware virtualization*. In the area of reconfigurable architectures hardware virtualization is still an emerging field without a generally accepted terminology. In (Plessl & Platzner, 2004) we have presented a survey of different approaches and

have proposed a taxonomy. In our research we have focussed on two approaches which we denote as *virtualized execution* and *temporal partitioning*.

- **Virtualized Execution.** The motivation for virtualized execution is to achieve a certain level of device-independence within a device family. An application is specified in a programming model that defines some atomic unit of computation. This unit is commonly called a hardware page. Hence, an application is specified as a collection of tasks (that fit into a hardware page) and their interactions. The execution architecture for such an application is defined as a whole family of devices. All devices support the abstractions defined by the programming model, that is, the hardware page and the interactions (communication channels). The members of a device family can differ in the amount of resources they provide, for example, the number of hardware pages that are executing concurrently, or the number of tasks that can be stored on-chip. Since all implementations of the execution architecture support the same programming model, an application can run on any member of the device family without resynthesis. In this respect, this approach is comparable to the device independence achieved for microprocessors by the definition of an instruction set architecture. The resulting independence of the device size allows the designer to trade off performance for cost. Furthermore, the forward compatibility lets us exploit advances in technology that result in larger and faster devices.

- **Temporal Partitioning.** The motivation for this virtualization approach is to enable the mapping of an application of arbitrary size to a reconfigurable device with insufficient hardware capacity. Temporal partitioning splits the application into smaller parts, each of which fits onto the device, and runs these parts sequentially. Conceptually, this approach is similar to paged virtual memory, where applications can use an arbitrary amount of memory, which is divided into pages that are loaded into the processor on demand. Temporal partitioning was the first virtualization style that has been studied. It was a necessity when reconfigurable devices were too small for many interesting applications, but it is still of importance with today's multi-million gate FPGAs—in particular in embedded systems—for saving chip area and thus cost.

ZIPPY DYNAMICALLY RECONFIGURABLE PROCESSOR ARCHITECTURE

In this section we introduce a new dynamically reconfigurable processor architecture named Zippy. Zippy is not a single, concrete architecture but an architectural simulation model of a dynamically reconfigurable processor. The model integrates an embedded CPU core with a coarse-grained *reconfigurable processing unit (RPU)*. Such architectures are commonly known as Reconfigurable Processors or hybrid CPUs (Compton & Hauck, 2002).

The design of the Zippy architecture is guided by two objectives. First, we want to provide an experimentation framework to study the use of coarse-grained, dynamically reconfigurable CPUs and the associated design tools in the embedded system domain. Hence, for exploring a wide variety of architectures, we have designed a widely parametrized architectural model that specifies a whole family of reconfigurable CPUs. Second, we aim at investigating dynamic reconfiguration and hardware virtualization in an embedded systems context. Hardware virtualization demands that circuits are partitioned into a number of

smaller communicating sub-circuits at compile-time and that these sub-circuits are executed on reconfigurable hardware in a time-multiplexed way at runtime. Although hardware virtualization can be used with any reconfigurable architecture, an efficient implementation requires support by dedicated hardware components in the reconfigurable architecture, namely: 1. fast reconfiguration, 2. fast, repeated activation of a fixed sequence of configurations, and 3. efficient data-transfers between configurations.

The Zippy architecture supports these operations with the following architectural features:

1. multi-context configuration architecture, that is, several configurations are stored on-chip concurrently. The activation of a stored configuration happens within a single cycle
2. dedicated context sequencers that autonomously activate a programmable sequence of configurations for a given time, and
3. data-transfer register-files that are shared between different configurations for communicating data within the reconfigurable array, and FIFO memory-queues for communication between configurations and with the reconfigurable processor's CPU core.

System Architecture

Zippy is a reconfigurable processor composed of two main units: the *CPU core* and the *reconfigurable processing unit (RPU)*. Figure 1 presents a schematic drawing of the Zippy system architecture. The RPU acts as a coprocessor to the CPU, that is, the CPU's coprocessor interface is attached to the RPU's register interface. All data-transfers between the CPU and the RPU are performed via this coprocessor interface. Additionally, the various functions of the RPU (for example, configuration loading, context sequencer programming or synchronization of CPU and RPU) are exposed to the CPU via read and write operations on the

Figure 1. The Zippy system architecture comprises a CPU core and a Reconfigurable Processing Unit (RPU)

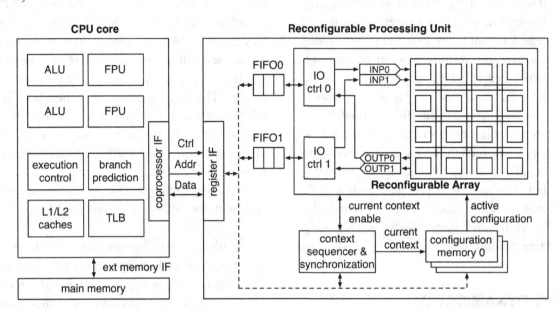

register interface. We assume that the CPU and the RPU use the same clock.

For the CPU core of the Zippy architecture we use the SimpleScalar PISA architecture, as defined by the SimpleScalar CPU simulator. Thus the CPU core is not a real CPU core, but a cycle-accurate simulation model (Austin, Larson, & Ernst, 2002). SimpleScalar is a well established tool for CPU architecture research and provides a highly configurable 32-bit super-scalar RISC architecture that allows for configuring the number of functional units (integer, floating-point, and multipliers), the degree of super-scalar processing, branch prediction, cache hierarchies and much more. These configuration parameters allow for customizing the CPU to model a broad range of architectures, from small low-end CPUs with a single integer ALU and small caches to powerful super-scalar CPU architectures with multi-level cache hierarchies.

Attached to the CPU via a co-processor interface is the RPU that features a coarse-grained reconfigurable array as a computational resource. To provide the reconfigurable array with con-

figurations and data, the RPU offers memories for storing the configurations and FIFO memory queues for data-transfers between CPU and RPU. For supporting efficient hardware virtualization, dedicated context sequencers allow for switching between different configurations during runtime. Just as the CPU core, the RPU architecture model is also highly configurable which enables us to explore and evaluate a whole family of reconfigurable processors. Customizable RPU parameters include the width of the data-path, the size of the memory queues, number of configuration contexts, dimensions of the reconfigurable array and the interconnect between the cells of the array.

Reconfigurable Processing Unit Architecture

A schematic diagram of the reconfigurable processing unit is shown in Figure 1. Zippy is a multi-context architecture, i.e., several configurations can be stored concurrently on-chip in the configuration memory. The RPU can switch rapidly between these configurations. The activation and sequencing of configurations is controlled by the context sequencer. The FIFOs are accessible by both, the reconfigurable array and the CPU core and are used to pass input data and results between the CPU core and the reconfigurable array and also between different configurations (contexts) of the RPU. The register interface provides the CPU with access to the RPU function blocks.

Reconfigurable Array

The *reconfigurable array* is the core unit of the Zippy architecture. It is organized as an array of uniform, coarse-grained reconfigurable cells, which are connected by two programmable interconnection structures: a local interconnect and a bus interconnect. The reconfigurable array has two input and two output ports and that connect the internal buses to the IO-controllers of the RPU. The bit-width of the ALU in the cells, the interconnection wires, and the FIFOs can be configured. Typically, the bit-width is set to 16 bit or 24 bit, which are common bit-widths for many fixed-point signal processing algorithms.

Interconnection Network

The Zippy architecture uses two interconnection structures: a local interconnect between neighboring cells, and a bus interconnect, between cells in the same row or column. The local interconnect allows each cell to read the output data from all of its 8 immediate neighbors. To make the array's interconnect fully symmetric and uniform, the local interconnect is cyclically continued at the edges. For the bus interconnect, the array provides three types of horizontal buses: the horizontal north buses that connect cells in adjacent rows, horizontal south buses that connect cells in the same row, and the memory buses that connect all cells in a row to one on-chip memory block per row. Additionally, vertical buses provide connectivity between the cells in the same column. An example for the schematic of the interconnect is shown in Figure 6.

Reconfigurable Cell

The *reconfigurable cell* is composed of three main structures: a versatile input structure with overall three inputs, an operator block, and an output structure. Figure 2 presents a detailed schematic of the cell.

The function of all shaded parts is controlled by the configuration. As Zippy is a multi-context architecture every context has a distinct configuration for these parts. In addition to the inputs, the current context selector is also fed into the cell to control the input multiplexers of the input and output register-files.

The input multiplexers (*inpX select*) connects each input (*inpX*) to either of six sources: to one of the cell's inputs (horizontal bus, vertical bus, any local neighbor), to a configurable constant, to the cell's output register (feedback path), or to one of the registers of the input register-file. The input register-file provides a dedicated register per input and context, which stores the selected bus or local input. The input register-files can be used for transferring data between the contexts; since the input multiplexer (inX select) has also access to input registers that have been written in all different contexts.

The operator block is based on a fixed-point ALU and performs the cell's computation. The operator takes up to three inputs and computes one output value. Figure 2 includes a table of supported cell operations.

Most arithmetic and logical operations are self-explaining. The *pass* operation forwards the unmodified input value to the output, which can be useful for routing purposes. The *testbitat* operations are used for bit-tests. The *mux(sel,a,b)* operator is a ternary operator that forwards input *a* or input *b* to the output, depending on the value of the least-significant bit of *sel*. Each row of cells has access to a shared ROM memory block The *rom(addr)* operation of a cell reads the contents at address *addr* of the ROM associated with this cell.

Like the input register-file, the output register-file provides a dedicated register per context. The

Figure 2. Reconfigurable Processing Unit: Cell architecture (shaded parts are controlled by the configuration)

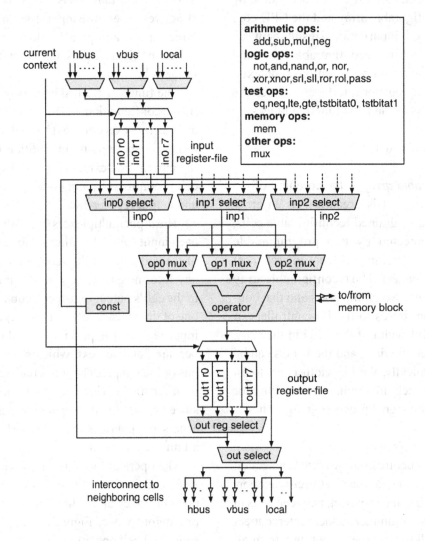

output of the operator block is stored in a dedicated register of the output register-file. The output of the cell can be selected either as the combinational output of the operator block, or as the contents of an output register. Since the output multiplexer has access to all output registers it can also be used for data-transfers between different contexts.

Memory Blocks

Each row of the reconfigurable array has an associated ROM memory block. The depth of the ROM is an architecture parameter, the content of the ROM is defined by the configuration.

FIFO Memory Queues and IO controllers

The RPU provides two FIFO memory queues. The depth of the FIFOs is parametrized. The FIFOs are used for transferring input data from the CPU to the RPU and for reading the results back to the CPU after processing. As the FIFOs are accessible from any context they can be also used for passing data between contexts. This is particularly important for the virtualized execution hardware virtualization mode, where FIFOs are used to pass intermediate data from one context to the next.

The reconfigurable array accesses the FIFO contents via input and output buses that are connected to IO ports, that is, input ports (INP0/1) and output ports (OUTP0/1), as well as to the bus interconnect. For controlling the access to the FIFOs, the architecture provides dedicated IO controllers, which are simple yet effective controllers for generating many important FIFO activation sequences. For example, the controllers can generate repetitive activation sequences, for example, enabling the FIFO in every fourth cycle. Additionally, the controllers can generate more complex activation schemes that depend on the number of execution cycles without fixing this number at circuit compilation time. For example, writing to a FIFO can be stopped a given number of cycles before the end of the last cycle. This activation mode is important for pipelined circuits when the transient data-samples, caused by filling and clearing the pipeline, shall be discarded.

Register Interface

The *register interface* implements the interface from the CPU's coprocessor port to the RPU and vice versa. It is accessed with the coprocessor instructions that we have added to SimpleScalar. Table 1 provides an overview of the commands supported by the register interface.

The FIFO functions offer FIFO read and write access to the CPU, further the FIFO's fill-level can be queried. The *configuration memory command* initiates the upload of a configuration to a context memory. The *cycle count* command sets the number of execution cycles if the cycle-counter context sequencer is used. This register is also polled by the CPU for detecting the end of the execution. *Context select* activates a context for execution. Optionally, the registers in the cell's register-files that are associated with the selected context can be reset on activation. The remaining *context sequencer commands* are used for select-

Table 1. Register Interface: Commands

RPU coprocessor register	CPU access
FIFO {1,2}	R/W
FIFO {1,2} level	R
configuration memory {1...n}	W
RPU reset	W
cycle count	R/W
context select	W
context sequencer mode	W
context sequencer temporal partitioning contexts	W
context sequencer start	W
context sequencer status	R
context sequence store {1...s}	W

ing the context sequencer mode and setting the sequencer's parameters.

Context Sequencers for Hardware Virtualization

Hardware virtualization requires the execution of a sequence of configurations (contexts) where each context is executed for a predefined number of cycles. Efficient context sequencing is a precondition for efficient hardware virtualization, but has so far not been explicitly targeted in related work. The requirements on the efficiency depend on the hardware virtualization approach (see Section BACKGROUND). Hardware virtualization using temporal partitioning requires a context switch in every cycle and hence demands for a context sequencer with low timing overhead. If the virtualized execution hardware virtualization method is used, the execution can tolerate longer context switching overheads, since context switches occur less frequently. Hence, the context sequencing could be controlled either by the reconfigurable processor's CPU core or a dedicated sequencer. However, a dedicated sequencer as it is provided in the Zippy architecture increases the performance.

The Zippy architecture offers a choice of *three different context sequencers* that are designed to match the requirements for hardware virtualization: the cycle-counter sequencer, the virtualized execution sequencer, and the temporal partitioning sequencer. These sequencers handle the activation and switching of contexts without CPU intervention and thus relieve the CPU from this task.

Figure 3 shows the activation sequences that are generated by the sequencers with timing-diagrams.

a) **Cycle-Counter Context Sequencer.** The Cycle-Counter Context sequencer is the basic form of a context sequencer. It executes a single context for a configurable number of cycles, after which the execution is stopped. This sequencer is very similar to the mechanism proposed by Hauser to control the execution of the GARP architecture (Hauser, 1997). Figure 3(a) illustrates the generated activation patterns. In this example, context 0 is activated for 128 cycles. The CPU detects the end of the execution phase by polling the cycle down register for reaching zero.

b) **Virtualized Execution Context Sequencer.** The Virtualized Execution Context Sequencer executes a programmable sequence of contexts. After a context has been executed, the next context is activated and executed, until the whole sequence of contexts has been processed. The duration of the execution can be configured per context. Figure 3(b) shows an example for a virtualized execution sequencer with 3 contexts: Context 0 is executed for 128 cycles, then context 2 is executed for 2 cycles, and finally, context 1 is executed for 64 cycles. The termination of the sequence is detected by polling the context sequencer status register.

c) **Temporal Partitioning Context Sequencer.** The Temporal Partitioning Context Sequencer is specifically designed for hardware virtualization through temporal partitioning. Temporal partitioning requires a very specific, cyclic execution sequence.

Figure 3. Context sequencers

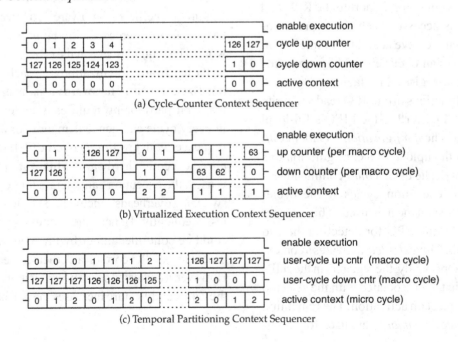

90

Each context is executed for a single cycle, after which the next context is activated and executed. After the last context, the sequence is cyclically repeated. Due to the frequent context switches, a context sequencer with low switching overhead is mandatory for efficient temporal partitioning. Our design allows for switching contexts in a single cycle, that is, without any timing overhead. Figure 3(c) shows an example with 3 contexts that are repeated 128 times. Note, that this sequencer has no overhead for context switching in contrast to the virtualized execution sequencer (see Figure 3(b)).

Multi-Context Architecture

In order to support rapid reconfiguration, we have designed Zippy as a multi-context architecture. Multi-context architectures concurrently store several configurations—denoted as contexts—on-chip and allow for switching rapidly between these configurations. While multi-context devices do not decrease the time for initial loading a configuration, they can dramatically reduce the reconfiguration time because they allow for fast switching between preloaded contexts. All contexts share the computation elements in the data-path, but each context has its own set of registers. This allows us to store and share intermediate results generated by a context until the next context invocation. These registers eliminate memory to store this data and render time-consuming context store and restore phases unnecessary.

Configuration Architecture

The configuration architecture of Zippy is similar to the configuration architecture of fine-grained FPGAs. The configurations are stored in the configuration memory (SRAM) and determine the function of the cells and the IO controllers, and configure the interconnection network. If the active configuration is switched, for example, by the context sequencer, the configurations of all cells change at once.

The configuration bitstream is uploaded from the CPU to the RPU via the register interface. The RPU supports the download of full and partial configurations for any of the contexts. A partial reconfiguration can be used to make small changes to a configuration and prevents the overhead of loading a full configuration.

The size of a configuration depends on the architecture parameters, for example, the size of the array, the bit-width, the size of the on-chip memory blocks, etc. Given an array instance with 4×4 cells, a data-width of 24 bits, 2 horizontal north buses, 2 horizontal south buses, 2 vertical buses and a 128x24bit ROM per row, the configuration size of a context is 1784 bytes.

TOOL FLOWS

For implementing hardware accelerated applications on the Zippy architecture, we have developed an automated hardware and software tool flow which is graphically outlined in Figure 4.

The starting point of the tool flow is an application specification as C source code. In a manual codesign process the application is decomposed into a hardware part, a software part, and a context sequencer configuration. The software part is specified as C source code and uses a communication and reconfiguration library for accessing the RPU. The hardware part is a circuit that uses the resources of the reconfigurable array and is specified as a netlist. In the subsequent hardware implementation tool flow, an automated placement and routing process determines a valid implementation of the circuit on the reconfigurable array. This implementation is transformed into configuration data that is downloaded to the RPU. When implementing applications that use hardware virtualization, the placement and routing process is repeated for every sub-circuit. In a final step, the software part

Figure 4. Outline of the application implementation tool flow

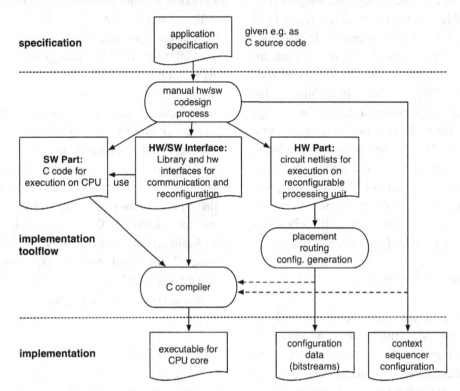

of the application is compiled into an executable with a C compiler.

Hardware Tool Flow

In this section, we provide a brief overview over the Zippy hardware tool flow, which transforms the specification of a circuit into configuration for the reconfigurable array. A detailed discussion of the hardware tool flow can be found in (Plessl, 2006).

We assume that the circuit to be implemented is defined as a netlist of technology-mapped coarse-grained operators that can be implemented by the cells of the reconfigurable array. The netlist is a directed graph composed of the following elements: primary inputs, primary outputs, coarse-grained cells, and registers. Given the coarse grained nature of the cells, the netlist can be obtained easily from signal-flow diagrams, which are a frequently used specification formalism in digital

signal processing. Figure 5 presents an example for a graphical representation of the netlist of a first order FIR filter, which is a canonical signal processing application.

For mapping the components of the circuit's netlist to the coarse-grained reconfigurable array, we have developed an automated placement and routing tool named *zroute*. zroutes builds on core methods and algorithms from the VPR (versatile place and route) tool (Betz, Rose, & Marquardt, 1999) which is the most widely used academic placement and routing framework for fine-grained FPGAs. Just like VPR, we place netlists with a randomized placement procedure and use simulated annealing to optimize the placement. For routing we use an algorithm that is an adapted version of the Pathfinder algorithm (Ebeling, McMurchie, Hauck, & Burns, 1995). Our modifications to the place and route algorithms (for details see (Plessl, 2006)) mainly concern the

Figure 5. Netlist specification of a first order FIR filter (signal-flow diagram)

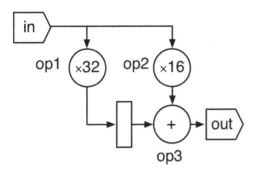

factor that coarse-grained architectures like Zippy have much sparser routing resources than fine-grained FPGAs, hence the placer and router have been adapted with different heuristics to reduce the likelihood of creating placements that result in infeasible routings.

The configuration of the reconfigurable array is determined by the results of the placement and routing process which determines the locations to which each netlist element is mapped and the settings for the programmable switches, multiplexers, and cell input/output blocks. The configuration for the reconfigurable array is specified as a hierarchical VHDL data-structure which can be directly used by the VHDL simulation model of the RPU in the performance evaluation framework (see Section SYSTEM-LEVEL CYCLE-ACCURATE CO-SIMULATION). We use VHDL as the native configuration format because it is human readable and allows for manual modification. Additionally, our tool flow implements an automated translation from the VHDL configuration data structures to a compact binary format and vice versa. This binary configuration bitstream is the data that is finally stored in the configuration memory. Figure 6 shows the place and routed FIR filter on a 2x2 cell instance of the Zippy architecture.

Software Tool Flow

This section introduces the software tool flow for the Zippy architecture. The result of the software tool flow is the executable for the reconfigurable processor's CPU core. The executable incorporates the software parts of the application, the configuration for the context sequencers, and the configuration bitstreams that have been created by the preceding hardware tool flow.

Our software tool flow is based on the GNU C compiler tool chain for the SimpleScalar PISA architecture. Since we have extended the PISA instruction set with new co-processor instructions for accessing the RPU we need to extend the code generation capabilities to support these instructions. As modifying the assembler and compiler with support for new instructions requires significant modifications of the code, we have developed a pragmatic approach for code generation that avoids any modification of the assembler and the compiler. Instead we use the unmodified compilation tools and extend the standard compilation flow with additional pre and post processing steps.

We exploit the fact that the C compiler passes any inline assembler instructions directly to the assembler. This mechanism allows us to pass arbitrary, pseudo-instructions to the assembler without modification. The GNU C compiler simplifies this task by supporting powerful *inline-assembler macros*. These macros can create high-level wrappers around inline-assembler commands that can be used like ordinary C functions. The assembler code within these macros can interact with surrounding C code and can access variables using their symbolic names. The application thus never calls a coprocessor instruction directly, but always uses the function wrappers which are provided to the developer as a communication and configuration library allowing to conveniently access the RPU's functions.

While the proposed method enables the C compiler to issue the new coprocessor instructions,

Figure 6. Implementation of a first order FIR filter on a 2x2 instance of the reconfigurable array

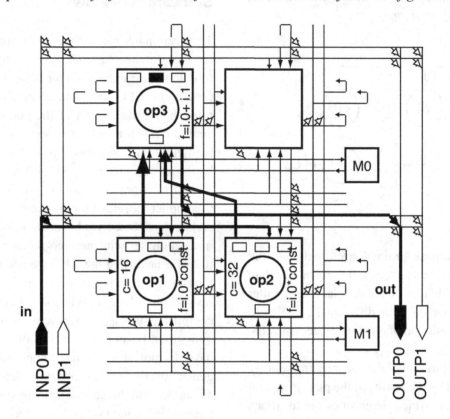

the assembler still cannot process them, because they are not part of the PISA instruction set. We solve this problem by splitting the compilation process into two phases: the compilation phase and the assembly phase. In an intermediate processing step (instruction encoding) the coprocessor instructions are replaced by instructions that are understood by the assembler. The coprocessor instructions in the application's assembly code serve as pure pseudo-instructions that cannot be directly executed. But, although the instructions are not executable, the inline-assembler has determined the register allocation for the instruction's operands. The final instruction encoding step removes these pseudo-instructions from the assembly and replaces them with the binary instruction encoding for the instructions and their register operands. The instruction encoding is specified with a .*word* assembler directive, which

can insert arbitrary data in the assembled object code. Figure 7 depicts the augmented software tool flow and presents the implementation of the *RU_readfifo* function wrapper which reads the contents of a FIFO on the RPU.

SYSTEM-LEVEL CYCLE-ACCURATE CO-SIMULATION

In this section we introduce our co-simulation framework for accurately assessing the performance of the reconfigurable processor architecture, which we have introduced in (Enzler et al., 2003a, 2005). The design of a reconfigurable processor involves a multitude of design decisions related to finding an optimal architecture of the reconfigurable processing unit (RPU) and a suitable system integration of the CPU and

Figure 7. Tool-Flow for generating software executables running on the CPU

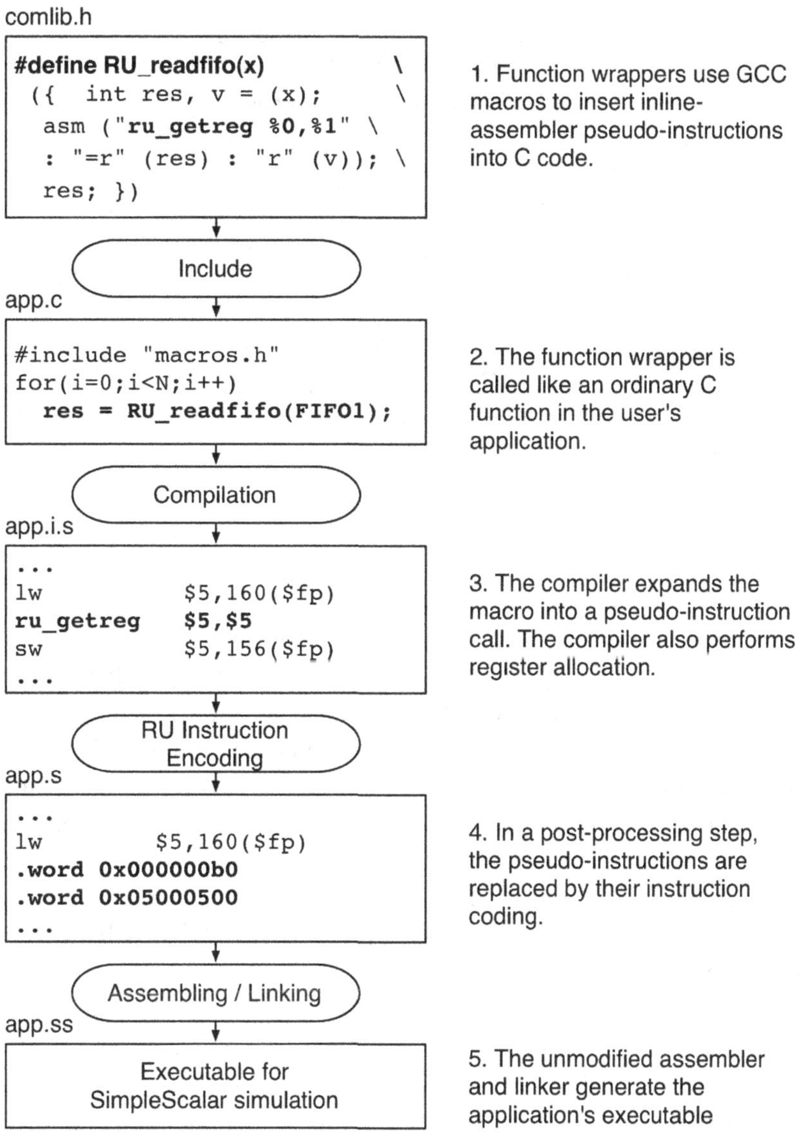

comlib.h

```
#define RU_readfifo(x)            \
({  int res, v = (x);             \
  asm ("ru_getreg %0,%1"          \
  : "=r" (res) : "r" (v));        \
  res; })
```

1. Function wrappers use GCC macros to insert inline-assembler pseudo-instructions into C code.

Include

app.c

```
#include "macros.h"
for(i=0;i<N;i++)
  res = RU_readfifo(FIFO1);
```

2. The function wrapper is called like an ordinary C function in the user's application.

Compilation

app.i.s

```
...
lw           $5,160($fp)
ru_getreg    $5,$5
sw           $5,156($fp)
...
```

3. The compiler expands the macro into a pseudo-instruction call. The compiler also performs register allocation.

RU Instruction Encoding

app.s

```
...
lw           $5,160($fp)
.word 0x000000b0
.word 0x05000500
...
```

4. In a post-processing step, the pseudo-instructions are replaced by their instruction coding.

Assembling / Linking

app.ss

Executable for SimpleScalar simulation

5. The unmodified assembler and linker generate the application's executable

the RPU. The design decisions for the RPU (for example, the type of reconfigurable logic cells, interconnect, configuration architecture), the CPU (for example, the kind of execution units, degree of parallelism, memory and cache architectures), and the bandwidth and latency characteristics of the interface have complex interactions. Also dynamic effects in the CPU core, variable delay for communication between CPU and RPU, and possibly data-dependent processing times in the

RPU, render pure functional RPU models for the performance evaluation of the reconfigurable processor inaccurate because the raw (best-case) performance of the RPU and the actual performance when integrated in a reconfigurable processor can differ significantly.

To address this performance evaluation we have created an execution based performance evaluation method based on co-simulation. Instead of writing a single simulator that simulates

Figure 8. Co-simulation framework integrating the SimpleScalar and ModelSim simulators

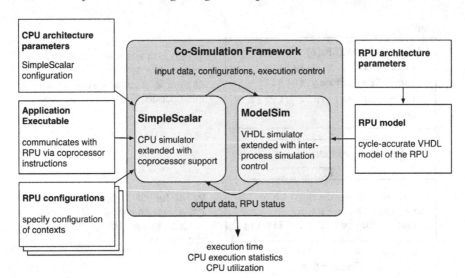

the whole architecture, we combine two existing cycle-accurate simulators, the cycle-accurate SimpleScalar CPU simulator and the ModelSim simulator, which executes a cycle-accurate VHDL model of the RPU. This co-simulation strategy allows us to perform system-level performance evaluation and to use the most productive simulation tool for each simulation task. Figure 8 shows the architecture of the co-simulation framework.

CPU Simulation Model

As introduced in Section SYSTEM ARCHITECTURE we use the SimpleScalar CPU simulator (Austin et al., 2002) for simulating the CPU core and the memory hierarchy of the Zippy architecture. Since SimpleScalar is available in source code and can be easily extended with new instructions and even functional units, it is well suited for building a functional-simulation-based simulator for a reconfigurable processor. We have extended SimpleScalar with a coprocessor interface, which is modeled as a functional unit, and with instructions for accessing the coprocessor interface.

Conceptually, the RPU coprocessor is attached to this coprocessor interface. But while

the coprocessor interface is modeled within SimpleScalar, the RPU itself is modeled outside of SimpleScalar with a VHDL simulator that executes a cycle-accurate VHDL model of the RPU. The co-simulation framework takes care of bridging the coprocessor access of SimpleScalar to the external VHDL simulator and returning results from the VHDL simulation to SimpleScalar again.

RPU Simulation Model

The RPU is modeled as a cycle-accurate VHDL model. We prefer using VHDL over other discrete event simulation approaches, since VHDL supports the modeling at different levels of abstraction ranging from high-level behavioral modeling over register transfer level modeling down to structural modeling. In spite of these different levels of abstraction, VHDL allows for retaining overall cycle accuracy, while using the expressiveness of behavioral modeling for parts of the model. Further, a VHDL model can not only be used for a system-level co-simulation of the reconfigurable processor, but the same model can be refined to the synthesizable VHDL subset from which a prototype VLSI chip implementation can be generated. Hence, we can get a perfect match of the architecture simulation model and the architecture implementation.

We use the ModelSim simulator (*ModelSim SE User Manual*, 2005) for executing the RPU's VHDL model. ModelSim is a powerful mixed-language simulator supporting VHDL, Verilog, and SystemC. ModelSim provides the programmer with direct access to the simulation kernel via the foreign language interface (*ModelSim SE Foreign Language Interface*, 2004). This extension interface allows for loading user-defined shared libraries with access to ModelSim's simulation kernel into the simulator. We use this extension interface to integrate SimpleScalar and ModelSim into a common co-simulation environment.

Co-Simulation Framework

The system-level co-simulation framework for the Zippy architecture combines the cycle-accurate simulation models for the CPU core and the RPU into a common simulator.

The main result obtained from the co-simulation is the application's execution time measured in cycles. Since the co-simulation is execution-based, the execution of the application includes also the process of loading the configurations to the RPU, transferring data between CPU and RPU and switching between configurations. Additionally, SimpleScalar collects a multitude of execution statistics for the CPU core, for example, cycles per instruction, cache and branch-prediction miss-rates, and dispatch rates for the instruction fetch, load-store and register updated units. Assuming a certain CPU clock rate, the CPU utilization (load) can be computed as a derived metric. The CPU utilization is of interest for applications that demand for fixed-rate processing (for example real-time audio signal processing) instead of throughput maximization.

In the co-simulation framework, both simulators run in parallel as separate processes that communicate using a shared memory area. The

SimpleScalar simulator acts as the master of the simulation and exerts complete control over the RPU simulation via ModelSim's foreign language interface. Whenever SimpleScalar encounters a coprocessor instruction, it relays the corresponding command to ModelSim, which executes the RPU's VHDL model and transfers the results back to SimpleScalar.

HARDWARE VIRTUALIZATION ON THE ZIPPY PROCESSOR

In this section we present case studies that demonstrate the use of hardware virtualization on the Zippy architectures. While the virtualization techniques introduced in Section INTRODUCTION can be generally used with any dynamically reconfigurable architecture, hardware virtualization can lead to very high performance penalties when used on arbitrary architectures. The key to efficient hardware virtualization is to provide mechanisms for fast reconfiguration, for automated low overhead activation of configurations sequences, and support for storing the state of a previous context while another context is active. When designing the Zippy architecture, we have addressed exactly these features in order to provide a reconfigurable architecture that is tailored for hardware virtualization.

In the following, we elaborate how the Zippy architecture supports the virtualized execution and temporal partitioning virtualization techniques and we present case studies that demonstrate and evaluate these hardware virtualization modes.

Virtualized Execution

Virtualized execution mainly asks for two architectural features: a basic unit of computation (called operator, or hardware page), and a mechanism for communication between these operators.

In the Zippy architecture, a configuration of the reconfigurable array can be treated as the operator. The multi-context support can be used to hold several operators concurrently on-chip, without reloading them. Since each context has a dedicated set of registers, the contexts can operate without interfering with each other.

Since all configurations have access to the FIFOs on the RPU, these FIFOs can be used to implement the communication between the operators. Hence, the Zippy architecture is appropriate to implement applications that use a coordination model based on tasks communicating via FIFOs, for example, applications specified as a process network.

Virtualized execution works at the task level and sequencing between configurations is required rather infrequently. Thus, context switching and sequencing performance is less critical than in the case of temporal partitioning where a context switch is required in every cycle. Hence, the run-time system can be implemented in software on the CPU core and a dedicated context sequencer is not strictly required.

Case Study: Virtualized Execution of a Digital Filter

In this case we study an application of *hardware virtualization by virtualized execution* on the Zippy architecture. Virtualized execution is suited for data streaming applications that map well to (macro-)pipelines where each pipeline stage is implemented by one configuration of the reconfigurable array. Hence, the basic unit of computation (hardware page) in this example is a 4×4 instance of the Zippy reconfigurable array. Macro-pipelining is a special case of virtualized execution and restricts the communication between the subcircuits to forward pipelining, hence feedback exists only within a subcircuit.

As an example, we present the partitioning and mapping of Finite Impulse Response (FIR) filters (see for example, Oppenheim & Schafer, 1999) which are important building blocks in many digital signal-processing applications. We show how FIR filters of arbitrary order—that are too large to fit entirely into an RPU configuration—can be implemented with virtualized execution. We consider the implementation on three architectural variants of the Zippy architecture: an implementation that uses only the CPU core, an implementation on a single-context RPU, and an implementation on a multi-context RPU with 8 contexts.

FIR Filter Partitioning and Mapping

Macro-pipelined virtualized execution requires that the application is split into a sequence of operators with forward-pipelining between operators only. For FIR filters it is possible to split a large filter into a sequence of communicating subfilters with algebraic manipulations of the transfer function. The answer $Y(z)$ of an FIR filter, specified by its transfer function $H(z)$, to an input signal $X(z)$ can be computed as $Y(z)=H(z) \cdot X(z)$. $H(z)$ is defined as a polynomial in z^{-1}:

$$H(z) = h_0 + h_1 z^{-1} + \ldots + h_m z^{-m} = \sum_{i=0}^{m} h_i \cdot z^{-i},$$

and can be factorized into polynomials $H_i(z)$ of a lower degree, that is, $H(z) = (H_1(z) \cdot H_2(z) \cdot \ldots \cdot H_l(z))$. Each of these polynomials represents an FIR filter of lower order. Hence, this algebraic manipulation splits up the initial FIR filter into a cascade of FIR filters (subfilters), where each subfilter implements a part of the factorized transfer function. If the input data-stream is filtered through a cascade of these subfilters, the initial FIR filter function is computed.

In this case study we implement a 56th-order FIR filter as a cascade of eight 7th-order filter stages. Each stage is implemented in the so-called 'transposed direct form'. Figure 9 shows a simplified schematic of the mapping of one of these stages onto the reconfigurable array. The filter coefficients are part of the configurations and are computed by factorizing the initial transfer function of the filter.

Each FIR subfilter comprises delay registers (see Figure 9), which form the *state* of the RPU context. At the next invocation of the context, the subfilter requires that the state, that is, the register contents, is restored before the context is executed again. Figure 10 illustrates the execution schedule for the application on the single-context and the 8-context implementation.

In the single-context implementation, each execution of a subfilter is preceded by a configuration load, switch (activation), and restore phase. The execution phase can run for an arbitrary number of cycles. The output of a subfilter is intermediately stored in a FIFO of the RPU and constitutes the input data for the subsequent subfilter. The length of an execution phase is bounded by the size of the FIFOs.

The restore phase restores the delay registers to their values at the end of the last execution. The restore phase is needed, since the single-context architecture provides only a single set of registers whose contents are overwritten if a different configuration is executed. We implement the restore operation by overlapping subsequent data blocks (Oppenheim & Schafer, 1999), which results in an execution overhead. In the case of the 8-context implementation the state is preserved automatically and no overlapping of data blocks

Figure 9. One 8-tap FIR filter stage mapped to the reconfigurable array

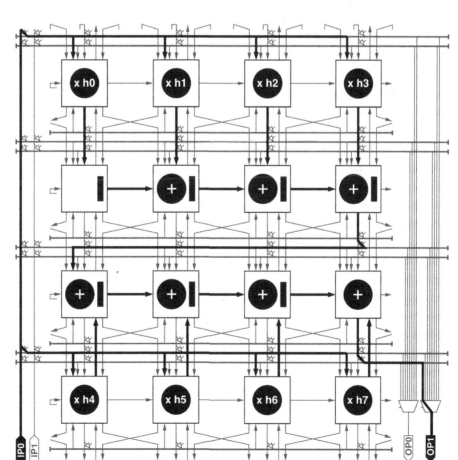

Figure 10. Execution schedule for the virtualized FIR Filter implementation

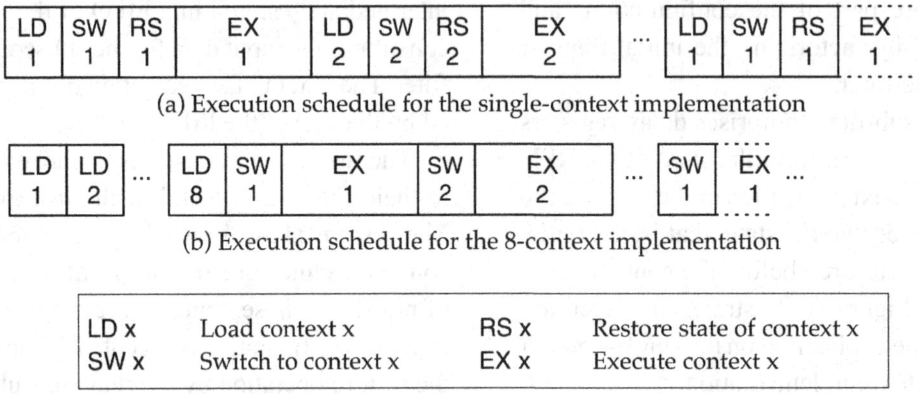

(a) Execution schedule for the single-context implementation

(b) Execution schedule for the 8-context implementation

LD x	Load context x	RS x	Restore state of context x
SW x	Switch to context x	EX x	Execute context x

is required since each context has a dedicated set of registers.

Experimental Setup

In total, we process 64k samples organized in data blocks in each simulation run. The size of the data blocks is a simulation parameter and corresponds to the depth of the FIFO buffers available on the RPU. We vary the depth of the FIFOs between 128 and 4k words. A data block is written to the RPU, processed sequentially by the eight FIR subfilter stages, and finally the result is read back from the RPU.

A control task running on the CPU core controls the loading and activation of contexts according to Figure 10. In the case of the 8-context implementation, each context is loaded only once at initialization. In the single-context implementation the configurations must be loaded at each invocation of a context. Further, the delay registers of the context are restored by overlapping the data-blocks by 57 samples (filter taps of the non-virtualized FIR filter).

The RPU architecture in this example features a 4×4 instance of the Zippy architecture with 2 horizontal north buses, 1 horizontal south bus and no vertical buses. The parameters of the CPU core are summarized in Table 2.

Results and Discussion

The simulation results, that depend on the implementation architecture and on the FIFO buffer size, are presented in Table 3 and Figures 11 and 12.

Table 3 shows the execution time in cycles for the various architectures. For comparing the performance of the implementation, the table also shows the execution time normalized to *cycles/*

Table 2. CPU configurations of the embedded CPU model

Parameter	Embedded CPU
Integer units	1 ALU, 1 Multiplier
Floating point units	1 ALU, 1 Multiplier
L1 I-cache	32-way 16k
L1 D-cache	32-way 16k
L2 cache	none
Memory bus width	32 bit
Memory ports	1
Instruction fetch queue size	1
Register update unit size	4
Load/store queue size	4
Decode width	1
Issue width	2
Commit width	2
Execution order	in-order
Branch prediction	static (not-taken)

Table 3. Execution time and efficiency for virtualized execution case study

Architecture	Buffer	Execution time	Normalized Performance
	[words]	[cycles]	$[cyc/(tap \cdot sample)]$
CPU only	4096	110'672'354	29.63
	2048	110'654'459	29.61
	1024	110'646'831	29.62
	512	110'643'416	29.62
	256	110'643'924	29.62
	128	110'650'685	29.62
single-context	4096	14'325'169	3.83
	2048	14'923'289	3.99
	1024	16'147'674	4.32
	512	18'778'091	5.02
	256	25'163'909	6.74
	128	45'520'990	12.12
8-context	4096	11'669'279	3.12
	2048	11'687'130	3.13
	1024	11'730'940	3.14
	512	11'801'405	3.16
	256	12'014'197	3.22
	128	12'368'245	3.31

Figure 11. Relative speedup of reconfigurable processor implementation in the virtualized execution case study

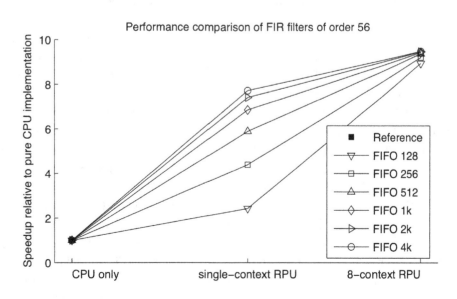

Figure 12. Relative CPU load of reconfigurable processor implementation in the virtualized execution case study

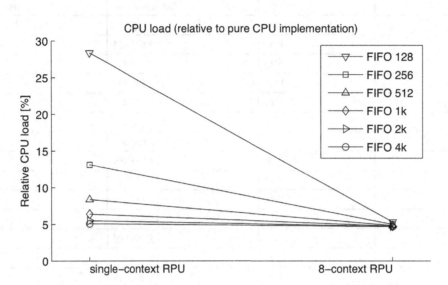

CPU load (relative to pure CPU implementation)

(*tap·sample*). The execution time of the filter for the pure CPU implementation varies only slightly with the block size and amounts to 110.65 million cycles on average. Figure 11 shows the speedups relative to this execution time.

Figure 12 presents the CPU load on the CPU core for the different architectures. For computing the CPU load, we assume a real-time system that filters blocks of data samples at a given rate. When the filter computation is moved from the CPU to the reconfigurable array, the CPU is relieved from these operations and can use this capacity for running other tasks. However, the CPU still has to transfer data to and from the FIFOs, load the configurations to the RPU on demand, and control the context switches. The load given in Figure 12 determines the spent CPU cycles normalized to the CPU only system.

This case study shows, that we can not only implement the large FIR filter, but also achieve two main benefits over a pure CPU implementation: First, the computation is accelerated, and secondly, the CPU is relieved from some operations and can devote the free capacity to other functions.

We point out the following observations:

- Using an RPU we achieve significant speedups, ranging from a factor of 2.4 for a 128 word FIFO single-context device up to a factor of 9.5 for an 8-context RPU with a 4096 word buffer.

- The system performance in terms of speed-up and CPU load depends on the length of the FIFO buffers. Enlarging the FIFOs increases the performance but also the filter delay. For instance, a single-context RPU using a FIFO with 1k words instead of 128 words improves the speedup from 2.43x to 6.85x (factor 2.82) and reduces the CPU load from 28.4% to 6.4% (factor 4.43). But at the same time, the latency is increased by a factor of 8. Practical applications, for example, real-time signal processing, could limit these potential gains by imposing delay constraints.

- Figures 11 and 12 shows that also a single-context implementation can provide decent speedups and CPU load reduction, if the application is not delay sensitive and large FIFO buffers are used. But if an 8-context implementation is used, the context loading and switching overheads are largely reduced and the performance becomes almost independent of the FIFO size. Hence, an 8-context implementation allows for low-latency processing.

- With increasing FIFO size, speedup and CPU load reach an asymptotic value of about 9.5x for the speedup, and 4.7% for the CPU load. For these asymptotic cases, the execution time is dominated by the data-transfers from the CPU to the RPU's FIFO and vice versa.

This case study shows, that *virtualized execution* is a useful technique for implementing a macro-pipelined application on the Zippy architecture. We have shown, that a large FIR filter can be partitioned and executed on the Zippy architecture. One configuration for the RPU corresponds to the hardware page required for virtual execution. The hardware pages communicate via the on-chip FIFOs that are accessible from all contexts. The runtime system for sequencing the contexts is implemented by the CPU core.

The results of the case study also emphasize the importance of the system-level cycle-accurate simulation for architectural evaluation and optimization. Only a system-level evaluation approach allows us to accurately quantify the design trade-offs.

Temporal Partitioning

An efficient implementation of temporal partitioned circuits demands for a modified hardware implementation tool flow and for additional dedicated hardware. The key requirements are: 1. fast switching between configurations, 2. fast cyclic sequencing of a pre-defined sequence of configurations, and 3. efficient and fast communication between contexts. Dedicated hardware support for all of theses requirements has been incorporated in the Zippy architecture:

1. Fast switching between configurations is enabled by the design as a multi-context architecture. Zippy allows for storing several configurations concurrently on-chip. After the configurations have been downloaded once, they can be activated quickly, within a single clock cycle.

2. The temporal partitioning sequencer implements the repeated cyclic sequencing of all temporal partitions. The temporal partitioning sequencer allows for switching between the individual configurations in every cycle without any time overhead. This sequencer is essential to leverage the capability of fast contexts switches provided by a multi-context architecture.

3. Efficient and fast communication between contexts is implemented with the input and output register files in the cells of the reconfigurable array. Each register file provides a dedicated register per context. This register is the target for register write operations. Read operations on an input or output register file can access also register contents written in other contexts, hence the register files can not only implement the actual delay registers (flip-flops) of the circuit, but can be also used for inter-context communication.

Case Study: Temporal Partitioning of an ADPCM Decoder

This case study illustrates hardware virtualization by temporal partitioning on the Zippy architecture. We compare the execution of an ADPCM application on a large instance of the Zippy architecture with the execution on a smaller instance of the same architecture. The large instance requires more area but allows to map the complete application into one configuration. The smaller instance requires temporal partitioning to run the application. For reference, we compare both implementations to a pure software implementation of the application running on the same CPU core.

Application

Adaptive Differential Pulse Code Modulation (ADPCM) is a speech coding algorithm which compresses the data rate by a factor of 4 while providing acceptable quality for voice signals. The decoder uses a simple predictor that predicts the next 16bit output value as the sum of the current output value and an increment. The increment is adapted based on a 4bit input signal using a non-linear function, which is defined by two look-up tables.

Figure 13. ADPCM: application netlist

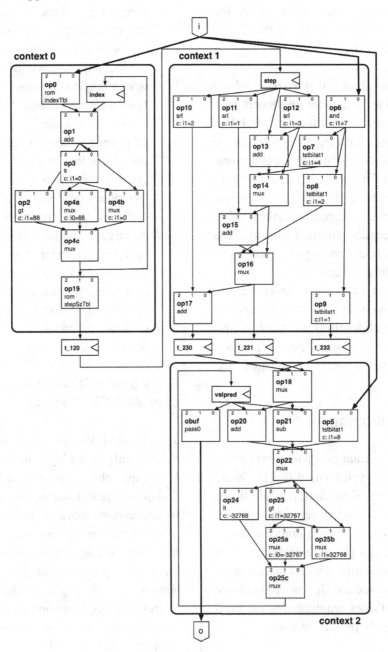

Based on a ADPCM reference implementation, we have designed a hardware implementation of the ADPCM decoder which is shown in Figure 13.

ADPCM uses 31 combinational operators (that can be directly implemented by a cell), 3 dedicated registers, 1 input, and 1 output port. The dedicated registers can be implemented within the input register files of the Zippy cells, see Figure 2. Thus the hardware implementation requires an execution architecture with at least 31 cells.

Experiments

We have performed three experiments:

A. For the *non-virtualized* implementation, we have chosen a reconfigurable array of size 7×7. Although a 6×6 array would provide a sufficient number of cells, the dense interconnect structure of the ADPCM netlist leads easily to congestion and makes placement and routing on a 6×6 array rather difficult. Using a 7×7 array relaxes the implementation constraints and allows the tools to quickly find a routable implementation.

B. For the *virtualized implementation* the full netlist has been manually partitioned into three smaller sub-netlists, such that each of them fits onto an array of size 4×4. Figure 13 presents the division of the initial netlist into three contexts. As previously explained, we use the output register files of the cells for inter-context communication. To simplify the hardware implementation process for this case study, we used dedicated cells with fixed placement as virtualization registers (denoted by t_x_y). For each sub-netlist a configuration is generated using the Zippy hardware implementation tool flow. The constraints for the fixed placement of the virtualization registers have been manually added to the sub-circuit's netlists. Figure 13 shows that for this temporal partitioned implementation of the ADPCM algorithm all feedback paths of the circuit stay within a single context. It must be emphasized that this is not a requirement for hardware virtualization by temporal partitioning. Thanks to the virtualization registers, arbitrary feedback cycles between contexts are possible.

C. The *pure software implementation* uses the C source code of the ADPCM reference implementation. The code has been compiled with SimpleScalar's GNU C compiler.

Table 4. Reconfigurable Processing Unit: configurable architecture parameters

Parameter	Description	Typical value
DATAWIDTH	width of the data-path	24bit
FIFODEPTH	depth of the FIFOs	4096 words
N_CONTEXTS	number of contexts	8
N_ROWS	number of rows	4
N_COLS	number of columns (cells per row)	4
N_IOP	number of input and output ports	2
N_HBUSN	number of horizontal north buses	2
N_HBUSS	number of horizontal south buses	2
N_VBUSE	number of vertical east buses	2
N_MEMDEPTH	depth of memory blocks	128 words
N_CELLINPS	number of inputs to a cell	3
N_LOCALCON	number of local connections of a cell	8

Table 5. Simulation Results for the ADPCM Decoder Case-Study

Architecture	No RPU, CPU only	Large RPU without temporal partitioning	Small RPU with temporal partitioning
Implementation results			
total cycles [k cycles]	39260	23941	24896
cycles/ sample [cycles]	157.0	95.8	99.6
rel. speedup	1	1.64	1.58
array size [cells]	0	49	16
Co-simulation results			
simulation time [s]	177	3767	15210
instruction rate [inst/s]	121543	3687	942
relative simulation time	1	21.3	85.9
relative instruction rate	1	0.0303	0.00775

Experimental Setup and Results

We have evaluated the performance of these three implementations using our system-level co-simulation framework. For the simulation of the CPU core we approximate an Intel StrongARM architecture by useing the same parameter settings as in the previous case study, see Table 2. For the RPU configuration we use the parameters shown in Table 4, the size of the array is set to 4×4 and 7×7, respectively.

We have used the software tool flow for creating the applications binaries. Since using memory-mapped IO for accessing the RPU requires to strictly retain the order of instructions, we have turned off compiler optimization for all three experiments to prevent any disarranging of instructions.

For performance evaluation we determine the execution time for decoding 250'000 AD-PCM samples, processed as 250 blocks of 1000 samples each. By averaging over 250 iterations we try to approximate the sustained application performance and to reduce the effect of the application setup phase.

The execution time is cycle-accurate on the system-level. That is, the execution time includes all overheads, such as reading the input data from memory, transferring data between CPU and RPU and vice versa, downloading the configurations, etc.

Table 5 summarizes the results of the case study and demonstrates the trade-off involved in hardware virtualization with temporal partitioning. We point out the following observations:

- Using a reconfigurable co-processor yields a speedup over the pure CPU implementation of 1.64 when using the large reconfigurable array without temporal partitioning, and a slightly reduced speedup of 1.58 for the temporal partitioned implementation. The rather small difference of 6% in the speedups for the temporal partitioned and the non-partitioned case suggests, that the zero-overhead temporal partitioning sequencer handles the context sequencing efficiently.

- Comparing only the raw performance of the hardware accelerated kernel can be seriously misleading. The non-partitioned ADPCM decoder decodes 1 sample per cycle, while the temporal partitioned implementation is 3 times slower (3 cycles per sample). While this large difference of raw-speedups (factor of 3) could lead to the expectation that the implementation without temporal partitioning performs significantly better, system-level simulation reveals that the actual performance gain is merely 6%. This observation strongly supports our claim that system-level performance analysis is a necessity for an accurate performance assessment of a reconfigurable processor application.

- The example also shows the trade-off between chip size and performance. In his dissertation (Enzler, 2004) Enzler estimates that adding a 4 context Zippy RPU with a 4×4 reconfigurable array to an embedded CPU core increases the chip area by about 25%. Hence with 25% increased chip area, the performance is increased by a factor of 1.58 when temporal partitioning is used. Without temporal partitioning, the hardware size for the RPU would be significantly larger (49 vs. 16 cells) while the additional performance gain is only 6%.

- Table 5 presents also data about the performance of the simulation environment. The total simulation time increases as a consequence of the additional RPU simulation by a factor of 21 for the experiment without temporal partitioning, and a factor of 86 for the temporal partitioned implementation. The temporal partitioning case is slower, since changing the active configuration of the RPU in every cycle leads to more signal transitions and the computational effort of discrete event simulation correlates with the number of signal changes.

With this case study we have demonstrated that hardware virtualization with temporal partitioning is feasible. We have studied the trade-offs between execution time and hardware requirements. We conclude that temporal partitioning offers a sensible approach to reduce the hardware requirements while still making use of the high

performance of application-specific accelerator circuits. The reduction in hardware requirements is in particular attractive for embedded systems, where chip area is scarce due to cost constraints.

FUTURE TRENDS

Our research in hardware virtualization for processors with attached coarse-grained reconfigurable arrays has shown that hardware virtualization is feasible with only moderate architectural modifications over a regular, single context array. While hardware virtualization is currently still in its infancy and a subject of academic research, the expected practical implications are manifold. We believe that hardware virtualization may be a valuable key technology for designing new energy-efficient processors for mobile computing that are better suited to exploit performance versus chip-area versus power consumption trade-offs.

One could argue that the current trend to homogeneous multi-core processors that applies also to the embedded processor domain could be a threat to reconfigurable processor architectures. Admittedly the development of applications for reconfigurable processors is more complex because of the necessity to deal with hard and software design and two different tool chains, whereas multi-core CPUs are programmed using standard compilers and well known programming models. Still, in our view reconfigurable co-processors have at least two distinctive advantages over multi-core CPUs: First, as Enzler has shown in his dissertation (Enzler, 2004) the reconfigurable co-processor outperforms a CPU core by large in computational density (performance/area). For example, for a digital filter application it has been shown that increasing the chip size by approximately 20% result in a 9x speedup, where—assuming linear speedup—a multi-core CPU would require an increase in chip size by 900% for the same performance gain. Second, a multi-core processor requires the application to exhibit thread-level parallelism to achieve any speedups. In contrast reconfigurable accelerators can exploit many forms of spatial parallelism and can be used to improve single-thread performance. Hence we consider reconfigurable accelerators not merely as a competing but as a complementary technology that can be used to build heterogeneous multi-core processors that combine the benefits of both worlds.

CONCLUSION

In this chapter we have presented our work on a coarse-grained reconfigurable processor architecture that was developed in the Zippy research effort at ETH Zürich and University of Paderborn. The design of this architecture was guided by the objective to support novel, innovative usage modes that are enabled by fast dynamic reconfiguration. A specific focus of our work, which we have presented in this chapter, is the investigation of hardware virtualization concepts. Hardware virtualization has been peripherally touched in related work, but has not been considered in a holistic approach for reconfigurable processors like ours that reaches from the fundamentals of hardware virtualization, over dedicated hardware units for increasing the efficiency of hardware virtualization, to design methods and tool flows for hardware virtualization.

In this chapter we have focused on the hardware architecture and have presented two detailed case study that demonstrate how these virtualization techniques can be applied and what benefits can be achieved. Our case studies underpin our proposition that coarse-grained reconfigurable processors are promising target architectures for embedded systems as they allow for significantly increasing the performance at a moderate increase in chip size. The hardware virtualization techniques introduced in this chapter show a new way for balancing performance and chip size which opens up new points the computer architecture design space.

In order to allow other researchers to take up, expand or contribute to our work, we have released the ZIPPY architecture model and all the associated tool flows as *open source software* under the permissive BSD license. The source code is available on http://github.com/plessl/zippy.

In our future work we plan to address the topic of design tools for hardware virtualization. While we have automated placement and routing, the process of creating the configurations for temporal partitioning and virtualized execution is still a manual process. For promoting hardware virtualization, the development of new methods and algorithms for decomposing application specifications into parts suitable for hardware virtualization and the integration of these methods into a coherent tool flow is highly desirable. For temporal partitioning, we have already presented initial work on a new design method (Plessl et al., 2006) that addresses this problem on the netlist level. An alternative approach is to address this problem in high-level synthesis tools. Since these tools operate on more abstract application specifications, for example, control data flow graphs, they have knowledge about the temporal behavior of the application which could be exploited to find the best contexts for virtualized execution. Finally, we plan to evaluate hardware virtualization with more benchmarks to show the applicability of the approach for a wide range of applications.

REFERENCES

Austin, T., Larson, E., & Ernst, D. (2002, February). SimpleScalar: An infrastructure for computer system modeling. *IEEE Computer*, *35*(2), 59–67.

Baumgarte, V., May, F., Nückel, A., Vorbach, M., & Weinhardt, M. (2001). PACT XPP – a self-reconfigurable data processing architecture. In *Proc. 1st Int. Conf. on Engineering of Reconfigurable Systems and Algorithms (ERSA)*, (pp. 64–70). Las Vegas, NV: CSREA Press.

Betz, V., Rose, J., & Marquardt, A. (1999). *Architecture and CAD for deep-submicron FPGAs.* Amsterdam: Kluwer Academic Publishers.

Compton, K., & Hauck, S. (2002, June). Reconfigurable computing: A survey of systems and software. *ACM Computing Surveys, 34*(2), 171–210. doi:10.1145/508352.508353

Ebeling, C., McMurchie, L., Hauck, S., & Burns, S. (1995, December). Placement and routing tools for the Triptych FPGA. *IEEE Trans. on Very Large Scale Integration (VLSI). Systems, 3*(4), 473–482.

Enzler, R. (2004). *Architectural trade-offs in dynamically reconfigurable processors.* PhD thesis, Diss., ETH No. 15423, ETH Zurich, Switzerland.

Enzler, R., Plessl, C., & Platzner, M. (2003a, June). Co-simulation of a hybrid multi-context architecture. In *Proc. Int. Conf. on Engineering of Reconfigurable Systems and Algorithms (ERSA)* (pp. 174–180). Las Vegas, NV: CSREA Press.

Enzler, R., Plessl, C., & Platzner, M. (2003b, September). Virtualizing hardware with multi-context reconfigurable arrays. In *Proc. Int. Conf. on Field Programmable Logic and Applications (FPL)* (Vol. 2778, pp. 151–160). Berlin: Springer.

Enzler, R., Plessl, C., & Platzner, M. (2005, April). System-level performance evaluation of reconfigurable processors. *Microprocessors and Microsystems, 29*(2–3), 63–73. doi:10.1016/j.micpro.2004.06.004

Hauser, J. R. (1997, October). *The Garp architecture* (Tech. Rep.). UC Berkeley, CA, USA.

Miyamori, T., & Olukotun, K. (1999, February). REMARC: Reconfigurable multimedia array coprocessor. *IEICE Trans. on Information and Systems. E (Norwalk, Conn.), 82-D*(2), 389–397.

ModelSim SE foreign language interface. (2004, November). Retrieved from http://www.model.com

ModelSim SE user manual. (2005, January). Retrieved from http://www.model.com

Oppenheim, A. V., & Schafer, R. W. (1999). *Discrete-time signal processing* (2nd ed.). New York: Prentice Hall.

Plessl, C. (2006). *Hardware virtualization on a coarse-grained reconfigurable processor.* ETH dissertation no. 16742, ETH Zurich, Switzerland.

Plessl, C., & Platzner, M. (2004, June). Virtualization of hardware – introduction and survey. In *Proc. Int. Conf. on Engineering of Reconfigurable Systems and Algorithms (ERSA)* (pp. 63–69). Los Vegas, NV: CSREA Press.

Plessl, C., & Platzner, M. (2005, July). Zippy – a coarse-grained reconfigurable array with support for hardware virtualization. In *Proc. IEEE Int. Conf. on Application-Specific Systems, Architectures, and Processors (ASAP)* (pp. 213–218). Washington, DC: IEEE Computer Society.

Plessl, C., Platzner, M., & Thiele, L. (2006, December). Optimal temporal partitioning based on slowdown and retiming. In *Int. Conf. on Field Programmable Technology (ICFPT)* (pp. 345–348). Washington, DC: IEEE Computer Society.

Salefski, B., & Caglar, L. (2001). Re-configurable computing in wireless. In *Proc. 38th Design Automation Conf. (DAC)* (pp. 178–183).

Singh, H., Lee, M.-H., Lu, G., Kurdahi, F. J., Bagherzadeh, N., & Chaves Filho, E. M. (2000, May). MorphoSys: An integrated reconfigurable system for data-parallel and computation-intensive applications. *IEEE Transactions on Computers, 49*(5), 465–481. doi:10.1109/12.859540

Chapter 5
Measurement–Based Timing Analysis for Reconfigurable Embedded Systems

Raimund Kirner
University of Hertfordshire, UK

Sven Bünte
Technische Universität Wien, Austria

Michael Zolda
Technische Universität Wien, Austria

ABSTRACT

Reconfigurable embedded computing opens many interesting possibilities for efficiency and reliability improvement. Still, it is necessary to verify whether the reconfigurable embedded computer system fulfills its timing requirements. Purely static worst-case execution time (WCET) analysis is not the best choice for verifying the timing behavior of reconfigurable embedded computer systems, as frequent re-modeling of different hardware configurations is not practicable. We describe measurement-based timing analysis as an approach that is better applicable for reconfigurable applications. Measurement-based timing analysis is a hybrid approach that combines static program analysis techniques, borrowed from static WCET analysis, with empirical learning of the application's timing behavior by performing systematic measurements. But even the MBTA approach is challenged by the reconfigurable computing paradigm by the need for adequate coverage of the reconfigurable fabric.

INTRODUCTION

Embedded computer systems have to meet the real-time requirements imposed by their envi-

ronment. To ensure that an embedded computer system can meet its deadlines, an upper bound of the execution time of all components must be known (Kirner & Puschner, 2005)(Wilhelm, et al., 2008). Because the determination of the ac-

DOI: 10.4018/978-1-60960-086-0.ch005

tual *worst-case execution time* (WCET) is a hard problem, estimates are usually used.

For safety-critical applications these estimates have to be safe, i.e., they must not underestimate the actual WCET. Such safe estimates are usually obtained through *static WCET analysis*. Depending on the complexity of the analyzed system, these analyses tend to introduce a high pessimism, i.e. the obtained estimates are overestimations. Moreover, the method depends on the availability of precise hardware models. The construction of such models is usually expensive, error-prone, and requires the availability of a complete hardware specification.

In *soft real-time systems* the miss of a deadline is assumed not to have catastrophic consequences. Due to a higher cost pressure compared to hard real-time systems, high hardware utilization is a top priority for soft real-time systems. In response to these needs, measurement-based timing analysis that employ a hybrid approach of systematic execution-time measurements and static program analysis has emerged, aiming for a good tradeoff between precision and flexibility (Wilhelm, et al., 2008)(Kirner, Wenzel, Rieder, & Puschner, 2006)(Bernat, Colin, & Petters, 2002). A primary strength of the approach is the relatively low retargeting effort when the new target hardware becomes available.

By *timing analysis* we mean the analysis of the execution time of a given program in a specific computational hardware environment. A real-time application can be a very complex system, where many individual computational *tasks* are concurrently running in a distributed system consisting of several computational nodes that communicate over a network infrastructure (Kopetz, 1997). Within such a system, it is the duty of the *task scheduler* to assign the computational resources to the individual tasks in such a way that the system can deliver its service in a timely manner. However, to fulfill its planning task, the scheduler must know the computational requirements of each task in advance.

Practical scheduling algorithms require information about the WCET of each task, where a *task* is defined as the execution of a sequential program that starts with reading some input data and terminates with the production of some output data.

The current state-of-the-art in WCET analysis is to examine tasks individually. This means that present analysis methods cannot handle *blocking tasks* (sometimes called *complex tasks*) that can be delayed by other tasks or external events. Rather, the fields of WCET analysis and scheduling usually adopt the concept of a *simple task* that cannot be blocked by outside events. As a consequence, the execution time of an individual task becomes independent of the interaction with other tasks and the outside world, and can be analyzed in isolation. It should be noted that it is, to a certain extent, possible to implement the behavior of a complex task by a set of simple tasks that communicate only via their input and output states.

Figure 1 illustrates the problem of analyzing the execution time of an individual task: Depending on the actual input that a task obtains when it is started, its execution time can vary. The figure depicts how a frequency distribution of execution times over all possible inputs can look like. There is a large concentration of mass on the left hand side, representing typical execution times. When running the program with random data, the observed execution time will likely be found in this range of the execution time spectrum. However, the figure also indicates a small, but relevant set of settings that yield a considerably higher execution time. Because they occur in relatively few situations, they are hard to trigger by random testing.

It is the duty of WCET analysis to determine this worst case behavior of a given program. Because it is generally intractable to determine the exact worst case execution time of the program, estimations are used. If a certain analysis method does, by design, consistently provide overestimations of the WCET, we call the method, as well as the obtained WCET estimate *safe*. Some

Figure 1. Example of a timing distribution. There is a large concentration of mass on the left hand side, representing typical execution times. Still, a few cases of considerable higher execution times can be spotted on the right hand side.

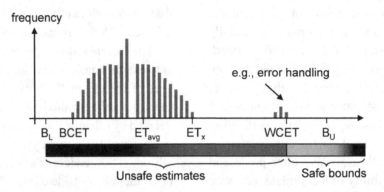

safety-critical applications demand safe WCET estimates for some or all tasks that are run. The reason for this is that with safe WCET estimates it is possible to design a real-time system in a way that all task deadlines are guaranteed to be met.

For practically usable WCET estimates, meeting the safety requirement is not enough. Due to technical and monetary limitations of the available hardware, WCET estimates must also be tight, i.e., they must be close to the actual WCET.

Safety is not always an indispensable requirement. For many applications, a sufficiently close, but not necessarily safe, estimate is enough. *Soft real-time* applications usually fall into this category. Another example are hard real-time systems that include an external safety mechanism that is always able to bring the systems into a safe state. For such a system, it is sufficient to use very tight WCET estimates that are never surpassed during an extensive testing phase. Thirdly, unsafe WCET estimates can be useful in an early design phase of a hard-real time system, to obtain a preliminary idea of how the system is going to behave.

The salient property of *reconfigurable computing* is the possibility to perform computations in reprogrammable hardware (Dutt & Choi, 2003) (Todman, Constantinides, E., Mencer, Luk, & K, 2005)(Compton & Hauck, 2002). The flexibility of reconfiguration offers new possibilities, like performance improvements through customized hardware, or higher robustness through dynamic reorganization. However, the application-specific modification of the hardware configurations and the possibility of dynamic reconfiguration open completely new challenges for WCET analysis.

The reconfigurable fabric is typically linked to a traditional host processor, and the challenges vary with the different types of coupling between them. Hauk et al. (Compton & Hauck, 2002) distinguish four different levels of coupling, c.f. Figure 2:

1. A **reconfigurable functional unit** of the host processor as a reconfigurable fabric. In this tight coupling the reconfigurable fabric is relatively small and is within the processing path of the host processor. Performing a timing analysis in the presence of this kind of coupling is relatively easy, because the part of the internal state space that is relevant for the timing behavior of the reconfigurable fabric is rather small.

2. A **coprocessor** as a reconfigurable fabric. Performing a timing analysis under this kind of coupling must consider the state space and parallel processing capability of the coprocessor.

3. An **attached reconfigurable processing unit** as a reconfigurable fabric, similar as

Figure 2. Levels of coupling in a reconfigurable system (Source(Compton & Hauck, 2002))

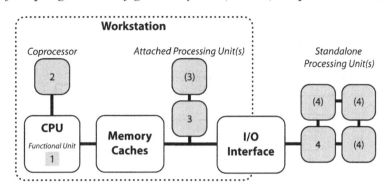

in multi-processor systems. Timing analysis for this kind of coupling might be done separately for the host processor and the reconfigurable fabric, since the two components tend to interact rarely.

4. An **external stand-alone processing unit** as a reconfigurable fabric, similar to networked workstations, which is the loosest form of coupling. A timing analysis for this kind of coupling must consider the timing characteristics of the I/O interface between the host processor and the reconfigurable unit. The bus arbitration is also important for the other kinds of coupling, but with the I/O interface one might have to consider additional external devices to estimate the communication timing.

In principle both, purely static and measurement-based analysis, can be used in a WCET analysis for reconfigurable systems. However, static WCET analysis requires the availability of a complete model of the timing behavior of all hardware components, including those that are reconfigurable. The creation of such a model for non-reconfigurable hardware is usually expensive, error-prone, and relies on the availability of a complete hardware specification. For reconfigurable components, a vendor of a WCET analysis tool can hardly predict what components the customer is going to construct. Even if these components

were known in advance, the modeling of each of these components can be expected to be prohibitively high.

A possible solution would be to develop WCET analysis tools with an open architecture such that the user can write plug-ins for timing-models of application-specific hardware. However, it is questionable whether this approach is realistic, since hardware modeling is a complex task that requires detailed knowledge of the timing behavior. Hence, static WCET analysis is applicable to reconfigurable systems in principle, but its commercial deployment is hindered by practical aspects. However, this will probably change as soon as further progress is made on automatic learning of hardware timing models from hardware description languages like, e.g., VHDL, or as tighter cooperation is established between vendors of synthesis and of WCET analysis tools.

Measurement-based timing analysis fits naturally to the reconfigurable computing paradigm, since here the timing model is learned empirically from the real system. When measurement-based timing analysis is applied, there is no need for manual modeling of timing behavior. However, the accuracy of measurement-based timing analysis relies on the quality of coverage reached by performing systematic execution time measurements.

The following section provides a quick overview on static WCET analysis, which should help in understanding the differences towards

Figure 3. Generic WCET analysis framework

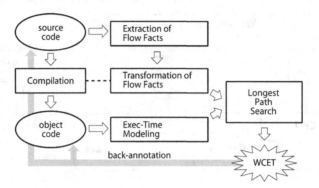

measurement-based timing analysis, which is presented in the subsequent section.

BACKGROUND: STATIC WORST-CASE EXECUTION-TIME ANALAYSIS

Research on static WCET analysis, which is aimed at providing safe upper bounds of the WCET of a program, started at the end of the 1980s (Puschner & Koza, 1989). Such a bound can be found using analytic techniques that calculate the execution path through a program that takes the maximum time to complete.

Contrary to popular belief, the undecidability of the halting problem is not the limiting factor of WCET analysis (Kirner, Zimmermann, & Richter, 2009). However, the complexity of a detailed timing analysis for hardware platform can be intractably high, forcing the analysis to employ approximations. The strength of static WCET analysis is the use of sound approximations. The WCET analysis is called sound if it is ensured by construction that the calculated WCET estimate may overestimate the real WCET but underestimate it.

A typical framework for a static WCET analysis is shown in Figure 3. The program code is usually written in a high-level programming language. To obtain a precise WCET estimate, the analysis should be performed at machine code level.

Explicit flow information is generally needed to calculate the WCET bound. If this information is specified at source-code level, it has to be transformed to mirror the code optimizations performed by the compiler. The machine code is analyzed during *exec-time modeling*, where each instruction is assigned timing information that is based on the hardware model of the target processor. The resultant *timed program model* is used together with the flow information to determine the execution path that takes maximal time, which in turn yields the WCET. The detailed timing information can be annotated back to the machine code or source code, to help the user to optimize the WCET of the program. In the following the different stages of static WCET analysis are explained in detail.

Elicitation of Flow Information

To calculate the WCET it is mandatory that the programs always terminate, i.e., all loops and recursions must have a finite iteration bound. Moreover, to obtain a precise WCET estimate, infeasible paths, i.e., paths that are valid from a static point of view, but which never actually occur during execution, have to be excluded from the longest path search. Both, loop bounds and infeasible paths, are specified by providing additional *flow information*, which consists of constraints that restrict the control flow (Kirner, Knoop, Prantl, Schordan, & Wenzel, 2007). To a limited extent flow information can be calculated automatically using program analysis techniques. For example, Healy et al. have proposed a method for inferring *loop bounds summation formula* for various loop patterns (Healy, Sjödin, Rustagi, Whalley, & Engelen, 2000). Gustafsson et al. have developed a tool that derives loop bounds via abstract interpretation (Gustafsson, Ermedahl, Sandberg, & Lisper, 2006). The latter method is more computation-intensive than the method of Healy et al., but tends to succeed for a larger number of loop patterns. If permitted by program complexity, exact verification techniques like bounded model checking (Clarke, Biere, Raimi, & Zhu, 2001) can be used to iteratively eliminate infeasible paths found by approximation techniques.

In practice, only a limited amount of flow information can be inferred automatically. One limiting factor is program complexity. Another reason can be the lack of essential meta-information on the program's environment, like value restrictions for input variables. Such additional information to guide the analysis can be provided by manual code annotations.

Transformation of Flow Information

Automatic extraction of flow information can be performed on different representational levels of the program. From the perspective of precision, elicitation at source-code level is preferable over extraction at machine code level, due to the higher level of abstraction. For example, the type systems found in typical high-level programming languages can support the analysis by restricting value ranges and possible uses of data items.

In the case of manual annotation, the source code level is also preferable, because the source-code representation is well-known by the developer[1]. In comparison, manual annotation at the machine code level can be extremely tedious, because the user has to deal with a large amount of low-level compiler-generated code that is com-

parably hard to understand and likely to change with every recompilation.

The challenge of source-code annotation is that the compiler may optimize the code in a way that invalidates flow information for the machine code. This requires the use of explicit transformation of flow information for each code optimization that affects the control flow (Kirner, 2008). So far, such an automatic transformation has only been realized in academic prototypes, but not in commercial compiler (Kirner, 2003).

State-of-the-art practical tools offer annotations at the machine-code level. As mentioned above, writing such annotations is labor-intensive and error-prone. Furthermore, they have to be adapted after every re-compilation if the code has been slightly modified or the compiler settings have been changed. The transformation of flow information is typically only an issue for static WCET analysis. However, a similar issue for measurement-based timing analysis is testing that the achieved coverage at source code level is also achieved at machine code level (Kirner, 2009).

Exec-Time Modeling

The biggest challenge in deploying static WCET analysis for reconfigurable systems is *exec-time modeling*, i.e., modeling of the target hardware in such a way that timing information can be associated with each code statement. Hardware features like pipelines, caches, or branch prediction have to be modeled precisely to keep WCET overestimation low. Accurate modeling is a labor-intensive and complicated task for complex processors (Heckmann, Langenbach, Thesing, & Wilhelm, 2003). Consequently, the community is looking for more predictable processors (Thiele & Wilhelm, 2004). Moreover, the hardware would have to be modeled for each configuration of a reconfigurable system. This is difficult in practice, as long as fully automatic extraction of timing information from a VHDL description is not available. The benefit of reconfigurable systems versus conventional systems is the freedom of turning hardware predictability in the time domain into a design goal, thus simplifying subsequent exec-time modeling. Both, static analysis and measurement-based timing analysis, would benefit from doing so.

Longest Path Search

The longest path search aims at finding the longest execution path through the timing-annotated program code. Usually the labeling is established in a separate exec-time modeling step. The three main search techniques are:

Tree-based search. This is the fasted technique, as it is based on simple hierarchical calculation rules (Puschner & Koza, 1989). For example, a loop of the form

WHILE cond DO body DONE

is translated into the following recursive *timing schema*, where *ULB* denotes the upper loop bound, i.e., upper bound of the iteration count, of the loop:

$$T_{while} = T(cond) \cdot (ULB+1) + T(body) \cdot ULB$$

A conditional of the form

IF cond THEN bthen ELSE belse ENDIF

is translated into the following recursive timing schema:

$$T_{if} = T(cond) + max(T(bthen), T(belse))$$

One serious disadvantage of the tree-based search is that rather complex adaptations would be required to include additional flow information for ruling out infeasible paths.

Path-based search. This technique calculates the timing in a bottom-up style over the hierarchy of nested scopes over the control flow structure. Within each scope, all paths are enumerated during the search for the longest one. When finished, the scope is replaced by a virtual instruction that has the same execution time as its longest local path. The computational costs of this approach depend on the exact definition of scopes. Typically loop borders are used as scope delimiters (Healy, Arnold, Mueller, Whalley, & Harmon, 1999). In that case, the efficiency of the approach depends on a reasonable local path count within loops.

The strong advantage of this technique is that it allows for the efficient modeling of timing effects that are caused by caches and pipelines. A disadvantage of the approach is that it cannot handle flow information across local scopes.

Implicit Path Enumeration Technique (IPET). This is the most powerful method with respect to flexible use of flow information to rule out infeasible paths. In IPET, we assume that a program is represented as a *control-flow graph* (CFG) with $CFG = \langle N,E,s,t \rangle$, where N is a set of program nodes (basic blocks) and $E \subseteq N \times N$ is a set of control-flow edges (Muchnick, 1997). Furthermore, we assume a unique entry node s, as well as a unique exit node t. Each edge $e_i = AB \in E$ denotes the passage of control-flow from node A to node B, and is labeled with its execution time τ_i. The flow (total execution count) through an edge $e_i \in E$ is denoted as f_i. The value of each flow variable has to be greater or equal to zero: $f_i \geq 0$. The WCET is expressed by the following target function, using the variables f_i and the constants τ_i:

$$WCET = \max \sum_{e_i \in E} f_i \cdot \tau_i$$

A flow variable f_i represents the overall execution count of the edge e_i after one execution of the program. The CFG itself is modeled by a set of constraints over the flow variables f_i. The incoming and outgoing edges for each CFG node $n \in N$ are denoted as $IN(n)$ and $OUT(n)$. Thus we have to add the following flow constraints to model the structure of the CFG:

$$\forall n \in N. \sum_{e_i \in IN(n)} f_i = \sum_{e_j \in OUT(n)} f_j$$

One can add additional constraints over flow variables to rule out infeasible paths. For example, if e_e is the entry edge of a loop and e_b is the starting edge of the loop body, we can add the following constraint to describe a loop bound:

$$f_e \cdot LLB \leq f_b \leq f_e \cdot ULB$$

Here *LLB* is a lower and *ULB* is an upper loop bound. Typically the flow constraints are linear constraints, enabling the application of integer linear programming solvers.

Even though static WCET analysis may not be the first choice for timing analysis of reconfigurable systems, understanding its processing steps is relevant, because some of them are also deployed within measurement-based timing analysis.

MEASUREMENT-BASED TIMING ANALYSIS

Measurement-based execution time analysis combines both static analysis and simple execution time measurements, and is therefore also referred to as *hybrid WCET analysis*. The basic idea is to find a trade-off between the inherent problems that come along with both techniques:

- Measuring a target system exhaustively is not feasible as there are too many input value combinations that lead to divergent execution times. Consequently, only a subset of all possible executions can be measured, leading to a high chance that the actual WCET is not included in this set and thereby underestimated. The analysis is therefore *unsafe*.
- Static analysis relies on a system model that includes the hardware. The construc-

tion such a model takes significant human effort and requires detailed knowledge of the hardware. Also, for complex hardware, static analysis potentially involves pessimism, i.e. the derived WCET estimate might be significantly higher than the actual WCET.

There is an analogy to the field of *functional verification*: random testing is likely to miss bugs, whereas formal verification becomes inaccessible or infeasible as the program gets more complex. In functional testing a common strategy is to improve the quality of a test bench by generating test data according to coverage-metrics (Ntafos, 1988). Adapting this approach to the analysis of temporal properties leads to measurement-based timing analysis, where the behavioral structure of the system under test is investigated in order to improve the quality of the results.

As shown in Figure 4, measurement-based timing analysis typically consists of the three consecutive phases *Analysis and Decomposition*, *Execution Time Measurement* and *Timing Composition*:

Analysis and Decomposition. The hybrid approach is based on a model that captures the different possible behaviors of the program. This behavioral model is usually a directed graph, where nodes represent individual operations, edges represent possible successive execution, and paths represent different possible runs on the program. The straightforward way to obtain an execution time profile of the complete program would be to first obtain a profile for each path, and then combine these profiles into an overall profile. However, practice shows that even coarse models contain a huge number of paths. Enumerating and measuring the execution time for all these paths is intractable. The graph model is therefore decomposed into tractable subgraphs that are analyzed separately.

Execution Time Measurement. Once the graph model has been decomposed, execution

Figure 4. The workflow of measurement-based timing analysis

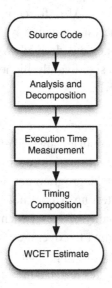

times are obtained for each subgraph by performing measurements on real physical hardware. The hardware is used as an oracle; expensive and error-prone modeling is not necessary.

Timing Composition. After systematic measuring for each subgraph, the results are composed to obtain timing information for the complete system.

Modeling the Structure of Reconfigurable Systems for MBTA

Prerequisite to the hybrid approach is a model that captures the different possible behaviors of the program. This behavioral model is usually a directed graph, where nodes represent individual operations, and where edges represent possible successive execution.

The prototype of such a graph is the *control flow graph* (CFG) of a program. In this model, each node represents a sequential code section that is always executed as a whole, and each directed edge represents a possible jump between such code sections. The CFG is therefore a software-centric model of the program that does not capture all variations in the behavior that can be found at the hardware level.

Following the machine model of Moore (Moore, 1956), the future behavior of a discrete machine is, at any instant in time, determined by its current *state*. For our purpose, the state of a computer system can be seen as the combination of the *software state* of the program and the *hardware state* of the executing platform.

The software state of a program comprises

- the content of all memory cells that can be accessed by the program, and
- the content of all processor registers, including the instruction counter.

The constituents of the hardware state depend on the specific hardware platform on which the program runs. For a classical, non-reconfigurable system it may, amongst others, comprise

- the content of instruction and data caches,
- the state of branch prediction units,
- the state of pipelines, and
- the state of functional units.

For reconfigurable systems, the hardware state does, in addition, include the *hardware configuration*.

Of all these constituents, the control flow graph of the machine code reflects the essential information from the instruction counter that determines the possible sequences of instructions that are executed during a run of the program.

The concrete sequence of instructions that are executed during an actual run of the program under scrutiny has a major impact on the execution time of the program. However, it is well-known that the hardware state, which is opaque in the CFG, can also have a big effect on the execution time (Kadlec & Kirner, 2007)(Lundqvist & Stenström, 1998)(Berg, 2006).

Figure 5. Control flow of the source code fragment in Listing 1.((a) Control Flow Graph (CFG). CFGs are simple behavioral models of an application that can be used in measurement-based timing analysis) ((b) Predicated variant that can distinguish the special case of multiplication with an 8-bit number. Predicated CFGs can be used to augment plain CFGs with additional software or hardware state information)

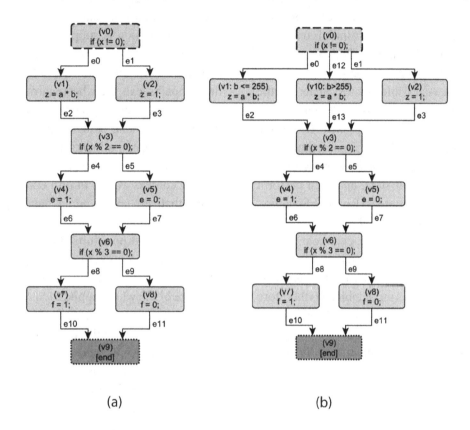

(a)   (b)

If needed, more fine grained graph models can be built. For instance, the execution time of arithmetic operations sometimes depends on the concrete operand values. A typical example are shift-and-add implementations of multiplication, where multiplications with small operand values can be performed faster than multiplications with big operand values. In this case, the CFG can be augmented by distinguishing such cases by tagging nodes with preconditions over program variables (on the source code level) or over memory contents (on the machine code level). Likewise, it is possible to add preconditions over hardware states.

Listing 1 shows a tiny source code fragment in a C-like language, featuring three conditional constructs in a row. The corresponding CFG in

Figure 5 (a) features three consecutive diamond-shaped structures, resulting in a total of eight possible paths. The graph in Figure 5 (b) is a predicated variant, where the multiplication node has been split into the case where the multiplier fits into an 8-bit register, and the complementary case, where the value representation requires at least 9 bits. The latter case would require at least two shift-and-add operations, whereas the former case could be handled with just one such operation, resulting in a shorter execution time.

In a graph model, each path represents a different end-to-end behavior of the program. The straightforward way to obtain an execution time profile of the complete program would therefore be to first obtain a profile for each path, and then combine these profiles into an overall profile. However, we face several complications here:

Path enforcement. To measure the execution time of a particular path, we have to force the program into the corresponding behavior. This requires the set up of appropriate initial conditions before the application is run. For the software state, this amounts to the preparation of suitable input data in the accessible memory areas and the register file. The generation of such input data is a crucial issue in the hybrid approach. To enforce a particular hardware state, it is sometimes necessary to apply *homing sequences* that guide the hardware into a known state, and then perform additional configuration steps (Rivest & Schapire, 1989)(Rivest & Schapire, 1993).

Path explosion. In practice, even coarse models, like the plain CFG, contain a huge number of paths. Enumerating and measuring the execution time for all these paths is intractable. It is therefore necessary to choose a meaningful subset of paths.

Listing 1. Source code fragment with three consecutive tests.

```
if (x != 0)
z=a * b;
else
z= 1;
if (x %2 == 0)
d= 1;
else
d= 0;
if (x %3 == 0)
e= 1;
else
e= 0;
```

Graph Segmentation

We first present the general ideas and concepts of graph segmentation, and later on present a concrete example.

Graph segmentation is a family of techniques for bundling structurally similar end-to-end paths, such that execution time analysis will no longer directly distinguish them. The obtained sets of end-to-end paths are called *abstract paths*. Ideally, segmentation is supposed to pack together paths that induce the same or at least very similar execution times on certain subpaths. In this case, the subpaths can then be regarded as *context-independent* with respect to the corresponding original end-to-end paths, in terms of execution time. This property allows the analysis to consider the execution time of the subpaths independently of their context, which in turn enables two principles that are important in handling the path explosion problem:

Timing compositionality. It is possible to measure the execution time of subpaths and later combine these times to obtain an execution time estimate of the whole application. This is in stark contrast to end-to-end measurements.

Context-independent measurement. It is not necessary to measure the execution time of a subpath under all possible contexts. Rather, it is possible to arbitrarily choose one of the corresponding end-to-end paths. This reduces the measurement burden and simplifies test data generation.

The two principles do, however, only apply fully if the segments have been arranged in such a way that all paths of an abstract path do in fact induce the same, or at least very similar execution times on the respective subpaths. However, because we cannot know the exact execution time of any given path before we have measured it, it is impossible to provide such a segment layout right from the beginning. It is therefore necessary to introduce an iterative refinement process that can gradually readjust the segment layout in such a way that the abstract paths converge to context-independence. This refinement process is a central issue for ongoing research.

In the past, different segmentation concepts have been proposed which offer various degrees of flexibility (Wenzel, Rieder, Kirner, & Puschner, 2005)(Wenzel, Kirner, Rieder, & Puschner, 2008)(Zolda, 2008)(Zolda & Kirner, 2008)(Zolda, Bünte, & Kirner, 2009). However, the concept of a segment basically boils down to two aspects:

Interface. The interface of a segment defines an interval within a graph model for which execution times should be obtained. As such, the interface defines clearly where measurements should begin, and where they should end.

Measurements. Any segment has associated execution times that refer to the execution of the application from a measurement starting point to a measurement ending point, as they are defined in the interface. This set or multi-set of execution times is sometimes referred to as *execution time profile*.

Before the actual analysis has started, the execution time profiles of all segments are empty, because no measurements have been performed at this point. During measurement, additional execution times are added to the profiles. No execution times are added in the case of subpaths that are infeasible during runtime, or in case that enforcing a corresponding run is intractable.

If the desired output of the analysis is a single value, like the WCET estimate, the execution time profile may also consist just of this single value. This can radically reduce high memory requirements.

It was mentioned above that the interface of a segment defines an interval for which execution time measurements should be performed. In terms of paths, this means that the interface of a segment implicitly or explicitly defines a set of *measurable subpaths*, i.e., subpaths for which the execution time should be determined by observation.

Various interface designs can be conceived that serve the above purpose. One simple interface design, proposed by Kirner et al., consists of markings of two nodes in the graph model, the *entry node* and the *exit node* (Wenzel, Rieder, Kirner, & Puschner, 2005)(Zolda, Bünte, & Kirner, 2009). In this case, the induced set of measurable

subpaths is the set of all subpaths that start in the entry node and end in the exit node. A more flexible, but also more complex interface can be obtained by allowing multiple entry and/or exit nodes. Such segments have been described in (Zolda & Kirner, 2008).

As an example, for the CFG in Figure 5 (a) we could define a segment with entry node v_4 and exit node v_9. Assuming the above-mentioned single entry-node/single exit-node interface, this segment would induce the measurable subpaths $\{v_4, v_6, v_7, v_9\}$ and $\{v_4, v_6, v_8, v_9\}$.

Besides the set of measurable subpaths, a segment moreover induces a set of end-to-end *context paths*, which is the set of all end-to-end paths that contain any of the induced measurable paths as a subpath. The example segment from the previous paragraph would therefore induce the context paths $\{v_0, v_1, v_3, v_4, v_6, v_7, v_9\}$, $\{v_0, v_1, v_3, v_4, v_6, v_8, v_9\}$, $\{v_0, v_2, v_3, v_4, v_6, v_7, v_9\}$, and $\{v_0, v_2, v_3, v_4, v_6, v_8, v_9\}$.

The context paths of a segment together form the abstract path that was mentioned at the beginning of the section, and the measureable subpaths are the subpaths that are assumed to be context-independent with respect to context paths. These semantics of a segment imply that the execution time of all dynamically feasible measureable subpaths must be determined for an application run that follows some arbitrary context path, in order to obtain an execution time profile for a segment. This means that application runs for measurements are always complete end-to-end runs, whereas the execution time measurements themselves are performed on subpaths as they cross through the respective segments.

The freedom of choosing a single arbitrary context path for measuring the execution time along a given measureable subpath renders analysis and measurement tractable:

Measurement overhead. As fewer measurements are needed, the overhead of input data generation and measurement runs is reduced. Moreover, fewer measurement results have to be processed.

Input data generation. Fewer computational resources are needed for input data generation, due to relaxation of path constraints.

It is important to note that any execution time profile of a segment that has been obtained this way is only guaranteed to be complete if the segment meets the criterion of context independence. As mentioned above, it is impossible to provide such a layout at the beginning of the analysis, since we cannot know the exact execution time of any given paths before we have measured it. It is, however, possible to design heuristic refutation algorithms that test the validity of a given segment layout. Segments that do not pass the test can subsequently undergo iterative readjustment, until the segment layout is valid with an appropriately high degree of confidence.

Timing Composition

To obtain the execution time of a complete application, the model is *segmented*, i.e., a segment layout is generated that covers the whole model. After the iterative segment readjustment that was sketched in the previous section, the execution times of the individual segments are put together to obtain the execution time for the complete application.

The method that is applied for composition depends on the concrete segment concept and analysis goal. For example, to obtain a WCET estimation using single entry-node/single-exit node segments, IPET can be used. The approach is similar to the more traditional IPET approach at CFG level that has been sketched earlier in this chapter.

To make the approach applicable for segments, we have to provide a CFG-like graph structure on segment level. An algorithm for generating such *segment graphs* has been described in (Zolda, Bünte, & Kirner, 2009).

Measurement Techniques

Execution times of particular program runs can be quantified either *actively* or *passively*. If the program's source code is modified in order to derive temporal information, the measurement is performed actively. On the other hand, if the hardware allows for collecting temporal information such that the source code can remain unmodified, the technique is called passive. Gathering temporal information dynamically (i.e. during runtime), as introduced in this section, is often referred to as *profiling*.

Active Measurement

A convenient, active procedure to perform measurements is to read from an internal processor cycle counter at user-defined program locations. This is probably the most widely used technique due to its accessibility, as almost all processors provide a cycle count register. Note that the execution time is counted in terms of processor cycles and not according to a physical clock. Any perturbation in the CPU frequency, for instance due to temperature fluctuation or frequency scaling features, can therefore not be reflected directly by this measurement technique.

Another active method is adding procedures to the program under test that raise specific hardware signal patterns. An external hardware device with an individual reference clock gets triggered by those signals and assigns timestamps in parallel with program execution. This setup does reflect frequency perturbations directly. However, it is less accessible than reading the local cycle count register due to the need for an additional hardware device.

The price for the convenience of active measurement techniques are probe effects that are inherent in both methods. Program certification reflects this well-known problem by demanding that instrumentation code remain in the final version of products if they have safety-critical temporal requirements.

Table 1. Processor-Specific Versions of the NEXUS Standard

Manu-facturer	Name of Tracing Device
Infineon	On-Chip Debug Support (OCDS) Level 2
ARM	Embedded Trace Macrocell (ETM)/ Program Trace Macrocell (PTM)
Altera	On-Chip Instrumentation (OCI®)
Xilinx	Xilinx MicroBlaze™ Trace Core (XMTC)

Keeping the number of instrumentation points low is an important goal in software design. Not only does this reduce the code size. Additional code might also considerably influence runtime performance, as it changes both memory layout and control flow of the program under investigation which in turn modifies the behavior of the processor's instruction cache.

Betts and Bernat show how the number of instrumentation points can be minimized while maintaining enough information to reproduce the unique corresponding CFG path for any execution run (Betts & Bernat, 2006).

Passive Measurement

A commonly used passive measurement technique is *instruction set simulation*. Here, the target system is simulated by software. Like for the technique of reading the cycle count register, the execution time can be derived in terms of execution cycles. Instruction set simulators are available for many microprocessors and microcontrollers. Although they are easily accessible and overcome trace probe effects, there is no guarantee that the simulator models the timing of the physical hardware correctly. Another disadvantage is the poor performance of software simulation which is usually worse than for execution on the target hardware system.

Some processors provide an on-chip debug interface that can enable *Hardware Trace Probing*, a powerful technique for passive measurement. The interface is defined by the *NEXUS (Class 2) standard* (IEEE-ISTO, 2003) and similar vendor-specific standards (see Table 1). It allows for the collection of high-resolution timing information at runtime, while minimizing temporal interferences due to probe effects. The execution's program flow can usually be reconstructed completely.

A general setup for hardware trace probing is illustrated in Figure 6. The host computer loads a program into the target processor, injects test data and trigger the execution via the *Joint Test Action Group (JTAG)* IEEE 1149.1 standard or a similar manufacturer-specific debugging interface. During execution an on-chip debugging module in the CPU collects timing and flow information from which an external *Trace Port Analyzer* reconstructs a *trace*, i.e., a sequence of program locations annotated with timestamps. After the trace has been built, it is passed to the host computer, where the developer or an application can analyze the collected data.

Measurement in Reconfigurable Systems

The major difference in the measurement of reconfigurable systems compared to fixed hardware systems is that not only the computation is to

Figure 6. Schematic hardware trace probing setup

be profiled, but also the reconfiguration phases. The more complex it gets to predict the temporal behavior of reconfigurations, e.g., if modification durations are data-dependent, the more beneficial reconfiguration profiles become for system evaluation and debugging.

The following paragraph will touch on how different reconfigurable architectures demand different measurement techniques. Here, we focus on systems in which a host microprocessor is coupled with areas of reconfigurable logic as described in (Compton & Hauck, 2002).

Figure 2 shows four different options on how reconfigurable logic can be coupled, each of which requiring specific measurement techniques:

Reconfigurable functions within the CPU. Provided that the duration of a reconfigurable instruction is fixed, or at least easy to predict statically, there are no ramifications concerning measurement. The system can be profiled in the usual manner as aforementioned. However, the amount of compatible instruction set simulators might be reduced, as they must not only simulate the (non-configurable) processor but also the behavior of the user-defined reconfigurable functional units.

Reconfigurable coprocessor. On the one hand a coprocessor is usually larger than a CPU-internal functional unit, which allows for the implementation of more complex logical behavior the execution of which takes more than one host processor cycle. On the other hand the coprocessor runs more independently of the host processor which can cause non-trivial temporal interferences due to concurrency. Those fine-grained effects are hard to observe with active measurements for it would take many instrumentation points and accumulate probe effects. Passive measurements are capable of catching low-level effects, provided that on-chip debug support is provided that is compliant to the interplay of the host processor and the coprocessor.

Attached processing unit(s). Concurrency and the ensuing level of temporal interference is even higher than for coupling type (2), as multiple computation units are potentially involved. Also, communication between the reconfigurable units and the host processor entails higher delays, and synchronization becomes a crucial issue. Consequently, measurements performed on individual computation units have to be synchronized and must reflect concurrent computing properly. For on-chip debug support this implies that traces of individual computation units have to be synchronized and merged either on-chip or by the external trace port analyzer. Even though the former option will ultimately increase the amount of hardware resources needed spent for trace probing, it will make adherence to standards such as NEXUS easier to achieve, hence increasing the amount of compatible trace port analyzers.

External stand-alone processing unit(s). The computation units are distributed, similar to networked workstations, and communication obtains an even higher delay and jitter. Profiling reconfigurable systems of this kind demands a considerably higher amount of effort compared to coupling levels (1), (2), and (3), because there are most likely no commercial off-the-shelf products for obtaining a global execution time profile, as the overall system configuration is too specific. However, if subsystems can be measured with any of the described techniques, system designers can integrate means into the system that assemble the profiles of all subsystems of interest to get a global view of the temporal behavior.

In summary, the concrete architecture of a reconfigurable system determines which techniques for temporal measurement are applicable. It does not only affect non-functional properties such as runtime, memory, and power, but also their analyzability.

Test Data Generation

Random test data generators are commonly used in practice. Although the generation process is easy to implement, the automatic localization of variables that can potentially affect the control

Figure 7. Measurements on random test data

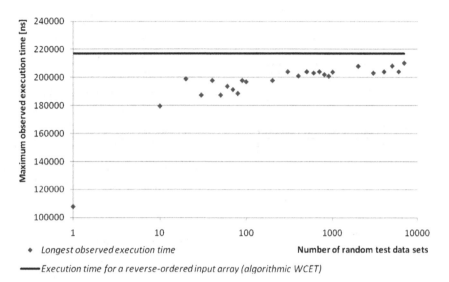

behavior and determination of their corresponding types demand a bit more effort. However, the convenience has its prize: finding the WCET of a program via randomly generated test data is in general infeasible. Figure 7 illustrates the WCET-search performance for the bubble sort implementation from the Mälardalen Benchmark Suite (Mälardalen Research and Technology Centre, 2006). For the purpose, the input array of the algorithm was reduced to 10 elements instead of 100, in order to speed up the experiments. Each mark in the diagram represents one experiment. The horizontal axis denotes the number of generated inputs *n*, and the vertical axis shows the longest observed execution time among the *n* corresponding measurements. Each experiment took approximately *n · 0.17s*, including test data generation, measurement, and examination. The horizontal line indicates the execution time for a reversed-ordered input array, which results in a long execution time for bubble sort as expected.

The figure indicates three important things:

• Since the horizontal axis is scaled logarithmically, the analysis effort to find higher

maximum execution times grows exponentially in the number of measurements.

• Even the longest observed execution time of 210 105 ns is below the execution time for a manually selected execution run (reversed-ordered input array) with 217 000 ns by more than 3%. The corresponding experiment took 20 minutes and involved 7 000 randomly generated inputs.

• The variance among the longest observed execution times is quite high, especially for experiments with up to 100 randomly generated inputs.

To conclude, random test data generation is not well-suited for reliably finding a good WCET estimate. However, the experiments also indicate that the program is investigated quite well in terms of temporal behavior, as the induced maximum observed execution times show a high jitter. Consequently, it can make sense to combine random test data generation with other methods. McMinn gives a good summary of some search-based test data generation techniques in (McMinn, 2004).

Wenzel et al. were the first to combine random test data generation, heuristic methods, and model

Figure 8. Test data generation hierarchy (Source (Wenzel, Kirner, Rieder, & Puschner, 2008))

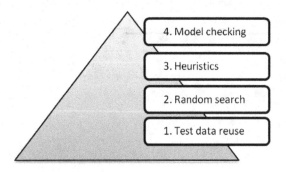

checking for WCET analysis (Wenzel, Kirner, Rieder, & Puschner, 2008). As depicted in Figure 8, they recycle test data from previous experiments for initial measurements. In a next step random test data is used, followed by heuristic methods, like genetic algorithms. Eventually model checking techniques are applied for the production of test data that enforces remaining uncovered execution paths, or to prove infeasibility. The remaining coverage gain on levels 1 through 4 is inversely proportional to resource consumption of the according test data generation techniques: reusing test data comes almost for free, whereas model checking is very resource consuming.

Still, model checking seems crucial for enforcing the execution of specific paths. The application of specific model checking techniques for the generation of input data for measurement is a topic of ongoing research (Holzer, Schallhart, Tautschnig, & Veith, 2008)(Holzer, Schallhart, Tautschnig, & Veith, 2009).

SUMMARY AND CONCLUSION

Reconfigurable embedded computing opens new challenges for worst-case execution time analysis. Most importantly, the timing of the hardware is partially undefined before programming. In case of dynamic reconfiguration, this challenge is am-

plified by the need to cover the timing behavior for the different configurations.

Static WCET analysis provides a safe approximation of the actual timing behavior, but relies on the provision of a correct timing model of the target hardware. Current tools for static WCET analysis do not yet fit into the domain of reconfigurable embedded computing, as the production channel for the reliable timing model is missing. This could possibly be fixed by providing WCET tools with an open architecture, such that the system developer can provide plug-ins that describe the timing behavior of custom hardware components. Furthermore, a close cooperation between developers of tools for hardware synthesis and WCET analysis may unleash the potential for automatic creation of the hardware timing models needed for static WCET analysis.

For the time being, the hybrid nature of measurement-based timing analysis seems to be the most attractive choice for timing analysis of reconfigurable embedded systems. The method employs systematic execution time measurements to learn the hardware behavior of the actual system. At the same time, it harnesses techniques from static program analysis for optimizing the achieved measurement coverage and to infer the final WCET estimate.

It is the system designer who has to ensure adequate coverage of the reconfigurable fabric, such that the measurement-based timing analysis technique is able to derive a WCET estimate of sufficient precision. The complexity of the coverage metric depends on the specific reconfigurable hardware architecture.

REFERENCES

Berg, C. (2006). PLRU Cache Domino Effects. In *Proc 6th Intl. Workshop on Worst-Case Execution Time (WCET) Analysis*.

Bernat, G., Colin, A., & Petters, S. M. (2002). WCET Analysis of Probabilistic Hard Real-Time Systems. In *Proc. 23rd IEEE Real-Time Systems Symposium*, (pp. 279-288).

Betts, A., & Bernat, G. (2006). Tree-Based WCET Analysis on Instrumentation Point Graphs. In *Proc. 9th IEEE International Symposium on Object-oriented Real-time distributed Computing.*

Clarke, E., Biere, A., Raimi, R., & Zhu, Y. (2001). Bounded Model Checking Using Satisfiability Solving. *Formal Methods in System Design, 19,* 7–34. doi:10.1023/A:1011276507260

Clarke, E., Kroening, D., & Lerda, F. (2004). A Tool for Checking ANSI-C Programs. In Jensen, K., & Podelski, A. (Eds.), *LNCS 2988* (pp. 168–176). Berlin: Springer.

Compton, K., & Hauck, S. (2002). Reconfigurable Computing: A Survey of Systems and Software. *ACM Computing Surveys, 34,* 171–210. doi:10.1145/508352.508353

Dutt, N., & Choi, K. (2003). Configurable Processors for Embedded Computing. *Computer, 36,* 120–123. doi:10.1109/MC.2003.1160063

Gustafsson, J., Ermedahl, A., Sandberg, C., & Lisper, B. (2006). Automatic Derivation of Loop Bounds and Infeasible Paths for WCET Analysis using Abstract Execution. In *Proc. 27th IEEE Real-Time Systems Symposium.*

Healy, C. A., Arnold, R. D., Mueller, F., Whalley, D., & Harmon, M. G. (1999). Bounding Pipeline and Instruction Cache Performance. In *IEEE Transactions on Computers, 48.*

Healy, C. A., Sjödin, M., Rustagi, V., Whalley, D., & Engelen, R. v. (2000). Supporting Timing Analysis by Automatic Bounding of Loop Iterations. In *Journal of Real-Time Systems*, (pp. 121-148).

Heckmann, R., Langenbach, M., Thesing, S., & Wilhelm, R. (2003). The Influence of Processor Architecture on the Design and Results of WCET Tools. *Proceedings of the IEEE, 91,* 1038–1054. doi:10.1109/JPROC.2003.814618

Holzer, A., Schallhart, C., Tautschnig, M., & Veith, H. (2008). FShell: Systematic Test Case Generation for Dynamic Analysis and Measurement. In *LNCS 5123* (pp. 209–213). Berlin: Springer.

Holzer, A., Schallhart, C., Tautschnig, M., & Veith, H. (2009). Query-Driven Program Testing. In *Proc. 10th Int'l Conference on Verification, Model Checking, and Abstract Interpretation,* N. D. Jones, & M. Müller-Olm (Ed.), *LNCS 5403,* (pp. 151-166). Berlin: Springer.

IEEE-ISTO. (2003). 5001-2003: The Nexus 5001 Forum Standard for a Global Embedded Processor Debug Interface. In *IEEE-ISTO Standard 5001-2003: The Nexus 5001 Forum Standard for a Global Embedded Processor Debug Interface.* IEEE-ISTO Standard.

Kadlec, A., & Kirner, R. (2007). On the Difficulty of Building a Precise Timing Model for Real-Time Programming. In *Proc. 14th Colloquium „Programmiersprachen und Grundlagen der Programmierung",* 99-105.

Kirner, R. (2003). *Extending Optimising Compilation to Support Worst-Case Execution Time Analysis.* PhD Thesis, Technische Universität Wien, Austria.

Kirner, R. (2008). *Compiler Support for Timing Analysis of Optimized Code: Precise Timing Analysis of Machine Code with Convenient Annotation of Source Code.* Berlin: VDM Verlag.

Kirner, R. (2009). Towards Preserving Model Coverage and Structural Code Coverage. In *EURASIP Journal on Embedded Systems.*

Kirner, R., Knoop, J., Prantl, A., Schordan, M., & Wenzel, I. (2007). WCET Analysis: The Annotation Language Challenge, In *Proc. 7th Intl. Workshop on Worst-Case Execution Time (WCET) Analysis*, 83-99.

Kirner, R., & Puschner, P. (2005). Classification of WCET Analysis Techniques. In *Proc. 8th IEEE International Symposium on Object-oriented Real-time distributed Computing*, (pp. 190-199).

Kirner, R., Wenzel, I., Rieder, B., & Puschner, P. (2006). In *Intelligent Systems at the Service of Mankind*. Berlin: UBooks Verlag.

Kirner, R., Zimmermann, W., & Richter, D. (2009). On Undecidability Results of Real Programming Languages. In *Proc. 15th Colloquium „Programmiersprachen und Grundlagen der Programmierung".*

Kopetz, H. (1997). *Real-Time Systems - Design Principles for Distributed Embedded Applications*. Amsterdam: Kluwer.

Lundqvist, T., & Stenström, P. (1998). Integrating Path and Timing Analysis using Instruction-Level Simulation Techniques. In *LNCS 1474* (pp. 1–15). Berlin: Springer.

Mälardalen Research and Technology Centre. (2006). The Worst-Case Execution Time (WCET) analysis project. *The Worst-Case Execution Time (WCET) analysis project.*

McMinn, P. (2004). Search-based software test data generation: a survey: Research Articles. In *Softw. Test. Verif. Reliab., 14*, (pp. 105-156).

Moore, E. F. (1956). Gedanken Experiments on Sequential Machines. In *Automata Studies* (pp. 129–153). Princeton, NJ: Princeton U.

Muchnick, S. S. (1997). *Advanced Compiler Design & Implementation*. San Francisco: Morgan Kaufmann Publishers, Inc.

Ntafos, S. C. (1988). A Comparison of Some Structural Testing Strategies. *IEEE Transactions on Software Engineering, 14*, 868–874. doi:10.1109/32.6165

Puschner, P., & Koza, C. (1989). Calculating the Maximum Execution Time of Real-Time Programs. In. *Journal of Real-Time Systems, 1*, 159–176. doi:10.1007/BF00571421

Rivest, R. L., & Schapire, R. E. (1989). *Inference of Finite Automata Using Homing Sequences*, In *Proc. 21st annual ACM symposium on Theory of Computing*. (pp. 411-420). New York: ACM.

Rivest, R. L., & Schapire, R. E. (1993). Inference of Finite Automata Using Homing Sequences. *Information and Computation, 103*(2), 299–347. doi:10.1006/inco.1993.1021

Thiele, L., & Wilhelm, R. (2004). Design for Timing Predictability. *Real-Time Systems, 28*, 157–177. doi:10.1023/B:TIME.0000045316.66276.6e

Todman, T. J., & Constantinides, G. A. E., S. J., Mencer, O., Luk, W., & K, P. Y. (2005). Reconfigurable Computing: Architectures and Design Methods. In *Proceedings on Computers and Digital Techniques, 152*, (pp. 193-207). Washington, DC: IEEE.

Wenzel, I., Kirner, R., Rieder, B., & Puschner, P. (2008). Measurement-Based Timing Analysis. In *Proc. 3rd Int'l Symposium on Leveraging Applications of Formal Methods, Verification and Validation.*

Wenzel, I., Rieder, B., Kirner, R., & Puschner, P. (2005). Automatic Timing Model Generation by CFG Partitioning and Model Checking. In *Proc. Design, Automation and Test in Europe (DATE)* (pp. 606–611). Washington, DC: IEEE.

Wilhelm, R., Engblom, J., Ermedahl, A., Holsti, N., Thesing, S., Whalley, D., et al. (2008). The Worst-Case Execution Time Problem - Overview of Methods and Survey of Tools. In *Transactions on Embedded Computing Systems (TECS), 7.* ACM.

Zolda, M. (2008). INFER: Interactive Timing Profiles based on Bayesian Networks. In *Proc. 4th International Symposium on Leveraging Applications*.

Zolda, M., Bünte, S., & Kirner, R. (2009). Towards Adaptable Control Flow Segmentation for Measurement-Based Execution Time Analysis. In *Proc. 17th International Conference on Real-Time and Network Systems (RTNS)*.

Zolda, M., & Kirner, R. (2008). Divide and Measure: CFG Segmentation for the Measurement-Based Analysis of Resource Consumption, In *Proc. Junior Scientist Conference,* (pp. 117-118).

ENDNOTE

[1] We are here considering source that was written by a human programmer. For source code that was generated by a code generator, it can be beneficial to additionally consider the original model for automatic extraction of flow information and manual annotation.

Chapter 6
Trends in Reconfigurable Embedded Systems

C. Valderrama
University of Mons, Belgium

L. Jojczyk
University of Mons, Belgium

P. Possa
University of Mons, Belgium

ABSTRACT

This chapter presents reconfigurable embedded systems by looking closely at three different but interrelated aspects: design tools, methodologies and architectures, paying special attention at reconfigurable interconnections. The authors will start having a closer look at the evolution of the latest design strategies, tools and methodologies facing challenges and user requirements. Reconfigurable interconnections will be analyzed, examining topologies, drawbacks, and capabilities, specially focusing on the reconfiguration potential. From the application point of view, the authors will resume with a case study regarding embedded systems, a Software-Defined Radio application highlighting the most significant technical features and design choices.

INTRODUCTION

Embedded systems are designed to perform dedicated specific tasks with real-time processing constraints. Such systems comprise complete devices ranging from portable such as video cameras and set-top boxes, to complex industrial controllers including mechanical parts.

Embedded systems complexity varies from a single microcontroller to several interrelated dedicated functional units, peripherals and network devices. Often they come with contradictory design constraints such as low power consumption and high performance. Indeed, mass production portable devices should be cheap and power efficient. On the other hand, they still need to support multiple, sometimes real-time, applications and

DOI: 10.4018/978-1-60960-086-0.ch006

standards. The wide spectrum of design requirements leads to complex architectures composed by several processors and customized hardware components. These multiprocessors System-on-chip (MpSoC) have now become the foundation of most common appliances such as digital TV, navigation systems and wireless devices.

One of the major challenges on embedded systems design is to obtain the necessary system performance with efficient utilization of hardware resources. To accomplish this goal, the system must be optimized in power consumption, size and cost, complying with flexibility, reliability and processing performance requirements. The architecture must support multiple applications and standards. Targeting the architecture to a single application prevents its evolution and flexibility. Accuracy at the early design stage is not an option; low level simulation suffers from low simulation speed and design effort. Such conflicting design requirements cannot be satisfied by traditional design methods (Pimentel, Lieverse, & Van der Wolf, 2001).

Classical hardware/software codesign methodology was typically based on system level specification refinement forcing the designer to make early decisions regarding system architecture (Coumeri & Thomas, 1995) (Kim, et al., 1995) (Bauer & Ecker, 1997) (Balarin, et al., 1997) (Hines & Borriello, 1997). A system-level model represents application behavior, architecture characteristics and the relation between application and architecture (application partitioning, mapping and resources utilization). One essential design task is to perform design space exploration at the early design stages. System level simulation is here used to provide a first estimate on system performance (for instance, power consumption or cost) and to make early decisions on various design parameters (Pimentel, Erbas, & Polstra, 2006) (Balarin, Watanabe, Hsieh, Lavagno, Passerone, & Sangiovanni-Vincentelli, 2003) (Stammermann, Kruse, Nebel, & Pratsch, Oct. 2001) (Gadient, Debardelaben, & Madisetti,

1997). Using a high abstraction level minimizes the modeling effort increasing simulation speed. Several possible implementations can be rapidly evaluated at the system-level prior to the refinement (at the instruction-level, cycle-accurate or register-transfer level) and synthesis.

Recent work, Y-chart methodology, recognizes a clear separation between application and architecture models: an explicit mapping step relates the application model to the architecture model (Balarin, et al., 1997) (Kienhuis, Deprettere, Vissers, & Van der Wolf, 1997) (Lieverse, Stefanov, Van der Wolf, & Deprettere, Nov. 2001) (Zivkovic, Van der Wolf, Deprettere, & De Kock, Oct. 2002) (Mohanty & Prasanna, 2002) (Balarin, Watanabe, Hsieh, Lavagno, Passerone, & Sangiovanni-Vincentelli, 2003). The application model describes only functional behavior of an application, independently of architecture characteristics or timing parameters. The application concerns are clearly separated in computational and communication events. The architecture model defines architecture resources, capturing timing characteristics and performance consequences of an application event. The latter involves simulation of programmable as well as reconfigurable or dedicated components. The mapping of each application onto an architecture instance is evaluated by a performance analysis. The resulting performance numbers may inspire the designer to improve the architecture, restructure the application, or change the mapping.

Design space exploration turned into the platform-based design (PBD) approach at the architecture level (Keutzer, Malik, Newton, Rabaey, & Sangiovanni-Vincentelli, 2000) (Carloni, De Bernardinis, Pinello, Sangiovanni-Vincentelli, & Sgroi, 2005) (Cooke, McNelly, & Martin, 1999). The platform is an abstraction layer hiding the details of several possible implementation scenarios. The approach makes use of a common platform and intellectual property (IP) blocks shared among multiple applications. An IP block is here characterized by a model representing its functionality and physical parameters. The library also contains interconnects and compatibility rules. A legal composition of blocks and interconnects is called a platform instance. In this context, the reuse of IP blocks reduces time-to-market and manufacturing costs by increasing productivity.

Network platforms and communication protocols experienced a great evolution both at the system and architectural level. That evolution started with bus-based communication architectures and protocols abstracted as part of the refinement process at the system level (Shin, Gerstlauer, Domer, & Gajski, 2005). Transaction-level modeling (TLM) appeared to improve simulation performance and modeling efficiency for early design space exploration (Shin, Gerstlauer, Peng, Domer, & Gajski, Oct. 2006). However, the interconnection infrastructure becomes harder to design due to the endless increase of the number of components and the performance requirement to deal with. Requirements regarding scalability and reconfiguration at the interconnection level were finally satisfied with the Network on Chip solution (NoC) (Marculescu, Ogras, Peh, Jerger, & Hoskote, 2009). The NoC interconnection architecture is a tradeoff between the two main interconnection strategies used in electronic design: the shared connection like the bus and the private connection like peer to peer.

The Network-on-Chip interconnection architecture is basically based on a set of routers driving the data exchange between a set of IP blocks. Their main advantage is to allow parallel data paths between separated IPs as well as reconfigurable connections. Moreover, by looking at chip design, regular NoC topologies are well suited to scalability concerns about the growing number of required IPs. In terms of execution time, reconfigurable interconnections are sometimes a better alternative compared to partial or dynamic reconfiguration once the required components being allocated (Mouhoub & Hammami, 2006). NoC is today a mature concern covering application modeling and optimization

(how to choose the best application/architecture combination that satisfies various performance and energy constraints), architecture topology and communication parameters (bandwidth, latency, area, power and reliability), architecture validation and synthesis.

In recent years, hardware reconfigurable architectures received increasing attention due to their flexibility and short design time. Field-programmable Gate Arrays (FPGAs) emerging in the '80's as a programmable interconnection between major components (Woods, McAllister, Lightbody, & Yi, 2008). Twenty years later, FPGAs became the most promising device for embedded system design. The main FPGA distinguishing feature is the possibility of changing the system hardware structure in the field, a process known as reconfiguration. Device reconfiguration enables the incremental development of systems, the correction of design errors after implementation, and the addition of new hardware functions (Lysaght & Rosenstiel, 2005). Years ago, FPGA vendors started combining general purpose processors and FPGA fabric on a single chip (Altera Corp., 2002) (Atmel Corp., 2009). The Excalibur solution from Altera (Altera Corp., 2002) included already the Nios soft embedded processor, the ARM9 processor and general purpose programmable logic into a single device. Xilinx embed IBM PowerPC hard and soft processor cores in Virtex FPGAs in addition to the Pico/MicroBlaze soft cores on Spartan-3 FPGA (Xilinx, 2004). Current FPGA technology allows the integration of one or more Generic Purpose Processors (GPPs), on-chip memory, peripheral devices, and complex IP cores (Pasricha & Dutt, 2008). Commercial FPGAs may implement an entire System-on-Chip (SoC) but offering that flexibility at the cost of large silicon area utilization and relevant power consumption (Bolsens, Challenges and Opportunities of FPGA Platforms, Sept. 2002).

To reduce the importance of the silicon area concern, the latest commercial FPGA platforms offer support for partial and dynamic hardware reconfiguration (Berthelot, Nouvel, & Houzet, 2006). Systems built with FPGAs can be statically or dynamically reconfigured. A static reconfigurable system is one where it is necessary to completely reconfigure it each time any change of the hardware is required. In this case, system execution stops during reconfiguration. A dynamic reconfigurable system (DRS) allows that part of the system be modified, while the rest of it continues to operate (Lysaght & Rosenstiel, 2005). Total and partial reconfiguration protocols are distinct. Thus, special features must be present in tools used to partially reconfigure FPGAs. Nevertheless, their main drawback remains the large reconfiguration latencies. In order to hide these latencies, compiler support is fundamental to automatically schedule and optimize the compiled application code for efficient reconfigurable hardware usage (Panainte, Bertels, & Vassiliadis, 2007).

Nowadays, the two main FPGA vendors, Xilinx and Altera, provide solutions to run-time reconfiguration (Gavrielov, 2009) (Altera Corp., 2009). FPGA partial reconfiguration (PR) is a Xilinx's design flow that attempts to create reconfiguration regions in an FPGA device, so that one region can be reconfigured while the remainder of the FPGA continues to operate in the system. Software programmable reconfiguration (SPR) is the Altera designed-in capability to modify digital logic flows through internal or external software commands. A control plane provides a path for control, configuration, and status of the implemented components, allowing dynamic reconfiguration and feedback of each function. It also allows commands to be sent to the streaming data switch fabric, reconfiguring the data path and allowing other functions to operate. Examples of run-time reconfigurable applications include Software-defined Radio (SDR), or the ability to adapt to varying waveforms, airborne applications, susceptibility to radiation-induced single event upsets (SEUs) makes it important to monitor and reconfigure devices with bit failures, or remote sensors, the ability to reconfigure devices that

are difficult to reach physically requiring "over the air" update.

This chapter presents reconfigurable embedded systems by looking closely at three different but inter-related aspects: design tools, methodologies and architectures, paying special attention at reconfigurable interconnections. First, we will start having a closer look at the evolution of the latest design strategies and methodologies facing challenges and user requirements. A plethora of commercial tools are now filling the gap to implementation applying these design strategies. To summarize, section 2 will go over some regular (Xilinx System Generator, Symplify, ImpulseC, Mentor CatapultC) and special (CoreUnifier, ReCoBus-Builder) tools. Afterward, we will explore reconfigurable architectures. Current FPGA architectures will be described regarding its flexibility, power, size and reconfiguration capabilities. As an alternative to reconfiguration requirements, on section 3, reconfigurable interconnections will be analyzed, examining topologies, drawbacks, and capabilities. In this section, we will draw up an adapted state of the art that will give an objective point of view about the use of NoC in new embedded design. Moreover, the analysis will specially focus on the reconfiguration potential. Finally, it will be impossible to conclude the section without analyzing the hot topics of the NoC application design. From the application point of view, section 4 will resume with a case study regarding embedded systems, a Software-Defined Radio application will be used as an example to highlight the most significant technical features and design choices.

FROM PLATFORM BASED TO DERIVATIVE SOC DESIGN

Design effort was reduced by customizing a common generic platform with a variety of accelerators, initially ASICs (Application-Specific ICs) and today regarding a SoC platform populated with IP (Intellectual Property) blocks.

Platform-based design is an IP reuse strategy that facilitates the rapid creation and verification of SoC designs containing sophisticated IP coming from different sources (Shaver, 2008). A platform is an abstraction layer that hides the details of several possible implementation refinements of the underlying layers (Carloni, De Bernardinis, Pinello, Sangiovanni-Vincentelli, & Sgroi, 2005). Platform design is the composition of IP library elements characterized by models representing their functionality and estimates of physical parameters. A legal composition of elements and interconnects is called a platform instance. The interplay of top-down constraints propagation and bottom-up performance estimation promotes a fast migration of a platform instance to one specific application. The successive refinement of specifications, ideally, will automate the non-differentiated aspects of a potential implementation, concentrating the effort on value added design. By following this procedure, domain specific platforms, such as network platforms for communication protocols design or fault-tolerant platforms for the design of safety critical applications, can quickly be differentiated.

Platform-based design is a good fit for the embedded software design style, but it is only a temporary solution for SoC designers (Smith, 2004). Once you change the architecture, you tend to disrupt your interfaces. That calls for a major effort in verification and in setting up the new standards required to keep the platform viable. It is still possible to do derivative SoC design by simply replacing cores, with a good architecture and a strict hierarchical design methodology. However, the SoC design style is used when your competitive advantage is in silicon design.

Market pressure encourages the use of pre-fabricated platforms. However, those platforms must be highly configurable to be useful for a variety of applications, and hence mass produced. The large diffusion of embedded systems raises very demanding requirements in terms of computing performance, power budgeting and functional flexibility. In particular, multimedia processing and high speed telecommunications impose real-time and quality constraints requiring intensive computation capabilities. Nevertheless, the continuous evolution of standards imposes a flexible architecture able to be adapted to new computation patterns after fabrication. Pure hardware reconfigurable architectures can hardly answer those requirements. For legacy and performance reasons, leading edge applications cannot migrate their functionality to reconfigurable hardware (Campi, et al., 2007).

The combined software and silicon technology provide a way to create and modify highly customized embedded systems applications (from prototyping to manufacturing) and develop cost-effective derivatives to address changing market demands at the price of a standard product. Hardware/software partitioning can increase software performance by implementing a critical software section on the FPGA fabric (Ernst, Henkel, & Benner, 1993) (Balboni, Fornaciari, & Sciuto, 1996) (Henkel, 1996) (Eles, Peng, Kuchinski, & Doboli, 1997) (Gajski, Vahid, Narayan, & Gong, 1998). Soft processor cores allow incorporating several processors within a single FPGA that can be configured or even customized (instructions set or data-path components) according to the application needs (Tensilica Xtensa, 2009). The Tensilica Xtensa LX3 high-performance data-plane processor (DPU), an application-specific instruction-set processor (ASIP), optimized for digital signal processing (DSP) offers a wide range of pre-verified DSP options ranging from a simple floating point accelerator to a 16-MAC (multiply accumulator) vector DSP powerhouse.

Embedded reconfigurable platforms combine the flexibility of software (standard programmable cores, DSP and ASIP) with the performance of configurable hardware (programmable logic) better adapted to different applications and legacy constraints (Mangione-Smith, et al., 1997) (De-

Hon, Apr. 2000). Recent commercial configurable platforms show a steady migration from application specific circuits to domain oriented platforms. The actual offer ranges from embedded FPGAs to reconfigurable processors and configurable SoC devices (M2000 Embedded FPGA) (Triscend, 2004) (eSilicon Embedded FPGA ASIC Design Services) (Abound Logic) (Singh, Lee, Lu, Kurdahi, Bagherzadeh, & Chaves Filho, 2000) (Arnold, Dec. 2005).

Flash-based FPGAs have reasonably performance and power consumption balance for embedded devices (Morris, 2007). In spite of having lower-density than SRAM-based, today Flash-based FPGAs allow a complete SoC to fit within a single device. Actel ProASIC3, Fusion, and Igloo Flash-based devices all have the capabilities to support the inclusion of soft-core embedded platforms into their FPGA programmable fabric. As an example, Actel CoreMP7 includes a 32-bit ARM core, real-time operating system (RTOS) and a variety of peripherals that can be connected via the AMBA bus, which provides wide-ranging IP interoperability. FPGA-based embedded platforms offer today a viable option for higher-volume cost-sensitive applications. The time-to-market and system flexibility advantages can be truly compelling when compared to fixed-hardware solutions.

Domain and service oriented platforms are becoming widespread. Many service oriented platforms are available with different characteristics and constraints. Most of today DSP processors are used in the wireless sector, especially in mobile handsets, and new applications such as mobile TV or high-speed Internet on mobile devices will increase the demand for more processing power and lower power consumption. That represents a shift from platform-oriented to domain-oriented, platform-independent development to distributed embedded systems. The telecom domain provides some examples of this move. A Software-Defined Radio (SDR) can be basically defined as a collection of hardware and software technologies that enable reconfigurable system architectures for wireless networks and user terminals (Perre, Craninckx, & Dejonghe, 2009). According to the SDR Forum, Software Defined Radio (SDR) is a radio in which some or all of the physical layer functions are Software Defined (SDR Forum, 2008). For a device that supports multi-mode multi-standard functionality, SDR offers an overall attractive solution to a very complex problem (Rouphael, 2009). Current SDR implementations mostly rely on reconfigurable hardware to support a particular standard or waveform while the algorithms and the various setups for other waveforms are stored in memory. Although application-specific integrated circuits lead to the most efficient implementation of a single-standard radio, the same cannot be said when addressing a multi-mode multi-standard device. For a device with such versatility, the ASIC could prove to be very complex in terms of implementation and inefficient in terms of cost and power consumption. For this reason, SDR designers have turned to FPGAs to provide a flexible and reconfigurable hardware that can support complex and computationally intensive algorithms used in a multitude of voice, data, and multimedia applications (Rouphael, 2009). In that case, one or more FPGAs are typically used in conjunction with one or more DSPs, and one or more general-purpose processors (GPPs) and/or microcontrollers to simultaneously support multiple applications. Unlike dedicated DSPs used in single standard solutions, SDR employs programmable DSPs that use the same computational kernels for all the baseband and control algorithms (Rouphael, 2009). FPGAs are typically configured at startup and with certain new architectures can be partially configured in real time. Similarly, DSPs and GPPs can also be programmed in real time from memory, allowing for a completely flexible radio solution. Despite all of their advantages, the industry still has not adopted fully reconfigurable FPGA platforms as the solution for handheld and portable devices due to their size, cost, and power consumption. However, to provide that hardware flexibility and scalability to ASICs, derivative SoC brought the NoC technology as a cost-effective, high performance and reliable interconnection solution. Example of that shift is the Spidergon topology from STMicroelectronics launched in 2005 (STMicroelectronics, 2005), a NoC based SoC solution providing reconfigurability at the interconnection level for embedded consumer devices.

MULTIPROCESSOR SYSTEM ON CHIP

Many cores programming is an interesting subject for high-performance applications. In addition to performance, splitting computation over multiple processing units also tackles the power dissipation problem. Indeed, processor clock speeds have stopped climbing while processor cores have multiplied.

Modern processing architectures are increasingly multi-core. Multi-core processors are today available within a single chip (for instance, dual core x86-based processors from AMD and Intel or 8-core SUN SPARC processor) with varying capabilities (network processors such as Intel IXP distributed processing architecture or IBM Cell processor) (Intel IXP425, 2006) (IBM Power XCell8i, 2008) (Walsh & Conway, 2008). Multicore DSP architectures appear today as a viable solution for high performance applications in packet telephony, 3G wireless and WiMax (Bhattacharyya, Bier, Gass, Krishnamurthy, Lee, & Konstatinides, 2008).

The growing number of applications written using multiple threads can benefit from multi-core parallelism (Gupta, Dutt, Gupta, & Nicolau, 2003) and FPGA-based accelerators (Jung & Ha, 2004) (Lysecky, Stitt, & Vahid, 2006). Thread optimizations include thread scheduling, dynamic detection of critical regions, run-time optimization and recompiling, etc. (Lu, Chen, Yew, & Hsu, 2004) (Zhang, Calder, & Tullsen, 2005). FPGAs bring

processing power at the additional cost of system level programming languages, such as SystemC, and Electronic System Level (ESL) design and verification tools (Grimpe & Oppenheimer, 2003) (Fin, Fummi, & Signoretto, 2001). Thread warping uses a single processor to dynamically synthesize single-processor single-thread into custom accelerator circuits on FPGAs (Stitt & Vahid, Thread Warping: A Framework for Dynamic Synthesis of Thread Accelerators, 2007). Warp processing dynamically remaps critical code regions from processor instructions to FPGA circuits using runtime synthesis. The technique, based on aggressive de-compilation, improves performances speeding up individual threads and allowing more threads to execute concurrently. Thread warping maintains the separation of function from architecture enabling portability of applications to architectures. The approach allows software designers to use any software language and compiler. The software binary de-compilation technique, translating from one instruction set architecture to another or to recover high-level code, is used here to convert binary code into a representation suitable for synthesis (Stitt & Vahid, 2005). Binary-level partitioning provides competitive results in terms of performance and energy (Lyseckey & Vahid, 2009).

Tomorrow's multi-core SoC designs will be pervasive with high-performance engines and standard accelerators outpacing front-end computations needed for communication and multimedia applications (Shaver, 2008). Consequently, we must understand how today's components (software and hardware) can be built on and integrated into other applications. More video and audio compression standards with higher compression ratios will increase content availability in all consumer devices. Video-processing features such as object recognition and tracking will become fully standards given their usefulness in a wide range of applications. Reliable wireless transport of HD (high-definition) video and standard wireless sensors interfaces will arise for high performance processors.

Future SoC will integrate multiple cores, processing units and storage elements, with performances highly dependent on interconnection facilities (Ho, Mai, & Horowitz, April 2001). The communication volume between cores will increase drastically, demanding highly efficient communication architectures (Rowson & Sangiovanni-Vincentelli, Getting the bottom of deep sub-micron, 1998). Derivative design will again motivate the selection and customization of standard communication architectures based on specific performance requirements. However, state-of-the-art on-chip bus topologies and protocols suffer from power and performance scalability limitations (Martin, 2009) (Loghi, Angiolini, Bertozzi, Benini, & Zafalon, Feb. 2004) (Sheynin, Suvorova, & Shutenko, 2006). Complex and multiple communication parameters (data traffic, topologies, protocols, clock speed, arbitration, packet sizes, and others) affecting system performance motivate a design paradigm shift of on-chip communication to transaction level modeling (TLM) of communication architectures, automatic synthesis of communication interconnects, and networks-on-chips (NoC) (Ayala, Lopez-Vallejo, Bertozzi, & Benini, 2009) (Henkel, Wolf, & Chakrandhar, On-Chip networks: a scalable, communication-centric embedded system design paradigm, Jan. 2004) (Benini & De Micheli, Networks on chip: a new SoC paradigm, 2002) (Pasricha, Dutt, & Ben Romdhane, 2007). As an example, the Intel's power efficient Teraflops Research Chip (Intel, 2007) includes a 2D mesh NoC and fine-grain power management (combining frequency scaling and multiple cores activation).

High performance computing (HPC) applications employ scalar processors supported by highly efficient communication architectures (IBM Power XCell8i, 2008) (Cell broadband engine, 2006). SIMD-based (Single Instruction, Multiple Data) data-parallel or vector architectures emerge today providing a unified programming environ-ment for parallel high-performance applications (NVidia Tegra, 2009). The Cell Broadband Engine exploits parallelism at all levels, including data and task level parallelism as well as SIMD parallelism optimization (Cell broadband engine, 2006). The platform includes a Power-Architecture processor and eight attached streaming processors with their own memory. Each processor has several SIMD units that can process from 2 double-precision floating-point values up to 16 byte-values per instruction.

The graphics programmable processor (GPU) is especially suited to data parallel computation with the same program executed on many data elements concurrently (NVidia Tegra, 2009). For instance, The NVidia Tegra family of computers-on-a-chip brings the power of advanced visual computing to a broad range of handheld and mobile platforms, from smart phones to mobile internet devices (NVidia Tegra, 2009). Embedded devices such as the Beagle Board platform also offer GPUs as a co-processor (beagleboard.org). Beagle board is a low power, low cost single board computer based on the OMAP3530 device, produced by Texas Instrument, including in the same die an ARM Cortex-A8 CPU, a TMS320C64x+ DSP, and an Imagination Technologies PowerVR SGX530 GPU (OMAP). GPU cores like Imagination Technologies PowerVR, NVidia, Yappa, ZiiLabs, Vivante, Takumi, or ATI, among others, are today present in several embedded SoCs.

The GPU has evolved into an increasingly convincing computational resource for non graphics applications. General Purpose Computing on Graphic Processor Units (GPGPU) can accelerate many applications such as search algorithms, data compression, cryptography, physical-based simulation, Grid computing or signal processing, by orders of magnitude over CPUs (Luebke & Harris, 2004). Using the CUDA programming environment, developers became more attracted to decompose algorithms that lend to explicit parallelism on GPUs (Bleiweiss, 2008). Apple operating system Snow Leopard, optimized for multi-core processors, exploits the computing power of GPUs (Apple Snow Leopard, 2008). Snow Leopard further extends GPU computing power with Open Computing Language (OpenCL Khronos, 2009). OpenCL is a parallel programming based on the C programming language proposed as an open standard by the Khronos group. Another general purpose GPU intended for the high performance computing market is the Tesla from NVidia (NVidia, 2007). For instance, the Tesla C1060 contains 240 thread processors providing a total processing power of almost one Tera FLOPS (floating point operations per second).

SIMD and GPU provide the advantage of a wide range of parallelism founded on a single compiler solution. The popularity of CPU-GPU programming environments like CUDA and OpenCL motivates to broaden that integration to FPGAs and DSPs. As an example, the FCUDA, a CUDA-based programming model for FPGAs, maps the coarse and fine grained parallelism of CUDA onto the reconfigurable fabric (Papakonstantinou, Gururaj, Stratton, Chen, Cong, & Hwu, 2009). The CUDA-to-FPGA flow employs AutoPilot, a high-level synthesis tool enabling high-abstraction FPGA programming (AutoPilot, 2009).

TRANSACTION LEVEL MODELING

For years, communication models were used for simulation purposes, thus, facilitating architecture design and exploration of implementation alternatives (Hines & Borriello, 1997) (Rowson & Sangiovanni-Vincentelli, Interface-based design, 1997) (Cai & Gajski, 2003). Assisted by communication models at different abstraction levels, interconnection topologies, communication mechanisms and synchronization primitives, several approaches treated various aspects of communication architectures, such as automatic generation (Bolsens, De Man, Lin, Van Rompaey, Vercauteren, & Verkest, 1997) (Cesario, Baghdadi,

Gauthier, Lyonnard, Nicolescu, & Paviot, 2002), optimization for specific applications (Gogniat, Auguin, Bianco, & Pegatoquet, 1998) (Knudsen & Madsen, 1998), synthesis (Ortega & Borriello, 1998) (Yen & Wolf, 1995) and refinement of system buses (Shin, Gerstlauer, Domer, & Gajski, 2005).

Transaction level models (TLM) appeared managing communication mechanisms and interface requirements at a high level of abstraction. TLM function calls model the communication hiding the intended hardware/or software implementation (Swan, 2006). For example, a TLM would represent a burst read or write transaction using just a single function call, with an object representing the burst request and another object representing the burst response. A hardware view of such a burst transaction becomes a series of signal read/write operations occurring on the wires of a bus.

As a consequence of the standardization process, widely used standard modeling languages such as SystemC and APIs appeared facilitating model exchange, IP reuse and interoperability (Ghenassia, 2005) (Swan, 2006). The adoption of TLM as a means of exchange of executable models between the diverse groups of engineers is helping to eliminate these problems and has been proven to significantly reduce the overall SoC design time (ConvergenSC, 2008) (CoCentric System Studio, 2008). TLM allows to model complex communication topologies including buses and NoCs (Caldari, Conti, Coppola, Curaba, Pieralisi, & Turchetti, 2003) (Boussctta, Abid, Layouni, & Pistrito, Dec. 2004) (Tsai, Y.-N., & Lin, 2008). SystemC brought TLM libraries initially for simulation purposes (Coppola, Curaba, Grammatikakis, & Maruccia, 2003) (Grotker, Liao, Martin, & Swan, 2002) (Ghenassia, 2005). The models can include parameters to be used for design exploration providing estimates on power consumption, bandwidth, clock speed, wire cost and other performance figures (Dumitrascu, Bacivarov, Pieralisi, Bnaclu, & Jerraya, 2006)

(Wieferink, Kogel, Leupers, Ascheid, & Meyr, 2004). TLM can be fully cycle accurate and still simulate much faster than its equivalent register transfer level (RTL) (Grotker, Liao, Martin, & Swan, 2002). However, in order to reduce modeling effort and to increase simulation speed, designers avoid the use of full cycle accurate models.

Regarding reconfigurable embedded systems, it is still required to capture the reactive nature of certain transactions (Doucet, Shyamasundar, Kruger, Joshi, & Gupta, 2007) (Moy, Maraninchi, & Maillet-Contoz, 2005) (Oliveira & Hu, 2002) (Siegmund & Muller, 2002). Reactive transactions are different from regular TLM transactions in the sense that the transaction can be killed or reinitialized before its completion. In that context, it is very valuable to simulate reactive transactions with the appropriated verification support to formally prove the correctness of the implementation choice (the design does not deadlock and is always responsive).

RECONFIGURABLE HARDWARE FOR EMBEDDED SYSTEMS

Reconfigurable platforms based on Field-programmable Gate Arrays (FPGAs) have quickly become the main option to address the flexibility of software with the performance of hardware into embedded systems designs. FPGA-based systems are faster than a pure software approach in terms of computational performance, and less static than traditional ASIC-based solutions and with better time-to-market (Rana, Santambrogio, & Sciuto, 2007). However, the introduction of reconfigurable platforms into embedded systems designs attaches more challenges to embedded systems designers. As part of these challenges, we can highlight the power constrains, the area constrains, and reconfiguration latencies. Moreover, the high cost per unit is also a barrier for an expansion of utilization of FPGAs in embedded systems.

The cost per unit of FPGA devices is still higher than ASIC's cost for high-volume applications. Though, the difference between FPGAs and ASICs costs has been attenuated by the current expansion of the FPGA market. This market is forecast to grow to $2,756.7 million by 2010, 68% larger than in 2005 (Worchel, 2006).

The power consumption is a key constrain for portable embedded system designs. This constrain has demanded many efforts from researchers around the world to improve the battery`s life. Despite the high power consumption of FPGA-based systems when compared to ASIC-based ones, many works have shown that reconfigurable hardware applications can dissipate less power than equivalent software running on embedded processors (Garcia, Compton, Schulte, Blem, & Fu, 2006) (Vaslin, Gogniat, Diguet, Tessier, Unnikrishnan, & Gaj, 2008). Also, new improvements of FPGA architecture claim that the new generation of FPGAs can reduce significantly the power consumption.

The technology used on FPGAs has also been improved. The already impressive 65 nm generation launched in 2006, now arrives at the 40 nm technology. With this new technology, the manufactures can produce devices with higher density, higher performance, and lower power consumption than the last generation. Considering the FPGA programmability, the technology most widely used on FPGAs is based on static RAM (SRAM) (Woods, McAllister, Lightbody, & Yi, 2008). Other technologies based on anti-fuse, EEPROM, and Flash will not be addressed in this text. For more information on these technologies the interested reader is referred to Kuon, Tessier, & Rose (2007) and Maxfield (2004).

Following, we will present an overview of classic FPGA architectures and the new features of modern FPGA devices. After that, we will discuss about tools and methodologies that can help embedded system designers to introduce a reconfigurable architecture in their work.

Figure 1. Generic FPGA architecture

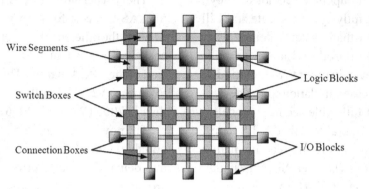

FPGA ARCHITECTURE

Field-programmable Gate Arrays (FPGAs) emerged in the '80's as a programmable inter-connection between major components (Woods, McAllister, Lightbody, & Yi, 2008). 25 years later, FPGAs became the most promising device for embedded system designs. The main FPGA distinguishing feature is the possibility of changing the system hardware structure in the field, a process known as reconfiguration. Device reconfiguration enables the incremental development of systems, the correction of design errors after implementation, and the addition of new hardware functions (Moraes, Calazans, Möller, Brião, & Carvalho, 2005).

Figure 1 presents a generic FPGA architecture based on three main components: logic blocks (LBs), I/O blocks (IOBs), and a programmable interconnection formed by horizontal and vertical wire segments, switch boxes, and connection boxes.

The LB, also called logic element (LE), is the key component for the FPGA reconfigurability. It is based on a look-up table (LUT), also called function generator, which is a programmable memory block containing all possible results of a specific Boolean function with a determined number of inputs. The LBs are arranged in an array of rows and columns on the FPGA device and can be associated to obtain more complex

functionalities. Figure 2 shows a basic LB structure with a 4-input LUT.

The IOBs are programmable blocks designed to provide communication between the internal circuits of FPGAs and the outside world signals. They are located on the device's periphery and basically can be configured as an input port, an output port, or a bidirectional port. A simplified IOB is shown in Figure 3.

A programmable interconnection, formed by wire segments, switch boxes, and connection boxes, provides routing tracks to connect one LB to another LB or to an IOB. The switch boxes are programmable switch matrices located on intersections of horizontal and vertical wire segments. They allow the connection between one wire segment to another. The connection boxes are programmable connection matrices which provide connections from LBs or IOBs to wire segments.

Figure 2. Basic LB formed from a 4-input LUT, a D flip-flop, and a multiplexer which forwards the registered or unregistered LUT output

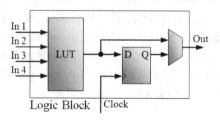

Figure 3. Simplified IOB structure

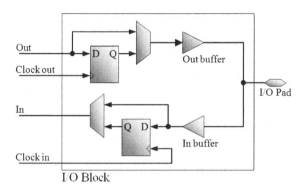

They are located on intersections of wire segments and LB or IOB connectors.

To program an FPGA device, configuration data, called bit-stream, is loaded from an external non-volatile storage device into SRAM configuration cells of LBs, IOBs, and interconnection programmable blocks (switch boxes and connection boxes). These memory cells define the LUT equations, signal routing, IOB configurations, and all other aspects of the user design (Xilinx, Inc., 2009a).

Current FPGAs have much more components and functions than the generic architecture just presented. Several hard blocks, such as memory blocks, DSP blocks, gigabit transceivers, and PCIe interfaces, were included in modern FPGAs in order to achieve better performance and lower

power consumption than equivalent soft core-based blocks. The newest family devices based on 40-nm technology from the two major FPGA manufacturers, Xilinx and Altera, provide similar resources (Altera Corp., 2009a) (Betz, 2009) (Xilinx, Inc., 2010).

Figure 4 shows a simplified chip view of the Altera Stratix IV GX family.

The major differences between the newest family from Xilinx and Altera are related to specific blocks characteristics. Here, we highlight the new LB architectures that have been claimed as the key to performance and power consumption improvements in the newest FPGA generations (Xilinx, Inc., 2009b) (Altera Corp., 2008) (Mansur, 2009). The 6-input LUT from Xilinx and the 8-input adaptive logic module (ALM) from Altera allow a reduction of resource utilization. This reduction is possible because more logic functions can be implemented in a unique LB, reducing the number of LBs, connections, and routing resources utilized by an application. Figure 5 and Figure 6 show high-level block diagrams of Xilinx Virtex-6 LB (6-input LUT) and Altera Stratix IV LB (ALM) respectively (Altera Corp., 2009a).

Another important feature of new FPGA architectures for embedded systems is the possibility to integrate one or more GPPs. These GPPs are divided into two classes: soft core processors and hard core processors. Soft core processors

Figure 4. Altera Stratix IV GX family structure (adapted from (Altera Corp., 2009a))

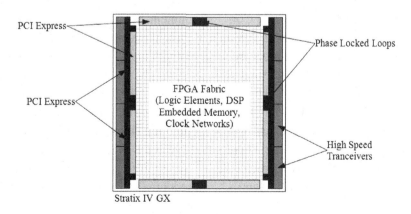

Figure 5. Architecture of the Xilinx Virtex-6 LB (adapted from (Xilinx, Inc., 2009b))

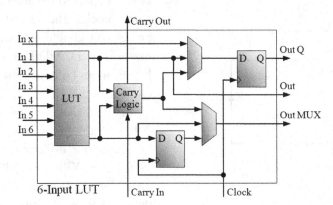

Figure 6. Architecture of the Altera Stratix IV LB (adapted from (Atmel Corp., 2009))

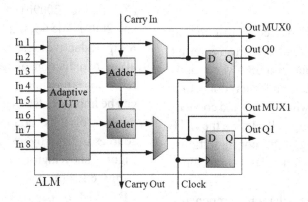

are formed by a group of logic blocks programmed to act as a processor (Maxfield, 2004). These processors are very flexible and can be found in many different sizes and architectures. They can also be implemented in almost any modern FPGA device. Two common examples of this class of processors are the Xilinx MicroBlaze (Xilinx, Inc., 2008a) and the Altera Nios II (Altera Corporation, 2009b). The work of Lysecky & Vahid (2009) is an illustration of the soft core processor flexibility, where a warp processor was designed from a MicroBlaze soft core. Hard core processors are dedicated hardware blocks inside of an FPGA device. They have better performance than soft core processors but they are not so flexible. There are few FPGA families with these dedicated blocks. An example is the Virtex-5 FXT family

with up to two IBM PowerPC 440 hard processors (Xilinx, 2009c).

FPGA manufacturers offer special tools that enable designers to create a complete embedded processor system for implementation in FPGAs. These tools have a set of IP cores, including core processors, buses, and peripherals, and a development environment to help the integration of these elements. Figure 7 shows a typical design integrating a GPP with some functional modules.

We can see that modern FPGAs include enough resources to build a complete embedded system on chip (SoC). However, most real-life applications are simply too large to fit in the logic available on a single chip (Rana, Santambrogio, & Sciuto, 2007). To demote the silicon area concern, modern FPGAs offer support for partial dynamic

Figure 7. Typical embedded processor system in a FPGA (GPP + Bus + Peripherals)

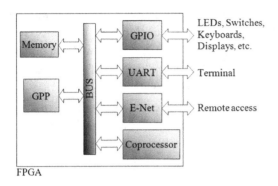

reconfiguration (PDR) (Berthelot, Nouvel, & Houzet, 2006). In the next topic, we will present an overview of the PDR technology.

PARTIAL DYNAMIC RECONFIGURATION

PDR is the most promising feature of modern FPGAs. This process can modify part of the FPGA, while the rest of it continues to operate (Moraes, Calazans, Möller, Brião, & Carvalho, 2005). The PDR allows utilizing a unique device to perform different tasks at different phases of an application's execution (Papadimitriou, Anyfantis, & Dollas, 2009). Figure 8 shows an example of

a Xilinx FPGA-based PDR structure for a video application.

In Figure 8, the FPGA is divided into two areas: a static region where are located all the modules not requiring to be reconfigured at run-time, and a dynamic region where the modules will be swapped according to the system needs. An embedded processor, PowerPC (PPC), is in charge of task scheduling process. The PowerPC receives information from the Video Processor Module and decides which module needs to be loaded from the Flash Memory into the dynamic region. The new module is transferred to the internal configuration access port (ICAP) that performs the reconfiguration of the dynamic region. The ICAP provides a bidirectional data bus interface to the FPGA configuration logic that can be used for both configuration and read-back (Xilinx, Inc., 2009a). The read-back is a reading operation of configuration memory cells, which can be used for verification and debugging. The interconnection of a reconfigurable module with another reconfigurable or fixed module has to be realized through a special communication interface called Bus Macro (Delahaye, Palicot, Moy, & Leray, 2007). For a detailed description of PDR theory and approaches, please refer to Bobda (2007), (Xilinx, Inc., 2008b), and Altera Corp., 2009c.

Figure 8. FPGA-based PDR structure for a video application

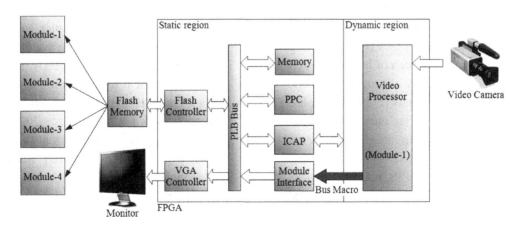

The main drawback in PDR remains the large reconfiguration latencies due to the time to download the partial bit-stream, which is known as reconfiguration overhead (Papadimitriou, Anyfantis, & Dollas, 2009). In order to hide these latencies, compiler support is fundamental to automatically schedule and optimize the compiled application code for efficient reconfigurable hardware usage (Panainte, Bertels, & Vassiliadis, 2007). Moraes et al (2005) also point to another drawback, the lack of tools to deal with the differences between a static system design flow and a dynamic system design flow. This turns more complex producing a reconfigurable system. Cardoso & Diniz (2009) believe that an efficient automatic compilation from high-level programming languages to reconfigurable architectures, which is a key to make this promising technology the dominant computing paradigm, still remains an elusive goal.

Several other reconfigurable dedicated architectures, e.g. reconfigurable arithmetic logic units (rALUs), have been developed by research teams of reconfigurable computer systems. Some important examples of these architectures are described in Hartenstein (2001) and Rosti, Campi, Bonnot, & Brelet (2009).

FPGA DESIGN TOOLS AND METHODOLOGIES

Traditional techniques to develop systems targeting FPGA devices are based on hardware description languages (HDLs) such as VHDL or Verilog. These languages use the idea of behavioral synthesis which describes how the algorithm works in terms of input and outputs (Fobel, Gréwal, & Morton, 2009). However, as mentioned earlier, nowadays embedded systems are getting more and more complex, as well as reconfigurable devices containing one or more GPPs, on-chip memory, high performance serial transceivers, and DSP blocks. At this level of complexity, it is extremely hard to design an entire system utilizing only the traditional HDLs.

High-level languages can accelerate the hardware/software development process. Their introduction in the design flow is widely believed as a key approach to the success of reconfigurable computing (Cardoso & Diniz, 2009).

Currently, there exists a plethora of tools available for embedded system designers, but, it is hard to choose which will fit the design needs in terms of usability, time-to-market, and results quality (e.g., low latency, small area, and low power consumption). Figure 9 shows a resume of design entry methods, design tools, and their interrelationship.

We can divide this picture in three levels. The first level is the 'Specification' where the design (hardware/software) is described according to the design entry method. The second level is the integrated design environment (IDE) where the design is synthesized, implemented (placed and routed - P&R), and verified. At this level, we also included the tools for DPR and embedded system design including its operating system (OS) and software development (C++). The last level is FPGA programming.

At the Specification level, we have six groups of design entry methods:

- **IP Library**: Many companies, e.g. Xilinx, Altera, Mentor Graphics, provide a large set of IP (soft/hard) cores for implementation and reuse. This methodology simplifies the work to design complex embedded system. An IP core can be used directly as entry of IDEs or as an HDL (VHDL/Verilog) block if the source code is available. Open IP repositories, such as the OpenCores.org (OpenCores, 2009), are available for embedded system designers. HDL and already synthesized blocks can be stored on the library and reused in different designs.

Figure 9. Resumed block diagram of design entry methods, design tools, and their interrelationship

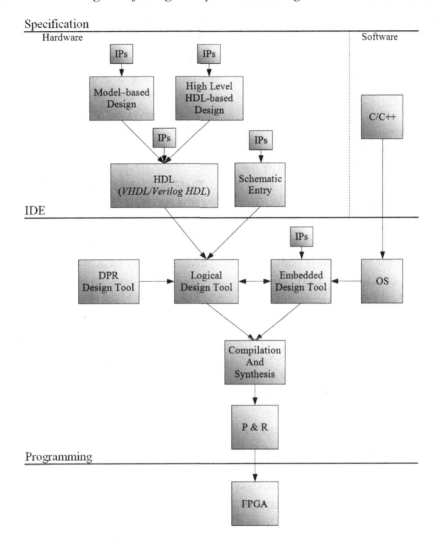

- **Model-based Design**: a high-level entry method based on MATLAB/Simulink. Basically, it is a block set in the Simulink environment that can be used to design a hardware application, simulate it, and translate it to VHDL or Verilog HDL. The System Generator (Xilinx), DSP Builder (Altera), and Synplify DSP (Synopsys) are examples of tools available at that level.
- **High-level HDL-based Design**: High-level entry method based on high-level programming languages, e.g. C/C++, Java,

and Phyton. This method brings a higher level of abstraction to HDLs helping embedded system designers to handle the complexity at the system level. In addition, this method enables non-hardware specialists to program FPGAs. The C-based languages such as SystemC (supported by AutoPilot from AutoESL, C-to-Silicon Compiler from Cadence, Catapult C from Mentor Graphics), Handel-C (supported by DK Design Suite from Agility), and Impulse C (supported by CoDeveloper from Impulse Accelerated Technologies) are the most popular languages of this category (Woods, McAllister, Lightbody, & Yi, 2008) (Pellerin & Thibault, 2005).

- **HDL (VHDL/Verilog languages)**: Traditional entry method for FPGAs programming.
- **Schematic Entry**: Entry method available in the IDEs where the embedded system designer draws a graphical diagram of the desired logical circuit.
- **C/C++**: Traditional entry method for the embedded processors.

At the IDE level, the main component is the Logic Design Tool (LDT). The LDT, such as Xilinx's Integrated Software Environment (ISE) and Quartus II, produced by Altera, receive the RTL specification and help the designer to implement logic circuits into FPGAs. The Logic Design Tool can also include auxiliary tools to create PDR systems (e.g., RecoBus from University of Erlangen-Nürnberg).

A special IDE is available to create a complete embedded processor platform. The Embedded Design Tool, e.g. EDK (Xilinx) and Nios II EDS (Altera), is an IDE where embedded system designers can integrate core processors, buses, and peripherals to be implement in an FPGA. On the software side, this tool includes compiler, debugger, and verification tools necessary to program the

embedded processor. Additional tools are required to work with embedded operational systems (OS), such as Linux (e.g., µCLinux from ArcTurus, Xilinx Open Source Linux from Xilinx, PetaLinux from PetaLogix, and BlueCat Linux from LynuxWorks) and real time operational systems (RTOS) (e.g., FreeRTOS from Real Time Engineers, and VxWorks from Wind River).

THE NETWORK ON CHIP COMMUNICATION PARADIGM

The Network-on-Chip (NoC) interconnection architecture is basically based on a set of routers driving the data exchange between a set of IP blocks, also called processing elements (PEs). Each PE is connected to the NoC by a local Router (R). PEs can have different size, clock frequency, communication protocol or different supply voltage. A Network Interface (NI) is placed between the PE and the local Router preserving the NoC from heterogeneous PEs. The NI acts as a bridge taking care of protocols, interfaces, data size, clock frequency and other PE specific characteristics. Figure 10 shows the basic elements of a standard NoC architecture.

The Network infrastructure allows parallel data paths between separated IPs as well as reconfigurable connections. Depending on how network components (router, links, …) are inter-

Figure 10. Typical NoC architecture

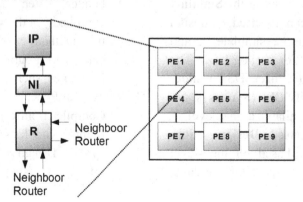

connected, the topology can be quite regular because the same pattern is repeated to create the architecture. Regular topologies are a valuable alternative for SoC design, well suited to scalability concerns about the growing number of required IPs (Dally & Towles, Principles and Practices of Interconnection, 2004). Scalable NoCs are needed to match increasing communication demands of large-scale MPSoCs for high-end wireless communications applications (Benini, 2006). The network can be flexible in the number of paths between PEs and communication parameters, but also customized according to application needs.

Application specific NoCs are the best alternative for on-chip heterogeneous architectures and energy efficiency requirements of wireless communications. In terms of execution time, reconfigurable interconnections are sometimes a better alternative compared to partial or dynamic reconfiguration once the required components being allocated (Mouhoub & Hammami, 2006).

NoC is today a mature concern covering application modeling and optimization (how to choose the best application/architecture combination that satisfies various performance and energy constraints), architecture topology and communication parameters (bandwidth, latency, area, power and reliability), architecture validation and synthesis. The on-chip context of NoC leads to some different choices that were adopted for the communication paradigm (Duato, Yalamanchili, & Ni, 2002).

To provide an overview of design techniques currently used, we will analyze the following NoC characteristics: switching technique, routing strategy, QoS, power and thermal management, reliability and fault tolerance.

Switching technique: As the network is shared by different IPs, data with different destinations will be present simultaneously in each router. The information to be send has to be structured to be manipulated easily. The solution mainly used is the WormHole switching. It consists in the encapsulation of the data in a packet. The data packet will also contain additional information like for instance the destination address. The major difference between WormHole and traditional packet switching is that the size of the packet is fixed. When the data is bigger than the size of a network packet called a flit, the data is split in several flits which are sent one after the other in the Network. This solution regulates the size of each buffer present in the Network and prevents a waste of memory space that occurs with packets of different sizes.

Another switching technique also used in certain NoC solutions is the circuit switching (Enright-Jerger, Peh, & Lipasti, May 2008). Here, the interconnection can be seen as a reconfigurable point to point connection. The virtual point to point connection is created by the configuration of the routers between the transmitter and the receiver. The data transmission is done in two phases. A transmitter/receiver private connection is firstly established. Then, the data can be sent through that connection directly without encapsulation. Latency overheads are due to the creation of the private channel; however, circuit switching allows a faster data transfer than packet switching at the cost of reducing the number of available channels.

Routing Strategy: In NoC solutions, there are multiple possible paths to send a data between two IPs. The routers will need a packet routing strategy to determine the best path for each data transfer. In this on-chip infrastructure, the use of a routing table is not the best choice; a routing table means allocation of additional memory to this purpose. Due to the hard area restrictions, on-chip networks commonly use an algorithmic routing strategy.

Two standard routing algorithms for NoCs are deterministic and adaptive routing (Dally & Towles, Principles and Practices of Interconnection, 2004) (Duato, Yalamanchili, & Ni, 2002). In deterministic solutions, the data path will only be determined by the destination address of the IP. In adaptive routing solutions, the router will take care of the network load. In that case, data can follow different paths to reduce traffic overload to some points of the network. Even if the adaptive solution is better in terms of routing, it requires more processing. Moreover, in adaptive routing, the packets don't necessary arrive in the right order. Deterministic routing requires less packet processing and will lead to a solution using fewer resources. Between these two standard solutions, there is semi-deterministic routing algorithm like the random and alternative routing (Hu & Marculescu, DyAD - Smart routing for networks-on-chip, Jun. 2004).

Quality of Service (QoS): Due to its network characteristics, the NoC architecture cannot avoid facing congestion problems. The main challenge is to guarantee the hard deadline of packet delivering while using as fewer resources as possible. Three mains techniques are used to control the QoS (Ogras & Marculescu, Analysis and optimization of prediction-based flow control in networks-on-chip, 2008): QoS-aware congestion control algorithms, which regulate the traffic at the NI, multiple priority level, to ensure the respect of hard deadline for critical data packets, and the insertion of virtual channels in the routers (Dally, 1992), which increase the number of buffers connected in parallel to one link. With more than one buffer attached to the router entry (Figure 11), the virtual channels insertion reduces the risk of network congestion and deadlock.

Power and thermal management: Several NoC prototypes showed that the Network uses between 30 and 40% of the system power (Taylor,

et al., 2002) (Vangal, et al., Feb. 2007). NoC flexibility significantly affects power consumption. During the design process, power minimization becomes the main parameter that rules the remaining implementation choices.

Reliability and fault tolerance: Nano-scale CMOS technology is sensitive to faults affecting circuit robustness in general, requiring additional techniques, different than those commonly found on communication networks. To guarantee NoC reliability, techniques such as time/space redundancy for sequential elements or dynamic faulty routers virtual channel reallocation were proposed (Mingjing & Orailoglu, 2007). (Neishaburi & Zilic, 2009).

DESIGNING A NETWORK ON CHIP APPLICATION

Application-specific NoCs must be supported by adequate design flows to reduce design time and effort (Benini, 2006). The application performance will depend on the NoC topology, and required flexibility. Embedded applications are subject to strong QoS and real-time requirements. The on-chip communication structure will impact the network energy efficiency as well as chip area. Five basic parameters can be established for NoC analysis and optimization. Two of them are application dependent performance metrics: communication bandwidth and network latency. The last three are cost metrics: area, power and reliability.

Figure 11. Virtual Channel Insertion

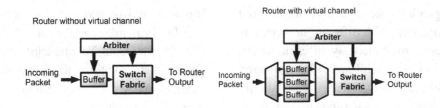

Due to its heterogeneous and distributed nature, it becomes very difficult to find the "best solution" minimizing all critical parameters. Some authors consider raising the abstraction level taking NoC as a whole (Lu & Haukilahti, 2003). The NoC is not treated as individual elements (resources, switches and interfaces) but as a programming model composed by communication primitives (message passing or shared memory) plus an operating system layer taking care of application process migration based on power consumption analysis. A competitive application specific NoC in terms of area, performance and power consumption, can be generated from TLM or a high level specification (Benini, 2006). Multi-objective analysis can be performed based on the applications set, firstly by looking at the execution architecture (IP cores where the application will be executed). The architecture exploration (if this one had not been defined yet) will provide the communication requirements (Lahiri, Raghunathan, & Dey, 2004).

To pass through this design problem and to allow designers to find quickly and efficiently a SoC application, the approximated formulation of the problem is to find a solution that matches the specifications required by the application. The required parameters can be basically divided in two groups: the parameters that belong to the application and the parameters belonging to the interconnection architecture. To understand their impact, those parameters will be detailed and evaluated.

NoC Architecture Parameters

NoC architecture parameters allow designers to fine tune a properly characterized application. An application is well characterized when the mapping of tasks to IP cores, the scheduling of each task and the data exchange between IPs is already known. In this context, it's possible to tune the NoC parameters for maximum efficiency.

Generally, the search for an optimal NoC starts with a basic topology and a set of parameters to be tuned (Taylor, Lee, Amarasinghe, & Agarwal, 2005). The following points will present all of the most important NoC parameters: the topology, the router design, the channel design and the clocking and power distribution (Marculescu, Ogras, Peh, Jerger, & Hoskote, 2009).

Topology design. The topology of the network defines the disposition of the router and the way routers are interconnected. Several topologies, different in regularity, were proposed with distinctive properties (Gratz, Kim, McDonald, Keckler, & Burger, 2006).

Generally, the first topology choices are 2D regular ones such as mesh or torus (Figure 12). The torus is just a variant of mesh topology with additional links connecting geometrically opposite routers. Topology regularity is synonym of simplicity and homogeneity. Regularity promotes scalability; the same pattern can just be repeated. Moreover, the square design is very compatible with traditional layout design which mainly consists in manipulating square or rectangular areas. Links between routers have the same length meaning that the network has a uniform latency just dependant on the IPs position.

In most of the cases, size and position of IPs is not uniform leading to irregular topologies and area overhead. However, regular topologies do not always bring optimal results depending on application data flow or task distribution, and a full custom topology can improve the overall performance.

Between these two extremes a lot of variants can be found. For instance, the semi custom technique called long range link insertion (Figure 12) (Ogras & Marculescu, 2005). By the insertion of additional links according to critical traffic values, the technique can improve the network load with minimum changes.

Router design. Router design parameters are: number of virtual channels, buffer size, switch design, control flow policy. The number and size

Figure 12. basic NoC topologies

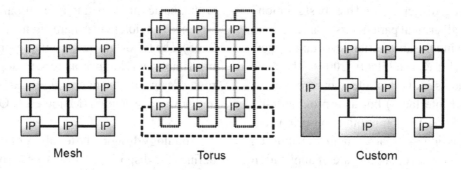

Mesh   Torus   Custom

of virtual channels depends on the number of simultaneous transfers and will affect somehow the buffers number and size. For area and energy concerns all buffers can be assigned to only one virtual channel but, when required, a performance balance can be obtained between buffer size and number of channels. The size of a buffer depends on the granularity of a network packet, or flit size. A bigger flit implies fewer transfers for one packet increasing QoS, but also area and consumption. Energy estimates can provide a good packet/flit balance (Starobinski, Karpovsky, & Zakrevski, 2003). The size of a switch will increase with the number of cores it is connected to, unless deadlock-free alternative routes can be provided for different traffic flows. The complexity of the control flow policy depends on QoS requirements, having a direct impact on the router size (buffer/ switch control signals).

Channel design. The efficient design of a channel, or link between routers, implies a compromise between area, reliability of transmitted data and bandwidth. Channel bandwidth will not just affect the width of a channel, but also the size and number of input buffers per router. Longer wires have also long latency in nanoscale technology. An alternative solution to small and short links is the use of repeaters (Pamunuwa, Öberg, Zheng, Millberg, Jantsch, & Tenhunen, Dec. 2003).

Clocking and power distribution. The design of a fully synchronous system with a global clock

implies a large design effort controlling skew and energy consumption. Moreover, a single clock isn't compatible with the heterogeneous philosophy of NOC architectures. This is why alternative clocking strategies are used. Two adequate clocking strategies are asynchronous and mesochronous clocking. In mesochronous clocking architectures (Bainbridge & Furber, 2001), the clock frequency is uniform, but NoC components can deal with phase shift. This component-based solution treats timing related errors avoiding a fully asynchronous deployment. By using a latency insensitive approach, it is possible to keep routers locally synchronous and globally decoupled. This solution profits from the synchronous design advantages. While complex in design effort, the fully asynchronous approach gives better results in terms of average packet latency, for a particular bandwidth, area and power consumption (Sheibanyrad, Panades, & Greiner, 2007). In addition to multiple clock frequencies, heterogeneous cores can have different power supply voltages. In this case, some approaches propose splitting the network in voltage islands (Ogras, Marculescu, Marculescu, & Jung, 2009).

Application Parameters

As in hardware/software codesign, the application can be decomposed to be executed by several IP cores like for instance GPPs or DSPs and data distributed between memories. A scheduling algorithm will split the application into a set of tasks, inserting communication links for data exchange or tasks synchronization. The mapping step will assign tasks to IP cores. Both operations, done statically or dynamically, can fundamentally infer a network topology or charge.

Application scheduling. The application scheduler is a program able to split the application into a set of tasks with its associated communication (Figure 13). The challenge of the scheduler is to find the optimal balance between decomposition of tasks and communication load. Splitting into many tasks to be executed in parallel can increase processing power. However, the communication overhead can increase latency.

The goal of scheduling algorithms used in real-time embedded systems is to meet the required hard deadline for the tasks that are executed. In the SoC context, energy aware schedulers, for NoC-based embedded systems, will minimize the overall (tasks and communication) required energy (Gruian, 2001) (Hu & Marculescu, 2004).

Application mapping. The assignment of tasks to processing elements provides information about the network load and router requirements. A mapping algorithm can balance router complexity, resources usage and energy consumption when an application with timing constraints is mapped to a NoC.

The mapping process will indicate to which router the IP will be connected and the communication that will be established (Figure 14). This mapping will dramatically influence the performances and the energy consumption of the network.

The complexity of the mapping algorithm will vary depending on the complexity of the topology. Latency and power consumption will be uniform on a regular network and only the communication between the tasks will be taken into account. In other cases, floorplaning information can contribute getting better results (Murali, Coenen, Radulescu, Goossens, & De Micheli, Mar. 2006).

NETWORK ON CHIP AND EMBEDDED SYSTEMS

Network on Chip was presented as a mature solution for on-chip and, in particular, embedded systems communication. As in Platform based design or derivative design, NoC must also be adapted to an application domain. TLM helped rising communication to the system level making possible the migration from bus-based to NoC architectures. In addition, TLM can help gathering information regarding concurrency/non-concurrency of communication transactions among cores.

Figure 13. The application scheduling challenge

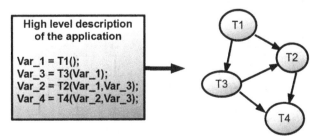

Task graph of the application

Control dominated applications cannot always profit from full NoC deployment. If the application does not require a big number of processing elements or when the communication between IPs is simple or not requiring overlap, adding a NoC to the architecture will not provide optimal performances. In those cases, a fast point-to-point or a shared bus connection will be a better option. Moreover, if the features of the network are not really exploited, the interconnection will just consume more power, area and latency than a basic one.

Scheduling/mapping algorithms can identify an efficient NoC implementation for highly parallel and regular structures present on multimedia or wireless applications. For instance, more than two IPs need to be interconnected, to exchange data simultaneously, or a flexible connection must be established. The algorithms can exploit the application specific information to distinguish pairs of cores which communicate and other pairs which never communicate to maximize communication flexibility and performance. Reliability can also be an important design parameter for deep sub-micron technology requiring the use of routing algorithms to cope with failures (Palesi, Holsmark, Kumar, & Catania, 2009).

Network on Chip on FPGAs

Due to their higher power consumption and speed limitations compared to ASICs, FPGAs are frequently used just for NoC prototyping. Moreover, the internal architecture of a FPGA is already a generic mesh interconnection network with primitive routers. A NoC mapping will create a network on top of this one with hard limitations. Indeed, the ASIC implementation can better exploit the flexibility and benefits of a NoC. The NoC parameters such as layout design, clocking strategy and power dispatching can be tuned to get optimal results.

Even if the FPGA is not a convenient place for NoC implementation, a mixture of FPGA and NoC will not only inherently support dynamic reconfiguration but will also replace the on-chip busses currently built with reconfigurable logic (Goossens, Bennebroek, Hur, & Wahlah, 2008). That alternative motivated other researchers to propose hardwired NoC on FPGA (Gindin, Cidon, & Keidar, May 2007). A hardwired NoC can be used for both the functional interconnect between IP blocks and the configuration interconnect that transports the bitstreams.

Network on Chip and Reconfiguration

A Network on Chip solution can deploy reconfigurable interconnections also attractive for embedded systems. The reconfiguration scheme can provide a change on the interconnection of IP blocks and a dynamic configuration of IPs

Figure 14. The application mapping challenge

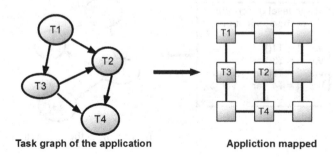

Task graph of the application   Appliction mapped

without disturbing the execution of the rest of the application.

NoC dynamic Packet reconfiguration: packets can be dynamically redirected following a task relocation policy. In that case, only the interconnection (the destination address of the data packet) between IPs will change.

NoC dynamic IP Reconfiguration: task scheduling also supports design reuse through dynamic configuration of IP blocks. That reconfiguration implies to send the task configuration data to the destination IP and sometimes to upgrade the IPs interconnection. A NoC can perform both operation dynamically with no execution overhead.

SDR APPLICATION: A CASE STUDY

Software defined radio (SDR) technology is gaining an increasing interest due to the flexibility and ease of adaptation properties (Sadiku & Akujuobi, 2004). The idea of the SDR is simple: to replace as much as possible specialized electronics, used to treat the radio signal, by programmable devices controlled by software. SDR enables running a set of waveform applications on the same radio platform, depending on the operational need. This leads to several benefits of SDR: (i) for subscribers, it is easy to achieve a seamless wireless connection if the terminal can support multiple wireless protocols; (ii) for a mobile network operator, it is easier to update the infrastructure and to provide new services without the need to purchase new costly and specialized equipment; (iii) for the manufacturers, it will reduce the time and cost to market (Huang, Jojczyk, Achille, & Valderrama, 2008).

One of the applications of SDR is in satellite communications (SATCOM). The use of SDR systems in SATCOM has many advantages, such as achieving the requirements of flexibility and interoperability, allowing frequency reuse between satellite beams, reducing the power requirements,

developing new services and applications. For instance, with the advent of the Galileo system in Europe, it is in great demand to develop a Global Navigation Satellite System (GNSS) to enable interoperability between Galileo and the existing Global Positioning System (GPS) (Girau, Tomatis, Dovis, & Mulassano, 2007).

SDR technology has been used in SATCOM systems supporting high data-rate modems in order to reduce hardware and software development costs. A SDR is a flexible hardware architecture typically consisting of a combination of GPPs, DSPs, and FPGA-based accelerators (Skey, Bradley, & Wagner, 2006). The use of GPPs in these systems answers not only the flexibility and programmability needs but also supports the Portable Operating System Interface (POSIX), in which the Common Object Request Broker Architecture (CORBA) can be used. However, for high data-rate waveforms in satellite communication systems, GPPs and DSPs may not be able to support the required high performance processing, and FPGAs have to be used to boost system processing power due to the high-parallel signal processing capabilities and reconfigurable properties.

Figure 15 shows a block diagram of an SDR strategy for waveform reconfiguration using FPGA and PDR. The interconnection architecture between different IP cores, which can be GPPs, FPGAs, or just interconnected IP blocks, is a critical issue for SDR design.

NoC is becoming one of the best alternatives to bus-based systems which are not flexible enough to provide reconfigurable interconnections of IP blocks. NoC architectures can benefit SDR implementations due to its scalability, reusability and reliable performance (Huang, Jojczyk, Achille, & Valderrama, 2008).

SDR applications that perform coding and decoding tasks are perfect case studies to illustrate the double level of reconfiguration that a NoC can offer. A coder and decoder can share resources and operations, used in different order. SDR generally

Figure 15. Block diagram of an SDR based on FPGA and PDR

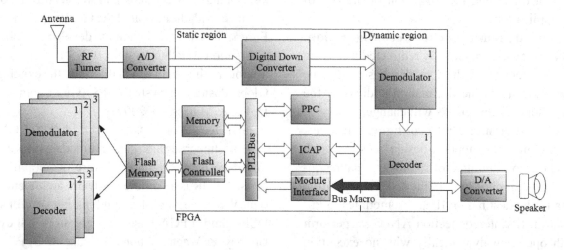

requires several different codecs depending on the operation scenario. Frequently, a codec must be upgraded. In addition, not all the codecs are required simultaneously.

Even though software libraries can provide all required codecs, a pure software or common platform will fail to provide a flexible and efficient implementation. To increase processing power, the codec functionality can be split over several basic processing elements working in parallel. Depending on the operation mode, the data must be redirected to a different processing element or transferred in a dissimilar order. In addition to what partial and dynamic reconfiguration can provide, this execution scenario demonstrates reconfiguration at the interconnection level. The interconnection reconfigurability provides efficiently (in terms of IP reuse, reconfiguration time and throughput) the required flexibility. By changing the data packet path a NoC can switch from coding to decoding. Moreover, individual processing elements can be reused or reconfigured through separated channels without affecting current execution.

Reusability is one of the essential requirements of SDR systems. To address these requirements, standardized interfaces have been defined for communication between IPs, e.g. OCP interface.

The OCP is one standard interface for IP cores or sockets that facilitates "plug and play" SoC design (OCP-IP Association, 2009). An IP core can be a simple peripheral core, a high-performance GPP, or an on-chip communication subsystem such as an NoC. With the use of the OCP interface, the application developer needs only to understand the OCP interface that exposes hardware, but not the hardware itself (Figure 16). Therefore, the application developer can focus on the development of IP cores, since they are independent of the architecture and design of the system used due to the OCP interface. As a result, reusability of the IP blocks is achieved, and the application's time to market will also be reduced.

In the architecture presented in Figure 15, the PDR can demote the area constrains of the system. However, a partial dynamic reconfigurable region does not grant the best area utilization but just the maximum allowed size for a reconfigurable block. In the case of a larger block, PDR must be supported by a scheduling tool helping on sequential execution partitioning (splitting the sequential execution flow into interchangeable execution segments). Task partitioning and scheduling based on Timed Petri Nets allow the optimal use of a reconfigurable region and storage components (Eskinazi, Lima, Maciel, Valderrama, Filho, &

Figure 16. Reconfigurable architecture based on NoC with OCP interface and PDR of IPs

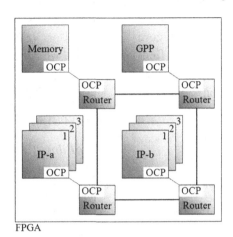

Nascimento, 2005). The methodology includes the generation of an embedded controller supporting the run-time scheduling process and self-reconfiguration.

CONCLUSION

In the last decade, the evolution of embedded systems was driven by multimedia applications and mobile devices. Continuous IC technology scaling facilitates the emergence of SoCs and the access to reconfigurable hardware. Today Multiprocessor architectures take care of flexibility and power consumption concerns. Dedicated hardware such as FPGAs, DSP, GPUs, reconfigurable processors and in general IP cores, are now part of the latest commercial MPSoCs.

System level languages, models and tools are also concerned due to the gap between architecture and application. ESL tools bring today a common view of hardware and software methodologies helping the refinement process and platforms creation. New abstractions like TLM motivate a move to communication abstraction, modeling and synthesis. Tools based on thread warping maintain the separation of function from architecture enabling portability of applications to architectures. The technique based on software

binary de-compilation improves performances speeding up individual threads and allowing more threads to execute concurrently.

The emergence of IP cores and heterogeneous MPSoCs is now experiencing a shift towards easy-of-use, regularity and scalability concerns. Regular and flexible architectures such as FPGAs, NoCs and GPUs are part of that move. The growing popularity of programming languages such as OpenCL and CUDA illustrates the request for a parallel programming consensus. Application oriented reconfigurable processors and synthesis tools based on the CUDA programming language are an example of mapping that parallelism onto a reconfigurable fabric. Performance improvements can be achieved working at the bit-stream level with FPGAs or at the instruction level in the case of reconfigurable processors as shown by the latest publications. By using the warp processing technique, single processor applications are remapped dynamically on custom accelerator FPGA circuits using runtime synthesis. An example of next generation of multi-core SoC is the Spidergon IPU (Interconnect Processing Unit) from STMicroelectronics illustrating a shift towards a programmable on-chip communication platform. The Spidergon NoC acts as a programmable distributed hardware/software set of services to design advanced application features. A similar approach was adopted by the Intel's power efficient Teraflops Research Chip, providing more than one Teraflops of performance. The multi-core Teraflops also includes a 2D mesh NoC and fine-grain power management (combining frequency scaling and multiple cores activation).

REFERENCES

M2000 Embedded FPGA. (n.d.). Retrieved from http://www.m2000.fr

Abound Logic. (n.d.). Retrieved from http://www.aboundlogic.com/

Alfke, P. (2009). *Xilinx Virtex-6 and Spartan-6 FPGA Families [PowerPoint slides]*. Retrieved October 20, 2009, from FPL 2009: http://fpl2009.org/

Altera Corp. (2002, january). Retrieved from Altera Excalibur™ Embedded Processor Solutions Gain Global Acceptance At Alcatel: http://www.altera.com

Altera Corp. (2008). *40-nm FPGAs: Architecture and Performance Comparison*. Retrieved October 20, 2009, from Altera.com: http://www.altera.com/

Altera Corp. (2009, June). *FPGA Run-Time Reconfiguration: Two Approaches*. Retrieved from www.altera.com.

Altera Corp. (2009a). *Stratix IV Device Handbook (Vol. 1)*. Retrieved October 20, 2009, from www.altera.com.

Altera Corporation. (2009b). *Nios II Processor Reference Handbook*. Retrieved October 20, 2009, from Altera.com: http://www.altera.com/

Apple Snow Leopard. (2008). Retrieved from Apple Previews Mac OS X Snow Leopard to Developers: http://www.apple.com/pr/library/2008/06/09snowleopard.html

Arnold, J. (Dec. 2005). S5: the architecture and development flow of a software configurable processor. *IEEE International Conference on Field-Programmable Technology*, (pp. 121-128).

Atmel Corp. (2009). Retrieved from FPSLIC™ (AVR with FPGA) http://www.atmel.com/products/FPSLIC/

AutoPilot. (2009). Retrieved from AutoESL: http://www.autoesl.com/

Ayala, J.-L., Lopez-Vallejo, M., Bertozzi, D., & Benini, L. (2009). SoC Communication Architectures: from interconnection busses to packet-switched NoCs. In Zurawski, R. (Ed.), *Embedded systems design and verification* (2nd ed., pp. 1–28). CRC Press.

Bainbridge, W.-J., & Furber, S.-B. (2001). Delay Insensitive System-on-Chip Interconnect using 1-of-4 Data Encoding. *7th International Symposium on Asynchronous Circuits and Systems ASYNC*, (p. 118). Salt Lake City, Utah.

Balarin, F., Sentovich, E., Chiodo, M., Giusto, P., Hsieh, H., & Tabbara, B. (1997). *Hardware-Software Co-design of Embedded Systems - The POLIS approach*. Kluwer Academic Publishers.

Balarin, F., Watanabe, Y., Hsieh, H., Lavagno, L., Passerone, C., & Sangiovanni-Vincentelli, A. (2003). Metropolis: An integrated electronic system design environment. *Computer*, *36*(4), 45–52. doi:10.1109/MC.2003.1193228

Balboni, A., Fornaciari, W., & Sciuto, D. (1996). Partitioning and exploration in the TOSCA co-design flow. In *Proceedings of the IEEE International Workshop on Hardware/Software Codesign CODES*, (pp. 62–69), Los Alamitos, CA.

Bauer, M., & Ecker, W. (1997). Hardware/software co-simulation in a VHDL-based test bench approach. In *Proc. of the Design Automation Conference DAC*, (pp. 774-779).

beagleboard.org. (n.d.). Retrieved from http://beagleboard.org

Benini, L. (2006). Application Specific NoC Design. In *Proceedings of the Design Automation & Test in Europe Conference DATE, 1*, (pp. 105), Munich, Germany.

Benini, L., & De Micheli, G. (2002, Jan.). Networks on chip: a new SoC paradigm. *IEEE Computer, 35*(1), 70–78.

Berthelot, F., Nouvel, F., & Houzet, D. (2006). Partial and dynamic reconfiguration of FPGAs: a top down design methodology for an automatic implementation. *International Parallel and Distributed Processing Symposium IPDPS, 20*.

Betz, V. (2009). *FPGA Challenges and Opportunities at 40nm and Beyond [PowerPoint slides]*. Retrieved October 20, 2009, from FPL 2009: http://fpl2009.org/

Bhattacharyya, S., Bier, J., Gass, W., Krishnamurthy, R., Lee, E., & Konstatinides, K. (2008, Nov.). Advances in hardware design and implementation of signal processing systems. *IEEE Signal Processing Magazine, 25*(6), 175–180. doi:10.1109/MSP.2008.929838

Bleiweiss, A. N. (2008). GPU Accelerated Pathfinding. In *Proceedings of the 23rd ACM SIGGRAPH/EUROGRAPHICS symposium on Graphics hardware*, (pp. 65-74). Sarajevo, Bosnia and Herzegovina.

Bobda, C. (2007). *Introduction to Reconfigurable Computing: Architectures, Algorithms, and Applications*. Dordrecht, Netherlands: Springer Netherlands.

Bolsens, I. (Sept. 2002). Challenges and Opportunities of FPGA Platforms. *in Proceedings of the 12th International Conference on Field-Programmable Logic and Applications FPL'02*, (pp. 39–392). Montpellier, France.

Bolsens, I., De Man, H.-J., Lin, B., Van Rompaey, K., Vercauteren, S., & Verkest, D. (1997, Mar). Hardware/software co-design of digital telecommunication systems. *Proceedings of the IEEE, 85*(3), 391–418. doi:10.1109/5.558713

Boussctta, H., Abid, M., Layouni, F., & Pistrito, C. (Dec. 2004). STBus transaction level models using SystemC 2.0. *Proceedings of the 16th International Conference on Microelectronics ICM*, (pp. 347- 350), Sfax, Tunisia.

Cai, L., & Gajski, D. (2003). Transaction-level Modeling: an Overview. In *Proc. of the Int. Conf. on Hardware/Software Codesign and System Synthesis* (pp. 19–24). New York: ACM Press.

Caldari, M., Conti, M., Coppola, M., Curaba, S., Pieralisi, L., & Turchetti, C. (2003). Transaction-Level Models for AMBA Bus Architecture Using SystemC 2.0. *Proceedings of the Design, Automation and Test in Europe conference DATE: Designers' Forum*, (p. 20026).

Campi, F., Deledda, A., Pizzotti, M., Ciccarelli, L., Rolandi, P., & Mucci, C. (2007). *A dynamically adaptive DSP for heterogeneous reconfigurable platforms* (pp. 9–14). Proceedings of Design Automation and Test in Europe DATE.

Cardoso, J. M., & Diniz, P. C. (2009). *Compilation Techniques for Reconfigurable Architectures*. New York, NY: Springer US.

Carloni, L., De Bernardinis, F., Pinello, C., Sangiovanni-Vincentelli, A.-L., & Sgroi, M. (2005). Platform-based design for embedded systems. In Zurawski, R., & Raton, B. (Eds.), *Embedded Systems Handbook* (pp. 1–26). Boca Raton, FL: CRC Press.

Cell broadband engine. (2006). Retrieved from IBM Research: Compiler Technology for Scalable Architectures: http://domino.research.ibm.com/comm/research_projects.nsf/pages/cellcompiler.index.html

Cesario, W. -0., Baghdadi, A., Gauthier, L., Ly-onnard, D., Nicolescu, G., & Paviot, Y. (2002). Component-based design approach for multicore SoCs. *In Proceedings of the Design Automation Conference DAC*, (pp. 789-794).

CoCentric System Studio. (2008). Retrieved from Synopsys: http://www.synopsys.com

Convergen, S. C. (2008). Retrieved from CoWare: http://www.coware.com

Cooke, C., McNelly, H., & Martin, T. (1999). *Surviving the SOC Revolution: A Guide to Platform-Based Design*. Boston, MA: Kluwer Academic Publishers.

Coppola, M., Curaba, S., Grammatikakis, M., & Maruccia, G. (2003). IPSIM: SystemC 3.0 enhancements for communication refinement. In *Proceedings of the Design Automation and Test Conference in Europe*, (pp. 106-111).

Coumeri, S., & Thomas, D. (1995). A simulation environment for hardware-software codesign. *In Proc. of the Int. Conference on Computer Design*, (pp. 58-63).

Dally, W.-J. (1992, Mar.). Virtual-channel flow control. *IEEE Transactions on Parallel and Distributed Systems*, 3(2), 194–205. doi:10.1109/71.127260

Dally, W.-J., & Towles, B. (2004). *Principles and Practices of Interconnection*. San Mateo, CA: Morgan Kaufmann.

DeHon, A. (2000, Apr.). The density advantage of configurable computing. *Computer*, 33(4), 41–49. doi:10.1109/2.839320

Delahaye, J.-P., Palicot, J., Moy, C., & Leray, P. (2007). *Partial Reconfiguration of FPGAs for Dynamical Reconfiguration of a Software Radio Platform*. Budapest: Mobile and Wireless Communications Summit.

Doucet, F., Shyamasundar, R.-K., Kruger, I.-H., Joshi, S., & Gupta, R.-K. (2007). Reactivity in SystemC Transaction-Level Models. *Haifa Verification Conference*, (pp. 34–50).

Duato, J., Yalamanchili, S., & Ni, L. (2002). *Interconnection Networks: An Engineering Approach*. San Mateo, CA: Morgan Kaufmann.

Dumitrascu, F., Bacivarov, I., Pieralisi, L., Bnaclu, M., & Jerraya, A. (2006). Flexible MPSoC platform with fast interconnect exploration for optimal system performance for a specific application. *Proceedings of the Design, automation and test in Europe conference DATE: Designers' forum*, (pp. 168-171). Munich, Germany.

Eles, P., Peng, Z., Kuchinski, K., & Doboli, A. (1997). System level hardware/software partitioning based on simulated annealing and tabu search. *Design Automation of Embedded Systems DAES*, 2(1), 5–32. doi:10.1023/A:1008857008151

Enright-Jerger, N., Peh, L., & Lipasti, M. (May 2008). Circuit-switched coherence. In *Proceedings of the Network-on-Chips International Symposium NoCs*, (pp. 193–202).

Ernst, R., Henkel, J., & Benner, T. (1993). Hardware-software cosynthesis for microcontrollers. *IEEE Design & Test of Computers*, 10(4), 64–75. doi:10.1109/54.245964

eSilicon Embedded FPGA ASIC Design Services. (n.d.). Retrieved from http://www.esilicon.com/

Eskinazi, R., Lima, M.-E., Maciel, P.-R., Valderrama, C., Filho, A. G.-S., & Nascimento, P.-S. (2005). A Timed Petri Net Approach for Pre-Runtime Scheduling in Partial and Dynamic Reconfigurable Systems. *Proceedings of the 19th IEEE International Parallel and Distributed Processing Symposium IPDPS*, *4*, p. 154a. Denver, Colorado.

Fin, A., Fummi, F., & Signoretto, M. (2001). SystemC: a homogenous environment to test embedded systems. In *Proceedings of Int. Workshop on Hardware/Software Codesign CODES*, (pp. 17-22).

Fobel, C., Gréwal, G., & Morton, A. (2009). Hardware accelerated FPGA placement. *Microelectronics Journal*, *40*(11), 1667–1671. doi:10.1016/j.mejo.2008.09.008

Forum, S. D. R. (2008). Retrieved from The Software Defined Radio Forum Cognitive Radio Definitions www.sdrforum.org

Gadient, A.-J., Debardelaben, J.-A., & Madisetti, V. K. (1997). Incorporating cost modeling in embeddedsystem design. *IEEE Design & Test of Computers*, *14*(3), 24–35. doi:10.1109/54.605989

Gajski, D., Vahid, F., Narayan, S., & Gong, J. (1998). SpecSyn: an environment supporting the specify-explore-refine paradigm for hardware/software system design. *IEEE Transactions on VLSI Systems*, *6*(1), 84–100. doi:10.1109/92.661251

Garcia, P., Compton, K., Schulte, M., Blem, E., & Fu, W. (2006). An Overview of Reconfigurable Hardware in Embedded Systems. *EURASIP Journal on Embedded Systems*, 19.

Gavrielov, M. (2009, Apr.). *FPGA targeted design platforms: Fulfilling the programmable imperative*. Retrieved from www.DSP-FPGA.com.

Ghenassia, F. (2005). *Transaction Level Modeling with SystemC*. Dordrecht, Netherlands: Springer. doi:10.1007/b137175

Gindin, R., Cidon, I., & Keidar, I. (May 2007). NoC-Based FPGA: Architecture and Routing. *in proceedings of the First International Symposium on Networks-on-Chip NOCS*, (pp. 253-264).

Girau, G., Tomatis, A., Dovis, F., & Mulassano, P. (2007). Efficient software defined radio implementations of GNSS receivers. *IEEE International Symposium on Circuits and Systems*, (pp. 27-30). New Orleans, LA.

Gogniat, G., Auguin, M., Bianco, L., & Pegatoquet, A. (1998). Communication Synthesis and HW/SW Integration for Embedded System Design. *Sixth International Workshop on Hardware/Software Co-Design CODES*, (pp. 49).

Goossens, K., Bennebroek, M., Hur, J.-Y., & Wahlah, M.-A. (2008). Hardwired Networks on Chip in FPGAs to Unify Functional and Confguration Interconnects. In *Proceeding of the International Symposium on Networks-on-Chip NOCS*.

Gratz, P., Kim, C., McDonald, R., Keckler, S.-W., & Burger, D.-C. (2006). Implementation and evaluation of on-chip network architectures. In *Proceedings of the International Conference on Computer Design ICCD*, (pp. 477-484), San Jose, CA.

Grimpe, E., & Oppenheimer, F. (2003). Extending the SystemC synthesis subset by object oriented features. In *Proceedings of Int. Conf. on Hardware/Software Codesign and System Synthesis CODES/ISSS*, (pp. 25-30).

Grotker, T., Liao, S., Martin, G., & Swan, S. (2002). *System Design with SystemC*. Amsterdam: Kluwer Academic Publishers.

Gruian, F. (2001). Hard real-time scheduling for low-energy using stochastic data and DVS processors. In *Proceedings of the International Symposium on Low Power Electronics and Design*, (pp. 46–51).

Gupta, S., Dutt, N., Gupta, R., & Nicolau, A. (2003). SPARK: a high-level synthesis framework for applying parallelizing compiler transformations. In *Proceedings of Int. Conf. on VLSI Design*.

Hartenstein, R. (2001). *A decade of reconfigurable computing: a visionary retrospective*. Munich, Germany: Design, Automation and Test in Europe.

Henkel, J. (1996). A low power hardware software partitioning approach for core-based embedded systems. In *Proceedings of the ACM Design Automation Conference DAC*, (pp. 122–127), New York.

Henkel, J., Wolf, W., & Chakrandhar, S. (Jan. 2004). On-Chip networks: a scalable, communication-centric embedded system design paradigm. *Proceedings of International Conference on VLSI Design*, (pp. 845-851), Mumbai, India.

Hines, K., & Borriello, G. (1997). Dynamic communication models in embedded system co-simulation. In *Proc. of the Design Automation Conference DAC*, (pp. 395-400).

Ho, R., Mai, R.-K., & Horowitz, M.-A. (2001, April). The future of wires. *Proceedings of the IEEE, 89*(4), 490–504. doi:10.1109/5.920580

Hu, J., & Marculescu, R. (Jun. 2004). DyAD - Smart routing for networks-on-chip. In *Proceedings of Design Automation Conference DAC*, (pp. 260–263).

Hu, J., & Marculescu, R. (2004). Energy-Aware Communication and Task Scheduling for Network-on-Chip Architectures under Real-Time Constraints. In *Proceedings of the Design, Automation and Test in Europe Conference DATE*, (pp. 10234).

Huang, M., Jojczyk, L., Achille, T., & Valderrama, C. (2008). A SDR architecture proposal for SATCOM applications. *International Design and Test Workshop*. Monastir, Tunisia.

Intel. (2007, February 11). *Intel's Teraflops Research Chip*. Récupéré sur Teraflops research Chip Overview: http://download.intel.com/pressroom/kits/Teraflops/Teraflops_Research_Chip_Overview.pdf

Intel IXP425. (2006). Retrieved from Embedded Computing Intel IXP425 Network Processor Product Brief intel.com/go/networkprocessors

Jung, H., & Ha, S. (2004). Hardware synthesis from coarse-grained dataflow specification for fast hw/sw cosynthesis. In *Proceedings of Int. Conf. on Hardware/Software Codesign and System Synthesis CODES/ISSS*, (pp. 24-29).

Keutzer, K., Malik, S., Newton, R., Rabaey, J., & Sangiovanni-Vincentelli, A. (2000). System level design: Orthogonalization of concerns and platform-based design. *IEEE Transactions on Computer-Aided Design of Circuits and Systems, 19*(12), 1523–1543. doi:10.1109/43.898830

Kienhuis, B., Deprettere, E., Vissers, K., & Van der Wolf, P. (1997). An approach for quantitative analysis of application-specific dataflow architectures. In *Proc. of the Int. Conf. Application-specific Systems, Architectures and Processors*, (pp. 338-349).

Kim, Y., Kim, K., Shin, Y., Ahn, T., Sung, W., Choi, K., et al. (1995). An integrated hardware-software cosimulation environment for heterogeneous systems prototyping. In *Proc. of the Conference Asia South Pacifc Design Automation*, (pp. 101-106).

Knudsen, P.-V., & Madsen, J. (1998). Integrating Communication Protocol Selection with Partitioning in Hardware/Software Codesign. In *Proceedings of the 11th international symposium on System synthesis*, (pp. 111-116), Hsinchu, Taiwan, China.

Kuon, I., Tessier, R., & Rose, J. (2007). FPGA Architecture: Survey and Challenges. *Foundations and Trends in Electronic Design Automation, 2*(2), 135–253. doi:10.1561/1000000005

Lahiri, K., Raghunathan, A., & Dey, S. (2004, June). Design space exploration for optimizing on-chip communication architectures. *IEEE Transactions on Computer-Aided Design of Integrated Circuits and Systems, 23*(6), 952–961. doi:10.1109/TCAD.2004.828127

Lieverse, P., Stefanov, T., Van der Wolf, P., & Deprettere, E. (Nov. 2001). System level design with Spade: an M-JPEG case study. In *Proc. of the Int. Conference on Computer Aided Design*, (pp. 31-38).

Loghi, M., Angiolini, F., Bertozzi, D., Benini, L., & Zafalon, R. (Feb. 2004). Analyzing on-chip communication in a MPSoC environment. In *Proceedings of IEEE Design Automation and Test in Europe Conference DATE*, (pp. 752-757), Paris, France.

Lu, J., Chen, H., Yew, P., & Hsu, W. (2004). Design and implementation of a lightweight dynamic optimization system. *Journal of Instruction-Level Parallelism*, *6*, 1–24.

Lu, Z., & Haukilahti, R. (2003). High level communication primitives and operating system services for power management. In Jantsch, A., & Tenhunen, H. (Eds.), *NoC Application Programming Interfaces* (*Vol. 3*, pp. 239–260). Berlin: Springer.

Luebke, D., & Harris, M. (2004). GPGPU: General Purpose Computing on Graphics Hardware. *International Conference on Computer Graphics and Interactive Techniques ACM SIGGRAPH*. Los Angeles, CA.

Lysaght, P., & Rosenstiel, W. (2005). *New Algorithms, Architectures and Applications for Reconfigurable Computing*. New York: Springer-Verlag. doi:10.1007/1-4020-3128-9

Lyseckey, R., & Vahid, F. (2009). Design and implementation of a MicroBlaze-based warp processor. *ACM Transactions on Embedded Computing Systems TECS*, *8*(3), 22.

Lysecky, R., Stitt, G., & Vahid, F. (2006). Warp processors. *ACM Transactions on Design Automation of Electronic Systems TODAES*, *11*(3), 659–681. doi:10.1145/1142980.1142986

Mangione-Smith, W., Hutchings, B., Andrews, D., DeHon, A., Ebeling, C., & Hartenstein, R. (1997, Dec.). Seeking solutions in configurable computing. *Computer*, *30*(12), 38–43. doi:10.1109/2.642810

Mansur, D. (2009). A New 40-nm FPGA and ASIC Common Platform. *IEEE Micro*, *29*(2), 46–53. doi:10.1109/MM.2009.22

Marculescu, R., Ogras, U., Peh, L.-S., Jerger, N., & Hoskote, Y. (2009). Outstanding Research Problems in NoC Design: System, Microarchitecture, and Circuit Perspectives. *IEEE Transactions on Computer-Aided Design of Integrated Circuits and Systems*, *28*(1). doi:10.1109/TCAD.2008.2010691

Martin, G. (2009). System-on-Chip design. In *Embedded systems design and verification* (pp. 13 1-18). Boca Raton, FL: CRC Press.

Maxfield, C. (2004). *The Design Warrior's Guide to FPGAs*. Orlando, FL: Elsevier.

Mingjing, C., & Orailoglu, A. (2007). Improving Circuit Robustness with Cost-Effective Soft-Error-Tolerant Sequential Elements. *Proceedings of the 16th Asian Test Symposium*, (pp. 307-312).

Mohanty, S., & Prasanna, V. (2002). Rapid system-level performance evaluation and optimization for application mapping onto SoC architectures. In *Proc. of the IEEE ASIC/SOC Conference*, (pp. 160-167).

Moraes, F., Calazans, N., Möller, L., Brião, E., & Carvalho, E. (2005). Dynamic and Partial Reconfiguration in FPGA SoCs: Requirements Tools and a Case Study. In Lysaght, P., & Rosenstiel, W. (Eds.), *New Algorithms, Architectures and Applications for Reconfigurable Computing* (pp. 157–168). Netherlands: Springer. doi:10.1007/1-4020-3128-9_13

Morris, K. (2007, Jan.). *Actel Activates Platforms*. Retrieved from Embedded Technology Journal: http://www.embeddedtechjournal.com/articles_2007/20070130_actel.htm

Mouhoub, R., & Hammami, O. (2006, Oct.). NoC Monitoring Hardware Support for Fast NoC Design Space Exploration and Potential NoC Partial Dynamic Reconfiguration. *International Symposium on Industrial Embedded Systems IES*, (pp. 1-10).

Moy, M., Maraninchi, F., & Maillet-Contoz, L. (2005). LusSy: A Toolbox for the Analysis of System-on-a-Chip at the Transactional Level. In *Proc. of the Int. Conf. on Application of Concurrency to System Design*.

Murali, S., Coenen, M., Radulescu, A., Goossens, K., & De Micheli, G. (Mar. 2006). A methodology for mapping multiple use-cases onto networks on chips. In *Proceedings of The International Design Automation and Test in Europe Conference*, (pp. 118–123).

Neishaburi, M.-H., & Zilic, Z. (2009). Reliability aware NoC router architecture using input channel buffer sharing. *Proceedings of the 19th ACM Great Lakes symposium on VLSI*, (pp. 511-516), Boston.

NVidia. (2007, June 5). *NVidia Tesla GPU Computing Technical Brief*. Récupéré sur NVidia Tesla Technical Brief: http://www.nvidia.com/docs/IO/43395/tesla_technical_brief.pdf

NVidia Tegra. (2009). Retrieved from NVidia: http://www.nvidia.com/page/handheld.html

OCP-IP Association. (2009). Open Core Protocol Specifications. [sur OCP-IP.]. *Consulté le, 10*, 20.

Ogras, U.-Y., & Marculescu, R. (2005). Application-Specific Network-on-Chip Architecture Customization via Long-Range Link Insertion. In *Proceedings of the IEEE/ACM International conference on Computer-aided design*, (pp. 246-253), San Jose, CA.

Ogras, U.-Y., & Marculescu, R. (2008, Jan.). Analysis and optimization of prediction-based flow control in networks-on-chip. *ACM Transactions on Design Automation of Electronic Systems TODAES, 13*(1), 1–28. doi:10.1145/1297666.1297677

Ogras, U.-Y., Marculescu, R., Marculescu, D., & Jung, E.-G. (2009, Feb./Mar.). Design and management of voltage–frequency island partitioned networks-on-chip. *IEEE Transactions on Very Large Scale Integration VLSI Networks-on-Chip Special Section*.

Oliveira, M., & Hu, A. (2002). High-level Specification and Automatic Generation of IP Interface Monitors. In *Proceedings of the Design Automation Conference DAC*.

OMAP. (n.d.). Retrieved from Texas Instruments, OMAP35x Applications Processors http://focus.ti.com/dsp/docs/dspcontent.tsp?contentId=53403

Open, C. L. *Khronos*. (2009). Retrieved from Khronos OpenCL The open standard for parallel programming of heterogeneous systems: http://www.khronos.org/opencl/

OpenCores. (2009). *OpenCores.org*. Retrieved October 23, 2009, from http://www.opencores.org/

Ortega, R.-B., & Borriello, G. (1998). Communication synthesis for distributed embedded systems. In *Proceedings of the International Conference on Computer-Aided Design*, (pp. 437-444).

Palesi, M., Holsmark, R., Kumar, S., & Catania, V. (2009, Mar.). Application Specific Routing Algorithms for Networks on Chip. *IEEE Transactions on Parallel and Distributed Systems, 20*(3), 316–330. doi:10.1109/TPDS.2008.106

Pamunuwa, D., Öberg, J., Zheng, L.-R., Millberg, M., Jantsch, A., & Tenhunen, H. (Dec. 2003). Layout, Performance and Power Trade-Offs in Mesh-Based Network-on-Chip Architectures. In *Proceeding of IFIP International Conference on Very Large Scale Integration*, (p. 362).

Panainte, E.-M., Bertels, K., & Vassiliadis, S. (2007). The Molen Compiler for Reconfigurable Processors. *ACM Transactions on Embedded Computing Systems, 6* (1).

Papadimitriou, K., Anyfantis, A., & Dollas, A. (2009). An Effective Framework to Evaluate Dynamic Partial Reconfiguration in FPGA Systems. *IEEE Transactions on Instrumentation and Measurement*.

Papakonstantinou, A., Gururaj, K., Stratton, J.-A., Chen, D., Cong, J., & Hwu, W.-M. (2009). FCUDA: Enabling Efficient Compilation of CUDA. *Proceedings of the 23rd international conference on Supercomputing*, (pp. 515-516). Yorktown Heights, NY, USA.

Pasricha, S., & Dutt, N. (2008). *On-chip communication architectures: system on chip interconnect*. San Francisco: Morgan Kaufmann.

Pasricha, S., Dutt, N., & Ben Romdhane, M. (2007). BMSYN: Bus matrix communication architecture synthesis for MPSoC. *IEEE Transactions on CAD, 8*(26), 79–85.

Pellerin, D., & Thibault, S. (2005). *Practical FPGA Programming in C*. Upper Saddle River, NJ: Prentice Hall PTR.

Perre, L.-V., Craninckx, J., & Dejonghe, A. (2009). *Green Software Defined Radios: Enabling seamless connectivity while saving on hardware and energy*. Berlin: Springer.

Pimentel, A. D., Erbas, C., & Polstra, S. (2006). A systematic approach to exploring embedded system architectures at multiple abstraction levels. *IEEE Transactions on Computers, 55*(2), 99–112. doi:10.1109/TC.2006.16

Pimentel, A.-D., Lieverse, P., & Van der Wolf, P.-H. (2001, Nov.). Exploring embedded-systems architectures with Artemis. *Computer, 34*(11), 57–63. doi:10.1109/2.963445

Power, I. B. M. *XCell8i*. (2008, Aug.). Retrieved from With Its New Power XCe l l 8i Product Line IBM Intends to Take Accelerated Processing into the HPC Mainstream http://www-03.ibm.com/technology/resources/technology_cell_IDC_report_on_PowerXCell.pdf

Rana, V., Santambrogio, M., & Sciuto, D. (2007). Dynamic Reconfigurability in Embedded System. *IEEE International Symposium on Circuits and Systems*, (pp. 2734-2737), New Orleans, LA.

Rosti, A., Campi, F., Bonnot, P., & Brelet, P. (2009). SoA of Reconfigurable Computing Architectures and Tools. In Dans N. Voros, A. Rosti, & M. Hübner, (eds.), *Dynamic System Reconfiguration in Heterogeneous Platforms* (pp. 13-27). Berlin: Springer.

Rouphael, T.-J. (2009). *RF and Digital Signal Processing for Software-Defined Radio: A Multi-Standard Multi-Mode Approach*. New York: Elsevier.

Rowson, J.-A., & Sangiovanni-Vincentelli, A. (1997). Interface-based design. *Proceedings of the 34th Design Automation Conference DAC, 34*, 178-183.

Rowson, J.-A., & Sangiovanni-Vincentelli, A. (1998). Getting the bottom of dccp sub-micron. In *Proceedings of the IEEE/ACM International Conference on Computer Aided Design ICCAD*, (pp. 203-211), San Jose, CA.

Sadiku, M. N., & Akujuobi, C. M. (2004). Software-defined radio: a brief overview. *IEEE Potentials, 23*(4), 14–15. doi:10.1109/MP.2004.1343223

Shaver, D. (2008). *Platform-based design in the year 2020*. Retrieved from TI E2E Community http://e2e.ti.com/blogs/video360/archive/2008/12/05/platform-based-design-inthe-year-2020.aspx

Sheibanyrad, A., Panades, I.-M., & Greiner, A. (2007). Systematic comparison between the asynchronous and the multi-synchronous implementations of a network-on-chip architecture. In *Proceeding of Design Automation and Test in Europe Conference DATE*, (pp. 1090–1095).

Sheynin, Y., Suvorova, E., & Shutenko, F. (2006). Complexity and low power issues for on-chip interconnections in MPSoC system level design. In *Proceedigns of the IEEE Computer Society Annual Symposium on Emerging VLSI Technologies and Architectures*, (p. 283), Karlsruhe, Germany.

Shin, D., Gerstlauer, A., Domer, R., & Gajski, D. (2005). Automatic generation of communication architectures. In Springer (Ed.), *From Specification to Embedded Systems Application* (Vol. 184). Boston: Book Series IFIP International Federation for Information Processing.

Shin, D., Gerstlauer, A., Peng, J., Domer, R., & Gajski, D. (Oct. 2006). Automatic Generation of Transaction Level Models for Rapid Design Space Exploration. In *Proceedings of the international conference on Hardware/software codesign and system synthesis*, (pp. 64-69).

Siegmund, R., & Muller, D. (2002). Automatic Synthesis of Communication Controller Hardware from Protocol Specification. *IEEE Design & Test of Computers*, *19*, 84–95. doi:10.1109/MDT.2002.1018137

Singh, H., Lee, M.-H., Lu, G., Kurdahi, F., Bagherzadeh, N., & Chaves Filho, E. (2000, May). MorphoSys: an integrated reconfigurable system for data-parallel and computation-intensive applications. *IEEE Transactions on Computers*, *49*(5), 465–481. doi:10.1109/12.859540

Skey, K., Bradley, J., & Wagner, K. (2006). A reuse approach for FPGA-based SDR waveforms. *Military Communications Conference*, (pp. 1–7), Washington, DC.

Smith, G. (2004). Platform Based Design: Does it Answer the Entire SoC Challenge? In *Proceedings of the 41st Design Automation Conference DAC*, (p. 407).

Stammermann, A., Kruse, L., Nebel, W., & Pratsch, A. (Oct. 2001). System level optimization and design space exploration for low power. In *Proceedings of the International Symposium on Systems Synthesis*, (pp. 142-146).

Starobinski, D., Karpovsky, M., & Zakrevski, L.-A. (2003, June). Application of network calculus to general topologies using turn-prohibition. In *IEEE/ACM Transactions on Networking TON*, *11*(3), 411-421.

Stitt, G., & Vahid, F. (2005). New decompilation techniques for binarylevel co-processor generation. In *Proceedings of IEEE/ACM International Conference on Computer-Aided Design ICCAD*, (pp. 547-554).

Stitt, G., & Vahid, F. (2007). Thread Warping: A Framework for Dynamic Synthesis of Thread Accelerators. In *Proceedings of the International Conference on Hardware/Software Codesign and System Synthesis CODES/ISSS*, (pp. 93-98), Salzburg, Austria.

STMicroelectronics. (2005, December 15). *STMicroelectronics Unveils Innovative Network-on-Chip Technology for New System-on-Chip Interconnect Paradigm*. Récupéré sur www.stm.com: http://www.stm.com/stonline/press/news/year2005/t1741t.htm

Swan, S. (2006). SystemC transaction level models and RTL verification. *Proc. of the Design Automation Conference DAC*, *43*, 90-92.

Taylor, M., Lee, W., Amarasinghe, S., & Agarwal, A. (2005, Feb.). Scalar operand networks. *IEEE Transactions on Parallel and Distributed Systems*, *16*(2), 145–162. doi:10.1109/TPDS.2005.24

Taylor, M.-B., Kim, J., Miller, J., Wentzlaff, D., Ghodrat, F., & Greenwald, B. (2002, Mar./Apr.). The RAW microprocessor: A computational fabric for software circuits and general-purpose programs. *IEEE Micro, 22*(2), 25–35. doi:10.1109/MM.2002.997877

Tensilica Xtensa. (2009). Retrieved from New Tensilica DPU Family Delivers 10 GigaMAC/sec DSP Performance, Tops 1 GHz Mark: http://www.tensilica.com/

Triscend. (2004). Retrieved from Xilinx: http://www.triscend.com

Tsai, T.-H. Y-N., P., & Lin, C.-H. (2008). An Electronic System Level Design and Performance Evaluation for Multimedia Applications. In *Proceedings of the 2008 International Conference on Embedded Software and Systems ICESS*, (pp. 621-624).

Vangal, S., Howard, J., Ruhl, G., Dighe, S., Wilson, H., Tschanz, J., et al. (Feb. 2007). An 80-tile 1.28TFLOPS network-on-chip in 65 nm CMOS. In *proceedings of the IEEE Solid-State Circuits International Conference ISSCC*, (pp. 98-589).

Vaslin, R., Gogniat, G., Diguet, J.-P., Tessier, R., Unnikrishnan, D., & Gaj, K. (2008). Memory security management for reconfigurable embedded systems. *International Conference on Field-Programmable Technology*, (pp. 153-160), Taipei, Taiwan.

Walsh, R., & Conway, S. (2008, Aug.). *With Its New Power XCe 1 1 8i Product Line IBM Intends to Take Accelerated Processing into the HPC Mainstream.* Retrieved from IBM Technology http://www-03.ibm.com/technology/resources/technology_cell_IDC_report_on_PowerXCell.pdf

Wieferink, A., Kogel, T., Leupers, R., Ascheid, G., & Meyr, H. (2004). A system level processor/communication co-exploration methodology for multi-processor system-on-chip platforms. In *Proceedings of the Design Automation and Test in Europe Conference DATE*, (pp. 21-258). Paris, France.

Woods, R., McAllister, J., Lightbody, G., & Yi, Y. (2008). *FPGA-based Implementation of Signal Processing Systems.* West Sussex, UK: John Wiley & Sons. doi:10.1002/9780470713785

Worchel, J. (2006). *The Field-Programmable Gate Array (FPGA): Expanding Its Boundaries.* Consulté le October 20, 2009, sur In-Stat: http://www.instat.com/abstract.asp?id=68&SKU=IN0603187SI

Xilinx, I. (2009c). *UG200: Embedded Processor Block in Virtex-5 FPGAs.* Retrieved October 20, 2009, from Xilinx.com http://www.xilinx.com/

Xilinx. (2004). Retrieved from Xilinx FPGA embedded solutions http://www.xilinx.com/prs_rls/ip/0492_cmpembedded.htm

Xilinx, Inc. (2008a). *UG081: MicroBlaze Processor Reference Guide.* Retrieved October 20, 2009, from Xilinx.com: http://www.xilinx.com/

Xilinx, Inc. (2008b). *UG208: Early Access Partial Reconfiguration.* Retrieved October 20, 2009, from Xilinx.com: http://www.xilinx.com/

Xilinx, Inc. (2009a). *UG360: Virtex-6 FPGA Configuration User Guide.* Retrieved October 20, 2009, from Xilinx.com: http://www.xilinx.com/

Xilinx, Inc. (2009b). *UG364: Virtex-6 FPGA Configurable Logic Block User Guide.* Retrieved October 20, 2009, from Xilinx.com: http://www.xilinx.com/

Xilinx, Inc. (2010, April 12). *DS150: Virtex-6 Family Overview.* Récupéré sur http://www.xilinx.com

Yen, T.-Y., & Wolf, W. (1995). Communication synthesis for distributed embedded systems. In *Proceedings of the International Conference on Computer-Aided Design*, (pp. 288-294).

Zhang, W., Calder, B., & Tullsen, D. (2005). An event-driven multithreaded dynamic optimization framework. In *Proceedings of Int. Conf. on Parallel Architectures and Compilation Techniques PACT*, (pp. 87-98).

Zivkovic, V., Van der Wolf, P., Deprettere, E., & De Kock, E.-A. (Oct. 2002). Design space exploration of streaming multiprocessor architectures. In *Proceedings of the IEEE Workshop on Signal Processing Systems*, (pp. 228-234).

Chapter 7

Reconfiguration of Uniprocessor Sporadic Real–Time Systems:
The Sensitivity Approach

Laurent George
University of Paris-Est – Val de Marne, France

Pierre Courbin
LACSC – ECE Paris, France

ABSTRACT

In this chapter the authors focus on the problem of reconfiguring embedded real-time systems. Such reconfiguration can be decided either off-line to determine if a given application can be run on a different platform, while preserving the timeliness constraints imposed by the application, or on-line, where a reconfiguration should be done to adapt the system to the context of execution or to handle hardware or software faults. The task model considered in this chapter is the classical sporadic task model defined by a Worst Case Execution Time (WCET), a minimum inter-arrival time (also denoted the minimum Period) and a late termination deadline. The authors consider two preemptive scheduling strategies: Fixed Priority highest priority first (FP) and Earliest Deadline First (EDF). They propose a sensitivity analysis to handle reconfiguration issues. Sensitivity analysis aims at determining acceptable deviations from the specifications of a problem due to evolutions in system characteristics (reconfiguration or performance tuning). They present a state of the art for sensitivity analysis in the case of WCETs, Periods and Deadlines reconfigurations and study to what extent sensitivity analysis can be used to decide on the possibility of reconfiguring a system.

1. INTRODUCTION

Real-time scheduling has been extensively studied over the last forty years. Feasibility Conditions (FCs) for the dimensioning of a real-time system enable a designer to ensure that timeliness constraints associated to an application run by the system are always met for all possible configurations. The goal of FCs is thus to ensure a deterministic respect of the timeliness constraints.

DOI: 10.4018/978-1-60960-086-0.ch007

Classical feasibility conditions do not consider possible deviations resulting from the reconfiguration of real-time systems. A reconfiguration can be decided either off-line or on-line. In the first case, the goal is to check whether several hardware platforms or several hardware configurations can be used to run a specific application while preserving the timeliness constraints of the tasks. In the second case, a reconfiguration might result from a system mode change to adapt the system to the context of its execution or to handle hardware or software faults.

It could be interesting to study the validity of FCs in the case of such reconfigurations. Sensitivity analysis aims at studying the ability to introduce greater flexibility in the specifications. In this paper, we study only one-dimension sensitivity analysis (one task parameter can evolve, the other task parameters are assumed to be constant).

Definition 1: The classical methodology to solve a real-time scheduling problem in the dimensioning phase (more formally described in LeLann (1996)) is as follows:

- (a) Identify the class of scheduling problem to solve, defined by the task model, the timeliness constraints and the scheduling models.
- (b) Identify for this class the possible scenarios of task activation request times.
- (c) Identify from those possible scenarios the subset of scenarios leading to the worst case conditions for the respect of the timeliness constraints.
- (d) Express for this subset the associated Feasibility Conditions (task parameters are used as variables).
- (e) Check that the FCs are met on a targeted architecture (the values of the task parameters are only used at this phase).

This methodology is valid for a given architecture. Sensitivity analysis aims at providing more robust feasibility conditions, valid for a set

of hardware platforms or able to tolerate on-line deviations in the specifications of a problem.

In this paper, we consider a preemptive uniprocessor scheduling. We focus on two scheduling policies: Fixed Priority highest priority first (FP) scheduling and Earliest Deadline First scheduling (EDF). The task model is the classical sporadic task model. A sporadic task set $\tau=\{\tau_1,\ldots,\tau_n\}$ is composed of n sporadic tasks, where a sporadic task τ_i is defined by:

- C_i: its worst-case execution time (WCET) on a given architecture.
- T_i: its minimum inter-arrival time (also called the minimum period).
- D_i: its relative deadline (any job of task τ_i with a request time t_i must be executed by its absolute deadline $t_i + D_i$).

We therefore consider timeliness constraints expressed as late deadlines on the worst case response time of a task, defined as the maximum possible time between the request time of a task and its termination time.

In classical FCs, the task parameters are assumed to be constant for all tasks instances at run time. In the following we discuss the problems that may occur in real systems.

- The WCET depends on the underlying architecture and on the conditions of execution (e.g.: type of memory or cache, frequency of the processor) leading to WCET that depend on the conditions of execution.
- Considering constant task parameters might not be suitable for every application and should be adapted to the situations at run time (e.g. a process should be run more frequently in a given situation to obtain more precision). This has therefore an impact on the periods of the tasks chosen at run time.
- Furthermore, new architectures propose variable speed processors to scale the per-

formances to the required performances, in order to reduce energy consumption when possible. Reducing the frequency of a processor leads to reducing the speed of the processor and to increase the WCETs of the tasks. It would be interesting to determine the effect of a change in the architectures characteristics. Should all the FCs computed for a given architecture in phase (e) of definition1 be recomputed? Can we extend the FCs obtained on a given architecture to another one obtained after a reconfiguration?

- FC enables us to ensure timeliness constraints are respected but another important parameter for control tasks and multimedia applications is the output jitter that results from the execution of a task. For example, if the scheduling algorithm chosen for the system assigns the task priority according to the deadlines of the task (e.g. Deadline Monotonic for fixed priority scheduling and Earliest Deadline First), then reducing the deadline of a task will reduce its worst case response time accordingly and thus reduce its output jitter. Adapting the deadlines of the tasks could result from a reconfiguration, to ensure the control loop stability of a control task.

It might therefore be interesting to study the temporal robustness of a real-time system in the case of a reconfiguration where the reconfiguration results in a change in the value of the task's parameters: WCET, deadline and period. This analysis can be achieved:

- At design time with an off-line approach. The reconfiguration of a system can be handled with a sensitivity analysis. The sensitivity analysis aims at defining the acceptable variations in the task configurations (WCETs, periods or deadlines) such that the scheduling problem is still feasible

(in phase (d) of definition 1). The first solution proposed by Bini & al. (2006) determines the maximum possible scaling factor to expand or reduce the tasks parameters such that the resulting task set is schedulable. The correction can either be applied to one task or to the entire task set. A similar approach tries to determine the maximum acceptable deviation on a task parameter and has been formally defined by George & al. (2007) as the allowance on the task parameter. An extension of this approach has been proposed in Bini, & al. (2006) with the notion of feasibility region characterization. The problem is then to find the equations characterizing a feasibility region. We identify, according to task parameters, the space of feasible WCETs, Periods and Deadlines denoted in the paper respectively the C-space, T-space and D-space. For any task set configuration in the feasibility region, the task set can be scheduled to meet all the deadlines of the tasks.

- On-line, if a reconfiguration of the system is required (e.g. a processor speed change), possibly leading to execution overruns faults, overload situations and deadline misses. Automatic reconfiguration algorithms should be implemented to deal with such situations, to stabilize the system and ensure its robustness.

Focusing on the problem of WCET reconfiguration, we observe that the current trend in real-time systems is to propose a temporal protection service to handle WCET overruns. If a WCET overrun occurs, an interrupt is raised and a service is called to handle the problem. The scaling factor or the C-space characterization could be used to determine on-line if the WCET reconfiguration is acceptable or if a correction should be undertaken (stop task or put it in background for example).

In this paper we study the different approaches for reconfiguring real-time systems while preserving the timeliness contraints of the tasks run by the system. We recall classical concepts and results for Fixed Priority scheduling and Earliest Deadline First in section 2. We then focus on the state of the art of sensitivity analysis in section 3. We consider the sensitivity of WCETs, periods and deadlines in the case of an off-line reconfiguration. We then focus on the state of the art of existing solutions for the reconfiguration of real-time systems at run time in section 4. Section 5 proposes future directions for this work. Finally, we give some conclusions in section 6.

2. CONCEPT AND NOTATIONS

We recall classical results in the uniprocessor context for real-time scheduling.

- A sporadic task τ_i (C_i, T_i, D_i) is an infinite collection of jobs having their request times constrained by a minimum inter-arrival time T_i, a WCET C_i and a relative deadline D_i.
- A real-time scheduling problem is said feasible if there is a least one scheduling policy able to meet the deadlines of all the tasks.
- A task set is said to be schedulable with a given scheduling policy if and only if no job of this task set ever misses its absolute deadline.
- A task is said to be valid with a given scheduling policy if and only if no job of this task ever misses its absolute deadline.
- A task is said to be non-concrete if its request time is not known in advance. In this paper, we only consider non-concrete request times, since the activation request times are supposed to be unpredictable (the request times of two successive jobs of a task are only constrained by a minimum-inter-arrival time)
- An idle time t is defined on a processor as a time such that there are no task released before time t pending at time t. An interval of successive idle times is called an idle period.
- A busy period is defined as a time interval $[a, b)$ such that there is no idle time in $[a, b)$ (the processor is fully busy) and such that both a and b are idle times.
- Given a non-concrete task set, the synchronous scenario corresponds to the scenario where all the tasks are first released at the same time.
- We consider a preemptive event driven scheduling. With an event driven scheduling, the scheduler is called at task activation or completion times. Examples of operating systems providing event driven scheduling are: in the industry: OSEK (Bimbard, F. & George, L. (2006)) for automotive applications and RTLinux (FSMLabs Corp., TimeSys Corp.), in open-source systems: TinyOS, RTAI and Xenomai.
- EDF is the preemptive version of Earliest Deadline First scheduling. EDF schedules tasks according to their absolute deadlines: the task with the shortest absolute deadline has the highest priority. Ties are broken arbitrarily.
- FP is a preemptive Fixed-Priority scheduling according to an arbitrary priority assignment.
- For FP:
  - $hp(i)$ denotes the subset of tasks with a fixed priority higher than or equal to that of τ_i except τ_i.
  - $lp(i)$ denotes the set of task having a lower priority than τ_i.
  - *Alevel*$_i$ busy period (see Lehoczky, J. (1990)) is a period of time during

which a processor is running only tasks in $\tau_i \cup hp(i)$. .

- $U = \sum_{i=1}^{n} \frac{C_i}{T_i}$ is the processor utilization factor, i.e., the fraction of processor time spent in the execution of the task set (Lui & al. 1973). If $U > 1$, then no scheduling algorithm can meet the task deadlines. $U \leq 1$ is a necessary condition for the feasibility of a scheduling problem.

- $W(t) = \sum_{i=1}^{n} \left\lceil \frac{t}{T_i} \right\rceil C_i$ is the workload demand resulting from the requests of all the tasks in the time interval *[0,t)*, in the synchronous scenario, where $\lceil x \rceil$ returns the nearest integer higher than or equal to *x*.

- $W_i(t) = C_i + \sum_{\tau_j \in hp(i)} \left\lceil \frac{t}{T_j} \right\rceil C_j$ is the workload demand resulting from the request of one task τ_i and of all the tasks in *hp(i)* in the time interval [0,t), in the synchronous scenario.

- The processor demand *h(t)* is the amount of processing time requested by all tasks, whose release times and absolute deadlines are in time interval *[0,t]* in the synchronous scenario (Baruah & al. (1990)). For a given task set τ, we have: $h(t) = \sum_{i=1}^{n} \max(0, 1 + \left\lfloor \frac{t - D_i}{T_i} \right\rfloor) C_i$, where $\lfloor x \rfloor$ returns the integer part of *x*.

- *P* is the least common multiple of the task periods i.e. $P = LCM(T_1, ..., T_n)$.

For Fixed-Priority (FP) scheduling, necessary and sufficient FCs have been proposed, based on the computation of the task worst-case response times (Joseph & al. (1986), Tindell & al. (1995)). The worst-case response time is obtained in the worst-case synchronous scenario and is computed by successive iterations for all task activations

of τ_i in its *level$_i$* (see Lehoczky, J. (1990)). A task set is then declared schedulable if the worst-case response time of any task requested in the synchronous scenario is less than or equal to its deadline.

In the case of deadlines less than or equal to periods for all tasks, the worst-case response time r_i of a task τ_i is obtained in the synchronous scenario for the first release of τ_i at time *0* and is the solution of the equation (Joseph & al. (1986)) $r_i = W_i(r_i)$. r_i can be computed by the recursive equation $r_i^{m+1} = W_i(r_i^m)$, with $r_i^0 = C_i$. The number of iterations is bounded by $1 + \sum_{\tau_j \in hp(i)} \left\lfloor \frac{D_i}{T_j} \right\rfloor$, the number of tasks requests in *hp(i)*, in the time interval *[0,D_i]*.

A necessary and sufficient FC for the a schedulable task set τ is then $\forall i \in [1, n], r_i \leq D_i$.

This FC, yet easy to use, is not the most appropriate feasibility condition for sensitivity analysis as it is recursive. Lehoczky & al. (1989) proposed a test in the case of deadlines equal to periods. This test was extended in Bini & al. (2005), in the case of deadlines less than or equal to periods as follows:

Theorem 1: Lehoczky & al. (1989) and Bini & al. (2005)

Given a task set $\tau = \{\tau_1, ..., \tau_n\}$, a task τ_i is valid if and only if $X_i = \min_{t \in S_i} \frac{W_i(t)}{t} \leq 1$ where

$$S_i = \left\{ kT_j, \tau_j \in hp(i), k = 1, ..., \left\lfloor \frac{D_i}{T_j} \right\rfloor \right\}$$

The task set is schedulable if: $\max_{i=1...n} X_i \leq 1$.

This test is interesting as it is non recursive but the number of times to consider even in the case of deadlines less than or equal to periods can potentially be high.

In the case of FP scheduling, the feasibility condition of theorem 1 has been significantly improved in Manabe et al. (1998). We describe in theorem 2 the same result, given with the formalism of Bini & al. (2004). For any task τ_i, it is possible to reduce the times to check to specific times in the time interval $[0, D_i]$, instead of

$$1 + \sum_{\tau_j \in hp(i)} \left\lceil \frac{D_i}{T_j} \right\rceil \text{ times, leading to at most } 2^{i-1} \text{ times}$$

for a task τ_i.

For a task τ_i, the times to consider are obtained from the recursive equation

$$P_i(t) = P_{i-1}\left(\left\lceil \frac{t}{T_i} \right\rceil T_i \right) \cup P_{i-1}(t),$$

where $P_0(D_i) = D_i$.

Theorem 2: Bini & al. (2006)

Given a task set $\tau = \{\tau_1, ..., \tau_n\}$, a task τ_i is valid if and only if $X_i = \min_{t \in P_{i-1}(D_i)} \dfrac{W_i(t)}{t} \leq 1$, where

$$P_i(t) = P_{i-1}\left(\left\lceil \frac{t}{T_i} \right\rceil T_i \right) \cup P_{i-1}(t) \text{ and } P_0(D_i) = D_i$$

The task set is schedulable if: $\max_{i=1...n} X_i \leq 1$.

When deadlines and periods are independent, Tindell & al. in (Tindell & al. (2005)) show that the worst-case response time of a periodic task τ_i is not necessarily obtained for the first activation request of τ_i at time 0. The number of activations

to consider is $1 + \left\lceil \dfrac{L_i}{T_i} \right\rceil$, where L_i is the length of the worst-case level$_i$ busy period defined in Lehoczky J. (1990) as the longest period of processor activity running tasks of priority higher than or equal to τ_i in the synchronous scenario. It can

be shown that $L_i = \sum_{\tau_j \in hp(i) \cup \tau_i} \left\lceil \dfrac{L_i}{T_j} \right\rceil C_j$. From its

definition, L_i is bounded by (see George & al. (1996)):

$$Min\left(\frac{C_j}{1 - \sum_{\tau_j \in hp(i) \cup \tau_i} \frac{C_j}{T_j}}, \sum_{\tau_j \in hp(i) \cup \tau_i} \frac{C_j}{T_j} \cdot P \right)$$

which leads to a pseudo-polynomial time complexity. It seems difficult from this test to propose a sensitivity analysis with an acceptable complexity.

For EDF scheduling, in Baruah & al. (1990), the authors show that a necessary and sufficient feasibility condition, valid for any configuration of periods and deadlines is

$$\forall t \in \bigcup_{i=1...n} \left\{ kT_i + D_i, k \in \mathbb{N} \right\} \cap [0, L), h(t) \leq t,$$

where L is the length of the first busy period in the synchronous scenario, solution of $L = W(L)$ when $U \leq 1$.

In the special case where $\forall \tau_i \in \tau, D_i = T_i, U \leq 1$ becomes a necessary and sufficient feasibility condition (see Baruah & al. (1990)).

3. SENSITIVITY ANALYSIS

Sensitivity analysis can be been as a solution to handle evolutions in the task parameters due to hardware or software reconfigurations. We recall existing sensitivity analysis results when considering WCETs, Periods and Deadlines changes, according to two approaches:

* Based on the allowance (the maximum acceptable deviation of a task parameter) or based on the maximum scaling factor computation on WCETs, periods or deadlines.
* Based on the characterization of the n dimensions X-space domain (X=C,T or D). Denoting respectively the space of feasible WCETs, Periods or Deadlines. The concept of feasibility domain, introduced in

Bini & al. (2004), is such that for any vector $\{X_1, ..., X_n\}$ in the X-space domain, the task set is schedulable.

3.1 Reconfiguration of the WCETs

3.1.1 Scaling Factor on WCETs for FP and EDF

Allowance and Scaling Factor of WCETs for FP Scheduling

In the case of deadlines equal to periods, Lehocsky & al. (1989) introduce the critical scaling factor α on the WCETs, computed for a fixed priority scheduling such that the WCET of a task τ_i is αC_i. This approach was extended in Vestal & al. (1994), where the authors show how to introduce slack variables in the response times of the tasks. They propose the concept of scaling factor applied to one task and to all the tasks.

In the case of deadlines less than or equal to periods Bougueroua & al. (2006) propose to compute the allowance on the WCETs of the tasks defined as the maximum extra duration that can be granted to a set of at most $k \leq n$ faulty tasks having an execution overrun, on a sliding window $W = \underset{i=1...n}{Min}(T_i)$, still meeting all the deadlines of the tasks. The allowance $A_{i,k}$ for a task τ_i assuming k faulty tasks is equal to the maximum extra duration that can be given to a faulty task without compromising the deadlines of the tasks. The $k-1$ tasks competing against a faulty task τ_i must be chosen to minimize the allowance given to τ_i. The allowance $A_{i,k}$ is the minimum solution of Equations (1) (2) and (3), where Equations (1) and (2) are respectively the worst case response times of τ_i (respectively of tasks in $lp(i)$) when the allowance $A_{i,k}$ is given to task τ_i and to other $k-1$ tasks minimizing the allowance $A_{i,k}$. Equation (3) is the processor utilization factor assuming that k faulty tasks (including task τ_i) use the allowance $A_{i,k}$.

$$r_i = C_i + A_{i,k} + \sum_{\tau_j \in hp(i)} \left\lceil \frac{r_i}{T_j} \right\rceil C_j + \sum_{\tau_j \in MinP(i,k)} \left\lceil \frac{r_i}{T_j} \right\rceil A_{i,k} \leq D_i \tag{1}$$

$$\forall \tau_j \in lp(i), r_j = C_j + \sum_{\tau_m \in hp(j)} \left\lceil \frac{r_i}{T_m} \right\rceil C_m + \sum_{\tau_m \in Max(i,k) \cup \tau_i} \left\lceil \frac{r_j}{T_m} \right\rceil A_{i,k} \leq D_j \tag{2}$$

$$\forall \tau_i \in [1, n], \tag{3}$$

Where $MinP(i,k)$ is the set of at most $k-1$ tasks in $hp(i)$ having the smallest periods.

A detailed analysis can be found in Bougueroua & al. (2007) where the authors consider different allowance repartition strategies according to an importance weight given to the tasks.

In the case of deadlines less than or equal to periods, Bini &al. (2006) show how to compute the maximum value of λ, where for any task τ_i, the WCET becomes $C_i + \lambda C_i$, such that increasing the WCETs of any task leads to a non schedulable task set. The complexity of the computation of λ is reduced due to the reduction of the number of times in the feasibility condition of FP, obtained from theorem 2. They show that:

$$\lambda = Min \underset{t \in P_{i-1}(D_i)}{Max} \left(\frac{t}{W_i(t)} - 1 \right) \text{ where } P_{i-1}(D_i) \text{ is}$$

defined in theorem 2.

Notice that the maximum scaling factor α is equal to $\lambda + 1$.

If $\lambda < 0$ then the initial task task set was not schedulable and the WCET of any task τ_i must be decreased by λC_i.

In the case of independent deadlines and periods, α can be computed by iterations, but the computation becomes more and more costly. Indeed, when α increases, the length of the level$_i$ busy period tends towards P as the load utilization tends towards 1. In that case, increasing the task WCETs requires to recompute the lengths of the level$_i$ busy periods which tend towards P, of potentially exponential length.

Allowance and Scaling Factor of WCETs with EDF

Balbastre & al. (2002) show how much a task can increase its computation time still meeting the system feasibility when tasks are scheduled EDF. They consider the case of only one task increasing its WCET. With EDF, a necessary and sufficient feasibility condition (see section 2) is: $\forall t \in [0, L), h(t) \leq t$. As for FP in the general case, increasing the duration of the WCET of a task increases U and L tends towards P when U tends toward 1. To find the maximum allowance that can be granted to a single task, we therefore have to consider the time interval $[0,P)$ for the computation of the maximum slack. The minimum allowance that can be granted for a single task τ_i is:

$$\underset{D_i \leq t < P}{Min} \frac{t - h(t)}{\left\lceil \dfrac{t + T_i - D_i}{T_i} \right\rceil}.$$

They introduce in Balbastre & al. (2002) the concept of Optional Computation Window (OCW) such that for any task τ_i, at most n_i activations of τ_i in a window N_i activations can request an extra duration. They show how to compute the extra duration that can be given to task τ_i when considering a window constrained execution time system. Only one task in τ follows an OCW.

In Bougueroua & al. (2007), the authors show how to compute the extra duration, denoted allowance, that can be given to faulty periodic tasks having WCET overruns. The allowance is computed in order to preserve the deadlines of all the tasks. They consider at most k faulty tasks (exceeding their WCET) over a sliding window $W = \underset{i=1...n}{\min}(T_i)$. They want to support either transient or permanent faults due to WCETs overruns. The allowance $A_{i,k}$ for a faulty task τ_i, assuming a fair allowance distribution among k faulty tasks, is the minimum solution of the following Equa-

tions (4) and (5) where Equation (4) is the processor utilization factor condition and Equation (5) is the processor demand feasibility test updated to take into account k faulty tasks(including task τ_i) using the allowance $A_{i,k}$ (see Bougueroua & al. (2007)):

$$U^* = U + \sum_{\tau_j \in \tau_i \cup MinP(i,k)} \frac{A_{i,k}}{T_j} \leq 1 \qquad (4)$$

$$\forall t \in \left[D_i, U^* P \right), \qquad (5)$$

Where:

- $$f_{i,k}(t) = \left(1 + \left\lfloor \frac{t - D_i}{T_i} \right\rfloor\right) + X_{i,k}(t) \qquad \text{with}$$

$$X_{i,k}(t) = \sum_{\tau_j \in MinD(i,k)} \left(1 + \left\lfloor \frac{t - D_j}{T_j} \right\rfloor\right)$$

- $MinP(i,k)$ is the set of at most $k-1$ tasks τ_j except τ_i, having the smallest periods

- $MinD(i,k)$ is the set of at most k-1 tasks τ_j except τ_i maximizing $\left(1 + \left\lfloor \frac{t - D_j}{T_j} \right\rfloor\right)$, with $t \geq D_j$.

Finally, in Hermant & al. (2007), the authors show how to compute the optimal scaling factor α that can be applied to the WCETs in the case of preemptive EDF for periodic or sporadic tasks. They show that:

$$\alpha = \frac{1}{Max\left(U, \underset{t \in [D_{min}, P)}{Sup} \dfrac{h(t)}{t}\right)}$$

where D_{min} is the minimum deadline and P the Least Common Multiple (LCM) of the periods.

If $\alpha<1$ then the task set is not schedulable with EDF and multiplying the WCET by α will reduce the WCETs to the maximum feasible WCETs. If

$\alpha \geq 1$ then the task set is schedulable with EDF and the WCETs can still be increased by at most a factor α still meeting the deadlines of the tasks.

Example of application of the scaling factor:

Consider the case of a plateforme reconfiguration in charge of running an application composed of three tasks τ_1, τ_2 and τ_3. We want to know if the reconfiguration is possible on the given new platform and what is the minimum processing power increase (or decrease) compared to new platform, to run the task set and meet the deadlines of all the tasks.

Assume that the task set has the following parameters when run on the new plateform:

- τ_1 (C_1=40, T_1=70, D_1=50)
- τ_2 (C_2=60, T_2=110, D_2=70)
- τ_3 (C_3=100, T_3=130, D_3=100)

We have for this task set: $U=C_1/T_1+C_2/T_2+C_3/T_3=1.89>1$. The task set is clearly not schedulable on the new platform. On this platform, we have

$$\alpha = \frac{1}{Max(U, \underset{i \in [D_{min}, P)}{Sup} \frac{h(t)}{t})} = \frac{1}{2}.$$ Hence, the pro-

cessing power of the platform should be 2 times the processing power of the new platform to obtain a schedulable task set. With such a platform, the WCETs of the tasks would be divided by 2.

3.1.2 C-space for FP and EDF

C-space Characterization for FP Scheduling

The improvement obtained in theorem 2 in the number of times to consider for the FC of FP scheduling can be used to characterize the C-space domain for a reasonable number of tasks. Any vector $C=\{C_1, ..., C_n\}$ of WCETs in the C-space corresponds to a schedulable task set. The C-space region is then defined in theorem 3 as follows:

Theorem 3: Bini & al. (2004) Let $\tau = \{\tau_1, ..., \tau_n\}$ be a set of periodic tasks indexed by decreasing priorities. The C-space region when

$\forall i \in [1, n], D_i \leq T_i$, is defined as the region such that $\forall C = \{C_1, ..., C_n\} \in R^{+n}$:

$\forall i = 1 ... n, \exists t \in \mathrm{P}_{i-1}(D_i)$ such that $W_i(t) \leq t$

where $\mathrm{P}_i(t)$ is defined from the recursive equation

$$\mathrm{P}_i(t) = \mathrm{P}_{i-1}(\left\lceil \frac{t}{T_i} \right\rceil T_i) \cup \mathrm{P}_{i-1}(t),$$

where $\mathrm{P}_0(D_i) = D_i$.

The C-space region is then defined by a set of at most $Card\left\{\bigcup_{i=1}^{n} \mathrm{P}_{i-1}(D_i)\right\}$ inequalities.

Notice that for a task t_i, times in $P_{i-1}(D_i)$ are in disjunction (at least one must be met). The sets $P_{i-1}(D_i)$ are in conjunction. We propose in this section an example of C-space characterization for FP and EDF scheduling.

The Space of Feasible WCETs with EDF

The space of feasible WCETs (C-space) has been characterized in George & al. (2009).

The following theorem 4 gives another formulation of the FC of EDF based on the processor demand function. This formulation helps characterizing the C-space:

Theorem 4: George & al. (2009)

A sporadic task set τ is schedulable with EDF if and only if:

$$Sup_{t \in R^+}\left(\frac{h(t)}{t}\right) = Max\left(U, Sup_{t \in M}\left(\frac{h(t)}{t}\right)\right) \leq 1$$

with

$$M = \bigcup_{j=1}^{n}\left\{D_j + k_j T_j, 0 \leq k_j \leq \left\lceil \frac{P - D_j}{T_j} \right\rceil - 1\right\}$$

The set M is composed of all the absolute deadlines of the tasks released in the synchonous scenario, in the time interval $[D_{min}, P]$. From theorem 4, they obtain a set of inequalities in disjunction characterizing the C-space. The number of inequalities can be significant (exponential in the worst case).

They propose a linear programming approach to reduce when possible the number of times in M thus reducing the number of inequalities characterizing the C-space. They show that the C-space is convex. It is thus possible to reduce the number of inequalities by applying the simplex algorithm on the identified linear programming problem.

The problem of defining if a time t_i in M is significant for the C-Space is characterized by the following linear programming problem for any time t_i in M:

Linear Programming problem LP1
For any time t_i in M
With WCETs as variables
Maximize the objective function h(ti)
With the Card(M)-1 constraints:

$$\bigcup_{t_j \in M, t_j \neq t_i} h(t_j) \leq t_j$$

Finding the maximum value of h(t_i) is done with the simplex. The simplex will find, considering all the possible configurations of WCETs, the one that maximizes the goal function h(t_i).

If the goal function $h(t)$ is such that $h(t) \leq t_i$ then t_i can be removed from the set M (the constraint is always met for any WCET satisfying the Card(M)-1 inequalities.

We now study the performance of the simplex for reduction of times in *M,* in the case of constrained deadlines ($\forall i, D_i \leq T_i$) with an exhaustive example considering more than 3500 constraints in the set M. The number of constraints in M depends more on the value of the periods than on the number of tasks (the number of constraints can be small even for a high number of tasks).

In order to evaluate the impact of the simplex, applied to solve LP1, on the reduction of times

in M, we produce one hundred systems of three tasks. For each system, we proceed as follows:

- The period of each task is uniformly chosen from [1,100]
- The deadline of any task τ_i is $D_i = \alpha T_i$ with $\alpha \in]0,1]$. α is discretized in the time intervals [0, 0.8] and [0.8, 1] with a granularity of respectively 0.1 and 0.025.

We focus on the influence of the ratio α on the number of remaining time t_i after the execution of the simplex on the linear programming problem LP1.

Figure 1 shows the results of our analysis. The number of time in M is represented by the solid line and associated to the left axis. The dotted line refers to the number of times obtained after the simplex applied to the linear programming problem LP1 and must be read according to the right axis.

We notice that the number of instant which curb the C-Space inch-up in [0.1, 0.6] then soar when α tends toward 1. If $\alpha=1$, we are in the special case of implicit deadlines where the only one constraint is the global utilization: $U \leq 1$.

In all the cases we have found that the number of constraints obtained before and after the simplex is respectively higher than 3570 and less than 12. This reduction of times is valid in our example for any processor load less than or equal to 1. This confirms that the C-space characterization could be considered on-line for determining if a WCET reconfiguration is possible.

A Comparison Example of C-space Obtained with FP vs EDF

In this section, we consider a sporadic task set $\tau = \{\tau_1, \tau_2, \tau_3\}$, composed of three sporadic tasks, where for any task τ_i, T_i and D_i are fixed, and $C_i \in R^+$ the WCET of task τ_i, is a parameter.

- τ_1: $(C_1, T_1, D_1) = (C_1, 7, 5)$;

Figure 1. Times in M before and after applying the simplex to LP1 according to α

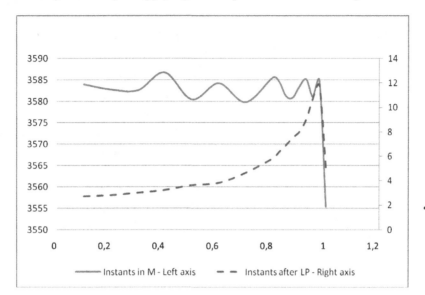

- τ_2: $(C_2, T_2, D_2) = (C_2, 11, 7)$;
- τ_3: $(C_3, T_3, D_3) = (C_3, 13, 10)$.

We have in this example $\forall i \in D_i \leq T_i$. In this context, an optimal algorithm exists, called Deadline Monotonic (DM) (see Leung & al. (1980)). With DM, the task having the smallest relative deadline has the highest priority. The optimality of DM is in the sense that if a feasible FP scheduling exists then DM will find one. Applying theorem 3, we obtain for DM scheduling the following times to consider:

- For τ_1, $P_0(D_1) = \{5\}$
- For τ_2, $P_1(D_2) = \{7\}$
- For τ_3, $P_2(D_3) = \{7,10\}$

Leading to the following set of inequalities characterizing the C-Space for DM:

- $C_1 \leq 5$

And

- $C_2 \leq 7$

And

- $C_1 + C_2 + C_3 \leq 7$ Or $2C_1 + C_2 + C_3 \leq 10$

And

- $C_1/7 + C_2/11 + C_3/13 \leq 1$ (processor utilization condition)

Considering EDF scheduling, we have: $D_{min} = 5$ and $P = 1001$. From Theorem 4, we have to consider the set M of times (absolute deadlines) for the computation of $h(t)/t$ in the time interval $[5, 1001)$, where M is given by: $M = \{5 + 7k_1, k_1 \in [0, 142]\} \cup \{7 + 11k_1, k_1 \in [0, 90]\} \cup \{10 + 13k_1, k_1 \in [0, 76]\}$, leading to 281 constraints. Applying the simplex on the linear programming problem LP1, we are able to reduce the set M to the set of only 5 times: $\{5, 7, 10, 12, 40\}$ (see George & al. (2009)).

The C-space for EDF is thus defined by the following set of inequalities $h(t_i) \leq t_i$ for $t_i \in \{5, 7, 10, 12, 40\}$ in conjunction:

- $C_1 \leq 5$

And

- $C_{1+}C_2 \leq 7$

And

- $C_{1+}C_2 + C_3 \leq 10$

And

- $2C_{1+}C_2 + C_3 \leq 12$

And

- $6C_{1+}4C_2 + 3C_3 \leq 40$

And

- $C_1/7 + C_2/11 + C_3/13 \leq 1$ (processor utilization condition)

In both cases, the C-space obtained with FP or EDF is composed of few inequalities.

In the case of a reconfiguration (e.g. processor frequency change) that would result in change of the WCETs of the tasks, it could be possible to use the C-space equations on line to decide whether the reconfiguration is possible or not.

3.2 Reconfiguration of Periods

Sensitivity analysis of periods is certainly more complex than sensitivity of WCETs and deadlines. We only present in this section results concerning FP scheduling. Concerning the sensitivity of the periods, as far as the author is aware, no result exists for EDF. Contrary to the case of WCETs and deadlines sensitivity analysis, no linear inequalities computed in a closed form can be obtained. The T-space (of f-space, f=1/T) domain has been studied in Bini, E. & Di Natale, M. (2006). They show that the T-space is composed of an infinite number of hyperplanes. Hence, computing the

sensitivity along a generic direction in the T-space domain is still an open problem.

In Bini, E. & Di Natale, M. (2005) and in Bini, E. & Di Natale, M. (2006), Bini & al. show how to determine for a task τ_i the minimum task period $T_i^{\min}$ such that any period smaller than $T_i^{\min}$ leads to a non schedulable task set.

The idea behind the solution lies from the following theorem 5 and is based on the worst case response time r_i of any task τ_i.

Theorem 5: (Bini, E. & Di Natale, M. (2005), Bini, E. & Di Natale, M. (2006))

Let $T_i^{\min}$ be the minimum feasible period such that task τ_i is valid. Then we have either:

(i) $T_i^{\min} = \dfrac{r_i}{\delta_i}$, where $\delta_i = \dfrac{D_i}{T_i} > 0$ or

(ii) there exists a lower priority task $\tau_j \in lp(i)$ such that the worst case response time r_j of τ_j is an integer multiple of $T_i^{\min}$.

The first condition comes from the necessary condition $r_i \leq D_i = \delta_i T_i$, the second condition tries to maximize the impact of τ_i by maximizing the number of possible activations of τ_i before the completion of a lower priority task τ_j. This number must be computed by iterations starting from $n_j^i = 1$ to $n_j^i = N_j^i$ interferences of τ_i such that $N_j^i + 1$ interferences would lead to a non valid task τ_j.

For a lower priority task τ_j, the worst case response time $r_j(n_j^i)$ of τ_j taking into account n_j^i activations of τ_i is:

$$r_j(n_j^i) = C_j + n_j^i C_i + \sum_{\tau_k \in hp(j), k \neq i} \left\lceil \frac{r_j(n_j^i)}{T_k} \right\rceil C_k.$$

Finally, the minimum period of task τ_i can be computed as follows:

$$T_i^{\min} = Max(\frac{r_i}{\delta_i}, Max_{\tau_j \in lp(i)}(Min_{n_j^i = 1...N_j^i} \frac{r_j(n_j^i)}{n_j^i})).$$

Determination of the Maximum Scaling Factor

In Bini, E. & Di Natale, M. (2005), Bini & al. show an interesting property concerning the schedulability of a task set in the C-space and in the T-space. This result is given in theorem 6.

Theorem 6: (Bini, E. & Di Natale, M. (2005)):

Let τ^C be the task set where every WCETs is multiplied by a scaling factor α. Let τ^T be the task set where every Task period is divided by α. The task set τ^C is schedulable if and only if the task set τ^T is schedulable.

The maximum scaling factor on the periods can therefore be computed from the maximum scaling factor on the WCETs (see section 3.1).

3.3 Reconfiguration of Deadlines

3.3.1 Computing the Minimun Deadlines

Few results have been proposed to deal with the deadline assignement problem. As far as the author is aware, no results are available for FP scheduling. In Baruah, S., Buttazo, G., Gorinsky, S. & Lipari, G. (1999), the authors propose to modify the deadlines of a task set to minimise the output, seen as a secondary criteria. In Cervin, A., Lincoln, B., Eker, J., Arzen, K. & G., B. (2004), the deadline are modified to guarantee close-loop stability of a real-time control system. In Marinca & al. (2004), a focus is done on the deadline assignment problem in distributed multimedia systems. The deadline assignment problem is formalized in term of a linear programming problem. The scheduling considered on every node is non-preemptive EDF or FIFO with a jitter cancelation applied on every node. A performance evaluation of several deadline assignment schemes is proposed.

In Balvastre & al. (2006), the authors propose an optimal deadline assignment algorithm for periodic tasks scheduled with preemptive EDF in the case of deadline less than or equal to periods. The goal is to find the minimum deadline reduction factor preserving all the deadlines of the tasks.

They first focus on the case of a single task deadline reduction. Let $D_i^{\min}$ denote the minimum deadline of task τ_i such that any deadline smaller than $D_i^{\min}$ for task τ_i would lead to a non schedulable task set. The principle is to compute for every task activations of τ_i in *[0,L)* (synchronous scenario), the minimum deadline for the validity of τ_i. The maximum number of activations of τ_i is

$$k_i = \left\lceil \frac{L}{T_i} \right\rceil.$$

$s_{i,j}$ (respectively $d_{i,j}$) denotes the jth activation request time (respectively absolute deadline) of τ_i at time *(j-1)T_i* (respectively *(j-1)T_i +D_i*). They show that $D_i^{\min}$ can be computed as follows with theorem 7:

Theorem 7: (Balvastre & al. (2006)):

Let τ be a schedulable task set of *n* periodic tasks. Let τ' be the modified task set such that task τ_i is assigned a deadline

$$D_i^{\min} = Max_{j=1...k_i}(d_{i,j}' - s_{i,j}),$$

where $d_{i,j}' = h(t_1) + C_i$ and t_1 is the smallest value if any such that $s_{i,j}+C_i \leq t_1 \leq d_{i,j}$ and $h(t_l)>t_l-C_i$ and $d_{i,j}' = C_i$ else. If τ is schedulable then τ' is schedulable.

From theorem 7, the following algorithm for the computation of $D_i^{\min}$ is proposed from Balvastre & al. (2006): (see Figure 2)

Remark 1: (Balvastre & al. (2006)) When considering the reduction of a single task τ_i, $D_i^{\min}$ is the worst case response time of task τ_i.

The maximum deadline reduction factor α_i for task τ_i is then: $\alpha_i = 1 - \dfrac{D_i^{\min}}{D_i}$.

Figure 2.

$$\begin{aligned}
&\tau = \{\tau_1, \ldots, \tau_n\} : \textbf{task set;}\\
&\text{L} \leftarrow \text{compute-L}(\tau) : \textbf{integer;}\\
&D_i^{min} \leftarrow C_i : \textbf{integer; deadline : integer;}\\
&k_i \leftarrow \left\lceil \frac{L}{T_i} \right\rceil : \textbf{integer;}\\
&\textbf{For } (p = 0; p < k_i; p++) \textbf{ do}\\
&\quad\Big| \quad t \leftarrow pT_i + D_i;\\
&\quad\Big| \quad deadline = C_i;\\
&\quad\Big| \quad \textbf{While } (t > pT_i + C_i) \textbf{ do}\\
&\quad\Big| \quad\quad\Big| \quad \textbf{If } (t = (\lceil \frac{t}{T_j} \rceil - 1)T_j + D_j) \textbf{ then}\\
&\quad\Big| \quad\quad\Big| \quad\quad\Big| \quad slack = t - h(t);\\
&\quad\Big| \quad\quad\Big| \quad\quad\Big| \quad \textbf{If } (slack < C_i) \textbf{ then}\\
&\quad\Big| \quad\quad\Big| \quad\quad\Big| \quad\quad\Big| \quad deadline = h(t) + C_i - pT_i;\\
&\quad\Big| \quad\quad\Big| \quad\quad\Big| \quad\quad\Big| \quad \text{exit-while;}\\
&\quad\Big| \quad\quad\Big| \quad\quad\Big| \quad \textbf{end If}\\
&\quad\Big| \quad\quad\Big| \quad \textbf{end If}\\
&\quad\Big| \quad\quad\Big| \quad t \leftarrow t - 1;\\
&\quad\Big| \quad \textbf{done}\\
&\quad\Big| \quad D_i^{min} = max(D_i^{min}, deadline)\\
&\textbf{end For}
\end{aligned}$$

In the case of a deadline reduction applied to *n* tasks:

The goal is to minimize all task deadlines assuming the same reduction factor for all the tasks (no preference regarding which task requires the greatest deadline reduction). In Balvastre & al. (2006), the authors show how to compute the maximum deadline reduction factor α applied to all the deadlines using an iterative algorithm. The principle is to compute the minimum slack t-*h(t)* for any time *t* in *[0,L)*, to determine the deadline reduction factor applied to all the tasks. (See Figure 3)

Notice nevertheless that with this algorithm, the property of remark 1 is no more true.

3.3.2 The Space of Feasible Deadlines: D-Space

To the author's knowledge, no result is available in the state of the art for FP scheduling.

We focus in this subsection on the result proposed by Bini & al. (2007) for the characterization of the D-space with EDF scheduling.

Figure 3.

$$\begin{aligned}
&\tau = \{\tau_1, \ldots, \tau_n\} : \textbf{task set;}\\
&\text{L} \leftarrow \text{compute-L}(\tau) : \textbf{integer; } \alpha \leftarrow 1 : \textbf{real}\\
&slack = min_{t \in [0,L)}(t - h(t)) : \textbf{real;}\\
&\textbf{While } (slack \neq 0) \textbf{ do}\\
&\quad\Big| \quad \alpha = min_{i=1\ldots n}(1 - \frac{slack}{D_i});\\
&\quad\Big| \quad \textbf{For } (i = 1; i < n; i++) \textbf{ do}\\
&\quad\Big| \quad\quad\Big| \quad D_i = \alpha D_i;\\
&\quad\Big| \quad \textbf{end For}\\
&\quad\Big| \quad slack = min_{t \in [0,L)}(t - h(t));\\
&\textbf{done}\\
&\text{Return } \alpha;
\end{aligned}$$

Bini & al. (2007) propose a sufficient feasibility domain included in the D-space. They show that this domain is convex.

A characterization of the D-space is obtained from a dual expression starting from the necessary and sufficient condition proposed in Baruah & al. (1990): $\forall t \geq 0, h(t) \leq t$.

Starting from the expression

$$h(t) = \sum_{i=1}^{n} K_i(t, D_i)C_i,$$

where $K_i(t, D_i) = Max\left(0, 1 + \left\lfloor \frac{t - D_i}{T_i} \right\rfloor\right),$

they express the constraints on any integer $K_i(t, D_i)$, for any time *t*:

$K_i(t, D_i) = 0$ If $t < D_i$

$$\frac{t - D_i}{T_i} < K_i(t, D_i) \leq \frac{t - D_i}{T_i} + 1 \text{ Else.}$$

This dual expression enables us to express the set of constraints associated to the domain of deadlines:

$$\forall t \geq 0, \forall k_i \in K_i(t, D_i):$$

$D_i > t$ If $k_i = 0$

$t - k_i T_i < D_i \leq t - (k_i - 1) T_i$ Else.

Let $K(t,D) = \{K_1(t,D_1),\ldots,K_n(t,D_n)\}$ be a vector of integers. The set of deadlines satisfying the constraints associated to the domain of deadlines is denoted $domD(t,k)$ and $domD^c(t,k)$ its complementary.

The authors show in Bini & al. (2007) that a necessary and sufficient condition for the schedulability with EDF, for a vector of deadlines $D = \{D_1,\ldots,D_n\}$ (with $C = \{C_1,\ldots,C_n\}$ a vector a WCETs) is:

$\forall k \in \mathbb{N}^n, \forall t \in [0, kC), D \in domD^C(t,k)$

The space of feasible deadlines (D space) is then the intersection of the feasibility domains $domD^c(t,k)$, $\forall k \in \mathbb{N}^n$ and $\forall t \in [0, kC)$.

The D-space is then defined by:

$$\bigcap_{t \in [0,kC)} domD^c(t,k) \qquad (6)$$

An expression that can be complex to use.

Bini & al. (2007) thus propose a sufficient feasibility region included in the D-space, defined by the set of deadlines satisfying Equation (7), with $U_i = \dfrac{C_i}{T_i}$:

$$\sum_{i=1}^{n} U_i D_i \geq \sum_{i=1}^{n} C_i - D_{\min}\left(1 - \sum_{i=1}^{n} U_i\right) \qquad (7)$$

4. RECONFIGURATION ISSUES AT RUN TIME

We now focus on the different mechanisms that can be proposed handle task parameters changes, to handle a reconfiguration at run time. Different situation can be considered at run time.

What happens if a reconfiguration is needed that modifies the task parameters? Can we allow some flexibility in the system to deal with WCETs or periods changes? System reconfiguration might result in temporal faults if not correctly handled.

The value of the WCETs can be influenced by the occurrence of faults in the system. Since faults are unavoidable, fault tolerance is necessary. Generally speaking, a fault-tolerant system can be made up of redundant components so that the system delivers correct services (i.e. is safe) despite faults. Faults can be classified according to their duration: permanent or intermittent faults. With permanent faults, a fault once revealed will last forever; intermittent faults appear and disappear at hard to predict times. The duration of a fault is variable. It might be interesting to reconfigure the system in the case of a permanent execution overrun fault.

Among such systems, we can cite the AUTOSAR specification used for automotive applications (Hladik & al. (2007)) and the Real-Time Specification for Java (RTSJ) (Bollela & al. (2000) and Bougueroua & al. (2006)) which specify such services (even if no solution is currently provided in real systems).

Taking into account execution overruns at run time is a current trend in new operating systems proposed in the industry:

- In the automotive industry, the AUTOmotive Open System Architecture (AUTOSAR) consortium aims at defining open standardized software architecture to improve the portability of the code with the concept of Run-Time Environment (RTE), a communication infrastructure between the application and the underlying operating system providing applications a hardware independent communication. In this environment, the AUTOSAR OS describes task management, Interrupts management and scheduling policies. AUTOSAR OS proposes a timing protection mechanism in the case of WCETs violations. This service triggers a user defined function that is called when a WCET overrun occurs. In this function could be implemented a reconfiguration strategy used at run time, to ensure a safe system reconfiguration in the case of WCETs overruns (see (Hladik & al. (2007))

- In the context of java industrial applications, the Real-Time Specification for Java (RTSJ) (Bollela & al. (2000) and Bougueroua & al. (2006)) aims at defining safe and portable java real-time applications. The abstract class ReleaseParameters describes in its constructor an Asynchronous Event Handler raised in the case of execution overrun. This handler can be also used to handle system reconfiguration in the case of WCET overruns.

The use of scalable architectures: some systems propose variable speed processor able to run applications at different frequencies. Reducing the frequency of a processor will increase the WCETs but might result in system overloads and possibly deadline miss. It could be interesting to reconfigure the periods in the case of overloads to come back to a normal load condition.

In the case of energy constraints, a variable speed processor can be used to adapt the frequency to the real-time constraints of the application. The problem is that most architecture proposes discrete voltage levels. It is therefore not always possible to fully adapt the frequency.

In process control applications, it would be interesting to introduce more flexibility in the choice of the periods at run time. In some situations, a task should be more frequent (e.g. the sampling rate of an altimetric sensor is a function of the altitude: the lower altitude, the higher sampling frequency). This situation does not lead to system fault but reduce the benefits of the use of a variable processor.

4.1 Dealing with WCET Overruns after a Reconfiguration

We can observe that an execution overrun fault does not necessarily mean a deadlines miss. With enough free CPU resources, a system can self stabilize and still meet the deadlines of all the tasks. The problem is to determine how long the execution overrun can be allowed, leading to sensitivity analysis to compute slack time or allowance that can be given to a faulty task (see section 3.1).

Two types of faults captured by the execution-overrun error and the deadline-miss error can happen. In the first case, the execution duration of the task exceeds its estimated WCET while in the second case the task does not meet its deadline. Yet, among all possible execution overruns, only those leading to a deadline miss, if nothing is done to correct the system, should be considered.

Notice that the exact allowance of a task obtained on-line in an arbitrary task release pattern could be higher than the static allowance computed with a sensitivity analysis defined in section 3.1. The exact on-line allowance computation cost could nevertheless be high if the number of execution overrun becomes important. Indeed, the exact allowance evolves at tasks release and completion times and has a pseudo polynomial complexity for EDF and for FP. The results obtained from the state of the art therefore mainly focus on static allowance.

The problem is now to detect when execution overruns occur in the system:

- Some systems propose a CostOverrun handler attached to every task (e.g. the Sun RTS 1.0 system). This requires being able to determine for every task, at any time, how much CPU has been used, to detect that the task duration exceeds its prescribed WCET plus its allowance.

- Many systems do not provide CostOverrun handlers but have only classical timers. A CostOverrun is then detected at a deadline miss (very pessimistic as a deadline miss of a task might cause cascading effects on lower priority tasks). Another approach introduced in Bougueroua & al. (2007) is to compute the worst case Latest Execution Time (LET) of a task used to set the timer of a task, such that any task exceeding its LET has exceeded its WCET plus its allowance. The LET is computed taking into account the allowance of the tasks (see section 3.1.1). If a task τ_i is released at time t, the LET of τ_i and of all the tasks already released of lower priority than τ_i is updated. The timers are also updated accordingly.

With the LET mechanism:

- For any task τ_j released at time t_j, the Latest Execution Time of t_j, denoted $LET_j(t_j)$, is updated only at task activations.
- If τ_i is the task released, the Latest Execution Time is recomputed only for tasks actually released in $\tau_i \cup lp(i)$ for FP and in $\tau_i \cup \{\tau_k, t_k + D_k \geq t_i + D_i\}$ for EDF.
- Upon task activation, the Latest Execution Time of the task is updated and the timer of the released tasks is updated accordingly.
- The unused allowance of a task τ_i can be recovered and given to other lower priority tasks.

Bougueroua & al. (2007) show how to compute the Latest Execution Time $LET_i(t_i)$ of a task τ_i having a request time t_i, based on the allowance of the tasks (see section 3.1.1) for FP (definition 2) and EDF (definition 3) schedulings.

Definition 2: Let task τ_i be a new task having a request time at time t_i. The Latest Execution Time $LET_i(t_i)$ of all the tasks released in $\tau_j \in \tau_i \cup lp(i)$ scheduled FP is computed as follows:

$$LET_i(t_i) = \max(t_i, \max_{\tau_j \in hp(i)}(LET_j(t_j)) + C_i + A_{i,k}$$
$$\forall \tau_j \in lp(i): \quad LET_j(t_j) = LET_j(t_j) + C_i + A_{i,k}$$

Definition 3: Let task τ_i be a new task released at time t_i. The Latest Execution Time of all the tasks in $\tau_j \in \tau_i \cup \{\tau_k, t_k + D_k \geq t_i + D_i\}$ released at time t_j scheduled EDF is computed as follows:

$$LET_i(t_i) = \max(t_i, \max_{\tau_j \in hp_i(t_i)}(LET_j(t_j)) + C_i + A_{i,k}$$
$$\forall \tau_j \in lp_i(t_i), LET_j(t_j) = LET_j(t_j) + C_i + A_{i,k}$$

Example of LET with FP scheduling:

In Table 1, we consider three task τ_1, τ_2 and τ_3 scheduled with FP, having decreasing priorities and we suppose at most k=n=3 faulty tasks. We give for any task τ_i, i=1…3, the values of allowance $A_{i,3}$.

Figure 4 shows the execution of three tasks $\{\tau_1, \tau_2, \tau_3\}$ in the synchronous scenario (that minimizes the allowance). The black arrows represent the task activation requests. We can notice that the first activation of task τ_3 can use three time units when it exceeds its WCET (C_3) instead of one granted by the allowance $A_{3,3}$. An execution overrun management that would stop

Table 1. Example of three tasks with FP

Tasks	C_i	D_i	T_i	$A_{i,3}$
τ_1	4	10	10	1
τ_2	2	16	16	1
τ_3	3	20	20	1

Figure 4. Example of LET with FP

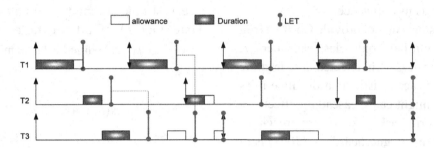

a faulty task just after it exceeds its WCET + allowance, based on the values the task allowance would not be the best solution compared to the LET mechanism if some instances of tasks don't use their allowance. With the LET mechanism, the unused allowance can be recovered by some other faulty tasks. In the example (Figure 2), the first instance of task τ_3 released at time 0 uses the unused allowance of the task τ_2 released at time 0 plus the allowance of the second instance of task τ_1.

4.2 Deadling with Deadline Miss

Why considering a deadline miss? A deadline miss can be due to the following cases:

- The deviation of the WCET of a task is too important and has effects on the tasks itself and on the lower priority tasks. This deviation can create an overload situation that must be taken into account.
- In the case of a variable speed processor, reducing the frequency will increase the WCETs of the tasks. This can create overloads situations that will result in deadline miss if not correctly handled.

We identify several approaches to deal with overloads conditions:

- Remove some tasks to come back to a normal load.
- Adapt the task parameters to come back to a normal load

In the first case, several solutions from the state of the art have been proposed:

- Stop the faulty task or put it in background. This is the solution used by most industrial systems. Probably not the best.
- Use an heuristic to remove some tasks. In Locke D. (1986), the author proposes to remove the task with the lowest importance. The importance is characterized by a Time Value Function (TVF) providing a statistical overload management with no guarantee to solve the overload problem.
- Applied for EDF scheduling, REDF (robust earliest deadline first) described in Butazzo & al. (1993) where a partitioning of critical real-time tasks and non-critical real-time tasks is proposed. The critical tasks should always meet their deadlines. The non critical tasks are removed if necessary according to their value density. A task τ_i has a value v_i and a value density $\frac{v_i}{C_i}\ldots$.

With this mechanism, for an identical value, the task having a long duration will be removed first.

- Applied for EDF scheduling, D-OVER proposed in Koren & al.(1992) where the authors assigns a Time Value Function (TVF) to every task. A value equal to 0 is equivalent to a deadline miss. The goal is to obtain the maximum value among all the tasks. They prove that their algorithm is optimal in the sense that it achieves the maximum possible benefit for an on-line algorithm (1/4 of an omniscient algorithm).

In the second case, the task parameters must be adapted on-line to cope with an overload. The idea is to adapt the periods of the tasks when needed to reduce the processor utilization. This approach has been proposed by Kuo & al. in the case of equally important tasks by gracefully adjusting the task periods. Other related papers are detailed in Buttazzo & al. (2002). In this paper, Buttazzo & al. introduce a novel scheduling framework to propose a flexible workload management at run time. They present the concept of elastic scheduling (introduced in Buttazzo & al. (1998)). The idea behind the elastic model is to consider the flexibility of a task as a spring able to increase or decrease its lenght according to workload conditions. The length of a spring is associated to the current processor utilization of its tasks. For a periodic task τ_i, the period T_i is the actual period and is supposed to range from T_i^{min} to T_i^{max}. The processor utilization of τ_i is C_i/T_i. The period adaptation is done with a new parameter: E_i defining an elastic coefficient. The greater E_i, the more elastic the task. Decreasing processor utilization result is applying a compression force on the spring that results in a period decrease. This model is well adapted to the case of deadlines equal to periods as it is possible in this case to derive sufficient feasibility for FP with Rate Monotonic algorithm (Liu & al. (1973) and Bini & al. (2003)) and necessary and sufficient feasibility conditions for EDF (Liu & al. (1973)) based on the processor utilization U. In this case,

determining if a task set is still schedulable after a task period change is not complex and can be done at run time.

In Buttazzo G. (2006), the author proposes to use also the elastic model to adapt the period of the tasks to reach high processor utilization in the case of discrete voltage levels in variable speed processors.

In soft real-time systems, another approach has been proposed, to bound the number of deadline miss. The (m,k)-firm approach introduced in Hamdaoui & al. (2005), can be used to specify that a task should have at least m consecutives instances over k meeting their deadlines. This algorithm, first conceived in the context of message transmission, is a best effort algorithm. In Bernat & al. (2001), the authors propose to extend the *(m,k)-firm* model with the *Weakly-hard* model, considering non consecutives deadline miss.

5. FUTURE RESEARCH DIRECTIONS

We have considered in this paper the benefits of sensitivity analysis for the reconfiguration of sporadic tasks when only one task parameter can evolve (WCET, Period or Deadline). Multi-dimensional sensitivity analysis has been considered by Racu & al. (2006) where a heuristic and a stochastic approach to deal with complex timing constraints is proposed. A stochastic approach could be considered in the case of multi-criteria reconfigurations.

In the case where applications are defined by several modes of execution, a reconfiguration consists of a mode change. A mode is defined by its task set. Changing the mode of an application changes the task set run by the system. The problem of mode change is to study if it is possible to end a mode and to start a new one while preserving all the timeliness constraints associated to all the tasks in both modes. Mode change is a current active research area and has been considered for e.g. in Nelis & al. (2009). Sensitivity analysis could be used to determine if a mode change results in acceptable WCET, period or deadline changes.

New architectures are more and more multiprocessor architectures. In this context, sensitivity approaches could help defining if a reconfiguration is possible or not. Multiprocessor scheduling is nevertheless much more complex. Two approaches have been investigated: the partitioned approach and the global scheduling approach. In the first case, tasks are statically assigned to a processor according to a partitioning heuristic (the general problem is a NP-hard bin packing problem). In the second case, task migration from one processor to another is possible. Global scheduling has been considered as it is viewed as a promising approach that could outperform partitioned scheduling approach. Nevertheless, it suffers from scheduling anomalies (see for e.g. Andersson & al. (2002)). A scheduling anomaly happens when a task set schedulable for given WCETs, periods and deadlines becomes non schedulable when tasks have smaller WCETs, higher periods or higher deadlines.

This case could not happen in the uniprocessor case for preemptive scheduling as it result in "easier" configurations. But this problem can happen in the global multiprocessor scheduling context. Baker & al. (2009) has introduced the concept of sustainability to handle this problem. A feasibility test is deemed to be sustainable when a task set, schedulable on a multiprocessor platform with global scheduling remains schedulable with smaller WCETs, higher period or higher deadlines. A reconfiguration is the context of global scheduling could be investigated with sensitivity and sustainability approaches.

The integration of real-time scheduling theory in real-time controlled systems is also an issue that should be considered. In a recent paper, Bini & al. (2008) has considered the problem of optimal static period assignment for multiple independent tasks run on the same system with Fixed Priority scheduling. The authors assume a linear cost function for the controllers. They show that the quality of control can be improved if the periods of task are chosen so as to minimize a goal function representing the control performance cost. The period of a task has an impact on the control delay that strongly affects the quality of control. A response analysis is used to solve the optimal period assignment problem. A better association of scheduling theory and control should be considered to improve the quality of a reconfiguration in the case of controlled systems.

6. CONCLUSION

In this chapter we have proposed to handle reconfigurations of sporadic tasks with a sensitivity approach. Sensitivity analysis permits to determine acceptable deviations on the WCETs, periods or deadlines of the tasks that can occur after a reconfiguration. The reconfiguration can be considered in a dimensioning phase to adapt an application to a new hardware platform or on-line to handle software fault or task parameter evolutions. We have given in this chapter a state of the art of existing sensitivity analysis for Fixed Priority scheduling and for Earliest Deadline First scheduling. We have shown how to compute acceptable deviations on task parameters with the allowance concept and with the maximum scaling factor preserving the schedulability of the tasks. We have then shown how to characterize the space of feasible WCETs and Deadlines (C-space and D-space) providing necessary and sufficient feasibility conditions valid for any WCETs or Deadlines reconfiguration. We have then focused on-line approaches to handle a reconfiguration that result in execution overruns and deadline misses.

REFERENCES

Andersson, B., & Jonsson, J. (2002). Preemptive Multiprocessor Scheduling Anomalies. In *International Parallel and Distributed Processing Symposium - Symposium Volume*, (pp. 0012).

Baker, T., & Sanjoy, B. (2009). Sustainable Multiprocessor Scheduling of Sporadic Task Systems. In *21st Euromicro Conference on Real-Time Systems (ECRTS'09)*, (pp. 141-150).

Balbastre, P., & Crespo, A. (2006). Optimal deadline assignment for periodic real-time tasks in dynamic priority systems. In *Proceedings of the 18th Euromicro Conference on Real-Time Systems (ECRTS'06)*, Dresden, Germany July 5-7.

Balbastre, P., & Ripoll, I. (2002). Schedulability analysis of window-constrained execution time tasks for real-time control. In *Proc. Of the 14th Euromicro Conference on Real- Time Systems (ECRTS'02)*.

Baruah, S., Buttazo, G., Gorinsky, S., & Lipari, G. (1999). Scheduling periodic task systems to minimize output jitter. In *6th Conference on Real-Time Computing Systems and Applications*, (pp. 62-69).

Baruah, S., Howell, R., & Rosier, L. (1990). Algorithms and complexity concerning the preemptive scheduling of periodic real-time tasks on one processor. *Real-Time Systems*, 2, 301–324. doi:10.1007/BF01995675

Bernat, G., & Burns, A. & A., L. (2001). Weakly Hard Real-Time Systems. *IEEE Transactions on Computers*, 50(4), 308–321. doi:10.1109/12.919277

Bimbard, F., & George, L. (2006, April). FP/FIFO Feasibility Conditions with Kernel Overheads for Periodic Tasks on an Event Driven OSEK System. In *9th IEEE International Symposium on Object and component-oriented Real-time distributed Computing (ISORC'06)*, Gyeongju, Korea.

Bini, E., & Buttazzo, G. (2003). Rate monotonic analysis: the hyperbolic bound. *IEEE Transactions on Computers*, 52(7). doi:10.1109/TC.2003.1214341

Bini, E., & Buttazzo, G. (2004). Schedulability Analysis of Periodic Fixed Priority Systems. *IEEE Transactions on Computers*, 53(11). doi:10.1109/TC.2004.103

Bini, E., & Buttazzo, G. (2007). The space of EDF feasible deadlines. In *Proceedings of the 19th Euromicro Conference on Real-Time Systems (ECRTS'07), Pisa, Italy July 4-6.*

Bini, E., & Cervin, A. (2008). Delay-Aware Period Assignment in Control Systems. In *Proceeding of IEEE Real-Time Systems Symposium (RTSS'2008), Barcelona, Spain.*

Bini, E., & Di Natale, M. (2005). Optimal Task Rateselection in Fixed Priority Systems. In *Proceedings of the 26th IEEE International Real-Time Systems Symposium (RTSS'05).*

Bini, E., Di Natale, M., & Buttazzo, G. (2006). Sensitivity Analysis for Fixed-Priority Real-Time Systems. In *Proceedings of the 18th Euromicro Conference on Real-Time Systems (ECRTS'06)*, Dresden, Germany, July 5-7.

Bollela, Gosling, Brosgol, Dibble, Furr, Hardin & Trunbull. (2000). *The Real-Time Specification for Java,* (1st ed.). Reading, MA: Addison & Wesley.

Bougueroua, L., George, L., & Midonnet, M. (2007). Dealing with execution-overruns to improve the temporal robustness of real-time systems scheduled FP and EDF. In *The Second International Conference on Systems (ICONS'07)*, Sainte-Luce, Martinique, France, April 22 - 28.

Bougueroua, L., George, L., & Midonnet, S. (2006). An execution overrun management mechanism for the temporal robustness of java real-time systems. In *The 4th International Workshop on Java Technologies for Real-time and Embedded Systems (JTRES 2006)*, 11-13 October 2006, *CNAM*, Paris, France.

Buttazzo, G. (2006). Achieving scalability in real-time systems. In *IEEE Computer*.

Buttazzo, G., Lipari, G., & Abeni, L. (1998). Elastic task model for adaptive rate control. In *proc. of the 19th IEEE Real- Time System Symposium*, Dec. 1998.

Buttazzo, G., Lipari, G., Caccamo, M., & Abeni, L. (2002). Elastic scheduling for flexible workload management. *IEEE Transactions on Computers*, *51*(3). doi:10.1109/12.990127

Buttazzo, G., & Stankovic, J. (1993). RED: A Robust Earliest Deadline Scheduling. In *3rd international Workshop on responsive Computing*, Sept.

Cervin, A., Lincoln, B., Eker, J., Arzen, K. & G., B. (2004). The jitter margin and its application in the design of real-time control systems. In *proceedings of the IEEE Conference on Real-Time and Embedded Computing Systems and Applications*.

George, L., Hermant, J.F., Characterization of the Space of Feasible Worst-Case Execution Times for Earliest-Deadline-First scheduling. Journal of Aerospace Computing, Information and Communication (JACIC), 6(11).

George, L., Rivierre, N. & Spuri, M. (1996, September). *Preemptive and non-preemptive scheduling real-time uniprocessor scheduling*. INRIA Research Report, No. 2966.

Hamdaoui, M., & Ramanathan, P. (1995, December). A dynamic priority assignment technique for streams with (m,k)-firm deadlines. *IEEE Transactions on Computers*, *44*, 1443–1451. doi:10.1109/12.477249

Hermant, J., & George, L. (2007). An optimal approach to determine the minimum architecture for real-time embedded systems scheduled by EDF. In 3rd IEEE International Conference on Self-Organization and Autonomous Systems in Computing and Communications (SOAS'07), September 2007.

Hladik, P., Déplanche, A., Faucou, S., & Trinquet, Y. (2007). Adequacy between AUTOSAR OS specification and real-time scheduling theory. In IEEE Second International Symposium on Industrial Embedded Systems (SIES '07), Lisbon, Portugal, July 4-6.

Joseph, M., & Pandya, P. (1986). Finding response times in a real-time system. *BCS Comp. Jour.*, *29*(5), 390–395. doi:10.1093/comjnl/29.5.390

Koren, G. & Shasha, D. (1992). D-over: An Optimal On-line Scheduling Algorithm for over loaded real-time system. Research report Num. 138, Feb. 1992.

Le Lann, G. (1996, March). A methodology for designing and dimensioning critical complex computing systems. IEEE Intl. symposium on the Engineering of Computer Based Systems, (pp. 332-339), Friedrichshafen, Germany.

Lehoczky, J. (1990). Fixed priority scheduling of periodic task sets with arbitrary deadlines. In Proceedings 11th IEEE Real-Time Systems Symposium, (pp. 201-209), Lake Buena Vista, FL.

Lehoczky, J., Sha, L., & Ding, Y. (1989). The Rate-Monotonic scheduling algorithm: exact characterization and average case behavior. In Proceedings of 10th IEEE Real-Time Systems Symposium, (pp. 166-172).

Leung, J. Y. T., & Merril, M. (1980). A note on premptive scheduling of periodic real-time tasks. *Information Processing Letters*, *11*(3). doi:10.1016/0020-0190(80)90123-4

Liu, L. C., & Layland, W. (1973). Scheduling algorithms for multi-programming in a hard real time environment. *Journal of the ACM*, *20*(1), 46–61. doi:10.1145/321738.321743

Lock, C. (1986). Best effort decision making for real-time scheduling. PhD thesis, Computer science department, Carnegie-Mellon University, Pittsburgh, PA.

Manabe, Y., & Aoyagi, S. (1998). A feasibility decision algorithm for rate monotonic and deadline monotonic scheduling. *Real-Time Systems, 14*(2), 171–181. doi:10.1023/A:1007964900035

Marinca, D., Minet, P., & George, L. (2004). *Analysis of deadline assignment methods in distributed real-time systems. Computer Communications*. New York: Elsevier.

Nelis, V., Goossens, J., & Andersson, B. (2009). Two Protocols for Scheduling Multi-mode Real-Time Systems upon Identical Multiprocessor Platforms. In 21st Euromicro Conference on Real-Time Systems (ECRTS'09), (pp. 151-160).

Racu, R., Hamann, A., & Ernst, R. (2006). A formal approach to multi-dimensional sensitivity analysis of embedded realtime systems. In proceedings of the 18th Euromicro conference on real-time systems (ECRTS'06).

Tindell, K., Burns, A., & Wellings, A. J. (1995). Analysis of hard real-time communications. *Real-Time Systems, 9*, 147–171. doi:10.1007/BF01088855

Vestal, S. (1994). Fixed-Priority Sensitivity Analysis for Linear Compute Time Models. *IEEE Transactions on Software Engineering, 20*(4). doi:10.1109/32.277577

Chapter 8
On Model–Driven Engineering of Reconfigurable Digital Control Hardware Systems

Tomás Balderas-Contreras
National Institute for Astrophysics, Optics and Electronics, Mexico

Gustavo Rodriguez-Gomez
National Institute for Astrophysics, Optics and Electronics, Mexico

René Cumplido
National Institute for Astrophysics, Optics and Electronics, Mexico

ABSTRACT

The continuous increase in the degree of design complexity during the development process of modern digital hardware systems, come into being due to the increasing demand of more and more functionality under strict design constraints, has led to designers trying to alleviate this complexity by increasing the level of abstraction when describing the functionality of a system. Recent proposals in the field of Electronic Design Automation intend to use common programming languages, like C, C++, and Java, or dialects derived from them, to describe the behavior of a digital hardware system and then generate a lower-level representation, closer to the hardware implementation platform, from such description. This phenomenon led us to firmly believe that the process of describing the functionality of a digital circuit resembles more and more the process of developing software; and, thus, it is possible to experiment with the application of the latest trends in software engineering, like the Model-Driven Engineering (MDE) paradigm, to design digital hardware systems. In this chapter we describe the basic principles of MDE, and provide some hints about the kind of languages and transformation tools needed to design algorithms in the domain of digital control that could be transformed into a digital circuit. We intend to open doors and encourage the research on the design of digital control systems at higher levels of abstraction and their implementations in different kinds of hardware platforms, including reconfigurable devices.

DOI: 10.4018/978-1-60960-086-0.ch008

INTRODUCTION

A digital control system is made up of a set of computer-based components whose mission is to coordinate, manage, and command the operation of another system. Examples of controlled systems include navigation systems for both terrestrial and aerial vehicles, specific-purpose industrial machinery, automated chemical and thermal processes, and other man-made artifacts and dynamic processes. The algorithms that perform these control operations are usually implemented in software running on special microprocessors known as microcontrollers, which are present in plenty of devices, vehicles, and machines that are common in our every-day live.

Figure 1 illustrates the organization of a generic closed-loop digital control system. It is built around a digital computer that receives, as input, a discrete signal $e(kT)$ that is the difference between the sampled versions of both the system's input ($r(t)$) and the controlled system's (the plant) output ($y(t)$). The computer produces another discrete signal ($u(kT)$) that, by means of a D/A converter and a zero-order hold (ZOH) module, is transformed into a continuous signal that controls the plant. The sample period is denoted as T in the figure.

According to (Wills, Heck, Prasad, Schrage, & Vachtsevanos, 2001), there are a number of capabilities demanded by modern software used by both civilian and military control systems. These capabilities are driven by modern technological trends and include the following:

- **Adaptability:** Depending on changes in the environment, changes in external inputs and/or the behavior of the system, the control software modifies its own behavior in a quick and seamless manner and without affecting the system's stability.

- **Extensibility:** The ability to include software components for new technologies (like control algorithms, sensors, or communication protocols) without redesigning the architecture of the control system software.

- **Interoperability:** Current control systems are distributed among a number of heterogeneous hardware/software platforms. These systems should be able to communicate with each other using different protocols and communication links, and meet a number of strict constraints related to response time and reliability.

This sort of software reconfigurability demands that the software architecture of the control system is flexible enough to support on-line changes without compromising the integrity of the system. There are a number of software technologies that might be useful to implement the previous capabilities, like component-based development (Kozaczynski & Booch, 1998) and self-adaptive software (Oreizy et al., 1999).

Alternatively, the control algorithms and operations performed by software may be implemented by a digital hardware system when strict performance and real-time requirements are a

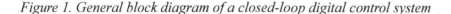

Figure 1. General block diagram of a closed-loop digital control system

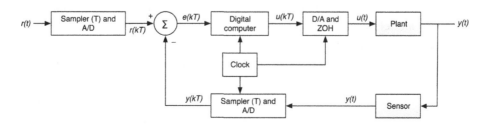

must. In this case, the capabilities listed above are still necessary features that must be supported in some manner by hardware-based control systems; thus, we can take advantage of the current advances in reconfigurable hardware to allow a hardware-based control system to load different configuration bit-streams on the fly to perform a different operation.

Designing any kind of digital hardware system, whether dedicated or reconfigurable, is not a straightforward task; there are a number of complexities in the development process that must be addressed properly. The mechanisms to implement dynamic reconfiguration are specific to the hardware platform and are generally invisible to the end user and, to some extent, to the designer. However, the developer does deal with the challenge of implementing numerous functional requirements of the system in shorter periods of time by meeting a number of operational constraints. This chapter discusses about the use of a model-driven principle to describe the functionality of hardware-based control systems at higher levels of abstractions, and to automatically synthesize a hardware implementation of those descriptions for either an Application-Specific Integrated Circuit (ASIC) or a reconfigurable platform. The intention is to alleviate design complexity and to increase development productivity.

In the following sections we focus our attention on the problem of digital design complexity and its direct consequence: the productivity gap phenomenon. We then describe modern approaches to raise the level of abstraction in the design process to increase productivity. Next, we describe how the model-driven paradigm for software development might help during the development process of digital hardware-based digital control systems by describing how to model difference equation block diagrams using a modeling language, and how these models could be implemented.

DESIGN COMPLEXITY

A computer-based system is a combination of hardware and software that implements a set of algorithms to automate the solution to a number of problems. Computer design technology transforms the designer's ideas and objectives into a number of representations describing software modules and hardware components that can be tested and manufactured (Semiconductor Industry Association, 2007). The design process is not straightforward; the developers always deal with the problem of alleviating the complexity of their designs to develop high-quality products within rigid time constraints. This problem arose as a consequence of the steady evolution of technology and the constant demand for new functionality.

Computer-based systems are not becoming easier to design as time goes by; on the contrary, the advancement of development and manufacturing technologies, and the need to meet new usage demand encourage the development of devices incorporating more and more functionality. This is a list of some key functionality aspects that have demanded attention from hardware/software engineers during the last years:

- **Communication.** A large number of computing devices must be connected to the Internet nowadays. This can be done by means of either broadband-wired Ethernet, or local wireless WiFi, or global wireless WiMax, or a cellular telephone network. It is common that a single device supports a set of the previous standards, which makes it more flexible but more challenging to design efficiently.

- **Security.** Several computer systems must implement mechanisms to cipher information, authenticate users, guarantee the integrity and confidentiality of data, and protect against a number of attacks. It is usually needed to cipher lots of information in a short amount of time, so hardware accelerators that increase performance of encryption algorithms are pervasive.

- **Power management.** Computers must run operating systems that switch idle hardware components to an operation mode that consumes less power when needed. Thus, the hardware components must implement a set of power states, each corresponding to a specific requirement of power consumption.

- **Multimedia processing.** A wide range of mobile devices, every single video game console, and some desktop computers, workstations, and servers must execute software to visualize video streams and files, produce high definition sound, process 2D images, and render 3D images. In almost every case, the software is aided by hardware accelerators to increase the performance of the algorithms that demand more computing power.

- **Fault tolerance.** High performance mission critical servers and supercomputers must incorporate algorithms to detect and correct errors, or, if the errors are uncorrectable, prevent them from spreading and compromising the whole system. In addition, those systems must implement algorithms to provide information redundancy and protect sensitive information as much as possible.

When designing the digital hardware of a computer-based system the developers must deal with the challenge of meeting a number of design constraints while implementing the required functionality. This is a list of the most common restrictions in hardware engineering:

- **Higher performance.** Very often it is not enough to solve a problem but to solve it fast. The functionality of the system must be implemented using algorithms that solve the corresponding problem with a

high degree of performance. Performance is measured in different ways depending on the application.

- **Power consumption efficiency.** Portable devices must meet their operational requirements while providing long battery life. In this case the systems must be designed with the goal of consuming less power as possible.

- **Low area.** When a large number of resources (such as transistors) are not available, the developer must conceive small designs that reutilize a component iteratively until completion.

It is not possible to optimize all of these parameters at the same time because some of them contradict to each other; thus, the designer must make trade-offs between them. For instance, an area-efficient hardware implementation of a block cipher algorithm for 3G cellular communications that reuses a basic function block iteratively until completion is able to encrypt information at a rate of 317.8 Mbps. (Balderas-Contreras, 2004), whereas a high-performance hardware implementation of the same algorithm that requires 6.3 times more hardware resources has a performance of 5.32 Gbps.

It is not possible to stop the evolution of technology or to prevent computer-based systems from implementing more and more functionality over time and becoming more complex. Hardware and software engineers are condemned to face the challenge of designing products that implement lots of functionality, while meeting difficult constraints, in shorter periods of time.

Productivity Gap

At this point we focus our attention on the challenging process of designing digital hardware systems that implement control systems, and propose a method to improve productivity during their functional description phase. These functional descriptions can be tested and implemented in semiconductor platforms like Application-Specific Integrated Circuits (ASIC) or Field Programmable Gate Arrays (FPGA).

In spite of having more resources to design with, design complexity imposes serious limits to the ability of designers to develop high quality products that fully meet their requirements in a short period of time; that is, to their productivity. The productivity gap is the challenge that arises when the number of available transistors grows faster than the ability to meaningfully design with them (Semiconductor Industry Association, 2007). Flynn et al. (Flynn & Hung, 2005) illustrate the considerable separation between the exponential increase in the number of transistors per chip along the last 28 years and the increase in design productivity along the same period of time.

Abstraction Levels

An effective way to alleviate design complexity and to reduce the productivity gap during the design of computer-based systems is to raise the level of abstraction at which developers carry out their activities. The goal is to design correct systems faster by making it easier to check for, identify, and correct errors.

The raise in the level of abstraction has been done many times in the past for both software and hardware development. The following is a brief description of the different levels of abstractions that have been used throughout the last decades to design digital hardware systems:

- **Transistor-level design.** The first solid-state computers were built using discrete transistors and other electronic components. These machines were relatively complex systems with little memory and consumed several kilowatts of power. As new architectural techniques to increase performance arose the hardware became so complex that turned design with discrete components impractical.

- **Schematic design.** When Medium-Scale Integration (MSI) and Large-Scale Integration (LSI) integrated circuits became pervasive the discrete components that made computer modules up were gathered together and encapsulated into a single silicon die. This allowed a high degree of miniaturization and the description of hardware components as a set of schematics specifying the interconnection of a number of integrated circuits.

- **Register-Transfer Level (RTL) design.** The behavior of a circuit is defined in terms of a flow of signals (data transference) between hardware registers, and the logical operations performed on those signals. This level of abstraction employs hardware description languages (like VHDL and Verilog) to create a more manageable description of a system. This representation can be transformed into a description of the electronic components that make up the system and the interconnections between them (net-list), which can be implemented in a Very Large Scale Integration (VLSI) silicon platform.

- **Electronic System Level (ESL) design.** The functionality of a digital hardware system is described by means of higher-level languages (some of them built from languages like C and Java) and graphical tools. The main goals are to achieve a high degree of comprehension and reutilization of the functional descriptions, and to fully automate the implementation process (Bailey, Martin, & Piziali, 2007).

In spite of their advantages to describe the functionality of digital hardware systems at higher levels of abstraction, some ESL technologies have important drawbacks that prevent them from being used to design some kind of devices, like low-power embedded hardware, efficiently. There is a strong need for very high-level design languages and tools that are customized for different application domains and help to alleviate design complexity. ESL is a recent research trend that has been neither fully explored nor fully standardized (Densmore, Passerone, & Sangiovanni-Vincentelli, 2006) and there is still room for important innovations.

At the ESL there are lots of similarities between the process of describing the functionality of a digital hardware systems and the process of developing software[1]. Thus, we can think of taking advantage of the recent advances in software engineering, like the Model-Driven Engineering paradigm (MDE) (Kent, 2002), to raise the level of abstraction even further, alleviate design complexity, increase reuse of existing designs, and automate the production of representations at lower levels of abstraction.

MODEL-DRIVEN ENGINEERING

MDE is a recent effort intended to raise the level of abstraction further when developing software systems. This approach is about conceiving the solution to a problem as a set of models expressed in terms of concepts in the problem's domain space, those that the designers and/or customers know very well, instead of concepts in the solution space, those related to software and hardware technologies. The intention is to translate the designer's models into the appropriate implementation for a specific platform[2], and to hide the complexities of such platform's hardware and software. The motivation of this paradigm is to improve both short-term productivity (increase functionality) and long-term productivity (lengthen longevity) during the development process (Atkinson & Kühne, 2003). Kent describes a set of general aspects that characterize MDE: high-level modeling, multiple modeling dimensions, processes, tools, transformations, and meta-modeling (Kent, 2002).

The Model-Driven Architecture (MDA) technology, proposed by the Object Management Group (OMG), is a realization of the MDE paradigm. It attempts to define an MDE-based framework using the OMG's standards, most notably the Unified Modeling Language[3] (UML), to improve the process of software development (Frankel, 2003; Miller & Mukerji, 2001). MDA separates a software system's functionality and requirement specification from the implementation of such functionality on a specific combination of hardware and software technologies (platform). The benefit of MDA is twofold: first, to enable the implementation of the same functionality on multiple computer platforms by means of automatic transformations; second, to allow the integration of different software systems by relating the corresponding models.

MDA categorizes models according to their level of abstraction, the only dimension in this MDE realization. A high-level functional model is called Platform-Independent Model (PIM), and its implementations, one for each particular platform, are called Platform-Specific Models (PSM). In a complete scenario, the designer should be able to create, execute, test and interchange PIMs before generating the corresponding PSMs. Figure 2 illustrates these concepts when applied to a number of software technologies based on Java, .NET, and CORBA. PIMs are usually built using dialects of UML called profiles, which customize the language to model abstractions within a specific application domain.

The way to the development of a full-fledged MDA design tool for developing digital hardware systems has been paved by the efforts of a number of people who have proposed the use of UML as a description language at different levels of abstraction during the process of designing digital hardware systems.

Figure 2. The MDA approach: transformation of PIMs into PSMs

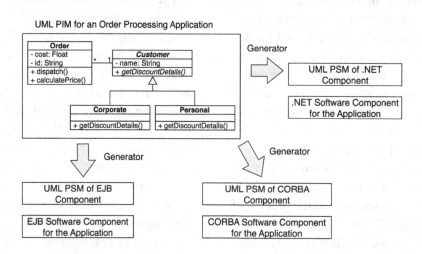

THE USE OF UML IN ESL DESIGN

Incipient areas of research involve the use of UML 2.0 as an ESL language to describe the functionality of a digital hardware system, and the use of software tools to implement this description. The following paragraphs describe the works identified so far that apply UML to model digital hardware systems.

UML for System on Chip

A System on Chip (SoC) is a computer-based system that integrates a number of processing elements, communication links, memory hierarchies and other electronic components, either digital or analog, within a single chip. The complexity of this kind of device has made the designers turn to UML to ease their design tasks.

The UML Profile for SoC, standardized by the OMG, extends UML to allow the hierarchical modeling of fundamental elements of SoCs like modules and channels, the description of information transfers between modules, and the support of both synchronous and asynchronous semantics (Object Management Group, 2006). This profile is built by defining extensions to the modeling elements in UML and adding constraints to them,

and by introducing specialized SoC structure diagrams. The profile's specification does not impose an implementation mechanism to derive a lower level representation and gives the designer freedom to implement the UML models.

Benkermi et al. describe a set of UML-based models for SoC platforms that include reconfigurable hardware components (Benkhermi, Benkhelifa, Chillet, Pillement, Prévotet, & Verdier, 2005). Every aspect of the system is modeled: the hardware architecture of the SoC, the so-called middleware (the operating system, communication protocols, and the tasks to be executed by either software or specialized hardware), and the high-level applications that may be implemented by software and/or hardware tasks in the middleware. The purpose of this project is to support the high-level exploration of the design space for reconfigurable SoCs and to enable the validation of the different design choices. There is no mention of any synthesis process going from the models to actual hardware or software implementation, though.

Mueller et al. and Riccobene et al. describe a UML profile for the SystemC language that is able to model the structural and behavioral features of SystemC using UML diagrams (Mueller et al., 2006; Riccobene, Scandurra, Rosti, & Bocchio,

A SoC Design Methodology Involving a UML 2.0 Profile for SystemC, 2005). The authors also propose a design flow to describe both the hardware and the embedded software of a SoC in terms of UML. UML improves the development process in three ways:

1. UML can be adopted to describe the SoC's overall functionality.
2. The UML profile for SystemC is used for hardware description at an abstraction level on top of an RTL representation of the hardware.
3. The software branch in the general flow may use UML profiles tailored for programming languages like C/C++ and Java.

The authors claim that modeling at the level of abstraction of UML has a number of advantages over writing SystemC code: visualization, reuse, integration, documentation, model analysis, and automatic generation of SystemC code. The authors' SystemC profile provides the user with the ability to "visualize" the SystemC language and to design in terms of building diagrams instead of writing code (Riccobene, Scandurra, Rosti, & Bocchio, A UML 2.0 Profile for SystemC. ST Microelectronics, Technical Report: AST-AGR-2005-3, 2005). Some of the profile's modeling constructs describe the structural aspects of the SystemC language, whereas the rest are used in UML behavioral diagrams to model SystemC's behavioral constructs.

The authors are strong advocates of extending UML by means of profiling to model any kind of system at any level of detail. They mention the suitability of the new features in UML 2.0 diagrams to carry out development tasks at the ESL. The authors also make an important assertion: "the use of profiles allows you to move from a description of a system in a given language to the description of the same system in another language, at the same level of abstraction or at a lower level of abstraction" (Riccobene, Scandurra, Rosti, &

Bocchio, A SoC Design Methodology Involving a UML 2.0 Profile for SystemC, 2005).

A more advanced UML-based infrastructure for SoC modeling is described in (Mellor, Wolfe, & McCausland, 2005). The authors first identify the following problems that occur during the design process of a SoC:

- **Partition.** Hardware and software engineers gather together at the beginning of the project to define the requirement specification. Prototypes of the system's hardware and software are needed, as soon as possible, to determine if both teams have the same understanding of the requirements.
- **Interface.** The only link between two separate teams with different skills working in parallel is a hardware/software interface specification written in natural language. A common failure occurs when a change in the interface occurs that is not reflected in its documentation.
- **Integration.** Correcting bugs whose origin is one of the previous problems is expensive and might represent a loss of market share. The engineers have to spend non-scheduled time to correct the errors.

The authors suggest the following solutions to the previous problems:

- **Build a single model of the application.** It is necessary to express the solution using a formal language in an implementation-independent manner. This description should be at a high level of abstraction to increase visibility and communication.
- **Build an executable model of the application.** The execution of models enables earlier feedback on desired functionality.
- **Do not model the structure of the implementation.** A set of mapping rules generates the descriptions for both hardware and software from the executable model, and

establishes the communication mechanisms between them.

The authors define the process of capturing an executable model of an application as the representation of a set of data, states and functions. The models can be executed independently of their implementation and exercised with a set of test benches to validate their functionality. Each component of the executable model can be marked with a tag indicating if the component is implemented in software or in hardware; thus, by assigning different sets of values to the tags we can experiment with different ways of partitioning the implementation into hardware and software.

Mapping from UML to VHDL

Björklund described a language called SMDL that can be used as an interface between high-level UML models and formal verification tools, simulators, and code synthesizers to implementation languages (Björklund, 2001). SMDL has formal semantics and incorporates high-level concepts like states, queues and events. The language statements' semantics are formally defined by structural operational rules.

Björklund et al. use SMDL as an intermediary to map UML state charts to the VHDL target language (Björklund & Lilius, 2002). UML edition tools store UML models using a standard XML-based representation called XML Metadata Interchange (XMI), which is translated into preliminary SMDL code. This code contains all the elements in the model: active states, transitions between states, event emission and concurrent states. This code is first reduced by removing trivial states and applying scheduling policies, and then transformed into Software Graphs (S-Graphs)[4] where a number of optimizations occur, like the removal of isomorphic nodes[5]; finally, VHDL code is generated from optimized S-graphs.

Coyle et al. describe a design flow consisting of a series of transformations going all the way from requirement specifications to hardware/software implementation (Coyle & Thornton, 2005). In the first phase of the flow two sets of UML models are generated from both functional and non-functional requirements. Functional requirements transform into UML structural and behavioral diagrams describing the basic functionality of the system to be implemented, whereas non-functional requirements are mapped into annotations that work as extensions to the functional UML models to indicate performance and timing restrictions. In the second phase of the flow a set of functional UML models are implemented as software components, whereas the rest are synthesized as hardware description language modules by means of a tool called MODCO. The UML models are first saved in XMI format; they are then processed by an XML parser module, and finally the data extracted by the parser is mapped to VHDL constructs by means of VHDL templates.

Discussion

The UML profile for the SystemC language described in (Mueller et al., 2006), (Riccobene, Scandurra, Rosti, & Bocchio, A SoC Design Methodology Involving a UML 2.0 Profile for SystemC, 2005), and (Riccobene, Scandurra, Rosti, & Bocchio, A UML 2.0 Profile for SystemC. ST Microelectronics, Technical Report: AST-AGR-2005-3, 2005) facilitates the development of descriptions in the SystemC language through visualization and automatic code generation. However, since the level of abstraction at which the developer conceives his/her solution is still that of the SystemC language, and not that of the problem domain, there is a risk of low productivity due to the investment of time in implementation details. Therefore, we believe that this kind of profile is not well-suited for high-level functional description of a SoC, but for its implementation phase.

The work in (Benkhermi, Benkhelifa, Chillet, Pillement, Prévotet, & Verdier, 2005) reports a set of models to describe both the hardware and software components of a reconfigurable SoC, but has serious limitations due to the lack of a transformation process going from the models to lower-level descriptions of the hardware and software components. Something similar occurs with the OMG's profile for SoC reported in (Object Management Group, 2006); it does not specify the mechanisms to implement the models built with it, although it is advantageous that there is a standard way to model SoCs using UML.

The works reported in (Coyle & Thornton, 2005), (Mellor, Wolfe, & McCausland, 2005) and (Riccobene, Scandurra, Rosti, & Bocchio, A SoC Design Methodology Involving a UML 2.0 Profile for SystemC, 2005) propose a flow based on UML to design and implement every aspect of a SoC, including both hardware and software. These design flows have a number of advantages: managing a single source for the whole project, modeling every component of the system using a consistent methodology and a single language, improving the communication between the software and hardware teams, and testing the whole system within the same development environment.

Schattkowsky et al. provide a number of important recommendations related to the application of UML for digital hardware design in general and for SoC design in particular (Schattkowsky, 2005):

- "UML is, by definition, a general-purpose modeling language that cannot be instantly applied to hardware design. It is necessary to tailor UML in a way that the domain-specific requirements can be met."
- "The real world things that need to be represented have to be identified and consistently put into the right context as UML elements."
- "The relation between the concepts used in UML and the real circuits has to be clarified. The application of different diagrams in the design process needs to be clarified."

In this chapter we use these recommendations as the foundations of a real model-driven design flow that includes extensions to UML providing modeling constructs that represent abstractions of a specific application domain.

PROPOSED MDA DESIGN FLOW

The following is a description of the main principles our proposed MDA-based design flow relies on:

- UML 2.0 (Object Management Group, 2007) has two main advantages that make it the best choice for building the modeling languages for our proposal: first, it was designed with the purpose of being extended and customized; second, its graphical nature allows a better comprehension degree than a textual language.
- A Domain-Specific Modeling Language (DSML) is necessary for the designer to describe functionality more effectively because it allows the use of terms and abstractions in the problem domain, instead of letting the designer deal with the awkward details belonging to the implementation domain. Mernik et al. state that "by providing notations and constructs tailored toward a particular application domain, the domain-specific languages offer substantial gains in expressiveness and ease of use compared to general-purpose languages for the domain in question, with corresponding gains in productivity and reduced maintenance costs" (Mernik, Heering, & Sloane, 2005). This DSML is conceived as an extension to UML 2.0, in the form of a profile.
- The functional description in DSML (a PIM in the jargon of MDA) is, in the long run, automatically transformed into a lower level representation in VHDL that,

Figure 3. Proposed MDA-based design flow

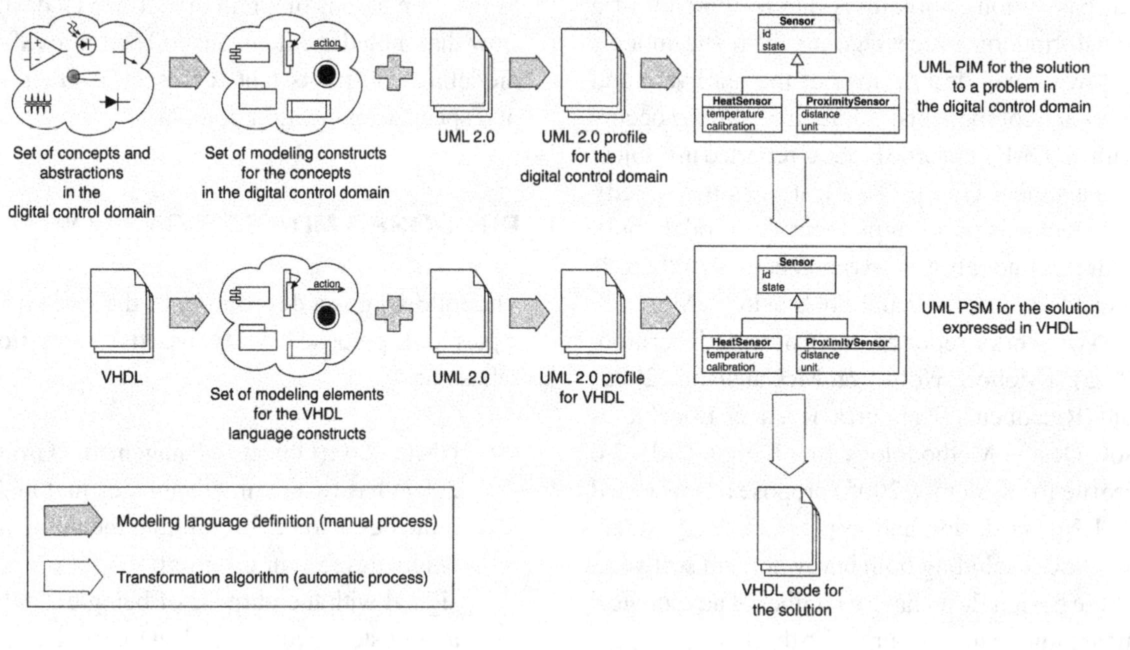

Set of concepts and abstractions in the digital control domain

Set of modeling constructs for the concepts in the digital control domain

UML 2.0

UML 2.0 profile for the digital control domain

UML PIM for the solution to a problem in the digital control domain

Sensor
id
state

HeatSensor
temperature
calibration

ProximitySensor
distance
unit

VHDL

Set of modeling elements for the VHDL language constructs

UML 2.0

UML 2.0 profile for VHDL

UML PSM for the solution expressed in VHDL

Sensor
id
state

HeatSensor
temperature
calibration

ProximitySensor
distance
unit

Modeling language definition (manual process)

Transformation algorithm (automatic process)

VHDL code for the solution

in turn, can be implemented on either an ASIC or an FPGA. In between these two representations it is possible to introduce another UML-based description whose modeling elements have the same semantics as the language constructs of VHDL, which describes the same functionality as the DSML model, and that allows the generation of VHDL code from it. The purpose of this description (a PSM in the jargon of MDA) is twofold: first, to ease the transformation process from DSML to VHDL by partitioning it into two simpler ones; second, to provide the user with a UML-based blueprint of the system that is closer to the final VHDL representation and allows a better comprehension of such VHDL code.

Figure 3 illustrates how the previous principles define a design flow similar to that in Figure 2. We can observe both the PIM and PSM abstraction levels along with the VHDL code that is the

ultimate result of the whole design approach. The DSML for a particular application domain, used to build the PIMs, is constructed by identifying the primitive abstractions and concepts relying at the foundations of every problem and solution in such domain; these abstractions are expressed as a set of modeling elements, or language constructs, that are added to the definition of an existing modeling language, like UML 2.0. Similarly, the VHDL profile is constructed by extending UML 2.0 with modeling elements corresponding to VHDL's language constructs. The designer might be able to fine-tune the models at this level before generating VHDL code from them; however, some people consider this an inappropriate practice. Figure 3 shows the procedure to define the DSML and the UML 2.0 profile for VHDL, as well as the two transformation algorithms that map high-level descriptions into lower level representations and that generate VHDL code.

The UML 2.0 profile should be suitable to allow the designer to explore multiple design alternatives in a shorter period of time. The main idea is that the developer builds an initial PIM of the structure of the application according to his/her architectural strategies, automatically synthesizes VHDL code from it, tests this code using a number of standard test benches, and computes the parameters of interest (performance, power consumption or area) to validate the design. If something goes wrong, or if the designer conceives a different architecture for the block cipher, it is always possible to directly manipulate the UML model to correct errors or to reorganize the architecture of the model, and then perform the test cycle again. The expectation is that handling domain-specific UML modeling elements and having a complete view of the design will be more productive than sketching the design and then writing the corresponding code in an implementation language like VHDL.

The architecture of the PIM depends heavily on the parameter the designer needs to optimize. For instance, if hardware resource area were a concern the designer would structure the model of the system in such a way that its functionality would be based on the iterative use of small components. If the requirement were to achieve higher level of performance then the developer would structure the model in such a way that it would exploit parallel processing, pipelining, memory caching, etc. Thus, the designer has full control of the architecture of the model and the algorithms it implements, and is able to directly modify it to meet the requirements and constraints imposed by the context of the problem.

This model-driven development approach plays an important role during reconfigurable control. The model-driven design flow may be customized to a number of application domains, including the digital control domain. Additionally, since the initial models are platform-independent, they can be synthesized to representations suitable to be laid out in a reconfigurable mesh, like an FPGA's. Some dynamic reconfiguration concepts, like configuration scheduling, might be included in the PIMs in a high-level fashion to add recon-

figuration policies to the model. This policies and the model's functionality may be implemented slightly different for each reconfigurable platform.

MODELING OF DIFFERENCE EQUATIONS

Consider a closed-loop digital control system, like the one in Figure 1, performing sampling operations with a period T. During the k-th sample, the digital computer has received the inputs e_0, e_1, e_2, ..., e_k and has produced the outputs u_0, u_1, u_2, ..., u_{k-1}; it computes the current output u_k by means of a difference equation, a linear combination of n previous inputs and m previous outputs:

$$u_k = -a_1 u_{k-1} - a_2 u_{k-2} - \ldots -a_m u_{k-m} + b_0 e_k + b_1 e_{k-1} + \ldots + b_n e_{k-n} \tag{1}$$

A specific example of a difference equation that can be programmed in the digital computer to perform a practical operation is the trapezoid rule used for numerical integration with a sample period of T:

$$u_k = u_{k-1} + \frac{T}{2}(e_k + e_{k-1}) \tag{2}$$

By using the feedback line, the control system computes each of the e_k inputs provided to the computer, which stores them along with its previous outputs u_k and uses them during execution of Equation 2. Thus, with every step the computer gets closer to the estimation of the integral for a continuous function $e(t)$. Figure 4 illustrates the block diagram corresponding to this trapezoid rule difference equation; it denotes the delays in both the input and output signals, the arithmetic operations needed to compute the output signal, and the coefficients required.

Figure 4. Block diagram for the trapezoid rule

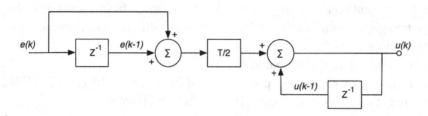

In this section we describe the first step of a process to implement simple difference equations into the computation engine of a digital control system by means of a model-driven development approach. To complete model-driven design process departs from block diagrams, like the one in Figure 4, and synthesizes either software to program a control system's digital computer, or VHDL code for a reconfigurable digital hardware platform for control applications. The block diagrams are first built using an extension to UML 2.0 Activity Diagram and then transformed automatically into software or VHDL code.

The UML 2.0 Profile

Current versions of UML include a formal definition of the language's constructs and abstract syntax that is called *meta-model* (a model of a model). The meta-model contains a set of meta-classes that define UML's modeling elements, and describes the relationships between meta-classes that indicate how the modeling elements are assembled together by the user to build models of a system using UML.

The use of meta-modeling during the specification of UML led to the definition of meta-levels that encompass all the existing categories for objects within a software system and their possible descriptions. Figure 5 illustrates the four meta-levels, denoted as M0, M1, M2 and M3, as well as the "instance of" relationship that exists between an entity at one specific level, and another entity at the level immediately above.

The meta-level M0 contains all of the objects that make up a software system, including all of the instances running within the program that contain data, exchange messages and make the processor to execute their methods. These software objects are instances of classes that describe them, which can be modeled in UML using the class diagram notation; it is possible to build UML diagrams that model the objects themselves. The UML models built by the designer to describe his/her software system are located at the meta-level M1 in the hierarchy, whereas the modeling elements used by the designer to build the UML diagrams, like the box representing a class as well as the attributes and operations within the box, are instances of a number of meta-classes that make up the meta-model of UML and are located at the meta-level M2 in the hierarchy. These meta-classes are, in turn, defined as instances of the meta-meta-classes located at the uppermost level in the hierarchy, the meta-level M3. The OMG's Meta-Object Facility (MOF) specification is located at the meta-level M3.

A profile is an extension mechanism for UML to get dialects that customize the language for particular platforms or application domains. Profiles are made up of stereotypes that extend particular meta-classes; tagged definitions that define additional attributes for the stereotypes; and restrictions that specify rules, pre- and post-conditions for the extended modeling elements.

The UML Activity Diagram is used to describe procedural logic, business processes, and work flows. This diagram is conceptually similar to a

Figure 5. Meta-levels and the "instance of" relationships between them

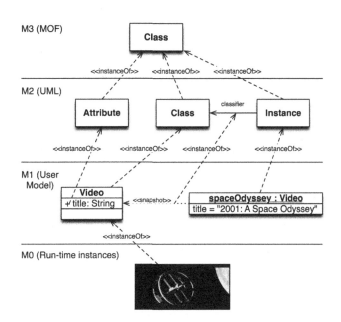

flowchart, but differs from it in its ability to describe parallel behavior and model both control and data flows; these two distinctions make this kind of diagram the most adequate one to model the data flows and the operations required by the block diagrams representing difference equations in a correct manner. The Activity Diagram's modeling elements include: actions representing behavior execution, input/output pins working as connection points for data or control going in or out the actions, edges indicating the flow of either data or control, decision elements to choose one out of several paths, fork nodes to initiate parallel paths, asynchronous signaling mechanisms, and constructions to elaborate a hierarchy of sub-activity diagrams. Our profile's stereotypes extend the meta-classes of these modeling elements to derive specialized modeling constructs representing the operations required by difference equations.

Figure 6 shows a UML 2.0 class diagram illustrating the hierarchy of meta-classes from which we derive our profile's stereotypes, which are indicated by the shaded class boxes. A stereo-type is a special kind of meta-class labeled with the keyword «stereotype» that is derived from an existing meta-class within the meta-model with the intention of extending its behavior. The stereotype's attributes shown in Figure 6 are called tagged definitions and define properties for the new modeling element that are additional to the ones contained in the extended meta-class. Our profile derives several stereotypes from the Action meta-class to model the operations that are common to difference equation block diagrams; it also derives a stereotype from the meta-class ObjectFlow to model edges transmitting data; and it also derives a stereotype from the meta-class ForkNode to either distribute data along two or more different paths, or to partition an n-bit datum into several data of different lengths. Table 1 provides a brief description of the semantics of the profile's modeling elements, or stereotypes. An UML Activity Diagram built using this profile is called a UML Block Diagram.

Figure 6. Fragment of the meta-model of UML 2.0 for Activity Diagrams extended with the stereotypes that make up the profile for modeling difference equation block diagrams

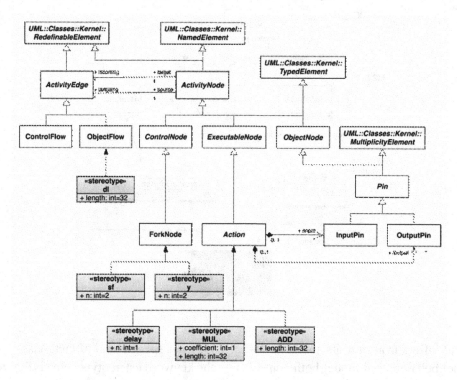

Table 1. Description of the modeling elements that make up the UML profile for difference equations

Modeling Element	Description
delay	Models a delay operation, denoted in block diagrams as Z^{-1}.
MUL	Models a multiplication by a coefficient operation.
ADD	Models an addition operation.
dl	Models a data line that transfers intermediate results between modeling elements.
y	Allows sending an intermediate result along two or more data lines.

Building UML Block Diagrams

Figure 7 shows the UML Block Diagram corresponding to the block diagram in Figure 4. The UML Block Diagram is enclosed within a main activity called TrapezoidRule having an integer input port to receive the sequence e_k, and an output port to send the output sequence u_k. There are two actions (delay_1 and delay_2) that perform the delay of the incoming datum, and this is known because these actions are denoted by the «delay» stereotype. Similarly, there are actions that perform integer addition, like add_1 and add_2, denoted by the «ADD» stereotype, and actions that perform integer multiplication, like T/2, denoted by the «MUL» stereotype. Every operation is a special kind of action of the UML Activity Diagram; thus, the operations have pins attached to them for input and output data.

A very important aspect to take into account when building UML Block Diagrams is to set each of the modeling element's attributes cor-

Figure 7. The UML Block Diagram for the trapezoid rule difference equation

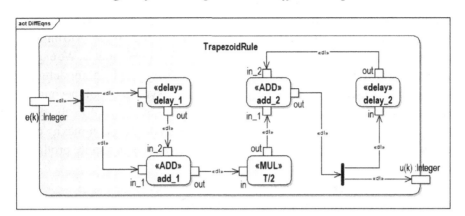

rectly. Figure 6 indicates that each delay modeling element has an attribute called n, whose default value is one, that indicates the delay steps performed by the action; in the UML Block Diagram in Figure 7 there is no need to set this attribute to a different value. The integer multiplication modeling element has two attributes: coefficient, whose default value is one, stores the value of the coefficient the input datum is multiplied by; and length, whose default value is 32, indicates the length in bits of the value in the attribute coefficient. In the diagram in Figure 7 there is no settings for the multiplication action that is different from the default values; do not confuse the action's label T/2 with the value of its coefficient. The modeling element representing integer addition has only one attribute related with the precision of its operands. Depending on the specific UML modeling tool, the values of the attributes can be shown along with the corresponding modeling element or not.

The data lines in the UML Block Diagram are modeling elements that are instances of the «dl» stereotype; they connect actions to one another by means of the actions' pins. The fork nodes that appear in the diagram allow sending the incoming data flow along two, or more, different data paths, which semantically represents the initiation of two or more parallel processes.

Synthesis of UML Block Diagrams

In this sub-section we provide a number of ideas about what we can do with the UML Block Diagrams, about where we can go to with these representations. To do this we must take into account the ideas discussed previously about the MDE paradigm, and its realization in the MDA technology. We will link the UML Block Diagrams to the design flow in Figure 3.

A UML Block Diagram, like the one in Figure 6, can be stored and exchanged by multiple UML tools by using a standard representation called XML Metadata Interchange (XMI). One can develop a number of software tools that take these XMI textual representations and work with them to transform them into a new representation at lower levels of abstractions.

On the one hand, the models can be transformed into software to be executed by the microcontroller under the following rules:

- The delay operations are mapped to memory accesses to retrieve the proper sequence element.
- The coefficients of the multiplication actions can be stored in the microcontroller's registers.
- The addition and multiplication actions can be synthesized to a number of multipli-

cation and accumulation operations whose operands come from the registers.

- Advanced processor micro-architectures might implement instruction-level parallelism mechanisms and the synthesis tools could produce code that exploits these micro-architectural features.

These rules apply when the synthesis process produces assembly language code. Alternatively, the synthesis tools might generate C code that can be compiled by the microcontroller's specific compiler, which could be a more portable solution.

On the other hand, a different synthesis tool might be able to build special-purpose hardware architectures from the UML Block Diagrams' XMI representation. In this case, the result of the synthesis process could be either a functional description in a language like VHDL, like in the design flow described previously, or a net-list for a specific semiconductor platform. The functionality of the customized hardware architecture may be fixed but it could be constructed to exploit parallelism and achieve higher performance. When implemented in platforms like FPGAs, it is possible to implement dynamic reconfiguration mechanism to change the functionality of the computing engine in the digital control system according to its environment.

CONCLUSION

In this chapter we reviewed the motivation for design methodologies and tools at higher levels of abstractions to develop digital control systems in hardware; we focused our attention in current trends at the ESL level. We examined the causes of the productivity gap phenomenon and suggested that the latest trends in software engineering, like the model-driven engineering paradigm, could have a positive impact on the improvement of productivity. We examined how the block diagrams for discrete difference equations could be

modeled using a dialect of UML 2.0, and provided some hints on the processes required to generate descriptions that are closer to implementation from such higher level models. We expect that this kind of high-level graphical modeling languages and automatic synthesis tools become pervasive in the near future, so they allow the designer to tackle the ever-increasing complexity of modern digital control systems in a more productive manner.

REFERENCES

Atkinson, C., & Kühne, T. (2003). Model-Driven Development: A Metamodeling Foundation. *IEEE Software*, *20*(5), 36–41. doi:10.1109/MS.2003.1231149

Bailey, B., Martin, G., & Piziali, A. (2007). *ESL Design and Verification: A Prescription for Electronic System Level Methodology*. San Francisco, CA: Morgan Kaufmann Publishers.

Balderas-Contreras, T. (2004). *Hardware/Software Implementation of the Security Functions for Third Generation Cellular Networks*. Masters Thesis, INAOE, Tonantzintla, Puebla, Mexico.

Benkhermi, I., Benkhelifa, A., Chillet, D., Pillement, S., Prévotet, J.-C., & Verdier, F. (2005). System-level Modelling for Reconfigurable SoCs. In *20th Conference on Design of Circuits and Integrated Systems (DCIS)*, Lisboa, Portugal.

Björklund, D. (2001). *The SMDL Statechart Description Language: Design, Semantics and Implementation*. Masters Thesis, Abo Akademi University, Finland.

Björklund, D., & Lilius, J. (2002). From UML Behavioral Descriptions to Efficient Synthesizable VHDL. In *Proceedings of the 20th IEEE Norchip Conference*, Copenhagen, Denmark.

Coyle, F. P., & Thornton, M. A. (2005). From UML to HDL: a Model Driven Architectural Approach to Hardware-Software Co-Design. In *Information Systems: New Generations Conference (ISNG)*, (pp. 88-93).

Densmore, D., Passerone, R., & Sangiovanni-Vincentelli, A. (2006). A Platform-Based Taxonomy for ESL Design. *IEEE Design & Test*, *23*(5), 359–374. doi:10.1109/MDT.2006.112

Flynn, M. J., & Hung, P. (2005). Microprocessor Design Issues: Thoughts on the Road Ahead. *IEEE Micro*, *25*(3), 16–31. doi:10.1109/MM.2005.56

Frankel, D. S. (2003). *Model-Driven Architecture: Applying MDA to Enterprise Computing*. Indianapolis, IN: Wiley Publishing, Inc.

Kent, S. (2002). *Model Driven Engineering*, (. *LNCS*, *2335*, 286–298.

Kozaczynski, W., & Booch, G. (1998). Guest Editors' Introduction: Component-Based Software Engineering. *IEEE Software*, *15*(5), 34–36. doi:10.1109/MS.1998.714621

Mellor, S. J., Wolfe, J. R., & McCausland, C. (2005). Why Systems-on-Chip Needs More UML like a Hole in the Head. In Martin, G., & Müller, W. (Eds.), *UML for SOC Design* (pp. 17–36). Berlin: Springer. doi:10.1007/0-387-25745-4_2

Mernik, M., Heering, J., & Sloane, A. M. (2005). When and How to Develop Domain-Specific Languages. *ACM Computing Surveys*, *37*(4), 316–344. doi:10.1145/1118890.1118892

Miller, J., & Mukerji, J. (2001). *Model Driven Architecture (MDA): Document number ormsc/2001-07-01*. Object Management Group.

Mueller, W., Rosti, A., Bocchio, S., Riccobene, E., Scandurra, P., Dehaene, W., & Vanderperren, Y. (2006). UML for ESL Design: Basic Principles, Tools, and Applications. In *Proceedings of the 2006 IEEE/ACM International Conference on Computer-Aided Design*, (pp. 73-80). San Jose, CA: ACM.

Object Management Group. (2006). *UML Profile for System on a Chip (SoC) V1.0.1. OMG Document Number: formal/06-08-01*. Object Management Group.

Object Management Group. (2007). *OMG Unified Modeling Language (OMG UML) Infrastructure V2.1.2. OMG Document Number: formal/2007-11-04*. Object Management Group.

Object Management Group. (2007). *OMG Unified Modeling Language (OMG UML) Superstructure V2.1.2. OMG Document Number: formal/2007-11-02*. Object Management Group.

Oreizy, P., Gorlick, M. M., Taylor, R. N., Heimbigner, D., Johnson, G., & Medvidovic, N. (1999). An Architecture-Based Approach to Self-Adaptive Software. *IEEE Intelligent Systems*, *14*(3), 54–62. doi:10.1109/5254.769885

Riccobene, E., Scandurra, P., Rosti, A., & Bocchio, S. (2005). A SoC Design Methodology Involving a UML 2.0 Profile for SystemC. In *Proceedings of the conference on Design, Automation and Test in Europe (DATE 2005)*, (pp. 704-709). Munich, Germany: IEEE Computer Society.

Riccobene, E., Scandurra, P., Rosti, A., & Bocchio, S. (2005). *A UML 2.0 Profile for SystemC. ST Microelectronics, Technical Report: AST-AGR-2005-3*. ST Microelectronics.

Schattkowsky, T. (2005). UML 2.0 - Overview and Perspectives in SoC Design. IN *Proceedings of the conference on Design, Automation and Test in Europe (DATE 2005)*, (pp. 832-833). Munich, Germany: IEEE Computer Society.

Semiconductor Industry Association. (2007). *International Technology Roadmap for Semiconductors: Design Chapter*. Semiconductor Industry Association.

Wills, L., Heck, B., Prasad, J. V., Schrage, D., & Vachtsevanos, G. (2001). An Open Platform for Reconfigurable Control. *IEEE Control Systems Magazine*, *21*(3), 49–64. doi:10.1109/37.924797

ENDNOTES

[1] However, the divergence point is at the moment of implementing the digital hardware system's descriptions into silicon.

[2] In this context a platform is defined as a combination of hardware and software technologies.

[3] UML is a graphical notation that has been used during the last decade to model and document object-oriented software systems. It allows specifying both the structural and the behavioral aspects of a software system. The last major revision of the language is the UML 2.0 revision.

[4] S-graphs are directed acyclic graphs that represent decision trees with assignment statements.

[5] Two nodes are isomorphic if they have the same level and their children are isomorphic.

Chapter 9
A Design Methodology of MIN–Based Network for MPPSoC on Reconfigurable Architecture

Y. Aydi
University of Sfax, Tunisia

M. Baklouti
University of Sfax, Tunisia & University of Lille, France

Ph. Marquet
University of Lille, France

M. Abid
University of Sfax, Tunisia

J.L. Dekeyser
University of Lille, France

ABSTRACT

Massive parallel processing systems, particularly Single Instruction Multiple Data architectures, play a crucial role in the field of data intensive parallel applications. One of the primary goals in using these systems is their scalability and their linear increase in processing power by increasing the number of processing units. However, communication networks are the big challenging issue facing researchers. One of the most important networks on chip for parallel systems is the multistage interconnection network. In this paper, we propose a design methodology of multistage interconnection networks for massively parallel systems on chip. The framework covers the design step from algorithm level to RTL. We first develop a functional formalization of MIN-based on-chip network at a high level of abstraction. The specification and the validation of the model have been defined in the logic of ACL2 proving system. The main objective in this step is to provide a formal description of the network that integrates architectural parameters which have a huge impact on design costs. After validating the functional model,

DOI: 10.4018/978-1-60960-086-0.ch009

step 2 consists in the design and the implementation of the Delta multistage networks on chip dedicated to parallel multi-cores architectures on reconfigurable platforms FPGA. In the last step, we propose an evaluation methodology based on performance and cost metrics to evaluate different topologies of dynamic network through data parallel applications with different number of cores. We also show in the proposed framework that multistage interconnection networks are cost-effective high performance networks for parallel SOCs.

INTRODUCTION

A large number of data parallel applications, especially multimedia, image processing and real time applications, ported to embedded systems require intensive computations. The complexity of these devices has lead to the appearance of parallel programming and parallel systems on a chip such as clusters, multiprocessor systems, grid systems, etc. These systems can satisfy the need for speed required by the data parallel applications due to their increasing complexity needed to compute the solution to the problem, the size of the data set to be processed, and the time constraint on when a solution to the problem must be attained. The SIMD (Single Instruction Multiple Data) parallel systems play a crucial role in the field of intensive signal processing (Meilander, Baker, M. J., 2003) because of their area and energy-efficiency. They are effective for applications that are highly parallelizable and require execution of the same operation over and over again. Massively parallel machines make use of fine-grained computational units, called Processing Elements (PEs) working in parallel to speed up computation. They are connected together in some sort of simple network topology, which often is custom-made for the type of application it's intended for (Flynn, 1972). In SIMD machines, a main processor is responsible for synchronously controlling the whole architecture. Targeting high-performance applications requires that developers create implementations that are fast enough to meet demanding processing requirements are developed quickly enough to reach the time to market and can easily be updated to provide a different functionality. Given the rich domain of parallel applications it is always possible to find a set of applications that perform well on a given parallel architecture. However, it is often difficult to determine which architecture is best for a given application. Reconfigurable architecture will therefore be a key step in the development of such systems. Nowadays we have a great variety of high capacity programmable chips, also called reconfigurable devices (FPGAs) where we can easily integrate complete SoCs architectures for many different applications. FPGA reconfigurability can be exploited to implement a reusable design, which can be adjusted for specific applications without altering the basic structure. While SIMD systems may have been out of fashion in the 1990s, they are now developed to make effective use of the millions of transistors available and to be based on the new design methodologies. By using VLSI technology based on the use of intellectual properties (IPs) and replication of components effectively; massively parallel processors can achieve high performance at low cost. Key issues are how the processor and memory are partitioned and replicated, and how the communications and IO are accomplished. In fact, for most the parallel systems, communication networks are considered as one of the challenges facing researchers. These parallel systems require a cost-effective yet high-performance interconnection scheme to provide the needed communications between processors. Thus, this interconnect system must support the entire inter-component data traffic and has a significant impact on the overall system performance (Pasricha, Dutt, Bozorgzadeh & Ben-Romdhane,

2005). As a promising alternative, Networks on Chip (NoCs) have been proposed by academia and industry to handle communication needs for the future multiprocessor systems-on-chip, in particular parallel processing SoCs (Benini & Micheli, 2002). In comparison with previous communication platforms (e.g., a single shared bus, a hierarchy of buses, dedicated point-to-point wires), NoCs provide enhanced performance and scalability. All NoCs advantages are achieved thanks to efficient sharing of wires and a high level of parallelism (Dally & Towles, 2001). The NoC is considered the trend for future generations of multi-core processors (Schack, Heenes & Hoffmann, 2009).

Multistage Interconnection Networks (MINs) have been used in many parallel systems. As an example MINs are used to assure the communication between processors and the IO data transfer in the parallel supercomputers (Siegel, Nation, Kruskal & Napolitano, 1989), the Mas-Par (Blank, 1972), CRAY Y-MP series (Cheung & Smith, 1986). Moreover, MINs are applied for networks-on-chip to connect processors to memory modules or processors to processors in parallel systems. MINs are also used to handle IO data transfers which are clearly a key issue in a massively parallel SoC. A MIN is defined by, its topology, switching strategy, routing algorithm, scheduling mechanism, fault tolerance (Kruskal & Snir, 1983), and dynamic reconfigurability (Aydi, Meftali, Abid, Dekeyser, 2007).

Developing a design methodology for networks-on-chip based interconnect architecture poses new challenges to designers (Orgas & Marculescu, 2005). In this context our goal is to provide a novel approach for the design of MIN-based network for a Massively Parallel Processing System on Chip, MPPSoC. Therefore, the framework starts from an informal description of network architecture at the algorithmic level and produces a complete implementation of on-chip network on programmable circuits. The approach discussed in the present paper covers two issues.

The first issue aims at the development of a functional formalism of MIN-based network. Its input is an informal model described in a functional style at a high level of abstraction and produces validate formal description of communication architecture based on multistage interconnection networks. This formalization validates architectural parameters such as, network topology, routing algorithm, and scheduling strategy which have a huge impact on design costs. Furthermore, this model constitutes the formal reference for future implementation by ensuring the quality of the design (Elleuch, Aydi, & Abid, 2008), improving the robustness of the system, and speeding up the development. The second issue consists in the design and the implementation of MIN-based network for MPPSoC. We will ensure the soundness of the proposed approach by using programmable logic circuits for faster performance evaluation by bringing the design to reality. We propose an evaluation methodology based on performance metrics, such as execution time and speed-up; and costs metrics, such as energy consumption and area. Hence, the easy programmability and the large integration capacity of FPGA provide evaluation through emulation which complements the formal verification process of the MIN-based communication architecture.

The rest of this paper is organized as follows. First, MIN architecture is introduced in the next section. Second, a functional formalization of MIN-based network is detailed in section 3. Third, the target MPPSoC system is highlighted with focus on its global network. The Modeling and implementation of the proposed communication architecture on FPGA based MPPSoC are described in section 4. Section 5 highlights the performances of the proposed parallel system as well as its MIN interconnection network in executing data parallel applications. Finally, some concluding remarks and future perspectives are presented.

BACKGROUND

Several interconnect architectures on FPGA ranging from busses (Wee, 2007), crossbars (Kapre, 2006), to networks on chip (Marescaux, 2003) have been reported in the literature. Parallel processing systems are more and more used to satisfy a wide range of data parallel applications needs. In the one hand, parallel systems require high-performance interconnection networks. On the other hand, designing high-performance interconnection networks becomes a critical issue to exploit the performance of parallel systems. Custom interconnection networks are designed to be adopted by most manufacturers for high-performance parallel computers such as Intel Paragon, Cray T3D and T3E, CM-5, SP2, Origin2000 and Blue Gene. MINs are also used for the Transputer system SC320, the CM-5 and the Meiko CS-2 machine (Meyer, Auf Der Heide, Monien & Rosenberg, 1992). MINs are good for constructing parallel systems with hundreds of processors and have been even used in some commercial parallel computers. They have been also widely proposed for SIMD architectures (Siegel & Smith, 1978) (Siegel, 1979). In (Stone, 1971), the perfect shuffle interconnection pattern has been demonstrated fundamental to achieve the communications in a parallel processor. It has been also shown that the shuffle interconnection scheme presents advantages over the near-neighbor (or cyclically symmetric) interconnection scheme (as used in the ILLIAC IV (Hord, 1982), (Schurz & Fey, 2007 and (Eklund, 2001)). We briefly describe below some communication architecture designs proposed recently for parallel systems.

A parallel routing mechanism for a MIN on the circuit-switching mode is described in (Ferreira, Laure, Beck, Lo, Rutzig & Carro, 2009). Only one-to-one and one-to-many permutations are considered. However, many-to-one and many-to-many permutations are not taken into account. In (Freitas & Navaux, 2008) a multi-cluster NoC architecture for parallel processing is proposed. It

is an indirect interconnection network that shows better performance than conventional NoCs. A multiprocessor architecture for the massively parallel GCA model is presented in (Schack, Heenes & Hoffmann, 2009). It integrates a number of processors connected through an omega network. The architecture shows better performances and can be adapted to different GCA algorithms. These results demonstrate the efficiency of MIN networks in multi-cores architectures. In (Sharma, Kahlon, Bansal & Singh, 2008), an irregular MIN, called Improved Four Tree, is proposed for large-scale parallel systems. Furthermore, other NoC architectures have been recently proposed. Kumar (Kumar, 2007) has proposed a reconfigurable Multi Processor Network on Chip architecture in which both the network and the processing nodes are fully configurable, and the network is designed to match the application requirements. An FPGA-based NoC design that consists of processors and reconfigurable components is presented in (Bartic, 2003). In (Huebner, 2004), a reprogrammable interconnect is implemented based on a LUT-based bus macro and is used to dynamically reconfigure the attached IPs. A design of an adaptable FPGA-based Network on Chip which is dynamically reconfigurable has been proposed by pionteck et al (Pionteck, 2006).

MAIN FOCUS OF THE CHAPTER

Basic MIN

In this section, we present an overview of the networks used for the design methodology of MIN-based communication architecture for MPSOCs.

MIN Components

The common multistage interconnection networks (MINs) used, have N inputs and N outputs nodes and are built using r×r switches. Such MINs have N/r switches at each stage, and $\log_r N$ stages of

Figure 1. A generic MIN model

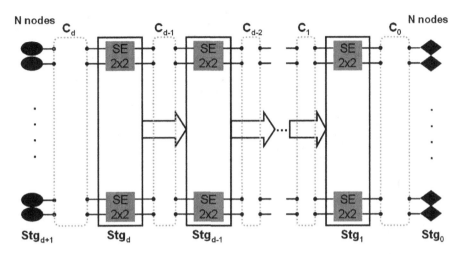

switches denoted by d. The different stages are connected by links generated by applying permutation functions. Figure 1 represents a generic model of MINs of size N×N using crossbars with r equals 2. In a MIN, a path between a source and a target is obtained by operating each corresponding switch of the stage i in a straight mode if the ith bit of the destination address is equal to 1, otherwise in exchange mode.

MIN with Banyan Property

In Figure 2, we propose a topological classification of MINs. A banyan MIN is a multistage interconnection network characterized by one and only one path between each source and destination. A banyan MIN of size N×N consists of r×r crossbars. An interesting subclass of Banyan MINs is composed of Delta networks (Patel, 1981). We denote by: oi the ith output of a crossbar in a MIN, and by Cj, a crossbar belonging to the stage j. So, the Delta property can be defined as follows: if an input of Cj is connected to the output o_i of Cj-1, then all other inputs of Cj must be connected to the stage (j-1) on outputs with the same index I Figure 2.

Delta Networks

The difference between each of the existing MINs is the topology of interconnection links between the crossbar stages. An equivalence study of a variety of Delta MINs (Figure 3) has been detailed in (Kruskal, 1986).

Table 1 shows the links permutation of the most popular Delta MIN: omega, baseline and butterfly. Common links permutation used in a multistage interconnection network using 2x2 crossbar elements are:

- The perfect shuffle denoted by σ is a bit-shuffling permutation where: $\sigma^\kappa(x_{n-1} x_{n-2} \cdots x_1 x_0) = x_{n-2} \cdots x_1 x_0 x_{n-1}$.
- The butterfly permutation denoted by β is a bit-shuffling permutation where: $\beta_i^\kappa(x_{n-1} x_{i+1} x_i x_{i-1} \cdots x_1 x_0) = x_{n-1} \cdots x_{i+1} x_0 x_{i-1} \cdots x_1 x_i$.
- The baseline permutation denoted by d δ is a bit-shuffling permutation where: $\delta_i^\kappa(x_{n-1} \cdots x_{i+1} x_i x_{i-1} \cdots x_1 x_0) = x_{n-1} x_{i+1} x_0 x_i x_{i-1} \cdots x_1$
- The identity permutation denoted by $\mathbf{I}$ is a bit-shuffling permutation where: $\mathbf{I}(x_{n-1} x_{n-2} \cdots x_1 x_0) = x_{n-1} x_{n-2} \cdots x_1 x_0$

Figure 2. Classification of MINs

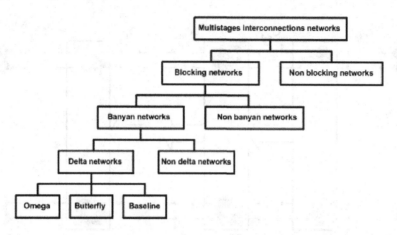

Figure 3. A Delta network (8,2)

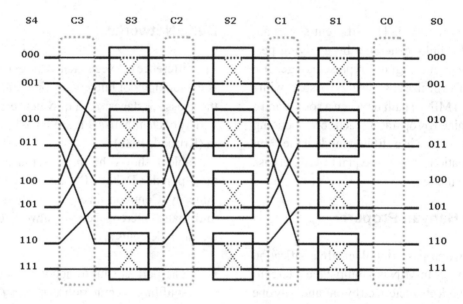

A Functional Formalization of MIN-Based Network

In this section, we describe the methodology adopted to identify the communication architecture based on multistage interconnection networks in formal notations. As a first step, we present the generic network on chip model denoted by GeNoC, and its implementation in the ACL2 theorem proving environment. Next, we detail a generic topology and extended routing components as

Table 1. Links permutation in Delta MINs

Links permutation	stage (d+1)	stage k ∈ [1..d]	stage 0
Omega	σ^κ	σ^κ	I
Baseline	I	$\delta_{(d-i)}^{\kappa}$	I
Butterfly	σ^κ	$\beta_{(d-i)}^{\kappa}$	I

extension of the generic model GeNoC. Finally, we validate this formalism in a Delta multistage interconnection networks case study.

Figure 4. GeNoC: a generic network on chip model

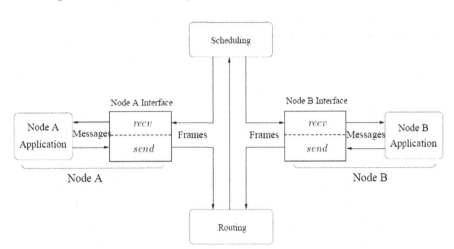

GeNoC Model Overview

The Generic Networks on Chip model denoted by GeNoC is based on a generic formalization (Borrione, Helmy, Pierre & Schmaltz, 2009). GeNoC takes into account the common components of any on-chip interconnection architecture, and models them in a functional style through four functions: "Send", "Recv", "Routing" and "Scheduling" (Figure 4). The two first functions describe the interfaces of any network, while "Routing" and "Scheduling" exemplify the routing algorithm and the switching technique respectively. Each of these functions does not have an explicit definition but is constrained by properties modelled by theorems, also called proofs obligation.

The main function of this model is recursive. Each recursive call represents one step of execution, where a message progresses by at most one hop. Such a step defines our time unit. It takes as arguments the list of requested communications (messages to send) and the characteristics of the network, and produces as results two lists: successful communications and aborted ones. The correctness of this function is guaranteed through a key theorem expressing that a sent message is always received by its right destination without any modification of its content. In other words, the theorem states that for all interfaces I, routing algorithm R, and scheduling technique S that satisfy associated constraints Po1, Po2, Po3, and Po4, GeNoC fulfils a correctness property THM. The corresponding formalization is as follows.

Theorem.

$$\forall\ I, \forall R, \forall\ S,$$
$$Po1(I) \wedge Po2(R) \wedge Po3(S)$$
$$\Rightarrow THM\ (GeNoC(I,R,S)).$$

The GeNoC model has been implemented in the ACL2 theorem proving environment. ACL2 (A Computational Logic for Applicative Common LISP) is a tool involving a mathematical logic of the first order and a theorem prover (Kaufmann & Moore, 1996). To demonstrate one theorem, ACL2 uses various techniques like rewriting, simplification by the repeated substitution of equals for equals, decision-making procedures, and mathematic induction. By applying the GeNoC approach, several NOCs were specified and validated (Schmaltz & Borrione, 2006). The GeNoC model has also been extended to verify the Hermes NoC (Borrione, Helmy & Schmaltz, 2008), and Octagon networks from ST Microelectronics (Schmaltz & Borrione, 2004).

Compared to previous formal works in the context of on-chip communications (Roychoudhury, Mitra, & Karri, 2003) and (Amjad, 2006), GeNoC is innovative. Verifying any instance of a given NoC is possible through the GeNoC approach, provided that the NoC components meet the generic constraints. Indeed, it has the specificity to be generic and it does not make any assumption on topology, routing algorithm and scheduling policy of the NoC.

The main objective is to extend the GeNoC model by involving the connection and the routing components, so that we describe a more realistic model of on-chip communications. The extension is possible by formally defining, at a generic level, abstract interconnection functions. After that, the network case study can be validated by applying the GeNoC model extended.

Specification of the Generic MIN-based Network

The following section presents the formalization of a generic network topology composed of nodes set and connections. As the nodes set was already defined in GeNoC, we focalize on the generalization of connections. We keep the same GeNoC notation of functions and predicates defined for the nodes.

Formulation of MIN Topology

The arrangement of the elements (nodes and links) of a network, especially the physical (real) and logical (virtual) interconnections between nodes, defines its topology. In general, the study of the network physical topology is assimilated to the study of a graph, whose vertices are the nodes of the network and its edges are the links connecting pairs of vertices. Traditionally, a graph (G) has been always defined statically by its collection of vertices (V) and its collection of edges (E). In contrast, the approach is based on adopting a direct graph for the topology, and identifying the

interconnection functions list. In a direct graph, the edges are oriented from one vertex to another. A vertex x of the graph can be connected to one or more other vertices. In general, to generate one edge or link from the vertex x, we have to apply a mathematical function designated by fp. Such a function expresses the relation between the vertex x and one of its outgoing edges. All outgoing edges from x are the result of the application of a list of functions denoted by $Lfpx$. For the validity of the generic topology model, we suppose that for each vertex, such a mathematical function list exists.

The main constraint to check on this graph topology is that a vertex v produced by a given function connection fp, is really in the nodes set (*NodeSet*). Figure 5 shows a topology graph of octagon network in which nodes are natural (*NodeSet* = (0,1,2,3,4,5,6,7)), and its connections which are described simultaneously by an incremental function fp = '+1', fp = '+N/2', fp = '-(N-1)'.

A few definitions regarding MIN-Based communication architecture that will be used later in the paper are detailed below.

Definition 1. A MIN-Based graph $G=G(V,E)$, is a directed graph, where each vertex $vi \in V$ represents a node (processor, or IP core, or memory, or switch port), and each directed edge $ei \in E$ characterizes a link from vertex vi to vertex vj. $Fp: V \rightarrow E$ is a function that generates one link $ei \in E$ form a vertex $vi \in V$.

In the ACL2 logic, we define the function denoted by *Gen*-Cnx which generates all the edges of a given vertex x. It takes as arguments

Figure 5. Octagon topology

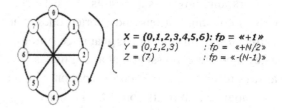

the vertex and the corresponding function list *lfpx*. The predicate *Validlfp* identifies a valid list *lfpx*. The first constraint on topology (*theorem* 1) expresses the correction of the function lfpx. Such a function is valid if, for every connection *cnx* generated from a node x (in *NodeSet*) and its corresponding list *lfpx,* the second extremity of *cnx* belongs to the *NodeSet*. The access to the second extremity of any connection *cnx* is possible through the function *ext2*. We also define the function denoted by *Gen-Top* which generates all network topology. It takes as argument a list denoted by pms-top which is a list consisting of pairs (X, Fp), where *fp* is the connection function that must be applied to all nodes contained in *X*. The *Gen-Top* function uses an intermediate function denoted *Gen-Top-1* which generates connections in each stage (definition2).

Definition 2.

Gen-Top (pms-top) = $\wedge$ (List (gen-top-1 (X, fp)))
X $\subseteq$ NodeSet
fp $\in$ Listfp

Theorem 1 serves as an intermediate lemma. In fact, for each connection *cnx* generated from a node in *NodeSet* and its corresponding list *lfpx*, the second extremity of *cnx* belongs to the *NodeSet*. The corresponding formalization is as follows.

Theorem 1. Validity of connection functions

$\forall$ x $\in$ NodeSet, $\forall$ lfpx, Validlfp (lfpx)
$\Rightarrow \forall$ cnx $\in$ Gen-Cnx (x, lfpx), ext2 (cnx) $\in$ NodeSet

Theorem 2. Validity of nodes generated by connection functions

$\forall$ pms, $\forall$ pms-top,
(ValidParamsp pms) $\wedge$ (ValidParamsp-top pms-top)
$\Rightarrow$ (ext2s-top (gen-top pms-top)) $\subseteq$ (Nodeset-Generator pms)

Theorem 2 is defined for all extremity nodes generating connection topology; the predicate *ValidParams-top* serves to verify the validity of the parameters of topology generation. The access to the extremity node of any connection is given by the function *ext2s-top*.

Theorem 3 is defined for the validity of the all network topology. Thus, for any parameter *pms-top* recognized by the predicate *ValidParams-top*, any connection generated by the function *gen-top* must be recognized by the predicate *ValidCnxp*. The validity of the topology is ensured via *Valid-Top* predicate. The corresponding formalization is as follows.

Theorem 3. Validity of network topology

$\forall$ x $\in$ NodeSet,$\forall$ pms-top, (ValidParamsp-top pms-top)
$\Rightarrow \forall$ cnx $\in$ Gen-Top (pms-top), ValidCnxp (cnx)

Extension of the Generic Routing Function

The generic routing function depends only on the set of nodes (*NodeSet*). For each missive (*message*) denoted by m from the set of missives *M*, "*Routing*" applies a function ρ that computes all possible routes between the origin of the missive (*OrgM*) and its destination (*DestM*). We have redefined the routing function so that it takes into account the whole topology (denoted by *Top*) which is composed of nodes and connections. In particular, the function ρ must take into consideration the *Top*. The new routing function is designated by *Ext-Routing* (definition 3). In this definition, we use *IdM, FrmM, OrgM, DestM* which are GeNoC functions giving access to the elements of a missive. A missive is a data type also defined in GeNoC. It represents a message having the form: "*id org frm dest*", where *id* is used to identify the message, *org* is its origin, *dest* denotes its destination and *frm* is the content of the message.

Definition 3. Redefinition of the generic function routing

Ext-Routing (Top,M)= $\wedge$ (List (IdM (m),FrmM(m),ρ-ext(OrgM (m),DestM (m), Top)) m ∈ M

GeNoC defines three routing function constraints. In the extended model, we focalize only on the first two constraints. The first constraint is related to the validity of computed routes which is expressed by the predicate *ValidRoutep*. It said that any route *r* produced by the function ρ must be valid. So, *r* is valid only if it starts from the source node (*OrgM* (*m*)), and terminates at the destination node (*DestM* (*m*)), all the nodes of the route r are included in *NodeSet*, and r includes at least two nodes. We also redefined *ValidRoutep* in order to involve the topology component. The new computed route *r* is no longer composed just of nodes but of connections. We denote the ith element of r by r[i], and by l the length of r. Thus, the new predicate *Ext-ValidRoutep* requires that the first element of r (function first) is equal to the origin of the missive (*OrgM* (m)), that r[i] is a connection *cnx* included in *Top*, and that *r* has a length l greater than or equal to 1. l is equal to 1 if the origin and the destination are directly connected (definition 4).

Definition 4. Redefinition of the route validity

Ext-ValidRoutep (r, m, Top) = $\wedge$ (First (r[0]) = OrgM (m)
r $\subseteq$ Top $\wedge$ (len(r) $\geq$ 1)

The constraint concerning the validity of routes is redefined in *theorem 4*. The GeNoC predicate denoted by *Mlstp* recognizes a valid list of missives. We have redefined it to include the topology *Top*, so this predicate must be satisfied by all routes produced by function ρ-ext.

Theorem 4. Validity of routes produced by ρ-ext

$\forall$ M, Mlstp (M, Top)
$\Rightarrow \forall$ m ∈ M, $\forall$ r ∈ ρ-ext (OrgM (m), DestM (m)), Ext-ValidRoutep (r, m, Top)

The constraint concerning the extended routing function will not have major changes. In fact, we substitute *NodSet* with *Top* for the *theorem 5*. The latter proves that function *Routing* denoted by *Ext-Routing* produces a valid travel list if the initial missive list is valid.

Theorem 5. Validity of Travel list

$\forall$ M, Mlstp (M,Top) $\Rightarrow$ Vlstp (Ext-Routing (M,Top))

Formal Specification and Verification of Delta MIN Based Network: A Case Study

In this section, we apply the extended GeNoC model to validate the Delta multistage interconnection networks. We insist on applying the generic topology to a Delta MIN case study that constitutes a concrete instance of the extended model.

Formalization of Delta-MIN Topology

The generic approach requires beginning by identifying the connection functions to apply to generate all the network connections. Once this list is identified, we have to check the three main constraints expressed at the generic level: one constraint defined in GeNoC for the validity of the nodes set; and the two constraints that we have defined for the connections (*theorem 1 and 2*). The Delta MIN topology as described above (Figure 3) is composed of nodes and connections.

Nodes specification: a pair of coordinates (x y) is used to represent a node in a Delta MIN. The coordinate x is decimal. It represents the stage of nodes to which belongs the node. The *Y* coordinate is binary and it describes the position of the node within the same stage. The function *gen-nodes-dmin* generates all nodes of the network. It takes as parameters *d*, the stage number of the network, *r* (r=2), the degree of switches, and the *network identifier*. The validity of these parameters is recognized by the predicate *ValidParamsp-dmin*. We also define another predicate called *valid-nodes-dmin* for the whole nodes validity. The nodes set generation is constrained by *theorem 6*.

Theorem 6. Nodes set generation

∀pms, ValidParamsp-dmin (pms)
⇒∀x∈ gen-nodes-dmin (pms), valid-nodes-dmin (x)

Connections specification: we represent a connection *cnx* in a Delta MIN by a list *((x px) (y py))*, where *x* is the origin of *cnx*, *px* is the port involved in *cnx*, y is the second extremity and *py* is the port of *y*. For example, the connection (((3) (0 1)) O0) (((2) (1 0)) I0) signifies that the port O0 of the switch ((3) (0 1)) is connected to the port I0 of ((2) (1 0)). In the case of Delta MIN, the connection functions are always a list of three permutations to apply on the first, the middle, and the last stage of connection, respectively. In the ACL2 logic, we define the function denoted by *gen-one-cnx* which generates the connection of the port *i* of *ext1*. It takes as arguments the node *ext1*, the connection port *i*, and the connection function *fp*. We present below the ACL2 simulation and the validation of the global function gen-top-dmin.

ACL2!> (*gen-top-dmin* (*params-top-t* '(3 2 omega))))
ACL2!> (valid-top-dmin (gen-top-dmin (params-top-t '(3 2 omega))))) >> T

Figure 6 presents the connections of a Delta MIN network generated by the global function *gen-top-dmin*.

The validity of the Delta MIN topology is ensured via *Valid-Top-dmin* predicate. The corresponding formalization is as follows.

Theorem 7. Validity of Delta MIN topology

∀ pms,∀ pms-t, (ValidParamsD pms) ∧ (ValidParamsp-t pms-t)
⇒ ∀ cnx ∈ gen- top-dmin (pms-t), valid-top-dmin (cnx)

Formalization of Delta MIN Routing Component

The routing algorithm used in Delta MINs is the self routing. It depends only on the destination address, also called control sequence. If the corresponding digit of the control sequence is equal to i, the message to deliver will be switched to the output i of the current crossbar. Here, the routing algorithm must take into account connections. Indeed, the only information of the port through which the message must be switched is not enough. Thus, we must look into the topology for the connection with the current switch as origin. As defined in ACL2, the routing function *routing-dmin* takes as arguments the list of missives to be routed through the Delta MIN, and the parameters to generate the whole topology. For each missive, *routing-dmin* calls the following function *compute-r*te (definition 5) to compute the route between the *origin* (*from*) and the *destination* (*to*).

Definition 5. Routing Function algorithm.

```
compute-routes-dmin (from dest top)
if (from = dest) /* destination reached */
then take the local port of the destination
else
if (dest [i] = 0) /* ith bit equals 0 */
then take the upper output of the switch at Si
from = rech_top (from top 0)
compute-routes-dmin (from dest top)
else /* ith bit equals 1 */
```

Figure 6. Delta-MIN topology generation

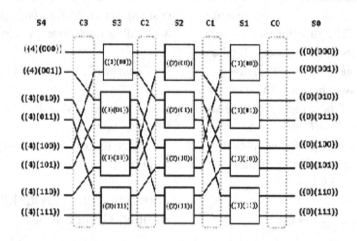

take the lower output of the switch at Si
from = rech_top (from top 1)
compute-routes-dmin (from dest top)

The ACL2 theorem proving environment also provides an execution engine. Thus, we can simulate the execution of the definitions. We present below a simulation of the function *routing-dmin* showing the progression of the list of missives (Table 2) through an omega network 8x8, using 2x2 crossbars. The simulation result of missives 1 and 2 are shown below. We can notice that the routing algorithm make use of connections like ((((3)(0 1))O1)(((2)(1 1))I0)), to compute a route.

The following Theorem is a valid instance of the generic theorem 4. The latter proves that the predicate *Ext-ValidRoutep* must be satisfied by all routes produced by the function *compute-routes-dmin*.

Theorem 8. Validity of routes produced by *compute-routes-dmin* function

∀ M, Mlstp (M,Top)
⇒ ∀ m ∈ M, ∀ r ∈ compute-routes-dmin (OrgM (m),DestM (m),Top), Ext-ValidRoutep (r,m,Top)

Theorem 4 is concretized through theorem 9. Therefore, the validity of travel list produced by the function *routing-dmin* is ensured via *Vlstp* predicate if the initial missive list is valid. The corresponding formalization is as follows.

Theorem 9. Validity of Travel list produced by routing-dmin function

∀ M, Mlstp(M,Top) ⇒ Vlstp(routing-dmin (M,Top))

MIN Networks for FPGA Based MPPSoC: Design and Implementation

After validating the functional model which constitutes the formal reference for an implementation of the network, we present in this section the design translated into low level layers. Therefore, we will deal with the part which relates to the design of the Delta multistage networks on chip dedicated to massively parallel architectures on reconfigurable platforms FPGA and their methodology. The main goal is to implement the MIN in an FPGA based massively parallel architecture and study the effectiveness of such networks to satisfy the data parallel applications.

Figure 7. missives routing

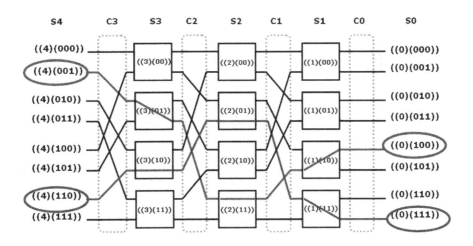

Table 2. The list of missives

id	origin	content	destination
1	((4) (001))	frm1	((0) (100))
2	((4) (110))	frm2	((0) (111))

Based on a reconfigurable parallel NoC, our aim is to vary topologies in order to find the most suitable to a given application and to compare the performances of the various types of the networks. First of all, the MPPSoC architecture will be briefly described with focus on its parallel NoC. Then, the implementation and evaluation of the MIN for the parallel system will be discussed.

MPPSoC Architecture

The proposed architecture is an SIMD architecture, close to the very well known MasPar (Blank, 1972). It is built based on opencore processor, miniMIPS in this work. As a basic architecture, it is composed of a parametric number of processing elements (the PEs), organized in a 2-D grid, working in a perfect synchronization. A small amount of local and private memory is attached to each PE. The PE is also potentially connected to

its eight neighbors in an Xnet network topology. Furthermore, each PE is connected to an entry of mpNoC, a massively parallel Network on Chip that potentially connects each PE to one another, performing efficient irregular communications. The mpNoC is responsible of managing point to point communications through different communication modes. It is based on switches to connect the required sources as well as the appropriate destinations and an interconnection network to assure data transfers. In this work, the Delta MIN is chosen as the mpNoC router. The system operating is organized by a control processor (the ACU, Array Control Unit) that accesses its own sequential memory which contains data and instructions. The ACU reads instructions and, according to the executed program, synchronously controls the whole MPPSoC system. In fact, the ACU is built as a modified processor which produces a micro-instruction at the end of the decode stage.

Figure 8.The proposed MPPSoC architecture

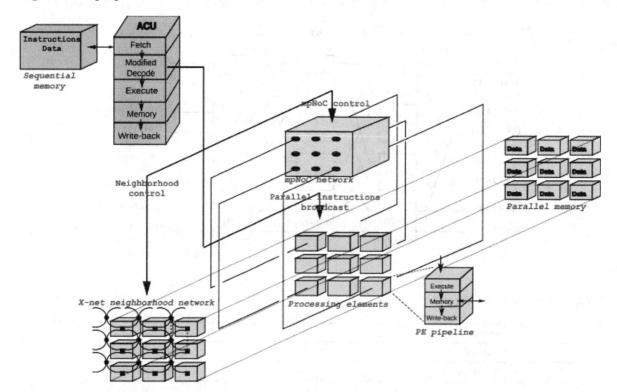

This micro-instruction is either executed locally by the ACU in the case of a sequential instruction, or is broadcasted to all the PEs in the case of a parallel instruction. So, the MIPS instruction set is modified by adding parallel instructions. The ACU is also responsible of controlling the networks, in particular determines the route of the irregular communications in the mpNoC. Figure 8 illustrates the MPPSoC architecture.

In this work, the mpNoC is based on a MIN network and can accomplish different functions. Firstly, the mpNoC is able to connect, in parallel, any PE with another one. Secondly, the mpNoC could connect the PEs to the MPPSoC devices. Thirdly, it is able to connect the ACU to any PE. The role of MIN is so to manage these various accesses and avoid conflicts. The MIN based mpNoC architecture is depicted in Figure 9.

This work focuses on the efficiency of integrating a MIN network in a parallel SoC. The Delta

MIN router architecture is fully described in the next paragraph.

Delta MIN Based mpNoC Router Architecture

The proposed Delta MIN router architecture, implemented as a packet-switched network, is primarily composed of different modules. In the following paragraphs the basic delta MIN architecture is firstly exposed. Then, the data packet is presented. Finally, the internal architecture of each MIN component is detailed.

Delta MIN Basic Architecture

Delta network consists of a^n sources and b^n destinations, n number of stages and the ith stage has $a^{n-1} b^{n-1}$ crossbar modules or Switching Elements (SE) of size a x b (in our case crossbars of size 2x2). The nodes pairs are connected to each other

Figure 9. MIN based mpNoC architecture

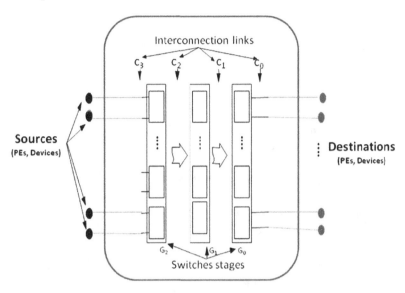

with switches which are dynamically set by control logic associated with interconnected network. Delta network possesses full access property since it is possible to connect every node (Ni) to the other (Nj). The basic building blocks of the Delta MIN are Switches Elements, connected by links. The goal is to have a communication infrastructure, in which the reach-ability of packets is ensured, independently of the changing topology which occurs when connections are changed on the MPPSoC. For enabling configuration in Delta MIN architecture, a link permutation manager is used to change the connections between stages for varying the topology of the network (omega, baseline, and butterfly) just by changing the links between the crossbar stages.

MIN Data Packet

The data communicated via the mpNoC are transferred as packets of length 65-bits. Each data packet contains:

- Header (1bit): contains the enable-read or -write signal to indicate the type of the communication (read or write).

- Message (32bits): the data to be exchanged.
- Queue (32 bits): contains the address of the source (processor, I/O device) and the memory address.

Figure 10 represents the MIN data packet structure.

Switch Element Architecture

The switch element is the key component in the MIN architecture. It is composed of two FIFO (First-In-First-Out buffer of size equal to eight) and a scheduler who decides when data is sent from particular inputs to their desired outputs following a round robin scheduling algorithm. The incoming packets are buffered in FIFO and held until they will be sent to their destinations. The scheduler's decision is determined by a scheduling algorithm which has to be fast, efficient, easy to implement in hardware, and fair in serving all the inputs.

There are various scheduling algorithms (McKeown & Anderson, 1998). We choose to use round robin algorithm. The scheduler plays the role of a router, arbiter and a temporary memorizing. He has two Inputs which receive the packets from

Figure 10. Delta MIN Packet structure

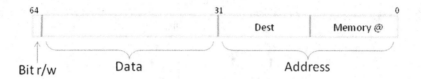

Figure 11. Switch element architecture

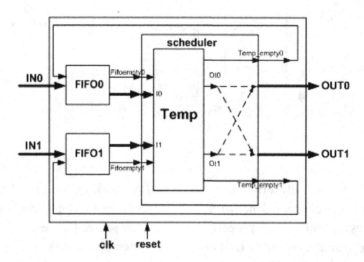

FIFOs. The latter will be held and stored until being forwarded according to their destination within a minimum time. The routing module in the Scheduler determines the output port to which the packet will be sent using its self routing algorithm. If two packets destined for the same output port arrive simultaneously at different input ports, the arbiter allows only one packet at a time to be transferred to output port (the other packet will be held in the temporary memory).

MIN Based mpNoC for FPGA Based MPPSoC: Implementation and Evaluation

Hardware Platform

The used development board is the Altera's DSP Development Kit equipped with a Stratix 2S-180 FPGA with 179k logic elements, 1 MB external

SRAM, 32 MB external SDRAM, and I/Os such as UART and Ethernet. The software tools used are the Quartus II V9.0 which is a synthesis and implementation tool (Altera, n.d.) used also to download the compiled program file onto the chip, and the Modelsim Altera 6.4a simulator to simulate and debug the implemented design. The MPPSoC architecture is run at 50MHz.

Synthesis Results

The described MPPSoC architecture is implemented integrating an mpNoC with a MIN interconnection network. The mpNoC is parametric so that it can be adapted to a parametric number of PEs in the system. Different sized MPPSoC architectures (with 4, 8, 16 and 32 PEs), as well as their MIN networks have been evaluated in terms of area and frequency. Table 3 shows the

Table 3. Delta MIN synthesis results

Number of PEs	Logic Utilization ALUT registers		Frequency (Mhz)
4	402	1404	126
8	1101	3885	120
16	1456	5401	109
32	2099	7746	89

Table 4. MPPSoC synthesis results

Number of PEs	Logic Utilization ALUT registers		Max. Frequency (Mhz)
4	10046	4305	54.3
8	17222	7176	53.46
16	27268	11481	51.77
32	51667	17231	41.68

synthesis results of the different Delta MIN networks designs varying the number of PEs.

As illustrated in the Table 3, the Delta MIN requires more FPGA resources when increasing the number of connected nodes in a proportional manner. The MIN with 32 nodes only occupies 6% of the total FPGA area. We clearly see from the above tabulated results that the frequency of the network decreases as the number of nodes increases. This is due to the increase of conflicts when the communicated nodes become larger. The MPPSoC configurations integrating a Delta MIN based mpNoC have been also evaluated in term of FPGA area, as presented in the Table 4.

We see that the MPPSoC configurations occupy more FPGA area when integrating more PEs. The MPPSoC architecture with 32 PEs only needs about 38% of the total FPGA surface. So we are able to integrate more PEs in the Stratix 2S-180 FPGA. Two aspects can be deduced from the measured frequency results. On the one hand, it is shown that a parallel architecture can increase the frequency of the used processor when integrating many processors working in parallel to achieve a given task (for example with 4 PEs we obtained 54.3 Mhz which is superior than 50 Mhz, the frequency of the miniMIPS processor). On the other hand, we see that when the architecture comprises more PEs, the frequency drops. This is due to the used network and the complexity of routing which increases with the increase size of the architecture.

To test the performance of the MPPSoC architecture and the efficiency of the proposed

Delta MIN network, two different representative data parallel applications have been tested. The experimental results are presented and analyzed in the next Section.

Data Parallel Applications: Performance Evaluation

The objective of this Section is to validate the functioning of the MPPSoC architecture and to test the reliability and the effectiveness of the used Delta MIN network to increase the performance of a parallel processing system. The reconfiguration aspect of the mpNoC is also tested to assure different communication modes needed to satisfy the application communication requirements. Different Delta MIN topologies are also evaluated in order to prove the flexibility of the architecture. In addition, based on the simulation results, suitable SIMD system with an adequate MIN topology can be chosen for the targeted application.

Two data parallel applications were tested: a picture rotation and a parallel reduction. These two applications are considered among the basic image processing operations. They necessitate different communication schemes between the processors and are good examples to test the implemented MIN network. The applications are written in the extended MIPS assembly code. In fact, the GNU MIPS assembler has been modified to generate a binary which can be directly integrated in the bit stream of the FPGA MPPSoC implementation. The assembly code can be then executed by MPPSoC.

Figure 12. MPPSoC programming

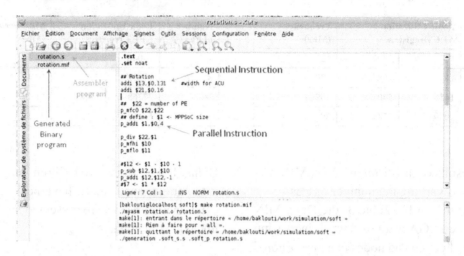

Figure 13. LENA picture rotation

The Figure 12 illustrates the environment to generate the binary MPPSoC programs.

Picture Rotation

This application consists on applying specific rotations on the LENA picture. So, 17161-pixel picture rotations are performed. The MIN seems to be a good network to manage the required irregular communications. The resulting images of Figure 13 were provided by an execution of binary programs on MPPSoC mapped to an FPGA.

The picture rotation application requires a non homogeneous data movement and I/O throughput requirements. For that purpose, the Delta MIN based mpNoC is used to assure communications between the processors and also to perform parallel data transfers to read pixels from the external Flash memory to the PEs and to display processed data from the PEs to the VGA screen based on its

reconfigurable communication mode. The used modes are: PE-PE, Flash memory-PE and PE-VGA driver. Furthermore, the parametricity of the MPPSoC architecture has been also validated while testing different sized configurations in terms of number of PEs as well as the PE data memory size, as highlighted in the Table 5.

The PEs are arranged in a 2D (p x p) grid. Each PE performs the rotation on its image sub-matrice of size (131/p x 131/p). The Figure 14 presents the performance results in term of computation cycles, varying the used MIN topology. In fact,

Table 5. Parametric MPPSoC configurations

Number of PEs	Memory size (bytes/PE)	FPGA Area (%)	Tested MIN topology
4	17424	8	Omega Butterfly Baseline
16	4356	21	
36	1936	46	

Figure 14. Simulation results

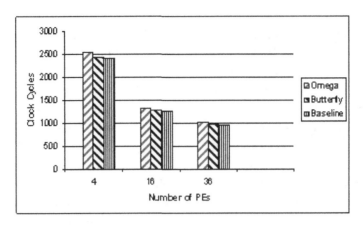

Figure 15. Energy consumption results

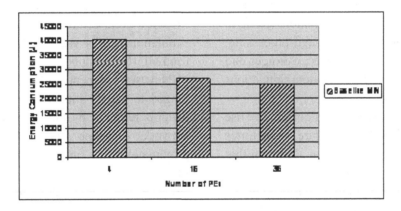

the three different MIN topologies differ in terms of the connection links between the crossbar based stages.

As illustrated by Figure 14, the speedup increases when increasing the number of PEs. We note that the architecture of the used parallel system has also a great impact on the speedup of a given application. With 36 PEs, the speedup is approximately 2.5 times higher than with 4PEs. It is also shown that the baseline topology is the most suitable to run a picture rotation application using a MIN network. These results demonstrate the flexibility of the MPPSoC architecture and the high efficiency achieved by establishing a well mapped network topology to one application.

The energy consumption is also measured for the baseline MIN based MPPSoC configurations (see Figure 15) to study the embedded system properties. The energy E is measured by: $E = T \times P$; where T is the execution time (s) and P (W) is the power consumption. The power is calculated by the synthesis tool using the PowerPlay power analysis tool.

The Figure 15 shows a decrease in the energy consumption for the different sized MPPSoCs while increasing the number of PEs working in parallel.

Parallel Reduction

The reduction algorithm (Siegel, Wang, So, & Maheswaran, 1994) presents one basic image processing operations. The reduction operation consists on computing the result of an associative operation (e.g. sum, product, min and max) on the data set. It is important to study parallel algorithms for reduction operations, because data elements are generally distributed across the PEs on parallel architectures (Zomaya, 1995). Reductions are used in many algorithms to compute error metrics and termination conditions for iterative algorithms. In addition, reduction may be itself be used in parallel as part of another algorithm for example in matrix multiplication. Reductions are also used extensively in Monte Carlo simulations (using in finance, computer graphics, image processing, and a variety of other fields) were averages and variances of a large number of random simulations need to be computed.

To implement the reduction algorithm we use the recursive doubling procedure, sometimes also called tree summing. It is an algorithm that combines a set of operands distributed across PEs (Stone, 1980). The Figure 16 illustrates the reduction computation using 8 PEs.

Consider the example of finding the sum of 4096 integers. Sequentially, this requires one load and 4095 additions, or approximately 4096 additions. However, if these 4096 integers are distributed across N = 4096 PEs, the parallel summing procedure requires $\log_2(N)=64$ transfer-add steps,

where a transfer-add is composed of the transfer of a partial sum to the PE and the addition of that partial sum to the PE's local sum. The described algorithm (sum of 4096 integers) is executed on different sized MPPSoC configurations (with 4, 8 and 16 PEs) and with topologically distinct mpNoC interconnection networks (baseline, butterfly, omega). Execution performances are then compared as presented in Figure 17.

We notice, as expected, that the parallel application achieves better results when computed with more processing elements. This proves that the performance of the MPPsoC scales with the number of processors. The speedup obtained with 16 PEs is 2.5 times higher than that with 4 PEs. This confirms the performance of the parallel MPPSoC architecture. The Figure 17 shows the simulation results varying the topology of the used MIN based mpNoC. The performance of the MIN network depends on how its stages are arranged to satisfy the different communication patterns required by the application. The three networks (baseline, butterfly and omega) approximately give similar results since they can satisfy the needed parallel communications. However, the recursive doubling procedure could not be executed using the butterfly MIN with 16 PEs. This is caused by the inefficiency of the butterfly network to respond to the needed communications as illustrated in the Figure 18. In fact, in the first step of the application, PE3 needs to communicate with PE2 (as PE7-PE6, PE9-PE8

Figure 16. Parallel reduction-addition with eight processing elements

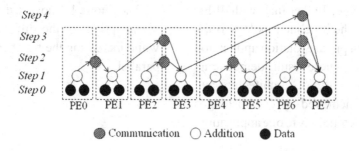

and PE13-PE12) which is not possible using the available butterfly connections (see Figure 18).

According to these results, we deduce that having a configurable and flexible network in a parallel system is very advantageous to satisfy the required communications for different data parallel applications.

The designer can choose the most suitable network, depending on his application, in order to optimize the whole system performances. In fact, the flexibility and configurability of the MPPSoC architecture, in particular its interconnection network, allow the designers to generate the most appropriate architecture satisfying the application needs. It is vital to have a flexible interconnection scheme that can be applied to the system design. The parameterization of the MPPSoC is also a key aspect to easily tailor the architecture according to HW as well as SW requirements.

Figure 17. Parallel reduction simulation results

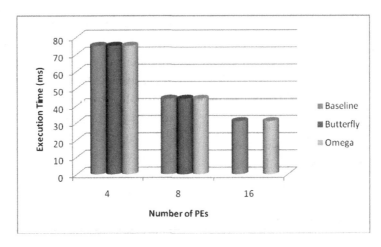

Figure 18. Inefficiency of the butterfly MIN network to satisfy the parallel reduction communications

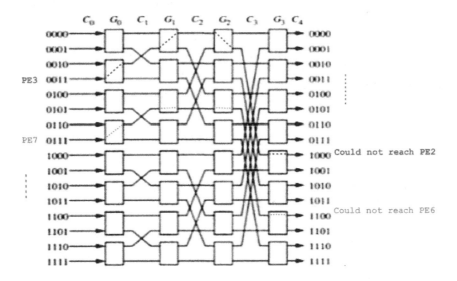

FIR Filter

FIR (Finite Impulse Response) filtering is one of the most popular DSP algorithms. It is well suited to be executed on SIMD systems. FIR filters are easy to design. On the other hand, they require increased number of multiplications and additions, and, what is also important, number of memory reads. A FIR filter is implemented with the following equation:

$$Y(n) = \sum_{k=0}^{M-1} b_k X(n-k)$$

X is the input signal and b_k are filter coefficients. M is the filter order or number of taps which is equal to 64. A 64-order FIR filter requires 64 multiplications and 64 additions for every output signal sample. It also requires 128 memory read operations; 64 of them is for input signal, the rest for them is for filter coefficients. In this work an adapted version of the difference equation called the Direct Form Structure (Figure 19), is implemented.

Different sized MPPSoC configurations using different MIN based mpNoC topologies are tested and evaluated.

The Figure 20 illustrates the clock cycles needed to run the FIR filter application on various MPPSoC configurations. The results are based on a 64-tap FIR and an impulse response with a length of 128.

Only two MIN topologies, omega and baseline, are used to compute the FIR filters since the butterfly topology is not suitable to achieve the de-

manded communications between PEs. Simulation results presented in Figure 20 shows the increasing performance of MPPSoC to compute a data parallel application when increasing the number of PEs working in parallel. We notice that the omega network is the most effective for the FIR application. These results highlight the advantages of using a flexible network in a parallel SoC; so that the designer would choose the best interconnect suited to his application.

FUTURE RESEARCH DIRECTIONS

The work presented in this chapter has proved that a multistage network on chip is suited to be integrated in a massively parallel system and can lead to sustained performance results. The design methodology proposed here is very important to prove the performances of the MIN and covers all design levels from a formal verification at the specification level to an FPGA implementation at the RTL level.

The described massively parallel processing system on chip has shown to be also efficient to run data parallel applications. Integrating a reconfigurable network which can be adapted according to the application requirements is an essential characteristic to achieve high performances. In fact, the FPGA implementation of the MIN based MPPSoC, with various configurations, has been validated on three significant simple data parallel applications which could easily be a component of a more complex, real-life MPPSoC application. According to the performances of

Figure 19. Direct form of FIR filters

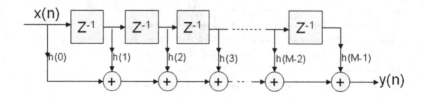

each configuration, the designer can choose the most appropriate one for the tested application. We have so demonstrated that it is vital to have a flexible interconnection scheme which can be applied to the system design. The flexibility of the architecture allows matching the design with the application, improving the performances and satisfying its requirements.

Future research will deal with the choice of the best suited network configuration while running the application. For that purpose an architecture exploration step is necessary in the MPPSoC design flow in order to automatically select the needed architectural configuration. The exploration can be done at a high abstraction level in order to speed-up the exploration process and then the appropriate MPPSoC configuration can be generated at the low level. A dynamic exploration at the implementation level can be also performed in order to assure the dynamic reconfiguration of the architecture taking into account the trade-off between flexibility and performance. To dynamically change the design implementation is efficient to meet and satisfy all the requirements of the system implementation.

CONCLUSION

In this paper, we presented a design and validation approach of multistage interconnection network for Massively Parallel Processing System on Chip. It starts with an informal description of network

architecture at the algorithmic level and produces a complete implementation of on-chip network on programmable circuits. The framework covers two issues.

We developed a functional formalization of MIN-Based network by identifying inherent properties of all topologies. These properties, which are also called constraints, have been validated using the ACL2 theorem proving environment. To achieve the routing extension, we have also formalized the general common relation between topology and routing. To validate our approach, we insist on the application of this formalism to a Delta MIN case study that constitutes a concrete instance of the model. After validating the functional model, we first described the modeling and the implementation of a MIN networks for FPGA-based MPPSoC. Second, we proposed an evaluation methodology based on performance and costs metrics for ensuring the compliance of the design with the initial specification. The analysis results prove the efficiency of the MIN networks to maintain a high performance in the parallel systems.

The main objective in the present work is to use several techniques to validate selected communication architecture in different level abstraction. The framework presented in this paper opens a promising trend for further development as complement to verification techniques. We plan to extend this work to employ formal notations to validate the implementation of the communication architecture based on multistage interconnection

Figure 20. FIR filters simulation results

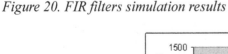

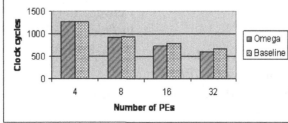

network. Another possible prospect is to develop a complete MPPSoC design framework helping the designer to perform an architecture exploration for a given application.

REFERENCES

Altera. (n.d.). Retrieved from http://www.altera.com

Amjad, H. (2006). Verification of AMBA Using a Combination of Model Checking and Theorem Proving. *Electronic Notes in Theoretical Computer Science, 145*, 45–61. doi:10.1016/j.entcs.2005.10.004

Aydi, Y., Meftali, S., Abid, M., & Dekeyser, J. L. (2007). Design and Performance Evaluation of a Reconfigurable Delta MIN for MPSOC. In Proc. of *the 19th International Conference on Microelectronics (ICM '07)*.

Bartic, T. A. (2003). Highly scalable network on chip for reconfigurable systems. In Proc. *Int. Symp. Syst.-on-Chip* (pp. 79-82).

Benini. L, & Micheli. G. D. (2002). Networks on chips: A new SoC paradigm. *Computer, 1 (35)*, IEEE Computer Society Press, Los Alamitos, California, 70-78.

Borrione, D., Helmy, A., & Schmaltz, J. (2008). Executable formal specification and validation of NOC communication infrastructures. Proc. of *the 21st annual symposium on Integrated circuits and system design*. Brazil.

Borrione. D., Helmy. A., Pierre. L., & Schmaltz. J. (2009). A Formal approach to the verification of networks on chip. *Eurasip Journal on Embedded Systems, (2009)*.

Cheung. T, & Smith. J. E. (1986). A simulation study of the CRAY X-MP memory system. *IEEE Transactions on Computers, 7 (35)*. IEEE Computer Society, Washington. 613-622.

Dally, W. J., & Towles, B. (2001). Route packets, not wires: on-chip interconnection networks. In Proc. of *the 38th conference on Design automation* (pp. 684-689). ACM Press, New York, USA.

Eklund, S. E. (2001). A Massively Parallel Architecture for Linear Machine Code Genetic Programming. In Proc. *4th International Conference on Evolvable Systems: From Biology to Hardware*. (pp. 216-224).

Elleuch, M., Aydi, Y., & Abid, M. (2008). Formal Specification of Delta MINs for MPSOC in the ACL2 Logic. In Proc. of *Forum on Design and specification Languages, FDL '08*.

Ferreira, R., Laure, M., Beck, A. C., Lo, T., Rutzig, M., & Carro, L. (2009). A Low Cost and Adaptable Routing Network for Reconfigurable Systems. In Proc. *IEEE International Symposium on Parallel & Distributed Processing IPDPS*. (pp. 1-8).

Flynn, M. J. (1972). Some computer organizations and their effectiveness. *IEEE Transactions on Computers, 21*, 948–960. doi:10.1109/TC.1972.5009071

Freitas, H. C., & Navaux, P. O. A. (2008). Evaluating On-Chip Interconnection Architectures for Parallel Processing. In Proc. *11th International Conference on Computational Science and Engineering – Workshops*. (pp. 188-193).

Hord. R. M. (1982). *The Illiac IV: The First Supercomputer*. Computer Science Press.

Huebner, M. (2004). Scalable Application-Dependent Network on Chip Adaptivity for Dynamical Reconfigurable Real-Time Systems. In *FPL*.

Jay Siegel. (1989). Using the Multistage Cube Network Topology in Parallel Supercomputers. In *Proc. IEEE, 12 (77) 1932–1953*. H., Nation. W. C., Kruskal. C. P., & Napolitano. L. M.

Kapre, N. (2006). Packet switched vs time multiplexed FPGA overlay networks. In *IEEE Symposium of Field-Programmable Custom Computing Machines*.

Kaufmann, M., & Moore, J. S. (1996). *ACL2: An industrial strength version of nqthm. IEEE Transactions on Software Engineering, 4 (23)* (pp. 23–34). New York: IEEE Press.

Kruskal. C. (1986). A unified theory of interconnection network. *Theoretical Computer Science, 1 (48)*. Elsevier Science Publishers Ltd., Essex. 75-94.

Kruskal. C.P., & Snir. M. (1983). The performance of multistage interconnection networks for multiprocessors. *IEEE Transactions on Computers, 12 (32)*. IEEE Computer Society, Washington. 1091-1098.

Kumar, A. (2007). *An FPGA design flow for reconfigurable network-based multi-processor systems on chip* (pp. 117–122). In DATE.

Marescaux, T. (2003). *Networks on chip as hardware components of an OS for reconfigurable systems*. In FPL.

McKeown, N., & Anderson, T. E. (1998). A quantitative comparison of scheduling algorithms for input-queued switches. *Computer Networks and ISDN Systems, 24*(30), 2309–2326. doi:10.1016/S0169-7552(98)00157-3

Meilander. W. C., Baker. J. W., & M. J. (2003). Importance of SIMD Computation Reconsidered. In Proc. *International Parallel and Distributed Processing Symposium.*

Meyer Auf Der Heide. F., Monien. B., & Rosenberg. A. L. (1992). Parallel Architectures and Their Efficient Use. In: Proc. *1ˢᵗ Heinz Nixdorf Symposium*. Germany.

Ogras, U. Y., & Marculescu, R. (2005). Key research problems in NOC design: A holistic perspective. In Proc. of *International conference hardware-software codesign system synthesis* (pp. 69-74).

Pasricha, S., Dutt, N., Bozorgzadeh, E., & Ben-Romdhane, M. (2005). Floorplan-aware automated synthesis of bus-based communication architectures. In Proc. of *the 42ⁿᵈ annual conference on Design automation* (pp. 565-570). ACM Press, New York.

Patel, J. (1981). Performance of processor-memory interconnections for multiprocessors. *IEEE Trans., C*(30), 771–780.

Pionteck, T. (2006). *A Dynamically Reconfigurable Packet-Switched Network-on-Chip* (pp. 136–137). In DATE.

Roychoudhury, A., Mitra, T., & Karri, S. R. (2003). *Using Formal Techniques to Debug the AMBA System-On-Chip Protocol. Proc. of the conference on Design, Automation and Test in Europe, 1* (pp. 828–833). Washington: IEEE Computer Society.

Schack, C., Heenes, W., & Hoffmann, R. (2009). A Multiprocessor Architecture with an Omega Network for the Massively Parallel Model GCA. In Proc. *9ᵗʰ International Workshop on Embedded Computer Systems: Architectures, Modeling, and Simulation*. (pp. 98-107).

Schmaltz, J., & Borrione, D. (2004). A Functional Specification and Validation Model for Networks on Chip in the ACL2 Logic. Proc. of *the 5ᵗʰ International Workshop on the ACL2 Theorem Prover and its Applications (ACL2'04)*. Austin.

Schmaltz, J., & Borrione, D. (2006). Towards a Formal Theory of Communication Architecture in the ACL2 Logic. Proc. of *the 6ᵗʰ international workshop on the ACL2 theorem prover and its applications*. ACM Press, New York. (pp. 47-56).

Schurz, F., & Fey, D. (2007). *A Programmable Parallel Processor Architecture in FPGAs for Image Processing Sensors*. In Proc. Integrated Design and Process Technology.

Sharma, S., Kahlon, K. S., Bansal, P. K., & Singh, K. (2008). Irregular Class of Multistage Interconnection Network in Parallel Processing. *Journal of Computer Science*, 4(3), 220–224. doi:10.3844/jcssp.2008.220.224

Siege1. H. J., Wang. L., So. J. E., & Maheswaran. M. (1994). *Data parallel algorithms*. ECE Technical Reports.

Siegel, H., & Smith, S. (1978). Study of Multistage SIMD Interconnection Networks. In Proc. *5th Annual Symposium on Computer Architecture*. New York (pp. 223-229).

Siegel, H. J. (1979). Interconnection Networks for SIMD Machines. *IEEE. Computer*, 6(12), 57–65. doi:10.1109/MC.1979.1658780

Stone, H. S. (1971). Parallel Processing with the Perfect Shuffle. *IEEE Transactions on Computers*, 20, 153–161. doi:10.1109/T-C.1971.223205

Stone, H. S. (1980). Parallel computers. In Stone, H. S. (Ed.), *Introduction to Computer Architecture* (2nd ed., pp. 363–425). Chicago, IL: Science Research Associates.

(1972). The MasPar MP-1 Architecture. In *Proc. IEEE Compcon Spring90. IEEE Society Press* (pp. 20–24). San Francisco, CA: Blank. T.

Wee, S. (2007). A Practical FPGA based Framework for Novel CMP Research. In *International Symposium on Field Programmable Gate Arrays*.

(1995). *Zomaya. A. Y* (1st ed.). Parallel and Distributed Computing Handbook. McGraw-Hill Professional.

KEY TERMS AND DEFINITIONS

Packet Switching Networks: the switching type of the proposed network.

Parallel Processing: the targeting application domain.

Hardware Evaluation: evaluate the hardware performance of the proposed network.

Network Model: Delta multi-stage network.

Parallel Processing Systems: the systems dedicated to run parallel applications.

Formal Model: the formal model proposed in the formal verification of the network.

ACL2: the used programming language for the NoC verification.

FPGA: Field Programmable Gate Arrays, the target implementation platform.

Chapter 10
Reconfigurable Embedded Control Systems

Mohamed Khalgui
Xidian University, China

Olfa Mosbahi
Martin Luther University, Germany

ABSTRACT

The chapter deals with distributed multi-agent reconfigurable embedded control systems following the component-based International Industrial Standard IEC61499 in which a Function Block (abbreviated by FB) is an event-triggered software component owning data and a control application is a distributed network of Function Blocks that have classically to satisfy functional and to meet temporal properties described in user requirements. The authors define a new reconfiguration semantic where a crucial criterion to consider is the automatic improvement of the system's performance at run-time, in addition to its protection when hardware faults occur. To handle all possible cases in industry, the authors classify thereafter the reconfiguration scenarios into three forms before the authors define an architecture of reconfigurable multi-agent systems where a Reconfiguration Agent is affected to each device of the execution environment to apply local reconfigurations, and a Coordination Agent is proposed for any coordination between devices in order to guarantee safe and adequate distributed reconfigurations. A Communication Protocol is proposed in our research work to handle coordinations between agents by using well-defined Coordination Matrices. The authors specify both the reconfiguration agents to be modelled by nested state machines, and the Coordination Agent according to the formalism Net Condition/Event Systems (Abbreviated by NCES) which is an extension of Petri nets. To verify the whole architecture, the author check by applying the model checker SESA in each device functional and temporal properties described in the temporal logic "Computation Tree Logic", but the authors have also to check any coordination between devices by verifying that whenever a reconfiguration is applied in a device, the Coordination Agent and other concerned devices should react as described in user requirements. The chapter's contributions are applied to two Benchmark Production Systems available in our research laboratory.

DOI: 10.4018/978-1-60960-086-0.ch010

INTRODUCTION

Nowadays in industry, the development of safety distributed embedded systems is not a trivial activity because a failure can be critical for the safety of human beings (e.g. air and railway traffic control, nuclear plant control, aircraft and car control). They have classically to satisfy according to user requirements, functional and temporal properties (Baruah, & Goossens, 2004), but their time to market should be shorter than ever. To address all these important requirements, the component-based approach is studied in several academic research works and also in industrial projects to develop modular embedded systems in order to control the design complexity and to support the reusability of already developed components (Goessler & Sifakis, 2002). Several component-based technologies have been proposed in industry to design the application (as a composition of components) (Crnkovic & Larsson, 2002). Among all these technologies, the International Standard IEC61499 is proposed by the International Electrotechnical Commission to design distributed control applications as well as corresponding execution environments (IEC61499, 2004),. A Function Block in this Standard is an event-triggered software component composed of an Interface and an Implementation where the interface contains data/event inputs/ outputs for external interactions with the environment. Events are responsible for the activation of the block, whereas data contain valued information. The Implementation of the block contains algorithms to execute when corresponding events occur. The selection of an algorithm to execute is performed by a state machine called Execution Control Chart (ECC) which is also responsible for sending output events at the end of the algorithm execution. An IEC61499 application is therefore a network of blocks that should meet functional as well as temporal properties defined in user requirements. Today in academia and industry, rich books have been written (Lewis, 2001), many

research works have been made, useful tools have been developed and finally real industrial platforms have been deployed while following this International Standard. In our research laboratory at Martin Luther University in Germany, two Benchmark Production Systems (FESTO and EnAS) are completely developed according to this component-based technology.

The new generation of industrial control systems is addressing today new criteria as flexibility and agility. To reduce their cost, these systems should be changed and adapted to their environment without disturbances. Several interesting academic and industrial research works have been made last years to develop reconfigurable control systems (Gehin & Staroswiecki, 2008). We distinguish in these works two reconfiguration policies: static and dynamic reconfigurations where static reconfigurations are applied off-line to apply changes before the system cold start (Angelov Sierszecki & Marian, 2005), whereas dynamic reconfigurations are applied dynamically at run-time. Two cases exist in the last policy: manual reconfigurations applied by users (Rooker, Sunder, Strasser, Zoitl, Hummer & Ebenhofer, 2007) and automatic reconfigurations applied by Intelligent Agents (Al-Safi & Vyatkin, 2007). We are interested in this chapter in automatic reconfigurations of industrial control systems following the International Standard IEC61499. We define at a first time a new reconfiguration semantic where a crucial criterion to consider is the automatic improvement of the system performance at run-time, in addition to its protection when hardware faults occur. To explain in detail this semantic, we give examples of automatic reconfigurations to be applied to the Benchmark Production Systems FESTO and EnAS. To cover all possible reconfiguration cases in industry, we define a classification of scenarios into three forms: the first deals with the system architecture, the second with the internal structure of blocks or with their composition, finally the third deals with the reconfiguration of data. To handle all possible reconfiguration scenarios to be automatically applied at run-time, we propose a multi-agent distributed architecture where a reconfiguration agent is affected to each device of the execution environment to handle local automatic reconfigurations, and a Coordination Agent is defined to manage distributed reconfigurations between devices because any uncontrolled automatic reconfiguration applied in a device can lead to critical problems or serious disturbances in others. We define therefore the concept of "Coordination Matrix" to define for each distributed reconfiguration scenario the behavior of all concerned agents that have to react simultaneously. To guarantee a deterministic behavior of the whole control system, we define for each matrix a priority level according to the emergency of the corresponding reconfiguration scenario. The Coordination Agent handles all matrices to coordinate between agents according to a well-defined communication protocol: when an agent applies in the corresponding device a highest-priority reconfiguration, the Coordination Agent informs concerned agents to react and to bring the whole system into safe and optimal behaviors. The reconfigurable embedded system is assumed to be implemented by a set of distributed FB networks such that only one network is executed when the corresponding scenario is applied by reconfiguration agents at run-time. Each FB network should meet functional and temporal properties according to user requirements. To check the whole distributed architecture, we model each reconfiguration agent Ag by nested state machines (i.e. states can be other state machines) according to the formalism Net Condition/Event Systems (NCES) proposed by Rausch and Hanisch as an extension of the well-know Petri nets, and we use the well-expressive temporal logic "Computation Tree Logic" (denoted by CTL) as well as its extensions (eCTL and TCTL) to specify functional and temporal properties that we verify with the model checker SESA on the nested state machines of Ag and also on the corresponding controlled Function Blocks. At

this step, the internal behavior in each device in checked, but the coordination between agents should be verified in order to avoid any critical problems at run-time. We propose therefore for each Coordination Matrix a NCES-based model and we apply the model checker SESA to check if all the system's agents react as described in user requirements to guarantee safe distributed reconfigurations.

In the next section, we analyze previous works on model checking, reconfigurable embedded systems and multi-agent systems, before we present in Section 3 the IEC61499 technology, the formalism NCES and the temporal logic CTL. We define in Section 4 a new reconfiguration semantic that we explain on the systems FESTO and EnAS to be considered as running examples in the following. We define in Section 5 a multi-agent architecture of reconfigurable embedded systems where a Coordination Agent and Coordination Matrices are proposed to guarantee safe distributed reconfigurations. We propose in Section 6 NCES-based models for reconfiguration agents and also for Coordination matrices before we apply SESA to verify eCTL-based functional and TCTL-based temporal properties described in user requirements. We finish the chapter with a conclusion and the presentation of our future work.

STATE OF THE ART

We present in this section well-known model checkers in academia and also in industry for verifications of functional and temporal properties, before we describe interesting previous research works on reconfigurations of embedded systems, and present thereafter some studies on multi-agent systems.

Model Checking

Finite state machines (abbr. FSM) are widely used for the modelling of control flow in embedded systems and are amenable to formal analysis like model checking. Two kinds of computational tools have been developed last years for model checking: tools like KRONOS (Daws, Olivero, Tripakis & Yovine, 1996), UPPAAL (Amnell, Behrmann, Bengtsson, D'Argenio, David, Fehnker, Hune, Jeannet, Larsen, Mller, Pettersson, Weise & Yi, 2001), HyTech (Henzinger, Ho & Womg-Toi, 1997) and SESA (SESA, 2008) which compute sets of reachable states exactly and effectively, whereas emerging tools like CHECKMATE (Chutinan & Krogh, 1999), d/dt (Asarin, Bournez, Dang & Maler, 2000) and level-sets (Mitchell & Tomlin, 2000) methods approximate sets of reachable states. Several research works have been proposed last years to control the verification complexity by applying hierarchical model checking for complex embedded systems. The authors propose in (Alur & Yannakakis, 1998) an approach for verifications of hierarchical (i.e. nested) finite state machines whose states themselves can be other machines. The straightforward way to analyze a hierarchical machine is to flatten and apply a model checking tool on the resulting ordinary FSM, but the authors show in this interesting research work that this flattening can be avoided by developing useful algorithms for verifications of hierarchical machines. We use SESA in our research work to validate multi-agent reconfigurable embedded systems following the technology IEC61499, where each agent is specified by nested Net Condition/Event Systems.

Reconfiguration of IEC61499 Embedded Systems

Nowadays, rich research works have been proposed to develop reconfigurable embedded systems following the Standard IEC61499. The authors propose in (Angelov, Sierszecki & Marian, 2005) reusable Function Blocks to implement a broad range of embedded systems where each block is statically reconfigured without any re-programming. This is accomplished by updating the supporting data structure, i.e. a state transition table, whereas the executable code remains unchanged and may be stored in permanent memory. The state transition table consists of multiple-output binary decision diagrams that represent the next-state mappings of various states and the associated control actions. The authors propose in (Rooker, Sunder, Strasser, Zoitl, Hummer & Ebenhofer, 2007) a complete methodology based on the human intervention to dynamically reconfigure control systems. They present in addition an interesting experimentation showing the dynamic change by users of a function block's algorithm without disturbing the whole system. The authors use in (Thramboulidis, Doukas & Frantzis, 2004) Real-time-UML as a meta-model between design models of IEC61499 and their implementation models to support dynamic user-based reconfigurations of control systems. The authors propose in (Brennan, Fletcher & Norrie, 2001) an agent-based reconfiguration approach to save the whole system when faults occur at run-time. Finally the authors propose in (Al-Safi & Vyatkin, 2007) an ontology-based agent to perform system reconfigurations that adapt changes in requirements and also in environment. They are interested to study reconfigurations of control systems when hardware faults occur at run-time. Although the applicability of these contributions in industry is clear and obvious, we believe in their limitation in particular cases (i.e. to resolve hardware faults or to add new functionalities like updates of algorithms in blocks) without studying all possible reasons to apply reconfigurations like improvements of system's performances. They do not consider in addition particular reconfiguration techniques that we can probably apply at run-time like additions of data/event inputs/outputs in control systems.

Multi-Agent Systems

Several research works have been done last years in academia and also in industry to define inter-agents communication protocols for multi-agent systems. The authors focus in (Pitt & Mamdani, 2000) on the communicative act between agents and define a general semantic framework for specifying a class of Agent Communication Language (ACLs) based on protocols. They introduce a small ACL denoted by sACL for different application domains and describe a development method to define an ACL for a particular application. The authors are interested in (Mailler & Lesser, 2003-a) in Distributed Constraint Satisfaction Problems (DisCSP) as an important area of research for multi-agent systems. The agents work together to solve problems that cannot be completely centralized due to security, dynamics, or complexity. The authors present an algorithm called asynchronous partial overlay (APO) for solving DisCSPs that is based on a mediated negotiation process. The same authors present in (Mailler, Lesser, Horling, 2003-b) a cooperative negotiation protocol that solves a distributed resource allocation problem while conforming to soft real-time constraints in a dynamic environment. A fully automated and knowledge-based organization designer for multi-agent systems called KB-ORG is proposed in the same research activities (Sims, Corkill & Lesser, 2008). Organization design is the process that accepts organizational goals, environmental expectations, performance requirements, role characterizations, as well as agent descriptions, and assigns roles to each agent. In (Corkill, Holzhauer & Koziarz, 2007), an agent-based power-aware sensor network called CNAS (Collaborative Network for Atmospheric Sensing) is proposed for ground-level atmospheric monitoring. The CNAS agents must have their radios turned off most of the time, as even listening consumes significant power. CNAS requires agent's policies that can intelligently meet operational requirements while communicating only during intermittent, mutually established, and communication windows. The authors describe in (Novak, Rollo, Hodik & Vlcek, 2003) the architecture and implementation of the security (X-Security) system, which implements authentification and secure communication among agents. The system uses certification authority (CA) and ensures full cooperation of secured agents and already existing (unsecured) ones. The authors propose augmenting in (Berna-koes, Nourbakhsh & Sycara, 2003) the capabilities of current multi-agent systems to provide the efficient transfer of low-level information, by allowing backchannels of communications between agents with flexible protocols in a carefully principled way.

In our research work, we are interested in communications and collaborations between agents to guarantee safe and adequate distributed reconfigurations of embedded control systems following the Standard IEC61499. These communications are handled by a Coordination Agent that coordinates between agents according to environment's evolutions, user requirements and also priorities of reconfigurations.

BACKGROUND

We describe in this section the main concepts of the International Standard IEC61499 before we present the formalism Net Condition/Event Systems and we describe thereafter the temporal logic Computation Tree Logic.

IEC61499 Standard

The component-based International Industrial Standard IEC61499 (IEC61499, 2004; Khalgui & Rebeuf, 2008; Khalgui, Rebeuf & Simonot-Lion, 2007; Khalgui & Hanisch, 2008; Khalgui & Thramboulidis, 2008; Khalgui, Carpanzano & Hanisch, 2008), is an extension of the previous one IEC61131.3 which is used for the development of Programmable Logic Controllers (IEC61131, 1993). According to IEC61499, a Function Block (FB) (Figure 1) is a unit of software that supports functionalities of an application. It is composed of an interface and an implementation such that the interface contains data/event inputs and outputs for external interactions with the environment. Events are responsible for the activation of the block while data contain valued information. The implementation of the block contains algorithms to execute when corresponding events occur. The selection of an algorithm to execute is performed by a state machine called Execution Control Chart (ECC) which is also responsible for sending output events at the end of the algorithm execution. The block BELT F B shown in Figure 1 is a FB used to control conveyer belts. It is activated by the input events INIT, OBJ_ARR, OBJ_LEFT and STOPI and responds to the environment by the output events INITO, CNF, MOVEF and STOPO. When the event OBJ_ARR occurs, the state OBJ_ARRIVED is activated as shown in Figure 2 to execute the algorithm Inc.Counter. Once such execution finishes, the ECC sends the output event CNF and activates the states MOVE OR START depending on the value of the internal variable Count. In particular, when the output event CNF should be sent, the block updates the corresponding output data COUNT and SPEED. A control application is specified in the Standard IEC61499 by a network of blocks where each event input (resp. output) of a block is linked to an event output (resp. input) by a channel. Otherwise, it corresponds to a global input (resp. output). Data inputs and outputs follow the same rules. The architecture of the execution environment is well-defined by a network of devices where each device is composed of one processing unit and interfaces (with sensors, actuators and the network).

NCES Formalism

The formalism of Net Condition/(Event Systems (NCES) is an extension of the well-known Petri net formalism. It was introduced by Rausch and Hanisch in (Rausch & Hanisch, 1995) and further developed through last years, in particular in (Hanisch & Luder, 1999), according to which

Figure 1. An IEC 61499 Function Block

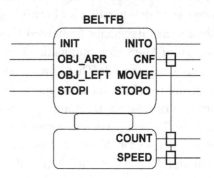

a fully composed NCES is a place-transition net formally represented by a tuple (Figure 3):

$$NCES = (P, T, F, CN, EN, C^{in}, E^{in}, C^{out}, E^{out}, B_c, B_e, C_s, D_t, m_0)$$ where,

- P (resp, T) is a non-empty finite set of places (resp, transitions),
- F is a set of flow arcs, $F: (P \, X \, T) \cup (T \, X \, P)$,
- CN (resp, EN) is a set of condition (resp, event) arcs, $CN \subseteq (P \, X \, T)$ (resp, $EN \subseteq (T \, X \, T)$),
- C^{in} (resp, E^{in}) is a set of condition (resp, event) inputs,
- C^{out} (resp, E^{out}) is a set of condition (resp, event) outputs,
- B_c (resp, B_e) is a set of condition (resp, event) input arcs in a NCES module,
- $B_c \subseteq (C^{in} \, X \, T)$ (resp, $B_e \subseteq (E^{in} \, X \, T)$),
- C_s (resp, D_t) is a set of condition (resp, event) output arcs,
- $C_s \subseteq (P \, X \, E^{out})$ (resp, $D_t \subseteq (T \, X \, E^{out})$),
- $m_0: P \rightarrow 0, 1$ is the initial marking,

The semantics of NCES are defined by the firing rules of transitions. There are several conditions to be fulfilled to enable a transition to fire. First, as it is in ordinary Petri nets, an enabled transition should have token concession. That means that all pre-places should be marked with at least one token. In addition to the flow arcs from places, a transition in NCES may have incoming condition arcs from places and event arcs from

Figure 2. The ECC of the FB BeltF B

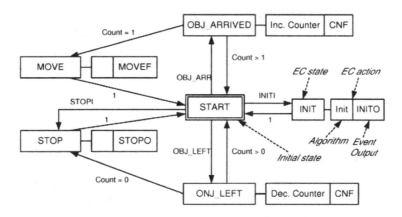

Figure 3. A module of Net Condition/Event Systems

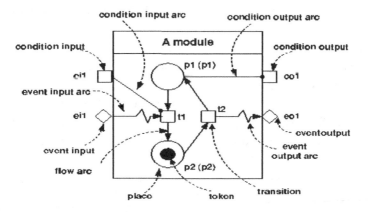

other transitions. A transition is enabled by condition signals if all source places of the condition signals are marked by at least one token. The other type of influence on the firing can be described by event signals which come to the transition from some other transitions. Transitions having no incoming event arcs are called spontaneous, otherwise forced. A forced transition is enabled if it has token concession and it is enabled by condition and event signals (Rausch & Hanisch, 1995). On the other hand, the NCES formalism is enriched in the last years to consider time constraints applied to the input arcs of transitions: to every pre-arc of a transition, an interval [eft,lft] of natural numbers is attached with $0 \leq eft \leq w$ (w is a fixed integer). The interpretation is as follows,

every place p bears a clock which is running iff the place is marked and switched off otherwise. All running clocks run at the same speed measuring the time the token status of its place has not been changed i.e. the clock on a marked place p shows the age of the youngest token on p. If a firing transition t is able to remove a token from the place p or adds a token to p then the clock of p is turned back to 0. In addition, a transition t is able to remove tokens from its pre-places (i.e. to fire) only if for any pre-place p of t the clock at place p shows a time $u(p)$ such that $eft(p; t) \leq u(p) \leq lft(p; t)$. Hence, the firing of transitions is restricted by the clock positions. We note finally that the model-checker SESA is a useful and rich tool to verify functional and temporal properties of NCES (Vyatkin & Hanisch, 2003). We propose to apply it in our work for verifications of reconfigurable control systems following the Standard IEC61499.

Temporal Logic

The "Computation Tree Logic" CTL offers facilities for specifications of properties to be fulfilled by the system behavior (Roch, 2000). We briefly present in this section this logic, its extension "Extended Computation Tree Logic" (denoted by eCTL) and the "Timed Computation Tree Logic" (denoted by TCTL).

Computation Tree Logic

In CTL, all formulae specify behaviors of the system starting from an assigned state in which the formula is evaluated by taking paths (i.e. sequence of states) into account. The semantics of formulae is defined with respect to a reachability graph where states and paths are used for the evaluation. A reachability graph M consists of all global states that the system can reach from a given initial state. It is formally defined as a tuple $M = [Z; E]$ where,

- Z is a finite set of states,
- E is a finite set of transitions between states, i.e. a set of edges $(z; z')$, such that z, $z' \in Z$ and z' is reachable from z.

In CTL, paths play the key role in the definition and evaluation of formulae. By definition, a path starting in the state z_0 is a sequence of states $(z_i) = z_0 z_1 ...$ such that for all $j \geq 0$ it holds that there is an edge $(z_j; z_{j+1}) \in E$. We denote in the following by (z_i) such path. The truth value of CTL formulae is evaluated with respect to a certain state of the reachability graph. Let $z_0 \in Z$ be a state of the reachability graph and φ a CTL formula, then the relation $|=$ for CTL formulae is defined inductively.

* *Basis:*

** $z_0 |= \varphi$ iff the formula ' holds in z_0,
** $z_0 |= true$ always holds,
** $z_0 |= false$ iff never holds,

* *Steps:*

** $z_0 |= EF\varphi$ iff there is a path (z_i) and $j \geq 0$ such that $z_j |= \varphi$,
** $z_0 |= AF\varphi$ iff for all paths (z_i) there exists $j \geq 0$ such that $z_j |= \varphi$,
** $z_0 |= AG\varphi$ iff for all paths (z_i) and for all $j \geq 0$ it holds $z_j |= \varphi$.

Extended Computation Tree Logic

In CTL, it is rather complicated to refer to information contained in certain transitions between states of a reachability graph. A solution is given in (Roch, 2000) for this problem by proposing an extension of CTL called Extended Computation Tree Logic eCTL. A transition formula is introduced in eCTL to refer to a transition information contained in the edges of the reachability graph. Since it is wanted to refer not only to state information but also to steps between states, the structure of the reachability graph $M = [Z; E]$ is changed as follows:

- Z is a finite set of states,
- E is a finite set of transitions between states, i.e. a set of labeled edges (z,s,z'), such that z, z' $\in$ Z and z' is reachable from z by executing the step s.

Let $z_0 \in Z$ be a state of the reachability graph, τ a transition formula and φ an eCTL formula. The relation $|=$ for eCTL formulae is defined inductively:

I.

° $z_0 |= E\tau X_\varphi$: iff there exists a successor state z_1 such that there is an edge $(z_0,$

s, z_1)$\in$E where (z_0, s, z_1) $|= \tau$ and $z_1 |=$ φ holds,

○ $z_0 |= E\tau X_\varphi$: iff $z_1 |= \varphi$ holds for all successors states z_1 with an edge (z_0, s, z_1) $\in$ E such that (z_0, s, z_1) $|= \tau$ holds.

Timed Computation Tree Logic

TCTL is an extension of CTL to model qualitative temporal assertions together with time constraints. The extension essentially consists in attaching a time bound to the modalities. We note that a good survey can be found in (Roch, 2000). For a reachability graph $M=[Z, E]$, the state delay D is defined as a mapping $D: Z \rightarrow N_0$ and for any state $z =[m, u]$ the number $D(z)$ is the number of time units which have to elapse at z before firing any transition from this state. For any path (z_i) and any state $z \in Z$ we put:

- $D[(z_i), z] = 0$, if $z_0 = z$,
- $D[(z_i), z] = D(z_0) + D(z_1) +... + D(z_{k-1})$, if $z_k = z$ and $z_0,..., z_{k-1} \neq z$.

With other words, $D[(z_i), z]$ is the number of time units after which the state z on the path (z_i) is reached the first time, i.e. the minimal time distance from z_0. Let $z_0 \in Z$ be a state of the reachability graph and φ a TCTL formula. The relation $|=$ for TCTL is defined as follows:

- $z_0 |= EF [l, h]_\varphi$, iff there is a path (z_i) and a j > 0 such that $z_j |= \varphi$ and $l \leq D((z_i), z_j) \leq h$,
- $z_0 |= AF [l, h]_\varphi$, iff for all paths (z_i), there is a j > 0 such that $z_j |= \varphi$ and $l \leq D((z_i, z_j) \leq h$.

AUTOMATIC RECONFIGURATION OF EMBEDDED CONTROL SYSTEMS

A crucial criterion to consider for the new generation of embedded systems is the automatic improvement of their performances at run-time. Indeed, these systems should dynamically and automatically improve their quality of service according to well-defined conditions. In addition, they should dynamically reduce the memory occupation and therefore the energy consumption in order to decrease the production cost. They have also to dynamically reduce the number of running controllers or also the traffic on used communication networks. We define in this section a new reconfiguration semantic that we apply to the Benchmark Production Systems FESTO and EnAS available in our research laboratory. To cover all possible reasons in industry, we define thereafter different reconfiguration forms that change the architectures, structures or data of the whole system to safe and preferment behaviors.

NEW RECONFIGURATION SEMANTIC

We define any dynamic reconfiguration of an embedded system as follows.

Definition. *A dynamic reconfiguration is any change according to well-defined conditions in software as well as hardware components to lead the whole embedded system at run-time to better and safe behaviors.*

According to the Standard IEC61499, we mean in this definition by a change in software components any operation allowing the addition, removal or also update of Function Blocks to improve the whole system behavior. We mean by a change in hardware components any operation allowing the addition, removal or also update of devices to be used in the execution environment. This new definition remains compatible with previous works on reconfigurations of control systems following the Standard IEC61499. Indeed, as defined in (Al-Safi & Vyatkin, 2007), the reconfiguration is applied to save the system when hardware problems occur at run-time. In this case, we have to apply changes in software as well as hardware components to bring the whole architecture to optimal and safe behaviors. In addition, as defined in (Rooker, Sunder, Strasser, Zoitl, Hummer & Ebenhofer, 2007), the reconfiguration is manually applied to add new functionalities in the system. Therefore, it corresponds also to changes in software and hardware components in order to bring the whole architecture to optimal behaviors. Finally, a dynamic reconfiguration will be in our research work any automatic action that saves the system, enriches its behaviors or also improves its performances at run-time. To our knowledge, this definition covers all possible reconfiguration cases in industry.

INDUSTRIAL CASE STUDIES: RECONFIGURATION OF BENCHMARK PRODUCTION SYSTEMS FESTO AND ENAS

We apply this new semantic of reconfiguration to two Benchmark Production Systems following the Standard IEC61499: FESTO and EnAS available in our research laboratory at Martin Luther University in Germany.

FESTO Manufacturing System

The Benchmark Production System FESTO is a well-documented demonstrator used by many universities for research and education purposes, and it is used as a running example in the context of this chapter (Figure 4). FESTO is composed of three units: the Distribution, the Test and the Processing units. The Distribution unit is composed of a pneumatic feeder and a converter. It forwards cylindrical work pieces from a stack to the testing unit which is composed of the detector, the tester and the elevator. This unit performs checks on work pieces for height, material type and color. Work pieces that successfully pass this check are forwarded to the rotating disk of the processing unit, where the drilling of the work

Figure 4. The FESTO modular production system

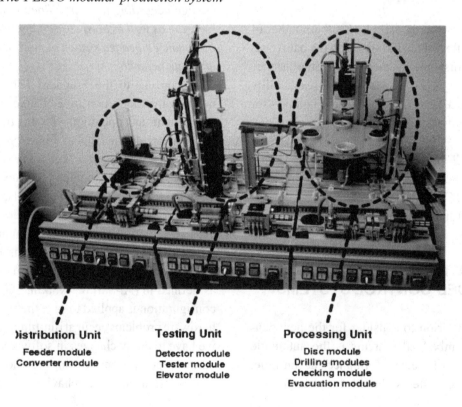

Distribution Unit
Feeder module
Converter module

Testing Unit
Detector module
Tester module
Elevator module

Processing Unit
Disc module
Drilling modules
checking module
Evacuation module

piece is performed. We assume in this research work two drilling machines *Drill machine*1 and *Drill machine*2 to drill pieces. The result of the drilling operation is next checked by the checking machine and the work piece is forwarded to another mechanical unit. We present in Figure 5 the Function Blocks-based design of this system. In our research laboratory, three production modes of FESTO are considered according to the rate of input pieces denoted by *number_pieces* into the system (i.e. ejected by the feeder).

- **Case 1: High production**. *If number_pieces* ≥ *Constant1*, Then the two drilling machines are used at the same time to accelerate the production. In this case, the Distribution and Testing units should forward two successive pieces to the rotating disc before starting the drilling with Drill_machine1 AND Drill_machine2. For this

production mode, the periodicity of input pieces is p = 11seconds.

- **Case 2: Medium production**. *If Constant2* ≤ *number_pieces* < *Constant1*, Then we use Drill_machine1 OR Drill_machine2 to drill work pieces. For this production mode, the periodicity of input pieces is p = 30seconds.

- **Case 3: Light production**. *If number_pieces* < *Constant2*, Then only the drilling machine Drill_machine1 is used. For this production mode, the periodicity of input pieces is p =50seconds.

On the other hand, if one of the drilling machines is broken at run-time, then we have to only use the other one. In this case, we reduce the periodicity of input pieces to p = 40seconds. The system is completely stopped in the worst case if the two drilling machines are broken. We present in Figure 5 the times to distribute, test, drill and

Figure 5. An IEC61499-based Design of FESTO

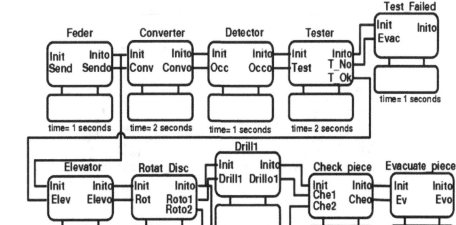

finally check work pieces (In particular, the drilling operation takes 5 seconds before forwarding the piece into the checking machine). According to the rate of input pieces, the dynamic reconfiguration is useful to:

- protect the whole system when hardware faults occur at run-time. Indeed, If Drill_machine1 (resp, Drill_machine2) is broken, then the drilling operation will be supported by Drill_machine2 (resp, Drill_machine1),
- improve the system productivity. Indeed, if the rate of input pieces is increased, then we improve the production from the Light to the Medium or from the Medium to the High mode.

This first example shows the new reconfiguration semantic in industry: we can change the system configuration to improve performances even if there are no faults.

ENAS Manufacturing System

The Benchmark Production System EnAS was designed as a prototype to demonstrate energy-antarcic actuator/sensor systems. For the sale of this contribution, we assume that it has the following behavior: it transports pieces from the production system (i.e. FESTO system) into storing units (Figure 6). The pieces in EnAS shall be placed inside tins to close with caps afterwards. Two different production strategies can be applied: we place in each tin one or two pieces according to production rates of pieces, tins and caps. We denote respectively by nb_{pieces}, $nb_{tins+caps}$ the production number of pieces and tins (as well as caps) per hour and by *Threshold* a variable (defined in user requirements) to choose the adequate production

Figure 6. EnAS-Demonstrator in Halle

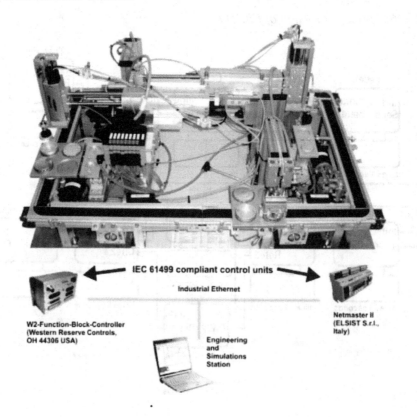

strategy. The EnAS system is mainly composed of a belt, two Jack stations (J1 and J2) and two Gripper stations (G1 and G2) (Figure 7). The Jack stations place new produced pieces and close tins with caps, whereas the Gripper stations remove charged tins from the belt into the storing units. We present in Figure 8 the design of the EnAS demonstrator according to the Function Block technology.

Initially, the belt moves a particular pallet containing a tin and a cap into the first Jack station J1. According to production parameters, we distinguish two cases,

- **First production policy:** If ($nb_{pieces}/nb_{tins+caps} \leq Threshold$), Then the Jack station J1 places from the production station a new piece and closes the tin with the cap. In this case, the Gripper station G1 removes the tin from the belt into the storing station St1 (Figure 9).

Figure 7. Distribution of the EnAS stations

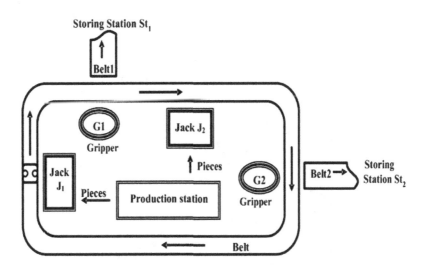

Figure 8. An IEC61499-based Design of EnAS

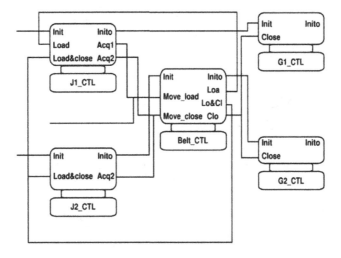

- **Second production policy**: If (nb_{pieces} / $nb_{tins+caps}$ > *Threshold*), Then the Jack station J1 places just a piece in the tin which is moved thereafter into the second Jack station to place a second new piece. Once J2 closes the tin with a cap, the belt moves the pallet into the Gripper station G2 to remove the tin (with two pieces) into the second storing station St2 (Figure 10).

We note that each piece (resp, tin and cap) costs 0.4= € (resp, 0.6= €). In addition, let us assume that *Threshold = 1.5*. According to produc-

tion parameters, we have to apply the best production policy as follows,

- If nb_{pieces} /$nb_{tins+caps}$ = *180/100 > Threshold*, Then,
- If we apply the first policy, Then we will charge 100 tins per hour that cost 100€/h,
- Else If we apply the second policy, Then we will only charge 90 tins per hour that cost 126€/h and the gain is 26%,
- If nb_{pieces} /$nb_{tins+caps}$ = *100/100 < Threshold*, Then,
- If we apply the first policy, Then we will charge 100 tins per hour that cost 100€/h,

Figure 9. Policy 1: production of a tin with only one piece

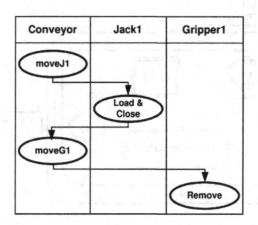

Figure 10. Policy 2: production of tins with double pieces

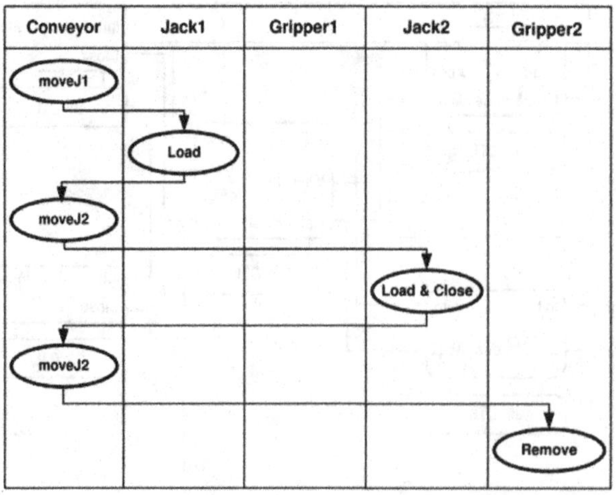

- Else If we apply the second policy, Then we will have 50 tins per hour that cost 70€/h and the loss is − 30%.

According to production parameters, the dynamic reconfiguration of the transportation system is useful to:

- protect the system when hardware problems occur at run-time. For example, if the Gripper G2 is broken, then we have to follow the first production policy by placing only one piece in each tin,
- improve the production gain when (*nb pieces /nb tins+caps > T hreshold*). In this case, we have to apply the second policy and we have therefore to apply changes in the system architecture and blocks to follow this policy.

In these Benchmark Production Systems FESTO and EnAS, the reconfiguration is not only applied to resolve hardware problems but also to improve system's performances by increasing the production gain or the number of produced pieces. This new semantic of reconfiguration will be a future issue in industry.

Classification of Reconfiguration Forms

We propose in this section a classification of all possible reconfiguration forms of embedded control systems:

- **First form.** deals with changes of the application's architecture that we consider as a com-position of Function Blocks. In this case, we have possibly to add, remove or also change the localization of Function Blocks (from one to another device). This reconfiguration form requires to load new (or to unload old) blocks in (from) the memory

Running example 1. In the FESTO manufacturing system, we distinguish two architectures:

- **First Architecture (Light production).** We implement the system with the first architecture if we apply the Light Production mode (i.e. number_pieces < Constante2). In this case, the Function Block Drill2 is not loaded in the memory.
- **Second Architecture.** We implement the system with the second architecture if we apply the high or also the medium mode (i.e. number_pieces ≥ Constante2). In this case, we load in the memory the Function Blocks Drill1 and Drill2.

Running example 2. In our EnAS manufacturing system, we distinguish two architectures:

- **First Architecture.** We implement the system with the first architecture if we follow the First Production Policy. In this case, we load in the memory the Function Blocks J1_CTL, Belt_CTL and G1_CTL,
- **Second Architecture** We implement the system with the second architecture if we follow the second production policy. In this case, we load in the memory the Function Blocks J1_CTL, J2_CTL, Belt_CTL and G2_CTL.

If we follow the first production policy and $nb_{pieces}/nb_{tins+caps}$ becomes higher than Threshold, then we have to load the function block G2_CTL in the memory to follow the second production policy.

- **Second form.** deals with reconfigurations of the application without changing its architecture (i.e. without loading or unloading Function Blocks). In this case, we apply changes of the internal structure of blocks or of their composition as follows:
  ○ we change the ECC structure,

- we add, update or also remove data/event inputs/outputs,
- we update algorithms,
- we change the configuration of connections between blocks.

Running example 1. In our FESTO system, we distinguish for the second architecture the following cases:

- **High production.** If number_pieces ≥ Constante1, Then we have to apply an automatic modification of ECC of Rotat_Disc in order to use the two drilling machines Drill_machine1 and Drill_machine2.
- **Medium production.** If Constante2 ≤ number_pieces < Constante1, Then we have to apply a new modification of ECC of Rotat_Disc to use one of these machines.

Running example 2. In our EnAS system, if we follow the second policy and the Jack station J2 is broken, then we have to change the internal behavior (i.e. the ECC's structure) of the block J1_CTL to close the tin with a cap once it places only one piece. The tin will be moved directly thereafter to the Gripper G2. In this example, we do not change the application architecture (e.g. loading or unloading blocks) but we just change the behavior of particular blocks.

- **Third form.** it simply deals with easy reconfigurations of application data (i.e. internal data of blocks or global data of the system).

Running example 1. In our FESTO system, If we apply the Medium production mode (i.e. the second architecture), Then the production periodicity is 30 seconds, whereas If we apply in the same architecture the High mode Then the periodicity is 11 seconds.

Running example 2. In our EnAS system, If a hardware problem occurs at run-time, Then we have to change the value of Threshold to a great number max_value. In this case we will not be interested in the performance improvement but in the rescue of the system to guarantee a minimal level of productivity.

MULTI-AGENT ARCHITECTURE FOR RECONFIGURABLE EMBEDDED SYSTEMS

We define a multi-agent architecture for distributed reconfigurable systems following the International Standard IEC61499. Each reconfiguration agent is affected in this architecture to a device of the execution environment to handle automatic reconfigurations of Function Blocks. It is specified by nested state machines that support all reconfiguration forms. Nevertheless, the coordination between agents in this distributed architecture is extremely mandatory because any uncontrolled automatic reconfiguration applied in a device can lead to critical problems, serious disturbances or also inadequate distributed behaviors in others. To guarantee safe distributed reconfigurations, we define the concept of "Coordination Matrix" that defines correct reconfiguration scenarios to be applied simultaneously in distributed devices and we define the concept of "Coordination Agent" that handles Coordination matrices to coordinate between distributed agents. We propose a communication protocol between agents to manage concurrent distributed reconfiguration scenarios (Figure 11).

Reconfiguration in a Device

We define for each device of the execution environment a unique agent that checks the environment's evolution and takes into account user requirements to apply automatic reconfiguration scenarios.

Running Example. In our Production Systems FESTO and EnAS where a reconfiguration agent is defined for each one of them, the reconfigura-

Figure 11. Multi-agent architecture of distributed reconfigurable embedded systems

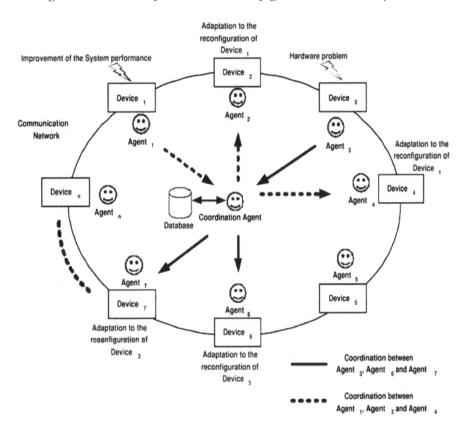

tion of the first can lead to a reconfiguration of the second in order to guarantee coherent productions in the platforms. This means:

- **If** Constant2 ≤ number_pieces, **Then** the FESTO agent should apply the Medium or the High Production Mode, and in this case the EnAS Agent should improve the productivity by applying the Second Production Policy in order to put two pieces in each tin.
- **If** Constant2 > number pieces, **Then** the FESTO Agent should decrease the productivity by applying the Light mode (i.e. only Drill_machine1 is used), and in this case, the EnAS Agent should also decrease the productivity by applying the First Production Policy in order to put only one piece in the tin.

On the other hand, when a hardware problem occurs at run-time in a platform, a reconfiguration of the other is required as follows:

- **If** one of the Jack stations J1 and J2 or the Gripper station G2 is broken in the EnAS Production System, **Then** the corresponding Agent should decrease the productivity by applying the First Production mode, and in this case the FESTO Agent should follow also the Light Production mode in order to guarantee a coherent behavior.
- **If** one of the drilling machines Drill_machine1 and Drill_machine2 is broken, **Then** the FESTO Agent should decrease the productivity, and in this case the EnAS Agent should follow the First Production mode where only one piece is put in a tin.

Architecture of the Reconfiguration Agent

We define the following units that belong to three hierarchical levels of the agent's architecture:

- **First level: (Architecture Unit)** this unit checks the system's behavior and changes its architecture (adds/removes Function Blocks) when particular conditions are satisfied. We note that Standardized Manager Function Blocks are used in this unit to load or unload such blocks into/from the memory (Lewis, 2001).
- **Second level: (Control Unit)** for a particular loaded architecture, this unit checks the system behavior and:
- reconfigures FB compositions (i.e. changes the configuration of connections),
- adds/removes data/event inputs/outputs,
- reconfigures the internal behavior of blocks (i.e. modification of the ECC structure or the update of algorithms),
- **Third level: (Data Unit)** this unit updates data if particular conditions are satisfied.

We design the agent by nested state machines where the Architecture unit is specified by an Architecture State Machine (denoted by ASM) in which each state corresponds to a particular architecture of the system. Therefore, each transition of the ASM corresponds to the load (or unload) of Function Blocks into (or from) the memory. We construct for each state S of the ASM a particular Control State Machine (denoted by CSM) in the Control unit. This state machine specifies all reconfiguration forms to possibly apply when the system architecture corresponding to the state S is loaded (i.e. modification of FB compositions or of their internal behavior). Each transition of any CSM should be fired if particular conditions are satisfied. Finally, the Data unit is specified also by Data State Machines (denoted by DSMs)

where each one corresponds to a state of a CSM or the ASM.

Notation. we denote in the following by,

- n_{ASM} the number of states in the *ASM* state machine (i.e. the number of possible architectures implementing the system). ASM_i ($i \in [1, n_{ASM}]$) denotes a state of ASM to encode a particular architecture (i.e. particular FB network). This state corresponds to a particular CSM state machine that we denote by CSM_i ($i \in [1, n_{ASM}]$),
- n_{CSMi} the number of states in CSM_i and let $CSM_{i,j}$ ($j \in [1, n\ CSMi]$) be a state of CSM_i,
  - n_{DSM} the number of Data State Machines corresponding to all possible reconfiguration scenarios of the system. Each state $CSM_{i,j}$ ($j \in [1, n_{CSMi}]$) is associated to a particular DSM state machine DSM_k ($k \in [1, n_{DSM}]$).
- n_{DSMk} the number of states in DSM_k. $DSM_{k,h}$ ($h \in [1, n_{DSMk}]$) denotes a state of the state machine DSM_k which can correspond to one of the following cases:
- one or more states of a *CSM* state machine,
- more than one *CSM* state machine,
- all the *ASM* state machines.

The agent automatically applies at run-time different reconfiguration scenarios where each scenario denoted by Reconfiguration$_{i,j,k,h}$ corresponds to a particular network of Function Blocks $fbn_{i,j,k,h}$ as follows:

- the architecture ASM_i is loaded in the memory,
- the control policy is fixed in the state $CSM_{i,j}$,
- the data configuration corresponding to the state $DSM_{k,h}$ is applied.

Running example 1. We present in Figure 12 the nested state machines that implement the

Figure 12. The architecture of the FESTO Agent with Nested State Machines

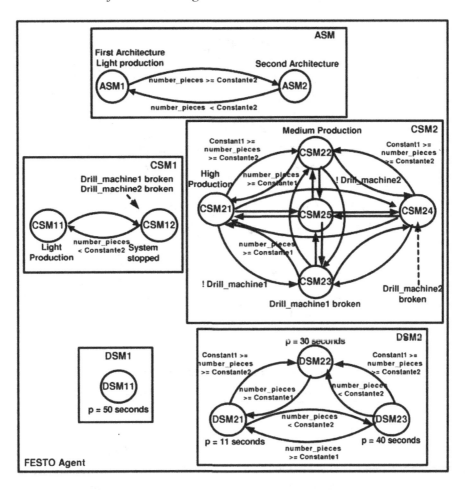

Agent in our FESTO system to handle automatic reconfigurations. The ASM state machine is composed of two states ASM1 and ASM2 corresponding to the first (i.e. the Light production mode) and the second (the High and Medium modes) architectures. The state machines CSM1 and CSM2 correspond to the states ASM1 and ASM2. In CSM2 state machine, the states CSM21 and CSM22 correspond respectively to the High and the Medium production modes (where the second architecture is loaded). To fire a transition from CSM21 to CSM22, the value of number_pieces should be in [Constant2, Constant1[. We note that the states CSM12 and CSM25 correspond to the blocking problem where the two drilling machines are broken. Finally the state machines

DSM1 and DSM2 correspond to the state machines CSM1 and CSM2. In particular, the state DSM21 encodes the periodicity when we apply the High production mode (i.e. the state CSM21 of CSM2), and the state DSM22 encodes the periodicity when we apply the Medium mode (i.e. CSM22 of CSM2). Finally, the state DSM23 corresponds to CSM23 and CSM24 when one of the drilling machines is broken.

Running example 2. We design the agent in our EnAS system by nested state machines as depicted in Figure 13. The first level is specified by the ASM where each state defines a particular architecture of the system (i.e. a particular composition of blocks to load in the memory). The state ASM 1 (resp. ASM 2) corresponds to the

Figure 13. The architecture of the EnAS Agent with Nested State Machines

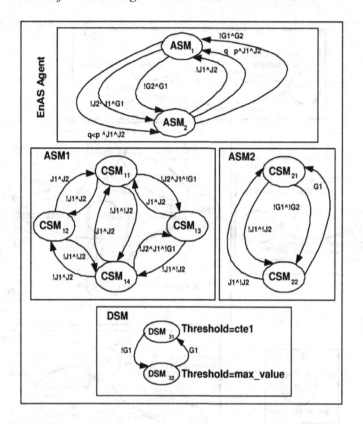

second (resp. first) policy where the stations J1, J 2 and G 2 (resp. only J 1 and G 1) are loaded in the memory. We associate for each one of these states a CSM in the Control unit. Finally, the data unit is specified with a DSM defining the values that Threshold takes under well-defined conditions. Note that if we follow the second production policy (state ASM 1) and the gripper G 2 is broken, then we have to change the policy and also the system architecture by loading the block G1_CT L to remove pieces into Belt1. On the other hand, we associate in the second level for the state ASM1 the CSM CSM1 defining the different reconfiguration forms to apply when the first architecture is loaded in the memory. In particular, when the state CSM11 is active and the Jack station J 1 is broken, then we activate the state CSM 12 in which the Jack station J 2 is running alone to place only one piece in the tin. In this case, the internal

behavior of the block Belt_CT L has to be changed (i.e. the tin has to be transported directly to the station J 2). In the same way, if we follow the same policy in the state CSM 11 and the Jack station J 2 is broken, then we have to activate the state CSM 13 where the J 1 behavior has to be changed to place a piece in the tin that has to be closed too (i.e. the ECC structure of the block J1_CT L has to be reconfigured). Finally, we specify in the data unit a DSM where we change the value of Threshold when the Gripper G1 is broken (we suppose as an example that we are not interested in the system performance when the Gripper G1 is broken). By considering this specification of the agent, we specify all possible reconfiguration scenarios that can be applied in a system: Add-Remove (first level) or Update the structure of blocks (second level) or just update data (third level).

System Behaviors

The different reconfiguration scenarios applied by the agent define all possible behaviors of the system when conditions are satisfied. We specify these behaviors by a unique System State Machine (denoted by SSM) in which each state corresponds to a particular Function Block.

Running example 1. In the system FESTO, we specify in Figure 14 the different types of system's behaviors that we can follow to resolve hardware problems or to improve performances. The branch Branch1 specifies the system behavior when Drill_machine1 or Drill_machine2 are broken or also when the Medium production mode is applied, Branch2 defines the system behavior when the High production mode is applied, and Branch3 defines the behavior when the Light production mode is applied.

Running example 2. In the system EnAS, we specify in Figure 15 the different system's behaviors that we can follow to resolve hardware problems or to improve system performances. In this example, we distinguish 4 traces encoding 4 types of different behaviors. The trace trace1 implements the system behavior when the Jack station J1 is broken. The trace trace2 implements the system behavior to apply the second production policy. The trace trace3 implements the system behavior when the Jack station J2 is broken. Finally the last scenario implements the system behavior when the Gripper G2 is broken or when we have to apply the first production policy. Note finally that each state corresponds to a particular behavior of a system block when the corresponding input event occurs.

Figure 14. The system's state machine of the FESTO Benchmark Production System: SSM(FESTO)

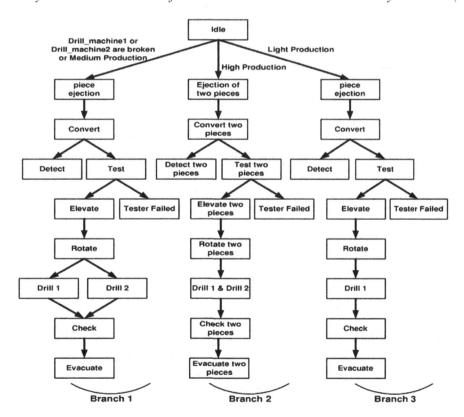

Reconfiguration in a Distributed Architecture

We are interested in automatic reconfigurations of Function Blocks to be distributed on a network of devices where coordinations between agents are well-mandatory because any uncontrolled automatic reconfiguration applied by any agent can lead to critical problems or serious disturbances in others. We define in this section the concept of "Coordination Matrix" to handle coherent reconfiguration scenarios in distributed devices and we propose thereafter an architecture of multi-agent distributed reconfigurable systems where a communication protocol between agents is defined to guarantee safe behaviors after distributed reconfigurations.

Distributed Reconfigurations

Let *Sys* be a distributed reconfigurable system of *n* devices, and let A_{g1},..., A_{gn} be *n* agents to handle automatic distributed reconfigurations of these devices. We denote in the following by *Reconfiguration* $a_{ia,ja,ka,ha}$ a reconfiguration scenario applied by A_{ga} ($a \in [1, n]$) as follows:

- the corresponding *ASM* state machine is in the state ASM_{ia}. Let $cond^a_{ia}$ be the set of conditions to reach this state,
- the *CSM* state machine is in the state $CSM_{ia,ja}$. Let $cond^a_{ja}$ be the set of conditions to reach this state,

- the *DSM* state machine is in the state $DSM_{ka,ha}$. Let $cond^a_{ka,ha}$ be the set of conditions to reach this state.

To handle coherent distributed reconfigurations that guarantee safe behaviors of the whole system *Sys*, we define the concept of "Coordination Matrix" of size $(n,4)$ that defines coherent scenarios to be simultaneously applied by different agents. Let *CM* be a such matrix that we characterize as follows: each line a ($a \in [1, n]$) corresponds to a reconfiguration scenario *Reconfiguration*$^a_{ia,ja,ka,ha}$ to be applied by A_{ga} as follows:

$$CM[a,1]=i_a ; CM[a,2]=j_a ; CM[a,3]=k_a ; CM[a,4]= h_a$$

According to this definition: **If** an agent A_{ga} applies the reconfiguration scenario *Reconfiguration*$^a_{CM[a,1],CM[a,2],CM[a,3],CM[a,4]}$, **Then** each another agent A_{gb} ($b \in [1, n] \setminus \{ a \}$) should apply the scenario *Reconfiguration*$^b_{CM[b,1],CM[b,2],CM[b,3],CM[b,4]}$ (Figure 16). We denote in the following by "idle agent" each agent Ag_b ($b \in [1, n]$) which is not required to apply any reconfigurations when the others perform scenarios defined in CM. In this case:

$$CM[b,1] = CM[b,2] = CM[b,3] = CM[b,4] = 0$$

$$cond^a_{CM[a,1]} = cond^a_{CM[a,2]} = cond^a_{CM[a,3],CM[a,4]} = True$$

We denote in addition by $\xi(Sys)$ the set of Coordination matrices to be considered for the reconfiguration of the distributed embedded sys-

Figure 15. The system's state machine of the EnAS Benchmark Production System: SSM(EnAS)

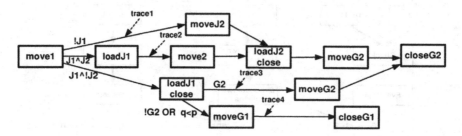

Figure 16. A Coordination Matrix

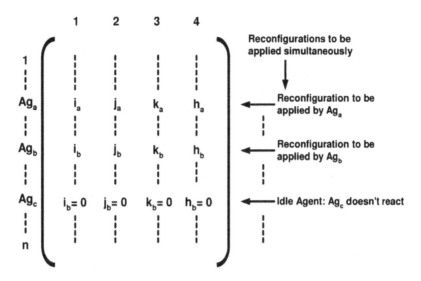

tem *Sys*. Each Coordination Matrix *CM* is applied at run-time if for each agent A_{ga} ($a \in [1, n]$) the following conditions are satisfied:

$$cond^a_{CM[a,1]} = cond^a_{CM[a,2]} = cond^a_{CM[a,3],CM[a,4]} = True$$

On the other hand, we define "Concurrent Coordination matrices", CM_1 and CM_2 two matrices of $\xi(Sys)$ that allows different reconfigurations of same agents as follows: $\exists b \in [1, n]$ such that:

- $CM_j[b, i] \neq 0 \; \forall j \in \{1, 2\}$ and $i \in [1,4]$,
- $CM_1[b, i] \neq CM_2[b, i] \; \forall i \in [1, 4]$.

In this case, the agent A_{gb} is disturbed because it should apply different reconfiguration scenarios at the same time. To guarantee a deterministic behavior when Concurrent Coordination matrices are required to be simultaneously applied, we define priority levels for them such that only the matrix with the highest priority level should be applied. We denote in the following by:

- *Concur(CM)* the set of concurrent matrices of $CM \in \xi(Sys)$,
- *level(CM)* the priority level of the matrix *CM* in the set *Concur(CM)* $\cup$ *{CM}*.

Running Example. In our Benchmark Production Systems FESTO and EnAS, we show in Figure 17 the Coordination Matrices to be applied in order to guarantee coherent distributed reconfigurations at run-time. According to Figures 5 and 6:

- the first matrix CM1 is applied when the FESTO Agent applies the Light Production mode (i.e. the states ASM1, CSM11 and DSM11 are activated and Reconfiguration$_{1,1,1,1}$ is applied) and the EnAS Agent is required to decrease the productivity by applying the First Production policy to put only one piece in each tin (i.e. the states ASM2, CSM21 are activated and Reconfiguration$_{2,1,0,0}$ is applied),
- the second matrix CM2 is applied when the FESTO Agent applies the High Production mode (i.e. the states ASM2, CSM21 and DSM21 are activated and Reconfiguration$_{2,1,2,1}$ is applied) and the EnAS Agent is required to increase the productivity by applying the Second Production mode to put two pieces into each tin (i.e. the states ASM1, CSM11

Figure 17. Coordination Matrices for the FESTO and EnAS Benchmark Production Systems

$$
\overset{\textbf{CM1}}{\begin{pmatrix} 1 & 1 & 1 & 1 \\ 2 & 1 & 0 & 0 \end{pmatrix}}
\overset{\textbf{CM2}}{\begin{pmatrix} 2 & 1 & 2 & 1 \\ 1 & 1 & 0 & 0 \end{pmatrix}}
\overset{\textbf{CM3}}{\begin{pmatrix} 2 & 2 & 2 & 2 \\ 1 & 1 & 0 & 0 \end{pmatrix}}
$$

$$
\overset{\textbf{CM4}}{\begin{pmatrix} 1 & 1 & 1 & 1 \\ 1 & 2 & 0 & 0 \end{pmatrix}}
\overset{\textbf{CM5}}{\begin{pmatrix} 1 & 1 & 1 & 1 \\ 1 & 3 & 0 & 0 \end{pmatrix}}
$$

$$
\overset{\textbf{CM6}}{\begin{pmatrix} 2 & 3 & 2 & 3 \\ 2 & 1 & 0 & 0 \end{pmatrix}}
\overset{\textbf{CM7}}{\begin{pmatrix} 2 & 4 & 2 & 3 \\ 2 & 1 & 0 & 0 \end{pmatrix}}
\overset{\textbf{CM8}}{\begin{pmatrix} 2 & 5 & 0 & 0 \\ 2 & 2 & 0 & 0 \end{pmatrix}}
$$

are activated and $Reconfiguration_{1,1,0,0}$ is applied),

- the third matrix CM3 is applied when the FESTO Agent applies the Medium Production Mode (i.e. the states ASM2, CSM22 and DSM22 are activated and $Reconfiguration_{2,2,2,2}$ is applied). In this case the EnAS System is required to apply the Second Production Policy (i.e. the states ASM1, CSM11 are activated and $Reconfiguration_{1,1,0,0}$ is applied),

- the fourth matrix CM4 is applied when the Jack station J1 in the EnAS system is broken (i.e. the states ASM1, CSM12 are activated and $Reconfiguration_{1;2;0;0}$ is applied). In this case the FESTO system has to decrease the productivity by applying the Light production mode (i.e. the states ASM1, CSM11 and DSM11 are activated and $Reconfiguration_{1,1,1,1}$ is applied),

- the matrix CM5 is applied when the Jack station J2 and the Gripper station G1 are broken in the EnAS system (i.e. the states ASM1;CSM13 are activated and $Reconfiguration_{1,3,0,0}$ is applied). In this case the FESTO system is required to decrease the productivity by applying the Light Production mode,

- the matrix CM1 is applied at run-time when the Gripper station G2 is broken (i.e. the states ASM2, CSM21 are activated and $Reconfiguration_{2,1,0,0}$ is applied). In this case the FESTO agent has also to decrease the productivity by applying the Light Production mode,

- the matrix CM6 is applied when the Drilling machine Drill machine1 is broken in FESTO (i.e. the states ASM2, CSM23 and DSM23 are activated and $Reconfiguration_{2;3;2;3}$ is applied). In this case EnAS system is required to decrease the productivity by applying the First Production mode (i.e. the states ASM2, CSM21 are activated and $Reconfiguration_{2,1,0,0}$ is applied),

- the matrix CM7 is applied at run-time when the second drilling machine is broken at run-time and in this case the EnAS system is required also the decrease the productivity by applying the First Production mode,

- finally, the matrix CM8 is applied at run-time to stop the whole production when the two drilling machines Drill_machine1 and Drill_machine2 are broken at run-time. In this case the EnAS Agent has to reach the halt state (i.e. the states ASM1, CSM14 are activated and $Reconfiguration_{1,4,0,0}$ is applied).

Coordination between Distributed Agents

We propose a multi-agent architecture for embedded control systems following the Standard IEC61499 to handle automatic distributed reconfigurations of devices. To guarantee a coherent behavior of the whole distributed system, we define a "Coordination Agent" (denoted by $CA(\xi(Sys))$) which handles the Coordination Matrices of $\xi(Sys)$ to control the rest of agents (i.e. Ag_a, $a \in [1, n]$) as follows:

- When a particular agent Ag_a ($a \in [1, n]$) should apply a reconfiguration scenario $Reconfiguration\ ^a_{ia,ja,ka,ha}$ (i.e. under well-defined conditions), it sends the following request to $CA(\xi(Sys))$ in order to obtain its authorization:

  request(Ag_a, CA(ξ(Sys)), Reconfiguration $^a_{ia,ja,ka,ha}$).

- When CA(ξ(Sys)) receives this request that corresponds to a particular coordination matrix CM $\in \xi$(Sys) and if CM has the highest priority between all matrices of Concur(CM) $\cup$ { CM }, then CA(ξ(Sys)) informs the agents that have simultaneously to react with Ag_a as defined in CM. The following information is sent from CA(ξ(Sys)):

  For each Ag_b, $b \in [1, n] \setminus \{a\}$ and $CM[b, i] \neq 0$, $\forall\ i \in [1, 4]$:

  reconfiguration($CA(\xi(Sys))$, Ag_b, Reconfiguration$^b_{CM[b,1],CM[b,2],CM[b,3],CM[b,4]}$)

According to well-defined conditions in the device of each Ag_b, the CA(ξ(Sys)) request can be accepted or refused by sending one of the following answers:

- If $cond^b_{ib}$ = $cond^b_{jb}$ = $cond^b_{kb,hb}$ = True, Then the following reply is sent from Ag_b to CA(ξ(Sys)):

  Possible_reconfig(Ag_b, CA(ξ(Sys)), Reconfiguration$^b_{CM[b,1],CM[b,2],CM[b,3],CM[b,4]}$).

- Else the following reply is sent from Ag_b to CA(ξ(Sys)):

  Not_possible_reconfig(Ag_b, CA(ξ(Sys)), Reconfiguration$^b_{CM[b,1],CM[b,2],CM[b,3],CM[b,4]}$).

  If CA(ξ(Sys)) receives positive answers from all agents, Then it authorizes the reconfiguration in the concerned devices:

For each Ag_b, $b \in [1, n]$ and CM[b,i] $\neq 0$, $\forall i \in [1, 4]$,
apply (Reconfiguration$^b_{CM[b,1],CM[b,2],CM[b,3],CM[b,4]}$) in device b.

Else If CA(ξ(Sys)) receives a negative answer from a particular agent, Then

If the reconfiguration scenario Reconfiguration$^a_{ia,ja,ka,ha}$ allows the optimization of the whole system behavior,
Then CA(ξ(Sys)) refuses the request of Ag_a by sending the following reply:
Refused_reconfiguration(CA(ξ(Sys)), Ag_a, Reconfiguration$^a_{CM[a,1],CM[a,2],CM[a,3],CM[a,4]}$)).

Running example. In our FESTO and EnAS Benchmark Production Systems, we show in Figure 18 interactions between the corresponding agents when number_pieces $\geq$ Constant1. In this case, the Coordination Agent uses the Matrix CM2 to coordinate between the agents in order to apply in FESTO the High production policy and in EnAS the second production mode. We show in Figure 19 the coordination between these agents when Drill_machine1 is broken in FESTO. In this case, the Coordination Agent uses the Matrix CM6 to decrease the productivity in EnAS. We

Figure 18. Coordination between the FESTO and EnAS agents to optimize their productivities

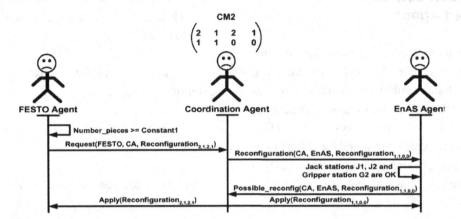

note that any reconfiguration scenario should be applied after the complete process of a piece in FESTO and EnAS.

Evaluation of the Proposed Multi-Agent Architecture

We evaluate in this section the proposed multi-agent architecture for automatic reconfigurations of distributed embedded control systems by counting the maximum number of exchanged messages between agents after distributed reconfiguration scenarios. We assume as a particular case that all Coordination Matrices are concurrent. We denote by $number^{coordination}_{messages}$ such number when we use a Coordination Agent to coordinate between distributed devices of the execution environment, and by $number_{messages}$ when we do not apply any coordinations. In this case, each agent should know priorities of matrices, and should inform all others before applying any reconfiguration scenarios in the corresponding device. Let $number_{reconfigurations}$ be the number of reconfigurations desired by distributed agents that control evolutions of the whole system.

- If we apply the proposed approach where a Coordination Agent is applied to coordinate between devices such that the highest-priority reconfiguration scenario is applied at run-time, Then $number^{coordination}_{messages}$ is as follows:

$$number^{coordination}_{messages} = number_{reconfigurations} + 3*(n-1)+1$$

Indeed, $number_{reconfigurations}$ among n agents desiring reconfigurations of corresponding devices send $number_{reconfigurations}$ messages to the Coordination Agent, but only the highest-priority message is accepted before a notification is sent to the rest (i.e. n-1) of agents. The Coordinator decides any scenario to be applied once answers are received from the distributed agents,

- If we apply an approach without coordinations where each agent should inform all others before applying reconfiguration scenarios, Then $number_{messages}$ is as follows:

$$number_{messages} = number_{reconfigurations} * 3 *(n-1)$$

In this case, each agent desiring reconfigurations sends messages to all others before waiting their answers and deciding the next scenario to be applied. The gain of our approach is then the decrease of these exchanged messages between distributed devices of the execution environment:

Figure 19. Coordination between the FESTO and EnAS agents when Drill machine1 is broken

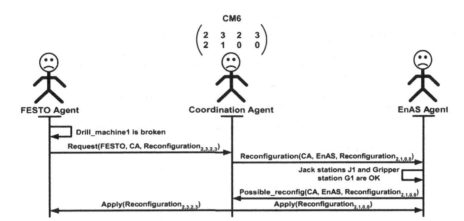

$$\text{Gain} = \text{number}^{\text{coordination}}_{\text{messages}} / \text{number}_{\text{messages}} =$$
$$1/(3*(n\text{-}1)) + 1/\text{number}_{\text{reconfigurations}} + 1 =$$
$$(\text{number}_{\text{reconfigurations}} * 3 * (n - 1))$$

Application. If $n = 100$ and number$_{\text{reconfigurations}}$ = 100, Then Gain = 0,01.

Running example. We use in this research work the Simulink environment to simulate both FESTO and EnAS as well as their coordination when hardware faults occur in the plant or when improvements of performances should be applied according to user requirements. We show in Figure 20 the behaviors of these benchmark platforms to be balanced between high, medium and light productions according to environment's evolutions. The figure shows also the different matrices to be used by the Coordination Agent to guarantee coherent distributed reconfigurations. In particular, the matrix CM2 is applied at t2 by the Coordination Agent to improve the productivity of FESTO and EnAS. The matrix CM4 is used at t3 to decrease this productivity under well-defined conditions. We show also in the same Figure how FESTO is stopped at t5 or at t7 when Drill1 and Drill2 or the Distribution and Tester units are broken.

NCES-BASED MODELLING AND SESA-BASED MODEL CHECKING OF DISTRIBUTED RECONFIGURABLE EMBEDDED SYSTEMS

We specify each reconfiguration agent affected to a particular device of the execution environment by nested (i.e. hierarchical) Net Condition/Event Systems that support all reconfiguration forms, and we specify also the different networks of Function Blocks that implement this device in different possible reconfiguration scenarios by NCES-based models, before we apply the model checker SESA to check eCTL-based functional and TCTL-based temporal properties described in user requirements. We specify in addition each Coordination Matrix by a NCES-based model and we apply SESA to check that any distributed reconfiguration scenario applied by agents brings the whole distributed architecture to safe and optimal behaviors.

NCES-Based Specification of a Reconfiguration Agent

We use in this research work the formalism Net Condition/Event Systems that provide useful facilities to specify synchronizations between

Figure 20. Evaluation of the multi-agent architecture by Varying the number of reconfigurations

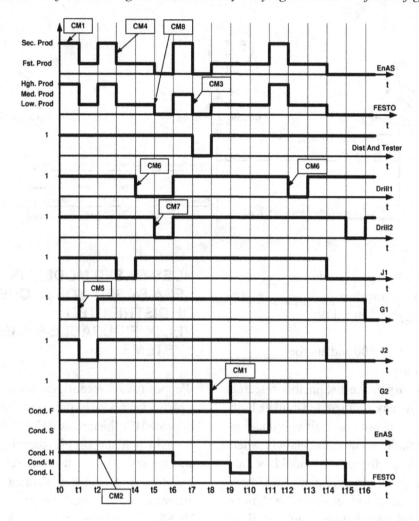

agents and Function Blocks. We use in particular event-condition signals from agents to activate traces of states in the SSM (i.e. a reconfiguration), and we use in addition event signals to synchronize the state machines: ASM, CSM and DSM of each agent.

Running example 1. We show in Figure 21 the agent model in FESTO according to the NCES formalism. In the ASM state machine, the place PF1 defines the Light production mode and corresponds to the state machine CSM1(PF1). The synchronization between these two machines is supported by an event signal ev1. On the other hand, the place PF2 defines the Medium or the

High mode and corresponds to the state machine CSM(PF2) (synchronization is supported by the event signal ev2). The place PF5 of CSM(P2) defines the High production mode and corresponds to the place PF12 when the period p = 11 seconds is applied. The place PF3 of CSM (PF2) defines the Medium production mode and corresponds to the place PF13 when the period p = 30 seconds is applied.

Running example 2. Figure 22 shows models of the agent and the system EnAS according to the formalism NCES. We specify temporal intervals in the transitions of the system's model according to user requirements. When the Jack

Figure 21. Design of the FESTO agent with the formalism NCES

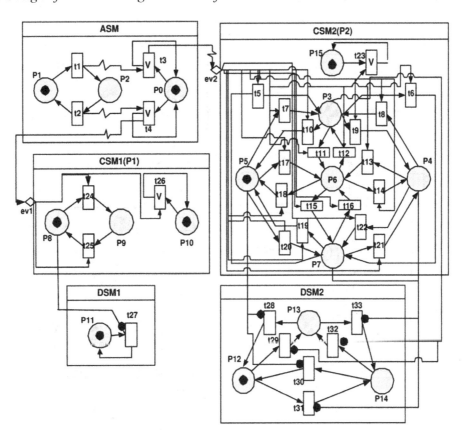

station J1 is broken, the agent activates the place PE12 and sends a condition signal to activate the trace trace1 in the system. Note that the architecture and control state machines are communicating by event signals to synchronize the agent's behavior. Finally, the state "Well" represents a deadlock in the system when the Jack stations J1 and J2 are broken.

SESA-Based Model Checking in a Device

We verify functional and extra-functional properties of reconfigurable control systems following the Function Block technology. We limit our research work to two types of extra-functional constraints namely: Temporal and QoS properties. We use the temporal logic CTL as well as

its extensions to specify these properties and the model checker SESA to check the system feasibility in each device of the execution environment.

Running example. In our EnAS system, we apply the model checker SESA to verify properties of its Function Blocks implementing the different reconfiguration scenarios. We generate with this tool different reachability graphs corresponding to these scenarios. We present in Figure 23 the graph that corresponds to the second production policy where the states State1,...State17 encode the behavior of the Agent as well as the system blocks when $nb_{pieces}/nb_{tins+caps} >$ Threshold.

Verification of Functional Properties

We verify functional properties of state machines that specify the agent to prove the correct adapta-

Figure 22. Design of the EnAS system with the NCES formalism

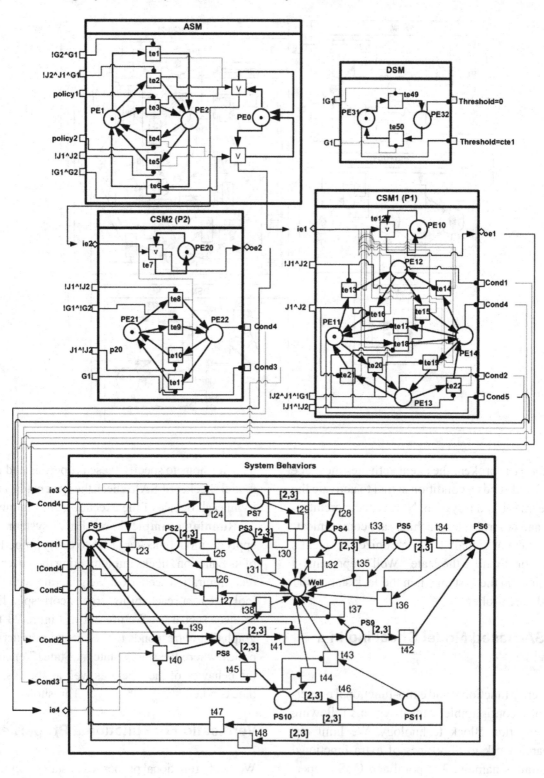

Figure 23. Reachability graph of the first production policy

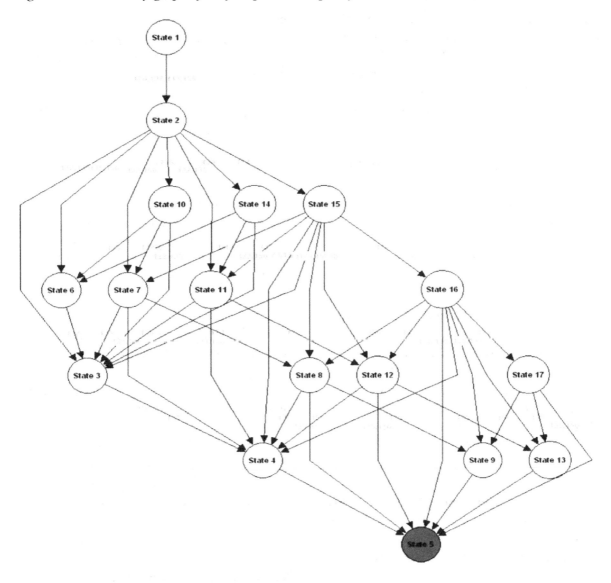

tion of the system to any change in the environment, and we verify the functional correctness of the different FB networks to validate the whole system behavior.

Running example. In our EnAS system, we check functional properties of the state machines encoding the Agent. In particular, we have to check if the system applies the second policy whereas the Gripper station G2 is broken. We propose the following eCTL formula:

z0 |= AGAte1XP S2

This formula allows to check with SESA that whenever a state transition fulfilling te1 is possible (e.g. G2 is broken), this transition leads to a successor state in which PS2 holds true in the reachability graph (e.g. we apply the second production policy). This formula is proven to be False. The following formula is proven to be True:

z0 | = AGAte1XP S8

Indeed, whenever the Gripper G2 is broken, the state PS8 of SSM is activated. On the other hand, to check the behavioral order of the SSM when the Gripper station G2 is broken (e.g. Load a piece and Close the tin in the Jack station J1, then move the Belt to the Gripper station G1 to remove the product to Belt1), we propose the following eCTL formula:

z0 |= AGA t40 XA FE t45 XA FE t46 X TRUE

This formula is proven to be True with the model checker SESA.

Verification of Temporal Properties

We verify TCTL-based temporal properties of the FB networks corresponding to the different reconfiguration scenarios as follows:

Running example. In our EnAS platform, we check temporal properties of the SSM model. When the Gripper station G2 is broken, we should check if the duration to activate the Gripper station G1 does not exceed 5 time units. Therefore, we propose to apply the following formula:

AF [2,5]PS11

This formula is proven to be True with the SESA Model checker. To check if the Gripper station is reachable in 3 time units, we should verify the following formula:

EF [2,3]PS11

It is proven to be False with the model checker SESA.

Verification of QoS Properties

The last property to be verified according to user requirements is the QoS where we check if the system provides the minimal accepted quality at run-time. We use in this case the CTL logic to specify the QoS formulas.

Running example. In our platform EnAS, we verify if the system provides the minimal accepted QoS. According to the value of nb_{pieces}/$nb_{tins+caps}$, we should verify if the system applies the best production policy. We propose to following eCTL formula,

z0 |= AGAte 3 XP S11

Indeed, we should verify if nb_{pieces}/$nb_{tins+caps} \leq$ Threshold (e.g. the first production policy should be applied), then the fourth trace of SSM should be activated (e.g. the state PS11 should be activated). By applying the tool SESA, we find that this formula is True.

SESA-Based Model Checking of the Coordination Agent

The model checking of a distributed reconfigurable system is mandatory to check the reactivity of distributed agents when reconfiguration scenarios should be applied in corresponding devices. We propose a NCES-based model for each Coordination Matrix to be handled by the Coordination Agent, and we propose thereafter the verification of the whole system behavior by applying the model checker SESA and the temporal logic CTL.

NCES-Based Modelling of the Coordination Agent

We model each Coordination Matrix CM $\in$ ξ(Sys) to be handled by the Coordination Agent CA(ξ(Sys)) by a NCES-based Coordination Model in which the conditions $cond^a_{ia}$, $cond^a_{ja}$ and $cond^a_{ka,ha}$ are verified for each non idle agent Ag_a (a $\in$ [1, n]) (i.e. application of the reconfiguration scenario Reconfiguration$^a_{ia,ja,ka,ha}$) before an authorization is sent to all non idle agents to effectively apply corresponding reconfigurations.

Running Example. We show in Figure 24 the Coordination Module Module(CM7,8) to be applied when the drilling machines Drill_machine1 or Drill_machine2 are broken (i.e. the states PF4 and PF7 of the CSM1(PF1)). In this case, the EnAS agent should reduce the productivity by applying the First Production Mode (i.e. the state PE2 of ASM(EnAS)). We show in Figure 25 the module Module(CM4,5) that defines the behavior of the Coordination Matrix when the Jack stations J1, J2 or the Gripper G1 are broken. In this case, the FESTO agent should reduce the productivity by applying the Light Production Mode (i.e. the state PF1 of ASM(FESTO)). We show in Figure

Figure 24. Automatic Distributed Reconfigurations in FESTO and EnAS when the drilling machines Drill_machine1 or Drill_machine2 are broken at run-time

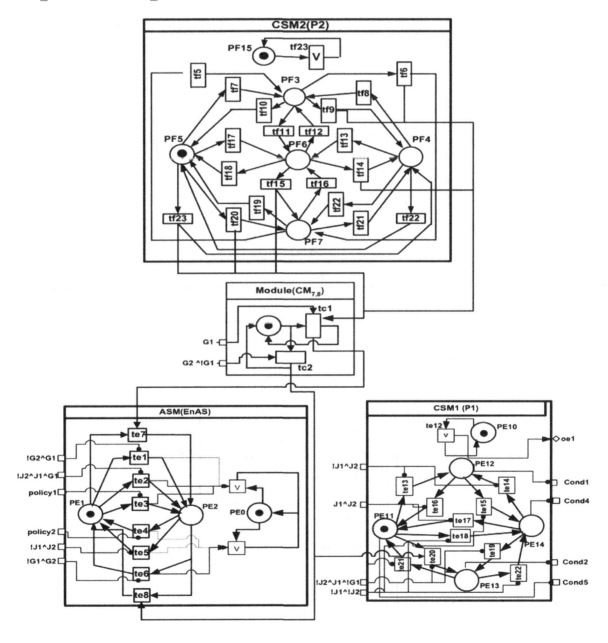

26 the module Module(CM1) that defines the behavior of the Coordination Matrix when the Light Production Mode is applied by the FESTO Agent (number$_{pieces}$ < Constant2). In this case, the EnAS agent should apply the First Production Mode in which only one piece is put in the tin. On the other hand, the module Module(CM2,3) defines the behavior of the Coordination Matrix when the FESTO Agent should apply the High or the Me-

dium modes. In this case the EnAS Agent should change the production strategy to the Second Production mode where two pieces are put in the tin. To manage concurrent coordination matrices, the resolution of hardware problems is assumed to have a higher priority than any optimization of the system productivity. Therefore, the Coordination Matrix CM7,8 (CM4,5, resp) has higher priority than CM1 (CM2,3, resp). According to Figure 26,

Figure 25. Automatic Distributed Reconfigurations in FESTO and EnAS when hardware problems occurs at run-time

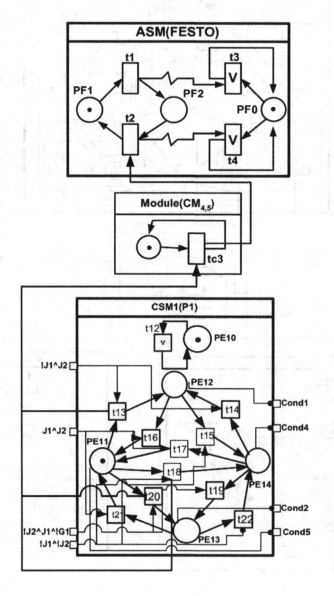

the matrix CM1 (CM2,3, resp) is applied if and only if the drilling machines Drill_machine1 and Drill_machine2 (the Jack stations J1, J2 and the Gripper station G1) are not broken.

SESA-Based Verification of Distributed Reconfigurations

We verify with the model checker SESA the behavior of the whole control system when distributed reconfigurations are applied by the Coordination Agent. Indeed, we have to check for each Coordination Matrix CM $\in \xi$(Sys) that whenever an Agent Ag$_a$ (a $\in$ [1, n]) applies a reconfiguration scenario under well-defined conditions, the others non-idle agents have to react by applying required reconfigurations.

Running Example. In our FESTO and EnAS Benchmark Production Systems, we apply the model checker SESA to verify the correct feasi-

Figure 26. Automatic Distributed Reconfigurations in FESTO and EnAS to regulate the whole system performance

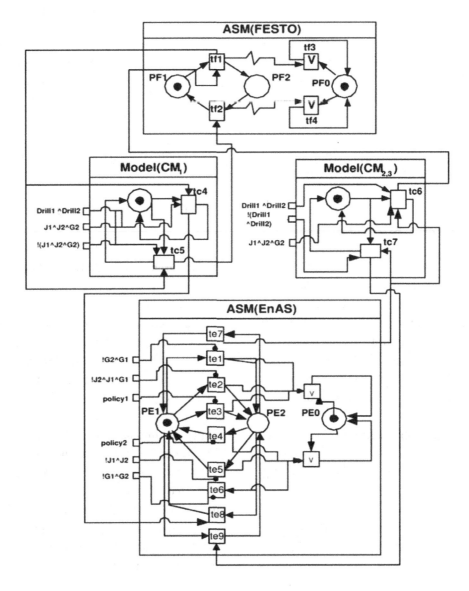

bility of distributed reconfiguration scenarios of NCES-based models of agents. Our objective is to check that whenever one of these demonstrators improves or decreases the productivity, the other applies the same strategy. We have in addition to check that each one reacts when any hardware problem occurs in the other. This verification is mandatory in order to guarantee coherent behaviors of these complementary demonstrators. The SESA model checker generates for the NCES-based models of the considered agents a reachability graph composed of 162 states. We specify the following functional properties according to the temporal logic CTL:

- **Property1:** whenever the drilling machines Drill_machine1 or Drill_machine2 are broken in the Benchmark System FESTO (i.e. the states PF7 or PF4 are reached), the EnAS system should therefore decrease the productivity (i.e. the state PE2 is reached). The following formulas are proven to be true by the model checker SESA:

  Formula1: $z0 \models AGAte7XAGAtc1XPF7$
  Formula2: $z0 \models AGAte7XAGAtc1XPF4$

- **Property2:** whenever the Jack stations J1 and J2 or the Gripper station G1 are broken in the EnAS Benchmark system. the FESTO system should react by decreasing the productivity to the Light production mode. The following formulas are proven to be true by the model checker SESA:

  Formula2 (J1 is broken): $z0 \models AGAtf2XAGAtc3XPF12$
  Formula3 (J2 and G1 are broken): $z0 \models AGAtf2XAGAtc3XPF13$

- **Property3:** If the condition number$_{pieces} \geq$ Constant2 is satisfied and the FESTO system improves in this case the productiv-

ity to the Medium or the High modes (i.e. the place PF2 is reached), the EnAS system should improve also the productivity by applying the second production policy where two pieces are put in each tin. The following formula is proven to be true by the model checker SESA:

Formula4: $z0 \models AGAtf8XAGAtc4XP F2$

- **Property4:** If the condition (nb$_{pieces}$ / nb$_{tins+caps}$ > Threshold) is satisfied and the EnAS system has to improve the productivity by applying the second mode (i.e. the place PE1 is reached), the FESTO system should also increase the productivity by applying the Medium or High modes (i.e. the state PF1 is reached). The following formula is proven to be true by the model checker SESA:

  Formula5: $z0 \models AGAtf1XAGAtc6XP E1$

CONCLUSION AND FUTURE WORKS

The chapter deals with distributed multi-agent reconfigurable embedded control systems following the component-based International Standard IEC61499. We define a new reconfiguration semantic where a crucial criterion to consider is the automatic improvement of performances at runtime. We classify thereafter the reconfiguration scenarios into three forms: the first deals with the system architecture, the second with the internal structure of blocks or with their composition, finally the third deals with the reconfiguration of data. We define an architecture of reconfigurable multi-agent systems where a reconfiguration agent is affected to each device of the execution environment to handle local automatic reconfigurations, and a Coordination Agent handling Coordination Matrices is defined to guarantee safe distributed reconfigurations. We specify each reconfiguration agent by nested state machines according to the formalism Net Condition-Event Systems. To meet user requirements in each device, we verify eCTL-based functional and TCTL-based temporal properties by applying the model checker SESA, and to validate the whole distributed architecture, we model each Coordination Matrix by a NCES-based model before we apply SESA to check that any distributed reconfiguration brings the whole distributed system into safe and optimal behaviors. The chapter's contributions are applied to two Benchmark Production Systems FESTO and EnAS available in our research laboratory at Martin Luther University in Germany. In our future work, we plan to study the schedulability of distributed and reconfigurable Function Blocks in order to meet real-time constraints, and we plan also to study the code generation of the whole control system. To a posteriori validate the implementa tion of the distributed architecture, a simulation of reconfigurable blocks should be applied where a technique based on fault-injections will be considered in order to improve such verification which is not exhaustive.

REFERENCES

Al-Safi, Y., & Vyatkin, V. (2007). An ontology-based reconfiguration agent for intelligent mechatronic systems. In *Third International Conference on Industrial Applications of Holonic and Multi-Agent Systems*. Berlin: Springer-Verlag.

Alur, R., & Yannakakis, M. (1998). Model checking of hierarchical state machines. In *Sixth ACM Symposium on the Foundations of Software Engineering*, (pp. 175-188).

Amnell, T., Behrmann, G., Bengtsson, J., D'Argenio, P.-R., David, A., Fehnker, A., et al. (2001). Uppaal - Now, Next, and Future. In F. Cassez, C. Jard, B. Rozoy, & M. Ryan (Eds.), *Proceedings of Modelling and Verification of Parallel Processes (MOVEP '2k)*, France, (LNCS Tutorial 2067, pp. 100-125).

Angelov, C., Sierszecki, K., & Marian, N. (2005). Design models for reusable and reconfigurable state machines. In L.T. Yang, et al. (Eds.), *EUC 2005*, (LNCS 3824, pp. 152-163). International Federation for Information Processing.

Asarin, E., Bournez, O., Dang, T., & Maler, O. (2000). Approximate reachability analysis of piecewise-linear dynamical systems. In *Hybrid Systems: Computation and Control, Third International Workshop*, (LNCS).

Berna-koes, M., Nourbakhsh, I., & Sycara, K. (2003). Communication efficiency in multiagent systems. *International Conference on Robotics and Automation*, April 26 - May 1, (Vol. 3, pp. 2129 - 2134).

Brennan, R.-W., Fletcher, M., & Norrie, D.-H. (2001). A holonic approach to reconfiguring real-time distributed control systems. In *Multi-Agent Systems and Applications: MASA'01*. Berlin: Springer-Verlag.

Chutinan, A., & Krogh, B.-K. (1999). Verification of Polyhedral-invariant hybrid automata using polygonal flow pipe approximations. In *Hybrid Systems: Computation and Control, Second International Workshop*, (LNCS).

Corkill, D.-D., Holzhauer, D., & Koziarz, W. (2007). Turn Off Your Radios! Environmental Monitoring Using Power-Constrained Sensor Agents. In *First International Workshop on Agent Technology for Sensor Networks (ATSN-07)*, Honolulu, Hawaii, (pp. 31-38).

Crnkovic, I., & Larsson, M. (2002). *Building reliable component-based software systems*. Boston: Artech House.

Daws, C., Olivero, A., Tripakis, S., & Yovine, S. (1996). The tool KRONOS. In *Hybrid Systems III, Verification and Control*, (LNCS 1066). Berlin: Springer-Verlag.

Goessler, G., & Sifakis, J. (2002). Composition for Component-Based Modeling. In *Proceedings of FMCO'02*, November 2002, Leiden, the Netherlands, (LNCS 2852, pp. 443-466).

Hanisch, H.-M., & Luder, A. (1999). Modular Modelling of Closed-Loop Systems. In *Colloquium on Petri Net Technologies for Modelling Communication Based Systems*, Germany, (pp. 103-126).

Henzinger, T.-A., Ho, P., & Womg-Toi, H. (1997). HyTech: the next generation. In *TACAS95: Tools and Algorithms for the Construction and Analysis of Systems*, (LNCS).

IEC61131. (1993). *Programmable Controllers Part 3*. Bureau Central de la commission Electrotechnique Internationale Switzerland.

IEC61499. (2004). *Industrial Process Measurements and Control Systems. International Electrotechnical Commission (IEC)*. Committee Draft.

Khalgui, M., Carpanzano, E., & Hanisch, H.-M. (2008). An optimised simulation of component-based embedded systems in manufacturing industry. *International Journal of Simulation and Process Modelling, 4*(2), 148–162. doi:10.1504/IJSPM.2008.022076

Khalgui, M., & Hanisch, H.-M. (2008). Automatic specification of feasible Control Tasks in Benchmark Production Systems. In *IEEE International Conference on Emerging Technologies and Factory Automation, ETFA08*.

Khalgui, M., & Rebeuf, X. (2008). An approach to implement a programmable logic controller from real-time software components. *International Journal of Industrial and Systems Engineering, 3*(6).

Khalgui, M., Rebeuf, X., & Simonot-Lion, F., (2007). A deployment method of component based applications on distributed industrial control systems. *European Jounal of Automated Systems, 41*(6).

Khalgui, M., & Thramboulidis, K. (2008). An IEC61499-based Development Approach for the Deployment of Industrial Control Applications. *International journal of Modelling* [IJMIC]. *Identification and Control, 4*(2), 186–204. doi:10.1504/IJMIC.2008.021096

Lewis, R.-W. (2001). *Modelling Control systems using IEC 61499*. Institution Of Engineering and Technology.

Mailler, R., & Lesser, V. (2003-a). A Mediation Based Protocol for Distributed Constraint Satisfaction. In *Fourth International Workshop on Distributed Constraint Reasoning*, (pp. 49-58).

Mailler, R., Lesser, V., & Horling, B. (2003-b). Cooperative Negotiation for Soft Real-Time Distributed Resource Allocation. In *Proceedings of Second International Joint Conference on Autonomous Agents and MultiAgent Systems (AAMAS 2003)*, (pp. 576-583). New York: ACM Press.

Mitchell, I., & Tomlin, C. (2000). Level set methods for computation in hybrid systems. In *Hybrid Systems: Computation and Control, Third International Workshop*, (LNCS).

Novak, P., Rollo, M., Hodik, J., & Vlcek, T. (2003). Communication Security in Multi-Agent Systems. In *Multi-Agent Systems and Aplications III* (pp. 454–463). Berlin: Springer-Verlag. doi:10.1007/3-540-45023-8_44

Pitt, J., & Mamdani, A. (2000). Communication Protocols in Multi-Agent Systems: A Development Method and Reference Architecture. In F. Dignum & M. Greaves (eds.), *Issues in Agent Communication*, (LNAI 1916, pp. 160-177). Berlin: Springer Verlag.

Rausch, M., & Hanisch, H.-M. (1995). Net condition/event systems with multiple condition outputs. *Symposium on Emerging Technologies and Factory Automation, 1*, 592-600.

Roch, S. (2000). Extended Computation Tree Logic: Implementation and Application. In *Proceedings of the AWPN2000 Workshop*, Germany.

Rooker, M.-N., Sunder, C., Strasser, T., Zoitl, A., Hummer, O., & Ebenhofer, G. (2007). Zero Downtime Reconfiguration of Distributed Automation Systems: The εCEDAC Approach. In *Third International Conference on Industrial Applications of Holonic and Multi-Agent Systems.* Berlin: Springer-Verlag.

SESA. (2008). *Signal/Net System Analyzer*. Retrieved from http://www.ece.auckland.ac.nz/vyatkin/tools/modelchekers.html

Sims, M., Corkill, D., & Lesser, V. (2008). Automated Organization Design for Multi-agent Systems. *Autonomous Agents and Multi-Agent Systems*, *16*(2), 151–185. doi:10.1007/s10458-007-9023-8

Thramboulidis, K., Doukas, G., & Frantzis, A. (2004). Towards an implementation model for FB-based reconfigurable distributed control applications. In *Proceedings of 7th IEEE International Symposium on Object-Oriented Real-Time Distributed Computing,* (pp. 193-200).

Vyatkin, V., & Hanisch, H.-M. (2003). Verification of Distributed Control Systems in Intelligent Manufacturing. *Journal of Intelligent Manufacturing*, *14*(1), 123–136. doi:10.1023/A:1022295414523

Chapter 11
Performance Analysis of FPGA Architectures Based Embedded Control Applications

Slim Ben Othman
National Institute of Applied Sciences and Technology (INSAT), Tunisia

Ahmed Karim Ben Salem
National Institute of Applied Sciences and Technology (INSAT), Tunisia

Slim Ben Saoud
National Institute of Applied Sciences and Technology (INSAT), Tunisia

ABSTRACT

The performances of System on Chip (SoC) and the Field Programmable Gate Array (FPGA) particularly, are increasing continually. Due to the growing complexity of modern embedded control systems, the need of more performance digital devices is evident. Recent FPGA technology makes it possible to include processor cores into the FPGA chip, which ensures more flexibility for digital controllers. Indeed, greater functionality of hardware and system software, Real-Time (RT) platforms and distributed subsystems are demanded. In this chapter, a design concept of FPGA based controller with Hardware/ Software (Hw/Sw) codesign is proposed. It is applied for electrical machine drives. There are discussed different MultiProcessor SoC (MPSoC) architectures with Hw peripherals for the implementation on FPGA-based embedded processor cores. Hw accelerators are considered in the design to enhance the controller speed performance and reduce power consumption. Test and validation of this control system are performed on a RT motor emulator implemented on the same FPGA. Experimental results, carried on a real prototyping platform, are given in order to analyze the performance and efficiency of discussed architecture designs helping to support hard RT constraints.

DOI: 10.4018/978-1-60960-086-0.ch011

INTRODUCTION

Nowadays, digital controllers are widely used in different industrial application areas such as motion control, power electronics, and motor control. Efficiency of control device technologies has been proven with the use of highly optimized DSP controllers. However, System on Chip (SoC) capability introduces new challenges in the design process. Codesign becomes a crucial issue where software and hardware must be developed together and different design and modeling techniques have been used.

In the last years, several research studies proved that Field Programmable Gate Array (FPGA), are an appropriate alternative to implement digital controllers in several application areas, such as motion control, power electronics, and motor control over pure software solutions (DSP, Microcontrollers) and analog solutions (Rodriguez-Andina, Moure, & Valdes, 2007; Yuen Fong, Moallem, & Wei, 2007). FPGA-based controllers offer advantages such as high speed, complex functionality, and low power consumption. Even, FPGA-based computing platforms, with embedded processors, have been more potential to implement extreme high-performance applications without the up-front risk of creating custom fixed function hardware (Seul & Sung su, 2007). One of the often-overlooked benefits of using embedded processors within FPGA is the ability to create a Hardware/Software (Hw/Sw) development target within a single programmable device. Different approaches were used to obtain more speed performance like the use of embedded MultiProcessor SoC (MPSoC) (Kumar, Fernando, Yajun, Mesman, & Corporaal, 2007) or specific Hw coprocessor accelerator (Pellerin & Shenoy, 2006).

Embedded control system designs are often complicated by strict performance, area, and power constraints (Carlos Paiz & Porrmann, 2007). The rigidity of the target architecture may lead to a very restricted application field or poor perfor-

mances (Zergainoh, Baghdadi, & Jerraya, 2004). The MPSoC remains a promising architecture to ensure a correct behavior of the embedded closed loop controller. Nevertheless, one of the most important issues in MPSoC design is the target architecture. In this chapter, different FPGA-based MPSoC architectures are proposed. The authors discuss the Hw/Sw flow design according to the InterProcessor Communication (IPC) supports, and analyze the impact of architecture models on embedded system performances.

However, modularity, flexibility and scalability are required to have an efficient application specific multiprocessor design flow (Carlos Paiz & Porrmann, 2007). This has led to the study of Hw/Sw codesign issues. These issues traditionally arise from applications where there are fixed constraints that cannot be met in software but do not warrant a fully Hw solution.

Considering the programmable logic inside the FPGA as an extension to the embedded processor, processing tasks of the application can be distributed conveniently and efficiently between hardware and software. This chapter also discusses the design of an application-specific MPSoC, including generation of Hw/Sw wrappers that adapts the processors to the on-chip control system applications and results to a great deal of performance.

As well, the rapid development of the fully embedded control system is pending on not only the SoC target knowledge and equipment needed to fabricate any prototype but also on the accurate modeling and simulation of the digital closed-loop controller in its power and analog context. It requires extensive testing before applying in real conditions.

The proposed wok, aims to define a new FPGA-based design flow that instantly allows validation and prototyping of the digital Controller Under Test (CUT). The proposed approach leads to an embedded simulation approach composed by the CUT and the Real Time (RT) process emulator implemented in the same SoC. Therefore, the implementation concept, will be used either for complete controller device validation at the designing and validation stage or for diagnosis at normal functioning stage.

Overall, in this chapter, we discuss various FPGA-based MPSoC architectures that can be supported for the design, implementation, and validation of digital control units. Thus, the design model for these architectures considers integration of a RT process emulator with controllers. The proposed design architectures are classified according to 1) the number of used processors, 2) the adopted network connections, 3) the use of Hw for Sw accelerators, 4) the integration of dedicated hardware for RT connectivity. Accordingly, the performance analysis is depicted for the case study of a DC machine speed control. This is a set of criteria that may eventually help in the choice of a suitable architecture model for other control systems.

BACKGROUND

We provide in this section an overview of well-known targets technologies used to implement digital control systems. Specifically, we discuss the design methodology and advanced features of FPGA-based electrical system controllers. In addition, we review the co-simulation concept of embedded control systems.

Implementations Targets Technologies of Digital Controllers

Digital controller implementations for power systems are nowadays more and more complex since they integrate sophisticated control algorithms and many additional tasks such as diagnosis and fault adaptive online. Additionally, several constraints are to be considered with these control device systems. The main constraints are, firstly, the time execution of the control algorithm and the time needed for conversion of analogue in-

formation to digital form. Secondly, the precision and especially the resolution of the I/O modules like the resolution of the used Analogue Digital Converters (ADC) components (number of bits), the resolution of the position/speed acquisition module (clock and number of bits) and the resolution of the PWM module...

Nowadays, Designing high performance modern controllers for electrical actuators is a complex task. It normally involves multiple talents and disciplines in different technology fields. The implementation targets of such systems demand a perfect satisfaction of the required performances, especially for critical industrial applications (Idkhajine, Prata, Monmasson, Bouallaga, & Naouar, 2008).

The aggressive evolution of the semiconductor industry, smaller process geometries, and higher densities, has provided design engineers, the means to create complex, high-performance digital components allowing implementation of more complex control algorithms. Indeed, improved reliability and performance of digital technologies, allowed digital control techniques to predominate over their analogue counterparts. They offer many advantages compared with traditional analogue control, such as power consumption reduction, time optimizations, flexibility to modify the control schemes, adaptability to different systems (Monmasson & Cirstea, 2007).

However, the efficient digital control of the electrical motor drive systems involves fast computational units. Signal processors and microprocessors are frequently used in such applications. Using universal microprocessors or signal processors enables obtaining high computational efficiency but significantly increases the costs of a drive application (Lis, Kowalski, & Orlowska-Kowalska, 2008).

Furthermore, various kinds of digital control methods were proposed for power electronics applications with DSP based Sw controller (e.g., sensorless motor drive control and estimators (Boussak & Jarray, 2005; Griva, Ilas, Eastham,

Profumo, & Vranka, 1997; Kaliamoorthy, Hima-vathi, & Muthuramalingam, 2006), neural network controller (Mohamadian, et al., 2003) and fuzzy logic (Singh, Singh, & Dwivedi, 2006). Generally, in the DSP based Sw controller, DSP treats the digital control schemes and ASIC or PLD treats the other logic control interfaces (Bosheng & Zhiqiang, 2005; Jezernik & Rodic, 2008; Lascu & Trzynadlowski, 2001). Nowadays, DSP has many features to deal with power electronics applications such as PWM generation logic and other gate control logic.

Moreover, in some application, the ASIC chips can be applied to replace the sets of interfaces offered by such processors. Such an approach enables developing custom-built digital interface as well as digital data processing blocks and sometimes-even integration of ADC converters into one integrated circuit.

In recent years, FPGA have become an alternative solution for the realization of digital control systems, which were previously dominated by general-purpose DSP systems (Yuen Fong, et al., 2007). FPGA-based programmable platforms have emerged as viable alternatives for many types of high-performance computing applications (Hongtao, Hairong, & Xiaoling, 2007). They have proven themselves in a broad range of Hw applications, including telecommunications, aerospace and defense, medical electronics, and consumer electronics (Idkhajine, et al., 2008).

However, new high-performance SoC digital control devices can also be considered as an appropriate solution in order to boost performances of controllers and consequently to reduce the gap between the analog and digital world. The new FPGA are considered as new trends in SoC (Seul & Sung su, 2007). As FPGA have grown in logic capacity, their ability to host high-performance Sw algorithms and complete applications has grown correspondingly. They integrate embedded processors with extremely fast computation capability. They also provide flexible and fast interconnect

options for interfacing peripherals and creating a multi-processors system (Kumar, et al., 2007).

Among industrial applications that use the SoC based-FPGA capabilities we quote: High-precision high-speed motor drives (Carbone, Colli, Stefano, Figalli, & Marignetti, 2009; Da & Hui, 2008; Kowalski, Lis, & Orlowska-Kowalska, 2007; Ying-Shieh & Ming-Hung, 2007), active filter applications (Abe, Arai, & Kawamata, 2005), control process for robotic and mechatronic systems (Astarloa, Làzaro, Bidarte, Jiménez, & Zuloaga, 2009; Simard, Beguenane, & Mailloux, 2008), image processing (Hongtao, et al., 2007)…

Contributions and Limits of FPGA-Based Control Systems

In the last years, FPGA is considered as an appropriate solution to implement digital controllers (Rodriguez-Andina, et al., 2007). In the following sections, the suitability of the different resources of modern FPGAs to fit the requirements of different electrical system controller applications are discussed, and their limitations are highlighted.

The first common strong point characterizing all the FPGA fabric is their significant integration density. The FPGA provides a much more flexible configurable architecture. A high number of programmable logic blocks is available, which can be individually connected by a programmable interconnect matrices. Additionally, programmable I/O blocks are available for interfacing. They also allow designing parallel architectures, based only on the specific needs of the targeted algorithm, which can considerably reduce the execution time and as consequence, ensure a quasi-analog treatment. Furthermore, their reprogramability ensures good controller flexibility (Idkhajine, et al., 2008). The controller based-FPGA can then be implemented exploiting its natural parallelism to achieve a higher throughput.

In addition, current FPGAs technologies based computing platforms with embedded processors (either hard or soft ones) and integrated memory blocks, have the potential to implement extreme high-performance applications without the upfront risk of creating custom fixed function hardware (Seul & Sung su, 2007). Therefore, these FPGA circuits serve as a powerful platform for prototype embedded system design, supporting easy integration and implementation of one or more processors, peripherals and data processing logic in a single configurable chip. Currently, various FPGA platforms with integrated hardcore processors (e.g. VirtexII-Pro from Xilinx, Excalibur from Altera) or FPGA circuits, suitable for implementation of softcore processor models (e.g. MicroBlaze from Xilinx, Nios from Altera) are available for supporting such SoC (Pellerin & Shenoy, 2006). These FPGA are also expected for resolving complex digital controller algorithm that requires a high speed sample time and intensive processing power. Thus it provides a lot of integrant embedded multipliers and DSP blocks, which allow complex arithmetic operations to be performed, expect parallel processing capabilities (e.g., distributed arithmetic), and also support processing for higher bandwidth data streams.

In the FPGA based computing, the specific algorithm functionalities can be developed and stored in libraries of Hw IP blocks for reuse in different applications (Salewski & Kowalewski, 2008). The Hw cores are tightly coupled with the CPU using very high speed, point to point links for fast data transfer. This allows them to act as accelerators (co-processors) for compute intensive portions of the applications such as floating point intensive calculations, discrete transformation algorithms (FFT, DWT, DCT, etc.), and also for other custom applications (Mitra, Zhi, Banerjee, & Najjar, 2006). Furthermore, Hw/Sw vendor development tools for FPGA (i.e. Embedded Development Kit from Xilinx, SOPC Builder IDE from Altera, the System Designer from Atmel...) are well developed to contribute easily to an embedded system codesign.

In order to respect high-integrated SoC implementation, FPGA devices, including ADC conver-

sion and actuation capabilities are also available from Actel company (Fusion FPGA SoC). This mixed treatment approach offers a new level of integration by allowing the use of heterogeneous functions in a same device. As consequence, the system cost and board space are reduced and, at the same time, the control reliability is improved (Idkhajine, et al., 2008).

More recently, FPGAs, using new design tools, have also provided support for partial reconfiguration. It consists of creating a system that can enable re-configuration of pre-assigned parts of the FPGA without affecting the static parts, or inducing a system-wide reset (Mitra, et al., 2006). This partial reconfiguration and in particular, the run time dynamic reconfiguration is a powerful tool to overcome the area limitation of a FPGA platform and to speed up the processing time achievement (C. Paiz, et al., 2009; Qu, Tiensyrjä, Soininen, & Nurmi, 2008).

In spite of the advantages that FPGA bring to the digital controller implementations, this technology remains often deferred by the control engineer. However, Sw-to-Hw tools (e.g. DK Design Suite from Celoxica, CoDeveloper from Impulse Accelerated Technologies, and Catapult C Synthesis from Mentor Graphics) as well as high-level Hw description tools (e.g., System Generator from Xilinx, DSP Builder from Altera, or Synplify DSP from Synplicity) help engineers to overcome the lack of expertise in digital Hw design (Schulz, et al., 2007; Simard, et al., 2008).

Nevertheless, because the efficient implementation of the algorithms largely depends on the designer experience, the codesign tools and methodologies need additional evolution to take the most possible advantage of dedicated resources and efficiently distribute tasks in hardware and software. These improvements allow addressing the minimization and also the accurate estimation of power consumption, which is a limiting requirement in many embedded applications (Rodriguez-Andina, et al., 2007).

Co-Simulation Concept of Embedded Control Systems

The design flow of the fully embedded control system leads with extensive testing before applying in real conditions. High-level computer off-line simulation tools such as Matlab/Simulink or PSpice could be used to develop the process model and the controller. However, in these simulation environments, control code is usually not developed keeping RT execution in mind. New Sw packages recently designed by FPGA manufacturers can cure to this problem. They enable the co-simulation inside off-line simulators (Han, et al., 2009) (e.g. System generator for Matlab-Simulink from Xilinx). This methodology takes the dynamics of electrical machine environments and models them using software to test newly designed controller performance (Han, et al., 2009; Ho & Xu, 2007). Corrective changes to the controller can be implemented and tested without fear of destroying expensive equipment.

This RT simulation concept is called Hw-in-the-Loop (HIL) simulation. It offers several distinct advantages. For example, the simulated motor drive can be tested with borderline conditions that would damage a real motor, often a costly prototype. The controller unit can be developed and tested without preliminary need of a physical process.

In some HIL platforms, the process model is designed for embedded SoC (in most cases an FPGA chip). This consists of designing an embedded RT emulator (Ben Saoud, 1996), that provides controller device validation at the designing and validation stage or for diagnosis at normal functioning stage.

This emulator should behave exactly like the physical system, in sense to make the control device believe that it is connected to the real process. Thereby it has to generate and receive information similarly to the physical process: it receives control signals and generates information about the system state in forms identical to those obtained by sensors. After this step, the control device is completely validated and can be switched for use with the physical process.

STATE OF THE ART

The literature contains several alternative approaches of HIL simulation with emulation concepts. Reference (R. Jastrzębski, et al., 2004) reports a Hw design of asynchronous motor emulator which allows testing and evaluation of the very fast motor controllers in RT. In (Laakkonen, Rauma, Saren, Luukko, & Pyrhonen, 2004), a dSPACE Hw target is used to simulate inverter and motor when the control algorithms run in FPGA circuit and control the completely emulated electric drive system. Others interesting works use the concept of emulation to reproduce only partial functions of the whole controller device. As in (Aggarwal & Kuhlman, 2007), authors depict the FPGA-based sensor emulators to allow designers to incorporate RT signals as early as possible in the design process. When in (Ruelland, Gateau, Meynard, & Hapiot, 2003), paper gives a power system co-simulation case by using an FPGA-based emulator for series multicell converters. Reference (National-Instruments, 2008) provides an overview of how the LabView FPGA and PXI reconfigurable I/O module platforms can help to design and deploy rapidly a HIL system. More recently FPGA-based distributed HIL simulator platform like RT-LAB (Christian, Jean, Vincent, & Simon, 2008) came to close the simulation loop by offering a powerful Hw platform and Sw libraries to run complex models with real-time constraints.

In our research works, we are focused on design methodologies of dedicated digital control systems on SoC. Our aims are to define a design flow, an effective validation, and efficient tools to help in the VLSI implementation of numerical controls on a mixed Hw/Sw platform. Reference (Ben Othman, Ben Salem, & Ben Saoud, 2008a) describes a hardcore single processing for implementing RT motor control loops with emulation concept. There are discussed several difficulties to the level of emulation routine latency and interrupt management (timing, partitioning, priorities...). These problems are partially resolved by using RTOS solutions to schedule the controller and the motor emulator into software tasks executed in an embedded processor (Ben Salem, Ben Othman, & Ben Saoud, 2008b). The last propositions are after completed by a comparison between the use of hard and soft core processors (PowerPC and MicroBlaze) (Ben Salem, Ben Othman, & Ben Saoud, 2008a). In opposite to single processor solution, a Multi-processor one is proposed by (Ben Othman, Ben Salem, & Ben Saoud, 2008). MPSoC implementation is carried using Micro-Blaze (MB) soft-cores and Mailbox IPC to divide computing time between two or three of them. In (Ben Othman, Ben Salem, & Ben Saoud, 2008b) authors present another solution to enhance controller performances based on coprocessor Hw with biprocessor architecture. All these works have been validated either by simple PI speed controllers for DC machines or by complex FOC control for induction machines (Ben Salem, Ben Othman, & Ben Saoud, 2010).

Finally, we note that all these related works propose a single or multiple processor architectures that are restricted to some specific resources on the FPGA target (bus, peripherals...). In contrast, the work proposed by this chapter book develops a wider architectural space exploration that may eventually help for the choice of a suitable architecture model according to the control system applications.

Similarly, these related works are limited to the implementation and validation of behavior control algorithms. In addition, we present in this chapter a fully integrated solution for motor control applications that adds real-world sensor functionalities to the emulator side and RT acquiring interfaces to the control unit side.

CONTRIBUTIONS

We propose in our book chapter a new design flow that aims to generate an embedded simulation platform based on HIL simulation and emulation concept. This approach is an interesting development environment for control engineering to be targeted on reconfigurable hardware. The designer can easily achieve the implementation of controller loops from the validation phase to the operational phase.

The design effort for this embedded simulation platform may be complemented by considering RT I/O data of sensors and actuators to reproduce the physical system functioning in real-time and with high accuracy. However, the designer can realize whether the controller, running on an FPGA actually works as expected by meeting all RT constraints.

Our design approach intends to switch control system functionalities to software instead of implementing all of them in hardware, which is not desirable for several reasons. On the one hand, some control heavy computation tasks are hard to parallelize and their Hw implementations yield low speed-up. On the other hand, some system tasks require little computation time and they can be executed on a processor with low utilization of FPGA area. Therefore, the goal of implementing controllers' functionalities in software is to save design/verification time with respecting RT performance, flexibility, and user-friendliness.

The remaining parts of the chapter are divided in the following way. The next section discusses the MPSoC concept and Hw design contributions. It introduces the IPC and bus interfaces available with the FPGA target platform. The "RT control application specification" section discusses the partitioning model for motor control application process, and presents a generic multiprocessor architecture supporting a mixed Hw/Sw codesign of controller devices. The two-followed sections propose different MPSoC architecture schemes based respectively on shared memory and mailbox

IPC. The "Hw controller coprocessor design" section considers the design of a Hw current controller and shows how to construct coprocessors in order to produce optimal system performance. In "Hw interfaces design" section, we detail the design flow of Hw control device peripherals. Thereafter, implementation results with thorough performance evaluation of described architectures are achieved. Future trends are discussed in the sequence followed by the main conclusions of this chapter.

MPSOC ARCHITECTURE TEMPLATES

Multiprocessor Systems

MPSoCs are the most recent challenge of the VLSI technologies (Palumbo, Secchi, Pani, & Raffo, 2008). New applications for embedded systems demand complex multiprocessor designs to meet RT deadlines while achieving other critical design constraints like low power consumption and low area (Nikolov, Stefanov, & Deprettere, 2006). With high consumer demand, the time-to-market has significantly reduced (Jerraya & Bouchhima, 2006). Furthermore, MPSoC have been proposed as a promising solution for all such problems (Jerraya & Wayne, 2004) to provide adequate processing capabilities at low power consumption (Limberg, Ristau, & Fettweis, 2008).

Indeed, the MPSoC consists of putting multiple CPU on a SOC, aiming to have a parallel programming application to take full advantages of the hardware (Schirrmeister, 2007). There are various factors, which can require a system to be designed using more than one processor such as performance, functionality, modularity ....

Moreover, a common scenario in a system is the presence of a clearly distinct set of RT and non RT tasks, such that a solution based on a single processor to handle both may cease to be responsive (Hubner, Paulsson, & Becker, 2005).

Furthermore, in certain cases, a single processor may just not provide enough performance and it may be hard to find clean boundaries at which the solution can be partitioned across multiple processors (Del valle, et al., 2006).

With MPSoC, the design may have multiple set of processing tasks to be performed with creating various processing modules that are completely independent (Kumar, et al., 2007). Each one is assigned a unique processor and peripheral set to cope with even more concurrent and dynamically changing applications.

Unfortunately programming such systems is not trivial (Lee, 2006). Understandable programming models, which utilize hardware effectively, are required, in order to get the maximum benefit out of parallel systems.

MPSoC-Based FPGA Target Platform

The used development platform consists of Xilinx ML310 board (Xilinx, 2005b). Its high performance Xilinx Virtex-II Pro XC 2VP30 FPGA combines more than 30,000 configurable logic blocks (CLB) and 2 IBM PowerPC 405 (PPC) hardcore processors on a single chip. The large amount of peripherals offers a variety of different interfaces.

The Xilinx Embedded Development Kit (EDK) environment provides the tools and libraries to integrate the PPC cores on chip, soft MicroBlaze (MB) cores, IBM CoreConnect buses, and customizable peripherals to design multiprocessor micro-architectures.

The Xilinx ML310 board provides a MPSoC FPGA design. Both the MB softcore processor and PPC hardcore processor offer some unique benefits through circuitry dedicated to interfacing with on-chip peripherals in the FPGA fabric. The topology of a multiprocessor system is defined by the interconnect infrastructure used to connect the various processing elements, memories and peripherals as shown in Figure 1.

Figure 1. Xilinx FPGA Multiprocessing Topology

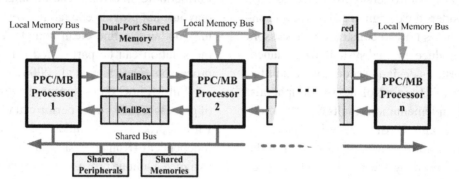

The only differences of interest between MB and PPC are the computing power and the maximum data rates. That is why it is not possible to make a decision between them without knowing the requirements of the implemented algorithm. Nevertheless, for the used target platform, the MB is the best solution because the ML310 board can only hold two PPC. Since the proposed MPSoC architectures uses several homogenous processors in most cases, PPC cannot be used. However, several architectural aspects (such as FSL link, Hw FPU...) available in the softcore versions are not allowed for PPC processors. For all these reasons, only MB MPSoC architectures are involved. The PPC designs will be evoked for comparing implementation results.

Hw Design Contribution in Processors-Based FPGA Architectures

In many Sw-defined applications, FPGAs are being used increasingly as a general-purpose computational fabric to implement Hw acceleration units that boost performance while lowering cost and power requirements (Hampel, Sobe, & Maehle, 2008).

Using FPGA resources for processor acceleration can be done in several ways. Whereas custom instructions are an extension of an ALU, which is relegated to a softcore processor (Hodjat, Batina, Hwang, & Verbauwhede, 2007), Hw acceleration coprocessors can be used to accelerate processors (either hard-core or soft-core processors) that are implemented on the FPGA. Thus, peripherals as coprocessors are ideal for extending the processors execution unit with custom Hw accelerators. Further, custom instructions can be added without change the optimized processor core to achieve the determined strict timing constraints defined for the CPU.

Situations where Hw acceleration coprocessors could be used over a custom instruction have one or more of the following common characteristics (Seely, 2005):

- Operations are more complex (often a subroutine in software),
- Algorithms do not use only register variables (non atomic),
- Transformation of data is done on a large data block.

This design strategy has many advantages in MPSoC architecture. When FPGAs are added to a multiprocessing environment, opportunities exist for improving both application-level and instruction-level parallelism (Rodriguez-Andina, et al., 2007). Using FPGAs, it is possible to create structures that can greatly accelerate individual operations, such as a simple multiply-accumulate or more complex sequences of integer or floating point operations, or that implement higher-level control structures such as loops. These parallel structures can themselves be replicated to create further degrees of parallelism, up to the limits of the target device's capacity (Cong, Gururaj, & Han, 2009).

Interprocessor Communication (IPC) Overview

Efficient communication between processors is critical in multiprocessor and multicore embedded designs. How the software will take advantage of the underlying Hw support structure is equally important. In multiprocessor environments, things get difficult when embedded designers encounter interprocessor connections designed to take advantage of a particular processor environment (Wong, 2006).

On FPGA processors, the most common communication schemes are Shared Memory and Mailbox based message passing (Kumar, et al., 2007). Each IPC method has its advantages and drawbacks. System designers must choose the most appropriate tool method for their application (Jerraya & Bouchhima, 2006).

Shared Memory IPC

Shared memory is the most common and intuitive way of passing information between processing subsystems. Shared memory is typically the fastest asynchronous mode of communication, especially when the information to be shared is large (>1000 bytes). It also offers high bandwidth and low latency.

This IPC scheme can be built out of on-chip local memory or on external memory connecting to a shared system bus or a point-to-point multiport memory connection. Both, OPB and LMB can be used to create shared memory segments. This scheme works by connecting memory controllers via local memory interfaces to the on-chip BRAM blocks.

The Sw designer defines the shared memory regions, based on some partitioning, and writes the Sw protocol that uses the memory regions to pass information between the processing subsystems.

Mailbox IPC

The mailbox tends to be used to exchange smaller packets of information. It also provides synchronization between processors (Asokan, 2007). The mailbox forms a channel through which messages are queued in a FIFO mode from one end by senders, and then dequeued at the other by the receiver. The FIFO is implemented using Hw logic or memory resources. The reception of the message at the end of the receiver may be done in a synchronous or asynchronous way. In the synchronous method, the receiver actively keeps polling the mailbox for new data. In the asynchronous method, the mailbox sends an interrupt to the receiver upon the presence of data in the mailbox.

The MB processors offer such FIFO style communication capabilities through the Fast Simplex Link (FSL) interface. FSL is a unidirectional point-to-point FIFO link. They have special instructions that allow a program to write to a given FSL channel with optional non-blocking and/or control semantics (Xilinx, 2005d). The point-to-point nature and the minimal Hw requirements are the greatest advantages of FSL. Because the FSL channels are dedicated, no arbitration or bus mastering is required. This allows an extremely fast interface to the processor. In addition, the latency of sending a message through this interface is very low (Schirrmeister, 2007).

Hw Peripheral Bus Interface

Bus interface logic is needed to bridge the gap between the I/O ports on the peripheral and the processor connection. In MB systems, there are three commonly available Hw/Sw interfaces: direct connection busses (FSL), processor local

Figure 2. FSL peripheral connections

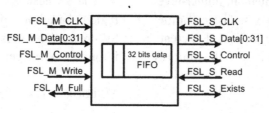

busses (LMB) and general-purpose system busses (OPB). Processor local busses are specific only for memories connections, and will not be considered as Hw peripherals support.

FSL Bus Interface

The FSL bus (Xilinx, 2005a), 32-bit wide and interfaced directly to MB, is dedicated unidirectional point-to-point data streaming interface. This interface, with no arbitration, can be used to send data in and out of the custom hardware. The performance of the FSL interface can reach up to 300 MB/sec and the throughput depends on the target device itself. The FSL bus has one master and one slave, and supports synchronous or asynchronous communication. Figure 2 shows the FSL interface with the available signals.

Each Master and Slave interface contains a data bus, a control bit, and an asynchronous clock signal. The control bit has no direct correlation to the data bus, as its context and value are dependent on its usage in software. The asynchronous clock signals provide separate clock domains for both the Master and Slave interfaces. The Master interface has Write and Full signals, while the Slave interface uses Read and Exists signals.

The MB with the FSL interface can dramatically enhance the speed and performance of the whole implemented system by employing the most time consuming software in hardware (Guo, Chen, & Schaumont, 2008). This makes the design flexible and changes at the last moment of the project is permissible making the whole development process less costly. Since the communication to

the FSL Hw accelerator is by way of a point-to-point non-arbitrated communication protocol, the FSL FPU is really an extension of the processor execution unit. This is a key benefit of customizable Hw platform, the ability to tailor hardware to meet the intended application.

OPB Bus Interface

An alternative to Hw accelerated cores accessible by way of the FSL ports on MB are peripheral components placed on the OPB. The OPB is a centrally arbitrated, shared peripheral bus. It is composed of masters, slaves, a bus interconnect, and an arbiter. The prime goal of OPB is to provide for a flexible connection path to peripherals and memory of various bus widths and transaction timing requirements while providing a minimal performance impact.

The Hw side of an OPB interface consists of a decoder for a memory-read or memory-write cycle on a selected address in the memory range mapped to the OPB. The decoded memory cycle is translated to a read-from or a write-into a register in the peripheral. The drawback of this interface is the low-speed connection between hardware and software. Even on an embedded core, a simple round-trip communication between software and hardware can run into several tens of CPU clock cycles (Schaumont & Verbauwhede, 2007).

The FPGA processing OPB peripheral can implement the following components as shown in Figure 3.

Figure 3. Peripheral OPB bus attachment overview

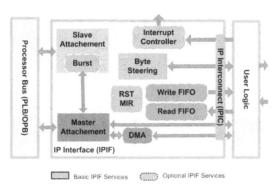

- *A Bus Interface:* A set of ports to connect the peripheral and the targeted bus.
- *The Intellectual Property Interface (IPIF) for OPB peripherals:* The bus interface connects to this component. Additionally, it provides functionality that FPGA processor peripherals need, including address decoding, addressable registers, interrupt handling, read/write FIFO, and DMA.
- *A component that implements the application-specific logic (user logic):* For OPB peripherals, this is the logic that cannot be implemented in the IPIF. The user logic interfaces to the IPIF through a set of ports called the Intellectual Property Interconnect (IPIC).

By residing on the OPB, additional bus arbitration latencies are introduced, which are not found at a lower Hw interface such as the FSL. Thus, FSL remain the ideal solution for extending the processors execution unit with custom Hw accelerators. However, the OPB bus stays useful like interfaces for the slow peripherals.

In the next sections, we discuss a design approach of Hw components that improve the Sw applications execution times and ensure a nearest test environment to the real functioning case.

RT CONTROL APPLICATION SPECIFICATION

Overview of Power Process Digital Controllers

A motor drive system is composed of 1) the process to control including the converter circuit, the electric motor and load components and the different used sensors and 2) the digital control unit which is composed of the digital controller based on a specific algorithm and the necessary interfaces for sensors outputs acquiring and control signals generation (Figure 4).

The control unit is modeled according to the applied CMS process (AC or DC) and to its target input. In this work, we seek of solutions, which enable us to implement controller unit and the CMS emulator on the same SoC.

MPSoC Partitioning Model

Considering that this work aims to implement the whole motor control loop components using a clearly-defined run-time behavior that can perform the best RT response, we have chosen to implement these different controller loops and the emulator using different Hw components and interrupts handling on multiprocessor architecture. This offers the possibility to manage the time

Figure 4. Motor drive block diagram

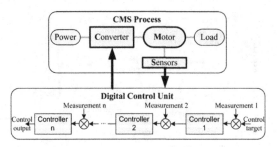

Figure 5. Generic partitioning model of a motor drive

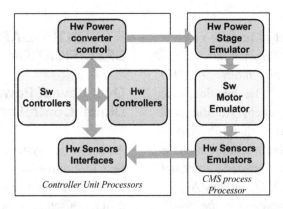

constraint for control loop independently of the controller devices and the emulator main tasks.

Hence, many partitioning models can be defined in this case. We have proposed to move the emulator functionality aside in a single processor. This allows the emulator to work on RT conditions at optimal processor execution time without affecting control unit interrupts working at a higher time. Therefore, depending on interrupts complexity, the control loops in the controller unit can be handled in another single processor or split on two or more processors otherwise mapped in Hw modules.

Figure 5 presents a generic approach of partitioning model for motor drive design. This model is based on Hw/Sw codesign with multiprocessor concept and specific Hw peripherals. The first one is to support Sw motor emulator and controllers. The second one is to accelerate Sw and to resolve power stage and sensors signals.

In order to validate our approach, we consider the case study of DC process speed controller. We assume that work on simple process templates allows us to validate our approach. However, it can be easily generalized to any other process control.

As shown in Figure 6, the process is based on two nested closed loops. The inner loop is in charge of current control while the external loop manages the motor speed. The used controllers for both loops are based on PI algorithms.

Therefore, as illustrated in Figure 7, speed and current controllers loops in the control unit can be achieved either by a single (Figure 7a) or double processor (Figure 7b). Another partitioning consideration consists of applying a Hw accelerator approach for the controller processor. In this case, the current PI controller is positioned in a Hw part and controlled by a Sw part.

Figure 6. General diagram of a motor control drive

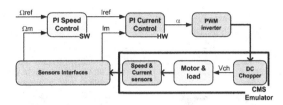

Figure 7. Specific partitioning models: (a) biprocessor model, (b) three processors model

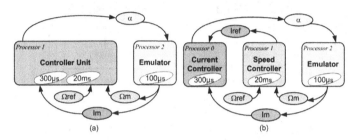

SHARED MEMORY BASED CONTROL SYSTEM DESIGN

Hardware Design

MB processor use LMB as the local memory interface. Slow peripherals such as timer, UART, and interrupt controller are available with the OPB main system bus interface.

Because all on-chip memory blocks on Xilinx FPGA are dual port memories, it is easy and efficient to employ dual port memory as communication channel between processors. Figure 8 depicts a case of two processors sharing an OPB/LMB dual ported BRAM.

Every processor connects two independent data memory blocks to its Instruction LMB (ILMB) and Data LMB (DLMB) bus. However, controller peripheral is used to interface memory block to its bus. Each port of the shared BRAM is connected to the respective bus (OPB or LMB) of two different processors and therefore constitutes a communication channel. Processors can then, access dual port memory via a normal memory access.

Other OPB slower peripherals are used in these architectures to ensure handling of software time routines, to analyzing software execution and to make an external communication. They consist of:

- UART peripheral is an RS232 serial connection that allows communication with a PC.
- GPIO peripheral was used to interface external logic analyzer to processors.
- Timer peripherals used to generate interrupts at varying intervals.
- Interrupt controller was used for handling the timer interrupts in the order of their priorities. It is required for connecting multiple interrupt signals to one processor.

Apart from OPB, LMB BRAM interface can also be used to create high-performance, guaranteed latency, shared memory segments.

However, the dual port Shared memory IPC solution leads to a bad architecture when they are used to interconnect more than two processors. Figure 9 depicts an architecture example of three processors sharing LMB dual port memories.

Figure 8. Shared dual port BRAM: (a) OPB controller, (b) LMB controller

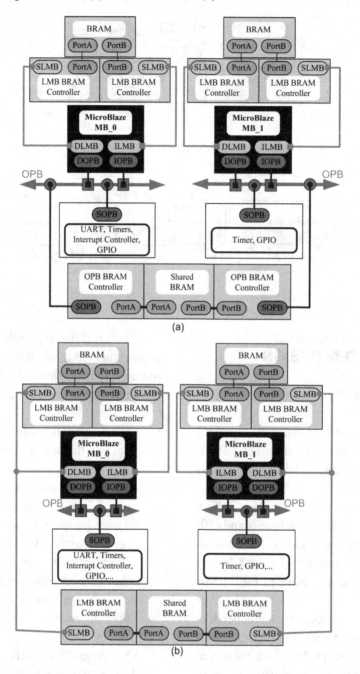

The last architecture has the limitation that the memory can be shared between a maximum of two master processors. It makes a complex Hw description with heavy synthesis process. It is also limited by the available memory resources in the FPGA target. Besides, this architecture needs a particular attention to the Sw application design.

The shared bus scheme becomes the typical solution of these inconvenient. In this case, the shared memory configurations use a single external memory controller connected via a shared

Figure 9. Three processors sharing LMB dual port memories

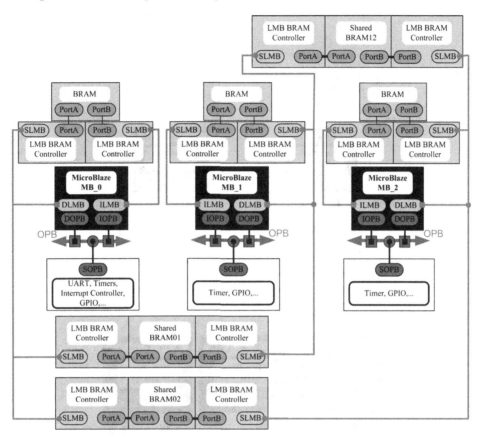

system bus. Because all the processors are on the same system bus, they automatically share this memory. Figure 10 present a Hw design example of an OPB Shared BRAM interfaced to a shared OPB bus. We note that LMB connections are used only to connect memories to one processor; they cannot achieve a shared bus.

The above method presents the same behavior than two MB processors sharing an OPB dual ported BRAM, but this one works well for any number of processors. Consequently, the shared Bram on the shared bus becomes the only shared memory solution to perform communication between three processors or more (the OPB bus support up to 16 master and 16 slave peripherals). Figure 11 shows three MB processors sharing the same memory.

Software Design

Case of Two Processors Architecture

Because the local memory interfaces on MB processors are point-to-point interfaces to BRAM, and the controllers live on different buses mastered by different processors, memory map for the shared region on each of the two processors could have different addresses and still refer to the same memory. However, to simplify our software design, the same memory address map is choosing as shown in Figure 12.

There is no inter-processor synchronization directly supported by dual port memory interconnection. Unless there is some sort of well-defined non-conflicting way in which each processor accesses the shared data, a synchronization protocol

Figure 10. Two MB processors sharing BRAM on a shared OPB bus

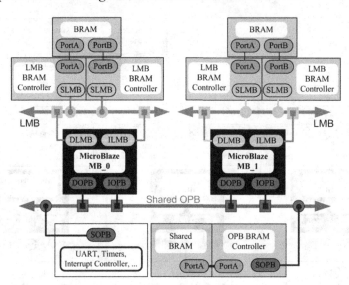

Figure 11. Three MB processors sharing OPB BRAM

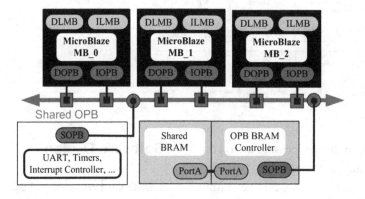

Figure 12. Dual MB processors memory map

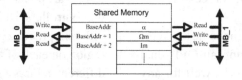

or construct is usually required to serialize accesses to the shared resource. Fortunately, there is no synchronization needed to access the shared memory because all the variables (α, Ωm and Im) are shared in read only access by one processor and write only access by the other (Figure 12).

Software systems in the two processors employed a looping construct for the main part of the application and used interrupts to handle time-critical events. Software routines have been configured with an interval timer using a real time interrupt clock as a peripheral device. MB_0

Figure 13. Three MB processors memory map

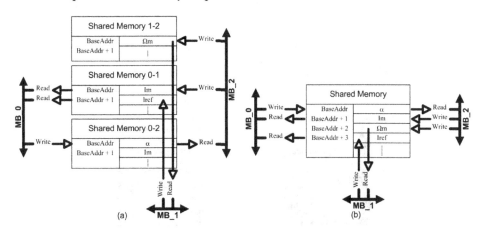

processor executes the controller unit algorithm. It is composed by the PI speed and PI current interrupt handler routines running at 20ms and 300μs. MB_1 processor runs the emulator interrupt handler code at 100μs.

Software on a processor can easily update the value of the shared variable and have it be visible to the other processor. All that is required is the address of the variable or a pointer into the shared region. The following code shows the shared global variables declarations in every software processors corresponding to the last memory map.

```
#define α *(float*) BaseAddr
#define Ωm *(float*) BaseAddr+1
#define Im *(float*) BaseAddr+2
```

Case of Three Processors Architecture

MB_0, MB_1, and MB_2 execute respectively current controller, speed controller, and emulator routines at the appropriate time delay. The three processors exchange four variables between them mapped in the shared memories according to the used Hw architecture (Figure 13).

In the first case (Figure 13a), processors can access dual port memories via normal memory access. The only restriction in the software design is the address of the variable or a pointer into the shared region. Furthermore, there is no synchronization requirement for the same reasons of last two processors architecture.

In the second case (Figure 13b), the processors share the same OPB bus as Master peripherals. This design causes the possibility of simultaneous requests on the bus and performs a concurrent bus access problem. This case cannot arise when only one single Master-Slave bus connection is possible (bus with only one Master and several slave connections). Consequently, the solution of this bus access problem implies to the arbitration concept: a dedicated Hw unit decides the priority assignment according to an arbitration algorithm (fixed priority, dynamic priority, bus parking, FIFO…).

In Xilinx FPGA, OPB system includes the Masters and Slaves interconnections and OPB arbiter core. The last one receives all the master request signals and asserts master grant signals based on a configurable arbitration algorithm. When OPB bus is shared by multiple MB processors, The Round-Robin behavioral remains the most recommended algorithm implementation, otherwise the highest priority processor will starve the others.

Figure 14. FSL dual MB processors interconnection

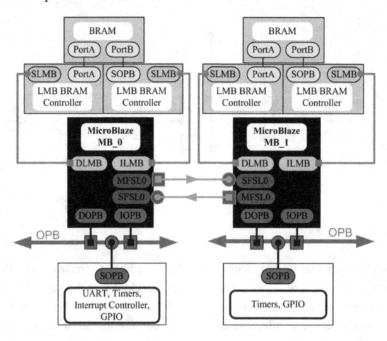

MAILBOX BASED CONTROL SYSTEM DESIGN

Hardware Design

The FSL channels are dedicated unidirectional point-to-point data streaming interfaces. The FSL Bus is a uni-directional point-to-point communication channel bus used to perform fast communication between any two design elements on the FPGA when implementing an interface to the FSL bus. MB consists of up to eight inputs and eight outputs 32 bits wide FSL interfaces. The interfaces are used to transfer data in two clock cycles to and from the register file on the processor to hardware running on the FPGA (can be another processor).

The put and get instructions of MB may be used to transfer the contents of a MB register onto the FSL bus and vice-versa. Figure 14 depicts a case of a two interconnected MB processors by FIFO.

Every processor connects two independent data memory blocks to its Instruction and Data

LMB bus. However, controller peripheral is used to interface memory block to its bus.

FIFO is connected to a processor via FSL bus. Thus, there are two more buses for every processor, FSL master (MFSL) and FSL slave (SFSL). In fact, FSL processor may be created as a Master or a Slave to the FSL bus. A processor connected to the MFSL bus pushes data and control signals onto the FSL. Further, a processor connected to the SFSL bus reads and pops data and control signals from the FSL.

In the case of three (or more) processors implementation, the design consists of two Master/Slave pairs of FSL bus on every MB processor. The Hw system design is shown in Figure 15.

OPB interface on processors can be done using independent OPB bus or shared one. Like in shared memory architecture, the OPB slower peripherals are used in this architecture to ensure handling of software time routines, to analyze software execution and to make an external communication.

Figure 15. FSL three MB processors interconnection

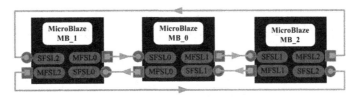

Figure 16. FSL link between two MB software processors

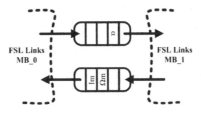

Software Design

Case of Two Processors Architecture

Software systems in the case of two processors architecture employed a looping construct for the main part of the application and used interrupts to handle time-critical events. Software routines have been configured with an interval timer using a RT interrupt clock as a peripheral device. MB_0 processor executes the controller unit algorithm. It is composed by the PI speed and PI current interrupt handler routines running at 20ms and 300μs. MB_1 processor runs the code of emulator interrupt handler at 100μs.

The software on each processor can queues or dequeues the shared variables on blocked or non-blocked mode according to the following Figure 16.

The read instruction in MB is used to transfer information from an FSL port to a general-purpose register. The write instruction is used for transfer in the opposite direction.

Because interrupt routines on every processor proceed in different sampled times, a synchronization device is necessary in order to ensure correct transfer of messages between the two processors.

This synchronization process is explained on the Figure 17.

With each interruption occurrence, the emulator routine starts by carrying out a non-blocking reading on FSL port, then checks if the data is valid. In this case, it updates the pulse-width value and sends the current and speed values to the MB_0 processor. On the MB_0 side, the current loop routine sends pulse-width value and then reads on the FSL port to update the current and speed values.

Case of Three Processors Architecture

MB_0, MB_1, and MB_2 execute respectively current controller, speed controller, and emulator routines at the appropriate time delay. The three processors exchange four variables between them by the different FSL links as shown in Figure 18.

Synchronization of exchanged messages between three processors is also required in this software design, but becomes more complex. However, we approve the same synchronization mechanism as previously.

MB_1 processor handles the speed routine at the biggest time period. When the interruption is occurred, the routine sends to MB_2 processor on

Figure 17. Two MB FSL synchronization process

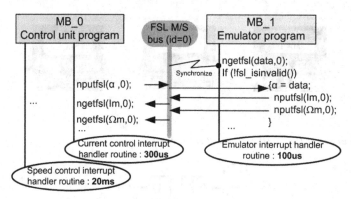

Figure 18. FSL link between three MB software processors

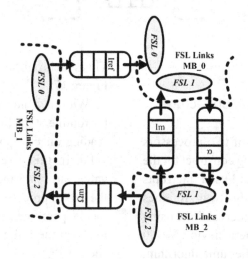

FSL2 port an ask-order of the speed value, and then reads this value. After that, it sends the *Iref* value to MB_0 on the FSL0 port.

In the MB_0 side, the current control routine sends the α value, and then reads the *Im* on the FSL1 port. It updates the *Iref* value if one given is sent on FSL0 port.

The emulator routine on MB_0 processor handles the fastest interrupt routine. It is synchronized with reception of pulse-width on the FSL1 port to send the current value. Moreover, it is synchronized with reception of an ask-order on the FSL2 port to send the speed value. Thus, this process of interprocessor communication is explained on the Figure 19.

HW CONTROLLER COPROCESSOR DESIGN

To achieve powerful processing capabilities in the controller unit, the fast loop controller algorithms will be implemented in the FPGA fabric in Hw, working in a parallel fashion. For that reason, we have considered a specific Hw accelerator approach for the controller unit by implementing the current PI controller in a Hw part and controlling it by a Sw part. The FSL based solutions were supported because they are the best access alternative to Hw accelerated cores on MB. Figure 20 illustrates the MB and necessary FSL connections for integrating the PI controller unit. In this

Figure 19. Three MB FSL synchronization process

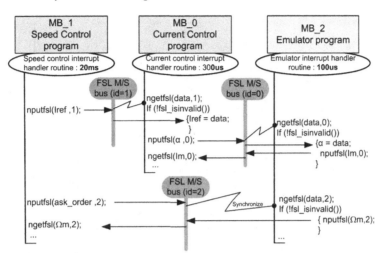

Figure 20. Hw PI controller FSL connections

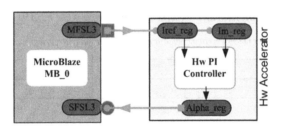

design, two FSL connections were implemented to provide bi-directional communication to write *Iref* and *Im* to the FSL peripheral, and to read α from this last.

PI Controller Data-Path

Because the Hw current controller is designed for integer form, the I/O *Iref_num*, *Im_num*, and α*num* are the numerical conversion of corresponding variables and are accessible by 16 bits registers.

The Hw PI controller is designed using a FSMD architecture model (Gajski, Zhu, Dömer, Gerstlauer, & Zhao, 2001) that combines a control unit with a datapath. As shown in Figure 21 the data path has two types of I/O ports. One type of I/O ports is data ports, which are used by the outside environment to send and receive data to and from

component (*Iref_num*, *Im_num*, α*num*). The other type of I/O ports is control ports that are used by the control unit to control the operations performed by the datapath and receive information about the status of selected registers in the datapath.

The control unit of the Hw PI description is described by a Finite State Machine (FSM). It carries out one computing cycle in 26 states. The designed FSMD architecture for this PI controller is optimized for surface while keeping a minimal latency (Table 1).

Because the maximum frequency supported by the Hw PI controller (135 MHz) is higher than the system clock rate (100 MHz), the Hw peripheral can be synchronized to the global system clock. In this case, the PI algorithm computing time is of 270ns.

Figure 21. FSMD high-level block diagram of Hw PI controller

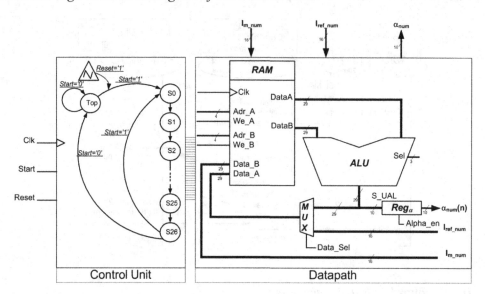

Table 1. Hw PI controller implementation results (Virtex2 Pro XC2VP30)

Number of External IOBs	50 (8%)
Number of SLICEs	1193 (8%)
Minimum period (ns)	7.386

PI Controller FSL Interface

The current PI controller is implemented as a FSL master/slave peripheral module. Figure 22 shows a protocol diagram outlining the FSL's operations. When data is written to the FSL, the *FSL_S_exist* is asserted to indicate that valid data indeed exists within the FSL. Peripheral reads data input, asserts the *FSL_S_read* signal and updates content of the corresponding register. After reading the *Im* and *Iref* data from the Master component, the Hw PI controller launches the computing process. When α value is ready, peripheral writes out the content of *alpha_reg* into the *FSL_M_data* while asserting the *FSL_M_write* signal.

PI Controller Sw Interface

As seen above, the FSL ports on MB are accessible via simple get and put assembly instructions (available in blocking and non-blocking varieties). C macro routines were used in the FSL PI controller drivers developed. This last one is consistent with the sequence in which data are read in and written out in the Hw peripheral. Both operands (*Im_num* and *Iref_num*) are written to the FSL peripheral with non-blocking calls, followed by a blocking read that stalls MB until the Hw PI controller returns a result. Since MB is an in-order execution machine, this penalty cannot be overcome.

Figure 22. Protocol diagram of FSL Hw PI controller

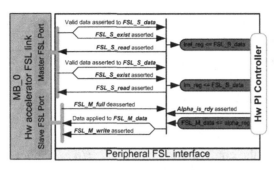

Figure 23. Hw/Sw controller devices interface

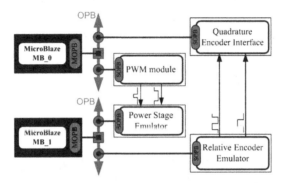

HW INTERFACES DESIGN

Hw Interfaces Data Paths

Hw interfaces consist of an extension to our MPSoC architecture to include support for sensor functionalities, pulse width generation, and power stage emulation.

These interfaces are associated to the corresponding processor of our MPSoC design as OPB slave peripherals. Each peripheral can then exchange data with processor via OPB bus or also with other peripherals through internal signal connections. An integration example of interfaced peripherals, in the case of two processors architecture, is shown in Figure 23.

The control unit associated to the MB_0 processor captures the speed information from the Quadrature Encoder Interface peripheral and orders the PWM module peripheral to generate the approved chopper drive signals. The motor emulator associated to the MB_1 processor recovers the order data from Power Stage Emulator peripheral, and then makes sensor speed signals by the Relative Encoder Emulator peripheral.

These modules are written in synthesizable VHDL language with configurable generic parameters. The resulting designs characteristics for required configuration are summarized in Table 2.

OPB IP Interface Core

Hw interfaces are implemented as an OPB slave peripheral modules. Interfacing with the OPB bus has been simplified by the use of a Xilinx IPIF. This provides a simpler interface standard, the Xilinx IPIC, for the user module.

Control and configuration of these modules are undertaken through a register write operations. Generic Hw control values are written to registers,

Table 2. Hw interfaces implementation results (Virtex2 Pro XC2VP30)

	Number of SLICEs	Minimum period (ns)
PWM Module	45 (0.3%)	5.875
Power stage emulator	25 (0.2%)	3.943
Relative encoder emulator	29 (0.2%)	5.229
Quadrature encoder interface	52 (0.4%)	4.825

which are again connected to the configuration inputs of the interface core. Depending on the Hw interface, registers are also provided for feeding device with operand inputs or for storing the operand outputs. The size of these registers must be the same as the data-width of the OPB bus (32 bits). This allows for a smaller implementation of the IPIF by optimizing out the implementation of the byte-steering logic (Xilinx, 2005c).

Peripheral Sw Drivers

The peripheral Sw drivers are automatically generated by the OPB IPIF template generation process. These drivers will make the IP registers interface visible to the Sw application running on the embedded system. The advantage of these drivers is that they are independent of the Hw user logic side. Therefore, the Sw drivers remain usable with the updated custom IP without any modification.

To add some high-level functionality that the custom IP can perform, new functions based on the Sw interface are added to the driver source codes. They consist of:

- *HWInit(peripheral_base_address,   init_ mask)*: Reset, Start or initialize peripheral at *peripheral_base_address*,
- *HW_PWM_drive(α):* Drive PWM module to generate output from corresponding pulse-width value,
- *float HW_pulse_update():* Get the output value from Power Stage Emulator Hw device and return resulting pulse-width value.

- *HW_Encoder_drive(RPM):* Order the Relative Encoder Emulator to generate *a* and *b* outputs corresponding to the actual *RPM* speed.
- *float HW_speed_update():* update speed *RPM* by reading *Direction* and *Speed_Val* from Quadrature Encoder Interface Hw device.

IMPLEMENTATION RESULTS

Experimental Setup

In order to evaluate the proposed MPSoC and codesigned architectures for electrical control applications, we based our experimental setup on the Xilinx ML310 board with the Virtex-II Pro FPGA. These various architectures are reported with acronyms illustrated by Table 3. The results analyses are more enhanced with implementation results of biprocessor based PPC architecture sharing an OPB dual port memory.

The basic setup is identical in all cases; the aim is to evaluate design architectures by improving the design cost, simulation results and timing analysis.

To achieve simulations results, an on-board simulation is launched along a fixed simulation time. During this time, embedded software applications store all simulation results in a memory table. At the end of this simulation, one processor starts to print results on a HyperTerminal computer via an associated UART interface. Simulations results can be then treated for curves displaying.

Table 3. *List of architectures acronyms*

Architecture acronym	Description
PPC2	2 PPC sharing an OPB BRAM
MB2	2 basic MB (without FPU) sharing an OPB BRAM
MB2_OBR	2 MB sharing an OPB BRAM
MB2_OBU	2 MB sharing an OPB Bus
MB2_LBR	2 MB sharing a LMB BRAM
MB2_COP	*MB2_LBR* architecture with Hw current controller
MB2_FSL	2 MB with FSL IPC
MB3_OBU	3 MB sharing an OPB Bus
MB3_LBR	3 MB sharing a LMB BRAM
MB3_FSL	3 MB with FSL IPC

The FPGA design cost is reported by synthesizing architecture with ISE synthesizer. This report features the FPGA utilization of logic cells, blocks RAM, Multipliers ... and summarizes the FPGA timing constraints.

With regard to the temporal analysis, a logical analyzer allows inspections of the propagation delays in every processor. The generated chronograms are controlled by software codes through GPIO peripherals connected to the analyzer.

Simulation Results

By applying the variety of MPSoC architectures studied previously, this section is focused in the analysis of controlled system behavior and the check of physical outputs (Current and Speed) evolution according to the target input. Figure 24 show curves examples obtained with a speed reference of 100rad/s.

Although, in Figure 24, the speed reached exactly the fixed chosen reference, we have recorded three categories of distinct curves: those obtained with MPSoC architectures of 2 MB, 3MB and 2 PPC. The difference is related to the behavior at the initial state (Figure 24a), which is not managed by our application programs. In order to find the same feedback responses with all architectures, it is necessary to schedule the occurred routines on the distinct processors (allocate a priority to each processor).

In the following sections, a study of the synthesis results as well as a temporal analysis will emphasize the performances of MPSoC architectures according to IPC and Hw accelerator.

FPGA Utilization

Figure 25 presents the design tool information regarding the logic mapping and layout of the peripheral logic needed on MPSoC architecture.

Considering the flexibility of the MB processor, the resource utilization depends primarily on the processor IP configuration. A basic configuration requires around 7% of entire FPGA space when an additional enabled FPU configuration involves more than 12%. This is in contrast to the memory controller and the OPB modules such as timers, controllers, dedicated controller devices..., which use together less than 8%. These numbers give indicators as to what additional peripheral could be added to a system.

The FPGA used resources of the considered designs are presented in Figure 26. The area is reported in terms of slices (each consisting of a two 4-input function generators, carry logic, arithmetic logic gates, wide function multiplexers and two storage elements), elementary RAM blocs

Figure 24. Comparison results between different MPSoC architectures, (a) speed response, (b) current response for 100rad/s speed target

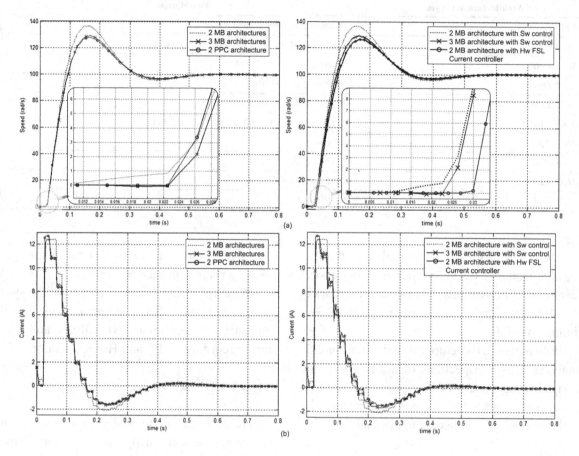

Figure 25. MPSoC Hw modules FPGA utilization

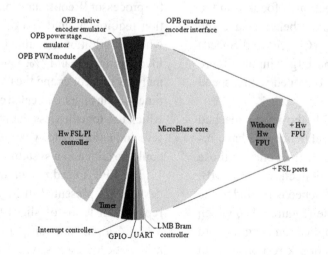

Figure 26. Synthesis results for MPSoC designs

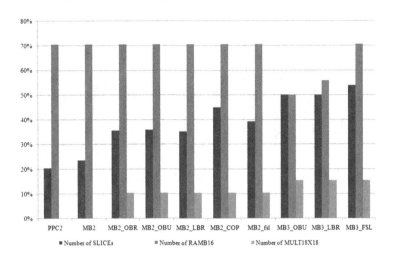

(18 Kb true dual-port RAM) and multiplier (18-bit by 18-bit 2's complement signed multiplier).

The two first column of Figure 26 depict a FPGA utilization comparison of PPC hardcore architecture and MB softcore architecture with similar configuration (without FPU, with same IPC...). Although the PPC is a hardcore processor, their area occupation is slightly less important than MB (4%). This is caused by the use of additional resources such as bus (PLB) and busses bridges.

However, the rest of architectures designs costs, depend, as mentioned previously, on the applied processors configuration and their occurrence.

Nevertheless, by comparing the MB2_LBR and MB2_COP architectures resources, there is only the number of slices that is affected. It is obvious that using Hw current controller increases the number of resources consumed by the design. However, the FSL PI controller used as Sw accelerator touches 8% of entire FPGA Space. In order to provide a fair comparison with software, performance of this FSL coprocessor should be measured using a weighting factor determined by the additional Hw resources of the peripheral. The resulting weighting factor (the ratio of Hw resources with pure Sw controller to the Hw resources with the FSL PI controller) is of 0.785.

The consumed blocks ram gives the total on-chip memory required by the processors. This memory size is dictated by the software program. Figure 27 illustrates the software memory size required by each architecture to store instructions (text sections) and data (data sections). On each design, about 20% to 23% of the available RAM Block is used by instruction and data software programs. The remaining memory block is managed by a synthesizer for other Hw components (FIFO FSL for example).

Since the current controller Sw routine is reduced to three processor instructions in the MB2_COP, the corresponding Sw program size is considerably decreased compared to the other architectures program size.

Timing Analysis

For comparing the performance of proposed MPSoC designs, this section inspects timing analysis of software handler routines (emulator, current controller and speed controller) dealing on two or three processors according to the design architecture.

Figure 28 displays the difference between hardcore and softcore architectures by comparing the performance times to execute software

Figure 27. FPGA Sw programs size

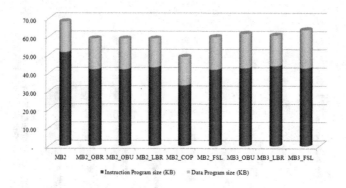

Figure 28. Hardcore vs. Softcore software execution time (us)

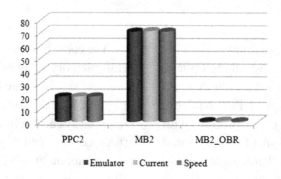

applications. With software only implementation, the PPC architecture increases in performance 3.5 times over MB architecture without considering the additional Hw resources highlighting by the softcore.

The performance of softcore is clearly improved when Hw FPU is added to MB core. This evolved architecture becomes 20 times better than a hardcore architecture. Table 4 reports the benefits of FPU to accelerate the execution time on processor in spite of the added cost of Hw resources.

Figure 29 depicts the processors time delays required to execute the speed, current, and emulator handle routines with the various MPSoC architectures studied previously. It shows the impact of multiprocessor partitioning on one hand

and IPC choice in MPSoC architecture on another hand.

When the same IPC is considered, the resulting software execution times are nearly equivalent for 3 processors architectures compared to biprocessor architectures (lower than 100ns) especially when the additional material resources and the software development difficulties are appreciated.

However, the benefits of three processors architectures can be better respected with more constraints in the control loops sampling times. Moreover, on Figure 30, which shows an example of execution with 2 MB architecture based on LMB, shared memory IPC, no mutual exclusion is observed in the control unit core between both current and speed interrupt handler routines. Consequently, in this application case, the biprocessor

Table 4. Processor times increase of FPU

	MB2 (us)	**MB2_OBR (us)**	**FPU times increase considering weighting factor (0,576)**
Emulator	70,960	0,958	42,665
Current	71,360	1,320	31,139
Speed	70,980	0,962	42,499

Figure 29. MPSoC architectures processors time delay (us)

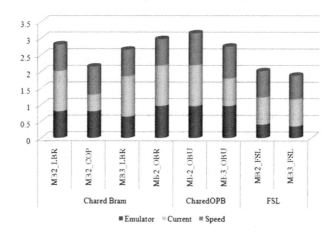

Figure 30. Timing analysis of 2 MB architecture based on LMB shared memory IPC

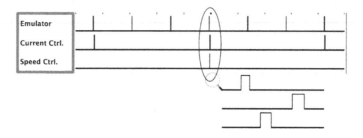

solution proves to be powerful with lower costs of Hw resources and design times.

The performance of MPSoC architectures depends also on the IPC choice. Figure 31 shows that best processor time is obtained with the Mailbox technique (ensured by the FSL bus) in spite of synchronization mechanism installation in FSL software applications. There is at least a gain of 500ns over the total software execution time. This performance comes at the point-to-point connection capability of the FSL bus, contrary to the shared memories techniques where the memory access implies important delays in the communication. However, the mailbox mechanism presents the drawback of forcing the programmer to deal with an explicit communication. A good attention must be granted for this support during the software development. Figure 31a shows an execution chronogram example, in which the current loop interrupt is blocked to synchronize

Figure 31. Timing analysis of 2 MB architecture based on FSL IPC (a) bad execution with a blocked interrupt (b) good execution without a blocked interrupt

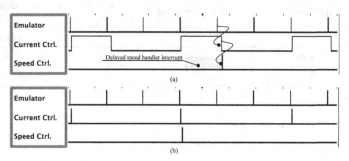

with emulator processor causing delays on the speed handler routine. This bad functioning is detected only by temporal analysis; it causes a falling in the architecture performance. An additional code in software application must be set up to cure this problem (Figure 31b).

This is not the case of the shared memory mechanisms that is fast to configure and simple to use. Thus, different MPSoC architectures based on shared memory IPC must to be distinguished. Within this framework, we tried out various architectures which are characterized by the sharing support (dual port memory / bus) and the bus type (LMB / OPB). Although the shared memory based on a shared bus (OPB) approach is the easiest method to design, it reveals more important execution time delays than shared dual port memory approach. Moreover, the best solution according to this temporal analysis is to use a shared dual port memory based on a LMB bus.

When running on the MB processor at 100MHz CPU clock frequency, the current PI controller algorithm delays about 1.2us for reaching the pulse width data output. This delay is extensively reduced to 0,5us when this current controller is performed in Hw design clocked at 100MHz (Figure 31). Consequently, the Hw design used as Sw accelerator proves to be very interesting to enhance the processor RT functioning, avoid the interrupt routines overhead, and also minimize memories and other processor resources. Subsequently, it leads to a more effective FPGA based

system with a more reduced consumption. Since hardware generally outperforms software methods, the added cost of Hw resources is weighed against the gains in performance. According to the computed weighting factor (0.785), the Hw FSL controller provides a 1.9 times of increase in performance to the PI control algorithms.

Figure 32 illustrates the temporal behavior of the FSL peripheral inside the current handler routine. The 2-read and 1-write operations of peripheral / processor communication occupy only 40ns. This much-reduced time explains the recourse to the FSL support to connect material accelerators, rather than with OPB bus.

FUTURE RESEARCH DIRECTIONS

FPGA circuits play a significant role to implement most recent control process. The quality of motion drives is directly related to the kind of controller structure and its implementation. The design methodology and architectures approach proposed in this chapter can be further improved by more complex controller structures with hard real-time requirements (e.g., sampling periods). Exploiting these platforms demands deep Hw conception skills and it is an important time consuming stage in a design flow. High Level Synthesis (HLS) technique avoids this bottleneck and increases designing productivity as witnessed by industrial specialists.

Figure 32. Timing analysis of Hw PI controller FSL

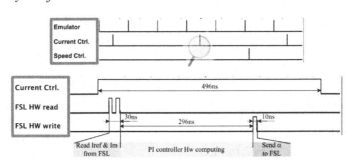

Therefore, FPGAs have a finite amount of reconfigurable resources, which constrains the size and the number of processing cores (either processors or coprocessors) that can be implemented concurrently. This imposes a constraint to software-based designs, since it is no longer possible to support any amount of functionality by sacrificing performance. Accordingly, the limitations imposed by the amount of configurable resources in FPGAs can be diminished by using run-time reconfiguration (Schulz, et al., 2007).

CONCLUSION

In this chapter, a MPSoC FPGA architecture for specific RT control applications based on Sw/Hw codesign was presented. Using FPGA Virtex2 Pro target, designs consisted of PI digital controllers linked to a motor emulator and controller devices. We have discussed several MPSoC architectures partitioned for two or three processors interconnected through shared memories or mailbox. Each architecture was tested and experimented on FPGA chip, demonstrating a good closed-loop response. However, the performance is affected by the use of hard or softcore, the use of different memory strategies and peripheral controllers or bus. Different requirements lead to make different trade-offs between performance and power, hardware and software, and so on.

The Hw contribution to SoC codesign solutions was also considered with this chapter. Hw solutions

are often imposed in such MPSoC architecture. This case is arisen when the behavior cannot be solved by Sw part. Control devices (PWM and quadrature encoder) and emulator devices (power stage and relative encoder emulator) are fitted in this Hw category. These peripherals are interfaced on the local buses of the processors (OPB), and are easily tested and exploited by the Sw code through high-level driver routines.

Another Hw category is related to the coprocessor peripherals. In the case study system, a Hw current PI controller is used as Sw accelerator in control unit processor. Although the usage of this peripheral was not crucial, because it can be easily solved by Sw, the obtained results have revealed a remarkable increase in the system performance. This solution can be considered as long as the Hw resources of coprocessors are lower than Hw resources of a new processor added to the MPSoC design.

REFERENCES

Abe, M., Arai, H., & Kawamata, M. (2005). *Design and FPGA implementation of a structure of evolutionary digital filters for hardware implementation*. Paper presented at the IEEE International Symposium on Circuits and Systems (ISCAS).

Aggarwal, V., & Kuhlman, R. (2007). *Simulating Sensors on FPGA Hardware*. Paper presented at the Embedded Systems Conferences, ESC-402.

Asokan, V. (2007). Dual Processor Reference Design Suite. *Xilinx application note, APP996.*

Astarloa, A., Làzaro, J. s., Bidarte, U., Jiménez, J., & Zuloaga, A. (2009). FPGA technology for multi-axis control systems. *Mechatronics, 19*(2), 258–268. doi:10.1016/j.mechatronics.2008.09.001

Ben Othman, S., Ben Salem, A. K., & Ben Saoud, S. (2008). *MPSoC Design of RT Control Applications based on FPGA SoftCore Processors.* Paper presented at the 15th IEEE International Conference on Electronics, Circuits and Systems, 2008. ICECS 2008., Ben Othman, S., Ben Salem, A. K., & Ben Saoud, S. (2008b). *RT Control Applications MPSoC based-FPGA Implementation using Hw Accelerator.* Paper presented at the International Conference on Embedded Systems and Critical Applications (ICESCA).

Ben Othman, S., Ben Salem, A. K., & Ben Saoud, S. (2008a). *FPGA HardCore Single Processor Implementation of RT Control Applications.* Paper presented at the 3rd IEEE International Conference on Design & Technology of Integrated Systems in Nanoscale Era (DTIS).

Ben Salem, A. K., Ben Othman, S., & Ben Saoud, S. (2008a). *Hard and soft-core implementation of embedded control application using RTOS.* Paper presented at the IEEE International Symposium on Industrial Electronics (ISIE 2008).

Ben Salem, A. K., Ben Othman, S., & Ben Saoud, S. (2008b). *MPSoC Embedded AC Machine Control Using RTOS.* Paper presented at the International Conference on Embedded Systems and Critical Applications (ICESCA).

Ben Salem, A. K., Ben Othman, S., & Ben Saoud, S. (2010). FPGA-Based System-on-Chip for RT Power Process Control [AJAS]. *American Journal of Applied Sciences, 7*(1), 127–139. doi:10.3844/ajassp.2010.127.139

Ben Saoud, S. (1996). *Emulateur temps réel d'associations Convertisseurs statiques / Machines électriques / Capteurs: Etude, conception et réalisation. ENSEEIHT.* France: INPT.

Bosheng, S., & Zhiqiang, G. (2005). A DSP-based active disturbance rejection control design for a 1-kW H-bridge DC-DC power converter. *IEEE Transactions on Industrial Electronics, 52*(5), 1271–1277. doi:10.1109/TIE.2005.855679

Boussak, M., & Jarray, K. (2005). A high-performance sensorless indirect stator flux orientation control of induction motor drive. *IEEE Transactions on Industrial Electronics, 53*(1), 41–49. doi:10.1109/TIE.2005.862319

Carbone, S., Colli, V. D., Stefano, R. D., Figalli, G., & Marignetti, F. (2009). *Design and Implementation of High performance FPGA Control for Permanent Magnet Synchronous Motor.* Paper presented at the 35th Annual Conference of the IEEE Industrial Electronics Society, IECON 2009.

Christian, D., Jean, B., Vincent, L., & Simon, A. (2008). *Real-Time Simulation on FPGA of a Permanent Magnet Synchronous Machine Drive Using a Finite-Element Based Model.* Paper presented at the International Symposium on Power Electronics, Electrical Drives, Automation and Motion (SPEEDAM 2008).

Cong, J., Gururaj, K., & Han, G. (2009). *Synthesis of reconfigurable high-performance multicore systems.* Paper presented at the Proceeding of the ACM/SIGDA international symposium on Field programmable gate arrays.

Da, Z., & Hui, L. (2008). A Stochastic-Based FPGA Controller for an Induction Motor Drive With Integrated Neural Network Algorithms. *Industrial Electronics. IEEE Transactions on, 55*(2), 551–561.

Del valle, P. G., Atienza, D., Magan, I., Flores, J. G., Perez, E. A., Mendias, J. M., et al. (2006). *A Complete Multi-Processor System-on-Chip FPGA-Based Emulation Framework*. Paper presented at the International Conference on Very Large Scale Integration, IFIP

Gajski, D. D., Zhu, J., Dömer, R., Gerstlauer, A., & Zhao, S. (2001). *SpecC: Specification language and methodology*. Amsterdam: Kluwer Academic Publishers, CECS.

Griva, G., Ilas, C., Eastham, J. F., Profumo, F., & Vranka, P. (1997). *High performance sensorless control of induction motor drives for industry applications*. Paper presented at the Power Conversion Conference, Nagaoka.

Guo, X., Chen, Z., & Schaumont, P. (2008). *Energy and Performance Evaluation of an FPGA-Based SoC Platform with AES and PRESENT Coprocessors*. Paper presented at the 8th international workshop on Embedded Computer Systems: Architectures, Modeling, and Simulation.

Hampel, V., Sobe, P., & Maehle, E. (2008). Experiences with a FPGA-based Reed/Solomon-encoding coprocessor. *Microprocessors and Microsystems*, *32*(5-6), 313–320. doi:10.1016/j.micpro.2008.03.003

Han, S.-I., Chae, S.-I., Brisolara, L., Carro, L., Popovici, K., Guerin, X., et al. (Writer) (2009). *Simulink®-based heterogeneous multiprocessor SoC design flow for mixed hardware/software refinement and simulation*. DOI: 10.1016/j.vlsi.2008.08.003.

He, S., & Xu, X. (2007, May 30 – June 1). *Hardware Simulation of an Adaptive Control Algorithm*. Paper presented at the 2007 Conference on Modelling and Simulation, Montreal, QC, Canada.

Hodjat, A., Batina, L., Hwang, D., & Verbauwhede, I. (2007). HW/SW co-design of a hyperelliptic curve cryptosystem using a microcode instruction set coprocessor. *Integration, the VLSI Journal*, *40*(1), 45-51.

Hongtao, D., Hairong, Q., & Xiaoling, W. (2007). Comparative Study of VLSI Solutions to Independent Component Analysis. *IEEE Transactions on Industrial Electronics*, *54*(1), 548–558. doi:10.1109/TIE.2006.885491

Hubner, M., Paulsson, K., & Becker, J. (2005). *Parallel and Flexible Multiprocessor System-On-Chip for Adaptive Automotive Applications based on Xilinx MicroBlaze Soft-Cores*. Paper presented at the 19th IEEE International Symposium on Parallel and Distributed Processing

Idkhajine, L., Prata, A., Monmasson, E., Bouallaga, K., & Naouar, M. W. (2008). *System on Chip controller for electrical actuator*. Paper presented at the IEEE International Symposium on Industrial Electronics (ISIE 2008).

Jastrzębski, R., Laakkonen, O., Rauma, K., Luukko, J., Sarén, H., & Pyrhönen, O. (2004, June 28 – 30, 2004). *Real-time Emulation of Induction Motor in FPGA using Floating Point Representation*. Paper presented at the IASTED International Conference on Applied Simulation and Modelling, Rhodes, Greece.

Jerraya, A. A., & Bouchhima, A. (2006). *Programming models and HW-SW interfaces abstraction for multi-processor SoC*. Paper presented at the 43rd annual conference on Design automation.

Jerraya, A. A., & Wayne, W. (2004). *Multiprocessor Systems on Chips*. San Francisco: Morgan Kaufmann.

Jezernik, K., & Rodic, M. (2008). *Torque sensorless control of induction motor*. Paper presented at the 13th Power Electronics and Motion Control Conference (EPE-PEMC 2008).

Kaliamoorthy, M., Himavathi, S., & Muthuramalingam, A. (2006, August 13-18 2006). *DSP based implementation of high performance flux estimators for speed sensorless induction motor drives using TMS320F2812*. Paper presented at the India International Conference on Power Electronics (IICPE 2006), Tokyo.

Kowalski, C. T., Lis, J., & Orlowska-Kowalska, T. (2007). *FPGA Implementation of DTC Control Method for the Induction Motor Drive*. Paper presented at the International Conference on Computer as a Tool (EUROCON 2007).

Kumar, A., Fernando, S., Yajun, H., Mesman, B., & Corporaal, H. (2007). *Multi-Processor System-Level Synthesis for Multiple Applications on Platform FPGA*. Paper presented at the International Conference on Field Programmable Logic and Applications (FPL 2007).

Laakkonen, O., Rauma, K., Saren, H., Luukko, J., & Pyrhonen, O. (2004). *Electric drive emulator using dSPACE real time platform for VHDL verification*. Paper presented at the 47th Midwest Symposium on Circuits and Systems (MWSCAS 2004).

Lascu, C., & Trzynadlowski, A. M. (2001). *A sensorless hybrid DTC drive for high-volume applications using the TMS320F243 DSP controller*. Paper presented at the IEEE Industry Applications Conference.

Lee, E. A. (2006). The problem with threads. *Computer magazine, 39,* 33-42.

Limberg, T., Ristau, B., & Fettweis, G. (2008). *A Real-Time Programming Model for Heterogeneous MPSoCs*. Paper presented at the 8th international workshop on Embedded Computer Systems: Architectures, Modeling, and Simulation.

Lis, J., Kowalski, C. T., & Orlowska-Kowalska, T. (2008). *Sensorless DTC control of the induction motor using FPGA*. Paper presented at the IEEE International Symposium on Industrial Electronics (ISIE 2008).

Mitra, A., Zhi, G., Banerjee, A., & Najjar, W. (2006). *Dynamic Co-Processor Architecture for Software Acceleration on CSoCs*. Paper presented at the International Conference on Computer Design (ICCD 2006).

Mohamadian, M., Nowicki, E., Ashrafzadeh, F., Chu, A., Sachdeva, R., & Evanik, E. (2003). A novel neural network controller and its efficient DSP implementation for vector-controlled induction motor drives. *IEEE Transactions on Industry Applications, 39*(6), 1622–1629. doi:10.1109/TIA.2003.819441

Monmasson, E., & Cirstea, M. N. (2007). FPGA Design Methodology for Industrial Control Systems-A Review. *IEEE Transactions on Industrial Electronics, 54*(4), 1824–1842. doi:10.1109/TIE.2007.898281

National-Instruments. (2008). *LabVIEW FPGA in Hardware-in-the-Loop Simulation Applications*.

Nikolov, H., Stefanov, T., & Deprettere, E. (2006). *Multi-processor system design with ESPAM*. Paper presented at the 4th international conference on Hardware/software codesign and system synthesis.

Paiz, C., Hagemeyer, J., Pohl, C., Porrmann, M., Rückert, U., Schulz, B., et al. (2009). *FPGA-Based Realization of Self-Optimizing Drive-Controllers*. Paper presented at the 35th Annual Conference of the IEEE Industrial Electronics Society, IECON 2009.

Paiz, C., & Porrmann, M. (2007). *The Utilization of Reconfigurable Hardware to Implement Digital Controllers: a Review*. Paper presented at the IEEE International Symposium on Industrial Electronics (ISIE 2007).

Palumbo, F., Secchi, S., Pani, D., & Raffo, L. (2008). A Novel Non-exclusive Dual-Mode Architecture for MPSoCs-Oriented Network on Chip Designs. In Heidelberg, S. B. (Ed.), *Embedded Computer Systems: Architectures, Modeling, and Simulation* (pp. 96–105). Berlin: SpringerLink. doi:10.1007/978-3-540-70550-5_11

Pellerin, D., & Shenoy, K. (2006). *C-Language techniques for FPGA acceleration of embedded software*. Paper presented at the Embedded Systems Conference (ESC-368).

Qu, Y., Tiensyrjä, K., Soininen, J.-P., & Nurmi, J. (2008). Design Flow Instantiation for Run-Time Reconfigurable Systems: A Case Study. *EURASIP Journal on Embedded Systems, 2008*(856756).

Rodriguez-Andina, J. J., Moure, M. J., & Valdes, M. D. (2007). Features, Design Tools, and Application Domains of FPGAs. *IEEE Transactions on Industrial Electronics, 54*(4), 1810–1823. doi:10.1109/TIE.2007.898279

Ruelland, R., Gateau, G., Meynard, T. A., & Hapiot, J. C. (2003). Design of FPGA-based emulator for series multicell converters using co-simulation tools. *IEEE Transactions on Power Electronics, 18*(1), 455–463. doi:10.1109/TPEL.2002.807104

Salewski, F., & Kowalewski, S. (2008). Hardware/Software Design Considerations for Automotive Embedded Systems. *IEEE Transactions on Industrial Informatics, 4*(3), 156–163. doi:10.1109/TII.2008.2002919

Schaumont, P., & Verbauwhede, I. (2007). *Hardware/Software Codesign for Stream Ciphers*. Paper presented at the Special workshop hosted by the ECRYPT Network of Excellence in Cryptology.

Schirrmeister, F. (2007). *Multi-core Processors: Fundamentals, Trends, and Challenges.* Paper presented at the Embedded Systems Conference, ESC-351.

Schulz, B., Paiz, C., Hagemeyer, J., Mathapati, S., Porrmann, M., & Bocker, J. (2007). *Run-time reconfiguration of FPGA-based drive controllers.* Paper presented at the European Conference on Power Electronics and Applications.

Seely, J. A. (2005). *Using Hardware Acceleration Units in Software Defined Radio Modem Functions.* COTS Journal Digital Edition.

Seul, J., & Sung su, K. (2007). Hardware Implementation of a Real-Time Neural Network Controller With a DSP and an FPGA for Nonlinear Systems. *IEEE Transactions on Industrial Electronics, 54*(1), 265–271. doi:10.1109/TIE.2006.888791

Simard, S., Beguenane, R., & Mailloux, J.-G. (2008). Performance Evaluation of Rotor Flux-Oriented Control on FPGA for Advanced AC Drives. *Journal of Robotics and Mechatronics, 21*(1), 113–120.

Singh, B., Singh, B. P., & Dwivedi, S. (2006). *DSP Based Implementation of Fuzzy Precompensated PI Speed Controller for Vector Controlled PMSM Drive.* Paper presented at the 1st IEEE Conference on Industrial Electronics and Applications.

Wong, W. (2006). *Basic of Design Embedded Processors.*

Xilinx (2005a). *Fast Simplex Link (FSL) Bus*: Xilinx Product Specification, DS449..

Xilinx (2005b). *ML310 User Guide, VirtexII pro Embedded Development Platform (UG068).*

Xilinx (2005c). *OPB IPIF*: Xilinx Product Specification, DS414.

Xilinx (2005d). *Standalone Board Support Package*: Xilinx EDK 7.1.

Ying-Shieh, K., & Ming-Hung, T. (2007). FPGA-Based Speed Control IC for PMSM Drive With Adaptive Fuzzy Control. *IEEE Transactions on Power Electronics, 22*(6), 2476–2486. doi:10.1109/TPEL.2007.909185

Yuen Fong, C., Moallem, M., & Wei, W. (2007). Design and Implementation of Modular FPGA-Based PID Controllers. *IEEE Transactions on Industrial Electronics, 54*(4), 1898–1906. doi:10.1109/TIE.2007.898283

Zergainoh, N. E., Baghdadi, A., & Jerraya, A. A. (2004). Hardware/Software Codesign of On-chip Communication Architecture for Application-Specific Multiprocessor System-On-Chip. *International Journal of Embedded Systems, 1*(12), 10.

KEY TERMS AND DEFINITIONS

Co-Simulation: is a simulation methodology that allows individual components to be simulated by different simulation tools running simultaneously and exchanging information in a collaborative manner.

Hardware-In-the-Loop (HIL) Simulation: is a form of real-time simulation with the addition of a real component in the loop.

Real-Time Emulator for Electromechanical Systems: is an electronic system design, which can reproduce the physical system functioning in real time and with high precision. The emulator should behave like the physical system in real time. It can provide an embedded HIL simulation platform.

Softcore Processor: is a processor core that can be wholly implemented using programmable logic synthesis.

Dual-Ported RAM: is a block RAM that allows multiple reads or writes to occur at the same time, or nearly the same time, unlike single-ported RAM which only allows one access at a time.

FIFO (First In/First Out): consists of a set of read and write pointers, storage and control logic. Storage may be BRAM, flip-flops, latches or any other suitable form of storage. This term refers to the way data stored in a queue is processed.

Hardware Acceleration: is the use of hardware to perform some function faster than software execution. Hardware accelerators are designed for computationally intensive software code.

Floating Point Unit (FPU): is a hardware accelerator unit designed to carry out operations on floating point numbers. Typical operations are addition, subtraction, multiplication, division, and square root.

Proportional-Integral (PI) Controller: is a feedback controller, which drives the process to be controlled with a weighted sum of the error (difference between the output and desired set-point) and the integral of that value.

Quadrature Encoder: is an optical relative rotary encoder. It is used to track motion and can be used to determine position and velocity.

Pulse Width Modulation (PWM): is a method of controlling the amount of power to a load without having to dissipate any power in the load driver. PWM works well with digital controls, which, because of their on/off nature, can easily set the needed duty cycle.

Chapter 12
FPGA–Based Accelerators for Bioinformatics Applications

Alba Cristina Magalhaes Alves de Melo
University of Brasilia, Brazil

Nahri Moreano
Federal University of Mato Grosso do Sul, Brazil

ABSTRACT

The recent and astonishing advances in Molecular Biology, which led to the sequencing of an unprecedented number of genomes, including the human, would not have been possible without the help of Bioinformatics. Bioinformatics can be defined as a research area where computational tools and algorithms are developed to help biologists in the task of understanding the organisms. Some Bioinformatics applications, such as pairwise and sequence-profile comparison, require a huge amount of computing power and, therefore, are excellent candidates to run in FPGA platforms. This chapter discusses in detail several recent proposals on FPGA-based accelerators for these two Bioinformatics applications, highlighting the similarities and differences among them. At the end of the chapter, research tendencies and open questions are presented.

1. INTRODUCTION

Bioinformatics is an interdisciplinary field that involves computer science, biology, mathematics and statistics (Mount 2004). Its main goal is to analyze biological sequence data and genome content in order to obtain the function/structure of the sequences as well as evolutionary information.

Once a new biological sequence is discovered, its functional/structural characteristics must be established. In order to do that, the newly discovered sequence is compared against the sequences that compose biological databases, in search of similarities. Sequence comparison is, therefore, one of the most basic operations in Bioinformatics. A sequence can be compared to another sequence (pairwise comparison), to a profile that describes a family of sequences (sequence-profile comparison) or to a set of sequences (multiple sequence comparison). The most accurate algorithms to execute pairwise and sequence-profile compari-

DOI: 10.4018/978-1-60960-086-0.ch012

sons are usually based on dynamic programming, with quadratic time and space complexity. This can easily lead to extremely high execution times and huge memory requirements, since biological databases are growing exponentially and biological sequences usually are extremely long.

Parallel processing can be used to produce results faster, reducing significantly the time needed to obtain results with dynamic programming-based algorithms. However, using parallel processing in Bioinformatics is not straightforward since the problems are often solved by complex methods, with a great amount of data dependencies. Moreover, it has been observed that, for some problems that involve really huge data sets, software-only parallel processing techniques are not able to reduce the execution time to reasonable limits. For instance, in order to use the dynamic programming exact method to compare the human chromosome 21 and the ape chromosome 22, with sizes 46 Million Base Pairs (MBP) and 34 MBP, respectively, it is estimated that a cluster with 2048 processors would take approximately one day (Batista et al., 2008). This shows clearly that new approaches and technologies must be used to further reduce such high execution times.

Designing specific hardware for such algorithms is a very attractive alternative to software-only solutions. Since the hardware will be tailored to execute a specific algorithm, drastic performance improvements can be achieved. This observation was made by many researchers in Bioinformatics in the 1990s, that led to a great variety of hardware-based solutions. Due to its flexibility, FPGAs (Field Programmable Gate Arrays) are the natural choice for these designs. In the last years, FPGAs have intensively been used to build specific circuits, especially targeted to accelerate compute-intensive Bioinformatics applications.

The goal of this chapter is to discuss in detail and compare the recent advances in FPGA-based accelerators for some classes of Bioinformatics applications. The problems discussed are two types of Biological Sequence Comparison: pairwise sequence comparison and sequence-profile comparison. The first one is widely used all over the world as a first step in the solution of complex problems such as the determination of the evolutionary history of the species. The second one is extremely important since it is used to decide if a recently sequenced protein belongs or not to a particular protein family/superfamily. For both problems, many FPGA-based accelerators have been proposed that obtained impressive speedups over the sequential and software-only parallel implementations.

The structure of this chapter is the following. In Section 2, we will introduce the Biological Sequence Comparison problem and present the most widely used algorithms to solve it. In Section 3, we discuss several state-of-the-art FPGA accelerators that tackle the pairwise sequence comparison problem. In Section 4, several state-of-the-art FPGA-based accelerators for the sequence-profile comparison problem are discussed. Finally, Section 5 concludes the chapter, presenting the future tendencies in this research area.

2. PAIRWISE COMPARISON AND SEQUENCE-PROFILE ALIGNMENT

2.1. Alignment and Score

A biological sequence is a single and continuous molecule of nucleic acid or protein. It is represented by a linear list of residues, which are nucleotide bases (for DNA sequences, for instance) or amino acids (for protein sequences). To compare biological sequences, we need to find the best alignment between them, which is to place one sequence above the other making clear the correspondence between similar residues from the sequences (Durbin et al., 1998).

Given an alignment between two sequences s and t, a score can be associated for it as follows. For each two residues in the same column, we associate (a) a punctuation *ma,* if the two characters are identical (*match*); or (b) a penalty *mi,* if the characters are different (*mismatch*); or (c) a penalty *g,* if one of the characters is a space (*gap*). The score is the sum of the values computed for each column. The maximal score is called the similarity between the sequences. Figure 1 illustrates an alignment.

If proteins are being compared, a substitution matrix of size 20×20 is used to store the match/mismatch punctuation. The most commonly used substitution matrices are PAM and BLOSUM (Durbin et al., 1998).

2.2. Pairwise Sequence Comparison

2.2.1. Needleman-Wunsh Algorithm (NW)

One of the first exact methods to globally align two sequences was NW (Needleman & Wunsh, 1970). It is based on dynamic programming and calculates a similarity matrix of size $m \times n$, where *m* and *n* are the sizes of sequences *s* and *t*, respectively. This algorithm has *O(mn)* time and space complexity. It is divided in two phases: create the similarity matrix and obtain the best global alignment.

The first phase receives input sequences *s* and *t*. The notation used to represent the *i*-th character of a sequence *seq* is *seq*[*i*] and, to represent a prefix with *i* characters, we use *seq*[1..*i*]. The similarity matrix is denoted *D*, where $D(i, j)$ contains the similarity score between prefixes *s*[1..*i*] and *t*[1..*j*].

At the beginning, the first row and column are filled with the values $g \times i$, where *i* is the size of the non-empty subsequence and *g* is the gap penalty. This represents the cost of aligning a non-empty subsequence with an empty one. Note that $D(0,0) = 0$. The remaining elements of *D* are obtained from Equation (1). In this equation, $p(i, j) = ma$ if *s*[*i*] = *t*[*j*] (match) or *mi* otherwise (mismatch). The similarity score between sequences *s* and *t* is the value contained in cell $D(m,n)$.

Figure 1. An alignment between sequences s = TTGGTGG and t = TTGTCGAGG, with score=+1. Values for matches, mismatches and gaps are ma=+1, mi=–1, g=–2, respectively

```
T   T   G   -   -   G   T   G   G
T   T   G   T   C   G   A   G   G   score
+1  +1  +1  -2  -2  +1  -1  +1  +1   +1
```

$$d(i, j) = \max \begin{cases} D(i, j-1) = g \\ D(i-1, j-1) + p(i, j) \\ D(i-1, j) + g \end{cases} \quad (1)$$

Figure 2 presents the NW similarity matrix between sequences *s* = TTGGTGG and *t* = TTGTCGAGG. The arrows indicate the cell from where the value was obtained.

Phase 2 is responsible to obtain the best global alignment. In order to do that, the algorithm starts from cell $D(m,n)$ and follows the arrows until cell $D(0,0)$ is reached. A left arrow in $D(i, j)$ (Figure 2) indicates the alignment of *s*[*i*] with a gap in *t*. An up arrow represents the alignment of *t*[*j*] with a gap in *s*. Finally, an arrow on the diagonal indicates that *s*[*i*] is aligned with *t*[*j*]. For the similarity matrix *D* illustrated in Figure 2, the global alignment retrieved is the one shown in Figure 1.

Note that many best global alignments may exist, since many arrows can exist in the same cell $D(i, j)$, indicating that the score value was produced from more than one cell. In Figure 2, we did not represent these multiple arrows because, in this case, we assumed that preference is given to the match/mismatch (diagonal).

2.2.2. Smith-Waterman Algorithm (SW)

To obtain the similarity between parts of the sequences, local alignment must be used. The exact algorithm that is most widely used in this case is the SW algorithm proposed by Smith &

313

Figure 2. Similarity matrix D to globally align sequences s=TTGGTGG and t=TTGTCGAGG, with score=+1. Values for matches, mismatches and gaps are ma=+1, mi=−1, g=−2, respectively

		T	T	G	G	T	G	G
	0	−2	−4	−6	−8	−10	−12	−14
T	−2	↖1	←0	←−2	←−4	←−6	←−8	←−10
T	−4	↖−1	↖2	←0	←−2	←−4	←−6	←−8
G	−6	↖−3	↑0	↖3	↖1	←−1	↖−3	↖−5
T	−8	↖−5	↖−2	↑1	↖2	↖2	↖0	←−2
C	−10	↑−7	↑−4	↑−1	↖0	↖1	↖1	↖−1
G	−12	↑−9	↑−6	↖−3	↖0	↖−1	↖2	↖2
A	−14	↑−11	↑−8	↑−5	↑−2	↖−1	↑0	↖1
G	−16	↑−13	↑−10	↖−7	↖−4	↖−3	↖0	↖1
G	−18	↑−15	↑−12	↖−9	↖−6	↖−5	↖−2	↖1

Waterman (1981). Like NW, SW is also based in dynamic programming with $O(mn)$ time and space complexity. However, there are three basic differences between them.

The first difference is on the initialization of the first row and column, which are filled with zeros in SW. In this way, gaps do not receive penalty if they are at the beginning of the alignment. The second difference involves the equation used to calculate the remaining cells since, in SW, no negative values are allowed. In order to do that, the value zero is included in Equation (1), generating Equation (2).

$$D(i, j) = \max \begin{cases} D(i, j-1) + g \\ D(i-1, j-1) + p(i, j) \\ D(i-1, j) + g \\ 0 \end{cases} \quad (2)$$

The third difference concerns the cell used to start the traceback process. To obtain the best local alignment, the SW algorithm starts from the cell which has the highest value, following the arrows until a zero-valued cell is reached.

Figure 3 presents the SW similarity matrix between sequences s = TTGGTGG and t = TTGTCGAGG.

2.2.3. Affine-gap Model and Divergence

The algorithms NW and SW assign a constant value to gaps. However, keeping gaps together generates more significant results, in a biological perspective (Durbin et al., 1998). For this reason, the opening of a gap must have a greater penalty than its extension. Based on this observation, Gotoh (1982) proposed an algorithm where the gap penalty is calculated with Equation (3), where k is the number of consecutive gaps, v is the penalty for opening a gap and u is the penalty for extending it (affine gap model).

$$w(k) = u \times k + v, \ k \geq 1 \quad (3)$$

In order to calculate gaps according to Equation (3), two matrices are needed (E and F), in addition to the similarity matrix D. These additional matrices are used to compute the cost of a set of gaps in sequences s and t, respectively. Even with this, time complexity remains $O(mn)$ (Gotoh, 1982). Equations (4), (5) and (6) present the recurrence relations of the Gotoh algorithm.

Figure 3. Similarity matrix D to locally align sequences s = TTGGTGG and t = TTGTCGAGG, with score=+3. Values for matches, mismatches and gaps are ma=+1, mi=–1, g=–2, respectively

		T	T	G	G	T	G	G
	0	0	0	0	0	0	0	0
T	0	↖1	↖1	0	0	↖1	0	0
T	0	↖1	↖2	↖0	0	↖1	↖0	0
G	0	0	↖0	↖3	↖1	0	↖2	↖1
T	0	↖1	↖1	↑1	↖2	↖2	0	0
C	0	0	0	↖0	↖0	↖0	0	0
G	0	0	0	↖1	↖1	0	↖1	↖1
A	0	0	0	0	0	0	0	0
G	0	0	0	↖1	↖1	0	↖1	↖1
G	0	0	0	↖1	↖2	0	↖1	↖2

$$D(i,j) = \max \begin{cases} D(i, j-1) + g \\ E(i,j) \\ D(i-1, j-1) + p(i,j) \\ F(i,j) \\ 0 \end{cases} \quad (4)$$

$$E(i,j) = \max \begin{cases} E(i, j-1) + gap\_extension \\ D(i, j-1) + gap\_opening \end{cases} \quad (5)$$

$$F(i,j) = \max \begin{cases} F(i-1, j) + gap + extension \\ D(i-1, j) + gap\_opening \end{cases} \quad (6)$$

The method proposed by Fickett (1984) is adequate to globally align similar sequences. It is based on the following observation: to follow the main diagonal is to align both sequences without gaps. As long as gaps are introduced, the alignment leaves the main diagonal. If the sequences are very similar, the alignment between them is near the main diagonal. Thus, in order to compute the best global alignment(s), it is sufficient to calculate only a small band (*k*-band) near the main diagonal.

This algorithm has time and space complexity $O(kn)$ and works as follows. First, the *k*-band is estimated and the algorithm is executed for this band. If the optimal alignment is outside the band,

a larger *k*-band is estimated, until the alignment is entirely retrieved.

Fickett's algorithm (Fickett, 1984) can be applied to a local alignment problem. To do that, it is sufficient to transform the global alignment problem into a local alignment one. First, the entire similarity matrices are calculated and the similarity score as well as the coordinates that determine the ending position of the optimal alignment ($D(i_{end}, j_{end})$) are obtained. After that, the similarity matrices are re-calculated over the reverses of the sequences, in order to obtain the coordinates where the optimal alignment starts ($D(i_{start}, j_{start})$). Having the coordinates $D(i_{start}, j_{start})$ and $D(i_{end}, j_{end})$, any algorithm designed for global alignment can be applied (Gusfield 1997).

Knowing that the entire matrices will be processed twice, as discussed in the above paragraph, Z-align (Batista et al., 2008) proposed the divergence concept, which enables the algorithm to obtain the exact *k*-band that contains the optimal alignment.

During the matrices calculation, it is also calculated how each possible alignment diverges from its beginning coordinates. As long as there are only matches or mismatches, there is no divergence and the alignment follows its main diagonal. When a gap is introduced, the alignment diverges from the diagonal. This divergence can be superior (DIV^{sup}) or inferior (DIV^{inf}), depending on the sequence where the gap is inserted. Therefore, we need

Figure 4. (a) A possible alignment between sequences s and t. (b) The divergences are initially calculated taking the main diagonal of the similarity matrix D as a basis. (c) Finally, the values DIV^{sup} and DIV^{inf} are adjusted to refer to the beginning of the alignment

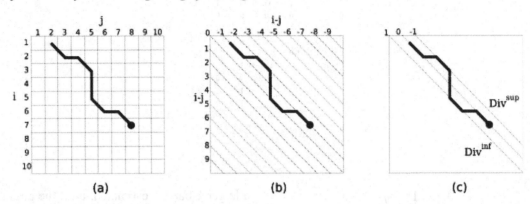

(a)   (b)   (c)

two additional dynamic programming matrices (DIV^{sup} and DIV^{inf}). At the end of the similarity matrix computation, the highest score and its coordinates (i,j) are obtained. The divergences for the optimal alignment can be found in $DIV^{sup}(i, j)$ and $DIV^{inf}(i, j)$, respectively. Figure 4 illustrates the divergence concept.

2.2.4. The DIALIGN Algorithm

DIALIGN (DIAGonal ALIGNment) (Morgenstern et al., 1998) is a method for sequence alignment that searches for *fragments* (or *diagonals*) that have no gaps and aligns them. In DIALIGN, a pairwise alignment is defined to be a chain of fragments. By doing that, it avoids the overhead of computing gap scores and discards low similarity regions out of diagonals. When compared to Smith-Waterman (Section 2.2.2), DIALIGN provides better results if there are more than one distinct regions with high similarity (Mount, 2004).

The algorithm works as follows. For each pairwise alignment, many diagonals can be found. Thus, it is necessary to calculate the relevance E of each diagonal before attempting to align them. This is done calculating the probability $P(l,sm)$ of a diagonal D of size l have at least sm matches and then using the negative natural logarithm of it ($E(l,sm) = -ln(P(l,sm))$) (Morgenstern et al., 1998).

For each candidate diagonal D, a weight $w(D)$ is assigned as $E(l,sm)$ if $E(l,sm)$ is above a given threshold T and 0, otherwise. A high $w(D)$ means that the probability of diagonal D occurrence by chance is small.

When the algorithm obtains a new significant diagonal, it tries to align it consistently with other previously calculated significant diagonals (Morgenstern et al., 1998). Figure 5 illustrates the cases when fragments can and cannot be consistently aligned.

In an alignment of k diagonals $D_1, D_2, ..., D_k$, the total score S is given by the addition of all weights $w(D_i)$, from D_1 to D_k. To discover the score S, a dynamic programming based strategy is used. Consider two sequences s and t, having sizes m and n, respectively. For each pair (i,j), it will be determined all integers k with $k \leq min(i,j)$ where the diagonal $(s_{i-k}t_{i-k}, ..., s_it_j)$ beginning at position $(i-k, j-k)$ and ending in position (i,j) has a positive weight w. For each position (i, j) is defined a *score*(i, j) for the alignment (chain of diagonals $D_1, D_2, ..., D_k$) in the prefixes $s[1..i]$ and $t[1..j]$.

According to Morgenstern et al. (1998), the last diagonal D_k aligned in position (i, j) is recovered by function $prec(i, j)$ (Equation (8)). The score is calculated as in Equation (7), where $\sigma(D_{i,j})$ is

Figure 5. DIALIGN consistency check: for each new significant fragment (or diagonal) calculated, a consistency check is made where the ending coordinates of a diagonal cannot overlap with the beginning coordinates of the next one

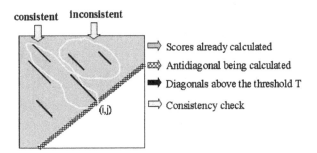

defined as the chain of diagonals ending at point (i, j) that has the highest score.

$$score(i, j) = \max \begin{cases} score(i-1, j) \\ score(i, j-1) \\ \sigma(D_{ij}) \end{cases} \quad (7)$$

$$prec(i, j) = \max \begin{cases} pre(i, j-1), \text{ if } score(i, j) = \\ score(i, j-1) \\ prec(i-1, j), \text{if } score(i, j-1) < \\ score(i, j) = score(i-1, j) \\ D_{ij}, \text{if } score(i, j-1), score(i-1, j) < \\ score(i, j) = \sigma(D_{ij}) \end{cases} \quad (8)$$

Two dynamic programming matrices are calculated, one for scores (Equation (7)) and the other for the preceding diagonal (Equation (8)). Once these matrices are calculated, the reverse path on the *prec* matrix gives the alignment. One example of such alignment is given in Figure 6. In Figure 6(a), the subsequences belonging to diagonals are shown in gray and the aligned diagonals are shown as lines. Figure 6(b) shows the final alignment.

2.3. Sequence-Profile Alignment

Profile analysis complements standard pairwise comparison methods for large-scale analysis of families of sequences. A sequence family is defined to be a set of sequences with similar function, similar 2D/3D structure, or a common evolutionary history (Hunter, 1993). Therefore, a newly identified sequence is often compared to several known families, in search of similarities. The comparison usually aligns the sequence to the representation of the family. This representation can be a profile, a consensus sequence or a signature (Gusfield, 1997).

We can build a multiple alignment of the sequences in a family and, based on the alignment, produce a profile representing the family. This profile keeps statistical information about the family, recording the residue distribution at each position of the multiple alignment, and describing statistically the variations in the family.

Given a sequence of interest and the profile modeling a sequence family, if the sequence-profile comparison results in high similarity, the sequence is usually identified to be member of the family. This identification is a very important step towards determining the function or/and structure of the sequence.

For instance, the PFAM database (Finn at al., 2008) is a huge collection of protein families represented as multiple sequence alignments, available via WWW servers that enable the comparison of protein sequences of interest against

Figure 6. Example of a DIALIGN alignment

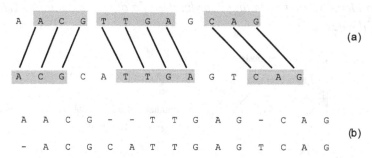

protein families, in search for additional remotely homologous sequences.

Our discussion will focus on profile representations of protein families, which are based on multiple sequence alignments. Nevertheless, the same techniques are also applicable to DNA sequences.

2.3.1. Hidden Markov Models

One of the most accepted probabilistic models to do sequence-profile comparisons is based on Hidden Markov Models (HMMs). HMMs, a statistical model based on Markov processes, have been applied to other research areas, such as speech recognition (Rabiner, 1989).

A profile HMM models a sequence family, representing the common similarities among the sequences in the family as discrete states, each one corresponding to an evolutionary possibility such as residue insertions or deletions, or matches between them.

Once a profile HMM is built to model a given sequence family (for instance, from the multiple alignment of the sequences in the family), it is commonly used to score how well a new sequence fits the family profile. For example, one could build a model for a number of proteins in a family, and then match sequences in a database to that model in order to try to find other family members.

Krogh et al. (1994) proposed a profile HMM structure for modeling protein families, consisting

of match (M), insert (I), and delete (D) states. This HMM usually has one state M for each consensus position in the multiple alignment of the sequences in the family. Each M state aligns to (emits) a single residue, with a probability score that is determined by the frequency that residues have been observed in the corresponding position of the multiple alignment. Therefore, each M state has 20 probabilities for scoring the 20 amino acids.

The states I and D model gapped alignments, that is, alignments including residue insertions and deletions. Each I state also emits a residue and has 20 probabilities for scoring the 20 amino acids. The D states do not emit any residues.

Besides the emission probabilities, there are transition probabilities associated to each transition from one state to another, that are set to capture specific information about each position in the multiple alignment of the family. The profile HMM allows position dependent insertion and deletion penalties, with different probabilities for entering different I and D states, modeling that certain regions of the multiple alignment tolerate insertions and deletions more than others. Also, we may have different transition probabilities for entering a particular insert state for the first time vs. staying in it, modeling affine gap penalties.

The Plan7 architecture (Eddy, 2003) is a modified profile HMM structure that augmented the simple model of Krogh at al. (1994) in order to enable global or local alignments, with respect to the model or to the sequence, and also multiple

Figure 7. A profile HMM with 4 nodes (with the Plan7 structure) and the transition probabilities

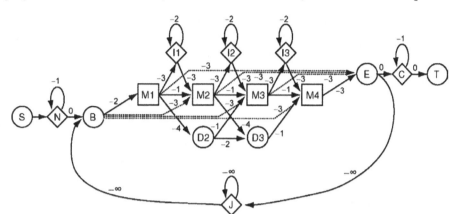

hit alignments. In addition to the original M, I and D states, the Plan7 HMM includes a set of flanking states.

The group of M, I, and D states corresponding to the same position in the multiple alignment is called a node of the HMM. The structure of a Plan7 HMM with four nodes is illustrated in Figure 7. The labels in the state transitions represent transition probabilities.

Local alignments with respect to the profile HMM are allowed by non-zero state transition probabilities from state B to internal M states, and from these states to state E. Local alignments with respect to the sequence are allowed by non-zero state transitions on the special insert states N and C. More than one hit to the HMM per sequence is allowed by transitions through the special insert state J.

2.3.2. Viterbi Algorithm

Given a query sequence and a profile HMM modeling a protein family, an alignment of the sequence to the model is an assignment of states to each residue in the sequence (represented as a path of the sequence over the states). There are many such alignments for a given sequence. Therefore, we need to find the best alignment of the sequence to the HMM, i.e., the one with the

highest probability. This can be done efficiently by a dynamic programming algorithm called the Viterbi algorithm (Rabiner, 1989). The algorithm finds the best alignment for that sequence and gives its probability.

The probability of an alignment is calculated by multiplying the transition and emission probabilities at each state in the path, and can be interpreted as a similarity score. If this score is sufficiently good, we can conclude that the sequence belongs to the family.

The probability parameters in a profile HMM are usually converted to additive log-odds scores. The transition and emission probabilities are converted into logarithms, and the log-odds score of the alignment is calculated by adding up these numbers, instead of multiplying the probabilities.

The Viterbi algorithm applied to Plan7 HMMs for aligning a sequence s of length n to a profile HMM with k nodes is shown in Equations (9), in the form of a set of recurrence equations. It calculates a set of score matrices of size $n \times k$ (corresponding to states M, I, and D) and vectors of size n (corresponding to states N, B, E, J, and C).(see Figure 8).

In these equations, $M(i, j)$ is the score of the best path aligning the subsequence $s[1..i]$ to the model up to state M_j, ending with s_i being emitted by state M_j. Similarly, $I(i,j)$ is the score of the best

Figure 8. Equation 9

$$M(i,0) = I(i,0) = D(i,0) = -\infty \quad \forall 1 \leq i \leq n$$
$$M(0,j) = I(0,j) = D(0,j) = -\infty \quad \forall 1 \leq j \leq k$$

$$M(i,j) = em(M_j,s_i) + \max \begin{cases} M(i-1,j-1) + tr(M_{j-1},M_j) \\ I(i-1,j-1) + tr(I_{j-1},M_j) \\ D(i-1,j-1) + tr(D_{j-1},M_j) \\ B(i-1) + tr(B,M_j) \end{cases} \quad \forall 1 \leq i \leq n, \forall 1 \leq j \leq k$$

$$I(i,j) = em(I_j,s_i) + \max \begin{cases} M(i-1,j) + tr(M_j,I_j) \\ I(i-1,j) + tr(I_j,I_j) \end{cases} \quad \forall 1 \leq i \leq n, \forall 1 \leq j \leq k$$

$$D(i,j) = \max \begin{cases} M(i,j-1) + tr(M_{j-1},D_j) \\ D(i,j-1) + tr(D_{j-1},D_j) \end{cases} \quad \forall 1 \leq i \leq n, \forall 1 \leq j \leq k$$

$$N(0) = 0$$
$$N(i) = N(i-1) + tr(N,N) \quad \forall 1 \leq i \leq n$$

$$B(0) = tr(N,B)$$
$$B(i) = \max \begin{cases} N(i) + tr(N,B) \quad \forall 1 \leq i \leq n \\ J(i) + tr(J,B) \end{cases}$$

$$E(i) = \max_{\forall 1 \leq j \leq k} \{ M(i,j) + tr(M_j,E) \} \quad \forall 1 \leq i \leq n$$

$$J(0) = -\infty$$
$$J(i) = \max \begin{cases} J(i-1) + tr(J,J) \quad \forall 1 \leq i \leq n \\ E(i) + tr(E,J) \end{cases}$$

$$C(0) = -\infty$$
$$C(i) = \max \begin{cases} C(i-1) + tr(C,C) \quad \forall 1 \leq i \leq n \\ E(i) + tr(E,C) \end{cases}$$

$$similarity\_score = C(n) + tr(C,T)$$

(9)

path ending with s_i being emitted by I_j, and $D(i,j)$ is the score of the best path ending in state D_j. The emission probability of the residue s_i at state₁ is denoted by $em(state_1,s_1)$, while $tr(state_1,state_2)$ represents the transition cost from state₁ to state₂.

As a result, the Viterbi algorithm finds the best (most probable) alignment and its score for the query sequence with the given model. The best alignment is represented as a path through the HMM, with a sequence of states that maximizes the probability of the query sequence being observed. The similarity score of the best alignment is given by $C(n) + tr(C,T)$. The best alignment itself can be obtained by tracking back on the Viterbi variables. This alignment can be used to add the sequence into the multiple alignment of the family.

This algorithm has $O(nk)$ time complexity. However, from Equations (9) we can see that it requires more computations per cell of the dynamic

programming matrices than the pairwise sequence comparison algorithms.

Given the profile HMM of Figure 7, the transition scores are shown in the figure, labeling the state transitions, and the emission scores for the M and I states are shown in Table 1. Figure 9 shows the score matrices and vectors computed by the Viterbi algorithm, when comparing the query sequence ACYDE to that profile HMM ($n = 5$ and $k = 4$). The best alignment has the similarity score of 22 and corresponds to the path (S,−)→ (N,−)→(B,−)→(M1,A)→(M2,C)→ (I2,Y)→(M 3,D)→(M4,E)→(E,−)→(C,−)→(T,−), which is shaded in Figure 9.

2.3.3. HMMER

The HMMER program suite developed by Eddy (2003) is a widely used software implementation of profile HMMs for biological sequence analysis. It is composed of several programs and can be

Table 1. Emission scores of amino acids for M and I states of profile HMM of Figure 7

State	A	C	D	E	F, I, L, M, V, W	G, K, N, P, S	H, Q, R, T	Y
M1	7	−1	−1	1	−1	2	1	−1
M2	−1	9	−1	1	−1	2	1	−1
M3	−1	−1	8	2	−1	2	1	−1
M4	−1	−1	3	9	−1	2	1	−1
I1	−1	−1	0	1	−1	0	1	2
I2	−1	−1	0	1	−1	0	1	2
I3	−1	−1	0	1	−1	0	1	2

Figure 9. Score matrices and vectors of the Viterbi algorithm for the comparison of the sequence ACYDE against the profile HMM of Figure 7: shaded cells represent the best alignment

i \ j	N	B	M					I					D					E	J	C
			0	1	2	3	4	0	1	2	3	4	0	1	2	3	4			
–	0	0	−∞	−∞	−∞	−∞	−∞	−∞	−∞	−∞	−∞	−∞	−∞	−∞	−∞	−∞	−∞	−∞	∞	∞
A	−1	−1	−∞	5	−4	−4	−4	−∞	−∞	−∞	−∞	−∞	−∞	−∞	1	−1	−∞	2	−∞	2
C	−2	−2	−∞	−4	13	−1	−3	−∞	1	−8	−8	−∞	−∞	−∞	−8	9	−∞	10	−∞	10
Y	−3	−3	−∞	−5	−3	11	7	−∞	1	12	2	−∞	−∞	−∞	−9	−7	−∞	8	−∞	9
D	−4	−4	−∞	−6	−3	17	13	−∞	−1	10	8	−∞	−∞	−∞	−10	−7	−∞	14	−∞	14
E	−5	−5	−∞	−5	−3	9	25	−∞	−2	9	15	−∞	−∞	−∞	−9	−7	−∞	22	−∞	22

used to build database search models from pre-existing alignments. HMMER software uses the Plan7 HMM structure in order to produce global or local alignments, with respect to the model or to the sequence, and also multiple hit alignments.

HMMER can take multiple alignments of sequence families and build the profile HMMs representing them. In particular, the program *hmmsearch* searches a sequence database for matches to a profile HMM, while the program *hmmpfam* searches a HMM database for matches to a query sequence. Both programs use the Viterbi algorithm to perform the sequence-profile comparison and generate the alignment of the sequence to the HMM and the corresponding similarity score. Experiments have shown that the function that implements the Viterbi algorithm is the most time consuming kernel of these programs (Sun et al., 2009).

3. FPGA-BASED ACCELERATORS FOR PAIRWISE COMPARISON

3.1. General Overview of the Proposed Solutions

In the literature, there are many proposals of FPGA-based architectures to accelerate pairwise sequence comparison applications by calculating the similarity matrix anti-diagonals in hardware, taking full advantage of the parallelism inherent in this computation. In this approach, an array processor with N elements is used, where each

Figure 10. A 4-element systolic array to calculate the dynamic programming matrix

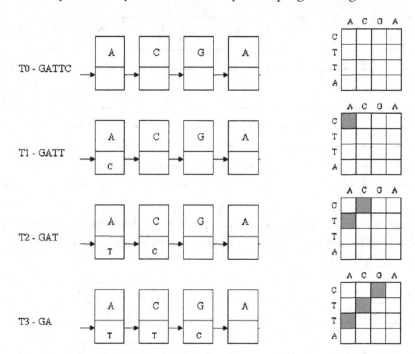

element is capable of calculating one matrix score per turn. Thus, when the wavefront is being processed by all elements, one processor array with N elements can generate N scores at a time.

Usually, systolic processor arrays (Kung, 1982) are used, where the processing elements operate in a lock-step basis. The seminal work of Lipton & Lopresti (1985) proposed a successful implementation of Smith-Waterman in a systolic array. Since then, variations of this design have been used in several different proposals. However, the $O(mn)$ space complexity of the SW algorithm is a great restriction. For this reason, most of the hardware solutions do not store the entire similarity matrix, obtaining only the similarity score.

Usually, the smallest sequence being aligned, called query sequence, is stored on the computing elements. The other sequence, called database sequence, can be of any size, since it "passes" through the FPGA.

At time T0 (Figure 10), the elements of the query sequence (A, C, G, and A) are already stored

in the processing elements (PEs). At T1, the first processing element compares A to C, using, for instance, the recurrence relation (2). At T2, two comparisons are made simultaneously (A to T and C to C) by the first and second processing elements, respectively. At T3, three cells are calculated in parallel, and so on. The wavefront is said to be at full processing when all PEs are processing simultaneously.

Frequently, the size of the query sequence is greater than the number of PEs contained in the FPGA. In this case, a partitioning technique is needed. To break query sequences, it is necessary to keep the scores of the last calculated column in the FPGA memory (usually a FIFO) to allow new scores to be calculated. Figure 11 illustrates the systolic array design with partitioning.

Some designs avoid the use of a FIFO by putting many query bases in the same computing element. The drawback of this approach is that to put more bases in each cell requires more registers per element and thus decreases the maximum

Figure 11. Systolic array composed by N PEs, with partitioning. The last column of each phase is stored in a FIFO and provided to the PE array as input to the next step

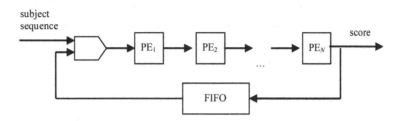

3.2. Some Early Approaches

In the last two decades, many proposals were made to execute pairwise sequence comparison applications in specific hardware. In this section, we will present briefly some of the relevant proposals made from 1992 to 2003.

A bidirectional systolic array was proposed by Hoang & Lopresti (1992). In this design, the database and query sequences are fed at the same time into the processing element array, in opposite sides and directions. Computation starts when the first characters of both sequences meet in the middle of the systolic array and continues until every character is compared. The sequences are processed twice and the alignment is output as a set of 2-bit representations that indicate (a) the alignment of both characters, (b) a gap in the first sequence or (c) a gap in the second sequence. Ten thousand alignments of 100-nucleotide sequences were performed in the SPLASH board, that is composed of 32 FPGA Xilinx XC3090. The total of 248 PEs was obtained.

Yamagutchi et al. (2002) proposed a unidirectional systolic array to compute the Smith-Waterman score and retrieve the alignment (Section 2.2.2), using the basic design illustrated in Figure 10. Sequence partitioning is achieved by a pipelined approach that calculates each diagonal in two steps: superior and inferior part.

The similarity matrix is stored in the FPGA and it is used to retrieve the alignment. Using the FPGA Xilinx XCV2000E, the alignment between sequences of 1KBP and 4KBP was obtained by 144 PEs. Speedups of 50 and 330 were obtained for the alignment retrieval and the score computation, respectively, when compared to a software implementation.

A systolic array architecture to run the SW algorithm at the OSIRIS board was proposed by Puttegowda et al. (2003). This board contains two FPGAs: one interfaces with the host machine whereas the other executes user-programmed hardware designs. Reconfiguration is used to generate custom circuit logic with the dynamic programming parameters and the query sequence. Four systolic arrays were implemented in the same FPGA, which enabled four comparisons to be made simultaneously. Sequence partitioning is achieved by using more than one PE array. In this design, the similarity matrix is calculated but the edit distance is obtained, instead of the SW score. A speedup of 500 was obtained when comparing sequences with up to 1750 nucleotides with a genomic database, with respect to a software solution.

3.3. Customized Smith-Waterman Accelerator

Oliver et al. (2005) proposed the use of a linear array of PEs to solve the pairwise SW-based local alignment problem with linear or affine gap functions. The proposed architecture computes the whole similarity matrix and outputs the highest score. Switching between the gap functions is done by static reconfiguration. Using reconfiguration, the size of the operands and other system parameters can also be specified for optimized circuit generation.

Moreover, the systolic array PEs are placed in the FPGA according to a zig-zag pattern, which provides a very good space occupation. Depending on the sizes of the sequences being compared, the FPGA can be reconfigured to compare more than one sequence at a time.

Several elements that compose the query sequence can be stored in the same PE. A FIFO is designed to accommodate the query sequence elements, as well as the substitution matrix column and the database sequence itself.

The architecture was programmed in Verilog and synthesized for the Virtex II XC2V6000 FPGA board. Query sequences of size that range from 1 to 1004 amino acids were compared with the Swiss-Prot database on a FPGA prototype with 252 PEs. Speedups of approximately 170 and 125 were achieved for the linear and affine gap functions, respectively, when compared to an optimized software program. This design imposes restrictions on the size of the query and database sequence. For the targeted FPGA, only sequences with less than 8192 amino acids can be compared.

3.4. Accelerator to Retrieve Highest Score and its Coordinates

Boukerche et al. (2007a) proposed a systolic array that computes the Smith-Waterman dynamic programming matrix (Section 2.2.2) for DNA sequences in linear space. A linear gap model is employed. The basic design discussed in Section 3.1 was used, where each PE calculates one column of the dynamic programming matrix. If the size of the query sequence is greater than the total number of PEs, sequence splitting is done

and the last column calculated is stored in the FPGA memory (Figure 11).

The particularity of this proposal is that it provides as output not only the highest score but also the coordinates in the dynamic programming matrix where the score occurs. These coordinates determine the position where the optimal score ends. In many parallel software-only approaches (Batista et al., 2008), this is the first phase of the SW algorithm. Having the highest score and its ending position, reprocessing can be done over the reverses of the sequences, in order to retrieve the beginning coordinates and the actual optimal alignment itself (Section 2.2.3).

Figure 12 presents the circuit executed in each PE. With the exception of the top right elements (*Bc, C1* and "+"), slight variations of this design are employed in most of the FPGA accelerators that implement SW.

To calculate each cell $D_{i,j}$ in the matrix, three cells are needed (Equation (2)): $D_{i,j-1}$, $D_{i-1,j}$ and $D_{i-1,j-1}$ (Figure 12). In each cycle, values $D_{i-1,j-1}$ and $D_{i,j-1}$, which are stored in registers, and value $D_{i-1,j}$, which is transmitted from the left PE, are used to calculate $D_{i,j}$. Two bases are compared: a query base $s[i]$, that is fixed in the PE and a database base $t[j]$ that comes from the left PE. If the bases are equal, it means that a match occurred and the coincidence punctuation *ma* is used. Otherwise, it is a mismatch and the substitution penalty *mi* is used. In parallel, values $D_{i,j-1}$ and $D_{i-1,j}$ are compared and the greater one is added to the gap penalty *g*. These values are compared and the greater one is compared to zero, as shown in Equation (2).

To calculate the best score, the new $D_{i,j}$ score is compared to the value stored in register *Bs* (Best score in that column so far). If the $D_{i,j}$ score is greater than *Bs*, it replaces the old value. To recover the anti-diagonal and therefore the row where the best score occurs, register *C1* is utilized. It is incremented by one each time a new score is calculated. If the current score is greater than the one stored in *Bs*, the writing on register *Bc* is

Figure 12. Circuit executed by each PE including the dynamic programming cell calculation and the highest score and its coordinates computation (Adapted from Boukerche et al., 2007a)

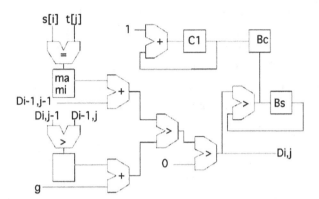

enabled and its value is replaced by the current value of *C1*. Therefore, *C1* stores the row where *Bs* occurs and, with the relative position of the PE itself, the column is obtained.

A prototype of this architecture was synthesized for the FPGA Xilinx XC2VP70. With this prototype, a speedup of 246.9 was achieved over an optimized C program, when comparing synthetic sequences of 10MBP (Millions of Base Pairs) and 10KBP (10 Kilo Base Pairs).

3.5. Pipelined Accelerator with Uneven Stages

Zhang et al. (2007) proposed the use of a unidimensional systolic array to execute the SW algorithm for protein and DNA sequences with both linear and affine gap function, i.e., SW and Gotoh gap penalties, respectively (Sections 2.2.2 and 2.2.3). As a result, the highest score is output. A partition technique is also used that compares parts of the query sequence with the entire database sequence in each phase. The elements of the last column computed in each phase are stored in the FPGA internal memory, as illustrated in Figure 11.

In order to achieve better performance, the authors propose a pipelined control mechanism, with uneven stage latencies. Four clocks with the same frequency are used, but there are different

phase delays between clocks. Also, intra-PE optimizations were proposed to reduce the number of *max* operations and to reduce the space needed to store the substitution matrix containing the mismatch penalties between every residue pair.

The proposed architecture was synthesized, targeted to run in the XD1000 platform. In this platform, the main processor is an AMD64 Opteron that is connected through HyperTransport to an Altera Stratix II FPGA. The main processor and the FPGA are located in the same board and the FPGA acts as a co-processor. A PE array of 384 elements that work at 66.7 MHz was implemented. Compared to an optimized C program, the proposed architecture achieved a speedup of 249.52 when comparing two sequences of 65,536 amino acids.

3.6. DIALIGN Accelerator

Boukerche et al. (2007b) proposed an FPGA-based accelerator for the DIALIGN algorithm (Section 2.2.4). The basic design discussed in Section 3.1 was used. If the query sequence has more elements than the PE array, the last column of each phase is stored in the FPGA internal memory (Figure 11).

The main difference between this proposal and the Smith-Waterman accelerators discussed so far is that the design of a PE that executes DIALIGN is totally different from the design of a PE that executes Smith-Waterman, with or without affine gap. This happens because the DIALIGN recurrence relations (Equations (7) and (8)) are more complex since they include conditional statements.

In order to obtain a high performance implementation of the DIALIGN algorithm in a processor array, some simplifications were made. First, the natural logarithm, that is used in the original DIALIGN equation, was replaced by log2. Second, the fragments are now defined to contain only matches. As soon as a mismatch is detected, the fragment is ended. This second simplification eliminates the dependence on the *k* last elements and, thus, makes it possible to use the generic processor array shown in Figure 10, in the DIALIGN implementation.

Also, this design includes a handshaking protocol between every two neighbor processing elements. Therefore, an asynchronous design is used instead of the traditional systolic approach. Inside the PEs that implement the DIALIGN recurrence relations, the size of the possible paths varies considerably and the path taken depends on the values being compared and on the best chain of fragments obtained so far. In this scenario, a systolic approach would have been targeted to the size of the largest path, limiting considerably the performance gains.

The proposed design was implemented in SystemC and compiled to Verilog by Forte (www.forteds.com). A processor array of 200 PEs was synthesized for the FPGA Altera Stratix 2 EP2S180F1508I4. A maximum speedup of 383.41 was achieved, when compared to an optimized software implementation.

3.7. Parameterized FPGA-Based Skeleton

Observing that there are many FPGA-based accelerators for pairwise sequence comparison that present the same general structure but differ in some characteristics such as type of sequence

compared, recurrence relation and/or output produced, Benkrid et al. (2009) proposed a parameterized skeleton for sequence comparison accelerators. In this work, the user can specify some parameters and a program is generated in Handel-C that executes the target architecture. The accelerators generated are systolic processor arrays that calculate the anti-diagonals in parallel (Figure 10).

Seven parameters do exist: sequence type (DNA, RNA or protein), query sequence length, maximum database sequence length, substitution matrix, gap penalty (linear or affine), matching algorithm (global, local or overlapped matching) and match score threshold. The query sequence length is used to determine the number of PEs. If this length is greater than a given value, a partition technique is implemented, where the last column is stored in the FPGA memory (Figure 11).

Using the proposed skeleton, an implementation was made of the SW with affine gap algorithm (Section 2.2.3), comparing proteins with the BLOSUM50 substitution matrix. The FPGA used was the XC2VP100-6 Virtex-II Pro. In this implementation, the systolic array had 135 processing elements, running at a clock frequency of 40MHz. When comparing a query sequence of 362 residues with a subset of the Swiss-Prot database, a speedup of 62 was achieved.

3.8. Comparative Overview

Table 2 presents a comparative overview of the proposals discussed in Sections 3.2 to 3.7.

The pairwise sequence comparison algorithm is shown in the second column (Table 2). As it can be seen, most of the papers implement the Smith-Waterman (SW) algorithm (Section 2.2.2). The more recent papers implement also the Gotoh algorithm (Section 2.2.3). Zhang et al. (2007), Oliver et al. (2005), and Benkrid et al. (2009) provide some kind of framework where different dynamic programming algorithms for pairwise sequence comparison can be implemented in a

Table 2. Comparative overview of the pairwise sequence comparison accelerators

Paper	Algorithm	Number of PEs	Clock rate (MHz)	Max query size compared	Speedup reported	Output
Hoang et al. (1992)	SW	248	Not reported	100	290.0	alignment
Yamagutchi et al (2002)	SW	144	40.0	4,096	330.0 / 50.0	score, alignment
Puttegowda et al (2003)	SW (edit distance)	4×1750	180.0	1,750	500.0	edit distance
Oliver et al. (2005)	SW/Gotoh	252	55.5	1,428	170.0	score
Boukerche et al (2007a)	SW	100	174.7	10,000	246.9	score, coordinates
Zhang et al. (2007)	SW/Gotoh	384	66.7	65,536	249.5	score
Boukerche et al (2007b)	DIALIGN	200	74.4	169,786	383.4	score
Benkrid et al. (2009)	SW/Gotoh/ NW/ overlap	135	40.0	362	62.0	score

simpler way. Only the accelerator proposed by Boukerche et al (2007b) implements the algorithm DIALIGN (Section 2.2.4).

The number of PEs (column 3 in Table 2) varies a lot and depends on both the complexity of each processing element and the capacity of the FPGA board used. In these designs, the number of PEs range from 100 to 384. An impressive result is obtained by Puttegowda et al. (2003), that were able to generate four systolic arrays with 1750 PEs each. This huge number of PEs can be explained by the algorithm implemented (edit distance), which is simpler than SW. Also, the best score was not stored, simplifying further the design of the PEs.

Column 4 presents the clock rate of each accelerator. With the exception of Boukerche et al. (2007a) and Puttegowda et al. (2003), the clock rates range from 40.0 to 74.4 MHz. It is surprising to see very similar clock rates in these accelerators since there is a gap of 27 years between the first accelerator discussed in this section and the last one. It must be noted, however, that, even though the capability of the FPGA boards have increased substantially from 1992 to 2009, the complexity of each PE has also increased. For instance, the designs of Hoang et al. (1992), Yamagutchi et al. (2002), and Puttegowda et al. (2003) compare DNA sequences and the other SW designs, with

the exception of Boukerche et al. (2007a), compare proteins. This makes a big difference in the design of each PE since a substitution matrix of size 20×20 must be stored, for the protein case. Also, most of the recent designs implement the Gotoh algorithm, that calculates three similarity matrices, instead of the one traditional SW matrix. This, of course, adds complexity to the design of the PE, increasing its size. In the same way, the simplicity in the design of each PE was a very important factor that determined the higher clock rates achieved by Puttegowda et al. (2003) and Boukerche et al. (2007a).

The size of the largest query sequence compared is illustrated in the fifth column. With the exception of Hoang & Lopresti (1992), all accelerators employ optimized partition techniques. This allowed query sequences of more than 10,000 elements to be compared in Boukerche et al. (2007b) and Zhang et al. (2007). Even though Benkrid et al. (2009) does use query sequence partition, their results used this feature in a restricted way, comparing small sequences of up to 362 amino acids.

Column 6 of Table 2 presents the speedup reported by each paper. In all cases, the FPGA implementations were compared to optimized software-only programs. Since different FPGA boards and desktops were used, a direct comparison among the accelerators cannot be made. But the speedup is an important indicator of the potential gains of the accelerators. The reported speedups range from 62 to 500 and, with the exception of Benkrid et al. (2009), all the accelerators were able to achieve speedups higher than 100, when compared to software. Impressive speedups, higher than 200, were achieved for most accelerators. In Benkrid et al. (2009), flexibility was obtained at the expense of performance. Even in this case, a speedup of 62 can be considered a good cost/benefit trade-off.

The output of each accelerator is shown in column 7. As it can be seen, the older approaches (1992 and 2002) provided the alignment as output. Nevertheless, in order to retrieve the alignment, the similarity matrix was stored in the FPGA internal memory and that severely restricted the size of the sequences being compared. Therefore, from 2003 to now, the pairwise sequence comparison accelerators act as filters, providing only the score as output. For the cases where the score is higher than a given threshold, the software will re-calculate the similarity matrix and generate the alignment using a software-only approach. In order to reduce this reprocessing time, the coordinates that determine the end of the optimal alignment are also retrieved by Boukerche et al. (2007a).

4. FPGA-BASED ACCELERATORS FOR SEQUENCE-PROFILE COMPARISON

4.1. General Overview of the Proposed Solutions

Since the Viterbi algorithm is the most time consuming part of the sequence-profile comparison, multiple attempts to optimize it have been made, including the implementation of FPGA-based accelerators. Studies have also shown that most of the execution time of the HMMER suite comparison programs is spent in processing poor scoring, and

consequently non significant, sequences (Maddimsetty et al., 2006).

In order to compute only the best alignment score it is not necessary to store the whole Viterbi matrices and vectors. In fact, only two rows of these structures are needed. On the other hand, to produce the best alignment a memory space of size $O(nk)$ is required, for a profile HMM with k nodes and a sequence of length n. This usually prevents the implementation of the alignment generation operation in hardware, given the memory limitations of current FPGAs and the long length of the biological sequences.

Therefore, most sequence-profile comparison solutions apply a first phase filter in order to discard poor scoring sequences, prior to full processing. The filter phase calculates only the similarity score (through the Viterbi algorithm) and is implemented in hardware, using FPGAs. Then, if the score is above a given threshold, the sequence is reprocessed in software in order to generate the corresponding alignment. In this reprocessing, the Viterbi algorithm is executed again, comparing the selected sequence against the profile HMM (using the HMMER software, for instance), but this time keeping information to produce the alignment.

Considering that hardware implementations can exploit the inherent fine- and coarse-grained parallelism of the algorithm and that only a small fraction of the sequences (the ones with high similarity) will be reprocessed in software, the FPGA filter can achieve performance gains when compared to the software-only implementation.

Figure 13 shows (with arrows) the data dependences for computing the cells (i,j) of the M, I, and D matrices in the Viterbi algorithm. These dependences determine which operations of the algorithm can be performed in parallel. The scores $M(i,j)$, $I(i,j)$, and $D(i,j)$ can be computed in parallel, since there are no data dependences between them. State J induces a feedback loop in the HMM (shown with dashed arrows in the figure) and creates data dependences which impose that the

Figure 13. Dependences of the Viterbi algorithm

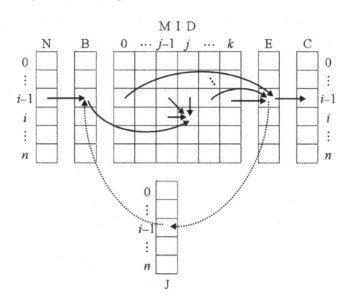

cells in each matrix must be computed one at a time in row-major order, limiting the parallelism.

In order to increase the available parallelism, most FPGA-based accelerators for the Viterbi algorithm (Benkrid et al., 2008; Oliver et al., 2009; Jacob et al., 2007) eliminate the state J of the Plan7 HMM. With this strategy, all cells in the same anti-diagonal of the Viterbi matrices become independent, yielding significant fine-grained parallelism. Therefore, a systolic array of processing elements (PEs) can be implemented so that each HMM node is mapped to one PE. Each PE calculates the score for the corresponding column of the dynamic programming matrices. At each time step, all PEs compute the cells in an anti-diagonal simultaneously, in a way similar to the approach used in pairwise sequence alignment (Section 3.1). However, the more resource intensive computations for each cell of the matrices, allied to the large number of parameters in a profile HMM, make it a challenging task to efficiently implement the Viterbi algorithm in hardware.

The state J removal strategy eliminates the Plan7 HMM ability to find multiple hit alignments such as several matches of subsequences of the query sequence to the profile HMM. It can result in loss of sensitivity for database searches, since sequences that would produce multiple hits, when limited to only one hit, can obtain a low score and be discarded. In order to match the sensitivity of a full Plan7 HMM with this simplified model, the threshold for accepting an alignment score is relaxed, at the cost of increasing the software reprocessing time.

The solution proposed by Eusse et al. (2009) uses a similar systolic array structure, eliminating the state J. However, besides computing the score, the PEs compute the alignment limits, in order to reduce the software reprocessing time. Maddimsetty et al. (2006) and Sun et al. (2009) also use the systolic array structure, but propose different techniques in order to reduce or correct the error induced by the J state elimination.

A different approach is presented in Oliver et al. (2008), where several sequences are compared to the same profile HMM at the same time, exploiting a coarse-grained parallelism. In this strategy, each PE implements the Viterbi algorithm for a complete Plan7 HMM, including the state J.

Derrien & Quinton (2007) proposed a mathematical model to represent the Viterbi algorithm applied to the comparison of multiple sequences against the same profile HMM, exposing the data dependences this problem presents. Using space-time mappings of the problem on the polyhedral model, they derive different parallelization schemes of the Viterbi algorithm for FPGAs.

The performance of most FPGA-based accelerators for the sequence-profile comparison is reported using the throughput measure CUPS (Cell Updates per Second), which indicates how many cells of the dynamic programming matrices are computed in one second. CUPS represent the peak performance that the hardware accelerator can achieve and usually does not include data communication time or initialization time. Therefore, it should be considered an upper-bound of the actual performance.

In the following sections, we describe in detail some solutions proposed to implement sequence-profile comparison on FPGAs. Section 4.8 presents a comparative overview of these solutions.

4.2. Systolic Array

Oliver et al. (2009) and Benkrid et al. (2008) proposed FPGA-based accelerators for the Viterbi algorithm in order to obtain the best alignment score between a profile HMM and a sequence. Oliver et al. (2009) use the HMM model of Krogh at al. (1994) consisting only of M, I, and D states (Section 2.3.1), while Benkrid et al. (2008) use the Plan7 HMM, but eliminate the state J. Therefore, their designs do not produce multiple hit alignments.

Both accelerators use the systolic array architecture described in Section 4.1, composed of a number of PEs interconnected in a linear structure. Each HMM node is mapped to one PE, which calculates the cells in the corresponding column of the matrices of the Viterbi algorithm. At each time step, each PE calculates one cell, in a way

that all cells in an anti-diagonal of the matrices are computed in parallel.

Figure 14 illustrates how the Viterbi matrices columns are mapped to the PEs in the systolic array, considering that the number k of profile HMM nodes is equal to the number of implemented PEs. In the figure, each anti-diagonal shows the cells that are computed simultaneously, at each time step. The shaded cells are calculated by their corresponding PEs, while a blank cell corresponds to an idle PE at that time step.

The systolic array is filled gradually as the query sequence elements are inserted until there are no idle PEs left. The sequence is processed, flowing through the systolic array, from left to right, one residue at each time step. The systolic array is also emptied gradually, until there are no more cells to compute, and then, it outputs the best alignment score. Assume we are aligning a sequence of length n to a profile HMM with k nodes on a systolic array of k PEs. Then, it takes $n+k-1$ time steps to completely shift the sequence through the array and to compute the alignment score with the Viterbi algorithm. Note that the structure of this design is very similar to the one presented for the pairwise sequence comparison accelerators (Section 3.1).

The parameters that define the particular profile HMM configuration are loaded in the systolic array, as a preprocessing step: the transition and emission probabilities of states M_j, I_j, and D_j are stored into PE_j, using memories or lookup tables of the FPGA. Each PE only interacts with its two adjacent neighbors. PE_j receives the values $M(i, j-1)$, $I(i,j-1)$, $D(i,j-1)$ and the residue s_i from its left neighbor PE_{j-1}, and sends the values $M(i,j)$, $I(i,j)$, $D(i,j)$ it calculated and the input residue to the right neighbor PE_{j+1}. All other required values are stored locally. The general structure of a PE (corresponding to HMM node j) is illustrated in Figure 15, with adders and maximum operators for computing the scores corresponding to states M, I, and D, according to the Viterbi algorithm (shown in Equations (9)). The design of the PE

Figure 14. Mapping of the columns of the dynamic programming matrices to the PEs in the systolic array

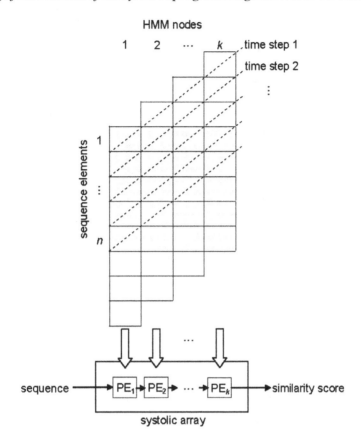

may also include the computation of the scores corresponding to states B and E.

Ideally, there would be one PE in the systolic array for each HMM node. In practice, this rarely happens, since the size of commercial FPGAs is limited and it is not practical to implement a system with a number of PEs that is equal to the number of nodes of the longest profile HMM in the databases. Since the length of the profile HMMs may vary, the computation must be partitioned to fit the fixed size systolic array.

The solution is to split the computation into several passes, similarly to the strategy used in pairwise sequence alignment (Section 3.1). Each pass computes a set of N adjacent columns of the dynamic programming matrices, where N is the maximum number of PEs that fits into the target FPGA. In the first pass, the first N nodes of the

profile HMM are assigned to the systolic array and the corresponding emission and transition probabilities are loaded. The entire query sequence is shifted through the array of PEs and the scores are calculated for the first set of adjacent columns. The M, I, and D scores computed by the last PE in each time step are output and stored, since they are the input to the next pass and will be consumed by the first PE. First-In First-Out (FIFO) memories are included in the implementation to store these partial results between passes. In the second pass, the next N nodes of the profile HMM are loaded into the systolic array. The sequence is shifted again through the array of PEs and the scores are computed for the second set of adjacent columns. This process is repeated until the end of the profile HMM is reached. Figure 16 shows the

Figure 15. Basic structure of a PE from the systolic array: $em(state_1, s_i)$ is the emission probability of amino acid s_i at $state_1$ and $tr(state_1, state_2)$ is the transition cost from $state_1$ to $state_2$

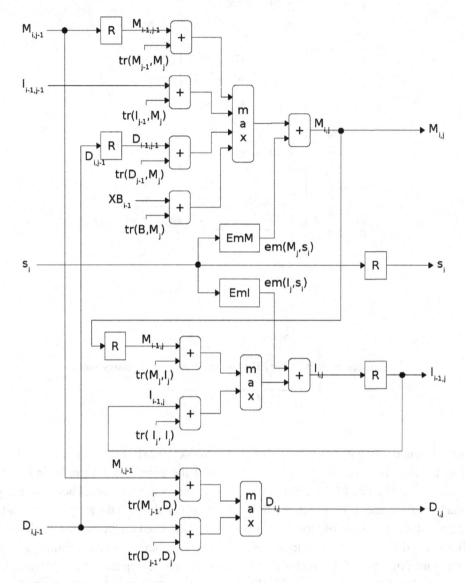

systolic array structure with N PEs and the FIFO memories that enable multiple passes.

The memory requirements for storing the transition and emission scores and implementing the FIFOs impose restrictions on the maximum number of PEs that can fit into the device, the maximum HMM length and the maximum sequence size.

Both Benkrid et al. (2008) and Oliver et al. (2009) implementations permit supplying the systolic array with a continuous stream of query sequences to be aligned to the profile HMM. The sequences are separated by a delimiter symbol that does not belong to the amino-acid alphabet. The purpose of this symbol is to define the start and finish boundaries of the sequences, so that each PE knows when it has to initialize its internal

Figure 16. Systolic array with N PEs and FIFOs to enable multiple passes

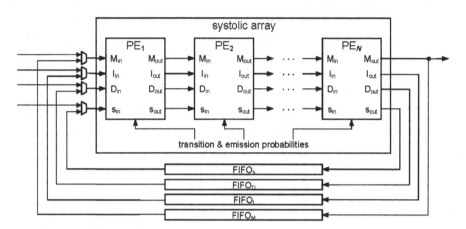

structures. After the last residue of a sequence enters the array, the first residue of the following sequence can be input in the next time step, after the delimiter symbol. Thus, all subject sequences of the database can be pipelined with only one time step delay between two consecutive sequences.

The systolic array proposed by Benkrid et al. (2008) has 90 PEs and is capable of comparing a sequence with 1024 residues against a 1440 nodes profile HMM. This solution was designed using Verilog and synthesized into a Virtex-II Pro 2VP100 FPGA with a 100MHz clock frequency, yielding a maximum performance of 5.2 GCUPS (GigaCUPS). Oliver et al. (2009) implemented their accelerator in Verilog, targeting the Xilinx Virtex-II XC2V6000 FPGA with a clock frequency of 74MHz. Their array has 72 PEs to process profile HMMs with up to 236 nodes against sequences of 8192 residues, achieving a performance of 3.95 GCUPS.

4.3. Systolic Array with Pipelined PE and Interleaved Sequences

Jacob et al. (2007) proposed a hardware accelerator for the Viterbi algorithm, also using the systolic array structure and eliminating the state J, as the works described in the previous section. The main contribution of their approach is that they divide each PE into pipeline stages, in order to increase the clock frequency of the design and, consequently, improve the performance of the accelerator.

The throughput of a FPGA-based implementation can be increased by pipelining its datapath, in order to reduce the clock period of the design. However, the data dependences of the Viterbi algorithm make it impossible to pipeline the PEs, while processing the cells of a single sequence-profile comparison. For example, assume the systolic array has pipelined PEs, each with several stages. If the anti-diagonal d enters the first stage of the PEs at cycle c, then at cycle $c + 1$ the computation for the cells in the anti-diagonal d proceeds to the second stage of the PEs. At the same cycle, the anti-diagonal $d + 1$ cannot enter the first stage, since it depends on the cells in d, which are still being computed.

The authors introduced an approach to pipeline the PEs and exploit parallelism inside them, while satisfying the Viterbi algorithm data dependencies. The pipelined systolic array of PEs simultaneously computes the Viterbi matrices cells of multiple sequences being compared against the same profile HMM. This way, the anti-diagonal d_s enters the first stage of the PE at cycle c, and anti-diagonal $d_{s'}$ at cycle $c + 1$, where s and s' are different sequences being processed. As long as there are as many sequences as is the number of stages in the PE, this approach is successful due to the lack of dependences between different sequences. The input residue stream must be modified in a pre-processing step in order to contain multiple sequences interleaved with each other.

The proposed architecture was implemented in VHDL and synthesized for the Xilinx Virtex-II 6000 FPGA and supports up to 68 four-stage PEs, processing a HMM with at most 544 nodes and a maximum sequence length of 1024 residues. They achieved a clock frequency of 180MHz and the performance of 10.6 GCUPS.

4.4. Systolic Array with Divergences

Like the designs discussed in the previous sections, the FPGA-based approach presented by Eusse et al. (2009) calculates the best alignment score and does not provide the alignment itself of the query sequence against the profile HMM. Nevertheless, the accelerator also produces the alignment limits, which determine the area in the dynamic programming matrices where the best alignment occurs. If the similarity score is significant enough, then the sequence is reprocessed in software to generate the alignment. However, in the software execution of the Viterbi algorithm it is not necessary to compute the whole dynamic programming matrices again. The alignment limits produced by the accelerator are used, in order to calculate only the cells inside the area where the best alignment occurs, saving memory space and execution time.

The alignment limits are obtained by adapting the divergence concept presented in Batista et al. (2008) (Section 2.2.3) to the Viterbi algorithm. Figure 17 illustrates the divergence concept. Given a profile HMM with k nodes and a query sequence of length n, the figure shows the matrices of the Viterbi algorithm. The best alignment of the sequence to the HMM is a path along the cells of the matrices. The limits of the best alignment are expressed by its initial and final rows and

superior and inferior divergences. The initial and final rows indicate the row of the matrices where the alignment starts and ends. The superior and inferior divergences represent how far the alignment departs from the main diagonal, in up and down directions, respectively. These divergences are calculated as the difference $i-j$ between the row (i) and column (j) coordinates of the matrix cell. The initial and final rows and the superior and inferior divergences of the alignment determine the alignment region, shown in shadow in the figure. This region contains the cells of the score matrices M, I, and D that must be computed in order to obtain the best alignment. The other Viterbi algorithm vectors are also limited by the initial and final rows, as well.

The proposed architecture consists of the systolic array of PEs, implementing a simplified version of the Viterbi algorithm without the state J. Besides computing the scores, each PE also calculates the alignment limits. These limits are computed as new dynamic programming matrices and vectors.

The accelerator was implemented with a parameterized VHDL code, in which the word bit-width, the number of PEs and the size of the memories can be modified at synthesis time. The system was designed in VHDL and prototyped on a Altera Stratix II EP2S180F1508C3 FPGA, obtaining a clock frequency of 67MHz for 85 PEs. The system can process HMMs with up to 2295 nodes and sequences with maximum length of 8192 amino acids, achieving a performance of 5.8 GCUPS.

4.5. Two-Pass Systolic Array

Maddimsetty et al. (2006) proposed a two-pass accelerator to reduce the error induced by the elimination of the J state. Their technique allows the detection of the sequences that would produce a multiple hit alignment when compared to a profile HMM, but, if limited to only one hit,

Figure 17. Alignment limits and alignment region for a HMM with k nodes and a sequence of length n (Eusse et al., 2009)

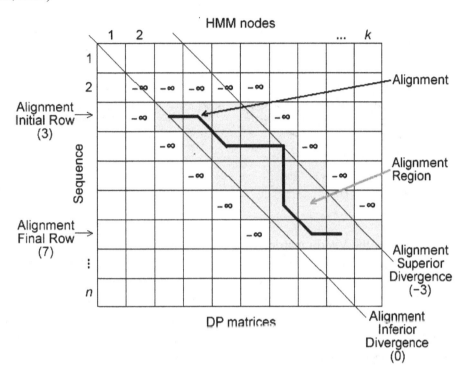

would obtain a low score and be discarded for not satisfying the threshold.

The profile HMM model is modified in order to compute the total score of the best two matches of subsequences of the query sequence to the original profile HMM. If this score is higher than the score obtained with only one hit, then the sequence is accepted, based on the assumption that it will produce a significant multiple hit alignment.

The two-pass accelerator can be viewed as running the Viterbi algorithm on a doubled version of the original profile HMM, without the state J. The two-pass profile HMM in showed in Figure 18 and consists of two copies of the original HMM (with the J state removed). The two copies are connected by a linker state L that permits skipping residues from the query sequence between the two matches. The accelerator can be implemented using a design similar to the systolic array structure.

Based on technology assumptions about current FPGAs, the authors evaluated the design of a systolic array of 50 PEs running at a clock frequency of 200MHz, and obtained an estimated performance of 5 to 20 GCUPS.

4.6. Systolic Array with Recalculation

Sun et al. (2009) proposed a FPGA accelerator to the Viterbi algorithm, based on a systolic array structure with special units to handle data access and recalculation, in order to correct the error caused by the elimination of the state J. The authors argue that the feedback loop induced by the J state rarely occurs in the sequence-profile comparison.

Their architecture speculatively computes all the cells in the same anti-diagonal in parallel (similar to the previous works), assuming that the feedback loop induced by the state J does not take place. After computing the scores of a

Figure 18. Two-pass profile HMM to reduce the error caused by J state elimination

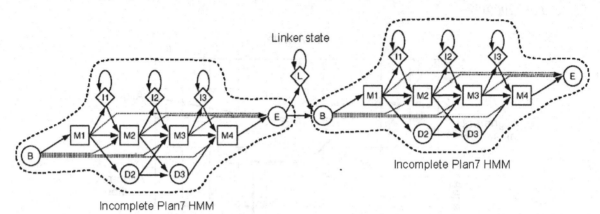

set of consecutive rows of the Viterbi matrices, the system checks if the feedback loop actually occurred. That is, the system detects if the best alignment so far should go through the state J and, consequently, the B state score should be calculated using the J state score.

If the feedback loop indeed occurred, a recalculation unit initiates a rollback mechanism to discard the scores of the cells computed with error, and updates the score of state B, this time considering the J state. It also restarts the computation in the systolic array, so that the PEs will recalculate the cells in the matrices rows with inaccurate scores. With this approach, the system ensures the correctness of the resulting similarity score.

The accelerator was coded in VHDL and synthesized to a Xilinx Virtex 5 110-T FPGA, with 25 PEs and clock frequency of 130MHz. The performance achieved was 3.2 GCUPS.

4.7. Complete Plan7 HMM

Oliver et al. (2008) proposed a FPGA-based accelerator that implements the Viterbi algorithm for the complete Plan7 HMM. Their accelerator acts as a filter that outputs the similarity score between a profile HMM and a sequence, as the previous solutions.

Because of the data dependences of the complete Plan7 Viterbi algorithm, low parallelism can be exploited inside the comparison of a sequence to a profile HMM. Therefore the authors propose to execute several comparisons in parallel, that is, to process different sequences against the same HMM at the same time. Since there are no data dependences between these comparisons, this approach exploits the coarse-grained parallelism inherent in the processing of different sequences.

Each PE computes all the cells of the matrices in the Viterbi algorithm, for a different sequence. All PEs are synchronized to process the same HMM state at the same clock cycle. This PE is more complex and resource demanding than those in the systolic array structure of previous works, since it computes the scores for all states in the profile HMM, including the state J.

The proposed accelerator was designed in Verilog and targeted to two FPGAs, Xilinx Spartan-3 XC3S1500 and XC3S4000, achieving a clock frequency of 70 MHz. In the first device, a system with 10 PEs was generated to process HMMs with up to 256 nodes, obtaining a performance of 700 MCUPS (MegaCUPS). In the second FPGA, 13 PEs were generated to process HMMs with up to 1024 nodes, achieving a performance of 910 MCUPS. In this last device, designs with 30 PEs were also generated to handle HMMs with

Table 3. Comparative overview of the sequence-profile comparison accelerators

Paper	Approach	Number of PEs	Max HMM nodes	Max sequence length	Clock rate (MHz)	Performance (GCUPS)	FPGA
Benkrid et al.(2008)	Systolic array without J state	90	1440	1024	100	5.2	Xilinx Virtex-II Pro 2VP100
Oliver et al. (2009)	Systolic array without J state	72	236	8192	74	3.95	Xilinx Virtex-II XC2V6000
Jacob et al. (2007)	Systolic array with interleaved sequences	68	544	1024	180	10.6	Xilinx Virtex-II 6000
Eusse et al. (2009)	Systolic array with alignment coordinates	85	2295	8192	67	5.8	Altera Stratix-II EP2S180F1508C3
Maddimsetty et al. (2006)	Two-pass systolic array	50	Not reported	Not reported	200 (estimated)	5 to 20 (estimated)	Not synthesized
Sun et al. (2009)	Systolic array with recalculation	25	Not reported	Not reported	130	3.2	Xilinx Virtex-5 110-T
Oliver et al. (2008)	Complete Plan7 HMM	10 to 30	256 to 1024	Not reported	70	0.7 to 2.1	Xilinx Spartan-3 XC3S1500/4000

at most 512 nodes, producing a performance of 2.1 GCUPS.

4.8. Comparative Overview

Table 3 summarizes the FPGA-based sequence-profile comparison proposals discussed in Sections 4.2 to 4.7 and presents a comparative overview of them.

The second column of Table 3 describes the main approach used in the corresponding accelerator. All accelerators act as filters and compute the alignment score, but do not produce the alignment itself. Only the solution proposed by Eusse et al. (2010) produces the alignment limits besides the score, reducing the computations that must be performed in software. All accelerators, except the last one, use the systolic array of PEs structure. Among the systolic array implementations, the solution of Jacobi et al. (2007) is the only one that implements a pipelined PE to process interleaved sequences. All systolic array accelerators eliminate the state J of the Plan7 HMM, however the systems proposed by Maddimsetty et al. (2006) and Sun

at al. (2009) reduce or correct the error produced by this simplification. Only Oliver et al. (2008) implement the complete Plan7 HMM Viterbi algorithm (including the state J).

The number of PEs implemented in each accelerator is indicated in the third column of the table. This number is limited by the FPGA capacity and by the memory banks available in the device. Considering the solutions based on the systolic array structure, the number of PEs ranges from 25 to 90. As expected, the accelerator with the greatest number of PEs (Benkrid et al., 2008) implements the basic approach of computing the anti-diagonals in parallel, without additional mechanisms. This way, the design of the PE is simple and consumes a reduced area in the FPGA, permitting the instantiation of many PEs. Eusse et al. (2010) were able to implement a good number of PE (85), considering that their PEs also include the alignment limits computation. Among the solutions that use the systolic array, the accelerator of Sun et al. (2009) has the smallest number of PEs. This was probably a consequence of the implementation of the special units for data access and recalculation, consuming a fraction of the FPGA capacity. Oliver at al. (2008) implemented a few PEs in their accelerator, which executes the complete Plan7 Viterbi algorithm. Their PE is more resource demanding than those in the systolic array solutions, since it computes the scores for all states in the profile HMM.

The size of the sequence-profile comparison problem is expressed by the number of nodes of the profile HMM and the sequence length. The maximum size supported by the proposed FPGA systems is informed in the fourth and fifth columns of Table 3. These values impose restrictions on the profile HMM models and sequences that can be processed in each accelerator. The system proposed by Eusse et al. (2010) supports profile HMM with many more nodes than the other solutions, and also handles long sequences.

The maximum clock frequency obtained by the system and the peak performance achieved (expressed in GCUPS) are shown in columns 6 and 7. Considering the designs that were synthesized to FPGAs, the clock frequency achieved ranges from 67 to 180 MHz.

The HMMER software (Section 2.3.3) is reported to achieve 24 MCUPs, running on a Pentium 4 processor with 3 GHz and 1 GB of RAM memory (Oliver et al., 2009). It can be considered a baseline solution for the performance evaluation. Comparing the performance of the FPGA implementations against the baseline solution, we see that most accelerators achieve a performance improvement of two orders of magnitude.

The accelerator described in Jacob et al. (2007) has the highest clock frequency (180 MHz), since the PE computation is divided into four stages of a pipeline. Consequently, it achieves the best performance among all solutions. Comparing the results produced by Benkrid et al. (2008) and Jacob et al. (2007), we see that the second yields a 2-fold increase in the performance, even though the first one has more PEs. These results demonstrate that exploiting pipelining is crucial to improve the performance of the system.

The system proposed by Sun et al. (2009) has the worst performance, among the solutions based on the systolic array, due to the small number of PEs implemented. A more accurate performance measurement may produce even worse results, since the reported performance ignored the recalculation overhead.

Oliver at al. (2008) report the worst performance among all accelerators, since their system has few PEs working in parallel. From the performance results, it becomes clear that without the data dependence induced by state J of the Plan7 HMM, better performances can be achieved, since much more parallelism can be exploited in the execution of the Viterbi algorithm.

Finally, the last column shows the target FPGA devices used for the synthesis of the accelerators. All proposed accelerators were synthesized to FPGAs, with the exception of the work of Maddimsetty et al. (2006), which estimated the clock frequency and the performance of the system.

5. CONCLUSION AND PERSPECTIVES

Many biological data analysis algorithms exhibit a great amount of fine-grained parallelism. The arithmetic is mostly composed of integer operations on small data width operands, and floating point operations are generally not required. Since FPGAs are suitable for implementing these regular structures, FPGA-based accelerators have exhibited extremely good performance for time consuming Bioinformatics algorithms related to DNA or protein sequence analysis over a huge volume of data. These accelerators have demonstrated that FPGAs can be a very attractive alternative compared or in complement to supercomputers or clusters in both academic and industrial projects dedicated to this domain. The BioXL/H system from Biocceleration (2009) and the DeCypher system from TimeLogic (2009) are two examples of commercial FPGA-based implementations available to Bioinformatics applications.

In this chapter, we discussed in detail several state-of-the-art accelerators for two fundamental problems in Bioinformatics: pairwise sequence comparison and sequence-profile comparison. As discussed in this chapter, most of the accelerators in the literature are designed as systolic arrays and they are able to accommodate up to 248 processing elements. Impressive speedups of up to 500 were obtained, when compared to the software-only based approach. This shows that FPGA-based designs are an extremely good alternative to increase drastically the performance of Bioinformatics algorithms.

5.1 Future Trends and Open Problems

Even though the first FPGA-based accelerators for Bioinformatics applications appeared in 1992 and impressive speedups have been obtained, this is still a very active research area, with many challenging problems yet to be solved.

A very important open problem that must be addressed is the reduction of the time needed to produce correct and functional code for FPGAs. This time is still very high, if compared to software-only approaches. Regarding this issue, a clear tendency for Bioinformatics applications is the focus on customizable designs or even skeletons where the structure of the basic systolic array processor is provided and the programmer can concentrate efforts on the distinguishing characteristics of his/her design. Combined with high-level languages such as System-C and Handel-C, the time to produce the accelerators can be substantially reduced.

Another very important issue is the exploitation of the FPGA's reconfiguration capabilities. Although current FPGA boards do support dynamic reconfiguration, most accelerators for pairwise or sequence-profile comparison do not exploit this characteristic. Usually, the parameters in the customizable designs are set statically, at synthesis time. Solutions that fully exploit this feature in order to enhance the system flexibility or capacity are yet to be proposed.

Another challenge in the design of FPGA-based accelerators for biological sequence analysis is that, in order to achieve large speedups, a high I/O bandwidth between the host system and the FPGA is needed. If the bandwidth to feed the FPGA with sequences and models is insufficient, the accelerator will likely remain bandwidth-constrained and will not be able to process data at its maximum potential capacity. The tendency is to overcome this issue using solutions with a strong coupling between the FPGA and the host system and/or a highly efficient communication interface between them.

Finally, most of the FPGA-based accelerators for either pairwise or sequence-profile comparison output only the score. As discussed throughout this chapter, the retrieval of the alignment is usually left to the software. Most authors argue that the retrieval of alignments in hardware would require the storage of the dynamic programming matrices in the FPGA internal memory, limiting severely the size of the sequences compared. This line of arguing contains a clear fallacy since, in the literature, there are algorithms, such as the one proposed by Myers and Miller (1988), that retrieve alignments in linear space. The basic idea of linear-space or memory-limited algorithms is the combination of limited matrix storage and reprocessing in order to produce the alignments. These algorithms were implemented successfully in software. Therefore, in our opinion, a crucial open question that is worth deeper investigation is the possibility of retrieving the alignment for long biological sequences efficiently in FPGAs. This is surely not an easy task since it will probably require the adaptation of existent algorithms or even the proposal of entirely new ones.

REFERENCES

Batista, R. B., Boukerche, A., & Melo, A. C. M. A. (2008). A parallel strategy for biological sequence alignment in restricted memory space. *Journal of Parallel and Distributed Processing, 68*(4), 548–561. doi:10.1016/j.jpdc.2007.08.007

Benkrid, K., Liu, Y. & Benkrid, A. (2009). A highly parameterized and efficient FPAG-based skeleton for pairwise biological sequence alignment. *IEEE Transactions on Very large Integration Systems, 17*(4), 561-570.

Benkrid, K., Velentzas, P., & Kasap, S. (2008). A high performance reconfigurable core for motif searching using profile HMM. In *NASA/ESA Conference on Adaptive Hardware and Systems,* (pp. 285-292).

Biocceleration. (2009). *BioXL/H*. Retrieved October 10, 2009, from http://www.biocceleration.com

Boukerche, A., Correa, J. M., Melo, A. C. M. A., Jacobi, R. P., & Rocha, A. F. (2007a). Reconfigurable architecture for biological sequence comparison in reduced memory space. In *IEEE International Parallel & Distributed Processing Symposium, Workshop NIDISC.*

Boukerche, A., Correa, J. M., Melo, A. C. M. A., Jacobi, R. P., & Rocha, A. F. (2007b). An FPGA-based accelerator for multiple biological sequence alignment with DIALIGN. In *International Conference on High Performance Computing,* (LNCS 4873, pp. 71-82).

Derrien, S., & Quinton, P. (2007). Parallelizing HMMER for hardware acceleration on FPGAs. In *International Conference on Application-specific Systems, Architectures and Processors,* (pp. 10-17).

Durbin, R., Eddy, S., Krogh, A., & Mitchison, G. (1998). *Biological Sequence Analysis*. Cambridge, UK: Cambridge University Press. doi:10.1017/CBO9780511790492

Eddy, S. (2003). *HMMER User's Guide*. Retrieved October 15, 2009, from http://hmmer.janelia.org

Eusse, J. F., Moreano, N., Melo, A. C. M. A., & Jacobi, R. P. (2010). A HMMER hardware accelerator using divergences. In *Design, Automation & Test in Europe Conference.*

Fickett, J. W. (1984). Fast optimal alignments. *Nucleic Acids Research, 12*(1), 175–179. doi:10.1093/nar/12.1Part1.175

Finn, R. D. (2008). The Pfam protein families database. *Nucleic Acids Research, 36,* 281–288. doi:10.1093/nar/gkm960

Gotoh, O. (1982). An improved algorithm for matching biological sequences. *Journal of Molecular Biology, 162,* 705–708. doi:10.1016/0022-2836(82)90398-9

Gusfield, D. (1997). *Algorithms on Strings, Trees, and Sequences: Computer Science and Computational Biology*. Cambridge, UK: Cambridge University Press. doi:10.1017/CBO9780511574931

Hoang, D. T., & Lopresti, D. P. (1992). FPGA implementation of systolic sequence alignment. In *Field-Programmable Gate Arrays: Architectures and Tools for Rapid Prototyping,* (LNCS 705, pp. 183-191). Berlin: Springer-Verlag.

Hunter, L. (1993). *Artificial Intelligence and Molecular Biology*. Cambridge, MA: MIT Press.

Jacob, A. C., Lancaster, J. M., Buhler, J. D., & Chamberlain, R. D. (2007). Preliminary results in accelerating profile HMM search on FPGAs. In *IEEE International Symposium on Parallel and Distributed Processing,* (pp. 1-8).

Jiang, X., Liu, X., Xu, L., Zhang, P., & Sun, N. (2007). A reconfigurable accelerator for Smith-Waterman algorithm. *IEEE Transactions on Circuits and Systems II, 54*(12), 1077–1081. doi:10.1109/TCSII.2007.909857

Krogh, A. (1994). Hidden Markov models in computational biology: applications to protein modeling. *Journal of Molecular Biology, 235*(5), 1501–1531. doi:10.1006/jmbi.1994.1104

Kung, H. T. (1982). Why systolic architectures? *IEEE Computer, 15*(1), 37–46.

Lipton, R. J., & Lopresti, D. (1985). A systolic array for rapid string comparison. In *Chapel Hill Conference on VLSI*, (pp. 363-376).

Maddimsetty, R. P., Buhler, J., Chamberlain, R. D., Franklin, M. A., & Harris, B. (2006). Accelerator design for protein sequence HMM search. In *International Conference on Supercomputing*, (pp. 288-296).

Morgenstern, B., Frech, K., Dress, A., & Werner, T. (1998). DIALIGN: Finding local similarities by multiple sequence alignment. *Bioinformatics (Oxford, England), 14*, 290–294. doi:10.1093/bioinformatics/14.3.290

Mount, D. (2004). *Bioinformatics: Sequence and Genome Analysis*. New York: C. S. Harbor Lab Press.

Myers, E. W., & Miller, W. (1988). Optimal alignments in linear space. *Computer Applications in the Biosciences, 4*(1), 11–17.

Needleman, S., & Wunsh, C. (1970). A general method applicable to the search for similarities in the amino acid sequence of two proteins. *Journal of Molecular Biology, 48*, 443–453. doi:10.1016/0022-2836(70)90057-4

Oliver, T., Schmidt, B., Jakop, Y., & Maskell, D. (2009). High speed biological sequence analysis with hidden Markov models on reconfigurable platforms. *IEEE Transactions on Information Technology in Biomedicine, 13*(5), 740–746. doi:10.1109/TITB.2007.904632

Oliver, T., Schmidt, B., & Maskell, D. (2005). Hyper customized processor for bio-sequence database scanning on FPGAs. In *ACM/SIGDA International Symposium on Field Programming Gate Arrays*, (pp. 229-237).

Oliver, T., Yeow, L. Y., & Schmidt, B. (2008). Integrating FPGA acceleration into HMMer. *Parallel Computing, 34*, 681–691. doi:10.1016/j.parco.2008.08.003

Puttegowda, K., Worek, W., Pappas, N., Dandapani, A., & Athanas, P. (2003). A run-time reconfigurable system for gene-sequence searching. In *International Conference on VLSI Design*, (pp. 561-566).

Rabiner, L. R. (1989). A tutorial on hidden Markov models and selected applications in speech recognition. *Proceedings of the IEEE, 77*(2), 257–286. doi:10.1109/5.18626

Smith, T. F., & Waterman, M. S. (1981). Identification of common molecular subsequences. *Journal of Molecular Biology, 147*(1), 195–197. doi:10.1016/0022-2836(81)90087-5

Sun, Y., Li, P., Gu, G., Wen, Y., Liu, Y., & Liu, D. (2009). Accelerating HMMer on FPGAs using systolic array based architecture. In *IEEE International Symposium on Parallel and Distributed Processing*, (pp. 1-8).

TimeLogic. (2009). *DeCypher FPGA Biocomputing Systems*. Retrieved October 10, 2009, from http://www.timelogic.com

Yamaguchi, Y., Maruyama, T., & Konagaya, A. (2002). High speed homology search with FPGAs. In *Pacific Symposium on Biocomputing*, (pp. 271-282).

Zhang, P., Tan, G., & Gao, G. R. (2007). Implementation of the Smith-Waterman algorithm on a reconfigurable supercomputing platform. In *Conference on High Performance Networking and Computing*, (pp. 39-48).

Chapter 13
Formal Analysis of Real–Time Systems

Osman Hasan
National University of Science and Technology (NUST), Pakistan

Sofiène Tahar
Concordia University, Canada

ABSTRACT

Real-time systems usually involve a subtle interaction of a number of distributed components and have a high degree of parallelism, which makes their performance analysis quite complex. Thus, traditional techniques, such as simulation, or state-based formal methods usually fail to produce reasonable results. The main limitation of these approaches may be overcome by conducting the performance analysis of real-time systems using higher-order-logic theorem proving. This chapter is mainly oriented towards this emerging trend and it provides the details about analyzing both functional and performance related properties of real-time systems using a higher-order-logic theorem prover (HOL). For illustration purposes, the Stop-and-Wait protocol, which is a classical example of real-time systems, has been considered as a case-study.

INTRODUCTION

Real-time systems can be characterized as systems for which the correctness of an operation is dependant not only on its functional correctness but also on the time taken. Some commonly used real-time system applications include embedded systems, digital circuits with uncertain delays, communication protocols and dynamic reconfigurable systems.

Until the last decade, real-time systems were analyzed using traditional techniques, such as paper-and-pencil proof methods or simulation. The paper-and-pencil based proof techniques usually have some risk of an erroneous analysis due to the human-error factor. Similarly, accuracy of analysis cannot be guaranteed in computer simulation as well since the fundamental idea in this approach is to approximately answer a query by analyzing a large number of samples. These inaccuracy limitations of paper-and-pencil proof methods and simulation techniques may lead to

DOI: 10.4018/978-1-60960-086-0.ch013

disastrous consequences in today's world, where real-time systems are extensively being used in safety critical and extremely sensitive applications such as medicine, military and transportation. In fact, some unfortunate incidents have already happened in this regard. One of the well-known incidents is the loss, in December 1999, of the Mars Polar Lander; a $165 million NASA space-craft launched to survey Martian conditions. The Mars Polar Lander is believed to be lost mainly because of its engine shutdown while it was still 40 meters above the Mars surface. The engine shutdown happened due to the vibrations caused by the deployment of the Lander's legs, i.e., a probabilistic behavior that gave false indication that spacecraft had landed. Some other such incidents related to inaccurate or inadequate analysis of real-time systems include the loss of $125 million Mars Climate Orbiter in 1998 and the performance degradation of Microsoft's IIS indexing service DLL due to a buffer overflow problem caused by the "Code Red" worm in 2001, which resulted in a loss of over $2 billion to the company. A more recent incident is the faulty operation of the fly-by-wire primary flight control real-time software of a Boeing 777, operated by the Malaysia Air-lines, in August 2005, which could have resulted in the loss of 177 passenger lives if the pilot had not manually taken over the autopilot program in time. All these incidents happened because the erroneous conditions were not caught during the analysis phase, due to the imprecise nature of the analysis techniques, and thus bugs appeared in the original product. Therefore, techniques like paper-and-pencil proof methods and simulation should not be relied upon for the analysis of real-time systems especially when they are used in safety or financial critical domains.

Formal methods are capable of conducting precise system analysis and thus overcome the above mentioned limitations. The main principle behind formal analysis of a system is to construct a computer based mathematical model of the given system and formally verify, within a computer,

that this model meets rigorous specifications of intended behavior. A number of elegant approaches for the formal analysis of real-time systems can be found in the open literature using state-based or theorem proving techniques (e.g., Alur, 1992; Cardell-Oliver, 1992; Amnell, 2001; Beyer, 2003; Kwiatkowska, 2002; Bucci, 2005; Kwiatkowska, 2007; Hasan, 2009). However, some of these existing formal verification tools are only capable of specifying and verifying hard deadlines, i.e., properties where a late response is considered to be incorrect. Whereas, in the case of performance analysis of real-time systems, soft deadlines, i.e., properties that provide the quality of service in terms of probabilistic quantities or averages, play a vital role. Also, the above mentioned state-based approaches are limited by reduced expressive power of their automata based or Petri net based specification formalism. On the other hand, the higher-order-logic theorem proving based technique [Hasan, 2009] tends to overcome the above mentioned limitations of existing formal real-time system analysis techniques.

The main principle behind the higher-order logic theorem proving based approach is to leverage upon the high expressiveness of higher-order logic to formally specify and reason about the temporal properties and random behaviors of the present age complex real-time systems. This approach is primarily based upon the previous work reported for the functional verification of hard real-time systems [Cardell-Oliver, 1992], the formalization of random variables [Hurd, 2002] and the verification of expectation properties for discrete random variables [Hasan, 2008]. The idea is to formally specify the given real-time system as a logical conjunction of higher-order-logic predicates [Cadell-Oliver, 1992], whereas each one of these predicates defines an autonomous component or process of the given real-time system, while representing the unpredictable or random elements in the system as formalized random variables [Hurd, 2002]. The functional correctness and the performance related properties for various parameters for this formal model can then be verified using an interactive theorem prover with the help of the useful theorems already proved in [Cadell-Oliver, 1992; Hurd, 2002; Hasan, 2008]. Since the analysis is conducted within the core of a mechanical theorem prover, there would be no question about the soundness or the precision of the results. Also, there is no equivalence verification required between the models used for functional verification and performance evaluation as the same formal model is used for both of these analyses in this approach.

The main focus of this chapter is on this theorem proving based real-time system analysis approach. In order to illustrate the utilization and practical effectiveness of the presented approach, the chapter includes the functional verification and performance analysis of a variant of the Stop-and-Wait protocol [Widjaja, 2004], which is a classical example of a real-time system. The Stop-and-Wait protocol utilizes the principles of error detection and retransmission and is a fundamental mechanism for reliable communication between computers. Indeed, it is one of the most important parts of the Internet's Transmission Control Protocol (TCP). The main motivation behind selecting the Stop-and-Wait protocol as a case study is its widespread popularity in the literature regarding real-time system analysis methodologies. The Stop-and-Wait protocol and some of its closely related variants have been checked formally for functional verification using theorem proving [Cadell-Oliver, 1992], state-based formal approaches (e.g. [Gallasch, 2006]) and a combination of both techniques (e.g. [Havelund, 1996]) and their performance has been analyzed using a number of innovative state-based formal or semi-formal techniques (e.g. [Wells, 2002]). In all of these previous works, only one aspect, i.e., either functional correctness or performance was analyzed. However, this chapter utilizes a single formal model of the Stop-and-Wait protocol and presents the analysis of its functional correctness

and performance by leveraging upon the expressiveness of higher-order logic.

The chapter is organized as follows. Section 2 provides some preliminaries including an overview of higher-order logic theorem proving and Stop-and-Wait protocol. The higher-order-logic theorem proving based technique for the analysis of real-time systems is outlined in Section 3. Next in Section 4, we present a higher-order-logic specification of the Stop-and-Wait protocol and formally verify its functional and performance related properties using a theorem prover in Sections 5 and 6, respectively. Finally, Section 7 will conclude the chapter.

PRELIMINARIES

In this section, we provide an overview of higher-order-logic theorem proving and the HOL theorem prover that will be used in the rest of this chapter. The intent is to provide a brief introduction to these topics along with some notation that is going to be used later.

Higher-Order-Logic Theorem Proving

Theorem proving [Gordon, 1989] is a widely used formal verification technique. The system that needs to be analyzed is mathematically modeled in an appropriate logic and the properties of interest are verified using computer based formal tools. The use of formal logics as a modeling medium makes theorem proving a very flexible verification technique as it is possible to formally verify any system that can be described mathematically. The core of theorem provers usually consists of some well-known axioms and primitive inference rules. Soundness is assured as every new theorem must be created from these basic axioms and primitive inference rules or any other already proved theorems or inference rules.

The verification effort of a theorem varies from trivial to complex depending on the underlying logic [Harrison, 2009]. For instance, first-order logic is restricted to propositional calculus and terms (constants, function names and free variables) and is semi-decidable. A number of sound and complete first-order logic automated reasoners are available that enable completely automated proofs. More expressive logics, such as higher-order logic, can be used to model a wider range of problems than first-order logic, but theorem proving for these logics cannot be fully automated and thus involves user interaction to guide the proof tools. For performance and probabilistic analysis, we need to formalize (mathematically model) random variables as functions and formalize characteristics of random variables, such as probability distribution functions and expectation, etc., by quantifying over random variable functions. Henceforth, first-order logic does not support such formalization and we need to use higher-order logic to formalize probabilistic analysis.

HOL Theorem Prover

In this chapter, we use the HOL theorem prover [Gordon, 1993] to conduct all the real-time system performance analysis related formalization and verification. HOL is an interactive theorem prover developed by Mike Gordon at the University of Cambridge for conducting proofs in higher-order logic. It utilizes the simple type theory of Church [Church, 1940] along with Hindley-Milner polymorphism [Milner, 1977] to implement higher-order logic. HOL has been successfully used as a verification framework for both software and hardware as well as a platform for the formalization of pure mathematics.

Secure Theorem Proving

In order to ensure secure theorem proving, the logic in the HOL system is represented in the strongly-typed functional programming language ML [Paulson, 1996]. An ML abstract data type is used to represent higher-order-logic theorems and the only way to interact with the theorem prover is by executing ML procedures that operate on values of these data types. The HOL core consists of only 5 basic axioms and 8 primitive inference rules, which are implemented as ML functions. Soundness is assured as every new theorem must be verified by applying these basic axioms and primitive inference rules or any other previously verified theorems/inference rules.

Terms

There are four types of HOL terms: constants, variables, function applications, and lambda-terms (denoted function abstractions). Polymorphism, types containing type variables, is a special feature of higher-order logic and is thus supported by HOL. Semantically, types denote sets and terms denote members of these sets. Formulas, sequences, axioms, and theorems are represented by using terms of Boolean types.

Theories

A HOL theory is a collection of valid HOL types, constants, axioms and theorems and is usually stored as a file in computers. Users can reload a HOL theory in the HOL system and utilize the corresponding definitions and theorems right away. The concept of HOL theory allows us to build upon existing results in an efficient way without going through the tedious process of regenerating these results using the basic axioms and primitive inference rules.

HOL theories are organized in a hierarchical fashion. Any theory may inherit types, definitions and theorems from other theories. Various mathematical concepts have been formalized and saved as HOL theories by the users. These theories are available to a user when he/she first starts a HOL session. The HOL theories of Booleans, lists, sets, positive integers, real numbers, measure and probability are some of the frequently used theories in

Figure 1. HOL symbols and functions

HOL Symbol	Standard Symbol	Meaning
$\wedge$	*and*	Logical *and*
$\vee$	*or*	Logical *or*
$\neg$	*not*	Logical *negation*
::	*cons*	Adds a new element to a list
++	*append*	Joins two lists together
hd L	*head*	Head element of list L
tl L	*tail*	Tail of list L
el n L	*element*	n^{th} element of list L
mem a L	*member*	True if a is a member of list L
length L	*length*	Length of list L
(a, b)	a x b	A pair of two elements
fst	fst (a, b) = a	First component of a pair
snd	snd (a, b) = b	Second component of a pair
λx.t	$\lambda x.t$	Function that maps x to $t(x)$
{x|P(x)}	$\{\lambda x.P(x)\}$	Set of all x such that $P(x)$
num	$\{0, 1, 2, \ldots\}$	Positive Integers data type
real	All Real numbers	Real data type
suc n	$n+1$	Successor of a *num*

analyzing the performance of real-time systems. In fact, one of the primary motivations of selecting the HOL theorem prover for this work was to benefit from these built-in mathematical theories.

HOL Symbols

Figure 1 provides the mathematical interpretations of some frequently used HOL symbols and functions in this chapter.

PROBABILISTIC THEOREM PROVING BASED METHODOLOGY

A real-time system and its environment may be viewed as a bunch of concurrent, communicating processes that are autonomous, i.e., they can communicate asynchronously. The behavior of these processes over time may be specified by higher-order-logic predicates on positive integers [Cadell-Oliver, 1992]. These positive integers represent the ticks of a clock counting physical time in any appropriate units, e.g., nanoseconds. The granularity of the clock's tick is believed to

be chosen in such a way that it is sufficiently fine to detect properties of interest. The behavior of a real-time system can now be formally specified by combining the corresponding process specifications (higher-order-logic predicates) using logical conjunction. In a similar way, additional constraints for the real-time system such as initial conditions or any assumptions, if required to ensure the correct behavior of the model, can also be defined as predicates and combined with its formal specification using logical conjunctions.

The performance analysis of real-time systems is primarily based on probability theory concepts. A hypothetical model of a theorem proving based real-time system performance analysis framework is given in Figure 2, with some of its most fundamental components depicted with shaded boxes. Like all traditional analysis problems, the starting point of performance analysis is also a system description and some intended system properties and the goal is to check if the given system satisfies these properties. For simplicity, we have divided system properties into two categories, i.e., system properties related to discrete

Figure 2. Theorem proving based real-time system performance analysis framework

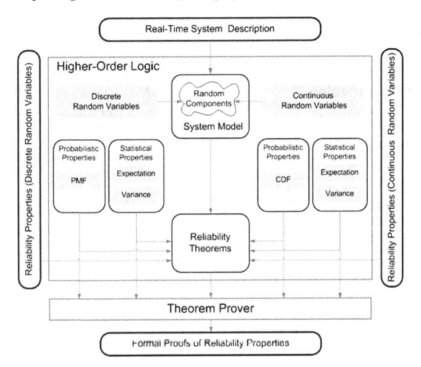

random variables and system properties related to continuous random variables.

The first step in the methodology illustrated in Figure 2 is to construct a model of the given real-time system in higher-order logic. For this purpose, we model the real-time system as a logical conjunction of processes as illustrated above while modeling the random components of the system by random variables. The foremost requirement for this step is the availability of infrastructures that allow us to formalize all kinds of discrete and continuous random variables as higher-order-logic functions, which in turn can be used to represent the random components of the given system in its higher-order-logic model. The second step is to utilize the formal model of the system to express system properties as higher-order-logic theorems. The prerequisite for this step is the ability to express probabilistic and statistical properties related to both discrete and continuous random variables in higher-order-logic. All probabilistic properties of discrete and

continuous random variables can be expressed in terms of their *Probability Mass Functions* (PMFs) and *Cumulative Distribution Functions* (CDFs), respectively. Similarly, most of the commonly used statistical properties can be expressed in terms of the expectation and variance characteristics of the corresponding random variable. Thus, we require the formalization of mathematical definitions of PMF, CDF, expectation and variance for both discrete and continuous random variables in order to be able to express the given system's performance characteristics as higher-order-logic theorems. The third and the final step for conducting performance analysis of a real-time system in a theorem prover is to formally verify the higher-order-logic theorems developed in the previous step using a theorem prover. For this verification, it would be quite handy to have access to a library of some pre-verified theorems corresponding to some commonly used properties regarding probability distribution functions, expectation and variance. Since, we can build upon such a library of theorems and thus speed up the verification process. The formalization details regarding the above mentioned steps are briefly described now.

Discrete Random Variables and the PMF

A random variable is called discrete if its range, i.e., the set of values that it can attain, is finite or at most countably infinite. Discrete random variables can be completely characterized by their PMFs that return the probability that a random variable X is equal to some value x, i.e., $Pr(X = x)$. Discrete random variables are quite frequently used to model randomness in performance analysis. For example, the Bernoulli random variable is widely used to model the fault occurrence in a component and the Binomial random variable may be used to represent the number of faulty components in a lot.

Discrete random variables can be formalized in higher-order-logic as deterministic functions with access to an infinite Boolean sequence B^∞; an infinite source of random bits with data type (*natural* → *bool*) [Hurd, 2002]. These deterministic functions make random choices based on the result of popping the top most bit in the infinite Boolean sequence and may pop as many random bits as they need for their computation. When the functions terminate, they return the result along with the remaining portion of the infinite Boolean sequence to be used by other functions. Thus, a random variable that takes a parameter of type α and ranges over values of type β can be represented by the function

$$F: \alpha \rightarrow B^\infty \rightarrow \beta \times B^\infty$$

For example, a Bernoulli(½) random variable that returns 1 or 0 with probability ½ can be modeled as

$$bit = \lambda s.\ (\text{if shd } s \text{ then } 1 \text{ else } 0,\ stl\ s)$$

where the variable s represents the infinite Boolean sequence and the functions *shd* and *stl* are the sequence equivalents of the list operations '*head*' and '*tail*'. A function of the form $\lambda x.\ t(x)$ represents a lambda abstraction function that maps x to $t(x)$. The function *bit* accepts the infinite Boolean sequence and returns a pair with the first element equal to either 0 or 1 and the second element equal to the unused portion of the infinite Boolean sequence.

The higher-order-logic formalization of the probability theory [Hurd, 2002] also consists of a probability function P from sets of infinite Boolean sequences to *real* numbers between 0 and 1. The domain of P is the set E of events of the probability. Both P and E are defined using the Caratheodory's Extension theorem, which ensures that E is a σ-algebra: closed under complements and countable unions. The formalized P and E can be used to formally verify all the basic axioms of probability. Similarly, they can also be used to prove probabilistic properties for random variables. For example, we can formally verify the following probabilistic property for the function *bit*, defined above,

$$P \{s\ |\ \text{fst (bit } s) = 1\} = ½$$

where $\{x|C(x)\}$ represents a set of all elements x that satisfy the condition C, and the function *fst* selects the first component of a pair.

The above mentioned infrastructure can be utilized to formalize most of the commonly used discrete random variables and verify their corresponding PMF relations. In this chapter, we will utilize the models for Bernoulli and Geometric random variables formalized as higher-order-logic functions *prob_bernoulli* and *prob_geom* and verified using the following PMF relations in [Hurd, 2002] and [Hasan, 2008], respectively.

Theorem 1:
$\forall$ p. $0 \le p \wedge p \le 1 \Rightarrow (P \{s\ |\ \text{fst (prob\_bernoulli } p\ s)\} = p)$

Theorem 2:

$\forall$ n p. $0 \leq p \wedge p \leq 1 \Rightarrow$ (P {s | fst (prob_geom p s) = (n + 1)} = p(1 - p)n)

The Geometric random variable returns the number of Bernoulli trials needed to get one success and thus cannot return 0. This is why we have *(n+1)* in Theorem 2, where *n* is a positive integer {0,1,2,3 …}. Similarly, the probability *p* in Theorem 2 represents the probability of success and thus needs to be greater than 0 for this theorem to be true as has been specified in the precondition.

Continuous Random Variables and the CDF

A random variable is called continuous if it ranges over a continuous set of numbers that contains all real numbers between two limits. Continuous random variables can be completely characterized by their CDFs that return the probability that a random variable X is exactly less than or equal to some value *x*, i.e., *Pr(X $\leq$ x)*. Examples of continuous random variables include measuring *T*, the arrival time of a data packet at a web server *(S$_T$ = {t | 0 $\leq$ t < ∞})* and measuring *V*, the voltage across a resistor *(S$_V$ = { v | -∞ < v < ∞ })*.

The sampling algorithms for continuous random variables are non-terminating and hence require a different formalization approach than discrete random variables, for which the sampling algorithms are either guaranteed to terminate or satisfy probabilistic termination, meaning that the probability that the algorithm terminates is 1. One approach to address this issue is to utilize the concept of the nonuniform random number generation, which is the process of obtaining arbitrary continuous random numbers using a Standard Uniform random number generator. The main advantage of this approach is that we only need to formalize the Standard Uniform random variable from scratch and use it to model other continuous random variables by formalizing the corresponding nonuniform random number generation method.

Based on the above approach, a methodology for the formalization of all continuous random variables for which the inverse of the CDF can be represented in a closed mathematical form is presented in [Hasan, 2007}. The first step in this methodology is the formalization of the Standard Uniform random variable, which can be done by using the formalization approach for discrete random variables and the formalization of the mathematical concept of limit of a *real* sequence [Harrison, 1998]. The formalization details are outlined in [Hasan, 2007].

The second step in the methodology for the formalization of continuous probability distributions is the formalization of the CDF and the verification of its classical properties. This is followed by the formal specification of the mathematical concept of the inverse function of a CDF. This definition along with the formalization of the Standard Uniform random variable and the CDF properties, can be used to formally verify the correctness of the Inverse Transform Method (ITM). The ITM is a well known nonuniform random generation technique for generating nonuniform random variables for continuous probability distributions for which the inverse of the CDF can be represented in a closed mathematical form. Formally, it can be verified for a random variable *X* with CDF *F* using the Standard Uniform random variable *U* as follows

Pr (F^{-1}(U) $\leq$ x) = F(x)

The formalized Standard Uniform random variable can now be used to formally specify any continuous random variable for which the inverse of the CDF can be expressed in a closed mathematical form as $X=F^{-1}(U)$. Whereas, the CDF of this formally specified continuous random variable, *X*, can be verified using simple arithmetic reasoning and the formal proof of the ITM. Based on this approach, Exponential, Uniform, Rayleigh and

Triangular random variables have been formalized and their CDF relations have been verified [Hasan, 2007].

Statistical Properties for Discrete Random Variables

In probabilistic analysis, statistical characteristics play a major role in decision making as they tend to summarize the probability distribution characteristics of a random variable in a single number. Due to their widespread interest, the computation of statistical characteristics has now become one of the core components of every contemporary probabilistic analysis framework.

The expectation for a function of a discrete random variable, which attains values in the positive integers only, is formally defined as follows.

$$\forall X.\ \text{expec } X = \text{suminf} (\lambda n.\ n\ P\ \{s \mid \text{fst } (X\ s) = n\})$$

where the mathematical notions of the probability function P and random variable X have been inherited from [Hurd, 2002], as presented in the previous section. The function *suminf* represents the HOL formalization of the infinite summation of a *real* sequence [Harrison, 1998]. The function *expec* accepts the random variable X with data type $B^{\infty} \rightarrow natural\ x\ B^{\infty}$ and returns a *real* number. The above definition can be used to verify the average values of most of the commonly used discrete random variables [Hasan, 2008]. For example, the average value of the Geometric random variable can be verified as the following theorem.

Theorem 3:
$\forall\ p.\ 0 \leq p \wedge p \leq 1 \Rightarrow (\text{expec } (\lambda s.\ \text{prob\_geom } p\ s) = 1/p)$

In order to verify the correctness of the formal definition of expectation and facilitate reasoning about expectation properties in probabilistic systems, many widely used expectation properties have been formally verified in the HOL theorem prover [Hasan, 2009a]. Namely being the linearity of expectation, Markov and Chebyshev's inequalities, variance and linearity of variance. In this chapter, we utilize the following linearity property out of this rich library of formally verified expectation properties.

Theorem 4:
$\forall\ a\ b\ X.\ \text{expec } (\lambda s.\ (a\ (\text{fst } (X\ s) + b,\ \text{snd } (X\ s)))) = a((\text{expec } X) + b)$

Statistical Properties for Continuous Random Variables

The expectation of a continuous random variable has been formally defined in [Hasan, 2009b] using the Lebesgue integral, which has strong relationship with the measure theory fundamentals [Galambos, 1995]. This definition is general enough to cater for both discrete and continuous random variables and is thus far more superior than the commonly used Rieman integral based definition that is only applicable to continuous random variables with well-defined PDF. Though, the main limitation of the Lebesgue integral based definition is the complex reasoning process involved for verifying expectation properties. This limitation has been tackled in [Hasan, 2009b] and the main idea is to verify two relatively simplified expressions for expectation by building on top of the Lebesgue integral based definition. The first expression is for the case when the given continuous random variable is bounded in the positive interval *[a,b]* and the second one is for an unbounded random variable. Both of these expressions are verified using the fundamentals from measure and Lebesgue integral theories but once verified, they can be utilized to verify expectation properties of any continuous random variable without applying these complex underlying concepts. The usage of these expressions is illustrated by verifying the expected values of Uniform, Triangular and Exponential random variables [Hasan, 2009b].

STOP-AND-WAIT PROTOCOL

This section provides a brief introduction to the Stop-and-Wait protocol [Widjaja, 2004], which will be used as case study for the formal analysis framework presented in the previous section. The Stop-and-Wait is a basic Automatic Repeat Request (ARQ) protocol that ensures reliable data transfers across noisy channels. In a Stop-and-Wait system, both sending and receiving stations have error detection capabilities. The operation is illustrated in Figure 3 using the following notation.

- t_f: Data message transmission time
- t_a: ACK message transmission time
- t_{prop}: One-way signal propagation delay between transmitter and receiver
- t_{proc}: Processing time required for error detection in the received message at both transmitter and receiver ends
- t_{out}: Timeout period

The transmitter sends a data message to the receiver and spends t_f time units in doing so. Then, it stops and waits to receive an acknowl-

Figure 3. Stop-and-Wait operation

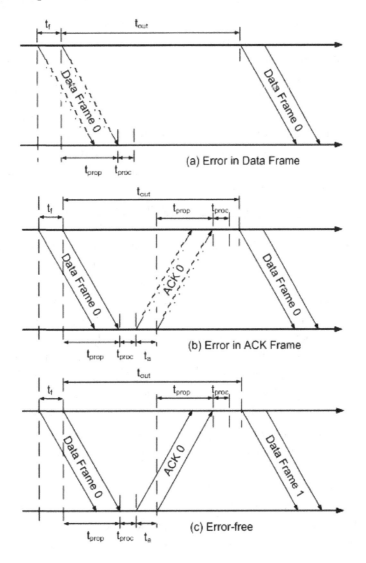

edgement (ACK) of reception of that message from the receiver. If no ACK is received within a given time out, t_{out}, period, the data message is resent by the transmitter and once again it stops and starts waiting for the ACK (Figure 3.a). If an ACK is received within the given t_{out} period then the transmitter checks the received message for errors during the next t_{proc} time units. If errors are detected then the ACK is ignored and the data message is resent by the transmitter after t_{out} expires and once again the transmitter stops and waits for the ACK (Figure 3.b). Thus, the main idea is that the transmitter keeps on retransmitting the same data message, after a pre-defined time-out period, t_{out}, until and unless it receives a corresponding error-free ACK message from the receiver. When an error-free ACK message is finally received then the transmitter transmits the next data message in its queue (Figure 3.c).

The receiver is always waiting to receive data messages. When a new message arrives, the receiver checks it for errors during the next t_{proc} time units. If errors are detected then the data message is ignored and the receiver continues to be in the wait state (Figure 3.a), otherwise it initiates the transmission of an ACK message, which takes t_a time units (Figure 3.b,c).

Under the above mentioned conditions, the ACK message cannot be received before t_{prop} + t_{proc} + t_a + t_{prop} + t_{proc} units of time after sending out a data message. It is, therefore, necessary to set $t_{out} \geq 2(t_{prop} + t_{proc}) + t_a$, i.e., the retransmission must not be allowed to start before the expected arrival time of the ACK is lapsed, for reliable communication between transmitter and receiver.

ARQ allows the transmitting station to transmit a specific number, usually termed as *sending window*, of messages before receiving an ACK frame and the receiving station to receive and store a specific number, usually termed as *receiving window*, of error-free messages even if they arrive out-of-sequence. Generally, both the *sending window* and the *receiving window* are assigned the same value, which is termed as the *window size* of the ARQ protocol. The *window size* for the Stop-and-Wait protocol is 1, as can be observed from its transmitter and receiver behavior descriptions given above.

In order to distinguish between new messages and duplicates of previous messages at the receiver or transmitter, a sequence number is included in the header of both data and ACK messages. It has been shown that, for correct ARQ operation, the number of distinct sequence numbers must be at least equal to twice the *window size*. Thus, the simplest and the most commonly used version of the Stop-and-Wait protocol uses two distinct sequence numbers (0 and 1) and is known as the Alternating Bit Protocol (ABP). The transmitter keeps track of the sequence number of the last data message it had sent, its associated timer and the message itself in case a retransmission is required. Whereas, the receiver keeps track of the sequence number of the next data message that it is expecting to receive. Thus, if an out-of-sequence data message arrives at the receiver, it ignores it and responds with the ACK for the data message that it is expecting to receive. On the other hand, when an in-sequence data message arrives at the receiver, it updates its sequence number by performing a modulo-2 addition with the number 1, i.e., 0 is updated to 1 and 1 is updated to 0. Similarly, if an out-of-sequence ACK message appears at the transmitter, it ignores it and retains the sequence number of the last data message it had sent. Whereas, in the case of the reception of an in-sequence ACK message, the sequence number at the transmitter is also updated by performing a modulo-2 addition by 1, which becomes the sequence number of the next data message as well. More details about sequence numbering in the Stop-and-Wait protocol can be found in [Widjaja, 2004].

The most widely used performance metric for the Stop-and-Wait protocol is the time required for the transmitter to send a single data message and know that it has been successfully received at the receiver. In the case of error-free or noiseless channels, which do not reorder or loose messages (Figure 3.c), the message transmission delay is given by

$$t_f + t_{prop} + t_{proc} + t_a + t_{prop} + t_{proc} \qquad (1)$$

On the other hand, in the presence of noise, every damaged or lost message (data or ACK) will cause a retransmission from the transmitter and thus wastes $t_f + t_{out}$ units of time (Figure 3a,b). Whereas, the final successful transmission will take the amount of time equal to the one given by Equation (1). In order to obtain more concise information about this delay, we consider the probability, p, of a message transmission being in error. This allows us to model the number of retransmissions in the Stop-and-Wait protocol in terms of a Geometric random variable, which returns the number of trials required to achieve the first success, with success probability $1-p$. Therefore, the delay of the Stop-and-Wait protocol can be mathematically expressed as

$$(t_f + t_{out}) (G_{(1-p)} - 1) + t_f + t_{prop} + t_{proc} + t_a + t_{prop} + t_{proc} \qquad (2)$$

where G_x denotes a Geometric random variable with success probability x. The above representation allows us to express the average delay of a single data message in a Stop-and-Wait protocol using the average or mean value of Geometric random variables as follows

$$(t_f + t_{out})p/(1-p) + t_f + t_{prop} + t_{proc} + t_a + t_{prop} + t_{proc} \qquad (3)$$

The main scope of the rest of the chapter is to formally specify the Stop-and-wait protocol, described in this section, as a real-time system and mechanically verify its functional correctness and average message delay relation, given in Equation (3), using the methodology described in the previous section.

FORMAL SPECIFICATION OF THE STOP-AND-WAIT PROTOCOL

Based on the formal probabilistic analysis methodology presented earlier, we formally specify the Stop-and-Wait protocol described in the previous section as a combination of six processes, as shown in Figure 2. The protocol mainly consists of three major modules, i.e., the sender or the transmitter, the receiver and the communication channel. Each one of these modules can be subdivided into two processes as both the sender and the receiver transmit messages and receive them and the channel between the sender and receiver consists of two logical channels: one carrying data messages from the sender to the receiver and one carrying ACK messages in the opposite direction.

Next we present the data type definitions of the six predicates, corresponding to each one of the processes in Figure 4, and finally the formal specification of the Stop-and-Wait protocol, which also includes the predicates for assumptions and initial conditions. We include the timing information associated with every action in these predicates so that the corresponding model can be utilized to reason about the message delay characteristic of the Stop-and-Wait protocol.

Type Definitions

The input to the Stop-and-Wait protocol, *source*, is basically a list of data messages that can be modeled in HOL by a list of *data elements

```
source: *data list
```

where *data list represents any concrete HOL data type such as a record, a character, an integer or an n-bit word. The output of the protocol, *sink*, is also a list of data messages that grows with time as new data messages are delivered to the receiver. It can be modeled in HOL as follows

```
sink: time → *data list
```

Figure 4. Logical structure of an ARQ protocol

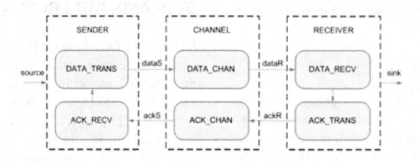

where *time* is assigned the HOL data-type for natural number and represents physical time in this case. This kind of variable, which is time dependant, is termed as a *history* in this chapter. The arrows in Figure 4 between processes represent information that is shared between the sender, channel and receiver. Data messages are transmitted from the sender to the receiver (*dataS, dataR*) and ACK messages are transmitted in the opposite direction (*ackR, ackS*). These messages are transmitted across the Stop-and-Wait protocol in a form of a packet, which can be modeled in HOL as a pair containing a sequence number and a message element

```
packet: natural x *data
```

where a *natural number* is used here for the sequence number and the **data* represents the message. Since we are dealing with an unreliable channel, the output of a channel may or may not be a packet. In order to model the no-packet case in HOL, a data-type *non_packet* is defined, which has only one value, i.e., *one*. Every message can either be of type *packet* or of type *non_packet*.

```
message: packet + non_packet
```

Data Transmission

The process *DATA_TRANS* in Figure 4 characterizes the data transmission behavior of the Stop-and-Wait protocol and the corresponding predicate is defined as follows in Box 1.

The variables *ws* and *sn* represent the *window size* and the number of distinct sequence numbers available for the protocol, respectively. By using these variables in our definitions, instead of their corresponding fixed values of 1 and 2 for the case of the Stop-and-Wait protocol, we attain two benefits. Firstly, it makes our definitions more generic as they can now be used, with minor updates, to formally model the corresponding processes of other ARQ protocols, such as Go-Back-N and Selective-Repeat [Garcia, 2004], as well. Secondly, this allows us to establish a logical implication between our definitions for the six processes (Figure 4) to the corresponding definitions for the Sliding Window protocol, given in [Cadell-Oliver, 1992]. This relationship can be used to inherit the functional correctness theorem, verified for the Sliding Window protocol in [Cadell-Oliver, 1992], for our Stop-and-Wait protocol model and thus saves us a considerable amount of verification time and effort. More details on this are given in the next section. It is important to note that in order to model the correct behavior for the Stop-and-Wait protocol; we will assign the values of 1 and 2 to the variables *ws* and *sn*, respectively, in an assumption that is used in all of the theorems that we verify for the Stop-and-Wait protocol.

The history *datas* represents the data messages transmitted by the sender at any particular time.

Box 1.

```
∀ ws sn dataS s rem i ackS tout tf dtout dtf.
    DATA_TRANS_STOP_WAIT ws sn dataS s rem i ackS tout tf dtout dtf =
      ∀ t. (if ~NULL (tli (i t) (rem t)) ∧ i t < ws then
        (if dtf t = 0 then
          (i (t + 1) = i t + 1) ∧ (dtout (t + 1) = tout - 1) ∧
          (dtf (t + 1) = tf) ∧
          (dataS t =
            new_packet (mod_n_add (s t) (i t) sn) (hdi (i t) (rem t)))
          else
            (i (t + 1) = i t) ∧ (dtout (t + 1) = tout) ∧
            (dtf (t + 1) = dtf (t - 1) ∧ (dataS t = set_non_packet))
      else
        (dtf (t + 1) = tf) ∧ (dataS t = set_non_packet)) ∧
        (if (dtout t = 1) ∨
          good_packet (ackS t) ∧
          mod_n_sub (label (ackS t)) (s t) sn < ws
        then
          (i (t + 1) = i t - 1) ∧ (dtout (t + 1) = tout)
        else
          (i (t + 1) = i t) ∧ (dtout (t + 1) = dtout t - 1))
```

The history s represents, modulo sn, the sequence number of the first unacknowledged data message. Data remaining to be sent at any time is represented by the history *rem* that has type *time→*data list*. whereas, the history i: *time→natural* is used to identify the number of data messages, at any particular time, that have been transmitted by the sender but are still unacknowledged by the receiver. the history *acks* represents the ack messages received by the sender at any particular time. the variables *tout* and *tf* hold the values for the t_{out} and t_f delays, respectively, defined in section 2, and histories *dtout* and *dtf* keep track of the timers associated with these delays.

The HOL functions *tli* and *hdi*, in the above definition, accept two arguments, i.e., a list l and a positive integer n, and return the tail of the list l starting from its nth element and the nth element of the list l, respectively. Whereas the functions *new_packet* and *set_non_packet* declare a mes-

sage of type *packet* (using its two arguments) and *non_packet*, respectively. The function *label* returns the sequence number of a *packet* and the predicate *good_packet* checks the message type of its argument and returns *False* if it is *non_packet* and *True* otherwise. The functions *mod_n_add* and *mod_n_sub* return the modulo-n, where n is their third argument, addition or subtraction results of their first two arguments, respectively.

The definition of *DATA_TRANS_STOP_WAIT* should be read as follows. At all times t, check for the transmission conditions, i.e., there is data available to be transmitted ~*NULL* (*tli* (*i t*) (*rem t*)) and the number of unacknowledged messages is less than the *window size* (*i t < ws*). If the transmission conditions are satisfied, then wait for the next t_f time units, i.e., decrement the timer *dtf* by one at every increment of the time until it reaches 0 and during this time maintain the values of histories *I* and *dtout* while holding the transmission of a new packet to the channel. Once t_f time units have elapsed, i.e., the contents of *dtf* timer become 0, then instantly transmit the *(i t)^(th)* message in the window *hdi (i t) (rem t))* using the sequence number *mod_n_add (s t) (i t) sn)* and increment the value of the history *i* by 1, activate the timer *dtout*, associated with the t_{out} delay, by decrementing its value by 1 and initialize the timer *dtf*, associated with the t_f delay, to its default value of t_f in the next increment of time *t*. On the other hand, for all times *t* for which one of the transmission conditions is not satisfied, no message is transmitted (*set_non_packet*) and the initial value of the *dtf* timer is maintained. The values of *i* and *dtout*, under the no transmission conditions, depend on the event if the timer *dtout* reaches 1 or an ACK message (*good_packet (ackS t)*) is received for a data message that has been sent and not yet acknowledged, i.e., if the difference between the label of (*ackS t*) and the sender's sequence number is less than *ws* (*mod_n_sub (label (ackS t)) (s t) sn < ws*). If this event happens, then the timer *dtout* is initialized to its default value *tout* and the value of *i* is decremented by 1 in the next increment of time *t*. Otherwise, we remain in the wait state until the timer *dtout* expires or a valid ACK is received, while maintaining the value of *i* and decrementing the timer *dtout* by one at every increment of the time *t*.

Data Reception

The process *DATA_RECV* in Figure 4 characterizes the data reception behavior, at the receiver end, of the Stop-and-Wait protocol and the corresponding predicate is defined as follows in Box 2, where the history *dataR* represents the data messages received by the receiver at any particular time. The history *r* represents, modulo *sn*, the sequence number of the data messages that the receiver is expecting to receive. The function *data* returns the data portion of a *packet* and ++ is the symbol for the list *cons* function in HOL.

The definition of *DATA_RECV_STOP_WAIT* should be read as follows. At all times *t*, if (*dataR t*) is not a *non_packet*, i.e., (*good_packet (dataR t)*), and the sequence field of the packet (*dataR t*) is equal to the next number to be output to the sink (*label (dataR t) = r t*), then the data part of the packet is appended to the *sink* list and *r* is updated to the sequence number of the next message expected, i.e., *(r (t + 1) = mod_n_add (r t) 1 sn)*. Otherwise if a valid data packet is not received then the output list *sink* and *r* retain their old values.

We have intentionally assigned a fixed value of 1 to the processing delay (t_p), which specifies the time required for processing an incoming message at the receiver end, in order to simplify the understandability of the proofs presented in the next two sections. If required, the processing

Box 2.

```
∀ sn dataR sink r.
    DATA_RECV_STOP_WAIT sn dataR sink r =
    ∀ t. (if good_packet (dataR t) ∧ (label (dataR t) = r t) then
        (sink (t + 1) = sink t ++ [ data (dataR t) ]) ∧
        (r (t + 1) = mod_n_add (r t) 1 sn)
      else
        (sink (t + 1) = sink t) ∧ (r (t + 1) = r t))
```

delay can be made a variable quantity by using a similar approach that we used for t_{out} and t_f delays in the predicate *DATA_TRANS_STOP_WAIT*.

ACK Transmission

The process *ACK_TRANS* in Figure 4 characterizes the ACK transmission behavior of the Stop-and-Wait protocol and the corresponding predicate is defined as follows in Box 3.

The history *ackR* represents the ACK messages transmitted by the sender. The history *ackty* represents the data part of the ACK message that could be used to specify properties of protocols, such as negative acknowledgements: a type of acknowledgement message which enables the sender to retransmit messages efficiently. The variable *ack_msg* represents a constant data field that is sent along with every ACK message by the receiving station, as in the Stop-and-Wait protocol the ACK messages do not convey any other information except the reception of a data message. The variable *ta* holds the value for the t_a delay, defined in Section 2 and the history *dta* keeps track of the timer associated with this delay. Whereas, the history *rec_flag* keeps track of the reception of a data message at the receiver until a corresponding ACK message is sent.

The definition of *ACK_TRANS_STOP_WAIT* should be read as follows. At all times *t*, the history *ackty* is assigned the value of the default ACK message for the Stop-and-Wait protocol, i.e., *ack_msg*. For all times *t*, if an in-sequence data message arrives at the receiver $\sim(r\ t = r\ (t - 1))$, then instantly transmit an ACK message if the contents of the timer *dta* are 0, otherwise do not issue an ACK and retain the information of receiving a valid data in the *rec_flag* while activating

Box 3.

```
∀ sn ackR r ackty ack_msg ta dta rec_flag.
    ACK_TRANS_STOP_WAIT sn ackR r ackty ack_msg ta dta rec_flag =
    ∀ t. (ackty t = ack_msg) ∧
      (if ~(r t = r (t - 1)) then
        (if dta t = 0 then
          (ackR t = new_packet (mod_n_sub (r t) 1 sn) (ackty t)) ∧
          (dta (t + 1) = ta) ∧ (rec_flag (t + 1) = F)
        else
          (ackR t = set_non_packet) ∧ (dta (t + 1) = dta t - 1) ∧
          (rec_flag (t + 1) = T))
      else
        (if rec_flag t then
          (if dta t = 0 then
            (ackR t = new_packet (mod_n_sub (r t) 1 sn) (ackty t)) ∧
            (dta (t + 1) = ta) ∧ (rec_flag (t + 1) = F)
          else
            (ackR t = set_non_packet) ∧
            (dta (t + 1) = dta t - 1) ∧ (rec_flag (t + 1) = T))
        else
          ackR t = set_non_packet) ∧ (dta (t + 1) = ta) ∧
          (rec_flag (t + 1) = F)))
```

the timer associated with t_a by decrementing its value by 1. On the other hand, for all times t for which no in-sequence data message arrives at the receiver, check if there exists a valid data message that has successfully arrived at the receiver but has not been acknowledged so far (*rec_flag t*). If that is the case, then if the timer associated with the delay t_a has expired (*dta t =0*) then instantly issue the respective ACK message while initializing histories *dta* and *rec_flag* to their default values of *ta* and *False*, respectively. Otherwise wait for the *dta* timer to expire while holding the ACK transmission and the value of history *rec_flag* and decrementing the value of the timer *dta* by 1. On the other hand, if there is no valid data arrival or no pending ACK transmission, then the receiver is not allowed to transmit an ACK message and it assigns the histories *dta* and *rec_flag* to their default values of *ta* and *False*, respectively.

ACK Reception

The process *ACK_RECV* in Figure 4 characterizes the ACK reception behavior, at the sending station, of the Stop-and-Wait protocol and the corresponding predicate is defined as follows in Box 4.

The sender checks the label of every ACK message it receives to find out if it is one of the messages that has been sent and not yet acknowledged, i.e., if the modulo-*sn* difference between the sequence number of (*ackS t*) and the sender's

sequence number is less than *ws*, i.e., (*mod_n_sub (label (ackS t)) (s t) sn < ws*). If this is the case, then the sender slides the window up by updating the sender's history (*s t*) to be the first message not known to be accepted: (*mod_n_add (label (ackS t)) 1 sn*) and by updating (*rem t*), the list of data remaining to be sent. Otherwise, both histories *s* and *rem* retain their previous values. Just like the receiver, we again assigned a fixed value of 1 to the processing delay (t_p).

Communication Channel

The processes *DATA_CHAN* and *ACK_CHAN* in Figure 4 characterize the communication channel connecting the sender and receiver in the Stop-and-Wait, respectively. In this chapter, we are dealing with a channel that has a fixed propagation delay (t_{prop}). We present two definitions for the communication channel for the Stop-and-Wait protocol; the first one models the channel that is noiseless and the second one models a noisy channel, which may lose packets. The noiseless channel predicate is defined as follows in Box 5, where the histories *in*, *out* and *d* represent the input message, output message and the propagation delay for the channel at a particular time, respectively. The variable *tprop* represents the fixed value of channel delay (*d t*) for all *t*. According to the above definition, the output from a channel at time *t* is a copy of the channel's input at time (*t - tprop*).

Box 4.

```
∀ ws sn ackS rem s.
    ACK_RECV_STOP_WAIT ws sn ackS rem s =
    ∀ t. (if good_packet (ackS t) ∧
        mod_n_sub (label (ackS t)) (s t) sn < ws
      then
        (s (t + 1) = mod_n_add (label (ackS t)) 1 sn) ∧
        (rem (t + 1) = tli (mod_n_sub (s (t + 1)) (s t) sn) (rem t))
      else
        (s (t + 1) = s t) ∧ (rem (t + 1) = rem t))
```

Box 5.

```
∀ in out d tprop.
    NOISELESS_CHANNEL_STOP_WAIT in out d tprop =
    ∀ t. (if t < tprop then
        out t = set_non_packet
      else
        out t = in (t - d t)) ∧ 0 < tprop ∧ (d t = tprop)
```

Next, we define a predicate that models a noisy channel that looses a message with probability *p*. (Box 6)

In Box 6, we utilized the formal definition of the Bernoulli(*p*) random variable to model the noise effect. The variable *p* represents the probability of channel error or getting a *True* from the Bernoulli random variable and the history *bseqt* keeps track of the remaining portion of the infinite Boolean sequence, explained in Section 3, after every call of the Bernoulli random variable. According to the above definition, a valid packet that arrives at input of the channel appears at the output of the channel after *tprop* time units with probability *1-p*.

Stop-and-Wait Protocol

We first define some constraints that are required to ensure the correct behavior of our Stop-and-Wait protocol specification, before giving the actual formalization of the protocol.

INITIAL CONDITIONS

In case of the formal specification of real-time systems in HOL, we need to assign appropriate values to the history variables as initial conditions. We use following initial conditions for the Stop-and-Wait protocol (Box 7).

Box 6.

```
∀ in out d tprop p bseqt.
    NOISY_CHANNEL_STOP_WAIT in out d tprop p bseqt =
    ∀ t. (if t < tprop then
        (out t = set_non_packet) ∧ (bseqt (t + 1) = bseqt t)
      else
        (if good_packet (in (t - d t)) then
          (if ~fst (prob_bernoulli p (bseqt t)) then
            (out t = in (t - d t)) ∧
            (bseqt (t + 1) = snd (prob_bernoulli p (bseqt t)))
          else
            (out t = set_non_packet) ∧
            (bseqt (t + 1) = snd (prob_bernoulli p (bseqt t))))
        else
          (out t = set_non_packet) ∧ (bseqt (t + 1) = bseqt t)) ∧
          0 < tprop ∧ (d t = tprop)
```

Box 7.

```
∀ source rem s sink r i ackR dtout dtf dta tout tf ta rec_flag bseqt bseq.
INIT_STOP_WAIT source rem s sink r I ackR dtout dtf dta tout tf ta rec_flag
bseqt bseq = (rem 0 = source) ∧ (s 0 = 0) ∧ (sink 0 [ ]) ∧ (r 0 = 0) ∧
    (i 0 = 0) ∧ (dtout 0 = tout) ∧ (rec_flag 0 = F) ∧ (ackR 0 = set_non_pack-
et) ∧
    (dtf 0 = tf) ∧ (dta 0 = ta) ∧ (bseqt 0 = bseq)
```

ASSUMPTIONS

Liveness or Timeliness: While verifying a system, which allows nondeterministic or probabilistic choice between actions, we often need to include additional constraints to make sure that events of interest do occur. This has been done by including a *timeliness* constraint in the specification of the Stop-and-Wait protocol: if the sender's state has not changed over an interval of *maxP* time units, then the sender assumes that the receiver or the channel has crashed and aborts the protocol. A predicate *ABORT* is defined that is *True* only when the protocol aborts and *False* otherwise. Now, the predicate *ABORT* characterizes which *abort* histories satisfy this constraint. (Box 8)

A protocol is said to be live if it is never aborted. This kind of liveness is *assumed* using the following constraint

```
LIVE_ASSUMPTION abort = ∀ t. ~(abort t)
```

Window Size and Sequence Numbers: As has been mentioned before, instead of using their exact values of 1 and 2, we use the variables *ws* and *sn* to represent the *window size* and distinct sequence numbers for the Stop-and-Wait protocol

in the above predicates. This has been done, in order to be able to establish logical implications between the predicates defined in this chapter and the corresponding predicates for the Sliding Window protocol, defined in [Cadell-Oliver_92]. Now, we assign the exact values to these variables in an assumption predicate as follows

```
∀ ws sn. WSSN_ASSUM_STOP_WAIT ws sn =
(ws = 1) ∧ (sn = 2)
```

The Stop-and-Wait protocol can now be formalized as the logical conjunction of the predicates defined in the preceding sections. We present two specifications corresponding to noiseless or ideal and noisy channel conditions. (Box 9)

The higher-order-logic predicate *STOP_WAIT_NOISELESS* formally specifies the behavior of the Stop-and-Wait protocol under ideal or noiseless conditions as the corresponding predicate for the channel has been used for both data and ACK channels. It is also important to note here that we do not initialize the history *bseqt* in the predicate *INIT_STOP_WAIT* as there is no need to use the infinite Boolean sequence in this case. Next, we utilize the noisy channel predicate

Box 8.

```
∀ abort maxP rem.
    ABORT abort maxP rem =
    ∀ t. abort t = (rem t = rem (t - maxP)) ∧ maxP ≤ t ∧ ~NULL (rem t)
```

Box 9.

```
∀ source sink rem s i r ws sn ackty maxP abort dataS dataR ackS ackR d
    tprop dtout dtf dta tf ack_msg ta tout rec_flag.
STOP_WAIT_NOISELESS source sink rem s i r ws sn ackty maxP abort dataS
      dataR ackS ackR d tprop dtout dtf dta tf ack_msg ta tout rec_flag =
    INIT_STOP_WAIT source rem s sink r I ackR dtout dtf dta tout tf ta rec_
flag ∧
    DATA_TRANS_STOP_WAIT ws sn dataS s rem i ackS tout tf dtout dtf ∧
    NOISELESS_CHANNEL_STOP_WAIT dataS dataR d tprop ∧
    DATA_RECV_STOP_WAIT sn dataR sink r ∧
    ACK_TRANS_STOP_WAIT sn ackR r ackty ack_msg ta dta rec_flag ∧
    NOISELESS_CHANNEL_STOP_WAIT ackR ackS d tprop ∧
    ACK_RECV_STOP_WAIT ws sn ackS rem s ∧
    ABORT abort maxP rem ∧ WSSN_ASSUM_STOP_WAIT ws sn
```

to formally specify the Stop-and-Wait protocol with a noisy channel as follows in Box 10.

In the above definition, the data channel has been made noisy while a noiseless channel is used for the ACK messages. This has been done on purpose in order to reduce the length of the performance analysis proof by avoiding some redundancy. On the other hand, this decision does not affect the illustration of the idea behind the performance analysis of the Stop-and-Wait protocol under noisy conditions as we present the complete handling of a noisy channel in one direction. The analysis can be extended to both noisy channels by choosing noisy channel predicates for both channels and then handling the ACK channel in a similar way as the noisy data channel is handled in this chapter.

FUNCTIONAL VERIFICATION OF THE STOP-AND-WAIT PROTOCOL

The job of an ARQ protocol is to ensure reliable transfer of a stream of data from the sender to the receiver. This functional requirement can be formally specified as follows [Cadell-Oliver, 1992].

```
∀ source sink.
    REQ source sink =
    (∃ t. sink t = source) ∧ ∀ n.
is_prefix (sink t) (sink (t + n))
```

where the predicate *is_prefix* is *True* if its first list argument is a prefix of its second list argument. According to the predicate *REQ*, an ARQ protocol satisfies its functional requirements only if there exists a time at which the *sink* list becomes equal to the original *source* list, i.e., a time when the data at the sender is transferred, as is, to the receiver, and the history *sink* is prefix closed.

In order to verify the functional correctness of our specification of the Stop-and-Wait protocol, we now define the predicates for the Stop-and-Wait protocol in such a way that they logically imply the corresponding predicates used for the formal specification of the Sliding Window protocol presented in [Cadell-Oliver, 1992]. This relationship allows us to inherit the functional correctness theorem verified for the specification of the Sliding Window protocol for our Stop-and-Wait protocol specification.

For illustration purposes, consider the example of the data transmission predicate. It has been

Box 10.

```
∀ source sink rem s i r ws sn ackty maxP abort dataS dataR ackS ackR d
    tprop dtout dtf dta tf ack_msg ta tout rec_flag bseqt bseq p.
    STOP_WAIT_NOISY source sink rem s i r ws sn ackty maxP abort dataS
      dataR ackS ackR d tprop dtout dtf dta tf ack_msg ta tout
      rec_flag bseqt bseq =
    INIT_STOP_WAIT source rem s sink r i
        ackR dtout dtf dta tout tf ta rec_flag bseqt bseq ∧
    DATA_TRANS_STOP_WAIT ws sn dataS s rem i ackS tout tf dtout dtf ∧ NOISY_
CHANNEL_STOP_WAIT in out d tprop p bseqt ∧
    DATA_RECV_STOP_WAIT sn dataR sink r ∧
    ACK_TRANS_STOP_WAIT sn ackR r ackty ack_msg ta dta rec_flag ∧
    NOISELESS_CHANNEL_STOP_WAIT ackR ackS d tprop ∧ ACK_RECV_STOP_WAIT ws sn
ackS rem s ∧
    ABORT abort maxP rem ∧
    WSSN_ASSUM_STOP_WAIT ws sn
```

defined in [Cadell-Oliver, 1992] for the Sliding Window protocol as follows in Box 11.

It can be easily observed, and we verified it in HOL using Boolean algebra properties, that the predicate DATA_TRANS_STOP_WAIT, given in the previous section, logically implies the above predicate

```
∀ ws ns dataS s rem i ackS tout tf
dtout dtf.
    DATA_TRANS_STOP_WAIT ws ns dataS
s rem i ackS tout tf dtout dtf ⇒
    DATA_TRANS_SW ws ns dataS s rem
i
```

In a similar way, we were able to prove logical implications between all the predicates used in the formal specification of the Sliding Window protocol and the corresponding predicates used for the formal specification of the Stop-and-Wait protocol (see Boxes 12 and 13). These relationships allowed us to formally verify the functional correctness of both of the formal specifications of the Stop-and-Wait protocol, given in the previous section, in HOL.

It is important to note that the generic specification of the Sliding Window Protocol in [Cadell-Oliver, 1992] is quite general and does not include many details, such as the precise conditions under which the messages are transmitted or acknowl-

Box 11.

```
∀ ws sn dataS s rem i.
    DATA_TRANS_SW ws sn dataS s rem i =
    ∀ t. (if ~NULL (tli (i t) (rem t)) ∧ i t < ws then
        (dataS t = new_packet (mod_n_add (s t) (i t) sn) (hdi (i t) (rem t))) ∨
        (dataS t = set_non_packet)
      else
        dataS t = set_non_packet)
```

Box 12. Theorem 5

```
∀ source sink rem s i r ws sn ackty maxP abort dataS dataR ackS
      ackR d tprop dtout dtf dta tf ack_msg ta tout rec_flag.
STOP_WAIT_NOISELESS source sink rem s i r ws sn ackty maxP abort dataS
    dataR ackS ackR d tprop dtout dtf dta tf ack_msg ta tout rec_flag ∧
LIVE_ASSUMPTION abort ⇒ REQ source sink
```

edged and the delays (t_{out}, t_f, t_d, etc.) associated with different operations. Therefore, it cannot be used for reasoning about message delays and thus performance related properties, as such. On the other hand, the formal specification of the Stop-and-Wait protocol, given in this chapter, is more specific and provides a detailed description of the protocol including the timing behavior associated with different operations.

Another major point that we would like to mention here is that in order to establish the logical implication between the two protocol models, we had to introduce some additional generality in our formal definitions, such as the usage of variables *ws* and *sn* instead of their exact values of 1 and 2, respectively.

Even though, such generalizations are not required for the functional description of the Stop-and-Wait protocol, they do not harm us in any way. They lead to a much faster functional verification, as has been illustrated in this section. On the other hand, they do not affect the formal reasoning related to the performance issues, since the exact values for these variables are assigned in an assumption (*WSSN_ASSUM_STOP_WAIT*)

that is a part of our Stop-and-Wait protocol specification, which is used for conducting the performance analysis as well.

PERFORMANCE ANALYSIS OF THE STOP-AND-WAIT PROTOCOL

In this section, we present the verification of the message delay relations for the Stop-and-Wait protocol, given in Equations 1 and 3, for noiseless and noisy channels, respectively. The verification is based on the two formal specifications of the Stop-and-Wait protocol, STOP_*WAIT_NOISELESS* and *STOP_WAIT_NOISY*, given earlier in the chapter.

Noiseless Channel Conditions

The first and the foremost step in verifying the message delay characteristic for the Stop-and-Wait protocol is to formally specify it. Informally speaking, the message delay refers to the time required for the transmitter to send a single data message and know that it has been successfully

Box 13. Theorem 6

```
∀ source sink rem s i r ws sn ackty maxP abort dataS dataR ackS
      ackR d tprop dtout dtf dta tf ack_msg ta tout rec_flag
        bseqt bseq p.
STOP_WAIT_NOISY source sink rem s i r ws sn ackty maxP abort dataS
    dataR ackS ackR d tprop dtout dtf dta tf ack_msg ta tout
    rec_flag bseqt bseq ∧
LIVE_ASSUMPTION abort ⇒ REQ source sink
```

received at the receiver. We specify this in higher-order-logic as follows

```
∀ rem source.
     DELAY_STOP_WAIT_NOISELESS rem
source =
     @ t. (rem t = TL source) ∧ (rem
(t - 1) = source)
```

where *TL* refers to the *tail* function for *lists* and *@x.t* refers to the Hilbert choice operator in HOL that represents the value of *x* such that *t* is *True*. Thus, the above specification returns the time *t* at which the *rem* list, which represents the data remaining to be sent at any time *t*, is reduced by one element from its initially assigned value of the *source* list. Indeed it is precisely equal to the message delay of the first data element in the *source* list.

Based on the above definition of the message delay and the delays associated with the formal specification of the Stop-and-Wait protocol (*STOP_WAIT_NOISELESS*), Equation 1 can be formally expressed in HOL as follows in Box 14.

It is important to note here that the processing delay, t_p, has been assigned a value of 1 in our model, as explained in the previous section. The two assumptions that we have added to Theorem 7 ensure that the source list is not an empty list, i.e., *~(NULL source)*, otherwise no data transfer takes place, and the time out period *tout* is always greater than or equal to its lower bound. Rewriting the proof goal of Theorem 7 with the formal

specification of the Stop-and-Wait protocol delay and removing the Hilbert Choice operator we get the following expression

```
(∃x. (rem x = TL source) ∧ (rem (x -
1) = source)) ∧
     ∀ x. (rem x = TL source) ∧ (rem
(x - 1) = source) ⇒
          (x = tf + tprop + 1 + ta +
tprop + 1
```

The above subgoal is a logical conjunction of two Boolean expressions and it can be proved to be *True* only if there exists a time *x* for which the conditions (*rem x = TL source*) and (*rem (x - 1) = source*) are *True* and the value of any variable *x* that satisfies these conditions is unique and is equal to *tf + tprop + 1 + ta + tprop + 1*.

We proceed with the proof of this subgoal by assuming the following expression

Lemma 1:

```
(rem (tf + tprop + 1 + ta + tprop +
1) = TL source) ∧
(rem ((tf + tprop + 1 + ta + tprop +
1) - 1) = source))
```

to be *True*, which we will prove later, under the given constraints for the Stop-and-Wait protocol. Lemma 1 leads us to prove the first Boolean expression in our subgoal as now we know an *x = (tf + tprop + 1 + ta + tprop + 1)* for which the

Box 14. Theorem 7

```
∀ source sink rem s i r ws sn ackty maxP abort dataS dataR ackS
     ackR d tprop dtout dtf dta tf ack_msg ta tout rec_flag.
STOP_WAIT_NOISELESS source sink rem s i r ws sn ackty maxP abort
dataS dataR ackS ackR d tprop dtout dtf dta tf ack_msg ta tout rec_flag ∧
~(NULL source) ∧ (tprop + 1 + ta + tprop + 1 ≤ tout) ⇒
     (DELAY_STOP_WAIT_NOISELESS rem source =
     tf + tprop + 1 + ta + tprop + 1)
```

given conditions are *True*. We verify the second Boolean expression in the subgoal by first proving the monotonically decreasing characteristic of the history *rem* under the given constraints of the Stop-and-Wait protocol, i.e.,

```
∀ a b. a < b ⇒ ∃c. c ++ rem b = rem a
```

where ++ represents the list *cons* function in HOL. Now, if there exists an *x*, that satisfies the conditions (*rem x = TL source*) and (*rem (x - 1) = source*), then it may be equal to, less than or greater than (*tf + tprop + 1 + ta + tprop + 1*). For the latter two cases, we reach a contradiction in the assumption list, based on the monotonically decreasing characteristic of the history *rem*, whereas, the case when *x = (tf + tprop + 1 + ta + tprop +1)* verifies our subgoal of interest, which concludes the proof of Theorem 7 under the assumption of Lemma 1.

Lemma 1 can now be proved in HOL using the definitions of the predicates in the formal specification of the Stop-and-Wait protocol under noiseless channels. The corresponding HOL proof step sequence is summarized in Figure 5.

Noisy Channel Conditions

The message delay, under noisy channel conditions, refers to the time required for the transmitter to send a single data message and know that it has been successfully received at the receiver. Though the delay, in this case, is a random quantity since its value is non-deterministic and depends on the outcomes of a sequence of Bernoulli trials, which are used to model the channel noise as can be seen in the definition of the predicate *NOISY_CHANNEL_STOP_WAIT*. Therefore, the message delay of the Stop-and-Wait protocol under noisy channel conditions needs to be formally specified as a random variable as follows in Box 15, where

Figure 5. HOL Proof Sequence for Lemma 1

Number	Formally Verified Statements
1	$\forall t. t \leq tf \Rightarrow (i(t) = 0)$
2	$\forall t. t < tf \Rightarrow (dataS\ t = set\_non\_packet)$
3	$\forall t. t < tf + tprop \Rightarrow (dataR\ t = set\_non\_packet)$
4	$\forall t. t < tf + tprop + 1 \Rightarrow (sink\ t = []) \wedge (r\ t = 0)$
5	$\forall t. t \leq tf + tprop + 1 \Rightarrow (rec\_flag\ t = F) \wedge (dta\ t = ta)$
6	$\forall t. t < tf + tprop + 1 + ta \Rightarrow (ackR\ t = set\_non\_packet)$
7	$\forall t. t < tf + tprop + 1 + ta + tprop \Rightarrow (ackS\ t = set\_non\_packet)$
8	$\forall t. t < tf + tprop + 1 + ta + tprop + 1 \Rightarrow (s\ t = 0) \wedge (rem\ t = source)$
9	$(dataS\ tf = new\_packet\ 0\ (HD\ source)) \wedge (i(tf + 1) = 1)$
10	$\forall t. tf < t \wedge t < tf + tprop + 1 + ta + tprop + 1 \Rightarrow (tout + tf - t \leq dtout\ t)$
11	$\forall t. tf < t \wedge t < tf + tprop + 1 + ta + tprop + 1 \Rightarrow$ $(i\ t = 1) \wedge (dataS\ t = set\_non\_packet)$
12	$dataR(tf + tprop) = new\_packet\ 0\ (HD\ source)$
13	$\forall t. tf + tprop < t \wedge t < tf + tprop + 1 + ta + tprop + 1 \Rightarrow$ $(dataR\ t = set\_non\_packet)$
14	$\forall t. tf + tprop + 1 \leq t \wedge t < tf + tprop + 1 + ta + tprop + 1 \Rightarrow (r\ t = 1)$
15	$\forall t. tf + tprop + 1 \leq t \wedge t < tf + tprop + 1 + ta \Rightarrow$ $(rec\_flag(t + 1)) \wedge (dta(t + 1) = ta - (t - (tf + tprop)))$
16	$ackR(tf + tprop + 1 + ta) = new\_packet\ 0\ ack\_msg$
17	$rem(tf + tprop + 1 + ta + tprop + 1) = TL\ source$

Box 15.

```
∀ rem source bseqt.
     DELAY_STOP_WAIT_NOISY rem source bseqt =
     ((@t. (rem t = TL source) ∧ (rem (t - 1) = source)),
     bseqt @t. (rem t = TL source) ∧ (rem (t - 1) = source))
```

history *bseqt t* represents the unused portion of the infinite Boolean sequence, explained in Section 2, after performing the required number of Bernoulli trials at any given time *t*. The above specification returns a pair with the first element equal to the time *t* that satisfies the two conditions (*rem t = TL source*) and (*rem (t - 1) = source*), and thus represents the random message delay of the first data element in the *source* list, and the second element equal to the unused portion of the infinite Boolean sequence at this time instant *t*.

As a first step towards the verification of the average value of the random delay specified in *DELAY_STOP_WAIT_NOISY*, we establish its relationship with the infamous Geometric random variable, which basically returns the number of trials to attain the first success in an infinite sequence of Bernoulli trials. This way, we can benefit from existing HOL theorems related to the average characteristic of Geometric random variable, such as Theorem 2, for the verification of the average value of the message delay of a

Stop-and-Wait protocol. This relationship, given in Equation 2 can be expressed in HOL using the formal specification of the Stop-and-Wait protocol *STOP_WAIT_NOISY* and the Geometric random variable *prob_geom* [Hasan, 2007], as follows in Box 16, where *p* represents the probability of channel error, i.e., getting a *True* from the Bernoulli random variable. The first argument of the function *prob_geom* [Hasan, 2007] represents the probability of success for the corresponding sequence of the Bernoulli trials, which, in the case of our definition of the noisy channel, is equal to the probability of getting a *False* from a Bernoulli trial. The above theorem is proved under the assumption that the value of the probability *p* always falls in the interval *[0,1)*. It is not allowed to attain the value 1, in order to avoid the case when the channel always rejects incoming packets and thus leads to no data transfers. The assumption, *LIVE_ASSUMPTION abort* ensures liveness as has been explained in Section 2. The other assumptions used in the above theorem are

Box 16. Theorem 8

```
∀ source sink rem s i r ws sn ackty maxP abort dataS dataR ackS ackR
     d tprop dtout dtf dta tf ack_msg ta tout rec_flag bseqt bseq p.
STOP_WAIT_NOISY source sink rem s i r ws sn ackty maxP abort dataS
     dataR ackS ackR d tprop dtout dtf dta tf ack_msg ta tout
     rec_flag bseqt bseq ∧
LIVE_ASSUMPTION abort ∧
0 ≤ p ∧ p < 1 ∧ ~NULL source ∧
tprop + 1 + ta + tprop + 1 ≤ tout ⇒
     (DELAY_STOP_WAIT_NOISY rem source bseqt =
          ((tf + tout) * (fst (prob_geom (1 - p) bseq) - 1) + tf +
          tprop + 1 + ta + tprop + 1, snd (prob_geom (1 - p) bseq)))
```

Box 17.

```
(∀ p bseq.
    BERNOULLI_TRIAL_F_IND 0 p bseq = ~fst (prob_bernoulli p bseq)) ∧
  ∀ n p bseq. BERNOULLI_TRIAL_F_IND (SUC n) p bseq =
    fst (prob_bernoulli p bseq) ∧
    BERNOULLI_TRIAL_F_IND n p (snd (prob_bernoulli p bseq))

(∀ p bseq. NTH_BERNOULLI_TRIAL_SND 0 p bseq = bseq) ∧
  ∀ n p bseq. NTH_BERNOULLI_TRIAL_SND (SUC n) p bseq =
    snd (prob_bernoulli p (NTH_BERNOULLI_TRIAL_SND n p bseq))
```

similar to the ones used for the verification of Theorem 7.

We proceed with the verification of Theorem 8 in HOL by first defining the following two recursive functions (see Box 17).

The first function, *BERNOULLI_TRIAL_F_IND* returns *True* if and only if its first argument, say *n*, represents the positive integer index of a trial, in a sequence of independent Bernoulli trials, that returns a *False* while all Bernoulli trials with lower index values than *n* have returned a *True*. The second function *NTH_BERNOULLI_TRIAL_SND* returns the value of the *snd* element of the nth Bernoulli trial in a sequence of independent Bernoulli trials, where *n* is the first argument of the function *NTH_BERNOULLI_TRIAL_SND*. In other words, it basically returns the unused infinite Boolean sequence after *n* independent Bernoulli trials have been performed using the given infinite Boolean sequence.

Under the given assumptions of Theorem 8, it can be shown that a data message available at the *source* list does finally make through the noisy channel at some time. This can be verified in HOL, for the top element of the *source* list, by proving that there exists some *n* for which the function *BERNOULLI_TRIAL_F_IND* returns a *True*

```
∃ n. BERNOULLI_TRIAL_F_IND n p bseq
```

for the given values of p and bseq. If a positive integer n exists that satisfies the above condition, then it can be verified in HOL that the Geometric random variable, which returns the number of trials to attain the first success in an independent sequence of Bernoulli(p) trials, with success probability equal to (1 - p) can be formally expressed as follows

```
∀ n p s.
    0 ≤ p ∧ p < 1 ∧ BERNOULLI_
TRIAL_F_IND n p s ⇒
      (prob_geometric_p (1 - p) s =
      (n + 1,NTH_BERNOULLI_TRIAL_SND
(n + 1) p s))
```

The HOL proof is based on the formal definition of the function *prob_geom* and the underlying probability theory principles, presented in [Hurd, 2002].

Based on the above results, the proof goal of Theorem 8 can be simplified using the definition of *DELAY_STOP_WAIT_NOISY* and removing the Hilbert choice operator as follows

```
(∃ x. (rem x = TL source) ∧ (rem (x -
1) = source)) ∧
    ∀ x.
      (rem x = TL source) ∧ (rem (x
- 1) = source) ⇒
        (x = (tf + tout) * n + tf +
```

Box 18. Lemma 3

```
∀ bseq v.
INIT_STOP_WAIT_GEN source rem s sink r i
      ackR dtout dtf dta tout tf ta rec_flag bseqt bseq v ∧
      BERNOULLI_TRIAL_F_IND n p bseq ⇒
      (rem (v + (tf + tout) * n + tf + tprop + 1 + ta + tprop + 1 - 1) = source) ∧
        (rem (v + (tf + tout) * n + tf + tprop + 1 + ta + tprop + 1) = TL
source)∧
          (bseqt (v + (tf + tout) * n + tf + tprop + 1 + ta + tprop + 1) =
NTH_BERNOULLI_TRIAL_SND (n + 1) p bseq)
```

tprop + 1 + ta + tprop + 1) ∧
    (bseqt x = NTH_BERNOULLI_TRI-
AL_SND (n + 1) p bseq)

The above subgoal is quite similar to the one that we got after simplifying the proof goal of Theorem 7. Therefore, we follow the same proof approach and assume the following expression

Lemma 2:

```
(rem ((tf + tout) * n + tf + tprop +
1 + ta + tprop + 1 - 1) = source) ∧
(rem ((tf + tout) * n + tf + tprop +
1 + ta + tprop + 1) = TL source) ∧
(bseqt ((tf + tout) * n + tf + tprop
+ 1 + ta + tprop + 1) =
    NTH_BERNOULLI_TRIAL_SND (n + 1)
p bseq)
```

to be *True*, which we will prove later, under the given assumptions of Theorem 8. Lemma 2 leads us to prove the first Boolean expression in the subgoal as now we know an $x = ((tf + tout) * n + tf + tprop + 1 + ta + tprop + 1)$ for which the given conditions (*rem x = TL source*) and (*rem (x - 1) = source*) are *True*. The second Boolean expression in the subgoal can now be proved using Lemma 2 along with the monotonically decreasing characteristic of the history *rem* in a similar way as we handled the counterpart while verifying Theorem 7.

The next step is to prove Lemma 2 under the assumptions given in the assumption list of Theorem 8. We proceed in this direction by verifying a more generalized lemma (Box 18), under the assumptions of Theorem 8, for which Lemma 2 is a special case when v=0.

The first assumption in Lemma 3, i.e., the predicate INIT_STOP_WAIT_GEN, provides the status of the histories used in the predicate STOP_WAIT_NOISY at time *v* and is defined as shown in Box 19.

It can be proved to be a logical implication of the predicate *INIT_STOP_WAIT*, which is included in the definition of *STOP_WAIT_NOISY* and is thus present in the assumption list of Theorem 8, for the case when v = 0.

Whereas, the second assumption of Lemma 3, i.e., *BERNOULLI_TRIAL_F_IND n p bseq* has already been shown to be a consequence of the assumptions of Theorem 8. Thus, Lemma 2 can be proved as a special case of Lemma 3 when the positive integer variable *v* is assigned a value of 0. Now, in order to complete the formal proof of Theorem 8 in HOL, we need to verify Lemma 3. We proceed with this proof by applying induction on the positive integer variable *n*. For the base case, i.e., *n* = 0, we get the following subgoal after some basic arithmetic simplification and using the function definitions of *BERNOULLI_TRIAL_F_IND* and *NTH_BERNOULLI_TRIAL_SND*.

Box 19.

```
∀ source rem s sink r i ackR dtout dtf dta tout tf ta rec_flag bseqt bseq v.
    INIT_STOP_WAIT_GEN source rem s sink r i ackR dtout dtf dta tout tf
      ta rec_flag bseqt bseq v =
    (i v = 0) ∧ (dtout v = tout) ∧ (dtf v = tf) ∧ (dta v = ta) ∧
    (bseqt v = bseq) ∧
    (∀ t.
      t ≤ v ⇒
      (rem t = source) ∧ (s t = 0) ∧ (sink t = [ ]) ∧ (r t = 0) ∧
      (rec_flag t = F) ∧ (ackR t = set_non_packet)) ∧
    ∀ t. v - (tout - 1) ≤ t ∧ t < v ⇒ (i t = 1))
```

```
INIT_STOP_WAIT_GEN source rem s sink
r i ackR dtout dtf dta tout tf ta
rec_flag bseqt bseq v ∧
~fst (prob_bernoulli p bseq) ⇒
    (rem (v + tf + tprop + 1 + ta +
tprop + 1 - 1) = source) ∧
    (rem (v + tf + tprop + 1 + ta +
tprop + 1) = TL source) ∧
    (bseqt (v + tf + tprop + 1 + ta
+ tprop + 1) =
        snd (prob_bernoulli p bseq))
```

The assumption ~*fst (prob_bernoulli p bseq)* ensures that the noisy data channel allows reliable transmission of the first data message in the first trial. Thus, the base case of Lemma 3 becomes similar to the case of a noiseless data channel, as far as the transmission of the first data element of the *source* list is concerned. Therefore, its proof can be handled in a similar way as the proof of Lemma 1, presented in the last section, as the only difference between the two is the fact that now the initial conditions are defined for an arbitrary positive integer *v* instead of *0*. The HOL proof step sequence is summarized in Figure 6. These proofs are based on the INIT_*STOP_WAIT_GEN* and the predicates corresponding to the six processes, given in Figure 4, for the Stop-and-Wait protocol under a noisy data channel.

In the step case for Lemma 3, we get the following subgoal after some simplifications using the function definitions of *BERNOULLI_TRIAL_F_IND* and *NTH_BERNOULLI_TRIAL_SND* (Box 20), which needs to be proved under the assumption list of Theorem 8 along with the statement of Lemma 3.

The above subgoal can be proved in a very straightforward manner by specializing Lemma 3 for the case when *bseq* and *v* are equal to *snd (prob_bernoulli p bseq)* and (*v + tf + tout*), respectively, if the given initial conditions in the predicate *INIT_STOP_WAIT_GEN* hold for *snd (prob_bernoulli p bseq)* and *(v + tf + tout)*, i.e.,

Lemma 4:

```
INIT_STOP_WAIT_GEN source rem s sink
r i ackR dtout dtf dta
tout tf ta rec_flag bseqt (snd (prob_
bernoulli p bseq)) (v + tf + tout)
```

under the assumptions of Theorem 8 and the step case of Lemma 3. In order to prove Lemma 4 we need to formally verify the behavior of the histories, used in the predicate INIT_STOP_WAIT_GEN, at various points in the interval [0, v + tf + tout]. Therefore, we again use the same approach that we used to prove Lemma 1 and the base case of Lemma 3, i.e., to verify the value of

Figure 6. HOL Proof Sequence for the base Case of Lemma 3

Number	Formally Verified Statements
1	$\forall t. v \leq t \wedge t \leq v + tf \Rightarrow (i(t) = 0)$
2	$\forall t. v - (tout - 1) \leq t \wedge t < v + tf \Rightarrow (dataS\ t = set\_non\_packet)$
3	$\forall t. v \leq t \wedge t < v + tf + tprop \Rightarrow (dataR\ t = set\_non\_packet)$
4	$\forall t. v \leq t \wedge t \leq v + tf + tprop \Rightarrow (bseqt\ t = bs)$
5	$\forall t. v \leq t \wedge t < v + tf + tprop + 1 \Rightarrow (sink\ t = [\,]) \wedge (r\ t = 0)$
6	$\forall t. v \leq t \wedge t \leq v + tf + tprop + 1 \Rightarrow (rec\_flag\ t = F) \wedge (dta\ t = ta)$
7	$\forall t. t < v + tf + tprop + 1 + ta \Rightarrow (ackR\ t = set\_non\_packet)$
8	$\forall t. v \leq t \wedge t < v + tf + tprop + 1 + ta + tprop \Rightarrow (ackS\ t = set\_non\_packet)$
9	$\forall t. v \leq t \wedge t < v + tf + tprop + 1 + ta + tprop + 1 \Rightarrow (s\ t = 0) \wedge (rem\ t = source)$
10	$(i(v + tf + 1) = 1) \wedge (dataS(v + tf) = new\_packet\ 0\ (HD\ source))$
11	$\forall t. v \leq t \wedge t \leq v + tf \Rightarrow (dtout\ t = tout)$
12	$\forall t. v + tf < t \wedge t < v + tf + tprop + 1 + ta + tprop + 1 \Rightarrow$ $v + tf + tout - t \leq dtout\ t$
13	$\forall t. v + tf + 1 \leq t \wedge t \leq v + tf + tprop + 1 + ta + tprop \Rightarrow$ $(i\ t = 1) \wedge (dataS\ t = set\_non\_packet)$
14	$dataR(v + tf + tprop) = new\_packet\ 0\ (HD\ source)$
15	$\forall t. v + tf + tprop < t \wedge t < v + tf + tprop + 1 + ta + tprop \Rightarrow$ $(dataR\ t = set\_non\_packet)$
16	$(r(v + tf + tprop + 1) = 1) \wedge (dta(v + tf + tprop + 1) = ta)$
17	$\forall t. v + tf + tprop + 1 < t \wedge t < v + tf + tprop + 1 + ta + tprop \Rightarrow (r\ t = 1)$
18	$\forall t. v + tf + tprop + 1 \leq t \wedge t < v + tf + tprop + 1 + ta \Rightarrow$ $(rec\_flag(t + 1)) \wedge (dta(t + 1) = v + ta - (t - (tf + tprop)))$
19	$ackR(v + tf + tprop + 1 + ta) = new\_packet\ 0\ ack\_msg$
20	$ackS(v + tf + tprop + 1 + ta + tprop) = new\_packet0ack\_msg$
21	$rem(v + tf + tprop + 1 + ta + tprop + 1) = TL\ source$
22	$\forall t. v + tf + tprop < t \wedge t < v + tf + tprop + 1 + ta + tprop + 1 + tprop \Rightarrow$ $(bseqt\ t = snd(prob\_bernoulli\ p\ bseq))$

Box 20.

```
INIT_STOP_WAIT_GEN source rem s sink r i ackR dtout dtf dta tout tf ta rec_flag
bseqt bseq v ∧
     fst (prob_bernoulli p bseq) ∧
     NTH_BERNOULLI_TRIAL_F n p (snd (prob_bernoulli p bseq)) ⇒
     (rem (v + (tf + tout) * (n + 1) + tf + tprop + 1 + ta + tprop + 1 - 1) =
source) ∧
     (rem (v + (tf + tout) * (n + 1) + tf + tprop + 1 + ta + tprop + 1) = TL
source) ∧
     (bseqt (v + (tf + tout) * (n + 1) + tf + tprop + 1 + ta + tprop + 1) =
         NTH_BERNOULLI_TRIAL_SND (n + 1) p (snd (prob_bernoulli p bseq)))
```

these histories using the initial conditions and the definitions of the predicates used for the formal specification of the Stop-and-Wait protocol. In fact, the first 11 proof lines, given in Figure 6, for the base case of Lemma 3 can be used as they are for the proof of Lemma 4 as well, since a message transmission cannot complete before v + tf + tprop + 1 + ta + tprop + 1 time units are lapsed and the first data message is issued at time v + tf in both cases. Hereafter, contrary to the base case of Lemma 3, where one of the assumptions assured the reliable transmission of the first data message, in the case of Lemma 4 we have the assumption fst (prob_bernoulli p bseq) that forces the channel to lose the first data message. Thus, the sender keeps on waiting for a valid ACK until the timer associated with the tout delay expires and this is how the initial state at time v is maintained until the time v + tf + tout. We were able to verify this result, and thus Lemma 4, using the first 11 proof lines, given in Figure 6, followed by the proof

sequence given in Figure 7. The proof of Lemma 4 concludes the proof of Lemma 3, which in turn leads to the proof of Theorem 8 as well.

Now, we are in the position of verifying the average message delay relation, given in Equation 3, for the Stop-and-Wait protocol under noisy channels. The corresponding theorem can be expressed in HOL as follows in Box 21.

The above proof goal can be reduced to the following subgoal using Theorems 4 and 8 and some arithmetic simplification

```
∀ p. 0 < p ∧ p ≤ 1 ⇒
  (expec
  (\.s. (fst (prob_geom p s) - 1,
    snd (prob_geom p s))) = (1 - p)
/ p)
```

which we were able to verify in HOL, using the formalization of the expectation theory and the Geometric random variable prob_geom, given in

Figure 7. HOL Proof Sequence for Lemma 4

Number	Formally Verified Statements
1	$\forall t. v + tf < t \land t < v + tf + tout \Rightarrow v + tf + tout - t \leq dtout\ t$
2	$\forall t. v + tf < t \land t < v + tf + tout \Rightarrow (i\ t = 1)$
3	$\forall t. v + tf < t \land t < v + tf + tout \Rightarrow (dataS\ t = set\_non\_packet)$
4	$\forall t. v \leq t \land t < v + tf + tout + tprop \Rightarrow (dataR\ t = set\_non\_packet)$
5	$\forall t. t < v + tf + tout + tprop + 1 \Rightarrow (sink\ t = []) \land (r\ t = 0)$
6	$\forall t. v \leq t \land t < v + tf + tout + tprop + 1 \Rightarrow (rec\_flag\ t = F) \land (dta\ t = ta)$
7	$\forall t. t < v + tf + tout + tprop + 1 \Rightarrow (rec\_flag\ t = F)$
8	$\forall t. t < v + tf + tout + tprop + 1 \Rightarrow (ackR\ t = set\_non\_packet)$
9	$\forall t. v \leq t \land t < v + tf + tout + tprop + 1 \Rightarrow (ackS\ t = set\_non\_packet)$
10	$\forall t. t < v + tf + tout + tprop + 1 \Rightarrow (s\ t = 0) \land (rem\ t = source)$
11	$\forall t. v + tf < t \land t \leq v + tf + tout \Rightarrow (dtf\ t = tf)$
12	$\forall t. v + tf + tprop < t \land t < v + tf + tout + tprop \Rightarrow$ $\quad (bseqt\ t = snd(prob\_bernoulli\ p\ bseq))$
13	$\forall t. v + tf < t \land t < v + tf + tout \Rightarrow (dtout\ t = v + tf + tout - t)$
14	$dtout(v + tf + tout) = tout$
15	$i(v + tf + tout) = 0$

Box 21. Theorem 9

```
∀ source sink rem s i r ws sn ackty maxP abort dataS dataR
ackS ackR d tprop dtout dtf dta tf ack_msg ta tout rec_flag bseqt bseq p.
(∀ bseq. STOP_WAIT_NOISY source sink rem s i r ws sn ackty maxP abort
    dataS dataR ackS ackR d tprop dtout dtf dta tf ack_msg ta tout
    rec_flag bseqt bseq) ∧
  (LIVE_ASSUMPTION abort) ∧
  (0 ≤ p ∧ p < 1) ∧ (~NULL source) ∧
  tprop + 1 + ta + tprop + 1 ≤ tout ⇒
    (expec (DELAY_STOP_WAIT_NOISY rem source bseqt) =
      ((tf + tout) * p/(1-p) + (tf + tprop + 1 + ta + tprop + 1)))
```

[Hasan, 2007], and the probability theory principles, formalized in [Hurd, 2002].

Theorem 9 specifies the average message delay relation of a Stop-and-Wait protocol in terms of individual delays of the various autonomous processes, which are the basic building blocks of the protocol. Thus, it allows us to tweak various parameters of the protocol to optimize its performance for any given conditions. It is important to note here that the result of Theorem 9 is not new and the performance analysis of Stop-and-Wait protocols, based on Equation 3, existed since the early days of their introduction, however, using theoretical paper-and-pencil proof techniques. On the other hand, to the best of our knowledge, this is the first time that such a relation has been mechanically verified without any loss in accuracy or precision of the results. It therefore provides a superior approach to both paper-and-pencil proofs and simulation based performance analysis techniques.

CONCLUSION

In this chapter, we presented a higher-order-logic theorem prover based approach for the functional verification and performance analysis of real-time systems. A real-time system and its environment can be formalized as a logical conjunction of higher-order-logic predicates on positive integers, whereas the positive integers represent the ticks of a clock counting physical time in any appropriate units. Higher-order-logic has been successfully used for the formalization of a significant amount of probability theories. This feature allows us to use random variables in our model to represent the random and unpredictable elements of a real-time system and its environment. The functional and performance related properties, such as average characteristics, of a real-time system can now be formally verified, using this model, in a higher-order-logic theorem prover. Due to the inherent soundness of the theorem-proving based analysis, the presented approach ensures accurate and precise results and thus can prove to be quite useful for the performance and reliability optimization of safety critical and highly sensitive real-time system application domains, such as medicine, military or space travel. Similarly, unlike other commonly used state-based formal techniques, which are severely affected by the state-space explosion problem, the presented approach is capable of handling any real-time system that can be expressed in a closed mathematical form due to the high expressive nature of higher-order-logic. Also, there is no equivalence verification required between the models used for functional verification and performance evaluation as the same formal model is used for both of these analysis in the approach presented in this chapter.

In order to illustrate the practical effectiveness of theorem proving in the domain of analyzing real-time systems, we have utilized it in this chapter to conduct the functional verification and performance analysis of a Stop-and-Wait protocol using the HOL theorem prover. A higher-order-logic specification for the Stop-and-Wait protocol is presented, with the noise effect modeled as a random variable. We also outlined the major steps in the verification of performance related theorems. The most significant result is the verification of the classical average message delay relation for the Stop-and-Wait protocol in HOL. To the best of our knowledge, formal verification of the average message delay relation for the Stop-and-Wait protocol cannot be handled by any other formal technique. Because of the fact that the Stop-and-Wait protocol bears most of the essential characteristics of the present day real-time systems, these results clearly demonstrate the usefulness of the proposed performance analysis approach.

The main limitation of the higher-order-logic theorem proving based performance analysis approach is the associated significant user interaction, i.e., the user needs to guide the proof tools manually since we are dealing with higher-order-logic. In the analysis of the Stop-and-Wait protocol, presented in this chapter, we tried to minimize the effect of this inherent limitation by taking a number of decisions, such as, building upon existing HOL theories, whenever possible, and choosing the discrete time domain for the analysis, which allows us to use the powerful induction technique for verification and thus minimize the proof effort considerably. The formalization and verification presented in this paper translated to approximately 6000 lines of HOL code and we had to spend about 300 man-hours on this project. Because of the interactive nature of the analysis, the proposed approach should not be viewed as an alternative to methods such as simulation and model-checking for the performance analysis of

real-time systems but rather as a complementary technique, which can prove to be very useful when precision of the results is of prime importance.

REFERENCES

Alur, R. (1992). *Techniques for Automatic Verification of Real-Time Systems*. PhD Thesis, Stanford University, Stanford, CA.

Amnell, T., Behrmann, G., Bengtsson, J., D'Argenio, P., David, A., Fehnker, A., et al. (2001). Uppaal - Now, Next, and Future. In Cassez, F., Jard, C., Rozoy, B., Ryan, M.D. (Eds.), *Modeling and Verification of Parallel Processes*, (LNCS Vol. 2067, pp. 99-124). Berlin: Springer.

Beyer, D., Lewerentz, C., & Noack, A. (2003). Rabbit: A Tool for BDD-based Verification of Real-Time Systems. In W.A. Hunt, Jr. & F. Somenzi (Eds.), *Computer Aided Verification*, (LNCS. Vol. 2725, pp. 122-125), Boulder, CO. Berlin: Springer.

Bucci, G., Sassoli, L., & Vicario, E. (2005). Correctness Verification and Performance Analysis of Real-Time Systems Using Stochastic Preemptive Time Petri Nets. *Transactions on Software Engineering*, *31*(11), 913–927. doi:10.1109/TSE.2005.122

Cardell-Oliver, R. (1992). *The Formal Verification of Hard Real-time Systems*. PhD Thesis, University of Cambridge, Cambridge, UK.

Church, A. (1940). A Formulation of the Simple Theory of Types. *J. of Symbolic Logic*, *5*, 56–68. doi:10.2307/2266170

Galambos, J. (1995). *Advanced Probability Theory*. New York: Marcel Dekker, Inc.

Gallasch, G., & Billington, J. (2006). A Parametric State Space for the Analysis of the Infinite Class of Stop-and-Wait Protocols. In *Model Checking Software*, (LNCS 3925, pp. 201-218). Berlin: Springer.

Garcia, A. L., & Widjaja, I. (2004). *Communication Networks: Fundamental Concepts and Key Architectures*. New York: McGraw-Hill.

Gordon, M. J. C & Melham T.F. (1993). *Introduction to HOL: A Theorem Proving Environment for Higher-Order Logic*. Cambridge, UK: Cambridge University Press.

Gordon, M. J. C. (1989). *Mechanizing Programming Logics in Higher-order Logic. Current Trends in Hardware Verification and Automated Theorem Proving* (pp. 387–439). New York: Springer.

Harrison, J. (1998). *Theorem proving with Real Numbers*. Berlin: Springer.

Harrison, J. (2009). *Handbook of Practical Logic and Automated Reasoning*. Cambridge, UK: Cambridge University Press. doi:10.1017/CBO9780511576430

Hasan, O., Abbasi, N., Akbarpour, B., Tahar, S., & Akbarpour, R. (2009b). Formal Reasoning about Expectation Properties for Continuous Random Variables. In A. Cavalcanti & D. Dams (Eds.), *Formal Methods*, (LNCS 5850, pp. 435-450). Berlin: Springer.

Hasan, O., & Tahar, S. (2007). Formalization of Continuous Probability Distributions. In F. Pfenning (Ed.), *Automated Deduction*, (LNCS Vol. 4603, pp. 2-18). Berlin: Springer.

Hasan, O., & Tahar, S. (2008). Using Theorem Proving to Verify Expectation and Variance for Discrete Random Variables. *Journal of Automated Reasoning*, *41*(3-4), 295–323. doi:10.1007/s10817-008-9113-6

Hasan, O., & Tahar, S. (2009). Performance Analysis and Functional Verification of the Stop-and-Wait Protocol in HOL. *Journal of Automated Reasoning*, *42*(1), 1–33. doi:10.1007/s10817-008-9105-6

Hasan, O., & Tahar, S. (2009a). Formal Verification of Tail Distribution Bounds in the HOL Theorem Prover. *Mathematical Methods in the Applied Sciences*, *32*(4), 480–504. doi:10.1002/mma.1055

Havelund, K., & Shankar, N. (1996). Experiments in Theorem Proving and Model Checking for Protocol Verification. *Industrial Benefit and Advances in Formal Methods*, (LNCS 1051, pp. 662-681). Berlin: Springer.

Hurd, J. (2002). *Formal Verification of Probabilistic Algorithms*. PhD Thesis, University of Cambridge, Cambridge, UK.

Kwiatkowska, M., Norman, G., & Parker, D. (2007). Stochastic Model Checking. In M. Bernardo and J. Hillston (Eds.). *Formal Methods for Performance Evaluation*, Bertinoro, Italy, (LNCS, 4486, pp. 220-270). Berlin: Springer.

Kwiatkowska, M., Norman, G., Segala, R., & Sproston, J. (2002). Automatic Verification of Real-Time Systems with Discrete Probability Distributions. *Theoretical Computer Science*, *282*(1), 101–150. doi:10.1016/S0304-3975(01)00046-9

Milner, R. (1977). A Theory of Type Polymorphism in Programming. *Journal of Computer and System Sciences*, *17*, 348–375. doi:10.1016/0022-0000(78)90014-4

Paulson, L. C. (1996). *ML for the Working Programmer*. Cambridge, UK: Cambridge University Press.

Wells, L. (2002). Performance Analysis Using Coloured Petri Nets. In *International Symposium on Modeling, Analysis, and Simulation of Computer and Telecommunications Systems*, (pp. 217-222). Washington, DC: IEEE Computer Society.

ADDITIONALREADING

Billington, J., Gallasch, G., & Petrucci, L. (2005). Fast Verification of the Class of Stop-and-Wait Protocols Modelled by Coloured Petri Nets. *Nordic Journal of Computing, 12*(3), 251–274.

Duflot, M., Fribourg, L., Herault, T., Lassaigne, R., Magniette, F., Messika, S., et al. (2004). Probabilistic Model Checking of the CSMA/CD Protocol using PRISM and APMC. *Workshop on Automated Verification of Critical Systems*, (pp.195-214). Elsevier Science.

Hasan, O. Abbasi & Tahar, S. (2009). Formal Probabilistic Analysis of Stuck-at Faults in Reconfigurable Memory Arrays; M. Leuschel and H. Wehrheim (Eds.), *Integrated Formal Methods, LNCS Vol.5423*, (pp. 277-291) Springer. Düsseldorf, Germany.

Hasan, O., & Tahar, S. (2007). Formalization of the Standard Uniform Random Variable. [Elsevier.]. *Theoretical Computer Science, 382*(1), 71–83. doi:10.1016/j.tcs.2007.05.009

Hasan, O., & Tahar, S. (2007). Verification of Probabilistic Properties in the HOL Theorem Prover, J. Davies and J. Gibbons (Eds.), *Integrated Formal Methods, LNCS Vol. 4591*, (pp. 333-352). Springer. Oxford, UK.

Hasan, O., & Tahar, S. (2008). Performance Analysis of ARQ Protocols using a Theorem Prover, *International Symposium on Performance Analysis of Systems and Software*, (pp. 85-94). IEEE Computer Society. Austin, Texas, USA.

Hasan, O., & Tahar, S. (2009). Probabilistic Analysis of Wireless Systems using Theorem Proving. [Elsevier.]. *Electronic Notes in Theoretical Computer Science, 242*(2), 43–58. doi:10.1016/j.entcs.2009.06.022

Suzuki, I. (1990). Formal Analysis of the Alternating Bit Protocol by Temporal Petri Nets. [IEEE.]. *Transactions on Software Engineering, 16*(10), 1273–1281. doi:10.1109/32.60315

Chapter 14
Formal Methods for Verifications of Reactive Systems

Olfa Mosbahi
Nancy University, France & Martin Luther University, Germany

Mohamed Khalgui
Xidian University, China

ABSTRACT

This chapter deals with the use of two verification approaches: theorem proving and model checking. The authors focus on the Event-B method by using its associated theorem proving tool (Click_n_Prove), and on the language TLA+ by using its model checker TLC. By considering the limitation of the Event-B method to invariance properties, the authors propose to apply the language TLA+ to verify liveness properties on a software behavior. The authors extend first the expressivity and the semantics of a B model (called temporal B model) to deal with the specification of fairness and eventuality properties. Second, they give transformation rules from a temporal B model into a TLA+ module. The authors present in particular, their prototype system called B2TLA+, that they have developed to support this transformation; then they can verify these properties thanks to the model checker TLC on finite state systems. For the verification of infinite-state systems, they propose the use of the predicate diagrams. The authors illustrate their approach on a case study of a parcel sorting system.

INTRODUCTION

Reactive systems are systems whose role is to maintain an ongoing interaction with their environment rather than produce some final values upon termination. Typical examples of reactive systems are Air traffic control systems, Programs controlling mechanical devices such as a train, a plane, or ongoing processes such as a nuclear reactor. Formal methods [Spivey,1988] is the term used to describe the specification and verification

DOI: 10.4018/978-1-60960-086-0.ch014

of these systems using mathematical and logical techniques. The main advantages of the formal approach to software construction [Dyba, Kampenes & Sjøberg, 2006; Pickard, Kitchenham & Jones, 1998; Wohlin, 2005; Wordsworth, 1987] is that, whenever applicable, it can lead to an increase of the reliability and correctness of the resulting programs by several orders of magnitude.

Several approaches for the verification of reactive systems are available, the most prominent are Algorithmic (model checking [Clarke, GRUM-BERG, Jha, Lu & Veith, 2001; Clarke, Emerson & Sistla, 1986; Clarke, 1994; Clarke, 1997; Clarke, Grumberg & Peled, 1999; Kaltenbach, 1994]) and Deductive verification (theorem-proving techniques [Hoare, 1969; Dijkstra, 1975; Kaufmann & Moore, 2004; Archer, Vito & Muno, 2003; Holzmann, 2003]). These approaches are used to establish the correctness of reactive programs relative to their temporal specifications. Verifying the correctness of a program involves formulating a property to be verified using a suitable logic such as first order logic or temporal logic.

The model checking problem [Clarke, GRUM-BERG, Jha, Lu & Veith, 2001; Clarke, Emerson & Sistla, 1986] involves the construction of an abstract model M, in the form of variations on finite state automata, and the construction of specification formulas ϕ, in the form of variations on temporal logic. The verification algorithm used in model checking involves exploring the set of reachable states of the model to ensure that the formula ϕ holds. It has gained popularity in industry because the verification procedure can be fully automated [Clarke, Emerson & Sistla, 1986] and counterexamples are automatically generated if the property being verified does not hold. Furthermore, model checkers rely on exhaustive state space enumeration to establish whether a property holds or doesn't hold. This approach to verification puts immediate limits on the state space of problems that can be explored by model checkers. This common problem, known as the state explosion problem, is an often cited drawback of verification by model checking.

Theorem proving is a very tedious process involving keeping in mind a multitude of assumptions and transformation rules. The calculi used in theorem proving is based on Hoare and Dijkstra theories [Dijkstra, 1975]. The first one describes a calculus to reason about program correctness in terms of pre and post conditions [Dijkstra, 1976; Dijkstra & Schweten, 1990]. Dijkstra extended Hoare's ideas in the concept of "*predicate transformers*" which, instead of starting with a pre-condition and post-condition, starts with a post-condition and uses the program code to determine the pre-condition that needs to hold to establish the post condition [Dijkstra, 1975; Dijkstra, 1995]. Hoare's approach to proving correctness introduced the concept of a "Hoare triple", which is a formula in the form: $\{\phi_{pre}\}\ P\ \{v_{post}\}$. This formula can be read as "if property $\{\phi_{pre}\}$ holds before program P starts, $\{\phi_{post}\}$ holds after the execution of P". The program P can refer to an entire program or to a single function call, depending on the unit that is being verified. In Hoare's calculus, axioms and rules of inference are used to derive $\{\phi_{post}\}$ based on $\{\phi_{pre}\}$ and P. The syntax of P described by Hoare corresponds to a simple imperative language with the usual constructs (assignment, conditional branching, looping, and sequential statements).

A key difference between the theorem approach to software verification and the model checking approach to software verification is that theorem provers do not need to exhaustively visit the program's state space to verify properties. Consequently, a theorem prover approach can reason about infinite state spaces and state spaces involving complex datatypes and recursion. This can be achieved because a theorem prover reasons about constraints on states, not instances of states. While theorem provers have distinct advantages over model checkers, namely in the superior size of the systems they can be applied to and their ability to reason inductively, deductive systems also have their drawbacks [Kaufmann & Moore, 2004]. An often cited drawback of theorem provers is that they require a great deal of user expertise and effort [Archer, Vito & Munoz, 2003]. This requirement presents perhaps the greatest barrier to widespread adoption and usage of theorem provers. Although theorem proving and model checking appear to be contradictory approaches to software verification, there has been considerable effort in the past 15 years to incorporate model checking and theorem proving [Shankar, 2000; Arkoudas, Khurshid, Marinov & Rinard, 2003]. Because theorem provers and model checkers each provide complementary benefits in terms of automation and scalability, it is likely that this trend will follow and that model checkers will continue to be useful on systems of manageable size while theorem provers will be used on large systems [Holzmann, 2003].

In this paper, we have chosen the use of the Event-B method [Abrial, 1996-a; Abrial, 1996-b; Abrial & Laffitte, 1996; Abrial, 2000] in the development of reactive systems because it supports development of programming language code from specifications. It has been used in major safety-critical system applications in Europe (such as the Paris Metro Line 14), and is attracting increasing interest in industry. It has robust, commercially available tool support for specification, design, proof and code generation, for example Click_n_Prove and Rodin Platform [Clearsy, 2004]. It focuses on refinement to code rather than just formal specification. The basic idea of refinement [Back & Wright, 1998; Back & Sere, 1989; Back, 1990] consists in successively adding implementation detail while preserving the properties required at an abstract level. In a refinement-based approach to system development, one proceeds by writing successive models, each of which introduces some additional detail while preserving the essential properties of the preceding model. Fundamental properties of a system can thus be established at high levels of abstraction, errors can be detected in early phases,

and the complexity of formal assurance is spread over the entire development process.

Our aim is to check that the model has an expected behavior, i.e., satisfies the safety and liveness requirements of an informal specification. For that, one can express the requirement as formal properties that are checked on the model. The notions of safety and liveness properties have been first introduced by Lamport [Lamport, 2002]. Informally, a safety property expresses that *"something (bad) will not happen"* during a system execution. Mutual exclusion and partial correctness are two prominent examples of safety properties. A liveness property expresses that eventually *"something (good) must happen"* during an execution. The most prominent example of a liveness property is termination. Lamport [Lamport, 2002] distinguishes two types of liveness properties: Eventuality and Fairness. Eventuality asserts that something good must eventually happen. Fairness means that if a certain event is enabled, then the program must eventually execute it.

The Event-B method provides us with techniques and tools for specifying, refining, verifying invariant properties and implementing systems; its scope is limited to invariant properties and it is not well suited to deal with liveness properties in reactive systems. By considering the limitation of the Event-B method to safety properties, we propose to apply the language TLA+ to verify liveness properties on a software behavior. The language TLA+ provides us with an abstract and powerful framework for modeling, specifying and verifying safety, eventuality and fairness properties of reactive systems. The combination of the Event-B method and the language TLA+ allows us to take benefits of the powerful tool of B to verify safety properties and to formulate in TLA+ more natural properties that are not straightforward to express with the Event-B method and to verify them with the TLC model checker on finite state systems. For the verification of liveness properties on infinite-state systems, we propose the use of the predicate diagrams. We propose in this paper to combine and apply two techniques with the goal being to take advantages of both: theorem proving, when possible, and model checking otherwise, in the construction and verification of safe reactive systems. The theorem prover concerned is part of the Click_n_Prove tool associated to the Event-B method and the model checker is TLC for TLA+ models.

The chapter is organized as follows: Section 2 gives an overview of some related works concerning B extensions for capturing and proving liveness properties, Section 3 presents a Background: the Event-B method, the language TLA+ and the predicate diagrams. Section 4 gives a description of the proposed approach: we extend the syntax of the Event-B method to deal with liveness properties, we give the semantics of these properties in terms of traces (*temporal B model*) and we give transformation rules from a temporal B model into a TLA+ module on which we can verify liveness properties. Section 5 presents an example to illustrate our approach. Finally, Section 6 ends with a conclusion and future work.

RELATED WORK

In this section we review some related works and we discuss the positioning of our work and the contribution of this paper. The works presented in this section have studied liveness properties in the context of program verification in the B event systems. The problem has been specified in the B event system methodology by Abrial and Mussat in [Abrial & Mussat, 1998], Bert and Barradas in [Ruiz Barradas & Bert, 2002], [Bert, 2001], [Bert & Cave, 2000] and Julliand, Masson and Mountassir in [Julliand, Masson & Mountassir, 2001; Julliand, Masson & Mountassir, 1999; Mountassir, Bellegarde, Julliand & Masson, 2000; Masson, Mountassir & Julliand, 2000].

The integration of temporal modalities to specify and to model reactive systems started with the work of Pnueli [Pnueli, 1977] and work

on temporal logics (linear-time temporal and branching-time temporal logics [Manna & Pnueli, 1992; Manna & Pnueli, 1995] model checking [Clarke, 1994; Clarke, 1997; Kaltenbach, 1994], theorem proving [**37**]). The temporal logic of actions TLA defined by Leslie Lamport [Lamport, 1994] is a linear temporal logic, combining actions as predicates in a temporal framework; TLA defines an action as primed and unprimed relation and allows one to state invariance properties using the □ (Always) temporal operator and eventuality properties stated with the ~> (Leads to) operator. TLA is a stuttering-closed logic and has semantics based on infinite traces. Refinement is simply defined as an implication: Φ_1 is refined by Φ_2, if $\Phi_2 \Rightarrow \Phi_1$. The main advantage of TLA is its simplicity and it has gathered the essence of invariance and eventuality properties together in an elegant way of specifying a system using the weak and strong fairness operators. In TLA, we can specify that some actions are executed under weak fairness and some others are executed under strong fairness. Eventuality asserts that something good must eventually happen. Fairness means that if a certain event is enabled, then the program must eventually execute it. Weak fairness stipulates that an event occurs infinitely often during a behavior if it is almost always enabled and strong fairness condition requires that an event must happen infinitely often during a behavior if it is infinitely often enabled. The TLA proof engine is powerful but tools are lucking in the order of animation. We will try to use TLA to improve the expressivity of the Event-B method. We consider that B and TLA+ are very close with respect to their foundations. Unity [Chandy & Misra, 1989] is another framework which is interesting with respect to the design of parallel programs and also to the development of distributed programs and real time aspects. The UNITY formalism is made up of a programming notation based on action systems and a specification language which is a fragment of the linear temporal logics and a proof system. The safety and liveness properties of an algorithm are specified using a particular temporal logic then, a UNITY program is derived by stepwise refinement of the specification. Temporal modalities express safety and eventuality properties in a very concise way, the refinement is implemented as a logical implication.

The Event-B method is mainly based on the predicate transformer, called generalized substitution, and it exists two options for carrying out the extension. The first option is to introduce eventuality properties in the formalism and to use the tools provided by B to prove the decreasing of natural numbers (the general case includes well founded relations). This option will not introduce any explicit notion of trace for expressing the semantics of a system, since we can introduce explicit traces. A second option is to consider that a system is considered as a set of events reading and writing variables: it is a state-to-state transformation. Now we can combine state-to-state transformation (or transitions) into traces. However, we have to define properties of traces in a predicate transformer-based approach:

- Stating fairness constraints,
- Stating eventuality properties.

Predicate transformers are the way to express a common semantics for programs and specifications. They are useful for building proof systems and for proving that these proof systems are sound. Mery has already studied predicate transformers for fairness assumptions [Méry, 198; Méry, 1987]. In the following, we will propose an extension of the Event-B methodology for fairness and eventuality properties.

In their paper, Abrial and Mussat make various proposals for introducing dynamic constraints in B. They all express, in different complementary ways, how a system is allowed to evolve. They proposed an extension consisting in a dynamic invariant clause containing linear temporal logic formulae (LTL). In order to allow verification by theorem proving, the users have to provide the

model with decreasing functions, a variant and a loop invariant. Such items are necessary for the prover but are indeed not part of the specification. Furthermore, finding variant and loop invariant is not an easy task. In other work [Abrial & Mussat, 1997], the authors have presented a way to use B for developing protocols without adding new language constructs to B but by introducing the explicit *time stretching* during the development; the solution is convincing and certainly in the spirit of B. The *time stretching* is also known as the *stuttering*.

Bert and Barradas have proposed a method for the specification and proof of liveness properties in B event systems under fairness assumptions. They give proof obligations in order to prove basic progress properties in B event systems under two types of assumptions: minimal progress and weak fairness. They define proof obligations in terms of *weakest preconditions*, which allow us to prove basic liveness properties as usual B proof obligations. They suggest the use of UNITY "Leadsto" operator to specify more general liveness properties. In this way, they integrated the UNITY logic in the specification and proof of B event systems. With this approach, they combine basic progress properties in order to prove more general liveness properties, instead of using model checking techniques as it is proposed in [Bert & Cave, 2000]. Moreover, the proof of liveness properties is not necessarily given by proving the decrement of a variant, in a way similar to a loop termination, as it is proposed in [Abrial & Mussat, 1998]. They dispose of the UNITY system rules which provide a variety of theorems, which can be used in the study and proof of properties in B event systems. They claim the use of weak fairness assumptions in order to have abstract specification without the introduction of schedulers. The semantics of these properties is defined in terms of *weakest preconditions* but in our work, we give a semantics in terms of *traces*.

Julliand et all [Julliand, Masson &Mountassir, 1999], [Masson, Mountassir & Julliand, 2000],

[Bellegarde, Chouali &Julliand, 2002] have proposed to extend the B event systems by allowing in B a specification of reactive systems under fairness hypotheses as it is currently done in other approaches [Julliand, Masson & Mountassir, 2001; Mountassir, Bellegarde, Julliand & Masson]. For that, he proposes a way to express fairness assumptions as events with optional additional guards so that some but not all of the activation of the events are fair. In this framework, he studies and compares two ways to model checking the PLTL property on a model which takes account of the fairness assumptions by noticing the fair exiting cycles in the model. To implement this approach, he needs the following:

1. to build a finite labelled transition system from the B event system. For that, he uses a formalism borrowed to constraint programming with a representation of states by a mapping between variables and set constraints [Bert & Cave, 2000].
2. to search for all fair exiting cycles in the reachability graph.
3. a model checker which uses the constrained model. To take account of the fairness assumptions, it is enough to pay no attention to fair exiting acceptation cycles, a minor extension to the already implemented constrained model checker.

In their work, they express fairness assumptions as events and they verify liveness properties by model checking of finite-state-systems but in our work, we show that the old recipe of Lamport together with Abrial's framework is very simple and powerful. In our approach, we propose to define the syntax and the semantics of the extension of a B model (called temporal B model) to deal with eventuality and fairness properties. As TLA+ is appropriate to the specification and the verification of such properties, we have extended the B notation and its semantics over traces in the same way as TLA+ does. We also give the trans-formation rules from a temporal B model into a TLA+ module and we present a prototype system called B2TLA+ supporting these transformation rules. Invariants are verified with Click n Prove and liveness properties are verified with TLC on a TLA+ module. Hence, the proposed method allows us to model the system by refinement to specify liveness properties. The model checker TLC is used for the verification of finite-state systems. For the verification of infinite-state systems, we propose the use of predicate diagrams. We suppose in our approach that the specifier is familiar with the use of the B technology and not with TLA+ modeling. Hence, the specifier uses the prototype system to translate a temporal B model into a TLA+ module and then he verifies liveness properties using the TLC model checker.

BACKGROUND

We present in this section, the well-known methods: the Event-B method, the language TLA+ and the predicate diagrams.

Overview of the Event-B Method

B is a formal method developed by Abrial [Abrial, 1996-a] to support the software development life cycle from specification to implementation. It is based on Zermelo-Fraenkel set theory and on generalized substitution. Sets are used for data modelling, Generalized Substitutions [Abrial & Laffitte, 1996; Abrial, 2000; Abrial, 2003] are used to describe state modification, the refinement calculus is used to relate models at varying abstraction levels.

Event-Based Modeling

The Event-B method [Abrial, 1996-b; Abrial & Mussat, 1998] is based on the B notation [Abrial, 1996]. It extends the methodological scope of basic concepts such as set-theoretical notations

Box 1.

```
MODEL ⟨name⟩
SETS ⟨sets⟩
CONSTANTS ⟨constants⟩
PROPERTIES ⟨properties of sets and constants⟩
VARIABLES ⟨variables x⟩
INVARIANT ⟨invariants I(x)⟩
ASSERTIONS ⟨A(x)⟩
INITIALISATION ⟨initialization of variables⟩
EVENTS ⟨events⟩
END
```

and generalized substitutions in order to take into account the idea of *formal models*. Roughly speaking, a formal model is characterized by a (finite) list *x* of *state variables* possibly modified by a (finite) list of *events*; an invariant *I(x)* states some properties that must always be satisfied by the variables *x* and maintained by the activation of the events. Generalized substitutions provide a way to express the transformations of the values of the state variables of a formal model. An event consists of two parts: a *guard* (denoted *grd*) and an action. A guard is a predicate built from the state variables, and an *action* is a generalized substitution (denoted *GS*).

An event can take one of the forms shown in the table below. Let $BA_e(x,x')$ be the before-after predicate associated with each event shape. This predicate describes the event as a logical predicate expressing the relationship linking the values of the state variables just before (x) and just after (x') the event "execution". In the table below, x denotes a vector build on the set of state variables of the model and P a predicate. In the general substitution $x: p(x_0, x)$, x denotes the *new value* of the vector, whereas x_0 denotes its *old value* and t represents a vector of distinct local variables.

Proof obligations are associated to events and state that the invariant condition *I(x)* is preserved. Their general form follows immediately from the definition of the before-after predicate, $BA_e(x,x')$ of each event:

$$I(x) \wedge BA_e(x,x') \Rightarrow I(x')$$

Note that it follows from the guarded forms of the events that this obligation is trivially discharged when the guard of the event is false.

The B model has the following form (see Box 1.)

An abstract B model has a name; the clause **SETS** contains definitions of sets; the clause **CONSTANTS** allows one to introduce information related to the mathematical structure to solve and the clause **PROPERTIES** contains the effective definitions of constants. The clause **ASSERTIONS** contains the list of theorems to be discharged by the proof engine. The clause **VARIABLES** contains a (finite) list of state variables possibly modified by a (finite) list of events; the clause **INVARIANT** states some properties that must always be satisfied by the variables and maintained by the activation of the events. The clause **EVENTS** contains all the system events which preserve the invariants.

Refinement

The refinement of a formal model allows us to enrich a model in a step-by-step approach, and is the foundation of our correct-by-construction approach. Refinement provides a way to strengthen invariants and to add details to a model. It is used to transform an abstract model into a more concrete version by modifying the state description. This is essentially done by extending the list of state variables, by refining each abstract event into a corresponding concrete version, and by adding new events. The abstract state variables, x, and the concrete ones, y, are linked together by means of a gluing invariant $J(x, y)$. A number of proof obligations ensures that (1) each abstract event is correctly refined by its corresponding concrete version, (2) each new event refines skip, (3) no new event takes control forever, and (4) relative deadlock-freeness is preserved.

Supported Tool: Click_n_Prove

Click_n_Prove tool is the new proactive interface of the interactive prover of Atelier B [ClearSy, 2002; Project IST, 2007] and its free version B4free [ClearSy, 2004] and it has been developed by Jean-Raymond Abrial and Dominique Cansell. The tool generates the proof obligations associated with a model or a refinement and it also provides automatic and iterative proof procedures to discharge these proof obligations.

THE LANGUAGE TLA+

TLA+ is a language intended for the high level specification of reactive, distributed, and in particular asynchronous systems. It combines the linear-time temporal logic of actions TLA [Lamport, 1994], and mathematical set theory. The language has a mechanism for structuring in the form of modules, either by extension, or by instance.

Temporal Logic TLA

The semantics of TLA is based on behaviors of state variables. It can be viewed as a logic built in an incremental way in three stages:

- predicates having as free variables rigid and flexible variables and whose semantics is based on states. A state s satisfies the predicate P (denoted as $s[|P|]$ being true). $s[|P|]$ is the value obtained by substituting in P variables by their values in the state s, (for instance $s[|x=0|] \equiv s[|x|]=0$), where $s[|x|]$ is the value of x in the state s,

- actions which are logical formulas having primed flexible variables as well as free variables and whose semantics is based on pairs of states. A pair of state $\langle s,t \rangle$ satisfies the action A if and only if $s[|A|]t$ is true. $s[|A|]t$ is the value obtained by substituting in A unprimed variables by their values in the state s and primed variables by their values in the state t. (for instance $s[|x'=x+1|]t \equiv t[|x|] = s[|x|] + 1$),

- temporal formulas of actions whose semantics is based on state behaviors of variables. We note that a behavior is an infinite sequence of states $\langle s_0, s_1,... \rangle$. $\langle s_0, s_1,... \rangle [|\Box T|]$ ($\Box T$ asserts that the formula T is always true) is true if and only if $\$ \forall n \in$ Nat: $\langle s_n, s_{n+1},... \rangle [|T|]$. $\langle s_0, s_1,... \rangle [|\Box[A]_x\}|]$ (a behavior $\langle s_0, s_1,... \rangle$ satisfies $\Box[A_x]$) is true if and only if $\forall n \in$ Nat $\langle s_n, s_{n+1},... \rangle [|[A]_x|]$, where A is an action, x is a state function and $[A]_x$ requires A to hold only if x changes value during transition. $\langle s_0, s_1,... \rangle [|\Diamond T|]$ ($\Diamond T$ asserts that T is eventually true) is true if and only if $\exists n \in$ Nat: $\langle s_n, s_{n+1},... \rangle [|T|]$. The formula $(F \rightsquigarrow G)$ asserts that any time F is true, G is true then or at some later time $(F \rightsquigarrow G = \Box (F \Rightarrow \Diamond G))$.

A TLA specification of a system denoted by *Spec(S)* looks like: *Init* $\land \Box[Next]_x \land L$ where:

- *Init* is the predicate which specifies initial states ($s_0 [|Init|]$),

- x is the list of all state variables and $\Box[Next]_x$ means that either two consecutive states are equal on x, $x'= x$ (*stuttering*), or *Next* is an action (a relation) that describes the next-state relation ($\forall\ n \in$ Nat: s_n [|*Next*|] s_{n+1}), usually written as a disjunction of more elementary actions,

- *L* is a fairness assumption (strong or weak) on actions. Fairness means that if an action is possible, then the program must eventually execute it. Weak fairness stipulates that an action occurs infinitely often during a behavior if it is almost always enabled and strong fairness condition requires that an action must happen infinitely often during a behavior if it is infinitely often enabled.

In TLA, we can state invariance properties ($Spec(S) \Rightarrow \Box I$), eventuality properties ($Spec(S) \Rightarrow \Diamond F$) or ($Spec(S) \Rightarrow (P \sim > Q)$) and refinement properties ($Spec(S_2) \Rightarrow Spec(S_1)$), where S_1 is an abstract specification and S_2 is its refinement.

Refinement

Unlike most other temporal logics, TLA is intended to support stepwise system development by refinement of specifications. A system S_1 is refined by a system S_2, when: $Spec(S2) \Rightarrow Spec(S_1)$ holds. A refinement S_2 preserves all TLA properties of an abstract specification S_1 if and only if for every formula F, if $Spec(S_1) \Rightarrow F$ is valid, then so is $Spec(S_2) \Rightarrow F$. This condition is in turn equivalent to requiring the validity of ($Spec(S_2) \Rightarrow Spec(S_1)$). Because $Spec(S_2)$ will contain extra variables to represent the lower-level detail, and because these variables will change in transitions that have no counter-part at the abstract level, stuttering invariance of TLA formulas is essential to make validity of implication a reasonable definition of refinement.

Proofs in TLA are carried out using proof rules [Lamport, 1996] and rules of the classical logic. It is clear that the main advantage is that everything is stated as a logical object and relations as refinement are stated using the logical implication.

The refinement states a property between logical formulas interpreted over external behavior.

TLA+

TLA+ [Lamport, 2002] is an extension of TLA with modules for structuring a specification. A module is a text containing a name, a list of definitions (constants, variables, operators, functions, predicates, assumptions, theorems, proofs). A specification is made up of several modules that are combined using EXTENDS and INSTANCE clauses. The clause EXTENDS imports the definitions of specified modules by a macro expansion mechanism; the clause INSTANCE provides the mechanism of parameterization and a bloc-like structure. A module TLA+ for our proposal extension of B is represented as follows: (see Box 2.)

SUPPORTED TOOL: TLC MODEL CHECKER

The TLC model checker [Lamport & Yu, 2003] can check a finite model of a specification obtained by instantiating the constant parameters and, if necessary, specifying constraints to make the set of reachable states finite. It assumes that the specification has the form of the formula ($Init \land \Box[Next]_x \land L$) and works by generating behaviors that satisfy the specification. With TLC, we can check that a specification satisfies invariance or liveness specifications and we can check refinement such that a TLA+ specification implies another one.

Predicate Diagrams

A predicate diagram [Cansell, Méry & Merz, 2001-a; Cansell, Méry & Merz, 2001-b] is a finite graph whose nodes are labelled with sets of literals. A node represents the set of states satisfying the formulas contained in the node label. Edges in the diagram represent possible state transitions

Box 2.

```
MODULE ⟨name⟩
CONSTANTS ⟨list of constants⟩
VARIABLES ⟨list of variables x⟩
ASSUME ⟨properties of constants⟩
TYPE INVARIANTINIT ⟨initialization of variables⟩
NEXT ⟨disjunction of actions⟩
FAIRNESS ⟨Fairness assumptions on actions⟩
SPEC ⟨Spec = Init ∧□[Next]ₓ ∧ FAIRNESS ⟩
INVARIANT ⟨Safety properties⟩
LIVENESS ⟨Liveness properties⟩
THEOREM
END
```

and are labelled with action names. A fairness condition (weak fairness or strong fairness) may be associated with each action name. Moreover, edges may be labelled with annotations of the form $(t, \prec)$ or $(t, \preceq)$ asserting that the term t decreases, or does not increase, with respect to the well-founded ordering. Formally, the definition of predicate diagrams is relative to finite sets P and A that contain the state predicates and the names of actions. A predicate diagram $G = (N, I, \delta, \zeta, o)$ over P and A consists of:

- a finite set N of nodes,
- a finite set $I \subseteq N$ of initial nodes,
- a family $(\delta_a)_{a \in A}$ of relations $\delta_a \subseteq N \times N$; we denote by δ the union of the relations δ_a,
- a mapping ζ: $\{NF, WF, SF\}$ that associates with each action name a fairness condition (no fairness, weak fairness, or strong fairness), and
- an edge labeling o that associates a finite set of pairs $\{(t_1, \prec_1),...,(t_k, \prec_k)\}$ of terms t_i and symbols $\prec_i$ to each edge in $(n,m) \in \delta$.

Predicate diagrams represent the possible runs of a system: a run through the diagram is an w-sequence of system states s_i, diagram nodes n_i, and actions A_i such that each state satisfies the label of n_i, A_i relates n_i and n_{i+1}, and all edge annotations are satisfied. Besides the transitions that correspond to edges in the diagram, we also allow for stuttering transitions that remain at a node, preserving all its predicates (but not necessarily the values of the underlying variables). Infinite stuttering is prevented by appropriate fairness assumptions. A trace through the diagram is an w-sequence of states for which there exists a run. The precise definition of runs and traces appears in [Cansell, Méry & Merz, 2001-a].

We say that a predicate diagram G conforms to a system specification Spec if every possible run of Spec is a trace through G. We can formally compare a predicate diagram G and a TLA+ system specification *Spec* that appears in a TLA+ module. In fact, a set of essentially non-temporal proof obligations expressing correct initialization, state consecution, and respect of ordering annotations are sufficient to establish conformance. Temporal reasoning may be required for proving that *Spec* implies the fairness assumptions of the diagram, however, in many cases, the same conditions appear in both models. On the other hand, correctness properties expressed in linear-time temporal logic (including TLA) and built from the atomic predicates in P, can be verified over a predicate diagram G by model checking. To do so,

G is considered as a finite-state transition system defining a set of fair runs.

The predicates in P are encoded as Boolean variables, and ordering annotations $(t, \prec)$ give rise to hypotheses which are an expression of the well-foundedness condition in temporal logic and can be verified in the finite-state representation by tracking, for every transition taken, whether it carries an annotation indicating that t decreases w.r.t. $\prec$ or $\preceq$.

Refinement of Predicate Diagrams

Beyond their use in system verification, predicate diagrams can also be employed to compare two models of the same system at different levels of abstraction. We say that a predicate diagram G_1 refines a predicate diagram G_2 if every trace through G_1 is also a trace through G_2. We assume that the sets of predicates, action names, and orderings underlying G_1 extend the corresponding sets underlying G_2.

The refinement of predicate diagrams require the transition graphs of the two diagrams to be closely related: node labels of G_1 imply those of the corresponding nodes of G_2 (1), initial nodes of G_1 are related to initial nodes of G_2 (2), transitions in G_1 must map to (possibly stuttering) transitions in G_2 (3), and ordering annotations already present in G_2 must be preserved in G_1 (4). In contrast, there are two conditions for weak and strong fairness assumptions (5) which ensure that fair runs through the refining diagram can be mapped to fair runs through the refined diagram without requiring a syntactic preservation of high-level fairness conditions. Establishing structural refinement relies on three kinds of verification, beyond the purely syntactic check of condition (1), the conditions (3),(4) and (5) can be verified by inspection of the graph structure and the annotations of the diagrams. Condition (2) requires (non-temporal) theorem proving, whereas the two conditions in (5) can be verified by model checking the finite transition systems generated from the diagrams. At any rate, structural refinement ensures refinement of traces, and thus preservation of temporal-logic properties [Spivey, 1988].

Supported Tool: DIXIT

DIXIT [Fejoz, Méry & Merz, 2005] is a toolkit to support the use of predicate diagrams for the verification of infinite-state systems, with a particular focus on proving liveness properties. Besides the verification of temporal logic properties, it also supports the stepwise development of a system by refinement. Temporal logic properties (expressed over the set of literals that appear in the node labels) can be verified by model checking. DIXIT generates a model for the SPIN model checker and has to verify an appropriate LTL formula. In addition, one can check that a predicate diagram is a correct refinement of another one, implying that all properties expressed in LTL are preserved. The proof obligations for establishing refinement require that the refining diagram faithfully reflects the transition structure of the abstract diagram. On the other hand, fairness conditions of the high-level diagram can be implemented in very flexible ways. Moreover, DIXIT can generate proof obligations that ensure that a predicate diagram conforms to (i.e., is a correct abstraction of) a TLA+ system specification.

Contribution

The Event-B method deals with safety properties, but there are applications, such as reactive or distributed systems, where liveness properties must be considered. TLA+ deals with safety, eventuality and fairness properties. We suggest the use of TLA+ because these two methods are very close with respect to their foundations. The main advantage of TLA is its simplicity and it has gathered the essence of invariance and eventuality properties together in an elegant way of specifying a system using the weak and strong fairness operators. In TLA, we can specify that some actions are executed under weak fairness and some others are executed under strong fairness. The TLA proof engine is powerful but tools are lucking in the order of animation. We will try to use TLA to improve the expressivity of the Event-B method. In this proposed method, we suppose that the specifier uses the Event-B method for developing reactive systems and he is not familiar with TLA+ modeling. He uses the prototype system B2TLA+, which we have developed to transform automatically a temporal B model into a TLA+ module, then he verifies liveness properties on finite state systems using the TLC model checker. Thereafter, the specifier uses the predicate diagrams to verify safety and liveness properties on infinite state systems. The translation into predicate diagrams

is not performed automatically but it is done by the specifier based on TLA+ modules.

Presentation of the Approach

The proposed approach [Mosbahi, 2008] as shown in Figure 1 uses the Event-B method, the language TLA+ and the predicate diagrams as follows:

- **Step 1:** at first, an abstract model of the system is given in the Event-B method where only invariance properties are considered,
- **Step 2:** invariance properties are verified with the Click_n_Prove tool,
- **Step 3:** liveness properties are added to the abstract B model when necessary. The

Figure 1.

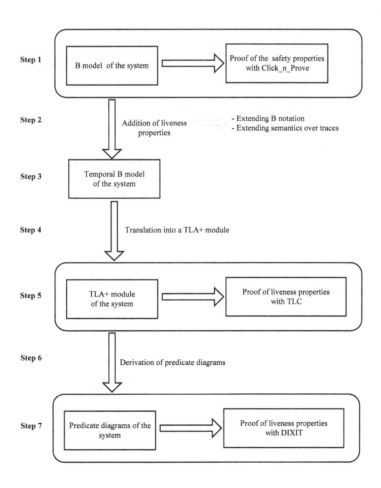

FAIRNESS clause is used for specifying fairness properties and EVENTUALITY clause for the specification of eventuality properties. The obtained model called temporal B model is as follows: (see Box 3.)

- **Step 4:** the temporal B model is then translated into a TLA+ module using the prototype system B2TLA+, which we have developed,
- **Step 5:** only liveness properties are checked with TLC,
- **Step 6:** derivation of predicate diagrams (PDs) for the verification of liveness properties on infinite state systems,
- **Step 7:** verification of liveness properties by DIXIT tool.

In each refinement step, we repeat the steps 2,3,4,5, 6 and 7 until satisfying all properties of the system. The refinement is shown in Figure 2.

In the sequel we will focus on two points. The first one concerns the expressivity extension of the Event-B method with liveness properties and their semantics (step 2 of Figure 1). The second one concerns the translation of the extended B model into a TLA+ module using the prototype B2TLA+ (step 4 of Figure 1).

ASSIGNING TEMPORAL MEANING TO B MODELS

This section defines an extension to Event-B in order to deal with temporal properties. The most important construction we need is the "*leads to*" eventuality operator as in TLA and Unity which expresses requirements on behaviors, i.e. sequence of states. In order to assess eventuality properties we must state assumptions on the fair occurrence of events. Such assumptions are stated using the TLA operators *WF* and *SF*. *WF(e)* assumes that the event *e* is weakly fair, i.e. the event *e* occurs infinitely often provided that it is eventually always enabled. *SF(e)* assumes that the event *e* is strongly fair, i.e. the event *e* occurs infinitely often provided that it is infinitely often enabled. We indeed integrate some pieces of TLA+ into the Event-B models and we deal with refinement and proof obligations of "temporal" B models.

In the following, we start with the syntax of the extension, then we give the semantics of liveness properties over traces as it is done in TLA+. We suggest the use of TLA+ operators because the two methods are very close with respect to their foundations.

Box 3.

```
MODEL   ⟨name⟩
SETS   ⟨sets⟩
CONSTANTS   ⟨constants⟩
PROPERTIES ⟨properties of sets and constants⟩
VARIABLES   ⟨variables x⟩
INVARIANT   ⟨invariants I(x)⟩
ASSERTIONS   ⟨A(x)⟩
INITIALISATION   ⟨initialization of variables⟩
EVENTS   ⟨events⟩
FAIRNESS⟨Fairness assumptions⟩
EVENTUALITY⟨Eventuality properties⟩
    END
```

Syntax of the Extension

In order to establish liveness properties we must assume some progress conditions on the system. As long as we have to verify that a event system satisfies safety properties, it is sufficient to refer to a pair of states (before and after states of a triggering event). But in order to prove temporal properties we need to introduce behaviors, sequences of states starting from the initial state and where two consecutive states s_i and s_{i+1} are such that some event enabled in s_i and leads to the state s_{i+1}.

Before defining the syntax of formulae which extends B expressivity, we start with some definitions.

State variables. The state of a system is composed of a denumerable set of flexible or state variables (V). Let (X) be a denumerable set of rigid variables. These variables are not modified by program transitions and hence keep the initially chosen value during a program run. A state is a valuation of flexible variables.

Terms and States. A term t is defined recursively as follows:

$t ::= c \mid x \mid f(t_1,...,t_n)$ where c is a constant, x is a variable ($x \in [V \cup X]$), $t_1,...,t_n$ are terms and f is a function symbol with arity n.

Atomic propositions. An atomic proposition ap is a formula of the form:

Figure 2.

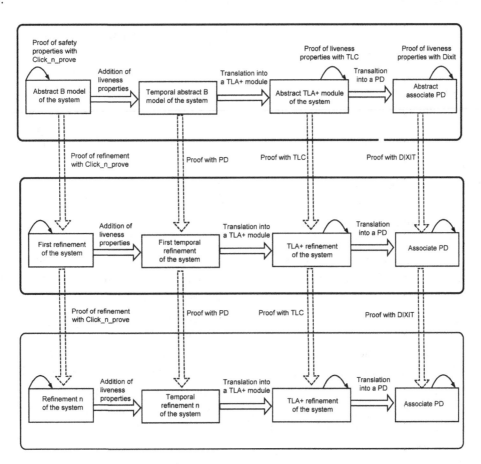

$ap ::= p(t_1,...,t_n)$ where p is a predicate symbol with arity n and $t_1,...,t_n$ are terms.

State predicates. A state predicate sp is a formula defined by the following grammar:

$$sp ::= ap \mid \neg sp \mid sp \lor sp \mid sp \land sp \mid sp \Rightarrow sp \mid sp \Leftrightarrow sp \mid \exists x\, sp \mid \forall x\, sp$$

In our extension, we introduce transition and liveness formulae.

Transition formulae. A transition formula describes state transitions. A transition formula ac is a formula of the form:

$$ac ::= GS(e) \mid [e]sp \mid \langle e \rangle sp$$ where e is an event, $GS(e)$ is its generalized substitution and sp is a state predicate.

Safety properties. Safety properties are formulae of the form:

$$F ::= \Box sp \mid \Box(sp \Rightarrow \Box sp),$$ where sp is a state predicate.

Liveness properties. Liveness properties (fairness and eventuality) are formulae defined as follows:

- *Eventuality properties* are expressed with formulae of the form: $F \rightsquigarrow G$ (*F leads to G*) defined as $\Box(F \Rightarrow \Diamond G)$ and means that every F will be followed by G, where F and G are formulae of the form: $F ::= sp \mid \Diamond F \mid \Box F \mid WF_f(e) \mid SF_f(e)$. Where sp is a state predicate, f is a state function, $WF_f(e)$ and $SF_f(e)$ are respectively the weak and strong fairness of the event e.

These properties are added in the clause EVENTUALITY as it is shown in the step 3 of the proposed method.

- *Fairness properties* are expressed with formulae of the form:

  ◦ For weak fairness of an event e: $WF_f(e)$ is defined as $\Diamond\Box grd(e) \Rightarrow \Box\Diamond GS(e)$ and means that the event e occurs infinitely often provided that it is eventually always enabled,

  ◦ For strong fairness of an event e: $SF_f(e)$ is defined as $\Box\Diamond grd(e) \Rightarrow \Box\Diamond GS(e)$ and means that the event e occurs infinitely often provided that it is infinitely often enabled.

These properties are added in the clause FAIRNESS as it is shown in the step 3 of the proposed method.

Where: e is a B event, $grd(e)$ is the guard of this event e (state predicate), $GS(e)$ is the generalized substitution of the event e (it is a transition formula containing both primed and unprimed occurrences of states variables, such as a before-after predicate).

Semantics of the Extension

In Event-B, an event e as it was shown in Table 1, is defined by a guard denoted $grd(e)$ and a generalized substitution $GS(e)$ ($e \equiv (grd(e), GS(e))$) and $BA_e(x,x')$ is the before-after predicate for an event; this is a first-order formula built from the constants declared for the system specification, the event's parameters, as well as primed and unprimed occurrences of the system variables V.

In our extension, we deal with properties over state sequences (fairness and eventuality properties). This is why we need semantics over a sequence of states and have to explain how we can view events as a relation over primed and unprimed variables and we will use this point to find the extension of the Event-B method. A system S is modeled as a set of possible events triggering actions, when guards are true. As in TLA, we can define an event e by a guard denoted *Enabled(e)* (condition for triggering or enabledness condition) and by a relation over a set of flexible variables

Table 1. Event forms

Event	Before-after predicate $BA_e(x,x')$	Guard
BEGIN x:P(x0,x) END	$P(x, x')$	*TRUE*
SELECT G(x) THEN *x:Q(x0,x') END*	$G(x) \land Q(x, x')$	$G(x)$
ANY t where G(t,x) THEN *x: R(x0,x,t) END*	$\exists t.(G(t,x) \land R(x,x',t))$	$\exists t.G(t,x)$

(*V*) denoted *Relation(e)* (relation stating the transformation of variables).

According a TLA+ module, we consider three kinds of properties:

- *State properties* which denote properties on states of the system *S* and are interpreted over states. These properties are state predicates,
- *Relational properties* which denote relations of *S* between pairs of states, which we call transition formulae,
- *Temporal Properties* state properties over traces and use state properties, relational properties and temporal operators ($\square,\diamond,\leadsto,...$), which we call liveness properties.

Properties are interpreted over traces (sequences of states). We introduce notations for characterizing systems:

- *V* is the set of flexible variables of the system *S*, *v* is a state variable; *x* is the current value of *v* and *x'* is the next value of *v*. $primed\_Var(S) = \langle x' \mid v \in V \rangle$ and $unprimed\_Var(S) = \langle x \mid v \in V \rangle$.
- *Val* is the set of values of the system variables.
- *States(S)* is the set of states of the system S and a state s_i is a function from *V* to *Val* ($s_i: V^e \rightarrow Val$).
- *Init(S)* specifies the initial values of flexible variables of the system *S*.

- The satisfaction of the state predicate *sp* in the state s_i of a system *S* is as follows:

$s_i, \xi \models sp$ where ξ is a valuation of the rigid variables of *S*.

- *Events(S)* specifies the set of possible events of *S*; it means that we list the possible events defined in Table 1.
  - $\underset{\rightarrow}{e}$ is a relation over *States(S)* simulating the execution of the system *S*.
- *Next(S)* is a formula over primed and unprimed variables of *S* corresponding to the relation over *States(S)*. Next has the following form:

$Next(S) \equiv R(e_1) (x,x') \lor ... \lor R(e_n) (x,x')$

Where $R(e_j)(x,x')$ is a TLA relation corresponding to one of the three types of B events defined in Table 1.

- $-P(x,x')$ (before-after predicate corresponding to the simple event)
- $-G(x) \land P(x,x')$ (before-after predicate corresponding to the guarded event)
  - $\exists t.(G(t,x) \land P(x,x',t))$ (before-after predicate corresponding to the indeterministic event)

We have: $(s_i, s_{i+1}), \xi \models Next(S) \equiv s_i \underset{\rightarrow}{e} s_{i+1}$. The formula $BA_e(x,x')$ and *Next(S)* express relation between primed and unprimed variables, so there is a semantic equivalence between $BA_e(x,x')$ and

Next(S). This implies that $BA_e(x,x')$ in B is interpreted by the formula *Next(S)* in TLA.

- *Invariants(S)* is a set of properties over *States(S)* invariant for *S*. φ is in *Invariants(S)*, if:
  1. Init(S) $\Rightarrow \varphi$
  2. $\forall s_0, s_i \in States(S): s_0, \xi \models$ Init(S) $\char94 (s_0 \rightarrow s_i) \Rightarrow s_i, \xi \models \varphi$
- *Traces(S)* is the set of traces generated from *Init(S)* using $\rightarrow$. A trace is denoted by $\sigma = \langle s_0, s_1,....., s_i,..... \rangle$ and satisfying the following constraints:
  1. $s_0, \xi \models$ *Init(S)* (the initial state s_0 satisfies the initial condition),
  2. $\forall i \in N: (s_i \rightarrow s_{i+1}) \vee (s_i = s_{i+1})$ any two successive states (s_i, s_{i+1}) either satisfy the before-after predicate $BA_e(x,x')$ for some event *e* and some variables *x*, or agree on the values of all system variables (called stuttering steps)

Let $\sigma \in$ *Traces(S)*, A property φ over states sequence of the system *S* is a state property, a relational property or a temporal property; the semantics over traces unified semantics over states and pairs of states as follows:

1. a state property φ is a trace property as follows: $\sigma, \xi \models \varphi$, if $s_0 \models \xi \varphi$
2. a relational property φ is also a trace property by extending the semantics over pairs of states into a semantics over traces as follows:

$$\sigma, \xi \models \varphi, \text{ if } (s_0, s_1), \xi \models \varphi$$

Temporal properties contains state properties, relational properties and temporal combination of these properties. Our extension is the same one than TLA+ and a system *S* is specified by the following temporal expression:

Specification(S) $\equiv$ Init(S) (1)
$\wedge \Box[Next(S)]_{\langle unprimed\_var(S) \rangle}$ (2)
$\wedge WF_{unprimed\_var(S)}$ (S) (3)
$\wedge SF_{unprimed\_var(S)}$ (S) (4)

(1) states initial conditions,
(2) states how traces are built,
(3) states the weak fairness assumption,
(4) states the strong fairness assumption.

$WF_{unprimed\_var(S)}$ (S) defines the condition of weak fairness over the system *S* and $SF_{unprimed\_var(S)}$ (S) defines the condition of strong fairness over the system *S*. The notation $[Next(S)]_{\langle unprimed\_var(S) \rangle}$ is equivalent to $Next(S) \vee (\forall x \in unprimed\_var(S):x=x')$.

TLA defines $WF_{unprimed\_var(S)}$ (S) and $SF_{unprimed\_var(S)}$ (S) as follows:

$$WF_{unprimed\_var(S)}(S) \equiv \wedge_{e \in WF\_EVENTS(S)} WF_{unprimed\_var(S)}(e)$$

$$SF_{unprimed\_var(S)}(S) \equiv \wedge_{e \in SF\_EVENTS(S)} SF_{unprimed\_var(S)}(e)$$

WF_EVENTS(S) is the set of weakly fair events and *SF_EVENTS(S)* is the set of strongly fair events. The two sets satisfy the following constraints:

WF_EVENTS(S) $\cap$ SF_EVENTS(S) = $\varnothing$.

$WF_{unprimed\_var(S)}$ (e) is the weak fairness associated to the event *e* and $SF_{unprimed\_var(S)}$ (e) is the strong fairness associated to the event *e*. Each event is associated with a fairness condition which will be a weak or strong or undefined.

When a system is viewed as a set of events, it is easy to characterize it by a TLA specification. However, when one develops a formal specification in TLA, one has to define *Init(S)*, *Next(S)*, *unprimed_var(S)*, $WF_{unprimed\_var(S)}$(S) and $SF_{unprimed\_var(S)}$ (S).

Let *unprimed_var(S)* be equal to *X*. A system *S* is specified as a set of events that are conditions/

Box 4.

$$\{\{\wedge_{e\in EVENTS(S)} \; Enabled(e) \Rightarrow Relation(e) \;\}\}_{\langle\langle x\rangle\rangle} \; =$$
$$\wedge_{e\in EVENTS(S)} \; Enabled(e) \Rightarrow Relation(e) \wedge ((\wedge_{e\in EVENTS(S)} \; \neg Enabled(e)) \Rightarrow (\forall x \in X: \; x=x'))$$

actions and we introduce a notation dual to the notation of Lamport $[N]_x$: (see Box 4)

Interpretation of Formulae

Let σ be a behavior, i.e. a sequence of states and ξ a valuation of the rigid variables of S. In the following, we denote by s_i, $\xi \models sp$ the satisfaction of the state predicate sp in the state s_i of a transition system and by σ, $\xi \, F$ the satisfaction of the temporal formula F over a trace $\sigma \in Traces(S)$.

Proposition Formulae

s_i, $\xi \models ap$ iff ap holds in the state s_i

State Formulae

s_i, $\xi \models sp$ iff sp holds in the state s_i

Boolean Formulae

s_i, $\xi \models \neg sp$ iff s_i, $\models \xi \; sp$ is false
s_i, $\xi \models sp_1 \wedge sp_2$ iff s_i, $\models \xi \; sp_1$ and $\models s_i$, $\xi \; sp_2$
s_i, $\xi \models sp_1 \vee sp_2$ iff s_i, $\xi \models sp_1$ or s_i, $\xi \models sp_2$
s_i, $\xi \models sp_1 \Rightarrow sp_2$ iff s_i, $\models \xi \; \neg sp_1$ or (s_i, $\xi \models sp_1$ and s_i, $\models \xi \; sp_2$)
s_i, $\xi \models sp_1 \Leftrightarrow sp_2$ iff s_i, $\models \xi \; sp_1 \Rightarrow sp_2$ and s_i, $\xi \models sp_2 \Rightarrow sp_1$
s_i, $\xi \models (\exists x) \; sp$ iff $(\exists x \in V): s_i, \models \xi \; sp$
s_i, $\xi \models (\forall x) \; sp$ iff $(\forall x \in V): s_i, \models \xi \; sp$

Transition Formulae

(s,s'), $\xi \models GS(e)$ iff $s \rightarrow s'$

Let $sp = [e]sp'$. $[e]sp'$ is the weakest precondition $wp(e,sp')$, where sp' is a state predicate. This formula is satisfied by a state which evolves to a state satisfying sp' for every performance of the event e.

s, $\xi \models [e]sp'$ iff for every execution of the event e, if s $\rightarrow$ s' then s', $\models \xi \; sp'$

Let $sp = \langle e \rangle sp'$. $\langle e \rangle sp'$ is the conjugate weakest pre-condition ($wp(e,sp) = \neg[e]\neg sp$). This formula is satisfied by a state which can evolve to a state satisfying sp' by performing the event e.

s, $\xi \models \langle e \rangle sp'$ it exists a performance of the event e, such that, if $s \rightarrow s'$ then s', $\models \xi \; sp'$

Temporal Formulae

We interpret a temporal formula on behaviors. In the definitions below, $\sigma|i, \xi \models F$ means that formula F holds of the suffix of σ from point i onwards.

σ, $\xi \models \Box F$ iff $\sigma|i$, $\models \xi \; F$ for all $i \in N$

The formula $\Box \; F$ asserts that F is true at all times during the behavior σ.

Leads-to property $F \leadsto G$

This formula asserts that every suffix satisfying the temporal property F is followed by some suffix satisfying the temporal property G.

σ, $\xi \models F \leadsto G$ iff for all $i \in N$, if $\sigma|i$, $\models \xi \; F$ then $\models \sigma|j$, $\xi \; G$ for some $j \geq i$
$F \leadsto G \equiv \Box(F \Rightarrow \Diamond G)$ where $\Diamond G = \neg \Box \neg G$

Weak Fairness Assumption

A behavior is weakly fair for some event e iff e occurs infinitely often provided that it is eventually always enabled ($WF_f(e) = \diamond\square grd(e) \Rightarrow \square\diamond GS(e)$)

$\sigma, \xi \models WF_f(e)$ iff it exists $j \in N$ such that for all $i \geq j$, $\sigma|i$, ξ $grd(e)$ then for all $n \in N$, it exists $m \in N$ such that for all $k \geq n+m$, $(s_i, \models s_k)$, ξ $GS(e)$.

Strong Fairness Assumption

A behavior is weakly fair for some event e iff e occurs infinitely often provided that it is eventually always enabled ($SF_f(e) = \square\diamond grd(e) \Rightarrow \square\diamond GS(e)$)

$\sigma, \xi \models SF_f(e)$ iff for all $i \in N$, it exists $j \in N$ such that for all $l \geq i+j$, $\sigma|l$, $\xi \models grd(e)$ then for all $n \in N$, it exists $m \in N$ such that for all $k \geq n+m$, (s_i, s_k), $\models \xi$ $GS(e)$.

Reasoning on Systems

When a system S is specified by a TLA specification, $Spec(S)$, temporal properties can be proved and can be stated in a very natural way. A set of rules is available. In [Mery & Petin, 1998], the authors have used the temporal language for modeling and verification of control systems. The invariance of I for S is simply stated as follows: $Spec(S) \Rightarrow \square\varphi$

1. $Init(S) \Rightarrow I$
2. $\forall e \in Events(S): I \wedge Enabled(e) \Rightarrow [e]I$
3. $I \Rightarrow \varphi$

The proof of the property is based on the use of an intermediate assertion starting the computation states.

An eventuality property for S is stated as follows:

$Spec(S) \Rightarrow (P \leadsto Q)$

When one wants to prove an eventuality property as above, we have to discover intermediate properties and state the largest set of states leading to Q. The semantical completeness of a set of rules for deriving eventuality properties under fairness assumptions is based on the definition of new predicate transformers. The use of proof lattices would help people to prove eventuality properties in a graphical notation.

Finally, proving systems is a crucial question when they exist but we can use a methodological approach for constructing systems based on new predicate transformers. A system S_1 is refined by a system S_2, when $Spec(S_2) \Rightarrow Spec(S_1)$.

The refinement relationship is simply an implication property; however, even if the statement is simple, the problem is to make as simple as possible the task of the user and the use of a theorem prover can be helpful. Proofs in TLA are carried out using proof rules and rules of the classical logic. It is clear that the main advantage is that every thing is stated as a logical object and relations as provability or refinement are stated using the logical implication. Nevertheless we have to define a methodology for developing specifications and refinement of specifications. The refinement states a property between logical formulae interpreted over external behavior.

We can summarize several remarks on the construction of a specification in TLA+ versus a B specification. It is clear that we need to define an invariant for the transition of the system as in B. However, we do not need to use explicit temporal sequences as Abrial and Mussat are using. TLA+ defines very abstract specifications, however, we can combine B and TLA: it is a very simple compromise and the two methods can win methodological gain from the other one. TLA stands as a semantical framework for an extension of B.

VERIFICATION RULES OF LIVENESS PROPERTIES IN TEMPORAL EVENT-B SYSTEMS

In this section, we give verification rules (WF, SF and $LATTICE$) to prove liveness properties under fairness assumptions.

Under Weak Fairness

Let S be an extended B event system and *WF_ EVENTS (S)* is the set of events of the system S satisfying the weak fair assumption. Let $[e]P$ be the weakest pre-condition which ensures that P is true after the execution of the event e. Let $\langle e \rangle P(\neg[e] \neg P)$ be the conjugate weakest pre-condition, i.e. the state from which it is possible for an event e to ensure P. The following rule is used to prove a leads-to formula under a weak fairness assumption.

$I \wedge P \wedge \neg Q \Rightarrow [e] (P \vee Q)$ for all event e of S
It exists an event e of S where:

$\qquad I \wedge P \wedge \neg Q \Rightarrow \langle e \rangle$ true $\wedge [e] Q$
$\qquad e \in WF\_EVENTS\ (S)$
WF. $\rule{5cm}{0.4pt}$
$\qquad S \models P \rightsquigarrow Q$

In this rule, P and Q are state predicates, I is the invariant of the B event system S. By the first premise, any successor of a state satisfying P has to satisfy P or Q, so P must hold for as long as Q has not been true. By the second premise, it exists a successor of a state satisfying P must satisfy Q and ensures that in every state, the event e is enabled ($\langle e \rangle$ true means the feasibility condition of the event e), and so the assumption of weak fairness ensures that e eventually occurs, unless Q has become true before. Finally, the third premise ensures that e is an event for which weak fairness is assumed.

Proof of a Liveness Property under Weak Fairness

To see why the rule is correct, assume that $\sigma = s_0, s_1, \dots s_i, \dots$ is a behavior satisfying $\Box I \wedge WF\_EVENTS(S)$, and that P holds in s_i. We have to show that Q holds of some states s_j with $j \geq i$. Let s_0 be the initial state and s_i satisfies P. Suppose that no next state satisfies Q, so all next states must satisfy P. By the second premise, it exists

a successor of a state satisfying P in which an event e is enabled and always its execution carry out in a state satisfying Q (contradiction). So, from a state s_i satisfying P, we can reach a state $s_j (j \geq i)$ satisfying Q with the execution of an event e under weak fairness.

Under Strong Fairness

Let S be a B event system and *SF_EVENTS(S)* is the set of strong fair events. As similar to the previous rule, the following rule is used to prove a leads-to formula from a strong fairness assumption.

$I \wedge P \wedge \neg Q \Rightarrow [e] (P \vee Q)$ for all event e of S.
It exists an event e of S where:
$I \wedge P \wedge \neg Q \Rightarrow [e] Q$
$S \models \Box(I \wedge P \wedge \neg Q) \Rightarrow \Diamond grd(e)$
$e \in SF\_EVENTS\ (S)$
SF. $\rule{5cm}{0.4pt}$
$S \models P \rightsquigarrow Q$

In this rule, P and Q are state predicates, I is again an invariant, e is an event for which strong fairness is assumed. We assume that σ is a behavior satisfying $\Box I \wedge SF(e)$ and that P holds of a state s_i. We have to show that Q holds of some s_j with $j \geq i$. By the first premise, any successor of a state satisfying P has to satisfy P or Q. By the second premise, it exists an event $e \in S$ where its execution from a state satisfying P evolves the system to a state satisfying Q. The third premise ensures that in all of these states, the event e is enabled, and so the assumption of strong fairness ensures that eventually e occurs, unless Q has become true before, in which case we are done. Finally, the last premise ensures that e is an event for which strong fairness is assumed.

Under LATTICE Rule

The Lattice rule is used to verify complex liveness properties using well-founded relations. $(S, <)$ is a binary relation such that there does not exist an infinite descending chain $x1 \prec x2, \dots$ of elements $xi \in S$. F and G are temporal formulae.

LATTICE

$(S, \prec)$ is a well-founded relation over S

$\forall x \in S: F(x) \sim> G \vee (\exists y \in S: (y \prec x) \wedge F(y))$

$(\exists x \in S: F(x)) \sim> G$ (x not free in G)

In this rule, x and y are rigid variables such that x does not occur in G and y does not occur in F. The second hypothesis of the rule is itself a temporal formula that requires that every occurrence of F, for any value $x \in S$, be followed either by an occurrence of G, or again by some F, for some smaller value y. Because the first hypothesis ensures that there cannot be an infinite descending chain of values in S, eventually G must become true. This rule allows us to derive liveness properties by induction over some well-founded ordering.

Other Verification Rules

These rules can be used to prove complex Leadsto formulas. (see Box 5)

REFINEMENT OF LIVENESS PROPERTIES IN TEMPORAL EVENT-B SYSTEMS

As the B refinement preserves invariance properties through refinement steps, we would like to get the reservation of eventuality properties.

B Refinement

$M \sqsubseteq_{EB} N \cong \forall \varphi \in \beta: [M]\varphi \Rightarrow [N]\varphi$. $[M]\varphi$ denotes the application of the generalized substitution M on φ and defines the weakest precondition of M with respect to φ. φ is an assertion and β is the assertion language used by the Event-B method.

Box 5.

$$\frac{P \sim> Q \quad Q \sim> R}{P \sim> R} \qquad (transition)$$

$$\frac{P \sim> Q}{(\exists x: P(x)) \sim> (\exists x: Q(x))} \qquad (exists)$$

$$\frac{P \sim> Q \quad R \sim> Q}{P \vee R \sim> Q} \qquad (disjunction)$$

$$\frac{P \Rightarrow Q}{P \sim> Q} \qquad (deduction)$$

Extended B Refinement

$M \sqsubseteq_{EB} N \cong$

1) $\sqsubseteq_B M N$
2) $\forall P \in \beta$, if $Spec(M) \Rightarrow P$ is valid then $Spec(N) \Rightarrow P$ is valid

The property $M \sqsubseteq_B N$ is supported by the B environment but the problem now is to prove that $\forall P, Q \in \beta: M$ satisfy $P \sim> Q \Rightarrow N$ satisfy $P \sim> Q$. Clearly, we can prove properties for a finite number of couples as (P, Q) but not for every couple.

Property 1. Let us consider the two following abstract systems M and N such that $M.\text{EVENTS} \cup \{P\} = N.\text{EVENTS}$, P is a new event that does not modify variables modified by events of M, the list of variables of M is X and the list of variables of N is X, y (P modifies only y). If $M.\text{INVARIANT}$ is the invariant of M, then it is also invariant for N.

Property 2. Let us consider the two following abstract systems M and N such that $M.\text{EVENTS} \cup \{P\} = N.\text{EVENTS}$, P is a new event that does not modify variables modified by events of M, the list of variables of M is X and the list of variables of N is X,y (P modifies only y). Then $M \sqsubseteq_{EB} N$

Property 3. Let us consider the two following abstract systems M and N such that $M.\text{EVENTS} = \{E1...En\}$, $N.\text{EVENTS} = \{E\|P:$ $E \in M.\text{EVENTS}\}$ P does not modify variables used by M. Then $M \sqsubseteq_{EB}$

The Event-B method requires that the number of events in the refinement system is equal to the number of vents in the refined events; we introduce the SKIP event that is implicit in the general noice of the events of every abstract system. SKIP preserves proof obligations of the refined system.

Property 4. Let M and N be two abstract systems, P does not modify variables used by M, $M.\text{EVENTS} = \{E1...En, skip\}$, $N.\text{EVENTS} = M.\text{EVENTS} \cup P$. Then $M \sqsubseteq_{EB} N$.

Property 5. Let M and N be two abstract systems such that:

1. $M.\text{EVENTS} = \{e1...en\}$, $N.\text{EVENTS} = \{p1... pn\}$
2. $\forall i \in \{1...n\}$: $ei \sqsubseteq_{EB} pi$
3. $\forall i \in \{1...n\}$: $trm(ei) = trm(pi)$

Then $\forall P, Q$: M satisfy $P{\sim}{>}Q \Rightarrow N$ satisfy $P{\sim}{>}Q$.

It is clear that if one strengthens an invariant in an abstract system we keep the leads to properties, because of the definition of the leadsto operator. *trm(ei)* denotes the termination of the event *ei*.

Property 6. Let M and N be two abstract systems such that:

1. $N.\text{INVARIANT} \Rightarrow M.\text{INVARIANT}$
2. $N.\text{EVENTS} = M.\text{EVENTS}$

Then $M \sqsubseteq_{EB} N$.

That ends our list of possible transformations on abstract systems to preserve properties as leads to properties. The main problem is related to the fairness assumption that does not allow a monotonic reasoning through the refinement. The fairness assumption at a defined level depends of the global system and if at abstract level, we have an event *e* executed with weak fairness assumption and at refined level, this event is refined into a set of events *e1*, *e2*, *e3* and *e*; then the activation of the event *e* at refined level depends of the other events and their activation. Then, an event with weak fairness assumption at abstract level can have a strong fairness assumption at refined level.

TRANSLATION RULES FROM A TEMPORAL B MODEL INTO A TLA+ MODULE

We present in this section just transformation rules from a temporal B model into a TLA+ module and we dot not give in this paper a proof that the translation between the B specification language and TLA+ is appropriate. This would consist in taking the formal semantics of the B specification language and the formal semantics of TLA+ and giving a proof that the proposed translation is semantics-preserving [Mosbahi, 2008]. The tables below show the correspondence between B syntax and TLA+ one.

- *Clauses key word correspondence.* In the table below, we will give the different clauses from a temporal B model translated in a TLA+ module.
- *Modeling of data.* Both B and TLA+ are based on Zermelo-Frankel set theory in which every value is a set. The modeling of data is based on constants, variables, sets, relations and functions. In the tables below, we will give the translation rules of data from a temporal B model to a TLA+ module.

The Event-B method has used a simplification of classical set theory. The only basic set classical theoretic constructs axiomatized are the most natural ones: cartesian product ($\times$), power-set (P) and set comprehension ($\{|\}$). The cartesian product

Table 2. Clauses Names in B and TLA+

B model	TLA+ module
SYSTEM	MODULE
REFINEMENT	MODULE
REFINES	EXTENDS
CONSTANTS	CONSTANTS
VARIABLES	VARIABLES
PROPERTIES	ASSUME
INVARIANT	INVARIANT
INITIALISATION	INIT
ASSERTIONS	THEOREM
FAIRNESS	FAIRNESS
EVENTUALITY	LIVENESS

of two sets s and t is the set whose members are all the ordered pairs whose two components are members of s and t respectively. The power-set of a set s is the set whose members are all the sets whose members belong to s. A set is defined in comprehension with respect to another set s when the members of the former are exactly the members of s satisfying a certain predicate. The set theory in TLA+ is based on the simple forms of the constructs $\{x \in S: P\}$ (the subset of S consisting of all elements x satisfying property P) and $\{e: x \in S\}$ (the set of elements of the form e, for all x in the set S) as primitives, and the more general forms are defined in terms of them. In TLA+, the two powerful operators of set theory

are UNION and SUBSET, defined as follows: UNION S is the union of the elements of S (in math $\cup_s$) and SUBSET S is the set of all subsets of S. $T \in$ SUBSET S iff $T \subseteq S$ (it is the power set of P(S) or 2^S). We find correspondence between the B and TLA+ set theories.

In the Table 4, we give correspondence between functions in B and TLA+. In this table, the symbols *TF*, *PF*, *TS*, *PS*, *TI* and *PI* describes respectively total and partial function, total and partial surjection and total and partial injection. We associate the value *undef* to the elements where the function is not defined because in TLA+ we have just total function. $f' = [f \text{EXCEPT} ![x] = y]$ means that the function f is equal to f except for x where $f[x] = y$.

- *Events.* Events in B method are actions in the language TLA+. In the following, we give the translation of the three event types B into TLA+ actions where X = *unprimed_var(e)*.
- *Safety properties.* The syntax of safety properties in B and TLA+ are quite similar because the two methods are based on the first order logic. The table VI provides a translation of safety formulae from B to TLA+.
- *Liveness properties.* The translation is obvious because the extension is inspired by the syntax of TLA+. In the following, we

Table 3. Constants, Variables and Sets Translation

B model	TLA+ module
c_1, c_2 in CONSTANTS	c_1, c_2 in CONSTANTS
v_1, v_2 in VARIABLES	v_1, v_2 in VARIABLES
E_1 in SETS $E_2 = \{x_1...,x_n\}$ in SETS	E_1 in CONSTANTS $x_1..,x_n$ in CONSTANTS and $E_2 = \{x_1...,x_n\}$ occurs after the clause ASSUME
$\{e_1,....,e_n\}$	$\{e_1,....,e_n\}$
$\{x \mid x \in S \wedge P\}$	$\{x \in S: P\}$
$\{e \mid x \in S\}$	$\{e: x \in S\}$
$P(S)$	SUBSET S

Table 4. Functions translation

B model	TLA+ module
$f(e)$	$f[e]$
$Dom(f)$	$Domain\ f$
$(\lambda\ x.x \in S \mid e)$ Lambda expression	$[x \in S \to e]$
$H\ TF\ K,\ H\ PF\ K,\ H\ TS\ K,$ $H\ PS\ K,\ H\ TI\ K,\ H\ PI\ K$	$[H \to K]$
$F_i: S\ PF\ T$ we have $F = F_u \cup F_i$ where $F_u: (S - dom(Fi))\ \_\ F$ and $F_u = (\lambda\ x.x \in S - dom(F_i)$ $\mid Undef)$	$[S \to T \cup Undef]$
$f[S]$	$Image(f, S) \equiv \{f[x]: x \in S\}$
$f(x):= y$	$f' = [f\ EXCEPT\ ![x] = y]$

give the translation rules of liveness properties from a B model to a TLA+ module where e is an event in B and an action in TLA+, *F* and *G* arc liveness properties.

PROTOTYPE SYSTEM B2TLA+

The transformation of a B model into a TLA+ module is based on the technique of syntax-directed translation, which adds semantics actions in the B grammar to obtain an equivalent TLA+ module. Based on our approach to ensure the verification of safety and liveness properties, we implement a prototype system. Figure 3 describes the architecture of the prototype system which is implemented using the Flex-Yacc tool. Liveness

Table 5. Events translation

B event	TLA+ action
$e \equiv BEGIN\ x:\ P(x_0,x)\ END$	$e \equiv \wedge P(x,x')$ $\wedge UNCHANGED\ \langle X \rangle$
$e \equiv SELECT\ G(x)\ THEN$ $x:\ Q(x_0,x)\ END$	$e \equiv \wedge G(x)$ $\wedge Q(x,x')$ $\wedge UNCHANGED\ \langle X \rangle$
$e \equiv ANY\ t\ WHERE\ G(t,x)$ $THEN\ x:\ R(x_0,x,t)\ END$	$e \equiv \exists\ t:\ \wedge G(t,x)$ $\wedge R(x,x',t)$ $\wedge UNCHANGED\ \langle X \rangle$

Table 6. Safety formulae translation

B formula	TLA+ formula
P	P
$\neg P$	$\neg P$
$P \wedge Q$	$P \wedge Q$
$P \vee Q$	$P \vee Q$
$P \Rightarrow Q$	$P \Rightarrow Q$
$P \Leftrightarrow Q$	$P \Leftrightarrow Q$
$!x.(P \Rightarrow Q)$	$\forall\ x: (P \Rightarrow Q)$
$!(x,y).(P \Rightarrow Q)$	$\forall\ (x,y): (P \Rightarrow Q)$
$\exists\ x.(P \wedge Q)$	$\exists\ x: (P \wedge Q)$

properties are given by the user who introduces fairness conditions and eventuality properties to be verified by the system model. The user has to give the fairness condition (weak fairness, strong fairness) for each event. These liveness properties are added into a B model in order to obtain a temporal B model.

Table 7. Liveness properties translation

B operators	TLA+ operators	Definition
WF(e)	WF(e)	weak fairness for e
SF(e)	SF(e)	strong fairness for e
$F \sim> G$	$F \sim> G$	F leads to G
$\Box F$	$\Box F$	F is always true
$\Diamond F$	$\Diamond F$	F is eventually true

Figure 3.

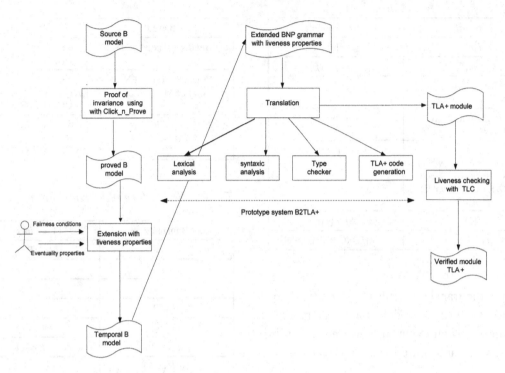

Figure 4.

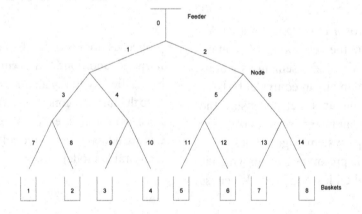

CASE STUDY: A PARCEL SORTING SYSTEM PSS

In this section, we present an example of reactive system: a parcel sorting device [Jaray & Mahjoub, 1996] which will

Informal Description of the System

The problem is to sort parcels into baskets according to an address written on the parcel. In order to achieve such a sorting function we are provided with a device made of a feeder connected to the root of a binary tree made of switches and pipes as shown in Figure 4. The switches are the nodes

Figure 5.

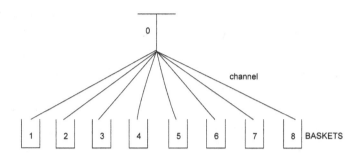

of the tree, pipes are the edges and baskets are the leaves. A parcel, thanks to gravity, can slide down through switches and pipes to reach a basket.

A switch is connected to an entry pipe and two exit pipes, a parcel crossing the switch is directed to an exit pipe depending on the switch position. The feeder releases one parcel at a time in the router, the feeder contains a device to read the address of the parcel to be released. When released, a parcel enters a first switch (the root of the binary tree) and slides down the router to reach a basket. The controller can activate the feeder and change the switches position. For safety reasons, it is required that switch change should not occur when a parcel is crossing it. In order to check this condition, sensors are placed at the entry and the exits of each switch.

Refinement-Based Verification of PSS

We define in this section at first time the abstract level of the PSS, before we describe thereafter the refinement based verification of the PSS.

Abstract Level

The seven steps proposed above (section 4.1) are applied in this section where the PSS abstract model of the system is given Figure 5.

Step 1: Abstract B model of the system.

Sorting device. The sorting device consists of a feeder and a sorting layout. The feeder has two functions: selection of the next parcel to be introduced into the sorting layout and gate opening (releasing a parcel in the sorting layout). We introduce the events *Select_parcel* and *Release* to capture the two functions. In order to produce the abstract model of the sorting layout, we have to notice that a given state of the switches forms a *channel* linking the entrance to a unique sorting basket. A basket is an element of a set named *BASKETS*. Channels and sorting baskets are in a one to one correspondence. Therefore, the abstract model of the sorting device can be reduced to a single variable *channel* taking the value of the sorting basket it leads to, namely a value in the set *BASKETS*. The *channel* value is changed by the event *Set channel*.

Parcels. Parcels, as part of the environment, are represented as elements of a set we name *PARCELS*. We use a total function (*adr*) from *PARCELS* to the interval *BASKETS* to refer to the parcels address. We give the status "*stored*" to the parcel which has reached a sorting basket. The variable (*stored*) is a function from *PARCELS* to *BASKETS*. The goal of the sorting system is to decrease the set of the parcels to sort. The variable *sorted* represents the set of sorted parcels. The remaining parcels are defined by the expression *PARCELS - sorted* named *TO_SORT*. As *next* is undefined when the sorting device is empty, we have introduced a set *EPARCELS* of which *PARCELS* is a proper subset; *next* is an element of *EPARCELS* and assignment of any value in *EPARCELS - PARCELS* stands for "undefined".

The expression *EPARCELS - PARCELS* will be referred as *UNDEF*. The selection of a parcel is an event which may be activated once the device is free and the variable *next* is undefined, which means that no parcel is processed. The variable *current* designs the current parcel in the sorting system. (see Box 6).

Controller. The controller has to ensure right parcel routing. Two events are added for the controller: *Set_channel* and *Release*. The event *Set_channel* assigns to channel the value of *adr_next*. The event *Release* changes the state of the sorting device from free to busy. (see Box 7 and Box 8).

Moving parcels. In our abstraction a parcel takes no time to travel from the feeder to a basket. A parcel arrives in the basket to which the channel leads up. When the event *Cross_sorting* occurs, the current parcel sorting is finished and then, of course, the current parcel becomes undefined. (see Box 9).

Simulation of the B model with ProB. We have used ProB [Leuschel & Butler, 2003], which is a simulator and model checker for the (B/Event-B) Method. It allows fully automatic animation of many B specifications, and can be used to systematically check a specification for errors. ProB's animation facilities allow users to gain confidence in their specifications, and unlike the animator provided by the B-Toolkit, the user does not have to guess the right values for the operation arguments or choice variables. ProB contains a model checker and a constraint-based checker, both of which can be used to detect various errors in B specifications. ProB enables users to uncover errors that are not easily discovered by existing tools.

Step 2: Verification of the B model by proof and model-checking.

For us, the primary way of verification is done by mechanical proof. But we also have used model-checking with ProB in order to make partial verifications and to find counter-examples.

Box 6.

```
Select_parcel =
  ANY p Where p ∈ TO_SORT ∧ current ∈ UNDEF ∧
  next ∈ UNDEF ∧ ready_to_sort = FALSE
  THEN
  Adr_next:= adr(p) || next:= p
  END;
```

Box 7.

```
Set_channel =SELECT
  Ready_ to_sort = FALSE ∧
  next ∈ PARCELS ∧
  current ∈ UNDEF
  THEN
  channel:= adr_next ||
  ready_to_sort:= TRUE
  END;
```

Box 8.

```
Release= SELECT
  next ∈ PARCELS ∧ current ∈ UNDEF ∧
  ready_to_sort = TRUE
  THEN
  current:= next || next: ∈ UNDEF ||
  ready_to_sort:= FALSE
  END;
```

In order to have a finite number of transitions with our models, we can not let some variable time increase indefinitely. Therefore, we define another version for the event which deals with these variables for model-checking. In any case, model-checking provides a convenient way to discover invariants and to test them before the proof. With the B prover the proof is cut into small "Proof Obligations" (PO). Some of those PO are automatically discharged and some need user interactions. The procedure of proof, with an invariant, leads to the discovery of an invariant strong enough to be inductive.

We can always start with a small invariant containing types of variables and some requirements for the refinements of data or events. If we start to do the proof with an invariant that is too weak then the proof will fail with an impossible interactive proof. With this failure we see the missing piece of information about the system state: we add it to the invariant and retry to prove. For verification purpose, we add the following invariants to help the prover. (see Box 10).

The model of the system has to verify the following invariant meaning that every arrival parcel reaches its corresponding basket. (see Box 11).

All generated proof obligations are verified with the B Click_n_Prove tool using the automatic and interactive provers.

Step 3: Requirement of liveness properties.

In our example, we need to consider the dynamics of the system. Our model must take into account the following properties:

1.   Every parcel introduced in the entry eventually reaches one of the baskets, this property is described with:

$$\forall p.(p \in TO\_SORT \twoheadrightarrow \Diamond stored(p) \in Baskets)$$

2.   Every parcel introduced in the entry must reach the basket corresponding to its destination

$$\forall p.(p \in TO\_SORT) \Rightarrow stored(p) = adr(p)$$

3.   Weak fairness conditions on the events is assumed.

These properties can not be specified in the clause INVARIANT. We need to extend the ex-

Box 9.

```
Cross_sorting = SELECT
  current ∈ PARCELS
  THEN
  stored(current):= channel ||
  sorted:= sorted ∪ { current} ||
  current: ∈ UNDEF
  END;
```

Box 10.

```
(read_ to_sort = TRUE ⇒ channel = adr_next) ∧
(current ∈ PARCELS ⇒ channel = adr(current)) ∧
(next ∈ PARCELS ⇒ adr_next = adr(next)) ∧
```

Box 11.

```
∀ p.(p ∈ PARCELS ∧ p ∈ dom(stored) ⇒ stored(p)= adr(p))
```

pressivity of Event-B to take into account such properties.

Step 4: Translation of the temporal B model into a TLA+ module.

In the following, we present the translation of the temporal B model into a TLA+ module using the prototype system B2TLA+ in order to check liveness properties.

B Specification

Boxes 12-19

Box 12.

```
MODEL Parcel_routing
SETS EPARCELS ; NODES
CONSTANTS
PARCELS, adr, BASKETS
PROPERTIES
PARCELS ⊂ EPARCELS ∧
PARCELS ≠ ∅ ∧
BASKETS ≠ ∅ ∧
adr ∈ PARCELS → BASKETS
```

Box 13.

```
DEFINITIONS
TO SORT == PARCELS - sorted ;
UNDEF == EPARCELS - PARCELS
```

Box 14.

```
VARIABLES
stored, channel, next, current,
sorted, ready_to_sort, adr_next
INVARIANT
stored ∈ PARCELS →BASKETS ∧ channel ∈ BASKETS ∧
next ∈ EPARCELS ∧
current ∈ EPARCELS ∧
ready_to_sort ∈ BOOL ∧
sorted ⊆ PARCELS ∧
adr_next ∈ BASKETS
```

Box 15.

```
INITIALISATION
stored:= {} ||
channel: ∈ BASKETS ||
next: ∈ UNDEF ||
current: ∈ UNDEF ||
sorted:= {} ||
ready_to_sort:= FALSE ||
adr_next: ∈ BASKETS
```

Box 16.

```
Select_parcel =
ANY p Where p ∈ TO_SORT ∧
next ∈ UNDEF
THEN
adr_next:= adr(p) || next:= p
END;
```

404

Box 17.

```
Set_channel =
SELECT
current ∈ UNDEF ∧
next ∈ PARCELS ∧
ready_to_sort = FALSE
THEN
channel:= adr_next ||
ready_to_sort:= TRUE
END;
```

Box 19.

```
Cross_sorting =
SELECT
current ∈ PARCELS
THEN
stored(current):= channel ||
sorted:= sorted ∪ {current} ||
current: ∈ UNDEF
END;
```

TLA+ Specification

Boxes 20-28.

The TLA+ module has to verify the following invariant:

The TLA+ specification is as follows: (see Box 29)

Step 5: Verification of the liveness properties with TLC.

The invariants are verified with the TLA+ specification. Let *I* be the set of all the invariants of a module TLA+. The TLA+ specification satisfy *I* ((*Spec* ⇒ □ *I*). Also, the TLA+ module satisfy liveness properties with the TLC model checker (*Spec* ⇒ *Liveness*).

Step 6: Associate predicate diagram.

The TLC model checker can check a finite model of a specification obtained by instantiating the constant parameters and, if necessary,

Box 18.

```
Release =
SELECT
current ∈ UNDEF ∧
next ∈ PARCELS ∧
ready_to_sort = TRUE
THEN
current:= next || next: ∈ UNDEF ||
ready_to_sort:= FALSE
END;
```

specifying constraints to make the set of reachable states finite. For the verification of infinite state systems, we have used the predicate diagrams [Cansell, Méry & Merz, 2001-a; Cansell, Méry & Merz, 2001-b].

In a first abstraction, we represent the state of the system by the variables *ready_to_sort*, *next*, *current*, *channel*, *sorted* and *stored*. The predicate diagram shown in Figure 6 describes the first abstraction of the system. The left-hand node, named *Init*, is labelled by the predicate *next* ∈ *UNDEF* indicating that no parcel is chosen, this is the initial node. The node *Selected_parcel* is labelled by the predicates *next* ∈ *PARCELS* and *adr_next=adr(p)* indicating respectively the selection of the next parcel to be introduced into the sorting layout and the memorization of the

Box 20.

```
MODULE    Parcel_routing
CONSTANTS
EPARCELS, PARCELS,
BASKETS, NODES, noBaskets, adr
ASSUME
PARCELS ⊆ EPARCELS
∧ PARCELS ≠EPARCELS
∧ PARCELS ≠ { }
∧ BASKETS ≠ { }
∧ noBaskets ∉ BASKETS
∧ adr ∈ [PARCELS →BASKETS]
```

Box 21.

```
TO SORT = PARCELS \ sorted
UNDEF = EPARCELS \ PARCELS
```

Box 23.

```
Init =
∧ stored= [p ∈ PARCELS → noBaskets ]
∧ channel = noBaskets
∧ next ∈ UNDEF
∧ current ∈ UNDEF
∧ sorted = { }
∧ ready_to_sort = FALSE
∧ adr_next = noBaskets
```

Box 24.

```
Select_parcel =
∧ next ∈ UNDEF
∧ ∃ p ∈ TO_SORT: ∧ next ' = p
                 ∧ adr_next'=adr(p)
∧ UNCHANGED ( channel, sorted,
stored, current, ready_to_sort )
```

Box 26.

```
Release =
∧ current ∈ UNDEF
∧ next ∈ PARCELS
∧ ready_to_sort = TRUE
∧ current' = next
∧ next' ∈ UNDEF
∧ ready_to_sort' = FALSE
∧  UNCHANGED (channel, stored,
sorted, adr_next)
```

destination address. The node *positioned_channel* is labelled by the predicates *channel=adr_next* and *ready_to_sort=TRUE* indicating respectively that

Box 22.

```
VARIABLES
stored, channel, next, current,
sorted, ready_to_sort, adr_next
TypeInvariant =
∧ stored ∈ PARCELS →BASKETS ∪ {no-
Baskets}
∧ channel ∈ BASKETS ∪ {noBaskets}
∧ next ∈ EPARCELS
∧ current ∈ EPARCELS
∧ ready_to_sort ∈ BOOLEAN
∧ sorted ⊆ PARCELS
∧ adr_next ∈ BASKETS
```

Box 25.

```
Set_channel =
∧ current ∈ UNDEF
∧ next ∈ PARCELS
∧ ready_to_sort = FALSE
∧ channel'= ad_ next
∧ ready_to_sort'= TRUE
∧ UNCHANGED ⟨stored, sorted, next,
current, adr_next⟩
```

the channel takes the value of the sorting basket it leads to and the system is ready to release a parcel. The node *Gate_opened* labeled by the predicates *current=next* and *next ∈ UNDEF* indicating that there is a parcel in the sorting system to be sorted. The node *Parcel_in_basket* is labelled by the predicates *NoParcelStored=FALSE* and sorted ≠ ∅ indicating that the parcel is arrived in the basket to which the channel leads up.

Step 7: verification of liveness properties by the DIXIT tool.

We require weak fairness for the actions *Select_parcel*, *Set_channel*, *Release* and *Cross_sorting*, and therefore every parcel introduced must reach the basket corresponding to its destination

Box 27.

```
Cross_sorting =
∧ current ∈ PARCELS
∧ stored'=[stored EXCEPT![current] =channel]
∧ sorted'=sorted ∪ {current}
∧ current' ∈ UNDEF
∧ UNCHANGED ⟨ channel,ready_to_sort,adr_next⟩
```

Box 28.

```
Invariant==
∧ ready_to_sort = TRUE ⇒ channel = adr_next
∧ current ∈ PARCELS ⇒ channel = adr[current]
∧ next ∈ PARCELS              ⇒ adr_next = adr[next]
∧ ∀ p ∈ PARCELS: p ∈ DOMAIN stored ⇒ stored[p] = adr[p]
```

```
Box 29.

Spec== Init ∧□[Next]_trvars ∧ Fairness ∧ Liveness
       - Next== Select_parcel ∨ Set_channel ∨ Release ∨ Cross_sorting
       - trvars == ⟨channel, current, next, stored, sorted, ready_to_sort,
adr_next⟩
       - Fairness ==    WF_trvars (Select_parcel) ∧ WF_trvars (Set_channel)
                               ∧ WF_trvars (Release) ∧ WF_trvars (Cross_sorting)
       - Liveness ==           ∧∀ p ∈ TO_SORT ~> stored[p] = adr[p]
                                ∧∀ p ∈ TO_SORT ⇒ ◇ stored[p] ∈ BASKETS
```

address. We can use the SPIN model checker to verify the formula ($\forall p \in TO\_SORT \Rightarrow stored[p] = adr[p]$) over the diagram and this property is guaranteed to be preserved by the subsequent refinement steps. With this diagram we associate the TLA+ module that fixes the interpretation of the terms and predicates of the predicate diagram.

First refinement:

Once the first abstract model is verified, the refinement process has to be recursively applied using the seven steps defined in the section 4.1.

Step 1: B model of the system.

In the abstract model, the physical device of the system is reduced to a single variable channel.

A channel value corresponds to a setting of nodes called switches which correspond to the intermediate nodes (*switches = NODES - BASKETS*).

In order to represent a more concrete sorting device, we introduce the elements: *NODES*, *switches*, *right_n*, *left_n* and *Access*. The set *NODES* designs the nodes of the tree and the leaves (terminal nodes) of the tree correspond to the baskets introduced in the abstract model. The constant function *right_n* corresponds to the right set of subsets of a node *nd* (*right_n* ∈ *switches* → *NODES*) and *left_n* corresponds to the left set of subsets of a node *nd* (*left_n* ∈ *switches* → *NODES*). The constant function access associ-

Figure 6.

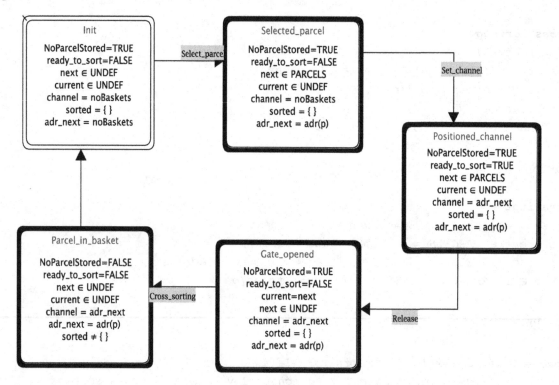

ates to each node the set of subsets of this node that corresponds to the set of baskets which it can attempt. The sorting device can be seen as a binary tree where nodes correspond to switches and edges to pipes connecting the nodes. To reach its destination basket, each parcel crosses a fixed number of switches which depend on its destination address. In the first refinement, we add details on the physical device. We add the new variables *exit*, *nd*, *rac* and *lng*. The variable *exit* designs the next node to be visited by the parcel and *nd* designs a node in the sorting device tree structure (the root node called *rac* is in the level 0). The variable *lng* models the level of a node *nd* in the sorting device (T corresponds to the depth of the tree).

i. **Invariant.** The first point to specify in an invariant is the type of the new variables (*exit*, *nd*, *rac*). In this refinement, the variable *channel* is not required any more because we

can deduce the channel from nodes. So, we can replace the abstract variable *channel* by the concrete variables *exit*, *rac* and *nd*. We call this "data refinement". For this we need a "gluing invariant" that relates the value of the abstract variable with the value of the concrete variables. (see Box 30)

This part of the invariant is the most important, but there are more things to express.

ii. **Events.** Events give properties over the transitions of the system. Here, we refine the old events and we add two new events *Set_switch* and *Cross_node*. The first one computes the next node to be visited by the current parcel. This event refines the *Set_channel* one. The choice of the next node depends on the value of *right_n* and *left_n* corresponding to the current node *nd*. If the destination basket (*adr_next*) is included in

Box 30.

```
Gluing Invariant:
(current ∈ PARCELS ∧ nd ∈ switches ∧ exit(nd) ∈ BASKETS ∧ nd ≠ rac ⇒ channel
= exit(nd))
```

the set *access*(*right*(*nd*)) then the next node to reach is the right son (*exit*(*nd*):=*right_n*(*nd*)), otherwise it is the left son. (see Box 31)

The event *Set_channel* is refined and the variable *channel* is refined by the *exit* one. (see Box 32)

In the abstract model, the crossing of the current parcel concerned a single event *Cross_sorting*, here we are concerned by the passing of the parcel through different nodes. The event *cross_node* is introduced to determine the next node to be visited which mean updating the current node

nd. The variable *lng* representing the current level is updated as well. (see Box 33)

The event *Cross_sorting* is refined by a successive occurrences of the event *Cross_node* which is executed since the parcel did not arrived to the destination address. (see Box 34)

Step 2: Verification of the B model.

The refinement model is verified and all the proof obligations including refinement proof obligations are verified automatically and interactively. The B refinement preserves the properties required of the preceding model. This controlled model is a refinement of the abstract

Box 31.

```
Set_switch =
ANY node WHERE node ∈ { right_n(nd),lef_n(nd) }∧
nd ∈ switches ∧ node ∉ BASKETS ∧
next ∈ PARCELS ∧ lng < T-1 ∧ current ∈ UNDEF ∧
adr_next ∈ access(node) ∧ ready_to_sort = FALSE
THEN
exit(nd):= node || nd:= node || lng:= lng+1
END;
```

Box 32.

```
Set_channel =
ANY node WHERE node ∈ { right_n(nd),left_n(nd) }∧
nd ∈ switches ∧ node ∈ BASKETS ∧ lng = T-1 ∧
adr_next = node ∧ next ∈ PARCELS ∧
current ∈ UNDEF ∧ ready_to_sort = FALSE
THEN
exit(nd):= adr_next || nd:= adr_next ||
ready_to_sort:= TRUE || lng:= lng+1
END;
```

Box 33.

```
Cross_node =
SELECT current ∈ PARCELS ∧
exit(nd) ∉ BASKETS ∧ lng < T-1
THEN
nd:= exit(nd) || lng:= lng+1
END;
```

one and all proof obligations are discharged by the prover. With the B prover the proof is cut into small "Proof Obligations" (PO). Some of those PO are automatically discharged and some need user interactions. The procedure of proof, with an invariant, leads to the discovery of an invariant strong enough to be inductive. We can always start with a small invariant containing types of variables and some requirements for the refinements of data or events. If we start to do the proof with an invariant that is too weak then the proof will fail with an impossible interactive proof. With this failure we see the missing piece of information about the system state: we add it to the invariant and retry to prove.

Step 3: Requirement of liveness properties.

Our model has to specify and verify dynamic properties. So, we begin by giving the fairness condition corresponding to each event. This property is described by the following formula: (see Box 35)

The refinement model has to verify the following formula: Every introduced parcel in the sorting system must reach the basket corresponding to its destination address. This property is refined as follows: (see Box 36)

Step 4: Translation of the temporal B model into a TLA+ module.

We use the prototype system B2TLA+ to obtain automatically the TLA+ module.

Step 5: Verification of the liveness properties with TLC.

TLC verifies on finite-state systems the required liveness properties and also the TLA+ modules refinement.

Step 6: Associate predicate diagram.

The predicate diagram in Figure 7 was obtained as a refinement of the diagram in Figure 6 by splitting the abstract node *Positioned_channel* to obtain *Positioned_channel* and *Path_positionned* nodes at the refinement level, and by adding the predicates concerning the variables *nd* and *exit* which we add to increase the state space of the system. Also, the node *Gate_opened* is splitted to obtain *Gate-opened* and *Crossing_node* nodes.

Box 34.

```
Cross_sorting =
SELECT current ∈ PARCELS ∧ exit(nd) ∈ BASKETS ∧ lng = T-1
THEN
stored(current):= exit(nd) || sorted:= sorted ∪ { current} ||
current: ∈ UNDEF || lng:= lng+1
END;
```

Box 35.

```
WF(Select_parcel) ∧ WF(Set_switch) ∧ WF(Set_channel) ∧
WF(Release) ∧ WF(Cross_node) ∧ WF(Cross_sorting).
```

Step 7: Verification of liveness properties by the DIXIT tool.

Using DIXIT, we can verify that the new diagram refines the previous one: first, a structural test confirms that initial nodes of the refining diagram are related to initial nodes of the refined diagram and that transitions at the lower level respect the transitions that existed before in particular, the new transition *Set_switch* refines a stuttering transition at the abstract level. Second, proof obligations are generated to show that the predicates appearing in the refined nodes imply those of the corresponding abstract nodes. In our

example, these obligations are trivially satisfied because we have only added new predicates. Third, model checking ensures that the abstract-level fairness properties are preserved.

CONCLUSION

We have proposed in this chapter a method for the specification and verification of safety and liveness properties for the development of reactive systems using the Event-B method, the language TLA+ and the predicate diagrams with

Box 36.

```
∀ p. (p ∈ TO_SORT ∧ (right_n(nd) ∈ BASKETS or left_n(nd) ∈ BASKETS) ~> stored(p)
= exit(nd)
```

Figure 7.

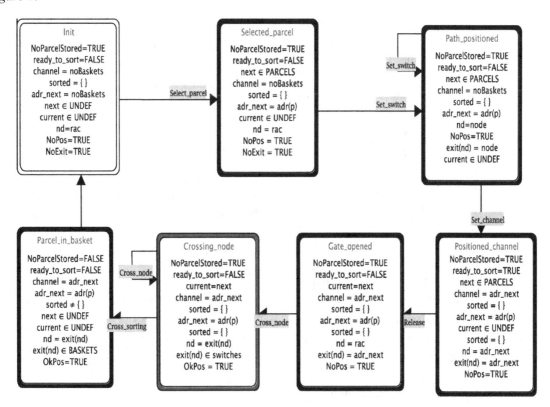

their associated tools. We have first extended the expressivity of the Event-B method to deal with fairness and eventuality properties. Second, we have proposed semantics of the extension over traces, in the same spirit as TLA+ does. Third, we have given verification rules in the axiomatic way of the Event-B method. Finally we have given transformation rules from a temporal B model into a TLA+ module and we have developed a prototype system (B2TLA+), which supports this translation. We have verified thereafter the liveness properties using the TLC model checker. TLC allows us to analyze finite state instances, this is why we have used DIXIT which is a graphical toolkit supporting the use of predicate diagrams for the verification of infinite state systems and, includes annotations for proving liveness properties. The toolkit also supports stepwise development of systems, based on a notion of refinement of predicate diagrams.

Our main idea is to start with an abstract B model of the system under development and then we verify all invariants using the proof tool (*Click_n_Prove*) which supports automatic and interactive proof procedures. For the expression and the verification of fairness and eventuality properties, we can not use the Event-B method because its semantics is expressed in the weakest precondition calculus. Our goal is to give a temporal meaning to a B model and then transform it to an equivalent TLA+ module. TLA+ and B are quite similar, both being based on simple mathematics and when a system is viewed as a set of events, it is easy to characterize it by a TLA+ specification. TLA+ stands as a semantical framework for an extension of B and the expression of fairness and eventuality constraints is a very powerful point of TLA+.

In future work, we plan to apply the paper contribution on real benchmark reactive systems. We plan also to define new required proof obligations. Moreover, the B prover may not be enough powerful for proving new proof obligations but proof engineering is evolving. Future work will explore also, the question of the refinement and the properties of refinement, within the extended language. There are questions on the scheduling policy to address. Tools are a very critical issue in the case of formal methods. The more technical and abstract a formal method is, the more well interfaced tools are needed. The B environments are probably a good starting point for experimenting our extension, but others are also usable like PVS, COQ, ISABELLE,...

ACKNOWLEDGMENT

I thank the researcher Stephan Merz and the professor Jacques Jaray for interesting comments on this paper.

REFERENCES

Abrial, J. R. (1996). *The B-Book: Assigning Programs to Meanings*. Cambridge, UK: Cambridge University Press. doi:10.1017/CBO9780511624162

Abrial, J. R. (1996). Extending B without changing it (for developing distributed systems). In H. Habrias, (Ed.), *Proceedings of the 1st Conference on the B method*, (pp. 169–191).

Abrial, J. R. (2000). Event driven circuit construction. In *MATISSE project*.

Abrial, J. R. (2003). B#:Toward a synthesis between Z and B. In D. Bert, J. P. Bowen, S. King, and Waldén, (eds.), *ZB'2003 – Formal Specification and Development in Z and B*, Turku, Finland, (LNCS 2651, pp. 168–177). Berlin: Springer-Verlag.

Abrial, J. R., & Laffitte, G. (1996). Higher-order mathematics in B. In *Formal Specification and Development in Z and B*.

Abrial, J. R., & Mussat, L. (1997). Specification and design of a transmission protocol by successive refinements using B. In M. Broy & B. Schieder, (eds.), *Mathematical Methods in Program Development,* (NATO ASI Series F: Computer and Systems Sciences vol. 158, pp 129–200). Berlin: Springer.

Abrial, J. R., & Mussat, L. (1998). Introducing dynamic constraints in B. In D. Bert, (Ed.), *B'98: The 2nd international B Conference,* (LNCS 1393, pp83–128). Berlin: Springer Verlag.

Archer, M., Vito, B., & Munoz, C. (2003). Developing user strategies in pvs: A tutorial. In *Proceedings of the First International Workshop on Design and Application of Strategies/Tactics in Higher Order Logics (STRATA).*

Arkoudas, K. Khurshid, S. Marinov, D. & Rinard, M. (2003). Integrating model checking and theorem proving for relational reasoning. In *Proceedings of the 7th International Seminar on Relational Methods in Computer Science (RelMiCS)* (LNCS 3015, pp. 21-33). Berlin: Springer-Verlag.

Back, R. J. (1990). Refinement calculus, part II: Parallel and reactive programs. In Stepwise Refinement of Distributed Systems, *(LNCS 430).* Berlin: Springer-Verlag.

Back, R. J., & Sere, K. (1989). Stepwise refinement of action systems. In *Mathematics of Program Construction* (pp. 115–1380). Berlin: Springer-Verlag.

Back, R. J., & Wright, J. v. (1998). *Refinement Calculus: A Systematic Introduction.* Berlin: Springer-Verlag.

Bellegarde, F., Chouali, S., & Julliand, J. (2002). Verification of dynamic constraints for B event systems under fairness assumptions. In *ZB'2002 – Formal Specification and Development in Z and B,* (LNCS 2272, pp. 477-496). New York: Springer-Verlag.

Bert, D. (2001). Preuve de propriétés d'équité en B: Preuve de l'algorithme d'arbitrage du bus SCSI-3. In *AFADL'2001* (pp. 221–241). ADER/LORIA.

Bert, D., & Cave, F. (2000). *Construction of finite labelled transistion systems from B abstract systems* (pp. 235–254). IFM.

Cansell, D., Méry, D., & Merz, S. (2001). Diagram refinements for the design of reactive systems. *Journal of Universal Computer Science*, 7(2), 159–174.

Cansell, D., Méry, D., & Merz, S. (2001). Formal analysis of a self-stabilizing algorithm using predicate diagrams. In *Workshop Integrating Diagrammatic and Formal Specification Techniques.*

Chandy, K. M., & Misra, J. (1989). *Parallel Program Design.* Austin, TX: Addison-Wesley.

Clarke, E., Grumberg, O., & Peled, D. (1999). *Model checking.* Cambridge, MA: MIT Press.

Clarke, E. M. (1994). Automatic verification of finite-state concurrent systems. In *Application and Theory of Petri Nets.*

Clarke, E. M. (1997). *Temporal logic model checking (abstract).* ILPS.

Clarke, E. M. GRUMBERG, O., Jha, S., Lu, Y., & Veith, H. (2001). Progress on the state explosion problem in model checking. In *Lecture Notes in Computer Science,* (vol. 2000pp. 176–194).

Clarke, E. M., Emerson, E. A., & Sistla, A. P. (1986). Automatic verification of finite-state concurrent systems using temporal logic specifications. *ACM Transactions on Programming Languages and Systems, 8*, 244–263. doi:10.1145/5397.5399

ClearSy. (2002). *Atelier B.* Technical Note, Version 3.6, Aix-en-Provence(F).

Clearsy. (2004). *B4free.* Technical Note, Version B3.7, http://www.b4free.com, Aix-en-Provence(F).

Clearsy.(2004). *B4free.* Aix-en-Provence(F), Technical Note Version B3.7. Retrieved from http://www.b4free.com/

Dijkstra, E. (1975). Guarded commands, non determinacy and formal derivation of programs. *Communications of the ACM, 18*(8), 453–457. doi:10.1145/360933.360975

Dijkstra, E. (1976). *A Discipline of Programming.* Englewood Cliffs, NJ: Prentice-Hall.

Dijkstra, E., & Schweten, C. (1990). *Predicate Calculus and Programm Semantics.* New York: Springer Verlag.

Dijkstra, R. M. (1995). An experiment with the use of predicate transformers in UNITY. *Information Processing Letters, 53*(6), 329–332. doi:10.1016/0020-0190(94)00215-K

Dybå, T., Kampenes, V. B., & Sjøberg, D. I. (2006). A systematic review of statistical power in software engineering experiments. *Information and Software Technology, 48*(8), 745–755. doi:10.1016/j.infsof.2005.08.009

Fejoz, L., Méry, D., & Merz, S. (2005). *DIXIT: a graphical toolkit for predicate abstractions.* [Online]. Retrieved from http://hal.inria.fr/inria-00000767/en/.

Hoare, C. (1969). An axiomatic basis for computer programming. *Communications of the ACM, 12*(10), 576–585. doi:10.1145/363235.363259

Holzmann, G. (2003). Trends in software verification. in *Proceedings of the Formal Methods Europe Conference (FME).*

Jaray, J., & Mahjoub, A. (1996). *Une méthode itérative de construction d'un modèle de système réactif.* TSI.

Julliand, J. Masson, P.A., & Mountassir, H. (1999). Modular verification of dynamic properties for reactive systems. In *IFM,* (pp. 89-108).

Julliand, J., Masson, P.A., & Mountassir, H.(2001). Vérification par model-checking modulaire des propriétés dynamiques introduites en B. *TSI (Technique et Science Informatiques), 20*(7), 927-957.

Kaltenbach, M. (1994). *Model checking for UNITY.* Technical Report CS-TR-94-31, The University of Texas at Austin, Department of Computer Sciences, Austin, TX.

Kaufmann, M., & Moore, J. (2004). Some key research problems in automated theorem proving for hardware and software verification. In *Spanish Royal Academy of Science (Vol. 98,* pp. 181–196). RAMSAC.

Lamport, L. (1994). The temporal logic of actions. *ACM Transactions on Programming Languages and Systems, 16*(3), 872–923. doi:10.1145/177492.177726

Lamport, L. (2002). *Specifying Systems, The TLA+ Language and Tools for Hardware and Software Engineers.* Reading, MA: Addison-Wesley.

Lamport, L., & Yu, Y. (2003). *TLC-The TLA+ Model Checker.* Redmond, WA: Microsoft Research. Retrieved from http://research.microsoft.com/users/lamport/tla/tlc.html

Leuschel, M., & Butler, M. (2003). ProB: A model checker for B. In K. Araki, S. Gnesi, & D. Mandrioli, (Eds.), *FME 2003: Formal Methods,* (LNCS 2805, pp. 855–874). Berlin: Springer-Verlag.

Manna, Z., Anuchitanukul, A., Bjorner, N., Browne, A., Chang, E., & Colon, M. L. de Alfaro, H., Devarajan, H., Sipma, T. & Uribe, T. (1994). *STeP: The Stanford Temporal Prover.* Technical Report CS-TR-94-1518, Stanford University, Department of Computer Science, Stanford, CA.

Manna, Z., & Pnueli, A. (1992). *The Temporal Logic of Reactive and Concurrent Systems: Specification.* Berlin: Springer-Verlag.

Manna, Z., & Pnueli, A. (1995). *Temporal Verification of Reactive Systems: Safety*. Berlin: Springer-Verlag.

Masson, P. A., Mountassir, H., & Julliand, J. (2000). *Modular verification for a class of PLTL properties* (pp. 398–419). IFM.

Méry, D. (1986). *A proof system to derive eventually properties under justice hypothesis* (pp. 536–544). MFCS.

Méry, D. (1987). Méthode axiomatique pour les propriétés de fatalité des programmes parallèles. In *ITA*, (3), 287-322.

Mery, D., & Petin, J. F. (1998). Formal Engineering methods for modelling and verification of control systems. In G. Morel & F. Vernadat, (Eds.), *9th Symposium On Information Control in Manufacturing INCOM*.

Mosbahi, O. (2008). *A formal development approach of automated systems*. Phd thesis, LORIA-Campus Scientifique, France.

Mountassir, H., Bellegarde, F., Julliand, J., & Masson, P. A. (2000). Coopération entre preuve et model checking pour vérifier modulairement des propriétés LTL. In *AFADL* (pp. 127–141). LSR/IMAG.

Pickard, L. M., Kitchenham, B. A., & Jones, P. W. (1998). Combining empirical results in software engineering. *Information and Software Technology, 40*(14), 811–821. doi:10.1016/S0950-5849(98)00101-3

Pnueli, A. (1977). The temporal logic of programs. In *focs77*, (pp. 46–57).

Project, I. ST-511599. (2007). RODIN: Rigorous Open Development Environment for Complex Systems. Technical Note, Retrieved from http://www.event-b.org/platform.html

Ruiz Barradas, H., & Bert, D. (2002). *Specification and proof of liveness properties under fairness assumptions in B event systems* (pp. 360–379). IFM.

Shankar, N. (2000). Combining theorem proving and model checking through symbolic analysis. In *Concurrency Theory (CONCUR)*, (LNCS 1877, pp. 1–16). Springer-Verlag.

Spivey, J. M. (1988). Understanding Z, A Specification Language and its Formal Semantics. In *Tracts in Theoretical Computer Science*. Cambridge, UK: Cambridge University Press.

Wohlin, C. (2005). An analysis of the most cited articles in software engineering journals. *Information and Software Technology, 47*(15), 957–964. doi:10.1016/j.infsof.2005.09.002

Wordsworth, J. (1987). Education in formal methods for software engineering. *Information and Software Technology, 29*(1), 27–32. doi:10.1016/0950-5849(87)90017-6

Chapter 15
Petri Net Based Deadlock Prevention Approach for Flexible Manufacturing Systems

Chunfu Zhong
Xidian University, People's Republic of China

Zhiwu Li
Xidian University, People's Republic of China

ABSTRACT

In flexible manufacturing systems, deadlocks usually occur due to the limited resources. To cope with deadlock problems, Petri nets are widely used to model these systems. This chapter focuses on deadlock prevention for flexible manufacturing systems that are modeled with S^4R nets, a subclass of generalized Petri nets. The analysis of S^4R leads us to derive an iterative deadlock prevention approach. At each iteration step, a non-max-controlled siphon is derived by solving a mixed integer linear programming. A monitor is constructed for the siphon such that it is max-controlled. Finally, a liveness-enforcing Petri net supervisor can be derived without enumerating all the strict minimal siphons.

BACKGROUND

Due to fierce market competition, flexible manufacturing systems (FMS) have been widely accepted by manufacturers so that they may be able to quick respond to market changes. In an FMS, resources, such as machine tools, automated guided vehicles, robots, buffers, and fixtures, are always shared by a number of jobs such that they may be made the best of. While different jobs are executed concurrently, they have to compete for the limited resources. If each of a set of two or more jobs keeps waiting indefinitely for the other jobs in the set to release resources, the jobs might never be finished. This situation, called deadlock, is highly undesirable in an FMS (Zhou Venkatesh, 1998). Deadlock and related blocking phenomena often cause unnecessary costs, such as long downtime and low use of some critical and

DOI: 10.4018/978-1-60960-086-0.ch015

expensive resources, and may lead to catastrophic results in some highly automated manufacturing systems (Fanti & Zhou, 2004), such as semiconductor production systems. Therefore, it is necessary to develop an effective FMS control policy to make sure that deadlocks will never occur in such systems. The problem of deadlock in an FMS has attracted many researchers' attention (Abdallah & ElMaraghy, 1998)(Ferrarini & Maroni, 1998) (Giua & Seatzu, 2002)(Hsieh & Chang, 1994)(Huang, Jeng, Xie & Chung, 2001) (Jeng, Xie & Chung, 2004)(Lawley, Reveliotis & Ferreira, 1998)(Li & Shou, 2004)(Li, Zhou & Wu, 2008)(Park & Reveliotis, 2001)(Reveliotis, 2003)(Roszkowska, 2004)(Uzam, 2002).

Petri nets have been widely used to model a variety of resource allocation systems including FMS. They are well suited to depict the behavior of an FMS, such as concurrency, conflict and causal dependency. A powerful feature of Petri nets is their ability to represent good behavior properties of the system such as liveness and boundedness (Abdallah & ElMaraghy, 1998)(Chu & Xie, 1997). Using Petri nets, there are mainly three approaches to deal with the problem of deadlocks in FMS: deadlock detection and recovery (Leung & Sheen, 1993), deadlock avoidance (Fanti, Maione, Mascolo & Turchiano, 1997)(Ferrarini & Maroni, 1998) (Hsieh & Chang, 1994)(Lawley, Reveliotis & Ferreira, 1998)(Park & Reveliotis, 2001)(Roszkowska, 2004)(Wu & Zhou, 2001) (Yim, Kim & Woo, 1997), and deadlock prevention (Abdallah & ElMaraghy, 1998)(Ezpeleta, Colom, & Martinez, 1995)(Giua & Seatzu, 2002)(Huang, Jeng, Xie & Chung, 2001)(Li & Shou, 2004) (Li, Uzam & Zhou, 2004)(Li & Zhou, 2006)(Li, Zhang & Zhao, 2007)(Li, Zhou & Wu, 2008)(Li & Zhao, 2008)(Uzam, 2002)(Uzam, 2004)(Zhou & DiCesare, 1992). In this chapter we focus on deadlock prevention.

Deadlock prevention is usually achieved by using an off-line computational mechanism to control the requests for resources to ensure that deadlocks never occur. Hence a deadlock prevention approach is to impose constraints on a system such that it can never reach deadlock states. For the Petri net model of a system, monitors and related arcs are added to the original net to realize such a mechanism (Abdallah & ElMaraghy, 1998)(Ezpeleta, Colom, & Martinez, 1995)(Li & Shou, 2004)(Li, Zhou & Wu, 2008). This implies that both a plant model and its supervisor are in a Petri net formalism.

As a special structure, siphons are related to the liveness of a Petri net model, which has been widely used in the characterization and prevention/ avoidance of deadlock situations. However, their computation can be very time-consuming or even impossible when a net is too large in size. Many researchers have considered a variety of ways for finding siphons, which are based on inequalities (Ezpeleta, Colom, & Martinez, 1995), logic equations (Kinuyama & Murata, 1986), linear algebra and invariants (Lautenbach, 1987), linear equations with slack variables (Ezpeleta, Couvreur & Silva, 1991), parallel algorithms (Tricas & Ezpeleta, 2006), and the direct application of the definition of siphons (traps) to the sign incidence matrix (Boer & Murata, 1994). However efficient computation of all the minimal siphons for a large-size net is still very difficult.

When all the strict minimal siphons are obtained, a deadlock prevention policy in (Ezpeleta, Colom, & Martinez, 1995) is developed based on the addition of a new monitor place for each strict minimal siphon to prevent the presence of unmarked siphons. Then a liveness-enforcing Petri net supervisor is derived. In the policy all the strict minimal siphons in a net model should be computed first. In (Li & Shou, 2004) Li and Zhou propose a method based on the concept of elementary and dependant siphons. The elementary siphons in a net model are explicitly controlled only, which greatly decrease the number of monitors. However they need compute all the strict minimal siphons. To avoid enumerating all the strict minimal siphons, in (Huang, Jeng, Xie & Chung, 2001) Huang et al. present an iterative approach consisting of two main phases. At each iteration step, a fast deadlock detection technique derived from mixed integer programming is used to find an unmarked maximal siphon. An algorithm is formalized that can efficiently obtain an unmarked minimal siphon from the maximal one. This first phase is called siphon control that deals with siphons in the plant net model and the second is called augmented siphon control that tackles siphons resulting from the addition of monitor places. Unfortunately, the policy can only be used for ordinary Petri nets.

In ordinary Petri nets, an unmarked siphon will never be marked again. When a siphon is empty, the transitions related it cannot fire again. Always a monitor is designed for such a siphon so that it will never be unmarked. The case in generalized Petri nets is much more complex than that in ordinary nets, since the fact that a siphon is marked might not be sufficient for the absence of dead transitions. In a generalized Petri net, the transitions related to a marked siphon may not be able to fire. Such a siphon is called an insufficiently marked siphon in a generalized Petri net. Barkaoui et al. (Barkaoui, Pradat-Peyre, 1996) put forward the concept of max-controlled siphons and prove its ability to deal with deadlock problem in a generalized Petri net.

Based on the concept of max-controlled siphons, this chapter presents an iterative deadlock prevention method for S^4R, a general class of Petri nets. In each iteration step, a mixed integer linear programming is solved to find a non-max-marked siphon. Then a P-invariant is constructed by the addition of a monitor to make the minimal siphon max-controlled. The addition of monitors does not generate new siphons in the resulting net. When there is no non-max-marked siphon, the net is live. This method usually ensures that only a few monitor places are added to the net but generating more permissive behavior. The other contribution of this chapter is that we improve the mixed integer linear programming in (Giua

& Seatzu, 2002) such that it can be applied to generalized Petri nets.

The rest of this chapter is organized as follows. Section 2 briefly reviews the basics of Petri nets used throughout this chapter. The definition of S^4R is shown in Section 3. A deadlock prevention method is developed in Section 4. Section 5 exemplifies the proposed method. Finally, Section 6 concludes this work.

PRELIMINARIES OF PETRI NETS

The basic definitions and properties of Petri nets are reviewed in this section. More details can be found in (Murata, 1989).

A Petri net is a four-tuple $N=(P, T, F, W)$, where P and T are finite, non-empty, and disjoint sets. P is a set of m places and T is a set of n transitions. $F \subseteq (P \times T) \cup (T \times P)$ is called the flow relation or the set of directed arcs. $W: (P \times T) \cup (T \times P) \rightarrow$ is a mapping that assigns a weight to an arc: $W(x, y) > 0$ if $(x, y) \in F$, otherwise $W(x, y)=0$, where $x, y \in P \cup T$ and. $N=(P, T, F, W)$ is ordinary, denoted as $N=(P, T, F)$, if $\forall f \in F$, $W(f)=1$. A self-loop free Petri net $N=(P, T, F, W)$ can be alternatively represented by its flow matrix or incidence matrix $[N]$, where $[N]$ is a $|P| \times |T|$ integer matrix with $[N](p, t)=W(t, p)-W(p, t)$. Alternatively, $[N]$ can be represented by *Post-Pre*, where $Pre(p, t)=W(p, t)$ and $Post(p, t)=W(t, p)$.

A marking is a mapping $M: P \rightarrow$. The set of all possible markings reachable from M_0 in (N, M_0) is denoted by $[M_0)$ or $R(N, M_0)$. We denote by $PR(N, M_0)$ the potentially reachable set, i.e., the set of all markings $M \in N^m$ for which there exists a vector $Y \in N^n$ that satisfies the state equation $M=M_0+[N]Y$, i.e., $PR(N, M_0)=\{M \in N^m: \exists Y \in N^n: M=M_0=[N]Y\}$. $M(p)$ indicates the number of tokens in p at M. p is marked by M if $M(p)>0$. A subset $D \subseteq P$ is marked by M if at least one place in D is marked by M. The sum of tokens in all places in D is denoted by $M(D)$ where $M(D)=\Sigma_{p \in D} M(p)$.

Given a node $x \in P \cup T$, ${}^{\cdot}x = \{y \in P \cup T | (y,x) \in F\}$ is called the preset of node x, while $x^{\cdot} = \{y \in P \cup T | (x,y) \in F\}$ is called the postset of node x. This notation can be extended to a set of nodes as follows: given $X \subseteq P \cup T$, ${}^{\cdot}X = \cup_{x \in X} {}^{\cdot}x$ and $X^{\cdot} = \cup_{x \in X} x^{\cdot}$. A string $x_1, \ldots, x_n$ is called a path of N if $\forall i \in \{1,2,\ldots,n-1\}: x_{i+1} \in x_i^{\cdot}$, where $\forall x \in \{x_1, x_2, \ldots, x_n\}$, $x \in P \cup T$. A simple path is a path whose nodes are all different (except, perhaps, x_1 and x_n). A simple path is denoted by $SP(x_1, x_n)$. A cycle is a simple path with $x_1 = x_n$.

Let (N, M_0) be a marked net. Transition is enabled at M if $\forall p \in {}^{\cdot}t, M(p) \geq W(p,t)$. Marking M' reached by firing t from M is defined by $M'(p) = M(p) - W(p,t) + W(t,p)$ which is denoted by $M[t\rangle M'$. Marking M' is said to be reachable from marking M if there exist a sequence of transitions $\sigma = t_0, t_1, \ldots, t_n$ and markings $M_1, M_2, \ldots$, and M_n such that $M[t_0\rangle M_1[t_1\rangle, \ldots, M_n[t_n\rangle M'$ holds, which is denoted as $M' = M + [N]\vec{\sigma}$, where $\vec{\sigma}: T \to N$ maps t in T to the number of occurrences of t in σ. A transition $t \in T$ is live at M_0 if $\forall M \in R(N,M)$, $\exists M' \in R(N,M_0)$, $M'[t\rangle$ holds. (N, M_0) is deadlock-free if $\forall M \in R(N,M_0)$, $\exists t \in T, M[t\rangle$ holds. (N, M_0) is live if $\forall t \in T$, t is live under M_0. (N, M_0) is bounded if $\exists k \in N, \forall M \in R(N,M_0), \forall p \in P, M(p) \leq k$ holds.

A $P(T)$-vector is a column vector $I(J): P(T) \to Z$ indexed by $P(T)$, where Z is the set of integers. I is a P-invariant (place invariant) if $I \neq 0$ and $I^T[N] = \mathbf{0}^T$ hold. P-invariant I is said to be a P-semiflow if every element of I is non-negative. $\|I\| = \{p \in P | I(p) \neq 0\}$ is called the support of I. If I is a P-invariant of (N, M_0) then $\forall M \in R(N, M_0)$, $I^T M = I^T M_0$. Let X be a matrix where each column is a P-semiflow of (N, M_0), and $I_X(N,M_0) = \{M \in N^M | X^T M = X^T M_0\}$ denote the set of invariant markings.

A nonempty set $S \subseteq P$ is a siphon (trap) if ${}^{\cdot}S \subseteq S^{\cdot} (S^{\cdot} \subseteq {}^{\cdot}S)$ holds. A siphon (trap) is minimal if there is no siphon (trap) contained in it as a proper subset. A minimal siphon is called strict if it does not contain a marked trap. A strict minimal siphon is denoted as SMS for short. A siphon S can also

be described by its characteristic vector $s \in \{0,1\}^m$ such that $s_i = 1$ if $p_i \in S$, else $s_i = 0$; thus $M(S) = s^T M$.

For economy of space, vectors and matrixes can be demonstrated as multisets or formal sum notations. For example, suppose that there is a Petri net with two places and two transitions, whose incidence matrix $[N] = [-1,0,0,1]$ can be denoted as $[N] = -p_1 t_1 + p_2 t_2$.

The following notations and properties of generalized Petri nets are from (Barkaoui, Pradat-Peyre, 1996). Given a place p, we denoted $\max_{t \in p^{\cdot}} \{W(p,t)\}$ by $\max_{p^{\cdot}}$.

Definition 1. (Barkaoui, Pradat-Peyre, 1996) Let (N,M_0) be a marked net and S be a siphon of N. S is said to be max-marked at a marking $M \in R(N,M_0)$ if $\exists p \in S$ such that $M(p) \geq \max_{p^{\cdot}}$.

Definition 2. (Barkaoui, Pradat-Peyre, 1996) Let (N,M_0) be a marked net and S be a siphon of N. S is said to be max-controlled if S is max-marked at any reachable marking.

Definition 3. (Barkaoui, Pradat-Peyre, 1996) A net (N,M_0) is said to be satisfying the max cs-property (controlled-siphon property) if each minimal siphon of N is max-controlled.

The cs-property is a concept that plays an important role in the development of the siphon-based deadlock prevention approach in this chapter. A siphon that is max-controlled can be always sufficiently marked to allow firing a transition once at least. Barkaoui *et al.* (Barkaoui, Pradat-Peyre, 1996) propose some results allowing to determine whether a given siphon is max-controlled, where the relationship of the cs-property and deadlock-freeness or liveness property is established.

Property 1. *(Barkaoui, Pradat-Peyre, 1996)* If (N,M_0) satisfies the cs-property, it is deadlock-free.

Property 2. *(Barkaoui, Pradat-Peyre, 1996)* If (N,M_0) is live, it satisfies the cs-property.

The net shown in Figure 1 is pure and bounded and there exist dead reachable states. Therefore it is not live. The net contains two strict minimal siphons: $S_1 = \{p_3, p_6, p_7, p_8\}$ and $S_2 = \{p_3, p_5, p_8\}$. If both of these two siphons are max-controlled, the net satisfies the max cs-property.

Figure 1. A small S^4R net $(N_{\mu 0}, M_{\mu 0})$

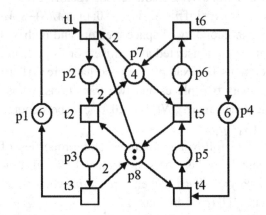

S^4R Nets

The definitions of S^4R nets are reviewed here (Abdallah & ElMaraghy, 1998). In (Park & Reveliotis, 2001) it is called S^3PGR^2. In fact they are equivalent.

Definition 4. Let $I_m = \{1, 2, ..., m\}$ be a finite set of indices. An S^4R is a generalized self-loop free net $N = O_{i \in I_m} N_i = (P, T, F, W)$, where

1) $N_i = (P_{A_i} \cup P_{R_i}, T_i, F_i, W_i) i \in I_m$;

2) $P = P_A \cup P^0 P_R$ is a partition of places such that (i)
$\forall p \in SP(p_6 p_1^0), p \notin Th_s; p_{10} \in p_9^{..}, \forall p \in SP(p_{10}, p_2^0),$
and $\forall i \neq j, P_{A_i} \cap P_{A_j} \neq \phi$; (ii) $P_R = \{r_1, r_2, ..., r_n\}$, n $\in N\backslash\{0\}$; (iii) $P^0 = \bigcup_{i \in_m} \{p_i^0\}$; (iv) The elements in P^0, P_A, and P_R are called idle, operation, and resource places, respectively; and (v) The output transitions of an idle place are called source transitions;

3) $T = \bigcup_{i \in_m} T_i, T_i \neq \phi, \forall i \neq j, T_i \cap T_j = \phi$;

4) $W = W_A \cup W_R$, where $W_A((P_A \cup P^0) \times T) \cup (T \times (P_A \cup P^0)) \rightarrow \{0,1\}$ such that $\forall i \neq j$, $((P_{A_j} \cup \{p_j^0\}) \times T_i) \cup (T_i \times (P_{A_j} \cup \{p_j^0\})) \rightarrow \{0\}$, and $W_R:(P_R \times T) \cup (T \times P_R) \rightarrow N^+$;

5) $\forall i \in I_m$ the subset N_i generated by $P_{A_i} \cup \{p_i^0\} \cup T_i$ is a strongly connected state

machine such that its every circle contains $\{p_i^0\}$;

6) $\forall r \in P_R, \exists$ a unique minimal P-invariant $I_r \in N^{|P|}$ such that $\{r\} = \|I_r\| \cap P_R, P^0 \cap \|I_r\| = \phi, P_A \cap \| \neq \phi$ and $I_r(r) = 1$. $P_A = \bigcup_{r \in P_R} \|I_r\| \backslash \{r\}$; and

7) N is pure and strongly connected.

Definition 5. Let $N = (P_A \cup P^0 \cup P_R, T, F, W)$ with $N = O_{i \in I_m} N_i$ and

$$N_i = (P_{A_i} \cup p_i^0 \cup P_{R_i}, T_i, F_i, W_i)$$

be an S^4R. An initial marking M_0 is acceptable for N if

1) $\forall i \in I_m, M_0(p_i^0) > 0$;

2) $\forall p = \in P_A, M_0(p) = 0$; and

3) $\forall r \in P_R, M_0(r) \geq \max_{p \in \|I_r\|} I_r(p)$.

The net shown in Figure 1 is an S^4R, where $p_1^0 = p_1, p_2^0 = p_4, P_{A_1} = \{p_2, p_3\}, P_{A_2} = \{p_5, p_6\}$ and $P_{R_1} = P_{R_2} = \{p_7, p_8\}$. There are four P-invariants: $I_1 = p_1 + p_2 + p_3$, $I_2 = p_4 + p_5 + p_6$, $I_3 = I_{p7} = 2p_2 + p_6 + p_7$, and $I_4 = I_{p8} = p_2 + 2p_3 + p_5 + p_8$.

Theorem 1. (Abdallah & ElMaraghy, 1998) Let S be a strict minimal siphon in an S^4R $N = (P_A \cup P^0 \cup P_R, T, F, W)$. Then $S = S^R \cup S^A$ satisfies $S \cap P_R = S^R \neq \phi$ and $S \cap P_A = S^A \neq \phi$.

Take a siphon in Figure 1 as an example. We have $S_1^R = S_1 \cap P_R = \{p_7, p_8\}$ and $S_1^A = S_1 \cap P_A = \{p_3, p_6\}$. If not proper controlled, a strict minimal siphon in an S^4R net system can lead to part or whole deadlock during its evolution.

Definition 6. A multiset Ω, over a non-empty set A, is a mapping $\Omega: A \rightarrow N^+$, which is represented as a formal sum $\Sigma_{a \in A} \Omega(a)a$.

In multiset Ω, non-negative integer $\Omega(a)$ is the coefficient of element $a \in A$, indicating the number of occurrences of a in Ω. It is said that a belongs to Ω, denoted by $a \in \Omega$, if $\Omega(a) > 0$. It does not belong to Ω, denoted by $a \notin \Omega$, if $\Omega(a)=0$. Let Ω_1 and Ω_2 be two multisets over A. The basic operations are defined as follows:

Definition 7. $\Omega_1 \cap \Omega_2 := \Sigma_{a \in A} min\{\Omega_1 (a), \Omega_2 (a)\}a$.

Definition 8. $\Omega_1 + \Omega_2 := \Sigma_{a \in A}(\Omega_1 (a), \Omega_2 (a))a$.

Definition 9. $\Omega_1 - \Omega_2 := \Sigma_{a \in A}(\Omega_1 (a) -. \ \Omega_1 \cap \Omega_2)$ $(a))a$.

Definition 10. Let r be a resource place and S be a strict minimal siphon in an S^4R. The holder of resource r is defined as the difference of two multisets I_r and r: $H(r)I_r$-r. As a multiset, $Th_s = \sum_{r \in S^R} H(r) - \sum_{r \in S^R, p \in S^A} I_r(p)p$ is called the complementary set of S.

Let $\Omega_1 = 5a+4c$ and $\Omega_2 = a+b+3c$ be two multisets over $A=\{a, b, c\}$. We have $\Omega_1 \cap \Omega_2 = a+3c$, $\Omega_1 + \Omega_2 = 6a+b+7c$ and $\Omega_1 - \Omega_2 = 4a+c$. Since $I_{p7} = 2_{p2} + p_6 + p_7$ and $I_{p8} = p_2 + 2_{p3} + p_5 + p_8$, for the siphon $S_1 = \{p_3, p_6, p_7, p_8\}$ in Figure 1, we have

$$Th_s = \sum_{r \in S_1^R} H(r) - \sum_{r \in S_1^R, p \in S_1^A} I_r(p)p =$$
$$I_{p_7} + I_{p_8} - \sum_{r \in S_1^R, p \in S_1^A} I_r(p)p = 3p_2 + p_5.$$

Theorem 2. (Abdallah & ElMaraghy, 1998) Let (N, M_0) be a marked S^4R net. It is live under M_0 if it satisfies max-cs property.

Proposition 1. (Barkaoui, Pradat-Peyre, 1996) Let (N, M_0) be a marked net and S be a siphon of N. S is max-controlled if there exists a P-invariant I such that $\forall p \in (\|I\|^- \cap S)$,

$$\max_{p^-} = 1, \left\| I \right\|^+ \subseteq S, \sum_{p \in P} I(p)M_0(p) > \sum_{p \in S} I(p)$$
$$(\max_{p^-} - 1).$$

From Theorem 2, if all the siphons in a marked S^4R net are max-controlled, the net is live. Proposition 1 demonstrates under what condition a siphon is max-controlled.

Deadlock Control Policy

In this section a definition and some propositions are first reviewed. Then an improved mixed integer linear programming problem for computing strict minimal siphons is derived. Finally a deadlock prevention algorithm is proposed.

Definition 11. (Li, Zhang & Zhao, 2007) Let S be a strict minimal siphon in an S^4R net $(N_{\mu 0}, M_{\mu 0})$, where

$$N_{\mu 0} = O_{i=1}^n N_i = (P^0 \cup P_A \cup P_R, T, F_{\mu 0}, W_{\mu 0}).$$

Let $\{\alpha, \beta, ..., \gamma\} \subseteq N_k$ be a set of positive integers, such that $\forall i \in \{\alpha, \beta, ..., \gamma\}, \left\| Th_s \right\| \cap P_{A_i} \neq \phi$, and $\forall j \in N_k \setminus \{\alpha, \beta, ..., \gamma\}, \left\| Th_s \right\| \cap P_{A_i} \neq \phi$. For S, a non-negative P-vector is constructed as follows:

- $\forall p \in P^0 \cup P_A \cup P_R, k_s(p) := 0$;
- $\forall p \in \|Th_s\|, k_s(p) := Th_s(p)$;
- $\forall i \in \{\alpha, \beta, ..., \gamma\}$, let $P_s \in \left\| Th_s \right\| \cap P_{A_i}$ be such a place that

$$\forall P_t \in SP(p_\mu, p_i^0), p_\mu \in p_s^{..}, p_t \notin \left\| Th_s \right\|.$$

- Suppose that there are m such places, $p_s^1, p_s^2, ...,$ and p_s^m. We have

$$p_s^k \left| k \in \mathbb{N}_m\right\} \subseteq Th_s \cap P_{A_i} \cdot \forall p_s^k,$$

- let $p_v \in SP(p_i^0, p_s^k)$ be such a place that $Th_S(p_v) \geq Th_S(p_w)$,

$$\forall p_w \in SP(p_i^0, p_s^k). \ \forall p_v, \ \forall p_x \in SP(p_i^0, p_v),$$
- $k_s(p_x) := Th_s(p_v)$. $\forall p_y \in \cap_{k=1}^m SP(p_i^0, p_s^k), ks(p_y) := Th_s(p_z^i)$, where $p_z^i \in \left\| Th_s \right\| \cap P_{A_i} \ p_z^i \in \left\| Th_s \right\| \cap P_{A_i}$, $\nexists p \in \left\| Th_s \right\| \cap P_{A_i}, Th_s(p) \geq Th_s(p_z^i)$. Let $K_S = \{p | k_s(p) \neq 0, p \notin \|Th_s\|\}$.

To clarify Definition 11, the net shown in Figure 2 is taken as an example. Let

$$P_{A_1} = \{p_1, p_2, ..., p_7, ...\}, \text{ and}$$
$$P_{A2} = \{p8, p9, ..., p_{10}, ...\}.$$

Suppose that in the net there is a siphon S *with* $Th_s=p_2+3_{p3}+p_5+2_{p9}$. *We have* $Th_s(p_2)=1$, $Th_s(p_3)=3$, $Th_s(p_5)=1$, *and* $Th_s(p_9)=2$.

First, $k_s(p_2)=1$, $k_s(p_3)=3$, $k_s(p_5)=1$, $k_s(p_9)=2$, and $\forall p \notin Th_s$, $k_s(p)=0$ according to Steps 1 and 2.

For

$$p_4 \in p_3^{\bullet\bullet}, \forall p \in SP(p_4, p_1^0), p \notin Th_s; p_6 \in p_5^{\bullet\bullet},$$
$$\forall p \in SP(p_6 p_1^0), p \notin Th_s; p_{10} \in p_9^{\bullet\bullet}, \forall p \in SP(p_{10}, p_2^0),$$
$$p \notin Th_s.$$

We have:

$$p_S^1 = p_3, p_S^2 = p_5, \text{ and } p_S^3 = p_9;$$

$$M(p_i) \max{}_{p_i^\cdot} - 1,;$$

$$k_s(p_2)=k_s(p_3)=3, k_s(p_5)=1,$$

and $k_s(p_8)=k_s(p_9)=2$.

$$p_1 \in SP(p_1^0, p_3) \bigcap SP(p_1^0, p_5), \forall p \in P_{A_i} \bigcap Th_s,$$
$$Th_s(p) \leq Th_s(p_3),$$

we hence have $p_z^1 = p_3$ and furthermore $k_s(p_1)=3$. Finally one gets $k_s=3_{p1}+3_{p2}+3_{p3}+p_5+2_{p8}+2_{p9}$.

Proposition 2. (Li, Zhang & Zhao, 2007) Let S be a strict minimal siphon in an S⁴R net $(N_{\mu 0}, M_{\mu 0})$, where $N_{\mu 0}=(P^0 \cup P^A \cup P_R, T, F_{\mu 0}, W_{\mu 0})$. A monitor is added to $(N_{\mu 0}, M_{\mu 0})$ by imposing that g_S is a P-invariant of the resulting net system $(N_{\mu 0}, M_{\mu 0})$, where $N_{\mu 1}=P^0 \cup P_A \cup P_R \cup \{V_S\}, T, F_{\mu 1}, W_{\mu 1})$; $\forall p \in P^0 \cup P_A \cup P_R, M_{\mu 1}(p)=M_{\mu 0}(p)$. Construct k_S due to **Definition 11.** Let $g_S = k_S + V_S$, $h_s = \sum_{r \in S^R} I_r - g_s$, and $M_{\mu 1}(V_S)=M_{\mu 0}(V_S)-\xi_S(\xi_S \in N^+)$. Then S is max-controlled if
$$\xi_S > \sum_{p \in S} h_s(p)(\max{}_{p^\cdot} - 1) = \sum_{p \in S^R}(\max{}_{p^\cdot} - 1)$$

It is obvious that $\forall p \notin P_R$, $\max{}_{p^\cdot} - 1 = 0$ holds in any S⁴R net. Therefore

$$\xi_S > \sum_{p \in S} h_s(p)(\max{}_{p^\cdot} - 1) = \sum_{p \in S^R}(\max{}_{p^\cdot} - 1)$$

Figure 2. S is a siphon with $Th_s=p_2+3_{p3}+p_5+2_{p9}$

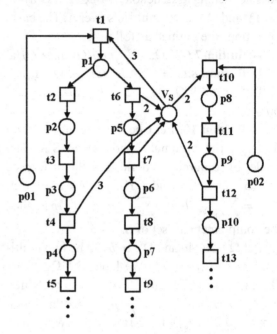

is true.

In Figure 1, $S_1=(p_3, p_6, p_7, p_8)$ is a strict minimal siphon in the net. *Since* $Th_{s_1} = \sum_{r \in S_R} H(r) \setminus S_1 = 3p_2 + p_5$, we have $Th_{s_1}(p_2) = 3$ and $Th_{s_1}(p_5) = 1$.

First we have $k_{S_1}(p_2) = 3, k_{S_1}(p_5) = 1$, and $\forall p \notin Th_{S_1}, k_{S_1}(p) = 0$ according to steps 1 and 2. Hence

$$k_{S_1} = 3p_2 + p_5, g_{S_1} = k_{S_1} + V_{S_1} = 3p_2 + p_5 + V_{S_1},$$

and $\xi_{S_1} > \sum_{p \in S_1} h_{S_1}(p)(\max{}_p - 1) = \sum_{p \in S_1^R}(\max{}_p - 1) = 2 - 1 = 1.$

Therefore we have

$$M_{\mu 1}(V_{S_1}) = M_{\mu 0}(S_1) - \xi_{S_1} = 6 - 2 = 4.$$

For the siphon $S_2 = \{p_3, p_5, p_8\}$, we accordingly have $k_{S_2} = p_2, g_{S_2} = k_{S_2} + V_{S_2} = p_2 + V_{S_2}$, and $M_{\mu 1}(V_{S_2}) = M_{\mu 0}(S_2) - \xi_{S_2} = 2 - 1 = 1.$

Proposition 3. (Li, Zhang & Zhao, 2007) Net system $(N_{\mu l},\ M_{\mu l})$ is an S^{4}R.

Proposition 4. (Li, Zhang & Zhao, 2007) The siphon control method in Proposition 2 does not generate new non-max-controlled siphons in $(N_{\mu l},\ M_{\mu l})$.

Non-Max-Marked Siphon

As a special structure object in a Petri net, siphons play an important role in the deadlock analysis and control of the systems modeled by Petri nets. However their number grows quickly and in the worst case grows exponentially with respect to the net size. Hence their computation is very time consuming or even impossible. It is interesting to avoid the computation of all the siphons and then fined a controlled net system. In (Giua & Seatzu, 2002), Basile and Giua propose an approach by solving a mixed integer linear programming problem to compute minimal siphons, which is shown as follows:

$$\begin{cases} \min 1^T s \\ s.t. K_1 Pre^T s \ge Post^T s \\ X^T M = k \\ K_2 s + M \le K_2 1 \\ 1^T s \ge 1 \end{cases} \tag{1}$$

where $s \in \{0,1\}^m$, $M \in R(N, M_0)$, Pre: $P \times T \rightarrow N$, $Post$: $P \times T \rightarrow N$, $[N] = Post\text{-}Pre$, $k = X^T M_0$, $K_1 = \max\{1^T Post(.,t) | t \in T\}$, $K_2 = \max\{M(p) | p \in P, M \in R(N, M_0)\}$ and X be the matrix whose columns are the P-semiflows of a net.

The integer linear programming problem in (1) can be applied to ordinary nets only. Next we improve it such that it can be used find a minimal siphon in a generalized net.

$$\begin{cases} \min 1^T s \\ s.t. K_1 Pre^T s \ge Post^T s \\ X^T M = k \\ K_2 s + M \le K_2 1 \\ 1^T s \ge 2 \end{cases} \tag{2}$$

where $L(i) = \max_{p_i} - 1 (i \in \mathbb{N}_m, P_i \in P)$.

The constraint $K_1 Pre^T s \ge Post^T s$ ensures that s is the characteristic vector of a siphon S. $X^T M = k$ means that M belongs to the set $I_x(N, M_0)$. Constraint $K_2 s + M - L \le K_2 1$ guarantees that $\forall P_i \in P$, $K_2 s(i) + M(p_i) - L(i) \le K_2$ holds, i.e., either $s(i)=1$ and $M(i) \ge 0$ or $s(i)=0$ and $M(i) \ge 0$. Constraint ensures that there are at least two places in a siphon. The integer linear programming problem in (2) ensures that non-max-marked siphons are computed only.

Theorem 3. Let (N, M_0) be a marked Petri net. A siphon S in (N, M_0) is a non-max-marked siphon at $M \in R(N, M_0)$ if its characteristic vector s satisfies *(2)*.

Proof: From (Giua & Seatzu, 2002), a set of places $S \subseteq P$ is a siphon if its characteristic vector s satisfies $K_1 Pre^T s \ge Post^T s$. It is unmarked at marking M if vector s satisfies $K_2 s + M - L \le K_2 1$. In a generalized Petri net, a siphon may never be emptied at any marking. However it still can cause deadlocks when it is insufficiently marked. Constraint $K_2 s + M - L \le K_2 1$ implies that given $I \in I_m$, if $s(i)=0$ (i.e. place p_i does not belong to the siphon), then no constraint exists on the marking of p_i since $K_2 = \max\{M(p) | p \in P, M \in R(N, M_0)\}$ and the constraint is satisfied for all reachable markings. Otherwise if $s(i)=1$ (i.e. place belongs to the siphon), then $M(p_i) - L(i) \le 0$ must be satisfied. Hence $M(p_i) \le L(i)$, i.e., $M(p_i) \max_{p_i} - 1$, the siphon is not max-marked. The theorem holds. □

In Figure 1, let $S^T = [x_1, x_2, \ldots x_8]$ and $M^T = [y_1, y_2, \ldots y_8]$, where $x_i \in \{0,1\}, y_i \in N, i=1,2,\ldots,8$. The initial marking of the net is $M_0^T = [6, 0, 0, 6, 0, 0, 4, 2]$. The matrix of the P-semiflows of the net is $X^T = [$

$1,1,1,0,0,0,0,0,0,0,0,1,1,1,0,0,0,1,2,0,1,0,0,1].$
Then $k=X^T M_0=[6,6,2,4]$. Others can be obtained as: $Pre+p_1t_1+p_2t_2+p_3t_3+p_4t_4+p_5t_5+p_6t_6+2p_7t_1+p_7t_1+p_7t_5+p_8t_1+p_8t_2+p_8t_4$, $Post+p_1t_3+p_2t_1+p_3t_2+p_4t_6+p_5t_4+p_6t_5+2p_7t_2+p_7t_6+p_7t_6+p_8t_3+p_8t_5$,
$K_1=\max\{1^T Post(.,t)|t\in T\}=3$,
$K_2=\max\{M(p)|p\in P, M\in R(N,M_0)\}=6$, and $L^T=[0,0,0,0,0,0,01,0]$.

They lead to the following mixed integer linear programming problem from (2):

$min\ \mathrm{x}_1+\mathrm{x}_2+...+\mathrm{x}_8$

subject to:

$3\mathrm{x}_1+6\mathrm{x}_7+3\mathrm{x}_8\geq\mathrm{x}_2$

$3\mathrm{x}_2+3\mathrm{x}_8\geq\mathrm{x}_3+2\mathrm{x}_7$

$3\mathrm{x}_3\geq+\mathrm{x}_1+2\mathrm{x}_8$

$3\mathrm{x}_4+3\mathrm{x}_8\geq\mathrm{x}_5$

$3x_5+3x_7\geq x_6+x8$

$3x_6\geq x_4+x_7$

$y_1+y_2+y_3=6$

$y_4+y_5+y_6=6$

$y_2+2y_3+y_5+y_8=2$

$2y_2+y_6+y_7=4$

$6\mathrm{x}_1+\mathrm{y}_1\leq6$

$6\mathrm{x}_2+\mathrm{y}_2\leq6$

$6\mathrm{x}_3+\mathrm{y}_3\leq6$

$6\mathrm{x}_4+\mathrm{y}_4\leq6$

$6\mathrm{x}_5+\mathrm{y}_5\leq6$

$6\mathrm{x}_6+\mathrm{y}_6\leq6$

$6\mathrm{x}_7+\mathrm{y}_7-1\leq6$

$6\mathrm{x}_8+\mathrm{y}_8\leq6$

$\mathrm{x}_1+\mathrm{x}_2+...+\mathrm{x}_8\geq2$

Solving it gives $min(\mathrm{x}_1+\mathrm{x}_2+...+\mathrm{x}_8)=3$, where $\mathrm{x}_3=1$, $\mathrm{x}_5=1$, and $\mathrm{x}_8=1$. The corresponding siphon is $S=\{p_3,p_5,p_8\}$. The siphon is not max-controlled.

Deadlock Prevention Algorithm

Here we derive an iterative procedure through which a liveness-enforcing Petri net supervisor for an S^4R net can be found.

Theorem 4. The controlled net $(N_{\mu 1}, M_{\mu 1})$ generated by Algorithm 1 is live.

Proof: At each iterative procedure of Algorithm 1, if a siphon S is obtained, a monitor is computed by Definition 11 and Proposition 1 such that the siphon is max-controlled. If no siphon is computed, From Theorem 2, the final net is live. Proposition 2 and Proposition 4 ensure that the algorithm eventually converges to a net that does not contain any non-max-marked siphon. From Theorem 2, the final net is live. □

To illustrate Algorithm 1, Figure 1 is taken as an example. In the first iterative procedure a siphon $S_1=\{p_3,p_5,p_8\}$ is obtained. We have $Th_{S_1}=p_2$ and $k_{S_1}=p_2$. Hence

$$g_{S_1}=k_{S_1}+V_{S_1}=p_2+V_{S_1},\xi_{S_1}>,$$
$$\sum_{p\in S_1}h_{S_1}(p)(\max_p-1)=$$
$$\sum_{p\in S_1^R}(\max_p-1)=1-1=0, \text{ and}$$
$$M_{\mu 1}(V_{S_1})=M_{\mu 0}(S_1)-\xi_{S_1}=2-\dot1=1.$$

Then we can find another siphon $S_2=\{p_3, p_6, p_7, p_8\}$ in the second iterative procedure. Similarly, we have $Th_{S_2}=2p_2+p_5$, and $k_{S2}=2p_2+p_5$.

Algorithm 1. Controlled system design for ($N_{\mu 0}$, $M_{\mu 0}$)

Input: an S⁴R net ($N_{\mu 0}$, $M_{\mu 0}$) with $N_{\mu 0=}(P^0 \cup P_A \cup P_R, T, F_{\mu 0}, W_{\mu 0})$

Output: a controlled net ($N_{\mu 1}$, $M_{\mu 1}$)

1: Let be the matrix whose columns are the *P*-semiflows of the S⁴R net ($N_{\mu 0}$, $M_{\mu 0}$)

2: Let $k:=X^T M_{\mu 0}$

3: Solve the integer linear programming problem in (2)

4: if ((2) has no solution, there is no non-max-marked siphon)

    $N_{\mu 1}:=N_{\mu 0}$, $M_{\mu 1}:=M_{\mu 0}$

    Go to 6

  end if

5: Let *S* be the siphon corresponding the solution s_0 of (2)

  Compute g_s and k_s by Definition 11 and Proposition 1

  Let V_s be the monitor of *S* and $M_{\mu 1}(V_S) := M_{\mu 0}(S) - (\max_{p\cdot} - 1) - 1$

  if $(M_{\mu 1}(V_S) < \max_{V_S})$

    $k_S := \sum_{p\in k_S} p, M_{\mu 1}(V_S) := 1$

    add a constraint $\sum_{S_0(i)\in S_0, S_0(i)=0} s(i) < \sum_{S_0(i)\in S_0} S_0(i)$ to (2)

  end if

Compute the incidence matrix of the monitor place: $N_c := -k_S^T[N]$

Let $\mathrm{Pre}:=\begin{bmatrix}\mathrm{Pre}\\\mathrm{Pre}_c\end{bmatrix}, Post := \begin{bmatrix}Post\\Post_c\end{bmatrix}, P_R := P_R \cup \{V_S\}, X := \begin{bmatrix}X\\g_s\end{bmatrix}, M_{\mu 0} := \begin{bmatrix}M_{\mu 0}\\M_{\mu 1}(V_S)\end{bmatrix}$, and $k:=X^T M_{\mu 0}$

  The resulting net is denoted by ($N_{\mu 0}$, $M_{\mu 0}$)

  go to 3

6: Output: a controlled net ($N_{\mu 1}$, $M_{\mu 1}$).

Then $g_{S_2} = k_{S_2} + V_{S_2} = 3p_2 + p_5 + V_{S_2}$ and

$\xi_{S_2} > \sum_{p\in S_2} h_{S_2}(p)(\max_{p\cdot} - 1) =$

$\sum_{p\in S_2^R}(\max_p - 1) = 2 - 1 = 1.$

$M_{\mu 1}(V_{S_2}) = M_{\mu 0}(S_2) - \xi_{S_2} = 6 - 2 = 4.$

As a result we get a liveness-enforcing Petri net supervisor for the net shown in Figure 1 as shown in Figure 3. The net has 24 live states. It is a supervisor with maximal permissiveness. However not all the monitors are necessary. For example, V_{S_1} is redundant with respect to V_{S_2}.

Figure 3. A controlled net ($N_{\mu 1}$, $M_{\mu 1}$) for the net shown in Figure 1

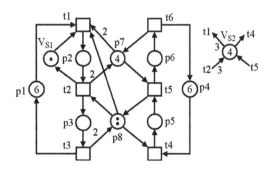

Theorem 5. Let $(N_{\mu I}, M_{\mu I})$ be the controlled net obtained by Algorithm 1 and $C = \{V_{S_i} \mid i \in \mathbb{N}_n\}$ be its monitors. If V_{S_1} is removed from $(N_{\mu I}, M_{\mu I})$ and there is no suitable solution for the integer linear programming problem in (2), then V_{S_1} is redundant.

Proof: Suppose that V_{S_1} is removed from $(N_{\mu I}, M_{\mu I})$ and there is no suitable solution for the integer linear programming problem in (2). Then there is no non-max-controlled siphon. From Theorem 2, the resulting net is live. Hence monitor V_{S_1} is redundant. □

Based on Theorem 5, we derive an iterative method such that the redundant monitors can be deleted. Then a liveness-enforcing Petri net supervisor with simple structure can be obtained. Let $V = \{V_{S_1} \mid i \in \mathbb{N}_n\}$ be a set of monitors, where V_{S_1} is the ith monitor computed in Algorithm 1.

Through Algorithm 2 we can delete redundant monitors. The last monitor derived from Algorithm 1 is necessary. Hence we only check the others.

For the supervisor in Figure 3, if we delete V_{S_1} from $(N_{\mu I}, M_{\mu I})$, there is no suitable solution for the integer linear programming problem in (2). The resulting net is live. Hence V_{S_1} is redundant with respect to V_{S_2}.

EXAMPLES

In this section two examples are presented to demonstrate the proposed methods. The first example is handled by the *P*-invariants based method. Since not all the output transitions of the monitors are source transitions, supervisors obtained by this approach have more permissive behavior. However it cannot always ensure a live supervisor. For the second example, we construct the monitors by Definition 11 and Proposition 1.

Example 1

Suppose that Figure 4 models an FMS with two production routings. Places p_9 and p_{11} represent

Algorithm 2. Identification of redundant monitors

```
Input: a liveness-enforcing Petri net supervisor with a set of monitors
C = {V_{S_i} | i ∈ ℕ_n}
Output: a set of monitors C_1 without redundant monitors
1: for j=1 to n-1 do
2:    Delete V_{S_1} from C
3:    Solve the integer linear programming problem in (2)
3:    if (there is no solution)
4:       V_{S_1} is redundant with respect to C
5:       C := {V_{S_i} | i ∈ ℕ_n} \ {V_{S_1}}
6:    end if
7: end for
8: C_1 := C
```

Figure 4. An S⁴R net

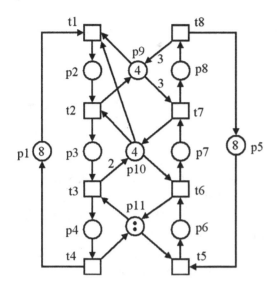

Figure 5. A liveness-enforcing Petri net supervisor for the net shown in Figure 4

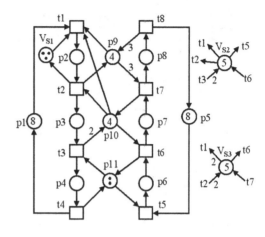

two robots. Place p_{10} represents a machine. Products are processed by two state machines. There are two raw product types. One of the product types is processed with production circle $(p_1 p_2 p_3 p_4 p_1)$. The other one is $(p_5 p_6 p_7 p_8 p_5)$. It is an S⁴R net, where $P^0\{p_1, p_5\}$, $P_R = \{p_9, p_{10}, p_{11}\}$. , $P_{A_2} = \{p_6, p_7, p_8\}$, and $P_R = \{p_9, p_{10}, p_{11}\}$.

In each iterative, by solving a mixed linear integer program, a non-max-marked siphon can be found. Then by Definition 11 and Proposition 1, a monitor is constructed. For details, we have

1: $S_1 = \{p_3, p_7, p_{10}\}$,

$Th_{S_1} = p_2$,

P-invariant $I_{V1} = p_2 + V_{S_1}$, and

$$M_0(V_{S_1}) = M_0(S_1) - \sum_{p \in S_1}(\max_{p.} - 1) - 1 = 4 - 1 = 3;$$

2: $S_2 = \{p_4, p_7, p_{10}, p_{11}\}$,

$Th_{S_1} = p_2 + 2p_3 + p_6$,

P-invariant: $I_{V2} = p_2 + 2p_3 + p_6 + V_{S_2}$, and

$$M_0(V_{S_3}) = M_0(S_3) - \sum_{p \in S_3}(\max_{p.} - 1) - 1 = 8 - 2 - 1 = 5.$$

3: $S_3 = \{p_3, p_8, p_9, p_{10}\}$,

$Th_{S_3} = 2p_2 + p_7$,

P-invariant: $I_{V3} = 2p_2 + p_7 + V_{S_3}$, and

$$M_0(V_{S_3}) = M_0(S_3) - \sum_{p \in S_3}(\max_{p.} - 1) - 1 = 8 - 2 - 1 = 5.$$

After three siphons are controlled, we cannot get any non-max-marked siphon. The resulting net is live as shown in Figure 5. It has 189 live states. An optimal supervisor for the net shown in Figure 4 has 194 live states.

From Algorithm 2, if V_{S_3} is removed from the controlled net, there is no suitable solution for the integer linear programming problem in (2). Hence V_{S_1} is redundant. If V_{S_2} is removed, the integer linear programming problem in (2) has $\min(x_1 + x_2 + \ldots x_{12}) = 4$, where $x_4 = x_7 = x_{10} = x_{11} = 1$, cor-

Figure 6. FMS layout

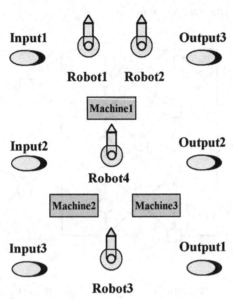

Figure 7. Production routings

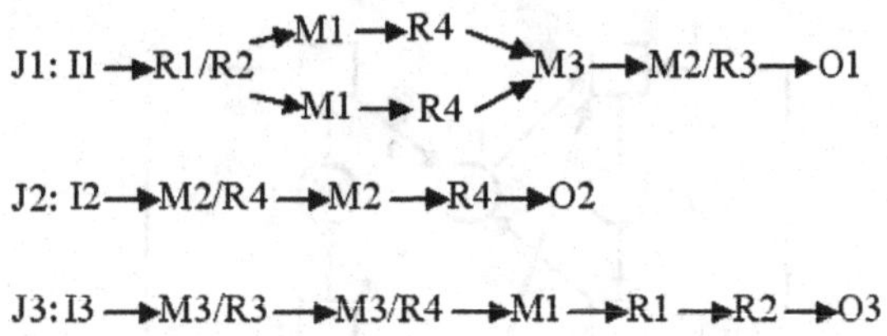

J1: I1 →R1/R2 →M1 →R4 →M3 →M2/R3 →O1
                →M1 →R4 →

J2: I2 →M2/R4 →M2 →R4 →O2

J3: I3 →M3/R3 →M3/R4 →M1 →R1 →R2 →O3

M2 to O2 by R4. A raw product J3 is taken from I3, processed by M3 and R3, and then by M3 and R4. After that, it is then processed by M1. Finally, after being processed by M1 it is then moved from M1 to O3 by R1 and R2 sequentially.

Figure 8 shows the net model of the FMS that may use a multi-set of resources at a work processing step. The system net is an S^{4}R, where

$$P^0 = \{p_8, p_{12}, p_{20}\}, \quad P_{A_3} = \{p_i \mid i = 13, 14, \cdots, 17\},$$

$$P_{R_1} = \{p_{18}, p_{19}, p_{20}, p_{21}, p_{22}, p_{23}, p_{24}, p_{25}\},$$

$$P_{A_3} = \{p_i \mid i = 13, 14, \cdots, 17\},$$

$$P_{R_1} = \{p_{18}, p_{19}, p_{20}, p_{21}, p_{22}, p_{23}, p_{24}, p_{25}\},$$

$$P_{R_2} = \{p_{24}, p_{25}\}, \text{ and}$$

$$P_{R_3} = \{p_{18}, p_{19}, p_{21}, p_{22}, p_{23}, p_{24}\}.$$

Places $p_{21}, p_{25}, p_{22}, p_{18}, p_{19}, p_{23}$ and p_{24} denote M1, M2, M3, R1, R2, R3, and R4, respectively. Initially, it is assumed that there are no parts being processed in the system. $M_{\mu0}(p_8) = M_{\mu0}(p_{12}) = M_{\mu0}(p_{20}) = 10$ represents the maximal number of concurrent activities that can take place for part types P1, P2 and P3.

If we use the same method for the first example, the process will not converge to a live net. Hence we control the siphons by the proposed algorithm. It proceeds in an iterative way and at each iteration step a non-max-marked siphon can be found and controlled.

responding a siphon $S = \{p_4, p_7, p_{10}, p_{11}\}$. We conclude that V_{S_1} is redundant with respect to V_{S_2} and V_{S_3}.

Example 2

Consider a hypothetical FMS whose layout is shown in Figure 6 and production routings in Figure 7. It consists of four robots R1-R4, each of which can hold one or three products at a time, and three machines M1-M3, each of which can process two or three products at a time. There are three loading buffers I1-I3 and three unloading buffers O1-O3 to load and unload the FMS. There are three raw product types, namely J1, J2 and J3, to be processed. For these raw product types the production cycles are shown in Figure 7. According to the production cycles, a raw product J1 is taken from I1 by R1 and R2 and put in M1. After being processed by M1 it is then moved to M3 by R4. Finally, after being processed by M3, it is processed by M2 and R3 and then moved to O1. A raw product J2 is taken from I2 and processed by M2 and R4, and then processed by M2 only. After being processed by M2 it is then moved from

Figure 8. An S⁴R net ($N_{\mu 0}$, $M_{\mu 0}$) modeling an FMS

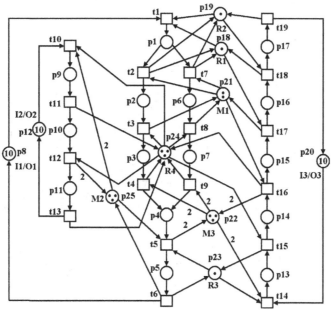

At each iteration step, a monitor is designed for a non-max-marked siphon such that it is max-controlled based on Definition 11 and Proposition 1. Take the control of $S_1 = \{p_2, p_6, p_{16}, p_{18}, p_{21}\}$ as an example.

We have $Th_{S_1} = p_1 + p_{15}$. For $P_{A_1}, p_s = p_1$, is true. For $P_{A_3}, p_s = p_{15}$. As a result we have $k_{S_1}(p_1) = 1$ 　 a n d $k_{S_1}(p_{13}) = k_{S_1}(p_{14}) = k_{S_1}(p_{15}) = 1$.
$\forall p \notin \{p_1, p_{13}, p_{14}, p_{15}\}$, $k_{S_1}(p) = 0$.

1: $S_1 = \{p_2, p_6, p_{16}, p_{18}, p_{21}\}$,

$$Th_{S_1} = p_1 + p_{15},$$

$$k_{S_1} = p_1 + p_{13} + p_{14} + p_{15},$$

$$g_{S_1} = p_1 + p_{13} + p_{14} + p_{15} + V_{S_1}, \text{ and}$$

$$M_{\mu 1}(V_{S_1}) = M_{\mu 0}(S_1) - \sum_{p \in S_3} (\max_{p\cdot} - 1) - 1 = 3 - 1 = 2$$

2: $S_2 = \{p_4, p_9, p_{11}, p_{14}, p_{22}, p_{24}\}$,

$$Th_{S_2} = p_3 + p_7 + 2p_{13},$$

$$k_{S_1} = p_1 + p_2 + p_3 + p_6 + p_7 + 2p_{13},$$

$$g_{S_2} = p_1 + p_2 + p_3 + p_6 + p_7 + 2p_{13} + V_{S_2}, \text{ and}$$

$$M_{\mu 1}(V_{S_2}) = M_{\mu 0}(S_2) - \sum_{p \in S_2} (\max_{p\cdot} - 1) - 1 = 6 - 1 - 1 = 4 \qquad ;$$

3: $S_3 = \{p_5, p_9, p_{11}, p_{14}, p_{22}, p_{24}, p_{25}\}$,

$$Th_{S_3} = p_3 + 2p_4 + p_7 + 2p_{10} + p_{11},$$

$$k_{S_3} = 2p_1 + 2p_2 + 2p_3 + 2p_4 + 2p_6 + 2p_7 + 2p_9 + 2p_{10} + 2p_{13},$$

$$g_{S_3} = 2p_1 + 2p_2 + 2p_3 + 2p_4 + 2p_6 + 2p_7 + 2p_9 + 2p_{10} + 2p_{13} + V_{S_3}, \text{ and}$$

$$M_{\mu 1}(V_{S_3}) = M_{\mu 0}(S_3) - \sum_{p \in S_2} (\max_{p\cdot} - 1) - 1 = 9 - 2 - 1 = 6.$$

Figure 9. A liveness-enforcing Petri net supervisor ($N_{\mu l}$, $M_{\mu l}$) for the net shown in Figure 8

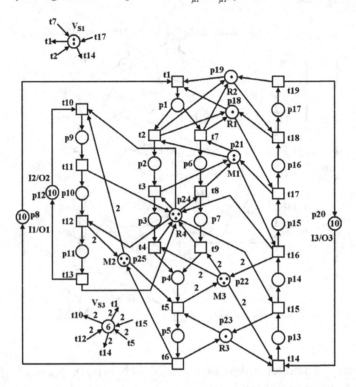

After three siphons are controlled, there is no non-max-marked siphon can be computed by the mixed integer linear programming problem in augmented net in Figure 9. All the siphons are max-controlled. From Theorem 2, the controlled net is live. Here we only add three control places and get 4,116 states. In (Li, Liang, Lu, & Wang, 2004) and (Li, Wang & Wei, 2006) there are only 2,570 and 2,654 states, respectively.

By Algorithm 2 the redundant of the monitors is checked. V_{S_2} is found to be redundant with respect to V_{S_1} and V_{S_3}. Hence only two monitors are necessary.

CONCLUSION

This chapter develops an iterative deadlock prevention approach for FMS that can be modeled by a class of Petri nets, S⁴R nets. To find a minimal

siphon that should be controlled in a plant net model and to avoid computing all the siphons, an improved mixed linear integer programming is proposed in this chapter, which is very efficient for siphon computation. By solving a mixed integer linear programming problem, a non-max-marked siphon in a net model can be derived directly. We just need to control the siphons that are explicitly computed. This leads to the successful avoidance of the complete siphon enumeration whose computation is expensive or even impossible when a large-sized net is dealt with. The redundant monitors are removed through an iterative method.

The proposed method in general cannot derive a maximally permissive supervisor. Since the monitors are designed based on the concept of max-controlled siphons, they are restrictive. Hence an open problem is to explore conditions under which a net has a maximally permissive supervisor. The way of adding monitors can be improved such that the resulting net contains more live states. In the future we will focus on how to construct the monitors.

REFERENCES

Abdallah, I. B., & ElMaraghy, H. A. (1998). Deadlock prevention and avoidance in FMS: A Petri net based approach. *International Journal of Advanced Manufacturing Technology, 14*(10), 704–715. doi:10.1007/BF01438223

Barkaoui, K., & Pradat-Peyre, J. F. (1996). On liveness and controlled siphons in Petri nets. In *Proceeding 17th International Conference on Applications and Theory of Petri Nets,* (LNCS 1091, pp.57–72).

Boer, E. R., & Murata, T. (1994). Generating basis siphons and traps of Petri nets using the sign incidence matrix. *IEEE Transactions on Circuits and Systems. I, Fundamental Theory and Applications, 41*(4), 266–271. doi:10.1109/81.285680

Chu, F., & Xie, X. L. (1997). Deadlock analysis of Petri nets using siphons and mathematical programming. *IEEE Transactions on Robotics and Automation, 13*(6), 793–804. doi:10.1109/70.650158

Ezpeleta, J., Colom, J. M., & Martinez, J. (1995). A Petri net based deadlock prevention policy for flexible manufacturing systems. *IEEE Transactions on Robotics and Automation, 11*(2), 173–184. doi:10.1109/70.370500

Ezpeleta, J., Couvreur, J. M., & Silva, M. (1991). A new technique for finding a generating family of siphons, traps, and st-components: Application to colored Petri nets. In G. Rozenberg (Ed.), *Advances in Petri Nets,* (LNCS 674, pp.126–147).

Fanti, M. P., Maione, B., Mascolo, S., & Turchiano, B. (1997). Event-based feedback control for deadlock avoidance in flexible production systems. *IEEE Transactions on Robotics and Automation, 13*(3), 347–363. doi:10.1109/70.585898

Fanti, M. P., & Zhou, M. C. (2004). Deadlock control methods in automated manufacturing systems. *IEEE Transactions on Systems, Man, and Cybernetics. Part A, 34*(1), 5–22.

Ferrarini, L., & Maroni, M. (1998). Deadlock avoidance control for manufacturing systems with multiple capacity resources. *International Journal of Advanced Manufacturing Technology, 14*(4), 729–736. doi:10.1007/BF01438225

Giua, A., & Seatzu, C. (2002). Liveness enforcing supervisors for railway networks using ES2PR Petri nets. In *Proceedings of the Sixth International Workshop on Discrete Event Systems,* (pp.55-60).

Hsieh, F. S., & Chang, S. C. (1994). Dispatching-driven deadlock avoidance controller synthesis for flexible manufacturing systems. *IEEE Transactions on Robotics and Automation, 10*(2), 196–209. doi:10.1109/70.282544

Huang, Y. S., Jeng, M. D., Xie, X. L., & Chung, S. L. (2001). Deadlock prevention policy based on Petri nets and siphons. *International Journal of Production Research, 39*(2), 283–305. doi:10.1080/00207540010002405

Jeng, M. D., Xie, X. L., & Chung, S. L. (2004). ERCN* merged nets for modeling degraded behavior and parallel processes in semiconductor manufacturing systems. *IEEE Transactions on Systems, Man, and Cybernetics. Part A, 34*(1), 102–112.

Kinuyama, M., & Murata, T. (1986). Generating siphons and traps by Petri net representation of logic equations. In *Proceeding of 2nd IECE Conf on Net Theory,* (pp. 93-100).

Lautenbach, K. (1987). Linear algebraic calculation of deadlocks and traps. In Voss, K., Genrich, H. J., & Rozenberg, G. (Eds.), *Concurrency and Nets* (pp. 315–336).

Lawley, M. A., Reveliotis, S. A., & Ferreira, P. M. (1998). A correct and scalable deadlock avoidance policy for flexible manufacturing systems. *IEEE Transactions on Robotics and Automation, 14*(5), 796–809. doi:10.1109/70.720355

Leung, Y. T., & Sheen, G. J. (1993). Resolving deadlocks in flexible manufacturing cells. *Journal of Manufacturing Systems, 12*(4), 291–304. doi:10.1016/0278-6125(93)90320-S

Li, Z. W. Liang, J.W. Lu, Y. Wang, A. R. (2004). A deadlock prevention method for FMS with multiple resource acquisitions. In *8th International Conference on Control, Automation, Robotics and Vision Conference*, (vol.3, pp.2117-2122).

Li, Z. W., Uzam, M., & Zhou, M. C. (2004). Comments on "Deadlock prevention policy based on Petri nets and siphons.". *International Journal of Production Research, 42*(24), 5253–5254. doi:10.1080/00207540412331330822

Li, Z. W., Wang, A. R., & Wei, N. (2006). Liveness-enforceing supervisors for flexible manufacturing systems with multiple resource acquisitions. In *Proceeding of the 2006 IEEE International Conference on Networking Sensing and Control*, (pp.710-714).

Li, Z. W., Zhang, J., & Zhao, M. (2007). Liveness-enforcing supervisor design for a class of generalized Petri net models of flexible manufacturing systems. *IET Control Theory and Applications, 1*(4), 955–967. doi:10.1049/iet-cta:20060218

Li, Z. W., & Zhao, M. (2008). On controllability of dependent siphons for deadlock prevention in generalized Petri nets. *IEEE Transactions on Systems, Man, and Cybernetics. Part A, 38*(2), 369–384.

Li, Z. W., & Zhou, M. C. (2004). Elementary siphons of Petri nets and their application to deadlock prevention in flexible manufacturing systems. *IEEE Transactions on Systems, Man, and Cybernetics. Part A, 34*(1), 38–51.

Li, Z. W., & Zhou, M. C. (2006). Two-stage method for synthesizing liveness-enforcing supervisors for flexible manufacturing systems using Petri nets. *IEEE Transactions on Industrial Informatics, 2*(4), 313–325. doi:10.1109/TII.2006.885185

Li, Z. W., Zhou, M. C., & Wu, N. Q. (2008). A survey and comparison of Petri net-based deadlock prevention policies for flexible manufacturing systems. *IEEE Transactions on Systems, Man, and Cybernetics. Part C, 38*(2), 173–188.

Murata, T. (1989). Petri nets: Properties, analysis, and applications. *Proceedings of the IEEE, 77*(4), 541–580. doi:10.1109/5.24143

Park, J., & Reveliotis, S. A. (2001). Deadlock avoidance in sequential resource allocation systems with multiple resource acquisitions and flexible routings. *IEEE Transactions on Automatic Control, 46*(10), 1572–1583. doi:10.1109/9.956052

Reveliotis, S. A. (2003). On the siphon-based characterization of liveness in sequential resource allocation systems. In W. M. P. van der Aalst and E. Best (Eds.), *Proc. Int. Conf. on Applications and Theory of Petri Nets,* (LNCS 2679, pp.241–255). Berlin: Springer.

Roszkowska, E. (2004). Supervisory control for deadlock avoidance in compound processes. *IEEE Transactions on Systems, Man, and Cybernetics. Part A, 34*(1), 52–64.

Tricas, F., & Ezpeleta, J. (2006). Computing minimal siphons in Petri net models of resource allocation systems: A parallel solution. *IEEE Transactions on Systems, Man, and Cybernetics. Part A, 36*(3), 532–539.

Uzam, M. (2002). An optimal deadlock prevention policy for flexible manufacturing systems using Petri net models with resources and the theory of regions. *International Journal of Advanced Manufacturing Technology, 19*(3), 192–208.

Uzam, M. (2004). The use of the Petri net reduction approach for an optimal deadlock prevention policy for flexible manufacturing systems. *International Journal of Advanced Manufacturing Technology*, *23*(3/4), 204–219. doi:10.1007/s00170-002-1526-5

Wu, N. Q., & Zhou, M. C. (2001). Avoiding deadlock and reducing starvation and blocking in automated manufacturing systems. *IEEE Transactions on Robotics and Automation*, *17*(5), 658–669. doi:10.1109/70.964666

Yim, D., Kim, J., & Woo, H. (1997). Avoidance of deadlocks in flexible manufacturing systems using a capacity designated directed graph. *International Journal of Production Research*, *35*(9), 2459–2475. doi:10.1080/002075497194606

Zhou, M. C., & DiCesare, F. (1992). A hybrid methodology for synthesis of Petri nets for manufacturing systems. *IEEE Transactions on Robotics and Automation*, *8*(3), 350–361. doi:10.1109/70.143353

Zhou, M. C., & Fanti, M. P. (Eds.). (2005). *Deadlock Resolution in Computer-Integrated Systems*. New York: MarcelDekker.

Zhou, M. C., & Venkatesh, K. (1998). *Modelling, Simulation and Control of Flexible Manufacturing Systems: A Petri Net Approach*. Singapore: World Scientific.

Chapter 16

Choosing the Optimized OS for an MPSoC Embedded System

Abderrazak Jemai
National Institute of Applied Science and Technology, Tunisia

ABSTRACT

This chapter provides a comparative study between recent operating systems, designed for embedded systems. Our study focuses, in particular, on systems designed for Multiprocessors implementations called MPSoC. An OS can be seen as abstract layer or an interface between the embedded application and the underlying hardware. In this chapter, we give a comparative study of main operating systems used in embedded systems. The originality of this chapter is that we specially focus on the OS ability to be optimized to support and manage a multiprocessor architecture. A multiprocessor system-on-chip is software driven and mastering the development complexity of the software part of MPSoC, is the key to reduce developing time factor. This opportunity could be reached through the use of a document giving a detailed description and analysis for criteria related to MPSoC. The wide diversity of existing operating systems, the huge complexity to develop an application specific or a general purpose, and the aggressive evolution of embedded systems makes the development of such a system a so difficult task. These considerations lead to the realization that a work that provides guidance for the MPSoC designers will be very beneficial for these communities.

INTRODUCTION

This chapter presents the basic services that an embedded OS should provide and gives a comparative study between recent operating systems designed for embedded systems. Our study focuses, in particular, on those designed for Multiprocessors implementations called MPSoC. The originality of this work is that we specially focus on the OS ability to be optimized to support and manage a multiprocessor architecture.

A multiprocessor system-on-chip is software driven and mastering the development complexity of the software part of MPSoC is the key to reduce developing time factor. This opportunity could be reached through the use of a document

DOI: 10.4018/978-1-60960-086-0.ch016

giving a detailed description and analysis for criteria related to MPSoC.

Basically, embedded system developers for MPSoC, start by defining the specification of their application and then turn to OS available on the market. If one of them gives good response to their application requirements, the selected OS will be chosen. Otherwise, developers may opt to develop a specific one. The hard work, in the first case, is to find a detailed and objective comparative study between existing OS to decide which one suits their application needs. Many studies may be found giving comparison between existing OS, but, the comparison should be based on today available OS and take into account new application requirements (QoS, Performance, energy consumption, memory footprint, parallel programming, multiprocessor management, etc.).

If no existing OS suits the application requirements, designers may opt to develop their own OS. In this case, the developed OS will contain the only needed services. This chapter details basic services that a minimal OS should have.

This chapter is structured as follows: Section II provides a number of definitions and descriptions that will help the reader to better understand the rest of this chapter. Section III presents the OS structure, Section IV presents the OS functions and services and section V presents a survey of existing operating systems that target embedded systems.

EMBEDDED SYSTEMS, RTOS AND SOC

Through this chapter, some concepts such as embedded systems, real-time systems, SoC, recur very frequently. It is useful to provide a number of definitions and descriptions that will help the reader to better understand the rest of this chapter.

A System (Hardware and Software) is considered embedded if it is a sub-component of a larger system and is used to receive events from and monitor that system, using special hardware devices.

A system is said to be on Chip if an entire embedded system is integrated in the same chip. These on chip systems (SoC: System on a Chip) need a specific design flow taking into account the limited space constraints, and the high speed transmission context. With classic systems, the hardware is already designed when designing the software part. In contrast, in SoC, the two parts are often designed in parallel in order to choose the best hardware function fitting the software requirements.

A real-time system is a system whose performance depends not only on the values of its outputs, but also on the time at which these values are produced. A real-time system can be defined also as one in which the correctness of the computations depends not only on the logical correctness of the computation but also on the time at which the result is produced. If the timing constraints of the system are not met, system failure is said to have occurred. The most important feature for a real-time system is not speed, but how much the individual timing constraints of each task are satisfied. We can distinguish hard real-time and soft real-time applications. In hard real time, there is no value of computation if it is late. The activities of the system must be completed on time. A soft real-time system can tolerate some late answers. It is important to note that in classic applications, we don't account for how late a computation is completed. A real-time operating system (RTOS) is an operating system able to provide a required service in a bounded response time.

OS STRUCTURE

An embedded OS is composed of five main layers: OS-API, Basic OS, Communication Layer, HALL-API and HALL.

- OS-API: It provides a flexible programming model for the application. It hides HW components particularities. To the application programmer's view point, it seems as if he is programming an embedded software on given platform.
- Basic OS: this layer contains basic OS functions such as scheduler, memory management, interruption management, etc.
- Communication layer: It provides different kinds of communication concepts such as message passing communication possibilities, FIFO, etc.
- Hall-API (also called platform API): It provides what hardware can offer to the OS and supports applications. This layer can be considered as a contract between OS development team and underlying hardware designer. This layer isolates the kernel from the hardware specificities and the platform characteristics..
- HALL: this layer gives the required services to HAL-API layer such that each HALL-API call will find as a return the needed service in HALL layer.

OS FUNCTIONS AND SERVICES

Basic Os Services

The OS can be viewed as an assembly of components: the designer will have to assemble together the needed components and eventually to parameterize them according to the application specification. OS services include task scheduling, synchronization, communication, and system call mechanism (Zuberi, Pillai & Shin, 1999).

Interruption

While the processor is running a task, an urgent event may occur. This event may come from peripheral devices or internal components. Two

Figure 1. OS Structure for MPSoC architecture

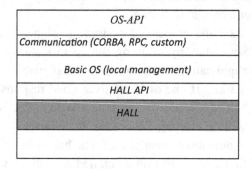

mechanisms are conceivable: asynchronous interrupt handling or continuously polling peripherals to see if an interruption request has occurred. Interrupts handling is an important part of the operating system. It takes a particular importance in embedded systems because of their need to react quickly to real-world (Zuberi, Pillai & Shin, 1999). When an interrupt is recognized, the CPU checks the priority of the event. If it has higher priority, the current running task is suspended, unless the task, or the OS, disables interrupts. When the external event is considered urgent (it has higher priority), the CPU saves the state of the current running task and loads a special routine called *Interrupt Service Routine* which has in charge to deal with the interruption request.

The Interrupt Service Routine, also called ISR, should have a short execution time. As a result of its execution, one or more tasks may change to a ready state. For this reason, the OS should verify if the interrupted task is still having the highest priority. If a higher priority task is made ready to run, the new highest priority task is selected. However, if as a result, all tasks fall in a waiting state, an idle task is executed.

The strategy to deal with the external event is not dictated by the compiler. For this reason, the embedded developer has to decide which interrupt architecture is more suitable for his application. Some approaches are to save the interrupted context on a secondary register file; another one is to preserve the context in a memory stack or a cache.

There is a maximum allowable time that can be delivered to the system to process an ISR. The interrupt service routine must do the just needed job. In other hand, the operating system must minimize the period during which interrupts are disabled. In some systems (e.g. QNX), interruptions can be nested and shared in that, the interrupts aren't disabled during the execution of an interrupt handler.

Task Management and Scheduling

Scheduling is the concept that determines which task is to be executed next time. In embedded systems, task set is statically well defined at the time of system generation. The number of tasks depends on whether concurrent invocations of a task are allowed or not. If not, we have no need to dynamic creation of task context. A task switches between two main states: active (ready to run or currently running) and inactive (suspended).

Depending on the OS features and the scheduling policies, a task can exist in one of the following states:

* Running: When the task is using the processor. The highest priority task is commonly chosen to run
* Ready: When a task is able to execute. A ready task is not currently executing because a higher priority task is already in the running state a takes control of the CPU.
* Waiting: When a task is waiting for a certain amount of time to expire. A running task may delay itself by using an OS delay function (e.g. OSTimeDly() for microC-OS/II). In that case, the current task is suspended and the next highest priority task is given control of the CPU. When the time delay expires, the delayed task is made back to the ready state. When all tasks are either waiting for time to expire or for an event, the operating system executes an

"idle task". This idle task is often set to the lowest priority level.

To switch to the next task, the operating system executes what we so call a context switch. The context switch consists of saving the valuable contents of CPU registers in a secure place to be copied back when the interrupted task resume. The CPU registers will be filled with values coming from a save stack corresponding to the new selected task. Different priority policies may be used to switch between tasks (Zuberi, Pillai & Shin, 1999). The chosen priority policy is often static in embedded systems.

Priority Setting and Management

In operating systems that support pre-emption, tasks could have priorities. A task that becomes ready to run can pre-empt an executing lower priority task. In most RTOSes a higher priority means a lower priority number. A task may have two different priorities: the base priority and the current priority. The base priority is the priority given to the task at the application level. The task may change priority at run time if it needs higher priority to be executed.

Synchronization and Communication

Tasks, almost, have to cooperate in order to make the application work. Two kinds of cooperation can be identified:

Synchronization and *Communication.*

Synchronization: In response to the application needs, and since time is important in real time systems, it can be important to synchronize tasks in order to make them execute in a predefined order. A task may wait on an event.

In other hand, synchronization service is used to let tasks share resources safely. In that case, synchronization can be done by means of mutexes, semaphores or conditions.

Communication: Often, tasks need to exchange information. To do this, tasks invoke communication primitives (such as send/receive). Synchronization can be viewed as a certain kind of Communication. But some communication primitives are used just to let a task communicate a certain result to another task. This mechanism can be achieved by using message passing or shared variable techniques.

Parallelism Management

When designing a multi-threaded kernel on an MPSoC, concurrent execution and parallelism management is a hard task. Two mechanisms are generally provided to deal with communication in parallel programming: message passing and shared memory (Yoo, Youssef, Bouchhima, Jerraya & Diaz-Nava, 2004). Communication using Message Passing technique has standardized by using MPI. This model of communication

This is a library specification for message-passing, proposed as a standard by a large committee of vendors and users. In a shared memory model, a memory is shared by different tasks in order to exchange data. This memory may be centralized or distributed. In the latter situation, address referencing and memory consistency are the major challenge.

System Call Mechanism and I/O

I/O management and device drivers are one of the three main OS services[1]. It is known that writing efficient device drivers requires knowledge of both hardware and software. The resulting device drivers become the keys issues to embedded system performance since they are called repeatedly. Device driver programming and its optimization dictates real-time performance in terms of response time, utilization of memory and other system resources (Stepner, et al, 1999).

Communication and Memory Abstraction

Communication between tasks differs whether tasks are within the same Processing Element (*PE*) or inter-PE communication tasks. Generally we use shared memory technique in communication within a PE (mutex, semaphores) and message passing technique to communicate between tasks running on different PE. Some implementations use shared memory to communicate in an inter-PE process. In that case, we have extra requirements to solve: external addressing memory and communication bandwidth. With the emergence of MPSoC, message passing technique becomes a solution to communicate between heterogeneous components within a chip (Poletti, Poggliali, & Marchal, 2005).

Memory abstraction is the concept responsible of accessing memory components. At application level, each task sees memory as a storing space. This space may be shared or not. Memory-APIs is a set of services (e.g. allocate/de-allocate) which reflects the available storage mechanism and hides the physical implementation mechanism.

In fact, data reside in RAMs (SRAM, SDRAM, flush) or ROM (EPROM). To be computed, data migrate to the CPU's task caller. Hence, data cross intermediate storage components and mechanism like caches and buffers to reside finally into the final register. To deal with this cross movement, many architectures and algorithms are used.

Algorithms like first fit and buddy-heap are not adapted for RTOS because, they are not-deterministic, and they have high Worst Case Execution TIME (WCET).

Management of on-chip memory may be:

- Static: allocation is determined at compile time. Static memory management can be simple or complex depending on three factors: memory structure, memory's software allocation functions and their suitability for the related application. Wolf (Li &

Wolf, 1999) gives a study of the impact of the memory management hierarchy on the performance and cost of RTOS on MPSoC.

- Dynamic: In Dynamic memory management (DMM) allocation is decided at runtime. This technique saves memory space but it is CPU time consumer. DMM can be manual or automatic. In the first case, allocation is dictated by the programmer (malloc, freemem) but in the latter, allocation and recuperation (garbage collector) is an inherent part of the OS. Automatic DMM can consume a great amount of CPU time and often has non deterministic behavior.

Most of SoC implementations focused on static allocation. This technique is inefficient if application memory requirements change during run-time and makes very difficult any system modification after implementation. Shalan noticed that manual dynamic allocation is more efficient for MPSoC (Shalan, 2003).

Message Passing

Communication using Message Passing (MP) is widely used on parallel architectures using a distributed memory. Communication using MP technique has standardized by using the MPI library. MPI lib is proposed as a standard by a broadly based committee of vendors and users. MPI is an abstract implementation of message-passing communication model. It provides a number of MPSoC requirements like parallelism and heterogeneity. Some MPI releases are fully asynchronous and provide overlapping communication. It achieves high-performance data exchange and at the same time reduces CPU overhead for communication.

Shared Memory

A memory is said to be shared if it is accessed by different tasks. Tasks may be distributed into different systems. There are two configurations of shared memory: centralized or distributed (Tanenbaum, 1995).

In distributed shared memory, many features have to be considered: data reference addressing, cache control and global consistency. In general purpose architecture, the Global consistency can be maintained by Hardware consistency components (e.g. MMU) using single bus multi-processor or switched multi-processor, or by software modules using page based DSM[2], shared variable DSM or object-based DSM (Tanenbaum, 1995). In the context of MPSoC where determinism is required this hardware mechanism is not very suitable.

Distributed Shared Memory

Resource management includes: task- management, memory management power management and inter-tasks communication management. Centralized resource management is a nightmare problem when thousands of processors and related resources have to coexist in the same chip. In that case Distributed Resource Management (DSM) should be the unique solution in order to avoid communication congestion and big response time.

In case of DSM, the designer has to solve different challenges: autonomy of different DSM units, extensibility and data coherence. To tackle these problems, policies and solutions used in Grid computing (Krauter, et al, 2002) seem to be applicable in the context of MPSoC. The use of NoC is widely used to address the interconnection and communication challenges.

OS CASE STUDIES

VxWorks

VxWorks was initially developed for pSOS and VRTX. Wind River VxWorks platforms support symmetric and asymmetric architectures (AMP, SMP) containing multicore nodes. VxWorks is a highly scalable real-time operating system

(RTOS). It is widely used in industrial applications, medical instruments, robotics, networking, and consumer electronics. This RTOS supports a full range of real-time features including multitasking, scheduling, inter-task synchronization/communication and memory management. Wind River has also added new features related to multi-OS interprocess communication (MIPC).

Developers using VxWorks can scale their solution to fit the just needed OS services which gives as a result a small footprint with a highest performance meeting cost and functionality requirements. A reduced footprint can be obtained by using VxWorks on ARM architecture.

In VxWorks, interruptions are nested and prioritized. To achieve the fastest possible response to external interrupts, interrupt service routine (ISR) run a special context outside of any thread's context. Hence there are no thread context switches involved. ISRs by default use a separate stack. But if the architecture doesn't allow separate stack of ISR then the stack of the interrupted task is used.

ECos

ECos is an open source real-time operating. Regarding its footprint, it can meet the requirements of the embedded space that other embedded OS cannot yet reach. It provides three abstraction layers: The first layer called "architecture HAL" can be seen as a platform wrapper. It abstracts the details of the current platform. We can find in this layer some services like context switching, and interrupt delivery. The second layer, called *"The platform HAL"* includes other services like I/O register access and interrupts controllers. The third layer, called *"The implementation HAL"* gives abstraction to on-chip devices and architecture variants. Three scheduling policies are provided: Bitmap, Multilevel and experimental lottery.

In response to interruption requests, ECos provides three kinds of ISRs:

- Interrupt Service Routines (ISRs) that are invoked in response to a hardware interrupt
- Deferred Service Routines (DSRs) that are invoked in response to request by an ISR; and
- Threads that are the clients of the driver.

The Ecos I/O package includes all classes of drivers from simple serial to networking stacks.

FreeRTOS

FreeRTOS is a scalable open source real-time system RTOS designed for small embedded systems. It was been developed by Richard BARRY. This OS can support up to 23 architectures including ARM Cortex M3, ARM9 and ARM7. It is designed to be small, simple and easy to use. The major part of FreeRTOS is written in C language and its footprint is approximately 4k to 9k bytes(Barry, 2010).

FreeRTOS provides different APIs targeting synchronization and communication such as Queues, semaphores and mutex.

Tasks can exist in one of the following states:

- **Running:** When a task is currently using the processor.
- **Ready:** when a task is able to execute but a different task with an equal or higher priority is already in the running state.
- **Blocked:** A task is said to be blocked if it is currently waiting for either a temporal of an eternal event. Temporal event may occur when a task calls a special APIs like vTaskDelay(). In that case, the current task is suspended until the delay period expires. In that case, the suspended task is added to a special list called *Delayed_List*. The scheduler visits this Delayed_List at every decision point to determine if any of the tasks have time-out. A task can also switch to a block state when it is waiting for semaphore events.

When a new task is created, it is immediately placed in a Ready state by adding it to the Ready List. FreeRTOS uses Round robin policy for serving CPU to tasks having the same priority level. Hence, multiple Ready Lists are used, one for each priority level. When the current task attempt to access to an unavailable resource, this task is immediately blocked and removed from the current Ready List. This operation includes attempts to obtaining other critical resources such as semaphores and queues.

MicroC/OS-II

μC/OS-II is an open source multitasking real-time system. It is developed by Jean Labrosse for microprocessors and micro controllers. This OS is written in highly portable ANSI C and some portions are written is assembly language. Theses portions target microprocessor specific code. We can port μC/OS-II on different hardware architectures like ARM, x86, PowerPC, etc (Altera, 2009).

μC/OS-II is a preemptive real-time kernel that can manage up to 64 tasks. A unique priority is assigned to each task which means that μC/OS-II cannot be a round robin scheduling. When an interrupt request occurs as soon as this current ISR and all nested interrupts complete the highest priority task is awakened and takes control of the CPU. Interrupts can be nested up to 255 levels deep. Interrupts should be written in an assembly language. The interrupt disable time dependents on the proprieties of processor and the ability of the compiler to manage these features at compile time.

Several mechanisms related to synchronization are present in μC/OS-II. For this purpose, developers can use semaphores, mutual exclusion semaphores, event flags, message mailboxes, and message queues.

μC/OS-II provides task management scheduling including creating, deleting, suspending and resuming tasks.

CONCLUSION

MPSoC is nowadays commonly used. Future embedded applications will continue to need more computation and real-time performance to meet their deadlines, but they need also extra requirements like low power and energy consumption and low cost. The use of hundreds or even thousands of PE within MPSoC at low clock rates for each PE gives some responses to reduce energy consumption and dissipation. But parallel modeling and programming on these PE still a big challenge. Some model like Khan process and SDF models address this problem in some kind of applications like Multimedia ones.

Existing OS often deliver basic requirements but their coexistence into the same chip in a heterogeneous environment with the combination of all the underlying requirements is a big challenge and requires new solutions.

This chapter gives a good guideline for designers searching for a response to their common question "Which OS is the best for our application?". However, in the context of MPSoC with hundreds or thousands of processors and components, a great work must be done by OS delivers such that their API takes into account the new requirements: Parallelism and Global Resource Management. In the case when the application developers' team will develop their proper OS for MPSoC; this chapter gives a good presentation of basic OS services and new useful ones for Global Management.

REFERENCES

Akgul, B. (2004). *The System-on-a-Chip Lock Cache*. PhD thesis, School of ECE, Georgia Institute of Technology, Atlanta, GA.

ALTERA Corporation. (2009, March). *MicroC/OS-II Real-Time Operating System, Nios II Software Developer's Handbook, NII52008-9.0.0*.

Ammari, A. C., & Jemai, A. (2009, January). Multiprocessor platform-based design for multimedia, Journal of Computers & Digital Techniques. *IET*, *3*(1), 52–61.

Barbalace, A. (2008, February). Performance Comparison of VxWorks, Linux, RTAI and Xenomea in a Hard Real-Time Application. *IEEE Transactions on Nuclear Science*, *55*(1), 435–439. doi:10.1109/TNS.2007.905231

Barry, R. (2010). *Using the FreeRTOS Real Time Kernel, NXP LPC 17xx Edition*. Real Time Engineers Ltd.

Baynes, K., Collins, C., Fiterman, E., Ganesh, B., Kohout, P., & Smit, C. (2003, November). The performance and energy consumption of embedded real-time operating systems. *IEEE Transactions on Computers*, *52*(11), 1454–1469. doi:10.1109/TC.2003.1244943

Culler, D. E., & Pal Singh, J. (1999). *Parallel Computer Architecture: A Hardware/Software Approach*. San Francisco: Morgan Kaufmann Publishers, Inc.

Jerraya, A., Tenhunen, H. & Wolf, W. (2005, July). Multiprocessors Systems-on-Chips. *IEEE Computer Society Magazine*, 36-40.

Krasner, J. (2003, July). Total cost of development: A COMPREHENSIVE COST estimation Embedded application design using a real-time OS. *Embedded Market forecasters*. Retrieved from www.embeddedforecast.com

Krauter, K. (2002). A taxonomy and survey of grid resource management systems for distributed computing. *Software, Practice & Experience*, *32*, 135–164. doi:10.1002/spe.432

Kwon, K.-S., Yi, Y.-M., Kim, D.-H., & Ha, S.-H. (2005). *Embedded Software Generation from System Level Specification for Multi-tasking Embedded Systems*. Washington, DC: IEEE, ASP-DAC.

Labrosse, J. J. (1999). *MicroC/OS-II The real-time Kernel*. Lawrence, KS: R&D Books.

Le Moigne, R., Pasquier, O., & Calvez, J.-P. (2004). A Generic RTOS Model for Real-time Systems Simulation with SystemC. In *Design, Automation and Test in Europe Conference and Exhibition Designers, DATE'04,* (Vol. 3, pp. 82 – 87).

Lee, J. (2004). *Hardware/Software Deadlock Avoidance for Multiprocessor Multi-resource System-on-a-Chip*. Ph.D. dissertation, Georgia Institute of Technology, Atlanta, GA.

Lee, J., & Mooney, V. (2005, March). Hardware/software partitioning of operating systems: Focus on deadlock detection and avoidance. [CDT]. *IEEE Computer and Digital Techniques*, *152*(2), 167–182. doi:10.1049/ip-cdt:20045078

Li, Q., & Yao, C. (2003). *Real-Time concepts for Embedded Systems*. Gilroy, CA: CMP Books.

Li, Y., & Wolf, W. (1999). Hardware/Software Co-Synthesis with Memory Hierarchies. *IEEE Transaction Computer-Aided Design of Integrated Circuits and Systems*, *18*(10), 1405–1417. doi:10.1109/43.790618

Liu, J. W. S. (2000). *Real-Time systems*. Upper Saddle River, NJ: Prentice Hall.

Park, J. C., Mooney, V., & Srinivasan, S. K. (2003, November). Combining data remapping and voltage/frequency scaling of second level memory for energy reduction in embedded systems. *Microelectronics Journal*, *34*(11), 1019–1024. doi:10.1016/S0026-2692(03)00170-8

Poletti, F., Poggiali, A., & Marchal, P., (2005). Flexible Hardware/Software Support for Message Passing on a Distributed Shared Memory Architecture. *DATE'05, 02*(2), 736-741.

Raghunathan, V. et al. (2005, February). Energy Aware Wireless Systems with Adaptive Power-Fidelity tradeoffs. *IEEE Transaction on very large scale integration (VLSI) systems, 13*(2), 211–225.

Semiconductor Industry Association. (2009). *International Technology Roadmap for Semiconductors (ITRS)*. Retrieved from http://www.itrs.net/Links/2009ITRS/Home2009.htm

Shalan, M. (2003). *Dynamic memory management for embedded real-time multiprocessor system-on-a-chip*. PhD thesis, School of ECE, Georgia Institute of Technology, Atlanta, GA.

Stepner, D., et al. (1999). Embedded application design using a real-time OS. In *DAC 99*, New Orleans, LA.

Stepner, D., et al. (1999). Embedded design using a real-time OS. In *DAC 99*, New Orleans, LA.

Tanenbaum, A. A. (1995). *Distributed Operation Systems*. New York: Prentice Hall.

Yoo, S., Youssef, M.-W., Bouchhima, A., Jerraya, A. A., & Diaz-Nava, M. (2004). Multi-Processor SoC Design Methodology using a Concept of Two-Layer Hardware-dependent Software. In *Proceedings of the Design, Automation and Test in Europe Conference and Exhibition (DATE '04)*, (pp. 1530-1591/04). Washington, DC: IEEE.

Zrida, H. K., Jemai, A., Ammari, A. C., & Abid, M. (2009). High Level H.264/AVC Video Encoder Parallelization For Multiprocessor Implementation. In *12th International conference Design, Automation & Test in Europe (DATE)*, 20-24 April 2009, Nice., Jemai, A., Kission, P., Jerraya, A.A., (1997, October). Combining Architectural Simulation and Behavioral Synthesis. *IEICE Transaction Fundamentals. E (Norwalk, Conn.), 80-A*(10), 1756–1766.

Zuberi, K. M., Pillai, P., & Shin, K. G. (1999). *AMERALDS-OSEK: A Small real-time Operating System for Automotive Control and Monitoring*. Warrendale, PA: Society of Automotive Engineers, Inc.

ENDNOTES

[1] Three categories of OS services: task management, synchronization/interrupt management (IT), and I/O (device drivers).
[2] DSM: Distributed Shared memory

Chapter 17
Specification and Validation of Real Time Systems

Olfa Mosbahi
Campus Universitaire, Tunisia

ABSTRACT

The chapter presents a specification technique borrowing features from two classes of specification methods, formal and semi-formal ones. Each of the above methods have been proved to be useful in the development of real-time and critical systems and widely reported in different papers (Bruel, 1996; Clarke & Wing, 1996; Cohen, 1994; Fitzgerald & Larsen, 1994; Ghezzi, Mandrioli & Morzenti, 1990). Formal methods are based on mathematical notations and axiomatic which induce verification and validation. Semi-formal methods are, in the other hand, graphic, structural and uer-friendly. Each method is applied on a suitable case study, that we regret some missing features we could find in the other class. This remark has motivated our work. We are interested in the integration of formal and semi-formal methods in order to lay out a specification approach which combines the advantages of theses two classes of methods. The proposed technique is based on the integration of the semi-formal method STATEMATE (Harel, 1997; Harel, 1987) and the temporal logic FNLOG (Sowmya & Ramesh, 1997). This choice is justified by the fact that FNLOG is formal, deals with quantitative temporal properties and that these two approaches have a compatibility which simplifies their integration (Sowmya & Ramesh, 1997). The proposed integration approach uses the notations of STATEMATE and FNLOG, defines various transformation rules of a STATEMATE specification towards FNLOG and extends the axiomatics of the temporal logic FNLOG by new lemmas to deal with duration properties. The chapter presents the various steps of our integration approach, the proposed extentions and illustrates it over a case of critical real-time systems: the gas burner system (Ravn, Rishel & Hansen, 1993).

DOI: 10.4018/978-1-60960-086-0.ch017

INTRODUCTION

Critical real-time systems are complex and require a high level of safety and reliability. To reduce this complexity and to reach a high required degree of reliability and safety, it would be quite interesting to lay out a specification approach which simplifies the requirement description, deals with mathematical notations inducing verification and validation, and allows the description of quantitative temporal properties. Thus, it comes the idea of integrating formal (Bruel, 1996; Bussow, Wolfgang & Grieskamp, 1998; Clarke & Wing, 1996; Jahanian & Mok, 1996; Ostroff, 1994) and semi-formal approaches in order to lay out a specification approach which combines the advantages of these two classes of methods. Semi formal methods are graphic, structural and user-friendly ; formal methods are based on mathematical notations and axiomatic inducing proofs. In this paper, we propose a specification technique integrating STATEMATE (Harel, 1987; Harel, 1997) as a semi-formal method and the temporal logic FNLOG (Sowmya & Ramesh, 1997) as a formal one. Several reasons justify the choice of these methods. STATEMATE (Harel, 1987) is a graphic formalism; covers the various aspects of a complex system (data, functionality, control and structure); deals with a tool allowing the checking of syntax and the validation by simulation. The temporal logic FNLOG (Sowmya & Ramesh, 1997) provides a requirement specification language that allows a concise expression of quantitative properties. The proposed specification and validation approach introduces an integration method using STATEMATE and FNLOG notations and proposes transformation rules, and an extension of FNLOG axiomatic to reason about duration properties.

The chapter is organized as follows: section 2 presents a backgroud for the used methods: STATEMATE and FNLOG. The reader interested by more details can be referred to papers (Harel, 1987; Harel, 1997 ; Harel, Pnueli, Schmidt & Sherman, 1987) for STATEMATE and to papers (Sowmya & Ramesh, 1997; Sowmya & Ramesh, 1992) for FNLOG. Section 3 presents the proposed method combining STTEMATE and FNLOG. Section 4 presents a case study illustrating the proposed method. We end by a cnclusion and a future work.

BACKGROUND

General View STATEMATE

STATEMATE is a graphic specification method for complex real-time reactive systems. In this section, we present a formal description of real-time reactive systems, an informal description of STATEMATE as a specification method. In STATEMATE, the descriptions used to capture the system specification are organized into three views, or projections, of the system: functional, behavioral and structural. The functional view describes the system's functions, processes and activities. The behavioral view describes the system's behavior over time. The structural view describes the subsystems, modules, or objects constituting the real system and the communication between them.

Activity-Charts

Activity-charts describes the system's functions, processes, or objects, also called activities. This view also includes the inputs and outputs of the activities, that is, the data-flow to and from the external environment of the system as well as the information flowing among the internal activities.

Statecharts

Statecharts describes the system's behavior over time, including the dynamics of activities, their control and timing behavior, the states and modes of the system, and the conditions and events that

Figure 1. Example of a Statechart specification

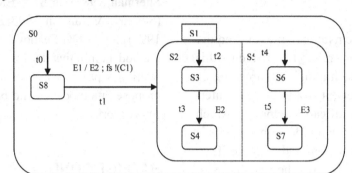

cause modes to change and other occurences to take place. It also provides answers to questions about causality, concurrency, and synchronization. In statecharts, conventional finite state machines (FSM) are extended by AND/OR decomposition of states, inter-level transitions and an implicit inter-component broadcast communication. A statechart specification can be visualized as a tree of states, where the basic states correspond to the conventional notion of states in FSM's. All other states are related by the superstate-substate property. The superstate at the top level is the specification itself. This relation imposes a natural concept of "depth" as a refinement of states. There are three types of states: AND, OR, and BASIC states. In Figure 1, for instance, S1 is an AND state, S0, S2, S5 are OR states, and S3, S4, S8 are BASIC states. States obey a hierarchical order. For instance, S2 and S5 are substates of state S1. Substates of an AND state are called parallel states. A configuration is a maximal set of states a system can simultaneousely reside in if an AND (OR) state is contained in a configuration, then all substates (only one of its substates) are (is) also contained in it. An OR–state consists of a number of substates and being in the OR-state means being in exactly one of its substates. An AND-state too comprises substates and being in an AND-state implies being in all its substates simultaneously.

Transitions. Transitions are specified by arcs originating at one (or more) state(s) and terminat-

ing at one (or more) state(s). A special default transition, which has no originality state, is specified in every superstate; this transition specifies the substate that is entered by default when the superstate is entered. Transitions may be labelled. Labels are of the form: **Event-part (condition-part) / Action-part**

Each component of the label is optional. The event-part is a boolean combination of atomic events, and it must evaluate to true before the transition can trigger. Additionally, the condition-part, which is again a boolean combination of conditions on the events, must be true for the transition to take place. The action-part is a boolean combination of events which will be generated as a result of taking the transition. States are entered and exited either explicity by taking a transition, or implicitly because some other states are entered/exited. In Figure 1, t0 is the default entry state of state S0. Similarly, t2 Hand t4 are the default entry states in S3 and S6 respectively.

Orthogonality. The substates of an AND-state, separated by dashed lines in the diagram, are said to be orthogonal. No transitions are allowed between the substates of an AND-state, which explains why they are said to be orthogonal. Since entering an AND-state means entering every orthogonal compoment of the state, orthogonality captures concurrency.

Events and Broadcasting. Atomic events are those generated by the environment in which the system functions or thoses generated within the system itself. Events act as signals to the system. Every occurence of any event is assumed to be broadcast throughout the system instantaneously. Entering and exiting states as well as a timeout, defined by tm(e, n) = n units of time since occurence of event e, are considered to be events. Broadcasting implies the events generated in one component are broadcast throughout the system, possibly triggering new transitions in other components, in general giving rise to a whole chain of transitions. By the synchrony hypothesis, explained below, the entire chain of transitions takes place simultaneousely in one time step. In Figure 1, the system can be in states S0 and S8 simultaneously.

Synchronization and Real-time. Statecharts incorporates Berry's (Berry & Coresserat, 1985) strong synchrony hypothesis: an execution machine for a system is infinitely fast (which defines synchrony) and control takes no time. This hypothesis facilitates the specification task by abstracting from internal reaction time. Real-time is incorporated in statecharts by having an implicit clock, allowing transitions to be triggered by timeouts relative to this clock and by requiring that if a transition can be taken, then it must be taken immediately. As mentioned already, by the synchrony hypothesis, the maximal chain of transitions in one time step takes place simultaneously. The events, conditions and actions are inductively defined, details of which appear in (Hooman, Ramesh & De Roever, 1990; Huizing, Gerth & De Roever, 1988) intuitively, there is a set of primitives events which may be composed using logical operators to obtain more complex events; there are also special events associated with entry into and exit from a state, called *enter (S)* and *exit (S)*, as well as a timeout event *timeout(e, n)*, which stands for n units of time elapsing since event e occured. Actions and conditions have corresponding definitions.

Semantics of Statechharts. Huizing et al.(Huizing, Gerth & De Roever, 1988) proposed an abstract semantics for statecharts, which was later refined by Hooman et al. (Hooman, Ramesh & De Roever, 1990; Hooman, Ramesh & De Roever, 1992). The semantic model associates with a statechart the set of all maximal computation histories representing complete computations. The semantics is a not-always semantics in which transitions labeled with ¬ e/e will never trigger, so that deadlock eventuates. Besides denotations for events generated at each computation step (the observables) and denotations for entry and exit, the computation history also specifies the set of all events generated by the whole system at every step, and a causality relation between the generated events. The semantic domain is the power set of all possible computation histories. For further details, the reader may consult (Sowmya & Ramesh, 1997; Hooman, Ramesh & De Roever, 19989; Hooman, Ramesh & De Roever, 1992; Huizing, Gerth & De Roever, 1988).

Module-Charts

Module-charts are used to describe the modules that constitute the structural view and the implementation of the system, its division into hardware and software blocks and their inner components, and the communication between them.

GENERAL VIEW OF FNLOG: A LOGIC-BASED FUNCTIONAL SPECIFICATION LANGUAGE

FNLOG is based on first-order predicate logic with arithmetic and first-order predicate temporal logic. Thus, it includes explicit time notations; this property is necessary in order to associate timing with the specification. Component behaviors of a real-time reactive system are specified in FNLOG by means of function relationships. FNLOG is also compositional in nature so that a specification may be stuctured in a manner analogous th the corresponding statecharts structure. FNLOG includes primitives inspired by the robotics field;

they permit the compositionality of specifications. Finally, both causal and temporal relationships may be specified in FNLOG.

Events and Activities. A specification in FN-LOG is built from events and activities occurring over time, connected by logical and temporal operators. Hence, an event is an instantaneous occurrence of a signal. An activity is defined as a durative happening with a beginning instant, an end instant, and a finite duration between the two instants. The status of all events and activities, which together specify the system, defines the system state at a given instant. At any instant t, an event occurs or does not occur; an activity is initiated, terminated, or still alive. In general, an event or activity is instantiated at a given time t, if the event holds or the activity is initiated at this time. Every event e and activity A is superscripted by a unique number i, written as e^i and A^i, which indicates that it is the occurrence of the event or activity in the current system instantiation. This notation permits the specification of repeated events and activities over time. With every activity A^i, is associated two special events: initiate-A^i (init-A^i)and terminate-A^i (term- A^i). Thus, any activity A^i is defined by:

$A^i \equiv$ *initiate-A^i ; durative component ; terminate-A^i* (where ' ;' stands for sequenscing in time).

Logical Operators. The logical operators $\wedge$, $\vee$, $\neg$, $\rightarrow$, $\leftrightarrow$ are included in FNLOG to facilitate composition of activities and events into higher level events as well as to enable logical assertions in the language. For this purpose, first order predicate logic and arithmetic are also included.

Relation betwwen events. It is assumed that the strong synchrony hypothesis holds, i.e, an execution machine for the system is infinitely fast and control takes no time. Thus, the instantiation of a single event at a given instant could cause a cascade of instantiations of other events synchronously. A reserved relational constant $<<$ is used to espress the relative order in which two simultaneous events occur. ($e^i_1 << e^j_2$) means that

even though both e^i_1 and e^j_2 occur at the same time n, e^i_1 precedes e^j_2 in relative order.

Temporal Operators. For the behavior specification, real-time is incorporated in statecharts by having an implicit clock and allowing transitions to be triggered by timeouts relative to this clock, and by requiring that if a transition can be taken, then it should be taken immediately. Very often timeouts alone are not sufficient to describe behaviors of a real-time reactive system. More complex temporal descriptions are required to capture relative and absolute time properties as well as that causal relationships over time.

Temporal logic already deals with the conceptual representation of time and is an obvious choice. The past temporal logic operators are described below:

The temporal operators are applicable to both events and activities. For an event e^i, $\odot_t (e^i)$ is true at the instant t when e^i occurs. For an activity A^i, $\odot_t (A^i)$ is true at time t if A^i is either initiated at t or previously initiated and not yet terminated at t. As implied above, the concept of time is that of an infinite sequence of descrete time instants. A duration or interval is thus defined by its initiating and terminating instants.

The existential and universal quantifiers are allowed to range over the time variable t in the logic-based function specification language. The quantified temporal operators are:

$\odot_{t-k} (e^i)$: e^i true k instants before time t, $t \geq k$

$\Diamond_t^{t-k} (e^i)$: e^i true at some instant in the interval (t-k, t), $t \geq k$

$\Box_t^{t-k} (e^i)$: e^i true at all instants in the interval (t-k, t), $t \geq k$

$\Diamond_t^{t-k} (e^j)$: $\exists$ i, t-k $\leq$ i $\leq$ t: $\odot_i(e^j)$, $t \geq k$

$\Box_t^{t-k} (e^j)$: $\forall$ i, t-k $\leq$ i $\leq$ t: $\odot_i (e^j)$, $t \geq k$.

Composition of events and activities. Hierarchical composition of events and activities are employed to derive the higher level events and activities. Higher level events and activities, which

Box 1.

$\odot_t$: true at instant t $\square_t$: true at all instants before t

$\ominus_t$: true at instant t-1 $\diamondsuit_t$: true at some instant before t

are of greater complexity than the primitive ones, are composed of logical and temporal predicates which directly or indirectly use the primitive events and activities. Thus, a hierarchy of events and activities may be built.

The temporal logic FNLOG refers to point time structure defining a precedence relation and a metric over a set of points. It deals with properties depending on points such as quantitative timing properties relating event occurrence: maximal distance between an event and its reaction, exact distance between events, bounded response time which imposes a maximal length to the interval allowed between two events. For instance, the property that an action A is followed by a response B before T time units or by C at time T is specified by the formula:

$$\odot t\text{-}d(\text{init-A}) \rightarrow \diamondsuit t^{t-d} (\text{init-B}) \vee \odot_t (\text{init-C}).$$

Proof System

The proof system for FNLOG was relatively the easy part. All deductive rules of first-order predicate logic and past temporal logic still hold. Additional rules arise from the axioms relating the events and activities, which have already been described. The rationale for these additional axioms and rules are as follows:

- The application level axioms (AL) relate the FNLOG primitives of events and activities directly and, hence, allow for more user-friendly and application-friendly proofs. They are not strictly necessary, since they may be derived from the axioms of arithmetic, which is included in FNLOG.

- The repeated occurence axioms (RO) disambiguate between multiple occurences of the same event or activity and are necessary.

The axioms give rise to rules of deduction in a natural manner. Appendix A contains a list of AL and RO axioms used.

THE PROPOSED SPECIFICATION AND VALIDATION METHOD

In this section, we present the proposed specification approach. We will begin first by presenting various steps in the method integrating STATEMATE and FNLOG. Then, we present the transformation rules and the proposed lemmas extending FNLOG axiomatic. The proposed integration method (Mosbahi, 2002) comprises mainly five great steps (Figure 2).

Step 1. Description of Requirements

This step consists on the description of system requirements by using FNLOG notation (Sowmya & Ramesh, 1997). They are liveness and safety properties specified at first by the system user as well as the experts.

Step 2. Specification with STATEMATE

The second step is a model construction. It consists on the description of system behavior using STATEMATE. This method reduces system complexity which is broken up into a hierarchy

Figure 2. Method of integration proposed using STATEMATE and FNLOG

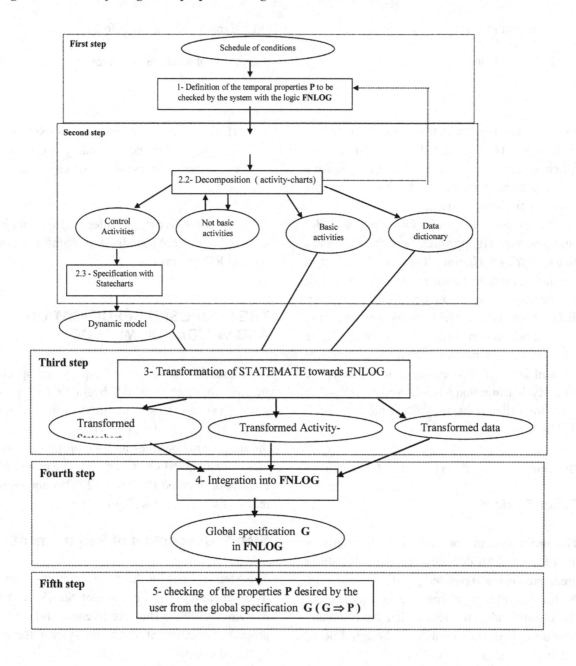

of activities, control and primitives activities, with statecharts and activity-charts; with this refinement, new specific properties are added at a given level to the already drawn up list. Here, three sub steps are proposed:

Development of the context diagram. We start with functional specification using activity-charts.

We generate the context diagram which consists on the main activity, some external processes and flows of information which connect the system to its environment.

Decomposition of the system with activity-charts. We break up the context diagram into a series of activities and date-store as well as control activity. For each activity, the refinement process is repeated until an acceptable level of detail is obtained. We then obtain a hierarchy of activities thus comprising a whole of not basic activities (activities requiring other decompositions), a whole of basic activities (activities not requiring other decompositions) and a whole of control activities (activities describing the behavior of their main activity).

Specification with statecharts. The control activities are associated with statecharts which describe the behavior of their main activity. The statecharts obtained constitute the dynamic model. Textual information on the statecharts (states, events, actions, conditions etc.) are arranged in the data dictionary. Thus, during the process of decomposition and elaboration of Statecharts, all the data, the events are saved in a data dictionary.

Step 3. Transformation of STATEMATE primitives to FNLOG

There is a compatibility and equivalent semantics between a statecharts and FNLOG specification (Sowmya & Ramesh, 1997). Based on this compatibility we have proposed some transformations rules from Statecharts and Activity-charts specifications to logical formulae in FNLOG. These transformation rules are presented in the following. At first we begin by presenting some compatibility aspects.

Compatibility. Statecharts and FNLOG uses the same primitives which are events, activities for FNLOG to which corresponds events and states for statecharts. Furthermore, we find in FNLOG as well as statecharts an hierarchical composition of events and activities (Sowmya & Ramesh, 1997). Also, one of the characteristics of statecharts is historisation and recovery; FNLOG also, is a past temporal logic then it's appropriate to the specification of system's behavior depending on historic.

Transformation from Statechart to FNLOG. The translation of a Statechart specification to an FNLOG specification consists on transforming states and transitions from the various levels of structure into FNLOG formulas and is based on primitive's transformations and composition's transformations given in Table 1.

To illustrate the transformations of statechart to FNLOG, we consider the example given in Figure 3. When a system is in state S, it is simultaneously in two substates, E and G. In state E, it can be in the state A, or in the state B; and in the state G, it can be also either in C, or in D. Here, is the specification of the system in Statecharts, then its transformation in FNLOG.

The transformation in FNLOG notation gives:

$\odot_t (S) \rightarrow \odot_t (E) \wedge \odot_t (G)$ (conjunction of two FNLOG formulae)

$\odot_t (E) \rightarrow \odot_t (A) \vee \odot_t (B)$ (disjunction of two FNLOG formulae)

$\odot_t (G) \rightarrow \odot_t (C) \vee \odot_t (D)$ (disjunction of two FNLOG formulae)

Transformation of a cycle encapsulating states. Other transformations are intended to specify state duration. Let us consider the example given in Figure 4. in which E is a state encapsulating two under states A and B. In the input of the state E, the variable D takes value 0. In the encapsulated substates, D is incremented with each clock tick. The exit from the state E occurs when D = K or when the event "e" occurs. We can then deduce that the duration of this cycle does not exceed K units of time.

Transformation of time expressions. Two classes of time expressions are found in statechart the event timeout and the action scheduled (Harel, 1997).

a: Timeout events

Timeout (E,T), abbreviated in tm (E,T), where E is an event and T an integer; defines a new event generated T units of time after the last occurrence of the event E.

Table 1. Transformation of statecharts's primitives to FNLOG

Statecharts	FNLOG
State	Activity
Action	Event
Event	Event
Event of input in a state: in(state)	Event
Event of output in a state: ex(state)	Event
Duration of activity	Duration of activity
Basic states	Functions FNLOG
OR of two states	Disjunction of 2 specifications FNLOG
AND of two states	Conjunction of 2 specifications FNLOG

b: Action scheduled

Schedule (G, T), abbreviated in Sc!(G, T), where G is an action and T an integer; defines the execution of G, T units of time after the execution of the primitive Sc. So if at one moment T the system is in state A, then after X time units there will be execution of action G.

Figure 3. Composition of basic states using AND and OR operators

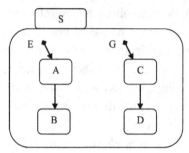

A, B, C and D : basic states

E and G : OR-states

S : AND-state

The transformation of these expressions is given in Figure 5.

Transformation of the activity-charts to FNLOG. The activity-charts complete the descriptions given by Statecharts by adding the description of data flow. An activity is defined with a begining instant, an end instant, and a finite duration between the two instants. In FNLOG also, an activity is characterised by two events, the event init-activity, the event term-activity and a

Figure 4. Transformation of a cycle encapsulating states

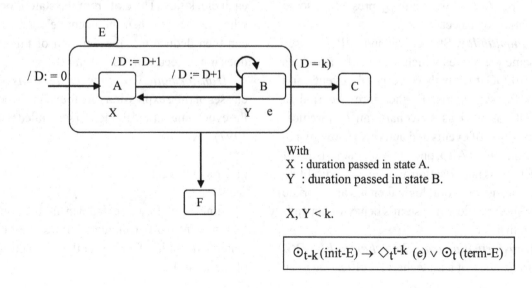

With
X : duration passed in state A.
Y : duration passed in state B.

X, Y < k.

$$\odot_{t-k}(\text{init-E}) \rightarrow \diamondsuit_t^{t-k}(e) \vee \odot_t(\text{term-E})$$

Figure 5. Transformation of time expressions from statecharts to FNLOG

Statecharts	FNLOG
A —— Tm (en (A), x) ——→ B	$\odot_{t-x}(\text{init-A}) \rightarrow \odot_t (\text{init-B})$
A —— Sc!(G, x) ——→ B	$\odot_{t-x}(\text{init-A}) \rightarrow \odot_t (G)$

Table. 2. Transformation of the activity-chart components to FNLOG

Activity_charts	FNLOG
Event	Event
Data	Expression of a number
Activity	Activity
Condition	Boolean expression

Figure 6. Example of relation between the Statechart AB_control and the Activity-chart A

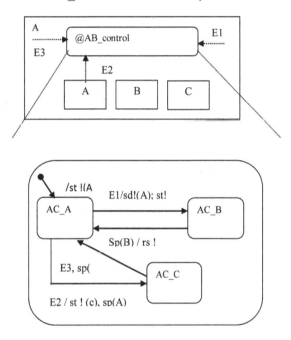

duration between the two events. The transformation of the activity-chart elements is illustrated in the following table:

Transformation of the relation between statecharts and activity-charts. Statecharts and Activity-charts are closely dependent. A statechart is associated with each activity. It describes the decomposition of an activity into sub activities, i.e. it describes the behavior of an activity by defining the instants when each subactivity must be started, stopped, suspended or resumed by respectively the events started (..), stoped (..), suspend (..) and resume (..). In the second sens and by sending an event, an activity causes states's transitions. Thus, relations between statecharts and activity-charts are transformed by the need of exchanged events.

In the example given in Figure 6., the statechart AB_control controls the activities A, B and C, it determines the instants when each activity must be started (St!(A)), suspended (sd!(A)), resumed (rs!((B)) or stopped (sp(B)). In the other way, the activity A causes by the event "E2" a transition from the state AC_A to the state AC_C.

Step 4. Composition in FNLOG

The fourth step is a composition of FNLOG formulae associated to basic and non basic activities obtained in the step 3. It is the conjunction of FNLOG formulae found at each level of the decomposition obtained at the steps 2 and 3. For each activity, we directly define the data and the sub activities in data and operations (or functions) in FNLOG and then we associate each of the statecharts to the corresponding controlled activity. In this step, we compose the activities and the events

Figure 7. Lemma 1

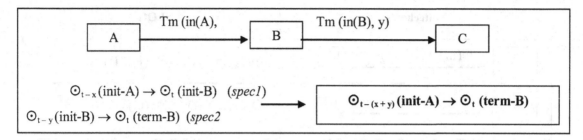

Box 2.

a- $\odot_{t-x}(init\text{-}A) \rightarrow \odot_t (term\text{-}A) \quad \forall t$	*spec1*
b- $\odot_{t-x-y}(init\text{-}A) \rightarrow \odot_{t-y}(term\text{-}A)$	*replace t by t-y*
c- $\odot_t (term\text{-}A) = \odot_t (init\text{-}B)$	*Axioms (17)*
d- $\odot_{t-y}(term\text{-}A) = \odot_{t-y}(init\text{-}B)$	*by replacing in c t by t-y*
e- $\odot_{t-y}(init\text{-}B) \rightarrow \odot_t (term\text{-}B)$	*spec2*
f- $\odot_{t-x-y}(init\text{-}A) \rightarrow \odot_{t-y}(init\text{-}B)$	*by replacing in b (term-A) by (init-B)*
g- $\odot_{t-x-y}(init\text{-}A) \rightarrow \odot_t (term\text{-}B)$	*by applying the rule $A \rightarrow B \wedge B \rightarrow C$*
	$\mid \overline{\qquad} \quad A \rightarrow C$

specified in FNLOG. This composition is based on the causality relation between them. We note that this step is used only if the system is complex and is refined on several levels.

Step 5. Validation

The fifth step is a validation step. It consists on proving that the behavior specification found in the fourth step implies the system's requirements specified in the first step. These requirements are in general safety or liveness properties depending on time consideration such as periodicity, time out, …(Harel, 1987; Henzinger, Manna & Pnueli, 1991). The temporal logic FNLOG refers to point time structure defining a precedence relation and a metric over a set of points. However a problem holds in the verification of such duration properties with the existing axiomatic. To simplify such verification, we extend the FNLOG axiomatic (Sowmya & Ramesh, 1997) by introducing two new lemmas presented below:

Lemma 1. *Duration over state sequence.*

The duration of an interval associated to a state sequence is the total length of the sub-intervals associated to each state.

We consider in Figure 7.three consecutive states A, B and C. A is followed by B and B is followed by C. A lasts x time units and B lasts y time units. The duration from the begenning of A to the begenning of C is x+y.

Lemma 2. *Reachability / Accessibility .*

If a property ϕ holds in an interval (t-k, t) with t > k, then it holds also in the interval (t-j, t) with $j \geq k$.

$$\diamondsuit_t^{t-k} (\phi) \Rightarrow \diamondsuit_t^{t-j} (\phi) \; \forall j \geq k$$

CASE STUDY 1. GAS-BURNER

We illustrate our approach through a version of a computer controlled gas burner (Ravn, Rishel & Hansen, 1993) (Figure 8). The gas burner is

Box 3.

$$\Diamond_t^{t-k}(\phi) \Rightarrow \exists\, i, t\text{-}k \le i \le t : \odot_i(\phi), t \ge k$$

$$\Downarrow$$

$$\exists\, j, t\text{-}j \le i \le t : \odot_i(\phi), j \ge k$$

$$\Downarrow$$

$$\Diamond_t^{t-j}(\phi)$$

So for any point $j \ge k$ we have : $\Diamond_t^{t-k}(\phi) \Rightarrow \Diamond_t^{t-j}(\phi)$

Figure 8. Gas burner example

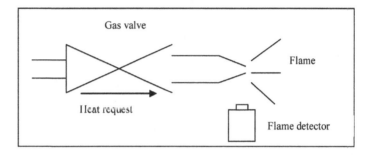

Box 4.

$$\odot_{t-60}(heat) \to \Diamond_t^{t-60}(flame) \lor \odot_t(\text{init-maintenance})$$
$$\odot_{t-60}(\neg\, heat) \to \Diamond_t^{t-60}(\neg flame)$$
$$\neg\,(\Diamond_t^{t-30}(d=4) \land \odot_t(\text{opened\_gas}) \land \odot_t(\neg\, flame))$$

controlled through a thermostat and can directly control the gas valve and monitor the flame. We can then say that the wish of the user consists of obtaining flame when the thermostat indicates if it is necessary to cause heat and extinding the combustion when the thermostat indicates that is necessary to cease heating.

Step 1. Description of the Requirements

The requirements are:

P1: Heat request shall after 60 seconds be followed by gas burning unless an ignition or flame failure has occurred.

P2: Heat request off shall result in the flame being after 60 seconds.

P3: For safety, gas must never leak for more than 4 seconds in any period of at most 30 seconds.

These requirements are specified in FNLOG by the following formulae:

Figure 9. The context diagram of the gas-burner system

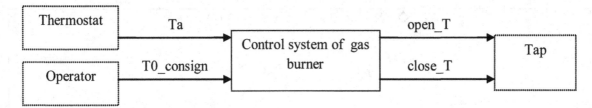

Figure 10. Refining level 1

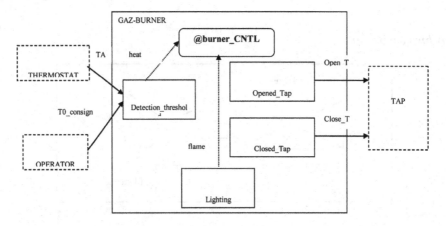

Step 2: Specification of the System with STATEMATE

Development of the Context Diagram

The system receives in input the ambient temperature Ta, and the temperature T0_consign starting from the operator. From the temperature Ta, the system indicates if it is necessary to heat or not; heat cost to ask the starting of the burner. At output, there is a signal allowing the opening of the tap, open_T and another signal for the closing of the tap close_T.

Decomposition of the System with Activity-Charts

For our example, the context diagram given previously is refined. This refinement (Figure 10) decomposes the principal activity into four sub activities: *Detection_threshold* for the acquisition of the temperature and its comparison with the temperature T0_consign, *Opened_Tap* allows the opening of the tap, *Closed_ Tap* allows the closing of the tap, *lighting* allows the lighting and the production of the flame and a control activity brûleur_CNTL (Figure 10).

Specification with Statecharts

In our example, the associated statechart is given in Figure 11. In the following, we consider a specific control function, where the system proceeds cyclically through the following phases with a local specification in each phase.

Idle: initially and after a complete cycle, gas is turned off. the system waits an ordering of heating (heat).

Figure 11.Statechart associated to the gas-burner system

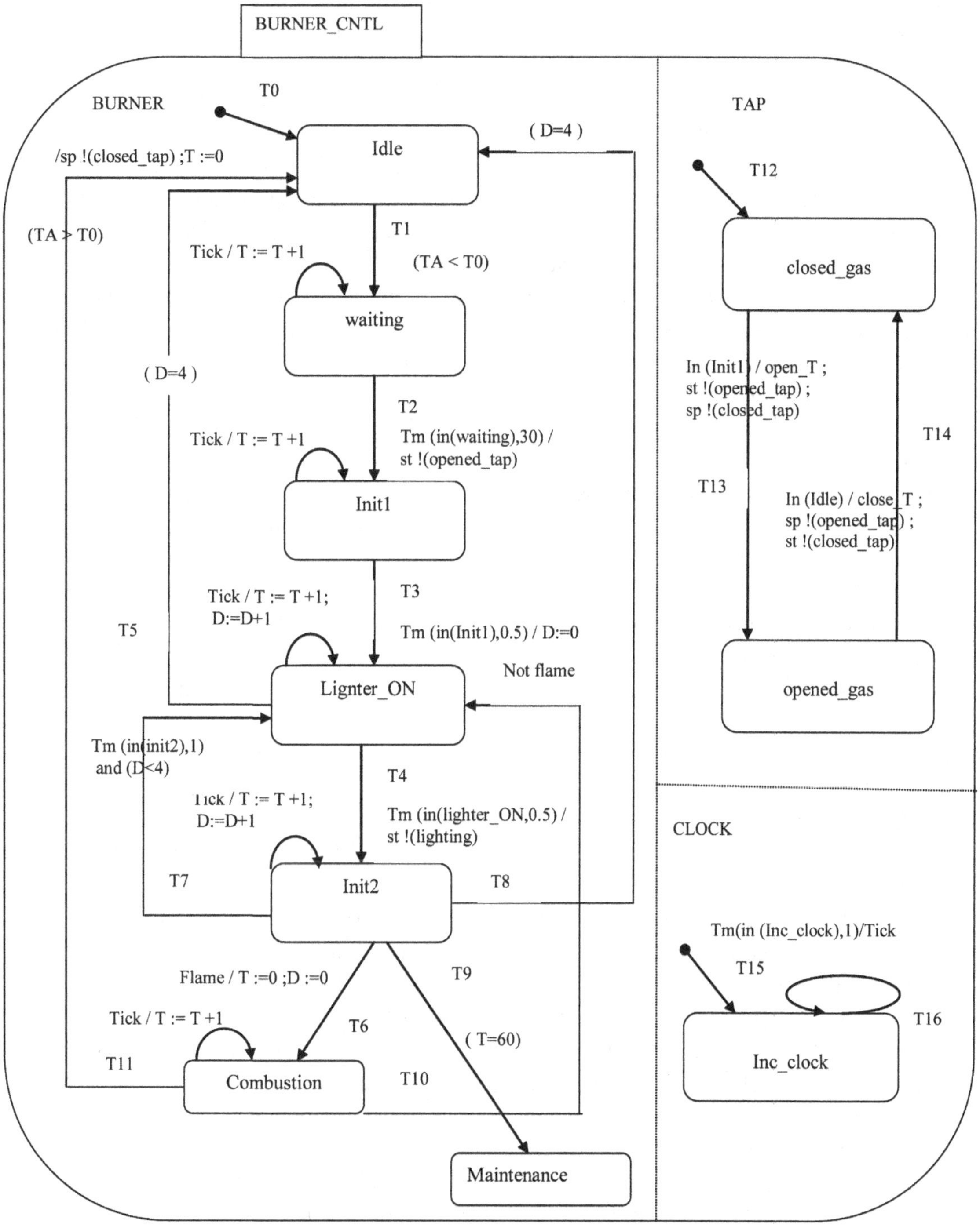

Waiting: After the request for heating, the system remains in this state 30 s without emission of gas.

Init 1: Gas is turned on, the system remains in this state 0.5 s.

lighter_ON : The igniter is activated during 0.5 s.

Init 2: The system procced to burn if flame is sensed, otherwise return to *lighter_ON* after 1 second if gas must never leak for more than 4 seconds in any period of at most 30 seconds or it passes to state *idle* if this duration reach the 4 seconds. And when time reaches the 60 S, the system passes to state *maintenance*.

Combustion: The system return to *lighter_ON* if flame is off or to *idle* if heat request is off.

Maintenance: the system passes in this state when time reaches 60s.

STATEMATE dispose also of a tool for generation code in ADA, to which the designer has the possibility to add programs simulating external environment, or establishing the basic activities being with the bottom of the hierarchy.

Step 3. Transformation of the STATEMATE Specification to an FNLOG Specification

The third step consists in transforming the specification STATEMATE which we obtained towards an FNLOG specification, by using the rules of transformation that we stated before.

We have using rules presented above, we have transformed Activity-charts and Statecharts given in Figure 10 and Figure 11 to FNLOG formulae.

According to Figure 11., the transformation of the Activity_charts gives:

a: $\odot_t$ (Detecion_threshold) $\wedge$ $\odot_t$ (heat) $\rightarrow$ $\odot_t$ (burner_CNTL)

b: $\odot_t$ (Open_T) $\rightarrow$ $\diamondsuit_t$ (Opened_tap)

c: $\odot_t$ (Close_T) $\rightarrow$ $\diamondsuit_t$ (Closed_tap)

d: $\odot_t$ (flame) $\rightarrow$ $\diamondsuit_t$ (Lighting)

According to Figure 11, the gas-burner system can be in three states at a given time T: burner, tap and clock.

1- L = $\odot_t$ (burner) $\wedge$ $\odot_t$ (clock) $\wedge$ $\odot_t$ (Tap)

When the system is in state burner, it can be either in state Idle, or in state waitnig, or in Init1, or in lighter_ON, or in Init2, or in Combustion.

2- $\odot_t$ (burner) = $\odot_t$ (Idle) $\vee$ $\odot_t$ (Wainting) $\vee$ $\odot_t$ (Init1) $\vee$ $\odot_t$ (lighter_ON) $\vee$ $\odot_t$ (Init2) $\vee$ $\odot_t$ (combustion)

The tap can be in two states: Tap_opened and Tap_closed.

3- $\odot_t$ (tap) = $\odot_t$ (opened_gas) $\vee$ $\odot_t$ (closed_gas)

In each clock tick, the clock is incremented of one unit of time.

4- $\odot_t$ (clock) = $\odot_t$ (Inc_clock)

Transformation of Idle

5- $\odot_t$ (init-burner) = $\odot_t$ (init-Idle)

6- $\odot_t$ (init-Idle) = $\odot_t$ (fire(T0)) $\vee$ $\odot_t$ (fire(T5)) $\vee$ $\odot_t$ (fire(T8)) $\vee$ $\odot_t$ (fire(T11))

7- $\odot_t$ (sp !(Closed-Tap)) = $\odot_t$ (fire(T0))

8- $\odot_t$ (term-Idle) = $\odot_t$ (fire(T1))

9- $\odot_t$ (term-Idle) = $\odot_t$ (init-waiting)

10- $\odot_t$ (T = 0) = $\odot_t$ (fire(T1))

10b - $\odot_t$ (init-Idle) $\rightarrow$ $\odot_t$ (init-closed_gas)

Transformation of waiting

11- $\odot_t$ (init-attente) = $\odot_t$ (fire(T1))

12- $\odot_t$ (term-attente) = $\odot_t$ (fire(T2))

13- $\odot_{t-30}$ (init- waiting) $\rightarrow$ $\odot_t$ (term- waiting)

14- $\odot_t$ (term- waiting) $\rightarrow$ $\odot_t$ (T=30)

15- $\odot_t$ (st !(Opened-Tap)) = $\odot_t$ (fire(T2))

16- $\odot_t$ (heat) = $\odot_t$ (init- waiting)

17- $\odot_t$ (term- waiting) $= \odot_t$ (init-Init1)

Transformation of Init1

18- $\odot_t$ (init-Init1) $= \odot_t$ (fire(T2))

19- $\odot_{t-0.5}$ (init-Init1) $\wedge \square_t^{t-0.5}$ (Init1) $\rightarrow \odot_t$ (term-Init1)

20- $\odot_t$ (term-Init1) $\rightarrow \odot_t$ (T:=T+0.5)

21- $\odot_t$ (term-Init1) $= \odot_t$ (fire(T3))

22- $\odot_t$ (init-Init1) $\rightarrow \odot_t$ (T =30)

23- $\odot_t$ (term-Init1) $= \odot_t$ (init-lighter_ON)

24- $\odot_t$ (d = 0) $= \odot_t$ (fire(T3))

Transformation of lighter_ON

25- $\odot_t$ (init- lighter_ON) $= \odot_t$ (fire(T3)) $\vee \odot_t$ (fire(T7)) $\vee \odot_t$ (fire(T10))

26- $\odot_t$ (term- lighter_ON) $= \odot_t$ (fire(T4))

27- $\odot_{t\ 0.5}$ (init- lighter_ON ^{1}) $\rightarrow \odot_t$ (term-lighter_ON)

28- $\odot_t$ (term- lighter_ON) $\rightarrow \odot_t$ (T:=T+0.5)

31- $\odot_{t-0.5}$ (init- lighter_ON ^{i}) $\wedge \square_t^{t-0.5}$ (d< 4) $\rightarrow \odot_t$ (init-Init2 ^{j}) avec i $\geq$ j

31b- $\odot_t$ (term- lighter_ON ^{i}) $\wedge \square_t^{t-0.5}$ (d< 4) $\rightarrow \odot_t$ (init-Init2 ^{j}) avec i $\geq$ j

Transformation of Init2

32- $\odot_t$ (init-Init2) $= \odot_t$ (fire(T4))

33- $\odot_t$ (term-Init2) $= \odot_t$ (fire(T6)) $\vee \odot_t$ (fire(T7)) $\vee \odot_t$ (fire(T8)) $\vee \odot_t$ (fire(T9))

34- $\odot_t$ (Init2) $\wedge \odot_t$ (d = 4) $\rightarrow \odot_t$ (init-Idle)

35- $\odot_{t-1}$ (init-Init2) $\wedge \square_t^{t-1}$ (Init2) $\wedge \odot_t$ (d < 4) $\rightarrow \odot_t$ (init-lignter_ON)

36- $\odot_t$ (Init2) $\wedge \odot_t$ (flame) $\rightarrow \odot_t$ (init-combustion)

37- $\odot_t$ (Init2) $\wedge \odot_t$ (T=60) $\rightarrow \odot_t$ (init-maintenance)

37b- $\odot_{t-60}$ (heat) $\rightarrow \odot_t$ (init-maintenance)

38- $\odot_{t-1}$ (init-Init2) $\rightarrow \diamondsuit_t^{t-1}$ (flame) $\vee \odot_t$ (init-lighter_ON) $\vee \diamondsuit_t^{t-1}$ (init-Idle)

39- $\odot_t$ (T = 0) $= \odot_t$ (fire(T5))

40- $\odot_t$ (d = 0) $= \odot_t$ (fire(T5))

41- $\odot_{t-1}$ (init-Init2 ^{j}) $\wedge \square_t^{t-1}$ ($\neg$ flame) $\wedge \square_t^{t-1}$ (d < 4) $\rightarrow \odot_t$ (init-lighter_ON ^{i}) avec i $\geq$ j

42- $\odot_{t-1}$ (init-Init2) $\rightarrow \diamondsuit_t^{t-1}$ (term-Init2)

43- $\odot_{t-1}$ (init-Init2 ^{j}) $\rightarrow \diamondsuit_t^{t-1}$ (flame) $\vee \diamondsuit_t^{t-1}$ (init-Idle) $\vee \odot_t$ (init- lighter_ON ^{i}) $\vee \diamondsuit_t^{t-1}$ (init-maintenance) i $\geq$ j

43b- $\odot_{t-4}$ (init- lighter_ON ^{1}) $\rightarrow \diamondsuit_t^{t-4}$ (flame) $\vee \odot_t$ (init-Idle)

Transformation of Combustion

44- $\odot_t$ (init-combustion) $= \odot_t$ (fire(T6))

45- $\odot_t$ (init-combustion) $= \odot_t$ (flame)

46- $\odot_t$ (term-combustion) $= \odot_t$ (fire(T10)) $\vee \odot_t$ (fire(T11))

47- $\odot_t$ (combustion) $\wedge \odot_t$ ($\neg$ flame) $= \odot_t$ (fire(T10))

48- $\odot_t$ (combustion) $\wedge \odot_t$ ($\neg$ flame) $\rightarrow \odot_t$ (init-ligher_ON)

49- $\odot_t$ (combustion) $\wedge \odot_t$ ($\neg$ heat) $= \odot_t$ (fire(T11))

50- $\odot_t$ (combustion) $\wedge \odot_t$ ($\neg$ heat) $\rightarrow \odot_t$ (init-Idle)

50b- $\odot_t$ ($\neg$heat) $\rightarrow \odot_t$ (combustion)

Transformation of the tap

51- $\odot_t$ (init-Tap) $= \odot_t$ (init-closed_gas)

52- $\odot_t$ (init-closed_gas) $= \odot_t$ (fire(T12)) $\vee \odot_t$ (fire(T14))

53- $\odot_t$ (closed_gas) $\wedge \odot_t$ (init-Init1)) $\rightarrow \odot_t$ (init-opened_gas)

54- $\odot_t$ (fire(T13)) $= \odot_t$ (Open_T) $\wedge \odot_t$ (st !(Opened_Tap)) $\wedge \odot_t$ (sp !(Closed_Tap))

55- $\odot_t$ (term-closed_gas) $= \odot_t$ (fire(T13))

56- $\odot_t$ (fire(T13)) $= \odot_t$ (closed_gas) $\wedge \odot_t$ (init-Init1))

57- $\odot_t$ (init-opened_gas) $= \odot_t$ (fire(T13))

58- $\odot_t$ (init-opened_gas) $= \odot_t$ (term-closed_gas)

59- $\odot_t$ (term-opened_gas) $= \odot_t$ (fire(T14))

60- $\odot_t$ (term-opened_gas) $= \odot_t$ (init-closed_gas)

61- $\odot_t$ (fire(T14)) $= \odot_t$ (opened_gas) $\wedge \odot_t$ (init-Idle))

62- $\odot_t$ (opened_gas) $\wedge \odot_t$ (init-Idle)) $\rightarrow \odot_t$ (init-closed_gas)

63- $\odot_t$ (fire(T14)) $= \odot_t$ (Close_T) $\wedge \odot_t$ (st !(Closed_Tap)) $\wedge \odot_t$ (sp!(Opened_Tap))

64- $\odot_t$ (init-closed_gas) $\rightarrow \odot_t$ ($\neg$flame)

Step 4: Composition in FNLOG

In our example, the system is refined on only one level so the problem of recombining levels is not considered.

Step 5: Checking of Properties of the System

In this step we have to verify that the specification given in the fourth step implies the system's requirements specified in the first step (see Boxes 5-9).

Box 5.

Property P1 :

P1 : $\odot_{t-60}$ *(heat)* $\rightarrow$ $\diamondsuit_t^{t-60}$ *(flame)* $\vee$ $\odot_t$ *(init-maintenance)*

Proof of P1 :

We have :

a-	$\odot_t$ *(heat)* = $\odot_t$ *(init-waiting)*	*spec 16*
b-	$\odot_{t-30}$ *(init- waiting)* $\rightarrow$ $\odot_t$ *(term- waiting)*	*spec 13*
c-	$\odot_t$ *(term- waiting)* $\rightarrow$ $\odot_t$ *(T=30)*	*spec 22*
d-	$\odot_{t-30}$ *(heat)* $\rightarrow$ $\odot_t$ *(term- waiting)*	*replace in b, init- waiting by*
		heat(b(-init- waiting | heat))
e-	$\odot_t$ *(term- waiting)* = $\odot_t$ *(init-Init1)*	*spec 17*
f-	$\odot_{t-30}$ *(heat)* $\rightarrow$ $\odot_t$ *(init-Init1)*	*d-(term- waiting \ init-Init1)*
g-	$\odot_t$ *(init-Init1)* $\rightarrow$ $\odot_t$ *(T=30)*	*c-(term- waiting \ init-Init1)*
h-	$\odot_{t-0.5}$ *(init- Init1)* $\rightarrow$ $\odot_t$ *(term- Init1)*	*spec 19*
i-	$\odot_t$ *(term- Init1)* $\rightarrow$ $\odot_t$ *(T :=T+0.5)*	*spec 20*
j-	$\odot_{t-30.5}$ *(heat)* $\rightarrow$ $\odot_t$ *(term- Init1)*	*to apply the lemma 1 to f and h*
		(lemma1 (f,h))
k-	$\odot_t$ *(term- Init1)* $\rightarrow$ $\odot_t$ *(T =30.5)*	*spec 20*
l-	$\odot_t$ *(term-Init1)* = $\odot_t$ *(init- lighter_ON)*	*spec 23*
m-	$\odot_{t-30.5}$ *(heat)* $\rightarrow$ $\odot_t$ *(init- lighter_ON)*	*j-(term-Init1\init- lighter_ON)*
n-	$\odot_t$ *(init- lighter_ON)* $\rightarrow$ $\odot_t$ *(T =30.5)*	*k-(term-Init1\init-lighter_ON)*
o-	$\odot_{t-0.5}$ *(init- lighter_ON)* $\wedge$ $\square_t^{t-0.5}$ *(d< 4)* $\rightarrow$ $\odot_t$ *(term- lighter_ON^1)*	*spec 27*
p-	$\odot_t$ *(term- lighter_ON^1)* $\rightarrow$ $\odot_t$ *(T =31)*	*spec 28*
q-	$\odot_{t-31}$ *(heat)* $\rightarrow$ $\odot_t$ *(term- lighter_ON)*	*lemma 1(m,o)*
r-	$\odot_t$ *(term- lighter_ON^i)* $\wedge$ $\square_t^{t-0.5}$ *(d< 4)* $\rightarrow$ $\odot_t$ *(init-Init2^j)*	*spec 31-b*
s-	$\odot_{t-1}$ *(init-Init2)* $\rightarrow$ $\diamondsuit_t^{t-1}$ *(term-Init2)*	*spec 42*
t -	$\odot_{t-1}$ *(init-Init2^j)* $\rightarrow$ $\diamondsuit_t^{t-1}$*(flame)* $\vee$ $\diamondsuit_t^{t-1}$ *(init-Idle)* $\vee$ $\diamondsuit_t^{t-1}$*(init-maintenance)* $\vee$	
	$\odot_t$ *(init- lighter_ON^i)* *with i ≥j*	*spec 43*
u-	$\odot_{t-4}$ *(init- lighter_ON^1)* $\rightarrow$ $\diamondsuit_t^{t-4}$ *(flame)* $\vee$ $\odot_t$ *(init-Idle)*	*spec 43-b*
v-	$\odot_{t-34.5}$ *(heat)* $\rightarrow$ $\diamondsuit_t^{t-4}$ *(flame)* $\vee$ $\odot_t$ *(init-Idle)*	*lema 1(m,u)*

Box 6.

So we have :

$$\begin{cases} v1 : \odot_{t-34.5}(heat) \rightarrow \diamondsuit_t^{\,t-4}(flame) \\ or \\ v2 : \odot_{t-34.5}(heat) \rightarrow \odot_t(init\text{-}Idle) \;\; \forall\, t \end{cases}$$

u- $\quad \odot_{t-60}(heat) \rightarrow \diamondsuit_t^{\,t-60}(flame)$ $\qquad\qquad\qquad$ *to apply the lemma 2 to*

$\qquad\qquad\qquad\qquad\qquad\qquad\qquad\qquad\qquad\qquad\qquad\qquad$ *v1(lemma2(v2))*

x- $\quad\quad \odot_{t-60}(heat) \rightarrow \odot_{(t-60)+34.5}(init\text{-}Idle)$ $\qquad\qquad$ *to replace t by (t-60+34.5)*

$\Rightarrow$x- $\odot_{t-60}(heat) \rightarrow \odot_{t-25.5}(init\text{-}Idle)$

x2- $\quad \odot_{t-60}(heat) \rightarrow \diamondsuit_t^{\,t-60}(flame) \vee \odot_{t-25.5}(init\text{-}Idle)$ $\qquad$ *to apply the rule*

$$\begin{array}{c} a \rightarrow b \;\wedge \\[2pt] \hline \\[-6pt] a \rightarrow c \end{array} \quad\Big|\!\!\!-\!\!\!-\!\!\!-\quad a \rightarrow b \vee c$$

If T = 60 time units, it is necessary to entry in state maintenance.

y- $\qquad \odot_t(Init2) \wedge \odot_t(T{=}60) \rightarrow \odot_t(init\text{-}maintenance)$ $\qquad$ *spec 37*

z- $\qquad \odot_{t-60}(heat) \rightarrow \odot_t(init\text{-}maintenance)$ $\qquad\qquad\qquad$ *spec37-b*

So we have :

$$\odot_{t-60}(heat) \rightarrow \diamondsuit_t^{\,t-60}(flame) \vee \odot_{t-25.5}(init\text{-}Idle) \vee \odot_t(init\text{-}maintenance)$$

Box 7.

<ins>**Proof of P2 :**</ins>

We have :

a- $\quad \odot_t(\neg heat) \rightarrow \odot_t(combustion)$ $\qquad\qquad\qquad\qquad$ spec 50-b

b- $\quad \odot_t(\neg heat) \rightarrow \odot_t(\neg heat) \wedge \odot_t(init\text{-}Idle)$

c- $\quad \odot_t(\neg heat) \wedge \odot_t(combustion) \rightarrow \odot_t(init\text{-}Idle)$ $\qquad$ spec 50

d- $\quad \odot_t(\neg heat) \rightarrow \odot_t(init\text{-}Idle)$ $\qquad\qquad$ to apply the rule

$$a \rightarrow b \wedge b \rightarrow c \quad\Big|\!\!-\!\!-\quad a \rightarrow c$$

e- $\quad \odot_t(opened\_gas) \wedge \odot_t(init\text{-}Idle) \rightarrow \odot_t(init\text{-}closed\_gas)$ $\qquad$ spec 62

f- $\quad \odot_t(init\text{-}Idle) \rightarrow \odot_t(init\text{-}closed\_gas)$ $\qquad\qquad\qquad$ spec 10-b

g- $\quad \odot_t(init\text{-}closed\_gas) \rightarrow \odot_t(\neg flame)$ $\qquad\qquad\qquad$ spec 64

h- $\quad \odot_t(\neg heat) \rightarrow \odot_t(init\text{-}closed\_gas)$ $\qquad\qquad$ transitivity (d, f)

i- $\quad \odot_t(\neg heat) \rightarrow \odot_t(\neg flame)$ $\qquad\qquad\qquad$ transitivity (g, h)

j- $\quad \odot_{t-60}(\neg heat) \rightarrow \odot_{t-60}(\neg flame)$ $\qquad\qquad$ to relpace t by t-60

So we have : $\quad \odot_{t-60}(\neg heat) \rightarrow \diamondsuit_t^{\,t-60}(\neg flame)$

Box 8.

Proof of P2 :

We have :

    a- $\odot_t (\neg heat) \rightarrow \odot_t (combustion)$ *spec 50-b*

    b- $\odot_t (\neg heat) \rightarrow \odot_t (\neg heat) \wedge \odot_t (init\text{-}Idle)$

    c- $\odot_t (\neg heat) \wedge \odot_t (combustion) \rightarrow \odot_t (init\text{-}Idle)$ *spec 50*

    d- $\odot_t (\neg heat) \rightarrow \odot_t (init\text{-}Idle)$ *to apply the rule*

                                  $a \rightarrow b \wedge b \rightarrow c \;\big|\!\!-\!\!-\;\; a \rightarrow c$

    e- $\odot_t (opened\_gas) \wedge \odot_t (init\text{-}Idle) \rightarrow \odot_t (init\text{-}closed\_gas)$ *spec 62*

    f- $\odot_t (init\text{-}Idle) \rightarrow \odot_t (init\text{-}closed\_gas)$ *spec 10-b*

    g- $\odot_t (init\text{-}closed\_gas) \rightarrow \odot_t (\neg flame)$ *spec 64*

    h- $\odot_t (\neg heat) \rightarrow \odot_t (init\text{-}closed\_gas)$ *transitivity (d, f)*

    i- $\odot_t (\neg heat) \rightarrow \odot_t (\neg flame)$ *transitivity (g, h)*

    j- $\odot_{t\text{-}60} (\neg heat) \rightarrow \odot_{t\text{-}60} (\neg flame)$ *to relpace t by t-60*

So we have : $\odot_{t\text{-}60} (\neg heat) \rightarrow \diamondsuit_t^{\,t\text{-}60} (\neg flame)$

CASE STUDY 2. A ROBOT EXAMPLE

Consider an assembly robot (Cox & Gehani, 1989) which is waiting at a conveyor belt and having specific but limited capabilities must act in response to a specific triggers, for example, a specific part arriving. As long as power is on, it must watch continuously for the occurences of various events. Some degree of concurrency is involved: for example, while lifting a part and moving it, the robot must avoid hitting other objects on the conveyor belt. Thus, the robot may be modeled as a real-time reactive system. In the case of an autonomous mobile robot, the case for the model is even stronger. The added capacity for mobility increases the real-time interactions with the environement, and concurrency needs arise. For example, a mobile robot conveying an object from one location to another in a real environment must have the following concurrent capabilities: pick up the object and hold it in a stable position, follow a path from source to destination, avoid collision with obstacles in the path and modify it

in real-time. Thus, the real-time reactive model captures the essential behavior of a robot system.

As a concrete example, we select a two-degree-of-freedom robot controller described by Cox and Gehani (Cox & Gehani, 1989). The robot possesses Cartesian XY motion, provided by a Sawyer motor in a single actuator. For control purposes, the Sawyer motor may be considered to be two independent stepper motors. The XY motion of the robot is provided by two orthogonal stepper motors. Each stepper motor controller produces the motion on receipt of the direction, distance and speed of travel. User requests to move the robot are received and the moves initiated by invoking the two motors concurrently. A new request for a move is accepted only after the robot has completed moving.

Figure 13 decribes the behavior of this robot controller using a statechart. It consists of orthogonal states corresponding to the two motors, namely *motor0* and *motor1*, as well as two other states called *main* and *robot*. The system is always in these four states concurrently. The state *main* initializes the robot hardware, and receives, and

Box 9.

Proof of P3 :

- Critical case:

In this case, we have successive requests for heating without production of flame. It is the case where the request for heating is started following 4s exhaust of gas.

$\forall$ [i , i +30] we have $\quad 0 \leq d \leq 4$

Where d is the time of gas flow without flame, on an interval of 30s. In fact d is the addition of time when there is escaped gas without flame during the formed cycle of the two states *marche_allumor* and *Init2*.

We have :

> 1- $\odot_t$ *(Init2)* $\wedge$ $\odot_t$ *(d=4)* $\rightarrow$ $\odot_t$ *(init-idle)*
> 2- $\odot_t$ *(Init2)* $\rightarrow$ $\odot_t$ *(opened-gas)*
> 3- $\odot_t$ *(Init2)* $\rightarrow$ $\odot_t$ *(¬flame)*
> *D'après 1, 2 et 3, nous avons*
> 4- $\odot_t$ *(opened-gas)* $\wedge$ $\odot_t$ *(¬flame)* $\wedge$ $\odot_t$ *(d=4)* $\rightarrow$ $\odot_t$ *(init-Idle)*

State Waiting :
Following a request for heating, the system returns in the state makes an attempt and remains there during 30 s, then leaves this state.

> 5- $\odot_{t-30}$ *(init-waitnig)* $\rightarrow$ $\odot_t$ *(term-idle)*
> 6- $\odot_t$ *(init-idle)* $\rightarrow$ $\odot_t$ *(d = 0)*
> 7- $\odot_t$ *(term-idle)* $\rightarrow$ $\odot_t$ *(d = 0)*
> 8- $\odot_{t-30}$ *(init-idle)* $\wedge$ $\odot_t$ *(term-idle)* $\rightarrow$ $\diamondsuit_t^{t-30}$ *(d = 0)*
> 9- $\odot_t$ *(idle)* $\rightarrow$ $\odot_t$ *(¬flame)* $\wedge$ $\odot_t$ *(closed-gas)*
> 10- $\odot_t$ *(waiting)* $\rightarrow$ $\odot_t$ *(¬flame)* $\wedge$ $\odot_t$ *(closed-gas)* $\wedge$ $\diamondsuit_t^{t-30}$ *(d = 0)*

Thus during the state makes an attempt we have:
> $\odot_t$ *(¬flame)* $\wedge$ $\odot_t$ *(closed-gas)* $\wedge$ $\diamondsuit_t^{t-30}$ *(d = 0)*
> ***So*** $\neg$ ($\diamondsuit_t^{t-30}(d = 4) \wedge \odot_t$ *(opened_gas)* $\wedge$ $\odot_t$ *(¬flame))*

State Init1 :
In the state Init 1, we have :
> 11- $\odot_t$ *(Init1)* $\rightarrow$ $\odot_t$ *(d = 0)*
> 12- $\odot_t$ *(term-Init1)* $\rightarrow$ $\odot_t$ *(d = 0)*
> 13- $\odot_{t-0.5}$ *(init-Init1)* $\wedge$ $\odot_t$ *(term-Init1)* $\rightarrow$ $\diamondsuit_t^{t-0.5}$ *(d = 0)*
> 14- $\odot_t$ *(Init1)* $\rightarrow$ $\odot_t$ *(¬flame)* $\wedge$ $\diamondsuit_t^{t-0.5}$ *(d = 0)*

In the cycle formed by the states *marche_allumor* and *Init2*, we have:

> $\odot_t$ *(Lighter_ON)* $\wedge$ $\odot_t$ *(d=4)* $\rightarrow$ $\odot_t$ *(init-idle)*
> $\odot_{t-4}$ *(init-Lighter_ON)* $\rightarrow$ $\diamondsuit_t^{t-4}$ *(flame)* $\vee$ $\odot_t$ *(init-idle)*

Thus during the cycle, d never exceeds the 4s.
> ***So*** $\neg$ ($\diamondsuit_t^{t-30}(d = 4) \wedge \odot_t$ *(opened_gas)* $\wedge$ $\odot_t(¬flame))$

responds to, user requests continuously. After the initialization phase, the system is either waiting for a move request from the environment (e_2) in state *InitiateMoves*, or taking action on a request in state *ProcessRequest*. The state *robot* moves the robot to the initial position in state *Rinit* and then synchronously moves the robot to the specified positions repeatedly. After the initialization, the system is always either waiting for an *accept request* signal (a_1) in state *Rwait*, or performing the move in state *move* by instructing the two motors to move (e_6). This instruction is caught by the two *motor* states and the move is actually realized. In the state *motor0* for example, after initialization, the system waits in state *Wait0* for a move instruction to be broadcast from *robot*. When it is received as signal e_6 from *robot* and of the distance to move is nontrivial (condition c_1), the hardware signal for moving the motor in the X-direction is issued by *motor0* as the signal a_2. While waiting for the instruction to be completed in the state *Xmove*, the *m0 move complete* signal (e_7) may be received from the environment. Then the *move0 complete* signal (e_3) is emitted and *wait0* is reentered, to wait for the next move instruction. *motor1* is identical for moves in the Y-direction.

Step 1. Description of the Requirements

Safety or Invariance Properties

A safety property states that all finite prefixes of a computation satisfy some requirements. If the computation is finite, then the requirements must also be satisfied by the entire computation. Thus, safey properties are expressed by a formula of the form A => □ B in temporal logic. Intuitively, a safety property states that "nothing bad will ever happen". Safety is expressed in FNLOG.

P1: A new request for moving is accepted only after the robot has completed initialization as well as the previous move.

$$\odot_t(moverequest^j) \wedge \neg\, \odot_t(Rinit^i) \wedge \neg\, \odot_t(move^i)$$
$$\rightarrow \odot_t(acceptrequest^i), \forall\ i \leq j$$

Liveness or Eventuality Properties

Liveness properties complement safety properties by requiring that certain properties hold at least once, infinitely many times, or continuously from a certain point. They may be falsified over finite time. In temporal logic, they are expressed as A => ◇ B.

P2: an accepted move request should be completed within finite time.

Figure 12.

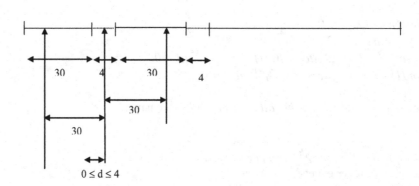

$$\odot_{t-k}(\text{accept-request}^i) \Rightarrow \Diamond_t^{t-k}(\text{movecomplete}^i)$$

Structural Properties

Structural properties are an effect of the decomposition adopted. For example, all the states in each of the sets {Hwinit, Rinit, M0init, M1init}, {InitiateMoves, Rwait, Wait0, Wait1} and {ProcessRequest, move, Xmove, Ymove} are entered

and exited at identical instants. This may be expressed in FNLOG; for example:

    P3: $\odot_t$ (HWinit) $\rightarrow \odot_t$ (Rinit)

    P4: $\odot_t$ (InitiateMoves^i) $\rightarrow \odot_t$ (Rwait^i)

Step 2: Specification of the System with STATEMATE

Figure 12 shows a statechart specification, in which the root state is an AND-state with four

Figure 13. Statechart for a single robot

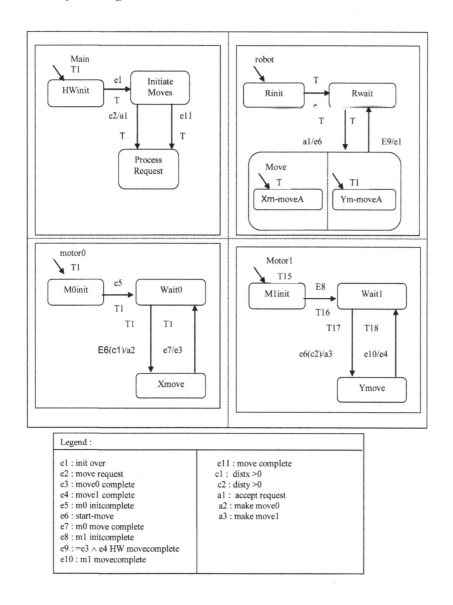

Legend :	
e1 : init over	e11 : move complete
e2 : move request	c1 : distx >0
e3 : move0 complete	c2 : disty >0
e4 : move1 complete	a1 : accept request
e5 : m0 initcomplete	a2 : make move0
e6 : start-move	a3 : make move1
e7 : m0 move complete	
e8 : m1 initcomplete	
e9 : =e3 ∧ e4 HW movecomplete	
e10 : m1 movecomplete	

components: *main*, *robot*, *motor0*, and *motor1*. Each of them is an OR-state. For example, main is an OR-state with components *HWinit*, *InitiateMoves* and *ProcessRequest*, while *robot* is an OR-state with components *Rinit*, *Rwait*, and *move*. Also, *move* is an AND-state with substates *xm-moveA* an *ym-moveA*, which correspond to move in the x- and y- directions. *HWinit* is the default entry state of state *main*, similarly, *Rinit*, *M0init*, and *M1init* are the default entry states in *robot*, *motor0*, and *motor1*, respectively.

Step 3: Tranformation to the STATEMATE Specification to an FNLOG Specification

we now give give a logic-based function specification, consisting of a sequence of event / action definitions, for the example of the two-degree-of-freedom robot.

At the top-level, the system is composed of four activities: *main*, *robot*, *motor0* and *motor1*. The system will be engaged in all these activities at a given time. Note the use of the same vocabulary as in the statecharts specification; also, entities with the same names in the two specifications correspond: informally, a state in statecharts is an activity in FNLOG, and an event/action in statecharts is an event in FNLOG. In a later section, this correspondence will be described in detail.

1. $L = \odot_t (main) \wedge \odot_t (robot) \wedge \odot_t (motor0) \wedge \odot_t (motor1)$

Transformation of the main activity with FNLOG

2. $\odot_t(main) = \odot_t(HWinit) \vee \odot_t(InitiateMoves) \vee \odot_t (ProcessRequest)$
3. $\odot_t (init\text{-}HWinit) = \odot_t(fire(T1))$
4. $\odot_t (fire(T1)) = \odot_t (init\text{-}main)$
5. $\odot_t (init\text{-}InitiateMoves) = \odot_t (fire(T2)) \vee \odot_t (fire(T4))$

6. $\odot_t (init\text{-}ProcessRequest) = \odot_t (fire(T3))$
7. $\odot_t (term\text{-}HWinit) = \odot_t (fire(T2))$
8. $\odot_t (fire(T2)) = \odot_t (HWinit) \wedge \odot_t (initover)$
9. $\odot_t (term\text{-}InitiateMoves) = \odot_t (fire(T3))$
10. $\odot_t (fire(T3)) = \odot_t (InitiateMoves) \wedge \odot_t (moverequest)$
11. $\odot_t (acceptrequest) = \odot_t (fire(T3))$
12. $\odot_t (term\text{-}ProcessRequest) = \odot_t (fire(T4))$
13. $\odot_t (fire(T4)) = \odot_t (ProcessRequest) \wedge \odot_t (movecomplete)$

Definition 1 is the top-level function. The activity *main* initiates the mobile robot and waits to accept user request. The activity *robot* initializes the system, initiates moves, and monitors their completion. The activity motor0 models the X motor and deals with performing moves and signaling their completion. Similarly motor1 models the Y motor.

Definition 2 is the top-level function for main. At this level, the system is performing one of three activities: hardware initialization (*Hwinit*), waiting to receive a move request (*InitiateMoves*), or is busy handling a move request (*ProcessRequest*).

Definitions 3 to 13 define the conditions under which each activity is initiated and terminated. Initiation and termination of an activity are defined by means of a condition of the form $\odot_t (fire(T))$, which may be treated at this stage as a syntactic label for the initiating / terminating event though it also has a semantic interpretation. For example, in definition 8, $\odot_t (fire(T2))$ is defined as occuring at time t when the activity *Hwinit* is on, and the event *initover* occurs, both at time t.

Now follow a set of definitions for the *robot* activity. The activity initializes and calibrates the hardware, initiates moves, and monitors the response.

Transformation of the acivity robot with FNLOG

14. $\odot_t (robot) = \odot_t (Rinit) \vee \odot_t (Rwait) \vee \odot_t (move)$

15. $\odot_t$ (init-Rinit) = $\odot_t$ (fire(T5))
16. $\odot_t$ (fire(T5)) = $\odot_t$ (init-robot)
17. $\odot_t$(init-Rwait) = $\odot_t$(fire(T6)) ∨ $\odot_t$(fire(T8))
18. $\odot_t$ (init-move) = $\odot_t$ (fire(T7))
19. $\odot_t$ (term-Rinit)) = $\odot_t$ (fire(T6))
20. $\odot_t$ (fire(T6)) = $\odot_t$ (Rinit) ∧ $\odot_t$ (initover)
21. $\odot_t$ (term-Rwait) = $\odot_t$ (fire(T7))
22. $\odot_t$(fire(T7)) = $\odot_t$(Rwait) ∧ $\odot_t$(acceptrequest)
23. $\odot_t$ (term-move) = $\odot_t$ (fire(T8))
24. $\odot_t$ (fire(T8)) = $\odot_t$ (move) ∧ $\odot_t$ (HW-movecomplete)
25. $\odot_t$ (movecomplete) = $\odot_t$ (fire(T8))

Definition 14 is the top-level function stating that *robot* comprises one of three activities: initialization, waiting to get a move signal, and actually performing the move. Definitions 18 and 22 state that *move* is initiated when the current activity is *Rwait* and an *accept request* signal arrives at that instant. Definitions 23 and 24 state the conditions under which move terminates. The other activities may be similarly understood.

The definitions of motor0 and motor1 are omitted to avoid tedium; they are similar in spirit to the definition of *main*. In these definitions, occurence counts are ommitted for simplicity. In general, all events / actions in the definitions are assumed to have associated occurence counts. For example, Definition 9 may be considered to be shorthand for:

∀ i ≥ 0: $\odot_t$ (term-InitiateMoves^i) → ∃ j > 0, $\odot_t$(fire^j (T3)) and

∀ i ≥ 0: $\odot_t$(fire^i (T3)) → ∃ j > 0, $\odot_t$ (term-InitiateMoves^i)

Transformation of the activity motor0 with FNLOG

26. $\odot_t$ (motor0) = $\odot_t$ (M0init) ∨ $\odot_t$ (Wait0) ∨ $\odot_t$ (Xmove)
27. $\odot_t$ (init-M0init) = $\odot_t$(fire(T11))
28. $\odot_t$ (fire(T11)) = $\odot_t$ (init-motor0)
29. $\odot_t$ (init-Wait0) = $\odot_t$ (fire(T12)) ∨ $\odot_t$ (fire(T14))

30. $\odot_t$ (init-Xmove) = $\odot_t$ (fire(T13))
31. $\odot_t$ (term-M0init) = $\odot_t$ (fire(T12))
32. $\odot_t$ (fire(T12)) = $\odot_t$ (M0init) ∧ $\odot_t$ (m0initcomplete)
33. $\odot_t$ (term-Wait0) = $\odot_t$ (fire(T13))
34. $\odot_t$(fire(T13)) = $\odot_t$(Wait0) ∧ $\odot_t$(start-move) ∧ $\odot_t$ (dist X > 0)
35. $\odot_t$ (make move0) = $\odot_t$ (fire(T13))
36. $\odot_t$ (term-Xmove) = $\odot_t$ (fire(T14))
37. $\odot_t$ (fire(T14)) = $\odot_t$ (Xmove) ∧ $\odot_t$ (move0 complete) ∧ $\odot_t$ (m0 movecomplete)

Transformation of the activity motor1 with FNLOG

38. $\odot_t$ (motor1) = $\odot_t$ (M1init) ∨ $\odot_t$ (Wait1) ∨ $\odot_t$ (Ymove)
39. $\odot_t$ (init-M1init) = $\odot_t$(fire(T15))
40. $\odot_t$ (fire(T15)) = $\odot_t$ (init-motor1)
41. $\odot_t$ (init-Wait1) = $\odot_t$ (fire(T16)) ∨ $\odot_t$ (fire(T18))
42. $\odot_t$ (init-Ymove) = $\odot_t$ (fire(T17))
43. $\odot_t$ (term-M1init) = $\odot_t$ (fire(T16))
44. $\odot_t$ (fire(T16)) = $\odot_t$ (M1init) ∧ $\odot_t$ (m1 initcomplete)
45. $\odot_t$ (term-Wait1) = $\odot_t$ (fire(T17))
46. $\odot_t$(fire(T17)) = $\odot_t$(Wait1) ∧ $\odot_t$(start-move) ∧ $\odot_t$ (dist Y > 0)
47. $\odot_t$ (make move1) = $\odot_t$ (fire(T17))
48. $\odot_t$ (term-Ymove) = $\odot_t$ (fire(T18))
49. $\odot_t$ (fire(T18)) = $\odot_t$ (Ymove) ∧ $\odot_t$ (move1 complete) ∧ $\odot_t$ (m1 movecomplete)
50. L = $\odot_t$ (main) ∧ $\odot_t$ (robot) ∧ $\odot_t$ (motor0) ∧ $\odot_t$ (motor1)

By repeated application of induction on the specification, we obtain an equivalent FNLOG specification which includes the occurrence counts. For main and robot, we have the following repeated occurrences version of the specification; whenever no occurence count is mentioned, the event / activity occurs exactly once, so that the default count is 1:

Transformation of the activity main with FNLOG

51. $\odot_t(\text{main}) = \odot_t(\text{HWinit}) \vee \odot_t(\text{InitiateMoves}^i) \vee \odot_t(\text{ProcessRequest}^j)$
52. $\odot_t(\text{init-HWinit}) = \odot_t(\text{fire}(T1))$
53. $\odot_t(\text{fire}(T1)) = \odot_t(\text{init-main})$
54. $\odot_t(\text{init-InitiateMoves}^1) = \odot_t(\text{fire}(T2))$
55. $\odot_t(\text{init-InitiateMoves}^i) = \odot_t(\text{fire}^{i-1}(T4))$, $i > 1$
56. $\odot_t(\text{init-ProcessRequest}^j) = \odot_t(\text{fire}^i(T3))$
57. $\odot_t(\text{term-HWinit}) = \odot_t(\text{fire}(T2))$
58. $\odot_t(\text{fire}(T2)) = \odot_t(\text{HWinit}) \wedge \odot_t(\text{initover})$
59. $\odot_t(\text{term-InitiateMoves}^i) = \odot_t(\text{fire}^i(T3))$
60. $\odot_t(\text{fire}^i(T3)) = \odot_t(\text{InitiateMoves}^i) \wedge \odot_t(\text{moverequest}^j)$ $i \leq j$
61. $\odot_t(\text{acceptrequest}^i) = \odot_t(\text{fire}^i(T3))$
62. $\odot_t(\text{term-ProcessRequest}^i) = \odot_t(\text{fire}^i(T4))$
63. $\odot_t(\text{fire}^i(T4)) = \odot_t(\text{ProcessRequest}^i) \wedge \odot_t(\text{movecomplete}^i)$

Transformation of the activity robot with FNLOG

64. $\odot_t(\text{robot}) = \odot_t(\text{Rinit}) \vee \odot_t(\text{Rwait}^i) \vee \odot_t(\text{move}^i)$
65. $\odot_t(\text{init-Rinit}) = \odot_t(\text{fire}(T5))$
66. $\odot_t(\text{fire}(T5)) = \odot_t(\text{init-robot})$
67. $\odot_t(\text{init-Rwait}^1) = \odot_t(\text{fire}(T6))$
68. $\odot_t(\text{init-Rwait}^i) = \odot_t(\text{fire}^{i-1}(T8))$, $i > 1$
69. $\odot_t(\text{init-move}^i) = \odot_t(\text{fire}^i(T7))$
70. $\odot_t(\text{term-Rinit}) = \odot_t(\text{fire}(T6))$
71. $\odot_t(\text{fire}(T6)) = \odot_t(\text{Rinit}) \wedge \odot_t(\text{initover})$
72. $\odot_t(\text{term-Rwait}^i) = \odot_t(\text{fire}^i(T7))$
73. $\odot_t(\text{fire}^i(T7)) = \odot_t(\text{Rwait}^i) \wedge \odot_t(\text{acceptrequest}^i)$
74. $\odot_t(\text{term-move}^i) = \odot_t(\text{fire}^i(T8))$
75. $\odot_t(\text{fire}^i(T8)) = \odot_t(\text{move}^i) \wedge \odot_t(\text{HW-movecomplete}^i)$
76. $\odot_t(\text{movecomplete}^i) = \odot_t(\text{fire}^i(T8))$

Transformation of the activity motor0 with FNLOG

77. $\odot_t(\text{motor0}) = \odot_t(\text{M0init}) \vee \odot_t(\text{Wait0}^i) \vee \odot_t(\text{Xmove}^j)$
78. $\odot_t(\text{init-M0init}) = \odot_t(\text{fire}(T11))$
79. $\odot_t(\text{fire}(T11)) = \odot_t(\text{init-motor0})$
80. $\odot_t(\text{init-Wait0}^1) = \odot_t(\text{fire}(T12))$
81. $\odot_t(\text{init-Wait0}^i) = \odot_t(\text{fire}^{i-1}(T14))$, $i > 1$
82. $\odot_t(\text{init-Xmove}^i) = \odot_t(\text{fire}^i(T13))$
83. $\odot_t(\text{term-M0init}) = \odot_t(\text{fire}(T12))$
84. $\odot_t(\text{fire}(T12)) = \odot_t(\text{M0init}) \wedge \odot_t(\text{m0initcomplete})$
85. $\odot_t(\text{term-Wait0}^i) = \odot_t(\text{fire}^i(T13))$
86. $\odot_t(\text{fire}^i(T13)) = \odot_t(\text{Wait0}^i) \wedge \odot_t(\text{start-move}^j) \wedge \odot_t(\text{dist X} > 0)$, $i \leq j$
87. $\odot_t(\text{make move0}^i) = \odot_t(\text{fire}^i(T13))$
88. $\odot_t(\text{term-Xmove}^i) = \odot_t(\text{fire}^i(T14))$
89. $\odot_t(\text{fire}^i(T14)) = \odot_t(\text{Xmove}^i) \wedge \odot_t(\text{move0complete}^i) \wedge \odot_t(\text{m0 movecomplete}^i)$

Transformation of the activity motor1 with FNLOG

90. $\odot_t(\text{motor1}) = \odot_t(\text{M1init}) \vee \odot_t(\text{Wait1}^i) \vee \odot_t(\text{Ymove}^j)$
91. $\odot_t(\text{init-M1init}) = \odot_t(\text{fire}(T15))$
92. $\odot_t(\text{fire}(T15)) = \odot_t(\text{init-motor1})$
93. $\odot_t(\text{init-Wait1}^1) = \odot_t(\text{fire}(T16))$
94. $\odot_t(\text{init-Wait1}^i) = \odot_t(\text{fire}^{i-1}(T18))$, $i > 1$
95. $\odot_t(\text{init-Ymove}^i) = \odot_t(\text{fire}^i(T17))$
96. $\odot_t(\text{term-M1init}) = \odot_t(\text{fire}(T16))$
97. $\odot_t(\text{fire}(T16)) = \odot_t(\text{M1init}) \wedge \odot_t(\text{m1 initcomplete})$
98. $\odot_t(\text{term-Wait1}^i) = \odot_t(\text{fire}^i(T17))$
99. $\odot_t(\text{fire}^i(T17)) = \odot_t(\text{Wait1}^i) \wedge \odot_t(\text{start-move}^i) \wedge \odot_t(\text{dist Y} > 0)$, $i \leq j$
100. $\odot_t(\text{make move1}^i) = \odot_t(\text{fire}^i(T17))$
101. $\odot_t(\text{term-Ymove}^i) = \odot_t(\text{fire}^i(T18))$
102. $\odot_t(\text{fire}^i(T18)) = \odot_t(\text{Ymove}^i) \wedge \odot_t(\text{move1 complete}^i) \wedge \odot_t(\text{m1 move-complete}^i)$

Box 10.

Proof of P1 :

$\odot_t (HWinit) \rightarrow \odot_t (Rinit)$
From Definition 1, since L is always true, the following are also always true :
$\odot_t (main), \odot_t (robot).$
So wa have :
$\odot_t (robot) \rightarrow \diamondsuit_t (init\text{-}robot)$ *by axiom AL1*
          $\rightarrow \diamondsuit_t (fire(T5))$ *from robot Definition 66*
          $\rightarrow \diamondsuit_t (init\text{-}Rinit)$ *from robot Definition 65*

Furthermore, $\odot_t (HWinit)$
          $\rightarrow \neg \diamondsuit_t (term\text{-}HWinit)$ *by axiom AL2*
          $\rightarrow \neg \diamondsuit_t (fire(T2))$ *by main Definition 57*
          $\rightarrow \neg \diamondsuit_t (initover)$ *by main Definition 58*
          $\rightarrow \neg \diamondsuit_t (term\text{-}Rinit))$ *by robot Definitions 70, 71*

Combinig the two results we have :
$\odot_t (HWinit) \rightarrow \diamondsuit_t (init\text{-}Rinit) \wedge \neg \diamondsuit_t (term\text{-}Rinit)$
          $\rightarrow \odot_t (Rinit)$ *from AL6*

So : $\boxed{\odot_t (HWinit) \rightarrow \odot_t (Rinit)}$

Step 4: Composition in FNLOG

Step 5: Checking of Properties of the System

An FNLOG specification may now be verified using the proof rules. Verification may take two forms. In the first, the entire specification itself may be subjected to consistency checks. In the second, system properties specified in FNLOG may be verified against the specification by logical derivation, using the rules (proofs in Boxes 10-13).

P1: $\odot_t (HWinit) \rightarrow \odot_t (Rinit)$
P2: $\odot_t (InitiateMoves^i) \rightarrow \odot_t (Rwait^i)$
P3: $\odot_t (moverequest^j) \wedge \neg \odot_t (Rinit^i) \wedge \neg \odot_t (move^i) \rightarrow \odot_t (acceptrequest^i), \forall i \leq j$
P4: $\odot_{t-k} (accept\text{-}request^i) \Rightarrow \diamondsuit_t^{t-k} (movecomplete^i)$

CONCLUSION

In this paper, a new technique for the specification and the validation of real-time and critical systems integrating the STATEMATE method (Harel, 1997; Harel, 1987; Harel, Pnueli, Schmidt & Sherman, 1987) and the FNLOG logic (Sowmya & Ramesh, 1997) has been proposed. The most distinctive characteristic of our approach is the simple way of specifying real-time system's behavior dealing with functional and behavioral aspects. Also, the use of FNLOG has allowed the validation of specification in STATEMATE. We have illustrate our appraoch through an industrial example: a version of a computer controlled gas burner (Mosbahi, 2002). We have at first described the system's requirements with FNLOG, the system's behavior with STATEMATE (starting by a decompositional specification with

Box 11.

Proof of P1 :

$\odot_t(HWinit) \rightarrow \odot_t(Rinit)$

From Definition 1, since L is always true, the following are also always true :

$\odot_t(main)$, $\odot_t(robot)$.

So wa have :

$\odot_t(robot) \rightarrow \Diamond_t(init\text{-}robot)$ *by axiom AL1*

     $\rightarrow \Diamond_t(fire(T5))$ *from robot Definition 66*

     $\rightarrow \Diamond_t(init\text{-}Rinit)$ *from robot Definition 65*

Furthermore, $\odot_t(HWinit)$

     $\rightarrow \neg\Diamond_t(term\text{-}HWinit)$ *by axiom AL2*

     $\rightarrow \neg\Diamond_t(fire(T2))$ *by main Definition 57*

     $\rightarrow \neg\Diamond_t(initover)$ *by main Definition 58*

     $\rightarrow \neg\Diamond_t(term\text{-}Rinit))$ *by robot Definitions 70, 71*

Combinig the two results we have :

$\odot_t(HWinit) \rightarrow \Diamond_t(init\text{-}Rinit) \wedge \neg \Diamond_t(term\text{-}Rinit)$

      $\rightarrow \odot_t(Rinit)$ *from AL6*

So : | $\odot_t(HWinit) \rightarrow \odot_t(Rinit)$ |

Box 12.

Proof of P3 :

$\odot_t(moverequest^j) \wedge \neg \odot_t(Rinit^i) \wedge \neg \odot_t(move^i) \rightarrow \odot_t(acceptrequest^i), \forall\ i \leq j$

We have :

    $\odot_t(InitiateMoves^i) \wedge \odot_t(moverequest^j) = \odot_t(fire^i(T3))\ i \leq j$ *from Definition 60*

We have also :

    $\odot_t(InitiateMoves^i) \rightarrow \odot_t(Rwait^i)$ *proof P2*

    $\rightarrow \odot_t(Rwait^i) \wedge \odot_t(moverequest^j) = \odot_t(fire^i(T3))\ i \leq j$

We have also :

    $\odot_t(robot) = \odot_t(Rinit) \vee \odot_t(Rwait^i) \vee \odot_t(move^i)$ *from Definition 64*

    $\rightarrow \odot_t(Rwait^i) \rightarrow \neg\odot_t(Rinit) \wedge \neg\odot_t(move^i)$

$\odot_t(moverequest^j) \wedge \neg\odot_t(Rinit) \wedge \neg\odot_t(move^i) = \odot_t(fire^i(T3))\ i \leq j$

nous avons: $\odot_t(acceptrequest^i) = \odot_t(fire^i(T3))$ *from Definition 61*

So : | $\odot_t(moverequest^j) \wedge \neg \odot_t(Rinit^i) \wedge \neg \odot_t(move^i) \rightarrow \odot_t(acceptrequest^i), \forall\ i \leq j$ |

Box 13.

Proof of P4 :

P4 : $\odot_{t-k}(\text{accept-request}^i) \Rightarrow \diamond_t^{t-k}(\text{movecomplete}^i)$

$\odot_t(\text{accept-request}^i) = \odot_t(\text{fire}^i(T3))$ *from Definition 61*

$\odot_t(\text{fire}^i(T7)) \rightarrow \odot_t(\text{accept-request}^i)$ *from Definition 73*

$\odot_t(\text{move-complete}^i) = \odot_t(\text{fire}^i(T8))$ *from Definition 76*

From Definitions 62 et 63, we have :

$\odot_t(\text{term-ProcessRequest}^i) \rightarrow \odot_t(\text{move-complete}^i)$

$\odot_t(\text{term-ProcessRequest}^i) \rightarrow \diamond_t(\text{ProcessRequest}^i)$ *AL*

$\odot_t(\text{init-ProcessRequest}^i) \rightarrow \odot_t(\text{accept-Request}^i)$

$\odot_t(\text{move-complete}^i) \rightarrow \diamond_t(\text{ProcessRequest}^i)$

$\rightarrow \diamond_t(\text{acceptRequest}^i)$

$\odot_t(\text{move-complete}^i) \rightarrow \odot_{t-k}(\text{accept-Request}^i)$

$\odot_t(\text{accept-Request}^i) \rightarrow \odot_t(\text{move-complete}^i) \vee \diamond_t(\text{move-complete}^i)$

$\odot_{t-k}(\text{accept-Request}^i) \rightarrow \diamond_t^{t-k}(\text{movecomplete}^i)$

So : $\odot_{t-k}(\text{accept-request}^i) \Rightarrow \diamond_t^{t-k}(\text{movecomplete}^i)$

Activity-charts then a behavioral specification with Statecharts). Then we have transformed STATEMATE specification to an FNLOG specification by a recomposition process (step 4) and we have verified that the behavior specification implies the requirements ones using the proof sytem of FNLOG and transformation rules given in step3. In order to develop formal technique for specifying and verifying real-time systems integrating STATEMATE and FNLOG, we have extended FNLOG axiomatic to reason about duration properties and proposed a transformation rules from STATEMATE to FNLOG (Sowmya & Ramesh, 1997). The axiomatization of our technique requests also a long term efforts and this paper represents a tentative attempts in this direction.

REFERENCES

Berry, G., & Coresserat, L. (1985). The ESTEREL sychronous programming language and its mathematical semantics, *in Seminar on Concurrency, ed. S. D. Brookes, A.W. Roscoe and G. Winskel* (pp.389-448). (Lecture Note in Computer Science, vol. 197.), Springer Verlag.

Bruel, J.-M. (1996). Fuze: Un environnement intégré pour l'analyse formelle de logiciels distribués temps réel, *thèse doctoral en informatique*, université Paul Sabatier, Toulouse, France.

Bucci, G. (1995). *CAMPANAI, G., &Nesi, P (Vol. 8*, pp. 117–172). Tools for Specifying Real-Time Systems.

Bussow, R., & Grieskamp, W. (1998). The ZETA System: Overview, *Technical Report*, Berlin.

Clarke, E. M., & Wing, J. M. (1996). Formal Methods: state of the art and Future Directions, *ACM computing survey* (pp. 626-643). Vol. 28, N0 4.

Cohen, B. (1994). A brief history of formal methods. *FACS Europe, 1*(0), 3.

Fitzgerald, J., & Larsen, P. G. (1997). *Modelling Systems: Practical Tools and Techniques in Software Development.* Cambridge University Press.

Ghezzi, C., Mandrioli, D., & Morzenti, A. (1990). A Logic Language for Executable Specifications of Real-Time Systems, *Journal of systems and software* (pp.107-123), vol. 12, no. 2.

Harel, D. (1997). *Modeling Reactive systems with Statecharts: The statemate approach.* USA: McGraw-Hill.

Harel, D. (1987). STATEMATE: the Languages of Statemate, *Technical Report*, USA.

Harel, D., Pnueli, A., Schmidt, J. P., & Sherman, R. (1987). On the formal Semantics of Statecharts, *Proc.2 nd I.E.E.E. Symposium on Logic in Computer Science*, Ithaca, NY, USA, (pp. 54-64).

Henzinger, T. A., Manna, Z., & Pnueli, A. (1991). *Temporal Proof Methodologies for Real-Time Systems, 18 th Ann. Syym on Principales of Programming Languages* (pp. 353–366). ACM Press.

Hooman, J., & Ramesh, S., & De Roever, W.P. (1989). A Compositional Semantics for Statecharts, *Proc. Formal Models of Concurrency*, Novosibirsk, USSR.

Hooman, J., Ramesh, S., & De Roever, W. P. (1990). *A compositional axiomatization of safety and liveness properties of statecharts*", proc. Int. BCS-FACS Workshop on Semantics for Concurency Univ. Of Leicester, UK.

Hooman, J., Ramesh, S., & De Roever, W.P. (1992). *A Compositional Axiomatization of Statecharts*, Theoretical Computer Science 101.

Huizing, C., Gerth, R., & De Roever, W. P. (1988). *Modelling statecherts behaviour in a fully abstract way*, Computing Science Notes, 88/07, Eindhoven Univ. Tech., Dept Math. Comp. Sci.

Jahanian, F., & Mok, A. K.-L. (1986). *Safety analysis of timing properties in Real-time systems*, I.E.E.E Trans (pp. 890-904). On soft. *Eng., 12*(0), 9.

Ostroff, J. S. (1994). *Formal Methods for the Specification and Design of Real-Time Safety Critical Systems,* I.E.E.E. Press book to be called "Tutorial on specification of Time".

Mosbahi, O. (2002). *Une technique de spécification et de validation basée sur la méthode STATEMATE et la logique FNLOG, mémoire de D.E.A en informatique.* Tunis, Tunisie: FST.

Ravn, A. P., Rishel, H., & Hansen, K.-M. (1993). Specifying and Verifying Requirements of Real-Time systems, *I.E.E.E. Transaction on Software Engineering* (pp. 41-55). Vol. 19, N0 1.

Sowmya, A., & Ramesh, S. (1992). Verification of Timing Properties in a Statecharts Based Model of Real-Time Reactive systems, *Distributed computer control systems, IFAC workshop series 1992*, N0. 3, H. Kopetz and M.G.Rodd, eds.Pergamon Press.

Sowmya, A., & Ramesh, S. (1997). A Semantics-Preserving Transformation of statecharts to FNLOG, Proc.14 th. *IFAC Workshop Distributed Computer Control systems*, Seoul, Korea.

Cox, I.-J., & Gehani, N.-H. (1989). *Concurrent Programming and Robotics*", Robotics Resolution, Vol. 8, N0 2, (pp. 3-16).

APPENDIX A: ADDITIONAL AXIOMS FOR THE FNLOG PROOF SYSTEM

We have the definitional axiom for all function definitions of the form $\odot_n(f) = $ tformula:

$$[\odot_n(f) = \text{tformula}] \leftrightarrow [\odot_n(f) \rightarrow \text{tformula} \wedge \text{tformula} \rightarrow \odot_n(f)]$$

The application level axioms (AL) relate events and activities temporally. We assume that the duration of an activity is at least one unit of time. The following axioms are true for all events and activities, without considering their repeated occurence:

1) $\odot_t(a^i) \rightarrow \diamond_t (\text{init-}a^i)$

2) $\odot_t(a^i) \rightarrow \neg \diamond_t (\text{term-}a^i)$

3) $\odot_t (\text{init-}a^i) \rightarrow \neg \odot_t (\text{term-}a^i)$

4) $\odot_t (\text{init-}a^i) \rightarrow \odot_t(a^i)$

5) $\neg \diamond_t (\text{init-}a^i) \rightarrow \odot_t(a^i)$

6) $\neg \diamond_t (\text{term-}a^i) \wedge \diamond_t (\text{init-}a^i) \rightarrow \odot_t(a^i)$

7) $\neg \odot_t(a^i) \rightarrow \neg \odot_t (\text{init-}a^i)$

8) $\odot_t (\text{term-}a^i) \rightarrow \odot_t(a^i)$

9) $\odot_t (\text{term-}a^i) \rightarrow \diamond_t (\text{init-}a^i)$

10) $\neg \diamond_t (\text{init-}a^i) \rightarrow \neg \odot_t(a^i)$

11) $\neg \diamond_t (\text{init-}a^i) \rightarrow \neg \diamond_t (a^i)$

12) $\neg \diamond_t (a^i) \rightarrow \neg \diamond_t (\text{init-}a^i)$

The repeated occurence axioms (RO) state that occurences of the same event / activity strictly follow each other, and at integral instants of time. The basic repeated occurence axioms are:

1) $\odot_t(a^i) \rightarrow t \geq 0, i \geq 1$

2) $\forall\ i,j,\ \odot_t(a^i) \wedge \odot_{t'}(a^j) \rightarrow (i < j \leftrightarrow t < t')$

The axioms that follow capture the basic property of repeated occurrences of a single event or activity, namely that the $i + 1$th occurence strictly follows the ith occurence in time.

3) $\odot_t(a^i) \rightarrow \neg \diamond_t (\text{init-}a^{i+1})$

4) $\odot_t(a^i) \rightarrow \neg \diamond_t (a^{i+1})$

5) $\odot_t(a^i) \rightarrow \neg \diamond_t (\text{term-}a^{i+1})$

6) $\odot_t(\text{init-}a^i) \rightarrow \neg \diamond_t (\text{init-}a^{i+1})$

7) $\odot_t(\text{init-}a^i) \rightarrow \neg \diamond_t (a^{i+1})$

8) $\odot_t(\text{init-}a^i) \rightarrow \neg \diamond_t (\text{term-}a^{i+1})$

9) $\odot_t(\text{term-}a^i) \rightarrow \neg \diamond_t (\text{init-}a^{i+1})$

10) $\odot_t(\text{term-}a^i) \rightarrow \neg \diamond_t (a^{i+1})$

11) $\odot_t(\text{term-}a^i) \rightarrow \neg \diamond_t (\text{term-}a^{i+1})$

12) $\odot_t(\text{init-}a^{i+1}) \rightarrow \diamond_t (\text{init-}a^i)$

13) $\odot_t(\text{init-}a^{i+1}) \rightarrow \diamond_t (a^i)$

14) $\odot_t(\text{init-}a^{i+1}) \rightarrow \diamond_t (\text{term-}a^i)$

15) $\odot_t(\text{term-}a^{i+1}) \rightarrow \diamond_t (\text{init-}a^i)$

16) $\odot_t(\text{term-}a^{i+1}) \rightarrow \diamond_t (a^i)$

17) $\odot_t(\text{term-}a^{i+1}) \rightarrow \diamond_t (\text{term-}a^i)$

18) $\odot_t(a^{i+1}) \rightarrow \diamond_t (\text{init-}a^i)$

19) $\odot_t(a^{i+1}) \rightarrow \diamond_t (a^i)$

20) $\odot_t(a^{i+1}) \rightarrow \diamond_t (\text{term-}a^i)$

Chapter 18

Flexible Implementation of Industrial Real–Time Servo Drive System

Ahmed Karim Ben Salem
National Institute of Applied Sciences and Technology, Tunisia

Hedi Abdelkrim
National Institute of Applied Sciences and Technology, Tunisia

Slim Ben Saoud
National Institute of Applied Sciences and Technology, Tunisia

ABSTRACT

The research presented in this chapter deals with the design and implementation of Real-Time (RT) control systems applying advanced Field Programmable Gate Array (FPGAs). The chapter proposes a promising flexible architecture that uses RT Operating System (RTOS) and ready-to-use Intellectual Properties (IPs). The authors detail an approach that uses software closed control loop function blocks (FB), running on embedded processor cores. These FBs implement the different control drive sub-modules into RTOS tasks of the execution environment, where each task has to be executed under well defined conditions. Two RTOSes are evaluated: μC-OS/II and Xilkernel. The FPGA embedded processor cores are combined with reconfigurable logic and dedicated resources on the FPGA. This System-on-Chip (SoC) has been applied to electric motors drive. A comparative analysis, in terms of speed and cost, is carried-out between various hardware/software FPGA-based architectures, in order to enhance flexibility without sacrificing performance and increasing cost. Case studies results validate successfully the feasibility and the efficiency of the flexible approach for new and more complex control algorithms. The performance and flexibility of FPGA-based motor controllers are enhanced with the reliability and modularity of the introduced RTOS support.

DOI: 10.4018/978-1-60960-086-0.ch018

INTRODUCTION

Nowadays, motor control researchers are increasingly developing new sophisticated control algorithms to increase performances and to optimize the efficiency of motors in a factory: i.e. sensorless control, neural network control, fuzzy logic control, Field Oriented Control (FOC), direct torque control, etc. These developments are always characterized by a growth of complexity. Indeed, the sophisticated control laws are constituted of heterogeneous functions because of the diversities in algorithm operations (memory storage, floating point arithmetic operations, trigonometric functions, integration, regulation, etc.) and differences in computation rate. Moreover, the control algorithms present always recursive computing that complicates the digital data coding. With this growing complexity of motor and motion control applications, there are larger computational requirements on the processor. The design challenge for embedded motors controlling machinery becomes how to integrate control complexities of high-sampling-frequency applications that can execute efficiently on limited resources and that meet not just higher performance but more flexibility as well. Many control applications require updated drive control algorithms and have to be changed and adjusted to their environment to reduce development costs.

So it becomes apparent that advanced Field Programmable Gate Array (FPGA), containing both reconfigurable logic blocks and embedded processor cores (Fletcher, 2005), offers significant advantages in the area of performance and flexibility. This Advanced FPGA technology (Rodriguez-Andina, Moure, & Valdes, 2007) becomes quite mature for high-speed power control applications (Ben Salem, Ben Othman, & Ben Saoud, 2008), since it has presented a good compromise between the programmable solution flexibility, and the efficiency and high-performance of a specific architecture. New FPGA capabilities have offered the means to create high-performance digital

components allowing implementation of more complex control applications. But the key issue in a System-on-Chip (SoC) (Eshraghian, 2006; Nurmi, 2007) design is to trade-off efficiency against flexibility. Therefore, there are a lot of challenges regarding SoC design methodologies and architectures styles. Nowadays SoC designers face important product development decisions in choosing Intellectual Property (IP) cores for SoC. Indeed, determining which core is most appropriate for a given SoC requires careful consideration. Decisions must be made about the type of core (soft vs. hard), the architecture to integrate this core, and the relationships between HardWare (HW) and SoftWare (SW).

In advanced FPGA design (Jóźwiak, Nedjah, & Figueroa, 2010), System-on-Programmable Chip (SoPC) for motion control results in very complex tasks involving SW and HW skilled developers. Therefore, there is a need to a co-design expertise to build a powerful digital embedded controller. But, the power of FPGAs has been made readily available to embedded system designers and SW programmers through the use of high-level HW description tools (Vega-Rodríguez, Sánchez-Pérez, & Gómez-Pulido, 2005). These co-design tools help engineers to overcome the lack of expertise in digital HW design.

Moreover, the implementation of digital control systems and RT systems belong together and they should be connected in the design process, as a substantial percentage of control applications have either timing critical or high throughput requirements. Therefore, embedded Real-Time (RT) control becomes a promising research domain. Control systems are commonly designed using a set of cooperating periodic sub-modules that must be able to perform assigned calculations within demanding timing constraints, in order to ensure a correct dynamic behavior of the closed loop controller. To achieve this goal, the previous FPGA-based platforms advantages should be combined with the modularity and predictability of an integrated SW Real-Time Operating System (RTOS).

This chapter proposes a flexible architecture that uses ready-to-use IPs, built in hardwired processors and RTOS support in FPGA-based platforms. The proposed design approach is suggested to be used to implement digital controllers in several application areas, such as motion control, power electronics, and motor control. It can be readily applied to any embedded control electric drive. Particularly, this ongoing work focuses on Alternative Current (AC) Induction Motors (IM) and Direct Current (DC) motors drive that are commonly used on industrial machinery.

Assuming that RT embedded control applications require higher performance without increasing cost, various processor architectures are considered and analyzed, using single and Multiprocessor SoC (MPSoC). Additionnaly, two RTOSes are evaluated: μC-OS/II and Xilkernel to ensure RT specifications. The experimental results compare both RTOSes varying the number of controllers and show the benefits of integrating such RTOSes in the SW design flow. Furthermore, a motor emulation concept is used to validate the controllers' functional correctness.

The chapter is organized as follows: Section Background introduces new trends in flexible and high performance digital controllers' design. Section State of the art discusses related works about digital implementation of control drive applications; it gives basic ideas about new challenges for control applications. In section Contribution, we present the problem and our adopted HW/SW design approach that is detailed in the next section Co-design approach. Section Embedded control case studies validate the proposed approach on two embedded motor control case studies. In section Experimental results, their main FPGA speed/area results are showed and discussed. Finally, future works are described and conclusions are given.

BACKGROUND

We describe in this section the advanced FPGA technology that is expanded by introducing programmable processors and ready-to-use IPs. The tackling of this FPGA technology is complicated by the need of HW/SW partitioning and design for complex algorithms at low cost. Therefore, we present next the FPGA-embedded processors technology and the co-design tools helping the full exploitation of this technology. Additionally, we detail the embedded RT scheduling concept and its benefit for embedded control drive.

Processor Cores

Nowadays, reconfigurable programmable logic devices offer two types of embedded processors: hardcore and softcore. Different options are available to a designer needing to select an embedded processor core. Some options provide more benefits over others; however, not all options are a fit for every application. The first solution is the "hard" processor core, which will be embedded in HW as dedicated silicon. The alternative solution is the embedded "soft" processor core where the processor is implemented in the primitives of an FPGA. The decision regarding the type of processor core used is typically based on a balance between computing time, unit cost, space constraints, toolset, and flexibility needs.

A hardcore processor is implemented directly in the FPGA integrated circuit transistors, so it has dedicated silicon on the FPGA. This allows it to operate with a core frequency and have a rating similar to that of a discrete microprocessor. Unfortunately, this hard implementation does not provide the ability to adjust the core for the application, nor does it allows for the flexibility of adding a hard-processor to an existing design or an additional hard-processor for more processing capabilities.

However, a softcore processor (Calderon & Vassiliadis, 2005) is implemented using the available FPGA's logic cells. It is an IP core representing a microprocessor fully described in SW, usually in a VHDL (VHSIC HW Description Language), and capable to be synthesized in programmable HW solution. Due to this implementation, the processor will not operate at the speeds or have the performance of a hardcore. But, in many embedded applications, the high performance achieved by the hardcore processor is not required, and performance can be traded for expanded functionality and flexibility through the configurable nature of the FPGA. Indeed, using a softcore processor alleviates many of the issues encountered due to changing requirements and enables further customization of the system to be performed (Dyer, Plessl, & Platzner, 2002). Furthermore, a softcore processor solution will prevent designers from being confined to a specific set of peripherals that may no longer fit the application as requirements change or new features are desired. Therefore, the use of a softcore processor offers a trade-off between price and performance, an easy integration in the FPGA, and an upgradeability. Consequently, it may be appropriate for a complex multiprocessor architecture.

Co-Design Tools

Advanced FPGAs present a mixed HW/SW structure. So FPGA-based applications require co-design tools (Wolf, 1993; Zhou, Xie, & Wang, 2005) to build a powerful SoC that can be readily modified to suit new requirements. Improvement in FPGA synthesis, place-and-route tools, and debug capabilities has made FPGA prototyping more available and practical to SoC designers than ever before.

The highest levels of abstraction achieved with the new Electronic Design Automation (EDA) tools help to work faster and produce more predictable solutions. These SW to HW tools (Vega-Rodríguez, et al., 2005) have improved the practicality of FPGA devices as SW-programmable computing platforms. On the one hand, SW to HW compiler tools accept high-level descriptions written in a language familiar to embedded SW programmers. Today's compilers have advanced to the point where writing assembly code is now rarely required and most mathematical functions can be written directly in a C environment. On the other hand, existing synthesis and place and route technologies are combined with system-level platform building tools, allowing designers to create optimized implementations based on specifications and to develop and target complete systems on programmable logic to specific development boards. Analysis and simulation tools are also used to evaluate cost, performance, and power consumption.

The Xilinx Embedded Development Kit (EDK) environment (Xilinx, 2009) is a one of the powerful co-design tools that provides a complete "embedded processing solution" for complex embedded processor applications. It includes a complete set of GNU-based SW tools as shown in Figure 1. From this high level design tool, the integration of a RTOS and a subset of libraries are managed.

Real-Time Scheduling

Nowadays, there has been an interest in enabling multiple embedded control applications to share a single processor and memory, such complex control systems involve sub-systems with different dynamics which must be further coordinated. Some parts of the control algorithm, e.g. controlling slow modes, can be executed slower than the one used for fast modes. The control system can be divided into subtasks that operate at different update rates depending on the available bandwidth. This can be achieved by a RT system that satisfies these various processing speeds. A RT system (Gambier, 2004) poses stringent requirements on precisely time-triggered synchronized actions in feedback loops.

In order to run multiple programs on a uniprocessor system with RT constraints, SW-based context switching is required. With RTOS, also

Figure 1. Embedded software tool architecture for XPS

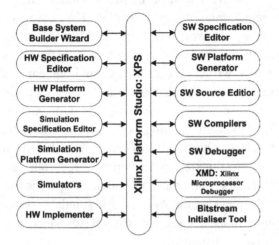

called a RT kernel, there has been a tendency to provide facilities for creating several tasks within the same program to have faster task switch, unrestricted access to shared memory and to simplify the communication and synchronisation. A RTOS allows applications to be easily designed and expanded in the sense that it simplifies the design process by splitting the application code into separate tasks, so functions can be added without requiring major changes to the SW. Multitasking simplifies coding, allowing a modularized solution and increasing code reuse. So application's performance is enhanced, regardless of its size and complexity. Therefore, RTOS feature insertion in the system level design process of an embedded system becomes an interesting design step, showing its benefits when applied to embedded processors in order to enhance modularity and determinism of the designed solution.

On the other hand, a run-time HW reconfiguration allows the implementation of various controllers without having to realize them all on the FPGA concurrently (Schulz, et al., 2007). However, the relative high reconfiguration time often represents an obstacle when using FPGA-based architectures for run-time reconfigurable systems. In order to overcome this barrier, A RTOS must be included

to explicitly respect the reconfiguration time. In such systems, the reconfiguration activities need to be carried out during run-time without causing the application tasks to miss their dead-lines.

Conventionally, the RTOS task manager is composed by the dispatcher and the scheduler. The dispatcher carries out the context switch and the scheduler has the function of selecting the task, which will obtain the processor as next. RT systems need special algorithms to schedule a set of tasks. Generally, scheduling algorithms can be classed in two types: static and dynamic algorithms.

- In a dynamic scheduling, the feasibility can be determined and changed in the configuration at run time. So this kind of scheduling can be planed either off-line if the complete scheduling problem is known a priori but with an on-line implementation, or on-line if the future is unknown or ignored. This class of scheduling offers a great degree of flexibility but it is poor in determinism.

- A static scheduling requires that the complete information about the scheduling problem (number of tasks, deadlines, priorities, periods, etc.) is known a priori. So it must always be planed off-line and this has a good advantage which is the determinism. But this kind of scheduling is inflexible.

There are various popular algorithms used in the literature (Buttazzo, 2005). But the effectiveness of RT scheduling algorithm depends on the guarantee that all deadlines are met.

STATE OF THE ART

Various approaches have been studied in this RT embedded control field in order to enhance industrial control systems performance (Dubey,

Agarwal, & Vasantha, 2007; Kiel & Lenze, 2002). The new requirements of power electronic control systems soon reveal that digital solutions based purely on microprocessors can not achieve the required specifications. These requirements exceed the capability of most common microprocessors (Cecati, 1999) to execute the new complex algorithm functions running in SW. The advent of the latest generation of Digital Signal Processors (DSP) has made it much less simpler to implement such algorithms (Singh, Singh, & Dwivedi, 2006). However, standalone DSPs can no longer answer this new generation of control applications that require not just higher performance but more flexibility as well without increasing cost and resources (Bhoot & Takahashi, 2003).

Furthermore, new complex control algorithms need to be partitioned in code for HW and code for SW. Certain time critical or speed sensitive tasks need to be implemented in HW while other complex functions that are computing intensive or require a large amount of memory should be embedded in SW using processors. A few years ago, new flexible platforms based on several common interconnected devices in the same board: such as an Application Specific Integrated Circuit (ASIC) to implement HW tasks with a general processor or DSP for SW tasks (Aguirre, et al., 2005), could be an alternative solution ensuring higher performance and more flexibility as explained in (Bueno, et al., 2009). However, the use of mixed devices adds cost and introduces complex functional partitioning or communication latencies.

Nowadays, thanks to novel gate-array integration levels and cost, SoC solution based on single programmable device is considered as an appropriate solution in order to boost performances of controllers. Commonly used SoC devices are FPGA chips. FPGAs for industrial drives started appearing since a decade (Monmasson & Chapuis, 2002). Several development activities have been conducted in recent years using these devices for high-speed control (Idkhajine, Monmasson, Naouar, Prata, & Bouallaga, 2009; Kariyappa &

Uttara Kumari, 2008; Martin, Bueno, Rodriguez, & Saez, 2009; Monmasson & Cirstea, 2007; Yang, Liu, Cui, & Zhao, 2006), as FPGAs prices have come down in the last five years. The surge of development activities in FPGA-based control system has proved efficiency of these highly reconfigurable solutions. A comparison between DSP and FPGA-based control capabilities has been carried out in (Fratta, Griffero, & Nieddu, 2004), it has been demonstrated how FPGA-based digital control properties are better than DSP ones for any comparative term. With FPGA, the controller can be implemented exploiting its natural parallelism to achieve a higher throughput.

But the last FPGA-based designs and modelling techniques lack flexibility since these HW-dedicated implementations are fixed with no possibility of upgrade or use with another algorithm. So, the FPGA core-based approach, interconnecting pre-designed HW Intellectual Property (IP) cores around the reconfigurable logic blocks of the component and programmable embedded processors on the same chip, offers a good compromise between flexibility and performance. It has been recently applied, in few works, to Mechatronic systems design such as in (Astarloa, Lázaro, Bidarte, Jiménez, & Zuloaga, 2009; Kung, Fung, & Tai, 2009).

Moreover, the closed loop control system is the most common type of control application that has naturally hard RT requirements. This imposes a constraint to SW-based designs, since it is no longer possible to support any amount of functionality by sacrificing performance. So this brings another perspective: to design and implement a RT digital controller based on a powerful RTOS to ensure higher performance. Several recent research works have shown the benefits of having the RTOS activities integrated in embedded systems (Crespo, Ripoll, Gonzalez-Harbour, & Lipari, 2008; Engel, Kuz, Petters, & Ruocco, 2004; Theelen, Verschueren, Reyes Suarez, Stevens, & Nunez, 2003). However, in embedded RT control system literature, the RT system design is commonly treated from the optic of control engineering without to consider implementation aspects and benefits for reconfigurability as explained in (Gambier, 2004; Zhou, et al., 2005). (Simard, Mailloux, & Beguenane, 2009) have discussed a FPGA-based SoC SW application under embedded Linux RTOS that is highly integrated in Xilinx design tool. (Götz, Rettberg, Pereira, & Rammig, 2009) presents the main concepts and methods used to achieve a reconfigurable RTOS that is able to distribute itself over a hybrid architecture. However, our work aims to highlight the new opportunities of inserting other SW RTOSes in the system level design process of SoC embedded controllers. It also shows their gain in terms of modularity and RT execution for reconfigurable SoC. So, it is proposed a design and implementation of a control solution applying FPGA-based processors supporting RTOS feature.

CONTRIBUTION

FPGA offers significant advantages to control drive applications in the area of performance thanks to their parallelism feature. With an FPGA, calculations that would normally consume large amounts of CPU time when implemented in SW may be HW accelerated. However, the implementation of all control system functionalities in HW has several drawbacks: On the one hand, some control heavy computation tasks are hard to parallelise and their HW implementations yield low speedup. On the other hand, some system tasks require little computation and can be executed on a processor with low utilization of FPGA area (Fort, Capalija, Vranesic, & Brown, 2006). These FPGAs have also a finite amount of reconfigurable HW resources, which constrains the size and the number of algorithms that can be HW implemented concurrently. Furthermore, HW implementation assumes the design of a dedicated HW block for each sub-module of the control drive, without further customization possibility, which limits

the design flexibility and requires a lot of silicon space and a long design time.

Modular conception is generally used to reduce design cycle. This methodology is based on partitioning a large or complex design into sub-parts called modules that are more manageable, so that to maximize the reuse of already designed modules (Bensalem, Bozga, Sifakis, & Nguyen, 2008).

Since HW solutions suffer from the lack of flexibility, the reconfigurability and particularly Dynamic Partial Reconfiguration (DPR) offers important benefits for the implementation of designs, in the sense of adding more flexibility to the interesting performance of HW solutions. Using a modular design, we can consider different reconfigurable controllers modules for the electric motor. Then, the commutation between different types of controller (e.g. PID, fuzzy, neuronal) can be done, on the fly, without turning off the motor. So, using a modular design structure allows control designers to work on different control law modules independently, respecting some restrictive clauses.

A second more flexible solution that we have adopted has as objective to switch control system functionalities to SW instead of implementing all of them in HW and to decide which critical functionality should be implemented in HW. The goal of switching to SW is to alleviate the need to design a dedicated HW block for a module, which saves design/verification time and reduces chip area. When using SW platforms, there is less size challenge due to the complexity and number of algorithms, as long as there is enough memory with new available platforms. At the same time, implementing system functionalities in SW allows reuse of already available SW libraries and tasks. This accelerates the development schedule by simplifying the HW porting effort and enhancing product flexibility. Having a motor control FPGA-based platform that is reprogrammable in SW allows for easy tweaking of systems to increase efficiency and flexibility.

The efficient IP integration constitutes the main difficulty from HW perspective while in SW

Figure 2. HW/SW partionning and design flow

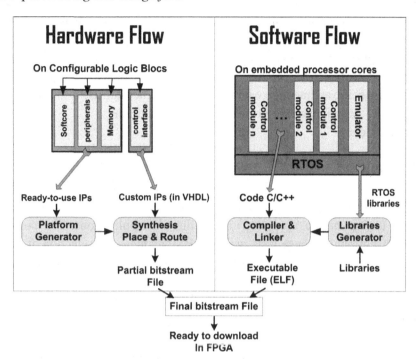

side the issue is the complexity of developing and coding the SW that runs under RTOS, in real HW.

CO-DESIGN APPROACH FOR MOTOR CONTROL

The control system was built using Xilinx Platform Studio (XPS) design SW with EDK Base System Builder toolchain, as illustrated in Figure 2. Taking into account, the EDK support of RTOS and high level languages for RT applications description, the selection of the previous FPGA technology offers a powerful framework for complex control applications definitions. The co-design approach is then based on the reusability of IP cores and RT programmable solution.

In the proposed FPGA-based design, both programmable embedded processor cores and ready-to-use IPs were used in varying combinations so that architecture can be tested for performance and low cost. The design is selectively partitioned into portions suitable for the HW or for SW resources on the FPGA, and the best suitability between the algorithm to implement and the chosen HW architecture is considered. As depicted in Figure 2, peripheral devices, memories, and designed interfaces were implemented in HW using the Configurable Logic Blocks (CLBs) around the embedded processor. They were integrated in the design as configurable ready-to-use IPs and custom IPs. While the closed control loop model, developed in SW, is implemented on top of a RTOS on embedded processors. SW configuration was implemented as Executable and Linking Format (ELF) file. However, HW configuration was implemented by a partial bitstream, a file representation of the CLBs.

This RT programmable solution combines the time predictability and the great flexibility. It could be efficiently exploited for motion control applications to allow an easy modification of the advanced control laws through short-design time. Furthermore, this SoC proposed design allows integrating a full control system in a single chip, avoiding external components. This offers smaller size and fewer suppliers improving both performance and design time and additionally reducing cost and complexity.

Such FPGA-based specific architecture with a high integration density is optimized for performance and energy efficiency.

Emulation Concept

Control system development of electrical drives requires extensive testing before applying in real conditions. Conventionally, these tests are performed on motor drive models built in SW simulation environments (off-line simulation tools) so that simulation and implementation phases are performed on two different platforms. Consequently, in these simulation environments, control code is usually not developed keeping RT execution in mind and the approach is somewhat lengthy due to code adaptation required to move from the simulation platform to the implementation one. So to remain closer to the real physical process, it is proposed to develop code in a rapid control prototyping HW environment, which emulates the real behaviour of the set Converter/ Motor/Sensor (CMS) directly on the same RT control platform. This code, under operating conditions, can reproduce the real physical system functioning in RT and with high precision. It will be similar to that of an actual motor.

This digital system, called emulator (Ben Saoud & Gajski, 2001), represented with a few simple and idealistic embedded equations, will be used for both of the control device validation and of diagnosis. Emulator can also contribute in the post-validation of the embedded control system. Indeed, before using the control device on the physical system, and in order to avoid any design surprise; the control device is validated on the emulation step where it is connected to the emulator. This emulator should behave exactly like the physical system, in sense to make the

control device believe that it is connected to the real CMS system. Thereby, it has to generate and receive information similarly to the physical process. After this opportunity of extensive testing, the control device is completely validated and can be switched for use with the physical process in real conditions.

Software Design

There are two major parts to SW design, configuring the Board Support Project (BSP) and writing the SW applications. The configuration of the BSP includes the selection of device drivers and libraries. For the proposed SW design, the control application was written in C to perform the following computing: motor emulating and motor controlling. It is running on top of an embedded RTOS on the same processor to perform calculations within demanding timing constraints. So, closed control loop Function Blocks (FB) implement the different control drive sub-modules into RTOS tasks of the execution environment. These FBs meets timing constraints like periods and latencies, which can be expressed as deadlines. In RT scheduling, theory priorities are principally applied to control loop periodic activities (Gambier, 2004). Therefore, it is opted to static priority based preemption mechanism. In this static scheduling, each task has a fixed priority which is computed pre-run time. The runnable tasks are executed in the order determined by their priorities. The scheduler should be triggered by a timer generating interrupts at a fixed time interval called the time tick. Hence, the system requires a scheduling interrupt handler routine.

The most important consideration when choosing a RTOS for control applications is reliable performance. So, to find the right RTOS for a control application, many features must be considered such as: control algorithm integration, robust scheduling algorithms, fast context-switch, I/O support, small code footprint, communication, etc. The Xilinx Xilkernel and μC-OS/II are the two RTOS choices that have been adopted; they can be included in the user application's SW platform as a BSP. Most of the routines in the RTOS library are written in C and can be ported to any platform. The Library Generator configures the libraries for a specific embedded processor, using the attributes defined in the Microprocessor Software Specification (MSS) file. As detailed in the SW flow of Figure 2, the user application source files must link with the RTOS library to access its functionality. The image linking the RTOS to the application becomes an ELF file that will be merged with the HW partial bitstream file to generate the final bitstream file that can be downloaded and debugged in the FPGA device.

Both RTOSes have been chosen among various existing RTOSes due to their interesting features detailed in the following.

Xilkernel

Xilkernel (Xilinx, 2006) is highly integrated with the Platform Studio™ framework and is a free SW library that can be got with Xilinx's EDK. It is easy to incorporate into any project using EDK, It is also a small light-weight (16 to 32kb with PPC405) easy to use kernel, and it works on both the MicroBlaze and PowerPC405 (PPC405) processors. This makes it a good candidate for testing purpose, before porting an application to more advanced OS.

The Xilkernel is an efficient multi-threaded OS that supports either simple round-robin scheduling or priority-driven, preemptive scheduling, with time slicing. This makes it perfect for priority based multithreaded RT control.

Xilkernel allows a great degree of customization, so that it is a flexible and modular kernel. It is modular in the sense that only the functions needed in the target system needs to be included, which helps keeping the size of the OS small.

Xilkernel is more a thin library which provides minimalist but essential services than a complete OS, it provides features like scheduling, threads,

interrupts, inter process communication and synchronization with an effectively POSIX subset interface, which is a common standard SW interface between C code and multithreaded RTOS.

μC-OS/II

μC-OS/II RTOS (Labrosse, 2002) is a very popular RTOS that has been widely used in several applications and can be delivered as a pre-certifiable SW component for safety-critical systems, including avionics RTCA DO-178B where failure could result in catastrophic loss of the aircraft, DO-178B Level A Class III medical devices where failure could result in loss of life for the patient, and transportation and nuclear systems standard IEC 61058 (Vargas, Piccoli, Alecrim, Moraes, & Gama, 2006).

μC-OS/II is a highly portable, very scalable, RT multitasking kernel. It is portable since it has been written in ANSI C and contains a small portion of assembly language code to adapt it to different processor architectures. μC-OS/II has been ported to different processor architectures, among them, the PPC405 and Microblaze. In order to achieve timeliness, priority scheduling is supported. μC-OS/II provides low latencies for the kernel services, and preemption is supported in order to perform a time-critical function.

μC-OS/II is a small RT kernel with a small memory footprint of about 20kB for space-constrained embedded designs. It is a good candidate for application specific RTOS configuration, since it can be scaled down in footprint if the application does require fewer features (down to 2Kb of code space) according to (Labrosse, 2002).

μC-OS/II is freeware for academic purpose and very reasonable royalty-free licensing. It is provided with all source code, which is 100% portable ANSI C. Easily scaled because of the modular nature of the source code. It has a well-documented source code that is organized into three segments:

- *Application Specific Code* contains the user specific application SW as well some code related to the µC-OS/II. This includes initializing and starting the kernel as well as using the kernel specific API.
- *Processor-Independent Code* is the main code of the µC-OS/II kernel and is independent of the target processor. It provides the kernel services for task management, time management, interprocess communication and synchronisation, scheduling policy and memory management.
- *Processor-Specific Code* contains an adaptation layer: the port to the selected target processor, which varies with processors. This code typically manipulates directly individual processor registers (e.g for contexts switch).

For the implementation, both first available segments have been used and the last one has been adapted to the FPGA embedded processors.

Hardware Design

Platform: ML-310 Evaluation Board

The development platform consists of Xilinx ML310 board (Xilinx, 2009) with a SoC FPGA. Its Xilinx Virtex-II Pro XC2VP30 FPGA combines more than 30,000 logic cells, and dual IBM PPC405 hardcore processors on a single chip. The large amount of peripherals offers a variety of different interfaces. The Virtex II Pro can be partially and dynamically reconfigured.

The Xilinx EDK 7.1i environment provides the tools and libraries to integrate the PPC405 cores on chip, soft Microblaze cores, IBM Core-Connect buses and customizable peripherals to design Multi-Processor SoC (MPSoC) micro-architectures.

Design Contents

The constructed platforms utilize both hard-coded PPC405 and softcore Microblaze processors (Xilinx, 2009). Both processors offer some unique benefits through circuitry dedicated to interfacing with on-chip peripherals in the FPGA fabric.

The embedded PPC405 core (Xilinx, 2007) is a 32-bit Harvard architecture processor with integrated functional units such as cache unit (separate 16 KB instruction and data L1 caches) and memory management unit. Most instructions execute in a single cycle. It is capable of more than 400mhz clock frequency. Considering that PPC405 has instruction and data cache built into the silicon of the hard processor, so enabling the cache is almost always a performance advantage for the design.

The Microblaze core (Xilinx, 2005) is a 3-stage pipeline 32-bit RISC Harvard architecture with 32 general purpose registers, logic unit, and a rich instruction set optimized for embedded application. There are different processor versions from which to choose: the smaller three-stage Microblaze v4.0 core is ideal for cost-focused applications. On the other hand, the Microblaze cache architecture is different than the PPC405 because the cache memory is not dedicated silicon. The instruction and data cache controllers are selectable parameters in the Microblaze configuration. When these controllers are included, the cache memory is built from Block RAM (BRAM). Therefore, enabling the cache consumes BRAM that could have otherwise been used for local memory.

Both previous Xilinx embedded processors are contained in a processor block. The latest also contains on-chip memory controllers and integration circuitry compatible with IBM core-connect bus architecture that enables the compliant IP cores to integrate with this block. The core-connect architecture provides various buses for interconnection of hard and soft IP cores.

For Microblaze, the Local Memory Bus (LMB) interface is designed to connect rapid components

Figure 3. Reference Design block diagram

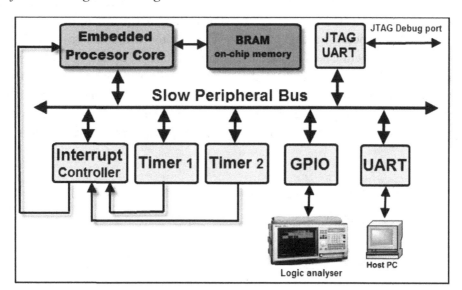

and thus to allow fast memory access. The program (code, data, stack etc.) can be located in both LMB-SRAM and external On-chip Peripheral Bus (OPB) SRAM. But, there is a trade-off: LMB is faster but it has lower capacity. The instruction side LMB provides two-cycles pipelined read access from BRAM for an effective access rate of one instruction per clock. However, instruction fetches on the OPB are slower than fetches from BRAM on the LMB. So, overall processor performance is lower than implementations using LMB. However, to enhance speed performance, the Microblaze can be configured to cache instructions or data over the OPB interface.

For PPC405, the Processor Local Bus (PLB) interface is designed to allow fast memory access. An OPB is also designed to connect slow peripherals and large external memories. The OPB is connected to the PLB through a PLB-to-OPB bridge.

For the designed architectures, the slow peripherals are the following (Figure 3):

- UART interface (RS232 serial channel), used to interface a Hyper Terminal on a host PC.

- General Purpose Input Output (GPIO), used for time execution measurements on logic analyser
- 2 timers: timer1 is used to synchronize the RT scheduling of the RTOS and timer2 is used for applications profiling
- Interrupt controller, used to connect the interrupt output of the timer1 and timer2 to the interrupt input of the processor

Different FPGA HW architectures have been designed, depending on the complexity of the power control case. These FPGA architectures are straightforward, and can be applied to any motor drive application.

In the monoprocessor architectures of Figure 4, the HW design block diagram is based on a single processor connected to ready-to-use IP cores via fast or slow buses. Such monoprocessor architecture is suitable for a simple closed loop motor control implementation. The first architecture of Figure4a outlines a hardcore PPC405 based design. The processor is connected to its own BRAM memory via a fast PLB. While, in the second architecture of Figure4b, the softcore

Microblaze is used. It is connected to its own BRAM memories via a fast LMB.

However, in the dual-processor architecture of Figure 5, a MPSoC architecture has been used for implementation. This HW design is dedicated to a more complex control algorithm. Indeed, the emulator functionality, previously implemented on the same processor used for controllers, should

be ported on a second processor core. The goal of locking a separate processor core to the specific motor emulation task is to obtain more predictability. This allows motor emulator working on RT conditions (with an optimal time period). On the other hand, this configuration aims to reduce the context switch latencies for processor supporting complex controllers. Referring to

Figure 4. Design block diagram for monoprocessor architecture

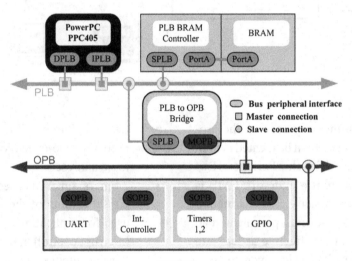

a. PPC405 based.

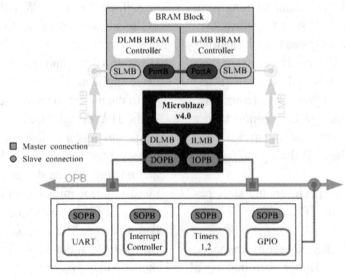

b. Microblaze based.

Figure 5, both PPC405 embedded processors interchange data parameters via a small shared BRAM. Additionally, each processor has its own BRAM to implement its specific portion of code. Such MPSoC configuration allows each processor to integrate its own RTOS, in order to support its allocated SW tasks.

EMBEDDED CONTROL CASE STUDIES

The proposed design methodology has been applied to electric motors drive implementation. The motors drive are used in significant number of industrial applications. Two standard electric motor drives have been used: firstly, a simple case of a DC motor driven by Proportional Integral (PI) controllers. Secondly, a generalization of the first study to a common complex AC machinery

drive consisting of an IM driven by a FOC. This 3 phase AC IM has been the major workhouses in industrial for variable-speed application (Bose, 2007). The aim of this second case experiment is to analyse the capability of SoC in ensuring RT performance for complex and sophisticated algorithms running in SW.

DC-Motor Drive

DC motor control systems are simple control applications commonly used for motion control applications. PI Derivative (PID) control is the most applied control strategy around the world usually for DC Motor. Generally, the PID controller is formulated in the continuous-time domain. Therefore, to implement the controller as a computational algorithm, the controller equations have been discretized. The DC motor control loop, based on two PI controllers and a process

Figure 5. Design block diagram for dual-processor architecture

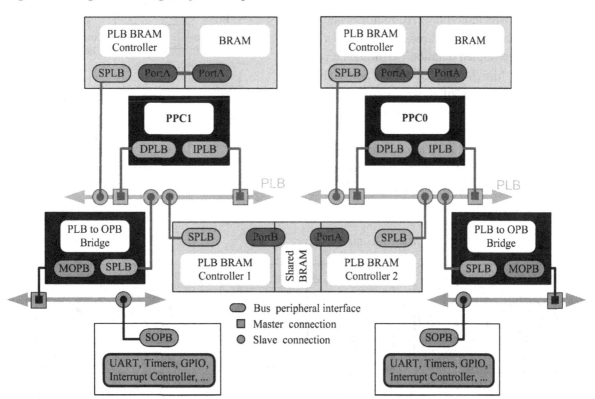

emulator, has been used for this case study. The control loop diagram is illustrated in Figure 6. Both PI controllers tasks have been interfaced with the motor emulator task on a single embedded processor using clearly-defined run-time behaviour on top of a RTOS. The multiple concurrent control tasks communicate amongst themselves using global variables mechanism as shown in Figure 7.

Besides, by providing the high CPU computing power, SoC makes the use of DC machines obsolete in terms of power conversion efficiency and system reliability, when compared with AC machines. So a FOC for AC motor is presented in the next section to highlight the power of the proposed approach.

FOC for Induction Motor

The FOC was introduced along time ago by (Blaschke, 1972) to develop high torque control at very low speed for an IM. It constitutes a fundamental concept behind the modern technology of high-performance vector-controlled drive systems with three-phase AC motors. Many technical papers have appeared in the literature to improve the implementation performance of FOC (Lovati, Marchesoni, Oberti, & Segarich, 1998). The properties of these controllers are well known and have been presented by several authors (Bose, 2007; Novotny & Lorentz, 1985; Trzynadlowski, 1993), they are not the subject matter of this contribution. Instead of that, it is looked at the efficient implementation of this

advanced machine drive algorithm using FPGAs. The micro-electronic revolution of the last years has allowed the well implementation and the efficiently use of this concept.

Figure 8 details the control block diagram of FOC for IM. The key idea of the FOC algorithm

Figure 7. Memory layout for monoprocessor architecture

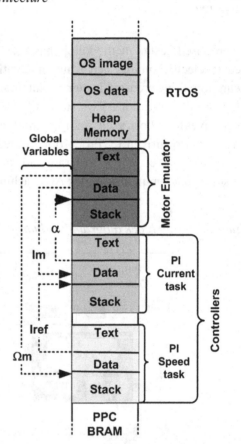

Figure 6. Control loop diagram for DC motor drive

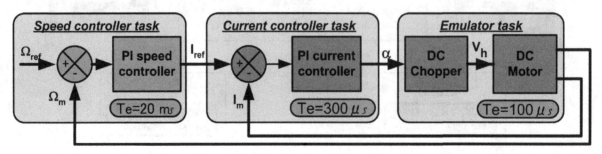

lays in performing basic transformations and rotations on the state variables of the asynchronous machine, in order to control the resulting machine like a separated excited DC machine. So the principle of the FOC method is to transform the equations of the three-phase IM in order to allow a separate control of both flux and torque. It senses 3-phase motor current *is1*, *is2* and *is3* and transforms into two variables, torque current (*Iq*) and flux current (*Id*), so that it simplifies the torque *Ce* control (1).

$$Ce = p \cdot M \left(Isq \cdot Ird - Isd \cdot Irq \right) = \frac{\Phi r}{K} \cdot Isq$$
(1)

Nomenclature

Ce: electromagnetic torque.
p: pole pairs number.
M: mutual inductance.

Isd, Isq: stator flux current, stator torque current.
Ird, Irq: rotor flux current, rotor torque current.
Φr: rotor flux.
K: constant.

Figure 8 depicts that the control device involves a set of FBs. Essentially, it contains two separate current control loops (D-current and Q-current) using PI strategy; the first one is for field current *isd* and the second one is for torque current *isq*. An additional speed controller could be used to produce the torque command Cem_{ref} in order to run the machine at a given speed (the speed set-point Ω_{ref}). It is also based on a slow mode PI regulator.

The Clarke transformation converts the 3-axis coordinates shifted by 120° (*is1, is2, is3*) into orthogonal 2-axis ones (*Ia, Ib*). In a second step, the Park transformation converts the fixed (*Ia, Ib*) coordinates into decoupled two-axis rotating coordinates (*Id, Iq*), which a PI controller can then control. The FOC system uses inverse Park and

Figure 8. Induction motor control using FOC

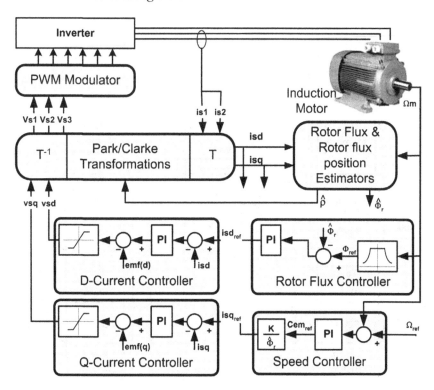

Clark transformation to bring them back into the fixed AC 3-phase frame of the stator windings. Both Park and inverse Park transformations need the rotor flux position ρ which is the core of the FOC, for the reason that if there is an error in this variable, the rotor flux is not aligned with d-axis, and *isd/isq* are incorrect flux/torque components of the stator current.

The control loops consist of several functions: Vector rotator, Park/Clarke transformations, PI, rotor flux and rotor flux position estimators and current and speed sensing. These functions are essential and involve complex mathematical computation (e.g trigonometric functions manipulation, integration, regulation, etc.) that cannot be done on pure analog components, and hence high speed processor is needed. Indeed, the computing power required to efficiently control IM is almost as impressive as the motor itself. The quality of this AC motor drive is directly related not only to the kind of controller structure but also to its imple-

mentation. Therefore, considering the complex general structure of this FOC algorithm, requiring a certain digital power computing, it should be embedded using the dual-processor architecture of Figure 5 to achieve the best speed performance.

Hence, the processor PPC1 runs separately the emulator code in order to track the real functioning of the IM, while the processor PPC0 runs the code of the controller. A RTOS has been used on top of the controller composite, where the controller is treated as one or several SW tasks as shown in Figure 9. The PI currents SW task consists of Clarke/Park transformations, the flux estimator, the rotor flux position computing and all the PI current controllers (torque and flux). For the motor emulator, the IM model has been partitioned in two FBs: electric and mechanic computing. The controller and the emulator, embedded on two different processors, interchange data via a small shared BRAM. SW on a processor can easily update the value of shared variables and

Figure 9. Memories layout for dualprocessor architecture

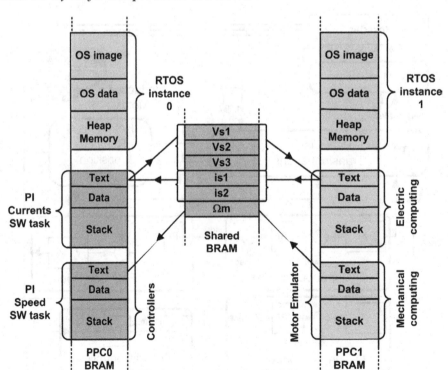

make them visible to the other processor using the variable address or its pointer into the shared memory. Figure 10 details the shared variables declaration in the global variable area of each processor own memory.

EXPERIMENTAL RESULTS

All experimental results were done on the ML310 board, where the Virtex-II Pro FPGA embedded processors were configured to run at 100 Mhz.

RTOS Scheduling Evaluation

These experimental results aim to evaluate scheduling mechanisms in terms of performance and latencies of some kernel services, using both μC-OS/II and Xilkernel RTOSes, to test their responsiveness. Precise time measurements have been carried out with the logic analyser, connected to the GPIO peripheral. The measurements were done using GPIO SW functions with set and reset of the different pins. For average execution time, during a certain testing period, the XTime_GetTime() routine has been used.

Every RTOS has a heart beat, which is configured with a HW interval timer using a RT interrupt clock. The HW timer periodically interrupts the processor to invoke the scheduler as detailed in Figure 11. It allows task control on a timed basis using a tick routine. Experimental results have shown that the best and lowest tick rate for both RTOSes is 100μs.

Testing codes for both μC-OS/II and Xilkernel RTOSes were developed to be as similar as possible to give good comparison values. However, the two kernels operate in such different ways and offer different functionalities, particularly for the task delay. μC-OS/II provides a service that allows the calling task to delay itself for a user specified number of clock ticks. This function is

Figure 10. Shared variable declaration for IM FOC

```
/*Shared Variables partagées*/
    vs1_g = (float *)XPAR_PLB_BRAM_PPC0_SHARED_BASEADDR;
    vs2_g = (float *)XPAR_PLB_BRAM_PPC0_SHARED_BASEADDR+1;
    vs3_g = (float *)XPAR_PLB_BRAM_PPC0_SHARED_BASEADDR+2;
    is2_g = (float *)XPAR_PLB_BRAM_PPC0_SHARED_BASEADDR+3;
    is3_g = (float *)XPAR_PLB_BRAM_PPC0_SHARED_BASEADDR+4;
     Wm_g = (float *)XPAR_PLB_BRAM_PPC0_SHARED_BASEADDR+5;
```

Figure 11. Standard RTOS scheduling process

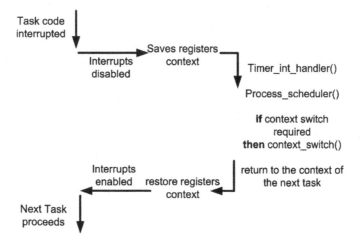

called OStimedelay (). Calling this function causes a context switch and forces μC-OS/II to execute the next highest priority task that is ready to run (Labrosse, 2002). However, Xilkernel uses the Sleep () routine that causes the calling task to enter a sleep state for a specified time, the granularity of this defined time depends on the system timer period. Xilkernel handles the main timer interrupt, using it as the kernel tick to perform scheduling. This same kernel pulse is also used to provide the sleep routine.

These experimental results have been conducted using the simple DC motor control case, implemented on the hardcore PPC405 with cache enabled. The task delay function allows each task, assigned to a certain FB of Figure 6, to be executed under a well defined sampling rate that was added manually. Both μC-OS/II and Xilkernel RTOSes use a fixed-priority scheduling. The 3 tasks should be executed in the order determined by their priorities: For the closed control loop components, the emulator task has the highest priority to be as closer as possible to the physical process and the control system task has a lower priority. Considering that the controller involves two sub-modules with different dynamics: a fast PI current controller and a slow PI speed controller, the current controller task should have a higher priority order compared to the speed controller task. The granularity of the highest priority task (emulator) should be sufficiently small than the time slice duration. Otherwise this active thread remains active for several iterations and consequently does not yield the processor. The RT scheduling of the adopted multitask case study is illustrated in Figure 12 using both RTOSes. Every kernel operates with its own way. As mentioned in the chronograms of Figure 12a, both parameters SCHEDU and ISREXI represent respectively task-level SCHEDUling and Interrupt Service Routine(ISR)-level scheduling which are done respectively by OS_Sched() and OSIntExit() routines of μC-OS/II. The last ISR is used to perform the context switch. However, for Figure 12b the SWITCH parameter represents the

process_scheduler including the context_switch (as explained in the RTOS mechanism between interrupting a task and starting a next task of Figure 11). Figure 12 describes clearly the respect of the defined task sampling rate and the fixed priority preemptive scheduling policy. The runnable tasks are executed in the order determined by their priorities. If no task is running, and all tasks are not in the ready state, the idle task executes. The idle task is always the lowest-priority task and can not be deleted or suspended by user tasks.

Hence, the RTOS allows a good periodic behaviour of the different closed loop FBs within defined sampling period. It introduces more predictability to control system response.

Furthermore, as shown in Table 1, each RTOS presents a different scheduling-context switch time. For μC-OS/II, the spreading time between the tick and the highest priority task ready to run represents only an ISR level scheduling of the tick interrupt handler without context switch. But the time spreading between tasks represents both an ISR level scheduling and a task level scheduling. This is more detailed in both last chronograms (SCHEDU and ISR) of Figure 12a. The table shows also more determinism with μC-OS/II. Indeed, Xilkernel consumes more time for scheduling mechanism than μC-OS/II. Consequently, μC-OS/II presents a more deterministic scheduling policy and it presents the right level of control for our embedded platform. But there is a trade-off since Xilkernel is free and highly integrated with Xilinx EDK.

Computation Time Analysis

Table 2 shows the comparisons of the throughputs for the different closed control loop FBs and their corresponding speedups. Tests were run both with and without cache for PPC405 on PLB. For MicroBlaze (Mblaze) core, tests were run on LMB as processor performance using LMB is faster than implementation using OPB, and the core can be configured to cache instructions only

Figure 12. The RT scheduling of a DC-motor closed control loop

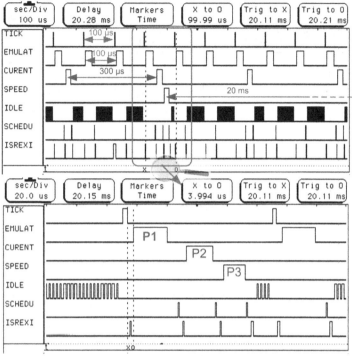

a. µC-OS/II RTOS support.

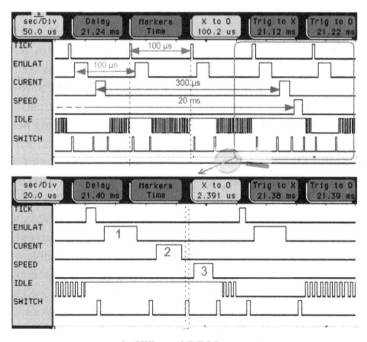

b. Xilkernel RTOS support.

Table 1. RTOS Scheduling Evaluation

RTOS	Spreading Time		
	Between the tick and the highest priority ready task	**Between tasks**	**Tick routine**
UC-OS/II	Best case: 3.2 us Worst case: 4.8 us	Best case: 4.8 us Worst case: 9 us	Average value during 1s execution: 1.7 µs
Xilkernel	Best case: 4.8 us Worst case: 6.4us	Best case: 5.5 us Worst case: 9.5us	Average value during 1s execution: 3.8 µs

Table 2. DC-Motor Case with µC-OS/II RTOS Support

Task	Task Processing Priority	Execution Time		
		On PPC405 PLB Bus cache disabled	**On Mblaze LMB Bus**	**On PPC405 PLB Bus cache enabled**
Emulator	1	~138us	~128us	22 us
PI Current Controller	2	~114us	~88us	16 us
PI Speed Controller	3	~85us	~78us	12-14 us

over the OPB interface. The presented timing results of Table 2 are for DC motor control using monoprocessor architecture, 3 tasks are running on top of µC-OS/II RTOS. Firstly, the speedups comparison highlights the great benefit of using cache in the design based on PPC405 processor. The system goes faster when the cache is enabled on PLB. This confirms the fact that enabling the cache is almost always a performance advantage. Secondly, assuming that Mblaze can not be configured to cache instructions or data over the LMB interface, the timing results confirm that the control drive implementation gives more speed performance on the hardcore PPC405 with cache enabled than on the softcore Mblaze.

Considering that the PPC405 processor with cache enabled gives a good compromise in terms of speed/area as illustrated by Table 2 and 4, the FOC for IM implementation was carried using PPC405 processor cores with cache enabled. The different timing analyses of Figure 13 have been done using µC-OS/II support. Figure 13 confirms that µC-OS/II and Xilkernel are preemptive RTO-

Ses and that they respond to clock tick interrupts right away. Both RTOSes allow the complex FOC algorithm to be partitioned into tasks that operate at different update rates. As illustrated in Figure 13b and c, PI currents controller task run every 700us and PI speed controller task runs every 4 times. But the PI currents controller task could not respect its sampling period of 300us. Its execution time exceeds this fixed period due to the fact that it includes Park/Clarke transformations and trigonometric functions that are computing intensive (Figure 13d). This leads to a relatively higher computing time (about 500us) as shown in Table 3. The table gives the average execution time of each sub-module of the FOC during 2s testing time. The electric computing task consumes about 260us as mentioned in Figure 13, but after several SW optimizations, the time computation has been reduced to 90us. This FOC for IM presents a sophisticated control algorithm that leads to a complex SW coding and consequently some control sub-modules should be switched to HW.

Table 3. Timing Analysis of a FOC for IM Case

		Execution time including intermediate tick routine		
		Xilkernel RTOS support	µC/OS-II RTOS support	
Number of controller tasks		2 tasks	2 tasks	1 task
Tick routine		2.25 us	1.74 us	1.52 us
Motor Emulator FBs	Electric computing (te*=100us)	90 us	90 us	90 us
	Mechanical computing (te*=100us)	6 us	6 us	6 us
Controller FBs	PI Currents (te*=300us)	540 us	520us	548.5 us
	PI Speed (te*=4* te_PIcurrent)	24 us	24 us	

te: the sampling period

Table 4. Device Utilization Summary

Type of processor core based	1 Mblaze	1 PPC405	2 PPC405
Number of occupied Slices	1,704 out of 13,696: **12%**	1,583 out of 13,696: **11%**	3089 out of 13,696: **22%**
Number of used Block RAMs	32 out of 136: **23%**	32 out of 136: **23%**	104 out of 136: **76%**
Total equivalent gate count for design	4,287,966 out of 30,000,000: **14.2%**	2,158,755 out of 30,000,000: **7%**	6,928,698 out of 30,000,000: **23%**

Comparison between Figure 13a and b (in the time shown in X to 0) demonstrates also that separating the control task into two separating tasks with different dynamics gives more speed performance.

Embedded Controllers Validation

These tests have been done to validate the controllers and evaluate the dynamic behaviours of the implemented motor control using the proposed architectures. A PC-based user interface has been used for data acquisition of different control variables. The PC communicates with the test board through the UART serial connection. Using the acquired data, the current (or torque) and speed responses have been plotted.

Firstly, we have focused on the DC motor control case. The behaviours of the feedback speed Ωm and the current Im have been analyzed. Using the monoprocessor PPC405 architecture with cache enabled, the waveforms of Figure 14 have been obtained. A comparative examination has been done between the throughputs of the PI control algorithm running on two different RTOSes, included in the SW design process: the µC-OS/II and the Xilkernel. The waveforms on the top depicts that the rotation speed Ωm is able to follow the speed reference $\Omega mref$ set to 100rad/s, with good dynamics and relatively low error, while the good motor current behaviour can be seen in the waveforms on the below. This is verified for both graphs of the two different RTOSes. Hence, these experimental results validate successfully the DC

Figure 13. Real-time execution of an AC motor FOC

a.
one control task using
µC-OS/II support.

b.
two control tasks using
µC-OS/II support.

c.
two control tasks using
Xilkernel support.

d.
Different sub-modules
of PI currents controller
task using µC-OS/II
support.

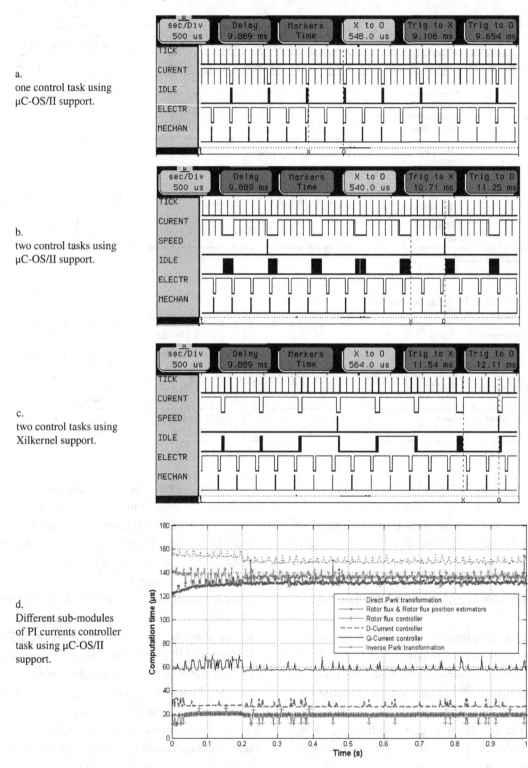

motor drive implementation with the proposed flexible SoC design.

Secondly, we have focused on FOC for IM case. Figure 15 details the graphs of the rotation speed response for IM. For Figure 15a, the algorithm implementation is done on dual PPC405 embedded processors using the SW/HW architecture of Figure 9 with two different RTOS supports (μC-OS/II and Xilkernel). The rotation speed graphs show that the two implementation waveforms reach exactly the speed reference assigned to 100rad/s at 0.2s and modified to -100rad/s at 1s time. The computation time waveforms (for the tick routine, the PI speed and PI currents) highlight clearly the gain with using μC-OS/II in terms of computation speed performance compared to Xilkernel.

For Figure 15b, we have varied the number of controllers and the HW platform, the algorithm implementation is done on a single and a dual processor architecture using PPC405. It is noted from the waveforms that the speed can track any fixed reference with good dynamic behaviour.

Different HW/SW architectures with μC-OS/II support have been used for controllers implementation. On the one hand, two different SW approaches have been analysed: The first one is using a unique control task (a single bloc control algorithm) and the second one is using two separate control tasks with different updating rates, scheduled by μC/OS-II RTOS: one task for PI current controllers with their related computing and the other one for PI speed controller. On the other hand, a dual-processor HW design (Figure 5), using two interconnected PPC405s, has been implemented to separate control algorithm from emulator functionality, the emulator uses a periodic interrupt handler routine whereas, the controllers are managed with μC-OS-II support. Figure 15b confirms that the dual PPC405 architecture gives more speed performance than the single PPC405 architecture. Furthermore, it is noted from graphs that the SW approach using two control tasks with different sampling rates instead of one control task gives a little more performance thanks to the RTOS support. The

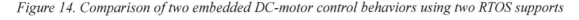

Figure 14. Comparison of two embedded DC-motor control behaviors using two RTOS supports

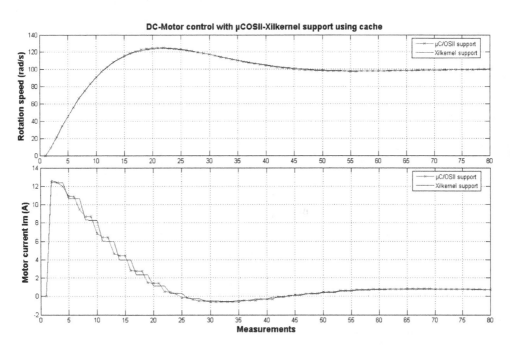

Figure 15. Comparison between different HW-SW design concepts for IM FOC case

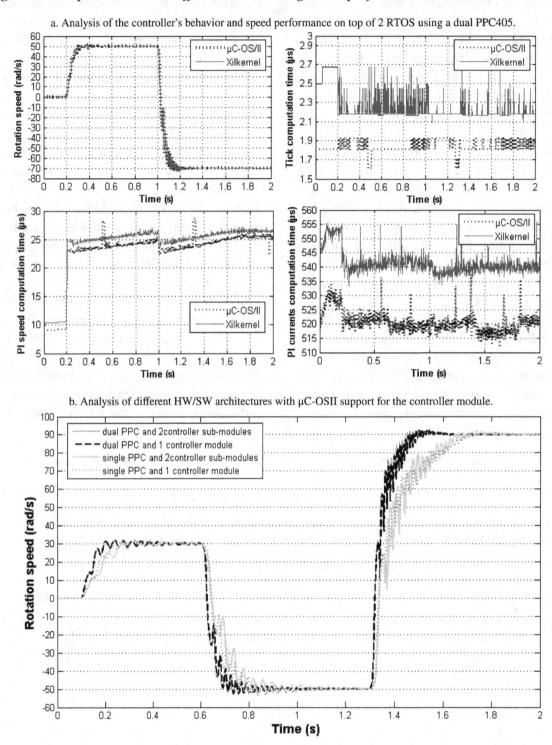

a. Analysis of the controller's behavior and speed performance on top of 2 RTOS using a dual PPC405.

b. Analysis of different HW/SW architectures with µC-OSII support for the controller module.

RTOS plays a major role in tasks scheduling and control loops synchronising and at the same time ensures the system modularity.

Logic Resources Utilization

The EDK synthesis report gives the following design summary exposed in Table 4. Systems were designed with only the required components, using the Virtex-II Pro FPGA XC2VP30,

It is noted from the total equivalent gate count summary that the design based on a single Mblaze consumes more logic area resources (14%) than the one using a single PPC405 (7%). This is to be expected, as the Mblaze softcore is built from logic units and it uses about 6% of total occupied slices which reduces the available area for logic. While the PPC405 hardcore is part of the FPGA fabric with no resource usage. Therefore, for the HW design of control drive, the use of PPC405 with cache enabled presents better performance than using Mblaze processor, assuming that the PPC405 cache unit is built into the silicon of the hard processor. It is also interesting to note that the overall HW summary shows a low HW costs for such an implementation (about 23% of total gate count in the worst case of a dual-processor

design). Assuming that there are available resources on the FPGA, it is still better to map time-critical tasks (such as Park transformations) onto the FPGA logic.

Furthermore, 64kb of BRAM size is used for all instruction and data storage for DC motor case using monoprocessor architecture and 192kb of BRAM size and 16kb of shared memory BRAM size are used for IM case applying the dual processor architecture. This has consequently increased the number of used BRAMs (about 75% of the total number for the 2 PPC405s architecture).

Figure 16 gives the design summary of the different components used in the monoprocessor HW architecture. It shows clearly the high cost in terms of slices for a HW timer component insertion. Therefore, when comparing our approach implementing different control drive sub-modules into RTOS tasks with another approach using periodic interrupts to handle the controller sub-modules (Ben Othman, Ben Salem, & Ben Saoud, 2008), we deduce that our approach using RTOS support presents a more flexible solution with a lower cost. Indeed, the periodic interrupts approach assumes that an interrupt handler routine and a HW Timer must be assigned for every control FB. If the control algorithm will be partitioned in

Figure 16. Device utilization summary for single PPC architecture

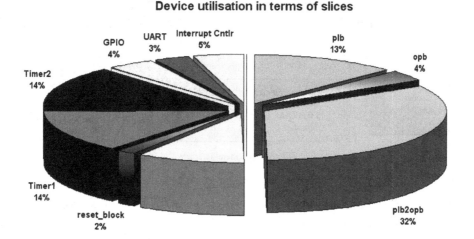

different FBs, they will need many HW Timers that will increase FPGA area cost. While the first approach needs only a unique HW timer for the RTOS tick routine.

FUTURE TRENDS

The designed architecture flexibility shortens design cycle time and allows for easy feature enhancements and customizations. Besides, it has been concluded from the previous execution time analysis of the closed control loop, in the FOC for IM, that control speed sensitive tasks such as PI current controllers require a relatively long execution time. So they should be fully or partially implemented in HW using logic cells to respond to new high sampling frequencies. Calculations that would normally consume large amounts of CPU time when implemented in SW may be HW accelerated. Since, all operations in FPGAs logic cells are in parallel, the controller's FBs can be

executed very fast and a high sampling rate can be sent for the controller. Such improvement can be performed, in the proposed flexible platform, by replacing speed sensitive SW computing with custom HW IP cores, connected to the PLB interface as shown in Figure 17. Xilinx FPGA gives a high bandwidth data transfer mechanism via the PLB of the PPC405 core. In the same direction, additional control application-specific interfaces such as Pulse Width Modulation (PWM), encoder, etc, can also be added as HW IP without major adapting. Applying the High-Level Synthesis (HLS) technique, the VHDL code of these HW IPs can be generated automatically from C code. The HLS technique consists of the conversion of an algorithm written in a high level language to practical and ready to implement circuit description in a HW language like VHDL (Coussy & Morawiec, 2008). Some emerging specialized HLS tools could be used such as Catapult C or Co-Developer tools (Ben Achballah, Ben Othman, & Ben Saoud, 2010).

Figure 17. Design block diagram for dual-processor architecture including custom HW IP

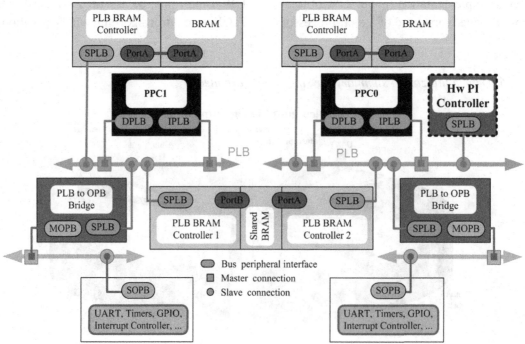

A second future work purpose is to implement a Reconfigurable SoC (RSoC) that will switch between various controllers applying different control laws, dedicated for electric machine control. A self reconfiguration will be performed in the system itself, so that the system is fully autonomous. For Virtex-II FPGA device, this self-reconfiguration is done through the Internal Configuration Port Access (ICAP) ready-to-use IP. Self-reconfiguration can be applied by simply giving a partial bitstream to the ICAP interface. In this case, the controller should be designed as a HW IP connected to the processor to simplify the reconfigurabiliy process. In this future work,

the RSoC will be based on the dual processor architecture of Figure 17. But, we should develop two HW controllers for the motor: a PI and Fuzzy one (Abdelkrim & Ben Saoud, 2008). The DPR consists in the successive execution of these two control laws on the same device. So, we will start the motor with HW fuzzy controller then, using the ICAP, the processor downloads automatically the partial bitstream of the HW PI. Both PI and fuzzy controllers reconfigurable modules have to be merged in one FPGA design using DPR flow (Figure 18). Each module represents a physical bounded part of the FPGA and communication between modules must be done through

Figure 18. Partial Reconfiguration Flow

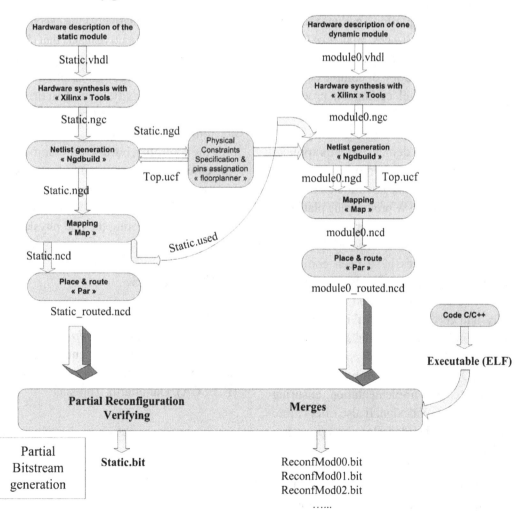

bus macro (Gregory, 2004). The dual processor architecture design needs to be prepared on EDK environment, and then it will be exported to ISE Xilinx tool (Xilinx, 2009) in order to prepare the partial bitstream of the whole design. The static module of Figure 18 is the exported design from EDK, describing the target board devices, while the reconfigurable modules are HW controllers (PI and fuzzy). Each module has to be described in a separate project.

CONCLUSION

This chapter suggests the use of advanced FPGA technology integrating embedded processor cores as Hw development platform for embedded control systems. The presented platform gathers the flexibility of SW and the high-performance of HW as shown in our results. The design methodology is based on the implementation of complex control algorithms, in high-level coding on processor cores. This flexible methodology supports the integration of ready-to-use IPs and RTOS, into a well-behaved system. It demonstrates its application to two electrical motor control case studies.

In this chapter, it is discussed the choice and use of the suitable HW-SW prototyping platform, for the design of RT SoC motor drive. Consequently, different processors core-based HW-SW architectures capabilities have been compared and contrasted. The selected architectures were successfully tested and validated, to show the feasibility and the efficiency of implementing embedded motor control on SoPC.

It has been described successfully that the use of a RTOS in handling embedded control tasks accelerates SW implementation, ensuring modularity for the SW design. It also offers more determinism for embedded closed loop control system. The simple case study of DC motor PI control implementation has shown the performance of the hardcore processor with cache enabled for handling embedded control system without

increasing cost. Using the same hardcore, the FOC for IM case study highlights the capacity of the proposed approach in producing a low cost solution for advanced 3-phase IM drive system, involving complex computing, with good precision.

The proposed design approach can be readily applied to any embedded electric drive. Indeed the FPGA-based development brings the possibility to add more stringent control strategy with a short development time. The designed control system is able to support both HW and SW customization, thanks to the HW reconfigurable feature and the modularity of the SW application that allows inserting additional interfaces and controllers as SW tasks or HW custom IPs. So that, this flexible design enable system re-use with various applications.

In spite of the relatively long execution time for some SW speed sensitive tasks, that should rather be implemented in HW, the SoPC FPGA-based flexible controllers are a good solution to deal with increasing complexity of modern drive systems.

Moreover, the interaction between validation and implementation phases, by implementing not only the controller, but also the controlled process (the emulator), are required to fine tune the controller. It allows detecting problems early in the development cycle and to correct them progressively before affecting the real physical process.

REFERENCES

Abdelkrim, H., & Ben Saoud, S. (2008, May). *Reconfigurable system On Chip (RSOC): Concepts & Applications*. Paper presented at the Int. Conf. on Embedded Systems & Critical Applications (ICESCA), Gammarth, Tunisia.

Aguirre, M. A., Tombs, J. N., Lecuyer, V. B., Mora, J. L., Carrasco, J. M., & Torralba, A. B. (2005). Microprocessor and FPGA interfaces for in-system co-debugging in field programmable hybrid systems. *Microprocessors and Microsystems, 29*(2-3), 75–85. doi:10.1016/j.micpro.2004.06.009

Astarloa, A., Lázaro, J., Bidarte, U., Jiménez, J., & Zuloaga, A. (2009). FPGA technology for multi-axis control systems. *Mechatronics, 19*(2), 258–268. doi:10.1016/j.mechatronics.2008.09.001

Ben Achballah, A., Ben Othman, S., & Ben Saoud, S. (2010, Mar.). *High Level Synthesis of Real Time embedded emulating system for motor controller.* Paper presented at the 5th Int. Conf. on Design & Technology of Integrated Systems in Nanoscale Era (DTIS), Hammamet, Tunisia.

Ben Othman, S., Ben Salem, A. K., & Ben Saoud, S. (2008, Mar.). *MPSoC Design of RT Control Applications based on FPGA SoftCore Processors.* Paper presented at the ICECS, Saint Julians, Malte.

Ben Salem, A. K., Ben Othman, S., & Ben Saoud, S. (2008, Jun.). *Hard and Soft-Core Implementation of Embedded Control Application Using RTOS.* Paper presented at the IEEE Int. Symposium on Industrial Electronics (ISIE), Cambridge, UK.

Ben Saoud, S., & Gajski, D. D. (2001). *Co-design of Emulators for Power electric Processes Using SpecC Methodology.* Technical Report ICS-TR, 01-46.

Bensalem, S., Bozga, M., Sifakis, J., & Nguyen, T. H. (2008). *Compositional verification for component-based systems and application.* Paper presented at the 6th Int. Symposium on Automated Technology for Verification and Analysis, ATVA.

Bhoot, J., & Takahashi, T. (2003, Summer 2003). Platform Delivers Fast, Flexible AC Servomotor-Control Designs. *Xcell Journal.*

Blaschke, F. (1972). The principle of field orientation as applied to the new transvektor closed-loop control system for rotating-field machines. *Siemens Review, 34*(5), 217–220.

Bose, B. K. (2007). *Modern Power Electronics and AC Drives.* Prentice Hall.

Bueno, E. J., Hernandez, Ã., Rodriguez, F. J., Giron, C., Mateos, R., & Cobreces, S. (2009). A DSP- and FPGA-Based Industrial Control With High-Speed Communication Interfaces for Grid Converters Applied to Distributed Power Generation Systems. *IEEE Transactions on Industrial Electronics, 56*(3), 654–669. doi:10.1109/TIE.2008.2007043

Buttazzo, G. C. (2005). Hard Real Time Computing Systems: Predictable Scheduling Algorithms and Applications. *Real-Time Systems, Springer, 23*(2).

Calderon, D. R. H., & Vassiliadis, S. (2005, Nov. 2005). *Soft core processors and embedded processing: a survey and analysis.* Paper presented at the ProRisc, Veldhoven, the Netherlands.

Cecati, C. (1999). Microprocessors for power electronics and electrical drives applications. *IEEE Industrial Electronics Society Newsletter, 46*(3), 5–9.

Coussy, P., & Morawiec, A. (2008). *High-Level Synthesis: From Algorithm to Digital Circuit.*

Crespo, A., Ripoll, I., Gonzalez-Harbour, M., & Lipari, G. (2008). Operating System Support for Embedded Real-Time Applications. *EURASIP Journal on Embedded Systems, 2.*

Dubey, R., Agarwal, P., & Vasantha, M. K. (2007). Programmable logic devices for motion control-a review. *IEEE Transactions on Industrial Electronics, 54*(1), 559–566. doi:10.1109/TIE.2006.885452

Dyer, M., Plessl, C., & Platzner, M. (2002). *Partially reconfigurable cores for xilinx virtex. In: Proceedings of the Reconfigurable Computing Is Going Mainstream*. Paper presented at the 12th Int. Conf. on Field-Programmable Logic and Applications, Montpellier, France.

Engel, F., Kuz, I., Petters, S. M., & Ruocco, S. (2004, Dec.). *Operating Systems on SoCs: A good idea*. Paper presented at the Embedded Real-Time Systems Implementation (ERTSI) Workshop, Lisbon, Portugal.

Eshraghian, K. (2006). SoC Emerging Technologies. *IEEE JPROC, 94*(6), 1197–1213. doi:10.1109/JPROC.2006.873615

Fletcher, B. H. (2005). *FPGA Embedded Processors, Revealing True System Performance*. Paper presented at the Embedded Systems Conference San Francisco, USA.

Fort, B., Capalija, D., Vranesic, Z. G., & Brown, S. D. (2006, Oct.). *A Multithreaded Soft Processor for SoPC Area Reduction*. Paper presented at the IEEE Symposium on Field-Programmable Custom Computing Machines (FCCM), Napa, CA.

Fratta, A., Griffero, G., & Nieddu, S. (2004, Nov.). *Comparative analysis among DSP and FPGA-based control capabilities in PWM power converters*. Paper presented at the IEEE IECON, Busan, Korea.

Gambier, A. (2004, Jul.). *Real-Time Control Systems: A Tutorial*. Paper presented at the 5th Asian Control Conference, Melbourne, Australia.

Götz, M., Rettberg, A., Pereira, C. E., & Rammig, F. J. (2009). Run-time reconfigurable RTOS for reconfigurable systems-on-chip. *Journal of Embedded Computing, 3*(1), 39–51.

Gregory, M. (2004, Nov.). *A module-based dynamic partial reconfiguration tutorial*. Paper presented at the Logic Systems Laboratory, EPFL.

Idkhajine, L., Monmasson, E., Naouar, M. W., Prata, A., & Bouallaga, K. (2009). Fully Integrated FPGA-Based Controller for Synchronous Motor Drive. *IEEE Transactions on Industrial Electronics, 56*(10), 4006–4017. doi:10.1109/TIE.2009.2021591

Jóźwiak, L., Nedjah, N., & Figueroa, M. (2010). Modern development methods and tools for embedded reconfigurable systems: A survey. *Integration, the VLSI Journal, 43*(1), 1-33.

Kariyappa, B. S., & Uttara Kumari, M. (2008). FPGA Based Speed Control of AC Servomotor Using Sinusoidal PWM. *Int. J. Computer Science and Network Security, 8*(10), 346–350.

Kiel, E., & Lenze, A. (2002, May). *Control electronics in drive systems micro controller, DSPs, FPGAs, ASICs from state-of-art to future trends*. Paper presented at the PCIM Conf, Nuremberg, Germany.

Kung, Y.-S., Fung, R.-F., & Tai, T.-Y. (2009). Realization of a Motion Control IC for $X\{-\}Y$ Table Based on Novel FPGA Technology. *IEEE Transactions on Industrial Electronics, 56*(1), 43–53. doi:10.1109/TIE.2008.2005667

Labrosse, J. J. (2002). *MicroC/OS-II: The Real-Time Kernel* (2nd Edn ed.): CMP Books.

Lovati, V., Marchesoni, M., Oberti, M., & Segarich, P. (1998). A Microcontroller-Based Sensorless Stator Flux-Oriented Asynchronous Motor Drive for Traction Applications. *IEEE Transactions on Power Electronics, 13*(4), 777–785. doi:10.1109/63.704156

Martin, P., Bueno, E., Rodriguez, F. J., & Saez, V. (2009, Nov.). *A Methodology for Optimizing the FPGA Implementation of Industrial Control Systems*. Paper presented at the IEEE IECON, Porto, Portugal.

Monmasson, E., & Chapuis, Y. A. (2002). Contributions of FPGA's to the control of electrical systems—A Review. *IEEE Industrial Electronics SoC Newsletter, 49*(4), 8–15.

Monmasson, E., & Cirstea, M. N. (2007). FPGA Design Methodology for Industrial Control Systems—A Review. *IEEE Transactions on Industrial Electronics, 54*(4), 1824–1842. doi:10.1109/TIE.2007.898281

Novotny, D. W., & Lorentz, R. D. (1985). *Introduction to Field Orientation and High Performance AC drives*. Paper presented at the Tutorial Course of the IEEE Industry Applications Society, Toronto, Canada.

Nurmi, J. (2007). *Processor Design, System-On-Chip computing for ASICS and FPGAs*. Berlin: Springer.

Rodríguez-Andina, J. J., Moure, M. J., & Valdes, M. D. (2007). Features, Design Tools, and Application Domains of FPGAs. *IEEE Transactions on Industrial Electronics, 54*(4), 1810–1823. doi:10.1109/TIE.2007.898279

Schulz, B., Paiz, C., Hagemeyer, J., Mathapati, S., Porrmann, M., & Bocker, J. (2007). *Run-time reconfiguration of FPGA-based drive controllers*. Paper presented at the 12th European Conf. on Power Electronics and Applications (EPE).

Simard, S., Mailloux, J. G., & Beguenane, R. (2009). Prototyping Advanced Control Systems on FPGA. *EURASIP Journal on Embedded Systems, 2009*.

Singh, B., Singh, B. P., & Dwivedi, S. (2006, July). *DSP Based Implementation of Hybrid Speed Controller for Vector Controlled Permanent Magnet Synchronous Motor Drive*. Paper presented at the IEEE Symp. on Industrial Electronics, Montreal, QC, Canada

Theelen, B. D., Verschueren, A. C., Reyes Suarez, V. V., Stevens, M. P. J., & Nunez, A. A. (2003). scalable single-chip multi-processor architecture with on-chip RTOS kernel. *Journal of Systems Architecture, 49*(12-15), 619–639. doi:10.1016/S1383-7621(03)00101-2

Trzynadlowski, A. M. (1993). *The Field Orientation Principle in Control of Induction Motors* (1st ed.). Berlin: Springer.

Vargas, F., Piccoli, L. B., Alecrim, A., Moraes, M., & Gama, M. (2006, Dec. 2006). *Summarizing a Time-Sensitive Control-Flow Checking Monitoring for Multitask SoCs*. Paper presented at the IEEE Int. Conf. Field Programmable Technology FPT, Bankok, India.

Vega-Rodríguez, A. M., Sánchez-Pérez, J. M., & Gómez-Pulido, J. A. (2005). Advances in FPGA tools and techniques. *Microprocessors and Microsystems, 29*(2-3), 47–49. doi:10.1016/j.micpro.2004.06.003

Wolf, W. (1993). *FPGA-Based System Design*. Upper Saddle River, NJ: Prentice-Hall.

Xilinx. (2005). *MicroBlaze Processor Reference Guide. UG081 (v5.1)*

Xilinx. (2006). *Xilkernel_V3_00_a, EDK 9.1i*.

Xilinx. (2007). *PowerPC Processor Reference Guide. UG011 (v1.2)*.

Xilinx. (2009). Retrieved Dec. 2009, from http://www.xilinx.com

Yang, G., Liu, Y., Cui, N., & Zhao, P. (2006, May 2006). *Design and implementation of a fpga-based ac servo system*. Paper presented at the 6th World Congress on Intelligent Control and Automation (WCICA)

Zhou, P., Xie, J., & Wang, L. (2005, Nov.). *Co-Design Of Embedded Real-Time Control Systems: A Feedback Scheduling Approach.* Paper presented at the Joint International Computer Conference (JICC), Chonqing, China.

KEY TERMS AND DEFINITIONS

Embedded Controller: it is simply a device that performs embedded control electric drive

SoPC: System on Programmable Chip describes any system implemented using a programmable logic device which contains a computation engine

Co-Design: two perspectives of hardware and software design are brought into a co-design process

RTOS: Real Time Operating System

Hardcore: hardware processor core

Softcore: software processor core

Chapter 19
A Model–Based Approach to Configure and Reconfigure Avionics Systems

Julien Delange
TELECOM ParisTech, France

Laurent Pautet
TELECOM ParisTech, France

Fabrice Kordon
Université P. & M. Curie, France

ABSTRACT

Aircraft manufacturers have been moving toward the Integrated Modular Avionics (IMA) approach to reduce the number of dedicated boxes in the aircraft. Standards such as as DO178B or ARINC 653 must be followed during design, configuration or certification of IMA systems. Productivity and costs must also be improved while preserving conformance to standards. For instance, development process of avionics systems involves several system representations and representation transformations are done manually. Moreover, the complexity of new generation of safety-critical systems has also increased the complexity of their development. The authors present their component-based approach which relies on an appropriate modeling language (AADL) combined with modeling patterns to represent, configure and deploy an IMA system. It reduces costs by detecting errors earlier and prevents specifications revisions. Their code generator reduces memory footprint and improves code coverage. One last benefit is a possible automatic certification.

INTRODUCTION

Historically, aircrafts have been designed and built using a federated design approach, where functions are isolated from others by confining them into dedicated boxes. However, in a recent past, aircraft manufacturers have been moving toward the Integrated Modular Avionics (IMA)

DOI: 10.4018/978-1-60960-086-0.ch019

approach with multiple functions running on a single processing unit.

A typical avionics system architecture is designed as a federated architecture of dedicated boxes. Each box can be a hardware/software configuration totally different to the others. The applications are physically protected from one another in such a way that failures of one or more applications do not affect others. However, such architectures are expensive to build in terms of space, weight, and power requirements. Moreover, adding new functions means adding new boxes. Thus, modifications and improvements usually convey serious drawbacks in terms of maintenance and operating costs.

To overcome those disadvantages, a new avionics architecture model, known as Integrated Modular Avionics (IMA), has been developed. IMA helps to reduce the number of dedicated boxes in the aircraft to a single computing platform running multiple applications. This approach reduces the space, weight, and power requirements of the aircraft, reduces spares holding, and therefore reduces complexity, costs, time, etc. In this environment, application code can be separated and tested independently, with the benefit of reducing the overall cost of software certification while maintaining safety requirements.

One of the major goals of the IMA approach is to enforce system configuration and incremental integration of new functionalities into a pre-existing system. Moreover, in order to exhibit fault tolerance in presence of errors giving any operational scenario, fault detection and health monitoring become a central point in IMA systems. Such systems must be reconfigurable to remain operational when a system component fails.

In order to provide an effective IMA system, standards have to be followed to allow for methodical development, validation and testing, as well as providing a standards-based Application Programming Interface (API) to allow for software portability and modularity. The ARINC 653 specification (Aeronautical Radio, Inc. 1997) is now a de-facto standard in Avionics. It provides a framework for building an operating system environment to support IMA. It specifies behavioral aspects such as scheduling and communications, as well as programming aspects such as an API set to call ARINC 653 methods.

However, it is currently hard to configure an IMA system. These safety-critical systems embed more and more functionalities year after year so that complexity of their development increases especially for design, configuration or certification. Due to their criticality, they must be carefully designed and comply against restrictive standards. For instance, adding new functions means reconfiguring the ARINC653 operating system environment so that both resource requirements and availability as well as integrity requirements are satisfied. It also means this new configuration has to be qualified and certified with regards to avionic software guidance documents (such as DO178B). This emerging complexity shows the need for a development and configuration process has to be defined to assist designers, developers or engineers and build the new generation of safety-critical systems.

To address these issues and ensure configuration correctness, requirements must be verified at the earliest stages of the development process to avoid errors traditionally detected during tests, integration or production. To do so, configuration is validated and its corresponding implementation code is automatically generated instead of being manually written by developers. This also avoids all errors introduced by "traditional" methods. In addition, generating configuration from validated artifacts eases their certification against standards (such as DO178B), and reduces their associated costs.

For that purpose, we design a dedicated process that automatically validates avionics system configuration, generates its code, builds the system and checks its requirements enforcement during its execution.

This chapter presents an approach for the specification, automatic generation and configuration of avionic systems. This innovative process uses a common modeling language as a backbone for each aspect of system development and thus, removes the use of different representation of the same system/requirements.

In the next sections, we first depict how to design a safety-critical architecture for avionics systems and, more specifically, we describe the ARINC653 standard. This highlights difficult issues in terms of development and configuration as this process based on different representations is manually conducted in most industrial projects. After presenting some related works, we describe our process based on a model-driven approach. We focus on the specification, automatic generation and configuration phases of our method. We first use a common modeling language (AADL) as a backbone for each aspect of system development. Then, we automatically generate the system configuration as well as the integration code (non function-specific code). We finally explain how to configure the whole system to validate the conformity to the initial requirements at design or execution time. Through these last sections, we illustrate our method with an example of an ARINC653 system architecture. We conclude and give some of our current research works.

CONTEXT

Avionics systems and more generally safety-critical systems embed more and more functionalities year after year so that complexity of their development increases especially for design, configuration or certification. To overcome the costs to build aircrafts in terms of space, weight, and power, a new avionics architecture model, known as Integrated Modular Avionics (IMA), has been developed. IMA federates multiple applications on a single computing platform. The ARINC 653 specification provides a framework

for building an operating system environment to support IMA. IMA environment and application software are not physically but logically isolated within the system. Logical interactions between applications and the IMA environment are also clearly identified.

This section gives an overview of the ARINC653 standard that are required to introduce the context of our work.

ARINC653 is a standard defining operating system services to support avionics software. ARINC653 operating systems isolate software applications into partitions and avoid errors propagation across partitions. Partitions are configured and executed as if they were running on an independent processor so that a partition at a given criticality level cannot impact partitions that run at a different criticality level.

ARINC653 Isolation Principles

ARINC653 partitions are isolated in terms of space and time.

Space isolation means that each partition has an exclusive access to a memory segment. One partition cannot read/write data from/to other partition memory segment to preserve data integrity and confidentiality.

Time isolation means that the system schedules partitions periodically. During their execution, partitions manage their resources and schedule their tasks.

ARINC653 operating systems use a hierarchical scheduler with two levels:

1. The first one corresponds to partitions scheduling. Partitions are activated with a fixed cyclic scheduler that repeats a preconfigured execution schema at a given rate (called the major time frame).
2. Second scheduling level deals with processes inside a partition. Partitions execute their processes by their own scheduling policy (Rate

Monotonic Scheduling, Earliest Deadline First, Round Robin, etc.).

ARINC653 Hierarchical Model

The ARINC653 hierarchical architecture defines three levels (or layers):

1. The **module layer** is composed of the partition manager that executes partitions and ensures time and space isolation enforcement. From a low-level point of view, it corresponds to a kernel that handles memory segments and executes partitions according to scheduling time slots. It is responsible to configure partitions execution time slots and allocate partitions memory.
2. The **partition layer** is composed of processes and resources for software execution. This layer has its own runtime for resources management (locking of shared variables, etc.).
3. The **process layer** is composed by a preemptive execution flow constrained by properties (period, deadline, priority, etc.). ARINC653 processes concept is similar to the task concept of actual real-time operating systems.

Communication Mechanisms

To exchange data across processes, ARINC653 defines the following mechanisms:

1. **Inter-partition communication** enables data exchanges between processes located in different partitions so that one partition can communicate with another. Only allowed partitions can exchange data: ARINC653 modules supervise communication to authorize or deny a communication channel.
2. **Intra-partition communication** defines communication and synchronization mechanisms between processes located in the same partition. In that case, partitions manage the resources required for these communications.

Inter-Partition Communication Mechanisms

ARINC653 defines two inter-partition mechanisms:

1. **Queuing ports** store every new instance of a data according to a preconfigured queuing policy. A sender process that sends data through queuing ports waits until queue is full. Similarly, receiver processes wait for new data when queue is empty.
2. **Sampling ports** store only latest data and act as a shared buffer: every new instance of a data replaces the old one. A freshness attribute is specified to specify data arrival rate.

Intra-Partition Communication Mechanisms

ARINC653 defines four intra-partition services:

1. **Buffers** are like queuing ports for intra-partition communication. As queuing ports, data instance are queued and sender/receiver waits when queue is full/empty.
2. **Blackboards** are similar to sampling ports but for intra-partition communications. Only latest received value is kept. A data freshness attribute also specify data arrival interval.
3. **Events** synchronize processes. It is a lightweight synchronization service, similar to mutex and barrier mechanisms available in UNIX systems. Processes wait or receive events, meaning that something happened in the partition. Receiver processes wait until a sender process sends the event.
4. **Semaphores** synchronize process with the counting semaphores mechanism. Compared to events, they provide enhanced synchro-

Figure 1. ARINC653 architecture example

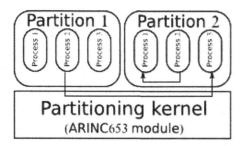

Figure 2. Scheduling example of an ARINC653 system

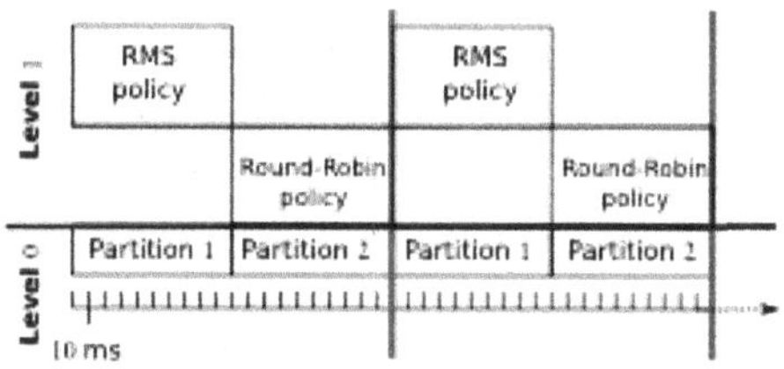

nization mechanisms since blocked tasks can be queued according to a preconfigured queuing policy (by priority, etc.).

Health Monitoring

ARINC653 defines a health monitoring service to identify and recover faults. It proposes mechanisms to identify faults and at each level of the hierarchical architecture (module, partition or process). When a layer detects a raised fault, it executes a preconfigured recovery procedure. It can report the error to the upper layer, which will be responsible to recover the new fault occurrence.

Error recovering strategy is statically configured in system specifications. For each error, the system designs assign a recovery procedure for its recovery.

Finally, ARINC653 proposes predefined errors types and recovery functions. However, each operating system vendor can redefine and extend them.

Illustration of ARINC653 Architecture

Figure 1 depicts an ARINC653 architecture with two partitions. illustrates the scheduling of this sample architecture. This example defines two partitions that run on top of an ARINC653 module. Each partition executes three processes. Process 2 of partition 1 and process 3 of partition 2 communicate through an inter-partition channel. First

and second processes of partition 2 exchange data using an intra-partition channel.

This example assumes that partitions have a 100ms time slice and a 200ms major time frame. Partition 1 schedules its processes using the RMS scheduling policy whereas partition 2 uses the Round-Robin scheduling policy. Figure 2 depicts the corresponding scheduling diagram that highlights the hierarchical scheduling: level 0 schedules partitions whereas level 1 schedules processes.

Summary

The ARINC653 architecture has strong requirements (in terms of isolation, fault containment, etc.). Mistakes in their specification or implementation could lead to critical errors in terms of safety and security. In consequence, they must be carefully specified, verified and configured.

The IMA concept permits much greater flexibility, as the system is able to fulfill different roles thanks to reconfiguration, as well as improving reliability and availability. However, if certification is difficult even in federated systems, it is even harder to demonstrate system safety on IMA due to the huge number of permutations of configurations. In order to deal with this complexity, we have to enrich the development process to assist designers, developers or engineers and build the new generation of safety-critical systems. The next section describes current problems with the development of ARINC653 systems and discusses

Figure 3. Traditional development process for safety-critical systems

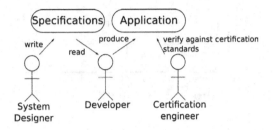

model-based approaches that would help addressing these issues.

PROBLEMS

ARINC653 systems have strong requirements that must be carefully designed and verified during their production.

Development Process

Development of avionics systems involves several engineers, each one being responsible of a particular role, as illustrated in Figure 3:

1. **System designers** write system configuration requirements. The configuration requirements include the configuration of partitions in terms of space and time isolation, the configuration of the partitions scheduling, the configuration of inter-partitions communications and so on. Each partition has also to be configured in terms of resource usage. For instance, the buffers needed for intra-partition communication have to be dimensioned. All these configurations are usually described in a text document.
2. **Developers** translate these requirements into configuration code. From the previous text document, developers configure manually the ARINC653 module taking into ac-

count the specificities of the final executive platform like input/output latencies. This configuration is much more detailed than the previous one as it takes into account data representation, code integration,... For instance, when the system configuration specifies the number of elements in a queue, this configuration requires specifying its size in terms of bytes.
3. **Certification engineers** review developers' code and designers' specifications to certify produced applications against a standard such as DO178B. Note that the conformance to the initial requirements is not a nice-to-have feature as a failure in the certification process prevents the aircraft from being authorized to fly.

This process is separated into loosely coupled steps and faces the following problems:

1. **Consistency and correctness**. Each role has its own system representation, which requires translation efforts (specification to code, tests, etc).
2. **Manual process**. Each step of the process is manually driven and can introduce potential errors.
3. **Costs**. Errors are detected in the later steps of the process and lead huge revision costs. An early validation process would help to detect problems. For instance, a schedulability analysis can be performed to roughly check that the system is not already overloaded.

System Complexity

These issues become particularly important since safety-critical systems functions increases significantly and led to a longer and expensive development. Figure 4 illustrates the evolution of avionics software for Airbus aircrafts: software size doubles every two years. This increasing size

Figure 4. Evolution of software size in civil airborne software. (from "System Architecture Virtual Integration: An Industrial Case Study" (Feiler, Hansson, de Niz & Wrage, 2009))

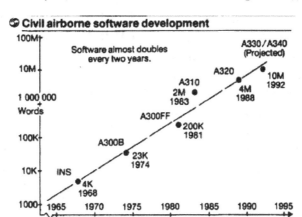

makes avionics software design and verification more complex.

For these reasons, new development methods must be introduced to improve configuration and development reliability. These new methods must help to make system design more consistent by representing system configuration with a single notation.

As functions complexity increases significantly, the development process can also require several iterations. For instance, adding a new function during the design of aircraft system is quite a frequent situation when such a process lasts for several years. However, it is difficult and costly to add a new function: it may require to add a new partition or to modify an existing one. Therefore, the development process has to be re-instantiated.

Development Techniques

One would think that the IMA approach could benefit from a component-based approach. Typically, an avionics system is composed from separate components, restricts component interactions and preserves some functional and non-functional component properties. The component models define what a component is, how it can be config-

ured, how it could be deployed on the execution platform, and how the components can interact via it. Such approaches promote reusability and increase the productivity of developers.

Furthermore, the properties of the resulting system can be determined from properties of the components and from these results several system analysis can be performed to improve the system reliability. Another benefit would be to take advantage of automatic code generation in order to improve both productivity and reliability. The component-based approach helps to automatically generate glue code binding the user-provided implementation to the execution platform. In such an approach, the potential impact of adding a new function can be reduced to the configuration and the deployment of a new component on a given hardware architecture.

However, these new development techniques have not been adapted to the avionics domain.

Modeling Techniques

Like new development techniques, new modeling techniques have not been adapted to the avionics domain.

The model-based approach consists in describing system configuration with its requirements and characteristics using a specific notation. Different aspects could be described through models: data flow, software components or system architecture. Appropriate tools process them to generate, validate and partially implement the system. The most known modeling language is UML that is mostly used to describe software aspects through several diagrams (class, use cases, collaboration, etc.).

But safety-critical systems' modeling is an issue: actual approaches are vendor-specific and no standardized solutions are used. As a consequence, there is no generic method to generate, validate and implement system requirements using models.

The use of a standardized notation would ease safety-critical systems configuration and development. It would be useful to verify system requirements at the earliest steps of the development process and avoids expensive revision costs. These models could also be processed to automatically create configuration and potentially verify it against certification standards. Finally, the automation of the process with dedicated tools avoids manual translations and their associated errors. A common modeling representation would help to understand the system.

Summary

So far, development process of avionics systems involves several steps and therefore system representations. Transformations from one representation to another are done manually. Functions in an avionics system increase even all along the development process. Productivity and costs must be improved and the use of COTS requires the conformance to new development and modeling techniques.

Next section gives an overview of our component-based approach. It relies on the AADL modeling language to represent, configure and deploy an ARINC653 system. It also provides a way to automatically validate and implement it.

RELATED WORK

Existing Approaches for ARINC653 Configuration

Actual ARINC653 development methods rely on the process illustrated in the previous section (Figure 3):

1. system designers write specification by hand,
2. developers translate them into code and integrate it with an execution platform,
3. engineers verify the produced application against certification standards.

To ease system development and avoid errors made by developers, ARINC653 introduces a standardized notation to describe configuration requirements, based on the XML file format. It represents system architecture (partitions, communication channels, etc.) and their characteristics (in terms of scheduling, memory or deployment). Appropriate tools rely on this description to produce configuration code. This translation ensures requirements enforcement, avoids developers mistakes and automates system development.

However, this notation is restricted and describes only requirements at a module-level. It does not provide any information on partitions content (such as tasks, intra-partition communication channels, etc) so that tools cannot configure partitions. As a result, their configuration is still written and verified manually, which is error-prone and costly.

In addition, this lack of description makes difficult system analysis from its specification, which can detect errors before implementation. For example, scheduling analysis could not be processed because the XML-notation does not describe tasks.

For these reasons, we need to represent ARINC653 systems architecture with another notation that describes the whole architecture (module and partitions). It would explicit partitions content (tasks, communication, etc.) with respect to their configuration requirements (period, deadline, data arrival rates, etc.). This new notation would then be used to automatically validate requirements, implement and certify systems configuration.

Research Initiatives for the Development of ARINC653 Systems

The AIDA project (Schoofs, Jenn, Leriche, Nilsen, Gauthier & Richard-Foy, 2009) aims at providing a generic execution platform for avionics systems. For that, it mimics ARINC653 concepts, defining safety and security development and certification for these architectures. However, the execution framework relies on the Java language, which makes difficult the analysis of the system. For example, analysis of memory allocation and usage by each thread is difficult due to the complexity of the runtime. In addition, the project focuses on development and certification aspects and does not provide any configuration analysis method that would prevent errors prior to development efforts.

In (Dubey, Karsia, Kereskenyi & Nagabhushan, n.d.), the authors detail their approach to deploy CCM (Object Management Group, n.d.) components on top of ARINC653 operating systems. They highlight the difficulty of this task due the strong requirements of such architectures (memory allocation on the stack, no task instantiation at run-time, etc.). They point the need to adapt current CCM frameworks to fulfill ARINC653 needs. Despite the description of these strong constraints, they do not provide any guidance for the configuration of ARINC653 architectures.

The European ADAMS project (ADAMS, Project, n.d.) consists in enhancing the UML MARTE (Petriu, Gérard & Medina, 2007) profile. Part of this work models ARINC653 services with UML in order to analyze the system (in terms of performance, scheduling, etc.). However, this work focuses on the applicative part of the system and does not provide any validation facility.

NEW APPROACH FOR SAFETY-CRITICAL SYSTEMS DEVELOPMENT

As presented in previous sections, ARINC653 systems development is difficult due to their strong and increasing requirements. We also highlighted the need for an automated development process based on a single description of the system.

This section gives an overview of our approach and its goals. It motivates our choice for the AADL modeling language as a backbone language for the specification, validation and implementation of ARINC653 systems. Finally, it introduces a case study that will be reused along the rest of the chapter to illustrate our approach.

Model-Based Approach for the Development of Safety-Critical Systems

Model-Based Approaches (MBA) (Schmidt, 2006), (Miller, Mukerji & OMG, 2003), (Lockheed Martin, 2005) rely on a language to represent system with its characteristics. They address issues of actual development methods by describing the system with a single notation that is used to drive each aspects of the development.

Our approach relies on the model-based approach concepts, as illustrated on Figure 5:

1. Designers define the requirements of their ARINC653 systems. These requirements are expressed as functions and properties associated to them.
2. They map these requirements into specifications using models. This description contains both module and partition-levels requirements.
3. Analyzers ensure configuration correctness. This step checks partitions and tasks schedulability, space and time isolation, validity of inter-partition error propagation, …
4. Code generator produces implementation code from validated models. This automatic

code generation produces configurations codes as well as integration code (glue code).

5. Certification tools check the reliability of the resulting system. We give only a brief description of this part of the process since it is not specifically related to configuration and reconfiguration issues.

This approach uses a single representation of ARINC653 for their analysis, validation, and implementation. Contrary to actual approaches, it cares of both layers (module and partition), ensuring their correctness along their development. The single representation of configuration requirements avoids costly translations (convert system representation from one format to another) and eases their traceability (Kannenberg & Saiedian, 2009).

Our model-based approach proposes solutions for ARINC653 development from AADL models. It shows that a modeling language can address the whole development (from specification to certification) of a standardized architecture.

Compared to other languages, the AADL offers an accurate and extensible semantics for safety-critical systems specifications. It defines a set of components with standardized property that may be refined or extended. In particular, the AADL comes with a specific annex for ARINC 653 systems. Moreover, it provides both graphical and textual representation formats. We think it's a great advantages compared to graphical-only languages (such as UML) since a textual notation is easier to process in a computer program. Finally, several tools already support the AADL for system modeling, validation and code generation. In fact, few safety-critical modeling approaches have an industrial tool support and no one provides a solution that covers the whole development process. In the case of AADL, industrial tools were already available and tested through different projects (such as AVSI (Chilenski, 2007), ASSERT or SPICES). If it shows the interest of the industrial community for this language and demonstrates

Figure 5. Overview of our model-based approach

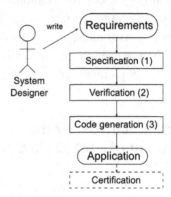

that, its semantics is appropriate for safety-critical systems development (Disseaux, 2004).

Next section provides more details of our AADL-based development approach and explains its use for ARINC653 architectures development.

Model-Based Approach for the Design of ARINC653 Systems with AADL

Our ARINC653-dedicated model-based relies on AADL to describe ARINC653 modules and partitions characteristics (e.g. time and space partitioning, communication channels, scheduling properties, etc.). It defines dedicated patterns for their modeling with the AADL. Then, appropriate tools process these AADL constructs in order to drive all development aspects (validation, implementation and certification).

Figure 6 illustrates this development process with AADL as a backbone language. As in Figure 5, it relies on four steps:

1. **Specification**: designers describe system architecture with their configuration requirements using appropriate modeling constructs. The AADL defines both hardware and software constructs. It helps to configure software components on hardware components but also provides solutions to define reconfiguration strategies using mode

Figure 6. Model-Based Development Process for the design of ARINC653 Architectures

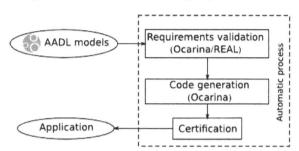

changes. For that purpose, the AADL provides a great modeling environment to deal with configuration of ARINC 653 systems. Moreover, through the ARINC 653 annex, we propose modeling patterns, which help to enforce classical constructs used in the avionic domain and to proceed with classical analysis techniques (like those coming from the schedulability theory for instance)

2. **Verification of configuration requirements**: model analyzers ensure configuration correctness and consistency. This part of the development is achieved with Ocarina and its associated constraint language, REAL. It provides a simple but efficient way to enforce the restrictions required in the avionic domain (such as those required by the DO-178B standard).

3. **Automatic code production**: generators create configuration code from validated models. Generated constructs enforce system requirements validated in models. The Ocarina AADL tool suite provides this part of the process. Thanks to fine-grained descriptions, the code generation is able to produce a code minimal and dedicated to the final system in order to ease code analysis, memory footprint reduction, efficient execution and certification.

4. **Automatic certification**: simulators execute generated applications and check their requirements enforcement during execution.

Modeling patterns standardize system specifications and ease their processing by tools for validation, implementation or certification purposes. The proposed process avoids any manual procedures, creates predictable applications and ensures requirements enforcement along the development. It also reduces its costs while increasing its reliability.

Case Study Description

Our AADL-based development approach is illustrated through this chapter with a case study that is used to detail each step (modeling, implementation and certification). It is a flight manager (Figure 7) composed of five partitions that run on the same processor:

1. **GPS partition handles** a GPS device and sends position data to the pilot partition and flight management partition. It cares about the position of the airplane.

2. **Passenger partition** sends non-critical data (ask for a service, ill passenger, etc.) to the pilot partition.

3. **Pilot information** partition displays information to the pilot and handles device to control of the airplane (manual control of the airplane).

4. **Flight management** partition computes yaw and speed values. It sets these values from manual input (data from the pilot partition)

Figure 7. Case study overview

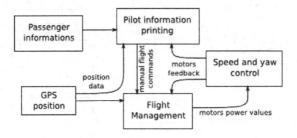

or automatically computes them from the GPS partition.

5. **Speed and Yaw control partition** controls speed and yaw motors according to values sent by the flight management partition. It also sends feedback signals to the pilot partition and the flight management partitions to detect navigation errors.

We also add additional requirements:

• Each partition is executed during 200ms. The major time frame is 1s.
• Data are shared using buffers so that new data instances replace old ones. On the contrary, the communication between pilot partition and flight management uses a queuing mechanism to avoid data loss.

From this requirements description, we deduce the following constraints:

1. Data from the information partition must not interfere with critical data (GPS position value, speed and yaw values).
2. The whole system must be schedulable so that each task meets its deadline.
3. Partitions memory capacity must be sufficient regarding partitions content
4. An error in a partition cannot affect another partition (fault isolation enforcement)

Using actual development methods, these issues are treated by different people:

• System designers write specifications (architecture, requirements and constraints). He also checks requirements and configuration feasibility, such as space and time isolation.
• Developers read specifications and translate them into executable code. Errors ("bugs" but also mistakes due to specifications misunderstanding) are usually introduced. Developers would also write bunch of tests to verify requirements enforcement.
• Certification engineers review developers' source code to verify that produced application enforces specification requirements and certification standards.

Through the rest of this chapter, we illustrate how our AADL-centered development approach faces these issues and make the development more consistent and reliable, avoiding multiple verifications of the same requirements, and costly manual development.

Next section details our ARINC653 patterns for the AADL and describes the modeling of our case studies with them.

ARCHITECTURE MODELING

This section presents the modeling of ARINC653 systems, highlighting the specification of their configuration requirements. It first introduces the modeling language we rely on (AADL) and then introduces our modeling patterns dedicated to the modeling of ARINC653 systems.

Overview of Architecture Analysis Design Language (AADL)

AADL is a standard published by the Society of Automotive Engineers (SAE). It defines a component-centric language for the modeling of both software and hardware concerns. It focuses on the definition of block interfaces, and separates the implementations from these interfaces.

An AADL description is made of components. The language defines three kinds of components software components, hardware components and hybrid components. Next paragraphs describe each of them.

Software Components

- **Subprogram** components model application code. Since it is not an architectural element, its purpose consists in a reference to a piece of code (e.g. C functions).
- **Thread** components model the active part of an application (such as POSIX threads). It represents an instructions flow with memory and scheduling constraints (e.g. stack size, period, execution time, etc.).
- **Process** components model address spaces containing thread components. It is similar to the concept of UNIX processes.

Hardware Components

- **Processor** components model microprocessors and the execution platform (operating system) it executes. It defines configuration of the platform (scheduling policy, communication functionalities, etc.)
- **Virtual processor** components model a part of the physical processor. For example, if a processor component models a dual-core microprocessor, it contains virtual processor sub-components to model each code. In that case, we can specify configuration requirements of each core by adding annotations on contained virtual processor components.
- **Memory** components model physical and logical memories. In case of physical memories, it represents hard disks, RAM, etc. In case of logical memory, it describes a part of a physical memory (for example, a memory segment).
- **Bus** components model physical networks (for example, the Ethernet network).
- **Virtual bus** components are logical buses. They are contained or associated with bus components for several purposes: protocol stack modeling, security layers specification, etc.
- **Device** components model physical devices, such as sensors or actuators. Software that manages the hardware (the device driver) can be bound to them.

Hybrid Component

System components represent composite components that are made up of hardware or software components or a combination of the two. For example, a system may represent a board with multiple processors and memory chips. Most of the time, a system component contains at least one process with several thread components and one processor for their execution.

AADL Model Syntax and Structure

Components hierarchy of an AADL model is composed of several components and sub-components. The topmost component is an AADL system (called *root system*) that contains process, processor and other architecture components.

The interface specification of a component corresponds to its type. It declares features to interact with other components. They represent communication channels (ports that send or receive data) or accesses to other components. Components communicate one with another by connecting their features (the connections section).

Each component describes its internals: subcomponents, connections between these sub-components, etc. An implementation of a thread or a subprogram can specify call sequences to other subprogram, thus describing the interaction with application concerns.

Since there can be different implementations of a given component type, it is possible to select the actual components to be put into the architecture, without having to change the other components. Thus, it provides a convenient approach to application configuration.

AADL allows properties to be associated with AADL model elements. Properties represent name/value pairs that specify characteristics and constraints of a component. Examples are the period and execution time of thread component, the implementation language of a subprogram component, etc. The AADL standard includes a pre-declared set of properties that are commonly used by most of system designers. In addition, users can introduce their own properties through property definition declarations.

AADL models can integrate other languages by mean of annex libraries. These annex languages are added on each component to describe their aspects. Several annex languages were already published, such as the behavior annex (Frana, Bodeveix, Filali & Rolland, 2007) or the error model annex (Rugina, Feiler, Kanoun & Kaaniche, 2008). The behavior annex adds information about components behavior (operations, states, etc.). It refines the model and introduces a finer modeling of the runtime architecture. The error model annex annotates AADL models to analyze errors, faults and their propagation. It defines components states in terms of errors, their potential faults, errors and propagation through components hierarchy.

AADL provides two major benefits for building safety-critical systems. First, compared to other modeling languages, AADL defines low-level abstractions including hardware descriptions. Second, the hybrid system component helps refining the architecture as they can be detailed later on during the design process.

For interested readers, there is a large documents collection about the AADL, including technical reports, tutorials or case studies. Most of them are available on the official AADL portal[1]. Others can be found on our AADL portal at TELECOM ParisTech[2]. For interested readers who want to have a complete presentation of the language and its syntax, designers of the language published (Feiler, Gluch & Hudak, 2005) an introduction about the AADL.

Existing Toolset

AADL has an extended toolset to model, validate and implement safety-critical systems. The OSATE (Open Source AADL Tool Environment) (Software Engineering Institute - Carnegie Mellon University, 2006) provides a complete integration of AADL (SAE, 2008) into the Eclipse modeling framework. Other tools (such as (WW Technology Group, 2008)) rely on OSATE functionalities for AADL models processing and analysis.

Additional plug-ins that run on top of OSATE provide validation functionalities (flow latency analysis, security analysis) to check architecture correctness. Other tools validate specific requirements in AADL models (such as scheduling policy with the Cheddar (Singhoff, Legrand, Nana & Marcé, 2004) scheduling simulator).

Code generation tools (such as Ocarina (Zalila, Hugues & Pautet, 2007)) automatically produce code from AADL specifications. It processes models components and requirements to manage resources (data, buffers, threads ...), configure the targeted operating systems and execute application-level code. Ocarina plugs this application level code (legacy C code or application models such as Simulink) on top its architecture-level generated code. Ocarina supports several languages and standards and generates Ada (Hugues, Zalila, Pautet & Kordon, 2008), RTPOSIX/ C (Delange, Hugues, Pautet & Zalila, 2008) or ARINC653-compliant C code (Delange, Pautet & Kordon, 2008). Thanks to careful optimizations, the generated applications have low memory footprint and complexity (Delange, Hugues, Pautet & Zalila, 2008).

ARINC653 Architectures Modeling with AADL

This section presents our modeling patterns for the specification of ARINC653 (Aeronautical Radio, Inc. 1997) architectures with AADL. This description is organized as the presentation of the ARINC653 standard. This work is included in the ARINC653 annex document of the AADL.

ARINC653 Module and Partitions

An ARINC653 module is specified in AADL by means of a processor component. It models the underlying ARINC653 module that provides isolation functionalities and contains partitions runtime (virtual processor component). From a configuration perspective, this component defines the partition-level scheduling policy (time slots allocated to each partition).

ARINC653 Partitions

ARINC653 partition modeling is achieved with two AADL components: virtual processor and process components:

- The virtual processor component models the partition runtime and its associated configuration (task-level scheduling policy). It is contained in a processor component to model the association of an ARINC653 partition and its ARINC653 module.
- The process component models the address space that contains data and code of the

partition. It defines the amount of memory required to store the partition.

The AADL property Actual_Processor_Binding associates virtual processor and process components. We also model memory segments allocation, associating a process component with a memory component (with the Actual_Memory_Binding property). It describes space isolation configuration (memory segments addresses, size, etc.).

ARINC653 Processes Modeling

AADL thread components model ARINC653 processes. Both represent the same concept: an instruction flow constrained by configuration requirements (period, deadline, execution time and so on). These requirements are specified on a AADL thread component by means of AADL properties. AADL thread components (ARINC653 processes) are contained in AADL process components (ARINC653 partitions).

Thread [event] data ports model ARINC653 intra- or inter-partition communications ports. When two connected threads belong to the same process, we assume the connection models an intra-partition communication mechanism. When the connected AADL thread components are contained in different AADL process components, we consider this channel relies on an ARINC653 inter-partition communication mechanism.

Intra-Partition Communications Modeling

We propose the following mapping rules to model ARINC653 intra-partition communication mechanisms with AADL:

1. AADL event data ports that connect two AADL thread components model an ARINC653 buffer. Its configuration (queue

and data size, timeout, etc.) is specified using dedicated properties.

2. AADL data ports that connect two AADL thread components model an ARINC653 blackboard. AADL data ports do not use queuing mechanisms; thus, their semantics is equivalent to the concept of ARINC653 blackboards (a shared memory space between ARINC653 processes that contains the latest written data). Data size and arrival rate is added with new properties.

3. AADL event port connected to other AADL thread components model an ARINC653 event port. AADL event ports transport and queue signals without any data and thus, fit with the definition of ARINC653 events.

4. An AADL shared data across several AADL thread components located in the same AADL process component models an ARINC653 semaphore. For that, the locking policy must specify the use of a semaphore and the AADL component can specify additional properties to model its behavior (queuing policy, etc.).

Inter-Partitions Communications Modeling

ARINC653 defines two communication mechanisms to exchange data across partitions: queuing ports and sampling ports. We propose the following mapping rules:

1. ARINC653 queuing ports correspond to AADL event data ports connected across AADL process components. AADL event data ports queue each new incoming data and thus correspond to the concept of ARINC653 queuing ports. Dedicated properties specify its configuration requirements (queue size, queuing policy, timeout, etc.).

2. ARINC653 sampling ports correspond to AADL data ports connected across several AADL process components. AADL data

ports do not queue data: new data instance overwrite older ones. Thus, AADL data port concept is similar to ARINC653 sampling ports. Dedicated AADL properties also specify port requirements (refresh period, etc.).

Health Monitoring Mapping

The ARINC653 health monitoring service detects and recovers faults in each layer of the ARINC653 partitioned architecture (module, partition, process). This modeling pattern is able to specify the configuration of health-monitoring mechanisms by specifying recovered faults and their associated recovery procedures. To do so, properties are added in each layer (AADL processor, virtual processor and thread components that correspond to the module, partition or process layer of ARINC653):

1. The ARINC653::HM Errors property specifies handled errors.

2. The ARINC653::HM Actions property specified recovery actions.

These properties are added to each level of the ARINC653 architecture so that we can precisely know where faults are handled and which fault would be recovered at run-time. These properties are then used to model analyzer or code generator to detect error in fault recovery mechanisms or generate appropriate recovery handler for each layer of the architecture.

Basic Example of an ARINC653 Architecture

An AADL model of an ARINC653 architecture is illustrated in Figure 8 (graphical representation) and Listing 1 (textual). It defines a producer/consumer architecture (one task sends data to another) based on our ARINC653 modeling patterns.

It contains one ARINC653 module (*arincmodule*) with two partitions and each one executing

Figure 8. ARINC653 producer/consumer with AADL

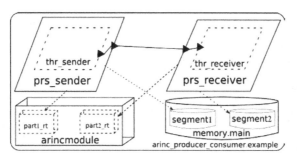

an ARINC process. Partitions are specified using AADL processes (*prs_sender* and *prs_receiver*) and AADL virtual processor components (*part1_rt* and *part2_rt* subcomponents of the *module* component).

ARINC653 processes are specified with AADL thread components. We add one thread component in each AADL process to model ARINC653 process allocation across partitions. Due to lack of space, we do not specify application concerns (it could be done by adding AADL subprogram components and subprogram calls to AADL threads).

The AADL mem component specifies the main memory (e.g. RAM) while its two sub-components (segment1 and segment2) describe its separation in segments. Address spaces allocation to ARINC653 partitions (AADL process components) is specified using a dashed arrow (graphical version) or the Actual_Memory_Binding property (textual version).

Partition runtime (AADL virtual processor components) are also associated with partitions (AADL process components) by a dashed arrow (graphical version) or the Actual_Processor_Binding property (textual version).

Communication ports are specified on ARINC653 partitions (AADL process) and ARINC653 processes (AADL thread), defining data flow across the overall architecture. In this example, connected AADL ports are located on different partitions and thus, model an inter-partition communication channel. Due to the nature

of the port (data ports), it represents ARINC653 sampling ports.

The graphical notation of AADL does not include components properties. For example, our textual specification defines the memory segments size. This information cannot be specified with the graphical version since the graphical notation of AADL properties is not standardized. For this reasons, most designers prefer to begin with the graphical representation to have a simple overview of the architecture and refine it later the architecture with the textual specification.

Apply Modeling Patterns to the Case Study

Figure 9 illustrates the modeling of our case with our AADL/ARINC653 modeling patterns. For each partition, we use three components: a process bound to a memory and a virtual processor. GPS, passenger and flight management partitions contain only one process. On the contrary, pilot and speed/yaw partitions use two processes to separate partitions functions. In the pilot partition, one process displays received information while the other handles manual control of the airplane. In the case of the speed and yaw controls partition, one thread controls the speed motor and another controls yaw motors.

Communication channel between the pilot information and flight management partitions uses an AADL event data port. It corresponds to an

Listing 1. Textual representation of our basic example

Content of sender partition	Content of receiver partition
thread thread_send features dataout: out data port integer_type end thread_send; thread implementation thread_send.i -- subprogram specification not -- described here end thread_send.i; process process_send features dataout: out data port integer_type; end process_send; process implementation process_send.i **subcomponents** thr_sender: thread thread_send.i; **connections** port thr_sender.dataout -> dataout; end process_send.i;	thread thread_recv features datain: in data port integer_type; end thread_recv; thread implementation thread_recv.i -- subprogram specification not -- described here end thread_recv.i; process process_recv features datain: in data port integer_type; end process_recv; process implementation process_recv.i subcomponents thr_receiver: thread thread_recv.i; connections datain -> thr_receiver.datain; end process_recv.i;

Types definition data integer_type properties Data_Model::Data_Representation => integer; end integer_type;	**Memory specification** memory memory_segment properties Byte_Count => 500000 Byte; end memory_segment; memory implementation memory_segment.i
Partitions runtime & ARINC module spec. virtual processor partition_runtime end partition_runtime; processor implementation arinc_module.i subcomponents part1: virtual processor partition_runtime; part2: virtual processor partition_runtime; end arinc_module.i;	end memory_segment.i; memory main_memory end main_memory; memory implementation main_memory.i subcomponents segment1: memory memory_segment.i; segment2: memory memory_segment.i; end main_memory.i;

System specification, components aggregation
system arinc_producer_consumer end arinc_producer_consumer; system arinc_producer_consumer.example subcomponents mem: memory main_memory.i; module: processor arinc_module.i; prs_sender: process_send.i; prs_receiver: process_recv.i; properties Actual_Memory_Binding => reference (mem.segment1) applies to prs_sender; Actual_Memory_Binding => reference (mem.segment2) applies to prs_receiver; Actual_Processor_Binding => reference (module.part1) applies to prs_sender; Actual_Processor_Binding => reference (module.part2) applies to prs_receiver; end arinc_producer_consumer.example;

ARINC653 queuing port that keeps all received data instance.

The other inter-partitions ports use sampling port mechanisms and thus, are specified using an AADL data port. Instead queuing ports, it keeps only the most recent data.

We associate properties to components to model configuration requirements of each partition. In particular we specify:

Figure 9. AADL representation of our case study

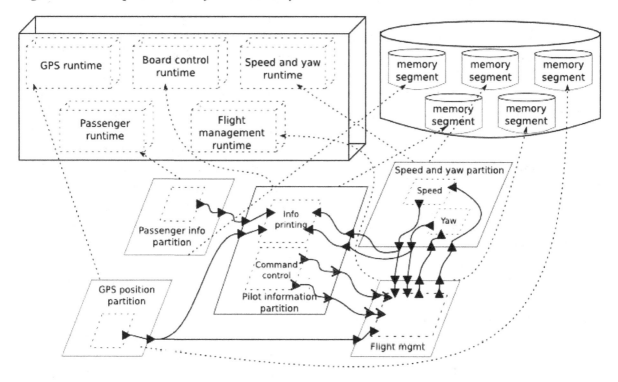

- **Scheduling properties:** timing constraints specification of thread and virtual processor components (ARINC653 process period/deadline, partitions time slots). In this model, all tasks have a period/deadline of one second and an execution time of 10 ms. Each partition is executed during 200ms and the major time frame is 1s.

- **Memory properties**: modeling of memory segments size and memory requirements of each software component (thread, subprogram, …)

- **Fault recovery properties**: representation of handled faults and recovery actions (Health Monitoring service) in each layer of the ARINC653 architecture: module (AADL processor), partition (virtual processor) and process (thread).

Next section details the validation of this model regarding ARINC653 configuration requirements,

ensuring their correctness at a model-level, before implementation efforts.

CONFIGURATION REQUIREMENTS ENFORCEMENT WITH AADL

Model analysis tools check configuration requirements correctness by processing models and detect potential issues (for example, error in flows (Feiler & Hansson, 2007)). This step is really helpful to system designers and developers, finding any configuration error before code production. This is of special interest since a study reports that more than 70% of design errors are introduced in system specifications (National Institute of Standards and Technology, 2006) and could be detected before development.

In the following, we detail such an analysis for the validation of ARINC653 configuration requirements. It relies on languages (such as OCL(OMG, n.d.) or REAL (Gilles & Hugues, 2008)) that check models according to predefined rules.

Next sections present our ARINC653-dedicated validation rules. At first, we explain benefits and limitations of model-based validation and then, detail each rule we designed for AADL model validation, detailing their relevant components and properties.

Benefits and Limitations of Model Validation

Architecture analysis assists designers for validating systems before implementation. Analysis of AADL model allows engineers to check requirements enforcement at a model-level.

However, AADL focuses on architecture aspects and do not include application concerns. Consequently, it could be necessary to an additional analysis on the application level, particularly if requirements are disseminated in both software and hardware layers. For example, scheduling requirements may seem to be feasible at an architecture level (tasks meet their deadlines) while application code may break this requirement (execution time too important). In that case, it makes sense to verify both architecture and application requirements.

In the following, we detail validation we made at the architecture using AADL models.

Ensure ARINC653 Architecture Correctness

Our first analysis validates the consistency of the overall architecture. It ensures that components hierarchy is valid property values are correct. To do so, we process models and check the enforcement of our ARINC653 modeling patterns, ensuring that it specifies a partitioned architecture. It also detects missing components or illegal components association.

However, it does not provide guarantees about configuration requirements correctness. Other analysis tools provide these functionalities; we detail them in next paragraphs.

Verification of Memory Configuration

ARINC653 systems isolate partitions in memory segments to ensure space isolation across partitions. To do so, system designers configure system memory and associate each partition with one memory segment. Segments size must be greater than the size of the partition; otherwise, it will create an error at the initialization of the partition.

This memory requirement can be verified with the following rule:

size (associated memory segment) > partition memory requirements

AADL components describe properties and requirements of partitions and memory segments so that we can verify this rule. Memory requirements of a partition can be deduced from its contained sub-components. ARINC653 partitions (AADL process components) contain ARINC653 processes (AADL thread components) and data (ARINC653 blackboards, semaphores, and shared data between threads that are specified with AADL data components), which size is specified with properties (Source_Stack_Size, Source_Data_Size ...). ARINC653 partitions also contain a runtime to manage resources and processes, which size is provided by the operating system provider.

Consequently, partition memory requirements are computed with the following formula:

$$\textit{Partition memory requirements} = \textit{Size}_{sharedresourcesp} + \textit{Size}_{rocessesrequirements} + \textit{Size}_{partitionruntime}$$

Memory size of shared data is deduced using the Source_Data_Size property on AADL data components, which indicates the actual memory size required to store this data.

Memory requirements of an AADL thread component are computed by adding Source_Data_Size, Source_Stack_Size and Source_Code_Size properties. By making the sum of these properties, we can compute the memory requirements of an ARINC653 process located in a partition. Thus, for any partition P, its contained shared data components D and its contained thread components T, we assume that:

$$\forall Data \in Partition_{Data}, \forall Process \in Partition_{Process}, \square$$
$$MemoryRequirements_{Partition} =$$
$$\sum SourceDataSize\left(Data\right) +$$
$$\sum SourceDataSize\left(Process\right) +$$
$$\sum SourceStackSize\left(Process\right) +$$
$$Size\_PartitionRuntime$$

Finally, size of a memory segment is deduced from AADL properties on a memory component. In AADL, the size of a memory component is specified by the Byte_Count property specify the size of the memory component, so that:

$$MemorySize_{memory} = Byte\_Count_{memory}$$

Checking that a partition P can store its data in its associated memory segment M, is done with:

$$MemorySize_M \geq MemoryRequirements_P$$

Verification of Error Handling Configuration

One major goal in safety-critical systems (and especially in ARINC653 systems) consists in ensuring that system configuration recover potential faults to enforce damage limitation. Our current model analysis enforces faults recovery.

Faults and recovery mechanisms that are potentially raised at run-time in each level of the layered architecture (ARINC654 module, parti-

tion or process layers) are specified with AADL with properties on processor, virtual processor or thread components. An analysis tool can use this property to compute the list of handled fault for each process of the architecture and ensure that all faults are handled for each one.

When an ARINC653 system executes a process, three layers are involved: module, partition, and process. A process belongs to a partition, which is also associated to a module. Consequently, the list of all recovered errors during the execution of a process is deduced with:

$$recoverederrors_{process} =$$
$$handlederrors_{process} \bigcup handlederrors_{partition} \bigcup handlederrors\_module$$

Where *partition* corresponds to the partition that executes the *process* and *module* is the ARINC653 module that contains the partition. Consequently, verification or error handling by all processes is done by this formula:

$$\forall\ process \in processes\ list : recoverederrors_{process} =$$
$$errorlist$$

Where *errorlist* corresponds to the list of all errors we want to recover at execution of each process. These formulas ensure errors recovering at run-time. Thus, they assist the system designer in the verification of its architecture, detecting errors in the configuration of the *Health-Monitoring* service.

Verification of Scheduling Requirements Configuration

Scheduling is a particular concern from a safety point of view: a missed deadline can have significant impacts on the system (data omission, execution avoidance of some tasks, etc.). Consequently, engineers must carefully design and test the configuration of the scheduling policy.

This is of particular interest in the context of ARINC653 systems and its hierarchical scheduling model: ARINC653 modules schedule partitions, which schedules their processes. Two model analyses could be issued to perform scheduling requirements: validation of major time frame and scheduling simulation. Next paragraphs discuss both topics.

Verification of the Major Time Frame

ARINC653 modules schedule partitions using a cyclic scheduling policy repeated at a given rate called the *major time frame*. It corresponds to the sum of partitions time slots. So, verification of major time frame correctness consists in checking that:

$$major\ time\ frame_{module} = \sum partitions\ slots_{module}$$

In AADL models, the AADL processor components model ARINC653 modules. It specifies the major time frame with the ARINC653::Module_Major_Frame property and partitions slots with the ARINC653::Partitions_Slots property. Then, verification is major time frame compliance on all ARINC653 modules is achieved with the following formula:

$$\forall processor \in processor\ list, major\ time\ frame_{processor} = \sum partitions\ slots_{processor}$$

Where *processor list* corresponds to the list of all AADL processor components. and *partitions_slots* to the list of slots the processor allocates to its partitions.

Scheduling Simulation with Cheddar

In the context of AADL modeling, the Cheddar tool (Singhoff, Legrand, Nana & Marcé, 2004),

(Dissaux, Legrand, Plantec & Singhoff, 2008) aims at helping scheduling validation, providing scheduling analysis. It processes AADL models and performs scheduling simulation and feasibility tests. It is able to process layered architectures (such as ARINC653 ones) and their hierarchical scheduling policies (Singhoff & Plantec, 2007).

Figure 10 shows a simulation sample produced by the Cheddar tool. It automatically produces the scheduling diagram from AADL models and giving the ability to system designers to check scheduling configuration feasibility.

ARINC653 Requirements Validation of Our Case Study

We implement our validation rules using the Requirements Enforcement Analysis Language (Gilles & Hugues, 2008) (REAL), available in our Ocarina (Zalila, Hugues & Pautet, 2007) AADL tool suite. It automatically processes and verifies models using theorems. However, other modeling frameworks (such as OSATE (Software Engineering Institute - Carnegie Mellon University, 2006) could be used to process AADL models and implement our verification rules. In the following, we discuss our experience of ARINC653 validation from AADL specifications using this method.

Architecture Consistency

Verification of architecture consistency is made by analyzing the model and look for erroneous declaration in the components hierarchy. For that, the verification tool explores AADL declarations, processes each component declaration and raises an error when it finds an invalid statement (for example, a process that is not bound to a virtual processor).

In the ARINC653 architecture, it will consist in:

1. Verifying components declarations and aggregation: each process is bound to a memory

Figure 10. Cheddar scheduling analysis tool

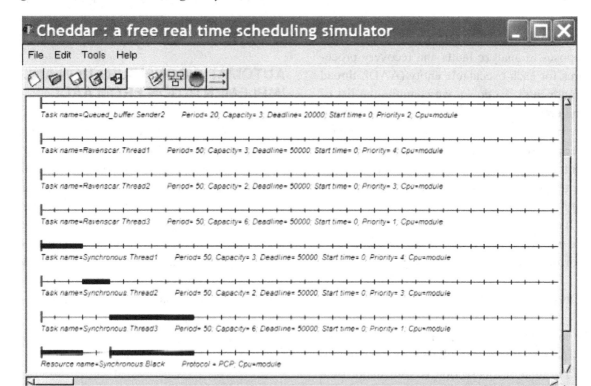

and a virtual processor. In addition, each virtual processor is contained in a processor,

2. Verifying properties values: memory properties (size of memory segments, threads/subprograms required size), scheduling requirements (processor major time frame, thread period/deadline/execution time) or health monitoring requirements (errors are set in each level of the layered architecture), etc ...

Properties of our architecture depicted in Figure 9 are correct. However, if we change the model and bind two partitions to the same memory segment, an error is raised by the analysis (for example, the information and the pilot partitions are bound to the same memory segment). In that case, the tool reports that space isolation is not enforced in this architecture.

Memory Validation

By applying our formula, we propose in this section, memory constraints verification is made by checking that partitions memory requirements are less than the size of their memory segment. For each partition (pilot, passenger, yaw/speed,…), we compute required memory size (from the Source_Data_Size and Source_Code_Size properties) and compare it to their associated memory segment.

Error Handling

Error handling verification formula of this section proposes to analyze faults and recovery procedures for each executable entity (AADL thread components). To do so, we compute the list of handled fault for each executable thread. In our case study, this analysis is processed one time for three partitions (GPS, Passenger, Flight Management: these partitions have only one thread) and two times for two partitions (Yaw/speed and pilot that have two threads).

It relies on properties of each level of the layered architecture. It analyzes the list of handled error for each thread and recovery procedures.

Scheduling Requirements

We verify the major time frame compliance of the ARINC653 module as well as tasks schedulability. Formula of this section verifies major time frame compliance. In this model, each partition is executed during 200ms so that the major time frame is 1 s (we have five partitions). This value corresponds to the one set in the processor component.

The Cheddar tool also verifies tasks schedulability. It automatically processes AADL models and makes a scheduling simulation based on tasks and partitions scheduling specifications. Our experience shows that our model is schedulable.

Summary

This section details ARINC653 configuration requirements validation from AADL models. It ensures configuration correctness prior to implementation, reducing potential errors in produced applications. Code generators to implement this configuration policy then process validated models. Produced configuration code would be correct by construction because it is generated from verified specifications. Next section presents such a process, detailing its code generation patterns that transform validated specifications into executable code.

AUTOMATIC CONFIGURATION AND IMPLEMENTATION FROM AADL

This section presents our automatic code generation process that transforms validated configuration into executable code. It first introduces the process itself, detailing its different steps and components. Then, it describes our code generation patterns that translate AADL models into code and introduces the executive designed for its execution. Finally, this section concludes with an application of this process on our case study, highlighting its benefits in the context of ARINC653 systems.

Code Generation Process

Overview

The code generation consists in translating AADL components that describe configuration requirements into executable code. Produced code creates and manages resources system resources according to model requirements and thus, enforces their requirements (tasks period, data protection, etc.). The process traverses the AADL components hierarchy and translates each one into code. It also integrates application-level code that implements AADL subprogram components (code executed by AADL thread components).

Generated code is generic in order to be adapted on different ARINC653 operating systems (O/S). In fact, most O/S use specific configuration declarations and we adapt the generated code to each one with an adaptation layer.

The code generation process integrates generic code, the adaptation layer and the application code. As a result, it produces a binary that executes applications on top of an ARINC653 operating system automatically configured.

Figure 11 illustrates this, highlighting each step. The code generator (Ocarina (Zalila, Hugues & Pautet, 2007)) produces the generic code from AADL models. Then, the compilation process integrates it with the abstraction layer and the application code (legacy C code or application-level models such as Scade or Simulink). It produces an executable binary that runs on embedded targets.

During our experiments, we run AADL-generated systems on embedded platforms (such as the LEON3, PowerPC or ARM processors used in avionics or aerospace domains). The abstraction layer adapts the generated code with real-time O/S such as RTEMS (OARCorp, n.d.).

Next subsections detail our AADL-to-code transformation patterns and our AADL/ARINC653 adaptation layer.

Code Generation Patterns for ARINC653 Systems

Code generation patterns are mapping rules that translate AADL components into code that enforces their configuration requirements (deduced from their properties, sub-components, etc.).

Figure 12 illustrates the code generation process workflow: the code generator traverses the

Figure 11. Overview of the code generation process

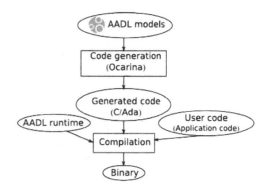

AADL model and translates each component into code that instantiates resources (communication, shared data) and creates partitions and tasks.

Table 1 details our code generation patterns that transform each AADL component into configuration code. Each pattern adapts a fixed block of code according to the requirements of a component, making generated applications predictable. Designers or engineers can deduce the impact of an AADL component in terms of memory (memory consumption) and performance (computation capacity required).

This is especially important because embedded platforms have limited memory resources and computation capacity. In addition, this could be

Figure 12. AADL to ARINC653/C code workflow

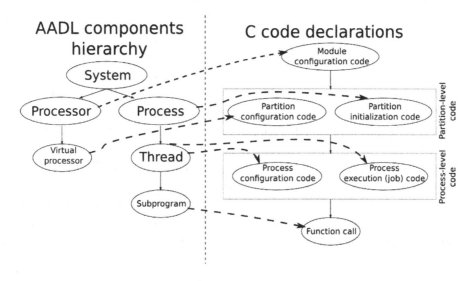

Table 1. AADL-to-ARINC653/C code generation patterns

AADL Component	Translation into C code
Processor	• Configure partitions memory requirements • Configure partitions scheduling policy • Configure inter-partitions ports • Associate partitions with their memory segments
Virtual Processor	• Configure partition processes scheduling policy • Configure partition memory allocator
Process	• Instantiate partition resources (processes, data, etc.) • Initialize of inter-partition communication channels • Configure and initialize intra-partition communication channels
Thread	• Create process job that sends/receives data and executes application-level code and enforces scheduling requirements (period, deadline, etc)
Data	• Create data type that corresponds to the AADL data component
Memory	• Configure memory segments
Subprogram	• Configure potentially application-level models • Make function calls to external code

very important for certification standards that care about computation and memory overhead.

Runtime for the Generated Code

As detailed in the introduction of this section and Figure 11, an abstraction layer (or runtime) adapts the generated code to a specific operating system. In the context of ARINC653 O/S, we design our own operating system, POK (Delange, n.d.) that automatically integrates generated code.

There are two main concerns in the implementation of this abstraction layer:

1. Its services must comply with the semantics of AADL and our dedicated ARINC653 modeling patterns.
2. It must avoid useless services or functionality to reduce memory overhead and fit with avionics certification standards (such as DO178B (RTCA, n.d.)).

POK follows the semantics of both AADL and ARINC653 and supports the semantics of our AADL/ARINC653 modeling rules. For this reason, it also automatically integrates code gener-

ated from AADL models and thus, avoids a very costly and error-prone integration step.

In addition, POK services are restricted according to configuration requirements. During code production, our generation patterns AADL models requirements and configure the system to embed only required services. For example, if no connection is declared in the AADL model, the system will be configured without communication service. By doing so, we reduce memory overhead and improve code coverage, which is suitable for certification standards (RTCA, n.d.).

Benefits

We identify three major benefits in the use of our code generation process: code predictability, optimization and the automatic integration of architecture and application concerns. We detail each one in a dedicated section.

Safe and Predictable Code

At first, our automatic code generation process does not require any manual code production, avoiding errors traditionally found with bunch testing. The second interest is code predictability. Our patterns create code adapts fixed code blocks according to system requirements so that produced code can be deduce from AADL specifications.

In addition, generated code enforces safety-critical development best practices. For example, our Ada code generator automatically enforces Ravenscar (Burns, Dobbing & Vardenegra, 2003) requirements. Our ARINC653-compliant code generator restricts memory and computation overhead. Consequently, designers can write and verify best practices enforcement from system requirements.

These two interesting benefits were experienced during the ASSERT project in coordination with the European Space Agency (ESA). During this project, we demonstrate that we can automatically generate predictable applications that fit with the Ravenscar (Burns, Dobbing & Vardenegra, 2003) profile.

Optimization

The integration of AADL-generated code with its associated abstraction layer relies on system requirements to select only required services and remove useless ones. This optimization step ensures avoids dead code, memory overhead and improve code coverage.

This is a great interest for the industrial community, which uses embedded devices with limited resources and must comply with strong certification requirements. During our experiments, we highlight the benefits of a such requirements-driven code generation approach and demonstrate that generated applications size decrease significantly compared to previous implementation that use traditional component approaches such as CCM (Object Management Group, n.d.). In fact, these systems include useless services and introduce a significant memory overhead. It shows that traditional code production methods would be avoided and code generation approaches will be heavily used in a near future.

Automatic Integration of Application Code

The code generation process automatically integrates application-level code on top of the architecture-level generated code. AADL specifications reference application-level code through subprogram components, so that the code generation process automatically configures the runtime for its inclusion. This avoids a manual integration traditionally performed by dedicated engineers that configures the system for application execution.

This was experienced during the ASSERT project by the European Space Agency where architecture-generated code is automatically integrated with Simulink models. The generation process creates code from AADL and auto-integrates Simulink models on top of it.

Experiments With Our Case Study

Our code generation patterns dedicated where experienced on our case-study. The code generator (Ocarina) produces configuration and implementation code from the AADL models validated using our verification rules. This code is integrated on top of POK, our ARINC653-compliant O/S. In the following, we detail code generation benefits on this case study.

Table 2 - Performance of generated code in terms of memory and time reports the impact of the generated code using three metrics:

1. Generated Source Line of Code (SLOC) describes the amount of code derived from AADL specifications. The less this number is, the best it is (overhead reduction).
2. Time overhead corresponds to the time consumed to handle application concerns (communication, tasks handling, etc.). The table does not provide information about time overhead in the kernel layer since it is considered as a "passive" component

Table 2. Performance of generated code in terms of memory and time

Component	Generated SLOC	Time overhead	Size (Kbytes)
Kernel	121	N/A	23 kB
Partition GPS	113	2 ms	14 kB
Partition information	114	2 ms	14 kB
Partition pilot	139	5 ms	21 kB
Partition flight Management	141	5 ms	17 kB
Partition yaw/speed	125	3 ms	18 kB

and its generated code mostly consists in configuration code.

3. Memory size corresponds to the size of the generated code with the abstraction layer. It is the required amount of memory required by the architecture-level generated code to call the application code.

Enforcing Embedded Real-Time Requirements

Table 2 reports our metrics for each component of our model. They are considered as small: most of the time, size of a complete real-time embedded system is about (at least) 100Kbytes. For example, real-time systems that use RTEMS (OARCorp, n.d.) have a consequent overhead (more than 100 Kbytes) due to the size of the underlying runtime.

In this case study, size of kernel and partitions is always under 20Kbytes. Memory consumption is as small because the code generator reduces functionalities according to system requirements and thus, avoids potential overhead.

These metrics show us that:

1. Model-Based Engineering methods produce compliant with embedded requirements
2. Configuration from system requirement (AADL specifications) avoids useless services and thus, reduces memory overhead.

In addition to these memory limitations, performances seem to meet embedded requirements.

In this case, introduced overhead does not break scheduling requirements. In fact, timing overhead is proportional to the requirements (communication, use of shared data, etc.) for each partition/task. It shows code compliance against specifications and does not introduce calls that may break scheduling requirements.

Predictable by Construction

Generated code is said to be predictable, meaning that we can deduce introduced overhead from the architecture description. These metrics illustrates that: introduced overhead grows according to the number of services (e.g.: communication channels) or resources (e.g.: tasks). For example, the information partition (one thread and one communication channel) consumes less time and memory than the speed/yaw partition (two threads and four communication channels).

This demonstrates that developers and designers can deduce timing and memory overhead from AADL specifications, because required memory size and execution time can be precisely described through architecture requirements.

PERSPECTIVES

This chapter presents our approach to represent, validate and implement the configuration of ARINC653 systems. Our modeling patterns describe configuration requirements using a standardized notation, easing their processing by validation and code generation tools. Our validation rules and code generation patterns ensure configuration correctness and automatically implement code that enforces the checked requirements.

However, there is still ongoing work on this topic. Due to the strong requirements of ARINC653 software in terms of representation, validation, implementation or certification, our approach could be enriched to assess system configuration aspects before its production. In particular, we think there are three relevant improvements vectors:

1. better analysis of the specifications that includes the behavior of the system,
2. a code generation that meets avionics standards, in particular, its code coverage,
3. a model-based certification process

Next paragraphs discuss each item, describing their potential benefits in the production process of ARINC653 systems.

Better Analysis and Validation of Configuration Requirements

Our validation rules validate different aspects of the system. They rely on our modeling patterns and check ARINC653 configuration requirements by analyzing AADL components and their properties. We present describe rules that address the validation of faults, scheduling and system consistency.

However, analysis tools could check other configuration aspects related to system behavior (for example, the way synchronization is managed) and include more flexibility (for example, by letting system designers introduce their own types of faults). This is not possible at this time due to the lack of expressiveness of the AADL language; some requirements could not be described through standard mechanisms (e.g. properties). Other modeling languages (such as UML/MARTE,

introduced in the related work section) have the same pitfall and are not able to provide to model these aspects.

Ongoing revisions of the AADL standard would address these issues by adding new features to the language by means of annex languages. In our context, two annex languages seem relevant for the specification and the validation of ARINC653 configuration: the error-model annex and the behavior annex.

The error-model annex enriches AADL models by defining potential error and error states for each component. It gives the ability to system designers to design their own types of faults and their recovery policies. However, the current version of the annex (Rugina, Feiler, Kanoun & Kaaniche, 2008) is oriented to system engineering and is not suitable for the specification of software errors, the ones specified in ARINC653 systems configuration. To address this issue, this annex is currently under revision and would support the modeling of software faults and recovery procedures. Using this new feature, validation tools would be able to process and validate user-defined faults for each level of ARINC653 systems. It would introduce a more flexible modeling and validation process.

The behavior annex extends the language by adding modeling constructs to specify the behavior of each component. For example, it is able to describe how concurrency between tasks is handled. Such a precise description of component internals would lead to a more precise modeling and validation of configuration concerns (for example, by configuring locking aspects of partitions runtime). However the semantics of the current behavior-model annex (Frana, Bodeveix, Filali & Roland, 2007) lacks of precision for the specification of such concerns. In addition, due to its restriction to the first version of the AADL language, it could not be associated to our modeling patterns. As for the error model annex, a revision is currently in progress. This new version should be compatible with the second version of the AADL and bring an appropriate semantics.

Improve Generated Code Coverage

Our implementation process, described in the last section, creates configuration and execution code from system specifications (AADL models). Thus, it ensures configuration correctness and avoids mistake introduced by traditional development methods (manual code production, etc.). However, due to its criticality, this code must meet several requirements, such as code coverage. If our code generation patterns are helpful at reducing the memory overhead, they are not able to fully fit with all the requirements of avionics standards. For example, the DO178B (RTCA, n.d.) certification standard requires that all critical code is fully covered.

To address this issue, the code production process needs to reduce software functionalities and remove all useless function calls. This could be achieved by adding more information (such as the one of the behavior annex) in all AADL components and precisely specify their requirements. Enriched components would then be used by the code generator to produce only required code artifacts and remove useless functions.

Towards a Model-Based Certification Process

As well as for code production, avionics systems configuration and execution need to be certified against certification standards (such as DO178B (RTCA, n.d.)). Most of the time, the certification process is manually achieved and consists in ensuring that system implementation is compliant with its specification. Due to the time required to inspect and track each requirement from a text document (specifications) to corresponding piece of code, this is a very costly and error-prone. We think that model-based approaches could be helpful in this context.

Indeed, our modeling patterns specify configuration requirements more formally than a text-document. Dedicated certification tools would then be able to track each requirement from the specifications (AADL models) and check for their enforcement during system execution. For example, tracking scheduling events during system execution and comparing them with the simulation issued from the specifications would be amenable to certify schedulability concerns. Such a process would automate the certification process and make it more reliable and affordable.

CONCLUSION

This chapter presents a model-based approach for ARINC653 systems configuration. It addresses actual problems of safety-critical systems development by validating configuration requirements as early as possible and enforcing them along the process. To do so, it relies on an appropriate modeling language (AADL) combined with ARINC653-specific modeling patterns. These are then processed by appropriate tools to validate, generate implementation code and certify system configuration.

This new configuration approach has many benefits. In particular, it reduces costs by detecting errors earlier and avoids specifications or code revisions. The automation of the process makes it also more reliable and robust by enforcing requirements at each development step. Finally, it creates safety-critical compliant code: our AADL-to-ARINC653 code generator generates only required code, reducing memory footprint and increasing code coverage. This feature is essential in the safety-critical domain, where memory and computation are very constrained.

One particular interest is the automatic certification of the system. Our tool-chain based on Ocarina (Zalila, Hugues & Pautet, 2007), checks scheduling correctness and analyses its code coverage of generated applications. In addition, these verifications are achieved on generated applications without manual modifications, similar to the one used during production. However, a complete certification process requires more tests. These experiments show the relevance of a model-based approach for that purpose.

This approach focuses on avionics systems by defining a modeling framework for ARINC653. However, it can support other critical domains such as medicine or aerospace and could be translated to fit with these domains.

REFERENCES

ADAMS project. (n.d.). Retrieved from http://www.adams-project.org

Aeronautical Radio, Inc. (1997). *Avionics Application Software Standard Interface*. Technical report.

Barnes, W. (2004). ARINC *653 and why is it important for a safety-critical RTOS*. Retrieved from http://www.embedded-control-europe.com/c_ece_knowhow/424/basapr04p16.pdf

Bellard, F. (2005). QEMU, a fast and portable dynamic translator. In *ATEC '05: Proceedings of the annual conference on USENIX Annual Technical Conference*.

Bernardi, S., Merseguer, J., & Petriu, D. (2008). *An UML profile for dependability analysis and modeling of software systems. Technical report*. Spain: University of Zaragoza.

Burns, A., Dobbing, B. & Vardenega, T. (2003). Guide for the use of the Ada Ravenscar Profile in high integrity systems. *ACM SIGAda Ada Letters*.

Burns, A., Dobbing, B., & Vardenega, T. (2003). *Guide for the use of the Ada Ravenscar Profile in high integrity systems*.

Chilenski, J. (2007). *Aerospace Vehicle Systems Institute Systems and Software Integration Verification Overview*. AADL Safety and Security Modeling Meeting.

Delange, J. (n.d.). *POK, ARINC653-compliant operating system*. Retrieved from http://pok.gunnm.org

Delange, J., Hugues, J., Pautet, L., & Zalila, B. (2008). Code generation strategies from aadl architectural descriptions targeting the high integrity domain. In *4th European Congress ERTS*.

Delange, J., Pautet, L., & Kordon, F. (2008). Code Generation Strategies for Partitioned Systems. In *29th IEEE Real-Time Systems Symposium (RTSS'08)*, (pp. 53–56), Barcelona, Spain, December 2008. Washington, DC: IEEE Computer Society.

Demathieu, S., Thomas, F., André, C., Gérard, S., & Terrier, F. (2008). First Experiments Using the UML Profile for MARTE. In *ISORC '08: Proceedings of the 2008 11th IEEE Symposium on Object Oriented Real-Time Distributed Computing*.

Dissaux, P., Legrand, J., Plantec, A., & Singhoff, F. (2008). *AADL performance analysis with Cheddar: a summary*. SAE AADL Working Group meeting, Sevilla.

Disseaux, P. (2004). Using the AADL for mission critical software development. In *2nd European Congress ERTS, Embedded Real Time Software*.

Dubey, A., Karsai, G., Kereskenyi, R., & Nagabhushan, M. (n.d.). A Real-Time Component Framework: Experience with CCM and ARINC-653. In *IEEE International Symposium on Object-Oriented Real-Time. Distributed Computing*.

Feiler, P. H., Gluch, D. P. & Hudak, J. J. (2005). *The Architecture Analysis and Design Language (AADL): An Introduction*. Technical report.

Feiler, P. H., & Hansson, J. (2007). *Flow Latency Analysis with the Architecture Analysis and Design Language (AADL). Technical report*. Software Engineering Institute.

Feiler, P. H., Hansson, J., de Niz, D., & Wrage, L. (2009). *System architecture virtual integration: An industrial case study. Technical report*. Software Engineering Institute.

Frana, R. B., Bodeveix, J.-P., Filali, M., & Rolland, J.-F. (2007). The AADL behaviour annex -- experiments and roadmap. In *12th IEEE International Conference on Engineering Complex Computer Systems*.

Frana, R. B., Bodeveix, J.-P., Filali, M., & Rolland, J.-F. (2007). The AADL behaviour annex -- experiments and roadmap. In *12th IEEE International Conference on Engineering Complex Computer Systems*.

Gilles, O., & Hugues, J. (2008). Validating requirements at model-level. *Ingénierie Dirigée par les modèles (IDM'08)*, Mulhouse, France, (pp. 35-49).

Hayhurst, K., Veerhusen, D. S., Chilenski, J. J. & Rierson, L. K. (2001). *A Practical Tutorial on Modified Condition/Decision Coverage*. Technical Report.

Hugues, J., Zalila, B., Pautet, L., & Kordon, F. (2008). *From the Prototype to the Final Embedded System Using the Ocarina AADL Tool Suite. ACM Transactions in Embedded Computing Systems*. TECS.

Kannenberg, A., & Saiedian, H. (2009). *Why Software Requirements Traceability Remains a Challenge. Crosstalk - The Journal of Defense Software*. Jul/Aug.

Karcich, R. M., Skibbe, R., & Garg, P. (1996). On Software Reliability and Code Coverage. In *proceedings of the Aerospace Applications Conference, 1996*.

Liedtke, J. (1996). Toward real Microkernels. *Communications of the ACM*.

Medvidovic, N. & Taylor, R. N. (2000). A classification and comparison framework for software architecture description languages. *IEEE Transactions on Software Engineering*. FAA. (2001). *An investigation of Three Forms of the Modified Condition/Decision/Coverage (MCDC) Criterion*. Technical Report.

Miller, J. & Mukerji, J., Object Management Group (OMG). (2003). *MDA Guide Version 1.0.1*. Technical Report. Lockheed Martin. (2005). *Lockheed Martin (MDA SUCCESS STORY)*. Technical report.

National Institute of Standards and Technology (NIST). (2002). *The Economic Impacts of Inadequate Infrastructure for Software Testing*. Technical Report.

OARCorp. (n.d.). *RTEMS*. Retrieved from http://www.rtems.com

Object Management Group. (n.d.). *CORBA Component Model Specification*.

OMG. (2007). *Systems Modeling Language (SysML)*.

OMG. (2008). *UML Profile for Modeling and Analysis of Real-time and Embedded Systems*. MARTE.

OMG. (n.d.). *OCL 2.0 Specification*. Retrieved from http://www.omg.org/docs/ptc/05-06-06.pdf

Petriu, D., Gérard, S., & Medina, J. (2007). MARTE: A New Standard for Modeling and Analysis of Real-Time and Embedded Systems. In *19th Euromicro Conference on Real-Time Systems (ECRTS 07)*.

RTCA. (n.d.). *Software considerations in airborne systems and equipment certification*. DO178B.

Rugina, A., Feiler, P. H., Kanoun, K., & Kaaniche, M. (2008). Software dependability modeling using an industry-standard architecture description language. In *Proceedings of 4th European Congress ERTS*, Toulouse.

SAE. (2008). *Architecture Analysis & Design Language v2.0 (AS5506)*.

Schmidt, D. C. (2006). Guest Editor's Introduction: Model-Driven Engineering. *Computer journal Model-Driven Engineering, 39*(2), 25-31.

Schoofs, T., Jenn, E., Leriche, S., Nilsen, K., Gauthier, L., & Richard-Foy, M. (2009). Use of PERC Pico in the AIDA avionics platform. In *JTRES '09: Proceedings of the 7th International Workshop on Java Technologies for Real-Time and Embedded Systems*.

Singhoff, F., Legrand, J., Nana, L., & Marcé, L. (2004). Cheddar: a flexible real time scheduling Framework. *ACM SIGAda Ada Letters, 24*(4), 1–8. doi:10.1145/1046191.1032298

Singhoff, F., & Plantec, A. (2007). AADL modeling and analysis of hierarchical schedulers. In *SIGAda '07: Proceedings of the 2007 ACM international conference on SIGAda annual international conference*.

Software Engineering Institute - Carnegie Mellon University. (2006). *Open source AADL tool environment*. Technical report.

Sokolsky, O., Lee, I., & Clark, D. (2006). Schedulability Analysis of AADL models. In *International Parallel and Distributed Processing Symposium*.

Vestal, S. (1998). *Metah user's manual, version 1.27*. Technical report.

WW Technology Group. (2008). *EDICT toolsuite*. Retrieved from http://www.wwtechnology.com/

Zalila, B., Hugues, J., & Pautet, L. (2007). *Ocarina user guide*. Technical Report.

ENDNOTES

[1] http://www.aadl.info

[2] http://aadl.telecom-paristech.fr

Chapter 20
Iterative Knowledge Based Embedded Systems Development Framework

Goh Kiah Mok
Singapore Institute of Manufacturing Technology, Singapore

Benny Tjahjono
Cranfield University, UK

Ding Wei
Penn State University, USA

ABSTRACT

Developing an embedded software solution can be time consuming and challenging especially for non-software trained engineers. This is because traditionally, embedded software is programmed manually in proprietary computer languages such as C, C++, Java and assembly languages, meaning that the developers have to be familiar with at least one of these languages. In addition, most of the embedded software design environments do not cater for both microprocessors-based and Field Programmable Gate Array (FPGA) based embedded computing environments, making the development process even more difficult without the assistance of a common method. This chapter proposes a design of a new embedded system code generator framework which is based on the International Electrotechnical Commission (IEC) 61499 Function Block, XML and EBNF. Along with this code generator, an Iterative Knowledge Based Code Generator (IKBCG) is presented to improve the accuracy of the target codes.

1. INTRODUCTION

An embedded system is a special-purpose, small size hardware device and software systems com-monly used in standalone products or added on to other equipment to enhance their functionalities. Examples include consumer products and industrial control equipment often found in manufacturing or aerospace sectors. By using embedded systems, both complexity and flexibility of equipment can

DOI: 10.4018/978-1-60960-086-0.ch020

be fulfilled mainly because embedded systems developers need to focus only on specific functions requested in order to optimize the solution.

Developing an embedded software solution is a challenging task and can be time consuming especially for non-software trained engineers such as automation and control engineers. Most of the non-software trained engineers or stakeholders cannot participate in the design and development of embedded system. Traditionally, software that runs on an embedded system is programmed manually in various proprietary computer languages such as C, C++, Java and assembly languages and the executable file is downloaded onto the hardware platform. This means the developers of embedded systems have to be familiar with many proprietary computer languages that support multiple embedded platforms. However, these proprietary languages are not compatible with each other, making it difficult to reuse the source codes. For example, although C and C++ are similar, they are not fully compatible with some of the subset embedded computer languages like SystemC, HandelC, and SpecC. In order to facilitate a more effective and efficient development of embedded systems solutions, a common embedded systems development framework for various embedded systems platforms is therefore needed.

The International Electrotechnical Commission (IEC) has proposed the IEC 61499 standard (IEC, 2000) which provides a modelling method aimed at manufacturing and automation domain experts. The standard allows encapsulation of control logic into function blocks that represent sequence of execution, based on process state, communication, control, event and dataflow using both networks and composite function blocks. The IEC61499 also encapsulates the low level source codes and makes low level coding independent from design. Although the IEC 61499, to a large extent, has been endorsed by automation and manufacturing engineers (Vyatkin et. Al., 2005), it does not address the lower level embedded system software issues such as the limited defi-

nition in handling the low level code generation. The overall purpose of the work described in this paper is therefore to explore the use of the IEC 61499 as a system design method for embedded systems and to extend its capability to address the aforementioned issues within the embedded systems design framework.

The paper is structured as follows. Having briefly introduced the topic of the paper, Section 2 describes the background of the research and its related work. Section 3 discusses the proposed framework for embedded system development. Section 4 presents the development environment and the chain of tools which leads to Section 5 that illustrates the validation test of the methodology using simple light switches. Section 6 discusses the code generation of SystemC using XML, and the IKBCG before the conclusions and future work.

2. BACKGROUND AND RELATED RESEARCH

This section presents the current embedded system environments and recent research on standard-based methodologies for embedded systems code generator.

2.1 Embedded System Environments

Embedded systems are typically developed using Microprocessor, FPGA and Application Specific Integrated Circuits (ASIC) hardware platforms. Figure 1 shows the different types of embedded systems development processes, design methodologies, tools and approaches for microprocessor, FPGA and ASIC. ASIC design methodologies involve a wide variety of complex tasks in the placement and routing step, such as placement of circuit and physical optimization, clock tree synthesis, signal integrity and routing. In the placement and routing step, both FPGA and ASIC development processes consist of defining the design specifications such as input/output

Figure 1. Comparison of microprocessors, FPGA and ASIC development process (adapted from Aslam, 2006; Klingman, 2006)

Development Process	Embedded System Hardware Platforms		
	Microprocessor	FPGA	ASIC
System level development methodologies	UML or IEC 61499 Lack of common standard	Lack of common standard	Lack of common standard
High level languages	↓ C++, C, Java etc	↓ SystemC, Handel C	↓ SystemC, Handel C
Low level languages	↓ Assembly language	↓ Verilog, VHDL	↓ Verilog, VHDL
Compilation	↓ Compile program into object code	↓ Compile program into RTL	↓ Compile program into RTL
	↓ Link objects into executable file	↓ Synthesise program into EDIF timing and area optimisation	↓ Synthesise program into EDIF timing & power analysis
	↓	↓	↓ Test synthesis (scan, insertion, synthesis)
Placement & routing	↓	↓ Placement and route the logic components and interconnection	↓ Placement and physical optimisation
	↓	↓	↓ Clock tree synthesis
	↓	↓	↓ Routing
Load & configuration	↓ Load program into ROM	↓ Load configuration file (.bit) to configure the FPGA	↓ Signal integrity
Debug & test	↓ Debug software	↓ Debug software	↓ Test the chip

standards, memory requirements and selection of hardware and platform.

At the compilation step, different FPGA and ASIC vendors support different Input/Output standards and different numbers of input/output pins. Vendors will provide specific tools for their own products.

FPGA and ASIC are generally developed using low level languages such as Verilog and VHDL (Very high speed integrated circuit Hardware Description Language) for RTL (Register Transfer Level) coding, specification of the external and internal memory. High level languages such as SystemC and Handel C are commonly used for both platforms.

Currently, there are no design tools, methodologies or standards for FPGA and ASIC design at the systems level. Most of the designers will focus

on single chip level design and do not consider distributed solutions, because the designers tend to have a very specific knowledge on low level gates, I/Os and electronics circuits rather than systems level application.

Compared to FPGA and ASIC, microprocessor development is similar to PC-based applications which produce object files and usually invoke the linker after compiling to provide linking object files and library files to form an executable file. The executable file provides instructions to control the sequence of logic in the microprocessor. UML is commonly used as the systems level design tool for PC-based software design. Operational functions are described in class diagrams, use case diagrams, and UML software tools translate them into the high level programming languages such as C++ or Java. For each compilation in the microprocessor-based development environment, a binary file is produced. After the compilation, the linker is usually invoked to link the library files into an executable file. The compiled microprocessor program controls the sequence of the logic gates, which is used to write data into data buses, latches and registers and across channels.

2.2 Related Research

Research at the systems level design for embedded systems has been one of the key areas in recent years. A literature review in this area has categorised them into UML based, IEC 61499 based and others.

2.2.1 UML Based Methodologies:

UML is a well known modelling method for PC-based software solutions. Many researchers (for example Coyle & Thornton, 2005; Wang et. al., 2006; Tan et. al. (2004); Nguyen et. al., 2007) extended the UML standard by using XML as an intermediate language to convert UML design to either SystemC or HDL for a single processor environment. In addition, Kangas et. al. (2007) further explored UML as a modelling method for multi-processor and FPGA environments. The above shows that there is a lot of interest in using software engineering-based modelling methodologies for FPGA application. The adoption of XML shows that the research is moving towards open standards. UML is commonly used for modelling and design of software systems as it comprises a collection of diagrams used for software design specifications. However, UML lacks representation for gates, I/Os, timing as well as distributing and interconnecting through multiple controllers. As a consequence, new diagrams and representations are needed to enhance the UML standards for FPGA-based embedded systems. In a survey by Graaf et. al. (2003), it was found that UML is not the common practice adopted by most embedded system developers. Projects that employed diagrams are mostly using free-form and box-line diagrams.

2.2.2 IEC 61499 Based Environment:

The Open Object-Oriented kNowledge Economy in Intelligent inDustrial Automation (OOONEIDA or O3NEIDA) initiated research on reconfigurable industrial control and automation objects (Vyatkin et. al, 2005). It strongly supports the IEC 61499 Function Block. Woll (2007) claimed that IEC 61499 is "simple, cost effective and repeatable' to meet the industry demand of mass customization and 24/7 industry".

Thramboulidis et. al. (2005) developed the Common Object-Oriented Real-Time Framework for Unified Development (CORFU) Engineering Support System (ESS) to translate UML to IEC 61499 and to generate Java code for embedded controller, although it does not address the need for the FPGA-based embedded systems.

In addition, there is a publicly available free Function Block Development Kit (FBDK) (Holobloc,2008) for IEC 61499 development environment written in Java. Although FBDK can generate XML and Java codes, it neither generates C or C++ codes nor addresses FPGA-based embedded platforms.

The only commercial product that uses IEC 61499 is ISaGRAF (ISaGRAF, 2008) but it does not interoperate with FBDK, CORFU. In addition, it does not support FPGA-based environments.

There is a lot of research focusing on the microprocessor-based development environments, the semantics, modelling and verification using IEC 61499 for example Torero (2010), Microns (2010), Khalgui et. al. (2004), Thramboulidis (2006), Dubinin & Vyatkin (2006). In addition, Zoitl et. al. (2007) summarised that most of the current research is on design and execution environment, definition of semantics, application scenarios and coding tools. Most of the IEC 61499 tools are for microprocessors-based solutions and do not address other types of embedded controllers including FPGA or hybrid of FPGA and Microprocessor.

2.2.3 Other Methodologies

Statecharts and Petri Nets have also been explored as code generator by many researchers, for example Mura (2007), Gomes et. al. (2004), Nunes et. al. (2007), Hagge& Wagner (2005). Gomes et. al. (2004), Nunes et. al (2007) use Petri Nets as a modelling method to capture the design and to convert XML-based intermediate language to C and potentially VHDL. The research interest is to provide a system level design using open standard, XML-alike tools for embedded system.

The aforementioned work has been exploring XML as an intermediate language for code generation. However, IEC 61499 based development environment for FPGA based embedded system is still lacking. Future research should therefore be focusing on IEC 61499-based embedded system development environment for both FPGA and microprocessor that would make the development environment more accessible by industrial engi-

neers and thereby increasing the adoption of embedded systems within manufacturing industries.

3. PROPOSED DESIGN OF THE ENVIRONMENT

As mentioned earlier, this paper proposes an embedded development framework for both microprocessor and FPGA using industry standard methodologies that are suitable for industrial engineers. Figure 2 shows the proposed framework. The following subsections will briefly describe the components of the framework.

Requirements (Stage A): This stage captures the technical and application requirements from the users (industrial engineers). There are numerous software engineering methodologies and tools available that can be used at this stage, for instance UML. IEC 61499 is another industrial automation standard that is explored in this research.

Structuring (Stage B): This stage aims to convert the system requirements into various hardware and software components, systems level architecture and reusable components structure. These

Figure 2. Proposed Embedded Development Framework

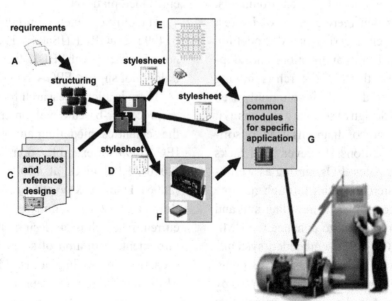

components will become the building blocks for the application. The components could be FPGA-based, microprocessor-based or a combination of both. Each component will have its functions, attributes, interface and control.

Templates and reference design (Stage C): This is a repository of various Extended Backus-Naur Form (EBNF) definitions of the target language, software templates, reference design and implementation, either from past implementation or from other external sources. The functionality needs to be encapsulated into reusable portable blocks. EBNF definitions define the style of the target application languages such as C, HTML, C++, or VHDL languages. EBNF definitions will allow potential code generators to generate the source codes. The templates and reference designs can be reconfigured to new users' application requirements. This will help in speeding up the development cycle.

Hardware/software partitioning and iterative knowledge based code generator (Stage D): In this stage, system designers are required to decide which part of the components should be developed using hardware-based, software-based or a hybrid approach. The interactive knowledge based code generator (IKBCG) that generates the codes will be based on the XML document from IEC 61499 Function block, the Extended Backus-Naur Form (EBNF) file of the target language and the Iterative Knowledge Base Data Library (IKBDL).

Reconfigurable hardware based solution (Stage E): In this stage, the use of Field Programmable Gate Arrays (FPGA), a chip that has many reconfigurable logic gates, is proposed. The FPGA gates can be configured into various circuits. Some of the circuits can be processed in parallel in order to speed up complex algorithm computation. This solution is more affordable nowadays as the cost of the FPGA chip has dropped significantly over the last few years and it is suitable for computational intensive processing.

Microprocessor-based solution (Stage F): This solution is similar to a PC-based solution embed-

ded in a small device with a smaller microprocessor. It requires an operating system and a software application. The system could also have databases, web servers, or standard software applications such as desktop computers. The only drawback of this solution is that the processing depends on the speed of the microprocessor, which could be much slower than PCs.

Specific applications (Stage G): The final applications could be, once again, an FPGA-based embedded system, a microprocessor-based embedded system or a combination of both. The system will be small in size and ready to add on to existing machines or equipment.

Prognostics services (Stage H): The embedded application could be in the form of a small box, added on to the equipment or it could be standalone or handheld. The embedded solution can have various sensors and algorithms to process raw data at the source and it can also communicate with other systems.

4. THE DEVELOPMENT ENVIRONMENT

Figure 3 shows the development environment and the tools chain for the proposed framework.

Stage A is the stage where the technical and application requirements from the users are captured. Stage B is the structuring stage which aims to convert the system requirements into the system level architecture. The first two stages can be addressed by IEC 61499 Function Block. Stage C, the templates and reference design stage is the repository of previous defined Extended Backus-Naur Form (EBNF) representation of the target language. Stage D is the parser stage which can be addressed by Interactive Knowledge Based Code Generator (IKBCG). Stage E is to generate source code for FPGA which can be addressed by generating SystemC codes or other high level codes such as Impulse C and Handel C. Various commercial and open source tools can convert

Figure 3. Development environment

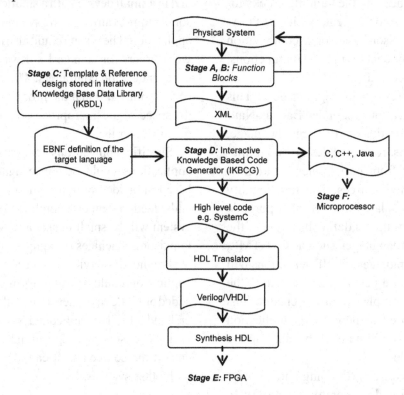

high level C codes into Verilog for FPGA. Stage F could be addressed by generating source codes in C, C++ or Java which are the common embedded system languages. In our validation testing, we use simple light switches to demonstrate an application that can be controlled by FPGA. The following sub-sections will discuss some of the key components of the framework.

4.1 IEC 61499 Function Blocks

IEC technical committee 65 (TC65) defines the IEC 61499 Function Block standard for distributed, programmable, dynamically configurable control. Function Blocks can be easily used for modelling a wide range of manufacturing problems and solutions ranging from small scale logic gates to large scale distributed systems. A Function Block is a 'functional unit of software application' that has its own internal data and algorithms. It allows functions to run on different resources so that distributed control systems can be constructed. Smaller elementary Function Blocks can be created and could be interconnected one another to form a composite Function Blocks for more complex problems. As shown in Figure 4, a Function Block consists of two parts: an algorithm part and an execution control part.

The top part of the block is the execution control, which is defined in terms of a state machine. Upon arrival of an event, the state machine will enter into a new state which will activate the algorithms within the block. Algorithms and internal data are hidden within the block which is represented in the lower part of the Function Block. A Function Block can have more than one algorithm sharing the same internal data. The Function Block will be mapped onto the actual resource, process interface and communication for deployments.

Figure 4. IEC 61499 Function Block

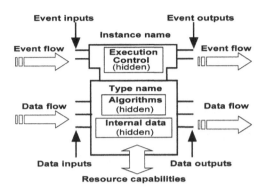

IEC 61499 is the component-based open standard function block model that helps both the design functionality of the system and the integration of various systems. Function block shares many features with Unified Modelling Language (UML) objects. Objects may contain data which are also instances of other objects. Likewise, function blocks may contain instances of other function blocks. Objects can be used for invocation with the methods with arguments and return values. Meanwhile function blocks use input and output variables and events. Data can be synchronized with events in function blocks. It can be used for capturing both current and future system requirements as in Stage A and can also be used as building blocks for applications. Non-software industrial system specialists who are familiar with connecting physical devices together can use these encapsulated function blocks, link them together to develop the system solutions. Function Blocks can be easily used for modelling a wide range of manufacturing problems and solutions ranging from small scale logic gates to large scale distributed systems.

A function block is a 'functional unit of software application' that has its own internal data and algorithms. Function blocks allow functions to run on different resources so that distributed control systems can be constructed. Smaller elementary function blocks can be created like software librar-ies and can be interconnected into larger function blocks for more complex problems.

4.2 XML Tree and Function Blocks

XML is an open, simple, flexible text format originally designed for a large-scale electronic publishing. XML is standardized by World Wide Web Consortium (W3C) and is jointly developed by IBM, Microsoft and Sun Micro Systems. In this paper, XML is used as the meta-language to define the set the function block. The XML format has flexible features which support easier custom code development or code generators in application development using corresponding parser to convert XML format into other textual formats.

IEC 61499 uses XML as intermediate language. The hierarchy XML tree representation of data will match to the EBNF tree of the target language which makes the automatic code generation feasible.

In IEC61499, there are six kinds of function block types: FB Type, Device Type, Resource Type, System Type, Data Type and Adapter Type (IEC 61499-2, 2005)corresponding to six kind of generated XML documents. In other words, the template for each function block type can be predefined. For each template, comparing with the customized XML document from IEC61499, the difference lies on the node's attribute especially more nodes with the same name to be inserted. In the following piece of XML codes, more nodes named "VarDeclaration" can be inserted in the design and this name will not be changed. "VarDeclaration" is meaningless for the target codes' generation. The valuable information lies in the nodes' attributes like "name" and "type" (see Example 1).

Therefore, the node's attribute should be considered as a leaf node for further data extraction. In this paper, the XML tree's leaf node is the attribute node. The XML tree is illustrated in Figure 5.

Example 1.

```
</InterfacList>
   <InputVars>
      <VarDeclaration Name="IN1" Type="BOOL" />
      <VarDeclaration Name="IN2" Type="BOOL" />
   </InputVars>
   <OutputVars>
      <VarDeclaration Name="OUT" Type="BOOL" Comment="Result" />
   </OutputVars>
</InterfacList>
```

Figure 5. XML tree construction

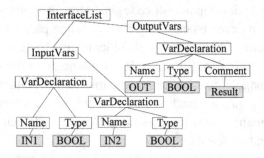

4.3 EBNF Tree Construction

Backus-Naur Form (BNF) and EBNF (Grammar, 2008) is used as syntax definition of programming languages. EBNF is more convenient to express the syntax. It consists of four operators: "|" which indicates alternatives, "[ ]" stands for option, "{ }" for repetition and "()" for grouping.

Basically, each language's EBNF has a start symbol-the root of the EBNF Tree. Each production rule's Left Hand Side (LHS) can be considered as a tree node and the Right Hand Side (RHS) can be thought as the children of this node. For the production rule:

decl-begin::= 'SC_MODULE' '(' module-name ')'

The LHS "decl-begin" is a tree node and the RHS "'SC_MODULE'", "(", "module-name" and ")" are its children.

IKBCG's EBNF tree contains three kinds of leaf nodes: the language's identifier node, the language's keyword node and the EBNF keyword node. The leaf node (which is also the attribute node) in XML tree corresponds to the language's identifier node in EBNF tree.

4.4 Graphical User Interface

Fully automatic language translation from XML to various other computer languages is not realistic (Kuikka et. al. 2002). IEC61499 will generate XML document and the target computer languages EBNF definition can be found from the compiler suppliers. However, only these data is not enough to generate the desired code. EBNF only defines the syntax of the language but lack of semantic rules. For example, production rules for Java's modifier are defined as:

modifier::= public | private | protected | static | final

| native | synchronized | abstract

The XML attribute corresponds to which modifier cannot be determined without additional semantic information. CodeWorker (2010) uses script language to define additional semantic information of the target language. Comparing with script language, provide interactive GUI

Figure 6. IKBCG Windows

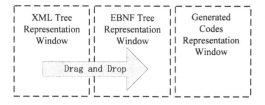

can simplify the user's operations without using additional script languages. Figure 6 shows the IKBCG's interactive GUI design framework.

IKBCG, can also specify this corresponding to achieve the same objective, which requires appropriate rules. The framework of code generator's working process is shown in Figure 7. It is separated into two parts - the front part and the end part. In front part, intermediate XML (iXML) is formed by merging the two inputs, XML and EBNF. Then the iXML is used as input to the end part to produce the desired codes through an interpreter. This part is independent from the source XML and target language's EBNF.

There are several benefits of the process. Firstly, it separates the whole process of code translation into two parts- the front part and end part. The front part merges EBNF and source XML together, unconcerned about what the target

codes will looks like (or how to form the target codes). In this part, IKBCG forms by abstracting the useful information both in EBNF and XML. As a text based language, IKBCG is easy for users to read and understand. Secondly, the end part from IKBCG to target language is independent from the EBNF and source XML and only relates to IKBCG itself.

4.5 Basic Elements

Rule-based blocks (RBB) can be divided into two main parts: the data type conversion part and the code generation part both of which contains several basic tags and attributes with fixed names, called basic elements. Code generation part consists of several RBBs. A RBB can also be embedded in another RBB. In this way, the hierarchy of the function blocks can be represented. Each block has a header indicates the assigned production rule for certain sub-structure or elements. The body of RBB contains information on how to translate such sub-structure or elements. Besides the basic elements, there are also some tags and attributes exist in each RBB with flexible name, name of which production rule being chosen. A general structure of RBB file is shown in Figure 8.

Figure 7. Process of code generator

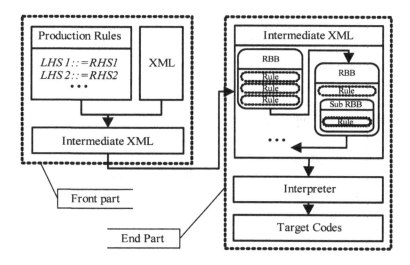

Figure 8. General structure of an RBB file

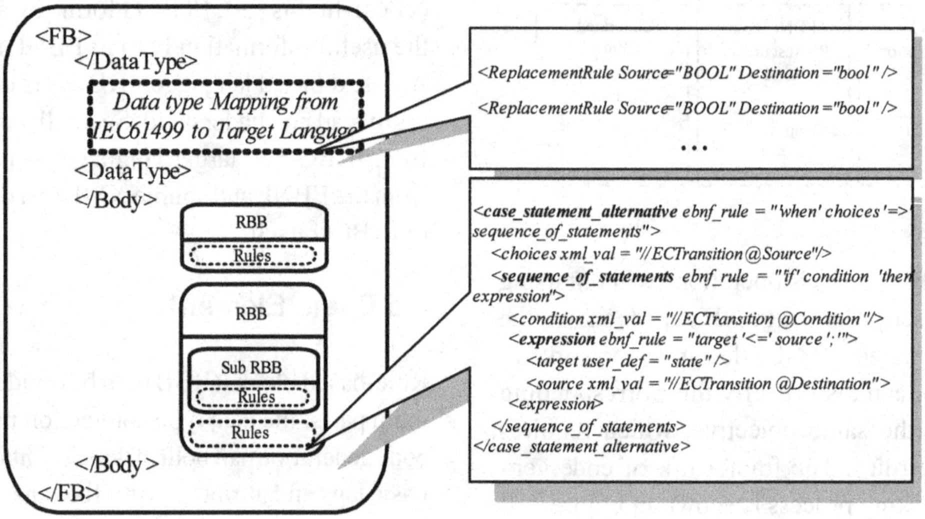

4.6 Interpret Process

The whole interpreting process has two steps, the pre-process and the parsing process. Pre-process makes modifications on XML. Those modifications only refer to change the structure of source XML and add the required information to facilitate the parsing process. Parsing process concerns how to generate the desired code. The whole interpreting process is illustrated in Figure 9.

4.7 Pre-Process

Pre-process executes before the iXML being parsed. This process is required mainly because the translation rule of data types is unknown and the format of connections between events, or ports, or states in source iXML does not enough support IKBCG. In this section, four pre-treatment rules will be given to facilitate the parsing process.

4.7.1 Pre-Process: Data Types

As mentioned before, different language has different data type definition. Even though some data

types have the same meaning, the forms different languages express can be difference.

Generally, there are two kinds of data types, one is those exist both in IEC 61499 and target language, the other is those exist either in IEC 61499 or target language. The latter one is meaningless for language translation. Now we give the pre-treatment rule for data types.

4.7.2 Pre-Treatment Rule 1

For the data types both exist both in IEC61499 and target language, assume the data type in IEC61499 is "A", the one with the same meaning in target language is "B". Insert the following tag as the child of <DataType>.

<ReplacementRule Source="A" Destination="B" />

It means that during the translation process, any value equals to "A" in the source XML will be translated into "B".

Figure 9. Sub- processes inside interpreter

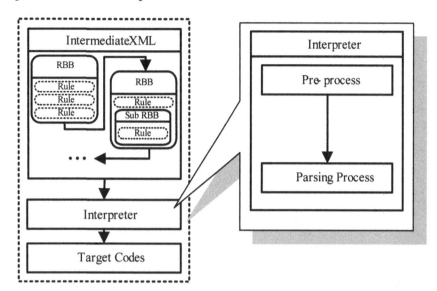

Pre-Process: Ports Connecting to the Physical Devices

Any system or function block should indicate input, output ports and its values.

4.7.3 Pre-Treatment Rule 2

Those ports and event, whose values are not assigned in function blocks, will be considered as the output event variables and output data variables and their tag names will be changed into <Input>/<Output>.

Therefore, once the input port or output port are recognized, a conversion will be taken. See Example 2.

4.7.4 Pre-Process: Connections between Function Blocks

<Connection> is a special tag in the XML definition of IEC61499. It means an event connection, data connection or adapter connection as defined in IEC 61499-1 (2005). It is the only tag relates to two function blocks as one connection from source to destination. There are three kinds of connection:

Connection type 1: <Connection Source="S.a" Destination="D.b" />, which means 'a connection exists from the variable a in function block "S" to the variable "b" in function block D'. Both composite function block and system function block have this connection type.

Connection type 2: <Connection Source="a" Destination="D.b" />, which means 'a connection exists from the variable an in current composite function block to the variable "b" in its sub-function block "D" '. A will be considered as the input variable.

Connection type 3: <Connection Source="S.a" Destination="b" />, which means 'a connection exists from the variable "a" in function block "S" which belongs to current composite function block to the variable "b" in this composite function block'. "b" will be considered as the output variable.

Connection type 1 and 2 only exist in composite function block.

The expression of connections in IEC61499 is not well designed for code generation. The reason relates to the code generating process, and it will be discussed in section 4.9.

Example 2.

```
In the following example, "IN" is recognized as the input, so conversion oc-
curs
from:
<FB Name="switch_2" Type="IN_BOOL" x="650.0" y="1255.5555">
<Parameter Name="QI" Value="1" />
<Parameter Name="IN" />
</FB>
to:
<FB Name="switch_2" Type="IN_BOOL" x="650.0" y="1255.5555">
<Parameter Name="QI" Value="1" />
< Input Name="IN" Id ="in1" Type = "BOOL" />
</FB>
```

4.7.5 Pre-Treatment Rule 3

a. For each tag in the form of <Connection Source="S.a" Destination="D.b" />, add a child under the tag <FB> whose attribute "Name" is "S":

<Connection Id="X" Name="a" Type="T" Dir="Source" />

And add a child under the tag <FB> whose attribute "Name" is "D":

<Connection Id="X" Name="b" Type="T" Dir=" Destination" />

b. In composite unction block, for each tag in the form of <Connection Source="S.a" Destination="b" />, add a child under the tag <FB> whose attribute "Name" is "S":

<Connection Id="X" Name="a" Type="T" Dir="Source" />

And add an attribute of the child under the tag < OutputVars> whose value of "Name" is "b":

<VarDeclaration Name="b" Type="BOOL" Id = "X" Dir = "Destination" />

c. For each tag in the form of <Connection Source="a" Destination="D.b" />, add an attribute of the child under the tag <InputVars> whose value of "Name" is "a":

<VarDeclaration Name="a" Type="BOOL" Id = "X" Dir = "Source" />

And add a child under the tag <FB> whose attribute "Name" is "D":

<Connection Id="X" Name="b" Type="T" Dir=" Destination" />

The attribute Id indicates these two tags belong to the same connection. The attribute "Type" tells what data type this variable should be. It complies with the data type declaration in the corresponding function block. The attribute "Dir" points out the direction of this connection. It indicates whether this variable is the source or destination in this connection.

4.8 Assumption to Source XML

The concept of "similarity" needs to be clarified to identify similarity between two nodes in the XML tree. Since node name cannot used as identifier of a unique node, a path consists of several node names from the root node cannot identify a unique node, neither. Nodes with the same path are the "equality node" which will be parsed with same operation. If a RBB includes more than one kind of equality nodes, the number of nodes for each kind is the same with other kinds', or else, they are enclosed by <ForEach> separately.

In function blocks, it is not allowed to connect an event output to more than one event input of other blocks while data connection allows. Both data and event connection are not allowed to connect one or more outputs to one input. As a result, the connection number in target codes is not simply equal to the number of <Connection>. Maybe two <Connection> tags both point to one connection. For example, the following codes illustrate two <Connection> tags:

<Connection Source="switch_3.out1" Destination="light_1.in1" />

<Connection Source="switch_3.out1" Destination="and.in1" />

In target codes, such as SystemC, these two tags will be translated into one channel type:

```
sc_singal <bool> sig1;
switch_3->out1(sig1);
light_1->in1(sig1);
and->in1(sig1);
```

In the last three lines, an EBNF production rule is used:

```
port_binding::= block_name '->' port_name '('
singal_name ');'
```

The number of block_name is not simply equal to the number of singal_name. Figure out their relationship, that is, number of block_name equals the sum of the value of attribute "Source" and "Destination" before "." without reduplicate, number of singal_name equals to the number of the value of attribute "Source" before "." without reduplicate. Although this calculation can be done by <ForEach>, besides that, assigning the correct singal_name into the port needs more work. Note that now there is only one channel, if the number

is more than one, how the parser knows which channel corresponds to the correct port? And now only data connection emerges; event connection has not been taken into account yet. Meanwhile port bindings in various languages may differ. All these evince <Connection> is not appropriated for parsing IKBCG. Since it has fixed format, only changing the structure of <Connection> but retaining the information as Pre-treatment Rule 3 does to facilitate the parsing process is more feasible.

4.9 Code Generation

4.9.1 Parsing EBNF File

The main problem for EBNF parsing is the repetition. Repetition has the formats of EBNF syntax {a}, a{, a} and {a, }a respectively. The repeat times can be found by recognizing how many similar nodes there are for a specified EBNF node. The priority exists in this matching. When several similar nodes being found in the XML tree, EBNF node needs to be associated first is always the one outside the curly brackets. Take a{, a} for example, assume there is no similar XML node to be found which means there is only one node to match the corresponding EBNF node. If the first "a" is not assigned to this XML node, the result becomes ", a" while the expected result is "a".

Searching similar nodes for specified XML node happens in repetition as identifying whether repeat EBNF nodes need to be added only occurs on the tree level which contains "{" and "}". The value of this node's corresponding EBNF node will be replaced but the other similar nodes' corresponding to newly added EBNF nodes will not. The causation is that this EBNF node itself cannot tell where its newly added EBNF nodes locate. Only the nodes on the level where "{ }" lies know that. One solution is appending a reference for this EBNF node, telling it where its "similar" nodes are. This is a recursive way starting from the nodes on the level which "{ }" lies to their children.

Figure 10. Similar attribute identification

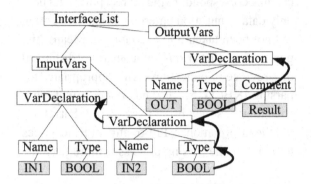

Figure 11. Similarity searching in IKBDL

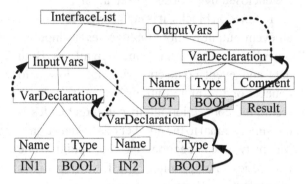

4.9.2 Similar Attribute Identification

When an attribute is assigned to the corresponding EBNF node, similar attribute can be recognized by searching the attribute node's parent node. Figure 10 below illustrates the procedure.

If there is a specified node called "VarDeclaration", and then any node named "VarDeclaration" will be regarded as the similar node. Here we introduce a concept named "similarity" which means how similar between two nodes. The usage will be discussed in the next section.

4.10 Iterative Knowledge Based Data Library

Interactive GUI cannot guarantee the accuracy of the codes. The IKBDL is designed to makeup this drawback by adding the "experience" gradually into a knowledge base.

4.10.1 Similarity Searching

Complex semantic rule cannot be handled automatically in the first. Take the previous piece of XML codes for example, the "IN1" and "IN2" is the input variable and "OUT" is the output variable. Different language will deal with them in different way. In SystemC, sensitive list should be like "sensitive <<IN1 <<IN2" while the first time using GUI will result "sensitive <<IN1 <<IN2

<<OUT". The problem lies on how similar among these three nodes. On the level "VarDeclaration", they seem to be the same. While forward to one more parent node, which is marked in dashed arrows in Figure 11 below, the difference appears. If forward for one more parent again, they are all convergence to "InterfaceList". Until now, it is clear to see their similarity. "IN1" and "IN2" are the "most" similar – they will be handled in the same way while "OUT" is a "less" similar node which may be treated in a different way in certain place.

The algorithm to determine the nodes' similarity is as follows:

1. Find those nodes whose parent's parent node has the same name. Put them in a group and set their similarity to 0.
2. Look up one more parent node for each node and take each node itself as the reference. Compare this node itself with the rest nodes one by one. Those nodes which have the parents with the same name will stay their original similarity for this node. Those whose parents have different names will add their similarity by 1.

Repeat step 2 until all these nodes are convergence to the same parent.

4.10.2 Correspond Similarity to EBNF

The similarity tells how "far" to look up in order to determine which node should be considered as the similar node. The similar node will be treated in the same way to meet the EBNF node. This is an iterative way. The first time when a new XML template is loaded, the parser will start from the attribute node's first non-attribute parent to determine the similarity. In other words, it will only look up to the first non-attribute parent node. After user interactive configuration on the EBNF node, previous similar nodes group will be divided into several sub-groups. Forward searching one level by one level until these XML tree nodes also meet the same or the most similar grouping. Then the desired similarity is found. Next time when the same template is loaded, the parser will obey this similarity to determine the similar nodes for each node.

The corresponding relationship between XML node and EBNF node will be stored so that next time, the desired codes will be generated directly. This kind of corresponding is not invariable due to the changes of user's requirement. Therefore, a knowledge base is proposed to record these changes. Assume there are currently k types of similarity grouping for node N, The information attached (I) on N consists of the node name n, the similarity groupings g = (g1, g2... gk), the corresponding EBNF node c, and the weight w which specify how frequency this similarity grouping is used. w will be increased by a factor as this grouping is used every time. Such that I = (n, g, c, w). As g = (g1, g2... gk), each gi is a kind of similarity grouping. Each grouping consists of several sub-groupings and each sub-grouping consists of several nodes. IKBDL will always pick up the most frequently used similarity group as the default matching. In this way, the accuracy will be corrected with the experience increasing.

Figure 12. Data types matching in IKBDL

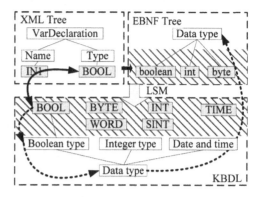

4.10.3 Data Types Matching

The standard data types defined in IEC61499 include integer types, floating types, boolean types, string types and date & time (Vyatkin, 2007). For each of those types, it contains several sub-types. E.g., integer type contains "BYTE", "WORD", "INT" and so on. User can also define various derived data types. The data storage can be in an XML format (Vyatkin, 2007).

In IKBDL, every language's data type follows the data type classification in IEC61499. The framework in Figure 12 shows how data types' auto-matching works. After drag and drop the XML node "BOOL" into EBNF node "boolean", IKBDL will record the corresponding between the two roots. In semantic level, it means this EBNF node and all its sibling nodes are data type definition in this language and correspond to those defined in IEC61499. Then Longest Substring matching (LSM) starts between EBNF data types' nodes and IEC61499 data types' nodes.

LSM only need to work from EBNF tree to IKBDL as the data types transfer from XML tree to the specified language. E.g. "int" in the EBNF tree can match "INT", "SINT" and so on. It doesn't matter what exactly it matches because this information already enough to know "INT" and "SINT" corresponds to "int" in this language.

The first time result may have some inaccurate matching. Modification is required but only

Figure 13. Language comparison

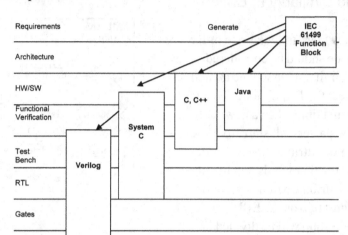

needs once. Then the corresponding will store in IKBDL for further work. As different language has different data type definition, there may have several data types missed matching, this kind will need manual appending into IKBDL.

4.5 SystemC

SystemC is an open standard system modelling language that supports hardware/software co-design and co-simulation using C++. It is used in both electronic and non-electronic systems designs. SystemC can provide higher levels of abstraction for all system components and the advantages of C++ class library constructs with timing, concurrency and reactive behaviours. Figure 13 shows IEC 61499 Function Block can be used as the system level design tool. IEC 61499 generate difference languages for various embedded environment. SystemC is used instead of Verilog because SystemC allows designs to be expressed and verified at high levels of abstraction and implemented in the lower level hardware. This approach helps system designer to design and simulate both the hardware and software behaviours of the system.

5. VALIDATION TEST IMPLEMENTATION

This section presents the validation test of IEC 61499-based implementation that will generate SystemC codes which will subsequently be converted to Verilog for FPGA. For simplicity, a switch and light system Fischer & Boucher (2010) is used to model and simulate using IEC 61499 function blocks.

5.1 Switch and Light System

Switch1 and Switch2 are the inputs and Light1 and Light2 are the outputs. In this system, Light1 and Light2 will be ON when Switch1 is turned ON while Switch2 is OFF. Only Light1 will be ON when both Switch1 and Switch2 are turned ON. Since Switch1 is the main switch, when Switch1 is turned OFF, both lights will be OFF.

Boolean logic, such as AND and NOT operators, is used in order to implement this system. The logic is

$$Light1 = Switch1$$

$$Light2 = Switch1 \ \overline{AND} \ Switch2$$

Figure 14. Function blocks of the switch and light system

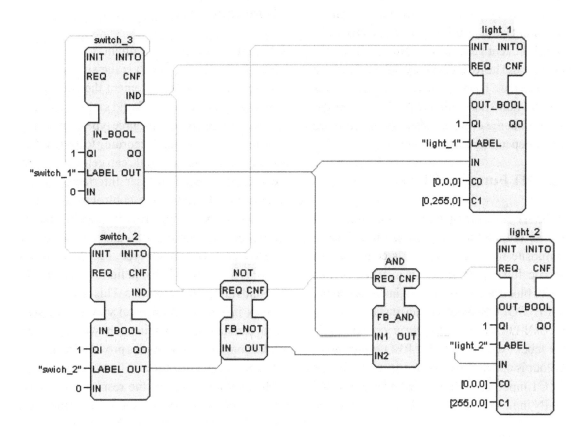

The system is modelled using a network of basic function blocks. The switch and light control system will be controlled by NOT and AND function blocks which are the main function block of the network. The model has 7 function blocks: START, (Switch) IN_BOOL, (Light) OUT_BOOL, NOT and AND as shown in Figure 8.

5.2 START Function Block

The START function block shown in Figure 14, is necessary for the system. This block is used to control the start and stop of the chain of function blocks. E_RESTART block has only three start events: COLD, WARM and STOP. The COLD start event is used to initially start the system and the WARM start event is used to restart the system after it has already been started. The STOP event is used to end the system. E_RESTART block is usually the first function block in the network of function blocks since it is controlling the start and stop of the system. Figure 14 depicts the time sequence diagram for COLD, WARM and STOP of E_RESTART function block respectively.

5.3 SWITCH Function Block

SWITCH function block shown in Figure 14 serves as input function block. Regarding to the system, switch may be ON or OFF therefore it is a Boolean input function block. The Boolean input 0 or 1 is set by the value of IN input where 0 means switch is OFF and 1 means switch is ON. In this system, input will be 0 at the initial state. There are two input events and three output events in IN_BOOL function block. In the switch and light system, two inputs INIT, REQ and two outputs INITO, IND are used. INIT event initializes the input variable used by the function blocks and INITO event generates output on successful initialization. The REQ event reads the value from the IND event. There are two switches in this system: Switch 3 and Switch 2. Both have similar behaviour but the event and data connections are different depending on the system.

5.4 LIGHT Function Block

The LIGHT function block shown in Figure 14 serves as output function block. OUT_BOOL is composite function block. It is composed of two basic function blocks. An instance of this function block type utilizes an instance of the FB_SEL_COLOR type and an instance of the OUT_COLOR type to display a colour circle with a label. According to the REQ event input, the colour is updated to the value specified by the C0 or C1 input depending on whether the value of the IN input is FALSE or TRUE, respectively.

5.5 FB_NOT Function Block

The FB_NOT function block in Figure 14 simply operates as the NOT logic operator that is TRUE if its operand is FALSE and is FALSE if its operand is TRUE. There will be one input true or false into IN. The OUT output will generate true or false according to the input.

5.6 FB_AND Function Block

The FB_AND function block in Figure 14 operate as an AND logic that returns a value of TRUE if both of its operands are TRUE and returns FALSE if otherwise. One output true or false will be generated according to the input value of IN1 and IN2.

5.7 Modelling and Simulation Using FBDK

Among other IEC-compliant tools, Holobloc FBDK (Holobloc, 2008) is the simplest and the most stable tool to implement the design. It is a freeware and enables to build and test data types, function block types, resource types, device types, system configurations according to the IEC 61499 standard. Holobloc FBDK can generate the XML codes and Graphical User Interface (GUI). By using FBDK editor, the control system can be configured by adding properties such as Function block name, identification and version and then define devices by their type, FRAME_DEVICE type is used for switch and light system and their bounds and grid parameters. This kind of function block provides a high level view of the system that can serve as a container (shown Figure 15) for GUI components or frames provided by instances of appropriate resource or function block types. The simulation shows the result of the applications and its operations. Once the application is tested correctly, then it can be converted to other embedded platform like FPGA. The next step is to map the function blocks to the proper resources in the device.

6. GENERATION OF SYSTEMC USING XML AND IKBCG

Most embedded system programmers will have to master many computer languages such as C, C++ and Java which consequently needs extensive training. Many embedded systems have proprietary programming languages. Code generation can give a better solution for engineers who are not expert in programming languages. They can use function block to 'draw' and 'link' the application and code generator will then generate the right source codes according to the embedded system language requirements.

Figure 15. Testing switch and light system

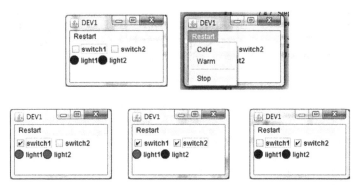

Figure 16 demonstrated IKBCG code generation example. In this case, it shows the code generation from a Basic Function Block named "FB_AND.fbt" to SystemC codes. Developer could select the data type (Figure 16a), modify the name (Figure 16b) and simply generate the systemC code (Figure 16c).

Choosing the right tool to perform code generation is critical. XML is the metafile for web and data representation and XSL is the style sheet that defines the resulting format of the XML. Software developers can create XSL style sheet to define the required language template. As shown in Figure 4, XML parser (e.g. Microsoft's MSXSL) can process the XML source and convert it to the target language based on the XSL.

6.1 Compile and Simulate SystemC

By using Microsoft Visual C++ or other compilers, the header and system files can be compiled into an executable file. The compiler needs to link the SystemC header file (SystemC.h) and the library file (SystemC.lib) with the Run-Time Type Information (RTTI) enabled. RTTI provides the run time type information of dynamic variables that are necessary for systems which are using dynamic variable with multiple inheritances and dynamic type casting as well as the template classes. SystemC library files are heavily dependent on the Run Time Type Information. The executable file will show output in console but will not be accurate as a real system due to the existence of the delta delay problem in SystemC which is commonly found in embedded systems. To solve this problem, tf=sc_create_vcd_trace_file ("sl_trace") needs to be added into the SystemC testbench to generate the Value Change Dump (VCD) files that can be viewed in a wave form viewer (e.g. SystemC Win) as shown in Figure 10. A VCD file is an ASCII file which consists of header information, variable definitions and the value changes for all variables specified in the task calls. VCD is a standard format that is compatible with many waveform viewers. The VCD file eliminates the need to know the internal logic of the system.

6.2 Verilog Code Generation

SystemC is the hardware modelling language based on the C++ language. SystemC provides the APIs and the simulation kernel to design and test electronic systems with high level of abstraction. However SystemC is a new hardware modelling language and the tools to convert SystemC into Electronic Data Interchange Format (EDIF) for FPGA are still lacking. It is therefore necessary to convert SystemC into other hardware description languages such as Verilog. This is because Verilog has been supported as the hardware description

Figure 16. IKBCG code generation example

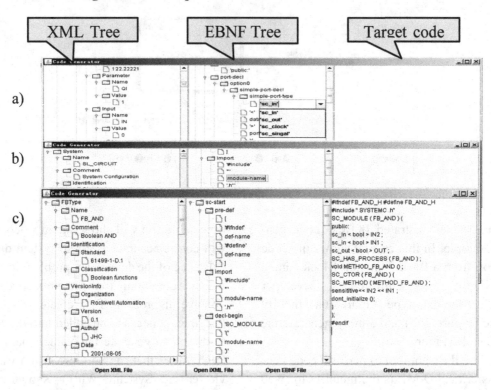

Figure 17. Simulated digital wave form

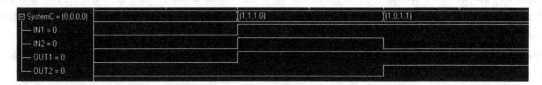

language for many years and there are numerous tools available to convert Verilog into EDIF.

The SC2V (SystemC to Verilog) (SC2V,2008) converter is a software tool which translates the SystemC source codes into the Verilog-equivalent ones. SC2V is based on the Lexical Analyzer Generator (LEX) and Yet Another Compiler-Compiler (YACC). LEX is a lexical processor for character input streams whereas YACC uses the code generated by the LEX and builds the parse tree. SC2V checks whether the input program is syntactically correct or not. Both LEX and YACC are the fundamental component for compiler construction.

SC2V it is an open source tool but it does not support In/Out ports and global variables for SystemC and, at the moment, it can only support a very limited data type for SystemC such as bool, sc_int, sc_bigint, sc_uint and sc_biguint. SC2V does not allow any C standard data types such as int, char, long and etc. Each module must have a header file with.h format including the declarations of ports, signals, processes and there must be a.cpp file which includes the implementation code of the processes. There are some expensive

Figure 18. Testing switch and light system on Spartan FPGA Board

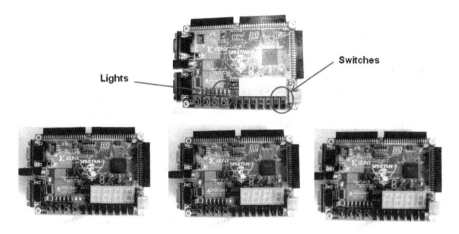

commercial tools available to convert SystemC to Verilog. They are Forte Cynthesizer (Forte, 2010), Synopsys Cocentric System Studio (Synopsis, 2008) and Agility Compiler (Agility, 2008). Once the Verilog file is generated, it could be easily converted into Electronic Data Interchange Format (EDIF) using the development environment from FPGA's vendor, e.g. Xilinx's ISE, to do the placement, routing and BIT file for configuring the FPGA chip. Figure 11 shows the Switch and Light System on a XLINIX Spartan FPGA Board.

7. CONCLUSION AND FUTURE RESEARCH

In this paper, an embedded system development framework has been proposed and a validation test has been discussed. The framework adopts the IEC 61499 for systems level design, XML, EBNF standards for source codes generation. The framework also includes the EBNF definitions for different computer languages, an IKBCG that generates different source codes and a converter from SystemC source codes to Verilog codes for FPGA-based embedded systems. The framework provides a flexible embedded software develop-

ment environment that could be use together with new or existing tools within the tool chain.

A simple case of switch and light system has been modelled in function blocks using the FBDK tool which supports XML. In this case, the various language formats are defined by the EBNF definitions to generate source codes for both microprocessor-based (e.g. C++, C, Java) and FPGA-based (e.g. SystemC). In order to implement the control system on FPGA, the switch and light system must be in HDL format because it is the only format capable of describing the circuit's operation, design and organization, in order to test and verify the operation by means of simulation. Among many hardware description languages, Verilog is chosen because there are a number of both free and commercial tools available to synthesize and route to FPGA. The function block is found to be more user-friendly for non-software specialists to design embedded systems compared to learning different programming languages and to manually code the systems.

As this research is still in an early stage, there are some limitations of the IEC 61944. First, the designer still needs to deal with many parameters and interface points in complex design. Second, the IEC 61499 does not define the detail of the metadata representation which may cause compatibility issues between different tools. Third, existing commercial tools are not cost effective whereas freeware tools chain are not integrated, not fully tested and not user friendly.

There is a potential improvement for a fully integrated tool chain. There are more research opportunities in areas such as the automated partition and optimization code from IEC 61499 to microprocessor-based, FPGA-based on hybrid solution, the automated style sheet creation, as well as the automated conversion from the traditional source codes to function block components.

REFERENCES

Aelfred. (2008). *Aelfred Parser*. Retrieved 10 October 2008, from http://saxon.sourceforge. net/aelfred.html

Agility. (2008). *Agility Compiler*. Retrieved 10 October 2008, from http://www.celoxica.com/ products/agility/default.asp

Aslam, N. (2006). *A low-cost solution for FPGA-based PCI Express Implementation*. Altera Corp. Retrieved March 09, 2007, from http://www. pldesignline.com/shared/article/showArticle. jhtml?articleId=187003208

Chen, X., et al. (2005). Modelling SystemC Design in UML and Automatic Code Generation. In *Conference on Asia South Pacific Design Automation*, (pp. 932-935).

Clark, D. P., Chen, M., & Tucker, J. V. (2004). Automatic Program Translation-A Third Way. In *IEEE Sixth International Symposium on Multimedia Software Engineering*.

Codeworker. (2010). *A universal parsing tool & a source code generator*. Retrieved 13 April 2010, from http://codeworker.free.fr/

Coyle, F. P., & Thornton, M. A. (2005). From UML to HDL: a Model Driven Architectural Approach to Hardware-Software Co-Design. In *Information Systems: New Generations Conference (ISNG)*, April 4-6, (pp. 88-93).

Dubinin, V., & Vyatkin, V. (2006). Towards a Formal Semantic Model of IEC 61499 Function Blocks. In *4th IEEE International Conference on Industrial Informatics (INDIN)*, Singapore, August 2006.

Dubinin, V., Vyatkin, V., & Hanisch, H.-M. (2006). Modelling and Verification of IEC 61499 Applications using Prolog. In *11th IEEE Conference on Emerging Technologies and Factory Automation*, Prague, September.

EBNF. (2010). *Extended Backus Naur For m*. Retrieved 13 April 2010, from http://en.wikipedia. org/wiki/Extended_Backus_Naur_For m

Fischer, J., & Boucher, T. O. (2010). *Workbook for Designing Distributed Control Applications using Rockwell Automation's HOLOBLOC Prototyping Software*. Working paper, 05-017.

Forte. (2008). *Forte Cynthesizer*. Retrieved 10 October 2008, from http://www.forteds.com/ products/cynthesizer.asp

Gomes, L., Barros, J. P., & Costa, A. (2004). Structuring Mechanisms in Petri Net Models: From specification to FPGA based implementations. In *Design of embedded control systems*. Amsterdam: Kluwer.

Graaf, B., Lormans, M., & Toetenel, H. (2003). Embedded Software Engineering: The State of the Practice. *IEEE Computer Society IEEE Software*, *20*(6), 61–69.

Grammar. (2008). *Grammar type*. Retrieved 10 October 2008, from http://www-cgi.uni-regensburg.de/~brf09510/ grammartypes.html

Hagge, N., & Wagner, B. (2005, November). A New Function Block Modelling Language Based on Petri Nets for Automatic Code generation. *IEEE Transactions on Industrial Informatics, 1*(4), 226–237. doi:10.1109/TII.2005.857614

Holobloc. (2008). *Holobloc FBDK*. Retrieved 10 October 2008, from http://www.holobloc.com.

IEC. (2000). *IEC 61499 Industrial-Process Measurement and Control Specification. IEC Technical Committee TC65/WG6*. IEC Draft.

IEC 61499-1. (2005). *Function blocks-part 1: Architecture*, (pp. 77-83).

IEC 61499-2. (2005). *Function blocks-part 2: Software tools requirements*.

ISaGRAF. (2008). *ICS Triplex ISaGRAF*. Retrieved 10 October 2008, from http://www.icstriplex.com/

Kangas, T., Kukkala, P., Orsila, H., Salminen, E., Hännikäinen, M., & Hämäläinen, T. D. (2007). UML-based Multi-Processor SoC Design Framework. *ACM Transactions on Embedded Computing Systems, 5*(2), 281–320. doi:10.1145/1151074.1151077

Khalgui, M., Rebeuf, X., & Simonot-Lion, F. (2004). A behaviour model for IEC 61499 function blocks. In *Third Workshop on Modelling of Objects, Components and Agents 2004 - MOCA'04*, (pp. 71-87).

Klingman, E. (2006). *FPGA programming step by step*. Retrieved September 07, 2006 from http://www.embedded.com/showArticle.jhtml?articleID=18201956

Kuikka, E., Leinonen, P. & Penttonen, M. (2002). *Towards Automating of Document Structure Transformations*, DocEng'02.

Megginson. (2008). *Megginson Parser*. Retrieved 10 October 2008, from http://www.megginson.com

Microns. (2010). *Micro holon for next generation embedded automation*. Retrieved 10 October 2008, from http://www.microns.org/

Microsoft. (2008). *Microsoft's DOM Parser*. Retrieved 10 October 2008, from http://msdn.microsoft.com/xml/

Mura, M., Paolieri, M., Negri, L., & Sami, M. G. (2007). StateCharts to systemc: a high level hardware simulation approach. In *Proceedings of the 17th great lakes symposium on Great lakes symposium on VLSI*, Stresa-Lago Maggiore, Italy, (pp. 505 – 508).

Nunes, R., Gomes, L., & Barros (2007). A Graphical Editor for the Input-Output Place-Transition Petri Net Class. In *12th IEEE International Conference on EWmerging Technologies and Factory Automation ETFA07*, Sept 25-28, (pp. 788-791).

SC2V. (2008). *SystemC to Verilog Converter*. Retrieved 10 October 2008, from http://www.opencores.org/projects.cgi/web/sc2v

Synopsis. (2008). *Synopsis CoCentric SystemC Compiler*. Retrieved 10 October 2008, from http://www.synopsys.com/products/cocentric_systemC/cocentric_systemC_ds.html

Tan, W. H., Thiagarajan, P. S., Wong, W. F., Zhu, Y., & Pilakkat, S. K. (2004). *Synthesizable SystemC Code from UML Models*. Presented at International Workshop on UML for SoC Design (USOC 2004), Sponsored by Design Automation Conference, June. Nguyen, K.D., Thiagarajan, P.S. & Wong, W.F. (2007). A UML-based Design Framework for Time-triggered Applications. In *28th IEEE Real-Time Systems Symposium (RTSS 07)*, Tucson, AZ.

Thramboulidis, K. (2006). *IEC 61499 in Factory Automation. Advances in Computer, Information and Systems Sciences and Engineering* (pp. 115–124). Amsterdam: Springer. doi:10.1007/1-4020-5261-8_20

Thramboulidis, K. (2005). Model-integrated mechatronics - toward a new paradigm in the development of manufacturing systems. *IEEE transactions on Industrial Informatics, 1*(1), 54- 61.

Top. (2008). *Top 10 Challenges in Logic Control for Manufacturing Systems*. Retrieved 10 October 2008, from http://www.personal.umich.edu/~tilbury/logiccontrol/

Torero. (2010). *Total life cycle web-integrated control*. Retrieved 13 April 2010, from http://www.uni-magdeburg.de/iaf/cvs/torero/

Vyatkin, V. (2007). *IEC 61499 Function Blocks for Embedded and Distribute Control Syatems Design* (pp. 50–54). ISA.

Vyatkin, V.V., Christensen, J.H., Lastra, J.L.M. (2005). OOONEIDA: An Open, Object-Oriented Knowledge Economy for Intelligent Industrial Automation. *IEEE transactions on Industrial Informatics, 1*(1), 4-17.

Wang, Y., Zhou, X. G., Zhou, B., Liang, L., & Peng, C. L. (2006). A MDA based SoC Modelling Approach using UML and SystemC. In *Proceedings of The Sixth IEEE International Conference on Computer and Information Technology (CIT'06)*.

Woll, D. (2007). *Setting the Stage for the Next Generation of Automation Control System Software: A Discussion of IEC 61499, ARC Insights, Insight# 2007-13M*. Retrieved 10 October 2007, from http://www.arcweb.com/Featured%20Research/IEC-61499-Ins13M.pdf

Zoitl, S. T., Hall, K., Staron, R., Sünder, C. & Favre-Bulle, B. (2007). The Past, Present and Future of IEC 61499. In *Holonic and Multi-Agent Systems for Manufacturing*, (LNCS 4659, pp. 1-14). Berlin: Springer.

Compilation of References

Abdallah, I. B., & ElMaraghy, H. A. (1998). Deadlock prevention and avoidance in FMS: A Petri net based approach. *International Journal of Advanced Manufacturing Technology*, *14*(10), 704–715. doi:10.1007/BF01438223

Abdelkrim, H., & Ben Saoud, S. (2008, May). *Reconfigurable system On Chip (RSOC): Concepts & Applications.* Paper presented at the Int. Conf. on Embedded Systems & Critical Applications (ICESCA), Gammarth, Tunisia.

Abe, M., Arai, H., & Kawamata, M. (2005). *Design and FPGA implementation of a structure of evolutionary digital filters for hardware implementation.* Paper presented at the IEEE International Symposium on Circuits and Systems (ISCAS).

Abele, E., Wörn, A., Stroh, C., & Elzenheimer, J. (2005). *Multi Machining Technology Integration in RMS.* Proceedings of the CIRP sponsored 3rd Conference on Reconfigurable Manufacturing, University of Michigan, Ann Arbor, MI, USA.

Abrial, J. R. (1996). *The B-Book: Assigning Programs to Meanings.* Cambridge, UK: Cambridge University Press. doi:10.1017/CBO9780511624162

Abrial, J. R. (1996). Extending B without changing it (for developing distributed systems). In H. Habrias, (Ed.), *Proceedings of the 1st Conference on the B method*, (pp. 169–191).

Abrial, J. R. (2000). Event driven circuit construction. In *MATISSE project*.

Abrial, J. R. (2003). B#:Toward a synthesis between Z and B. In D. Bert, J. P. Bowen, S. King,and Waldén, (eds.), *ZB'2003 – Formal Specification and Development in Z and B,* Turku, Finland, (LNCS 2651, pp. 168–177). Berlin: Springer-Verlag.

Abrial, J. R., & Laffitte, G. (1996). Higher-order mathematics in B. In *Formal Specification and Development in Z and B*.

Abrial, J. R., & Mussat, L. (1997). Specification and design of a transmission protocol by successive refinements using B. In M. Broy & B. Schieder, (eds.), *Mathematical Methods in Program Development,* (NATO ASI Series F: Computer and Systems Sciences vol. 158, pp 129–200). Berlin: Springer.

Abrial, J. R., & Mussat, L. (1998). Introducing dynamic constraints in B. In D. Bert, (Ed.), *B'98: The 2nd international B Conference,* (LNCS 1393, pp83–128). Berlin: Springer Verlag.

Acharya, S., & Mahapatra, R.-N. (2008). A dynamic slack management technique for real-time distributed embedded systems. *IEEE Transactions on Computers*, *57*(2).

Aelfred. (2008). *Aelfred Parser*. Retrieved 10 October 2008, from http://saxon.sourceforge.net/aelfred.html

Aeronautical Radio, Inc. (1997). *Avionics Application Software Standard Interface*. Technical report.

Aggarwal, V., & Kuhlman, R. (2007). *Simulating Sensors on FPGA Hardware*. Paper presented at the Embedded Systems Conferences, ESC-402.

Agility. (2008). *Agility Compiler*. Retrieved 10 October 2008, from http://www.celoxica.com/products/agility/default.asp

Aguirre, M. A., Tombs, J. N., Lecuyer, V. B., Mora, J. L., Carrasco, J. M., & Torralba, A. B. (2005). Microprocessor and FPGA interfaces for in-system co-debugging in field programmable hybrid systems. *Microprocessors and Microsystems, 29*(2-3), 75–85. doi:10.1016/j.micpro.2004.06.009

Ahmadinia, A., Bobda, C., Fekete, S.-P., Teich, J., & Van Der Veen, J.-C. (2007). Optimal free-space management and routing-conscious dynamic placement for reconfigurable devices. *IEEE Transactions on Computers, 56*(5).

Akgul, B. (2004). *The System-on-a-Chip Lock Cache*. PhD thesis, School of ECE, Georgia Institute of Technology, Atlanta, GA.

Alfke, P. (2009). *Xilinx Virtex-6 and Spartan-6 FPGA Families [PowerPoint slides]*. Retrieved October 20, 2009, from FPL 2009: http://fpl2009.org/

Al-Safi, Y., & Vyatkin, V. (2007). An ontology-based reconfiguration agent for intelligent mechatronic systems. In *Third International Conference on Industrial Applications of Holonic and Multi-Agent Systems*. Berlin: Springer-Verlag.

Altera Corp. (2002, january). Retrieved from Altera Excalibur™ Embedded Processor Solutions Gain Global Acceptance At Alcatel: http://www.altera.com

Altera Corp. (2008). *40-nm FPGAs: Architecture and Performance Comparison*. Retrieved October 20, 2009, from Altera.com: http://www.altera.com/

Altera Corp. (2009, June). *FPGA Run-Time Reconfiguration: Two Approaches*. Retrieved from www.altera.com.

ALTERA Corporation. (2009, March). *MicroC/OS-II Real-Time Operating System, Nios II Software Developer's Handbook, NII52008-9.0.0*.

Alur, R., & Dill, D. (1994). A theory of Timed Automata. *Theoretical Computer Science, 126*(2), 183–235.

Alur, R. (1992). *Techniques for Automatic Verification of Real-Time Systems*. PhD Thesis, Stanford University, Stanford, CA.

Alur, R., & Yannakakis, M. (1998). Model checking of hierarchical state machines. In *Sixth ACM Symposium on the Foundations of Software Engineering*, (pp. 175-188).

Amjad, H. (2006). Verification of AMBA Using a Combination of Model Checking and Theorem Proving. *Electronic Notes in Theoretical Computer Science, 145*, 45–61. doi:10.1016/j.entcs.2005.10.004

Ammari, A. C., & Jemai, A. (2009, January). Multiprocessor platform-based design for multimedia, Journal of Computers & Digital Techniques. *IET, 3*(1), 52–61.

Amnell, T., Behrmann, G., Bengtsson, J., D'Argenio, P., David, A., Fehnker, A., et al. (2001). Uppaal - Now, Next, and Future. In Cassez, F., Jard, C., Rozoy, B., Ryan, M.D. (Eds.), *Modeling and Verification of Parallel Processes*, (LNCS Vol. 2067, pp. 99-124). Berlin: Springer.

Andersson, B., & Jonsson, J. (2002). Preemptive Multiprocessor Scheduling Anomalies. In *International Parallel and Distributed Processing Symposium - Symposium Volume*, (pp. 0012).

Andrews, D., Niehaus, D., & Ashenden, P. J. (2004). Programming Models for Hybrid CPU/FPGA Chips. *IEEE Computer, 37*(1), 118–120.

Andrews, D., Sass, R., Anderson, E., Agron, J., Peck, W., & Stevens, J. (2008, January). Achieving Programming Model Abstractions For Reconfigurable Computing. *IEEE Transactions on Very Large Scale Integration (VLSI). Systems, 16*(1), 34–44.

Angelov, C., Sierszecki, K., & Marian, N. (2005). Design models for reusable and reconfigurable state machines. In L.T. Yang, et al. (Eds.), *EUC 2005*, (LNCS 3824, pp. 152-163). International Federation for Information Processing.

Apple Snow Leopard. (2008). Retrieved from Apple Previews Mac OS X Snow Leopard to Developers: http://www.apple.com/pr/library/2008/06/09snowleopard.html

Archer, M., Vito, B., & Munoz, C. (2003). Developing user strategies in pvs: A tutorial. In *Proceedings of the First InternationalWorkshop on Design and Application of Strategies/Tactics in Higher Order Logics (STRATA)*.

Arcticus. (2009). *Rubus OS Reference Manual*. Retrieved from Arcticus Systems, http://www.arcticus-systems.com/

Arkoudas, K. Khurshid, S. Marinov, D. & Rinard, M. (2003). Integrating model checking and theorem proving for relational reasoning. In *Proceedings of the 7th International Seminar on Relational Methods in Computer Science (RelMiCS)* (LNCS 3015, pp. 21-33). Berlin: Springer-Verlag.

Arnold, J. (Dec. 2005). S5: the architecture and development flow of a software configurable processor. *IEEE International Conference on Field-Programmable Technology*, (pp. 121-128).

Asarin, E., Bournez, O., Dang, T., & Maler, O. (2000). Approximate reachability analysis of piecewise-linear dynamical systems. In *Hybrid Systems: Computation and Control, Third International Workshop*, (LNCS).

Aslam, N. (2006). *A low-cost solution for FPGA-based PCI Express Implementation*. Altera Corp. Retrieved March 09, 2007, from http://www.pldesignline.com/shared/article/showArticle.jhtml?articleId=187003208

Asokan, V. (2007). Dual Processor Reference Design Suite. *Xilinx application note, APP996*.

Astarloa, A., Làzaro, J. s., Bidarte, U., Jiménez, J., & Zuloaga, A. (2009). FPGA technology for multi-axis control systems. *Mechatronics*, *19*(2), 258–268. doi:10.1016/j.mechatronics.2008.09.001

Atkinson, C., & Kühne, T. (2003). Model-Driven Development: A Metamodeling Foundation. *IEEE Software*, *20*(5), 36–41. doi:10.1109/MS.2003.1231149

Atmel Corp. (2009). Retrieved from FPSLIC™ (AVR with FPGA) http://www.atmel.com/products/FPSLIC/

Austin, T., Larson, E., & Ernst, D. (2002, February). SimpleScalar: An infrastructure for computer system modeling. *IEEE Computer*, *35*(2), 59–67.

AutoPilot. (2009). Retrieved from AutoESL: http://www.autoesl.com/

Ayala, J.-L., Lopez-Vallejo, M., Bertozzi, D., & Benini, L. (2009). SoC Communication Architectures: from interconnection busses to packet-switched NoCs. In Zurawski, R. (Ed.), *Embedded systems design and verification* (2nd ed., pp. 1–28). CRC Press.

Aydi, Y., Meftali, S., Abid, M., & Dekeyser, J. L. (2007). Design and Performance Evaluation of a Reconfigurable Delta MIN for MPSOC. In Proc. of *the 19th International Conference on Microelectronics (ICM '07)*.

Back, R. J. (1990). Refinement calculus, part II: Parallel and reactive programs. In *Stepwise Refinement of Distributed Systems, (LNCS 430)*. Berlin: Springer-Verlag.

Back, R. J., & Sere, K. (1989). Stepwise refinement of action systems. In *Mathematics of Program Construction* (pp 115–1380). Berlin: Springer-Verlag.

Back, R. J., & Wright, J. v. (1998). *Refinement Calculus: A Systematic Introduction*. Berlin: Springer-Verlag.

Bailey, B., Martin, G., & Piziali, A. (2007). *ESL Design and Verification: A Prescription for Electronic System Level Methodology*. San Francisco, CA: Morgan Kaufmann Publishers.

Bainbridge, W.-J., & Furber, S.-B. (2001). Delay Insensitive System-on-Chip Interconnect using 1-of-4 Data Encoding. *7th International Symposium on Asynchronous Circuits and Systems ASYNC*, (p. 118). Salt Lake City, Utah.

Baker, T., & Sanjoy, B. (2009). Sustainable Multiprocessor Scheduling of Sporadic Task Systems. In *21st Euromicro Conference on Real-Time Systems (ECRTS'09)*, (pp. 141-150).

Balarin, F., Sentovich, E., Chiodo, M., Giusto, P., Hsieh, H., & Tabbara, B. (1997). *Hardware-Software Co-design of Embedded Systems - The POLIS approach*. Kluwer Academic Publishers.

Balarin, F., Watanabe, Y., Hsieh, H., Lavagno, L., Passerone, C., & Sangiovanni-Vincentelli, A. (2003). Metropolis: An integrated electronic system design environment. *Computer, 36*(4), 45–52. doi:10.1109/MC.2003.1193228

Balbastre, P., & Crespo, A. (2006). Optimal deadline assignment for periodic real-time tasks in dynamic priority systems. In *Proceedings of the 18th Euromicro Conference on Real-Time Systems (ECRTS'06)*, Dresden, Germany July 5-7.

Balbastre, P., & Ripoll, I. (2002). Schedulability analysis of window-constrained execution time tasks for real-time control. In *Proc. Of the 14th Euromicro Conference on Real- Time Systems (ECRTS'02)*.

Balboni, A., Fornaciari, W., & Sciuto, D. (1996). Partitioning and exploration in the TOSCA co-design flow. In *Proceedings of the IEEE International Workshop on Hardware/Software Codesign CODES*, (pp. 62–69), Los Alamitos, CA.

Balderas-Contreras, T. (2004). *Hardware/Software Implementation of the Security Functions for Third Generation Cellular Networks*. Masters Thesis, INAOE, Tonantzintla, Puebla, Mexico.

Barbalace, A. (2008, February). Performance Comparison of VxWorks, Linux, RTAI and Xenomea in a Hard Real-Time Application. *IEEE Transactions on Nuclear Science, 55*(1), 435–439. doi:10.1109/TNS.2007.905231

Barkaoui, K., & Pradat-Peyre, J. F. (1996). On liveness and controlled siphons in Petri nets. In *Proceeding 17th International Conference on Applications and Theory of Petri Nets*, (LNCS 1091, pp.57–72).

Barnes, W. (2004). ARINC *653 and why is it important for a safety-critical RTOS*. Retrieved from http://www.embedded-control-europe.com/c_ece_knowhow/424/basapr04p16.pdf

Barry, R. (2010). *Using the FreeRTOS Real Time Kernel, NXP LPC 17xx Edition*. Real Time Engineers Ltd.

Bartic, T. A. (2003). Highly scalable network on chip for reconfigurable systems. In Proc. *Int. Symp. Syst.-on-Chip* (pp. 79-82).

Baruah, S., Howell, R., & Rosier, L. (1990). Algorithms and complexity concerning the preemptive scheduling of periodic real-time tasks on one processor. *Real-Time Systems, 2*, 301–324. doi:10.1007/BF01995675

Baruah, S., Buttazo, G., Gorinsky, S., & Lipari, G. (1999). Scheduling periodic task systems to minimize output jitter. In *6th Conference on Real-Time Computing Systems and Applications*, (pp. 62-69).

Batista, R. B., Boukerche, A., & Melo, A. C. M. A. (2008). A parallel strategy for biological sequence alignment in restricted memory space. *Journal of Parallel and Distributed Processing, 68*(4), 548–561. doi:10.1016/j.jpdc.2007.08.007

Bauer, M., & Ecker, W. (1997). Hardware/software co-simulation in a VHDL-based test bench approach. In *Proc. of the Design Automation Conference DAC*, (pp. 774-779).

Baumgarte, V., May, F., Nückel, A., Vorbach, M., & Weinhardt, M. (2001). PACT XPP – a self-reconfigurable data processing architecture. In *Proc. 1st Int. Conf. on Engineering of Reconfigurable Systems and Algorithms (ERSA)*, (pp. 64–70). Las Vegas, NV: CSREA Press.

Baynes, K., Collins, C., Fiterman, E., Ganesh, B., Kohout, P., & Smit, C. (2003, November). The performance and energy consumption of embedded real-time operating systems. *IEEE Transactions on Computers, 52*(11), 1454–1469. doi:10.1109/TC.2003.1244943

Bellard, F. (2005). QEMU, a fast and portable dynamic translator. In *ATEC '05: Proceedings of the annual conference on USENIX Annual Technical Conference*.

Bellegarde, F., Chouali, S., & Julliand, J. (2002). Verification of dynamic constraints for B event systems under fairness assumptions. In *ZB'2002 – Formal Specification and Development in Z and B*, (LNCS 2272, pp. 477-496). New York: Springer-Verlag.

Ben Achballah, A., Ben Othman, S., & Ben Saoud, S. (2010, Mar.). *High Level Synthesis of Real Time embedded emulating system for motor controller.* Paper presented at the 5th Int. Conf. on Design & Technology of Integrated Systems in Nanoscale Era (DTIS), Hammamet, Tunisia.

Ben Jmaa Derbel, H., (2007). On the pid control of systems with large delays. *International Journal of Modelling, Identification and Control (IJMIC), 2*(1).

Ben Othman, S., Ben Salem, A. K., & Ben Saoud, S. (2008, Mar.). *MPSoC Design of RT Control Applications based on FPGA SoftCore Processors.* Paper presented at the ICECS, Saint Julians, Malte.

Ben Salem, A. K., Ben Othman, S., & Ben Saoud, S. (2010). FPGA-Based System-on-Chip for RT Power Process Control [AJAS]. *American Journal of Applied Sciences, 7*(1), 127–139. doi:10.3844/ajassp.2010.127.139

Ben Salem, A. K., Ben Othman, S., & Ben Saoud, S. (2008, Jun.). *Hard and Soft-Core Implementation of Embedded Control Application Using RTOS.* Paper presented at the IEEE Int. Symposium on Industrial Electronics (ISIE), Cambridge, UK.

Ben Saoud, S. (1996). *Emulateur temps réel d'associations Convertisseurs statiques / Machines électriques / Capteurs: Etude, conception et réalisation. ENSEEIHT.* France: INPT.

Ben Saoud, S., & Gajski, D. D. (2001). *Co-design of Emulators for Power electric Processes Using SpecC Methodology.* Technical Report ICS-TR, 01-46.

Benini, L. (2006). Application Specific NoC Design. In *Proceedings of the Design Automation & Test in Europe Conference DATE, 1,* (pp. 105), Munich, Germany.

Benini. L., & Micheli. G. D. (2002). Networks on chips: A new SoC paradigm. *Computer, 1 (35),* IEEE Computer Society Press, Los Alamitos, California, 70-78.

Benkhermi, I., Benkhelifa, A., Chillet, D., Pillement, S., Prévotet, J.-C., & Verdier, F. (2005). System-level Modelling for Reconfigurable SoCs. In *20th Conference on Design of Circuits and Integrated Systems (DCIS),* Lisboa, Portugal.

Benkrid, K., Liu, Y. & Benkrid, A. (2009). A highly parameterized and efficient FPAG-based skeleton for pairwise biological sequence alignment. *IEEE Transactions on Very large Integration Systems, 17*(4), 561-570.

Benkrid, K., Velentzas, P., & Kasap, S. (2008). A high performance reconfigurable core for motif searching using profile HMM. In *NASA/ESA Conference on Adaptive Hardware and Systems,* (pp. 285-292).

Bensalem, S., Bozga, M., Sifakis, J., & Nguyen, T. H. (2008). *Compositional verification for component-based systems and application.* Paper presented at the 6th Int. Symposium on Automated Technology for Verification and Analysis, ATVA.

Berg, C. (2006). PLRU Cache Domino Effects. In *Proc 6th Intl. Workshop on Worst-Case Execution Time (WCET) Analysis.*

Berna-koes, M., Nourbakhsh, I., & Sycara, K. (2003). Communication efficiency in multiagent systems. *International Conference on Robotics and Automation,* April 26 - May 1, (Vol. 3, pp. 2129 - 2134).

Bernardi, S., Merseguer, J., & Petriu, D. (2008). *An UML profile for dependability analysis and modeling of software systems. Technical report.* Spain: University of Zaragoza.

Bernat, G., & Burns, A. & A., L. (2001). Weakly Hard Real-Time Systems. *IEEE Transactions on Computers, 50*(4), 308–321. doi:10.1109/12.919277

Bernat, G., Colin, A., & Petters, S. M. (2002). WCET Analysis of Probabilistic Hard Real-Time Systems. In *Proc. 23rd IEEE Real-Time Systems Symposium,* (pp. 279-288).

Berry, G., & Coresserat, L. (1985). The ESTEREL sychronous programming language and its mathematical semantics, *in Seminar on Concurrency, ed. S. D. Brookes, A. W. Roscoe and G. Winskel* (pp.389-448). (Lecture Note in Computer Science, vol. 197.), Springer Verlag.

Bert, D., & Cave, F. (2000). *Construction of finite labelled transistion systems from B abstract systems* (pp. 235–254). IFM.

Bert, D. (2001). Preuve de propriétés d'équité en B: Preuve de l'algorithme d'arbitrage du bus SCSI-3. In *AFADL'2001* (pp. 221–241). ADER/LORIA.

Berthelot, F., Nouvel, F., & Houzet, D. (2006). Partial and dynamic reconfiguration of FPGAs: a top down design methodology for an automatic implementation. *International Parallel and Distributed Processing Symposium IPDPS, 20.*

Betts, A., & Bernat, G. (2006). Tree-Based WCET Analysis on Instrumentation Point Graphs. In *Proc. 9th IEEE International Symposium on Object-oriented Real-time distributed Computing.*

Betz, V., Rose, J., & Marquardt, A. (1999). *Architecture and CAD for deep-submicron FPGAs.* Amsterdam: Kluwer Academic Publishers.

Betz, V. (2009). *FPGA Challenges and Opportunities at 40nm and Beyond [PowerPoint slides].* Retrieved October 20, 2009, from FPL 2009: http://fpl2009.org/

Beyer, D., Lewerentz, C., & Noack, A. (2003). Rabbit: A Tool for BDD-based Verification of Real-Time Systems. In W.A. Hunt, Jr. & F. Somenzi (Eds.), *Computer Aided Verification,* (LNCS. Vol. 2725, pp. 122-125), Boulder, CO. Berlin: Springer.

Bhattacharyya, S., Bier, J., Gass, W., Krishnamurthy, R., Lee, E., & Konstatinides, K. (2008, Nov.). Advances in hardware design and implementation of signal processing systems. *IEEE Signal Processing Magazine, 25*(6), 175–180. doi:10.1109/MSP.2008.929838

Bhoot, J., & Takahashi, T. (2003, Summer 2003). Platform Delivers Fast, Flexible AC Servomotor-Control Designs. *Xcell Journal.*

Bimbard, F., & George, L. (2006, April). FP/FIFO Feasibility Conditions with Kernel Overheads for Periodic Tasks on an Event Driven OSEK System. In *9th IEEE International Symposium on Object and component-oriented Real-time distributed Computing (ISORC'06),* Gyeongju, Korea.

Bini, E., & Buttazzo, G. (2003). Rate monotonic analysis: the hyperbolic bound. *IEEE Transactions on Computers, 52*(7). doi:10.1109/TC.2003.1214341

Bini, E., & Buttazzo, G. (2004). Schedulability Analysis of Periodic Fixed Priority Systems. *IEEE Transactions on Computers, 53*(11). doi:10.1109/TC.2004.103

Bini, E., & Buttazzo, G. (2007). The space of EDF feasible deadlines. In *Proceedings of the 19th Euromicro Conference on Real-Time Systems (ECRTS'07), Pisa, Italy July 4-6.*

Bini, E., & Cervin, A. (2008). Delay-Aware Period Assignment in Control Systems. In *Proceeding of IEEE Real-Time Systems Symposium (RTSS'2008),* Barcelona, Spain.

Bini, E., & Di Natale, M. (2005). Optimal Task Rateselection in Fixed Priority Systems. In *Proceedings of the 26th IEEE International Real-Time Systems Symposium (RTSS'05).*

Bini, E., Di Natale, M., & Buttazzo, G. (2006). Sensitivity Analysis for Fixed-Priority Real-Time Systems. In *Proceedings of the 18th Euromicro Conference on Real-Time Systems (ECRTS'06),* Dresden, Germany, July 5-7.

Biocceleration. (2009). *BioXL/H.* Retrieved October 10, 2009, from http://www.biocceleration.com

Björklund, D. (2001). *The SMDL Statechart Description Language: Design, Semantics and Implementation.* Masters Thesis, Abo Akademi University, Finland.

Björklund, D., & Lilius, J. (2002). From UML Behavioral Descriptions to Efficient Synthesizable VHDL. In *Proceedings of the 20th IEEE Norchip Conference,* Copenhagen, Denmark.

Blaschke, F. (1972). The principle of field orientation as applied to the new transvektor closed-loop control system for rotating-field machines. *Siemens Review, 34*(5), 217–220.

Bleiweiss, A. N. (2008). GPU Accelerated Pathfinding. In *Proceedings of the 23rd ACM SIGGRAPH/EUROGRAPHICS symposium on Graphics hardware,* (pp. 65-74). Sarajevo, Bosnia and Herzegovina.

Bobda, C. (2007). *Introduction to Reconfigurable Computing: Architectures, Algorithms, and Applications.* Dordrecht, Netherlands: Springer Netherlands.

Boer, E. R., & Murata, T. (1994). Generating basis siphons and traps of Petri nets using the sign incidence matrix. *IEEE Transactions on Circuits and Systems. I, Fundamental Theory and Applications*, *41*(4), 266–271. doi:10.1109/81.285680

Bollela, Gosling, Brosgol, Dibble, Furr, Hardin & Trunbull. (2000). *The Real-Time Specification for Java*, (1st ed.). Reading, MA: Addison & Wesley.

Bolsens, I., De Man, H.-J., Lin, B., Van Rompaey, K., Vercauteren, S., & Verkest, D. (1997, Mar). Hardware/software co-design of digital telecommunication systems. *Proceedings of the IEEE*, *85*(3), 391–418. doi:10.1109/5.558713

Bolsens, I. (Sept. 2002). Challenges and Opportunities of FPGA Platforms. *in Proceedings of the 12th International Conference on Field-Programmable Logic and Applications FPL'02*, (pp. 39–392). Montpellier, France.

Borrione, D., Helmy, A., & Schmaltz, J. (2008). Executable formal specification and validation of NOC communication infrastructures. Proc. of *the 21ˢᵗ annual symposium on Integrated circuits and system design*. Brazil.

Borrione. D., Helmy. A., Pierre. L., & Schmaltz. J. (2009). A Formal approach to the verification of networks on chip. *Eurasip Journal on Embedded Systems, (2009)*.

Bose, B. K. (2007). *Modern Power Electronics and AC Drives*. Prentice Hall.

Bosheng, S., & Zhiqiang, G. (2005). A DSP-based active disturbance rejection control design for a 1-kW H-bridge DC-DC power converter. *IEEE Transactions on Industrial Electronics*, *52*(5), 1271–1277. doi:10.1109/TIE.2005.855679

Bougueroua, L., George, L., & Midonnet, M. (2007). Dealing with execution-overruns to improve the temporal robustness of real-time systems scheduled FP and EDF. In *The Second International Conference on Systems (ICONS'07)*, Sainte-Luce, Martinique, France, April 22 - 28.

Bougueroua, L., George, L., & Midonnet, S. (2006). An execution overrun management mechanism for the temporal robustness of java real-time systems. In *The 4th International Workshop on Java Technologies for Real-time and Embedded Systems (JTRES 2006)*, 11-13 October 2006, *CNAM*, Paris, France.

Boussak, M., & Jarray, K. (2005). A high-performance sensorless indirect stator flux orientation control of induction motor drive. *IEEE Transactions on Industrial Electronics*, *53*(1), 41–49. doi:10.1109/TIE.2005.862319

Boussctta, H., Abid, M., Layouni, F., & Pistrito, C. (Dec. 2004). STBus transaction level models using SystemC 2.0. *Proceedings of the 16th International Conference on Microelectronics ICM*, (pp. 347- 350), Sfax, Tunisia.

Brennan, R. W., Fletcher, M., & Norrie, D. H. (2002). An agent-based approach to reconfiguration of real-time distributed control systems. *IEEE Journal on Robotics and Automation*, *18*(4), 444–451. doi:10.1109/TRA.2002.802211

Brennan, R. W., Zhang, X., Xu, Y., & Norrie, D. H. (2002). A reconfigurable concurrent function block model and its implementation in real-time java. *Integrated Computer-Aided Engineering*, *9*, 263–279.

Brennan, R.-W., Fletcher, M., & Norrie, D.-H. (2001). A holonic approach to reconfiguring real-time distributed control systems. In *Multi-Agent Systems and Applications: MASA'01*. Berlin: Springer-Verlag.

Brinkschulte, U., Schneider, E., & Picioragá, F. (2005). Dynamic real-time reconfiguration in distributed systems: timing issues and solutions. In *Proceedings of the Eighth IEEE International Symposium on Object-Oriented Real-Time Distributed Computing, ISORC 2005*, Seattle, WA, (pp. 174–181).

Bruel, J.-M. (1996). Fuze: Un environnement intégré pour l'analyse formelle de logiciels distribués temps réel, *thèse doctoral en informatique*, université Paul Sabatier, Toulouse, France.

Bucci, G., Sassoli, L., & Vicario, E. (2005). Correctness Verification and Performance Analysis of Real-Time Systems Using Stochastic Preemptive Time Petri Nets. *Transactions on Software Engineering, 31*(11), 913–927. doi:10.1109/TSE.2005.122

Bucci, G. (1995). *CAMPANAI, G., &Nesi, P (Vol. 8*, pp. 117–172). Tools for Specifying Real-Time Systems.

Bueno, E. J., Hernandez, Ã., Rodriguez, F. J., Giron, C., Mateos, R., & Cobreces, S. (2009). A DSP- and FPGA-Based Industrial Control With High-Speed Communication Interfaces for Grid Converters Applied to Distributed Power Generation Systems. *IEEE Transactions on Industrial Electronics, 56*(3), 654–669. doi:10.1109/TIE.2008.2007043

Burmester, S. (2004). Modeling reconfigurable mechatronic systems with mechatronic UML. *MDAFA - Model Driven Architecture: Foundations and Applications*.

Burns, A., Dobbing, B. & Vardenega, T. (2003). Guide for the use of the Ada Ravenscar Profile in high integrity systems. *ACM SIGAda Ada Letters*.

Bussmann, S., & McFarlane, D. (1999). *Rationales for Holonic Manufacturing Control*. In 2nd International Workshop on Intelligent Manufacturing Systems. New York: Leuven.

Bussow, R., & Grieskamp, W. (1998). The ZETA System: Overview, *Technical Report*, Berlin.

Butenhof, D. R. (1997). *Programming with POSIX threads*. Boston: Addison-Wesley Longman Publishing Co. eCosCentric. (2008). *eCos*. Retrieved from http://ecos.sourceware.org

Buttazzo, G., Lipari, G., Caccamo, M., & Abeni, L. (2002). Elastic scheduling for flexible workload management. *IEEE Transactions on Computers, 51*(3). doi:10.1109/12.990127

Buttazzo, G. (2006). Achieving scalability in real-time systems. In *IEEE Computer*.

Buttazzo, G. C. (2005). Hard Real Time Computing Systems: Predictable Scheduling Algorithms and Applications. *Real-Time Systems, Springer, 23*(2).

Buttazzo, G., & Stankovic, J. (1993). RED: A Robust Earliest Deadline Scheduling. In *3rd international Workshop on responsive Computing*, Sept.

Buttazzo, G., Lipari, G., & Abeni, L. (1998). Elastic task model for adaptive rate control. In *proc. of the 19th IEEE Real- Time System Symposium*, Dec. 1998.

Cai, L., & Gajski, D. (2003). Transaction-level Modeling: an Overview. In *Proc. of the Int. Conf. on Hardware/Software Codesign and System Synthesis* (pp. 19–24). New York: ACM Press.

Caldari, M., Conti, M., Coppola, M., Curaba, S., Pieralisi, L., & Turchetti, C. (2003). Transaction-Level Models for AMBA Bus Architecture Using SystemC 2.0. *Proceedings of the Design, Automation and Test in Europe conference DATE: Designers' Forum*, (p. 20026).

Calderon, D. R. H., & Vassiliadis, S. (2005, Nov. 2005). *Soft core processors and embedded processing: a survey and analysis*. Paper presented at the ProRisc, Veldhoven, the Netherlands.

Campi, F., Deledda, A., Pizzotti, M., Ciccarelli, L., Rolandi, P., & Mucci, C. (2007). *A dynamically adaptive DSP for heterogeneous reconfigurable platforms* (pp. 9–14). Proceedings of Design Automation and Test in Europe DATE.

Cansell, D., Méry, D., & Merz, S. (2001). Diagram refinements for the design of reactive systems. *Journal of Universal Computer Science, 7*(2), 159–174.

Cansell, D., Méry, D., & Merz, S. (2001). Formal analysis of a self-stabilizing algorithm using predicate diagrams. In *Workshop Integrating Diagrammatic and Formal Specification Techniques*.

Carbone, S., Colli, V. D., Stefano, R. D., Figalli, G., & Marignetti, F. (2009). *Design and Implementation of High performance FPGA Control for Permanent Magnet Synchronous Motor*. Paper presented at the 35th Annual Conference of the IEEE Industrial Electronics Society, IECON 2009.

Cardell-Oliver, R. (1992). *The Formal Verification of Hard Real-time Systems*. PhD Thesis, University of Cambridge, Cambridge, UK.

Cardoso, J. M., & Diniz, P. C. (2009). *Compilation Techniques for Reconfigurable Architectures*. New York, NY: Springer US.

Carloni, L., De Bernardinis, F., Pinello, C., Sangiovanni-Vincentelli, A.-L., & Sgroi, M. (2005). Platform-based design for embedded systems. In Zurawski, R., & Raton, B. (Eds.), *Embedded Systems Handbook* (pp. 1–26). Boca Raton, FL: CRC Press.

Cecati, C. (1999). Microprocessors for power electronics and electrical drives applications. *IEEE Industrial Electronics Society Newsletter, 46*(3), 5–9.

Cell broadband engine. (2006). Retrieved from IBM Research: Compiler Technology for Scalable Architectures: http://domino.research.ibm.com/comm/research_projects.nsf/pages/cellcompiler.index.html

Cervin, A., Lincoln, B., Eker, J., Arzen, K. & G., B. (2004). The jitter margin and its application in the design of real-time control systems. In *proceedings of the IEEE Conference on Real-Time and Embedded Computing Systems and Applications*.

Cesario, W. -0., Baghdadi, A., Gauthier, L., Lyonnard, D., Nicolescu, G., & Paviot, Y. (2002). Component-based design approach for multicore SoCs. *In Proceedings of the Design Automation Conference DAC*, (pp. 789-794).

Chandy, K. M., & Misra, J. (1989). *Parallel Program Design*. Austin, TX: Addison-Wesley.

Chen, X., et al. (2005). Modelling SystemC Design in UML and Automatic Code Generation. In *Conference on Asia South Pacific Design Automation*, (pp. 932-935).

Cheung. T, & Smith. J. E. (1986). A simulation study of the CRAY X-MP memory system. *IEEE Transactions on Computers, 7 (35)*. IEEE Computer Society, Washington. 613-622.

Chilenski, J. (2007). *Aerospace Vehicle Systems Institute Systems and Software Integration Verification Overview.* AADL Safety and Security Modeling Meeting.

Christensen, J. H. (2009). *Holobloc Inc. - Resources for the New Generation of Automation and Control.* Retrieved November 2, 2009 from http://www.holobloc.com

Christian, D., Jean, B., Vincent, L., & Simon, A. (2008). *Real-Time Simulation on FPGA of a Permanent Magnet Synchronous Machine Drive Using a Finite-Element Based Model.* Paper presented at the International Symposium on Power Electronics, Electrical Drives, Automation and Motion (SPEEDAM 2008).

Chu, F., & Xie, X. L. (1997). Deadlock analysis of Petri nets using siphons and mathematical programming. *IEEE Transactions on Robotics and Automation, 13*(6), 793–804. doi:10.1109/70.650158

Church, A. (1940). A Formulation of the Simple Theory of Types. *J. of Symbolic Logic, 5,* 56–68. doi:10.2307/2266170

Chutinan, A., & Krogh, B.-K. (1999). Verification of Polyhedral-invariant hybrid automata using polygonal flow pipe approximations. In *Hybrid Systems: Computation and Control, Second International Workshop*, (LNCS).

Clark, D. P., Chen, M., & Tucker, J. V. (2004). Automatic Program Translation-A Third Way. In *IEEE Sixth International Symposium on Multimedia Software Engineering.*

Clarke, E., Biere, A., Raimi, R., & Zhu, Y. (2001). Bounded Model Checking Using Satisfiability Solving. *Formal Methods in System Design, 19,* 7–34. doi:10.1023/A:1011276507260

Clarke, E., Grumberg, O., & Peled, D. (1999). *Model checking*. Cambridge, MA: MIT Press.

Clarke, E. M. (1997). *Temporal logic model checking (abstract).* ILPS.

Clarke, E. M., Emerson, E. A., & Sistla, A. P. (1986). Automatic verification of finite-state concurrent systems using temporal logic specifications. *ACM Transactions on Programming Languages and Systems, 8,* 244–263. doi:.doi:10.1145/5397.5399

Clarke, E., Kroening, D., & Lerda, F. (2004). A Tool for Checking ANSI-C Programs. In Jensen, K., & Podelski, A. (Eds.), *LNCS 2988* (pp. 168–176). Berlin: Springer.

Clarke, E. M. (1994). Automatic verification of finite-state concurrent systems. In *Application and Theory of Petri Nets*.

Clarke, E. M. GRUMBERG, O., Jha, S., Lu, Y., & Veith, H. (2001). Progress on the state explosion problem in model checking. In *Lecture Notes in Computer Science*, (vol. 2000pp. 176–194).

Clarke, E. M., & Wing, J. M. (1996). Formal Methods: state of the art and Future Directions, *ACM computing survey* (pp. 626-643). Vol. 28, N0 4.

ClearSy. (2002). *Atelier B*. Technical Note, Version 3.6, Aix-en-Provence(F).

Clearsy. (2004). *B4free*. Technical Note, Version B3.7, http://www.b4free.com, Aix-en-Provence(F).

Clearsy.(2004). *B4free*. Aix-en-Provence(F), Technical Note Version B3.7. Retrieved from http://www.b4free.com/

CoCentric System Studio. (2008). Retrieved from Synopsys: http://www.synopsys.com

Codeworker. (2010). *A universal parsing tool & a source code generator*. Retrieved 13 April 2010, from http://codeworker.free.fr/

Cohen, B. (1994). A brief history of formal methods. *FACS Europe*, *1*(0), 3.

Compton, K., & Hauck, S. (2002). Reconfigurable Computing: A Survey of Systems and Software. *ACM Computing Surveys*, *34*, 171–210. doi:10.1145/508352.508353

Cong, J., Gururaj, K., & Han, G. (2009). *Synthesis of reconfigurable high-performance multicore systems*. Paper presented at the Proceeding of the ACM/SIGDA international symposium on Field programmable gate arrays.

Convergen, S. C. (2008). Retrieved from CoWare: http://www.coware.com

Cooke, C., McNelly, H., & Martin, T. (1999). *Surviving the SOC Revolution: A Guide to Platform-Based Design*. Boston, MA: Kluwer Academic Publishers.

Coppola, M., Curaba, S., Grammatikakis, M., & Maruccia, G. (2003). IPSIM: SystemC 3.0 enhancements for communication refinement. In *Proceedings of the Design Automation and Test Conference in Europe*, (pp. 106-111).

Corkill, D.-D., Holzhauer, D., & Koziarz, W. (2007). Turn Off Your Radios! Environmental Monitoring Using Power-Constrained Sensor Agents. In *First International Workshop on Agent Technology for Sensor Networks (ATSN-07)*, Honolulu, Hawaii, (pp. 31-38).

Coumeri, S., & Thomas, D. (1995). A simulation environment for hardware-software codesign. *In Proc. of the Int. Conference on Computer Design*, (pp. 58-63).

Coussy, P., & Morawiec, A. (2008). *High-Level Synthesis: From Algorithm to Digital Circuit*.

Cox, I.-J., & Gehani, N.-H. (1989). *Concurrent Programming and Robotics*", Robotics Resolution, Vol. 8, N0 2, (pp. 3-16).

Coyle, F. P., & Thornton, M. A. (2005). From UML to HDL: a Model Driven Architectural Approach to Hardware-Software Co-Design. In *Information Systems: New Generations Conference (ISNG)*, April 4-6, (pp. 88-93).

Crespo, A., Ripoll, I., Gonzalez-Harbour, M., & Lipari, G. (2008). Operating System Support for Embedded Real-Time Applications. *EURASIP Journal on Embedded Systems*, 2.

Crnkovic, I., & Larsson, M. (2002). *Building reliable component-based software systems*. Boston: Artech House.

Culler, D. E., & Pal Singh, J. (1999). *Parallel Computer Architecture: A Hardware/Software Approach*. San Francisco: Morgan Kaufmann Publishers, Inc.

Da, Z., & Hui, L. (2008). A Stochastic-Based FPGA Controller for an Induction Motor Drive With Integrated Neural Network Algorithms. *Industrial Electronics. IEEE Transactions on*, *55*(2), 551–561.

Dally, W.-J. (1992, Mar.). Virtual-channel flow control. *IEEE Transactions on Parallel and Distributed Systems*, 3(2), 194–205. doi:10.1109/71.127260

Dally, W.-J., & Towles, B. (2004). *Principles and Practices of Interconnection*. San Mateo, CA: Morgan Kaufmann.

Dally, W. J., & Towles, B. (2001). Route packets, not wires: on-chip interconnection networks. In Proc. of *the 38th conference on Design automation* (pp. 684-689). ACM Press, New York, USA.

Daws, C., Olivero, A., Tripakis, S., & Yovine, S. (1996). The tool KRONOS. In *Hybrid Systems III, Verification and Control, (LNCS 1066)*. Berlin: Springer-Verlag.

DeHon, A. (2000, Apr.). The density advantage of configurable computing. *Computer*, 33(4), 41–49. doi:10.1109/2.839320

Del valle, P. G., Atienza, D., Magan, I., Flores, J. G., Perez, E. A., Mendias, J. M., et al. (2006). *A Complete Multi-Processor System-on-Chip FPGA-Based Emulation Framework*. Paper presented at the International Conference on Very Large Scale Integration, IFIP

Delahaye, J.-P., Palicot, J., Moy, C., & Leray, P. (2007). *Partial Reconfiguration of FPGAs for Dynamical Reconfiguration of a Software Radio Platform*. Budapest: Mobile and Wireless Communications Summit.

Delange, J. (n.d.). *POK, ARINC653-compliant operating system*. Retrieved from http://pok.gunnm.org

Delange, J., Hugues, J., Pautet, L., & Zalila, B. (2008). Code generation strategies from aadl architectural descriptions targeting the high integrity domain. In *4th European Congress ERTS*.

Delange, J., Pautet, L., & Kordon, F. (2008). Code Generation Strategies for Partitioned Systems. In *29th IEEE Real-Time Systems Symposium (RTSS'08)*, (pp. 53–56), Barcelona, Spain, December 2008. Washington, DC: IEEE Computer Society.

Demathieu, S., Thomas, F., André, C., Gérard, S., & Terrier, F. (2008). First Experiments Using the UML Profile for MARTE. In *ISORC '08: Proceedings of the 2008 11th IEEE Symposium on Object Oriented Real-Time Distributed Computing*.

Densmore, D., Passerone, R., & Sangiovanni-Vincentelli, A. (2006). A Platform-Based Taxonomy for ESL Design. *IEEE Design & Test*, 23(5), 359–374. doi:10.1109/MDT.2006.112

Derrien, S., & Quinton, P. (2007). Parallelizing HMMER for hardware acceleration on FPGAs. In *International Conference on Application-specific Systems, Architectures and Processors*, (pp. 10-17).

DIGI. (2009). *DIGI Connect ME development boards*. Retrieved November 2, 2009 from http://www.digi.com

Dijkstra, E. (1975). Guarded commands, non determinacy and formal derivation of programs. *Communications of the ACM*, 18(8), 453–457. doi:.doi:10.1145/360933.360975

Dijkstra, E. (1976). *A Discipline of Programming*. Englewood Cliffs, NJ: Prentice-Hall.

Dijkstra, E., & Schweten, C. (1990). *Predicate Calculus and Programm Semantics*. New York: Springer Verlag.

Dijkstra, R. M. (1995). An experiment with the use of predicate transformers in UNITY. *Information Processing Letters*, 53(6), 329–332. doi:.doi:10.1016/0020-0190(94)00215-K

Dissaux, P., Filali Amine, M., Michel, P., & Vernadat, F. (Eds.). (2005). Architecture Description Languages. In *IFIP TC-2 Workshop on Architecture Description Languages (WADL), World Computer Congress*, (Vol. 176).

Dissaux, P., Legrand, J., Plantec, A., & Singhoff, F. (2008). *AADL performance analysis with Cheddar: a summary*. SAE AADL Working Group meeting, Sevilla.

Disseaux, P. (2004). Using the AADL for mission critical software development. In *2nd European Congress ERTS, Embedded Real Time Software*.

Doucet, F., Shyamasundar, R.-K., Kruger, I.-H., Joshi, S., & Gupta, R.-K. (2007). Reactivity in SystemC Transaction-Level Models. *Haifa Verification Conference*, (pp. 34–50).

Duato, J., Yalamanchili, S., & Ni, L. (2002). *Interconnection Networks: An Engineering Approach*. San Mateo, CA: Morgan Kaufmann.

Dubey, R., Agarwal, P., & Vasantha, M. K. (2007). Programmable logic devices for motion control-a review. *IEEE Transactions on Industrial Electronics*, *54*(1), 559–566. doi:10.1109/TIE.2006.885452

Dubinin, V., & Vyatkin, V. (2006). Towards a Formal Semantic Model of IEC 61499 Function Blocks. In *4th IEEE International Conference on Industrial Informatics (INDIN)*, Singapore, August 2006.

Dubinin, V., Vyatkin, V., & Hanisch, H.-M. (2006). Modelling and Verification of IEC 61499 Applications using Prolog. In *11th IEEE Conference on Emerging Technologies and Factory Automation*, Prague, September.

Dumitrascu, F., Bacivarov, I., Pieralisi, L., Bnaclu, M., & Jerraya, A. (2006). Flexible MPSoC platform with fast interconnect exploration for optimal system performance for a specific application. *Proceedings of the Design, automation and test in Europe conference DATE: Designers' forum*, (pp. 168-171). Munich, Germany.

Durbin, R., Eddy, S., Krogh, A., & Mitchison, G. (1998). *Biological Sequence Analysis*. Cambridge, UK: Cambridge University Press. doi:10.1017/CBO9780511790492

Dutt, N., & Choi, K. (2003). Configurable Processors for Embedded Computing. *Computer*, *36*, 120–123. doi:10.1109/MC.2003.1160063

Dybå, T., Kampenes, V. B., & Sjøberg, D. I. (2006). A systematic review of statistical power in software engineering experiments. *Information and Software Technology*, *48*(8), 745–755. doi:.doi:10.1016/j.infsof.2005.08.009

Dyer, M., Plessl, C., & Platzner, M. (2002). *Partially reconfigurable cores for xilinx virtex. In: Proceedings of the Reconfigurable Computing Is Going Mainstream*. Paper presented at the 12th Int. Conf. on Field-Programmable Logic and Applications, Montpellier, France.

Ebeling, C., McMurchie, L., Hauck, S., & Burns, S. (1995, December). Placement and routing tools for the Triptych FPGA. *IEEE Trans. on Very Large Scale Integration (VLSI). Systems*, *3*(4), 473–482.

EBNF. (2010). *Extended Backus Naur For m*. Retrieved 13 April 2010, from http://en.wikipedia.org/wiki/Extended_Backus_Naur_For m

Eddy, S. (2003). *HMMER User's Guide*. Retrieved October 15, 2009, from http://hmmer.janelia.org

Edwards, S. A. (2006). The Challenges of Synthesizing Hardware from C-Like Languages. *IEEE Design & Test of Computers*, *23*(5), 375–386. doi:10.1109/MDT.2006.134

Eklund, S. E. (2001). A Massively Parallel Architecture for Linear Machine Code Genetic Programming. In Proc. *4th International Conference on Evolvable Systems: From Biology to Hardware*. (pp. 216-224).

Eles, P., Peng, Z., Kuchinski, K., & Doboli, A. (1997). System level hardware/software partitioning based on simulated annealing and tabu search. *Design Automation of Embedded Systems DAES*, *2*(1), 5–32. doi:10.1023/A:1008857008151

Elleuch, M., Aydi, Y., & Abid, M. (2008). Formal Specification of Delta MINs for MPSOC in the ACL2 Logic. In Proc. of *Forum on Design and specification Languages, FDL '08*.

Engel, F., Kuz, I., Petters, S. M., & Ruocco, S. (2004, Dec.). *Operating Systems on SoCs: A good idea*. Paper presented at the Embedded Real-Time Systems Implementation (ERTSI) Workshop, Lisbon, Portugal.

Enright-Jerger, N., Peh, L., & Lipasti, M. (May 2008). Circuit-switched coherence. In *Proceedings of the Network-on-Chips International Symposium NoCs*, (pp. 193–202).

Enzler, R., Plessl, C., & Platzner, M. (2005, April). System-level performance evaluation of reconfigurable processors. *Microprocessors and Microsystems, 29*(2–3), 63–73. doi:10.1016/j.micpro.2004.06.004

Enzler, R. (2004). *Architectural trade-offs in dynamically reconfigurable processors.* PhD thesis, Diss., ETH No. 15423, ETH Zurich, Switzerland.

Ernst, R., Henkel, J., & Benner, T. (1993). Hardware-software cosynthesis for microcontrollers. *IEEE Design & Test of Computers, 10*(4), 64–75. doi:10.1109/54.245964

Eshraghian, K. (2006). SoC Emerging Technologies. *IEEE JPROC, 94*(6), 1197–1213. doi:10.1109/JPROC.2006.873615

eSilicon Embedded FPGA ASIC Design Services. (n.d.). Retrieved from http://www.esilicon.com/

Eskinazi, R., Lima, M.-E., Maciel, P.-R., Valderrama, C., Filho, A, G,-S., & Nascimento, P.-S. (2005). A Timed Petri Net Approach for Pre-Runtime Scheduling in Partial and Dynamic Reconfigurable Systems. *Proceedings of the 19th IEEE International Parallel and Distributed Processing Symposium IPDPS, 4,* p. 154a. Denver, Colorado.

European Commission. (2004). *MANUFUTURE A Vision for 2020.* Report of the High-Level Group.

Eusse, J. F., Moreano, N., Melo, A. C. M. A., & Jacobi, R. P. (2010). A HMMER hardware accelerator using divergences. In *Design, Automation & Test in Europe Conference.*

Ezpeleta, J., Colom, J. M., & Martinez, J. (1995). A Petri net based deadlock prevention policy for flexible manufacturing systems. *IEEE Transactions on Robotics and Automation, 11*(2), 173–184. doi:10.1109/70.370500

Ezpeleta, J., Couvreur, J. M., & Silva, M. (1991). A new technique for finding a generating family of siphons, traps, and st-components: Application to colored Petri nets. In G. Rozenberg (Ed.), *Advances in Petri Nets,* (LNCS 674, pp.126–147).

Fanti, M. P., Maione, B., Mascolo, S., & Turchiano, B. (1997). Event-based feedback control for deadlock avoidance in flexible production systems. *IEEE Transactions on Robotics and Automation, 13*(3), 347–363. doi:10.1109/70.585898

Fanti, M. P., & Zhou, M. C. (2004). Deadlock control methods in automated manufacturing systems. *IEEE Transactions on Systems, Man, and Cybernetics. Part A, 34*(1), 5–22.

Feiler, P. H., & Hansson, J. (2007). *Flow Latency Analysis with the Architecture Analysis and Design Language (AADL). Technical report.* Software Engineering Institute.

Feiler, P. H., Hansson, J., de Niz, D., & Wrage, L. (2009). *System architecture virtual integration: An industrial case study. Technical report.* Software Engineering Institute.

Feiler, P. H., Gluch, D. P. & Hudak, J. J. (2005). *The Architecture Analysis and Design Language (AADL): An Introduction.* Technical report.

Fejoz, L., Méry, D., & Merz, S. (2005). *DIXIT: a graphical toolkit for predicate abstractions.* [Online]. Retrieved from http://hal.inria.fr/inria-00000767/en/.

Ferrarini, L., & Maroni, M. (1998). Deadlock avoidance control for manufacturing systems with multiple capacity resources. *International Journal of Advanced Manufacturing Technology, 14*(4), 729–736. doi:10.1007/BF01438225

Ferreira, R., Laure, M., Beck, A. C., Lo, T., Rutzig, M., & Carro, L. (2009). A Low Cost and Adaptable Routing Network for Reconfigurable Systems. In Proc. *IEEE International Symposium on Parallel & Distributed Processing IPDPS.* (pp. 1-8).

Fickett, J. W. (1984). Fast optimal alignments. *Nucleic Acids Research, 12*(1), 175–179. doi:10.1093/nar/12.1Part1.175

Fin, A., Fummi, F., & Signoretto, M. (2001). SystemC: a homogenous environment to test embedded systems. In *Proceedings of Int. Workshop on Hardware/Software Codesign CODES,* (pp. 17-22).

Finn, R. D. (2008). The Pfam protein families database. *Nucleic Acids Research, 36*, 281–288. doi:10.1093/nar/gkm960

Fischer, J., & Boucher, T. O. (2010). *Workbook for Designing Distributed Control Applications using Rockwell Automation's HOLOBLOC Prototyping Software*. Working paper, 05-017.

Fitzgerald, J., & Larsen, P. G. (1997). *Modelling Systems: Practical Tools and Techniques in Software Development*. Cambridge University Press.

Fletcher, B. H. (2005). *FPGA Embedded Processors, Revealing True System Performance*. Paper presented at the Embedded Systems Conference San Francisco, USA.

Flynn, M. J., & Hung, P. (2005). Microprocessor Design Issues: Thoughts on the Road Ahead. *IEEE Micro, 25*(3), 16–31. doi:10.1109/MM.2005.56

Flynn, M. J. (1972). Some computer organizations and their effectiveness. *IEEE Transactions on Computers, 21*, 948–960. doi:10.1109/TC.1972.5009071

Fobel, C., Gréwal, G., & Morton, A. (2009). Hardware accelerated FPGA placement. *Microelectronics Journal, 40*(11), 1667–1671. doi:10.1016/j.mejo.2008.09.008

Fort, B., Capalija, D., Vranesic, Z. G., & Brown, S. D. (2006, Oct.). *A Multithreaded Soft Processor for SoPC Area Reduction*. Paper presented at the IEEE Symposium on Field-Programmable Custom Computing Machines (FCCM), Napa, CA.

Forte. (2008). *Forte Cynthesizer*. Retrieved 10 October 2008, from http://www.forteds.com/products/cynthesizer.asp

Forum, S. D. R. (2008). Retrieved from The Software Defined Radio Forum Cognitive Radio Definitions www.sdrforum.org

Frana, R. B., Bodeveix, J.-P., Filali, M., & Rolland, J.-F. (2007). The AADL behaviour annex -- experiments and roadmap. In *12th IEEE International Conference on Engineering Complex Computer Systems*.

Frankel, D. S. (2003). *Model-Driven Architecture: Applying MDA to Enterprise Computing*. Indianapolis, IN: Wiley Publishing, Inc.

Fratta, A., Griffero, G., & Nieddu, S. (2004, Nov.). *Comparative analysis among DSP and FPGA-based control capabilities in PWM power converters*. Paper presented at the IEEE IECON, Busan, Korea.

Freitas, H. C., & Navaux, P. O. A. (2008). Evaluating On-Chip Interconnection Architectures for Parallel Processing. In Proc. *11th International Conference on Computational Science and Engineering – Workshops*. (pp. 188-193).

Gadient, A.-J., Debardelaben, J.-A., & Madisetti, V. K. (1997). Incorporating cost modeling in embedded system design. *IEEE Design & Test of Computers, 14*(3), 24–35. doi:10.1109/54.605989

Gajski, D., Vahid, F., Narayan, S., & Gong, J. (1998). SpecSyn: an environment supporting the specify-explore-refine paradigm for hardware/software system design. *IEEE Transactions on VLSI Systems, 6*(1), 84–100. doi:10.1109/92.661251

Gajski, D. D., Zhu, J., Dömer, R., Gerstlauer, A., & Zhao, S. (2001). *SpecC: Specification language and methodology*. Amsterdam: Kluwer Academic Publishers, CECS.

Galambos, J. (1995). *Advanced Probability Theory*. New York: Marcel Dekker, Inc.

Gallasch, G., & Billington, J. (2006). A Parametric State Space for the Analysis of the Infinite Class of Stop-and-Wait Protocols. In *Model Checking Software*, (LNCS 3925, pp. 201-218). Berlin: Springer.

Gambier, A. (2004, Jul.). *Real-Time Control Systems: A Tutorial*. Paper presented at the 5th Asian Control Conference, Melbourne, Australia.

Gamma, E., & Beck, K. (2003). *Contributing to Eclipse: Principles, Patterns, and Plugins* (1st ed.). Boston: Addison-Wesley Professional.

Garcia, A. L., & Widjaja, I. (2004). *Communication Networks: Fundamental Concepts and Key Architectures.* New York: McGraw-Hill.

Garcia, P., Compton, K., Schulte, M., Blem, E., & Fu, W. (2006). An Overview of Reconfigurable Hardware in Embedded Systems. *EURASIP Journal on Embedded Systems*, 19.

Gavrielov, M. (2009, Apr.). *FPGA targeted design platforms: Fulfilling the programmable imperative.* Retrieved from www.DSP-FPGA.com.

Gehin, A-L., & Staroswiecki, M., (2008). Reconfiguration analysis using generic component models. *IEEE Transactions on Systems, Machine and Cybernetics, 38*(3).

George, L., Hermant, J.F., Characterization of the Space of Feasible Worst-Case Execution Times for Earliest-Deadline-First scheduling. Journal of Aerospace Computing, Information and Communication (JACIC), 6(11).

George, L., Rivierre, N. & Spuri, M. (1996, September). *Preemptive and non-preemptive scheduling real-time uniprocessor scheduling.* INRIA Research Report, No. 2966.

Ghenassia, F. (2005). *Transaction Level Modeling with SystemC.* Dordrecht, Netherlands: Springer. doi:10.1007/b137175

Ghezzi, C., Mandrioli, D., & Morzenti, A. (1990). A Logic Language for Executable Specifications of Real-Time Systems, *Journal of systems and software* (pp.107-123), vol. 12, no. 2.

Gilles, O., & Hugues, J. (2008). Validating requirements at model-level. *Ingénierie Dirigée par les modèles (IDM'08)*, Mulhouse, France, (pp. 35-49).

Gindin, R., Cidon, I., & Keidar, I. (May 2007). NoC-Based FPGA: Architecture and Routing. *in proceedings of the First International Symposium on Networks-on-Chip NOCS*, (pp. 253-264).

Girau, G., Tomatis, A., Dovis, F., & Mulassano, P. (2007). Efficient software defined radio implementations of GNSS receivers. *IEEE International Symposium on Circuits and Systems*, (pp. 27-30). New Orleans, LA.

Giua, A., & Seatzu, C. (2002). Liveness enforcing supervisors for railway networks using ES2PR Petri nets. In *Proceedings of the Sixth International Workshop on Discrete Event Systems*, (pp.55- 60).

Goessler, G., Graf, S., Majster-Cederbaum, M., Martens, M., & Sifakis, J. (2007). An approach to modeling and verification of component based systems. In *Current Trends in Theory and Practice of Computer Science, SOFSEM'07, (LNCS 4362)*. Berlin: Springer.

Goessler, G., & Sifakis, J. (2002). Composition for Component-Based Modeling. In *Proceedings of FMCO'02*, November 2002, Leiden, the Netherlands, (LNCS 2852, pp. 443-466).

Gogniat, G., Auguin, M., Bianco, L., & Pegatoquet, A. (1998). Communication Synthesis and HW/SW Integration for Embedded System Design. *Sixth International Workshop on Hardware/Software Co-Design CODES*, (pp. 49).

Gomes, L., Barros, J. P., & Costa, A. (2004). Structuring Mechanisms in Petri Net Models: From specification to FPGA based implementations. In *Design of embedded control systems*. Amsterdam: Kluwer.

Goossens, K., Bennebroek, M., Hur, J.-Y., & Wahlah, M.-A. (2008). Hardwired Networks on Chip in FPGAs to Unify Functional and Confguration Interconnects. In *Proceeding of the International Symposium on Networks-on-Chip NOCS.*

Gordon, M. J. C. (1989). *Mechanizing Programming Logics in Higher-order Logic. Current Trends in Hardware Verification and Automated Theorem Proving* (pp. 387–439). New York: Springer.

Gordon, M. J. C & Melham T.F. (1993). *Introduction to HOL: A Theorem Proving Environment for Higher-Order Logic*. Cambridge, UK: Cambridge University Press.

Gotoh, O. (1982). An improved algorithm for matching biological sequences. *Journal of Molecular Biology, 162*, 705–708. doi:10.1016/0022-2836(82)90398-9

Götz, M., Rettberg, A., Pereira, C. E., & Rammig, F. J. (2009). Run-time reconfigurable RTOS for reconfigurable systems-on-chip. *Journal of Embedded Computing, 3*(1), 39–51.

Graaf, B., Lormans, M., & Toetenel, H. (2003). Embedded Software Engineering: The State of the Practice. *IEEE Computer Society IEEE Software, 20*(6), 61–69.

Grammar. (2008). *Grammar type*. Retrieved 10 October 2008, from http://www-cgi.uni-regensburg.de/~brf09510/grammartypes.html

Gratz, P., Kim, C., McDonald, R., Keckler, S.-W., & Burger, D.-C. (2006). Implementation and evaluation of on-chip network architectures. In *Proceedings of the International Conference on Computer Design ICCD*, (pp. 477-484), San Jose, CA.

Gregory, M. (2004, Nov.). *A module-based dynamic partial reconfiguration tutorial*. Paper presented at the Logic Systems Laboratory, EPFL.

Grimpe, E., & Oppenheimer, F. (2003). Extending the SystemC synthesis subset by object oriented features. In *Proceedings of Int. Conf. on Hardware/Software Codesign and System Synthesis CODES/ISSS*, (pp. 25-30).

Griva, G., Ilas, C., Eastham, J. F., Profumo, F., & Vranka, P. (1997). *High performance sensorless control of induction motor drives for industry applications*. Paper presented at the Power Conversion Conference, Nagaoka.

Grotker, T., Liao, S., Martin, G., & Swan, S. (2002). *System Design with SystemC*. Amsterdam: Kluwer Academic Publishers.

Gruian, F. (2001). Hard real-time scheduling for low-energy using stochastic data and DVS processors. In *Proceedings of the International Symposium on Low Power Electronics and Design*, (pp. 46–51).

Guler, M., Clement, S., Wills, L. M., Heck, B. S., & Vachtsevanos, G. J. (2003). Transition management for reconfigurable hybrid control systems. *IEEE Control Systems Magazine, 23*(1). doi:10.1109/MCS.2003.1172828

Guo, X., Chen, Z., & Schaumont, P. (2008). *Energy and Performance Evaluation of an FPGA-Based SoC Platform with AES and PRESENT Coprocessors*. Paper presented at the 8th international workshop on Embedded Computer Systems: Architectures, Modeling, and Simulation.

Guo, Z., Buyukkurt, B., Najjar, W., & Vissers, K. (2005 March). *Optimized Generation of Data-Path from C Codes*., Agron, J., Peck, W., Anderson, E., Andrews, D., Komp, E., Sass, R., Baijot, F., & Stevens, J. (2006, December). Run-Time Services for Hybrid CPU/FPGA Systems On Chip. In *Proceedings of the 27th IEEE International Real-Time Systems Symposium (RTSS)*.

Gupta, S., Dutt, N. D., Gupta, R. K., & Nicolau, A. (2003, January). SPARK: A High-Level Synthesis Framework For Applying Parallelizing Compiler Transformations. In *International Conference on VLSI Design*, (pp. 461–466).

Gupta, S., Dutt, N., Gupta, R., & Nicolau, A. (2003). SPARK: a high-level synthesis framework for applying parallelizing compiler transformations. In *Proceedings of Int. Conf. on VLSI Design*.

Gusfield, D. (1997). *Algorithms on Strings, Trees, and Sequences: Computer Science and Computational Biology*. Cambridge, UK: Cambridge University Press. doi:10.1017/CBO9780511574931

Gustafsson, J., Ermedahl, A., Sandberg, C., & Lisper, B. (2006). Automatic Derivation of Loop Bounds and Infeasible Paths for WCET Analysis using Abstract Execution. In *Proc. 27th IEEE Real-Time Systems Symposium*.

Hagge, N., & Wagner, B. (2005, November). A New Function Block Modelling Language Based on Petri Nets for Automatic Code generation. *IEEE Transactions on Industrial Informatics, 1*(4), 226–237. doi:10.1109/TII.2005.857614

Hamdaoui, M., & Ramanathan, P. (1995, December). A dynamic priority assignment technique for streams with (m,k)-firm deadlines. *IEEE Transactions on Computers, 44*, 1443–1451. doi:10.1109/12.477249

Hampel, V., Sobe, P., & Maehle, E. (2008). Experiences with a FPGA-based Reed/Solomon-encoding coprocessor. *Microprocessors and Microsystems*, *32*(5-6), 313–320. doi:10.1016/j.micpro.2008.03.003

Han, S.-I., Chae, S.-I., Brisolara, L., Carro, L., Popovici, K., Guerin, X., et al. (Writer) (2009). *Simulink®-based heterogeneous multiprocessor SoC design flow for mixed hardware/software refinement and simulation*. DOI: 10.1016/j.vlsi.2008.08.003.

Hanisch, H.-M., Khalgui, M., & Carpanzano, E. (2008). An optimised simulation of component-based embedded systems in manufacturing industry. *International Journal of Simulation and Process Modelling*, *4*(2).

Hanisch, H.-M., & Luder, A. (1999), *Modular modelling of closed-loop systems*. In *Colloquium on Petri Net Technologies for Modelling Communication Based Systems*, (pp. 103-126), Germany.

Happe, M., Luebbers, E., & Platzner, M. (2009 December). An Adaptive Sequential Monte Carlo Framework with Runtime HW/SW Repartitioning. In *Proceedings of the 2009 International Conference on Field-Programmable Technology (FPT)*.

Harel, D. (1997). *Modeling Reactive systems with Statecharts: The statemate approach*. USA: McGraw-Hill.

Harel, D. (1987). STATEMATE: the Languages of Statemate, *Technical Report*, USA.

Harel, D., Pnueli, A., Schmidt, J. P., & Sherman, R. (1987). On the formal Semantics of Statecharts, *Proc. 2 nd I.E.E.E. Symposium on Logic in Computer Science*, Ithaca, NY, USA, (pp. 54-64).

Harrison, J. (1998). *Theorem proving with Real Numbers*. Berlin: Springer.

Harrison, J. (2009). *Handbook of Practical Logic and Automated Reasoning*. Cambridge, UK: Cambridge University Press. doi:10.1017/CBO9780511576430

Hartenstein, R. (2001). *A decade of reconfigurable computing: a visionary retrospective*. Munich, Germany: Design, Automation and Test in Europe.

Hasan, O., & Tahar, S. (2008). Using Theorem Proving to Verify Expectation and Variance for Discrete Random Variables. *Journal of Automated Reasoning*, *41*(3-4), 295–323. doi:10.1007/s10817-008-9113-6

Hasan, O., & Tahar, S. (2009). Performance Analysis and Functional Verification of the Stop-and-Wait Protocol in HOL. *Journal of Automated Reasoning*, *42*(1), 1–33. doi:10.1007/s10817-008-9105-6

Hasan, O., & Tahar, S. (2007). Formalization of Continuous Probability Distributions. In F. Pfenning (Ed.), *Automated Deduction*, (LNCS Vol. 4603, pp. 2-18). Berlin: Springer.

Hauser, J. R. (1997, October). *The Garp architecture* (Tech. Rep.). UC Berkeley, CA, USA.

Havelund, K., & Shankar, N. (1996). Experiments in Theorem Proving and Model Checking for Protocol Verification. *Industrial Benefit and Advances in Formal Methods*, (LNCS 1051, pp. 662-681). Berlin: Springer.

Hayhurst, K., Veerhusen, D. S., Chilenski, J. J. & Rierson, L. K. (2001). *A Practical Tutorial on Modified Condition/ Decision Coverage*. Technical Report.

He, S., & Xu, X. (2007, May 30 – June 1). *Hardware Simulation of an Adaptive Control Algorithm*. Paper presented at the 2007 Conference on Modelling and Simulation, Montreal, QC, Canada.

Healy, C. A., Arnold, R. D., Mueller, F., Whalley, D., & Harmon, M. G. (1999). Bounding Pipeline and Instruction Cache Performance. In *IEEE Transactions on Computers, 48*.

Healy, C. A., Sjödin, M., Rustagi, V., Whalley, D., & Engelen, R. v. (2000). Supporting Timing Analysis by Automatic Bounding of Loop Iterations. In *Journal of Real-Time Systems*, (pp. 121-148).

Heckmann, R., Langenbach, M., Thesing, S., & Wilhelm, R. (2003). The Influence of Processor Architecture on the Design and Results of WCET Tools. *Proceedings of the IEEE, 91*, 1038–1054. doi:10.1109/JPROC.2003.814618

Henkel, J. (1996). A low power hardware software partitioning approach for core-based embedded systems. In *Proceedings of the ACM Design Automation Conference DAC*, (pp. 122–127), New York.

Henkel, J., Wolf, W., & Chakrandhar, S. (Jan. 2004). On-Chip networks: a scalable, communication-centric embedded system design paradigm. *Proceedings of International Conference on VLSI Design*, (pp. 845-851), Mumbai, India.

Henzinger, T. A., Manna, Z., & Pnueli, A. (1991). *Temporal Proof Methodologies for Real-Time Systems, 18 th Ann. Syym on Principales of Programming Languages* (pp. 353–366). ACM Press.

Henzinger, T.-A., Ho, P., & Womg-Toi, H. (1997). HyTech: the next generation. In *TACAS95: Tools and Algorithms for the Construction and Analysis of Systems*, (LNCS).

Hermant, J., & George, L. (2007). An optimal approach to determine the minimum architecture for real-time embedded systems scheduled by EDF. In 3rd IEEE International Conference on Self-Organization and Autonomous Systems in Computing and Communications (SOAS'07), September 2007.

Hines, K., & Borriello, G. (1997). Dynamic communication models in embedded system co-simulation. In *Proc. of the Design Automation Conference DAC*, (pp. 395-400).

Hladik, P., Déplanche, A., Faucou, S., & Trinquet, Y. (2007). Adequacy between AUTOSAR OS specification and real-time scheduling theory. In IEEE Second International Symposium on Industrial Embedded Systems (SIES '07), Lisbon, Portugal, July 4-6.

Ho, R., Mai, R.-K., & Horowitz, M.-A. (2001, April). The future of wires. *Proceedings of the IEEE, 89*(4), 490–504. doi:10.1109/5.920580

Hoang, D. T., & Lopresti, D. P. (1992). FPGA implementation of systolic sequence alignment. In *Field-Programmable Gate Arrays: Architectures and Tools for Rapid Prototyping*, (LNCS 705, pp. 183-191). Berlin: Springer-Verlag.

Hoare, C. (1969). An axiomatic basis for computer programming. *Communications of the ACM, 12*(10), 576–585. doi:.doi:10.1145/363235.363259

Hodjat, A., Batina, L., Hwang, D., & Verbauwhede, I. (2007). HW/SW co-design of a hyperelliptic curve cryptosystem using a microcode instruction set coprocessor. *Integration, the VLSI Journal, 40*(1), 45-51.

Holobloc. (2008). *Holobloc FBDK*. Retrieved 10 October 2008, from http://www.holobloc.com.

Holzer, A., Schallhart, C., Tautschnig, M., & Veith, H. (2008). FShell: Systematic Test Case Generation for Dynamic Analysis and Measurement. In *LNCS 5123* (pp. 209–213). Berlin: Springer.

Holzer, A., Schallhart, C., Tautschnig, M., & Veith, H. (2009). Query-Driven Program Testing. In *Proc. 10th Int'l Conference on Verification, Model Checking, and Abstract Interpretation*, N. D. Jones, & M. Müller-Olm (Ed.), *LNCS 5403*, (pp. 151-166). Berlin: Springer.

Holzmann, G. (2003). Trends in software verification. in *Proceedings of the Formal Methods Europe Conference (FME)*.

Hongtao, D., Hairong, Q., & Xiaoling, W. (2007). Comparative Study of VLSI Solutions to Independent Component Analysis. *IEEE Transactions on Industrial Electronics, 54*(1), 548–558. doi:10.1109/TIE.2006.885491

Hooman, J., Ramesh, S., & De Roever, W. P. (1990). *A compositional axiomatization of safety and liveness properties of statecharts"*, proc. Int. BCS-FACS Workshop on Semantics for Concurrency Univ. Of Leicester, UK.

Hord. R. M. (1982). *The Illiac IV: The First Supercomputer*. Computer Science Press.

Hsieh, F. S., & Chang, S. C. (1994). Dispatching-driven deadlock avoidance controller synthesis for flexible manufacturing systems. *IEEE Transactions on Robotics and Automation, 10*(2), 196–209. doi:10.1109/70.282544

Hsiung, P.-A., Chen, Y.-R., & Lin, Y.-H. (2007). Model checking safety-critical systems using safecharts. *IEEE Transactions on Computers, 56*(5).

Hu, H.-S., & Li, Z.-W. (2009). Clarification on the computation of liveness-enforcing supervisor for resource allocation systems with uncontrollable behavior. *IEEE Transactions on Automation Science and Engineering*, *6*(2).

Hu, J., & Marculescu, R. (Jun. 2004). DyAD - Smart routing for networks-on-chip. In *Proceedings of Design Automation Conference DAC*, (pp. 260–263).

Hu, J., & Marculescu, R. (2004). Energy-Aware Communication and Task Scheduling for Network-on-Chip Architectures under Real-Time Constraints. In *Proceedings of the Design, Automation and Test in Europe Conference DATE*, (pp. 10234).

Huang, Y. S., Jeng, M. D., Xie, X. L., & Chung, S. L. (2001). Deadlock prevention policy based on Petri nets and siphons. *International Journal of Production Research*, *39*(2), 283–305. doi:10.1080/00207540010002405

Huang, M., Jojczyk, L., Achille, T., & Valderrama, C. (2008). A SDR architecture proposal for SATCOM applications. *International Design and Test Workshop*. Monastir, Tunisia.

Hubner, M., Paulsson, K., & Becker, J. (2005). *Parallel and Flexible Multiprocessor System-On-Chip for Adaptive Automotive Applications based on Xilinx MicroBlaze Soft-Cores*. Paper presented at the 19th IEEE International Symposium on Parallel and Distributed Processing

Huebner, M. (2004). Scalable Application-Dependent Network on Chip Adaptivity for Dynamical Reconfigurable Real-Time Systems. In *FPL*.

Hugues, J., Zalila, B., Pautet, L., & Kordon, F. (2008). *From the Prototype to the Final Embedded System Using the Ocarina AADL Tool Suite. ACM Transactions in Embedded Computing Systems*. TECS.

Huizing, C., Gerth, R., & De Roever, W. P. (1988). *Modelling statecherts behaviour in a fully abstract way*, Computing Science Notes, 88/07, Eindhoven Univ. Tech., Dept Math. Comp. Sci.

Hunter, L. (1993). *Artificial Intelligence and Molecular Biology*. Cambridge, MA: MIT Press.

Hurd, J. (2002). *Formal Verification of Probabilistic Algorithms*. PhD Thesis, University of Cambridge, Cambridge, UK.

Idkhajine, L., Monmasson, E., Naouar, M. W., Prata, A., & Bouallaga, K. (2009). Fully Integrated FPGA-Based Controller for Synchronous Motor Drive. *IEEE Transactions on Industrial Electronics*, *56*(10), 4006–4017. doi:10.1109/TIE.2009.2021591

Idkhajine, L., Prata, A., Monmasson, E., Bouallaga, K., & Naouar, M. W. (2008). *System on Chip controller for electrical actuator.* Paper presented at the IEEE International Symposium on Industrial Electronics (ISIE 2008).

IEC. (2000). *IEC 61499 Industrial-Process Measurement and Control Specification. IEC Technical Committee TC65/WG6.* IEC Draft.

IEC 61499-1. (2005). *Function blocks-part 1: Architecture*, (pp. 77-83).

IEC 61499-2. (2005). *Function blocks-part 2: Software tools requirements.*

IEC61131. (1993). 3. In *International Standard IEC 1131-3. Bureau Central de la commission Electrotechnique Internationale.* Switzerland: Programmable Controllers Part.

IEC61131. (1993). *Programmable Controllers Part 3.* Bureau Central de la commission Electrotechnique Internationale Switzerland.

IEC61499. (2004). *Industrial Process Measurements and Control Systems. International Electrotechnical Commission (IEC).* Committee Draft.

IEC61499-1. (2003). *Function Blocks for Industrial Process Measurements and Control Systems.* International Standard IEC-TC65-WG6.

IEEE-ISTO. (2003). 5001-2003: The Nexus 5001 Forum Standard for a Global Embedded Processor Debug Intertace. In *IEEE-ISTO Standard 5001-2003: The Nexus 5001 Forum Standard for a Global Embedded Processor Debug Intertace*. IEEE-ISTO Standard.

Intel IXP425. (2006). Retrieved from Embedded Computing Intel IXP425 Network Processor Product Brief intel.com/go/networkprocessors

Intel. (2007, February 11). *Intel's Teraflops Research Chip.* Récupéré sur Teraflops research Chip Overview: http://download.intel.com/pressroom/kits/Teraflops/Teraflops_Research_Chip_Overview.pdf

International Electrotechnical Commission - IEC. (2003). *IEC 61131-3: Programmable controllers - Part 3: Programming languages,* (2nd Ed.). Geneva: IEC Press, International Standard. kirchner SOFT GmbH. (2009). *logiCAD - The IEC 61131 Technology Platform.* Retrieved November 2, 2009 from http://www.logicals.com

International Electrotechnical Commission - IEC. (2005). *IEC 61499: Function Blocks - Part 1,2, &3* (1st ed.). Geneva: IEC Press, International Standard.

ISaGRAF. (2008). *ICS Triplex ISaGRAF.* Retrieved 10 October 2008, from http://www.icstriplex.com/

Jacob, A. C., Lancaster, J. M., Buhler, J. D., & Chamberlain, R. D. (2007). Preliminary results in accelerating profile HMM search on FPGAs. In *IEEE International Symposium on Parallel and Distributed Processing,* (pp. 1-8).

Jahanian, F., & Mok, A. K.-L. (1986). *Safety analysis of timing properties in Real-time systems,* I.E.E.E Trans (pp. 890-904). On soft. *Eng., 12*(0), 9.

Jaray, J., & Mahjoub, A. (1996). *Une méthode itérative de construction d'un modèle de système réactif.* TSI.

Jastrzębski, R., Laakkonen, O., Rauma, K., Luukko, J., Sarén, H., & Pyrhönen, O. (2004, June 28 – 30, 2004). *Real-time Emulation of Induction Motor in FPGA using Floating Point Representation.* Paper presented at the IASTED International Conference on Applied Simulation and Modelling, Rhodes, Greece.

Jay Siegel. (1989). Using the Multistage Cube Network Topology in Parallel Supercomputers. In *Proc. IEEE, 12 (77) 1932–1953.* H., Nation. W. C., Kruskal. C. P., & Napolitano. L. M.

Jeng, M. D., Xie, X. L., & Chung, S. L. (2004). ERCN* merged nets for modeling degraded behavior and parallel processes in semiconductor manufacturing systems. *IEEE Transactions on Systems, Man, and Cybernetics. Part A, 34*(1), 102–112.

Jerraya, A. A., & Wayne, W. (2004). *Multiprocessor Systems on Chips.* San Francisco: Morgan Kaufmann.

Jerraya, A. A., & Bouchhima, A. (2006). *Programming models and HW-SW interfaces abstraction for multiprocessor SoC.* Paper presented at the 43rd annual conference on Design automation.

Jerraya, A., Tenhunen, H. & Wolf, W. (2005, July). Multiprocessors Systems-on-Chips. *IEEE Computer Society Magazine,* 36-40.

Jezernik, K., & Rodic, M. (2008). *Torque sensorless control of induction motor.* Paper presented at the 13th Power Electronics and Motion Control Conference (EPE-PEMC 2008).

Jiang, X., Liu, X., Xu, L., Zhang, P., & Sun, N. (2007). A reconfigurable accelerator for Smith-Waterman algorithm. *IEEE Transactions on Circuits and Systems II, 54*(12), 1077–1081. doi:10.1109/TCSII.2007.909857

Jigang, W., Srikanthan, T., & Wang, X. (2007). Integrated row and column rerouting for reconfiguration of vlsi arrays with four-port switches. *IEEE Transactions on Computers, 56*(10).

Joseph, M., & Pandya, P. (1986). Finding response times in a real-time system. *BCS Comp. Jour., 29*(5), 390–395. doi:10.1093/comjnl/29.5.390

Jóźwiak, L., Nedjah, N., & Figueroa, M. (2010). Modern development methods and tools for embedded reconfigurable systems: A survey. *Integration, the VLSI Journal, 43*(1), 1-33.

Julliand, J. Masson, P.A., & Mountassir, H. (1999). Modular verification of dynamic properties for reactive systems. In *IFM,* (pp. 89-108).

Julliand, J., Masson, P.A., & Mountassir, H.(2001). Vérification par model-checking modulaire des propriétés dynamiques introduites en B. *TSI (Technique et Science Informatiques), 20*(7), 927-957.

Jung, H., & Ha, S. (2004). Hardware synthesis from coarse-grained dataflow specification for fast hw/sw cosynthesis. In *Proceedings of Int. Conf. on Hardware/Software Codesign and System Synthesis CODES/ISSS*, (pp. 24-29).

Kaliamoorthy, M., Himavathi, S., & Muthuramalingam, A. (2006, August 13-18 2006). *DSP based implementation of high performance flux estimators for speed sensorless induction motor drives using TMS320F2812.* Paper presented at the India International Conference on Power Electronics (IICPE 2006), Tokyo.

Kaltenbach, M. (1994). *Model checking for UNITY.* Technical Report CS-TR-94-31, The University of Texas at Austin, Department of Computer Sciences, Austin, TX.

Kangas, T., Kukkala, P., Orsila, H., Salminen, E., Hännikäinen, M., & Hämäläinen, T. D. (2007). UML-based Multi-Processor SoC Design Framework. *ACM Transactions on Embedded Computing Systems, 5*(2), 281–320. doi:10.1145/1151074.1151077

Kannenberg, A., & Saiedian, H. (2009). *Why Software Requirements Traceability Remains a Challenge. Crosstalk - The Journal of Defense Software.* Jul/Aug.

Kapre, N. (2006). Packet switched vs time multiplexed FPGA overlay networks. In *IEEE Symposium of Field-Programmable Custom Computing Machines.*

Karcich, R. M., Skibbe, R., & Garg, P. (1996). On Software Reliability and Code Coverage. In *proceedings of the Aerospace Applications Conference, 1996.*

Kariyappa, B. S., & Uttara Kumari, M. (2008). FPGA Based Speed Control of AC Servomotor Using Sinusoidal PWM. *Int. J. Computer Science and Network Security, 8*(10), 346–350.

Kaufmann, M., & Moore, J. S. (1996). *ACL2: An industrial strength version of nqthm. IEEE Transactions on Software Engineering, 4 (23)* (pp. 23–34). New York: IEEE Press.

Kaufmann, M., & Moore, J. (2004). Some key research problems in automated theorem proving for hardware and software verification. In *Spanish Royal Academy of Science* (*Vol. 98*, pp. 181–196). RAMSAC.

Keutzer, K., Malik, S., Newton, R., Rabaey, J., & Sangiovanni-Vincentelli, A. (2000). System level design: Orthogonalization of concerns and platform-based design. *IEEE Transactions on Computer-Aided Design of Circuits and Systems, 19*(12), 1523–1543. doi:10.1109/43.898830

Khalgui, M., & Rebeuf, X. (2008). An approach to implement a programmable logic controller from real-time software components. *International Journal of Industrial and Systems Engineering, 3*(6).

Khalgui, M., & Thramboulidis, K. (2008). An IEC61499-based Development Approach for the Deployment of Industrial Control Applications. *International journal of Modelling* [IJMIC]. *Identification and Control, 4*(2), 186–204.

Khalgui, M., Carpanzano, E., & Hanisch, H.-M. (2008). An optimised simulation of component-based embedded systems in manufacturing industry. *International Journal of Simulation and Process Modelling, 4*(2), 148–162.

Khalgui, M., & Hanisch, H.-M. (2008). Automatic specification of feasible Control Tasks in Benchmark Production Systems. In IEEE International Conference on *Emerging Technologies and Factory Automation, ETFA08.*

Khalgui, M., Rebeuf, X., & Simonot-Lion, F., (2007). A deployment method of component based applications on distributed industrial control systems. *European Jounal of Automated Systems, 41*(6).

Khalgui, M., Rebeuf, X., & Simonot-Lion, F. (2004). A behaviour model for IEC 61499 function blocks. In *Third Workshop on Modelling of Objects, Components and Agents 2004 - MOCA'04*, (pp. 71-87).

Kiel, E., & Lenze, A. (2002, May). *Control electronics in drive systems micro controller, DSPs, FPGAs, ASICs from state-of-art to future trends.* Paper presented at the PCIM Conf, Nuremberg, Germany.

Kienhuis, B., Deprettere, E., Vissers, K., & Van der Wolf, P. (1997). An approach for quantitative analysis of application-specific dataflow architectures. In *Proc. of the Int. Conf. Application-specific Systems, Architectures and Processors*, (pp. 338-349).

Kim, Y., Kim, K., Shin, Y., Ahn, T., Sung, W., Choi, K., et al. (1995). An integrated hardware-software cosimulation environment for heterogeneous systems prototyping. In *Proc. of the Conference Asia South Pacifc Design Automation*, (pp. 101-106).

Kinuyama, M., & Murata, T. (1986). Generating siphons and traps by Petri net representation of logic equations. In *Proceeding of 2nd IECE Conf on Net Theory*, (pp. 93-100).

Kirner, R. (2008). *Compiler Support for Timing Analysis of Optimized Code: Precise Timing Analysis of Machine Code with Convenient Annotation of Source Code*. Berlin: VDM Verlag.

Kirner, R. (2003). *Extending Optimising Compilation to Support Worst-Case Execution Time Analysis*. PhD Thesis, Technische Universität Wien, Austria.

Kirner, R. (2009). Towards Preserving Model Coverage and Structural Code Coverage. In *EURASIP Journal on Embedded Systems*.

Kirner, R., & Puschner, P. (2005). Classification of WCET Analysis Techniques. In *Proc. 8th IEEE International Symposium on Object-oriented Real-time distributed Computing*, (pp. 190-199).

Kirner, R., Knoop, J., Prantl, A., Schordan, M., & Wenzel, I. (2007). WCET Analysis: The Annotation Language Challenge, In *Proc. 7th Intl. Workshop on Worst-Case Execution Time (WCET) Analysis*, 83-99.

Kirner, R., Wenzel, I., Rieder, B., & Puschner, P. (2006). In *Intelligent Systems at the Service of Mankind*. Berlin: UBooks Verlag.

Klingman, E. (2006). *FPGA programming step by step*. Retrieved September 07, 2006 from http://www.embedded.com/showArticle.jhtml?articleID=18201956

Knudsen, P.-V., & Madsen, J. (1998). Integrating Communication Protocol Selection with Partitioning in Hardware/Software Codesign. In *Proceedings of the 11th international symposium on System synthesis*, (pp. 111-116), Hsinchu, Taiwan, China.

Kopetz, H. (1997). *Real-Time Systems - Design Principles for Distributed Embedded Applications*. Amsterdam: Kluwer.

Koren, Y., Heisel, U., Jovane, F., Moriwaki, T., Pritshow, G., Ulsoy, G., & van Brussel, H. (1999). Reconfigurable Manufacturing Systems. [CIRP]. *Annals of the International Institution for Production Engineering Research*, *48*(2), 527–539.

Koren, G. & Shasha, D. (1992). D-over: An Optimal On-line Scheduling Algorithm for over loaded real-time system. Research report Num. 138, Feb. 1992.

Kowalski, C. T., Lis, J., & Orlowska-Kowalska, T. (2007). *FPGA Implementation of DTC Control Method for the Induction Motor Drive*. Paper presented at the International Conference on Computer as a Tool (EUROCON 2007).

Kozaczynski, W., & Booch, G. (1998). Guest Editors' Introduction: Component-Based Software Engineering. *IEEE Software*, *15*(5), 34–36. doi:10.1109/MS.1998.714621

Krasner, J. (2003, July). Total cost of development: A COMPREHENSIVE COST estimation Embedded application design using a real-time OS. *Embedded Market forecasters*. Retrieved from www.embeddedforecast.com

Krauter, K. (2002). A taxonomy and survey of grid resource management systems for distributed computing. *Software, Practice & Experience*, *32*, 135–164. doi:10.1002/spe.432

Kreuzinger, J., Schulz, A., Pfeffer, M., Ungerer, T., Brinkschulte, U., & Krakowski, C. (2000, December). Real-time Scheduling on Multithreaded Processors. In *Proceedings of the 7th International Conference on Real-Time Computing Systems and Applications (RTCSA)*, (pp. 155–159), Cheju Island, South Korea.

Krogh, A. (1994). Hidden Markov models in computational biology: applications to protein modeling. *Journal of Molecular Biology, 235*(5), 1501–1531. doi:10.1006/jmbi.1994.1104

Kruskal. C. (1986). A unified theory of interconnection network. *Theoretical Computer Science, 1 (48).* Elsevier Science Publishers Ltd., Essex. 75-94.

Kruskal. C.P., & Snir. M. (1983). The performance of multistage interconnection networks for multiprocessors. *IEEE Transactions on Computers, 12 (32).* IEEE Computer Society, Washington. 1091-1098.

Kuikka, E., Leinonen, P. & Penttonen, M. (2002). *Towards Automating of Document Structure Transformations*, DocEng'02.

Kumar, A. (2007). *An FPGA design flow for reconfigurable network-based multi-processor systems on chip* (pp. 117–122). In DATE.

Kumar, A., Fernando, S., Yajun, H., Mesman, B., & Corporaal, H. (2007). *Multi-Processor System-Level Synthesis for Multiple Applications on Platform FPGA.* Paper presented at the International Conference on Field Programmable Logic and Applications (FPL 2007).

Kung, H. T. (1982). Why systolic architectures? *IEEE Computer, 15*(1), 37–46.

Kung, Y.-S., Fung, R.-F., & Tai, T.-Y. (2009). Realization of a Motion Control IC for $X\{-\}Y$ Table Based on Novel FPGA Technology. *IEEE Transactions on Industrial Electronics, 56*(1), 43–53. doi:10.1109/TIE.2008.2005667

Kuon, I., Tessier, R., & Rose, J. (2007). FPGA Architecture: Survey and Challenges. *Foundations and Trends in Electronic Design Automation, 2*(2), 135–253. doi:10.1561/1000000005

Kwiatkowska, M., Norman, G., Segala, R., & Sproston, J. (2002). Automatic Verification of Real-Time Systems with Discrete Probability Distributions. *Theoretical Computer Science, 282*(1), 101–150. doi:10.1016/S0304-3975(01)00046-9

Kwiatkowska, M., Norman, G., & Parker, D. (2007). Stochastic Model Checking. In M. Bernardo and J. Hillston (Eds.). *Formal Methods for Performance Evaluation,* Bertinoro, Italy, (LNCS, 4486, pp. 220-270). Berlin: Springer.

Kwon, K.-S., Yi, Y.-M., Kim, D.-H., & Ha, S.-H. (2005). *Embedded Software Generation from System Level Specification for Multi-tasking Embedded Systems.* Washington, DC: IEEE, ASP-DAC.

Laakkonen, O., Rauma, K., Saren, H., Luukko, J., & Pyrhonen, O. (2004). *Electric drive emulator using dSPACE real time platform for VHDL verification.* Paper presented at the 47th Midwest Symposium on Circuits and Systems (MWSCAS 2004).

Labrosse, J. J. (1999). *MicroC/OS-II The real-time Kernel.* Lawrence, KS: R&D Books.

Labrosse, J. J. (2002). *MicroC/OS-II: The Real-Time Kernel* (2nd Edn ed.): CMP Books.

Lahiri, K., Raghunathan, A., & Dey, S. (2004, June). Design space exploration for optimizing on-chip communication architectures. *IEEE Transactions on Computer-Aided Design of Integrated Circuits and Systems, 23*(6), 952–961. doi:10.1109/TCAD.2004.828127

Lamport, L. (1994). The temporal logic of actions. *ACM Transactions on Programming Languages and Systems, 16*(3), 872–923. doi:.doi:10.1145/177492.177726

Lamport, L. (2002). *Specifying Systems, The TLA+ Language and Tools for Hardware and Software Engineers.* Reading, MA: Addison-Wesley.

Lamport, L., & Yu, Y. (2003). *TLC-The TLA+ Model Checker.* Redmond, WA: Microsoft Research. Retrieved from http://research.microsoft.com/users/lamport/tla/tlc.html

Lascu, C., & Trzynadlowski, A. M. (2001). *A sensorless hybrid DTC drive for high-volume applications using the TMS320F243 DSP controller.* Paper presented at the IEEE Industry Applications Conference.

Lastra, J. Martinez, Lobov, A. Godinho, & L. Nunes, A. (2004). *Function Blocks for Industrial-Process Mesaurement and Control Systems. Institute of Production Engineering*, Report 67. Tampere University of Technology.

Lautenbach, K. (1987). Linear algebraic calculation of deadlocks and traps. In Voss, K., Genrich, H. J., & Rozenberg, G. (Eds.), *Concurrency and Nets* (pp. 315–336).

Lawley, M. A., Reveliotis, S. A., & Ferreira, P. M. (1998). A correct and scalable deadlock avoidance policy for flexible manufacturing systems. *IEEE Transactions on Robotics and Automation, 14*(5), 796–809. doi:10.1109/70.720355

Le Lann, G. (1996, March). A methodology for designing and dimensioning critical complex computing systems. IEEE Intl. symposium on the Engineering of Computer Based Systems, (pp. 332-339), Friedrichshafen, Germany.

Le Moigne, R., Pasquier, O., & Calvez, J.-P. (2004). A Generic RTOS Model for Real-time Systems Simulation with SystemC. In *Design, Automation and Test in Europe Conference and Exhibition Designers, DATE'04,* (Vol. 3, pp. 82 – 87).

Lee, D.-U., & Villasenor, J.-D. (2009). Optimized custom precision function evaluation for embedded processors. *IEEE Transactions on Computers, 58*(1).

Lee, J., & Mooney, V. (2005, March). Hardware/software partitioning of operating systems: Focus on deadlock detection and avoidance. [CDT]. *IEEE Computer and Digital Techniques, 152*(2), 167–182. doi:10.1049/ip-cdt:20045078

Lee, E. A. (2006). The problem with threads. *Computer magazine, 39,* 33-42.

Lee, J. (2004). *Hardware/Software Deadlock Avoidance for Multiprocessor Multi-resource System-on-a-Chip.* Ph.D. dissertation, Georgia Institute of Technology, Atlanta, GA.

Lehoczky, J. (1990). Fixed priority scheduling of periodic task sets with arbitrary deadlines. In Proceedings 11th IEEE Real-Time Systems Symposium, (pp. 201-209), Lake Buena Vista, FL.

Lehoczky, J., Sha, L., & Ding, Y. (1989). The Rate-Monotonic scheduling algorithm: exact characterization and average case behavior. In Proceedings of 10th IEEE Real-Time Systems Symposium, (pp. 166-172).

Leung, J. Y. T., & Merril, M. (1980). A note on premptive scheduling of periodic real-time tasks. *Information Processing Letters, 11*(3). doi:10.1016/0020-0190(80)90123-4

Leung, Y. T., & Sheen, G. J. (1993). Resolving deadlocks in flexible manufacturing cells. *Journal of Manufacturing Systems, 12*(4), 291–304. doi:10.1016/0278-6125(93)90320-S

Leuschel, M., & Butler, M. (2003). ProB: A model checker for B. In K. Araki, S. Gnesi, & D. Mandrioli, (Eds.), *FME 2003: Formal Methods,* (LNCS 2805, pp. 855–874). Berlin: Springer-Verlag.

Lewis, R.-W. (2002). *Modelling control systems using iec 61499, Applying function blocks to distributed systems, (Control Engineering Series).* Stevenage, UK: Institution Of Engineering and Technology.

Lewis, R. W. (2001). *Modeling control systems using IEC 61499.* Washington, DC: IEE Publishing.

Li, Z.-W., Zhou, M.-C., & Jeng, M.-D. (2008). A maximally permissive deadlock prevention policy for fms based on Petri net siphon control and the theory of regions. *IEEE Transactions on Automation Science and Engineering, 5*(1).

Li, Z. W., Uzam, M., & Zhou, M. C. (2004). Comments on "Deadlock prevention policy based on Petri nets and siphons.". *International Journal of Production Research, 42*(24), 5253–5254. doi:10.1080/00207540412331330822

Li, Z. W., Zhang, J., & Zhao, M. (2007). Liveness-enforcing supervisor design for a class of generalized Petri net models of flexible manufacturing systems. *IET Control Theory and Applications, 1*(4), 955–967. doi:10.1049/iet-cta:20060218

Li, Z. W., & Zhao, M. (2008). On controllability of dependent siphons for deadlock prevention in generalized Petri nets. *IEEE Transactions on Systems, Man, and Cybernetics. Part A, 38*(2), 369–384.

Li, Z. W., & Zhou, M. C. (2004). Elementary siphons of Petri nets and their application to deadlock prevention in flexible manufacturing systems. *IEEE Transactions on Systems, Man, and Cybernetics. Part A, 34*(1), 38–51.

Li, Z. W., & Zhou, M. C. (2006). Two-stage method for synthesizing liveness-enforcing supervisors for flexible manufacturing systems using Petri nets. *IEEE Transactions on Industrial Informatics, 2*(4), 313–325. doi:10.1109/TII.2006.885185

Li, Z. W., Zhou, M. C., & Wu, N. Q. (2008). A survey and comparison of Petri net-based deadlock prevention policies for flexible manufacturing systems. *IEEE Transactions on Systems, Man, and Cybernetics. Part C, 38*(2), 173–188.

Li, Q., & Yao, C. (2003). *Real-Time concepts for Embedded Systems*. Gilroy, CA: CMP Books.

Li, Y., & Wolf, W. (1999). Hardware/Software Co-Synthesis with Memory Hierarchies. *IEEE Transaction Computer-Aided Design of Integrated Circuits and Systems, 18*(10), 1405–1417. doi:10.1109/43.790618

Li, Z. W. Liang, J.W. Lu, Y. Wang, A. R. (2004). A deadlock prevention method for FMS with multiple resource acquisitions. In *8th International Conference on Control, Automation, Robotics and Vision Conference*, (vol.3, pp.2117-2122).

Li, Z. W., Wang, A. R., & Wei, N. (2006). Liveness-enforceing supervisors for flexible manufacturing systems with multiple resource acquisitions. In *Proceeding of the 2006 IEEE International Conference on Networking Sensing and Control*, (pp.710-714).

Liedtke, J. (1996). Toward real Microkernels. *Communications of the ACM*.

Lieverse, P., Stefanov, T., Van der Wolf, P., & Depretere, E. (Nov. 2001). System level design with Spade: an M-JPEG case study. In *Proc. of the Int. Conference on Computer Aided Design*, (pp. 31-38).

Limberg, T., Ristau, B., & Fettweis, G. (2008). *A Real-Time Programming Model for Heterogeneous MPSoCs*. Paper presented at the 8th international workshop on Embedded Computer Systems: Architectures, Modeling, and Simulation.

Lipton, R. J., & Lopresti, D. (1985). A systolic array for rapid string comparison. In *Chapel Hill Conference on VLSI*, (pp. 363-376).

Lis, J., Kowalski, C. T., & Orlowska-Kowalska, T. (2008). *Sensorless DTC control of the induction motor using FPGA*. Paper presented at the IEEE International Symposium on Industrial Electronics (ISIE 2008).

Liu, L. C., & Layland, W. (1973). Scheduling algorithms for multi-programming in a hard real time environment. *Journal of the ACM, 20*(1), 46–61. doi:10.1145/321738.321743

Liu, J. W. S. (2000). *Real-Time systems*. Upper Saddle River, NJ: Prentice Hall.

Lock, C. (1986). Best effort decision making for real-time scheduling. PhD thesis, Computer science department, Carnegie-Mellon University, Pittsburgh, PA.

Loghi, M., Angiolini, F., Bertozzi, D., Benini, L., & Zafalon, R. (Feb. 2004). Analyzing on-chip communication in a MPSoC environment. In *Proceedings of IEEE Design Automation and Test in Europe Conference DATE*, (pp. 752-757), Paris, France.

Lorentz, K. (2006). *Torero newsletter no. 2, TORERO Consortium*. Retrieved March 3, 2006 from http://www.uni-magdeburg.de/iaf/cvs/torero

Lovati, V., Marchesoni, M., Oberti, M., & Segarich, P. (1998). A Microcontroller-Based Sensorless Stator Flux-Oriented Asynchronous Motor Drive for Traction Applications. *IEEE Transactions on Power Electronics, 13*(4), 777–785. doi:10.1109/63.704156

Lu, J., Chen, H., Yew, P., & Hsu, W. (2004). Design and implementation of a lightweight dynamic optimization system. *Journal of Instruction-Level Parallelism, 6*, 1–24.

Lu, Z., & Haukilahti, R. (2003). High level communication primitives and operating system services for power management. In Jantsch, A., & Tenhunen, H. (Eds.), *NoC Application Programming Interfaces* (*Vol. 3*, pp. 239–260). Berlin: Springer.

Luebbers, E., & Platzner, M. (2009, August). Cooperative Multithreading in Dynamically Reconfigurable Systems. In *Proceedings of the 19th International Conference on Field Programmable Logic and Applications (FPL)*.

Luebke, D., & Harris, M. (2004). GPGPU: General Purpose Computing on Graphics Hardware. *International Conference on Computer Graphics and Interactive Techniques ACM SIGGRAPH*. Los Angeles, CA.

Lundqvist, T., & Stenström, P. (1998). Integrating Path and Timing Analysis using Instruction-Level Simulation Techniques. In *LNCS 1474* (pp. 1–15). Berlin: Springer.

Lysaght, P., & Rosenstiel, W. (2005). *New Algorithms, Architectures and Applications for Reconfigurable Computing*. New York: Springer-Verlag. doi:10.1007/1-4020-3128-9

Lyseckey, R., & Vahid, F. (2009). Design and implementation of a MicroBlaze-based warp processor. *ACM Transactions on Embedded Computing Systems TECS, 8*(3), 22.

Lysecky, R., Stitt, G., & Vahid, F. (2006). Warp processors. *ACM Transactions on Design Automation of Electronic Systems TODAES, 11*(3), 659–681. doi:10.1145/1142980.1142986

Lysne, O., Montanana, J.-M., Flich, J., Duato, J., Pinkston, T.-M., & Skeie, T. (2008). An efficient and deadlock-free network reconfigurable protocol. *IEEE Transactions on Computers, 57*(6).

M2000 Embedded FPGA. (n.d.). Retrieved from http://www.m2000.fr

Maddimsetty, R. P., Buhler, J., Chamberlain, R. D., Franklin, M. A., & Harris, B. (2006). Accelerator design for protein sequence HMM search. In *International Conference on Supercomputing*, (pp. 288-296).

Mailler, R., & Lesser, V. (2003-a). A Mediation Based Protocol for Distributed Constraint Satisfaction. In *Fourth International Workshop on Distributed Constraint Reasoning*, (pp. 49-58).

Mailler, R., Lesser, V., & Horling, B. (2003-b). Cooperative Negotiation for Soft Real-Time Distributed Resource Allocation. In *Proceedings of Second International Joint Conference on Autonomous Agents and MultiAgent Systems (AAMAS 2003)*, (pp. 576-583). New York: ACM Press.

Mälardalen Research and Technology Centre. (2006). The Worst-Case Execution Time (WCET) analysis project. *The Worst-Case Execution Time (WCET) analysis project*.

Manabe, Y., & Aoyagi, S. (1998). A feasibility decision algorithm for rate monotonic and deadline monotonic scheduling. *Real-Time Systems, 14*(2), 171–181. doi:10.1023/A:1007964900035

Manna, Z., & Pnueli, A. (1992). *The Temporal Logic of Reactive and Concurrent Systems: Specification*. Berlin: Springer-Verlag.

Manna, Z., & Pnueli, A. (1995). *Temporal Verification of Reactive Systems: Safety*. Berlin: Springer-Verlag.

Manna, Z., Anuchitanukul, A., Bjorner, N., Browne, A., Chang, E., & Colon, M. L. de Alfaro, H., Devarajan, H., Sipma, T. & Uribe, T. (1994). *STeP: The Stanford Temporal Prover*. Technical Report CS-TR-94-1518, Stanford University, Department of Computer Science, Stanford, CA.

Mansur, D. (2009). A New 40-nm FPGA and ASIC Common Platform. *IEEE Micro, 29*(2), 46–53. doi:10.1109/MM.2009.22

Marculescu, R., Ogras, U., Peh, L.-S., Jerger, N., & Hoskote, Y. (2009). Outstanding Research Problems in NoC Design: System, Microarchitecture, and Circuit Perspectives. *IEEE Transactions on Computer-Aided Design of Integrated Circuits and Systems, 28*(1). doi:10.1109/TCAD.2008.2010691

Marescaux, T. (2003). *Networks on chip as hardware components of an OS for reconfigurable systems.* In FPL.

Marinca, D., Minet, P., & George, L. (2004). *Analysis of deadline assignment methods in distributed real-time systems. Computer Communications.* New York: Elsevier.

Martin, G. (2009). System-on-Chip design. In *Embedded systems design and verification* (pp. 13 1-18). Boca Raton, FL: CRC Press.

Martin, P., Bueno, E., Rodriguez, F. J., & Saez, V. (2009, Nov.). *A Methodology for Optimizing the FPGA Implementation of Industrial Control Systems.* Paper presented at the IEEE IECON, Porto, Portugal.

Masson, P. A., Mountassir, H., & Julliand, J. (2000). *Modular verification for a class of PLTL properties* (pp. 398–419). IFM.

Maxfield, C. (2004). *The Design Warrior's Guide to FPGAs.* Orlando, FL: Elsevier.

McKenzie, F-D., Petty, M-D. & Xu, Q. (2004). Usefulness of software architecture description languages for modeling and analysis of federates and federation architectures. *SCS Simulation journal.*

McKeown, N., & Anderson, T. E. (1998). A quantitative comparison of scheduling algorithms for input-queued switches. *Computer Networks and ISDN Systems, 24*(30), 2309–2326. doi:10.1016/S0169-7552(98)00157-3

McMinn, P. (2004). Search-based software test data generation: a survey: Research Articles. In *Softw. Test. Verif. Reliab., 14*, (pp. 105-156).

Medvidovic, N. & Taylor, R. N. (2000). A classification and comparison framework for software architecture description languages. *IEEE Transactions on Software Engineering.* FAA. (2001). *An investigation of Three Forms of the Modified Condition/Decision/Coverage (MCDC) Criterion.* Technical Report.

Megginson. (2008). *Megginson Parser.* Retrieved 10 October 2008, from http://www.megginson.com

Meilander. W. C., Baker. J. W., & M. J. (2003). Importance of SIMD Computation Reconsidered. In Proc. *International Parallel and Distributed Processing Symposium.*

Mellor, S. J., Wolfe, J. R., & McCausland, C. (2005). Why Systems-on-Chip Needs More UML like a Hole in the Head. In Martin, G., & Müller, W. (Eds.), *UML for SOC Design* (pp. 17–36). Berlin: Springer. doi:10.1007/0-387-25745-4_2

Mens, T., Wermelinger, M., Ducasse, S , Demeyer, S., Hirschfeld, R., & Jazayeri, M. (2005). Challenges in software evolution. In *Proceedings of the Eighth International Workshop on Principles of Software Evolution,* (pp. 13–22).

Mernik, M., Heering, J., & Sloane, A. M. (2005). When and How to Develop Domain-Specific Languages. *ACM Computing Surveys, 37*(4), 316–344. doi:10.1145/1118890.1118892

Méry, D. (1986). *A proof system to derive eventually properties under justice hypothesis* (pp. 536–544). MFCS.

Méry, D. (1987). Méthode axiomatique pour les propriétés de fatalité des programmes parallèles. In *ITA,* (3), 287-322.

Mery, D., & Petin, J. F. (1998). Formal Engineering methods for modelling and verification of control systems. In G. Morel & F. Vernadat, (Eds.), *9th Symposium On Information Control in Manufacturing INCOM.*

Meyer Auf Der Heide. F., Monien. B., & Rosenberg. A. L. (1992). Parallel Architectures and Their Efficient Use. In: Proc. *1st Heinz Nixdorf Symposium.* Germany.

Microns. (2010). *Micro holon for next generation embedded automation*. Retrieved 10 October 2008, from http://www.microns.org/

Microsoft. (2008). *Microsoft's DOM Parser*. Retrieved 10 October 2008, from http://msdn.microsoft.com/xml/

Miller, J., & Mukerji, J. (2001). *Model Driven Architecture (MDA): Document number ormsc/2001-07-01*. Object Management Group.

Miller, J. & Mukerji, J., Object Management Group (OMG). (2003). *MDA Guide Version 1.0.1*. Technical Report. Lockheed Martin. (2005). *Lockheed Martin (MDA SUCCESS STORY)*. Technical report.

Milner, R. (1977). A Theory of Type Polymorphism in Programming. *Journal of Computer and System Sciences, 17*, 348–375. doi:10.1016/0022-0000(78)90014-4

Minghui, W., Shugen, M., Bin, L., & Yuechao, W. (2009). Reconfiguration of a group of wheel-manipulator robots based on msv and csm. *IEEE Transactions on Mechatronics, 14*(2).

Mingjing, C., & Orailoglu, A. (2007). Improving Circuit Robustness with Cost-Effective Soft-Error-Tolerant Sequential Elements. *Proceedings of the 16th Asian Test Symposium*, (pp. 307-312).

Mitchell, I., & Tomlin, C. (2000). Level set methods for computation in hybrid systems. In *Hybrid Systems: Computation and Control, Third International Workshop*, (LNCS).

Mitra, A., Zhi, G., Banerjee, A., & Najjar, W. (2006). *Dynamic Co-Processor Architecture for Software Acceleration on CSoCs*. Paper presented at the International Conference on Computer Design (ICCD 2006).

Miyamori, T., & Olukotun, K. (1999, February). RE-MARC: Reconfigurable multimedia array coprocessor. *IEICE Trans. on Information and Systems. E (Norwalk, Conn.), 82-D*(2), 389–397.

ModelSim SE foreign language interface. (2004, November). Retrieved from http://www.model.com

ModelSim SE user manual. (2005, January). Retrieved from http://www.model.com

Mohamadian, M., Nowicki, E., Ashrafzadeh, F., Chu, A., Sachdeva, R., & Evanik, E. (2003). A novel neural network controller and its efficient DSP implementation for vector-controlled induction motor drives. *IEEE Transactions on Industry Applications, 39*(6), 1622–1629. doi:10.1109/TIA.2003.819441

Mohanty, S., & Prasanna, V. (2002). Rapid system-level performance evaluation and optimization for application mapping onto SoC architectures. In *Proc. of the IEEE ASIC/SOC Conference*, (pp. 160-167).

Monmasson, E., & Cirstea, M. N. (2007). FPGA Design Methodology for Industrial Control Systems-A Review. *IEEE Transactions on Industrial Electronics, 54*(4), 1824–1842. doi:10.1109/TIE.2007.898281

Monmasson, E., & Chapuis, Y. A. (2002). Contributions of FPGA's to the control of electrical systems—A Review. *IEEE Industrial Electronics SoC Newsletter, 49*(4), 8–15.

Monmasson, E., & Cirstea, M. N. (2007). FPGA Design Methodology for Industrial Control Systems—A Review. *IEEE Transactions on Industrial Electronics, 54*(4), 1824–1842. doi:10.1109/TIE.2007.898281

Moore, E. F. (1956). Gedanken Experiments on Sequential Machines. In *Automata Studies* (pp. 129–153). Princeton, NJ: Princeton U.

Moraes, F., Calazans, N., Möller, L., Brião, E., & Carvalho, E. (2005). Dynamic and Partial Reconfiguration in FPGA SoCs: Requirements Tools and a Case Study. In Lysaght, P., & Rosenstiel, W. (Eds.), *New Algorithms, Architectures and Applications for Recofigurable Computing* (pp. 157–168). Netherlands: Springer. doi:10.1007/1-4020-3128-9_13

Morgenstern, B., Frech, K., Dress, A., & Werner, T. (1998). DIALIGN: Finding local similarities by multiple sequence alignment. *Bioinformatics (Oxford, England), 14*, 290–294. doi:10.1093/bioinformatics/14.3.290

Morris, K. (2007, Jan.). *Actel Activates Platforms*. Retrieved from Embedded Technology Journal: http://www.embeddedtechjournal.com/articles_2007/20070130_actel.htm

Mosbahi, O. (2002). *Une technique de spécification et de validation basée sur la méthode STATEMATE et la logique FNLOG, mémoire de D.E.A en informatique*. Tunis, Tunisie: FST.

Mosbahi, O. (2008). *A formal development approach of automated systems*. Phd thesis, LORIA-Campus Scientifique, France.

Mouhoub, R., & Hammami, O. (2006, Oct.). NoC Monitoring Hardware Support for Fast NoC Design Space Exploration and Potential NoC Partial Dynamic Reconfiguration. *International Symposium on Industrial Embedded Systems IES*, (pp. 1-10).

Mount, D. (2004). *Bioinformatics: Sequence and Genome Analysis*. New York: C. S. Harbor Lab Press.

Mountassir, H., Bellegarde, F., Julliand, J., & Masson, P. A. (2000). Coopération entre preuve et model checking pour vérifier modulairement des propriétés LTL. In *AFADL* (pp. 127–141). LSR/IMAG.

Moy, M., Maraninchi, F., & Maillet-Contoz, L. (2005). LusSy: A Toolbox for the Analysis of System-on-a-Chip at the Transactional Level. In *Proc. of the Int. Conf. on Application of Concurrency to System Design*.

Muchnick, S. S. (1997). *Advanced Compiler Design & Implementation*. San Francisco: Morgan Kaufmann Publishers, Inc.

Mueller, W., Rosti, A., Bocchio, S., Riccobene, E., Scandurra, P., Dehaene, W., & Vanderperren, Y. (2006). UML for ESL Design: Basic Principles, Tools, and Applications. In *Proceedings of the 2006 IEEE/ACM International Conference on Computer-Aided Design,* (pp. 73-80). San Jose, CA: ACM.

Mura, M., Paolieri, M., Negri, L., & Sami, M. G. (2007). StateCharts to systemc: a high level hardware simulation approach. In *Proceedings of the 17th great lakes symposium on Great lakes symposium on VLSI*, Stresa-Lago Maggiore, Italy, (pp. 505 – 508).

Murali, S., Coenen, M., Radulescu, A., Goossens, K., & De Micheli, G. (Mar. 2006). A methodology for mapping multiple use-cases onto networks on chips. In *Proceedings of The International Design Automation and Test in Europe Conference*, (pp. 118–123).

Murata, T. (1989). Petri nets: Properties, analysis, and applications. *Proceedings of the IEEE, 77*(4), 541–580. doi:10.1109/5.24143

Myers, E. W., & Miller, W. (1988). Optimal alignments in linear space. *Computer Applications in the Biosciences, 4*(1), 11–17.

Najjar, W. A., Bohm, W., Draper, B. A., Hammes, J., Rinker, R., Beveridge, J. R., et al. (2003, August). High-Level Language Abstraction for Reconfigurable Computing. In *IEEE Computer*, (pp. 63–69).

National Institute of Standards and Technology (NIST). (2002). *The Economic Impacts of Inadequate Infrastructure for Software Testing*. Technical Report.

National-Instruments. (2008). *LabVIEW FPGA in Hardware-in-the-Loop Simulation Applications*.

Needleman, S., & Wunsh, C. (1970). A general method applicable to the search for similarities in the amino acid sequence of two proteins. *Journal of Molecular Biology, 48*, 443–453. doi:10.1016/0022-2836(70)90057-4

Neishaburi, M.-H., & Zilic, Z. (2009). Reliability aware NoC router architecture using input channel buffer sharing. *Proceedings of the 19th ACM Great Lakes symposium on VLSI*, (pp. 511-516), Boston.

Nelis, V., Goossens, J., & Andersson, B. (2009). Two Protocols for Scheduling Multi-mode Real-Time Systems upon Identical Multiprocessor Platforms. In 21st Euromicro Conference on Real-Time Systems (ECRTS'09), (pp. 151-160).

Nikolov, H., Stefanov, T., & Deprettere, E. (2006). *Multi-processor system design with ESPAM*. Paper presented at the 4th international conference on Hardware/software codesign and system synthesis.

Novak, P., Rollo, M., Hodik, J., & Vlcek, T. (2003). Communication Security in Multi-Agent Systems. In *Multi-Agent Systems and Aplications III* (pp. 454–463). Berlin: Springer-Verlag. doi:10.1007/3-540-45023-8_44

Novotny, D. W., & Lorentz, R. D. (1985). *Introduction to Field Orientation and High Performance AC drives*. Paper presented at the Tutorial Course of the IEEE Industry Applications Society, Toronto, Canada.

Ntafos, S. C. (1988). A Comparison of Some Structural Testing Strategies. *IEEE Transactions on Software Engineering, 14*, 868–874. doi:10.1109/32.6165

Nunes, R., Gomes, L., & Barros (2007). A Graphical Editor for the Input-Output Place-Transition Petri Net Class. In *12th IEEE International Conference on EWmerging Technologies and Factory Automation ETFA07*, Sept 25-28, (pp. 788-791).

Nurmi, J. (2007). *Processor Design, System-On-Chip computing for ASICS and FPGAs*. Berlin: Springer.

NVidia Tegra. (2009). Retrieved from NVidia: http://www.nvidia.com/page/handheld.html

NVidia. (2007, June 5). *NVidia Tesla GPU Computing Technical Brief*. Récupéré sur NVidia Tesla Technical Brief: http://www.nvidia.com/docs/IO/43395/tesla_technical_brief.pdf

OARCorp. (n.d.). *RTEMS*. Retrieved from http://www.rtems.com

Object Management Group. (2006). *UML Profile for System on a Chip (SoC) V1.0.1. OMG Document Number: formal/06-08-01*. Object Management Group.

Object Management Group. (2007). *OMG Unified Modeling Language (OMG UML) Infrastructure V2.1.2. OMG Document Number: formal/2007-11-04*. Object Management Group.

Object Management Group. (n.d.). *CORBA Component Model Specification*.

OCP-IP Association. (2009). Open Core Protocol Specifications. [sur OCP-IP.]. *Consulté le, 10*, 20.

Ogras, U.-Y., & Marculescu, R. (2008, Jan.). Analysis and optimization of prediction-based flow control in networks-on-chip. *ACM Transactions on Design Automation of Electronic Systems TODAES, 13*(1), 1–28. doi:10.1145/1297666.1297677

Ogras, U. Y., & Marculescu, R. (2005). Key research problems in NOC design: A holistic perspective. In Proc. of *International conference hardware-software codesign system synthesis* (pp. 69-74).

Ogras, U.-Y., & Marculescu, R. (2005). Application-Specific Network-on-Chip Architecture Customization via Long-Range Link Insertion. In *Proceedings of the IEEE/ACM International conference on Computer-aided design*, (pp. 246-253), San Jose, CA.

Ogras, U.-Y., Marculescu, R., Marculescu, D., & Jung, E.-G. (2009, Feb./Mar.). Design and management of voltage–frequency island partitioned networks-on-chip. *IEEE Transactions on Very Large Scale Integration VLSI Networks-on-Chip Special Section*.

Oliveira, M., & Hu, A. (2002). High-level Specification and Automatic Generation of IP Interface Monitors. In *Proceedings of the Design Automation Conference DAC*.

Oliver, T., Schmidt, B., Jakop, Y., & Maskell, D. (2009). High speed biological sequence analysis with hidden Markov models on reconfigurable platforms. *IEEE Transactions on Information Technology in Biomedicine, 13*(5), 740–746. doi:10.1109/TITB.2007.904632

Oliver, T., Yeow, L. Y., & Schmidt, B. (2008). Integrating FPGA acceleration into HMMer. *Parallel Computing, 34*, 681–691. doi:10.1016/j.parco.2008.08.003

Oliver, T., Schmidt, B., & Maskell, D. (2005). Hyper customized processor for bio-sequence database scanning on FPGAs. In *ACM/SIGDA International Symposium on Field Programming Gate Arrays*, (pp. 229-237).

OMAP. (n.d.). Retrieved from Texas Instruments, OMAP35x Applications Processors http://focus.ti.com/dsp/docs/dspcontent.tsp?contentId=53403

OMG. (2008). *UML Profile for Modeling and Analysis of Real-time and Embedded Systems*. MARTE.

OMG. (n.d.). *OCL 2.0 Specification.* Retrieved from http://www.omg.org/docs/ptc/05-06-06.pdf

Open, C. L. *Khronos*. (2009). Retrieved from Khronos OpenCL The open standard for parallel programming of heterogeneous systems: http://www.khronos.org/opencl/

OpenCores. (2009). *OpenCores.org*. Retrieved October 23, 2009, from http://www.opencores.org/

Oppenheim, A. V., & Schafer, R. W. (1999). *Discrete-time signal processing* (2nd ed.). New York: Prentice Hall.

Oreizy, P., Gorlick, M. M., Taylor, R. N., Heimbigner, D., Johnson, G., & Medvidovic, N. (1999). An Architecture-Based Approach to Self-Adaptive Software. *IEEE Intelligent Systems, 14*(3), 54–62. doi:10.1109/5254.769885

Ortega, R.-B., & Borriello, G. (1998). Communication synthesis for distributed embedded systems. In *Proceedings of the International Conference on Computer-Aided Design*, (pp. 437-444).

Ostroff, J. S. (1994). *Formal Methods for the Specification and Design of Real-Time Safety Critical Systems*, I.E.E.E. Press book to be called "Tutorial on specification of Time".

Pagilla, P-R., Dwivedula, R-V. & Siraskar, N-B. (2007). A decentralized model reference adaptive controller for large-scale systems. *IEEE Transactions on Mechatronics, 12*(2).

Paiz, C., & Porrmann, M. (2007). *The Utilization of Reconfigurable Hardware to Implement Digital Controllers: a Review*. Paper presented at the IEEE International Symposium on Industrial Electronics (ISIE 2007).

Paiz, C., Hagemeyer, J., Pohl, C., Porrmann, M., Rückert, U., Schulz, B., et al. (2009). *FPGA-Based Realization of Self-Optimizing Drive-Controllers*. Paper presented at the 35th Annual Conference of the IEEE Industrial Electronics Society, IECON 2009.

Palesi, M., Holsmark, R., Kumar, S., & Catania, V. (2009, Mar.). Application Specific Routing Algorithms for Networks on Chip. *IEEE Transactions on Parallel and Distributed Systems, 20*(3), 316–330. doi:10.1109/TPDS.2008.106

Palumbo, F., Secchi, S., Pani, D., & Raffo, L. (2008). A Novel Non-exclusive Dual-Mode Architecture for MPSoCs-Oriented Network on Chip Designs. In Heidelberg, S. B. (Ed.), *Embedded Computer Systems: Architectures, Modeling, and Simulation* (pp. 96–105). Berlin: SpringerLink. doi:10.1007/978-3-540-70550-5_11

Pamunuwa, D., Öberg, J., Zheng, L.-R., Millberg, M., Jantsch, A., & Tenhunen, H. (Dec. 2003). Layout, Performance and Power Trade-Offs in Mesh-Based Network-on-Chip Architectures. In *Proceeding of IFIP International Conference on Very Large Scale Integration*, (p. 362).

Panainte, E.-M., Bertels, K., & Vassiliadis, S. (2007). The Molen Compiler for Reconfigurable Processors. *ACM Transactions on Embedded Computing Systems, 6* (1).

Papadimitriou, K., Anyfantis, A., & Dollas, A. (2009). An Effective Framework to Evaluate Dynamic Partial Reconfiguration in FPGA Systems. *IEEE Transactions on Instrumentation and Measurement*.

Papakonstantinou, A., Gururaj, K., Stratton, J.-A., Chen, D., Cong, J., & Hwu, W.-M. (2009). FCUDA: Enabling Efficient Compilation of CUDA. *Proceedings of the 23rd international conference on Supercomputing*, (pp. 515-516). Yorktown Heights, NY, USA.

Park, J., & Reveliotis, S. A. (2001). Deadlock avoidance in sequential resource allocation systems with multiple resource acquisitions and flexible routings. *IEEE Transactions on Automatic Control, 46*(10), 1572–1583. doi:10.1109/9.956052

Park, J. C., Mooney, V., & Srinivasan, S. K. (2003, November). Combining data remapping and voltage/frequency scaling of second level memory for energy reduction in embedded systems. *Microelectronics Journal, 34*(11), 1019–1024. doi:10.1016/S0026-2692(03)00170-8

Pasricha, S., & Dutt, N. (2008). *On-chip communication architectures: system on chip interconnect.* San Francisco: Morgan Kaufmann.

Pasricha, S., Dutt, N., & Ben Romdhane, M. (2007). BM-SYN: Bus matrix communication architecture synthesis for MPSoC. *IEEE Transactions on CAD*, 8(26), 79–85.

Pasricha, S., Dutt, N., Bozorgzadeh, E., & Ben-Romdhane, M. (2005). Floorplan-aware automated synthesis of bus-based communication architectures. In Proc. of *the 42nd annual conference on Design automation* (pp. 565-570). ACM Press, New York.

Patel, J. (1981). Performance of processor-memory interconnections for multiprocessors. *IEEE Trans.*, C(30), 771–780.

Paulson, L. C. (1996). *ML for the Working Programmer.* Cambridge, UK: Cambridge University Press.

Pellerin, D., & Thibault, S. (2005). *Practical FPGA Programming in C.* Upper Saddle River, NJ: Prentice Hall PTR.

Pellerin, D., & Shenoy, K. (2006). *C-Language techniques for FPGA acceleration of embedded software.* Paper presented at the Embedded Systems Conference (ESC-368).

Perre, L.-V., Craninckx, J., & Dejonghe, A. (2009). *Green Software Defined Radios: Enabling seamless connectivity while saving on hardware and energy.* Berlin: Springer.

Petriu, D., Gérard, S., & Medina, J. (2007). MARTE: A New Standard for Modeling and Analysis of Real-Time and Embedded Systems. In *19th Euromicro Conference on Real-Time Systems (ECRTS 07).*

Pickard, L. M., Kitchenham, B. A., & Jones, P. W. (1998). Combining empirical results in software engineering. *Information and Software Technology*, 40(14), 811–821. doi:.doi:10.1016/S0950-5849(98)00101-3

Pimentel, A. D., Erbas, C., & Polstra, S. (2006). A systematic approach to exploring embedded system architectures at multiple abstraction levels. *IEEE Transactions on Computers*, 55(2), 99–112. doi:10.1109/TC.2006.16

Pimentel, A.-D., Lieverse, P., & Van der Wolf, P.-H. (2001, Nov.). Exploring embedded-systems architectures with Artemis. *Computer*, 34(11), 57–63. doi:10.1109/2.963445

Pionteck, T. (2006). *A Dynamically Reconfigurable Packet-Switched Network-on-Chip* (pp. 136–137). In DATE.

Pitt, J., & Mamdani, A. (2000). Communication Protocols in Multi-Agent Systems: A Development Method and Reference Architecture. In F. Dignum & M. Greaves (eds.), *Issues in Agent Communication*, (LNAI 1916, pp. 160-177). Berlin: Springer Verlag.

Plessl, C. (2006). *Hardware virtualization on a coarse-grained reconfigurable processor.* ETH dissertation no. 16742, ETH Zurich, Switzerland.

Plessl, C., & Platzner, M. (2004, June). Virtualization of hardware – introduction and survey. In *Proc. Int. Conf. on Engineering of Reconfigurable Systems and Algorithms (ERSA)* (pp. 63–69). Los Vegas, NV: CSREA Press.

Plessl, C., & Platzner, M. (2005, July). Zippy – a coarse-grained reconfigurable array with support for hardware virtualization. In *Proc. IEEE Int. Conf. on Application-Specific Systems, Architectures, and Processors (ASAP)* (pp. 213–218). Washington, DC: IEEE Computer Society.

Plessl, C., Platzner, M., & Thiele, L. (2006, December). Optimal temporal partitioning based on slowdown and retiming. In *Int. Conf. on Field Programmable Technology (ICFPT)* (pp. 345–348). Washington, DC: IEEE Computer Society.

Pnueli, A. (1977). The temporal logic of programs. In *focs77,* (pp. 46–57).

Poletti, F., Poggiali, A., & Marchal, P., (2005). Flexible Hardware/Software Support for Message Passing on a Distributed Shared Memory Architecture. *DATE'05*, 02(2), 736-741.

Power, I. B. M. *XCell8i.* (2008, Aug.). Retrieved from With Its New Power XCe l l 8i Product Line IBM Intends to Take Accelerated Processing into the HPC Mainstream http://www-03.ibm.com/technology/resources/technology_cell_IDC_report_on_PowerXCell.pdf

Project, I. ST-511599. (2007). RODIN: Rigorous Open Development Environment for Complex Systems. Technical Note, Retrieved from http://www.event-b.org/platform.html

Puschner, P., & Koza, C. (1989). Calculating the Maximum Execution Time of Real-Time Programs. In. *Journal of Real-Time Systems, 1*, 159–176. doi:10.1007/BF00571421

Puttegowda, K., Worek, W., Pappas, N., Dandapani, A., & Athanas, P. (2003). A run-time reconfigurable system for gene-sequence searching. In *International Conference on VLSI Design*, (pp. 561-566).

QNX Software Systems. (2009). *QNX Neutrino RTOS Overview*. Retrieved from http://www.qnx.com/products/neutrino_rtos/

Qu, Y., Tiensyrjä, K., Soininen, J.-P., & Nurmi, J. (2008). Design Flow Instantiation for Run-Time Reconfigurable Systems: A Case Study. *EURASIP Journal on Embedded Systems, 2008*(856756).

Quadros Systems Inc. (2007). *RTXC 3.2 real-time kernel*. Retrieved from http://www.quadros.com/products/operating-systems/rtxc-32/, Trimberger, S. (2007). *FPL 2007 Xilinx Keynote Talk - Redefining the FPGA*. Retrieved from http://ce.et.tudelft.nl/FPL/trimbergerFPL2007.pdf

Rabiner, L. R. (1989). A tutorial on hidden Markov models and selected applications in speech recognition. *Proceedings of the IEEE, 77*(2), 257–286. doi:10.1109/5.18626

Racu, R., Hamann, A., & Ernst, R. (2006). A formal approach to multi-dimensional sensitivity analysis of embedded realtime systems. In proceedings of the 18th Euromicro conference on real-time systems (ECRTS'06).

Raghunathan, V. et al. (2005, February). Energy Aware Wireless Systems with Adaptive Power-Fidelity tradeoffs. *IEEE Transaction on very large scale integration (VLSI) systems, 13*(2), 211 – 225.

Rana, V., Santambrogio, M., & Sciuto, D. (2007). Dynamic Reconfigurability in Embedded System. *IEEE International Symposium on Circuits and Systems*, (pp. 2734-2737), New Orleans, LA.

Rasche, A., & Polze, A. (2005). Dynamic reconfiguration of component-based real-time software. In *Proceedings of the 10th IEEE International Workshop on Object-Oriented Real-Time Dependable Systems, WORDS 2005*, Sedona, Arizona, (pp. 347–354).

Rausch, M., & Hanisch, H.-M. (1995). Net condition/event systems with multiple condition outputs. In *Symposium on Emerging Technologies and Factory Automation*, (Vol.1, pp.592-600).

Ravn, A. P., Rishel, H., & Hansen, K.-M. (1993). Specifying and Verifying Requirements of Real-Time systems, *I.E.E.E. Transaction on Software Engineering* (pp. 41-55). Vol. 19, N0 1.

Reveliotis, S. A. (2003). On the siphon-based characterization of liveness in sequential resource allocation systems. In W. M. P. van der Aalst and E. Best (Eds.), *Proc. Int. Conf. on Applications and Theory of Petri Nets*, (LNCS 2679, pp.241-255). Berlin: Springer.

Riccobene, E., Scandurra, P., Rosti, A., & Bocchio, S. (2005). *A UML 2.0 Profile for SystemC. ST Microelectronics, Technical Report: AST-AGR-2005-3*. ST Microelectronics.

Riccobene, E., Scandurra, P., Rosti, A., & Bocchio, S. (2005). A SoC Design Methodology Involving a UML 2.0 Profile for SystemC. In *Proceedings of the conference on Design, Automation and Test in Europe (DATE 2005)*, (pp. 704-709). Munich, Germany: IEEE Computer Society.

Rivest, R. L., & Schapire, R. E. (1993). Inference of Finite Automata Using Homing Sequences. *Information and Computation, 103*(2), 299–347. doi:10.1006/inco.1993.1021

Rivest, R. L., & Schapire, R. E. (1989). *Inference of Finite Automata Using Homing Sequences*, In *Proc. 21st annual ACM symposium on Theory of Computing*. (pp. 411-420). New York: ACM.

Roch, S. (2000). Extended computation tree logic. In *Proceedings of the CESP2000 Workshop*, (Vol. 140, pp. 225-234). Berlin: Informatik Berichte.

Roch, S. (2000). Extended computation tree logic: Implementation and application. In *Proceedings of the AWPN2000 Workshop*, Germany.

Roch, S. (2000). Extended Computation Tree Logic: Implementation and Application. In *Proceedings of the AWPN2000 Workshop*, Germany.

Rockwell. (2006). *Rockwell automation*. Retrieved from http://www.holobloc.com

Rodriguez-Andina, J. J., Moure, M. J., & Valdes, M. D. (2007). Features, Design Tools, and Application Domains of FPGAs. *IEEE Transactions on Industrial Electronics*, *54*(4), 1810–1823. doi:10.1109/TIE.2007.898279

Rooker, M.-N., Sunder, C., Strasser, T., Zoitl, A., Hummer, O., & Ebenhofer, G. (2007). Zero downtime reconfiguration of distributed automation systems: The εcedac approach. In *Third International Conference on Industrial Applications of Holonic and Multi-Agent Systems*. Berlin: Springer-Verlag.

Rosti, A., Campi, F., Bonnot, P., & Brelet, P. (2009). SoA of Reconfigurable Computing Architectures and Tools. In Dans N. Voros, A. Rosti, & M. Hübner, (eds.), *Dynamic System Reconfiguration in Heterogeneous Platforms* (pp. 13-27). Berlin: Springer.

Roszkowska, E. (2004). Supervisory control for deadlock avoidance in compound processes. *IEEE Transactions on Systems, Man, and Cybernetics. Part A*, *34*(1), 52–64.

Rouphael, T.-J. (2009). *RF and Digital Signal Processing for Software-Defined Radio: A Multi-Standard Multi-Mode Approach*. New York: Elsevier.

Rowson, J.-A., & Sangiovanni-Vincentelli, A. (1997). Interface-based design. *Proceedings of the 34th Design Automation Conference DAC, 34*, 178-183.

Rowson, J.-A., & Sangiovanni-Vincentelli, A. (1998). Getting the bottom of deep sub-micron. In *Proceedings of the IEEE/ACM International Conference on Computer Aided Design ICCAD*, (pp. 203-211), San Jose, CA.

Roychoudhury, A., Mitra, T., & Karri, S. R. (2003). *Using Formal Techniques to Debug the AMBA System-On-Chip Protocol. Proc. of the conference on Design, Automation and Test in Europe, 1* (pp. 828–833). Washington: IEEE Computer Society.

Ruelland, R., Gateau, G., Meynard, T. A., & Hapiot, J. C. (2003). Design of FPGA-based emulator for series multicell converters using co-simulation tools. *IEEE Transactions on Power Electronics*, *18*(1), 455–463. doi:10.1109/TPEL.2002.807104

Rugina, A., Feiler, P. H., Kanoun, K., & Kaaniche, M. (2008). Software dependability modeling using an industry-standard architecture description language. In *Proceedings of 4th European Congress ERTS*, Toulouse.

Ruiz Barradas, H., & Bert, D. (2002). *Specification and proof of liveness properties under fairness assumptions in B event systems* (pp. 360–379). IFM.

Sadiku, M. N., & Akujuobi, C. M. (2004). Software-defined radio: a brief overview. *IEEE Potentials*, *23*(4), 14–15. doi:10.1109/MP.2004.1343223

SAE. (2008). *Architecture Analysis & Design Language v2.0 (AS5506)*.

Salefski, B., & Caglar, L. (2001). Re-configurable computing in wireless. In *Proc. 38th Design Automation Conf. (DAC)* (pp. 178–183).

Salewski, F., & Kowalewski, S. (2008). Hardware/Software Design Considerations for Automotive Embedded Systems. *IEEE Transactions on Industrial Informatics*, *4*(3), 156–163. doi:10.1109/TII.2008.2002919

SC2V. (2008). *SystemC to Verilog Converter*. Retrieved 10 October 2008, from http://www.opencores.org/projects.cgi/web/sc2v

Schack, C., Heenes, W., & Hoffmann, R. (2009). A Multiprocessor Architecture with an Omega Network for the Massively Parallel Model GCA. In Proc. *9th International Workshop on Embedded Computer Systems: Architectures, Modeling, and Simulation*. (pp. 98-107).

Schattkowsky, T. (2005). UML 2.0 - Overview and Perspectives in SoC Design. IN *Proceedings of the conference on Design, Automation and Test in Europe (DATE 2005)*, (pp. 832-833). Munich, Germany: IEEE Computer Society.

Schaumont, P., & Verbauwhede, I. (2007). *Hardware/Software Codesign for Stream Ciphers*. Paper presented at the Special workshop hosted by the ECRYPT Network of Excellence in Cryptology.

Schirrmeister, F. (2007). *Multi-core Processors: Fundamentals, Trends, and Challenges*. Paper presented at the Embedded Systems Conference, ESC-351.

Schmaltz, J., & Borrione, D. (2004). A Functional Specification and Validation Model for Networks on Chip in the ACL2 Logic. Proc. of *the 5th International Workshop on the ACL2 Theorem Prover and its Applications (ACL2'04)*. Austin.

Schmaltz, J., & Borrione, D. (2006). Towards a Formal Theory of Communication Architecture in the ACL2 Logic. Proc. of *the 6th international workshop on the ACL2 theorem prover and its applications*. ACM Press, New York. (pp. 47- 56).

Schmidt, D. C. (2006). Guest Editor's Introduction: Model-Driven Engineering. *Computer journal Model-Driven Engineering, 39*(2), 25-31.

Schnakenbourg, C., Faure, J.-M., & Lesage, J.-J. (2002). Towards IEC 61499 function block diagrams verification. In *Proceedings of the IEEE International Conference on Systems, Man and Cybernetics*, Nashville, TN.

Schoofs, T., Jenn, E., Leriche, S., Nilsen, K., Gauthier, L., & Richard-Foy, M. (2009). Use of PERC Pico in the AIDA avionics platform. In *JTRES '09: Proceedings of the 7th International Workshop on Java Technologies for Real-Time and Embedded Systems*.

Schulz, B., Paiz, C., Hagemeyer, J., Mathapati, S., Porrmann, M., & Bocker, J. (2007). *Run-time reconfiguration of FPGA-based drive controllers*. Paper presented at the European Conference on Power Electronics and Applications.

Schulz, B., Paiz, C., Hagemeyer, J., Mathapati, S., Porrmann, M., & Bocker, J. (2007). *Run-time reconfiguration of FPGA-based drive controllers*. Paper presented at the 12th European Conf. on Power Electronics and Applications (EPE).

Schurz, F., & Fey, D. (2007). *A Programmable Parallel Processor Architecture in FPGAs for Image Processing Sensors*. In Proc. Integrated Design and Process Technology.

Seely, J. A. (2005). *Using Hardware Acceleration Units in Software Defined Radio Modem Functions*. COTS Journal Digital Edition.

Semiconductor Industry Association. (2007). *International Technology Roadmap for Semiconductors: Design Chapter*. Semiconductor Industry Association.

Semiconductor Industry Association. (2009). *International Technology Roadmap for Semiconductors (ITRS)*. Retrieved from http://www.itrs.net/Links/2009ITRS/Home2009.htm

SESA. (2008). *Signal/Net System Analyzer*. Retrieved from http://www.ece.auckland.ac.nz/ vyatkin/tools/modelchekers.html

Seul, J., & Sung su, K. (2007). Hardware Implementation of a Real-Time Neural Network Controller With a DSP and an FPGA for Nonlinear Systems. *IEEE Transactions on Industrial Electronics, 54*(1), 265–271. doi:10.1109/TIE.2006.888791

Shalan, M. (2003). *Dynamic memory management for embedded real-time multiprocessor system-on-a-chip*. PhD thesis, School of ECE, Georgia Institute of Technology, Atlanta, GA.

Shankar, N. (2000). Combining theorem proving and model checking through symbolic analysis. In *Concurrency Theory (CONCUR)*, (LNCS 1877, pp. 1–16). Springer-Verlag.

Sharma, S., Kahlon, K. S., Bansal, P. K., & Singh, K. (2008). Irregular Class of Multistage Interconnection Network in Parallel Processing. *Journal of Computer Science, 4*(3), 220–224. doi:10.3844/jcssp.2008.220.224

Shaver, D. (2008). *Platform-based design in the year 2020*. Retrieved from TI E2E Community http://e2e.ti.com/blogs/video360/archive/2008/12/05/platform-based-design-inthe-year-2020.aspx

Sheibanyrad, A., Panades, I.-M., & Greiner, A. (2007). Systematic comparison between the asynchronous and the multi-synchronous implementations of a network-on-chip architecture. In *Proceeding of Design Automation and Test in Europe Conference DATE*, (pp. 1090–1095).

Sheynin, Y., Suvorova, E., & Shutenko, F. (2006). Complexity and low power issues for on-chip interconnections in MPSoC system level design. In *Proceedigns of the IEEE Computer Society Annual Symposium on Emerging VLSI Technologies and Architectures*, (p. 283), Karlsruhe, Germany.

Shin, D., Gerstlauer, A., Domer, R., & Gajski, D. (2005). Automatic generation of communication architectures. In Springer (Ed.), *From Specification to Embedded Systems Application* (Vol. 184). Boston: Book Series IFIP International Federation for Information Processing.

Shin, D., Gerstlauer, A., Peng, J., Domer, R., & Gajski, D. (Oct. 2006). Automatic Generation of Transaction Level Models for Rapid Design Space Exploration. In *Proceedings of the international conference on Hardware/software codesign and system synthesis*, (pp. 64-69).

Siege1. H. J., Wang. L., So. J. E., & Maheswaran. M. (1994). *Data parallel algorithms*. ECE Technical Reports.

Siegel, H. J. (1979). Interconnection Networks for SIMD Machines. *IEEE. Computer*, 6(12), 57–65. doi:10.1109/MC.1979.1658780

Siegel, H., & Smith, S. (1978). Study of Multistage SIMD Interconnection Networks. In Proc. *5th Annual Symposium on Computer Architecture*. New York (pp. 223-229).

Siegmund, R., & Muller, D. (2002). Automatic Synthesis of Communication Controller Hardware from Protocol Specification. *IEEE Design & Test of Computers, 19*, 84–95. doi:10.1109/MDT.2002.1018137

Simard, S., Beguenane, R., & Mailloux, J.-G. (2008). Performance Evaluation of Rotor Flux-Oriented Control on FPGA for Advanced AC Drives. *Journal of Robotics and Mechatronics, 21*(1), 113–120.

Simard, S., Mailloux, J. G., & Beguenane, R. (2009). Prototyping Advanced Control Systems on FPGA. *EURASIP Journal on Embedded Systems, 2009*.

Sims, M., Corkill, D., & Lesser, V. (2008). Automated Organization Design for Multi-agent Systems. *Autonomous Agents and Multi-Agent Systems, 16*(2), 151–185. doi:10.1007/s10458-007-9023-8

Singh, H., Lee, M.-H., Lu, G., Kurdahi, F., Bagherzadeh, N., & Chaves Filho, E. (2000, May). MorphoSys: an integrated reconfigurable system for data-parallel and computation-intensive applications. *IEEE Transactions on Computers, 49*(5), 465–481. doi:10.1109/12.859540

Singh, B., Singh, B. P., & Dwivedi, S. (2006). *DSP Based Implementation of Fuzzy Precompensated PI Speed Controller for Vector Controlled PMSM Drive*. Paper presented at the 1st IEEE Conference on Industrial Electronics and Applications.

Singhoff, F., Legrand, J., Nana, L., & Marcé, L. (2004). Cheddar: a flexible real time scheduling Framework. *ACM SIGAda Ada Letters, 24*(4), 1–8. doi:10.1145/1046191.1032298

Singhoff, F., & Plantec, A. (2007). AADL modeling and analysis of hierarchical schedulers. In *SIGAda '07: Proceedings of the 2007 ACM international conference on SIGAda annual international conference*.

Skey, K., Bradley, J., & Wagner, K. (2006). A reuse approach for FPGA-based SDR waveforms. *Military Communications Conference*, (pp. 1–7), Washington, DC.

Smith, T. F., & Waterman, M. S. (1981). Identification of common molecular subsequences. *Journal of Molecular Biology, 147*(1), 195–197. doi:10.1016/0022-2836(81)90087-5

Smith, G. (2004). Platform Based Design: Does it Answer the Entire SoC Challenge? In *Proceedings of the 41st Design Automation Conference DAC*, (p. 407).

Software Engineering Institute - Carnegie Mellon University. (2006). *Open source AADL tool environment.* Technical report.

Sokolsky, O., Lee, I., & Clark, D. (2006). Schedulability Analysis of AADL models. In *International Parallel and Distributed Processing Symposium.*

Song, I., Kim, S., & Karray, F., (2008). A real-time scheduler design for a class of embedded systems. *IEEE Transactions on Mechatronics, 13*(1).

Sowmya, A., & Ramesh, S. (1992). Verification of Timing Properties in a Statecharts Based Model of Real-Time Reactive systems, *Distributed computer control systems, IFAC workshop series 1992*, N0. 3, H. Kopetz and M.G.Rodd, eds.Pergamon Press.

Spivey, J. M. (1988). Understanding Z, A Specification Language and its Formal Semantics. In *Tracts in Theoretical Computer Science*. Cambridge, UK: Cambridge University Press.

Stammermann, A., Kruse, L., Nebel, W., & Pratsch, A. (Oct. 2001). System level optimization and design space exploration for low power. In *Proceedings of the International Symposium on Systems Synthesis*, (pp. 142-146).

Stanica, M., & Guèguen, H. (2004). Using Timed Automata for the Verification of IEC 61499 Applications. In *Proceedings of the Workshop on Discrete Event Systems*, Reims, France.

Starobinski, D., Karpovsky, M., & Zakrevski, L.-A. (2003, June). Application of network calculus to general topologies using turn-prohibition. In *IEEE/ACM Transactions on Networking TON, 11*(3), 411-421.

Stepner, D., et al. (1999). Embedded application design using a real-time OS. In *DAC 99*, New Orleans, LA.

Stewart, D.-B., Volpe, R.-A., & Khosla, P.-K. (1997). Design of dynamically reconfigurable real-time software using port-based objects. *IEEE Transactions on Software Engineering, 23*(12), 759–776.

Stitt, G., & Vahid, F. (2005). New decompilation techniques for binarylevel co-processor generation. In *Proceedings of IEEE/ACM International Conference on Computer-Aided Design ICCAD*, (pp. 547-554).

Stitt, G., & Vahid, F. (2007). Thread Warping: A Framework for Dynamic Synthesis of Thread Accelerators. In *Proceedings of the International Conference on Hardware/Software Codesign and System Synthesis CODES/ISSS*, (pp. 93-98), Salzburg, Austria.

STMicroelectronics. (2005, December 15). *STMicroelectronics Unveils Innovative Network-on-Chip Technology for New System-on-Chip Interconnect Paradigm.* Récupéré sur www.stm.com: http://www.stm.com/stonline/press/news/year2005/t1741t.htm

Stone, H. S. (1971). Parallel Processing with the Perfect Shuffle. *IEEE Transactions on Computers, 20*, 153–161. doi:10.1109/T-C.1971.223205

Stone, H. S. (1980). Parallel computers. In Stone, H. S. (Ed.), *Introduction to Computer Architecture* (2nd ed., pp. 363–425). Chicago, IL: Science Research Associates.

Strasser, T., Zoitl, A., Auinger, F., & Sünder, C. (2005). *Towards engineering methods for reconfiguration of distributed automation systems based on the reference model of IEC 61499*. Proceedings of the 2nd International Conference on Industrial Applications of Holonic and Multi-Agent Systems. Copenhagen, Denmark, Aug. 22–24.

Sun, Y., Li, P., Gu, G., Wen, Y., Liu, Y., & Liu, D. (2009). Accelerating HMMer on FPGAs using systolic array based architecture. In *IEEE International Symposium on Parallel and Distributed Processing*, (pp. 1-8).

Sünder, C., Zoitl, A., Favre-Bulle, B., Strasser, T., Steininger, H., & Thomas, S. (2006). Towards reconfiguration applications as basis for control system evolution in zero-downtime automation systems. *Proceedings of the IPROMS NoE Virtual International Conference on Intelligent Production Machines and Systems, IPROMS, 2006*(June), 3–14.

Swan, S. (2006). SystemC transaction level models and RTL verification. *Proc. of the Design Automation Conference DAC, 43*, 90-92.

Synopsis. (2008). *Synopsis CoCentric SystemC Compiler.* Retrieved 10 October 2008, from http://www.synopsys.com/products/cocentric_systemC/cocentric_systemC_ds.html

Takahashi, J., Yamaguchi, T., Sekiyama, K., & Fukuda, T. (2009). Communication timing control and topology reconfiguration of a sink-free meshed sensor network with mobile robots. *IEEE Transactions on Mechatronics, 14*(2).

Tan, W., Fan, Y., & Zhou, M. (2009). A Petri net-based method for compatibility analysis and composition of web services in business process execution language. *IEEE Transactions on Automation Science and Engineering, 6*(1).

Tan, W. H., Thiagarajan, P. S., Wong, W. F., Zhu, Y., & Pilakkat, S. K. (2004). *Synthesizable SystemC Code from UML Models.* Presented at International Workshop on UML for SoC Design (USOC 2004), Sponsored by Design Automation Conference, June. Nguyen, K.D., Thiagarajan, P.S. & Wong, W.F. (2007). A UML-based Design Framework for Time-triggered Applications. In *28th IEEE Real-Time Systems Symposium (RTSS 07),* Tucson, AZ.

Tanenbaum, A. A. (1995). *Distributed Operation Systems.* New York: Prentice Hall.

Tang, H., Weng, L., Dong, Z-Y., & Yan, R., (2009). Adaptive and learning control for si engine model with uncertainties. *IEEE Transactions on Mechatronics, 14*(1).

Taylor, M., Lee, W., Amarasinghe, S., & Agarwal, A. (2005, Feb.). Scalar operand networks. *IEEE Transactions on Parallel and Distributed Systems, 16*(2), 145–162. doi:10.1109/TPDS.2005.24

Taylor, M.-B., Kim, J., Miller, J., Wentzlaff, D., Ghodrat, F., & Greenwald, B. (2002, Mar./Apr.). The RAW microprocessor: A computational fabric for software circuits and general-purpose programs. *IEEE Micro, 22*(2), 25–35. doi:10.1109/MM.2002.997877

Tensilica Xtensa. (2009). Retrieved from New Tensilica DPU Family Delivers 10 GigaMAC/sec DSP Performance, Tops 1 GHz Mark: http://www.tensilica.com/

Theelen, B. D., Verschueren, A. C., Reyes Suarez, V. V., Stevens, M. P. J., & Nunez, A. A. (2003). scalable single-chip multi-processor architecture with on-chip RTOS kernel. *Journal of Systems Architecture, 49*(12-15), 619–639. doi:10.1016/S1383-7621(03)00101-2

Thiele, L., & Wilhelm, R. (2004). Design for Timing Predictability. *Real-Time Systems, 28,* 157–177. doi:10.1023/B:TIME.0000045316.66276.6e

Thramboulidis, K. (2006). *IEC 61499 in Factory Automation. Advances in Computer, Information and Systems Sciences and Engineering* (pp. 115–124). Amsterdam: Springer. doi:10.1007/1-4020-5261-8_20

Thramboulidis, K. (2005). Model-integrated mechatronics - toward a new paradigm in the development of manufacturing systems. *IEEE transactions on Industrial Informatics, 1*(1), 54- 61.

Thramboulidis, K., Doukas, G., & Frantzis, A. (2004). Towards an implementation model for FB-based reconfigurable distributed control applications. In *Proceedings of the 7th IEEE International Symposium on Object-Oriented Real-Time Distributed Computing,* Vienna, Austria, (pp. 193–200).

TimeLogic. (2009). *DeCypher FPGA Biocomputing Systems.* Retrieved October 10, 2009, from http://www.timelogic.com

Tindell, K., Burns, A., & Wellings, A. J. (1995). Analysis of hard real-time communications. *Real-Time Systems, 9,* 147–171. doi:10.1007/BF01088855

Todman, T. J., & Constantinides, G. A. E., S. J., Mencer, O., Luk, W., & K, P. Y. (2005). Reconfigurable Computing: Architectures and Design Methods. In *Proceedings on Computers and Digital Techniques, 152,* (pp. 193-207). Washington, DC: IEEE.

Top. (2008). *Top 10 Challenges in Logic Control for Manufacturing Systems.* Retrieved 10 October 2008, from http://www.personal.umich.edu/~tilbury/logiccontrol/

Torero. (2010). *Total life cycle web-integrated control.* Retrieved 13 April 2010, from http://www.uni-magdeburg.de/iaf/cvs/torero/

Tricas, F., & Ezpeleta, J. (2006). Computing minimal siphons in Petri net models of resource allocation systems: A parallel solution. *IEEE Transactions on Systems, Man, and Cybernetics. Part A, 36*(3), 532–539.

Triscend. (2004). Retrieved from Xilinx: http://www.triscend.com

Trzynadlowski, A. M. (1993). *The Field Orientation Principle in Control of Induction Motors* (1st ed.). Berlin: Springer.

Tsai, T.-H. Y-N., P., & Lin, C.-H. (2008). An Electronic System Level Design and Performance Evaluation for Multimedia Applications. In *Proceedings of the 2008 International Conference on Embedded Software and Systems ICESS*, (pp. 621-624).

Tsui, W., Masmoudi, M-S., Karray, F., Song, I., & Masmoudi, M. (2008). Soft-computing-based embedded design of an intelligent wall/lane-following vehicle. *IEEE Transactions on Mechatronics, 13*(1).

Uzam, M. (2002). An optimal deadlock prevention policy for flexible manufacturing systems using Petri net models with resources and the theory of regions. *International Journal of Advanced Manufacturing Technology, 19*(3), 192–208.

Uzam, M. (2004). The use of the Petri net reduction approach for an optimal deadlock prevention policy for flexible manufacturing systems. *International Journal of Advanced Manufacturing Technology, 23*(3/4), 204–219. doi:10.1007/s00170-002-1526-5

Van Ommering, R. (2002). Building product populations with software components. In *Proceedings of the 24th international Conference on Software engineering*, (pp. 255- 265). New York: ACM Press.

Vangal, S., Howard, J., Ruhl, G., Dighe, S., Wilson, H., Tschanz, J., et al. (Feb. 2007). An 80-tile 1.28TFLOPS network-on-chip in 65 nm CMOS. In *proceedings of the IEEE Solid-State Circuits International Conference ISSCC*, (pp. 98-589).

Vargas, F., Piccoli, L. B., Alecrim, A., Moraes, M., & Gama, M. (2006, Dec. 2006). *Summarizing a Time-Sensitive Control-Flow Checking Monitoring for Multi-task SoCs.* Paper presented at the IEEE Int. Conf. Field Programmable Technology FPT, Bankok, India.

Vaslin, R., Gogniat, G., Diguet, J.-P., Tessier, R., Unnikrishnan, D., & Gaj, K. (2008). Memory security management for reconfigurable embedded systems. *International Conference on Field-Programmable Technology*, (pp. 153-160), Taipei, Taiwan.

Vega-Rodríguez, A. M., Sánchez-Pérez, J. M., & Gómez-Pulido, J. A. (2005). Advances in FPGA tools and techniques. *Microprocessors and Microsystems, 29*(2-3), 47–49. doi:10.1016/j.micpro.2004.06.003

Vestal, S. (1994). Fixed-Priority Sensitivity Analysis for Linear Compute Time Models. *IEEE Transactions on Software Engineering, 20*(4). doi:10.1109/32.277577

Vestal, S. (1998). *Metah user's manual, version 1.27.* Technical report.

Vyatkin, V. (2007). *IEC61499 Function Blocks for Embedded and Distributed Control Systems Design.* Research Triangle Park, NC: ISA Publisher.

Vyatkin, V., & Hanisch, H.-M. (2003). Verification of distributed control systems in intelligent manufacturing. *International Journal of Manufacturing, 14*(1), 123–136.

Vyatkin, V., & Hanisch, H.-M. (2003). Verification of Distributed Control Systems in Intelligent Manufacturing. *Journal of Intelligent Manufacturing, 14*(1), 123–136. doi:10.1023/A:1022295414523

Vyatkin, V., & Hanisch, H.-M. (1999). *A Modeling Approach for Verification of IEC1499 Function Blocks using Net Condition/Event Systems.* Proceedings of IEEE International Conference on Emerging Technologies and Factory Automation, ETFA 1999, Barcelona, Spain.

Vyatkin, V.V., Christensen, J.H., Lastra, J.L.M. (2005). OOONEIDA: An Open, Object-Oriented Knowledge Economy for Intelligent Industrial Automation. *IEEE transactions on Industrial Informatics, 1*(1), 4-17.

Walsh, R., & Conway, S. (2008, Aug.). *With Its New Power XCe l l 8i Product Line IBM Intends to Take Accelerated Processing into the HPC Mainstream.* Retrieved from IBM Technology http://www-03.ibm.com/technology/ resources/technology_cell_IDC_report_on_PowerXCell. pdf

Wang, Y., Zhou, X. G., Zhou, B., Liang, L., & Peng, C. L. (2006). A MDA based SoC Modelling Approach using UML and SystemC. In *Proceedings of The Sixth IEEE International Conference on Computer and Information Technology (CIT'06).*

Wazlowski, M., Agarwal, L., Lee, T., Smith, A., Lam, E., Athanas, P., et al. (1993). PRISM-II Compiler and Architecture. In *Proceedings of the IEEE Workshop on FPGAs for Custom Computing Machines,* (pp. 9–16).

Wee, S. (2007). A Practical FPGA based Framework for Novel CMP Research. In *International Symposium on Field Programmable Gate Arrays.*

Wells, L. (2002). Performance Analysis Using Coloured Petri Nets. In *International Symposium on Modeling, Analysis, and Simulation of Computer and Telecommunications Systems,* (pp. 217-222). Washington, DC: IEEE Computer Society.

Wenzel, I., Rieder, B., Kirner, R., & Puschner, P. (2005). Automatic Timing Model Generation by CFG Partitioning and Model Checking. In *Proc. Design, Automation and Test in Europe (DATE)* (pp. 606–611). Washington, DC: IEEE.

Wenzel, I., Kirner, R., Rieder, B., & Puschner, P. (2008). Measurement-Based Timing Analysis. In *Proc. 3rd Int'l Symposium on Leveraging Applications of Formal Methods, Verification and Validation.*

Wermelinger, M. (1997). A hierarchic architecture model for dynamic reconfiguration. In *Proceedings of the Second International Workshop on Software Engineering for Parallel and Distributed Systems,* Boston, (pp. 243–254).

Wieferink, A., Kogel, T., Leupers, R., Ascheid, G., & Meyr, H. (2004). A system level processor/communication co-exploration methodology for multi-processor system-on-chip platforms. In *Proceedings of the Design Automation and Test in Europe Conference DATE,* (pp. 21-258). Paris, France.

Wilhelm, R., Engblom, J., Ermedahl, A., Holsti, N., Thesing, S., Whalley, D., et al. (2008). The Worst-Case Execution Time Problem - Overview of Methods and Survey of Tools. In *Transactions on Embedded Computing Systems (TECS), 7.* ACM.

Wills, L., Heck, B., Prasad, J. V., Schrage, D., & Vachtsevanos, G. (2001). An Open Platform for Reconfigurable Control. *IEEE Control Systems Magazine, 21*(3), 49–64. doi:10.1109/37.924797

Wind River. (2007). *VxWorks 6.x.* Retrieved from http://www.windriver.com/products/run-time_technologies/ Real-Time_Operating_Systems/VxWorks_6x/

Wohlin, C. (2005). An analysis of the most cited articles in software engineering journals. *Information and Software Technology, 47*(15), 957–964. doi:.doi:10.1016/j. infsof.2005.09.002

Wolf, W. (1993). *FPGA-Based System Design.* Upper Saddle River, NJ: Prentice-Hall.

Woll, D. (2007). *Setting the Stage for the Next Generation of Automation Control System Software: A Discussion of IEC 61499, ARC Insights, Insight# 2007-13M.* Retrieved 10 October 2007, from http://www.arcweb.com/Featured%20Research/IEC-61499-Ins13M.pdf

Woods, R., McAllister, J., Lightbody, G., & Yi, Y. (2008). *FPGA-based Implementation of Signal Processing Systems.* West Sussex, UK: John Wiley & Sons. doi:10.1002/9780470713785

Worchel, J. (2006). *The Field-Programmable Gate Array (FPGA): Expanding Its Boundaries.* Consulté le October 20, 2009, sur In-Stat: http://www.instat.com/abstract.asp?id=68& SKU=IN0603187SI

Wordsworth, J. (1987). Education in formal methods for software engineering. *Information and Software Technology, 29*(1), 27–32. doi:.doi:10.1016/0950-5849(87)90017-6

Wu, N. Q., & Zhou, M. C. (2001). Avoiding deadlock and reducing starvation and blocking in automated manufacturing systems. *IEEE Transactions on Robotics and Automation, 17*(5), 658–669. doi:10.1109/70.964666

WW Technology Group. (2008). *EDICT toolsuite.* Retrieved from http://www.wwtechnology.com/

Xilinx, Inc. (2010, April 12). *DS150: Virtex-6 Family Overview.* Récupéré sur http://www.xilinx.com

Xilinx. (2004). Retrieved from Xilinx FPGA embedded solutions http://www.xilinx.com/prs_rls/ip/0492_cmpembedded.htm

Xilinx. (2005). *MicroBlaze Processor Reference Guide. UG081 (v5.1)*

Xilinx. (2006). *Xilkernel_V3_00_a, EDK 9.1i.*

Xilinx. (2007). *PowerPC Processor Reference Guide. UG011 (v1.2).*

Xilinx. (2009). Retrieved Dec. 2009, from http://www.xilinx.com

Yamaguchi, Y., Maruyama, T., & Konagaya, A. (2002). High speed homology search with FPGAs. In *Pacific Symposium on Biocomputing*, (pp. 271-282).

Yang, G., Liu, Y., Cui, N., & Zhao, P. (2006, May 2006). *Design and implementation of a fpga-based ac servo system.* Paper presented at the 6th World Congress on Intelligent Control and Automation (WCICA)

Yen, T.-Y., & Wolf, W. (1995). Communication synthesis for distributed embedded systems. In *Proceedings of the International Conference on Computer-Aided Design*, (pp. 288-294).

Yim, D., Kim, J., & Woo, H. (1997). Avoidance of deadlocks in flexible manufacturing systems using a capacity designated directed graph. *International Journal of Production Research, 35*(9), 2459–2475. doi:10.1080/002075497194606

Ying-Shieh, K., & Ming-Hung, T. (2007). FPGA-Based Speed Control IC for PMSM Drive With Adaptive Fuzzy Control. *IEEE Transactions on Power Electronics, 22*(6), 2476–2486. doi:10.1109/TPEL.2007.909185

Yoo, S., Youssef, M.-W., Bouchhima, A., Jerraya, A. A., & Diaz-Nava, M. (2004). Multi-Processor SoC Design Methodology using a Concept of Two-Layer Hardware-dependent Software. In *Proceedings of the Design, Automation and Test in Europe Conference and Exhibition (DATE'04)*, (pp. 1530-1591/04). Washington, DC: IEEE.

Yuen Fong, C., Moallem, M., & Wei, W. (2007). Design and Implementation of Modular FPGA-Based PID Controllers. *IEEE Transactions on Industrial Electronics, 54*(4), 1898–1906. doi:10.1109/TIE.2007.898283

Zalila, B., Hugues, J., & Pautet, L. (2007). *Ocarina user guide.* Technical Report.

Zergainoh, N. E., Baghdadi, A., & Jerraya, A. A. (2004). Hardware/Software Codesign of On-chip Communication Architecture for Application-Specific Multiprocessor System-On-Chip. *International Journal of Embedded Systems, 1*(12), 10.

Zhang, P., Tan, G., & Gao, G. R. (2007). Implementation of the Smith-Waterman algorithm on a reconfigurable supercomputing platform. In *Conference on High Performance Networking and Computing*, (pp. 39-48).

Zhang, W., Calder, B., & Tullsen, D. (2005). An event-driven multithreaded dynamic optimization framework. In *Proceedings of Int. Conf. on Parallel Architectures and Compilation Techniques PACT*, (pp. 87-98).

Zhou, M. C., & DiCesare, F. (1992). A hybrid methodology for synthesis of Petri nets for manufacturing systems. *IEEE Transactions on Robotics and Automation, 8*(3), 350–361. doi:10.1109/70.143353

Zhou, M. C., & Fanti, M. P. (Eds.). (2005). *Deadlock Resolution in Computer-Integrated Systems*. New York: MarcelDekker.

Zhou, M. C., & Venkatesh, K. (1998). *Modelling, Simulation and Control of Flexible Manufacturing Systems: A Petri Net Approach*. Singapore: World Scientific.

Zhou, P., Xie, J., & Wang, L. (2005, Nov.). *Co-Design Of Embedded Real-Time Control Systems: A Feedback Scheduling Approach.* Paper presented at the Joint International Computer Conference (JICC), Chonqing, China.

Zhuo, L., & Prasanna, V.-K. (2008). High-performance designs for linear algebra operations on reconfigurable hardware. *IEEE Transactions on Computers, 57*(8).

Zivkovic, V., Van der Wolf, P., Deprettere, E., & De Kock, E.-A. (Oct. 2002). Design space exploration of streaming multiprocessor architectures. In *Proceedings of the IEEE Workshop on Signal Processing Systems*, (pp. 228-234).

Zoitl, A. (2008). *Real-Time Execution for IEC 61499*. Research Triangle Park, NC: International Society of Automation - ISA, ISA Press.

Zoitl, S. T., Hall, K., Staron, R., Sünder, C. & Favre-Bulle, B. (2007). The Past, Present and Future of IEC 61499. In *Holonic and Multi-Agent Systems for Manufacturing*, (LNCS 4659, pp. 1-14). Berlin: Springer.

Zolda, M. (2008). INFER: Interactive Timing Profiles based on Bayesian Networks. In *Proc. 4th International Symposium on Leveraging Applications*.

Zolda, M., & Kirner, R. (2008). Divide and Measure: CFG Segmentation for the Measurement-Based Analysis of Resource Consumption, In *Proc. Junior Scientist Conference,* (pp. 117-118).

Zolda, M., Bünte, S., & Kirner, R. (2009). Towards Adaptable Control Flow Segmentation for Measurement-Based Execution Time Analysis. In *Proc. 17th International Conference on Real-Time and Network Systems (RTNS)*.

Zrida, H. K., Jemai, A., Ammari, A. C., & Abid, M. (2009). High Level H.264/AVC Video Encoder Parallelization For Multiprocessor Implementation. In *12th International conference Design, Automation & Test in Europe (DATE),* 20-24 April 2009, Nice., Jemai, A., Kission, P., Jerraya, A.A., (1997, October). Combining Architectural Simulation and Behavioral Synthesis. *IEICE Transaction Fundamentals. E (Norwalk, Conn.), 80-A*(10), 1756–1766.

Zuberi, K. M., Pillai, P., & Shin, K. G. (1999). *AMER-ALDS-OSEK: A Small real-time Operating System for Automotive Control and Monitoring*. Warrendale, PA: Society of Automotive Engineers, Inc.

About the Contributors

Mohamed Khalgui is a researcher at Xidian University in China. He was a full-time researcher in computer science at Martin Luther University in Germany, a part-time researcher at ITIA-CNR Institute in Italy, a collaborator with SEG Research Group in Greece, and a temporary lecturer at Henri Poincaré University in France. Dr. Khalgui obtained the Bachelor degree in Computer Science at Tunis University in 2001. The master degree was obtained in telecommunication and services at Henri Poincaré University in 2003. He made research activities in computer science at INRIA Institute to obtain the PhD at the French Polytechnical Institute of Lorraine in 2007. Dr. Khalgui activates in several European Projects and also in other interesting international collaborations. He's currently the Head of ICTICA.

Hans-Michael Hanisch is Professor and Head of Research Laboratory on Automation Technology at Martin Luther University in Germany. He obtained in 1982 the diploma degree on Chemical Engineering (Specialization Process Systems Engineering) with Excellent, and in 1987 the PhD diploma with "summa cum laude" on "Mathematical Modeling of Discrete Control Tasks in Chemical Process Systems" at Polytechnical Institute of Leuna Merseburg in Germany. Between 1991 and 1993, Prof. Hanisch followed researches at the Process Control Laboratory at University of Dortmund in Germany to prepare the Habilitation which is successfully obtained in 1995 on "Modeling, Analysis, and Controller Design in Hierarchical Discrete Control Systems". Prof. Hanisch is an active member in several scientific international organizations and supervizes different R&D projects. He wrote more than 200 papers in reviewed known Journals and Conference Proceedings. In his research laboratory, more than 15 PhD students finished or are following research activities.

* * *

Hedi Abdelkrim was born in Tunisia in 1979. He received the National engineer degree in applied science and technology in industrial computer and automatic and MS degree at the National Institute of Applied Science and Technology (INSAT), Tunisia, in 2004. Currently, he is pursuing the Phd degree at Laboratoire d'Etude et de Commande Automatique de Processus (LECAP), INSAT, Tunisia. Since 2006, he has been a higher education assistant in the department of electrical engineering, Higher Institute of Medical Technologies (ISTMT), Tunisia. His main research interests include Co-Design of Reconfigurable SoC with real time systems specific to the electrical machine drive and FPGA-based controllers.

Mohamed Abid received the Ph. D. degree from the National Institute of Applicated Sciences, Toulouse (France) in 1989 and the "thèse d'état" degree from the National School of Engineering of Tunis

(Tunisia) 2000 in the area of Computer Engineering & Microelectronics. He is working now as Professor in the department of Electrical Engineering at National School of Engineering of Sfax (Tunisia). Currently he is founding member and responsible of doctoral degree «computer system engineering» at ENIS since 2003. In 1992, he was founding responsible of Electronic Systems Synthesis Group at Laboratory of Electronic and Micro-Electronic in Sciences Faculty in Monastir (Tunisia). Since 2000 he is founding member of System on Chip at Computer, Electronic and Smart engineering system Laboratory at National School of Engineering of in Sfax (Tunisia). Since 2005, he has occupied the director position of the laboratory. His current research interests include: hardware-software co-design, System on Chip, Reconfigurable System, and Embedded System, etc. He has also been investigating the design and implementation issues of FPGA embedded systems. Recently, He is General Co-chair of SensorNetSchool'09, Vice General Co-chair of IDT'09, Special Session Co-chair of ICECS'09 December 2009. He is also Joint Editor of Specific Issues in two International Journals. He is served also as Guest professor at several international universities and is served as a Consultant to research & development in Telnet Incorporation.

Jason Agron received his B.S. and M.S. degrees in computer engineering from the University of Kansas in 2004 and 2006, respectively, and a Ph.D. degree in computer engineering from the University of Arkansas, Fayetteville, in 2010. His research interests include hardware/software co-design, embedded operating systems, heterogeneous & reconfigurable computing, parallel programming, and domain-specific language design. He is currently a Software Engineer at Intel in Santa Clara, California working on next generation binary translation technology.

David Andrews is a Professor and holds the Mullins Endowed Chair of Computer Engineering in the Computer Science and Computer Engineering Department at the University of Arkansas. Dr. Andrews received the B.S.E.E. and M.S.E.E. degrees from the University of Missouri, and the PhD in Computer Science from Syracuse University. Dr. Andrews has held positions in General Electric's Electronics Laboratory, and faculty positions at the University of Kansas and University of Arkansas. His research interests include parallel and distributed architectures, real time operating systems, and reconfigurable computing. Dr. Andrews is a senior member of the IEEE.

Yassine Aydi received the engineering and M.S. degrees from the National Engineering School of Sfax, Sfax, Tunisia in 1994 and 2005, respectively. He is currently working toward the Ph.D. degree in Department of Computer Science at National Engineering School of Sfax, Sfax, Tunisia. His research interests include hardware/software co-design, Networks-on-Chip design.

Mouna Baklouti received the engineering and M.S. degrees from the Tunisian Polytechnic School, Tunis, Tunisia in 2006 and 2007, respectively. She is currently working toward the Ph.D. degree in Department of Computer Science at National Engineering School of Sfax, Sfax, Tunisia and University of Lille, Lille, France. Her research interests include hardware/software co-design, massively parallel systems design and System-on-Chip design.

Tomás Balderas-Contreras is a PhD student in Computer Science at Instituto Nacional de Astrofísica, Óptica y Electrónica in Mexico. His areas of interested are: Computer Architecture, Software Engineering, and Reconfigurable Computing. He has previously worked, both in academia and in industry, in the development and testing of instruction set simulators, hardware implementations of block ciphers, and firmware for multiprocessor systems. He is currently working towards the design and implementation of digital hardware systems by means of model-driven development methods. He has authored and co-authored a number of publications in national conferences, international conferences, and journals.

Slim Ben Othman was born in 1980 (Tunisia). He received the engineer degree and the MA in industrial computer and automatic at National Institute of Applied Sciences and Technology (INSAT), Tunisia in 2004. Currently, he is pursuing his PhD at LECAP laboratory (Laboratoire d'Etude et de Commande Automatique de Processus) and he is an Assistant Professor in the electrical engineering department of Higher Institute of Medical Technologies (ISTMT). His main research interests include the co-design of high performance and MPSoC FPGA-based controllers applied to electrical motor drive.

Ahmed Karim Ben Salem graduated in Industrial Computer and Automatic Engineering from INSAT institute of Tunis in 2004. Born in 1979 (Tunisia), he received the MA in industrial computer in 2004. Currently, he is pursuing his PhD at LECAP laboratory in Tunis Polytechnic School (EPT) and he is an Assistant Professor in the electrical engineering department of Higher Institute of Medical Technologies (ISTMT), in Tunisia. His main research interests include the co-design of real time FPGA-based controllers applied to electrical motor drive.

Slim Ben Saoud (1969) received the electrical engineer degree from the High National School of Electrical Engineering of Toulouse/France (ENSEEIHT) in 1993 and the PhD degree from the National Polytechnic Institute of Toulouse (INPT) in 1996. From April 1997 to September 1997, he was with UNISYS-Tunisia as a Hardware support Engineer. He joined the department of Electrical Engineering at the National Institute of Applied Sciences and Technology of Tunis (INSAT) in 1997 as an Assistant Professor. He is now Professor and the Leader of the "Embedded Systems Design Group" at INSAT. His research interests include Embedded Systems Architectures, real-time solutions and applications to the Co-Design of digital control systems and SpaceWire modules.

Sven Bünte is working as a researcher in the FWF project "Formal Timing Analysis Suite (FORTAS)" and is a PhD student at Vienna University of Technology since 2007. He received both his master and bachelor degree at Universität des Saarlandes in Saarbrücken, Germany. His research interests include performance analysis, communication protocols, and cyber-physical systems.

René Cumplido holds a B.Sc. in Computer Systems from ITQ, Mexico (1995), a M.Sc. in electrical engineering from CINVESTAV, Mexico (1997), and a PhD in electrical engineering from Loughborough University, UK (2001). In 2002, he joined the FPGA Research Group at INAOE, Mexico. In 2009, he was an invited researcher at the communications research group at Intel Labs in Guadalajara, Mexico. His research interests are Reconfigurable Computing for DSP and Digital Communications, FPGA Technologies, Custom Architectures for Scientific Computing, and Software Radio. He has published more than 50 scientific papers in international conferences and journals. He is co-founder and general chair of the International Conference on Reconfigurable Computing and FPGAs, ReConFig. He is the founder and editor-in-chief of the International Journal of Reconfigurable Computing, IJRC, and associate editor of the journals Computers & Electrical Engineering, CEE, and Journal of Electrical and Computer Engineering, JECE. He is also active in a number of technical committees of international conferences.

Jean-Luc Dekeyser received his PhD degree in computer science from the University of Lille in 1986, he was a fellowship at CERN Geneva. After a few years at the Supercomputing Computation Research Institute in Florida State University, where he worked on high performance computing for Monté-Carlo methods in High Energy Physics, he joined in 1988 the University of Lille in France as an assistant professor. There he worked on data parallel paradigm and vector processing. He created a research group working on High Performance Computing in the CNRS lab in Lille. He is currently Professor in computer science at University of Lille. He is heading the DaRT Inria project. His research interests include embedded systems, System on Chip co-design, synthesis and simulation, performance evaluation, high performance computing, model driven engineering.

Julien Delange, PhD, is a Software Engineer in the Software Systems Division at the European Space Agency. He has authored several articles in the area of safety-critical systems, model-based engineering and automatic code generation. He is also the author of the ARINC653 annex of the Architecture Analysis and Design Language (AADL) standard for the description and modeling of avionics architectures. Julien Delange holds a Master Degree in Computer Science from Université Pierre & Marie Curie (Paris VI) and a doctorate in computer science from TELECOM ParisTech.

Wei Ding received the B.Sc. degree in Software Engineering from Wuhan University, Wuhan, China, in 2007 and got the M.Sc. Degree in Computer Integrated Manufacturing from Nanyang Technological University, Singapore, in 2009. He is currently a PhD student in the department of computer science and engineering at Pennsylvania State University, Pennsylvania, United State. His research interests are compiler optimizations and high performance computing.

Pierre Courbin is a PhD Student at UPEC university (Créteil, France), associate member of LISSI lab. (University Paris-Est) and member of LACSC lab. (ECE-Paris Engineering). Pierre obtained in 2009 a master of research in information technology and systems at University of Paris-Sud (Orsay, France). The same year he received his master in engineering at ECE-Paris Engineering, with a specialization in embedded systems. Since Sept. 2009, he is involved in a PhD whose subject is on real-time scheduling for multiprocessor systems, with a focus and sensitivity analysis and parallel systems. Pierre is also a teacher in real-time embedded at ECE.

Laurent George obtained his PhD on real-time embedded and distributed systems in 1998 at University of Versailles, France. He received the habilitation to direct research (HDR) in Nov 2008 at university of Nantes, France. His habilitation thesis was on temporal robustness of embedded and distributed real-time systems. He is now assistant professor at UPEC university (Créteil, France), teacher in network and embedded systems. Until 2010, he has published more than 80 international journal and conference papers. He has been involved in the program committee of more than 30 international conferences as reviewer. He is reviewer for more than 10 international journals focusing on real-time systems including RTS journal, IEEE Transactions on Industrial Informatics, AIAA Journal of Aerospace Computing, Information, and Communication, IEEE Transaction on Software Engineering.His current research interests focus on feasibility conditions for the dimensioning of hard real-time multiprocessor and distributed systems for automotive and aerospace applications. He is also interested in real-time sensor networks for the Internet of things.

Kiah Mok Goh is a Research Scientist of Singapore Institute of Manufacturing Technology (SIMTech). He has assumed various responsibilities of group manager, centre manager, programme leader, research team leader, project leader, principal research engineer and senior research fellow. His research focuses on topics related to system development framework, stochastic manufacturing modelling, optimisation, intelligent factory control and has published over 40 research papers.

Osman Hasan received the BEng (Hons) degree from the N-W.F.P University of Engineering and Technology, Pakistan, in 1997, and the MEng and PhD degrees from Concordia University, Montreal, Quebec, Canada, in 2001 and 2008, respectively. He worked as a postdoctoral fellow at the Hardware Verification Group (HVG) of Concordia University for one year until August 2009. Currently, he is an assistant professor with the School of Electrical Engineering and Computer Science, National University of Science and Technology, Islamabad, Pakistan. His current research interests include formal methods, higher order logic theorem proving, probabilistic analysis, and real-time systems.

Abderrazak Jemai received an Engineer degree from the University of Tunis, Tunisia in 1988 and the DEA and "Doctor" degrees from the University of Grenoble, France, in 1989 and 1992, respectively, all in computer sciences. From 1989 to 1992 he prepared his thesis on simulation of RISC processors and parallel architectures. Since 1993, his interests are focused on high level synthesis and simulation at behavioral and system levels within AMICAL and COSMOS at TIMA Laboratory in Grenoble. Dr Jemai became an assistant professor at the ENSI university in Tunis in 1993 and a Maitre-Assistant Professor at the INSAT university in Tunis since 1994. He was the principal investigator for the "Synthesis and Simulation of VLSI circuits" project at the ENSI/Microelectronic group. He was the principal investigator of the simulation module in AMICAL at TIMA in Grenoble. He is also the principal investigator for the "Performance evaluation of MPSoC" project in LIP2/FST Laboratory in Tunis. Dr Jemai is also working on Security of embedded systems.

Ir. Laurent Jojczyk received the electrical engineering degrees from the Faculty of engineering of Mons, Belgium in 2007. He is presently Phd. Student in the Electronic and Microelectronics Department at the University of Mons, in Mons, Belgium. His primary research interests include EDA and Network on Chip architecture. His research activity is supported by several publications.

Raimund Kirner is a Principal Lecturer at the Compiler Technology and Computer Architecture group of the University of Hertfordshire. The research focus of Kirner is on system reliability, especially worst-case execution time analysis of real-time programs, including compiler support and design methodologies to make systems predictable. He has published several papers on WCET analysis and was involved in two projects funded by the European Commission (SETTA, NEXT TTA). From 2003-2005 Raimund Kirner has worked on the FIT-IT project MoDECS, and from 2005-2007 he worked on the FIT-IT project TeDES, both funded by the Federal Ministry of Transport, Innovation, and Technology (BMVIT). Currently, Raimund Kirner is principal investigator of the following projects: "Compiler-Support for Timing Analysis" (COSTA), "Formal Timing Analysis Suite" (FORTAS), and "Sustaining Entire Code-Coverage on Code Optimization" (SECCO). He is a member of the IEEE Computer Society, the ACM, the IFIP WG 10.2 (Embedded Systems) and the Austrian Computer Society (OCG).

Zhiwu Li (M'06–SM'07) received the B.S., M.S., and Ph.D. degrees in mechanical engineering, automatic control, and manufacturing engineering, respectively, from Xidian University, Xi'an, China, in 1989, 1992, and 1995, respectively. He joined Xidian University, in 1992, where he is currently a Professor of School of Electro-Mechanical Engineering. From 2002 to 2003, he was a Visiting Professor at the Systems Control Group, Department of Electrical and Computer Engineering, University of Toronto, Toronto, ON, Canada. Since February 2007, he has been a Visiting Scientist at the Laboratory for Computer-Aided Design (CAD) & Lifecycle Engineering, Department of Mechanical Engineering, Technion–Israel Institute of Technology, Technion City, Haifa, Israel. He is the author or coauthor of over 100 publications including a book chapter in Deadlock Resolution in Computer-Integrated Systems (Marcel Dekker, 2005). His current research interests include Petri net theory and application, supervisory control of discrete event systems, workflow modeling and analysis, and systems integration. Prof. Li cochaired the session on Manufacturing and Automation in the First Asian Symposium on Mechatronics, September 24–27, 2004, Xi'an, China. He was invited to coorganize a special session on Petri Nets and Discrete Event Systems in the 33rd Annual Conference of the IEEE Industrial Electronics Society (IECON 2007), November 5–8, 2007, Taipei, Taiwan, R.O.C. He served as a member of the Program Committee of the 2005 IEEE International Conference on Networking, Sensing, and Control, Tucson, AZ, March 19–22, the 2007 IEEE International Conference on Systems, Man and Cybernetics, Montreal, QC, Canada, October 7–10, the 2008 IEEE International Conference on Networks, Sensing, and Control, Sanya, China, April 6–8, and the 29th International Conference on application and Theory of Petri Nets, Xi'an, China, June 23–27, 2008. He is the General Co-Chair of the IEEE International Conference on Automation Science and Engineering, August 23–26, Washington, DC, 2008. He is a member of Discrete Event Systems Technical Committee of the IEEE Systems, Man, and Cybernetics Society. He serves as a frequent reviewer for more than 15 international journals including a number of the IEEE Transactions as well as many international conferences. He is a recipient of Alexander von Humboldt Research Grant, Alexander von Humboldt foundation, Germany.

Philippe Marquet is currently an assistant professor at the University of Lille, France and a researcher within the INRIA, the French institute for research in computer science. Philippe MARQUET received a Ph.D. in Computer Science from the University of Lille in 1992. His research interests include the design of parallel, embedded and reconfigurable architectures, the definition of programming models, languages and compilers dedicated to parallel computing. He also worked on the definition and implementation of real-time operating systems for SMP architectures. He (co-)advised 10 Ph.D thesis.

Alba Cristina M. A de Melo received the BS degree in Computer Science from UnB, Brazil, in 1986, the MsC in Computer Science from UFRGS, Brazil, in 1991 and the PhD in Computer Science from the Institut National Polytechnique de Grenoble, France, in 1996. She is currently an Associate Professor at the University of Brasilia (UnB). Her current research interests include high performance computing, bioinformatics and application-specific accelerators. She has advised 15 graduate students in these research areas and published several papers in prestigious international journals and conferences. She is a Senior member of the IEEE Society.

Olfa Mosbahi is a researcher in Computer Science at University of Tunis El-Manar in Tunisia. She was a part time researcher at INRIA in France and a temporary lecturer at Nancy II University. Dr. Olfa obtained the Bachelor degree in Computer Science at Tunis University in 1999. The master degree was obtained at the same institution in 2002. She made research activities in Computer Science at IN-RIA Institute to obtain the PhD at the French Polytechnical Institute of Lorraine in 2008. Dr. Mosbahi activates in several European Projects and also in other interesting international collaborations. She's currently the Head deputy of ICTICA.

Nahri Moreano received the BS degree in Informatics from UFRJ, Brazil, in 1990, the MsC in Systems and Computer Engineering from UFRJ, Brazil, in 1994 and the PhD in Computer Science from the University of Campinas, Brazil, in 2005. She was awarded the 2006 CAPES Theses Award for her PhD work. She is currently an Assistant Professor at the Federal University of Mato Grosso do Sul (UFMS). Her main research interests include high performance computing, computer architecture and application-specific accelerators. She has published papers in prestigious international journals and conferences.

Laurent Pautet is a full professor at Télécom ParisTech, member of the CNRS laboratory LTCI. His research is mainly concerned with design and validation of distributed real-time embedded systems (component-based modelling, verification of non-functional properties, automatic code generation, application dedicated middleware). He is the coordinator of several international free software projects (DSA/GNAT/GCC, PolyORB, Ocarina, POK) and he is also an active member of AADL standard committee. He has co-authored about 15 communications in international journals and 70 communications in international conferences. He participates in the Program committee of numerous conferences dedicated on distributed real-time embedded systems.

Marco Platzner is Professor for Computer Engineering at the University of Paderborn. Previously, he held research positions at the Computer Engineering and Networks Lab at ETH Zurich, Switzerland, the Computer Systems Lab at Stanford University, USA, the GMD - Research Center for Information Technology (now Fraunhofer IAIS) in Sankt Augustin, Germany, and the Graz University of Technology, Austria. Marco Platzner holds diploma and PhD degrees in Telematics (Graz University of Technology, 1991 and 1996), and a "Habilitation" degree for the area hardware-software codesign (ETH Zurich, 2002).

Marco Platzner is senior member of the IEEE, member of the ACM, member of the board of the Paderborn Center for Parallel Computing and faculty member of the International Graduate School Dynamic Intelligent Systems of the University of Paderborn and of the Advanced Learning and Research Institute (ALaRI) at Universita della Svizzera Italiana (USI), in Lugano. His research interests include reconfigurable computing, hardware-software codesign, and parallel architectures.

Christian Plessl is a postdoctoral research associate and lecturer at the University of Paderborn, where he is leading a research group in the area of "Custom Computing and Manycores" at the Paderborn Center for Parallel Computing (PC²). He earned a PhD degree (Dr. sc. ETH) in Computer Engineering from ETH Zurich in 2006, and a MSc degree in Electrical Engineering in 2001, also from ETH Zurich. Before joining University of Paderborn in fall 2007, he held a postdoc position in the Computer Engineering Group at ETH Zurich. Dr. Plessl is a member of the IEEE and an affiliate member of the EU FP7 HiPEAC Network of Excellence. He is a regular reviewer for major scientific journals and conferences, and serves on the program committee of international conferences. His current research interests include custom computing for high-performance computing and design-methods for reconfigurable architectures.

Ir. Paulo Possa received the electronic engineering degree from the University of Passo Fundo (UPF), Passo Fundo, Brazil, in 2005. He received his MSc degree from the Federal University of Santa Catarina (UFSC), Florianópolis, Brazil, in 2008, concentrating on biomedical engineering. He currently is an Electrical Engineering PhD Student at the University of Mons (UMons), Mons, Belgium, under the advisement of Dr. Carlos Valderrama. His current research is focused on novel reconfigurable hardware architectures for embedded systems.

Gustavo Rodríguez-Gómez received the Bachelor degree and Master degree in Mathematics from the National Autonomous University of Mexico (UNAM). He has a PhD in Computer Science from the National Institute of Astrophysics, Optics and Electronics (INAOE). His current research interests include the development of scientific software with design patterns, the numerical solution of partial differential equations with radial basis functions and ordinary differential equation with multirate integration methods also called subcycling methods.

Martijn Rooker received his PhD in Computer Science at the Jacobs University Bremen, with the focus on mobile robotics. At PROFACTOR, he is responsible for distributed communication control concepts and distributed control automation in flexible assembly lines. In the last few years, he gained great expertise in the areas by collaborating in various national and international research projects. He holds about 25 publications in the above mentioned areas. Dr. Rooker has participated in the European FP6 IP DECOS, and the national founded projects εCEDAC and VIBELESS within Austria's FIT-IT program. Currently, he is participating in the European FP7 STREP MEDEIA project; the FIT-IT project FRONTICS and is sub-project coordinator for training and dissemination in the FP6 IP PISA.

Thomas Strasser holds a Ph.D. degree in Mechanical Engineering with focus on automation and control theory from Vienna University of Technology. Currently he is working as researcher at the AIT Austrian Institute of Technology in the domain of Electrical Energy Systems (i.e. Smart Grids and Distributed Generation) in the Energy Department. He was working for over 6.5 years as a senior researcher at PROFACTOR GmbH in the field of advanced automation systems. He was the coordinator of various national (e.g. FIT-IT μCrons, FIT-IT eCEDAC) and international projects (e.g. MEDEIA, 4DIAC) in the domain of embedded and advanced automation systems. In addition he is an evaluator of R&D proposals for the Swiss National Science Foundation and he is member of the IEC SC65B/WG15 for the IEC 61499 standard on distributed automation and control systems. Thomas Strasser is also member of IEEE, especially of IEEE-IES and IEEE-SMC. Furthermore he is member of the IEEE-IES TC-IA IEEE-IES TC-SG and IEEE-SMC TC-DIS.

Sofiène Tahar received the diploma degree in computer engineering from the University of Darmstadt, Germany, in 1990, and the PhD degree with distinction in computer science from the University of Karlsruhe, Germany, in 1994. Currently, he is a professor with the Department of Electrical and Computer Engineering, Concordia University, Montreal, Quebec, Canada. He is the founder and director of the Hardware Verification Group at Concordia University. He has made contributions and published papers in the areas of formal hardware verification, microprocessor and system-on-chip verification, analog and mixed signal circuits verification, VLSI design automation, and probabilistic, statistical, and reliability analysis of systems. He has been organizing and involved in program committees of various international conferences in the areas of formal methods and design automation. In 1998, he received the Canada Foundation for Innovation (CFI) Researcher Award. From 2001 to 2006, he held a junior Concordia University research chair in Formal Verification of Microelectronics Systems. In 2007, he was appointed senior Concordia University research chair in Formal Verification of System-on-Chip.

Benny Tjahjono is a Senior Lecturer in Manufacturing Systems Engineering and the Director of the Manufacturing Masters programme at Cranfield University. His degrees in Electrical Engineering and Manufacturing Systems Engineering have guided his research interest in the area of simulation modelling and condition/health monitoring of machines in the production lines. He has successfully completed over 20 industrial research projects funded by global companies such as Ford and Airbus and has published over 40 research papers. He has also been invited to deliver lectures and to present his research at a number of universities and companies throughout Europe.

Carlos Valderrama received the electrical engineering and M.Sc degrees from the Universidad Nacional de Cordoba (UNC), Cordoba, Argentina, in 1989, and from the Universidade Federal do Rio de Janeiro (UFRJ – COPPE), Rio de Janeiro, Brazil in 1993. In 1998, he received the PhD. Degree from the Institut National Polytechnique de Grenoble, Grenoble, France. He is presently the head of the Electronic and Microelectronics Department at the University of Mons, in Mons, Belgium, where he lectures on embedded systems, analog and system level design. His primary research interests include wireless communication, reconfigurable architectures, EDA and system level design validation and synthesis of embedded architectures. Dr. Valderrama serves as committee member of the RAW, FPL, SPL, ISQED, HiberChip and the NoC conference among others. From 1999 to 2003, he was with CoWare NV., Belgium, an EDA/ESL company, managing the hardware design team. In 1998 and 2003, he was invited professor at the Universidade Federal de Pernambuco, and at the Universidade Federal do Rio Grande do Norte, both located in Brazil. He won two Best Paper Awards on renowned international IEEE conferences SBCCI in 2002 and ED&TC in 1995. His research activity is supported by several publications, books chapters, and tutorials. Dr. Valderrama is IEEE Senior member.

Chunfu Zhong received the B.S. degree from Xidian University, Xi'an, China, in 2005. He is currently a Ph.D. student in Xidian University. His research interests include supervisory control of discrete event systems and Petri nets.

Alois Zoitl holds a PhD degree in Electrical Engineering with the focus on dynamic reconfiguration of real-time constrained control applications and a Master degree in Electrical Engineering with the focus on distributed industrial automation systems from Vienna University of Technology. Currently he is the head of the Agile Control Group at Automation and Control Institute (ACIN), Vienna University of Technology. There he is responsible for a group of 9 re-searchers. He is co-author of 79 publications and the co-inventor of 4 patents in the mentioned areas. Alois Zoitl conducted and lead several industry founded projects and participated in the national FIT-IT embedded systems projects μCrons and εCEDAC. Furthermore he is currently the coordinator of the FIT-IT semantic systems project OntoReA and works in the FP7 embedded systems project MEDEIA, in the national FIT-IT embedded systems project FRONTICS as well as in the FFG bridge project logi.diag. Alois Zoitl is a founding member O³neida automation network, a member of the IEEE, the PLCopen user organization as well as the IEC SC65B/WG15 for the distributed automation standard IEC 61499.

Michael Zolda received his master degree in computer science from Vienna University of Technology in 2005, in the area of computational logic. During his studies he was awarded the studentship for excellence from the faculty. He is currently working as a researcher on the FWF project "Formal Timing Analysis Suite" (FORTAS). His research focus is in dependable embedded systems. Particular research topics include timing analysis of real-time systems and robustness of embedded systems.

Index

A

Abstract B model 401

abstract paths 120

ACL2 209, 214, 215, 216, 219, 220, 221, 231, 232, 233, 234

ADAMS project 517, 539

Adaptability 191

Adaptive Differential Pulse Code Modulation (ADPCM) 104, 105, 106

adaptive logic module (ALM) 141

affine gap model 314

Agent Communication Language (ACLs) 239

AIDA project 517

Alternative Current (AC) 478, 489, 490, 492, 498, 505, 506, 507

ALU 86, 87, 88, 100, 282

Analogue Digital Converters (ADC) 276, 277, 278

Analysis and Decomposition 117

an appropriate modeling language (AADL) 509, 511, 516, 517, 518, 519, 520, 521, 522, 523, 524, 525, 526, 527, 528, 529, 530, 532, 533, 534, 535, 536, 537, 538, 539, 540, 541

AND-state 446, 465

application level axioms (AL) 449, 474

Application mapping 151

Application Programmer Interfaces (APIs) 32, 33, 34, 35, 36, 38, 510

Application scheduling 151

Application Specific Code 486

application-specific instruction-set processor (ASIP) 134

Application Specific Integrated Circuits (ASIC) 31, 52, 133, 136, 139, 152, 192, 194, 200, 481, 543, 544

Architecture Description Languages (ADL) 1, 2, 4, 10, 27, 28

Architecture State Machine (ASM) 12, 13, 14, 25, 252, 253, 254, 256, 262, 267

Architecture Unit 4, 12

Arcticus Systems 3, 28

ARINC 653 509, 510, 511, 512, 513, 514, 516, 517, 518, 519, 520, 521, 523, 524, 525, 526, 527, 528, 529, 530, 532, 533, 534, 535, 536, 537, 538, 539

Array Control Unit (ACU) 221, 222

asynchronous partial overlay (APO) 239

Atomic propositions 389

attached reconfigurable processing unit 112

Automation and Control Institute (ACIN) 74, 81

AUTOmotive Open System Architecture (AUTOSAR) 181, 182, 188

B

B2TLA+ 376, 381, 387, 388, 399, 404, 410, 412

Backus-Naur Form (BNF) 550

Basic OS 435, 436

Benchmark Production Systems 235, 236, 243, 244, 249, 257, 258, 259, 260, 269, 272

Bioinformatics applications 311, 312, 339

blocking tasks 111

Block RAM (BRAM) 38, 39, 41, 283, 287, 288, 289, 290, 299, 310, 486, 487, 488, 489, 492, 501

Board Support Project (BSP) 484, 485